UNDERSTANDING BANKRUPTCY
Second Edition

LexisNexis

LexisNexis Law School Publishing Advisory Board

UNDERSTANDING BANKRUPTCY
Second Edition

Jeff Ferriell
Professor of Law
Capital University Law School

Edward J. Janger
Professor of Law
Brooklyn Law School

ISBN#: **978-1-4224-7440-2**

NOTE TO USERS
To ensure that you are using the latest materials available in this area, please be sure to periodically check the LexisNexis Law School web site for downloadable updates and supplements at www.lexisnexis.com/lawschool

Library of Congress Cataloging-in-Publication Data

Ferriell, Jeffrey Thomas, 1953-
Understanding bankruptcy / Jeff Ferriell, Edward J. Janger. --2nd ed.
p. cm. --(Understanding series (New York, N.Y.))
Includes index.
ISBN 1-4224-1182-6 (soft cover)
1. Bankruptcy--United States. I. Janger, Edward J. II. Title.

KF1524.F47 2007
346.7307'8--dc22
2007026154

Editorial Offices
744 Broad Street, Newark, NJ 07102 (973) 820-2000
201 Mission St., San Francisco, CA 94105-1831 (415) 908-3200
701 East Water Street, Charlottesville, VA 22902-7587 (434) 972-7600
www.lexis.com

(Pub.00709)

PREFACE

This book is designed to provide a basic introduction to bankruptcy and related state debtor/creditor law. It will be useful for students taking an introductory course in Creditors' Rights that emphasizes bankruptcy; a free-standing Bankruptcy course; or an advanced course in Bankruptcy Reorganization. While it does not and cannot pretend to anticipate every question that may arise, it does provide a reasonably detailed discussion of the issues most likely to arise in these courses. It is as up-to-date as possible, given the fast-changing nature of the law it examines. The 2d edition incorporates detailed discussion of the so-called "Bankruptcy Abuse Prevention and Consumer Protection Act of 2005" and refers to some of the first cases to analyze its provisions.

The primary goal of this book is to bring order and clarity to a body of law that sometimes has neither. Its focus is on the newcomer to bankruptcy, who has little or no knowledge of bankruptcy law or practice. In addition, it provides a basic explanation of much of the state commercial law and debtor-creditor law that operates in the background of a bankruptcy proceeding. It is impossible, for example, to understand many key provisions of the Bankruptcy Code without having at least some knowledge of the state law regarding mortgages, deeds of trust, and security interests.

We hope it provides a useful supplement to other primary materials: the bankruptcy code, the bankruptcy rules, and the cases decided under them. Students using this book will still need to study these more fundamental materials in detail. In many situations, they will find it useful to put this book down, pick up the Bankruptcy Code, and read the relevant statutory provision carefully. A full understanding requires facility with the Code, the Rules, and the cases.

In the last three decades, bankruptcy has evolved from a somewhat obscure specialty to one of the dominant bodies of American law. Traditionally, the bankruptcy bar was divided into two groups — the rather small group that did consumer and small business bankruptcy, and the tiny group that worked on larger business reorganizations. Each had certain elements of a club; indeed, many bankruptcy practitioners retain a degree of nostalgia for the days when insolvency lawyers, if somewhat isolated from the profession as a whole, enjoyed (in much of the country at least) the kind of (perhaps imaginary) camaraderie that is usually associated with lawyers in a small community.

Much of this has changed. Bankruptcy has become a boom area of practice, one of interest to a growing number of large firms. The annual rate of bankruptcy filings has grown rapidly, reaching a recent peak of over one-and-a-half million. The administrative and judicial structure of bankruptcy has become elaborate and formalized; the scope of bankruptcy has grown in unexpected directions. Bankruptcy is now a serious matter not only for commercial and insolvency lawyers, but also for tax lawyers, environmental lawyers, tort lawyers, and labor lawyers, as well as those involved in business and personal injury litigation generally.

There are many reasons for this transformation. On the consumer side, some say the change is attributable to the fact that bankruptcy once carried with it the stigma of failure and dishonesty, but it does so no longer. Others attribute this shift to changes in the consumer credit industry, especially the advent of subprime lending and lenders who can lend profitably to much riskier borrowers. On the business side, some alternatives to bankruptcy, especially state insolvency proceedings, have withered away or are ineffective in the face of national and multinational business enterprises. The Bankruptcy Code itself is in part responsible; it contains a number of legal devices that permit people and companies to achieve — or at least to try to achieve — goals that are simply not achievable under any other body of law. For example, bankruptcy is practically the only method of dealing with "mass torts" in a single consolidated proceeding.

Along with the explosion of bankruptcy litigation has come a parallel explosion of academic interest in bankruptcy. Not long ago, most law schools had little more in their curriculum than a single course in Creditor's Rights, only part of which was taken up by bankruptcy law. Today, many schools have several courses, covering not only basic bankruptcy but reorganization bankruptcy, bankruptcy tax, bankruptcy environmental law, and the like. Similarly, for many years there was only one important secondary source — Collier on Bankruptcy, a venerable treatise first published in 1898 (the 15th edition of is still the leading authority).[1] Now there are many sources; of special interest to the law school community are the multiple law reviews that specialize in bankruptcy law, and the many articles on bankruptcy published in non-specialist law journals. We have tried to include a fair sampling of these other sources, to which students should turn for further discussion when they find themselves excited by a particular topic.[2]

Bankruptcy has also become a hot topic among legal theorists. Nothing that touches so large a part of the American economy and American society can exist for long without triggering efforts to fit it within larger structures of economic and political thinking. While this book is primarily aimed at giving a basic overview of bankruptcy, it also introduces the reader to the most important theoretical perspectives. Bankruptcy is an area in which

[1] Not coincidentally, Collier's is a LexisNexis publication.

[2] The suggestion that one might find bankruptcy law interesting and exciting brings to mind the teenage daughter of one of your author's friends. She found her father's amateur radio hobby both interesting and exciting, but when she passed her FCC amateur radio licensing exam, and thus became a "ham radio" operator, she made her father (W8HI) and his law professor friend (K8ZDA), promise not to tell any of her peers.

there is often little separation of theory and practice, not least because Congress is constantly returning to basic principles as it writes and rewrites bankruptcy law.

Bankruptcy law in this country is federal law. The substantive parts are found almost entirely in the Bankruptcy Code (Title 11 of the United States Code); procedural provisions are found mainly in the Federal Rules of Bankruptcy Procedure and in various parts of Title 28 of the United States Code (the "judicial code"). A few provisions are in Title 18 of the United States Code (the "criminal code"). Although some state law is directly incorporated into the Code, and other state law indirectly affects rights in bankruptcy, any conflict between state law and bankruptcy is resolved in favor of the latter.

One of the features of federal law is that a wealth of legislative history underlies it. Insofar as the Code is concerned, the primary sources of that history are the House and Senate Reports that accompanied its original enactment. There was also extensive floor debate on some provisions; and most of the subsequent amendments to the Code are supported by similar reports and debates. The weight to be given these sources is today controversial. Several members of the Supreme Court, most noticeably Justice Antonin Scalia, largely reject the use of legislative history in statutory interpretation and sometimes seems to use the bankruptcy code as a laboratory to test out his theories of statutory interpretation.

We end by suggesting one final reason why we think you will find this one of the most exciting courses you will take in law school. In a practical, if not a de jure, sense, bankruptcy is the court of last resort. In virtually every bankruptcy, there are far more claims than there are assets. Not only is there no free lunch; there is not enough lunch to feed everybody. In bankruptcy there is only so much to go around; it is not sufficient; yet it is all there is or will ever be. This means that bankruptcy law must make choices that are both unsatisfactory and final. How should the limited pool be divided up? How do we, how should we, decide between the claim of the mortgage holder to whom the debtor owes money on a loan and the maimed victim of the debtor's intentional tort? How do we also fit in the tax collector, the utility company, the credit card company, and the debtor's unpaid housekeeper? Bankruptcy law again and again forces us to make the hard, disagreeable choices that are otherwise too often ignored. You may agree or disagree with the choices that have been made, but you should understand them; you should also understand that a choice is unavoidable.

With all this said, I hope you will find your study of bankruptcy exciting and intriguing. I hope as well you will find this book a helpful guide. Good luck!

ACKNOWLEDGMENTS

Our first debt of gratitude must be to Rev. Michael J. Herbert of the Roman Catholic Diocese of Richmond, Virginia. Father Herbert provided the authors with no direct spiritual assistance (at least that we know of), but instead with the benefit of the considerable expertise in bankruptcy and related commercial law he acquired, prior to his ordination, as a member of the University of Richmond Law School faculty, and as the sole author of the first edition of this book. Although his ecclesiastical duties made it necessary for him to refuse to be named as a third co-author of the second edition of Understanding Bankruptcy, its basic structure, format, and indeed many of its passages reflect work he did in the early 1990s. Without the benefit of his earlier work, our task would have been much harder. Any mistakes, of course, are ours alone.

Thanks are also owed to Dean Joan Wexler and the Dean's research fund at Brooklyn Law School and to Dean Jack Guttenberg and Capital University Law School's research funds. Our able research assistants Mary Daugherty and Carla Cheung, as well as Keith Moore at LexisNexis, have provided the necessary encouragement and patient editorial work.

We also owe a debt of gratitude to those who first introduced us to bankruptcy and commercial law, Profs. Gary Neustadter and former Prof. Sheridan Downey of Santa Clara University (now a successful coin dealer in Oakland, California), former University of Illinois Prof. Jonathan Landers (now at the New York office of Gibson, Dunn & Crutcher), and Professor Douglas Baird of the University of Chicago.

Finally, thanks are also owed, in connection with both this work and every aspect of our lives, to our parents, Merlin and Frances Ferriell and Inez and Allen Janger, as well to our wives, Victoria Eastus and Cheryl Hacker.

TABLE OF CONTENTS

Page

Page

Page

Chapter 17 Liquidation Under Chapter 7

Chapter 18 Rehabilitation of Individuals With Regular Income

Chapter 19 Reorganization Under Chapter 11

Page

TABLE OF CONTENTS

Page

Chapter 1 General Principles Underlying Insolvency Law

Page

Page

Page

Page

Page

Chapter 6 Commencement of the Case

Page

Page

Page

Chapter 10 Claims and Interests

Page

Chapter 12 Preserving Assets: Exemptions, Reaffirmation, and Redemption

Chapter 13 Discharge

Page

Chapter 15 Preferences

Page

Page

Page

Chapter 19 Reorganization Under Chapter 11

Page

Page

Page

Page

Page

Chapter 21 Role of Professionals in Bankruptcy Proceedings

Chapter 22 International Bankruptcy

Chapter 1

General Principles Underlying Insolvency Law

§ 1.01 The Nature of Insolvency Law

[A] Introduction: Debtors or Deadbeats?

At the heart of insolvency law lie two intractable problems: (1) balancing the interests of insolvent debtors in a fresh start against those of their creditors who wish to be paid; and (2) balancing the interests of competing creditors with meritorious claims against a pile of assets that is, by definition, too small. Remarkably, bankruptcy law often succeeds reasonably well at both, providing a way out of trouble for hopelessly swamped debtors, while also providing a reasonably efficient means to adjust creditors' claims. Nonetheless, what for debtors is an escape is often regarded by creditors as a swindle. By the same token, creditors' efficient collection may be the debtor's peonage.

The arguments about the nature of bankruptcy debtors, their reasons for filing, and their innocence or blameworthiness are old. During the Civil War, it was argued that a pro-debtor law was needed to preserve loyalty to the Union:

> Of what advantage can it be to creditors or to the country that so many tens of thousands of the active men of this country should be held in thralldom? . . . The law formerly in force by which the creditor could keep his debtor in prison for an indefinite period, without relief, has been abolished in all Christian countries. But there may be a punishment of death without the knife, and an imprisonment without the bolts and bars of the jail . . . . What to [the debtors] are the guarantees of the Constitution? Why should they love the Government and yield it a hearty allegiance?[1]

Recent empirical data suggests that debtors do not file for bankruptcy lightly.

> The average bankrupt debtor or debtor family has a ratio of non-mortgage debt to income of approximately 2.12. That means that it would take them more than two years to pay all their debts, ignoring home mortgages . . . pretending that interest stopped running . . . [, and even if] they devoted every penny of their

[1] Cong. Globe, 38th Cong., 1st Sess. 2638 (1864) (statement of Rep. Jenckes).

> current incomes to debt payment and got someone else to support them.[2]

From the debate over the 2005 amendments to the Bankruptcy Code, which significantly restricted access of consumer debtors to the bankruptcy discharge, comes a passionate but anecdotal statement of the opposite point of view:

> Mr. Chairman, for the last couple of years in going home, I have been getting many complaints from the owners of small businesses about the large number of persons taking bankruptcy. It was pointed out to me that a number of these persons taking bankruptcy had good jobs. They could pay their obligations, but it was the easier route to go chapter 7 and take bankruptcy and not worry about their debts . . . . Well, something is wrong when the bankruptcy laws encourage people to take bankruptcy and then a small businessman goes before the courts and they tell him, "We can't help you at all."[3]

Indeed, two proponents of the 2005 Amendments characterized bankruptcy as an opportunity to get out of jail free, stating that:

> [B]ankruptcy should not merely be a means of violating promises willy-nilly. A promise to repay money is an important legal and moral obligation, neither lightly to be undertaken nor lightly cast away. Filing bankruptcy represents a decision to repudiate promises made in exchange for goods, services, and other promises. Of such promises and reciprocity is the fabric of civil society woven.[4]

The recent legislation appears to accept this critique of consumer bankruptcy and rigorously restricts debtors' access to the bankruptcy system. One of this book's co-authors has published his views on this aspect of the amendments.[5]

In addition to the struggle between debtor and creditor, there is a perpetual struggle over which creditors should be given the first crack at obtaining whatever few assets the debtor has. There are several tools that result in better treatment to some creditors than others; these include enforcing creditors' liens, giving priority to some unsecured creditors, and making all or part of certain debts non-dischargeable. Over the years, Congress has given favored treatment to an amazing variety of creditor groups and articulated a congeries of reasons for doing so. These include, among others, labor unions, retirees, victims of drunk (or drugged) drivers, government agencies that guarantee student loans, consumers who buy on layaway

[2] Elizabeth Warren & Jay Westbrook, The Law of Debtors and Creditors at 119 (2005).

[3] 130 Cong. Rec. H1812 (daily ed. March 21, 1984) (statement of Rep. G.V. Montgomery).

[4] Edith H. Jones & Todd J. Zywicki, *It's Time for Means-Testing*, 1999 BYU L. Rev. 177, 181 (1999).

[5] Edward J. Janger & Susan Block-Lieb, *The Myth of the Rational Borrower: Behaviorism, Rationality and the Misguided Reform of Bankruptcy Law*, 84 Tex. L. Rev. 1481 (2006); Edward J. Janger, *Crystals and Mud in Bankruptcy Law: Judicial Competence and Statutory Design*, 43 Arizona L. Rev. 559 (2001).

plans, ex-spouses, landlords, shopping mall operators, farmers, and the Federal Reserve Bank. There is sometimes little coherent logic, other than raw political power, used to decide who qualifies for a favorable position. Moreover, there is little consistency in the types of favors granted. For example, some tax claims are protected by giving them priority and by making them non-dischargeable in some forms of bankruptcy. Wage claims are given priority but are dischargeable. Drunk-driving claims are given no priority but are not dischargeable. Student loan claims have no priority but are sometimes dischargeable and sometimes not. Labor contracts are protected in an entirely different way: unlike most other contracts, the debtor must honor them or engage in a process of court supervised bargaining. Creditors with security interests must be paid the full value of their secured claim at the expense of creditors who never obtained a security interest.

A number of recurring themes run through bankruptcy law; some of these are introduced in the next sections of this chapter. Often these themes conflict and recur. They are often balanced, but never fully reconciled or synthesized. Given the relative completeness of the legislative record, it is possible to trace many of the horse-trades and policy tradeoffs that have given the Bankruptcy Code its current shape; this can be amusing for the amateur student of the legislative process and excellent fodder for more rigorous (or at least more elaborate) schools of analysis, such as public choice.[6]

In this book, our analysis is necessarily limited. Readers should keep in mind that the rationale stated in support of one provision may be contrary to the rationale stated in support of another seemingly parallel provision. This is due to the way in which bankruptcy law, like nearly all law, is inevitably made.[7]

[B] Bankruptcy as a Debtors' Remedy: Fresh Start for Honest Debtors

The historic concept of the "fresh start" for an honest but unfortunate debtor is central to modern American insolvency law.[8] The debtor

[6] *See, e.g.*, David A. Skeel Jr., Debt's Dominion: A History of Bankruptcy Law in America (2003).

[7] *Compare* Edward J. Janger, *The Locus of Lawmaking: Uniform State Law, Federal Law, and Bankruptcy Reform,* 74 Am. Bankr. L.J. 97 (2000), *with* Edward J. Janger, *Predicting When the Uniform Law Process Will Fail: Article 9, Capture, and the Race to the Bottom*, 83 Iowa L. Rev. 569 (1998).

[8] *See* Charles G. Hallinan, *The "Fresh Start" Policy in Consumer Bankruptcy: A Historical Inventory and an Interpretative Theory*, 21 U. Rich. L. Rev. 49 (1986); Margaret Howard, *A Theory of Discharge in Consumer Bankruptcy*, 48 Ohio St. L.J. 1047 (1987); Thomas H. Jackson, *The Fresh-Start Policy in Bankruptcy Law*, 98 Harv. L. Rev. 1393 (1985); Charles Jordan Tabb, *The Scope of the Fresh Start in Bankruptcy: Collateral Conversions and the Dischargeability Debate*, 59 Geo. Wash. L. Rev. 56 (1990) (reviewing the literature).

The term "fresh start" is derived from *Local Loan Co. v. Hunt*, 292 U.S. 234, 244 (1934),

surrenders his or her non-exempt assets to the trustee and receives a second chance to make a go of things. Some discussions of the fresh start principle take on almost a mystical quality: bankruptcy is seen as a financial rebirth. After the debtor's "estate"[9] is administered and the debts are discharged, the debtor begins a new financial life, unencumbered by his previous debts.

This fresh start is provided via two principal mechanisms: the discharge from debts and the ability to retain limited "exempt" property deemed necessary for life in modern society. For consumer debtors, discharge is frequently the most important aspect of bankruptcy. Eligible debtors are relieved from most of their debts.[10] Freed from their past obligations, debtors have a renewed incentive to engage in economically productive efforts knowing that they will be able to retain the fruits of their revived efforts. Provisions permitting debtors to retain property as "exempt" enhance the effect of the discharge by providing debtors with the tools they need to continue in life.[11]

However, a fresh start is available only to "honest debtors." This limitation reflects a moralistic strain in fresh start analysis that cannot be ignored. This moralistic strain is reflected in the hostility toward debtors reflected in the recent amendments to the Bankruptcy Code that restrict the number of debtors who are entitled to a fresh start. Most of the major amendments to the Bankruptcy Code since its original enactment in 1978 have been broadly pro-creditor.[12] The 2005 Amendments continued this pattern by limiting access to bankruptcy relief generally, imposing additional costs on those who remain eligible for relief, and strengthening the rights of secured creditors.

Whether these changes are desirable depends largely on one's assumptions. If a substantial number of bankrupts enjoy previously untapped capacity to pay their debts, then the recent changes to the Code are likely to open these spigots of cash to creditors.[13] Conversely, if, as recent studies show, debtors are, for the most part, truly unable to pay, keeping them out

where the Court indicated that bankruptcy gives "the honest but unfortunate debtor who surrenders for distribution the property which he owns at the time of bankruptcy, a new opportunity in life and a clear field for future effort, unhampered by the pressure and discouragement of preexisting debt." *See also* Williams v. United States Fid. & Guar. Co., 236 U.S. 549, 554–55 (1915).

[9] The filing of a bankruptcy petition results in the creation of an "estate" comprised of all of the debtor's pre-petition property. Bankruptcy Code § 541(a); *see* Chapter 7, Property of the Estate, *infra*. Bankruptcy operates as the financial death of the debtor, and at the some time creates the opportunity for a renewed financial existence, free from many if not all of the liabilities that led to its demise.

[10] *See* Chapter 13, Discharge, *infra*.

[11] Bankruptcy Code § 522; *see* § 12.02 Exemptions in Bankruptcy, *infra;* William J. Woodward, Jr., *Exemptions, Opting Out, and Bankruptcy Reform*, 43 Ohio St. L.J. 335 (1982).

[12] Paul M. Black & Michael J. Herbert, *Bankcard's Revenge: A Critique of the 1984 Consumer Credit Amendments to the Bankruptcy Code*, 19 U. Rich. L. Rev. 845 (1985).

[13] *E.g.*, Todd J. Zywicki, *An Economic Analysis of the Consumer Bankruptcy Crisis*, 99 Nw. U.L. Rev. 1463 (2005).

of bankruptcy court does not, by itself, put dollars in creditors' pockets.[14] Limiting access to a discharge only encourages creditors to continue to engage in costly and fruitless efforts to collect. At worst, it may destroy any incentives debtors have to invest whatever available resources they have to improve their financial condition and economic productivity. In this way, restricting relief may impose costs on society without a corresponding return in increased collections from overextended debtors.

Moreover, even when bankruptcy is available to clear off most existing debts, it does not provide debtors with an untarnished fresh start. Generally, private companies may discriminate against debtors who have sought bankruptcy protection, by denying them credit altogether, by charging them higher fees and interest, or by insisting on collateral. The fact of bankruptcy may be kept in the debtor's credit report for 10 years,[15] which may reduce the debtor's access to additional credit. Bankruptcy is thus by no means cost-free, even to debtors who have no assets to lose in the bankruptcy process.

[C] Bankruptcy as a Creditor's Remedy

Long before providing honest debtors with a fresh start was considered part of the purpose of insolvency law, bankruptcy was available as a creditor's remedy. Even when bankruptcy law supplied no redemption for the debtor, it was designed to provide an efficient and orderly system to collect and distribute an insolvent debtor's assets among competing creditors. These purposes remain intact. Bankruptcy procedures are designed to preserve the value of a consumer or business debtor's assets and to divide them equitably among creditors.

[1] Preserving Existing Value

Although few consumer debtors have substantial assets, financially troubled business debtors usually have some property available to distribute to creditors. Some may have enough assets to pay creditors in full, even though they are experiencing cash flow difficulties that make them unable to make regular payments as their debts become due. Some businesses may be solvent, or not, depending on whether they are valued as a going concern or based on the value that their individual assets would have generated

---

[14] Gordon Bermant & Ed Flynn, *Incomes, Debts, and Repayment Capacities of Recently Discharged Chapter 7 Debtors,* Executive Office for U.S. Trustees, U.S. Dept. Justice (Jan. 1999); Marianne B. Culhane & Michaela M. White, *Taking the New Consumer Bankruptcy Model for a Test Drive: Means-Testing Real Chapter 7 Debtors*, 7 Am. Bankr. Inst. L. Rev. 27 (1999); *but see* Ernst & Young, *Chapter 7 Bankruptcy Petitioners' Ability to Repay: The National Perspective, Policy Economics and Quantitative Analysis Group* (March 1998); Ernst & Young, *Chapter 7 Bankruptcy Petitioners' Ability to Repay: Additional Evidence from Bankruptcy Petition Files, Policy Economics and Quantitative Analysis Group* (Feb. 1998); Ernst & Young, *Chapter 7 Bankruptcy Petitioners' Repayment Ability Under H.R. 833: The National Perspective, Policy Economics and Quantitative Analysis Group* (March 1999).

[15] Fair Credit Reporting Act § 605(a)(1), 15 U.S.C. § 1681c(a)(1) (2000).

if they were sold item by item at a liquidating auction. When debtors retain valuable assets, bankruptcy seeks to provide an orderly procedure to collect and distribute them in a way that maximizes their value for the benefit of creditors. For a debtor whose business plan is destined to fail, maximizing the value available for creditors may require piecemeal liquidation of the debtor's property. For a debtor with a viable business plan but more debt than the business's cash flow can sustain, keeping the business in operation may produce greater payment to creditors than closing the doors and selling the assets.

Collection through the state law system is characterized by a race among creditors for the lion's share of the spoils. Left unrestrained, eager creditors may liquidate the debtor's assets one by one without regard to whether this maximizes the remaining value for all creditors. Unrestrained, individual creditors pay little heed to the desirability of preserving financial value for creditors who have lagged behind in their efforts to collect. After all, the first vulture to arrive on the scene of a fresh carcass cares little for whether later arrivals eat their fill.[16] In some cases, creditors' overreactions to a debtor's precarious financial condition might lead creditors into precipitous action to obtain payment which might tip the debtor over a brink that could have been avoided if the debtor had been permitted to retain its assets and deploy them in an effort to stave off eventual financial ruin.

Bankruptcy attempts to preserve value for all creditors and to ensure that creditors are paid on an equal basis. Bankruptcy procedures to preserve the value of a financially troubled debtor help ensure that the highest possible proportion of a debtor's total obligations is paid from the available resources.

[2] Equal Treatment of Creditors of the Same Class

Bankruptcy serves the interests of creditors not only by preserving the debtor's financial value, but by ensuring that creditors share whatever value remains in an equitable fashion. Thus, a frequently articulated goal of bankruptcy is to ensure "equal treatment of creditors of the same class."[17] This distinguishes bankruptcy from the state collection system which usually results in better treatment of creditors who act quickly to collect, leaving those who are inclined to permit the debtor to attempt to resolve its financial difficulties largely in a lurch. As will be seen, the equal treatment policy advances the purposes of the Bankruptcy Code to maximize the debtor's value by discouraging overly aggressive collection efforts that might lead to a debtor's premature financial demise.

[16] Douglas G. Baird, *A World Without Bankruptcy*, 50 Law & Contemp. Probs. 173 (1987).

[17] Thomas H. Jackson, The Logic and Limits of Bankruptcy Law 2–4 (1986); Elizabeth Warren, *A Principled Approach to Consumer Bankruptcy*, 71 Am. Bankr. L.J. 483, 483 (1997); Alan N. Resnick, *The Future of the Doctrine of Necessity and Critical-Vendor Payments in Chapter 11 Cases,* 47 B.C. L. Rev. 183, 184 (2005); H.R. Rep. No. 95-595, at 177–78 (1978), *reprinted in* 1978 U.S.C.C.A.N. 5787, 5963, 6137–39.

The equal treatment policy is reflected in numerous important provisions of the Bankruptcy Code. In liquidation proceedings, § 726(b) requires creditors' claims to be paid "pro rata among claims of the [same] kind."[18] In reorganization proceedings, § 1123 requires a Chapter 11 plan to "provide the same treatment for each claim or interest of a particular class, unless the holder . . . agrees to a less favorable treatment,"[19] and § 1129 prevents a plan from discriminating unfairly among classes of creditors who have not agreed to the terms of the plan.[20] Provisions in Chapters 12 and 13 impose similar requirements. Moreover, the bankruptcy trustee's ability to recover certain pre-bankruptcy payments and other kinds of property transfers to creditors that would disrupt the equal treatment policy apply in both liquidation and reorganization proceedings.[21]

§ 1.02 Modern Theories of Insolvency Law[22]

For many years, bankruptcy law existed without much theoretical context. There was only one broadly recognized history of bankruptcy law: Charles Warren's Bankruptcy in United States History, published in 1935.[23] This masked a sporadic and informal legal literature that was found in cases, occasional articles, and speeches. Studies were made from the perspective of other disciplines, however, formal efforts to draw together the disparate strands of bankruptcy thinking, at least as far as lawyers were concerned, were rare.

This is no longer true. There has been a renewed interest in bankruptcy history,[24] and a new effort to gather empirical data about bankruptcy practice and the substantive impact of bankruptcy law on real-world behavior.[25]

---

[18] Bankruptcy Code § 726(b).

[19] Bankruptcy Code § 1123(a)(4).

[20] Bankruptcy Code § 1129(b)(1).

[21] Bankruptcy Code § 547; *see generally* Chapter 15, Avoidable Preferences, *infra*.

[22] Douglas G. Baird, *Bankruptcy's Uncontested Axioms*, 108 Yale L.J. 573 (1998).

[23] Charles Warren, Bankruptcy in United States History (1935).

[24] Bruce H. Mann, Republic of Debtors: Bankruptcy in the Age of American Independence (2003); David A. Skeel, Jr., Debt's Dominion: A History of Bankruptcy Law in America (2003); Vern Countryman, *A History of American Bankruptcy Law*, 81 Com. L.J. 226, 226–32 (1976); Rhett Frimet, *The Birth of Bankruptcy in the United States*, 96 Com. L.J. 160, 163–63 (1991); Nathalie Martin, *The Role of History and Culture in Developing Bankruptcy and Insolvency Systems: The Perils of Legal Transplantation*, 28 B.C. Int'l & Comp. L. Rev. 1, 20–25 (2005); Charles Jordan Tabb, *The History of the Bankruptcy Laws in the United States*, 3 Am. Bankr. Inst. L. Rev. 5 (1995).

For just a few of the many articles that have blended historical review with analysis of contemporary bankruptcy problems, see John C. McCoid, II, *Pendency Interest in Bankruptcy*, 68 Am. Bankr. L.J. 1 (1994); John C. McCoid, II, *Setoff: Why Bankruptcy Priority?*, 75 Va. L. Rev. 15 (1989); Thomas E. Plank, *The Constitutional Limits of Bankruptcy*, 63 Tenn. L. Rev. 487, 500–17 (1996) (discussing the development of bankruptcy law in England); Charles Jordan Tabb, *Rethinking Preferences*, 43 S.C. L. Rev. 981 (1992).

[25] For a few of the most recent efforts in this regard, see Teresa A. Sullivan, Elizabeth Warren & Jay Lawrence Westbrook, *The Persistence of Local Legal Culture: Twenty Years of Evidence From the Bankruptcy Courts*, 17 Harv. J.L. & Pub. Pol'y 801 (1994); Paul B. Lackey,

For the theorist, the historian, and the pragmatist, there is now a wealth of material tackling bankruptcy from almost every conceivable perspective and nearly every mode of legal writing, from the dryly statistical to the vividly narrative.[26] Almost every current in present legal thought is now present in the bankruptcy literature.[27]

Unfortunately, it is impossible to sample the full range of this literature here. Instead, we will briefly describe the two most influential strains of bankruptcy theory. These two principal strains, characterized in the first edition of this work as "economic" and "social," have since come to be widely known as "proceduralist" and "traditionalist" views.[28] Both strains directly influence court opinions and congressional enactments.[29] While other approaches have their own distinct merits, they have not yet had much impact on the nitty-gritty of day-to-day bankruptcy work.

[A] "Proceduralist" Theories of Bankruptcy[30]

Proceduralist scholars advance the view that bankruptcy law should not create bankruptcy specific entitlements. This may lead to forum shopping into bankruptcy.[31] These scholars contend that bankruptcy law should not alter the non-bankruptcy entitlements of creditors and shareholders in order to rehabilitate firms. Instead, bankruptcy is simply a procedural mechanism to distribute the debtor's assets, based on non-bankruptcy entitlements, in an economically efficient manner. They further contend that entitlement holders, rather than bankruptcy judges, are in the best position to distinguish between debtors who are likely to be rehabilitated

---

An Empirical Survey and Proposed Bankruptcy Code Section Concerning the Propriety of Bidding Incentives in a Bankruptcy Sale of Assets, 93 Colum. L. Rev. 720 (1993); Ian Domowitz & Thomas L. Eovaldi, *The Impact of the Bankruptcy Reform Act of 1978 on Consumer Bankruptcy*, 36 J. Law & Econ. 803 (1993); *see also* Teresa A. Sullivan, Elizabeth Warren & Jay Lawrence Westbrook, As We Forgive Our Debtors: Bankruptcy and Consumer Credit in America (1989).

[26] For an example of a work that contains both the statistics and their dramatization, see Teresa A. Sullivan, Elizabeth Warren & Jay Lawrence Westbrook, As We Forgive Our Debtors: Bankruptcy and Consumer Credit in America (1989); *see also* Elizabeth Warren & Amelia Warren Tyagi, The Two-Income Trap: Why Middle-Class Mothers and Fathers Are Going Broke (2003).

[27] *See, e.g.*, Charles W. Mooney, Jr., *A Normative Theory of Bankruptcy Law: Bankruptcy as (Is) Civil Procedure*, 61 Wash. & Lee L. Rev. 931 (2004).

[28] This taxonomy can be traced to Douglas G. Baird, *Bankruptcy's Uncontested Axioms*, 108 Yale L.J. 573, 576–79 (1998); *see also* Edward J. Janger, *Crystals and Mud in Bankruptcy Law: Judicial Competence and Statutory Design*, 43 Ariz. L. Rev. 559, 566 (2001); Charles W. Mooney, Jr., *A Normative Theory of Bankruptcy Law: Bankruptcy as (Is) Civil Procedure*, 61 Wash. & Lee L. Rev. 931 (2004).

[29] Mark Bradshaw, Comment, *The Role of Politics and Economics in Early American Bankruptcy Law*, 18 Whittier L. Rev. 739 (1997).

[30] Thomas H. Jackson, The Logic and Limits of Bankruptcy Law (1986); Douglas G. Baird, *A World Without Bankruptcy*, 50 Law & Contemp. Probs. 173 (1987); Douglas G. Baird, *Bankruptcy's Uncontested Axioms*, 108 Yale L.J. 573, 578 (1998).

[31] Thomas H. Jackson, The Logic and Limits of Bankruptcy Law (1986).

from those who are likely to fail, and that as a general proposition, "rehabilitation" is not an independent goal of bankruptcy.[32]

Therefore, bankruptcy should do nothing more than preserve value for creditors by seeking to eliminate the inefficiencies that are inherent in atomistic state collection proceedings. When an individual creditor sues a debtor, that creditor's only interest is maximizing its own recovery, regardless of whether this is consonant with the greatest possible recovery for creditors as a whole. However, if creditors act collectively, proceduralists argue, then they become concerned about overall recovery. It simply makes more sense for creditors to share evenly in larger pools of assets from many debtors than to take their chances at being able to seize a disproportionate number of assets from a smaller pool of assets owned by a few debtors.

For example, imagine creditors A, B, and C; each is owed $1,000 by debtor X, $1,000 by debtor Y, and $1,000 by debtor Z. The value of each debtor's total assets depends on the way with which those assets are dealt. Imagine further a typical situation: the value is only $1,000 each if the debtors are liquidated in a piecemeal fashion, but it is $2,000 if the debtors are either liquidated in an orderly fashion or reorganized to preserve their ongoing concern value.

If creditors A, B, and C act independently, each will attempt to seize all available assets of each debtor. This will cause a disorderly liquidation that will limit the value of the assets to $1,000 per debtor. Independent action makes it impossible for the debtors to reorganize or to conduct an orderly liquidation. This reduces the value of each debtor's assets, which in turn reduces the total payout to the creditors as a whole.

To further illustrate, suppose A gets lucky in its independent action against X and collects the entire $1,000 X owes to A. X's assets will have been completely consumed in satisfaction of A's claim; B and C will receive nothing from their efforts to collect. A has obtained full payment on one debt, and if it gets equally lucky in its actions against Y and Z, it will be paid in full on all three of its debts. The corrolary of this is that if A is three times lucky, B and C get nothing at all from X, Y, or Z.

In the example given, it is easy to see why B and C would prefer orderly liquidations, but why would A? The reason is that A has no guarantee that it will be lucky once, let alone three times in a row. Assuming B and C are equally situated, A's chance of getting lucky in any action is 1 in 3; its chance of getting lucky in all (and thus being paid in full) is only 1 in 9. There is a considerable chance, 8 in 27, that A will get nothing at all.

By contrast, assume collective action of the three creditors would permit the debtors to reorganize or liquidate in an orderly fashion and thereby increase the value of each debtor's assets to $2,000. Moreover, assume the $2,000 would be equally divided among the three creditors. In that case, each creditor would receive two-thirds of its claims. This would directly

---

[32] *See* Edward J. Janger, *Crystals and Mud in Bankruptcy Law: Judicial Competence and Statutory Design*, 43 Ariz. L. Rev. 559, 566 (2001).

benefit the creditors, who would exchange a remote chance of full payment and a real chance of no payment for a certainty of substantial payment. It would indirectly benefit the rest of the economy: the risk and uncertainty faced by lenders would be reduced, and they would in turn be able to make better (and cheaper) decisions about their lending.

For practical reasons, the three creditors acting on their own outside of a coordinated bankruptcy proceeding are likely to find it difficult, if not impossible, to agree on an efficient model of collective action. Bankruptcy fills this gap by making the choice for them. It leaves them with their existing rights, thus avoiding an increase in uncertainty, but forces them to exercise those rights in a manner that in every case benefits them as a whole and over time benefits them individually. This model, which proceduralists support, is often called the "creditor's bargain," because it is the deal creditors would make if they could. Indeed, it is presumably a deal that they would have been willing to agree to at the time they initiated the credit, if all creditors had been gathered at the inception of the debtor's business and asked to agree on a regime to govern the debtor's insolvency. This bargain is imposed because of the often insuperable practical barriers to their making it for themselves once the business has found itself in difficulty.[33]

[B] "Traditionalist" Theories of Bankruptcy[34]

Bankruptcy scholars generally agree that preserving value is a key goal of bankruptcy. No one would dispute the suggestion that if greater value can be generated by keeping a firm afloat than by permitting it to be dismantled, then keeping the business alive is an appropriate use of bankruptcy. Both proceduralist and traditionalist bankruptcy scholars would want bankruptcy to be used to avoid a piecemeal liquidation of a debtor if rehabilitation or an orderly liquidation could double the value that could be retrieved from the business.[35] A key difference between the proceduralists and the traditionalists concern whether bankruptcy should be used to advance the goals of stakeholders other than creditors.

Traditionalists support rules that are designed not just to enhance and allocate a firm's value among existing entitlement holders; they approve of some rules that protect other creditor and non-creditor groups who are likely to have been particularly harmed by the debtor's financial failure but who might not be entitled to any of the debtor's value under normal

[33] Thomas H. Jackson, *Bankruptcy, Non-Bankruptcy Entitlements, and the Creditors' Bargain*, 91 Yale L.J. 857 (1982); *see also* Barry E. Adler, *Bankruptcy and Risk Allocation*, 77 Cornell L. Rev. 439 (1992); Douglas G. Baird, *Loss Distribution, Forum Shopping, and Bankruptcy: A Reply to Warren*, 54 U. Chi. L. Rev. 815 (1987); Thomas H. Jackson & Robert E. Scott, *On the Nature of Bankruptcy: An Essay on Bankruptcy Sharing and the Creditors' Bargain*, 75 Va. L. Rev. 155 (1989).

[34] Elizabeth Warren, *Bankruptcy Policy*, 54 U. Chi. L. Rev. 775 (1987).

[35] Thomas H. Jackson, *Bankruptcy, Non-Bankruptcy Entitlements, and the Creditors' Bargain*, 91 Yale L.J. 857, 861–68 (1982).

collection or priority rules. These groups might include current and retired employees, victims of the debtor's tortious conduct, and other members of the community,[36] even though they do not have substantive legal rights that are protected by the state law collection system. Traditionalist scholars view bankruptcy as carrying out a "deliberate distributional policy in favor of all those whom a business failure would have hurt."[37]

Using the above example, if bankruptcy procedures can be used to enhance the amount that would have been obtained for creditors using traditional state court collection procedures from $1,000 to $2,000, traditionalist scholars, unlike proceduralists, would not insist on distributing the additional value to those who would have received it under state collection law.

Traditionalists might say that additional value should be distributed to stakeholders like employees whose lives and fortunes would be disrupted if the debtor's business were allowed to fail. Proceduralists would agree to allocate payment to employees for their unpaid wages, but not for their relocation expenses or lost housing values, caused by the closing of a big business in a small town. Traditionalists prefer rehabilitation to avoid these additional losses (what economists would call "negative externalities") to those indirectly affected by the debtor's financial difficulties.

Traditionalists would also provide bankruptcy judges with leeway to adjust pre-bankruptcy entitlements, with a goal of either rehabilitating a financially troubled debtor or pursuing fairness.[38] In the traditionalist view, judges play a more central role in the administrative process.[39]

§ 1.03 Interpretation of the Bankruptcy Code

For several generations, it has been a commonplace view that the traditional rules of statutory interpretation have outlived their usefulness.[40] Chief among these is what has commonly been known as the "plain meaning" rule of statutory construction. Traditionally, if the text of a statute has a plain, unambiguous meaning that does not produce an absurd or unconstitutional result, that meaning controls and the court will not

[36] Ted Janger, *Crystals and Mud in Bankruptcy Law: Judicial Competence and Statutory Design*, 43 Ariz. L. Rev. 559, 566 (2001); *see generally* Karen Gross, Failure and Forgiveness: Rebalancing the Bankruptcy System (1997); Donald R. Korobkin, *Rehabilitating Values: A Jurisprudence of Bankruptcy*, 91 Colum. L. Rev. 717 (1991); Elizabeth Warren, *Bankruptcy Policy*, 54 U. Chi. L. Rev. 775 (1987); Elizabeth Warren & Jay Lawrence Westbrook, *Searching for Reorganization Realities*, 72 Wash. U. L.Q. 1257 (1994).

[37] Elizabeth Warren, *Bankruptcy Policy Making in an Imperfect World*, 92 Mich. L. Rev. 336, 355 (1993).

[38] Ted Janger, *Crystals and Mud in Bankruptcy Law: Judicial Competence and Statutory Design*, 43 Ariz. L. Rev. 559, 573 (2001).

[39] Ted Janger, *Crystals and Mud in Bankruptcy Law: Judicial Competence and Statutory Design*, 43 Ariz. L. Rev. 559, 574–75 (2001).

[40] Adrian Vermeule, Judging Under Uncertainty (2005); *see* Antonin Scalia, A Matter of Interpretation (1997).

consider other sources such as committee reports, floor debate, and other legislative history. While the court will attempt to make sense of the entire statutory text and fit the meaning of words and phrases within the entire body of the statute, only in rare cases will it go outside of the text. It is analogous to a strict application of the parol evidence rule in the law of contracts.

Critics of the plain meaning rule are many. The rule has been attacked as absurd. It has been seen as a block to the rational development of bankruptcy law, because Congress cannot constantly revise the statute to make its meaning clearer. Innumerable studies have attacked it as unworkable or incoherent, if for no other reason than that no English word or phrase is without ambiguity. Indeed the great majority of academic commentary on the rule is hostile.[41] Federal courts, which, unlike most state courts, have abundant legislative history available, have largely rejected the plain meaning rule. In the specific context of bankruptcy, the plain meaning rule has been seen as a block to the rational development of bankruptcy law because Congress cannot constantly revise the statute to make its meaning clearer. Thus, there has been a long tradition of paying minimal heed to the statute and maximum attention to perceived bankruptcy policy.

Over the past two decades, however, the plain meaning rule has been revitalized,[42] particularly in bankruptcy cases, and particularly by Justice Scalia. With an occasional exception,[43] the Supreme Court's bankruptcy decisions have insisted on the primacy of enacted text to determine what bankruptcy law is.[44] In a number of cases, the Court has added to its discussion of the statutory text a review of the legislative history despite Justice Scalia's insistence that references to the legislative history are a waste of thought, ink and paper. However, it must be said that the plain meaning rule is an honored method of interpretation. dThroughout this book, we will consider whether the plain meaning revival will affect

[41] Lee Dembart & Bruce A. Markell, *Alive at 25? A Short Review of the Supreme Court's Bankruptcy Jurisprudence, 1979-2004*, 78 Am. Bankr. L.J. 373, 386, 390–91 (2004); Walter A. Effross, *Grammarians at the Gate: The Rehnquist Court's Evolving "Plain Meaning" Approach to Bankruptcy Jurisprudence*, 23 Seton Hall L. Rev. 1636 (1993); Robert M. Lawless, *Legisprudence Through a Bankruptcy Lens: A Study in the Supreme Court's Bankruptcy Cases,* 47 Syracuse L. Rev. 1, 106-07 (1996); Robert K. Rasmussen, *A Study of the Costs and Benefits of Textualism: The Supreme Court's Bankruptcy Cases*, 71 Wash. U. L.Q. 535 (1993); Alan Schwartz, *The New Textualism and the Rule of Law Subtext in the Supreme Court's Bankruptcy Jurisprudence*, 45 N.Y. L. Sch. L. Rev. 149, 151 (2000-2001); Charles Jordan Tabb & Robert M. Lawless, *Of Commas, Gerunds, and Conjunctions: The Bankruptcy Jurisprudence of the Rehnquist Court*, 42 Syracuse L. Rev. 823 (1991); Ned Waxman, *Judicial Follies: Ignoring the Plain Meaning of Bankruptcy Code § 109(g)(2)*, 48 Ariz. L. Rev. 149 (2006).

[42] *E.g.*, William N. Eskridge, Jr., *The New Textualism*, 37 UCLA L. Rev. 621 (1990).

[43] *See* Dewsnup v. Timm, 502 U.S. 410 (1992) (Court used a "settled" preexisting practice to justify making a complete hash of the phrase "allowed secured claim").

[44] *See* Taylor v. Freeland & Kronz, 503 U.S. 638 (1992); Patterson v. Shumate, 504 U.S. 753 (1992); Toibb v. Radloff, 501 U.S. 157 (1991); United States v. Ron Pair Enter., 489 U.S. 235 (1989).

unsettled questions, particularly those that will inevitably arise under the cumbersome prose in the 2005 Amendments to the Bankruptcy Code.

§ 1.04 Constitutional Limits on Bankruptcy Law[45]

For all of the significance of bankruptcy law, there is little delineation of its constitutional boundaries. In a way, this is surprising. The power given by the Constitution to Congress to enact uniform laws on the subject of bankruptcy[46] carries with it potential powers nearly as broad as those contained in the Commerce Clause. However, this is not a power without limits. Most significantly, the same Constitution that permits bankruptcy also protects property rights.[47] At some point substantive bankruptcy law may impermissibly deprive creditors' property rights.[48] Courts have generally tried to dodge the constitutional issue, however, by interpreting the statutory language in a way that avoids the problem. The general assumption is that Congress may do virtually anything under its Bankruptcy Clause power that is reasonably related to dealing with insolvents, provided it acts prospectively.

§ 1.05 Basic Commercial Law Concepts & Bankruptcy Terminology

[A] Basic Concepts of Commercial & Related Business Law

This section contains a brief description of some very basic concepts about business and finance law that may be helpful to students who have no background in either. These concepts are an important background to bankruptcy law.

[1] "Debt" Claims and "Equity" Interests[49]

Broadly speaking, the financial structure of any business entity is divided into debt and equity. In its most basic form, debt is an absolute obligation

---

[45] Julia Patterson Forrester, *Bankruptcy Takings*, 51 Fla. L. Rev. 851 (1999); Thomas E. Plank, *The Constitutional Limits of Bankruptcy*, 63 Tenn. L. Rev. 487 (1996); Kurt Nadelmann, *On the Origin of the Bankruptcy Clause*, 1 Am. J. Legal Hist. 215 (1957); James S. Rogers, *The Impairment of Secured Creditors' Rights in Reorganization: A Study of the Relationship Between the Fifth Amendment and the Bankruptcy Clause*, 96 Harv. L. Rev. 973 (1983); Charles Jordan Tabb, *The History of the Bankruptcy Laws in the United States*, 3 Am. Bankr. Inst. L. Rev. 5 (1995).

[46] U.S. Const. art. I, § 8, cl. 4.

[47] U.S. Const. amend. V.

[48] *E.g.*, Louisville Joint Stock Land Bank v. Radford, 295 U.S. 555, 591–92, 601–02 (1935); James Steven Rogers, *The Impairment of Secured Creditors' Rights in Reorganization: A Study of the Relationship Between the Fifth Amendment and the Bankruptcy Clause*, 96 Harv. L. Rev. 973 (1983); Francis F. Gecker, Comment, *The Recovery of Opportunity Costs as Just Compensation: A Takings Analysis of Adequate Protection*, 81 Nw. U. L. Rev. 953 (1987).

[49] Apologies to those with a background in accounting.

owed to another entity. The obligation is "absolute" because it is owed regardless of the entity's financial health. Even if the entity is losing money, a debt must be paid according to its terms. By contrast, equity is the ownership of whatever value is left after all debts have been paid. If there is nothing left, the equity holder owns nothing. Owning equity is more of a risk than owning debt, because equity comes behind debt in the pecking order. On the other hand, equity holders have a chance to earn greater profits than debt holders.

For example, if you lent $1000 to Wal-Mart in 1970 at 7% interest for 40 years you would still receive a steady $70 per year and would reasonably expect repayment of your $1000 principal in 2010. If you had purchased Wal-Mart stock in the same year, your investment would probably be worth much more than what you paid for it and the dividends alone might well exceed your initial investment. In short, equity enjoys the unlimited benefits of success while bearing the greatest risk; debt enjoys lower risk at the cost of limited gain.

"Equity" is also used in business and related commercial and bankruptcy law in another important and related sense: in connection with the debtor's interest in a specific asset. When an asset is subject to a creditor's mortgage or security interest, the debtor's "equity" refers to the value of the asset in excess of the amount of the unpaid debt secured by the asset. Thus, if the debtor owns a building worth $1 million but subject to an outstanding $700,000 mortgage, the debtor is said to have "equity" worth $300,000 in the asset. Like the equity of a corporation, represented by the value of the corporation in excess of its debts, the equity a debtor owns in each of its individual assets is the amount by which the value of the asset exceeds the amount of debt secured by that particular asset.

[2] "Fiduciary Duty"

Most of our law is based on the notion that people are free to act in their own self-interest, as long as certain fundamental rules are obeyed. For example, every adult is obligated to act as a reasonably prudent person: you do not have the right to poison Uncle Mortimer's tea just because he has left you his vast fortune. However, in some relationships, often business relationships, one person owes another a fiduciary duty of loyalty, which means he or she must subordinate his or her own self-interest and act in the best interest of the person owed the duty.

In bankruptcy, this issue becomes important because both the trustee[50] and the debtor-in-possession[51] owe a fiduciary duty to the bankruptcy estate. They are supposed to devote their efforts to the best possible liquidation or reorganization: "best possible" being largely synonymous with maximum return to creditors.

---

[50] *See* § 1.05[B][36] "Trustee," *infra.*

[51] *See* § 1.05[B][16] "Debtor-in-Possession," *infra.*

[3] "Legal Entity" — Corporations and Partnerships

Under our law, living breathing human beings are not the only persons with property and other rights. Artificial entities, created primarily for business purposes (although including non-profits and municipalities), are also "persons" or "entities" with names, rights, and obligations. The most obvious example is a business corporation, organized under the law of a state or other type of government. Corporations may own property and act in their own right, although those actions, obviously, must be through the agency of human beings, or increasingly, computers.[52] Corporations are owned by their stockholders; however, with rare exceptions, these stockholders are not personally liable for the corporation's debts.[53]

Partnerships are another example. Although partnerships are often considered legal entities separate from their owners, partnerships are only partially independent of their owners. While a partnership can own property and act in its own right, ultimately, its general partners are personally liable for the partnership's debts. If the partnership has limited partners, however, those partners are more like stockholders in a corporation; they are not personally liable for partnership debts. There are many variations of these basic structures. A recently developed, and very popular one is the limited liability partnership. The exact attributes of the various types of legal entity, and the circumstances under which an owner is liable for an entity's debts, vary slightly from state to state.

Things are quite different if the business and the owner are one and the same. A business operated by a sole proprietor is not a separate legal entity. The business and its owner are legally identical. The Jeff Ferriell who files a Schedule "C" (business) tax form with his annual income tax return and receives an occasional small royalty from Lexis/Nexis is indistinguishable from the Jeff Ferriell who goes to the grocery store around the corner eight times a week[54] and sends a monthly check to the bank that holds the mortgage on his personal residence. Even though he might carefully keep his business income and expenses separate from his other financial affairs, this is purely for his own convenience. If he incurs liability to someone in pursuit of his business activities, his business creditors will be able to pursue any or all of his other non-exempt personal assets. Likewise, credit card companies who loan him money to finance a vacation, will be able, if necessary, to seek recovery from the assets (a computer and a couple of books) used to operate his publishing business. Further, the mere fact that Ferriell might give his business operations some sort of trade name, does not, by itself, change the fact that there is still only one legal entity involved: the living breathing human being born as the only son of Merlin and Frances Ferriell.

In bankruptcy, these rules remain. The stockholders of a bankrupt corporation are nearly always immune from personal liability for the

[52] *See* Model Bus. Corp. Act § 3.02 (2002).

[53] *E.g.*, Model Bus. Corp. Act § 6.22 (2002).

[54] He would go less frequently if the store were further than three blocks from his home.

corporation's debts. Limited partners are similarly immune from the partnership's obligations. General partners remain residually liable for the partnership's unpaid debts, although the bankruptcy of the partnership does not directly involve the partners, and vice-versa. A sole proprietorship bankruptcy is the bankruptcy of the individual who operates the sole proprietorship. His personal and business debts, as well as his personal and business assets, are treated together. There are a few significant differences between the bankruptcy of a sole proprietorship and a consumer bankruptcy, but these do not relate to nature of the legal entity who is the debtor.

[B] Terms of Art in Bankruptcy and Related Commercial Law[55]

In addition to these general business concepts, bankruptcy and related commercial law have a jargon all their own. What follows attempts to catalog the most important terms with which bankruptcy lawyers must be familiar.

[1] "Abuse"

In the context of early twenty-first century American bankruptcy law, "abuse" is used in reference to consumer debtors who are able to pay their debts but who nevertheless seek to discharge them through bankruptcy. The term is used in § 707(b), which permits the court to dismiss a Chapter 7 liquidation proceeding if the court finds that granting relief to the debtor would be "an abuse" of Chapter 7.[56] Whether a particular debtor's effort to use Chapter 7 would constitute such an abuse depends on a maddeningly complex calculation that seeks to determine if the debtor's income is sufficient, after deducting some of his presumed and actual living expenses, to pay what Congress has determined is a meaningful amount to his creditors. Chapter 7 cases filed by debtors who have the financial means to make meaningful payments to their creditors are to be dismissed and their lawyers possibly sanctioned.[57]

[2] "Adequate Protection"

"Adequate protection" refers to the protection given to secured creditors whose property rights might otherwise be impaired by delays or other procedures inherent in the bankruptcy process. In general, the Bankruptcy Code requires protection against a decline in the value of a secured creditor's collateral.

The most common situation in which the issue of adequate protection arises is in connection with the automatic stay of § 362. In general, § 362

[55] *See* Richard I. Aaron, *Hooray for Gibberish! A Glossary of Bankruptcy Slang for the Occasional Practitioner or Bewildered Judge*, 3 DePaul Bus. & Com. L.J. 141 (2005).

[56] Bankruptcy Code § 707(b)(1).

[57] *See* § 17.03[B] Dismissal of Consumer Cases Due to Abuse, *infra*.

prevents creditors from taking action outside of bankruptcy court, such as foreclosure, that might interfere with the bankrkuptcy process. However, if the debtor's property threatens to decline in value, the creditor's rights in the debtor's property may be harmed due to the delay caused by the bankruptcy proceeding. In this situation and others, a secured creditor may obtain relief from the automatic stay in the form of court permission to go ahead with a foreclosure proceeding, unless the creditor's rights in the debtor's property can be "adequately protected." Protection might take the form of cash payments, an insurance policy, additional collateral, or some other rights that protect the secured creditor from the threatened decline in the value of its collateral.[58]

Questions of adequate protection also arise if a business debtor wants to use one creditor's collateral as collateral for a loan from another creditor,[59] or if the debtor wants to sell or otherwise dissipate the creditor's collateral, such as inventory or cash.[60]

Many attorneys, particularly those who represent secured creditors, first encounter the Bankruptcy Code when they seek relief from the automatic stay and request the court's permission to foreclose on collateral, due to a lack of adequate protection.

[3] "Administrative Expense"

Administrative expenses are the "actual, necessary costs and expenses of preserving the [debtor's] estate, including wages, salaries, or commissions for services rendered after commencement of the case."[61] An administrative expense is given priority over other unsecured claims against the estate.[62] After all, the bankruptcy process, like lunch, isn't free. The costs of handling a bankruptcy case might include a wide variety of items that will be characterized as claims for administrative expenses, including claims of creditors who provide goods and services to the estate while the debtor's case is pending. Significantly, they include court-approved professional fees owed to the debtor's attorneys, accountants, investment bankers, and others involved in handling the bankruptcy case. They also include similar professional fees incurred by an official creditors' committee or a bankruptcy trustee, in a case where one is appointed.

Administrative expenses receive the highest priority among the claims entitled to any kind of priority under § 507. In a bankruptcy case with limited available assets, qualification for treatment as an administrative expense claim may easily determine whether the creditor receives any payment at all from the debtor's estate.

---

[58] Bankruptcy Code § 361.

[59] *See* Bankruptcy Code § 364.

[60] *See* Bankruptcy Code § 363; § 9.03 Use, Sale, or Lease of Estate Property, *infra*.

[61] Bankruptcy Code § 503(b)(1)(A).

[62] Bankruptcy Code § 507(a)(1); *see* § 10.04[A][2] Administrative Expense Claims, *infra*.

[4] "After Notice and a Hearing"

Numerous provisions of the Bankruptcy Code permit the court to enter an order or provide some other sort of relief "after notice and a hearing." Although the phrase suggests formal service to all interested parties and an in-court hearing in which these parties will be heard, nothing could be further from the truth. Bankruptcy Code § 102(1) indicates that the phrase "after notice and a hearing" means only "after such notice as is appropriate in the particular circumstances, and such opportunity for a hearing as is appropriate in the particular circumstances."[63] The definition "authorize[s] an act *without* an actual hearing if such notice is given properly and if (i) such a hearing is not requested timely by a party in interest; or (ii) there is insufficient time for a hearing to be commenced . . . and the court authorizes such act."[64] In other words, "after notice and a hearing" means some form of notice to someone and court authorization with or without a hearing, depending on whether someone insists on a hearing and on the exigencies involved in the circumstances.[65]

[5] "Allowed Claim"

A claim is a right to a legal or equitable remedy.[66] An "allowed claim" is a claim that is entitled to participate in the administration of the debtor's bankruptcy. As the modifier suggests, not all claims are allowed. Some are disallowed completely; others are limited.[67]

[6] "Bankruptcy Act" and "Bankruptcy Code"

When bankruptcy lawyers refer to the Bankruptcy Code, or more frequently, simply the Code, they mean the Bankruptcy Code that was adopted in 1978 and became effective in 1979, as it has been amended and is currently in force.[68] The Code's predecessor, originally enacted in 1898, was known as the "Bankruptcy Act." Because so many of the basic principles of the Bankruptcy Code are based on concepts and provisions found in the Bankruptcy Act, the Act and cases decided under it are still frequently relevant to questions that arise under the Code.

In reading cases, it is usually easy to determine whether the court is referring to the Act or to the Code. The Bankruptcy Act applied only to bankruptcy cases filed before October 1, 1979. The Bankruptcy Code applies to cases filed on or after that date. Of course, many cases filed before the transition from the old to the new law were pending and were still governed by the Act after the Code went into effect. In rare cases of doubt, or as a simple rule of thumb, cases decided under the Act can be easily detected

---

[63] Bankruptcy Code § 102(1)(A).

[64] Bankruptcy Code § 102(1)(b).

[65] *See, e.g.*, Fed. R. Bankr. P. 6004.

[66] Bankruptcy Code § 101(5).

[67] Bankruptcy Code § 502; *see* § 10.02[C] Allowance of Claims, *infra*.

[68] Bankruptcy Reform Act of 1978, Pub. L. No. 95-598, 92 Stat. 2629 (1977).

by their references to chapters of the bankruptcy law by Roman numerals, instead of by Arabic style numbers. Thus, liquidation cases governed by the old Bankruptcy Act refer to Chapter VII of the Act; liquidation cases governed by the current Bankruptcy Code refer to Chapter 7. Reorganization cases decided under the Act refer to Chapters X, XI, or XII; those handled under the Code cite to Chapters 11, 12, and 13.

[7] "Bankruptcy Administrator"

In two judicial districts, Alabama and North Carolina, the United States Trustee program does not operate. Instead, Bankruptcy Administrators perform the duties of the United States Trustee. Unlike the United States Trustee, which is an office in the United States Department of Justice and part of the Executive Branch, Bankruptcy Administrators are officers of the Judicial Branch and operate pursuant to regulations of the Judicial Conference of the United States, guidelines of the Administrative Office of the United States Courts, local rules, and court orders.

[8] "BAPCPA"

"BAPCPA" is the acronym used to refer to the 2005 amendments to the Bankruptcy Code, the Bankruptcy Abuse Prevention and Consumer Protection Act of 2005.[69] Every good piece of bankruptcy legislation needs an acronym. Though it is hard to pronounce, "BAPCPA"[70] stands for the "Bankruptcy Abuse Prevention and Consumer Protection Act of 2005."[71] It contains the most recent set of significant amendments to the Bankruptcy Code.[72] Most of BAPCPA's provisions went into effect on April 20, 2005.[73]

[9] "Cash Collateral"

"Cash collateral" is defined in § 363(a) as "cash, negotiable instruments, documents of title, securities, deposit accounts, or other cash equivalents whenever acquired in which the estate and an entity other than the estate have an interest."[74] This nearly always describes a situation in which a creditor, as an "entity other than the estate," has a security interest in these types of highly liquid assets. Because these types of assets are so easily spent or stolen, § 363 imposes restrictions on a debtor's ability to dispose of them without the creditor's consent.[75] Instead, court approval is

[69] Pub. L. No. 109-8, 119 Stat. 216 (2005).

[70] Pronounced "bap -cee -pa"

[71] Bankruptcy Abuse Prevention and Consumer Protection Act of 2005, Pub. L. No. 109-8, 119 Stat. 23 (2005).

[72] Some commentators have suggested that the absence of any evidence to show that there was extensive abuse of the Bankruptcy Code before BAPCPA, and the statute's failure to provide meaningful protection for consumers, makes the name misleading.

[73] Bankruptcy Abuse Prevention and Consumer Protection Act of 2005 § 1501, Pub. L. No. 109-8, 119 Stat. 23, 216 (2005).

[74] Bankruptcy Code § 363(a).

[75] *See* § 9.03[B] Use of "Cash Collateral," *infra*.

required, and is usually only granted if the creditor's interest is adequately protected.

[10] "Claim"

A "claim" is defined by the Bankruptcy Code as a creditor's right to payment or some other remedy.[76] The term is broadly defined in § 101(5) to embrace a creditor's right, regardless of whether the right is "reduced to judgment, fixed, contingent, matured, unmatured, disputed, undisputed, secured, or unsecured."[77] This broad definition of "claim" reflects the effect of a bankruptcy case on creditor's rights that otherwise might not yet be due or that might be subject to some contingency other than the passage of time. Thus, if a debtor files a bankruptcy petition six months before a debt to one of its creditors becomes due, the creditor has a claim, even though the debt has not yet matured. Likewise, a guarantor of one of the debtor's obligations has a claim even though the debtor's liability to the guarantor remains contingent on the guarantor making some payment to the creditor on the debt the creditor guaranteed.

The breadth of the definition of a "claim" reflects the significance of its role in the Bankruptcy Code. Bankruptcy proceedings provide the debtor with relief from "claims" and are intended to operate as a comprehensive proceeding to resolve all of the debtor's financial difficulties. Any limitation on the scope of the definition of a claim would operate as a limitation on the scope of relief provided by a bankruptcy case. Accordingly, the Supreme Court has consistently applied the term broadly, reflecting the position that the Bankruptcy Code "contemplates that all legal obligations of the debtor . . . will be able to be dealt with in a bankruptcy case."[78] This has been interpreted to include claims held by those who are not yet aware of the injuries they have suffered.

[11] "Consumer Debt"

Several provisions of the Bankruptcy Code provide special rules that apply only to "consumer debts." A consumer debt is a "debt incurred by an individual primarily for a personal, family, or household purpose."[79]

[12] "Current Monthly Income"

"Current monthly income" is a new term, added as part of the 2005 Bankruptcy Code Amendments[80] as a foundation for "means testing"[81] to

---

[76] Bankruptcy Code § 101(5); *see* § 11.02[A] Definition of Claim, *infra;* Johnson v. Home State Bank 501 U.S. 78 (1991) (creditor's right to foreclose mortgage to satisfy discharged debt); Pennsylvania Dept of Pub. Welfare v. Davenport, 495 U.S. 552 (1990) (obligation to make restitution as condition of probation); United States v. Kovacs, 469 U.S. 274 (1985) (state court judgment requiring the removal of hazardous waste).

[77] Bankruptcy Code § 101(5).

[78] Pennsylvania Dept. of Pub. Welfare v. Davenport, 495 U.S. 552, 558 (1990).

[79] Bankruptcy Code § 101(8).

[80] Bankruptcy Code § 101(10A).

[81] *See* § 1.05[B][26] "Means Testing," *infra.*

determine if the debtor is eligible for Chapter 7 relief.[82] It is also sometimes used in reference to the process of determining the amount of projected disposable income a Chapter 13 debtor is required to pay to his unsecured creditors through his Chapter 13 rehabilitation plan.[83] According to § 101(10A), a debtor's current monthly income is determined by dividing the total income earned during the six-month period immediately prior to the bankruptcy petition by 6.[84]

[13] "Debt"

"Debt" simply means "liability on a claim."[85] Thus, if a creditor holds a claim, the debtor's obligation to pay that claim is a debt. This "obligation to pay" is vulnerable to discharge in a bankruptcy proceeding.[86]

[14] "Debt Relief Agency"[87]

In 2005, the Bankruptcy Code imposed new regulations on attorneys who represent consumer debtors. It imposes these same restrictions on others who, though they are not licensed attorneys, assist consumer debtors in preparing bankruptcy petitions. These regulations apply to anyone who qualifies as a "debt relief agency." The term applies to "any person who provides any bankruptcy assistance to an assisted person in return for the payment of money or other valuable consideration, or who is a bankruptcy petition preparer."[88] An "assisted person" is any person whose debts are primarily consumer debts, incurred for personal, family, or household purposes,[89] with non-exempt property worth less than $150,000.[90] The term "debt relief agency" expressly excludes officers, directors, employees or agents of debt relief agencies, non-profit organizations, creditors, banks, and authors of books such as this one.[91] For the most part, the term applies to those who used to be called "consumer bankruptcy lawyers."

By characterizing them as debt relief agencies, the Bankruptcy Code subjects many bankruptcy attorneys to a wide variety of new regulations. They are required to enter into express written contracts with their client[92]

---

[82] *See* § 1.05[B][1] "Abuse," *supra.*

[83] *See* § 18.08[E][2] Debtor's Projected Disposable Income, *infra.*

[84] *See* § 17.03[B][2][a] Current Monthly Income, *infra.*

[85] Bankruptcy Code § 101(12).

[86] United States v. Kovacs, 469 U.S. 274 (1985) (state court judgment requiring the removal of hazardous waste was discharged).

[87] Terry Carter, *The Exodus Begins: Lawyers Wonder Whether Chapter 7 Will be a Viable Practice Area under New Law,* 91 A.B.A. J. 12 (2005); Gary Neustadter, *A Consumer Bankruptcy Odyssey,* 39 Creighton L. Rev. 225 (2006); Catherine E. Vance & Corrine Cooper, *Nine Traps and One Slap: Attorney Liability Under the New Bankruptcy Law,* 79 Am. Bankr. L.J. 283 (2005).

[88] Bankruptcy Code § 101(12A).

[89] Bankruptcy Code § 101(8).

[90] Bankruptcy Code § 101(3).

[91] Bankruptcy Code § 101(3).

[92] Bankruptcy Code § 528(a)(1).

and provide them with a set of very specific disclosures and training.[93] If they advertise the availability of their services, they are required to include a set of very specific disclosures in the text of their advertisements.[94] In addition, they are exposed to liability if they fail to meet certain explicit professional responsibilities that must be performed by attorneys and others who provide bankruptcy assistance to clients.[95]

[15] "Debtor"

"Debtor" has several closely related meanings, depending on the context in which the term is used. In its more general sense, it simply refers to a person who owes a debt, such as a person who has borrowed money to buy a house or a car or to expand or operate a business. When used in this generic way, it might also refer to a person who is liable for a tort. A person whose obligation has been adjudicated by a court might be referred to as a "judgment debtor."

"Debtor" is also used in a more precise manner by Article 9 of the Uniform Commercial Code to refer either to a person who owns an interest in personal property or fixtures used as collateral for a loan, or to the seller of "accounts, chattel paper, promissory notes, or payment intangibles," as those terms are further defined by Article 9.[96] When used in this context, the person to whom the term refers might not be obligated to pay a debt. For example, if Bill grants his brother Jim's Bank a security interest in his car as collateral for a loan that the bank made to Jim, Article 9 would refer to Bill as a debtor even though Bill has no obligation to repay Jim's debt. Likewise, if Autohaus sells its accounts receivable to the Merchant's Finance Company, Article 9 labels Autohaus a debtor, even though it did not borrow money from the finance company and owes no debt as a result of the sale.

When it appears in Bankruptcy Code, "debtor" refers to the entity that is the subject of a bankruptcy case.[97] The term that used to refer to the subject of a bankruptcy filing was the "bankrupt." However, because of the stigma attached to the term, it does not appear anywhere in the Bankruptcy Code. Thus, an individual, partnership, or corporation who files a bankruptcy case is consistently referred to merely as the debtor.

[16] "Debtor-in-Possession"

The filing of every bankruptcy case results in the creation of an estate which is comprised of the property owned by the debtor when the case began.[98] In liquidation cases, a trustee is appointed to liquidate the assets

[93] Bankruptcy Code § 527.

[94] Bankruptcy Code § 528(a)(3)-(4), (b).

[95] Bankruptcy Code § 526.

[96] U.C.C. § 9-105(1)(d) (2003).

[97] Bankruptcy Code § 101(13).

[98] Bankruptcy Code § 541(a).

of the estate and to distribute the proceeds to creditors. In chapter 11 cases, the appointment of a trustee is rare. Instead, the debtor remains in possession of the estate. Thus, "debtor-in-possession" or "DIP"[99] literally means "the debtor" in a Chapter 11 case.[100]

Although referring to the debtor as the "debtor-in-possession" might seem superfluous, it reflects the fact that the filing of a petition has resulted in the creation of a new legal entity, the estate. Although the estate's name and address might remain the same as that of the debtor, the estate is a separate legal entity that is governed by procedures that do not apply to entities who are not the subject of a bankruptcy case. In this respect, referring to the debtor as the "debtor-in-possession" helps not only to distinguish chapter 11 cases in which a trustee has been appointed, but also reminds the individuals responsible for managing the estate that they have a set of responsibilities that are different from those they had when their duties ran only to the debtor's shareholders, and not to its creditors.

In smaller Chapter 12 reorganization cases involving family farmers and family fishermen,[101] and in Chapter 13 reorganizations involving individuals with regular income,[102] a trustee is appointed but does not take possession or control of all of the property of the estate. Instead, the debtor remains in possession of these assets and is thus a "debtor-in-possession" in the literal (if not the technical) sense of the term. Because Chapter 12 cases always involve the operation of a business, Chapter 12 debtors are formally accorded the title "debtor-in-possession" and are supplied with most of the rights that would otherwise be exercised by the trustee.[103]

[17] Domestic Support Obligation

Domestic support obligations are defined broadly to include nearly every imaginable type of support obligation[104] owed to the debtor's spouse, a former spouse, the debtor's child, a parent or guardian of the debtor's child, or even to a governmental unit.[105] Domestic support obligations cannot be discharged in a liquidation case and must be paid in full as priority claims in reorganization cases.

[18] "Estate"

When a bankruptcy case is filed, an "estate" is created much as it is when a person dies.[106] Just as a decedent's estate is comprised of all of the

---

[99] When abbreviated in this fashion, the term is usually pronounced as "dee, eye, pea" rather than as a single syllable word, "dip."

[100] Bankruptcy Code § 1101(1).

[101] *See* Chapter 20, Family Farmer and Family Fisherman Reorganization, *infra.*

[102] *See* Chapter 18, Rehabilitation of Individuals with Regular Income, *infra.*

[103] Bankruptcy Code § 1203; *see* § 20.03[A] Chapter 12 Debtor-in-Possession, *infra.*

[104] Section 101(14A)(B) includes any such debt that is "in the nature of alimony, maintenance, or support (including assistance provided by a governmental unit . . . whether such debt is expressly so designated." Bankruptcy Code § 101(14A)(B).

[105] Bankruptcy Code § 101(14A)(A).

[106] Bankruptcy Code § 541(a).

property owned by the decedent at the time of his death, a bankruptcy estate is comprised of all of the property owned by the debtor when the bankruptcy case was commenced.[107] In reorganization cases, the debtor's estate includes property acquired by the debtor after the case has begun.

[19] "Executory Contract"

In the law of contracts, a contract is regarded as "executory" if some material duties of the contract have not yet been performed. In bankruptcy law, an "executory contract" is one in which, at the time the bankruptcy petition was filed, *both* parties had material duties remaining to be performed.[108] Thus, if a contractor has finished building an addition to the debtor's home, but has not yet been paid, the contract would not be regarded by the Bankruptcy Code as an executory contract, even though the debtor's obligation remains executory. Instead, the contractor would have an unsecured claim. Likewise, if the debtor had paid the contractor in advance, but the contractor had not yet substantially performed its duty to build the addition, the contract would not be an executory contract under the bankruptcy code, even though contract law would regard the contractor's duty as executory in the ordinary sense. Instead, the debtor would have the right to enforce the non-debtor's obligation under the applicable contract law. But, if neither party had performed all of its duties at the time of the debtor's bankruptcy petition, the contract would be governed by the Code's rules dealing with executory contracts.

Subject to many exceptions and qualifications, the bankruptcy trustee, or the debtor-in-possession in a reorganization case, has the right to either assume (perform) or reject (breach) both executory contracts and unexpired leases to which the debtor was a party at the time its petition was filed.[109] If the contract is rejected, the other party has a claim against the estate for breach. If the contract is assumed, the estate becomes bound by the contract and any subsequent breach gives rise to a priority claim. In some cases, the debtor may assume an executory contract, but then assign it to some other person who becomes obligated to the non-debtor party, and the debtor is relieved from responsibility for performing the contract as if there had been a novation.

[20] "Exemption"

"Exemption" refers to the right of individual debtors to keep some of their property away from both creditors and the bankruptcy trustee. In bankruptcy, a debtor's exemption rights, which usually apply to property deemed necessary for the routine aspects of life, are an important part of the debtor's fresh start.[110]

[107] Bankruptcy Code § 541(a); *see* Chapter 7, Property of the Estate, *infra.*

[108] *See* § 11.02[A] "Executory Contract" Defined, *infra.*

[109] Bankruptcy Code § 365; *see* § 10.01 Right to Assume or Reject; Assignment, *infra.*

[110] *See* § 12.02 Exemptions in Bankruptcy, *infra.*

All states provide debtors with some exemption rights. In state collection proceedings, property covered by a state exemption statute is immune from collection by a judgment creditor who does not have a mortgage, security interest, or statutory lien on the property protected by the exemption. Exemption statutes generally ensure that creditors do not leave debtors with nothing but the shirts on their backs, or nothing at all.

Although a wide variety of types of property are protected by state exemptions, most states provide some protection for a limited quantity of clothing, furniture, and household appliances.[111] Likewise, most states provide exemptions for at least one motor vehicle, limited tools of a debtor's trade, and any medically necessary health aids. In addition, the traditional American dream of home ownership is so powerful that most states provide at least limited protection for a debtor's equity in a home,[112] even though renters do not receive similar protection for equivalent assets.

Exemptions are preserved in bankruptcy. Section 522(b) supplies most debtors with the same set of exemption rights in bankruptcy that they would enjoy in a collection proceeding in state court. In some states, whose legislatures have not "opted-out" of the federal exemption scheme,[113] debtors enjoy a choice between the exemptions provided by their own state's exemption statute and a set of federal exemptions set out in the Bankruptcy Code.[114]

As explained more fully elsewhere, exemptions generally do not provide the debtor with protection from security interests and mortgages that the debtor has voluntarily granted to creditors. With very limited exceptions,[115] exemptions only protect a debtor's assets from the claims of unsecured creditors. A debtor who has voluntarily granted a creditor a security interest in what otherwise would have been an exempt asset, is not entitled to assert the exemption to prevent the creditor from foreclosing its security interest against the collateral.[116]

[21] "Fraudulent Transfer"

The classic definition of "fraudulent transfer" is a transfer by a debtor made with the "intent to hinder, delay, or defraud" its creditors.[117] The

---

[111] *See, e.g.*, Ohio Rev. Code § 2329.66 (LexisNexis Supp. 2006).

[112] *See* Joseph McKnight, *Protection of the Family Home from Seizure by Creditors: The Sources and Evolution of a Legal Principle*, 86 S.W. Hist. L.Q. 364 (1983). Differences in the extent of this protection, from one state to the next, are dramatic. In Ohio, a debtor may exempt up to $5,000 of equity in real estate used as the debtor's residence. Ohio Rev. Code § 2329.66 (LexisNexis Supp. 2006). In Texas, which since its inception as the Lone Star Republic has been regarded as a debtor's haven, debtor's may retain up to 10 acres of land in an urban area and up to 200 acres in a rural location. Tex. Prop. Code Ann. § 41.0002 (Vernon 2000).

[113] *See* § 12.02[B] State or Federal Exemptions; Opt-Out, *infra*.

[114] Bankruptcy Code § 522(d).

[115] *See* § 12.07 Avoiding Liens on Exempt Property, *infra*.

[116] *See* § 12.05[B] Liens on Exempt Property, *infra*.

[117] Unif. Fraudulent Trans. Act § 4(a)(1) (1984); *see* § 16.02[A] Actual Fraud, *infra*.

most obvious example occurs when a debtor transfers possession of her property to a close friend or family member so that it can be hidden from her creditors.

A transfer might also be treated as fraudulent, despite the lack of any evil intent on the debtor's part, if the transfer was made by an insolvent debtor for inadequate consideration.[118] Thus, the transfer is also fraudulent if the price for which it was sold deprives the debtor's creditors of its value, even if the debtor lacked any intent to deprive the creditors of its value. In a bankruptcy case, the trustee usually has the right to recover property fraudulently transferred by the debtor before his bankruptcy petition was filed for the benefit of all of the debtor's creditors.[119]

[22] "Interest"

In the context of a book on debt collection and bankruptcy, it might be thought that the term "interest" would most commonly be used to refer to a finance charge imposed by a creditor for a loan, usually at some specific annual percentage rate. This, of course, is an important and common meaning of the word.

"Interest" is also used to refer to property interests of all types. In the Bankruptcy Code, it is used in this general sense, but in a more technical way, to refer to an ownership interest in a debtor, such as stock or a partnership interest. Thus, a stockholder who owns shares of a corporation in bankruptcy would be regarded as the holder of an interest in the debtor.[120] Likewise, the individual partners of a partnership hold an interest in the partnership.

[23] "Letter of Credit"

A "letter of credit" is an irrevocable guarantee of payment of a sum of money to its beneficiary, subject to certain very precise conditions. Documentary letters of credit are commonly issued by banks and other financial institutions to facilitate payment to the buyer in a related contract for the sale of goods. The issuer of the letter of credit promises in writing to pay a sum of money to the beneficiary if the beneficiary supplies the issuer with a specific set of documents. When used in connection with a sale of goods, these documents usually include a draft ordering the buyer to pay for the goods, a bill of lading or other document of title showing that the goods have been delivered to a carrier for transportation to the buyer's location, any necessary customs documents showing that the goods have not been smuggled into the country, and sometimes inspection certificates indicating that the goods in the seller's shipping containers are what they purport to be. If the documents comply with the requirements of the letter of credit,

---

[118] Unif. Fraudulent Trans. Act § 5(a) (1984); *see* 16.03 Constructive Fraud, *infra*.

[119] *See* Chapter 15, Avoidable Preferences, *infra*.

[120] *See* Bankruptcy Code § 1111.

the issuer is, in most cases, obligated to pay. Usually, the documents are in order and the issuer provides payment to the beneficiary in due course.

Letters of credit are also frequently used in the place of a commercial bond. Unlike documentary letters of credit, these "standby" letters of credit are to be drawn on only if something occurs to disrupt the underlying transaction or to impair payment or performance of the parties' underlying obligations. Standby letters of credit are commonly used in construction contracts to ensure payment by the owner of the project or performance by the contractor. For example, if the contractor fails to substantially perform its duties, the owner will demand payment from the issuer of the credit, usually by presenting a certificate from the owner's architect or perhaps from some independent consulting firm or even a government agency, indicating that the contractor's work is incomplete or deficient. As with documentary letters of credit, the issuer's obligation to pay depends on whether the presented documents comply with the terms of the letter of credit, not on whether the contractor's performance was actually substandard.

Because letters of credit supply an alternative source of payment for obligations for which a bankrupt debtor might otherwise be responsible, they frequently play a role in bankruptcy proceedings.

[24] "Lien"

A "lien" is an interest in specific property that secures payment or performance of an obligation.[121] A creditor with a lien usually has the right to have the property subject to the lien sold and the resulting proceeds used to satisfy the debt secured by the lien. Assume, for example, that Merchant's Bank has a lien on Bart's $18,000 car, securing Bart's obligation to pay a $15,000 debt. Merchant's Bank has the right to have the car sold and to have the first $15,000 of the amount received from the sale allocated to payment of Bart's debt to the bank. Because the bank does not own the car outright, but only holds a lien on the vehicle, the $3,000 surplus remaining after payment of Bart's debt must be remitted to Bart upon the conclusion of the sale.

Liens arise from one of three possible sources. Consensual liens, like mortgages and Article 9 security interests that arise by agreement between the parties. The Bankruptcy Code refers to all such contractually created liens as "security interests."[122] Second, judicial liens are imposed on a debtor's property by a court, usually pursuant to a judgment obtained by the creditor against the debtor.[123] Third, statutory liens are imposed by the legislature, usually to benefit a favored class of creditors, such as

---

[121] *See* Bankruptcy Code § 101(37) (defining a lien as a "charge against or interest in property to secure payment of a debt or performance of an obligation").

[122] Bankruptcy Code § 101(51).

[123] The Bankruptcy Code defines it as a "lien obtained by judgment, levy, sequestration, or other legal or equitable process or proceeding." Bankruptcy Code § 101(36).

mechanics, contractors and subcontractors in the construction industry, or tax authorities, like the IRS.[124]

[25] "Lien Stripping"

"Lien stripping" is a colloquial term used by bankruptcy lawyers that refers to the reduction of the amount of a secured claim to the value of the collateral. For example, if a creditor is owed $10,000 but the collateral for the debt is worth only $7,000, the claim is only partially secured. If the creditor foreclosed, it would receive the $7,000 value of the collateral, plus whatever it could otherwise recover on account of the $3,000 deficiency. If the debtor was insolvent, the deficiency claim might result in little or no recovery. In some situations, debtors are permitted to "strip the lien" away from the collateral for all but the secured portion of the debt.

There is considerable controversy over the extent to which the Bankruptcy Code should permit lien stripping, particularly in reorganization settings where the debtor retains possession of the collateral. If, after making partial payment, the debtor defaults on the terms of its reorganization plan, the collateral would remain subject to the creditor's lien only for the amount of the unpaid balance of the secured claim, even though the unsecured portion of the original debt might remain unpaid. Conversely, if the lien is not stripped away from the unsecured portion of the debt, the creditor could use the collateral, to the extent of whatever value it retains, to satisfy the entire outstanding balance of both portions of the original debt. Lien stripping also deprives the creditor of any appreciation in the value of the collateral. Even worse, it deprives the creditor of any higher value of the collateral that the bankruptcy court might mistakenly have failed to recognize when it permitted the lien to be stripped down in the first place.

Lien stripping is an issue not only in reorganization cases under Chapters 11, 12, and 13, but also in liquidation cases where the debtor seeks to redeem the collateral from a security interest by paying the creditor the amount of the allowed secured claim. Lien stripping is unavailable in some situations, most notably with respect to mortgages on residential real estate. In addition, the 2005 amendments prevent lien stripping in connection with purchase money security interests on motor vehicles the debtor purchased during the two-and-a-half-year period immediately prior to the debtor's bankruptcy petition.

[26] "Means Testing"

"Means testing" refers generally to the eligibility for bankruptcy relief for debtors who have sufficient financial "means" to pay a portion of their debts. Under BAPCPA, means testing denies access to Chapter 7 to debtors

---

124 *See* Bankruptcy Code § 101(53).

whom the statute deems able to make meaningful payments to their creditors from their future income.[125]

More specifically, "means testing" refers to the complicated formula added to the Bankruptcy Code in 2005 that is used to determine whether a debtor's attempt to discharge her debts in a Chapter 7 liquidation case would be an "abuse" and thus whether the debtor's case should be dismissed.[126] When used in the context of a Chapter 13 bankruptcy case, it refers to the similar standards used to determine how much of a debtor's anticipated future income must be paid to her unsecured creditors under the terms of a Chapter 13 rehabilitation plan.[127]

[27] "No Asset Case"

"No asset case" refers to a Chapter 7 liquidation case in which no assets are available for distribution to unsecured creditors. The overwhelming majority of consumer liquidation cases are no asset cases. In these cases, all of the debtor's property is either exempt or subject to valid security interests and mortgages, leaving no non-exempt equity for the trustee to sell and distribute to creditors. The only compensation the trustee receives is a portion of the debtor's filing fee. The notice that is sent to creditors in these cases, formally advising them of the debtor's petition, alerts them to the fact that there are no assets available for distribution. It instructs them not to waste their time filing a proof of claim.

[28] "Preference"

A "preference" is a payment or other transfer to a creditor on the eve of bankruptcy, which enables the creditor to receive more than it otherwise would have received in the debtor's bankruptcy case.[128] The bankruptcy trustee enjoys the right to recover such pre-petition transfers so that the recovered property may be shared with all of the debtor's creditors. Left unrecovered, pre-petition preferences would frustrate the equal treatment policy of the Bankruptcy Code and give creditors an incentive to act aggressively to recover payment from a debtor before a bankruptcy case is filed.

[29] "Present Value"

"Present value" refers to the current value of a stream of future payments. It is a particularly important concept in reorganization and rehabilitation cases under chapters 11, 12 and 13 of the Bankruptcy Code. Present value is simply a way of describing the value today of payments that are to be

[125] Gary Neustadter, *A Consumer Bankruptcy Odyssey,* 39 Creighton L. Rev. 225, 271–300 (2006); Eugene W. Wedoff, *Means Testing in the New 707(b)*, 79 Am. Bankr. L.J. 231, 235 (2005).

[126] *See* § 17.03[B] Dismissal of Consumer Cases due to Abuse, *infra.*

[127] *See* § 18.08[E][2] Debtor's Projected Disposable Income, *infra.*

[128] Bankruptcy Code § 547(b); *see* Chapter 15, Avoidable Preferences, *infra.*

made in the future. One million dollars today is worth more than one million dollars received a year from now. Likewise, five annual $200,000 payments made over a five-year period are worth less than $1 million received right away.[129]

The reason for this is simple: $1,000 invested today will usually earn a future return in the form of interest, dividends, rents, or other profits. The same amount of money received a year from today cannot be invested until it is received. Thus, $1,000 received a year from today has a present value of less than $1,000 received today. If we assume that we could make an investment today and get a total of 5% per annum income, then the present value of $1,000 to be received one year from today is only $952.38. To put it the other way, if you invest $952.38 today at 5% per annum simple interest (that is, not compounded) then exactly one year from today you will have $1,000.[130]

At the most basic level, the calculation of present value is relatively easy, thanks to personal computers and electronic calculators. The difficult part is determining the appropriate "discount rate" to reduce a stream of future payments to their present value. The discount rate should represent the expected yield that would be produced by investment of the property. There are two problems in setting this yield. First, is that investment yields are not stable over time. They vary with supply and demand and are significantly affected by inflation rates.[131] It is sometimes difficult to predict interest rates for a five-week period, let alone for five years. The best a court can do is make a reasonable estimate. Inevitably there will be a degree of error in the calculation; and the error generally increases with time. Thus, the chance that payments made over a long period of time will in fact have a present value equal to the stated dollar amount is vanishingly small.[132] For this reason, courts have often been influenced by any interest rate previously agreed to by the parties.

Second, yields vary according to the risk involved in the investment, including the risk of non-payment. Quite high nominal rates of return can be earned on investments that have a high probability of going into default. The appropriate method for taking these risks into account has been cast into significant doubt by the Supreme Court's recent decision in *Till v. SCS*

---

[129] Readers who doubt this should contact the authors, either of whom would probably be interested in entering into a long-term business transaction with the doubter.

[130] Note that this example, like others used in this book, ignores tax effects of the investment. At times, it is necessary to make adjustments to offset differences in the tax treatment of the basic payment and the income on that payment. This is a simplifying assumption that does not change the basic point regarding the time value of money.

[131] Roughly speaking, high inflation tends to cause investment to move from financial instruments to tangibles, such as real property and non-perishable goods; when the supply of investment capital available to borrowers shrinks, the price of money, in the form of the rate of interest, rises.

[132] One way to avoid this problem, although it appears not to be widely used in bankruptcy cases, is for the future payments to include a variable rate of interest that increases or decreases in accordance with a set standard, such as the prime rate.

Credit.[133] *Till* will be discussed further in the chapters on confirming Chapter 11 and 13 plans.

[30] "Priority Claim"

A "priority claim" is an unsecured claim that is entitled to priority under one of the categories of priority in Bankruptcy Code § 507.[134] As the term suggests, priority claims receive better treatment in bankruptcy than "general" or "non-priority" claims. In liquidation cases under Chapter 7, priority claims are paid after secured claims have been satisfied but before general unsecured claims. In reorganization and rehabilitation cases under Chapters 11, 12 and 13, priority claims are entitled to payment in full. Moreover, in Chapter 11 reorganization cases, most priority claims are entitled to payment in full in cash as soon as the plan is consummated.

A few limited claims are entitled to super-priority treatment; they are to be paid ahead of all other priority claims in a very specific order of priority. At the bottom of this highest rung of the priority ladder are super-priority claims under § 507(b), designed to compensate creditors whose "adequate protection" turned out not to be so adequate. One step higher are super-duper-priority claims under § 363(c)(1) for post-petition credit, approved by the court for this treatment. At the very top rung are super-super-duper priority claims of a liquidating chapter 7 trustee under § 726(b) for expenses incurred in liquidating the debtor after a failed attempt to reorganize its affairs under chapter 11.[135] This complicated hierarchy of claims matters little, except of course when the estate is too small to satisfy claims on one of the lower tiers. When few assets are available to satisfy claims of priority creditors, even super-priority claims may end up unpaid due to the size of claims entitled to more senior priority.

[31] "Reaffirmation"

Reaffirmation refers to the process through which Chapter 7 debtors sometimes enter into a new legally enforceable agreement to repay a discharged debt. Debtors enter into reaffirmation agreements so that they can keep the collateral that secures the underlying debt. Although bankruptcy discharges secured debts, it does not usually impair creditors' security interests in property supplied as collateral for these debts. Thus, even though the debt is discharged, the creditor may repossess the collateral. If the debtor wishes to keep the property he must usually enter into a settlement agreement with the secured creditor, "reaffirming" his promise to pay the debt. Reaffirmation agreements usually call for the debtor to make regular monthly installment payments, over a period of time, in full satisfaction of the debt owed to the creditor, even if the collateral is worth less than the amount owed. Because reaffirmination agreements can leave

---

133 Till v. SCS Credit Corp., 541 U.S. 465 (2004).

134 Bankruptcy Code § 507; *see* § 10.04[A] Priority Claims, *infra.*

135 *See* § 10.04[B] Super-Priority Claims, *infra.*

a debtor in as much financial trouble as before he or she filed for bankruptcy, they are regulated by § 524(c), as more fully described elsewhere.

[32] "Redeem" and "Redemption"

"Redeem" and "redemption" refer to a debtor's right to recover collateral that secures a debt by paying the creditor a lump sum in satisfaction of all or part of the secured debt. Under state law, a debtor usually has the right to redeem his property from a lien by paying the full amount of the debt secured by the lien.[136]

Under the Bankruptcy Code, debtors sometimes have the right to redeem their property from a lien by paying the creditor the amount of the debt or the value of the collateral, whichever is lower. Thus, if the debtor owns a lawn tractor worth $800, subject to a security interest securing a $1000 debt, the debtor might redeem by paying only $800, rather than the full $1000 he would need to pay under state law. Although this seems like a considerable advantage, few bankrupt debtors have enough cash available to exercise this right. These debtors must either enter into a reaffirmation agreement with the creditor on whatever terms the creditor is willing to accept, or turn the collateral over to the creditor.

[33] "Secured Claim"

A "secured claim" is a key concept in bankruptcy. It refers to the secured portion of a creditor's claim, as determined by § 506 of the Bankruptcy Code. Under § 506, a claim is secured "to the extent of the value of such creditor's interest in the estate's interest in such property."[137] Any remaining claim of the creditor, beyond the value of the creditor's interest in the property, is usually treated as an unsecured claim.

The secured portion of a creditor's claim is the amount of the outstanding debt secured by the claim or the value of the collateral, whichever is lower. For example, if Capital Manufacturing owes Brooklyn Bank $100,000, which is secured by Capital's equipment worth only $70,000, then the bank's secured claim would be $70,000. The bank would have an unsecured claim for the remaining $30,000. If the equipment was worth $120,000, then Brooklyn's secured claim would be $100,000 and would be considered "fully secured."

This example illustrates the importance of the value of the collateral in determining whether a claim is fully secured or only partially secured. In many cases where the debtor plans to continue using the collateral, its value, based on what it could be sold for on the open market, will be indeterminable. Without conducting such a sale, the true value of the collateral and thus the amount of the secured claim depends on the court's determination of its value, based on the best available expert testimony,

---

[136] *See, e.g.*, U.C.C. § 9-623 (2003).

[137] Bankruptcy Code § 506(a).

using the applicable valuation standard. In most cases, expert testimony will conflict.

Moreover, which legal standard should be used to determine the value of the collateral may not be certain. Most types of property have different values, depending on the market in which they will be sold. As anyone who has attempted to trade in a used car knows, the retail value of the car may far outstrip its wholesale or trade-in value. Moreover, the value of the vehicle at the time of forced auction in a liquidation sale may be dramatically different from the replacement cost of a similar item.[138]

[34] "Security Interest"

The term "security interest" usually refers to a lien in personal property or fixtures, created by agreement and governed by Article 9 of the Uniform Commercial Code.[139] In Article 9, it also refers to the interest of a buyer of accounts, chattel paper, promissory notes, or payment intangibles.[140]

When the term "security interest" appears in the Bankruptcy Code, it refers to a lien on any kind of property that was created by agreement.[141]

[35] "Surety" (or "Guarantor")

A "surety," or "guarantor," is someone who is obligated to pay a debt primarily owed by someone else.[142] Family members commonly agree to become sureties for a relative's debts. For example, parents might enter into an agreement with a bank to repay a loan made to one of their children in the event that the child fails to pay the loan when it becomes due. In this situation, the guarantee is little more than a gift.[143] In a business setting, the controlling shareholders of a private corporation might personally guarantee a debt owed by the corporation. Without such a guarantee from the persons responsible for the success of the corporation, a bank may be unwilling to provide financing to the corporation. In other situations,

---

[138] One of your authors was once dismayed to learn that the value of his recently deceased mother's car, a "low-mileage teal-green Audi A-4, with a standard transmission" was considerably lower than he expected. According to the auctioneer, the color made it a "chick car" while the standard 4-speed transmission made it a "guys car." The men who showed up for the auction didn't want to drive a teal-green car, and the women who expressed an initial interest were turned off by the standard transmission. If he'd had any sense, your co-author, who liked the teal-green color, would have kept the car for himself and his wife, both of whom who happen to prefer driving a car with a standard transmission. They now own a royal blue BMW 325xi, with a standard transmission. Your other author's parents are alive and well.

[139] U.C.C. § 1-201(b)(35) (2003).

[140] U.C.C. § 1-201(b)(35) (2003).

[141] Bankruptcy Code § 101(51).

[142] *See* Restatement (Third) of Suretyship and Guaranty § 1 (1996). When a person signs a negotiable instrument, such as a promissory note, in order to facilitate a loan to someone else who is also liable on the instrument, the guarantor is also referred to, by Article 3 of the U.C.C., as an "accommodation party." U.C.C. § 3-419(a) (2003).

[143] When the loan is conditioned on the parent's guarantee, the loan to the child is the consideration for the parent's promise to pay the debt.

commercial sureties, who are in the business of providing guarantees, may supply a payment or performance bond similar to an insurance policy in return for a fee.

A surety's liability for the debt is usually, though not always, contingent on the principal debtor's failure to fulfill an obligation when it becomes due. If required to pay the debt, a surety has a right of reimbursement from the principal debtor. Thus, even before the surety is called upon to make payment, she is regarded as a creditor with a contingent claim against the principal debtor. So, a shareholder who has guaranteed a debt owed by the corporation he owns has a contingent claim against the corporation.

In addition, a surety who makes payment to the creditor obtains, through the doctrine of "equitable subrogation," whatever rights the creditor originally had against the principal debtor. If the creditor held a security interest in the principal debtor's property and the surety pays the debt to the creditor, the surety is subrogated to the creditor's rights in the collateral. Thus, the surety's right to reimbursement will be secured to the same extent as the claim of the original creditor.

[36] "Trustee"

In liquidation cases under Chapter 7, a "trustee" is appointed to administer the estate.[144] The trustee's responsibilities include collecting and liquidating the estate's property, investigating the financial affairs of the debtor, examining and possibly objecting to claims filed by creditors, providing information about the debtor's affairs to creditors, and, where appropriate, operating the debtor's business.[145] These duties encompass responsibility for recovering pre-petition transfers of property made by the debtor through fraudulent conveyances, avoidable preferences, or otherwise. If warranted, the trustee may object to the debtor's discharge.

Although the Code permits creditors to elect a trustee,[146] in the overwhelming majority of cases, the interim trustee appointed by the court at the outset of the case,[147] and is selected from an available panel of private trustees in the district in which the case is filed,[148] and serves as the trustee for the duration of the case.[149]

Likewise, in cases under Chapters 12 and 13, a standing trustee is appointed to administer the case.[150] The standing trustee is usually a local attorney or accountant who serves as the trustee for all Chapter 12 and 13 cases in the area in which the court is located.[151] In many areas, serving

[144] Bankruptcy Code § 701; Fed. R. Bankr. P. 2001.

[145] Bankruptcy Code § 704.

[146] Bankruptcy Code § 702(b).

[147] Bankruptcy Code § 701.

[148] *See* 28 U.S.C. § 586 (2000).

[149] Bankruptcy Code § 702(d).

[150] *See* Bankruptcy Code §§ 1202, 302.

[151] 28 U.S.C. § 586(b) (2000).

as the standing trustee for cases under chapters 12 and 13 provides full-time, year-round employment for the trustee, who is likely to have staff members available to assist him in fulfilling his duties.

The nature of most Chapter 12 and 13 cases, in which the debtor voluntarily makes payments to creditors pursuant to a court approved repayment plan, means that the trustees duties are different in some respects from those of a Chapter 7 trustee. Unlike Chapter 7 cases, in which the trustee must assemble and sell the debtor's non-exempt assets, most cases under Chapters 12 and 13 do not involve the liquidation of any assets. Instead, the trustee's job consists primarily of administering the payments supplied by the debtor.[152]

A Chapter 12 or 13 trustee also plays an important role in reviewing the debtor's financial affairs to determine whether the debtor's plan should be confirmed by the court. If a debtor's plan does not satisfy the requirements for confirmation, it is the trustee's job to object.[153] In most judicial districts, attorneys who regularly represent debtors in cases under Chapters 12 and 13 are well aware of the types of circumstances that are likely to attract the standing trustee's attention and draw an objection. Moreover, trustees who fail to object to unconfirmable plans will eventually be confronted by the United States Trustee's office, which is responsible for supervising trustees who serve in individual cases.

Appointment of a trustee in cases under Chapter 11 is extraordinarily rare. In most cases, the debtor's estate is administered by the debtor-in-possession who enjoys all of the same rights, powers, and duties of a trustee.

[37] "United States Trustee"

The "United States Trustee" is an appointed federal official, who works for the United States Department of Justice and has administrative responsibility for the bankruptcy system in a specified geographic region. The United States Trustee approves individuals to serve as standing and panel trustees, monitors fee applications by attorneys and others who provide professional services in bankruptcy cases, appoints and supervises creditors' committees, reviews reorganization plans, and generally ensures that cases progress efficiently through the bankruptcy system.[154]

[38] "Unsecured Claim"

"Unsecured claim" refers to a claim in a bankruptcy case for which there is no available collateral. A claim may be unsecured either because the creditor does not have a lien on any of the debtor's assets, or because the value of the assets that serve as the collateral for the claim will be

---

[152] *See* Bankruptcy Code § 1202(b)(1).

[153] Bankruptcy Code §§ 1202(a)(3)(B), 1302(a)(2)(B).

[154] *See* 28 U.S.C. § 586(a) (2000). Despite these tasks, many bankruptcy lawyers are unenthusiastic about the role of the United States Trustee and believe that the bankruptcy system worked better before the agency was created.

exhausted before they can be used to satisfy the claim in question. In consumer cases, most creditors have claims that are completely unsecured, typically including credit card companies, health care providers, utility companies, and landlords. In business cases, creditors with unsecured claims usually include utility companies, trade creditors, bond holders, unpaid employees, and tax authorities.

In both consumer and business cases, there may be creditors with claims that are partially secured and partially unsecured, due to the inadequacy of the value of their collateral to fully secure their claims. Thus, a creditor with a perfected security interest in the debtor's $8,000 car, securing a $12,000 debt, will have a secured claim of $8,000 and an unsecured claim for the $4,000 balance.

[39] "Value"

The "value" of property is critical in a number of situations, including determining the allowed amount of a secured claim, determining whether a creditor has adequate protection or is entitled to relief from the automatic stay, calculating when a debtor is insolvent, and determining whether payments provided for in a reorganization would result in creditors receiving at least what they would have obtained if the debtor had been liquidated.

Despite its importance, the term has no fixed definition; instead, the value of a debtor's property is determined contextually. Consider a simple example: what is the value of an inventory of 5,000 widgets? It might be $50,000 (the retail price), $37,000 (the wholesale price), $34,000 (the expected price the debtor would receive for them in an orderly liquidation), or $20,000 (the expected price that the debtor would receive in a quick, knock-down liquidation). Any of these prices might be the value of the inventory in bankruptcy, depending on the context in which the question is being raised. If the debtor is a reorganizing retailer with good prospects, the highest price might be correct; if it is a collapsed wholesaler undergoing an immediate liquidation, the lowest more likely applies.

Chapter 2
Creditors' Collection Rights

§ 2.01 Source of Creditors' Collection Rights[1]

The law of creditors' and debtors' rights has traditionally been left to the states. All of the basic procedures used by creditors to collect debts owed to them are established by state law. Most of these procedures are derived from the common law, but are now mostly codified.[2]

Despite this, the United States Bankruptcy Code casts a long shadow over these state procedures and represents an obvious intrusion of federal power into creditors' rights.[3] Moreover, in recent decades, creditors' state law collection procedures became regulated by federal legislation, especially with respect to consumer debtors. The most obvious examples of these federal interventions are the Fair Debt Collection Practices Act,[4] the Fair Credit Reporting Act,[5] and Federal Restrictions on Wage Garnishment,[6] all of which are parts of the Consumer Credit Protection Act.

Despite these federal statutes, most creditors' remedies remain primarily creatures of state rather than federal law. It is those remedies that are the usual stuff of traditional law school courses on creditors' rights, and thus they are the subject of this chapter. This is a massive subject in itself, and cannot be fully explored in this book.[7] However, this chapter will identify the most important issues, or at least the issues that are most likely to arise in the background of a subsequent bankruptcy proceeding.

Creditors' rights can be divided into two broad categories. The first category deals with property rights obtained by creditors by contract that protect their interest in receiving payment. These rights include mortgages, deeds of trust, and security interests under Article 9 of the Uniform Commercial Code. Also included in this chapter is a brief review of personal property leases. Leases, like mortgages and security interests, create divided interests in property; one purpose of that division is to protect the lessor's right to be paid the promised rent. Although not liens in the usual

---

[1] Arthur A. Leff, *Injury, Ignorance and Spite — The Dynamics of Coercive Collection*, 80 Yale L.J. 1 (1970).

[2] "The forms of action we have buried, but they still rule us from their graves." Frederic William Maitland, The Forms of Action at Common Law 1 (Cambridge ed. 1962).

[3] Richard M. Hynes, *Why (Consumer) Bankruptcy*?, 56 Ala. L. Rev. 121 (2004).

[4] *See* § 2.15[C] Fair Debt Collection Practices Act, *infra*.

[5] *See* § 2.15[D] The Fair Credit Reporting Act, *infra*.

[6] *See* § 2.12[A][4][a] Federal Restrictions on Wage Garnishment, *infra*.

[7] Indeed, most law school courses on creditors' rights de-emphasize these state law collection rules, in favor of more coverage of the Bankruptcy Code.

sense of the word, lessors' rights have some of the same characteristics as liens and are given somewhat similar treatment in bankruptcy. A discussion of creditors' right of setoff, which is treated much like a lien, is also included in this chapter. The rights of the offsetting creditor are treated by the Bankruptcy Code as virtual liens; it is therefore appropriate in this introductory material to group them together.

The second category deals with creditors' property rights that are created by law rather than by contract. These are sometimes referred to as "involuntary" property rights, even though this characterization is somewhat misleading. They are involuntary in the sense that the debtor did not explicitly grant them to the creditor. However, in many cases, they arise as a consequence of a voluntary transaction between the debtor and the creditor. For example, a simple construction contract, formed through the consent of the parties, might easily lead to the involuntary imposition of a construction lien if the owner of the project fails to pay for the contractor's services. Likewise, a debtor's failure to make payments due under a credit card agreement might lead to the credit card company obtaining a judgment lien against the cardholder's real estate or an order to garnish the debtor's wages.

§ 2.02 Consensual Liens and Other Interests

There are three basic types of liens: consensual liens, judicial liens, and statutory liens. They are created in different ways, are enforced through different procedures, and are accorded different priorities.[8]

Consensual liens are created by the agreement of the person granting the lien. The most familiar examples are home mortgages and purchase money security interests in new automobiles and household furnishings. Those who have studied the law of secured transactions under Article 9 of the Uniform Commercial Code will have encountered a wide array of similar transactions using inventory, equipment, receivables, and other property as collateral. In all of these transactions, the debtor who voluntarily grants the creditor a lien is exchanging a limited property interest for some accommodation from the transferee — typically a loan or other extension of credit. The creditor who obtains the lien is almost always seeking greater security for payment or performance of the debtor's obligation.

In its simplest terms, a bank that makes a mortgage loan might supply $100,000 to the borrower in exchange for the borrower's promise to repay the loan (with interest of course) together with a mortgage in the borrower's real property. If the debtor defaults on his promise to pay, the bank may obtain a judgment of foreclosure and have the house sold to obtain the cash necessary to satisfy the loan.

A security interest in personal property operates in the same way. Instead of securing a loan with real property (the house), a finance company

---

[8] *See* Justice v. Valley National Bank, 849 F.2d 1078, 1085 n.7 (8th Cir. 1988) (distinguishing judicial liens, statutory liens, and consensual liens).

might secure a corporate loan with the debtor's drill press. The debtor grants the finance company a security interest in his drill press as collateral, thus securing his promise to make regularly monthly installment payments on the loan. If the debtor defaults, the finance company has the right to take possession of the drill press and to have it sold to satisfy the debt.[9]

In these examples, both the bank (with its mortgage on the borrower's land) and the finance company (with its security interest in the debtor's drill press) are said to have priority over other creditors. As we will explain in more detail below, priority means that the creditor with seniority has the right to receive payment from a sale of the collateral before the collateral may be used to satisfy the claims of other creditors.

[A] Real Estate Mortgages and Deeds of Trust

[1] Basic Operation of Mortgages and Deeds of Trust

[a] Mortgages

Generally speaking, interests in real estate collateral are established either through a mortgage or through a deed of trust. In a traditional mortgage, the borrower (the "mortgagor") transfers a property interest (a "mortgage") in his land to the creditor (the "mortgagee"). Upon default by the mortgagor, the mortgagee has the right to obtain a judgment in court that will result in the property being sold by the county sheriff. The proceeds derived from that sale are used to satisfy the mortgagor's debt. Generally, if the property is sold for less than the debt, the mortgagee can obtain a judgment against the mortgagor personally for the amount of the deficiency; though some states have adopted anti-deficiency statutes which protect owners of residential real estate from liability on any such shortfall in the selling price of the land.[10] If in an extraordinarily rare circumstance, the property sells for more than the amount necessary to pay the outstanding debt, the surplus is paid to the mortgagor.[11]

---

[9] U.C.C. § 9-609 (2002).

[10] *E.g.,* Cal. Civ. Proc. Code § 580b (1976); *see generally* Robert M. Washburn, *The Judicial and Legislative Response to Price Inadequacy in Mortgage Foreclosure Sales*, 53 S. Cal. L. Rev. 843 (1980). Anti-deficiency statutes also sometimes apply with respect to security interests in consumer goods. *See, e.g.,* Unif. Consumer Credit Code § 1.106 (1974); Ind. Code Ann. § 24-4.5-5-103(2) (2006).

[11] Originally, a mortgage was nothing more than a fee simple on condition subsequent. The borrower conveyed a deed to the lender and the lender's deed was subject to a condition subsequent that would revest ownership (or "seisin") in the borrower upon repayment of the debt. The borrower's right of repayment operated to defeat the lender's title only if the borrower made the required payment on "law day." If the borrower paid the debt, the lender's interest would terminate and title in fee simple absolute would revert to the borrower. However, the borrower's failure to make the payment on law day destroyed the contingency on the lender's title and irretrievably vested title in fee simple absolute in the lender. The potential unfairness of this outcome led seventeenth century English chancery courts to permit a borrower who

[b] Deeds of Trust[12]

Deeds of trust, which are more common in western states, operate in a similar manner, except no judicial action is necessary to complete the foreclosure process. Unlike a mortgage, a deed of trust involves three parties: the borrower, the lender, and a trustee. The borrower conveys an interest in the property to a trust, with the lender as the beneficiary of the trust. The trustee of the trust, sometimes a bank employee, and sometimes a third party, is given the power to sell the property if the borrower defaults. Under the terms of the trust, the trustee sells the property and remits the proceeds of the sale to the lender, but only to the extent necessary to pay the borrower's debt.[13] As with a mortgage, any surplus resulting from the sale must be paid to the borrower.[14] The deed of trust device originated as an attempt to work around the cumbersome judicial procedures for foreclosure, in particular, the lengthy redemption periods that are frequently available to the mortgagor under the laws of many states.

As a result, deeds of trust are generally not enforceable without court action unless they are validated by a state statute. Where they are, the procedures required are similar to, but more streamlined than, those employed in a traditional judicial foreclosure action. They ensure that the borrower has adequate notice of the nature of his default, the time and place of the sale, the amounts received from the sale, and how the amounts were distributed. They also establish waiting periods and publicity requirements that must be followed when conducting the sale.

[c] Installment Land Contract

A variation used in some states is the installment land contract, sometimes called a "contract for deed."[15] In an installment land contract, the buyer takes possession of the land and makes regular installment payments. The seller retains title until the payments are complete. Traditionally, the contract for deed gave the vendor an exceptionally broad remedy: if the buyer (sometimes called the "vendee") defaulted, the seller (the "vendor") could keep all payments made and recover the property. This rule,

had defaulted on law day to redeem the property from the lender by paying the balance of the obligation due, despite the default, and thus avoid a loss of both the property and the payments that had previously been made. Eventually, procedures were developed to permit the lender to petition the chancery court to "foreclose" the equity of redemption by putting the property up for sale, with the buyer's rights invulnerable to attack by the borrower. Marshall E. Tracht, *Renegotiation and Secured Credit: Explaining the Equity of Redemption*, 52 Vand. L. Rev. 599 (1999); *see* Grant S. Nelson & Dale A. Whitman, Real Estate Finance Law 7–8 (4th ed. 2001).

12 Grant S. Nelson & Dale A. Whitman, *Reforming Foreclosure: The Uniform Nonjudicial Foreclosure Act*, 53 Duke L.J. 1399 (2004).

13 *E.g.*, In re Krohn, 52 P.3d 774 (Ariz. 2002).

14 Grant S. Nelson & Dale A. Whitman, Real Estate Finance Law 11 (4th ed. 2001).

15 Grant S. Nelson, *The Contract for Deed as a Mortgage: The Case for the Restatement Approach*, 1998 BYU L. Rev. 1111 (1998); Grant S. Nelson & Dale A. Whitman, Real Estate Finance Law 70–71 (4th ed. 2001).

which amounted to a forfeiture of the buyer's partial payments, has been whittled away by legislative actions and court decisions[16] similar to the rules that provided mortgagees with an equity of redemption in seventeenth century England. If the seller defaulted, and refused to convey legal title to the land, the buyer could obtain specific performance.

[2] Two Step Process: Contract and Recordation

Mortgages, deeds of trust, and other similar mechanisms involve a two-step process. The first step is execution and delivery of the document containing the parties' agreement. This establishes the rights between the immediate parties: the creditor and the debtor. In most cases, a second step — proper recording of the document — is required to establish rights against third parties, including most subsequent purchasers (including secured parties)[17] of the property, including other holders of consensual or non-consensual liens.[18]

Ordinarily, the mortgage or deed of trust document itself must be recorded in the real estate records of the county in which the real property is located. If the mortgage is not recorded, the creditor's interest in the property remains vulnerable to the rights of a good faith purchaser for value. It also remains vulnerable to the rights of a subsequent mortgagee, a creditor who obtains a judicial lien on the property, and to "avoidance" in a bankruptcy proceeding by the bankruptcy trustee, who has the power of a hypothetical bona fide purchaser of real estate.[19]

[3] Priority of Mortgages and Deeds of Trust

Priorities among competing mortgage holders are generally established on a first-in-time, first-in-right basis. Who is first-in-time is determined by the state's recording statute. Interests in the property that are recorded first are generally given first priority. But this is a broad generalization with many variations. For example, depending on the jurisdiction, a person who has notice of a previous unrecorded interest might take subject to it, despite the failure to record.[20] However, insofar as bankruptcy is concerned, recordation of the transfer is a virtual necessity, because the bankruptcy trustee's lack of notice is conclusively presumed by the statute.[21]

---

[16] *See* Grant S. Nelson & Dale A Whitman, Real Estate Finance Law 70-124 (4th ed. 2001).

[17] In colloquial language, "purchaser" is usually understood as a synonym of "buyer." In commercial law, it refers to anyone who obtains a voluntarily created interest in the property. *See* U.C.C. § 1-201(32), (33) (2002). In this technical sense, both buyers and secured lenders are purchasers. *E.g.*, In re Arlco, Inc., 239 B.R. 261, 268–69 (Bankr. S.D.N.Y. 1999).

[18] *See generally* 14 Richard R. Powell & Michael Allan Wolf, Powell on Real Property §§ 82.01-82.04 (2000).

[19] *See* § 14.02 Strong-Arm Clause, *infra.*

[20] *See generally* 14 Richard R. Powell & Michael Allan Wolf, Powell on Real Property §§ 82.02[1] (2000).

[21] Bankruptcy Code § 544(a)(3); *see* § 14.02 Strong-Arm Clause, *infra.*

[B] Security Interests in Personal Property

The system for creating and recording consensual liens in personal property is quite different from the system used for liens on real estate. Personal property, unlike real estate, tends to move around, making the location of the collateral far less significant. Moreover, many types of personal property, such as accounts, intellectual property, and other intangible rights, have no physical location. In the United States, consensual liens on all types of personal property are governed by Article 9 of the Uniform Commercial Code, which has been adopted in all American jurisdictions.

[1] Security Interests Under Article 9 of the Uniform Commercial Code[22]

[a] Scope of Article 9

Most aspects of the law regarding security interests in personal property and fixtures (but not real estate) are governed by Article 9 of the Uniform Commercial Code (UCC). The coverage of Article 9 is determined by the economic substance of the underlying transaction rather than by the label the parties attach to it. Article 9 governs if the interest is granted in order to secure payment or performance of an obligation (usually a money debt).[23]

The parties to a security interest sometimes try to disguise the nature of their transaction by characterizing it as a lease. This is sometimes done for tax or accounting purposes, and sometimes to obtain better treatment in bankruptcy.[24] However, if the "lessor" does not retain any valuable reversionary rights in the leased property, the transaction is regarded a sale to the "lessee," with the lessor retaining nothing more than a security interest.[25] For example, if the lease allows the lessee to buy the goods for nominal consideration at the end of the lease term, then the lease is probably not a lease at all but a security interest governed by Article 9.[26] Likewise, if the lease is for the entire anticipated useful economic life of the goods, whatever reversionary rights the lessor retains are economically meaningless and the transaction is a security interest, not a true lease.[27]

---

[22] Note that the discussion of Article 9 security interests is more extensive than that of other liens; this is because many bankruptcy casebooks use more cases and questions drawn from Article 9 than from other bodies of state law creditors' rights.

[23] U.C.C. § 1-201(b)(35) (2003). The obligation is not always a money debt. One of your authors recalls examining an agreement entered into between a pet breeder and one of its customers. The agreement specified that the customer was not permitted to have the kitten "declawed," and that the seller retained the right to retake possession of the cat if the buyer breached this promise. The obligation was to preserve the claws of the cat intact.

[24] The reasons for this are complicated, but turn on the difference between the treatment a personal property lessee receives under Bankruptcy Code § 365(d)(10), and the treatment a secured creditor receives under §§ 361, 362 and 363.

[25] *See generally* Corinne Cooper, *Identifying a Personal Property Lease Under the UCC*, 49 Ohio St. L.J. 195 (1988).

[26] U.C.C. § 1-203(b)(4) (2003).

[27] U.C.C. § 1-203(b)(1) (2003).

In bankruptcy this distinction is of critical importance. In most cases, a security interest creates a lien that is valid against the bankruptcy trustee only if the security interest is "perfected" — usually by a filed Article 9 "financing statement."[28] No such filing is required to preserve a lessor's rights in bankruptcy. Moreover, apart from the risk of avoidance by the trustee, the Bankruptcy Code provides far better treatment to lessors than it does to secured parties, particularly where the value of the property involved is worth less than the obligation the debtor owes.[29]

Article 9 also applies to many transactions that do not involve the use of property as collateral for a loan. It applies to most outright sales of accounts, chattel paper, payment intangibles, and promissory notes, even when the transfer of this kind of property is not made to secure an obligation.[30] When Article 9 applies, buyers of this type of property will find it necessary to comply with Article 9's attachment and perfection procedures in order to protect their rights from the claims of competing transferees — particularly the debtor's creditors and the bankruptcy trustee — in the event the seller of the property files a bankruptcy petition.

Article 9 also applies to certain "consignments," certain statutory "agricultural liens" and security interests arising under other articles of the Uniform Commercial Code.[31]

[b] Attachment of Security Interests

The basic enforceability of a security agreement is referred to as "attachment." Attachment requires three elements: a security agreement between the debtor and the creditor, value given by the secured party to the debtor, and the rights in the collateral that the debtor has the power to convey to the creditor.[32] An Article 9 security interest arises only by agreement between the debtor and the secured party. Further, unless the secured creditor takes physical possession of the collateral, the security agreement must be in writing, be signed by the debtor, and have an adequate description of the collateral.[33] If the collateral is timber to be cut, the security agreement must also include a description of the land on which the timber is located.[34]

In addition, the secured party must give value.[35] Usually this consists of a sale of goods on credit or a loan. "New value" is not required, as long

[28] U.C.C. § 9-310(a) & cmt. 2 (2003).

[29] A debtor who wants to continue to "use" collateral that is subject to a security interest needs only provide the creditor with adequate protection against a decline in the value of the collateral. An undersecured creditor is not entitled to interest to compensate it for the delay in its foreclosure. United Savings Assn. of Texas v. Timbers of Inwood Forest Associates, Ltd., 484 U.S. 365 (1988). By contrast, a lessee is entitled to timely payments under the lease if the debtor wishes to retain the leased property. Bankruptcy Code § 365(d)(10).

[30] U.C.C. § 9-109(a)(3) (2003).

[31] U.C.C. § 9-109(a) (2003).

[32] U.C.C. § 9-203(a) (2003).

[33] U.C.C. § 9-203(b)(3)(A) (2003).

[34] U.C.C. § 9-203 (2003).

[35] U.C.C. § 9-203(1)(b) (2003).

as value has been given at some time. If the security interest is given by the debtor to secure a debt that the debtor already owes to the secured party, the secured party has given value for it.[36]

Finally, the debtor must have rights in the collateral.[37] The debtor may be the owner of the collateral or a co-owner. The key question is whether the debtor has some transferable property interest in the collateral. In a bankruptcy setting, it sometimes becomes critical to determine when, rather than whether, the debtor acquired rights in the collateral.[38]

The security agreement may provide for "after-acquired" property. After-acquired collateral is property that the debtor does not have at the time of the agreement, but subsequently acquires.[39] The security interest does not attach until the debtor obtains some rights in the property, but when the debtor does obtain rights, the security interest attaches automatically without the need for any further documentation.

The security agreement may also provide that future advances made to the debtor are to be secured by both existing and after-acquired collateral.[40] Thus, a single security agreement can cover any number of loans made by the lender at different times, and these loans may be secured by collateral acquired by the debtor at different times.

Attachment fixes the rights of the secured party against the debtor. Most importantly, it establishes the secured party's right to repossess the property if the debtor defaults and to resell it to satisfy the amount of the debt.

[c] Perfection of Security Interests

Attachment, while sufficient to provide the creditor with rights against the debtor, does not protect the secured party's rights against competing claims of the debtor's other creditors. Nor will it protect against the avoiding powers of the bankruptcy trustee. Other creditors may assert a property interest in the same collateral. These may include judgment lien-holders, other secured creditors, buyers of the collateral, and the like.

To gain priority over these third parties, a secured party must "perfect" its security interest. Perfection occurs in some cases "automatically" upon attachment. For example, a purchase money security interest in consumer goods (other than motor vehicles and other goods subject to a certificate of title statute) is automatically perfected.[41] This means the secured party need not take any other step beyond attachment to establish its priority.

However, in most types of secured transactions, perfection requires additional steps, such as "possession," "control," or "filing."[42] These further

[36] U.C.C. § 1-201(44) (2003).

[37] U.C.C. § 9-203(1)(c) (2003).

[38] *See* Bankruptcy Code § 547(e).

[39] U.C.C. § 9-204(1) (2003).

[40] U.C.C. § 9-204(3) (2003).

[41] U.C.C. § 9-302(1)(d) (2003).

[42] *See* U.C.C. § 9-310 (2003).

steps are designed to give notice to third parties of the existence of the security interest and thus to avoid the possibility that subsequent lenders or purchasers might be misled by the debtor's apparent ownership of the collateral.[43]

To perfect a security interest in tangible types of collateral, such as goods, the secured party may perfect by taking physical possession of the collateral.[44] However, in most cases it would be highly impractical for the secured party to take possession of the goods, as this would deprive the debtor of their use. Debtors engaged in manufacturing need their machinery; debtors involved in selling retail goods need to have immediate access to their inventory. And, no-one would even think of buying a car on credit if he or she were unable to drive the car until all of the payments were made. Accordingly, possession is used only very infrequently to perfect a security interest.

For some types of collateral, such as deposit accounts, investment property, and electronic chattel paper, "control" is another means to perfect.[45] For example, a creditor with a security interest in a debtor's bank account, might obtain "control" by entering into an agreement with the debtor and its bank that requires the bank to follow any instructions it receives from the creditor regarding the disposition of funds in the account, without the need for further permission from the debtor.[46]

Security interests in most types of collateral can be perfected by filing,[47] and filing is the only permissible method of perfecting security interests in some types of collateral, such as accounts.[48] Indeed, filing a financing statement, with the office of the secretary of state, in the state where the debtor is located, is the most common method of perfecting a security interest.

The financing statement contains a limited range of information about the transaction. It requires the debtor's name, the secured party's name, and a description of the collateral.[49] This is usually enough information to permit other prospective lenders to determine, perhaps after conducting a further investigation, whether items of the debtor's property are already subject to a competing creditor's security interest.

Special perfection rules apply to some types of collateral. Most notably, security interests in motor vehicles, and in many states boats — or "watercraft"[50] — are nearly always governed by the state's certificate of

[43] In this respect in particular, Article 9 and its public notice filing procedures are closely related to the law of fraudulent conveyances.

[44] U.C.C. § 9-313 (2003).

[45] U.C.C. § 9-310(b)(8) (2002).

[46] U.C.C. § 9-104(2) (2003).

[47] U.C.C. § 9-310 (2003).

[48] U.C.C. § 9-310 (2003).

[49] U.C.C. § 9-502 (2003). The filing office may insist on additional information. *See* U.C.C. § 9-516(b) (2003).

[50] *See, e.g.*, Ohio Rev. Code Ann. § 1548.21 (Page 2006).

title statute, which requires perfection by having the security interest noted on the certificate of title covering the goods.[51] Federal law also prescribes special means of perfecting security interests in airplanes, certain vessels, and some types of intellectual property. Since the U.C.C. is state law, these federal rules supersede the U.C.C. where they apply.[52]

[d] Priority Rules under U.C.C. Article 9

Broadly speaking, Article 9 adheres to a first-in-time, first-in-right approach to priority: rights perfected prior in time are senior. Generally, if the security interest was perfected or an authorized financing statement was filed before the competing claim arose, the security interest has priority.[53] For example, if a finance company's security interest in a debtor's equipment was perfected on January 1, and the bank's judicial lien attached on January 5, the security interest held by the finance company prevails. When the equipment is sold, the proceeds are first applied to the debt secured by the security interest. Any surplus is applied to the debt secured by the bank's junior judgment lien.

Insofar as bankruptcy is concerned, the most crucial priority rule in Article 9 is that contained in § 9-301(1)(b). It states that an *unperfected* security interest is subordinate to the rights of "a person who becomes a lien creditor before the security interest is perfected."[54] The bankruptcy trustee enjoys all of the same rights as a judicial lien creditor as of the moment of the filing of the bankruptcy petition.[55] This means that an unperfected security interest is subordinate to the rights of, and can be avoided by, a bankruptcy trustee.

[e] Enforcement of Security Interests

As indicated above, an Article 9 security interest gives the secured party something that general creditors do not enjoy: an actual property interest in the debtor's property. This property interest coexists with the interest held by the debtor. The debtor is usually in possession of the property and is free to use it in the ordinary course of its business or financial affairs. However, if the debtor defaults, the secured party may seize and sell the property. In many cases, no court action is required to establish or enforce the secured party's rights to the collateral. Instead, it may be taken by self-help, as long as there is no breach of the peace in the process of repossession.[56]

In a bankruptcy case, a creditor with a perfected security interest has an even more valuable right. Although the secured creditor is by no means

[51] *E.g.*, Ohio Rev. Code Ann. § 4505.13 (Page 2006).

[52] U.C.C. § 9-109(c)(1) (2003).

[53] U.C.C. §§ 9-317 & 9-322 (2003).

[54] U.C.C. § 9-317(a)(2) (2003).

[55] *See* § 14.02 Strong-Arm Clause, *infra*.

[56] U.C.C. § 9-609 (2003). If self-help cannot be accomplished peaceably, the secured party must resort to judicial action, generally by seeking the remedy of replevin or detinue.

unaffected by the bankruptcy case and has no certainty of receiving payment in full, it is almost certain to obtain a much greater payout than is received by unsecured creditors. In Chapter 7 liquidation proceedings. secured creditors are frequently able to repossess and sell their collateral just as if the bankruptcy case had not been filed.[57] Even if it is not permitted to sell the collateral on its own, a protected secured party is entitled to receive the proceeds from the bankruptcy trustee's sale of the collateral up to the amount necessary to satisfy the secured party's claim. However, if the results of the sale are inadequate to pay the claim in full, the creditor's deficiency claim is, at least to that extent, unsecured.

In reorganization and rehabilitation proceedings, secured parties are entitled to "adequate protection" of their property interests while the case is pending and are entitled to receive payment, under the terms of the debtor's plan in an amount equal to the amount of their secured claims.

[2] Superseding Federal Law

There are several federal statutes that deal with consensual security interests in personal property. Some of them work in conjunction with Article 9; others operate independently of it.

Federal admiralty law governs security interests in registered vessels. In order for a preferred ship mortgage to have priority over the bankruptcy trustee, it must satisfy a number of formalities quite alien to Article 9.

Other federal laws only partially preempt Article 9. Security interests in aircraft, for example, are largely covered by the U.C.C., but perfection is governed by federal law, which requires notice of the security interest to be recorded in the F.A.A. Registry in Oklahoma City.

The law governing perfection of security interests in various forms of intellectual property is particularly uncertain and complex: filing under Article 9 is sufficient to perfect a security interest in a trademark;[58] filing with the Copyright Office is necessary to perfect a security interest in a registered copyright;[59] filing under Article 9 may be required to perfect a security interest in an unregistered copyright,[60] though under an earlier decision it had been held to be neither necessary nor sufficient;[61] and dual filings under both Article 9 and with the Patent and Trademark Office may

---

[57] The filing of a bankruptcy case operates as an "automatic stay" against virtually every type of creditor action, including repossession and sale by a secured creditor. Thus, even where secured creditors have the right to foreclose, they are required to obtain permission from the bankruptcy court, in the form of "relief from the automatic stay." *See* § 8.06[B] Relief From the Stay on Request of a Party, *infra*.

[58] Matter of Roman Cleanser Co., 43 B.R. 940 (Bankr. E.D. Mich. 1984), *aff'd*, 802 F.2d 207 (6th Cir. 1986).

[59] *See* In re Peregrine Entm't, 116 BR. 194 (C.D. Cal. 1990).

[60] In re World Auxiliary Power Co., 303 F.3d 1120 (9th Cir. 2002).

[61] In re Avalon Software, Inc., 209 B.R. 517 (Bankr. D. Ariz. 1997).

be necessary to fully protect a security interest in a patent against both the bankruptcy trustee and a subsequent purchaser of the patent.[62]

§ 2.03 Leases

[A] Real Estate Leases

Generally, long-term leases of real estate must be recorded to protect the rights of the lessee against third partes. Short-term leases need not be recorded. For example, in New York, leases of fewer than three years need not be recorded, while leases of three years or more must be recorded to be effective against a subsequent purchaser.[63] In addition, Article 2A of the U.C.C. provides special filing rules for leases of "fixtures" which apply regardless of the duration of the lease.[64]

In general, the rights of both the lessor and the lessee are determined on a first-in-time, first-in-right basis. Third party rights in the property that exist prior to the lease (or prior to the recording of the lease, if recording is necessary) are senior to those of the parties to the lease; subsequently arising rights are subordinate. Thus, if after the lease, the creditors of the lessor obtain a lien on the leased property, that lien will not affect the rights of the lessee.

If a long-term lease is not recorded, the rights of the lessee may be subject to those of a bona fide purchaser. If they are, then the lease may be avoided in bankruptcy because of the bankruptcy trustee's status as a bona fide purchaser of real estate.[65] In addition, there are a number of rules in the Bankruptcy Code that deal with the ability of a bankrupt lessee to retain possession of the property leased.[66]

[B] Personal Property Leases

Article 2A of the U.C.C. governs leases of personal property.[67] Its provisions include those regarding relative rights of the lessor and the lessee's creditors in the leased goods. Those provisions directly and indirectly affect the status of the various interests in bankruptcy.

---

[62] *Compare* In re Cybernetic Serv., Inc., 252 F.3d 1039 (9th Cir. 2001) (filing under Article 9 sufficient for protection against a lien creditor and thus arguably against the bankruptcy trustee), *with* City Bank & Trust Co. v. Otto Fabric, Inc., 83 B.R. 780 (D. Kan. 1988) (filing with the Patent and Trademark Office required for protection against a subsequent purchaser of the patent).

[63] N.Y. Real Prop. Law Ann. § 291-c (McKinney 2006); *see generally* 14 Richard R. Powell & Michael Allan Wolf, Powell on Real Property § 82.02[3][a][I] (2000).

[64] U.C.C. § 2A-307(4) (2002).

[65] Bankruptcy Code § 544(a)(3); *see, e.g.,* In re Huffman, 369 F.3d 972 (6th Cir. 2004).

[66] *See* Chapter 11, Executory Contracts and Unexpired Leases, *infra.*

[67] U.C.C. §§ 2A-102 & 2A-103(1)(j) (2002). As of August 1, 2006, forty-nine states, the District of Columbia, and the U.S. Virgin Islands have adopted Article 2A. It has not been adopted in Louisiana.

Of primary importance, at least to the lessor, is that lessors need not record their lease or file a financing statement to be protected from claims of the lessee's creditors. So long as the lease is a "true lease" and not a disguised security interest in goods that have really been sold to the lessee, and if the lease is not a lease of fixtures, recording is not necessary. Thus, the typical personal property lease is a one-step transaction. If the lease is enforceable between the lessor and the lessee, no additional steps are required to protect the lessor's rights against the rights of the lessee's creditors.

The only significant exception to this deals with a lease of goods that become fixtures.[68] A fixture is created when personal property is so affixed to realty that it becomes part of the realty.[69] For a fixture lessor to have priority over certain competing third parties, the lessor must file a "fixture filing."[70] Note, however, that even if there is no filing, the rights of the lessor are superior to the rights of a creditor who obtained a judgment lien after the lease contract became effective.[71] Thus, the lessee's bankruptcy trustee cannot avoid the lessor's interest in the fixture under its power as a hypothetical lien creditor.[72] However, the fixture lessor who has not filed remains vulnerable to other lien creditors, such as the holder of a mortgage or deed of trust on the entire property of which the fixture is a part.

Insofar as other Article 2A leases are concerned, the general rule is first-in-time, first-in-right. Broadly speaking, the rights of both the lessor and the lessee are prior to the rights of subsequent creditors, including subsequent lien creditors. Thus, a bankruptcy of the lessee does not ordinarily affect the property rights of the lessor, or vice-versa. However, the ability of a bankrupt lessor or lessee to assume or transfer the contract rights is regulated by §§ 363 and 365 of the Bankruptcy Code.[73]

§ 2.04 Judgments

Obtaining a judgment is the first step a creditor usually must take in attempting to use the courts to collect a debt. As most law students discover in Civil Procedure, a judgment may be obtained in several ways.[74]

---

[68] U.C.C. § 2A-309 (2002).

[69] U.C.C. § 2A-309 (2002); *see* Teaff v. Hewitt, 1 Ohio St. 511 (1853).

[70] U.C.C. § 2A-309(1)(b), (4) (2002).

[71] U.C.C. § 2A-309(5)(b) (2002).

[72] Bankruptcy Code § 544(a)(1). Note that the trustee also has the rights of a hypothetical bona fide purchaser of real estate — but only of real estate other than fixtures. *Id.* § 544(a)(3).

[73] *See* Chapter 11, Executory Contracts and Unexpired Leases, *infra.*

[74] At early common law, enforcement of a judgment was limited to one of several writs: fieri facias, which directed the sheriff to seize the judgment debtor's goods and to sell them to satisfy the judgment; levari facias, which ordered the sheriff to seize both the debtor's goods and profits from his land (but not the land itself); elegit, which ordered delivery of the debtor's goods to the creditor at an appraised value in satisfaction of the debt, and if necessary to further satisfy the debt, gave the creditor possession of (but not title to) one half of the debtor's lands until the judgment was paid; or of capias ad satisfaciendum, which imprisoned the debtor until

[A] Obtaining a Judgment

[1] Default Judgments

If the defendant fails to answer the plaintiff's complaint within the time period permitted to file a responsive pleading, judgment may be entered by default.[75] This usually requires compliance with the Federal "Servicemembers Civil Relief Act," which prohibits default judgments against members of the armed forces who are on duty away from home, where they might not receive actual notice of the suit, and even with notice, they might find it difficult to make arrangements to defend against the creditor's claim.[76]

[2] Summary Judgment

If the defendant files an answer to the complaint, summary judgment may be entered without a trial if no material fact is in dispute and if the plaintiff is entitled to judgment as a matter of law.[77] In collection cases, where the debtor is in default and generally has no defense, summary judgment is commonly available, even if the defendant files an answer, unless the defendant supplies some evidence contesting the creditor's right to a judgment.

[3] Consent Judgments

Judgment also may be entered by consent. This frequently occurs as a result of settlement negotiations between the parties while the case is pending but before a trial is complete.

[4] Judgment by Confession (Cognovit Judgments)

In some situations, a creditor may be permitted, without filing a complaint against the debtor, to enter a confessed or "cognovit" judgment against the debtor pursuant to the debtor's prior written consent. Judgment by confession is an ancient device[78] by which the debtor agrees in advance

---

the debt was paid. *See* Thomas E. Plank, *The Constitutional Limits of Bankruptcy*, 63 Tenn. L. Rev. 487, 515 (1996); William Blackstone, 3 Commentaries on the Laws of England *414, *417–19 (1979).

[75] *See* Fed. R. Civ. P. 55.

[76] Servicemembers Civil Relief Act, 2003, Pub. L. No. 108–189, § 1, 117 Stat. 2835 (2003) (codified at 50 U.S.C.S. app. §§ 501-596) (LexisNexis Supp. 2006) (formerly known as the Soldiers' and Sailors' Relief Act); *see* George C. Thompson, *The Servicemembers Civil Relief Act*, 48 Res Gestae 13 (Sept. 2004); Roger M. Baron, *Staying Power of the Soldiers' and Sailors' Civil Relief Act,* 32 Santa Clara L. Rev. 137 (1992).

[77] *See* Fed. R. Civ. P. 56.

[78] *See* William Blackstone, Commentaries on the Laws of England *397 (1979); Don Hopson, Jr., *Cognovit Judgments: An Ignored Problem of Due Process and Full Faith and Credit,* 29 U. Chi. L. Rev. 111 (1961); Robert M. Hunter, *The Warrant of Attorney to Confess Judgment*, 8 Ohio St. L.J. 1 (1941).

to permit the creditor to obtain a judgment against the debtor without formal notice or a hearing, sometimes through an attorney designated by the creditor, who purportedly acts on the debtor's behalf.[79] This was described by one court as "the written authority of the debtor and his direction . . . to enter judgment against him."[80]

The facts in a famous confession of judgment case, *D.H. Overmeyer Co. v. Frick,*[81] explain how judgment by confession works. After the debtor fell into default on its obligations to Frick, the parties entered into settlement negotiations, which resulted in the execution of a new promissory note. The new note specified:

> The undersigned hereby authorize any attorney designated by the Holder hereof to appear in any court of record in the State of Ohio, and waive this [sic] issuance and service of process, and confess a judgment against the undersigned in favor of the Holder of this Note, for the principal of this Note plus interest if the undersigned defaults in any payment of principal and interest and if said default shall continue for the period of fifteen (15) days.[82]

Overmeyer stopped making payments on the note that contained this cognovit provision, asserted that Frick was in breach of contract, and brought an action against Frick to resolve the dispute. In response, and without any prior notice to Overmeyer, Frick engaged a lawyer to make an appearance on behalf of Overmeyer[83] " 'by virtue of the warranty of attorney' in the second note." The lawyer waived the issuance and service of process and confessed a judgment for the amount of the note in Frick's favor. Overmeyer was completely unacquainted with the lawyer who was acting solely on the authority of the above-quoted language in the promissory note that Overmeyer had previously signed.[84]

The Supreme Court ruled that the cognovit provision was sufficient as a knowing and intelligent waiver of Overmeyer's constitutional rights to due process.[85] Although the Court believed that cognovit provisions "may well serve a proper and useful purpose in the commercial world," it cautioned that the procedure might not be constitutional "where the contract is one of adhesion, where there is great disparity in bargaining power, and where the debtor receives nothing for the cognovit provision."[86]

---

[79] D.H. Overmeyer Co. v. Frick, 405 U.S. 174, 176 (1972).

[80] Blott v. Blott, 290 N.W. 74, 76 (Iowa 1940).

[81] 405 U.S. 174 (1972).

[82] 405 U.S. at 180–81.

[83] That's right, the debtor, Overmeyer. One party is permitted to act on its own to enter a judgment against the other.

[84] 405 U.S. at 181.

[85] The confession of judgment provision was specifically negotiated between the parties, Overmeyer was represented by counsel in the negotiation of the provision, Overmeyer was aware of the meaning and significance of the provision, both parties were merchants, and the provision was included in the wake of an earlier default by Overmeyer.

[86] 405 U.S. at 188.

However, in the commercial setting presented by the parties, the judgment entered against Frick was valid, despite the absence of prior notice or an opportunity to be heard.

Judgment by confession has been eliminated by many states.[87] Others prohibit its use in consumer transactions.[88] Where it may still be used, it is frequently regulated with disclosure requirements and provisions for prompt notice from the court after the judgment has been entered.[89]

The Federal Trade Commission has adopted rules making a cognovit provision an unfair trade practice in a variety of consumer transactions.[90] Likewise, the Federal Consumer Credit Protection Act prohibits use of a cognovit provision without specific disclosures to the consumer.[91]

Where judgment by confession survives, the debtor may usually take action to reopen the judgment through the same mechanisms used to reopen other types of judgments. In many states, judgments entered by confession are easier to reverse than other judgments, sometimes merely upon a showing that there was a meritorious defense.[92] Thus, although a judgment might be easily obtained by confession, a debtor with a defense usually has the means to have the merits of his defense adjudicated.

[5] Judgment after Trial

Judgment also may be entered after a trial.[93] This may take anywhere from several hours to several days or weeks. In extreme cases it may take several years.

Most of the time, collection efforts can begin while any appeals are pending. For example, the Chapter 11 bankruptcy case of petroleum giant Texaco was precipitated by an $11 billion jury verdict in favor of Pennzoil for intentional interference with Pennzoil's merger agreement with Getty Oil Co.[94] When Texaco could not afford to file a bond to enjoin Pennzoil from filing liens against Texaco's assets while Texaco appealed Pennzoil's judgment, it was forced to file for bankruptcy to take advantage of the automatic stay.[95]

---

[87] *E.g.,* Fla. Stat. Ann. § 55.05 (2006).

[88] *See, e.g.*, N.Y.C.P.R. 3201 (McKinney 2005) (consumer goods); Ohio Rev. Code Ann. § 2323.13(E) (LexisNexis 2005) (consumer transactions).

[89] Ohio Rev. Code Ann. § 2323.13(E) (LexisNexis 2005).

[90] 16 C.F.R. § 429.1 (2004) (door-to-door sales); 16 C.F.R. § 444.2(a)(1) (2004) (retail installment sales).

[91] *See, e.g.*, McCoy v. Harriman Util. Bd., 790 F.2d 493 (6th Cir. 1986); Goldberg v. Delaware Olds, Inc., 670 F. Supp. 125 (D. Del. 1987).

[92] *E.g.*, Bates v. Midland Title of Ashtabula County, Inc., 2004 Ohio App. LEXIS 6325 (Ohio Ct. App. Nov. 26, 2004); Advanced Clinical Mgmt., Inc. v. Salem Chiropractic Ctr., Inc., 2004 Ohio App. LEXIS 113 (Ohio Ct. App., Jan. 12, 2004).

[93] *See* Fed. R. Civ. P. 54.

[94] Texaco Inc. v. Pennzoil Co., 729 S.W.2d 768, 784 (Tex. Ct. App. 1987).

[95] *See* Pennzoil Co. v. Texaco, Inc., 481 U.S. 1 (1987); In re Texaco Inc., 76 B.R. 322 (Bankr. S.D.N.Y. 1987); Thomas Petzinger, Oil & Honor: The Texaco-Pennzoil Wars 414–26 (1987).

[B] Dormancy, Renewal, and Revival of Judgments

Once obtained, a judgment does not last forever. States impose limits, similar to statutes of limitation, on the durability of judgments.[96] Creditors who have obtained a judgment must take steps to ensure that it remains viable. Otherwise, efforts to use the judgment to seize the debtor's assets may be fruitless, even tortious. Once this limitations period (which is usually quite long) has passed, the judgment may not be enforced.[97]

At common law, a judgment became dormant if the creditor failed to make an effort to collect through a writ of execution within a year and a day of the time the judgment was issued.[98] Once it became dormant, it could either be "renewed" by obtaining a second judgment based on the dormant judgment or "revived" by obtaining a court order permitting the issuance of a new writ of execution on the original judgment.[99]

The effect of dormancy on a judgment lien varies tremendously from one state to the next. Some states permit continuation of the lien with its original priority intact if the judgment is revived; others extinguish the lien, its priority, or both, when the judgment upon which it is based becomes dormant.[100] Renewal may either extend the priority of the original lien (or more likely) result in a new judgment lien with priority based on the time the second judgment is docketed or recorded.

[C] Judgment Based on a Judgment in Another State

Collection of a judgment through judicial process presupposes that the creditor has a judgment against the debtor *in the state* in which these post-judgment collection procedures are pursued. In this respect, collection is little more than post-judgment civil procedure. To pursue assets located in a state other than the one in which a judgment was obtained, a judgment creditor must establish the validity of its judgment in the state in which the debtor's assets are located.[101]

This process is facilitated by the Full Faith and Credit Clause of the United States Constitution. It provides: "Full Faith and Credit shall be given in each State to the public Acts, Records, and judicial Proceedings of every other State."[102] Thus, states are constitutionally required to enforce the valid judgments of their sister states.

---

[96] *See generally* Stefan A. Riesenfeld, Creditors' Rights and Debtors' Protection 59 (4th ed. 1987).

[97] *E.g.*, Hazel v. Van Beek, 954 P.2d 1301, 1307 (Wash. 1998) (10 years); Wyo. Stat. Ann. § 1-16-503 (LexisNexis 2005) (10 years with longer periods if the plaintiff is a minor or if the judgment involved is for child support).

[98] *See* Stefan A. Riesenfeld, *Collection of Money Judgments in American Law — A Historical Inventory and a Prospectus*, 42 Iowa L. Rev. 155, 172 (1957).

[99] *E.g.*, Leroy Jenkins Evangelistic Ass'n, Inc. v. Equities Diversified, Inc., 580 N.E.2d 812 (Ohio Ct. App. 1989) (explaining Ohio procedure to revive dormant judgment).

[100] *E.g.*, Aetna Fin. Co. v. Schmitz, 849 P.2d 1083 (Okla. 1993).

[101] *See, e.g.*, Keeton v. Hustler Magazine, Inc., 815 F.2d 957 (2d Cir. 1987).

[102] U.S. Const. art. IV, § 1.

The normal method to enforce a judgment obtained in another state is to file a lawsuit in the second state, alleging that a judgment was obtained against the defendant in the first state. Unless the judgment was invalid in the state in which it was originally obtained and thus subject to collateral attack (due to lack of personal jurisdiction over the defendant, for example), the defendant will have no defenses and the court in the second state will be obliged to enter a second judgment against the defendant based on the original judgment. Once this second judgment is obtained, it can be enforced in the same manner as other judgments obtained in the courts of the second state.

Several states have adopted the Uniform Enforcement of Foreign Judgments Act. It supplies a system for the "registration" of judgments, which makes it unnecessary to obtain a second judgment simply to enforce the first in another state. Courts consistently rule that judgment debtors may not re-litigate the merits of a sister-state judgment when enforcement is sought under the UEFJA.[103]

Procedures for enforcement of judgments obtained in foreign countries also vary from state to state. The creditor with the foreign judgment must sue in the United States, and the U.S. court will determine whether to give effect to the foreign judgment. Many states have enacted another uniform statute, the Uniform Foreign Money-Judgments Recognition Act.[104] Its 2005 replacement, the Uniform Foreign-Country Judgments Recognition Act, as of mid-2007, has been enacted in only Idaho and Nevada.[105]

§ 2.05 Judicial Liens[106]

Having obtained judicial recognition of its right to a specific sum of money, a judgment creditor can pursue several routes to collect the amount of its judgment. If the judgment debtor has insurance, the insurance carrier may simply write a check to satisfy the judgment in full. If the debtor is not insured, the size of the judgment and the debtor's financial condition may result in the creditor sending a barrage of letters and making a multitude of phone calls to the debtor, demanding payment. If the judgment debtor owns valuable property but remains unwilling to voluntarily pay, a judgment creditor may take additional steps to obtain a judicial lien on the

[103] Sara L. Johnson, Annotation, *Validity, Construction and Application of Uniform Enforcement of Judgments Act*, 31 A.L.R.4th 762 (1984).

[104] Uniform Foreign Money Judgments Recognition Act (1962), 13 (pt 2) U.L.A. 149 (1986) available online at www.nccusl.org/Update/uniformact_factsheets/uniformacts-fs-ufmjra.asp (last viewed May 7, 2007).

[105] Uniform Foreign-Country Judgments Recognition Act (2005), 13 (pt. 2) U.L.A. 43 (Supp. 2006) available online. *See* www.nccusl.org/Update/uniformact_factsheets/uniformacts-fs-ufcmjra.asp (last viewed May 28, 2007).

[106] Stefan A. Riesenfeld, *Collection of Money Judgments in American Law*, 42 Iowa L. Rev. 155 (1957); *see* Stefan A. Riesenfeld, *Enforcement of Money Judgments in Early American History*, 71 Mich. L. Rev. 691, 694 (1973); Clinton W. Francis, *Practice, Strategy, and Institution: Debt Collection in the English Common-law Courts, 1740-1840*, 80 Nw. U. L. Rev. 807 (1987).

debtor's property and then foreclose on the lien to obtain payment. Sometimes this is the only way for a judgment creditor to obtain payment from a recalcitrant debtor. On other occasions, the threat or actual imposition of a lien induces the debtor to pay voluntarily, without the necessity of incurring the expense of obtaining or enforcing a lien.

Judicial liens are involuntary liens that are available to creditors who have obtained a judgment against a debtor. They are involuntary because they are imposed without the consent of the debtor whose property is subject to the lien. Judicial liens are created to give tangible effect to a money judgment and to assist judgment creditors in obtaining payment.

There are numerous subtle features to the rules regarding these procedures which vary considerably from state to state. In most jurisdictions, a lien on real property is obtained by docketing or recording the judgment in the county where the debtor's land is located. A judicial lien on tangible personal property is obtained by having the local sheriff's department levy on the asset pursuant to a court order. Obtaining a judicial lien on intangible property through "garnishment" is more complicated and may require the initiation of an ancillary lawsuit against a person who owes money to the judgment debtor.

It is impossible in the limited space available here to consider every variation on these procedures, and law students taking a course in basic debtor-creditor law only rarely delve into the details of these procedures, even with respect to the law in their own state.[107] Accordingly, the following section merely identifies the most frequently encountered issues and sketches the most common rules.

[A] Judgment Liens on Real Estate

A judicial or "judgment" lien[108] on real estate is ordinarily established either by "docketing" the judgment or by recording the judgment in the county where the real estate is located.[109] In many states, formal entry of the judgment on the court's records alone may be sufficient for the judgment to operate as a lien on property belonging to the debtor and located in the same county in which the judgment was entered.[110] However, in other states, the judgment creditor to record notice of the judgment in the county real estate records, similar to the way a creditor would record a mortgage on the debtor's land. Recording the judgment protects third parties who might otherwise obtain an interest in the property, by giving them notice of the encumbrance. Likewise, it protects the creditor's lien

[107] Collection lawyers, on the other hand, become thoroughly familiar with them.

[108] Judgment liens were known to the common law as the writ of "elegit."

[109] *See, e.g.*, Cal. Civ. Proc. Code § 674 (West Supp. 2006).

[110] *See, e.g.*, N.Y. C.P.L.R. § 5018 (McKinney 1992).

from subsequent attack by the bankruptcy trustee in the event that the debtor files a bankruptcy petition.[111]

If the debtor owns land in several counties, the judgment must be recorded in each county in which the debtor's land is situated for the creditor's lien to extend to that land. Assume, for example, that Merchant's Bank has a $300,000 judgment against Titanic Industries and Titanic owns land in both Jefferson County, where the judgment was obtained, and another parcel in Madison County, in the same state. To obtain a judgment lien on the Jefferson County property, Merchant's Bank will usually find it necessary to docket the judgment or to record it in the real estate records in Jefferson County. To obtain a judgment lien on the debtor's Madison County land, Merchant's Bank will have to record the Jefferson County judgment in the real estate records maintained by the Madison County Recorder's office.

Judgment liens on real estate normally have priority over subsequently arising interests in the land, and are subordinate to previously recorded interests, other than ownership interests of the judgment debtor himself. Existing interests may or may not include the interests of a person who has an unrecorded interest but is in possession of the property — this varies from state to state.

Whether a judicial lien extends to real estate acquired by the debtor after the lien was recorded — "after-acquired" property — also varies from state to state, with most states permitting a judgment lien recorded in a county's real estate records to encumber real estate acquired by the debtor in the same county after the judgment was recorded.[112] However, the lien may not enjoy seniority over subsequently recorded judgment liens. In some states, judgments are entitled to pro-rata priority with respect to such after-acquired land. Assume, for example, that as of May 2005, Franklin Manufacturing, Inc. owns Blackacre, located in Wood County. If in June 2005, River Bank obtains and records a judgment in Wood County, the lien will apply to Blackacre. If in September, 2005 Merchant's Finance Co. obtains and records a judgment against Franklin in Wood County, Merchant's will also have a lien on Blackacre, but it will be subordinate in priority to River Bank's lien, which was recorded first. But, if Franklin subsequently inherits Redacre, which is also located in Wood County, the judgment liens of River Bank and Merchant's Finance will likely share priority over this newly acquired land. Other states, however, would preserve River's priority in Redacre, based on the time its judgment was originally recorded.

Insofar as bankruptcy is concerned, a judicial lien on real property has the same status as most other kinds of liens. If the judgment is recorded

[111] Note, however, that if the lien is acquired within the ninety day period immediately before bankruptcy is commenced, the lien may still be vulnerable to attack by the trustee as a voidable preference. This may lead wise creditors to delay foreclosure of the lien, which may precipitate a bankruptcy filing, until the 90-day period has expired. *See generally* Chapter 15, Preferences, *infra*.

[112] In re Estate of Robbins, 346 N.Y.S.2d 86 (N.Y. Sur. 1973); *see also* David Grey Carlson, *Simultaneous Attachment of Liens on After-Acquired Property*, 6 Cardozo L. Rev. 505 (1985).

before the bankruptcy case is filed, the judgment creditor is likely to have a secured claim. However, if the lien was recorded, or the asset became subject to a previously perfected lien, sometime in the ninety days immediately preceding the debtor's bankruptcy petition, it will likely be set aside by the bankruptcy trustee as an avoidable preference.[113]

[B] Judicial Liens on Tangible Personal Property

Imposing a judicial lien on personal property, especially goods, generally requires several steps beyond obtaining and docketing a judgment. Recording the judgment in the county where the debtor's goods are located, or even where the debtor resides, usually means nothing with respect to the judgment debtor's goods.[114] Instead, a judgment creditor must "levy" or "execute" on the goods, probably through physical seizure by the local sheriff pursuant to a court order.

Historically, a debtor's property could be seized by the sheriff and sold to satisfy a judgment pursuant to a writ of fieri facias, which is still commonly abbreviated and known colloquially in states where it is used as a "fi fa."[115] The procedure involved to obtain a modern writ of attachment or execution on a judgment debtor's goods is not appreciably different from that used to obtain a fi fa. After judgment, the creditor requests an order from the court directing the sheriff to locate and seize the debtor's property. After the writ is delivered to the sheriff, deputies are dispatched to comply with the instructions contained in the writ. Naturally, the more information the judgment creditor supplies to the sheriff's department, the more likely that the deputies assigned to the task will be able to successfully locate and seize the judgment debtor's property. The debtor, of course, can be expected to resist the sheriff's efforts, though not usually with force.[116]

Sometimes, the seizure may be merely symbolic. It might be accomplished by attaching some sort of official notice to the property, indicating that the property has been seized by the sheriff's department. Some states do not require this rather minimal form of seizure, and treat the property as having been attached if it came within the "view and control" of the sheriff.[117] Thus, in *Credit Bureau of Broken Bow v. Moninger*,[118] a truck was successfully levied on when a duly authorized deputy " 'grabbed ahold

---

[113] *See* Chapter 15 Avoidable Preferences, *infra*.

[114] *E.g.*, In re Tropicana Graphics, Inc., 24 B.R. 381 (Bankr. C.D. Cal. 1982) ("Unlike real property, a judgment lien has no analogue that reaches personal property.").

[115] Del. Code Ann. tit. 10, § 5041 (1999); *see* United States v. Crittenden, 563 F.2d 678, 680 n.4 (5th Cir. 1977) (the court jokingly noted that the facts did not require the court to determine whether the judgment debtor, the FHA, "could have attacked Crittenden's fi. fa. with a fo fum or whether the result would be different if Crittenden had English blood.").

[116] *See, e.g.*, Hickey v. Couchman, 797 S.W.2d 103 (Tex. Ct. App. 1990) (illustrating the debtor's delaying tactics).

[117] *But see* Socony Mobil Oil Co. v. Wayne County Produce Co., 196 N.Y.S.2d 729 (N.Y. Sup. Ct. 1959) (property viewed through a window, but not under the sheriff's dominion and control).

[118] 284 N.W.2d 855 (Neb. 1979).

of the pickup' and stated: 'I execute on the pickup for the County of Custer,' " even though he neither took the vehicle into his possession nor even acquired a set of keys to it.

The sheriff's failure to make a successful levy has several potential consequences. Most importantly, it deprives the judgment creditor of the priority it would have achieved over subsequent creditors who obtain a statutory, judicial, or consensual lien on property the sheriff might have seized.[119] If efforts to make an effective levy fail due to the deputy's deviation from the sheriff's statutory duties, the judgment creditor might be able to recover the amount of its judgment from the sheriff in an "amercement" action.[120] Sheriff's departments are usually bonded against liability for such mistakes.

In most states, a judgment creditor's priority over other creditors dates from the time the debtor's property was physically seized.[121] This provides the greatest possible protection for good faith purchasers and other creditors, who otherwise might be misled by the debtor's apparent unfettered ownership of the property subject to the lien. On the other hand, unless the sheriff has a duty to execute writs in the order in which he has received them,[122] it might make priority dependent upon the order in which assignments are made in the sheriff's department. This could lead to abuse due to political favoritism, or even bribery.

In other jurisdictions, priority relates back to the time the writ was delivered to the sheriff,[123] or possibly back to the time it was issued by the court.[124] These procedures prevent manipulation by the sheriff's office but permit the imposition of secret liens in the period between the date the writ is delivered to the sheriff, but before the property is actually seized.

A few states take a completely different approach to the matter. California, for example, permits a judgment creditor to obtain a judicial lien on the business debtor's personal property, both tangible and intangible, by filing notice of the judgment in the state's U.C.C. records. This is much in the same way that a lien on the debtor's real estate would be obtained, except notice of the judgment is filed with the office of the California Secretary of State instead of the county recorder's office.[125] The property

---

[119] *See* U.C.C. § 9-317(a)(2) (2003) (security interest); Illi, Inc. v. Margolis, 296 A.2d 412 (Md. Ct. App. 1972) (competing fi fa).

[120] Ryan v. Carter, 621 N.E.2d 399 (Ohio 1993); Vitale v. Hotel Cal., Inc., 446 A.2d 880 (N.J. Super. Ct.), *aff'd*, 455 A.2d 508 (N.J. App. Div. 1982); *see* Frank B. Wyatt, *Amercement of Sheriffs*, 10 Wake Forest L. Rev. 237 (1974).

[121] *E.g.*, Cal. Civ. Proc. Code § 697.710 (2005); *see generally* D.E. Murray, *Execution Lien Creditors Versus Bona Fide Purchasers, Lenders and Other Execution Lien Creditors: Charles II and the Uniform Commercial Code*, 85 Com. L.J. 485 (1980).

[122] *E.g.*, Ohio Rev. Code Ann. § 2329.10 (LexisNexis 2005).

[123] *E.g.*, N.Y. C.P.L.R. 5234(b) (McKinney Supp. 2005); 735 Ill. Comp. Stat. Ann. 5/12-111 (2003).

[124] Tenn. Code Ann. § 26-1-109 (LexisNexis 2000).

[125] *See* Cal. Civ. Proc. Code. Ann. § 697.510 (West 1987).

still must be seized in order to be sold, but the creditor's priority over competing claims is determined by the date of filing.

[C] Garnishment of Property Under the Control of Third Parties[126]

Property under the control of third parties is generally acquired by the creditor through garnishment proceedings.[127] This property usually consists of money owed to the judgment debtor, such as wages, bank accounts, and less frequently, accounts receivable. Although courts sometimes suggest that garnishment is purely a creature of statute and a stranger to the common law,[128] it had its origin in European cities during the middle ages in a procedure then known as "foreign attachment."[129]

Garnishment is usually initiated through service of a court order on a person in control of the debtor's property, directing that person to deliver the debtor's property to the creditor — at least to the extent necessary to satisfy the creditor's judgment.[130] In this respect, garnishment sometimes resembles a lawsuit within a lawsuit. The garnishment proceeding is little more than a cause of action alleging that the third party owes money (or some other form of property) to the judgment debtor.

Wage garnishment is one of the most common examples of garnishment proceedings. In a wage garnishment, the judgment creditor brings an ancillary action against the judgment debtor's employer. The creditor alleges that the judgment debtor is an employee of the defendant, who is usually referred to as the "garnishee,"[131] and that the employer owes money to the judgment debtor. The remedy sought is for the employer to pay the wages owed to the employee to his judgment creditor, instead of paying them to the employee. The garnishee may defend the action the way any defendant might — by denying the allegations of the complaint (such as where the judgment debtor is no longer employed by the defendant and owes the debtor no wages).

---

[126] Jonathan Glusman, Note, *Garnishment of Receivables in Chinese Law*, 3 Wash. U. Global Stud. L. Rev. 455 (2004).

[127] Garnishment can also be used to recover tangible property in the hands of a third party, but it is most commonly used to recover amounts owed to the judgment debtor by a third party.

[128] *E.g.*, Western v. Hodgson, 494 F.2d 379 (4th Cir. 1974).

[129] *See* Ownbey v. Morgan, 256 U.S. 94, 104–05 (1905); Stefan A. Riesenfeld, Creditors' Remedies and Debtors' Protection 240 (4th ed. 1987); *see* Nathan Levy, Jr., *Attachment, Garnishment and Garnishment Execution,*, 5 Conn. L. Rev. 399, 405 (1972).

[130] Peggy Coleman, Warren Ross & John P. Finan, Note, *Creditor's Rights in Ohio: An Extensive Revision (Introduction),* 16 Akron L. Rev. 487 (1983).

[131] "Garnishee" is a noun, which refers to the person against whom the garnishment action is brought — in a wage garnishment proceeding, the employer. "Garnishee" is frequently misused by those uneducated in the law of creditors' rights, as if it were a verb referring to the act of garnishment itself. The proper verb in this setting is "garnish." Black's Law Dictionary 702 (8th ed. 2004). Properly speaking, a person's wages are "garnished"; they are not "garnisheed." "Garnisheed" is not a word.

As required by federal law, all states impose significant limits on the percentage of a person's wages that are subject to garnishment. The Consumer Credit Protection Act generally prevents judgment creditors from garnishing more than 25% of a person's wages.[132]

Garnishment proceedings are also frequently brought to recover funds on deposit in a judgment debtor's bank account. As with a wage garnishment proceeding, the bank, as garnishee, has the opportunity to defend the lawsuit by denying allegations that it has any of the judgment debtor's funds on deposit.

Bank accounts present attractive targets for enforcement of a judgment. Unlike real estate or tangible personal property, the funds in a bank account are highly liquid. Moreover, a bank that fails to properly respond to a garnishment proceeding may find itself liable to the judgment creditor for the entire debt its banking customer owes to the creditor.[133] Banks tend to pay their debts.

Judgment creditors sometimes find that the bank in which a debtor's funds are deposited is one of the judgment debtor's other creditors. In this case, an effort to garnish the debtor's bank account is likely to persuade the bank to exercise its right of setoff against the debtor's account. For example, if Titanic Industries owes money to both Island Bank and to Merchant's Finance Co. and keeps its funds in an account at Island Bank, any effort by Merchant's Finance to garnish Titanic's account at Island will likely induce Island to exercise its right of setoff against the account. This inevitably raises questions about the propriety of the bank's exercise of its right of setoff and of the relative priority of a garnishing judgment creditor and the bank's equitable or statutory right of setoff.[134] Most of the time, the bank's right of setoff prevails.[135]

§ 2.06 Statutory, Common Law, and Equitable Liens

Statutory, common law, and equitable liens arise without any court action. They are imposed automatically by operation of law, usually as a result of the nature of the transaction involved between the debtor and the creditor. The most common example is a statutory construction lien, which operates for the benefit of someone who has supplied goods or services in connection with improvements to the debtor's land. Other examples include artisan's liens in favor of individuals who perform repairs on motor vehicles and other personal property, landlords liens, veterinarians liens, and even common law "charging liens" in favor of attorneys, which are sometimes

---

[132] 15 U.S.C. §§ 1671-1677 (2000); *see* § 2.12[A][4][a] Federal Restrictions on Wage Garnishment, *infra;* § 12.03[D][1] Wage Exemptions, *infra.*

[133] *E.g.*, Tenn. Code Ann. § 26-2-209 (LexisNexis 2000); *see generally* Robert Laurence, *The Supreme Court and the Defaulting Garnishee: An Essay on* Metal Processing, Inc. v. Plastic & Reconstructive Associates, Ltd. *and a Few of its Predecessors*, 40 Ark. L. Rev. 1 (1986).

[134] *See* § 2.07 Setoff, *infra.*

[135] *See* § 2.07 Setoff, *infra.*

imposed on the proceeds of successful litigation in which the attorneys have engaged. These various statutory and common law liens provide leverage to the creditor who may use the lien to obtain voluntary payment, and if necessary, to ensure the availability of a source of payment. Some are rooted in the concept of unjust enrichment. Others have deep historical roots. Others are the product of legislative lobbying efforts on behalf of participants in the industry who are protected by the lien.

Another important example is the tax lien, granted by the government in favor of itself, to enhance its ability to collect taxes owed by the debtor.[136]

Except for construction liens on real estate and tax liens, most of these statutory liens require the lien holder to have physical possession of the property subject to the lien. A creditor who relinquishes possession of the goods loses its lien. In most other respects, the details of these statutory and common law liens vary tremendously from state to state. Nevertheless, some common patterns exist.

[A] Construction or "Mechanic's" Liens

A construction lien (also sometimes known as a "mechanic's," "materialman's," or "laborer's" lien) is a statutory lien designed to protect those who supply goods and services in connection with a construction project from the risk of non-payment by the landowner, or default by the prime contractor. Protection provided to these suppliers is thought to reduce the cost of construction by eliminating some of the credit risk that the parties otherwise face.[137]

In most construction projects, the construction process is managed by a "general" or "prime" contractor who is responsible for completing the building or other improvement for the owner. Usually this prime contractor is the only person who deals directly with and who is in contractual privity with the owner of the land. The prime contractor parcels out portions of the job to various subcontractors and material suppliers. For example, one subcontractor will do the plumbing, another the electrical work, and a third the interior design. The actual goods used in the project will be acquired from building supply companies. Since the plumber, the electrician, the designer, and the supply company do not have a direct contract with the owner of the project, they cannot sue the owner directly if they are not paid by the prime contractor. Construction lien laws protect these parties by giving them liens on the improved real estate for the goods and services they have provided in connection with the improvements. Typically, these liens arise when construction begins. The lien is generally perfected by a system of notice to both the public and to the owner, generally involving recording notice of the lien in real property records and making personal service on the owners.

---

[136] *See* 26 U.S.C. § 6321 (2000).

[137] *See* Chesebro-Whitman Co. v. Edenboro Apartments, Inc., 207 A.2d 186, 188 (N.J. Super. Ct. 1965).

Notice to the owner plays an important role in protecting the owner from the risk of being obligated to pay twice. Without notice of the subcontractor or supplier's claim the owner may pay the prime contractor for the work provided before the prime contractor has paid the sub or supplier. Construction liens are neither limited to the amount required to be paid by the owner to the prime contractor nor affected by payments from the owner to the prime contractor who is supervising the overall project. Thus, owners incur a serious risk of having to pay twice for the same work if the owner pays the prime contractor without obtaining some sort of protection against the risk that the prime contractor has not remitted payment to others who have contributed to the project. This protection is normally secured either by obtaining a payment bond from the prime contractor or by obtaining releases from the subcontractors and suppliers.

It is usually necessary for the lien holder to record notice of the lien in the real estate records in the county where the land is located.[138] Notice may also be required to be published in a newspaper or served on the owner.[139] Once recorded, priority usually relates back to the time the overall construction project began,[140] though many states date the lien holder's priority from the time it began work or provided materials, even though the overall project began earlier.[141]

Construction lien statutes typically permit lien holders to provide owners with a "waiver" of their liens. Prudent owners and construction lenders will insist on obtaining waivers before making final payment for work that has been completed on the project. Similarly, purchasers of new construction should insist on evidence that work performed during the lien's relation back period has been paid for, before advancing their own funds.

[B] Repair Liens

Repair liens operate in favor of persons who have repaired personal property, such as an automobile, and who have not been paid. They are designed to protect service providers from the risk of non-payment by the owner. Such liens are also referred to as "mechanics" or "artisans" liens but they should not be confused with construction liens which also sometimes bear these labels. They might arise under the common law or rules of equity but today are nearly always statutory. Accordingly, both their scope and priority depend upon the provisions of the state statute under which they arise. As with most aspects of state collection law, they vary widely from state to state.

Repair liens almost always require the lien holder to remain in possession of the repaired property. An auto repair shop that relinquishes possession

---

[138] *See generally* Grant S. Nelson & Dale A. Whitman, Real Estate Finance Law 979 (4th ed. 2001).

[139] *See generally* Grant S. Nelson & Dale A. Whitman, Real Estate Finance Law 979 (4th ed. 2001).

[140] *E.g.*, Mich. Comp. Laws Ann. § 570.1119 (1996).

[141] *E.g.*, Northwest Nat'l Bank v. Metro Ctr., Inc., 303 N.W.2d 395, 398 (Iowa 1981).

of the car it has worked on usually loses its lien on the vehicle. Accordingly, repair shops rarely relinquish possession of goods they have repaired, without being paid, but it has been known to occur.

The most commonly recurring priority issue deals with conflicts between a creditor with a statutory lien and a competing creditor with an Article 9 security interest in the same property. Under U.C.C. § 9-333, a creditor with a "possessory lien" in goods that secures payment of an obligation for services or materials supplied to the debtor in the ordinary course has priority over a conflicting security interest in the same goods, unless the state statute that created the possessory lien provides otherwise. Loss of possession by the lien holder results in loss of this priority.[142]

[C] Common Law Liens[143]

Although most of the liens discussed in this section are creatures of state statutes, a few common law liens persist. Like statutory liens, they usually operate in favor of a creditor based on his or her status as a landlord, an auctioneer,[144] or a warehouseman. They usually arise to prevent unjust enrichment of the debtor whose property has been improved as a result of the efforts of the creditor for whose benefit the lien operates.[145] Again, they nearly always depend on the lien holder's continued possession of the goods subject to the lien.[146]

[D] Equitable Liens

Equitable liens are only imposed where the creditor has no adequate remedy at law.[147] They are usually awarded only when there is specific property to which the creditor's claim is related. For example, in *Palm Beach Savings. & Loan Ass'n v. Fishbein,*[148] the court granted an equitable lien to a bank whose mortgage was invalid because the debtor's former husband forged her signature on the loan documents. The lien was limited to the extent the proceeds of the bank's loan were used to satisfy a preexisting mortgage and taxes on the property, for which the wife had been liable. Because she had benefitted from the loans, imposing a lien on her property was not unfair. As *Fishbein* illustrates, equitable liens are frequently imposed in situations where there was an unsuccessful attempt to

---

142 U.C.C. § 9-330 (2003).

143 Ray Andrews Brown, The Law of Personal Property § 107 at 512 (2d ed. 1955); *see* Richard L. Barne, *UCC Article Nine Revised: Priorities, Preferences, and Liens Effective Only in Bankruptcy*, 82 Neb. L. Rev. 607, 627 (2004).

144 *E.g.*, Thoroughbred Horsemen's Ass'n of Tex. Inc. v. Dyer, 905 S.W.2d 752 (Tex. Ct. App. 1995) (common law auctioneer's lien).

145 *E.g.*, Burns v. Miller, 714 P.2d 1190 (Wash. Ct. App. 1986), *rev'd in part*, 733 P.2d 522 (Wash. 1987).

146 *E.g.*, Central Contractors Serv., Inc. v. Ohio County Stone Co., 255 S.W.2d 17 (Ky. 1952).

147 *See, e.g.*, In re Broadview Lumber Co., Inc., 118 F.3d 1246, 1253 (8th Cir. 1997).

148 619 So. 2d 267 (Fla. 1993).

obtain a consensual lien, and where the denial of relief would result in the debtor's unjust enrichment at the creditor's expense.[149]

Most jurisdictions now disfavor equitable liens because of their inherently secret nature. Without notice of the lien, other creditors may be misled into believing that the debtor's property is unencumbered. Given the ease of obtaining a security interest in personal property, the drafters of Article 9 of the U.C.C. attempted to eliminate equitable liens.[150] However, their efforts have not been completely successful, and courts still sometimes impose them.[151]

[E] Seller's Right of Reclamation

In some cases, sellers have a right to reclaim goods delivered to an insolvent buyer. U.C.C. § 2-702(2) provides a limited right of reclamation in credit sales. Section 2-507 gives sellers a similar right in cash sales where payment is not completed, usually as a result of dishonor of the buyer's check.

[1] Credit Sales

U.C.C. Article 2 gives sellers who have delivered goods on credit to an insolvent buyer with a limited right to reclaim them. U.C.C. § 2-702 gives a seller the right to reclaim the goods if:

- the goods were sold to the buyer on credit;
- the debtor was insolvent when it received the goods; and
- the seller demands return of the goods within ten days after the buyer received them.[152]

Section 2-702's right of reclamation only applies if the goods were sold on credit. If the transaction was intended to be a cash sale, with payment to be made with cash or a check, § 2-507's similar right applies instead.

Section 2-702 limits the right of reclamation to situations where the buyer is insolvent at the time it receives the goods. If the buyer is solvent at the time the goods are delivered, and becomes insolvent later, when payment is due, § 2-702 does not apply.

In most cases, the seller must assert its right to reclaim the goods within ten days after the buyer received them. However, if the buyer gave the seller

[149] *E.g.*, Washington Metro. Area Transit Auth. v. Reid, 666 A.2d 41 (D.C. 1995) (employers who paid workers' compensation benefits to employee entitled to equitable lien against employee's tort recovery to prevent unjust enrichment of the employee).

[150] U.C.C. § 9-203 cmt. 5 (2003) ("Since this Article reduces formal requisites to a minimum, the doctrine [of equitable liens] is no longer necessary or useful. More harm than good would result from allowing creditors to establish a secured status by parol evidence after they have neglected the simple formality of obtaining a signed writing.").

[151] *E.g.*, In re Carpenter, 252 B.R. 905 (E.D. Va. 2000); In re Czebotar, 5 Bankr. 379 (B.A.P. 9th Cir. 1980).

[152] U.C.C. § 2-702(2) (2002).

a written misrepresentation of his financial condition within the three-month period before delivery of the goods, the ten-day limit does not apply.[153]

[2] Cash Sales

In cash transactions, where the buyer's check bounces, § 2-507 gives the seller a similar right to reclaim the goods. It provides: "Where payment is due and demanded on the delivery to the buyer of goods or documents of title, his right as against the seller to retain or dispose of them is conditional upon his making the payment due."[154]

Section 2-507 permits the seller to reclaim regardless of whether the buyer is insolvent. Although § 2-507 does not mention a time limit on the seller's right to reclaim in a cash transaction, some courts have applied § 2-702(2)'s ten-day limit by analogy.[155] The Code's official comments, which originally suggested that § 2-702's time limit should be applied, were changed to indicate that no such limit should be imposed in a cash sale.[156]

[3] Priority of Right of Reclamation

These rights to reclaim goods delivered to a buyer are highly vulnerable to the competing claims of third parties who obtain an interest in the goods. Competing claimants might include a buyer in the ordinary course, who purchased them from the buyer, or another good faith purchaser, such as a creditor with a security interest in the buyer's inventory.

[a] Priority of Buyer in the Ordinary Course of Business

Section 2-702 explicitly provides that the seller's right to reclaim goods delivered to an insolvent buyer are subject to the rights of a buyer in the ordinary course and to the rights of a good faith purchaser. Thus, if the buyer is a seller of goods of the kind and resells the goods to a buyer in the ordinary course, the downstream buyer obtains them free of the unpaid seller's right to recover them.

Consider, for example, a credit sale of shingles from Century Slate to a Ron's Roofing, a roofing contractor. Ron was insolvent at the time the goods

---

[153] U.C.C. § 2-702(2) (2002). The 2003 revision to U.C.C. Article 2 remove the ten-day limit and require the seller assert its right to reclaim the goods within a "reasonable time" after the buyer receives them. U.C.C. § 2-702(2) (2003). These revisions are not expected to be widely adopted. As of mid-2006, they have not been adopted by any state. *See* www.nccusl.org/Update/uniformact_factsheets/uniformacts-fs-ucc22A03.asp (last visited June 7, 2006).

[154] U.C.C. § 2-507(2) (2002).

[155] *Compare* Szabo v. Vinton Motors, 630 F.2d 1 (1st Cir. 1980) (ten-day limit imposed by analogy), *with* Burk v. Emmick, 637 F.2d 1172 (8th Cir. 1980) (no limit).

[156] The proposed revisions to Article 2, if adopted anywhere, would make the rights of reclamation in §§ 2-507 and 2-207(2) identical, requiring the seller to assert its right to reclaim the goods within a reasonable time.

were delivered, but he immediately resold the shingles to Julie, in the ordinary course of installing a new roof on her house. Julie's rights as a buyer in the ordinary course of business takes priority over Century Slate's right to reclaim them from Ron's Roofing.

[b] Priority of a Good Faith Purchaser for Value (Secured Party)

Likewise, the seller's rights are vulnerable to the claim of a good faith purchaser from the buyer. Because a creditor with a security interest in the goods is regarded as a purchaser, unpaid sellers are vulnerable to the competing claims of the customer's secured lenders. If, for example, instead of immediately installing them on Julie's house, Ron simply adds the shingles to his inventory of roofing materials, they may become subject to a security interest held by Contractor's Finance Co., if it holds a security interest in Ron's "existing and after-acquired inventory." Under U.C.C. § 2-702(3), the seller's right of reclamation is expressly subject to the competing rights of such a "purchaser."[157] And, although § 2-507 makes no mention of a purchaser's superior rights, most courts addressing the issue have ruled that the buyer's secured lender prevails over the seller's right of reclamation.[158] Moreover, Bankruptcy Code § 546(c) expressly makes a reclaiming seller's rights subject to the "prior rights of a holder of a security interest in such goods or the proceeds thereof."[159]

[4] Bankruptcy Code Limits on Seller's Right of Reclamation

These rights of reclamation are also subject to limits imposed by the Bankruptcy Code. Since nearly all reclamations occur in the context of an insolvent buyer, there is a strong likelihood that the seller's rights will be subject to the Bankruptcy Code's restrictions. Thus, the seller's rights under Article 2 must be read in conjunction with Bankruptcy Code § 546(c).

Section 546(c) generally validates a seller's right to reclaim, but adds a further requirement that the seller's demand for the return of the goods be made in writing. In addition, it limits the seller's right of reclamation to goods the buyer received within forty-five days before commencement of the buyer's bankruptcy case.[160] Further, as explained in more detail elsewhere,[161] § 546(c) also imposes limits on the timing of the seller's

[157] U.C.C. § 2-702(3) (2002).

[158] *E.g.*, In re Dairy Mart Convenience Stores, Inc., 302 B.R. 128, 134–36 (Bankr. S.D.N.Y. 2003); Genesee Merchants Bank & Trust Co. v. Tucker Motor Sales, 372 N.W.2d 546 (Mich. Ct. App. 1985); *see also* In re Samuels & Co., 510 F.2d 139 (5th Cir. 1975), *rev'd en banc*, 526 F.2d 1238 (1976).

[159] Bankruptcy Code § 546(c)(1); *see* Simon & Schuster, Inc. v. Advanced Marketing Services, Inc. (In re Advanced Marketing Services, Inc.), No. 06-11480 (CSS), Adv. Proc. No. 07-50004 (CSS), 2007 Bankr. LEXIS 135 (Bankr. D. Del. 2007).

[160] Bankruptcy Code § 546(c)(1).

[161] § 14.08[C] Sellers' Reclamation Rights, *supra*.

demand for the return of the goods, requiring the demand to be made within forty-five days of the time the buyer receives the goods or, if the bankruptcy case commences before expiration of this forty-five day period, within twenty days of the commencement of the case.[162]

[5] Seller's Administrative Priority

The 2005 Amendments to the Bankruptcy Code gave unpaid sellers what is perhaps a more important right than that supplied in U.C.C. § 2-207. Section 546(c) now gives unpaid sellers who deliver goods to a debtor within twenty days of the debtor's bankruptcy petition a right to administrative priority for their claim for the unpaid price.[163]

[F] Tax Liens[164]

An important area of creditors' rights law that is sometimes overlooked in law school, although never in the rest of the world, is the power of government to attach and foreclose on property for unpaid tax obligations. Tax liens, particularly federal tax liens, are of great concern to those who own or who have extended credit to financially troubled businesses. As one might expect, governments tend to award themselves sweeping rights that can even be superior to those of existing private-sector creditors.

Although individual debtors in bankruptcy frequently have unpaid income tax obligations that result in the imposition of a lien, taxes on a debtor's income are usually not a problem for a financially troubled business. Financially troubled businesses typically suffer from too little income and too many deductible expenses, rather than from a surplus of income in excess of expenses.[165] The tax problems encountered by failing businesses more commonly arise as a result of unpaid payroll and sales taxes, owed to the IRS or to state and local tax authorities. Collecting but failing to remit these is a common problem for financially troubled business debtors.

[162] Bankruptcy Code § 546(C)(1)(A)-(B).

[163] Bankruptcy Code § 503(b)(9).

[164] William T. Plumb, Federal Tax Liens (1972).

[165] Businesses end up in financial difficulty as a result of selling goods and services below what the goods and services cost to provide. As many bankrupt businesses quickly discover, this is a problem that cannot be solved but is in fact exacerbated by increased sales. For a business engaged in this tactic, expanded sales of the holiday season accelerate the decline into insolvency.

[1] Federal Tax Liens[166]

The law governing federal tax liens is codified in the Federal Tax Lien Act, a part of the Internal Revenue Code.[167] Tax liens, like most other liens, are imposed through a two-step process. The first step establishes the government's rights against the taxpayer; the second step establishes the government's priority over third parties who have competing claims to the debtor's assets.

The first step involves the assessment of a tax — the formal method to determine the IRS' claim that the taxpayer has not paid all taxes due. Once a tax has been assessed, the lien is imposed on the taxpayer's property.[168]

The second step is filing a public notice of the lien. As is true of other filing requirements, the public notice is designed to alert buyers and creditors to the existence of the lien and thus of the IRS' interest in the taxpayer's property. Notice of the lien is filed on a statewide basis, at a place determined by state law.[169]

The scope of federal tax liens is especially broad. They apply to virtually every imaginable type of property interest owned by a delinquent taxpayer. Moreover, although subject to previously perfected liens of all types, a properly filed tax lien usually has priority over all subsequently arising liens, including many of those on after-acquired collateral and those which secure advances made after notice of the tax lien has been filed.

This priority creates headaches, even for existing creditors. For example, Article 9 of the U.C.C. generally permits a security interest to attach to after-acquired property.[170] However, if the debtor acquires property after notice of a federal tax lien has been filed, the IRS' lien will frequently have priority over the lien on the after-acquired collateral, even though the Article 9 creditor filed its financing statement before the tax lien arose.[171] Similar rules protect the IRS from security interests that increase in amount as a result of subsequent advances of credit from the Article 9 lender.[172]

---

[166] William H. Baker, Drye *and* Craft — *How Two Wrongs Can Make a Property Right*, 64 U. Pitt. L. Rev. 745 (2003); Peter F. Coogan, *The Effect of the Federal Tax Lien Act of 1966 Upon Security Interests Created Under the Uniform Commercial Code*, 81 Harv. L. Rev. 1369 (1968); Lance Staricha, *Giving and Taking Notice: The Relative Priority and Enforceability of the Federal General Tax Lien Versus the State's Specific Real Property Tax Lien*, 21 Hamline L. Rev. 469 (1998); Timothy R. Zinnecker, *Resolving Priority Disputes Between the IRS and the Secured Creditor under Revised U.C.C. Article 9: And the Winner Is . . . ?*, 34 Ariz. St. L.J. 921 (2002); Timothy R. Zinnecker, *When Worlds Collide: Resolving Priority Disputes Between the IRS and the Article Nine Secured Creditor*, 63 Tenn. L. Rev. 585 (1996).

[167] I.R.C. §§ 6321-6323 (2000).

[168] I.R.C. § 6321 (2000).

[169] I.R.C. § 6323(f) (2000).

[170] U.C.C. § 9-204 (2003).

[171] I.R.C. § 6323(c)-(d) (2000).

[172] I.R.C. § 6323(c)-(d) (2000).

For example, suppose that as of June 1, 2007, Shady Dealings, Inc. owed River Bank $100,000 for a loan it made a year earlier, and that River Bank has an Article 9 security interest in all of Shady Dealing's existing and after-acquired equipment as collateral for the debt. On July 10, 2007, the IRS filed notice of its federal tax lien against Shady Dealing's property. A few days later, on July 15, Shady paid cash for and acquired a new machine to use in its factory. Afterwards, on July 20, River Bank loaned Shady an additional $30,000 for working capital. This advance was secured under an optional future advance clause in the parties' original security agreement.

River Bank will have priority for the entire $130,000, but only in the equipment that Shady owned before the IRS filed notice of its lien. If that equipment is only worth $90,000, River Bank will not be able to use the value of the new machine acquired by Shady on July 15 to satisfy the unpaid balance. Instead, the IRS will have priority over the new machine because it was acquired after the IRS filed its notice.[173]

There are some additional variations to how these rules operate, depending on the nature of the collateral. These complex provisions give significant protection to creditors like River Bank who have security interests in after-acquired inventory and receivables. However, even those rules accord priority to the IRS over collateral acquired by the taxpayer more than forty-five days after notice of the tax lien was filed and with respect to advances made by the lender after that period. A detailed examination of their provisions is beyond the scope of this section.[174]

In a bankruptcy case, a federal tax lien's priority depends first on whether the IRS has filed notice of its lien. Filing establishes the IRS' rights against third parties and thus indirectly against the bankruptcy trustee. If notice of the tax lien was not filed before bankruptcy, the IRS is left with an unsecured claim. Its unsecured claim may be entitled to priority[175] and may be non-dischargeable, but it will not be secured.

[2] State and Local Tax Liens

State and local tax laws also provide for the imposition of liens on a taxpayer's property if his taxes are not paid when due. States universally have the authority to impose a tax lien on a taxpayer's real estate for unpaid state real estate taxes.[176] They also impose tax liens for unpaid income, franchise, withholding, sales and use taxes. Most of these laws are less sweeping than an IRS lien. In many states, for example, only real property is subject to the lien. As with state construction and repair liens, many variations exist from state to state regarding the scope and priority of these liens.

---

[173] Treas. Reg. §§ 301.6321-1 to 301.6323 (2006).

[174] The Treasury Regulations accompanying the Tax Lien Act provide an exhaustive (and exhausting) explanation of the operation of the priority rules in the Act. Treas. Reg. §§ 301.6321-1 to 301.6323 (2006).

[175] *See* § 10.04[A][8] Tax Claims, *infra*.

[176] *See* Frank S. Alexander, *Tax Liens, Tax Sales, and Due Process*, 75 Ind. L.J. 747 (2000).

§ 2.07 Setoff[177]

[A] Creditors' Right of Setoff

There may be no right of creditors that is more obvious or ancient than the right of setoff. This historic right is rooted in Roman law where it was based on the obvious notion that if debtors are obligated to one another, each should be permitted to reduce the obligation it owes by the obligation it is owed.[178] For example, if Max owes Roberta $25 and Roberta owes Max $10, the right of setoff permits Max to offset Roberta's $10 debt to him and pay Roberta only the $15 balance.

In a commercial context, the exercise of a creditor's right of setoff can have a dramatic impact on a debtor's business. It has, as a practical matter, the same effect as a security interest in the debtor's property, and indeed, is a remarkably efficient form of self help. For example, if Franklin Manufacturing owes $60,000 to Peninsula Bank and has an account at the bank containing $100,000, the bank's right of setoff effectively makes it a secured creditor, with the funds in the account as the collateral. Peninsula can exercise its right of setoff against the $100,000 in Franklin's account debiting the account in the amount of Peninsula's $60,000 claim. This will satisfy the debt Franklin owes and reduce the size of Franklin's bank account to $40,000. If Franklin had planned to use the $100,000 in its account to pay its employees, its inability to do so is likely to have a devastating effect on its ability to stay in business.

The right of setoff permits parties who owe money to one another to net out their mutual debts.[179] It is routinely used in a cooperative way between merchants who regularly buy and sell from one another, but it has its most important application when exercised by a bank against funds held on deposit by one of its loan customers.

Funds on deposit with a bank represent a debt owed by the bank to its customer.[180] If the customer borrows money from a bank and then defaults,

---

[177] *See* Barkley Clark, *Bank Exercise of Setoff: Avoiding the Pitfalls*, 98 Banking L.J. 196 (1981); Randal Lawson Dunn, *Banker's Lien and Equitable Setoff: Constitutional and Policy Considerations for Protecting Bank Customers*, 27 Stan. L. Rev. 1149 (1975); Lawrence Kalevitch, *Setoff and Bankruptcy*, 41 Clev. St. L. Rev. 599 (1993); Alan M. Keeffe, *Setoffs and Security Interests in Deposit Accounts*, 17 Colo. Law. 2107 (1988); William H. Loyd, *The Development of Set-off*, 64 U Pa. L. Rev. 541 (1916); John C. McCoid II, *Setoff: Why Bankruptcy Priority?*, 75 Va. L. Rev. 15 (1989); D.E. Murray, *Banks Versus Creditors of Their Customers: Set-offs Against Customers' Accounts*, 82 Com. L.J. 449, 463 (1977); Stephen L. Sepinuck, *The Problems with Setoff: A Proposed Legislative Solution*, 30 Wm. & Mary L. Rev. 51 (1988); John Teshelle, *Banker's Right of Setoff — Banker Beware*, 34 Okla. L. Rev. 40 (1981).

[178] William H. Loyd, *The Development of Set-Off*, 64 U. Pa. L. Rev. 541, 541 (1916); Michael E. Tigar, Comment, *Automatic Extinction of Cross-Demands: Compensation from Rome to California*, 53 Calif. L. Rev. 224, 229–30 (1965).

[179] *E.g.*, Minnesota Voyageur Houseboats, Inc. v. Las Vegas Marine Supply, Inc., 708 N.W.2d 521, (Minn. 2006); *see generally* 2 Barkley Clark & Barbara Clark, The Law of Bank Deposits, Collections and Credit Cards, ¶ 18.01, at 18–2 (Rev. ed. 2006); Barkley Clark, *Bank Exercise of Setoff: Avoiding the Pitfalls*, 98 Banking L.J. 196 (1981).

[180] We sometimes discuss money we have deposited in a bank account as if it is still "our

the bank is likely to seek to exercise its right of setoff against funds it holds on deposit for the customer.[181] This right is derived from the contract between the depositor and the bank. It is such a useful right that banks frequently require borrowers to keep a minimum amount of funds on deposit as a form of additional security.[182]

The two most important limitations on the right of setoff are the requirements that the debts be both "mutual" and "matured." In addition, setoff may be limited either by statute or based on an express or implied agreement between the parties.

[1] Setoff Limited to Mutual Debts

Only mutual debts may be offset. For debts to be mutual, they must be owed "in the same right and between the same parties, standing in the same capacity, and [of the] same kind or quality."[183] In the context of setoff by a bank, the debt owed by the bank's customer must be owed in the same capacity in which the customer holds his account with the bank. For example, if Dan Darrow owes $10,000 to Merchant's Bank, arising from Dan's use of his personal credit card, funds he holds on deposit with the bank as trustee for his niece are not owed to him by the bank in the same capacity as that in which his personal debt to the bank is owed. These are not "mutual" debts, and the bank has no right of setoff against the trust account.[184]

There are other settings where the mutuality requirement limits a bank's right to any setoff. It sometimes imposes a barrier to setoff when the debt is owed by one of the bank's customers and the account involved is jointly owned by two customers.[185] The mutuality requirement also prevents setoff against a deposit that the bank knows is dedicated to some special purpose,

money," subject to some sort of bailment with the bank as the bailee — like goods stored at a warehouse. This, of course, is mistaken. Money loaned to a bank as part of a deposit transaction belongs to the bank. The deposit is really a loan to the bank, accompanied by the bank's corresponding obligation to repay the loan. All the depositor owns is a right to have this loan repaid. *E.g.*, Crocker-Citizens Nat'l Bank v. Control Metals Corp., 566 F.2d 631, 637 (9th Cir. 1977).

[181] Lawrence Kalevitch, *Setoff and Bankruptcy*, 41 Clev. St. L. Rev. 599 (1993); Gary D. Spivey, Annotation, *Bank's Right of Setoff, Based on Debt of One Depositor, against Funds in Account Standing in Names of Debtor and Another*, 68 A.L.R.3d 192 (1976).

[182] *E.g.*, First Nat'l City Bank v. Herpel (In re Multiponics, Inc.), 622 F.2d 725 (5th Cir. 1980). Such a requirement also raises the effective rate of interest on the loan, by permitting the bank to earn interest on the amount required to be kept on deposit with the bank.

[183] Boston & Maine Corp. v. Chicago Pac. Corp., 785 F.2d 562, 566 (7th Cir. 1986); *see* In re Hal, Inc., 196 B.R. 159 (B.A.P. 9th Cir. 1996); *see generally* Barkely Clark, *Bank Exercise of Setoff: Avoiding the Pitfalls*, 98 Bank. L.J. 191 (1981); Stephen L. Sepinuck, *The Problems with Setoff: A Proposed Legislative Solution*, 30 Wm. & Mary L. Rev. 51, 71 (1988).

[184] *But see* Pope v. First of Am., 699 N.E.2d 178 (Ill. App. Ct. 1998).

[185] *See* Gary D. Spivey. Annotation, *Bank's Right of Setoff, Based on Debt of One Depositor, Against Funds in Account Standing in Names of Debtor and Another,* 68 A.L.R.3d 192 (1976).

such as for paying taxes, meeting payroll, or making payments to an employees' retirement fund.[186]

[2] Setoff of Matured Debts

It is equally necessary that both offsetting debts have matured when they are set off against one another. In other words, a creditor may not exercise its right of setoff on behalf of a debt that is not yet due from the debtor.[187] Assume, for example, that Franklin Manufacturing has $120,000 on deposit with Citizen's Bank and is obligated on an $80,000 promissory note to the bank, which becomes due on March 15, 2010. Citizen's Bank may not set off the promissory note against the account until March 15, 2010 — the date the note matures. However, the due date of the note is subject to acceleration and Citizen's Bank properly accelerates the note, making it due immediately,[188] the obligation represented by the note will have matured and it may be set off against Franklin Manufacturing's deposit.[189] On the other hand, if the note had been payable on demand instead of at a definite time, the bank could exercise its right of setoff at anytime, because a demand note is matured anytime after it has been issued.[190]

[3] Statutory Restrictions on Setoff

Federal and state consumer protection statutes impose some limits on a bank's right of setoff. For example, the Federal Fair Credit Billing Act prevents a bank from setting off debts arising from use of a credit card against a consumer's deposit account.[191] Likewise, some state statutes restrict setoff in similar ways.[192]

---

[186] *See, e.g.*, Nationsbank v. Ames Sav. & Loan Ass'n (In re First Am. Mortgage Co., Inc.), 212 B.R. 479 (Bankr. D. Md. 1997).

[187] *See* Wenneker v. Physicians MultiSpeciality Group, Inc., 814 S.W. 294 (Mo. 1991).

[188] Promissory notes and other obligations may be accelerated, if provided for in the parties' agreement, at any time the creditor in good faith deems itself insecure. *See* U.C.C. § 1-309 (2003).

[189] *See* Boyle v. American Sec. Bank, 531 A.2d 1258 (D.C. Ct. App. 1987); Minnesota Voyageur Houseboats, Inc. v. Las Vegas Marine Supply, Inc., 708 N.W.2d 521 (Minn. 2006).

[190] Marion Ins. Agency, Inc. v. Fahey Banking Co., 572 N.E.2d 124 (Ohio Ct. App. 1988) (formal demand not required to trigger maturity of a "demand" note prior to exercising setoff); Allied Sheet Metal Fabricators, Inc. v. People's Nat'l Bank, 518 P.2d 734 (Wash. Ct. App. 1974) (right of action against maker of demand note arises immediately upon delivery, and no express demand is required to mature the note).

[191] 15 U.S.C. § 1666h (2000).

[192] *See generally* 2 Barkley Clark & Barbara Clark, The Law of Bank Deposits, Collections and Credit Cards, ¶ 18.02, at 18–3 to 180–5 (Rev. ed. 2006).

[B] Priority of Right of Setoff[193]

A creditor's right of setoff is nearly always accorded senior priority over the rights of competing creditors. A bank's right of setoff thus defeats a claim of the payee of a check drawn on the account that had not been finally paid when the setoff was exercised.[194] It also defeats a competing judgment creditor of the customer who serves a writ of garnishment on the bank in an attempt to obtain the funds in the customer's account.[195] Likewise, the bank's right of setoff usually achieves priority over a creditor with a competing security interest in the account.[196] The principal exception to a bank's setoff priority involves competing claims of the IRS and other tax authorities, which are usually governed by express statutory authority that accords priority to the government.[197]

Setoff rights are largely preserved under the Bankruptcy Code, although the exercise of those rights may be postponed by the Code's automatic stay of actions against the debtor and the debtor's property.[198] Indeed, setoff rights are treated as if they were secured claims. In addition, a setoff that permits the offsetting creditor to improve its secured position during the last ninety days before the debtor's bankruptcy petition was filed is avoidable under Bankruptcy Code § 553 to the extent of the improvement in position.[199]

§ 2.08 Foreclosure Proceedings[200]

Foreclosure is the primary method used by various types of secured creditors to enforce their rights against the debtor's collateral. Methods of foreclosure against collateral vary depending on the type of collateral and the jurisdiction. However, the basic pattern is the same regardless of these differences. In nearly all cases, the collateral is sold and the proceeds are used to satisfy the debt owed to the foreclosing creditor.

A wide variety of mechanisms are used in an effort to ensure that the sale is conducted in a reasonable way. The debtor and others with an interest in the collateral, such as junior lien holders, are entitled to notice

---

[193] Stuart D. Albea, Commentary, *Security Interests in Deposit Accounts and the Banking Industry's Use of Setoff*, 54 Ala. L. Rev. 147 (2002); John C. McCoid II, *Setoff: Why Bankruptcy Priority?*, 75 Va. L. Rev. 15 (1989).

[194] U.C.C. § 4-303 (2003) (setoff priority vis-a-vis checks presented against account).

[195] *E.g.*, Wenneker v. Physicians MultiSpeciality Group, Inc., 814 S.W. 294 (Mo. 1991).

[196] U.C.C. § 9-340 (2003). However, the bank's right of setoff is subordinate to the competing secured creditor's interest, if the secured creditor has obtained "control" of the deposit account by becoming the "customer" on the account. U.C.C. § 9-340(c) & cmt. 2 (2003).

[197] United States v. Cache Valley Bank, 866 F.2d 1242 (10th Cir. 1989); Peoples Nat'l. Bank v. United States, 777 F.2d 459 (9th Cir. 1985) (unexecuted right of setoff does not defeat tax lien).

[198] *See* § 8.02[F] Exercise of Right of Setoff, *infra*.

[199] Bankruptcy Code § 553; *see* § 15.06 Setoff Preferences, *infra*.

[200] Debra Pogrund Stark, *Facing the Facts: An Empirical Study of the Fairness and Efficiency of Foreclosures and a Proposal for Reform*, 30 U. Mich. J.L. Ref. 639 (1997).

of the sale. The sale must usually be advertised and the method of sale is usually regulated.

Any surplus resulting from the sale is paid to any junior lien-holders and, if any funds remain, to the debtor. If the sale of the collateral does not produce sufficient funds to satisfy the debt owed to the secured creditor, the debtor is usually liable for any deficiency.

[A] Real Estate Foreclosure[201]

There are three primary methods real estate foreclosure: judicial foreclosure, private foreclosure under a power of sale, and strict foreclosure. As the name suggests, judicial foreclosure is initiated by filing a complaint and obtaining a court order for the sale of the land. Private foreclosure is accomplished without judicial action, under a power of sale, or under the terms of a deed of trust which permit the trustee to sell the property for the benefit of the creditor. Strict foreclosure permits the creditor to simply keep the property in satisfaction of the debt, without a sale; it is rarely permitted, at least without important procedural limitations, or the consent of the debtor.

[1] Judicial Foreclosure[202]

The most common method to foreclose on real estate is judicial foreclosure.[203] As with most creditors' remedies, apart from those governed by the U.C.C., the details of the procedures vary considerably from state to state. Nevertheless, they adhere to a common pattern.[204] The process involves judicial action culminating in a sheriff's auction sale of the encumbered property and distribution of the proceeds from the sale to the foreclosing creditor in an amount sufficient to satisfy the secured debt.

Foreclosure is initiated in the same way as any other lawsuit — by filing a complaint and serving process on anyone with an interest in the land that will be affected by the foreclosure. The debtor, any co-owner of the property, and anyone with a lien on the property that is junior to the interest being foreclosed are joined in the action. Junior lien holders may be creditors with second mortgages, judicial lien holders, or creditors with statutory or

---

[201] Steven Wechsler, *Through the Looking Glass: Foreclosure by Sale as De Facto Strict Foreclosure — An Empirical Study of Mortgage Foreclosure and Subsequent Resale*, 70 Cornell L. Rev. 850 (1985).

[202] Debra Pogrund Stark, *Facing the Facts: An Empirical Study of the Fairness and Efficiency of Foreclosures and a Proposal for Reform*, 30 U. Mich. J.L. Ref. 639 (1997).

[203] Harold L. Levine, *A Day in the Life of a Residential Mortgage Defendant*, 36 J. Marshall L. Rev. 687 (2003).

[204] *See generally* Debra Pogrund Stark, *Facing the Facts: An Empirical Study of the Fairness and Efficiency of Foreclosures and a Proposal for Reform*, 30 U. Mich. J.L. Reform 639, 644 (1997); Grant S. Nelson & Dale A. Whitman, *Reforming Foreclosure: The Uniform Nonjudicial Foreclosure Act*, 53 Duke L.J. 1399, 1403 (2004); Section of Real Property, Probate and Trust Law, American Bar Association, Foreclosure Law & Related Remedies: A State-By-State Digest (Sidney A. Keyles ed., 1995) (summarizing the foreclosure laws and processes in every state).

common law liens against the property. These parties have the opportunity to raise defenses, but it is rare for them to have one. Judgment is frequently entered by default.

Once a foreclosure judgment has been entered, a time and place for a sale of the encumbered property is scheduled. The procedures that govern the time, place, and manner of the sale are statutory; they usually require the property to be sold via public auction conducted by the county sheriff's department. The sale is usually required to be held in a public place, sometimes on the courthouse steps.[205] Notice of the time and place of the sale must be given to the debtor and to anyone else with an interest of record in the real estate that will be affected by the foreclosure. Typically, notice of the sale must be advertised, usually in a manner prescribed by statute.[206]

Between the time of the judgment of foreclosure and the time of the sale, the debtor has an equitable right to redeem the property by paying the entire obligation owed to the foreclosing creditor in a lump sum. This equitable right of the debtor to redeem the property from the mortgage is what is actually "foreclosed" in what is habitually (and imprecisely) described as a "mortgage foreclosure" action.[207] The equitable right to pay the mortgage after default — the debtor's "equity of redemption" — was routinely recognized by early English chancery courts to avoid the risk that the debtor would forfeit the value of the property above the amount of the debt.[208]

Sale of mortgaged property vests good title in the buyer, who usually receives a "sheriff's deed" that reflects her purchase of the property. The foreclosure judgment and sale cuts off the rights of the debtor, as well as the rights of any creditor whose interest is junior to that of the foreclosing creditor (provided, of course, that they were notified of the foreclosure action in the first place). Assume, for example, that Citizen's Bank holds a senior mortgage on land owned by Franklin Manufacturing, Inc. and that the land is also subject to a junior mortgage in favor of Merchant's Finance Co. If Citizen's Bank brings a foreclosure action to enforce its senior mortgage,

---

205 *E.g.*, Tex. Prop. Code Ann. § 51.002(a) (Vernon 2000); *see* Alex M. Johnson, Jr., *Critiquing the Foreclosure Process: An Economic Approach Based on the Paradigmatic Norms of Bankruptcy*, 79 Va. L. Rev. 959, 973 n. 46 (1993); Basil H. Mattingly, *The Shift from Power to Process: A Functional Approach to Foreclosure Law*, 80 Marq. L. Rev. 77, 87 (1996).

206 *E.g.,* Ohio Rev. Code Ann. §§ 2329.26, 2329.27 (LexisNexis 2006); Tex. Prop. Code Ann, § 51.002(b) (Vernon 2000).

207 Marshall E. Tracht, *Renegotiation and Secured Credit: Explaining the Equity of Redemption*, 52 Vand. L. Rev. 599, 607 n.22 (1999); *see* Black's Law Dictionary 646 (6th ed. 1990).

208 Grant S. Nelson & Dale A. Whitman, Real Estate Finance Law § 1.4 at 8–10 (4th ed. 2001); *e.g.,* Perry v. Miller, 112 N.E.2d 805 (1953)*; see generally* Abraham Bell & Gideon Parchomovsky, *A Theory of Property*, 90 Cornell L. Rev. 531, 609–11 (2005); Trauner v. Lowrey, 369 So. 2d 531, 534 (Ala. 1979) ("Execution of a mortgage passes legal title to the mortgagee . . . . The mortgagor is left with an equity of redemption, but upon payment of the debt, legal title revests in the mortgagor.").

sale of the land to Global Industries, Inc. cuts off both Franklin's title to the land and Merchant's junior lien.

In the unusual instance of foreclosure by a junior mortgagee, senior liens remain intact and the buyer's title remains subject to the senior lien. Thus, if Merchant's Finance Co. conducted a foreclosure sale to enforce its junior mortgage on Franklin Manufacturing's land, a sale of the land to Global Industries would not affect Citizen Bank's senior mortgage. Of course the existence of the senior mortgage would reduce the price Global would likely be willing to pay for the land. For example, if the land were worth $350,000 and Citizen Bank's senior mortgage secured a $200,000 debt, no sensible person with knowledge of the bank's lien would pay more than $150,000 for the land at a foreclosure sale conducted by a junior mortgagee like Merchant's Finance Co.[209]

In many instances, the foreclosing creditor will purchase the property at its own foreclosure sale. The foreclosing creditor has several distinct advantages over other prospective buyers. For example, it may be more familiar with the property than other bidders. More importantly, the foreclosing creditor can pay for the property by bidding in the amount of the mortgage debt owed to the creditor, without having to pay cash. Other bidders must have ready cash or available funding.

It is generally recognized that foreclosure sale procedures are time consuming and expensive.[210] Moreover, they rarely yield the same price that could be expected to be obtained from a conventional sale of the property on the broader real estate market, facilitated by the services of a broker.[211] This is not surprising. Most buyers of residential real estate do not look for a new home by combing the newspaper for property scheduled to be sold at upcoming mortgage foreclosure sales. The market of prospective buyers of property in foreclosure is predictably smaller than the market of interested real estate buyers in general. Moreover, buyers who are willing to consider buying property at a foreclosure sale may have difficulty making arrangements to view the house, which is usually still occupied by the debtor. A professional inspection of the premises is nearly always out of the question. Further, debtors who are unable to make their regular monthly mortgage payments are not likely to have kept the property in good repair, making the transaction even more risky for a

---

[209] Further, because of the risk that the senior mortgage debt would increase, due to accumulating interest, collection costs, late fees, and other charges, the amount someone would be willing to pay would likely be even less.

[210] *See generally* Grant S. Nelson & Dale A. Whitman, Real Estate Finance Law § 7.11 (4th ed. 2001); Comment, *Cost and Time Factors in Foreclosure of Mortgages*, 3 Real Prop. Prob. & Tr. J. 413 (1968).

[211] *See* Grant S. Nelson & Dale A. Whitman, *Reforming Foreclosure: The Uniform Nonjudicial Foreclosure Act*, 53 Duke L.J. 1399, 1419–22 (2004); Marshall E. Tracht, *Renegotiation and Secured Credit: Explaining the Equity of Redemption*, 52 Vand. L. Rev. 599, 607 (1999); Steven Wechsler, *Through the Looking Glass: Foreclosure by Sale as De Facto Strict Foreclosure — An Empirical Study of Mortgage Foreclosure and Subsequent Resale*, 70 Cornell L. Rev. 850, 853 (1985).

prospective buyer, who must face the very real possibility that the structure is laden with hidden defects. The terms of the sale are "as is." These factors make buying property at foreclosure far too risky for most prospective buyers to tolerate.[212]

Various mechanisms are imposed by state statutes to ensure that foreclosure does not deprive residential owners of any financial equity in their homes.[213] These include statutorily prescribed methods of advertising the sale to the public;[214] giving the debtor a temporary right to "cure" a default, de-accelerate the obligation, and reinstate the mortgage debt according to its original terms;[215] extending delays between the time of a foreclosure judgment and the time of a sale; and requiring the sale to be "confirmed" by the court.[216] Some states require a court to establish a minimum or "upset price" based on an appraisal of the property, imposing a floor below which the property may not be sold.[217]

In some states, the debtor and junior lien holders have an additional statutory period of redemption, during which they may purchase the property from the person who bought it at the foreclosure sale by paying the purchaser the amount it paid at the sale.[218] Although this right was implemented to discourage buyers from paying too little for the property, it has the effect of driving down foreclosure sale prices by subjecting buyers to the risk that they will lose the property they have bought.[219] Moreover, there is broad consensus that this right has little practical impact on a debtor's ability to actually recover her property.[220] If she was unable to

---

[212] Grant S. Nelson & Dale A. Whitman, *Reforming Foreclosure: The Uniform Nonjudicial Foreclosure Act*, 53 Duke L.J. 1399, 1421–22 (2004); *see* Carteret Sav. & Loan Ass'n v. Davis, 521 A.2d 831, 835 (N.J. 1987).

[213] Patrick B. Bauer, *Judicial Foreclosure and Statutory Redemption: The Soundness of Iowa's Traditional Preference for Protection over Credit*, 71 Iowa L. Rev. 1 (1985); J. Douglass Poteat, *State Legislative Relief for the Mortgage Debtor During the Depression*, 5 Law & Contemp. Probs. 517 (1938); Michael H. Schill, *An Economic Analysis of Mortgagor Protection Laws*, 77 Va. L. Rev. 489 (1991); James B. Hughes, Jr., *Taking Personal Responsibility: A Different View of Mortgage Antideficiency and Redemption Statutes*, 39 Ariz. L. Rev. 117 (1997).

[214] *E.g.*, N.Y. Real Propr. Acts. § 231(2) (McKinney Supp. 2006).

[215] *E.g.*, Or. Rev. Stat. § 86.753 (2006) (debtor may cure up to 5 days before the sale); 41 Pa. Cons. Stat. Ann. § 404 (1999) (debtor may cure until one hour before sale of residential property); *see* Unif. Nonjudicial Foreclosure Act § 202(c) (2002), *available at* www.law.upenn.edu/bll/ulc/uFBPOSA/2002final.pdf (last visited May 7, 2007).

[216] *E.g.*, Hazel v. Van Beek, 954 P.2d 1301, 1307 (Wash. 1998).

[217] *E.g.*, Wash. Rev. Code Ann. § 61.12.060 (2004).

[218] *E.,g.*, Cal. Civ. Proc. Code §§ 729.010-090, 726(e) (West Supp. 2006); *see generally* 4 Richard R. Powell & Michael Allan Wolf, Powell on Real Property § 37.46 (2006); Patrick B. Bauer, *Judicial Foreclosure and Statutory Redemption: The Soundness of Iowa's Traditional Preference for Protection over Credit*, 71 Iowa L. Rev. 1 (1985).

[219] Edgar Noble Durfee & Delmar W. Doddridge, *Redemption From Foreclosure Sale — The Uniform Mortgage Act*, 23 Mich. L. Rev. 825, 841 n.51 (1925); Grant S. Nelson & Dale A. Whitman, *Reforming Foreclosure: The Uniform Nonjudicial Foreclosure Act*, 53 Duke L.J. 1399, 1439 (2004); Robert M. Washburn, *The Judicial and Legislative Response to Price Inadequacy in Mortgage Foreclosure Sales*, 53 S. Cal. L. Rev. 843, 931 (1980).

[220] George M. Platt, *Deficiency Judgments in Oregon Loans Secured by Land: Growing Disparity Among Functional Equivalents*, 23 Willamette L. Rev. 37 (1987).

redeem the property before the sale, there is little reason to believe that she will be able to do so after it has occurred, unless she is able to locate a lender or buyer of her own.

If the amount received from the foreclosure sale is insufficient to satisfy the debt fully, the mortgagor usually has the right to recover the unpaid balance as a "deficiency." Some states, in an effort to protect mortgagors from persistently low foreclosure sale prices, have enacted anti-deficiency legislation, which prohibits mortgagees from recovering deficiencies in certain types of transactions (usually residential mortgages).[221]

[2] Private Foreclosure Under a Power of Sale[222]

In roughly half of the states, particularly where deeds of trust are customarily used instead of traditional mortgages, foreclosure is accomplished without judicial intervention.[223] In these transactions, a deed of trust or mortgage agreement grants the creditor a "power of sale," permitting a third person, acting as a trustee, to sell the property and pay the proceeds from the sale to the creditor in satisfaction of the debt. Just as in a traditional judicial foreclosure proceeding, any surplus from the sale is paid to the debtor. Likewise, the debtor usually remains liable for any deficiency, although she may be protected from this by an anti-deficiency rule.

Though it does not require judicial action, a power of sale foreclosure is potentially subject to the judicial review. A debtor who believes that she has a legal defense, justifying her default, can either seek to enjoin the sale or wait until after the sale and use her defense to resist being ejected from possession of the property.[224]

Unlike self-help repossession of personal property, power of sale foreclosure laws require substantial prior notice to the mortgagor of its default,[225] and they frequently provide the debtor with an opportunity to cure a default and reinstate the debt according to its original terms. The trustee usually conducts an auction sale of the property, and provides the buyer with a trustee's deed. This deed is similar to the sheriff's deed that the buyer would obtain following a traditional judicial foreclosure sale. Although the sale does not have to be confirmed by a court, there is usually a short statute

---

[221] J. Douglass Poteat, *State Legislative Relief for the Mortgage Debtor During the Depression*, 5 Law & Contemp. Probs. 517 (1938); Marshall E. Tracht, *Renegotiation and Secured Credit: Explaining the Equity of Redemption*, 52 Vand. L. Rev. 599, 609 (1999); Robert M. Washburn, *The Judicial and Legislative Response to Price Inadequacy in Mortgage Foreclosure Sales*, 53 S. Cal. L. Rev. 843 (1980); *e.g.*, Cal. Civ. Proc. Code § 580b (West Supp. 2006) (dwelling of up to four families occupied by purchaser); Fla. Stat. Ann. § 702.06 (West 1994) (purchase money mortgage).

[222] Grant S. Nelson & Dale A. Whitman, *Reforming Foreclosure: The Uniform Nonjudicial Foreclosure Act*, 53 Duke L.J. 1399 (2004).

[223] Grant S. Nelson & Dale A. Whitman, Real Estate Finance Law 581–82 (4th ed. 2001).

[224] Grant S. Nelson & Dale A. Whitman, Real Estate Finance Law 605–08 (4th ed. 2001).

[225] *See generally* Grant S. Nelson & Dale A. Whitman, Real Estate Finance Law 581–85, 615–20 (4th ed. 2001).

of limitations imposed on the debtor's ability to object to the sale. Thus, private foreclosure pursuant to a power of sale bears a close resemblance to judicial foreclosure, but it does not require the initiation of a court proceeding.

[3] Strict Foreclosure[226]

At one time, the debtor's right to redeem the property from a mortgage was terminated simply by the establishment of a deadline after which the debtor's equity of redemption was "foreclosed." This vested indefeasible title in the mortgagee.[227] This became known as "strict foreclosure" and is distinguishable because the creditor is not required to conduct a sale of the mortgaged property.

Strict foreclosure persists in a few states[228] but is highly regulated and severely limited, particularly with respect to debtors' homes.[229] It is also preserved in Article 9 of the U.C.C., with respect to personal property. There, the debtor must be given notice of the secured party's proposal to retain the collateral in satisfaction of the debt and has the right to compel the secured party to conduct a sale.[230]

[B] Self-Help Repossession of Goods[231]

Both Article 2A and Article 9 of the U.C.C. permit self-help repossession of goods, without court action. Article 2A gives a lessor the right to seize leased goods upon the lessee's default.[232] Likewise, Article 9 permits a secured party to take possession of the collateral any time after a debtor's default,[233] though some states have limited or eliminated this right with respect to some consumer goods.[234]

---

[226] James Geoffery Durham, *In Defense of Strict Foreclosure: A Legal and Economic Analysis of Mortgage Foreclosure*, 36 S.C. L. Rev. 461 (1985); Sheldon Tefft, *The Myth of Strict Foreclosure*, 4 U. Chi. L. Rev. 575 (1937).

[227] *See generally* Grant S. Nelson & Dale A. Whitman, Real Estate Finance Law 581–85, 554–58 (4th ed. 2001); 4 Richard R. Powell & Michael Allan Wolf, Powell on Real Property § 37.46 (2006).

[228] *See* Abacus Mortgage Ins. Co. v. Whitewood Hills Dev. Corp., 479 A.2d 1231 (Conn. Ct. App. 1984); Great Lakes Mortgage. Corp. v. Collymore, 302 N.E.2d 248 (Ill. App. Ct. 1973); Stowe Ctr., Inc. v. Burlington Sav. Bank, 451 A.2d 114 (Vt. 1982).

[229] *See* Grant S. Nelson & Dale A. Whitman, Real Estate Finance Law 555–58 (4th ed. 2001).

[230] U.C.C. § 9-620 (2003).

[231] Jean Braucher, *The Repo Code: A Study of Adjustment to Uncertainty in Commercial Law*, 74 Wash. U. L.Q. 549 (1997); William C. Whitford & Harold Laufer, *The Impact of Denying Self-Help Repossession of Automobiles: A Case Study of the Wisconsin Consumer Act*, 1975 Wis. L. Rev. 607.

[232] U.C.C. § 2A-525(2), (3) (2003).

[233] U.C.C. § 9-609 (2003).

[234] *See, e.g.*, Ohio Rev. Code Ann. § 1317.13 (LexisNexis 2002) (prohibiting repossession of consumer goods, other than motor vehicles and mobile homes, if the debtor has paid 75% of the cash price of the goods).

"Self-help" means repossession may be accomplished without notice, a hearing, a court order, a bond, the sheriff, or any immediate post-seizure judicial review. Because no state action is involved in self-help, it does not run afoul of the Fourteenth Amendment's Due Process Clause.[235]

There is one key statutory limitation on self-help: the creditor must not commit a breach of the peace.[236] This restriction has engendered volumes of decisions dealing with the parameters of the conduct in which a repossessing party may engage without breaching the peace. Broadly speaking, a secured party may neither engage in nor threaten any type of violence.[237] It may not enter the debtor's house without permission, and it must discontinue its efforts to repossess if the debtor resists or verbally objects to an ongoing attempt to repossess.[238] The secured party must not take any illegal action,[239] break into a locked area,[240] or continue an immediate attempt to repossess after someone resists in any tangible way.

In general, the debtor can prevent a self-help repossession simply by telling the repossessor to "go away." However, if there is no verbal resistance, the repossession may go forward, even if the debtor successfully blocked the creditor's earlier attempt to take the collateral.[241]

If self-help repossession cannot be accomplished without a breach of the peace, then the secured party or lessor must use judicial means to obtain possession — usually replevin.[242] Failure to cease and desist when a breach of the peace is on the verge of occurring may subject the repossessing creditor to liability to the debtor.[243] It may also prevent the creditor from

[235] *See, e.g.*, Adams v. Southern Cal. First Nat'l Bank, 492 F.2d 324 (9th Cir. 1973); Alan R. Madry, *State Action and the Due Process of Self-help;* Flagg Bros. *Redux*, 62 U. Pitt. L. Rev. 1 (2000); *Cf.* Flagg Bros., Inc. v. Brooks, 436 U.S. 149 (1978) (imposition of statutory warehouseman's lien not state action); *see also* Soia Mentschikoff, *Peaceful Repossession Under the Uniform Commercial Code: A Constitutional and Economic Analysis*, 14 Wm. & Mary L. Rev. 767 (1973); Robert E. Scott, *Constitutional Regulation of Provisional Creditor Remedies: The Cost of Procedural Due Process*, 61 Va. L. Rev. 807 (1975); James J. White, *The Abolition of Self-Help Repossession: The Poor Pay Even More*, 1973 Wis. L. Rev. 503 (1973); *see generally* Gary D. Spivey, Annotation, *Validity, Under Federal Constitution and Laws, of Self-Help Repossession Provision of Sec. 9-503 of Uniform Commercial Code*, 29 A.L.R. Fed. 418 (1976).

[236] U.C.C. §§ 2A-525(3), 9-609 (2003).

[237] Morris v. First Nat'l Bank & Trust Co., 254 N.E.2d 683 (Ohio 1970) (creditor's representatives surrounded the debtor's son, making him fearful of being beaten).

[238] Over a period of years, the father of one of your co-authors made himself quite popular with hourly employees at the factory where he worked, by walking out to the parking lot under his office window to express his objection to any attempted repossession of any of the other employee's vehicles parked in the company lot.

[239] *See* Morris v. First Nat'l Bank & Trust Co., 254 N.E.2d 683 (Ohio 1970).

[240] *E.g.*, Laurel Coal Co. v. Walter E. Heller & Co., 539 F. Supp. 1006 (W.D. Pa. 1982).

[241] *See, e.g.*, Wade v. Ford Motor Credit Co., 668 P.2d 183 (Kan. Ct. App. 1983) (debtor, who was armed at the time, told repo man that if she saw him near her car again she would "leave him laying right where she saw him." The car was later repossessed without incident during the middle of the night, and the court found that there was no breach of the peace).

[242] *See* § 2.08[C] Replevin, *infra*.

[243] U.C.C. § 9-625 (2003).

obtaining a judgment for any deficiency.[244] In extreme cases, punitive damages may be awarded for an improper self-help repossession.[245]

[C] Replevin

The common law writ of replevin (and, in a few states, detinue, sequestration, or "claim and delivery") is a long-established method to obtain possession of property that is wrongfully detained by the defendant. In the context of state creditors' rights, its primary significance is as a judicial alternative to self-help repossession of goods that are subject to a security interest. Historically, replevin was an action to recover possession of the goods themselves; the related writ of detinue was an action to recover either the goods or their value.[246] Because of the expense involved in a replevin action and the risk of mistakes in following the statutory procedures, creditors with security interests usually prefer to repossess goods through self-help; they resort to replevin only when self-help is either impossible without a breach of the peace or statutorily prohibited.

Once a creditor obtains possession through a judgment of replevin or one of its common law or statutory cousins, the creditor is usually required to sell the property in accordance with the procedures detailed in Article 9 of the U.C.C.

[D] Sales of Collateral under U.C.C. Article 9

Under Article 9, collateral is ordinarily sold by the secured party rather than by the sheriff. Article 9 specifies: "After default, a secured party may sell, lease, license, or otherwise dispose of any or all of the collateral."[247] The sale may be by either "public" auction or a "private" sale.[248] Every aspect of the sale must be accomplished in a commercially reasonable manner.[249] In nearly all cases, the secured party must supply advance notice to the debtor, and in some cases, the secured party must also give notice to competing secured parties whose rights may be affected by the sale.[250]

The proceeds of the sale are distributed first to cover the costs of the repossession and sale, second to satisfy the secured debt, and third to satisfy

---

[244] U.C.C. § 9-626 (2003).

[245] *See* Big Three Motors, Inc. v. Rutherford, 432 So. 2d 483 (Ala. 1983).

[246] Frederic William Maitland, The Forms of Action at Common Law: A Course of Lectures (A.H. Chaytore & W.J. Whitaker eds., 1968); *see* Roy Ryden Anderson, *Of Hidden Agendas, Naked Emperors, and a Few Good Soldiers: The Conference's Breach of Promise . . . Regarding Article 2 Damage Remedies*, 54 SMU L. Rev. 795, 838 (2001); George Lee Flint, Jr. & Marie Juliet Alfaro, *Secured Transactions History: The First Chattel Mortgage Acts in the Anglo-American World*, 30 Wm. Mitchell L. Rev. 1403 (2004).

[247] U.C.C. § 9-610(a) (2003).

[248] U.C.C. § 9-610(b) & cmt. 7 (2003).

[249] U.C.C. § 9-610(b) & cmt. 2 (2003).

[250] U.C.C. § 9-611 (2003).

any junior debts secured by the collateral, in their order of priority.[251] In rare cases where a surplus remains, it must be paid to the debtor.[252] More commonly, the collateral sells for less than the amount of the outstanding debt, leaving the debtor personally liable for a deficiency.[253]

In rare cases, a secured party may propose to strictly foreclose and keep the property in full satisfaction of the debt, while giving up the right to a deficiency.[254] The debtor always has the right to receive advance notice of the secured party's proposal to strictly foreclose and may require the secured party to sell the collateral.[255]

Debtors have a limited right to redeem the collateral by paying the secured debt any time before the secured party has either disposed of the collateral, entered into a contract to dispose of the collateral, or discharged the secured debt through strict foreclosure.[256] To redeem, the debtor must tender full payment of the outstanding obligation, together with any accrued interest; all of the reasonable expenses the secured party incurred as a result of the default; and any agreed reasonable attorney's fees and legal expenses.[257] This right to redeem may be waived, but only in a writing executed after the debtor defaulted. Any attempted waiver of redemption rights contained in the original security agreement is unenforceable.[258]

The requirement that the debtor pay the entire debt, plus the creditor's expenses, and in many cases, legal fees in a single lump sum, is almost always an insuperable barrier. As is true in real estate mortgage foreclosure proceedings, debtors who have access to that much cash rarely default in the first place. Moreover, to redeem, the debtor may have to pay much more than the goods are worth. As will be described elsewhere, the Bankruptcy Code provides a considerably more favorable form of redemption for debtors, where they need only pay the value of the collateral, rather than the full amount of the debt.[259]

Creditors who fail to adhere to the foreclosure procedures specified in Article 9 may find themselves precluded from recovering a deficiency judgment from the debtor. Many states have common law or non-uniform statutory rules that prohibit secured creditors who fail to follow the rules from recovering a deficiency.[260] Some states take a more generous approach

---

[251] U.C.C. § 9-615 (2003).

[252] U.C.C. § 9-615 (2003).

[253] U.C.C. § 9-615 (2003).

[254] U.C.C. § 9-620 (2003).

[255] U.C.C. § 9-620 (2003).

[256] U.C.C. § 9-623 (2003).

[257] U.C.C. § 9-623 (2003).

[258] U.C.C. § 9-624(c) (2003).

[259] Bankruptcy Code § 722; *see* § 12.08[A] Lump Sum Redemption by Debtor, *infra*.

[260] Herman Ford-Mercury, Inc. v. Betts, 251 N.W.2d 492 (Iowa 1977); Aimonetto v. Keepes, 501 P.2d 1017, 1019 (Wyo. 1972); Robert M. Lloyd, *The Absolute Bar Rule in U.C.C. Foreclosure Sales: A Prescription for Waste*, 40 UCLA L. Rev. 695 (1993).

to defective foreclosures and permit the debtor to offset against the outstanding balance any additional amount for which the collateral would have sold if the foreclosure had been conducted properly.[261] In other states, and in cases not involving consumer goods, creditors who fail to comply with the foreclosure procedures outlined in Article 9 are denied a deficiency unless the they are able to prove that the property would have sold for the same amount, even if they had followed the prescribed statutory procedures.[262] This "rebuttable presumption" rule presumes that the property would have sold for an amount sufficient to satisfy the entire debt if the sale had been conducted properly, but it gives the creditor the right to prove otherwise. In many cases, particularly those involving foreclosure sales of motor vehicles, the creditor will find it relatively easy to prove that any technical deficiencies in the foreclosure process had no effect on the price received for the property.

§ 2.09 Pre-Judgment Seizure[263]

Unsecured creditors are not usually permitted to seize a debtor's property before obtaining a judgment. However, these creditors are sometimes fearful that a debtor's assets many be squandered, hidden, or transferred to others before a judgment can be obtained. In this situation, they would like to seize the debtor's assets or at least block the debtor from transferring them while an action to obtain a judgment against the debtor is pending.

In extraordinary circumstances, pre-judgment seizure may be available. Not surprisingly, the Due Process Clause of the Fourteenth Amendment imposes constitutional restrictions on any effort to seize a debtor's property prior to judgment. This section reviews the patterns found in modern pre-judgment seizure statutes and explains how the Due Process Clause imposes limits on these procedures and their use.

[A] Pre-Judgment Seizure Procedures

[1] Attachment

Attachment is a pre-judgment remedy that deprives the debtor of possession of its property to preserve it while the creditor's lawsuit is pending. It has also been used to acquire quasi-in-rem jurisdiction over non-resident

[261] *E.g.*, Greene v. Associates (In re Greene), 248 B.R. 583 (Bankr. N.D. Ala. 2000); Chapman v. Field, 602 P.2d 481, 486 (Ariz. 1979); *see generally* Robert M. Lloyd, *The Absolute Bar Rule in U.C.C. Foreclosure Sales: A Prescription for Waste*, 40 UCLA L. Rev. 695, 699 (1993).

[262] U.C.C. § 9-696 (2003).

[263] *See generally* Steve H. Nickles, *Creditors' Provisional Remedies and Debtors' Due Process Rights: Attachment and Garnishment in Arkansas*, 31 Ark. L. Rev. 607 (1978); Doug Rendleman, *The New Due Process: Rights and Remedies*, 63 Ky. L.J. 531 (1975); Robert E. Scott, *Constitutional Regulation of Provisional Creditor Remedies: The Cost of Procedural Due Process*, 61 Va. L. Rev. 807 (1975).

defendants by attaching property owned by the defendant and located in the forum state by a resident of the forum state.[264]

Modern pre-judgment attachment procedures closely resemble post-judgment execution procedures. Like execution procedures, the mechanics of pre-judgment attachment statutes vary considerably from state to state but share many common features. They usually supply a set of statutory grounds to justify the seizure; mandate a court-ordered writ of attachment that directs the sheriff to seize a defendant's property and preserve it pending the outcome of the suit; and specify procedures for the debtor to recover possession of the property.

[a] Grounds for Attachment

The statutory grounds to obtain a writ of attachment vary but are usually targeted at circumstances that create a risk that the debtor's assets might be dissipated while the underlying suit progresses through the courts. Thus, it is common for attachment to be available if the creditor can show that the debtor's departure from the state is imminent, or that she will likely transfer, remove, or conceal her property in an effort to defraud her creditors.

Ohio's statute supplies a good example. It specifies that a plaintiff may obtain a writ of attachment if, among other things:

> [t]he defendant has absconded with the intent to defraud creditors; . . . the defendant has left the county of the defendant's residence to avoid the service of a summons; . . . the defendant is about to remove property, in whole or part, out of the jurisdiction of the court, with the intent to defraud creditors; the defendant is about to convert property, in whole or part, into money, for the purpose of placing it beyond the reach of creditors; the defendant has property or rights in action, which the defendant conceals; the defendant has assigned, removed, disposed of, or is about to dispose of, property, in whole or part, with the intent to defraud creditors; the defendant has fraudulently or criminally contracted the debt, or incurred the obligations for which suit is about to be or has been brought; or . . . [incongruously] that the claim is for work or labor.[265]

Further, to obtain attachment without giving prior notice to the defendant, the plaintiff must demonstrate that the plaintiff will suffer "irreparable injury" if the attachment is delayed until after the defendant has had the opportunity for a hearing. If this showing is made and a writ of attachment

---

[264] *See* Pennoyer v. Neff, 95 U.S. 714 (1878); Harris v. Balk, 198 U.S. 215 (1905). The utility of this use of attachment was, of course, seriously limited by the Supreme Court's decision in *Shaffer v. Heitner*, 433 U.S. 186 (1977). The discussion here will be limited to the use of attachment to preserve the availability of assets for the creditor to foreclose upon once a judgment is obtained.

[265] Ohio Rev. Code Ann. § 2715.01 (LexisNexis 1999).

is issued, the court must immediately notify the defendant of the issuance of the writ, and, upon request, the court must provide the defendant with the opportunity for a hearing.[266] In addition, like most states, Ohio requires the plaintiff to post a bond to protect the defendant against any loss that may be caused due to wrongful attachment.[267]

[b] Seizure of the Defendant's Property

Following issuance of a writ of attachment, the sheriff levies on the defendant's property, much as it would pursuant to a post-judgment writ of execution. Naturally, the sheriff will want to be sure that he operates within the strict requirements of the state's attachment procedure; and most importantly, that he only seizes property that belongs to the defendant. Wrongful seizure of someone else's property exposes the sheriff to liability for wrongful seizure.

Following physical seizure of the property, the sheriff must preserve it pending the outcome of the underlying litigation.[268] The sheriff is also usually required to supply the court with a "return" — a report that contains information regarding the results of the seizure, probably including a descriptive "inventory" of the property that was seized.[269]

[c] Release of the Property from Attachment

The defendant may usually recover possession of her property by posting a bond sufficient to cover its value.[270] Alternatively, the debtor might demonstrate at a hearing that the statutory grounds for attachment were not met.[271] In addition, the defendant is usually permitted to demonstrate that the seized assets are exempt and thus should be released from attachment.[272]

[d] Liability for Wrongful Attachment

The plaintiff may find itself liable to the defendant if pre-judgment attachment was wrongful. Liability may accrue due to the plaintiff's failure to subsequently obtain a judgment against the defendant, the inadequacy of the plaintiff's motion or bond, seizure of property that is exempt under the state's exemption statute,[273] seizure of more property than was

---

[266] Ohio Rev. Code Ann. § 2715.042 (LexisNexis 1999).

[267] Ohio Rev. Code Ann. § 2715.044 (LexisNexis 1999) (twice the amount of the value of the property to be seized); Fla. Stat. Ann. § 76.12 (LexisNexis 2004).

[268] *E.g.*, N.Y. C.P.L.R. 6218 (McKinney 1980).

[269] *E.g.*, Ohio Rev. Code Ann. § 2715.18 (LexisNexis 1999); Cal. Civ. Proc. Code § 488.130(b) (West Supp. 2006); *see also* Rodriguez v. Biron, 510 A.2d 1321 (Vt. 1986) (attachment defective due to failure of sheriff to include list of property seized in the return to the court).

[270] Ohio Rev. Code Ann. § 2715.26 (LexisNexis 1999).

[271] *E.g.*, Mitchell v. Lavigne, 770 A.2d 109 (Me. 2001).

[272] *See* § 2.12 Property Beyond the Reach of Creditors, *infra*.

[273] *See* § 2.12 Property Beyond the Reach of Creditors, *infra*.

necessary to satisfy the plaintiff's claim,[274] or any number of common tort claims, including trespass, conversion, abuse of process, or more simply "wrongful attachment."[275]

If attachment is undertaken pursuant to an unconstitutional state attachment statute, the creditor may be liable for violating the defendant's civil rights.[276] Moreover, the Supreme Court has ruled that private parties who invoke a pre-judgment seizure procedure that is subsequently held unconstitutional are not entitled to qualified immunity from liability for offending the defendant's civil rights.[277]

[2] Lis Pendens

Lis pendens is similar to pre-judgment attachment but is available only in proceedings, like mortgage foreclosure actions, regarding the right to ownership or possession of real property. As one court explained:

> Lis pendens is a legal doctrine — literally "a pending lawsuit." It means that the filing of a lawsuit concerning specific property gives notice to others of the claim alleged in the lawsuit and that a purchaser of the property may take the property subject to the outcome of the lawsuit.
>
> Lis pendens is not a substantive right. It does not create a lien, but "charges the purchaser with notice of the pending action." . . . If applicable, it does not prevent persons from transacting an interest in the property subject to litigation. Any conveyed interest, however, becomes subject to the outcome of the pending litigation. The purpose of lis pendens is to protect the plaintiff's interest in the subject property. Under the doctrine, "no interest can be acquired by third persons in the subject of the action, as against the plaintiff's title."[278]

Although lis pendens developed as a common law doctrine, today it is largely statutory.[279] It is distinguishable from a writ of attachment in that it provides no mechanism to liquidate the plaintiff's claim; it merely preserves the priority of the plaintiff's interest in the disputed property.

[B] Constitutional Limits on Pre-Judgment Seizure

Before 1969, pre-judgment seizures of a debtor's property were permitted with scant due process protection against unwarranted seizures.[280] The

---

[274] *E.g.*, White Lighting Co. v. Wolfson, 438 P.2d 345 (Cal. 1968) (abuse of process).

[275] *E.g.*, Neri v. J.I. Case Co., 566 N.E.2d 16 (Ill. App. Ct. 1991).

[276] Guzman v. Western State Bank of Devil's Lake, 540 F.2d 948 (8th Cir. 1976).

[277] Lugar v. Edmonson Oil Co., 504 U.S. 158 (1992).

[278] Cincinnati ex rel. Ritter v. Cincinnati Reds, L.L.C., 782 N.E.2d 1225 (Ohio Ct. App. 2002).

[279] *See, e.g.*, Minn. Stat. § 557.02 (West 2000); Ill. Comp. Stat. Ann. 5/2-1901 (U.C.C. § 9-623) (West 2003).

[280] *See, e.g.*, McKay v. McInnes, 279 U.S. 820 (1929).

Supreme Court's 1969 decision in *Sniadach v. Family Finance*[281] led to a series of decisions that imposed considerable limits on the practice of pre-judgment seizure.

Sniadach itself was a wage garnishment case. The state statute permitted a plaintiff to garnish a defendant's wages prior to judgment without a hearing or even notice to the defendant about the impending garnishment. The debtor could be reimbursed for her garnished wages only after prevailing at trial on the creditor's underlying claim.[282] The Court's decision emphasized the unfairness of this procedure, as well as the devastating impact that wage garnishment would have on a family that was living, as most families are, from paycheck to paycheck.[283] In a famous passage, Justice William O. Douglas indicated that wage garnishment of the type contemplated by the state statute could "drive a wage-earning family to the wall."[284] The Court's emphasis on this aspect of the case raised questions about whether a creditor could ever seize a debtor's wages prior to judgment. It also raised questions about the pre-judgment seizure of other types of property anytime prior to judgment, even if the state statute provided some measure of protection against unwarranted seizures.

Three years later, in *Fuentes v. Shevin*, the Court expanded the scope of the protection against pre-judgment seizures.[285] *Fuentes* involved two state pre-judgment replevin statutes, each of which allowed secured creditors to obtain a writ that permitted the sheriff to seize collateral without prior notice to the debtor. Finding the procedures unconstitutional, the Court emphasized that the state statutes did not provide an opportunity for a meaningful hearing before the debtor's property was seized. The fact that the debtor could retrieve his or her property by posting a bond, did not rescue the procedure from its defects.

After *Fuentes*, it seemed that pre-judgment seizure procedures that lacked any notice to or opportunity for the debtor to be heard prior to the seizure could not pass constitutional muster.[286] However, this impression was dispelled two years later by the Court's decision in *Mitchell v. W.T. Grant Co.*[287] *Mitchell* involved a Louisiana sequestration procedure that

[281] 395 U.S. 337 (1969).

[282] Former Wis. Stat. § 267.18(2)(a); *see* Sniadach v. Family Fin. Co., 395 U.S. 337, 340 (1969).

[283] *See generally* Elizabeth Warren & Amelia Warren Tyagi, The Two-Income Trap: Why Middle-Class Mothers and Fathers Are Going Broke (2003).

[284] 395 U.S. at 341. Although he is most widely known for his decisions about citizens' civil rights, before he was appointed to the Court, Justice Douglas was the principal author of what we now know as Chapter 11 of the Bankruptcy Code. Before becoming Chairman of the Securities Exchange Commission, he was a professor at Yale Law School where he taught the course in "Creditors' Rights." *See* www.oyez.org/oyez/resource/legal_entity/79/background (last visited on May 7, 2007).

[285] 407 U.S. 67 (1972).

[286] *E.g.*, Barkley Clark & Jonathan M. Landers, Sniadach, Fuentes *and Beyond: The Creditor Meets the Constitution*, 59 Va. L. Rev. 335 (1973).

[287] 416 U.S. 600 (1974).

permitted a secured creditor[288] to have its collateral seized by the sheriff without prior notice or a hearing if the creditor posted a bond with the court and supplied a sworn affidavit, specifying the alleged facts that entitled it to possession. The Court ruled that these facts, together with the requirement that a judge rather than a court clerk issue the writ and the fact that the debtor was entitled to an immediate post-seizure hearing and to damages if the property was improperly seized, provided sufficient protections for the debtor to justify the pre-judgment seizure.[289] In reaching its decision, the Court noted that the debtor was not the only one with a property interest at stake, and that the risk of loss of the creditor's rights in the collateral needed to be balanced against the property rights of the debtor.[290]

After *Mitchell*, it seemed that a secured creditor's pre-judgment seizure statute for secured creditors would satisfy the requirements of the Fourteenth Amendment if it contained the procedural protections that had saved the Louisiana statute.[291] First, the statute must provide for a judge, rather than a clerk to issue the writ. Second, the plaintiff must supply a sworn affidavit, detailing the circumstances that gave it a right to possession of the debtor's property. Third, the creditor must post a bond to ensure payment of any damages caused by an improper seizure. Finally, there must be an opportunity for an immediate post-seizure hearing regarding the propriety of the seizure.

The final decision in the series,[292] *North Georgia Finishing Co. v. Di-Chem*,[293] involved an attempted pre-judgment garnishment of a commercial debtor's bank account. *Di-Chem* ratified the protections that had sustained the pre-judgment seizure in *Mitchell*. The Court distinguished the Georgia garnishment statute before it from the Louisiana procedure in *Mitchell*, explaining:

---

[288] At the time, Louisiana had not yet adopted Article 9 of the U.C.C. The creditor retained a common law "seller's lien" on property it had sold to the debtor on credit.

[289] 416 U.S. 600, 605–06 (1974). A majority of the Court seemed to announce that *Fuentes*, which had been a 4-3 decision by an incomplete Court, was overruled. Justices Rehnquist and Powell had only recently been appointed to the Court at the time of the *Fuentes* decision, and took no part in it. They joined with the three Justices who had dissented in *Fuentes* to form the majority in *Mitchell*. The concurring decision of Justice Powell, 416 U.S. at 623, the dissenting opinion of Justice Stewart, which was joined by Justices Marshall and Douglas, 416 U.S. at 635 (Stewart, J., dissenting), and the dissenting opinion of Justice Brennan, 416 U.S. at 636, expressed the notion that *Fuentes* stood overruled. Thus, a full majority of the Court indicated that *Fuentes* had been overruled.

[290] 416 U.S. at 604.

[291] Steinheimer, *Summary Prejudgment Creditors' Remedies and Due Process of Law: Continuing Uncertainty After* Mitchell v. W.T. Grant Co., 32 Wash & Lee L. Rev. 79 (1975); *The Supreme Court, 1973 Term*, 88 Harv. L. Rev. 41 (1974).

[292] These four cases used to be a staple of law school courses in debtor-creditor law. Because they were also sometimes assigned in courses on civil procedure and constitutional law, they were, for a time, some of the most widely studied cases in the law school curriculum.

[293] 419 U.S. 601 (1975).

> The writ of garnishment is issuable on the affidavit of the creditor or his attorney, and the latter need not have personal knowledge of the facts . . . . The affidavit, like the one filed in this case, need contain only conclusory allegations. The writ is issuable, as this one was, by the court clerk, without participation by a judge. Upon service of the writ, the debtor is deprived of the use of the property in the hands of the garnishee. Here a sizable bank account was frozen, and the only method discernible on the face of the statute to dissolve the garnishment was to file a bond to protect the plaintiff creditor. There is no provision for an early hearing at which the creditor would be required to demonstrate at least probable cause for the garnishment. Indeed, it would appear that without the filing of a bond the defendant debtor's challenge to the garnishment will not be entertained, whatever the grounds may be.[294]

In the wake of *Sniadach*, *Fuentes*, *Mitchell*, and *Di-Chem*, most states amended their pre-judgment seizure statutes to meet these requirements. Many of these statutes now also require the creditor to show that there is some unusual risk that the debtor's property will be lost unless it is seized prior to judgment. Moreover, as a result of the strong language in *Sniadach*, pre-judgment wage garnishment is largely a thing of the past.

These changes to state statutes left the issue dormant for many years. The Court did not revisit the issue directly until its 1991 decision in *Connecticut v. Doehr.*[295] *Doehr* was distinguishable from the circumstances in *Fuentes* and *Mitchell*, both of which involved seizure by a creditor with a pre-existing security interest in the property it sought to have seized. In this regard, *Doehr* more closely resembled the pre-judgement garnishment statutes at issue in *Sniadach* and *Di-Chem*. However, it was unlike any of the Court's previously decided cases in that the creditor merely sought to obtain a pre-judgment attachment lien on the debtor's home, without depriving the debtor of either possession or use of the property while the underlying action progressed.

In *Doehr*, the Court applied a balancing test based on its 1976 decision in *Mathews v. Eldridge*,[296] which permitted the government to terminate state disability benefits without an evidentiary hearing. This balancing test weighed the interest of the creditor in obtaining an immediate provisional remedy against the risk that the defendant would be wrongly deprived of his or her property rights. In particular, the court examined: (1) the private interests of both parties that would be affected by the prejudgment remedy; (2) the risk that the defendant's interests would be erroneously deprived as a result of the procedures involved in the provisional remedy, together with the relative value of additional or alternative safeguards that might be employed; and (3) the ancillary interest the government may have in

---

[294] 419 U.S. at 607.

[295] 501 U.S. 1 (1991); *see generally* Linda Beale, Note, Connecticut v. Doehr *and Procedural Due Process Values: The* Sniadach *Tetrad Revisited*, 79 Cornell L. Rev. 1603 (1994).

[296] 424 U.S. 319 (1976).

making the provisional remedy available and avoiding the added burdens of additional protections for the defendant.[297]

Applying the first factor, the Court explained that the defendant's interests were considerable, even though he was not deprived of possession of his land while the case was pending. It explained, "[a]ttachment ordinarily clouds title; impairs the ability to sell or otherwise alienate the property; taints any credit rating; reduces the chance of obtaining a home equity loan or additional mortgage; and can even place an existing mortgage in technical default where there is an insecurity clause."[298]

With respect to the second factor, the Court emphasized that a trial judge could not meaningfully evaluate the plaintiff's likelihood of success on the underlying merits of his claim, supported merely by the "one-sided, self-serving, and conclusory submissions" on which the plaintiff's request for the provisional remedy was based. Even if pre-judgment attachment required "a detailed affidavit, [this] would give only the plaintiff's version of the [facts on which liability was based]."[299]

Moreover, the procedural safeguards provided by the statute did not, according to the Court, adequately guard against the risk of erroneous attachment. The attachment statute in question provided for a prompt post-seizure hearing, an opportunity for an interlocutory appeal of the results of the hearing, and double damages if the underlying suit had been commenced without probable cause; however it did not require the plaintiff to post a bond to ensure that any damages assessed as a result of an erroneous seizure would be paid. The Court also explained that the pre-judgment sequestration procedure in *Mitchell*, where similar procedures had been found adequate, involved a situation unlike the one in *Doehr*, in which the creditor had a property interest in the sequestered property. In addition, the nature of the underlying tort action in *Doehr* did not lend itself to resolution by the type of documentary evidence that would frequently be dispositive in cases like *Mitchell*, which involved missed installment payments.

Finally, the Court explained that any substantive interests the state has in protecting the plaintiff's rights do not outweigh the defendant's property rights.[300] This conclusion distinguishes the pre-judgment attachment involved in *Doehr* from emergency seizure procedures provided in statutes, like the ones the Court had mentioned favorably in *Fuentes*, that apply in disputes where public health or safety is at stake.[301]

The *Doehr* decision leaves many issues unresolved. Most significantly, it leaves undecided whether additional protections for the defendant, such as requiring the plaintiff to post an indemnity bond or limiting the

[297] *Doehr,* 501 U.S. at 11.

[298] *Doehr,* 501 U.S. at 11.

[299] *Doehr,* 501 U.S. at 12.

[300] *Doehr,* 501 U.S. at 16.

[301] Fuentes v. Shevin, 407 U.S. 67, 90–92 (1971).

availability of the seizure to exigent circumstances, would have saved the statute. Justice White's opinion indicated that he would not sustain a pre-judgment seizure hearing unless it required the plaintiff to post a bond, was limited to situations involving exigent circumstances that necessitated an immediate seizure, and provided for an immediate post-seizure hearing.[302] However, only three other Justices joined in this part of the opinion,[303] leaving the issue open for subsequent resolution.

The other major issue left unresolved by *Doehr* is the extent to which pre-judgment attachment is permitted in cases where the defendant's liability might be resolved by documentary evidence that can be examined by the court on an ex parte basis before authorizing the seizure. The *Doehr* Court specified that the difficulty of resolving factual issues on an ex parte basis in an intentional tort claim was one of the factors that contributed to the likelihood of an erroneous seizure. Moreover, the balancing test used in *Doehr* was based on the Court's earlier decision in *Mathews* in which the Court permitted a pre-hearing termination of social security disability payments, partially because of the relative ease of using documentary evidence to determine the defendant's right to continue receiving the benefits in question.[304]

Since *Doehr*, lower courts have upheld the constitutionality of lis pendens[305] and construction liens,[306] both of which might be imposed without an advance hearing. However, in *Grupo Mexicano de Desarrollo, S.A. v. Alliance Bond Fund, Inc.*,[307] the Supreme Court struck down a pre-judgment procedure that permitted use of a preliminary injunction to "freeze" a debtor's assets pending trial. The Court's reasoning did not, however, turn on the adequacy of the process, but whether a federal court's equity power extended to the procedures at issue.

---

302 *Doehr,* 501 U.S. at 18–23.

303 Even though the judgment of the Court was unanimous, only Justices O'Connor, Stevens, and Marhsall joined in Part IV of Justice White's opinion, dealing with the impact of these additional protections. Because most states' pre-judgment seizure statutes require a bond and an immediate post-seizure hearing and are limited to situations involving exigent circumstances, resolution of this issue is not imminent.

304 Mathews v. Eldridge, 424 U.S. 319, 345 (1976). Termination of the benefits had been based on agency review of documentary information supplied by the patient and his treating physicians.

305 New Destiny Dev. Corp. v. Piccione, 802 F. Supp. 692 (D. Conn. 1992) (lis pendens); *cf.* Aronson v. City of Akron, 116 F.3d 804, 811 (6th Cir. 1997) (criminal corrupt activity forfeiture proceeding); *see generally* Janice Gregg Levy, *Lis Pendens and Procedural Due Process: A Closer Look After* Connecticut v. Doehr, 51 Md. L. Rev. 1054 (1992).

306 *E.g.*, Gem Plumbing & Heating Co., Inc. v. Rossi, 867 A.2d 796 (R.I. 2005); Connecticut Natural Gas Corp. v. Miller, 684 A.2d 1173 (Conn. 1996); Haimbaugh Landscaping, Inc. v. Jegen, 653 N.E.2d 95 (Ind. Ct. App. 1995). Indeed, the *Doehr* opinion itself indicated that mechanics liens are not unconstitutional. *Doehr*, 501 U.S. at 11–13.

307 527 U.S. 308 (1999).

§ 2.10 State Insolvency Proceedings

Although federal bankruptcy cases are the most important proceedings that attempt to resolve the claims of multiple creditors in the same forum, state collective insolvency proceedings are also available.[308] The principal distinguishing feature of a federal bankruptcy proceeding is the availability of a discharge for the debtor, though other less significant differences abound. The two most important types of state insolvency proceedings are assignments for the benefit of creditors and state court receiverships. In addition, state statutes frequently provide for regulatory receiverships of insurance companies and similar financial institutions that are beyond the scope of the Bankruptcy Code. And, of course, federal laws other than the Bankruptcy Code regulate the rehabilitation of federally insured banks through the Federal Deposit Insurance Corporation (FDIC).

[A] Assignments for Benefit of Creditors[309]

An assignment for the benefit of creditors is a debtor's voluntary transfer of all of its nonexempt property in trust to an assignee, who liquidates the debtor's assets and distributes the proceeds to creditors in accordance with their relative priorities.[310] The debtor's property is efficiently liquidated, but the debtor receives no discharge (though if the debtor is a corporation, the discharge may not be necessary).[311]

Some states have attempted to use assignments for the benefit of creditors to provide debtors with a fresh start by limiting creditors' right to participate in the distribution of the debtor's assets unless they enter into a binding agreement to waive any remaining claims against the debtor. If they are unwilling to supply the waiver, they do not receive a share of the debtor's assets and remain free to pursue the debtor and any assets she subsequently acquires through litigation.

Another alternative for creditors who are uninterested in cooperating with an assignment for the benefit of creditors is to initiate an involuntary bankruptcy proceeding against the debtor. Under Bankruptcy Code § 303(b)(2), the appointment of a custodian, trustee, or agent with authority to take charge of all of the debtor's assets, provides creditors with grounds to impose a bankruptcy proceeding on an unwilling debtor.[312]

---

308 Interpleader is in many respects similar to bankruptcy and other insolvency proceedings. Both rule and statutory interpleader involve competing claims to a limited fund.

309 Melanie Rovner Cohen & Joanna L. Challacombe, *Assignment for Benefit of Creditors: A Contemporary Alternative for Corporations*, 2 De Paul Bus. L.J. 269 (1990); Benjamin Weintraub, Harris Levin & Eugene Sosnoff, *Assignments for the Benefit of Creditors and Competitive Systems for Liquidation of Insolvent Estates*, 39 Cornell L.Q. 3, 5 (1953).

310 *E.g.*, Compagnia Distribuzione Calzature, S.R.L. v. PSF Shoes, Ltd., 613 N.Y.S.2d 931 (A.D.2d 1994).

311 *See* International Shoe v. Pinkus, 278 U.S. 261 (1929) ("The power of Congress to establish uniform laws on the subject of bankruptcies throughout the United States is unrestricted and paramount.").

312 Bankruptcy Code § 303(b)(2); *see* § 6.03 Commencement of an Involuntary Case, *infra*.

Today, most assignments for the benefit of creditors are governed by state statute;[313] however, where statutory procedures are not available, an assignment can still be made using ordinary trust principles.[314]

Assignments for the benefit of creditors were once prevalent, but they fell into disuse for many years before experiencing a recent (though modest) revival.[315] They can be an effective means to liquidate a debtor's assets in an orderly manner, without the added expense of bankruptcy. This is particularly true for corporate debtors for whom receiving a discharge is less important.[316]

[B] Equitable Receiverships[317]

State court receiverships operate in a manner similar to assignments for the benefit of creditors, except they are involuntary. They are initiated by creditors, either acting alone or in concert with one another.

Receiverships were originally equitable proceedings designed to preserve a debtor's property from being dissipated by the debtor. These "equity receiverships" were initiated by creditors when the normal legal remedy of executing against the debtor's assets was at risk of becoming unavailable because of the debtor's mishandling, destruction, concealment, or dissipation of its assets. Receiverships are now largely statutory, though they remain viable as equitable remedies in some states.

Equity receiverships were an early precursor to modern Chapter 11 bankruptcy reorganization cases. Before the early 1930s and the enactment of the original reorganization provisions of the Bankruptcy Act,[318] equity receiverships were the primary mechanism to reorganize large complicated businesses, such as railroads, with diverse assets stretched across a broad range of territory.[319] However, they are rarely used today.[320]

---

[313] *See* Ohio Rev. Code Ann. §§ 1313.01-1313.59 (LexisNexis 2002) (designated as "Voluntary Assignments") (assignment to be filed with the probate court).

[314] *See, e.g.*, Tribune Co. v. Canger Floral Co., 37 N.E.2d 906 (Ill. App. Ct. 1941) .

[315] *E.g.*, Consolidated Pipe & Supply Co., Inc. v. Rovanco Corp., 897 F. Supp. 364 (N.D. Ill. 1995); *see generally* Melanie Rovner Cohen & Joanna L. Challacombe, *Assignment for Benefit of Creditors: A Contemporary Alternative for Corporations*, 2 DePaul Bus. L.J. 269 (1990).

[316] *See* § 13.02[B][1] Eligibility for Discharge — Individual Debtors, *infra*.

[317] Bruce A. Markell, *Owners, Auctions, and Absolute Priority in Bankruptcy Reorganizations*, 44 Stan. L. Rev. 69, 74–87 (1991); E. Merrick Dodd, Jr., *Reorganization Through Bankruptcy: A Remedy for What?*, 48 Harv. L. Rev. 1100, 1100–10 (1935); Roger S. Foster, *Conflicting Ideals for Reorganization*, 44 Yale L.J. 923 (1935); James N. Rosenberg, *A New Scheme of Reorganization*, 17 Colum. L. Rev. 523 (1917).

[318] Bankruptcy Act of March 3, 1933, ch. 204, § 77, 47 Stat. 1467, 1474 (1933); Bankruptcy Act of June 7, 1934, ch. 424, § 77B, 48 Stat. 911, 912 (1934).

[319] Bruce A. Markell, *Owners, Auctions, and Absolute Priority in Bankruptcy Reorganizations*, 44 Stan. L. Rev. 69, 75–84 (1991); David A. Skeel, Debt's Dominion: A History of Bankruptcy Law in America 57–60 (2001).

[320] Indeed, these remedies have fallen into such disuse that some trial court judges have refused to allow their use. *See* First Nat'l State Bank v. Kron, 464 A.2d 1146 (N.J. Super Ct. App. Div. 1983) (trial court judge gave, as one reason for refusal to appoint a receiver, that the receivership statute had been forgotten and was no longer viable).

[C] Regulatory Receiverships

By contrast to ordinary equitable receiverships, state and federal regulatory receiverships are common. However, they are largely unaffected by bankruptcy law. By long tradition, many financial institutions, especially insurance companies, have been regulated by state rather than federal authorities. Other financial institutions, such as FDIC-insured banks, are subject to a separate set of federal insolvency laws. Insurance companies and FDIC-insured financial institutions are not permitted to file bankruptcy. Those companies must be liquidated or reorganized under the relevant state or federal regulatory laws.

§ 2.11 Compositions and Workouts[321]

Workouts and compositions are non-judicial methods of dealing with debt that are rooted in the common law of contracts. The term "workout" refers to an agreement between the debtor and a single creditor or, more likely, a group of creditors. "Composition" refers to an agreement between the debtor and all of its creditors, or at least all of its significant creditors. A distinction is sometimes also made between a composition, in which creditors agree to reduce the amount owed by the debtor and an extension in which the amortization period and the due date for payment is extended. The terms, however, have no precise legal significance and are not used consistently. The key to these mechanisms is not the terminology but the legal substance, which is a contract that extends or partially discharges one or more of a debtor's obligations.

Historically, there have been two major conceptual problems with workouts and compositions: common law consideration, and the effect of these agreements on third parties. First, consider a bilateral workout between a debtor, Titanic Industries, and one of its principal creditors, Atlantic Consulting Corp. Assume that Titanic has been receiving consulting and repair services from Atlantic on 30-day open account credit and now owes Atlantic a total of $50,000. Of this amount, $40,000 is overdue, and the remaining $10,000 will become due within 30 days. Titanic proposes that Atlantic agree to reduce the amount of the total debt to $35,000, and Titanic will make a $10,000 cash payment to Atlantic within the next month and pay the $25,000 balance in monthly $1,000 installments over several years. Titanic agrees to pay for any future services in cash at the time the services are rendered.

While Titanic may be financially capable of performing this agreement, the deal may be unenforceable due to lack of consideration. Atlantic has modified its rights, but Titanic has promised to do nothing more than perform a portion of its pre-existing duties. If Atlantic had been supplying goods, modification would probably be enforceable under U.C.C. § 2-209,

---

321 Winton E. Williams, *Resolving the Creditor's Dilemma: An Elementary Game — Theoretic Analysis of the Causes and Cures of Counterproductive Practices in the Collection of Consumer Debt*, 48 Fla. L. Rev. 607 (1996).

despite the absence of consideration; however, since services were involved, consideration is necessary.[322] Absent consideration, the workout agreement is unenforceable by Titanic unless Titanic relied to its detriment in some way on Atlantic's promise to reduce the amount owed. That might make the modification enforceable on a theory of promissory estoppel.

A few adjustments to the terms of the workout could supply the necessary element of exchange. If Titanic agreed to give Atlantic some collateral in exchange for Atlantic's forbearance from requiring immediate payment of the full amount, such as a second mortgage on its warehouse and office buildings, or a security interest in its inventory or accounts receivable, the necessary element of a bargain would be present and the agreement would be enforceable. At the same time, however, the mortgage and security interest would be vulnerable to avoidance as a preference if Titanic filed a bankruptcy proceeding within the ninety day period following the transfer.[323] This would ultimately deprive Atlantic of the principal benefit of the bargain. To deal with this, many workout agreements do not release the debtor from its full obligations until 90 days after the last payment is made under the agreement.

A multilateral composition agreement between a debtor and several of its creditors is more complicated. Some of the creditors are bound to be secured while others are unsecured. These creditors are likely to be distrustful of both the debtor and of each other. And their suspicions may be warranted. After all, the debtor may be an important customer of some creditors, who will be facing their own financial difficulties if the debtor's business fails. Likewise, some creditors may be key suppliers to the debtor's business, without whose cooperation the debtor would be doomed. Unsecured creditors may be skeptical about the value placed on the collateral claimed by a secured creditor and worried that secured creditors should be making greater sacrifices, since they face a lesser risk if the debtor falls into bankruptcy. This mixture of factors leads to a variety of attitudes and motives among the participants concerning whatever deal is hammered out.

One thing should be clear: when creditors make agreements with one another, consideration is not a problem. When one creditor agrees to reduce the amount of his claim, in exchange for another creditor's agreement to do the same, the necessary element of a bargain is present; the promise is enforceable, with the debtor as a third-party beneficiary of the deal.

Instead, the principal drawback is the practical difficulty of obtaining all of the creditors' consent. Holdouts with the power to frustrate the workout might demand a larger payment than the debtor can afford. In addition, the agreement may provide that it is not enforceable against any of the parties unless everyone's agreement is obtained. Even without this provision, one key holdout, who is doubtful of the debtor's ability to pay, may disrupt everyone else's plans by continuing to pursue the debtor for the

---

322 U.C.C. § 2-209 (2002).

323 *See* Chapter 15, Avoidable Preferences, *infra*.

entire debt and by eventually seizing assets that the debtor needs to keep its business running. This holdout problem is one of the key weaknesses of workouts as a solution to a debtor's general default on its debts.

Although Chapter 11 of the Bankruptcy Code includes mechanisms to deal with these dissenters, as well as ways to evaluate the value of the debtor's assets, compositions retain important potential advantages over Chapter 11. Most importantly, the costs of a composition agreement are usually much lower than those of a Chapter 11 bankruptcy proceeding. Further, in Chapter 11, details of the debtor's financial difficulties are likely to be revealed to the general public. Moreover, a composition agreement is not subject to the kind of court or regulatory scrutiny that is involved in Chapter 11.

Compositions and bankruptcy reorganizations are not mutually exclusive. In some cases — often called "prepackaged" Chapter 11s — the debtor and the requisite majorities[324] of creditors agree to all or most of the reorganization plan before the debtor files its bankruptcy petition; the pre-negotiated plan is then presented to the court and the other creditors for confirmation.[325] Thus, in the right circumstances, a Chapter 11 plan (which is, after all, in the nature of a composition agreement) can be worked out in advance and taken to bankruptcy court for relatively swift approval.[326]

§ 2.12 Property Beyond the Reach of Creditors

Not all property is subject to creditors' claims. The popular image of a destitute debtor, left with nothing but an empty barrel held up by a pair of ratty suspenders, is pure hyperbole. All states have exemption statutes that provide a list of assets that are beyond the reach of creditors, unless the debtor has voluntarily encumbered them with a mortgage or a security interest. Further, some assets are immune even from security interests unless the security interest was granted as part of the deal that enabled the debtor to acquire the asset in the first place. Finally, limited types of assets are held in a form, such as a tenancy by the entirety or a valid spendthrift trust, that places them beyond the reach of even the debtor to encumber them.

---

[324] Bankruptcy Code § 1126.

[325] *See* § 19.09[E] Pre-Packaged Plans, *infra*.

[326] Ronald Barliant, Dimitri G. Karcazes & Anne M. Sherry, *From Free-Fall to Free-For-All: The Rise of Pre-Packaged Asbestos Bankruptcies*, 12 Am. Bankr. Inst. L. Rev. 441 (2004); *e.g.*, United Artists Theatre Co. v. Walton, 315 F.3d 217, 224 n.5 (3d Cir. 2003).

[A] Exemptions[327]

State law permits even the most impecunious debtor to retain some assets. These assets are "exempt" from attachment or execution; unsecured creditors seeking to enforce a judgment may not seize them. The fundamental reason for exemptions is the belief that even the most hopelessly insolvent debtors should not be deprived of the basic necessities of life. This tradition is also reflected in the Bankruptcy Code's "fresh start," which permits debtors to retain property that state laws exempt from execution.[328]

For many years, the exemption laws preserved a picture of nineteenth century rural American life. A debtor was allowed to keep cows, pigs, a spinning wheels, and a dozen or more dishes for *himself, his* wife and *their* children. In recent years, largely as a result of the influence of the 1978 overhaul of the Bankruptcy Code, exemptions have become more realistic; cars have replaced horses and pension rights have replaced acres of farm land.

Exemptions fall into three broad categories: the homestead exemption for residential real estate; exemptions for items of tangible personal property; and exemptions for various types of income. There are several key limits on exemption rights, which are explained below.

[1] Limitations on Exemptions

[a] Exemption in Debtor's Equity

The most important limit on a debtor's exemption rights is that they do not affect creditors' consensual liens, but apply only to the debtor's equity in her property.[329] For example, a debtor who owns a home worth $150,000 but that is subject to an outstanding $150,000 mortgage will not be able to claim an exemption for the home because she has no equity in it. Neither

---

[327] Wells M. Engledow, *Cleaning up the Pigsty: Approaching a Consensus on Exemption Laws*, 74 Am. Bankr. L.J. 275 (2000); Delmar Karlen, *Exemptions From Execution*, 22 Bus. Law. 1167 (1967); Marjorie Dick Rombauer, *Debtors' Exemption Statutes — Revision Ideas*, 36 Wash L. Rev. 484, 485 (1961); William T. Vukowich, *Debtors' Exemption Rights*, 62 Geo. L.J. 779 (1974); William T. Vukowich, *Debtors' Exemption Rights Under the Bankruptcy Reform Act of 1978*, 58 N.C. L. Rev. 769, 800–04 (1980); William J. Woodward, Jr., *Exemptions, Opting Out, and Bankruptcy Reform*, 43 Ohio St. L.J. 335 (1982); Richard C. Christenson, Comment, *Personal Property Exemptions and the Uniform Exemptions Act*, 1978 BYU L. Rev. 462, 466–67.

[328] Bankruptcy Code § 522(b). In some states, debtors may choose between the exemptions provided by their home state's exemption statute or a set of uniform exemptions in the Bankruptcy Code. *See* Bankruptcy Code § 523(d). Pursuant to authority delegated by Congress, most states have "opted-out" of this election, and left their residents with only the schedule of property exempted by the state exemption statute. Not surprisingly, most of the states that have opted out of the uniform federal exemptions are those with exemption statutes that are less generous toward debtors than those contained in the Bankruptcy Code. *See* § 12.02 Exemptions in Bankruptcy, *infra*.

[329] *See* In re Galvan, 110 B.R. 446 (B.A.P. 9th Cir. 1990); In re Rodriguez, 140 B.R. 562 (Bankr. D. Kan. 1992); Jungkunz v. Fifth-Third Bank, 650 N.E.2d 134 (Ohio Ct. App. 1994); Russell G. Donaldson, Annotation, *Avoidance under § 522(f)(1) of Bankruptcy Code of 1978 of Judicial Lien on Debtor's Exempt Personal Property*, 124 A.L.R. Fed. 465 (1995).

will the debtor's unsecured creditors be able to levy on the house, because all of the value would be eaten up by the secured creditor's claim. If the mortgage were $145,000, the debtor could claim an exemption of up to $5,000 in the property because that is the limit of her equity. Again, there would be no value available to unsecured creditors. However, if the mortgage debt were $130,000 and the state's homestead exemption were for only $8,000, the debtor could exempt $8,000. However, because the debtor's $20,000 in equity exceeds the amount of the available exemption, the unsecured creditors would be able to levy on the property in order to capture the excess $12,000 in equity. Thus, exemptions protect a limited amount of property from judicial liens, but they do not protect property from consensual liens like mortgages and security interests, or from statutory liens, like construction and repairmen's liens.[330]

[b] Limited Categories

Exemption rights are usually limited to very specific categories of property, such as "real or personal property used as the debtor's principal residence"; "one motor vehicle"; or "wearing apparel and household furnishings." Thus, the debtor's property must fit into one of the categories of property that qualify for an exemption.

Determining whether a particular item fits within a specified category is sometimes difficult. For example, some states' exemption statutes place an aggregate limit on the total value of "household furnishings" and "appliances" that may be exempted, but impose no limit on "wearing apparel." This may lead a debtor to claim that her MP3 player is wearing apparel, and not a household furnishing. The same sort of problem has arisen in connection with items that might be characterized either as "jewelry," which is usually subject to a more stringent restriction, or as "wearing apparel" for which most exemption statutes provide more liberal protection.[331] For example, in *In re Leva,*[332] the debtor's Rolex brand wristwatch qualified for a wearing apparel exemption, but his diamond "pinky ring" and gold bracelet did not.

Some states provide what has been characterized as a "wildcard" exemption, which permits the debtor to exempt any property, usually up to a specific dollar limit.[333] Following the example supplied by § 522(d)(5) of the Bankruptcy Code, the dollar limit of such exemptions varies, depending on the extent to which a debtor has used any available homestead exemption.[334]

---

330 The Internal Revenue Code has its own set of exemption provisions, which provide debtors with very limited protection from a statutory federal tax lien. I.R.C. § 6334 (2000).

331 *E.g.*, In re Fernandez, 855 F.2d 218 (5th Cir. 1988) (jewelry exempt as "clothing" under Texas exemption statute).

332 96 B.R. 723 (Bankr. W.D. Tex. 1989) (Texas has long been viewed as a debtor's haven).

333 *E.g.*, Ohio Rev. Code Ann. § 2329.66(A)(18) (LexisNexis Supp. 2006) ($400 "in any property"); 735 Ill. Comp. Stat. Ann. 5/12-1001(b) (2003) ($2000 "in any other property"); Mo. Stat. Ann. § 513.430(3) (West Supp. 2006) ($400 in "any other property of any kind").

334 Stephen F. Yunker, Comment, *The General Exemption of Section 522(d)(5) of the 1978 Bankruptcy Code*, 49 U. Chi. L. Rev. 564 (1982).

[c] Value Limits

Exemptions are nearly always limited in value. This limit may be imposed on each individual item, on categories of items, or more rarely, on the total amount of property that a debtor may claim as exempt. For example, the Ohio exemption statute limits the value of each item of a debtor's "wearing apparel" that may be claimed as exempt to $200 per item, but the statute imposes no overall limit on the value of the debtor's total portfolio of these items.[335] The debtor may exempt as many $199 shirts as he wants — though an aggressive creditor may inquire into how frequently the debtor "wears" each shirt and thus question whether all of them fit into this category.[336] Another provision of this illustrative statute permits debtors to protect individual items of "household furnishings" but limits the aggregate of such items that may be exempt to $2,000.[337] Clothing, it appears, is more important in Ohio than furniture.[338]

Value limitations supply another example of the omnipresent issue in debtor-creditor and bankruptcy law: valuation. The only real way to determine the value of an asset is to sell it. But selling the asset would frustrate the purpose of an exemption statute, which is to permit the debtor to keep the exempted property. Thus, the value of exempt property sometimes must be determined by expert appraisal testimony.[339] When the value of exempt property is contested, which generally occurs in a bankruptcy proceeding, fair market value is the governing standard, typically without any reduction for the amount that would have been consumed by the costs of the sale.[340] If the exempt asset is an intangible right, such as a cause of action, valuation may be particularly difficult.[341]

As a practical matter, bankruptcy trustees develop a fairly good sense of what common household items are worth. Most of the time they are worth very little — imagine the amount of cash you would expect to produce from a garage sale of all of your wearing apparel and household furnishings.[342]

---

335 The potential folly of this type of limitation was illustrated by the original bankruptcy code, which permitted debtors to keep an unlimited number of "household goods," so long as each item was worth no more than $200. In re Wahl, 14 B.R. 153 (Bankr. E.D. Wis. 1981). After several debtors exempted thousands of dollars of sets of silverware, each item of which was worth approximately $180, Congress amended the law to impose a ceiling on the total value of items of household goods that could be exempted. *See* In re Siegle, 257 B.R. 591 (Bankr. D. Mont. 2001); Margaret Howard, *A Theory of Discharge in Consumer Bankruptcy*, 48 Ohio St. L.J. 1047, 1078 n.212 (1987).

336 *See* In re Hazelhurst, 228 B.R. 199 (Bankr. E.D. Tenn. 1998) (engagement ring the debtor no longer wore was not reasonably necessary wearing apparel).

337 Ohio Rev. Code Ann. § 2329.66(A)(4) (LexisNexis Supp. 2006).

338 This is probably appropriate. There have been times in your author's lives when they owned no furniture and got along fine. Living without wearing apparel, on the other hand, might have been more difficult.

339 *E.g.*, In re Smith., 267 B.R. 568 (Bankr. S.D. Ohio 2001).

340 *See* In re Sumerell, 194 B.R. 818 (Bankr. E.D. Tenn. 1996); In re Mitchell, 103 B.R. 819 (Bankr. W.D. Tex. 1989).

341 *E.g.*, In re Ball, 201 B.R. 210 (Bankr. N.D. Ill. 1996).

342 Items of upholstered furniture, for example, are virtually worthless unless they are antiques.

The value of motor vehicles are readily determined from the automobile bluebook, commonly used by automobile dealers.[343] In many cases, the debtor's home is the only asset that might require a professional appraisal to determine its value. The value supplied by the debtor in the schedules she files with her bankruptcy petition will usually be relied on and may be dispositive in the absence of conflicting qualified evidence.

Alternatively, the value of some items can be indirectly limited by restricting the exemption to items that are "reasonably necessary for the support of the debtor."[344] For example, in *In re Sydlowski*, the court held that the married debtors could each exempt one TV and one VCR as reasonably necessary, and that a video game and library of video tapes were reasonably necessary for a custodial parent, and that a third TV and a lawn "edge trimmer" were not reasonably necessary and thus not entitled to an exemption for "household goods."[345] Another court ruled that a television and a VCR were reasonably necessary because of their customary usage in the home, but that "recreational equipment" not used inside the home such as "bowling balls, golf clubs, fishing equipment, [and] camping equipment" did not qualify for the exemption.[346]

Some particularly important items are sometimes exempt without regard to their value. The most obvious example is the exemption provided in most jurisdictions for "medically prescribed or medically necessary health aids."[347] The principal limitation here is that they must be "professionally prescribed" or "medically necessary."[348]

Categories of exempt property that contain no value limit are subject to potential abuse. In *In re Freelander*[349] the debtor was permitted to exempt

---

[343] *See* Kelly Blue Book *available at* kbb.com/ (last visited July 29, 2006). The "Kelly Bluebook," also sometimes known as "the bluebook," has nothing to do with The Uniform System of Citation published by the Harvard Law Review Association.

[344] *E.g.*, In re Walsh, 5 B.R. 239 (Bankr. D. Colo. 1980); Michael G. Hillinger, *How Fresh a Start?: What Are "Household Goods" For Purposes of Section 522(f)(1)(B)(I) Lien Avoidance?*, 15 Bank. Dev. J. 1 (1999); John D. Perovich, Annotation, *What Is "Necessary" Furniture Entitled to Exemption from Seizure for Debt*, 41 A.L.R.3d 607 (1972 & Supp. 1999).

[345] 186 B.R. 907 (Bankr. N.D. Ohio 1995).

[346] In re Biancavilla, 173 B.R. 930 (Bankr. D. Idaho 1994). Apparently, gear necessary for sedentary forms of recreation are reasonably necessary, but items necessary for more active types of recreation are not. *See also* In re Davis, 134 B.R. 34 (Bankr. W.D. Okla. 1991). Some states explicitly exempt various types of sporting goods. *E.g.,* Tex. Prop. Code § 42.002(3)(E) (Vernon 2000). Guns are sometimes explicitly exempt. *E.g.*, Tex. Prop. Code Ann. § 42.002(a)(7) (Vernon 2000); Idaho Rev. Code Ann. 11-605(7) (2004); *but see* In re Barnes, 117 B.R. 842 Bankr. D. Md. 1990) (firearms were sporting goods normally used outside and away from home and were not reasonably necessary for day-to-day existence of people in context of their homes, and thus not "household goods").

[347] *E.g.*, Ohio Rev. Code Ann. § 2329.66(A)(7) (LexisNexis Supp. 2006); Bankruptcy Code § 522(d)(8) ("professionally prescribed health aids for the debtor or a dependent of the debtor").

[348] *See* In re McCashen, 339 B.R. 907 (Bankr. N.D. Ohio 2006) (unmodified van that could accommodate debtor's physical size was neither professionally prescribed nor medically necessary); In re Hellen, 329 B.R. 678 (Bankr. N.D. Ill. 2005) (modifications to van made to accommodate disability were medically necessary).

[349] 93 B.R. 446, 450 (Bankr. E.D. Va. 1988).

his $640,000 thoroughbred race horse, under an archaic exemption statute that had been well suited to an agrarian lifestyle by permitting debtors to exempt their entire interest in "a horse."

Married debtors, who jointly own most of their property, are usually able to double the value limits imposed on exemptions. This is because most exemption statutes make "the debtor's interest" in the property exempt.[350] If property is jointly owned, each owner has an interest in it that can be exempted. Thus, a state statute that exempts up to $1,000 of an individual's interest in one motor vehicle could be used by a married couple who jointly own the car to exempt up to $2,000 equity in it.

This feature is particularly useful in connection with homestead exemptions on a debtor's residential real estate, especially where the debtors have not consumed the entire value of their house through the use of a "home equity credit line." It is also frequently useful in connection with exemptions for household items that might be worth more than the meager amount protected by the exemption statute. Of course, some valuable items, such as engagement rings, might not be jointly owned and thus are eligible for exemption only by the spouse who owns the item.[351]

In bankruptcy, a debtor may be able to set aside certain non-purchase money security interests that otherwise might impair her exemption in certain types of exempt property.[352] However, this ability to avoid security interests that impair an exemption applies only to debtors who are eligible for and can afford to file a bankruptcy case — an increasingly limited number of debtors.[353]

There has been a great deal of controversy over the effect of exemption laws. According to some scholars, generous exemption laws ought to lead to an increase in bankruptcies, because debtors will be able to shed debt without losing assets.[354] However, the available empirical evidence provides little support for this position.[355] It appears, instead, that few debtors are influenced by the amount of property they can retain in a bankruptcy

---

[350] *See, e.g.*, Ariz. Rev. Stat. Ann. § 33-1121.01 (West 2000).

[351] *Cf.* In re Gregorchik, 311 B.R. 52 (Bankr. W.D. Pa. 2004) (engagement ring not entireties property).

[352] Bankruptcy Code § 522(f); *see* § 12.07 Avoiding Liens on Exempt Property, *infra*.

[353] *See* § 6.02[B] Debtor Eligibility for Voluntary Relief, *infra*.

[354] *See* Michelle J. White, *Why It Pays to File for Bankruptcy: A Critical Look at Incentives Under US Bankruptcy Laws and a Proposal for Change*, 65 U. Chi. L. Rev. 685 (1998); Michelle J. White, *Why Don't More Households File for Bankruptcy?*, 14 J.L. Econ. & Org. 205 (1998); Reint Gropp, John Karl Scholz & Michelle White, *Personal Bankruptcy and Credit Supply and Demand*, 112 Q.J. Econ. 217 (1997).

[355] Susan Block-Lieb & Edward J. Janger, *The Myth of the Rational Borrower*, 85 Texas L. Rev. 1481, 1522-23 (collecting studies); Teresa Sullivan, Elizabeth Warren & Jay Lawrence Westbrook, As We Forgive Our Debtors: Bankruptcy and Consumer Credit in America 241–42 (1989); W.J. Woodward, Jr, *Exemptions as an Incentive to Voluntary Bankruptcy: An Empirical Study,* 88 Com. L.J. 309 (1983).

proceeding.[356] It may simply be that debtors do not have enough property for this to have an effect on their decision-making.[357]

[2] Homestead Exemptions on Residential Real Estate

As suggested by its name, homestead exemptions protect some or all of a debtor's equity in her home.[358] In most states, the amount of the homestead exemption is too small to permit the debtor to keep her home. Instead, it permits a debtor to keep a portion of the proceeds from the sale of her home, assuming it can be sold for its full market value. Ohio, with one of the smallest homestead exemptions in the country, protects only $5,000 of a debtor's equity "in one parcel or item of real or personal property that the person or a dependent of the person uses as a residence."[359] With the $161,000 median selling price of a house in Columbus, Ohio in April, 2007,[360] $5,000 does not even cover the amount necessary for a 10% down payment. The amount of the homestead exemption varies widely from a mere $5,000 in Ohio,[361] to $50,000 in New York,[362] to an unlimited amount in Texas[363] and a handful of other states where the extent of the exemption is measured in acres rather than dollars.

In a few states, to be eligible for a homestead exemption, debtors must file a "declaration of homestead" much in the way a creditor would file a

---

[356] Teresa Sullivan, Elizabeth Warren & Jay Lawrence Westbrook, As We Forgive Our Debtors: Bankruptcy and Consumer Credit in America 241–42 (1989); Susan Block-Lieb & Edward J. Janger, *The Myth of the Rational Borrower: Rationality, Behavioralism, and the Misguided "Reform" of Bankruptcy Law*, 84 Tex. L. Rev. 1481, 1523–24 & 1523 n.172 (2006).

[357] Richard M. Hynes, *Personal Bankruptcy in the 21st Century: Emerging Trends and New Challenges: Credit Markets, Exemptions, and Households with Nothing to Exempt,* 7 Theoretical Inquiries L. 493 (2006).

[358] The homestead exemption reputedly began in Texas. *See* United States. v. Johnson, 160 F.3d 1061 (5th Cir. 1998); 3 Laws of the Republic of Tex. 113 (1839). Indeed, along with a few other states, Texas has long been regarded as a debtor's haven. *See* Jean Braucher, *The Repo Code: a Study of Adjustment to Uncertainty in Commercial Law*, 75 Wash. U. L.Q. 549, 570 (1997); Julie B. Schroeder, Comment, *Perspectives on Urban Homestead Exemptions — Texas Amends Article XVI, Section 51*, 15 St. Mary's L.J. 603, 614–17 & 614 n.67 (1984) (referring to McKnight, *Protection of the Family Home from Seizure by Creditors: The Sources and Evolution of a Legal Principle*, 37 S.W. Hist. Quart. 369, 369–83 (1983), as outlining the early history and reputation of Texas in this regard).

[359] Ohio Rev. Code Ann. § 2329.66(A)(1)(b) (LexisNexis Supp. 2006). Ohio's homestead exemption statute goes one step further, and provides an unlimited exemption for a judgment debtor's interest in residential property, but only with respect to judgments held by health care providers. *Id.* § 2329.66(A)(1)(a). Moreover, the exemption merely operates to prevent the judgment creditor from foreclosing. When the property is voluntarily sold, the creditor is entitled to payment and the debtor's exemption is limited to the $5,000 amount provided for in § 2329.66(A)(1)(b).

[360] www.housingtracker.net/old_housingtracker/location/Ohio/Columbus/ (last viewed May 7, 2007).

[361] Ohio Rev. Code Ann. § 2329.66(A)(1) (LexisNexis Supp. 2006).

[362] N.Y.C.P.L. § 5206.

[363] Tex. Prop. Code Ann. § 41.002 (Vernon 2002) (10 acres of urban land, or up 200 acres in a rural area for a "family").

mortgage.[364] In other states, the exemption is not available to protect a debtor from some sorts of claims. It would not be surprising to find, for example, that the exemption could not be used by a "deadbeat dad" to protect his home from a claim for unpaid support.

The homestead exemption is usually only available for property used as the principal residence of the debtor or one of the debtor's dependents.[365] In most states, the exemption now applies to both personal property and real estate used as a residence, permitting mobile homes, trailers, and houseboats to quality for the protection. In rare circumstances,[366] a standard motor vehicle might qualify, though questions would arise regarding the debtor's ability to "stack" her motor vehicle exemption on top of her homestead exemption, and claim two exemptions for the car, one as a homestead, and the other as a motor vehicle.

[3] Personal Property Exemptions[367]

Many types of personal property are protected by exemption statutes. There are many common themes, but the differences from one state to the next sometimes seem staggering. In some states, a debtor's interest in her "seat or pew in any church or place of public worship" is exempt, while specific exemptions for firearms and livestock are more common in western states. In other states, exemptions are available for quantities of firewood,[368] assorted livestock, including sheep, cows, swine, and chickens,[369] and in at least one state, a liquor license.[370] In Louisiana, an exemption is available for "musical instruments played or practiced on by [the debtor] or a member of his family" apparently without regard to its value and regardless of whether it is used for the production of income.[371]

The most common exemptions for goods are those for household furnishings, wearing apparel, household appliances, motor vehicles, a limited amount of jewelry, and "tools of a debtor's trade or business." As explained above, exemptions for these categories of property are usually subject to limits. These limits are sometimes expressed as a limit on the value of

---

[364] *See, e.g.*, Va. Code Ann. § 34-14 (LexisNexis 2005); Zimmerman v. Morgan, 689 F.2d 471 (4th Cir. 1982) (debtor who failed to record notice of homestead exemption could not assert exemption in bankruptcy).

[365] *See* Holden v. Cribb, 561 S.E.2d 634 (S.C. Ct. App. 2002) (incarcerated debtor was not deprived of his homestead where he had been involuntarily removed from his residence and intended to return upon his release).

[366] A friend of one of your co-authors once lived in his long-haul truck cab.

[367] Michael G. Hillinger, *How Fresh a Start?: What Are "Household Goods" for Purposes of Section 522(f)(1)(B)(I) Lien Avoidance?*, 15 Bankr. Dev. J. 1 (1998).

[368] Me. Rev. Stat. Ann. tit. 14 § 4422(6)(c) (2003) ("10 cords of wood, 5 tons of coal, 1000 gallons of petroleum products or its equivalent").

[369] Mich Comp. Laws. Ann. § 600.6023(1)(d) (2000) (10 sheep, 2 cows, 5 swine, 100 hens & 5 roosters); Mass. Ann. Laws ch. 235 § 34 (2000) (12 sheep, 2 cows, 2 swine, no mention of hens or roosters).

[370] Idaho Code Ann. § 23-514 (LexisNexis 2001).

[371] La. Rev. State Ann. § 13:3881(A)(4)(d) (West Supp. 2006).

individual items, as an aggregate limit, or more ambiguously as a limit to whatever is "reasonably necessary."

[4] Exemptions for Sources of Income[372]

Wage garnishment exemptions protect a portion of most debtors' earnings from being garnished. Federal restrictions on wage garnishment establish an absolute limit on the extent of wages that states may permit creditors to seize. In addition, many states provide additional protection from wage garnishment, beyond the limits imposed by federal law.

Most states' exemption statutes protect a wide variety of sources of income, such as retirement funds, workers' compensation benefits, personal injury awards, disability benefits, veterans' benefits, alimony and support, unemployment insurance payments, and life insurance benefits. Such exemptions may be limited to the amount reasonably necessary for the support of the debtor and the debtor's dependents.

[a] Federal Restrictions on Wage Garnishment

The federal Consumer Credit Protection Act imposes limits on the amount of wages that states may permit creditors to garnish.[373] It provides:

> The maximum part of the aggregate disposable earnings of an individual for any workweek which is subject to garnishment may not exceed
>
> (1) 25 per centum of his disposable earnings for that week, or
>
> (2) the amount by which his disposable earnings for that week exceed thirty times the Federal minimum hourly wage prescribed by section 6(a)(1) of the Fair Labor Standards Act of 1938 in effect at the time the earnings are payable,
>
> whichever is less.[374]

For most employees, the maximum that may be garnished under this formula is 25% of weekly disposable income. However, if an employee's weekly disposable earnings are less than $206,[375] then only the amount that exceeds $175.50 (thirty times the current federal minimum wage of $5.85 per hour)[376] can be garnished. These numbers will change in July

[372] Sherwin P. Simmus, *Pension Plan Loans and Bankruptcy: The Great Debate and a New View*, 18 Bank. Dev. J. 373 (2002).

[373] 15 U.S.C. §§ 1671-1677 (2000). The restrictions apply to garnishment or any other type of proceeding used to seize wages for payment of a debt. 15 U.S.C. § 1672(c) (2000).

[374] 15 U.S.C. § 1673(a) (2000).

[375] This is a meager $10,300 per year, assuming a work week of 50 weeks with 2 weeks vacation. One of your authors remembers the day, in the early 1960s when his parents went out to dinner to celebrate his father's raise. His new annual salary was $10,000, an amount that as a college student immediately after World War II, he could not have imagined earning. As a "farm hand" before the war, he earned $1 a day.

[376] In May, 2007, legislation was enacted to increase the Federal minimum wage from $5.15 per hour to $5.85 per hour. It will increase again to $6.55 per hour in July, 2008, and to $7.25 per hour in July, 2009.

2008, and again in July 2009 when the minimum wage increases again to $6.55 per hour and $7.25 per hour respectively.[377]

A couple of simple examples illustrate how these rules apply. First, consider an employee whose weekly disposable earnings are $1,000. Twenty-five percent (25%) of $1,000 is $250. $1,000 of disposable earnings exceeds $175.50 (30 times the current minimum wage) by $824.50. The maximum amount subject to garnishment is the lesser of $824.50 or $250.[378]

However, consider an employee who earns $6.00 per hour, but who works only thirty-five hours per week. Her total gross earnings would be $210, but her disposable earnings, after deducting federal, state and local income taxes, social security taxes, and any applicable unemployment insurance taxes, required by law to be withheld, may be only $180. Although 25% of $180 is $45, $180 of weekly disposable earnings exceeds $175.50 (30 times the minimum wage) by only $4.50. The lower of these two amounts, $4.50, is the maximum weekly amount that can be garnished.[379]

These maximum amounts apply to weekly earnings. The Department of Labor has promulgated regulations that adapt these formulas with respect to employees who are paid on a biweekly or monthly basis.[380]

This 25% restriction does not apply to court-ordered support, state or federal taxes, or wage withholding orders in Chapter 13 bankruptcy cases.[381] Further, the 25% maximum is raised to varying amounts, up to 65% of an employee's disposable earnings for creditors whose wage garnishment orders are for unpaid support obligations. A support claimant can garnish 50% of an employee's disposable earnings if the employee has dependents other than those who are garnishing her wages to recover support, and 60% if the employee has no other dependents.[382] These amounts are increased to 55% and 65% for support obligations that are more than twelve weeks overdue.[383]

---

[377] The U.S. Troop Readiness, Veterans' Care, Katrina Recovery, and Iraq Accountability Appropriations Act, 2007, Pub. L. No. 110-28 § 8102(a), 121 Stat. 112, 188 (2007).

[378] When the minimum wage increases to $7.25 per hour in 2009, the exemption would still expose a debtor earning $1,000 per week to garnishment of only $250 per week. Thirty times the proposed new minimum wage of $7.25 per hour is $217.50. $1000 exceeds this amount by $782.50, which is more than 25% of the employee's disposable earnings ($250). Thus, $250 would still be the maximum that could be garnished.

[379] Under the $7.25 minimum wage that will be in effect in July 2009, the amount of such an employee's garnishable wages changes dramatically. Her gross earnings for 35 hours would be $235.75, with probably about $220 of disposable earnings. Although twenty-five percent of her disposable earnings is $55, she receives only $2.50 more than thirty times what the minimum wage will be at that time (30 x $7.25 = $217.50). Because $2.50 is less than $55, only $2.50 of her weekly earnings will be subject to garnishment. If she worked only 34 hours per week (instead of 35), none of her weekly earnings would be subject to garnishment.

[380] 29 C.F.R. § 870.10(c) (2004).

[381] 15 U.S.C. § 1673(b)(1) (2000).

[382] 15 U.S.C. § 1673(b)(2) (2000).

[383] 15 U.S.C. § 1673(b)(2) (2000).

As suggested above, an employee's "disposable earnings" are less than all of her gross earnings. Disposable earnings are " 'that part of the earnings of any individual remaining after the deduction from those earnings of any amounts required by law to be withheld.' "[384] Amounts required by law to be withheld include deductions for federal, state, and local income taxes, social security, medicare, and any applicable unemployment insurance taxes.

Deductions for health or life insurance, retirement benefits, and union dues are not "required by law to be withheld" and are part of an employee's disposable earnings.[385] Likewise, amounts withheld pursuant to a court-ordered wage assignment, made as part of a divorce decree, are not required by law to be withheld within the meaning of the statute.[386] However, such decrees are generally regarded as separate garnishments.[387] Otherwise, a judgment debtor whose wages are already subject to a court-ordered support decree might be left with very little income for her own living expenses.

[b] State Restrictions on Wage Garnishment

State wage garnishment statutes are preempted to the extent they conflict with the federal limits. Accordingly, some states simply conform to the federal limits and go no further.[388] Other states protect a larger percentage of wages from garnishment[389] or restrict wage garnishment claims to limited types of claims, such as those for support.[390]

[c] Exemptions for Other Sources of Income

Many state exemption statutes protect a wide variety of sources of income from garnishment. These include support payments, workers' compensation benefits, unemployment compensation insurance benefits, welfare benefits, and disability benefits.[391] Likewise, funds received due to a claim for lost wages due to personal injury or by a dependent of a decedent for her wrongful death are frequently exempt, though sometimes only to the extent

---

[384] 15 U.S.C. § 1672(b) (2000).

[385] Marshall v. District Court, 444 F. Supp. 1110 (E.D. Mich. 1978).

[386] *E.g.*, Marshall v. District Court, 444 F. Supp. 1110 (E.D. Mich. 1978).

[387] Long Island Trust Co. v. United States Postal Serv., 647 F.2d 336 (2d Cir. 1981); Marshall v. District Court, 444 F. Supp. 1110 (E.D. Mich. 1978).

[388] *E.g.*, N.Y. C.P.L.R. § 5295(d) (McKinney Supp. 2006) (90% exempt); Ohio Rev. Code Ann. § 2329.66(A)(13) (LexisNexis Supp. 2006) (75% exempt).

[389] *E.g.*, 735 Ill. Comp. Stat. 5/12-803 (West Supp. 2006) (15% maximum).

[390] *E.g.*, 42 Pa. Cons. Stat. Ann. § 8127 (West Supp. 2006) (support, limited "board," some actions brought by a landlord, for taxes, some retirement payments, union dues and health insurance premiums); Tex. Const. Ann. art. 16, § 28 (Vernon Supp. 2005) (only for child and spousal support).

[391] *E.g.*, Ohio Rev. Code Ann. § 2329.66(A)(9) (LexisNexis Supp. 2006); Bankruptcy Code § 522(d)(10).

necessary for the support of the debtor.[392] Annuities and life insurance policies are also sometimes exempt.[393]

Various types of pension benefits are usually exempt, at least to some extent.[394] And, under federal law, employees' ERISA pension funds are not generally subject to garnishment,[395] even for claims brought by the debtor's employer based on the employee's fraud.[396] Not surprisingly, however, pension funds are subject to garnishment for certain family support obligations.[397]

Individual retirement accounts, on the other hand, are not widely protected by state exemption statutes.[398] However, in 2005, the Supreme Court resolved a dispute over whether funds in an individual retirement account were covered by the exemption in § 522(d)(10) of the Bankruptcy Code. The decision in *Rousey v. Jacoway*[399] may give some debtors a reason to use the federal exemptions. The Court held that such funds fell under the protection of the federal exemption scheme. This decision is of limited applicability, because state legislatures retain the right to prevent debtors in their state from using the Bankruptcy Code's exemption scheme. Most states have "opted out" of the federal exemptions contained in § 522(d). Therefore, the *Jacoway* decision does not prevent state exemption statutes from taking a different and more limited approach, though it may yet have an influence on the interpretation of state exemption statues that use language similar to that in § 522(d)(10)(E).[400] Moreover, in 2005, Congress amended the Bankruptcy Code to provide even greater bankruptcy protection for funds in an IRA.[401]

[5] Tracing Exemptions

A key issue with respect to exemptions is the extent to which a debtor may trace an exemption in property after it is converted into another

---

[392] *E.g.*, Ohio Rev. Code § 2329.66(A)(12) (LexisNexis Supp. 2006); Bankruptcy Code § 522(d)(11).

[393] *E.g.*, Ohio Rev. Code § 2329.66(A)(6) (LexisNexis Supp. 2006); Bankruptcy Code § 522(d)(7) (any unmatured life insurance contract owned by a debtor, other than a credit life insurance contract).

[394] *E.g.*, Ohio Rev. Code Ann. § 2329.66(A)(10) (LexisNexis Supp. 2006); Bankruptcy Code § 522(d)(10)(E).; Darrell Dunjam, *Pensions and Other Funds in Individual Bankruptcy Cases,* 4 Bankr. Dev. J. 293 (1987).

[395] General Motors Corp. v. Buha, 623 F.2d 455 (6th Cir. 1980); *see also* Patterson v. Shumate, 504 U.S. 753 (1992) (ERISA funds are not part of a debtor's bankruptcy estate).

[396] Guidry v. Sheet Metal Workers Nat'l Pension Fund, 493 U.S. 365 (1990).

[397] *See* 29 U.S.C. § 1056(d)(3) (2000).

[398] *But see* Ohio Rev. Code Ann. § 2329.66(A)(10)(e) (LexisNexis Supp. 2006); In re Diguilio, 303 B.R. 144 (Bankr. N.D. Ohio 2003).

[399] Rousey v. Jacoway, 544 U.S. 320 (2005).

[400] *See* Farrar v. McKown (In re McKown), 203 F.3d 1188, 1189–90 & 1189 n.5 (9th Cir. 2000).

[401] *See* § 12.03[D][3] Retirement Funds, *infra*.

form.[402] Without the ability to trace exemptions, a large share of the protection provided by exemption statutes might be lost. On the other hand, once the debtor has converted exempt property into a form not deemed by the legislature to be necessary for financially troubled debtors, the reasons for protecting the property from seizure dissipates.

Exemptions for wages supply the most obvious example of this problem. On the one hand, if the 75% of a debtor's wages that are exempt from garnishment under the Consumer Credit Protection Act lose their exemption after an employee deposits them into her bank account, the protection provided by the Act loses its force. On the other hand, if wages remain exempt regardless of the form in which the debtor holds them, 75% of all of a debtor's assets might remain exempt, effectively negating the effect of other limitations on the types of property that a debtor may exempt from her creditors.

Consider, for example, a debtor whose disposable earnings are $1,000 per week. The most a creditor could garnish from her employer is $250. The remaining $750 is exempt. If the debtor cannot preserve this exemption after depositing her check into a bank account, the benefit of the exemption is lost: the debtor will not have the funds she needs to pay her ordinary living expenses. It seems clear that the wage exemption needs to be preserved, even after the debtor's wages have been deposited into a bank account, if the purpose of the wage exemption is to be fulfilled. However, the value tracing cannot be infinite.

For example, the debtor might use her wages to make payments on an automobile. Over time, she may acquire equity in the car beyond the amount protected by the state's motor vehicle exemption. Or she may use the funds to acquire luxury goods not considered necessary for life and thus not deemed worthy of exempt status. If the wage exemption were extended to these assets, the legislative purpose to limit exempt property to items reasonably necessary for the debtor to get along in life will have been frustrated.

Concern that the underlying purpose of wage exemption statutes would be frustrated if debtors were not permitted to trace their exemption after the property had been converted into an alternative form has led many courts to conclude that exempt wages do not lose their exempt status after they have been deposited into a bank account or some other liquid form in which they remain available for the debtor's ordinary living expenses. In *Daugherty v. Central Trust Co.*,[403] one state supreme court explained,

> [t]he legislature's purpose, in exempting certain property from court action brought by creditors, was to protect funds intended primarily for maintenance and support of the debtor's family . . . . This

[402] The related issue, whether debtors should be permitted to convert non-exempt property into an exempt form on the eve of bankruptcy or attachment, is discussed elsewhere. *See* § 12.02[E] Exemption Planning, *infra.*

[403] 504 N.E.2d 1100 (Ohio 1986).

> legislative intent would be frustrated if exempt funds were automatically deprived of their statutory immunity when deposited in a checking account which a depositor commonly maintains in order to pay by check those regular subsistence expenses he incurs.[404]

However, in *In re Schoonover*,[405] another court denied a debtor the right to exempt $80,000 deposited in a bank account that was traceable to Social Security benefits. There, the court said:

> [The state exemption statute] exempts "the debtor's right to receive" public benefits; it has nothing to do with funds on deposit long after their receipt and commingling with the debtor's other assets. Like the anti-alienation clauses in the federal benefits statutes themselves, this law ensures that recipients enjoy the minimum monthly income provided by the benefits laws; it does not entitle recipients to shield hoards of cash.[406]

As these excerpts reflect, there is little consistency in the approaches taken by states. As with many other aspects of state debt collection law, decisions in individual states need to be closely examined before one can draw any conclusions about the governing principles in that state.

[B] Other Property Immune from Creditors' Claims[407]

Apart from property declared by the legislature as exempt from execution, some types of property are, by their very nature, immune from the claims of creditors. Usually this is due to restrictions imposed by state law on the free transferability of the assets in question.[408] If the debtor is not free to transfer the property, her creditors are unable to seize it. Such assets primarily include spendthrift trusts and property held in a tenancy by the entirety.

[1] Spendthrift Trusts[409]

A spendthrift trust is a trust in which the beneficiary cannot transfer either the corpus (or "res") of the trust or her right to future payments of income from the trust. This non-transferability is accomplished through anti-alienation language in the documents that create the trust.[410] Because the beneficiary lacks the power under the terms of the trust to transfer these rights, they cannot be reached by the beneficiary's creditors.

---

404 504 N.E.2d at 1103.

405 331 F.3d 575 (7th Cir. 2003).

406 331 F.3d at 577.

407 Edward C. Halbach, Jr., *Creditors' Rights in Future Interests*, 43 Minn. L. Rev. 217 (1958); William T. Plumb, *The Recommendations of the Commission on the Bankruptcy Laws: Exempt and Immune Property*, 61 Va. L. Rev. 1, 77 (1975).

408 *E.g.*, N.Y. Civ. Prac. Law § 5201 (McKinney Supp. 2006).

409 Note, *Creditors' Rights Against Trust Assets*, 22 Real Prop., Prob. & Tr. J. 735 (1987).

410 *E.g.*, McColgan v. Walter Magee, Inc., 155 P. 995, 997 (1916) ("[T]he donor has the right to give his property to another upon any conditions which he sees fit to impose.").

Once the trustee has distributed funds from the trust to the beneficiary and the beneficiary acquires the full right to transfer the funds she has received, they become vulnerable to creditors' claims. However, if the property acquired with these funds is exempt, under the applicable state exemption statute, it will remain invulnerable to the creditors' claims.

The immunity from creditors' claims that spendthrift trusts enjoy does not usually extend to funds contributed to the trust by the trust's beneficiary. Most state laws do not generally recognize the enforceability of transfer restrictions on such "self-settled" trusts.[411] Accordingly, "self-settled trusts" remain vulnerable to the claims of creditors in most jurisdictions.[412] This is not surprising. If it were otherwise, debtors could protect their assets from seizure by their creditors through the simple expedient of transferring the assets to a trust maintained for the debtor's own benefit. Funds transferred to a spendthrift trust by the debtor's rich relative are protected, but funds the debtor deposits herself are not. There are a few notable exceptions, however. Alaska, Delaware and Nevada have enacted spendthrift trust statutes that permit the settlor to also be a beneficiary, without depriving the trust of its spendthrift characteristics.[413] Whether these trusts will stand up to a challenge in bankruptcy remains to be tested.

There is a key exception to this restriction on the immunity of self-settled trusts. Most pension plans are designed to qualify for favorable tax treatment under the federal Employee Retirement Income Security Act (ERISA).[414] ERISA-qualified pension plans frequently contain funds that were contributed by the employees for whose benefit the pension trusts were created. If the normal state rules regarding self-settled trusts applied, these retirement funds would be vulnerable to the claims of an employee's creditors. However, ERISA's preemptive effect makes the anti-alienation provisions of an ERISA qualified pension trust[415] immune from the claims of creditors, despite the limitations of state law that otherwise would render them vulnerable to those claims.

The full impact of ERISA's pre-emptive effect was realized in *Patterson v. Shumate*,[416] where the Supreme Court ruled that the spendthrift trust restrictions in an ERISA-qualified pension plan prevented funds in such a plan from becoming part of the employee's bankruptcy estate. *Patterson*'s holding, as well as the ERISA preemption of state law restrictions on self-settled trusts upon which it was based, depends on the retirement plans' compliance with ERISA's strict restrictions.[417] Funds contained in

---

[411] *E.g.*, In re Spenlinhauer, 182 B.R. 361 (Bankr. D. Me. 1995).

[412] *See, e.g.*, Cal. Civ. Proc. Code § 704.115 (West Supp. 2006).

[413] *See*, Stewart E. Sterk, *Asset Protection Trusts: Trust Law's Race to the Bottom?*, 85 Cornell L. Rev. 1035, 1042 (2000).

[414] 29 U.S.C. §§ 1001-1461 (2000 & Supp. III 2003).

[415] 29 U.S.C. § 1056(d)(1) (2000).

[416] 504 U.S. 753 (1992).

[417] The details of ERISA's requirements are far outside the scope of this work. *See generally* Charles E. Falk, Patterson v. Shumate: *A Five Year Legacy*, 9 BNA's Bankr. L. Rptr. 743 (1997).

retirement plans that fall outside the scope of ERISA's protection remain vulnerable to the claims of creditors, except to the extent they are protected by an express exemption statute.

[2] Tenancies by the Entirety[418]

As a general rule, property held in common by two or more people is just as vulnerable to the claims of creditors as any other type of property. An important exception to this general rule is property owned by a married couple in a "tenancy by the entirety."[419] Only about twenty-five states continue to recognize tenancies by the entirety, but those that do generally prevent a creditor of only one spouse from reaching that spouse's share in property jointly owned with the other spouse in a tenancy by the entirety.[420] This result is due to the legal fiction that a husband and wife are one person.[421] Because the property is owned by the couple as a single entity, it is vulnerable only to claims of creditors of both spouses.

Thus, entireties property owned by Dave and Kathy Morris may not be taken to satisfy a claim of a creditor of only one of them. If Dave owes a debt for which Kathy is not liable, neither the entireties property nor either of their interests in the entireties property is vulnerable to the creditor's claim. This effectively makes the property exempt from everyone except creditors to whom Dave and Kathy are jointly liable. If Dave and Kathy were both responsible for the debt, the entireties property could be taken to satisfy the creditor's claim.

Federal tax liens are an important exception to this rule. The Federal Tax Lien Act, using language similar to the Bankruptcy Code's definition of property of the estate,[422] imposes a federal tax lien "upon all property and rights to property, whether real or personal, belonging to [the taxpayer]."[423] In 2000, the United States Supreme Court interpreted this language and the functional attributes of a spouse's interest under Michigan law as sufficient to make an interest in entireties property subject to a tax lien imposed on entireties property.[424] Federal law determines whether

---

[418] Patrick J. Concannon, Note, *Bankruptcy and the Tenancy by the Entirety Property: Its Treatment under the Code and in the Courts*, 58 UMKC L. Rev. 501 (1990); *see* Steven R. Johnson, *After* Drye*: The Likely Attachment of the Federal Tax Lien to Tenancy-by-the-Entireties Interests*, 75 Ind. L.J. 1163 (2000); William H. Baker, Drye *and* Craft — *How Two Wrongs Can Make a Property Right*, 64 U. Pitt. L. Rev. 745 (2003); Lawrence Kalevitch, *Some Thoughts on Entireties in Bankruptcy*, 60 Am. Bankr. L.J. 141 (1986); Benjamin C. Ackerly, *Tenants by the Entirety Property and the Bankruptcy Reform Act*, 21 Wm. & Mary L. Rev. 701 (1980).

[419] 7 Richard R. Powell & Michael Allan Wolf, Powell on Real Property § 52.03[3] (2006).

[420] *E.g.*, In re Hutchins, 306 B.R. 82 (Bankr. D. Vt. 2004); In re Cross, 255 B.R. 25 (Bankr. N.D. Ind. 2000).

[421] *See* John V. Orth, *Tenancy by the Entirety: The Strange Career of the Common-Law Marital Estate*, 1997 B.Y.U. L. Rev. 35; William Blackstone, 2 Commentaries *179.

[422] Bankruptcy Code § 541(a).

[423] 26 U.S.C. § 6321 (2000).

[424] United States v. Craft, 535 U.S. 274 (2002).

entireties property, as defined by the law of a particular state, is "property" for purposes of the federal tax lien statute. Using the above example, if Dave owed a federal tax for which Kathy was not liable, his interest in the entireties property would be subject to a federal tax lien imposed on his property. Kathy's interest in the property could not be taken, but the government could recover the tax from Dave's interest just as it could recover any undivided interest in property held by joint tenants or tenants in common. Because the Supreme Court made this determination by examining the particulars of the Michigan law, this may or may not be the rule for entireties property in other states.

§ 2.13 Suretyship

A surety is someone who is obligated to pay a debt owed by someone else.[425] For example, if Mom and Dad promise Hybrid Motors Co. that they will pay Junior's debt, incurred for the purchase of his car, Mom and Dad are sureties who are obligated to pay Hybrid Motors if Junior fails to pay.[426] A surety might also be called a "guarantor,"[427] a "secondary obligor," or if the surety became liable by signing a negotiable instrument such as a promissory note, an "accommodation party."[428] Obtaining a surety is an alternative method to ensure payment, which can supplement or substitute for a consensual lien on the debtor's property.

In a business context, the owners of a corporation might guarantee a debt owed by the company they operate.[429] Or a commercial surety, who is in the business of providing guarantees in exchange for a fee, may provide a payment or performance bond.[430] These commercial sureties act, in effect, as insurers.

---

[425] Laurence P. Simpson, Handbook on the Law of Suretyship § 4 (1950); *see* Restatement (Third) of Suretyship and Guaranty § 1(a) (1996).

[426] Federal Trade Commission rules requires certain disclosures be made to consumer sureties. Michael J. Herbert, *Straining the Gnat: A Critique of the 1984 Federal Trade Commission Consumer Credit Regulations*, 38 S.C. L. Rev. 329, 355–59 (1987).

[427] Much has been made of the difference between a "surety" and a "guarantor." Although the terms are often used interchangeably, a surety is usually jointly and severally liable with the principal obligor, while a guarantor's liability is not usually triggered until the principal obligor has defaulted. Restatement (Third) of Suretyship and Guaranty § 1 cmt. c (1996).

[428] *See* U.C.C. § 3-419 (2003).

[429] *E.g.*, State Bank v. Owens, 502 P.2d 965 (Colo. Ct. App. 1972).

[430] For example, as part of the inducement by a general contractor, to persuade the owner to agree to hire the contractor to build a structure that the owner wishes to erect on his property, the contractor might pay a fee to a surety company in exchange for its agreement to pay all of the subcontractors and suppliers who contribute to the project, in the event the general contractor fails to pay them. This type of "payment bond" protects the owner against the risk that payments she makes to the contractor will not be distributed to these participants in the project. In this situation, the surety company is a secondary obligor on the general's contractual duty to pay the subcontractors and suppliers. *See* Restatement (Third) of Suretyship and Guaranty § 1 illus. 1 (1996).

[A] Basic Suretyship Principles

Suretyship transactions involve three parties: the principal debtor, the creditor, and the surety or secondary obligor. These arrangements can be very large or very small. Assume, for example, that Titanic Industries, Inc. borrowed $100,000 from North Atlantic Finance Co. Assume further that Harland Wolff, the sole shareholder of Titanic Industries, guaranteed payment by the corporation. Titanic Industries is the principal debtor, North Atlantic Finance Co. is the creditor, and Harland Wolff is the surety. It is no different, when Mom and Dad guarantee Junior's debt to Hybrid Motors. Junior is the principal debtor, Hybrid Motors is the creditor, and Mom and Dad are the sureties.

Suretyship transactions involve several separate contracts. The first contract, of course, is the one between the creditor and the principal debtor, sometimes referred to as the "underlying obligation."[431] This is Titanic Industries' agreement with North Atlantic Finance and Junior's agreement with Hybrid Motors.

The second contract is between the surety and the creditor: Harland Wolff's promise to North Atlantic and Mom and Dad's promise to Hybrid Motors. This is the suretyship contract, in which the surety makes a promise directly *to the creditor* to satisfy the principal debtor's obligation. This agreement may take one of several forms. For example, the surety may "cosign" the agreement entered into between the creditor and the principal debtor, agreeing to perform the same obligation as that of the principal debtor. Alternatively, the surety might enter into a separate suretyship agreement with the creditor, promising performance if the principal debtor fails to perform the underlying obligation.[432] Note that under most versions of the statute of frauds, the surety's promise to the creditor must be in writing.[433]

The third contract is the express or implied promise of the principal debtor to reimburse the surety for any amounts that the surety pays to the creditor.[434] The surety's right of reimbursement makes the surety a contingent creditor of the principal debtor, even before the surety has been called upon to perform its obligation. Thus, a shareholder who has guaranteed a debt owed by the corporation she owns has a contingent claim against the corporation. And, Mom and Dad, if they want to, have the right to recover from Junior any amounts they pay to Hybrid Motors.

A surety might make one of several types of agreements with the creditor. The normal obligation of a surety is to "guaranty payment." If the suretyship contract uses the word "guaranty" without any further limitation, the contract is normally construed to be a guaranty of payment. This means

[431] *See* Restatement (Third) of Suretyship and Guaranty § 1 cmt. d (1996).

[432] *See* Restatement (Third) of Suretyship and Guaranty § 1 cmt. g (1996).

[433] *E.g.*, Carey & Assoc. v. Ernst, 810 N.Y.S.2d 475 (N.Y. App. Div. 2006) (adult child's oral promise to pay parent's legal fees).

[434] Restatement (Third) of Suretyship and Guaranty § 22 (1996).

the creditor may pursue the guarantor as soon as the obligation is due, without having to first obtain a judgment against the principal.[435] Alternatively, a surety may merely "guaranty collection." When collection is guaranteed, the creditor in most cases must sue the principal and attempt to collect the debt from the principal's assets before pursuing the surety.[436] Finally, a surety may become an "accommodation party" by signing a promissory note made by the principal obligor, usually either as a co-maker or as an endorser of the note. An accommodation maker's contract is much like that of a guarantor of payment. If the debt is not paid when due, the accommodation maker may be sued immediately, without any prior recourse against the principal.[437] If the surety signs as an accommodation endorser, he will be liable only after the note is presented to and dishonored by the principal obligor as maker of the note.

In any event, it is important to stress that in each of these situations, the surety has a claim for full reimbursement from the principal. By contrast, the principal has no right of contribution or indemnification against the surety. The principal was supposed to pay the debt; if the principal does not do so, the surety is entitled to attempt to collect against it.[438]

In addition, a surety who pays the creditor obtains whatever rights the creditor originally had against the principal obligor under the doctrine of "subrogation."[439] If the creditor held a security interest in the principal obligor's property and the surety pays the debt to the creditor, the surety is subrogated to the creditor's rights in the collateral. Thus, the surety's right to reimbursement will be secured to the same extent as the claim of the original creditor.

[B] Suretyship Defenses

Sureties have a variety of potential defenses. They are usually based on the creditor's conduct either in its dealings with the principal obligor or with any collateral for the debt.

[1] Surety's Use of Principal's Defenses

A surety can assert most of the defenses that the principal obligor could have raised against the creditor. The most important exceptions are the debtor's incapacity or discharge of the principal debtor in bankruptcy.[440]

---

[435] Laurence P. Simpson, Handbook on the Law of Suretyship § 6 (1950).

[436] Laurence P. Simpson, Handbook on the Law of Suretyship § 6 (1950).

[437] U.C.C. §§ 3-419(b), 3-412 (2003).

[438] Laurence P. Simpson, Handbook on the Law of Suretyship §§ 47-48 (1950).

[439] Restatement (Third) of Suretyship and Guaranty § 27 (1996); Laurence P. Simpson, Handbook on the Law of Suretyship § 47 (1950); *see, e.g.*, In re Modern Textile, Inc., 900 F.2d 1184 (8th Cir. 1990).

[440] *See* U.C.C. § 3-305(d) (2003).

Since incapacity and discharge in bankruptcy are among the risks that led the creditor to obtain a surety in the first place, a surety may not use the incapacity or bankruptcy of the principal debtor as a defense.[441] Thus, if Mom and Dad promise Hybrid Motors that they will pay Junior's debt in the event of his default, they cannot assert Junior's status as a minor, or his discharge in bankruptcy as a defense, even though these defenses are available to Junior.

[2] Creditor's Impairment of the Collateral

If the guaranteed debt is secured, any action of the creditor that impairs the collateral discharges the surety to the extent of the impairment.[442] The collateral may be impaired in several ways, including failing to perfect or maintain the perfection of the security interest, releasing the collateral from the security interest without acquiring an adequate substitute, or acting in a way that results in a negligent diminution of the value of the collateral.[443]

Discharging the surety makes sense in these situations, particularly when considered in light of the surety's right of subrogation to the creditor's rights. If the creditor impairs the value of collateral supplied by the principal debtor, the surety's right to be subrogated to the creditor's security interest in the collateral would be prejudiced. This would expose the surety to a risk he thought he had avoided when he agreed to become a surety.

Consider an agreement by Kathy & Dave to serve as sureties for Friendly Finance Company's auto loan made to their son, Isaac. When the loan is made, Friendly Finance obtains a purchase money security interest in Isaac's new car but fails to take all of the steps necessary to perfect it. If Isaac defaults and files a bankruptcy petition, Friendly Finance would normally be able to recover the amount of the unpaid balance from Kathy and Dave. In turn, Kathy and Dave would normally be able to assert their right of subrogation and enforce the finance company's security interest in the car. But, because the security interest is unperfected, Isaac's bankruptcy trustee will be able to avoid the security interest and recover the non-exempt value of the car for the benefit of all of Isaac's creditors. The finance company's failure to perfect its security interest leaves Kathy and Dave with no recourse. His debt to them was discharged in bankruptcy, and the security interest in his car was avoided by the trustee. As a result, Kathy and Dave are relieved of their liability to the finance company, at least to the extent of the value of the car.[444]

---

441 *E.g.*, Murphy v. Bank of Dahlonega, 259 S.E.2d 670 (Ga. Ct. App. 1979).

442 Restatement (Third) of Suretyship and Guaranty § 42 (1996); *see* U.C.C. § 3-605(d) & cmt. 7 (2002).

443 Restatement (Third) of Suretyship and Guaranty § 42 (1996); *see* U.C.C. § 3-605(d) & cmt. 7 (2003).

444 *See* Restatement (Third) of Suretyship and Guaranty § 42 (1996); U.C.C. § 3-605(d) (2003).

[3] Release of the Principal Debtor

A creditor may find it useful to enter into a composition or other agreement that releases the principal obligor from all or part of the outstanding balance of a debt.[445] The principal may offer to make a partial or early payment of the creditor's claim, in exchange for release from the remainder of his liability. The creditor, concerned about the likelihood of receiving any payment from the obligor, is likely to agree to the proposed compromise.

The traditional rule was that a creditor's release of the principal obligor had an effect similar to the creditor's impairment of the collateral: the surety was discharged. However, savvy creditors could avoid discharge of the surety by following a strict set of rules that permitted them to "reserve the rights" of the surety against the principal obligor and thus avoid losing their own right to recover from the surety any portion of the debt left unpaid by the principal obligor.

However, these rules are now in transition. It has been recognized that little was achieved by insisting on the formal requirements of "reserving rights." Institutional creditors nearly always take the steps necessary to avoid discharge of the surety, leaving only inexperienced and casual lenders to be tripped up by their willingness to enter into compromise agreements with the principal obligor. Today, a creditor's release of the principal obligor discharges the surety's obligation to the same extent that the principal obligor's obligation was discharged.[446]

Thus, if Commerce Bank enters into an agreement with Titanic Industries, Inc., releasing Titanic from $20,000 of its $100,000 debt in exchange for an immediate cash payment of $10,000 and an increase in the interest rate on the remaining $70,000, the guarantor of the company's debt, Harlan Wolff, will also be released from $20,000 of his liability. Of course, Commerce Bank might refuse to release Titanic unless Wolff agrees to waive his right to be released, but whether the bank is able to elicit this agreement will depend on how desperate it is to receive the $10,000 cash payment and the increase in the applicable interest rate that Titanic is offering.

[4] Time Extension

The effect of a creditor's agreement to extend the due date of the principal's obligation is somewhat different from the effect of the creditor's release of the principal obligor. A time extension may harm the surety, such as where the debtor is solvent at the time of the extension but later becomes insolvent. However, the most common reason creditors grant a principal obligor additional time is that the principal is already unable to pay but anticipates a better financial condition in the future. If this is the case,

[445] *See* § 2.11 Compositions and Workouts, *supra*.

[446] Restatement (Third) of Suretyship and Guaranty § 39(b) (1996); U.C.C. § 3-605(a)(2) & cmt. 4 (2003).

granting an extension to the principal would have no impact on the surety's likelihood of recovery.

Because of this, time extensions granted to the principal obligor discharge a surety only if the surety is able to prove that the extension caused the surety to suffer a loss.[447] The burden of proof lies with the surety. On the other hand, if the principal obligor receives a time extension, the surety also enjoys the benefit of the extension and is not obligated to pay the debt until the extended due date.[448]

[5] Other Modifications

Other modifications, apart from releases, time extensions, and impairments of the collateral, such as changes in the interest rate, modifications of the conditions of default, or alterations of the schedule of payments (other than the ultimate date of maturity), also discharge the surety to the extent the surety can prove that the modification of the terms binding the principal obligor resulted in a loss to the surety.[449] As with time extensions, the surety's obligation is modified to the same extent as principal obligor's obligation is changed.[450]

[C] Suretyship Issues in Bankruptcy

Insofar as bankruptcy is concerned, there are several important suretyship issues. The first regards creditors' rights against bankrupt sureties. Ordinarily, a claim of a creditor against a bankrupt surety will be a general unsecured claim. However, if the surety has supplied its own collateral for the obligation, the creditor's claim against the surety is secured to the extent of the value of the collateral. Rules discharging the surety due to the creditor's impairment of collateral supplied by someone against whom the surety has a claim of reimbursement do not apply when it was the surety who provided the collateral.

Second, sureties who have satisfied the principal debtor's obligation have claims, due to their right of reimbursement, against a bankrupt principal. Ordinarily the surety's claim for reimbursement against a bankrupt principal enjoys the same status as the claim of the creditor. If the creditor's claim was a general unsecured claim, the surety's claim is unsecured. If the creditor had a security interest in the debtor/principal's property, the surety is subrogated to the creditor's security interest and has a secured claim to the extent the creditor's claim was secured.

---

[447] Restatement (Third) of Suretyship and Guaranty § 40 (1996); U.C.C. § 3-605(b) & cmt. 5 (2003).

[448] Restatement (Third) of Suretyship and Guaranty § 40 (1996); U.C.C. § 3-605(b)(1) & cmt. 5 (2003).

[449] Restatement (Third) of Suretyship and Guaranty § 41 (1996); U.C.C. § 3-605(c) & cmt. 6 (2003).

[450] Restatement (Third) of Suretyship and Guaranty § 41 (1996); U.C.C. § 3-605(c) & cmt. 6 (2003).

Third, a potential problem arises when the surety has not yet satisfied the creditor's claim when the principal's bankruptcy petition is filed. In that case, the surety's claim remains "contingent"; it is contingent on the surety's actual satisfaction of the creditor's claim. Placing a value on contingent claims, particularly for the purposes of voting on a Chapter 11 plan, is sometimes difficult.[451]

Finally, questions sometimes arise regarding the extent of protection that should be provided to sureties while the principal obligor's bankruptcy case is pending. As a general rule, the bankruptcy of the principal has no effect on the right of the creditor to sue the surety. Indeed, bankruptcy is one of the reasons why the creditor required a surety in the first place. However, in Chapter 12 and 13 cases, actions against some sureties are automatically stayed while the bankruptcy case is pending.[452] The court has some discretion to order a similar injunction when these automatic stay rules do not apply.[453] For example, in Chapter 11 reorganization cases, an injunction can sometimes be obtained restraining the creditor from pursuing a surety for payment until after the debtor's Chapter 11 plan has been confirmed and the case has been closed. Once confirmed, the plan itself might also affect a creditor's right to collect from those who have served as sureties for the principal obligor.[454]

§ 2.14 Supplemental Collection Proceedings

[A] Discovery: Examination of a Judgment Debtor

Before a creditor obtains a judgment on the underlying merits of its claim, information about the debtor's assets is usually beyond the permissible scope of discovery. However, once a judgment is obtained, discovery of this information becomes fair game.

State laws permit a judgment debtor to depose the debtor. Such a deposition is usually referred to as a "debtor's examination" or an "examination of a judgment debtor."[455] One such statute provides:

> A judgment creditor shall be entitled to an order for the examination of a judgment debtor concerning his property, income, or other means of satisfying the judgment upon proof by affidavit that such judgment is unpaid in whole or in part. Such order shall be issued by a probate judge or a judge of the court of common pleas in the county in which the judgment was rendered or in which the debtor

451 *See* § 10.02[C][1] Contingent & Unliquidated Claims, *infra*.

452 *E.g.*, Bankruptcy Code § 1302.

453 Bankruptcy Code §§ 1201 & 1301; *see* § 8.04 Automatic Co-Debtor Stay in Chapters 12 and 13, *infra*.

454 *See* § 8.05 Discretionary Stays, *infra*.

455 The word "examination" is not completely misleading. Sometimes debtors have the same difficulty in remembering what assets they own as students have in remembering, when questioned by their teachers, the material they were supposed to have studied the night before.

> resides, requiring such debtor to appear and answer concerning his property before such judge, or a referee appointed by him, at a time and place within the county to be specified in the order.[456]

A recalcitrant debtor may be compelled to provide sworn testimony about the nature, extent, and location of her assets. Since the examination is under oath, a lie by the debtor subjects her to prosecution for perjury. Even though prosecutions are extremely rare, the implied threat of jail induces most debtors to tell the truth.[457]

Upon disclosure of the existence and location of the debtor's assets, it may be possible to seize them immediately or the court may issue a turnover order. Your authors have heard of one young lawyer who was told by his supervising partner: "Ask the debtor 'how did you get to the court?' When he answers 'In my car,' ask the judge to order him to hand over the keys."[458] However, most of the time, creditors use information they obtain from the debtor through this process to facilitate collection through the normal mechanisms of attachment and garnishment. Procedures also exist for obtaining the testimony of third persons who are in possession of the debtor's property[459] or who may have information regarding the nature and location of the debtor's property.[460]

[B] Contempt Sanctions

Debtors who fail to cooperate with court ordered proceedings to locate their assets may be held in contempt for failing to obey the court's instructions. For example, Article 9 security agreements commonly require a defaulting debtor to assist the secured party in assembling the collateral.[461] If the debtor refuses to comply, the secured party may be able to get a court order for specific performance of the debtor's promise. Further refusal then becomes civil contempt; a court may order the debtor to pay a fine or even suffer imprisonment. Imprisonment would not violate prohibitions against imprisonment for debt, because the imprisonment is not on account of the debt but for contemptuous refusal to obey the court's order.

---

[456] Ohio Rev. Code Ann. § 2333.09 (LexisNexis 2005); *see also* N.Y. C.P.L.R. § 5223 (McKinney 1997); Cal Civ Proc. Code § 708.020 (West 2006) (written interrogatories); Cal. Civ. Proc. Code § 708.110 (West. Supp. 2006) (oral debtor's exam).

[457] The creditor conducting the examination must, of course, ask the right questions. Professors Lynn LoPucki and Elizabeth Warren describe the story of a defendant with $10,000 cash in his pocket who truthfully denied having any cash available in his house, his car, his office, the bank, or with his broker, and walked out of the debtor's exam having never been asked: "How much cash do you have with you here today?" Lynn M. LoPucki & Elizabeth Warren, Secured Credit: A Systems Approach 13-14 (4th ed. 2003).

[458] The practical utility of this maneuver depends on whether the auto is already encumbered by the claim of a secured creditor and the extent to which the debtor's equity is exempt. Moreover, the keys will not be nearly so helpful as the certificate of title to the car.

[459] Cal. Civ. Proc. Code § 708.120 (West Supp. 2006).

[460] Cal. Civ. Proc. Code § 708.130 (West 1987).

[461] *See* U.C.C. § 9-609(c) (2003).

§ 2.15 Common Law and Statutory Restrictions on Creditors' Collection Efforts

Overly aggressive creditors can be liable to the debtor as a result of belligerent actions. Creditors have been liable to debtors from whom they were trying to collect for committing a number of garden-variety torts, such as fraud, defamation, intentional infliction of emotional distress, or invasion of privacy. In addition, several "lender-liability" cases have held creditors liable for taking precipitous action to accelerate a debt or to terminate a line of credit that the debtor was relying on to operate its business. Some states have enacted legislation directed at creditors' overly aggressive out-of-court collection tactics. Likewise, there are federal restrictions on some of the most egregious activities of debt collectors, and on the activities of credit-reporting agencies and their customers.

[A] Common Law Tort Liability[462]

Creditors naturally have the right to take reasonable action to pursue debtors and collect the debts they owe.[463] However, creditors' informal collection methods sometimes are beyond the bounds of reason. When this happens, the roles of the parties can reverse, with the debtor obtaining a judgment against the creditor for its out-of-bounds conduct.

[1] Invasion of Privacy[464]

Courts sometimes impose liability on creditors for invading a debtor's privacy.[465] To establish a claim for invasion of privacy, a debtor must show that the creditor went beyond the reasonable steps that a creditor may take to persuade the debtor to pay. Creditors' attempts to collect may result in some intrusion on the debtor's privacy;[466] liability attaches only if the intrusions were unreasonable.

Unreasonable intrusion occurs as a result of harassing phone calls, particularly when made frequently, at all hours of the day and night, or

---

462 Michael M. Greenfield, *Coercive Collection Tactics — An Analysis of the Interests and the Remedies*, 1972 Wash U. L.Q. 1; Charles E. Hurt, *Debt Collection Torts*, 67 W. Va. L. Rev. 201 (1965); Arthur Allen Leff, *Injury, Ignorance and Spite — The Dynamics of Coercive Collection*, 80 Yale L.J. 1 (1970); Robert E. Scott, *Rethinking the Regulation of Coercive Creditor Remedies*, 89 Colum. L. Rev. 730 (1989); Myron M. Sheinfeld, *Current Trends in the Restriction of Creditors' Collection Activities*, 9 Hous. L. Rev. 615 (1972); William C. Whitford, *A Critique of the Consumer Credit Collection System*, 1979 Wis. L. Rev. 1047.

463 *E.g.*, Housh v. Peth, 133 N.E.2d 340, 340–41 (Ohio 1956); Jacksonville State Bank v. Barnwell, 481 So. 2d 863, 865–66 (Ala. 1985).

464 *See generally* Samuel D. Warren & Louis D. Brandeis, *The Right to Privacy*, 4 Harv. L. Rev. 193 (1890).

465 *See* Jeffrey F. Ghent, Annotation, *Unsolicited Mailing, Distribution, House Call, or Telephone Call as Invasion of Privacy*, 56 A.L.R.3d 457 (1974); J.L. Litwin, Annotation, *Public Disclosure of Person's Indebtedness as Invasion of Privacy*, 33 A.L.R.3d 154 (1970).

466 *E.g.*, Sears, Roebuck & Co. v. Moten, 558 P.2d 954 (Ariz. 1976); Household Finance Corp. v. Bridge, 250 A.2d 878 (Md. 1969); Gouldman Taber Pontiac, Inc. v. Zerbst, 100 S.E.2d 881 (Ga. 1957).

to the debtor's friends, relatives, and neighbors, or employer.[467] For example, in *Jacksonville State Bank v. Barnwell*,[468] a creditor who made several dozen phone calls to both the debtor's home and to his place of employment was characterized as having engaged in a "'systematic campaign of harassment,'" which, when combined with its use of "unequivocally coarse, inflammatory, malicious, and threatening language" at the debtor's place of employment, left the creditor liable for invading the debtor's privacy.[469]

In addition, creditors may become liable due to their unreasonable disclosure of private information about the debtor or regarding their claim against him in the course of pursuing their efforts to collect.[470] For example, in *Biederman's of Springfield, Inc. v. Wright*, a creditor was liable for invasion of the debtor's privacy because one of its agents complained loudly in a public restaurant about the debtor's failure to pay.[471] Similarly, in *Mason v. Williams Discount Center, Inc.*, a publicly posted list of customers from whom the creditor would not accept checks was actionable as an invasion of the debtor's privacy.[472]

[2] Intentional Infliction of Emotional Distress[473]

Creditors' overly aggressive conduct may result in liability under a theory of intentional infliction of emotional distress,[474] also sometimes called

[467] Malcom E. Calkins, Comment, *The Debtor v. Creditor Dilemma: When Does a Creditor's Communication With the Debtor's Employer Result in an Actionable Invasion of Privacy?*, 10 Tulsa L.J. 231 (1974).

[468] 481 So. 2d 863 (Ala. 1985).

[469] *Id. See also* Fernandez v. United Acceptance Corp., 610 P.2d 461 (Ariz. Ct. App. 1980) (creditor's agent threatened repossession without lawful right to do so and placed large number of telephone calls to debtor's place of employment and to debtor's neighbors); Housh v. Peth, 135 N.E.2d 440 (Ohio Ct. App.), *aff'd* 133 N.E.2d 340 (Ohio 1956) (systematic campaign of harassment, involving phone calls at all hours of the day and night to the debtor and to her employer).

[470] A convenience store, where your co-authors have sometimes stopped for refreshment in the middle of a veloconference (bike ride), regularly posts notices in the window with the names of several customers advising them to "come in and pick up your bounced checks." However, because neither of us has a license to practice law in the jurisdiction in which these signs appear, and we do not wish to wear out our welcome in this establishment, we have refrained from offering unsolicited legal advice about the potential liability associated with the sign. *See* Restatement (Second) of Torts § 652D, illus. 2 (1977).

[471] 322 S.W.2d 892 (Mo. 1959).

[472] 639 S.W.2d 836 (Mo. Ct. App. 1982).

[473] Michael M. Greenfield, *Coercive Collection Tactics — An Analysis of the Interests and Remedies*, 1972 Wash. U. L.Q. 1, 23; A.J.C., Comment, *Intentional Infliction of Mental Stress Within Debtor-Creditor Relationships,* 37 Alb. L. Rev. 797 (1973); Allan E. Korpela, Annotation, *Recovery for Emotional Distress or its Physical Consequences Caused by Attempts to Collect Debt Owed by Third Party*, 46 A.L.R.3d 772 (1972); Joel E. Smith, Annotation, *Recovery By Debtor, Under Tort of Intentional or Reckless Infliction of Emotional Distress, for Damages Resulting from Debt Collection Methods*, 87 A.L.R.3d 201 (1978).

[474] *See* Restatement (Second) of Torts § 46 & cmt. 3 (1976); *see, e.g.*, Champlin v. Washington Trust Co., 478. A.2d 985 (R.I. 1984); Hamilton v. Ford Motor Credit Co., 502 A.2d 1057 (Md. Ct. Spec. App. 1986); Sherman v. Field Clinic, 392 N.E.2d 154 (Ill. App. Ct. 1979).

"outrage."[475] To establish a claim of intentional infliction of emotional distress, the debtor must establish four elements: (1) the conduct of defendant must be intentional or in reckless disregard of plaintiff; (2) the conduct must be extreme and outrageous; (3) there must be a causal connection between defendant's conduct and plaintiff's mental distress; and (4) plaintiff's mental distress must be extreme and severe.[476]

Creditors' persistent efforts to persuade debtors to make additional payments are sometimes annoying, but they rarely rise to the level necessary either to constitute extreme and outrageous behavior[477] or to result in the type of extreme and severe emotional distress that the debtor must suffer from to have a claim for intentional infliction of emotional distress.

[3] Fraud

Creditors sometimes lie to a debtor as part of their efforts to persuade him to pay. Creditors who threaten action that they do not intend to take may be liable for fraud.[478] And, not surprisingly, creditors who unilaterally alter the language of their agreement with the debtor, in an attempt to remedy deficiencies in the documents memorializing their contract, are also liable for fraud.[479] Needless to say, attorneys who advance collection strategies based on this type of dishonorable behavior, with the knowledge of their client's dishonest conduct, run the risk of professional sanction, and also committing violations of the Federal Fair Debt Collection Practices Act which exposes them to their own personal liability.[480]

[4] Intentional Interference with Contractual Relations.

If the creditor's collection efforts interfere with the debtor's contractual relationship with a third person, the creditor may be held liable for intentional interference with a contractual relationship.[481] This might occur if the debtor loses her job as a result of the creditor's actions, or if one of the debtor's suppliers refuses to continue dealing with the debtor, in breach of an existing contract, because of the creditor's intentional actions. For example, in *Long v. Newby*,[482] a collection agent for one hospital, who happened to be a member of the board of trustees of the hospital where the debtor worked, induced the rest of the board to pass

[475] *E.g.*, Snyder v. Medical Serv. Corp., 35 P.3d 1158 (Wash. 2001).

[476] *See* Restatement (Second) of Torts § 46 (1965); *e.g.*, Caputo v. Professional Recovery Services, Inc., 261 F. Supp. 2d 1249 (D. Kan. 2003).

[477] *E.g.*, Public Finance Corp. v. Davis, 360 N.E.2d 765 (Ill. 1976).

[478] Third-party debt collection agencies and other "debt collectors" who engage in this type of dishonest behavior also violate the Fair Debt Collection Practices Act.

[479] Jacksonville State Bank v. Barnwell, 481 So. 2d 863, 865–66 (Ala. 1985).

[480] *See* § 2.14[D][1]Fair Debt Collection Practices Act, *infra*.

[481] *See* Restatement (Second) of Torts §§ 766-766B (1977); *see, e.g.*, Long v. Newby, 488 P.2d 719 (Alaska 1971).

[482] 488 P.2d 719 (Alaska 1971).

a resolution that required the debtor to be terminated from his employment if he did not repay the other hospital to which he was indebted. The employer hospital followed through on its resolution and fired the debtor when he failed to satisfy the other hospital's claim.[483]

Liability depends on the existence of the debtor's contract with the other party, the creditor's knowledge of the contract, his intent to induce a breach of the contract, and a resulting breach.[484] Thus, discharge of a debtor who is an "at will" employee is insufficient; this is not regarded as a breach of the employment contract.[485]

Even if the creditor has intentionally interfered with a contract of the debtor, the creditor is not liable if the creditor's actions were justified by his otherwise legal pursuit of his legitimate interests. Thus, a creditor's legitimate collection efforts, that cause the debtor to default on its other obligations, do not give rise to liability under this theory.

[5] Abuse of Process[486]

Creditors who improperly use the judicial system in their collection efforts can be liable for abuse of process.[487] A claim for abuse of process arises when a person has an ulterior motive to pursue some claim and commits a willful act in the use of the process that is not proper in the regular conduct of the proceedings.[488]

In the context of creditors' efforts to collect, claims for abuse have been successful where the creditor's wrongful actions consisted of wrongful attachment, either by levying on property that did not belong to the debtor or that was protected by an exemption, or by seizing more property than was necessary to satisfy the judgment.[489]

[6] Defamation

Creditors who disseminate false information about a debtor may incur liability for defamation if the false information damages the debtor's

---

[483] *See also* Troy v. Interfinancial Inc, 320 S.E.2d 872 (Ga. Ct. App. 1984) (plaintiff was terminated by his employer when defendant told employer he "could never expect to get anything out of this company again"); Hill Grocery Co. v. Carroll, 36 So. 789, 792 (1931) (employee discharged after creditor threatened debtor's new employer with loss of business if employer failed to either induce payment or fire debtor).

[484] Restatement (Second) of Torts § 766 (1979).

[485] *See* Frank J. Cavico, *Tortious Interference with Contract in the At-Will Employment Context*, 79 U. Det. Mercy L. Rev. 503 (2002).

[486] Dean Gloster, Comment, *Abuse of Process and Attachment: Toward a Balance of Power*, 30 UCLA L. Rev. 1218 (1983).

[487] Restatement (Second) of Torts § 682 (1977).

[488] Restatement (Second) of Torts § 682 (1977); *see* A.S. Klein, *Use of Criminal Process to Collect Debt as Abuse of Process*, 27 A.L.R.3d 1202 (1969); *e.g.*, Brown v. Kennard, 113 Cal. Rptr. 2d 891 (Cal. Ct. App. 2001).

[489] Dean Gloster, Comment, *Abuse of Process and Attachment: Toward a Balance of Power,* 30 UCLA L. Rev. 1218, 1228 (1983).

reputation or otherwise causes him harm.[490] A creditor who mischaracterizes the debtor's financial condition or publishes a false credit report regarding the debtor will be liable for harm the debtor suffers as a result.[491] Truth, of course, is a complete defense. In addition, the law of libel and defamation recognizes a mercantile privilege for credit reports, which requires the debtor to prove malice in order to be able to recover. This privilege virtually immunizes credit reporting agencies from liability for defamation, but may leave an individual creditor liable where it can be shown that it has some intent to harm the debtor, or for violations of the Fair Credit Reporting Act.[492]

[B] Lender Liability[493]

Loan agreements frequently give lenders some degree of discretion over the terms of the loan. For example, a creditor might have the right to insist on additional collateral, to raise the interest rate, to accelerate the due date, or to terminate or reduce a line of credit. This discretion is accompanied by an implied duty of good faith. A creditor who exercises its discretion in bad faith can be held liable for the harm suffered by the debtor as a result.[494]

K.M.C. Co., Inc. v. Irving Trust Co. is the most famous example of a lender being held liable for breaching its duty of good faith because of an exercise of its contractual discretion.[495] The court held that Irving Trust breached its duty of good faith when it refused to advance funds under a discretionary line of credit it had previously supplied to the borrower. At the time it refused the draw, the line was oversecured, and the debtor alleged that the reason for the denial arose out of a personality conflict between the debtor and the loan officer. The court ruled that under these circumstances, declining the draw without notice violated the implied duty of good faith.[496]

---

[490] Restatement (Second) of Torts § 559 (1977).

[491] Dun & Bradstreet, Inc. v. Greenmoss Builders, Inc., 472 U.S. 749, 757–63 (1985).

[492] Roger D. Blair & Virginia Maurer, *Statute Law and Common Law: The Fair Credit Reporting Act*, 49 Mo. L. Rev. 289, 297–300 (1984); Note, *Protecting The Subjects of Credit Reports*, 80 Yale L.J. 1035 (1971).

[493] Werner F. Ebke & James R. Griffin, *Lender Liability to Debtors: Toward a Conceptual Framework*, 40 Sw. L.J. 775, 795–98 (1986); Werner F. Ebke & James R. Griffin, *Good Faith and Fair Dealing in Commercial Lending Transactions: From Covenant to Duty and Beyond*, 49 Ohio St. L.J. 1237, 1241 (1989); Frances E. Freund et al., *Special Project, Lender Liability: A Survey of Common-Law Theories*, 42 Vand. L. Rev. 855 (1989).

[494] *See generally* Steven J. Burton, *Breach of Contract and the Common Law Duty to Perform in Good Faith*, 94 Harv. L. Rev. 369 (1980); E. Allan Farnsworth, *Good Faith Performance and Commercial Reasonableness Under the Uniform Commercial Code*, 30 U. Chi. L. Rev. 666, 669 (1963).

[495] K.M.C. Co. v. Irving Trust Co., 757 F.2d 752 (6th Cir. 1985).

[496] 757 F.2d at (6th Cir. 1985); *see also* Brown v. Avemco Invest. Corp., 603 F.2d 1367 (9th Cir. 1979).

Bankers everywhere were aghast at this decision. They argued that it would restrict the very discretion they had bargained for, and might lead to increased interest rates.[497]

K.M.C. Co., Inc. v. Irving Trust Co. elicited a considerable backlash.[498] Other courts have held that it cannot be a breach of good faith to take an action that is specifically permitted by the terms of the loan agreement. For example, in *Kham & Nate's Shoes No. 2, Inc. v. First Bank of Whiting* the court rejected the premise of *K.M.C. Co. v. Irving Trust* and ruled that:

> Firms that have negotiated contracts are entitled to enforce them to the letter, even to the great discomfort of their trading partners, without being mulcted for lack of "good faith." . . . When the contract is silent, principles of good faith . . . fill the gap. They do not block use of terms that actually appear in the contract.[499]

Lenders who take action as part of an effort to harm their borrowers may be held liable for the consequences of their actions, but otherwise creditors have no obligation to act in the best interests of their borrowers.[500]

[C] Federal Fair Debt Collection Practices Act[501]

In 1978, the inadequacy of existing common law restraints on the worst conduct of collection agencies led Congress to adopt the Fair Debt Collection Practices Act (FDCPA).[502] The Act "prohibits debt collectors from making false or misleading representations and from engaging in various abusive and unfair practices."[503] It applies primarily to collection agencies and lawyers, but has also had a significant impact on state courts' interpretations of state unfair and deceptive trade practices statutes and debt collection statutes.

[1] Scope of the FDCPA: Debt Collectors

The FDCPA restricts the conduct of debt collectors. A "debt collector" is defined in the statute as a person "who uses any instrumentality of

---

497 *See generally* Daniel R. Fischel, *The Economics of Lender Liability*, 99 Yale L.J. 131 (1989).

498 A. Brooke Overby, *Bondage, Domination, and the Art of the Deal: An Assessment of Judicial Strategies in Lender Liability Good Faith Litigation*, 61 Fordham L. Rev. 963, 997 & 1002 (1993).

499 Kham & Nate's Shoes No. 2, Inc. v. First Bank of Whiting, 908 F.2d 1351, 1357 (7th Cir. 1990); *see also* In re Clark Pipe and Supply Co., 893 F.2d 693, 702 (5th Cir. 1990) (noting that creditors have no fiduciary obligation to borrowers or to other creditors of the debtor with respect to efforts to collect the creditor's claim).

500 *See generally* Teri J. Dobbins, *Losing Faith: Extracting the Implied Covenant of Good Faith from (Some) Contracts*, 84 Or. L. Rev. 227, 251–62 (2005).

501 Elwin Griffith, *Fair Debt Collection Practices Act: Some Problems in Interpretation*, 27 Willamette L. Rev. 237 (1991).

502 15 U.S.C. § 1692-1692o (2000).

503 Heintz v. Jenkins, 514 U.S. 291 (1995).

interstate commerce or the mails in any business the principal purpose of which is the collection of any debts."[504] This language makes it applicable primarily to collection agencies, whose principal purpose is to collect debts.

The Act also applies to "any person who regularly collects or attempts to collect, directly or indirectly, debts owed or due or asserted to be owed or due another."[505] The key word in this definition is "another." The Act only applies to businesses who regularly try to collect debts that are owed to someone else. It does not apply to the efforts of the corner drugstore to collect unpaid bills from its own customers. Nor does it apply to efforts by large department stores to collect charges made to the store's proprietary credit card. However, it would apply if one of these businesses decided to expand its operations to collect debts owed to other businesses in town. Thus, the retailing giant Wal-Mart is not a debt collector if its collection efforts are limited to attempts to collect debts owed to Wal-Mart. But if it expands to include a division that "regularly" attempts to collect debts owed to other businesses, it would fit within the definition and be restricted by the act.

Although "debt collector" does not ordinarily include creditors who try to collect debts owed to themselves, the Act specifically provides that the term encompasses any creditor who, in the process of collecting his own debts, uses any name other than his own — this would indicate that a third person is collecting or attempting to collect such debts.[506] For example, in *Taylor v. Perrin, Landry, deLaunay & Durand*,[507] a lender fell within the definition of "debt collector," even though it was collecting its own debt, because it used a lawyer's letterhead and facsimile signature on the collection letters it sent to its borrower. The letters gave the impression that a third person was collecting the unpaid debt. Thus, if one in the direct employ of Corner Drugstore contacts the debtor using the name "City Revenue," the Act applies, even though Corner Drugstore is only attempting to collect debts owed by its own customers.

When originally adopted in 1978, the FDCPA contained an express exemption that insulated attorneys from the scope of the Act.[508] This exemption was removed in 1986.[509] Thus, attorneys whose entire practice consists of collection work are unquestionably subject to the Act's restrictions. Those who "regularly" engage in collection work for their clients are likewise covered by the Act.[510] Moreover, the Supreme Court's 1996 decision in *Heintz v. Jenkins*[511] concluded that attorneys who regularly

---

[504] 15 U.S.C. § 1692a(6) (2000).

[505] 15 U.S.C. § 1692a(6) (2000).

[506] 15 U.S.C. § 1692a(6) (2000).

[507] 103 F.3d 1232 (5th Cir. 1997).

[508] Pub. L. No. 95-109, § 803(6)(F), 91 Stat. 874, 875 (1978).

[509] Pub. L. No. 99-361, 100 Stat. 768 (1986).

[510] *See* Fox v. Citicorp Credit Serv. Inc., 15 F.3d 1507, 1513 (9th Cir. 1994).

[511] 514 U.S. 291 (1995).

attempt to collect debts "through litigation" are equally subject to the law.[512] The attorney in *Heintz* regularly engaged in traditional collection litigation, including sending pre-litigation collection letters to its clients' loan customers, in an effort to collect the claim prior to the initiation of suit. In addition, lawyers who regularly engage in attempts to collect unpaid rent owed to landlords are within the scope of the Act.[513]

The Act excludes some third-parties from its scope, including officers or employees of the creditor when they are attempting to collect for the creditor and using the creditor's name;[514] entities who are related by common ownership or affiliated control, so long as they only collect claims owed to an affiliated creditor and if their principal business is something other than the collection of debts;[515] governmental employees acting within the scope of their governmental authority;[516] process servers;[517] and non-profit consumer counseling agencies.[518]

[2] Debt Collectors' Communications with Debtor and Others

The FDCPA imposes a variety of restrictions on the timing and manner of a debt collector's efforts to communicate with both the debtor and third parties, such as the debtor's employer, her relatives, or her neighbors. It generally prohibits debt collectors from engaging in communications with persons other than the debtor, except to learn information about the debtor's location or to implement a post-judgment judicial remedy, such as garnishment.[519] In contacting the debtor's employer, neighbors, relatives, or others, debt collectors are prohibited from volunteering the reason for their efforts to get in touch with the debtor.[520] They are also prohibited from contacting third parties more than once.[521]

---

[512] *See also* Goldstein v. Hutton, Ingram, Yuzek, Gainen, Carroll & Bertolotti, 155 F. Supp. 2d 60 (S.D.N.Y. 2001) (firm whose income from collections was only 0.5% of its total annual gross revenue was not a debt collector within the FDCPA). *Compare* Fox v. Citicorp Credit Serv., Inc., 15 F.3d 1507 (9th Cir. 1994) (attorney who generated 70% of his legal fees from debt collection was a debt collector); Ditty v. CheckRite, Ltd., Inc., 973 F. Supp. 1320 (D. Utah 1997) (one-third to one-half was regular); Blakemore v. Pekay, 895 F. Supp. 972, 977 n.2 (N.D. Ill. 1995) (attorney who filed over 1,200 collection actions in the last year and was elected to Illinois Creditors Bar Association was a debt collector), *with* Nance v. Petty, Livingston, Dawson & Devening, 881 F. Supp. 223 (W.D. Va. 1994) (0.61% of partner's practice and 1.07% of firm's cases not sufficient to bring lawyer within scope of the act); *and* Mertes v. Devitt, 734 F. Supp. 872 (W.D. Wis. 1990) (attorney who averaged two collection matters per year which represented less than one percent of his practice was not a debt collector).

[513] Romea v. Heiberger & Assocs., 988 F. Supp. 715 (S.D.N.Y. 1998).

[514] 15 U.S.C. § 1692a(6)(A) (2000).

[515] 15 U.S.C. § 1692a(6)(B) (2000).

[516] 15 U.S.C. § 1692a(6)(B) (2000).

[517] 15 U.S.C. § 1692a(6)(B) (2000).

[518] 15 U.S.C. § 1692a(6)(B) (2000).

[519] 15 U.S.C. § 1692c(b) (2000).

[520] 15 U.S.C. § 1692b (2000).

[521] 15 U.S.C. § 1692b(3) (2000).

Moreover, written communications sent to a third party must not contain information on the outside that would reveal the nature of the debt collector's business, as this might reveal the debtor's financial woes to the mail carrier.[522] And, after the debt collector knows that the debtor is represented by counsel in connection with the debt and has information about how to contact that attorney, the creditor is prohibited from engaging in further efforts to communicate with third parties, at least until efforts to communicate with the debtor's attorney fail to elicit a response.[523]

Once the debt collector locates the debtor, its communications with the debtor must not occur at "any unusual time or place."[524] However, communications with the debtor after 8 a.m. or before 9 p.m. are presumed convenient.[525] Moreover, the debt collector must not communicate with the debtor at his place of employment if the debt collector has reason to know that the debtor is prohibited by his employer from receiving personal communications.[526] If the debt collector knows the debtor is represented by an attorney in connection with the debt, the debt collector is required to direct its communications regarding the debt to the debtor's attorney. After the debtor notifies the debt collector in writing, either that he is unwilling to pay the debt or that he wants the debt collector to cease its communications with the debtor, the debt collector is required, with a few exceptions, to end its stream of communications with the debtor.[527]

[3] Harassment or Abuse

The FDCPA prohibits debt collectors from engaging in any conduct that would have the natural consequence of harassing, oppressing, or abusing the debtor or any other persons, such as members of the debtor's family.[528] Specifically prohibited are threats of any crime or violence, obscene or profane language, publication or advertisement of lists of debtors who refuse to pay debts, incessant phone calls with the intent to annoy the debtor, or phone calls without full disclosure of the caller's identity.[529] These of course are all activities that many collection agencies routinely used before the Act was adopted.

---

[522] *See* 15 U.S.C. § 1692b (2000). Communication by post-card is absolutely prohibited. *Id.* § 1692b(4). Further, the outside of any envelope used by the debt collector must not "use any language or symbol . . . that indicates that the debt collector is in the debt collection business or that the communication relates to the collection of a debt." 15 U.S.C. § 1692b(5).

[523] *See* 15 U.S.C. § 1692b(6) (2000).

[524] *See* 15 U.S.C. § 1692c(a)(1) (2000).

[525] *See* 15 U.S.C. § 1692c(a)(1) (2000).

[526] *See* 15 U.S.C. § 1692c(a)(3) (2000).

[527] *See* 15 U.S.C. § 1692c(c) (2000); *see, e.g.*, Herbert v. Monterey Fin. Servs., Inc., 863 F. Supp. 76 (D. Conn. 1994) (phone call made after receiving a letter from the consumer's attorney stating the consumer refused to pay the debt).

[528] *See* 15 U.S.C. § 1692d (2000).

[529] *See* 15 U.S.C. § 1692d (2000); *see, e.g.,* Grassley v. Debt Collectors, Inc., 1992 U.S. Dist. LEXIS 22782 (D. Or. Dec. 14, 1992) (threat to have debtor "picked up").

[4] False or Misleading Representations

Debt collectors are prohibited from making false, deceptive, or misleading representations when attempting to recover an unpaid debt. Among the specific potentially misleading actions they may not take are:

- misrepresenting the "character, amount, or legal status of any debt;"[530]
- misrepresenting the amount or recoverability of fees in connection with their efforts to recover the debt;[531]
- representing or even implying that failure to pay the debt will result in the debtor's arrest or imprisonment;
- representing or implying that they will take any action that the creditor is legally prohibited from taking;[532]
- communicating or threatening to communicate to any third person information that is known to be false;[533]
- implying that any transfer of the claim against the debtor will result in the debtor's loss of any defense which he otherwise might have;[534]
- falsely implying that the debtor has committed any crime or other conduct that would disgrace the debtor.[535]

Moreover, the debt collector may not threaten legal action that it does not intend to take. This precludes false threats to file suit,[536] particularly if the debt collector's past practice of never actually filing suit belies its threats to do so,[537] or if the debt collector delays filing suit for a much longer time than the threat suggests.[538] However, communications falling short of a direct threat to initiate suit but indicating that the creditor may "consider" legal action have passed muster under the Act.[539]

In addition, debt collectors must accurately reveal their identity and the purpose for their communication.[540] They must not falsely imply that they

---

[530] 15 U.S.C. § 1692e(2)(A) (2000). Debt collectors therefore must be certain that they have accurate information about the amount owed by the debtor.

[531] 15 U.S.C. § 1692e(2)(B) (2000).

[532] 15 U.S.C. § 1692e(4) (2000).

[533] 15 U.S.C. § 1692e(8) (2000).

[534] 15 U.S.C. § 1692e(7) (2000).

[535] 15 U.S.C. § 1692e(7) (2000).

[536] 15 U.S.C. § 1692e(5) (2000); *e.g.,* Edwards v. National Business Factors, Inc., 897 F. Supp. 455 (D. Nev. 1995) (creditor had not yet authorized collection agency to bring suit).

[537] *Compare* United States v. National Financial Services, Inc., 820 F. Supp. 228 (D. Md. 1993), *aff'd,* 98 F.3d 131 (4th Cir. 1996) (attorney who threatened suit had not brought a single suit in collection matter in the past seven years), *with* Higgins v. Capitol Credit Services, Inc., 762 F. Supp. 1128, 1136–37 (D. Del. 1991) (where attorney had filed suit on regular occasions).

[538] *E.g.*, Trans World Accounts, Inc. v. FTC, 594 F.2d 212 (9th Cir. 1979).

[539] *E.g.*, Knowles v. Credit Bureau of Rochester, Div. of Rochester Credit Ctr., Inc., 1992 U.S. Dist. LEXIS 8349 (W.D.N.Y. May 27, 1992).

[540] 15 U.S.C. § 1692e(14) (2000).

are affiliated with a governmental agency[541] or that documents they provide to the debtor were issued or authorized by a court or other governmental body.[542] This rule prohibits them from using badges or uniforms that might indicate that the debt collector is a police officer or other public official.[543] They must also avoid representing that the communication is from an attorney, if it is not.[544] They may not falsely claim that any documents they provide to the debtor are "legal process."[545] They may not falsely represent that they are employed by a credit reporting agency.[546] Finally, debt collectors are affirmatively required to disclose, in their initial communication with the debtor, that they are "attempting to collect a debt and that any information obtained will be used for that purpose."[547]

[5] Unfair Practices

The FDCPA also prohibits any "unfair or unconscionable means to collect or to attempt to collect any debt."[548] Among the actions specifically restricted under this broad prohibition are:

- collecting any amount unless it is both authorized by the agreement with the debtor and permitted by law;[549]
- accepting a check from the debtor or anyone else that is post-dated by more than five days, without supplying that person with written notice of the debt collector's intent to deposit the check three to ten days before the deposit;[550]
- soliciting a post-dated check to subsequently threaten or institute a criminal prosecution should the check later be dishonored;[551]
- depositing or threatening to deposit any post-dated check before the date stated on the instrument;[552]
- causing any kind of charge to be made to any person for communications by concealing the purpose of the communications, such as by making a "collect" call to the debtor;[553]
- threatening to use self-help to take possession of the debtor's property, if there is no right to possession, no intent to take possession, or if the property involved is exempt;[554]

---

541 15 U.S.C. § 1692e(1) (2000).

542 15 U.S.C. § 1692e(9) (2000).

543 15 U.S.C. § 1692e(1) (2000).

544 15 U.S.C. § 1692e(3) (2000); *e.g.*, Russey v. Rankin, 911 F. Supp. 1449 (D.N.M. 1995).

545 15 U.S.C. § 1692e(13) (2000).

546 15 U.S.C. § 1692e(16) (2000).

547 15 U.S.C. § 1692e(11) (2000).

548 15 U.S.C. § 1692f (2000).

549 15 U.S.C. § 1692f(1) (2000).

550 15 U.S.C. § 1692f(2) (2000).

551 15 U.S.C. § 1692f(3) (2000).

552 15 U.S.C. § 1692f(4) (2000).

553 15 U.S.C. § 1692f(5) (2000).

554 15 U.S.C. § 1692f(6) (2000).

- communicating with the debtor via post card;[555]
- using any language or a symbol on an envelope or telegram that reveals the nature of the debt collector's business.[556]

It should be noted that the express statutory prohibitions are not an exclusive listing of the actions that may be held to be "unfair or unconscionable."

[6] Debt Validation

The FDCPA provides consumer debtors with the right to have validated a debt claimed to be owed by the debt collector.[557] Although it seems unimaginable to one of your co-authors, with tendencies toward obsessive compulsive behavior, your other co-author, who tends to be a bit scattered, is not the least bit surprised that consumer debtors sometimes lose track of debts they owe. The assignment of obligations from one creditor to another might make it difficult for debtors to keep track of the current owners of their obligations. Accordingly, within five days after any initial communication with a debtor in connection with the collection of a debt, the debt collector is required to send the consumer a written notification, containing (1) the amount of the debt; (2) the name of the creditor to whom the debt is owed; (3) a statement advising the debtor that the debt collector will assume that the debt is valid unless the debtor disputes its validity within thirty days; (4) a statement advising the debtor that if it disputes the debt within thirty days that the debt collector will obtain and mail to the debtor a verification of the debt; and (5) a statement that upon request within the thirty-day period, that the debt collector will supply the debtor with the name and address of the original creditor, if that person is different from the current creditor.[558]

Although debt collectors are permitted to continue efforts to collect from the debtor during this thirty-day period,[559] their efforts must not "overshadow" the debtor's right during this period to have the obligation verified.[560] For example, in *Rabideau v. Management Adjustment Bureau,* the court held that a statement in a communication from the debt collector asserting that "immediate payment would avoid further contact" from the collection agency, operated to contradict the validation notice because it implied that making payment was the only way to avoid subsequent contact from the collection agency.[561] It misled the debtor, who could have prevented subsequent contact from the collection agency, at least until verification of the debt was provided, by giving notice that it disputed the debt.

[555] 15 U.S.C. § 1692f(7) (2000).

[556] 15 U.S.C. § 1692f(8) (2000).

[557] Pub L. No. 95-109, 91 Stat 874 (1977).

[558] 15 U.S.C. § 1692g (2000).

[559] *E.g.*, Sprouse v. City Credits Co., 126 F. Supp. 2d 1083 (S.D. Ohio 2000).

[560] *E.g.*, Johnson v. Revenue Mgmt. Corp., 169 F.3d 1057 (7th Cir. 1999); Rhoades v. West Virginia Credit Bureau Reporting Servs., 96 F. Supp. 2d 528, 532 (S.D. W. Va. 2000).

[561] 805 F. Supp. 1086 (W.D.N.Y. 1992).

[7] FDCPA Remedies

Violations of the FDCPA permit the debtor to recover any actual damages it suffers as a result of the violations.[562] However, in many cases, actual damages are likely to be minimal or difficult to calculate. Therefore, the court has discretion to assess up to $1,000 in additional damages,[563] depending on the frequency and persistence of the debt collector's violations, the nature of its violations, and the extent to which its violations were intentional, negligent, or inadvertent.[564] Additional damages are available in class actions.[565] However, a debt collector is shielded from liability if it shows, by a preponderance of the evidence, "that the violation was not intentional and resulted from a bona fide error notwithstanding the [debt collector's] maintenance of procedures reasonably adapted to avoid any such error."[566]

In addition, the Federal Trade Commission may administratively enforce violations of the Act as violations of the Federal Trade Commission Act.[567] Administrative enforcement usually results in a "consent decree," which operates as an agreement by the debt collector not to engage in specific acts or practices that are spelled out in the order. The consent decree does not usually indicate that the respondent admitted any wrongdoing; this, of course, deprives it of any collateral estoppel effect in a private enforcement action; and, it limits its formal precedential effect. At the same time, the decree does provide a good indication of the position likely to be taken by the full Commission regarding the actions the respondent has agreed not to take in the future. Therefore, such consent decrees are a useful guide to the position of the FTC.

[D] Federal Fair Credit Reporting Act

Credit-reporting agencies collect, assemble, and report information concerning consumers to lenders, employers, landlords, insurers, and other businesses. The Fair Credit Reporting Act[568] regulates the activities of these agencies. It also regulates the conduct of their customers who receive credit reports, as well as the actions of those who supply information about consumers to credit-reporting agencies. In addition, the Act provides consumers with various rights that are designed to enable them to detect and correct inaccurate or outdated information that concerns them and their credit history.

The Act attempts to ensure that consumers have access to information contained in their credit reports by giving them the right, upon request,

[562] 15 U.S.C. § 1692k(a)(1) (2000).

[563] 15 U.S.C. § 1692k(a)(2)(A) (2000).

[564] 15 U.S.C. § 1692k(b)(1) (2000).

[565] 15 U.S.C. § 1692k(a)(2)(B) (2000).

[566] 15 U.S.C. § 1692k(c) (2000).

[567] 15 U.S.C. § 1692l(a) (2000).

[568] 15 U.S.C. §§ 1681-1691v (2000).

to one free copy of their credit report each year,[569] as well as to additional copies for a modest fee.[570] This facilitates consumers' detection of potentially inaccurate information in their credit reports. The Act also requires creditors, employers, and others who take "adverse action" with respect to a consumer that is at least partially based on information contained in a consumer credit report, to advise the affected consumer of the adverse action, the name and contact information of the credit reporting agency from whom the information was obtained, and the consumer's right to acquire a copy of the credit report on which the adverse decision was based.[571] After such an adverse decision, the consumer has a right to a free copy of the report that was supplied to the creditor, employer, insurer, or other person who took the adverse information.[572]

Upon receipt of a copy of his or her report, a consumer has the right to contest the accuracy of any information contained in the report and to compel the credit-reporting agency involved to conduct an "investigation" of the accuracy of the contested information.[573] The entity that supplied the contested information must participate in the agency's investigation.[574] If the contested information is inaccurate or cannot be verified, the credit-reporting agency is required to report the results of its investigation to the person who took adverse action against the consumer based on information contained in the report. Thus, if a prospective creditor denies credit to the debtor after receiving a report about the debtor and, after an investigation, the information in the credit report cannot be verified, the credit reporting agency must notify the creditor that the information it had previously provided could not be verified.

Of course, this investigation may or may not result in a reversal of the creditor's adverse action. A prospective creditor or employer may have had reasons for taking the adverse action that were not based on the inaccurate information in the credit report. Likewise, a prospective employer may have filled the available position in the meantime by hiring a different applicant. A landlord who received the incorrect credit report may have already rented the premises to someone else. Or, as litigators like to say about improperly admitted evidence, "It is impossible to unring a bell."

The extent to which these and other mechanisms in the Fair Credit Reporting Act provide consumers with meaningful relief from inaccurate information that might be contained in their credit reports remains open to question. In particular, the mechanisms to resolve disputes about the accuracy of information contained in consumer credit reports have been subject to severe criticism. However, exposing credit reporting agencies to

[569] 15 U.S.C. § 1681j(c) (2000).

[570] 15 U.S.C. § 1681j(a) (2000).

[571] 15 U.S.C. § 1681m (2000).

[572] 15 U.S.C. § 1681j(b) (2000).

[573] 15 U.S.C. § 1681i (2000).

[574] 15 U.S.C. § 1681s-2 (2000).

liability for defamation as a result of inaccurate information they disseminate might turn out to be overkill.

[E] State Consumer Protection Statutes[575]

A variety of state statutes exist to regulate the debt collection process. Foremost among them are the "Unfair and Deceptive Trade Practices" statutes, or "little FTC" acts, which many states have adopted, and which emulate the Federal Trade Commission Act's prohibition of "unfair and deceptive trade practices."[576]

In addition, a few states have adopted more specific statutes that emulate the Fair Debt Collection Practices Act, except they frequently govern not only collection agencies and other similar debt collectors, but also creditors themselves.[577]

Further, a few states have adopted the Uniform Consumer Creditor Code (UCCC), which prohibits creditors from engaging in "unconscionable conduct in collecting a [consumer] debt."[578] The UCCC defines unconscionable conduct to include a wide variety of tactics that the federal Fair Debt Collection Practices Act precludes collection agencies from deploying.[579]

Finally, states that have adopted the Uniform Consumer Sales Practices Act[580] have applied its prohibition against "unfair or deceptive acts or practices" and "unconscionable acts or practices" to prohibit creditors from engaging in the type of collection strategies that would violate the Fair Debt Collection Practices Act if engaged in by a third-party debt collector.[581]

The overall impact of these state statutes is to make actions by creditors that would violate the Fair Debt Collection Practices Act if engaged in by a third-party debt collector, a violation of the state statute. Debtors are usually provided with the right to recover actual damages[582] or rescind the transaction,[583] and also may be permitted to recover punitive damages.[584]

---

[575] 2 Howard J. Alperin & Roland F. Chase, Consumer Law 3560 (1986); Joel E. Smith, Annotation, *Validity, Construction, and Application of State Statutes Prohibiting Abusive or Coercive Debt Collection Practices*, 87 A.L.R.3d 786 (1978).

[576] *See* Federal Trade Commission Act § 5, 15 U.S.C. § 45 (2000); Debtor-Creditor Law § 8.09[3][a] (Theodore Eisenberg ed. 2006).

[577] *E.g.,* Iowa Debt Collections Practices Act, Iowa Code § 537.7101 (West 1998); Cal. Civ. Code §§ 1788-1788.32 (West Supp. 2006).

[578] Unif. Consumer Credit Code § 5.108(2) (1974).

[579] *See* Unif. Consumer Credit Code § 5.108(5) (1974).

[580] Unif. Consumer Sales Practices Act (1970); *e.g.*, Ohio Rev. Code Ann. § 1345.01-1345.13 (LexisNexis 2002).

[581] *E.g.,* Liggins v. May Company, 373 N.E.2d 404 (Ohio Ct. Com. Pleas 1977).

[582] *E.g.*, Ohio Rev. Code Ann. § 1345.09(A) (LexisNexis 2002).

[583] *E.g.*, Ohio Rev. Code Ann. § 1345.09(A) (LexisNexis 2002).

[584] *E.g.*, Ohio Rev. Code Ann. § 1345.09(B) (LexisNexis 2002).

Chapter 3

A Brief History of Bankruptcy[1]

§ 3.01 The Bankruptcy Clause[2]

The history of federal bankruptcy law starts with the drafting of the Constitution. Post-independence concerns about the weakness of the central government led to the drafting in 1787 of a new federal charter to replace the existing Articles of Confederation. Among the powers bestowed on the national government by the new Constitution was the power to enact "uniform laws on the subject of bankruptcies throughout the United States."[3] It was placed there, at least in part, at the behest of bankers concerned about their ability to collect debts in local courts. Like many of the other powers granted to the young federal government, the bankruptcy power remained largely dormant through most of the nineteenth century. And, like those other powers, it came into its own in the twentieth. Although it is the Commerce Clause that has been the primary vehicle for the expansion of federal power over trade and credit, the Bankruptcy Clause has played a substantial secondary role. To a large and growing degree, the law of debtors and creditors has been federalized; Congress' power over bankruptcies is a major reason why.

§ 3.02 Bankruptcy Law Prior to 1898[4]

During the nineteenth century, Congress exercised its Bankruptcy Power sporadically to meet the periodic crises of a growing market economy. Federal bankruptcy legislation was viewed as a temporary and emergency

---

[1] David A. Skeel, Jr., Debt's Dominion: A History of Bankruptcy Law in America (2001); Charles Warren, Bankruptcy in United States History (1935); Vern Countryman, *A History of American Bankruptcy Law*, 81 Com. L.J. 226 (1976); Charles Jordan Tabb, *The History of the Bankruptcy Laws in the United States,* 3 Am. Bankr. Inst. L. Rev. 5 (1995).

[2] Kurt H. Nadelman, *On the Origin of the Bankruptcy Clause*, 1 Am. J. Legal Hist. 215 (1957); Charles Jordan Tabb, *The History of the Bankruptcy Laws in the United States*, 3 Am. Bankr. Inst. L. Rev. 5 (1995).

[3] U.S. Const. art I, § 8, cl. 4; *see* Charles Jordan Tabb, *The History of the Bankruptcy Laws in the United States*, 3 Am. Bankr. Inst. L. Rev. 5, 12–14, 44–51 (1995).

[4] Peter J. Coleman, Debtors and Creditors in America: Insolvency, Imprisonment for Debt, and Bankruptcy 1607-1900 (1974); Vern Countryman, *A History of American Bankruptcy Law*, 81 Com. L.J. 226 (1976).

Regarding the history of English bankruptcy law, on which ours is predicated, *see* Jay Cohen, *The History of Imprisonment for Debt and its Relation to the Development of Discharge in Bankruptcy*, 3 J. Leg. Hist. 153 (1982); Ian P. Duffy, *English Bankrupts, 1571-1861*, 24 Am. J. Leg. Hist. 283 (1980); Louis E. Levinthal, *The Early History of English Bankruptcy*, 67 U. Pa. L. Rev. 1 (1919).

measure, only appropriate to deal with the aftermath of economic depression.[5] Temporary federal bankruptcy laws were in force from 1800 to 1803,[6] from 1841 to 1843,[7] and again from 1867 to 1878.[8]

In ordinary times, state creditors' rights law was viewed as sufficient to deal with the problems of debtor default. Routine adjustments to the relationship between debtors and creditors were left to the states. In the absence of federal bankruptcy legislation, however, the states were frustrated by their inability to grant debtors a discharge.[9] Relief was also provided through federal equity receiverships, which dealt primarily with the large railroad insolvencies of the late nineteenth century. The latter, combined with added protections to protect dissenting creditors, served as the basis for many of the features of the modern Chapter 11 reorganization.[10]

§ 3.03 The Bankruptcy Act of 1898[11]

The first permanent bankruptcy law in the United States was the Bankruptcy Act of 1898. Enacted in the aftermath of the 1893 depression, it endured for more than 80 years with only one major set of amendments. These amendments occurred in 1938 in the wake of the Great Depression of the first-half of the twentieth century. As was true of all the prior bankruptcy acts, the 1898 Act was born in controversy.

Two different groups were pressing Congress for a bankruptcy law. Debtors, including especially farmers, who were hit hard by the depression, wanted a voluntary act that would relieve debtors from creditor pressure. Creditors, especially commercial creditors, wanted an involuntary act that could be initiated by creditors and used to pry assets out of recalcitrant debtors. The resulting law represented an uneasy compromise between these two factions that created both voluntary and involuntary forms of bankruptcy (but protected farmers from the latter), provided both a fresh start for debtors and new collection tools for lenders, and became the basis

---

[5] Prior to the Great Depression of the 1930s, what we now know as economic "recessions" were referred to as "depressions." Reluctant to evoke images of the economic hardship the country suffered between the wars, politicians became reluctant to refer to these cyclical setbacks as depressions.

[6] Bankruptcy Act of 1800, ch. 19, 2 Stat. 19 (repealed 1803). This Act was a near copy of the English statute. Charles Jordan Tabb, *The History of the Bankruptcy Laws in the United States*, 3 Am. Bankr. Inst. L. Rev. 5, 14–15 (1995).

[7] Bankruptcy Act of 1841, 5 Stat. 440 (repealed 1843); *see* Charles Jordan Tabb, *The History of the Bankruptcy Laws in the United States*, 3 Am. Bankr. Inst. L. Rev. 5, 16–18 (1995).

[8] Bankruptcy Act of 1867, 14 Stat. 517 (repealed 1878); Charles Jordan Tabb, *The History of the Bankruptcy Laws in the United States*, 3 Am. Bankr. Inst. L. Rev. 5, 18–21 (1995).

[9] Sturges v. Crowninshield, 17 U.S. (4 Wheat.) 122 (1819).

[10] *See* Charles Jordan Tabb, *The History of the Bankruptcy Laws in the United States*, 3 Am. Bankr. Inst. L. Rev. 5, 21–23 (1995).

[11] David A. Skeel, Jr., *The Genius of the 1898 Bankruptcy Act*, 15 Bankr. Dev. J. 321 (1999); Charles Jordan Tabb, *The History of the Bankruptcy Laws in the United States*, 3 Am. Bankr. Inst. L. Rev. 5, 23–32 (1995).

for a body of substantive and procedural law that is far more important today than the Congress at the time could have imagined.

Although there were many amendments to the Act over the years (indeed, the first amendments were enacted just a couple of years after the Act was passed), the core of it remained intact until 1979, when the current Bankruptcy Code became law. There was one substantial set of amendments: the Chandler Act of 1938, which, in response to the Great Depression, added several chapters to the Act to deal with business and individual reorganization. The business reorganization chapters were denoted Chapter X, Chapter XI, and Chapter XII. Only the first two were of much significance (Chapter XII, according to some, was a piece of special legislation tailor-made for one specific company in a district represented by a powerful Congressman). Chapter X was designed for the reorganization of large, publicly owned companies. Chapter XI was designed for reorganizing small, closely-held corporations.

From at least the 1960s onward, there was growing dissatisfaction with the Act. Complaints were many and varied, including those about opaque language of the statute that had been so glossed by court decision and scholarly interpretation that the actual words of the Act were frequently ignored. The division of business reorganizations into Chapters X and XI was viewed as cumbersome and productive of unnecessary and expensive litigation. The debtors frequently died while the "doctors" argued about which "table" they should be on. Chapter XIII seemed to be a failure in all but a few districts. Moreover, the court system was clumsy, with jurisdictional provisions that defied rational justification. Indeed, the entire Act reflected a horse-and-buggy financial world far removed from contemporary American life.

The Burdick Commission, named after the Senator who sponsored its appointment, recommended revisions to the Act. The Commission was lightly staffed and funded but did a remarkable job of analyzing the existing law and proposing sensible changes. Although many of its recommendations did not survive the legislative process, but its report nevertheless served as the framework for Congress' eventual action.[12]

After much legislative wrangling over both the substance of the Code and its sweeping jurisdictional provisions, the Bankruptcy Reform Act of 1978, which included both the Bankruptcy Code and a number of related procedural and jurisdictional rules, was enacted.[13] The Bankruptcy Reform Act provides the framework for current bankruptcy law. This Bankruptcy Code, as amended and interpreted through the end of 2006, is the subject of the rest of this book.

---

[12] Report of the Commission on the Bankruptcy Laws of the United States, Rep. No. 93-137, pts. I and II (1973); *see* Charles Jordan Tabb, *The History of the Bankruptcy Laws in the United States*, 3 Am. Bankr. Inst. L. Rev. 5, 32 (1995).

[13] Bankruptcy Reform Act of 1978, Pub. L. No. 95-598, 92 Stat. 2549 (1978); *see* Kenneth N. Klee, *Legislative History of the New Bankruptcy Law*, 28 DePaul L. Rev. 941 (1979).

§ 3.04 The Bankruptcy Code[14]

Few laws that do not involve taxes have been greeted with as much anticipation as the Bankruptcy Code. During the final months of the Act, bankruptcy filings dwindled as lawyers waited to take advantage of the new law. A burst of pent-up filings greeted the Code when it came into effect. The most distinguished treatise in the field, Collier on Bankruptcy, was issued in a new (fifteenth) edition, specifically designed to deal with the new law.

The Code became effective on October 1, 1979,[15] and almost immediately became the subject of much debate and many calls for revision. The loudest complaints came from the consumer credit industry, which decried the Code as a virtual charter for deadbeats. Consumer creditors were concerned about the overall effect they saw on consumer borrowers' willingness to repay. It was not the fear of losing $100 in a particular case that spooked creditors, but the fear of losing $100 a million times over. If indeed the new Bankruptcy Code reduced the cost of defaulting on debts, then bad debts would rise, profits would fall, the price of credit would be pushed up.

Whether the Bankruptcy Code has significantly contributed to increased bankruptcy filings is not clearly established.[16] But, October 1, 1979, marked the beginning of a long period of generally rising bankruptcy filings. The years 1979 through 1982 included a period of considerable economic stress, with a burst of high inflation, followed by the worst recession since World War II. With greater prosperity in the mid-1980s, bankruptcy rates stabilized and then fell, although admittedly not to their pre-1979 levels. More economic trouble in the late 1980s and early 1990s led to another surge in bankruptcy petitions. The improvement in the economy after 1991 led to another plateau, and by 1994 filing rates were markedly down. After that, however, filings nearly doubled from 832,339 in 1994 to 1,597,462 in 2004, to over 2 million filings in 2005.[17] Most curiously, the filing rate increased during the mid 1990s, a time of relative economic prosperity.

It may be, however, that the increase in consumer bankruptcy reflects changes in the practices of consumer lenders. Another important event in 1978 was the Supreme Court's decision in the *Marquette National Bank* case.[18] There, the Supreme Court held that consumer lending contracts

---

[14] David A. Moss & Gibbs A. Johnson, *The Rise of Consumer Bankruptcy: Evolution, Revolution, or Both?*, 73 Am. Bankr. L.J. 311 (1999).

[15] Bankruptcy Reform Act of 1978, Pub. L. No. 95-598, tit. IV, § 402(a), 92 Stat. 2549, 2682 (1978).

[16] One of this book's co-authors has considerable doubts. *See*, Susan Block-Lieb & Edward J. Janger, *The Myth of the Rational Borrower: Behaviorism, Rationality and the Misguided Reform of Bankruptcy Law*, 84 TEX. L. REV. 1481 (2006).

[17] *See* Federal Judiciary Bankruptcy Statistics, www.uscourts.gov/bnkrpctystats/statistics.htm (last visited June 10, 2006). The increased number of filings in 2005 may be attributable to the number of debtors rushing to file before the 2005 Amendments went into effect.

[18] Marquette National Bank of Minneapolis v. First of Omaha Service Corp., 439 U.S. 299 (1978).

were governed by the law of the jurisdiction where the lending bank was located. This decision facilitated consumer lending by national banks, who, in many cases moved their credit card banks to favorable jurisdictions, such as South Dakota (Citibank), and Delaware (MBNA). Similarly, the growth of national credit reporting agencies such as Trans-Union, Equifax and Experian have improved the ability of consumer lenders to engage in risk-based pricing of consumer debt, and facilitated the growth of sub-prime consumer lending. In short, the increase in consumer bankruptcy has gone hand in hand with the expansion of consumer lending. Distinguishing the chicken from the egg may be difficult, but at least one of us has strong intuitions.[19] Borrowers might not be more feckless; rather, lenders may have found ways to lend profitably to higher risk borrowers.

In any event, the initial struggle over the original version of the Code came to a head in 1982. To the surprise of most observers, the United States Supreme Court held that the jurisdictional provisions of the Bankruptcy Reform Act were unconstitutional.[20] Suddenly, the country was faced with the possibility that there would be no bankruptcy system at all.

For two years, while the bankruptcy courts labored under a jury-rigged system of possibly unconstitutional jurisdictional rules, Congress fought over a revision of the Code. One of the main struggles concerned consumer bankruptcy. Many efforts were made to scale back the relief afforded to consumers, even to force some consumers to reorganize under Chapter 13 rather than to liquidate under Chapter 7.

The most draconian creditor proposals were defeated, at least for another two decades. However, the Bankruptcy Amendments and Federal Judgeship Act of 1984 ("BAFJA")[21] made several important changes, including an amendment to § 707, which permitted dismissal of a Chapter 7 petition to consumer debtors if providing relief would constitute "substantial abuse."[22] Of greater significance, at the time, was the new and highly complicated jurisdictional structure that seemed to herald a return to the complicated and expensive jurisdictional rules that reigned under the Bankruptcy Act.[23]

Almost two years later, the Bankruptcy Judges, United States Trustees and Family Farmer Bankruptcy Act of 1986 came into effect in October,

---

[19] *See*, Block-Lieb & Janger, *The Myth of the Rational Borrower: Behaviorism, Rationality and the Misguided Reform of Bankruptcy Law*, 84 Tex. L. Rev. 1481 (2006).

[20] Northern Pipeline Constr. Co. v. Marathon Pipe Line Co., 458 U.S. 50 (1982), *judgment stayed*, 459 U.S. 813 (1982); *see* § 5.03[A][3] The *Marathon Pipeline* decision, *infra*.

[21] Bankruptcy Amendments and Federal Judgeship Act of 1984, Pub. L. No. 98-353, tit. III, §§ 306, 453, 98 Stat. 353, 375 (1984).

[22] *See* § 17.03[B][3][a] Substantial Abuse Prior to 2005; *see, e.g.*, In re Walton, 866 F.2d 981, 984 (9th Cir. 1989) (debtor's "ability to pay" is the "crucial" factor in determining whether relief would be a substantial abuse); *see* Paul M. Black & Michael J. Herbert, *Bankcard's Revenge: A Critique of the 1984 Consumer Credit Amendments to the Bankruptcy Code*, 19 U. Rich. L. Rev. 845 (1985).

[23] *See* Charles Jordan Tabb, *The History of the Bankruptcy Laws in the United States*, 3 Am. Bankr. Inst. L. Rev. 5, 38–40 (1995).

1986.[24] The two most important provisions of this law were nationwide establishment of the previously experimental United States Trustee program, and the enactment of Chapter 12, for reorganization of family farms. Perhaps in reaction to the stingy spirit of BAFJA, or perhaps because there are a lot of farm-state senators, Chapter 12 is a thoroughly "pro-debtor" chapter.[25]

There were still many complaints about, and much tinkering with the Code. Dissatisfaction did not decrease. Instead, it increasingly focused on business rather than consumer bankruptcy. The hot issues from the mid 1980s through the early 1990s were the propriety of creative uses of bankruptcy to deal with mass torts, labor disputes, and declining real estate markets.

A number of ambitious proposals were made to revamp and even to jettison the Code. In the last days of the 103rd Congress, the Bankruptcy Reform Act of 1994 enacted an assortment of minor amendments.[26] It overturned a few controversial court cases,[27] strengthened the position of secured creditors on a variety of fronts,[28] and provided some assistance to institutional lenders.[29] However, despite the raw number of changes, the 1994 amendments did not have the sweep of the 1978 Act, 1984's BAFJA, or even the 1986 Amendments. It did not affect the basic structure of bankruptcy law in any significant way.

The 1994 Amendments provided for one potentially significant change: it created a new Bankruptcy Commission to study the Code and make recommendations.[30] The legislative history called upon the Commission to be cautious: "the Commission should be aware that Congress is generally satisfied with the basic framework established in the current Bankruptcy Code." The report eventually promulgated by this new Commission[31] was controversial and largely ignored by Congress in enacting subsequent legislation.[32]

---

[24] Pub. L. No. 99-554, 100 Stat. 3088 (1986*); see* Charles Jordan Tabb, *The History of the Bankruptcy Laws in the United States*, 3 Am. Bankr. Inst. L. Rev. 5, 40 (1995).

[25] *See* Chapter 20, Family Farmer and Family Fisherman Reorganization, *infra.*

[26] Bankruptcy Reform Act of 1994, Pub. L. No. 103-394, 108 Stat. 4106 (1994); *see generally* Robin E. Phelan, Richard E. Coulson, Stacey Jernigan & Alvin C. Harrell, *1994 Consumer Bankruptcy Developments: The Bankruptcy Reform Act of 1994*, 50 Bus. Law. 1193 (1995); Ned Waxman, *The Bankruptcy Reform Act of 1994*, 11 Bankr. Dev. J. 311 (1995).

[27] *See* Timothy R. Zinnecker, *Purchase Money Security Interests in the Preference Zone: Questions Answered and Questions Raised by the 1994 Amendments to Bankruptcy Code § 547*, 62 Mo. L. Rev. 47 (1997).

[28] *See* Kathryn R. Heidt, *The Effect of the 1994 Amendments on Commercial Secured Creditors*, Am. Bankr. L.J. 395 (1995).

[29] *See* Charles Jordan Tabb, *The History of the Bankruptcy Laws in the United States*, 3 Am. Bankr. Inst. L. Rev. 5, 42–44 (1995).

[30] Pub. L. No. 103-394, tit. VI, §§ 601-610, 108 Stat 4147 (1994).

[31] The commission's report was issued in 1997, Nat'l Bankr. Review Comm'n, *Bankruptcy: The Next Twenty Years, Final Report* (Oct. 20, 1997) govinfo.library.unt.edu/nbrc/reporttitlepg.html (last visited June 12, 2006).

[32] Gary Neustadter, *2005: A Consumer Bankruptcy Odyssey*, 39 Creighton L. Rev. 225, 230 & n.5 (2006).

In the mid 1990s, advocates for imposing more restrictions on consumer debtors' access to bankruptcy proposed new legislation which, among other things, would impose a financial "means test" for consumers' access to bankruptcy relief.[33] The impetus for these new restrictions originated in an empirical study of consumer debtors financed by the consumer credit industry, which concluded that approximately one-third of consumer debtors could pay a substantial part of their debts if all their income above the poverty level was applied to their debts over a five-year period.[34] While the conclusions of that report have been called into question,[35] after eight years of Presidential vetoes, pocket vetoes, and other legislative setbacks, this proposal was finally enacted, together with a variety of additional changes, as the "Bankruptcy Abuse Prevention and Consumer Protection Act of 2005" or "BAPCPA."[36] Most of its provisions went into effect on October 17, 2005, 180 days after it was adopted.

The 2005 legislation implemented controversial but sweeping changes in the role that bankruptcy will play in the lives of consumer debtors.[37] Most significantly, it imposes a stringent "means test," which, with a few qualifications that we will discuss later, blocks access to chapter 7 liquidation bankruptcy for consumers whose incomes are above their home states' medians. It forces these debtors into Chapter 13 rehabilitation plans, if they are to receive relief from their debts at all. At the same time, it uses this

[33] H.R. 3150, 105th Cong. § 101(4) (1995); *but see* Marianne B. Culhane & Michaela M. White, *Taking the New Consumer Bankruptcy Model for a Test Drive: Means-Testing for Chapter 7 Debtors*, 7 Am. Bankr. Inst. L. Rev. 27, 28 n.8 (1999); *see also* General Accounting Office, Personal Bankruptcy: The Credit Research Center Report on Debtors' Ability to Pay, GAO/GGD-98-47 (1998); General Accounting Office, Personal Bankruptcy: The Credit Research Center and Ernst & Young Reports on Debtors' Ability to Pay, GAO/T-GGD-98-79 (1998).

[34] Credit Research Ctr., Krannert Graduate Sch. of Mgmt., Purdue Univ., Monograph No. 23, Consumers' Right To Bankruptcy: Origins and Effects, Consumer Bankruptcy Study Vol. I (1982); Credit Research Ctr., Krannert Graduate Sch. of Mgmt., Purdue Univ., Monograph No. 24, Personal Bankruptcy: Causes, Costs and Benefits, Consumer Bankruptcy Study Vol. II (1982). The most important and influential conclusion of the Purdue study was that a large percentage of Chapter 7 debtors had sufficient post-bankruptcy income to make meaningful payments to their creditors. The "means test" of the 2005 legislation adopts a startlingly similar requirement. For a discussion of the merits of the scientific research in the Purdue study, see Teresa A. Sullivan, Elizabeth Warren & Jay Lawrence Westbrook, *Limiting Access to Bankruptcy Discharge: An Analysis of the Creditors' Data*, 1983 Wis. L. Rev. 1091; Charlene Sullivan, *Reply: Limiting Access to Bankruptcy Discharge*, 1984 Wis. L. Rev. 1069; Teresa A. Sullivan, Elizabeth Warren & Jay Lawrence Westbrook, *Rejoinder: Limiting Access to Bankruptcy Discharge*, 1984 Wis. L. Rev. 1087.

[35] Culhane & White, *Taking the New Consumer Bankruptcy Model for a Test Drive: Means-Testing for Chapter 7 Debtors*, 7 Am. Bankr. Inst. L. Rev. 27, 28 n.8 (1999).

[36] Pub. L. No. 109-8, 119 Stat. 23 (2005); *see generally* Susan Jensen, *A Legislative History of the Bankruptcy Abuse Prevention and Consumer Protection Act of 2005*, 79 Am. Bankr. L.J. 485 (2005); Gary Neustadter, *2005: A Consumer Bankruptcy Odyssey,* 39 Creighton L. Rev. 225, 228 n.2 (2006).

[37] Melissa B. Jacoby, *Ripple or Revolution? The Indeterminacy of Statutory Bankruptcy Reform,* 79 Am. Bankr. L.J. 169 (2005); Richard M. Hynes, *Non-Procrustean Bankruptcy*, 2004 U. Ill. L. Rev. 301, 361 (2004).

same means test to determine the amounts that must be paid to creditors under Chapter 13. It also mandates consumer credit counseling for consumer debtors as a condition of access to bankruptcy, and as a condition to discharge. The effective date of the 2005 legislation was preceded by a sharp spike in bankruptcy filings, and was followed by an equally sudden decline. At the time this book goes to press, however, the rate is rebounding slowly.[38] Part of the decline is due to the fact that many people who knew they were in financial difficulty rushed to file prior to the effective date of the new law. Part of the decline is also, no doubt, due to the fact that practice under the new law has not yet become routinized, so the cost of filing has increased, and the availability of qualified counsel has declined. Some of these changes are likely to be temporary. Others may be permanent. Whether these changes are desirable or not, largely depends on one's perspective.[39]

---

[38] The Administrative Office of the United States Courts publishes bankruptcy filing statistics on a quarterly basis. www.uscourts.gov/bnkrpctystats/statistics.htm#quarterly (last visited January 27, 2007).

[39] Walter W. Miller, Jr., *The Proposed "Bankruptcy Abuse Prevention and Consumer Protection Act of 2002,"* 22 Ann. Rev. Banking & Fin. L. 301, 308 (2003); Charles Jordan Tabb, *The Death of Consumer Bankruptcy in the United States?,* 18 Bankr. Dev. J. 1, 5–6 (2001); Catherine E. Vance & Paige Barr, *The Facts & Fiction of Bankruptcy Reform*, 1 DePaul Bus. & Com. L.J. 361 (2003); Richard M. Hynes, *Non-Procrustean Bankruptcy*, 2004 U. Ill. L. Rev. 301 (2004).

Chapter 4

Parties and Other Participants in Bankruptcy Cases

§ 4.01 Parties and Other Participants in the Bankruptcy Process

The number and role of the participants in a bankruptcy case depends on the nature and size of the proceeding. These participants always include the debtor and the debtor's creditors. The filing of a bankruptcy petition, much like the death of an individual, results in the creation of an estate, with all of the debtor's property vesting in the estate. The estate is administered by one of two participants: a trustee, or a "debtor-in-possession" of the estate. Creditors might be involved in the estate individually or may form into one or more "creditors' committees." Likewise, when a Chapter 11 debtor is a partnership or a corporation, owners of the bankrupt business (known as "interest" or "equity interest" holders) might form into "equity committees."

In Chapter 7 liquidation cases, a case trustee is appointed to collect and administer the debtor's property. However, because the overwhelming majority of consumer liquidation cases involve no assets for distribution to creditors, the trustee's role is frequently limited to reviewing the paperwork submitted by the debtor, in an effort to detect hidden assets or income that would make the debtor ineligible due to "abuse."[1]

In rehabilitation cases under Chapters 12 and 13, a trustee is involved, but he does not take control of all the estate's property. Instead, the trustee reviews the debtor's rehabilitation plan and receives and distributes payments the debtor makes pursuant to the terms of the debtor's court-approved payment plan. Appointment of a trustee in a Chapter 11 case is not the norm, but it does happen from time to time, usually where incumbent management has lost the confidence of the creditors or the bankruptcy judge. More typically, an "examiner" might be appointed to investigate the financial affairs of the debtor, and provide information to creditors and any creditors' committees that have been formed.

Several governmental officials might also become involved in a case. The United States Trustee is an administrative agency charged with monitoring bankruptcy cases on behalf of the United States government. This helps to maintain the financial integrity of a system that might otherwise be administered completely by the private parties who have a financial stake in the outcome of the case. And, of course, the bankruptcy court system

[1] *See* § 17.03[B] Dismissal of Consumer Cases Due to Abuse, *infra*.

will become involved in the case, with a full array of clerks, courtrooms, and judges.

§ 4.02 Debtors and Debtors-in-Possession

This book contains numerous references to both the "debtor" and the "debtor-in-possession." In most cases, the "debtor" is the one who initiates the case by filing a bankruptcy petition,[2] although creditors might also get the ball rolling by filing an involuntary petition.[3] In rehabilitation cases under Chapters 11, 12, and 13, where the debtor remains in possession of the property of the debtor's bankruptcy estate, the debtor morphs into a new entity: the "debtor-in-possession." The Code makes it clear, however, that where an estate is managed by a debtor-in-possession or "DIP," the DIP has all the statutory powers of the trustee in bankruptcy.[4]

[A] Debtor

The "debtor" is the subject of the bankruptcy case.[5] Under the old Bankruptcy Act, this person was referred to as "the bankrupt," but "debtor" is now used both for ease of reference and as a means to reduce the stigma suffered by a business debtor who is labeled "bankrupt."[6] The term "debtor" creates occasional ambiguity as to whether, in any particular context, it refers to an obligor in general or to an obligor who is the subject of a bankruptcy proceeding. After all, everyone in society who owes a debt is, in the general sense of the word, a debtor — and this includes nearly everyone.[7]

In a Chapter 7 liquidation case, the debtor is usually of little significance in the formal part of the case. Once the debtor files a petition and the accompanying paperwork regarding his financial affairs,[8] the debtor's only statutory role is to turn over his non-exempt property — if any exists — to the trustee, and receive a discharge. There are occasional exceptions to this limited role. For example, the case may involve litigation over the

[2] *See* § 6.01[A] Voluntary Commencement, *infra.*

[3] *See* § 6.01[B] Involuntary Commencement, *infra.*

[4] Bankruptcy Code § 1107.

[5] Bankruptcy Code § 101(13).

[6] H.R. Rep. 95-595, at 310 (1977), *reprinted in* 1978 U.S.C.C.A.N. 5963, 6267; Nathalie Martin, *The Role of History and Culture in Developing Bankruptcy and Insolvency Systems: The Perils of Legal Transplantation*, 28 B.C. Int'l & Comp. L. Rev. 1, 20–25 (2005); Gary Neustadter, *A Consumer Bankruptcy Odyssey*, 39 Creighton L. Rev. 225, 230–33 (2006). Even earlier, bankrupt debtors were considered criminals. *See* Charles J. Tabb, *The Historical Evolution of the Bankruptcy Discharge*, 65 Am. Bankr. L.J. 325, 329–30 (1991).

[7] It is virtually impossible to get along in life without incurring some obligations. Even those who abhor incurring debt and scrupulously avoid credit cards, auto loans, and even mortgages, usually owe money at the end of each month to the gas or electric company. The simple act of flipping on a light switch at home makes us debtors.

[8] *See* § 6.02[C] Petition and Schedules; Statement of Debtor's Affairs, *infra.*

dischargeability of a debtor's particular debts[9] or over whether the debtor should be granted a discharge at all.[10] However, especially in a consumer bankruptcy where there are few debts, fewer assets, and little likelihood of serious misconduct by the debtor, such litigation is rare.

In addition to filing the necessary schedules of property and debts, the debtor must cooperate with the trustee, surrender property of the estate and relevant records to the trustee, and appear at any examinations or hearings involved in the case.[11] Section 341 also requires the debtor to appear at a meeting of creditors. The meeting is convened under the authority of the United States Trustee, and usually presided over by the trustee appointed to administer the case.[12]

This meeting is sometimes referred to as the "341 meeting." No judge is present, and in consumer cases, it may not even really be a "meeting" in the normal sense of the word, as creditors rarely appear. When they do, they hardly ever conduct anything that might be characterized as a meeting. Instead, the event serves primarily as an opportunity for the trustee to ask the debtor questions about his or her financial affairs. This "examination" serves the same function as a state-law judgment debtor's examination.[13] It gives the trustee (and creditors if they choose to attend) the opportunity to probe for the location of assets and into other matters such as fraudulent conveyances,[14] preferences,[15] and the like.[16]

The debtor is required to appear at this meeting and to submit to an examination under oath.[17] The debtor may be questioned by the creditors, any indenture trustee, the case trustee, an examiner, or the United States Trustee.[18] The scope of the examination encompasses the debtor's "acts, conduct, or property, or to the liabilities and financial condition of the debtor, or to any matter which may affect the administration of the debtor's estate, or to the debtor's right to a discharge."[19] In a reorganization case, the examination may be more elaborate. It may:

> [R]elate to the operation of any business and the desirability of its continuance, the source of any money or property acquired or to be acquired by the debtor for purposes of consummating a plan, and the consideration given or offered to those who supplied these funds,

---

[9] *See* § 13.03 Non-Dischargeable Debts, *infra.*

[10] *See* § 12.02 Denial of Discharge, *infra.*

[11] Bankruptcy Code § 521; *see* § 6.02[C] Petition, Schedules, Statements, Certificates and Disclosures, *infra.*

[12] Bankruptcy Code § 341; Fed. R. Bankr. P. 2003.

[13] *See* § 2.14[A] Discovery: Examination of a Judgment Debtor, *supra.*

[14] *See* Chapter 16, Fraudulent Transfers, *infra.*

[15] *See* Chapter 15, Avoidable Preferences, *infra.*

[16] *See* Chapter 14, Trustee's General Avoiding Powers; Limits on Avoiding Powers, *infra.*

[17] Bankruptcy Code § 343; Fed. R. Bankr. P. 2004.

[18] Bankruptcy Code § 343; Fed. R. Bankr. P. 2004.

[19] Fed. R. Bank. P. 2004(b); *see* H.R. Rep. No. 95-595, at 332 (1977), *reprinted in* 1978 U.S.C.C.A.N 5963, 6288.

and any other matter relevant to the case or to the formulation of a plan.[20]

Thus, the examination must concern matters that are relevant to the bankruptcy case itself. The debtor also may be ordered to surrender books and records relating to his financial condition to the trustee at the 341 meeting.[21]

A debtor who has engaged in criminal activity may be reluctant to reveal information that might expose him to prosecution. Filing a bankruptcy petition does not operate as a waiver of the debtor's constitutional privilege against self incrimination. However, immunity from prosecution may be granted; if it is, the debtor must testify or run the risk of being denied a discharge.[22]

A consumer debtor must also file a statement of his or her intentions regarding encumbered property indicating whether the debtor intends to retain the property, surrender the property, claim the property as exempt, redeem the property, or reaffirm the debt that is secured by the property.[23]

This list of the debtor's duties is by no means exhaustive.[24] The remainder of this book will refer to various other duties that the debtor may have in both liquidation and rehabilitation cases.

[B] Debtor-in-Possession

A new entity, the "debtor-in-possession" (DIP)[25] is created whenever a debtor files a case under Chapter 11, 12, or 13. The debtor becomes a debtor-in-possession because there is normally no case trustee appointed to administer the debtor's estate. Literally, the debtor's management remains "in possession" of the estate's property and remains responsible for managing the estate's financial affairs while the case is pending.

The term technically applies to the debtor itself, but in corporate reorganization cases, it is universally used to describe the debtor's management. For example, when Titanic Industries, Inc. files a Chapter 11 case, its successor in the bankruptcy case is Titanic Industries, Inc., Debtor-in-Possession. But, when people refer to the DIP they may be referring to Harlan Wolff, the president of Titanic Industries, and the board of Directors, who ordinarily remain in control of the debtor's operations while the case is pending.

The DIP is a primary participant in all kinds of rehabilitation proceedings. The DIP has many of the powers and functions of the trustee[26] and

---

[20] Fed. R. Bank. P. 2004(b).

[21] Fed. R. Bankr. P. 2004(c).

[22] Bankruptcy Code § 344.

[23] Bankruptcy Code § 521(2)(A).

[24] *See* § 6.02[C] Petition, Lists, Schedules, Statements, Certificates and Disclosures, *infra*.

[25] This is usually pronounced "dee, eye, pee" rather than the possibly pejorative "dip."

[26] Bankruptcy Code §§ 1107, 1203, 1303.

conducts whatever negotiations precede the filing of a plan of reorganization. The DIP is responsible for deploying the estate's assets for the benefit of creditors. This may include bringing lawsuits to recover property for the benefit of the estate, including any actions against officers, directors, shareholders, and other insiders of a corporate debtor who might have received preferential transfers before the bankruptcy case began.[27]

§ 4.03 The Estate[28]

When a bankruptcy case is filed, an estate is created.[29] The estate becomes the owner of all of the debtor's property.[30] In this respect, the filing of a bankruptcy petition has some of the same legal effects as a person's death. The filing of the petition, like the death of a human being, instantaneously operates both to create an estate and to transfer all of the property belonging to the debtor to that estate.

The estate is not really a party to the case, but is rather a shorthand term for all of the property that is administered in the debtor's bankruptcy case. The debtor's estate is comprised primarily of whatever property the debtor owned at the time the bankruptcy case was filed, together with whatever additional income that property produces while the case is pending.[31] Included, as well, are assets recovered pursuant to the trustee's avoiding powers,[32] such as the power to avoid preferential pre-bankruptcy transfers to creditors,[33] fraudulent conveyances,[34] and other recoverable transfers.[35]

The value of the estate's property provides the baseline for distribution to creditors. In liquidation cases, the creditors receive either the estate's property or the value of the estate's property. In reorganization, the creditors are entitled to receive at least the value of the property that would have been available in the Chapter 7 estate.[36]

§ 4.04 Creditors and Creditors' Committees

Creditors sometimes participate in bankruptcy cases on their own. In Chapter 11 reorganization cases, they may organize themselves into one or more committees. A duly constituted committee is entitled to have its expenses, including attorney fees, reimbursed from the debtor's estate.

---

[27] *See* § 15.02[E] Preference Period, *infra*.

[28] *See* Chapter 7, Property of the Estate, *infra*.

[29] Bankruptcy Code § 541(a)(1); *see* § 7.01 Creation of the Debtor's Estate, *infra*.

[30] Bankruptcy Code § 541(a)(1).

[31] Bankruptcy Code § 541(a); *see* Chapter 7 Property of the Estate, *infra*.

[32] Bankruptcy Code § 541(a)(3).

[33] *See* Bankruptcy Code § 547; Chapter 15, Avoidable Preferences, *infra*.

[34] *See* Bankruptcy Code § 548; Chapter 16, Fraudulent Transfers, *infra*.

[35] *See* Chapter 14, General Avoiding Powers; Limits on Avoiding Powers, *infra*.

[36] *See* Bankruptcy Code §§ 1129(a)(7)(A)(ii), 1225(a)(4), 1325(a)(4); *see, e.g.*, § 18.08[E][1] Best Interests of Creditors, *infra*.

[A] Role of Creditors in Bankruptcy Cases

In nearly all bankruptcy cases, most of which involve consumer debtors with few assets, creditors play a passive role. Apart from filing a proof of claim[37] and perhaps receiving a small distribution, the typical creditor does nothing and pays little heed to what transpires in the debtor's case. Indeed, in most cases, creditors do not even bother filing a simple proof of claim form because there are no assets to distribute.

Accordingly, the bankruptcy value of the typical claim is negligible, and creditors who have already given up hope of collecting are rarely interested in sending good money after bad by participating in the case. With rare exceptions, only those creditors whose claims have real value in bankruptcy play an active part; and, in most cases, only secured creditors have claims with real value. In the vast majority of consumer cases, unsecured creditors' claims are worthless — the debtor has nothing to distribute to its unsecured creditors. In business cases, this may be different: priority, trade, and other unsecured creditors may have the opportunity for some meaningful payment from the debtor.

Creditors usually learn that the debtor has filed a bankruptcy case either directly from the debtor or in an official notice regarding the debtor's case, which is sent by the clerk of the bankruptcy court.[38] In consumer cases, where there are no assets available to distribute to creditors with unsecured claims, the notice will advise the debtor that there is no reason for the creditor to file a "proof of claim" form.[39] In Chapter 7 cases in which payment of a "dividend" to creditors seems likely, the notice sent to creditors listed on the schedule filed with the debtor's petition will include a simple proof of claim form that the creditor must submit to establish its claim to a share of the debtor's estate.[40] In a Chapter 11 case, however, the schedules filed with the debtor's petition establish the prima facie validity of creditors' claims, and no proof of claim need be filed if the creditor agrees with the amount and character of the claim as scheduled by the debtor.[41] If the creditor disagrees with the debtor's characterization of the claim, or with its amount, the creditor must file a proof of claim. This establishes the validity of the claim absent some further objection.

In reorganization cases, creditors play an additional role. They have the opportunity to object to the debtor's proposed plan of reorganization, and in Chapter 11 cases, creditors usually enjoy the right to vote to accept or reject the debtor's plan.[42] As a result of their right to vote, creditors with large claims are likely to actively negotiate the terms of a Chapter 11

[37] *See* § 10.02 Claims of Creditors, *infra*.

[38] Fed. R. Bankr. P. 2002(a).

[39] *See* Fed. R. Bankr. P. 2002(e).

[40] Bankruptcy Code § 502; Fed. R. Bankr. P. 3002(a).

[41] Fed. R. Bankr. P. 3003(b). The same is true in a Chapter 9 case involving a "municipality."

[42] *See* § 19.09 Acceptance of Plan by Holders of Claims and Interests: Disclosure and Voting, *infra*.

debtor's plan and may participate as members of an official creditors' committee.

[B] Creditors' Committees[43]

In some bankruptcy proceedings, creditors' committees may be organized to supervise the proceeding.[44] Creditors' committees are of greatest significance in Chapter 11 reorganization cases, where they may play a significant role in helping to formulate the terms of the debtor's proposed reorganization plan. However, creditors' committees are also occasionally used in complex Chapter 7 liquidation cases.[45]

The legal and other expenses of a creditors' committee (as committee members) are paid for, after approval by the court, from the debtor's estate. Thus, large creditors might choose to participate in a case through membership on a creditors' committee rather than by taking an active individual role, which would make it necessary for the creditor to pay this freight out of its own pocket.

§ 4.05 Trustees and Examiners

The appointment and role of a trustee or an examiner varies, depending on the type of bankruptcy case involved. In Chapter 7 liquidation cases, a trustee is appointed to administer or otherwise supervise the debtor's estate. In Chapter 12 family farmer and family fisherman reorganization cases and in Chapter 13 cases for the rehabilitation of an individual with regular income, a trustee is appointed but has a more limited role. In Chapter 11 reorganization cases, a trustee is appointed only rarely, but the court may appoint an independent "examiner" to inquire into the debtor's financial condition and to report the results of its investigation to creditors and the court, even though no trustee is appointed.

[A] Case Trustees

[1] Case Trustee in Chapter 7 Cases

In Chapter 7 liquidation cases, the debtor's estate is administered by a trustee.[46] Case trustees are also referred to as "panel" trustees, because

---

[43] Daniel J. Bussel, *Coalition-Building Through Bankruptcy Creditors' Committees*, 43 UCLA L. Rev. 1547 (1996); Andrew DeNatale, *The Creditors' Committee Under the Bankruptcy Code — A Primer*, 55 Am. Bankr. L.J. 43 (1981); Kenneth N. Klee & K. John Shaffer, *Creditors' Committees Under Chapter 11 of the Bankruptcy Code*, 44 S.C. L. Rev. 995 (1993); Lynn M. LoPucki, *The Debtor in Full Control — Systems Failure Under Chapter 11 of the Bankruptcy Code? (pts. 1 & 2)*, 57 Am. Bankr. L.J. 99, 247 (1983).

[44] Bankruptcy Code §§ 705, 901, 1102; *see* § 19.04 Role of Creditors and Creditors' Committees, *infra*.

[45] *See* § 17.07 Creditors' Committees, *infra*.

[46] Bankruptcy Code § 701.

they are appointed to serve in individual cases from a panel of those who have been qualified by the United States Trustee's office to serve as trustees. It is more precise to use the term "panel trustee" only when referring to those on the panel and "case trustee" when referring to the trustee in a particular case. In nearly all cases, the "interim trustee" appointed at the outset of a Chapter 7 case from among those on the panel of available trustees serves throughout the case as the permanent trustee. In rare cases, creditors may elect a different person to serve as a case trustee. It is only when creditors elect a different person to serve as trustee, or when this interim trustee loses his qualification or declines to serve, that a different person becomes the trustee.[47] Both circumstances are extraordinarily rare.

However, not all trustees serving in individual cases are appointed from the panel. In the rare circumstance that a trustee is appointed in a Chapter 11 reorganization case,[48] the trustee is not merely selected from among those who have qualified to be on the panel. Instead, the trustee is selected because of his or her experience in the industry in which the debtor participates. In Chapter 11 cases, trustees are appointed by the United States Trustee or are elected by the creditors. Although it is not necessary for a case trustee to be a lawyer,[49] most panel trustees are lawyers with substantial experience in bankruptcy cases.

A case trustee is generally responsible for locating, assembling, and liquidating the debtor's non-exempt assets.[50] Case trustees are also expected to pursue preferences, fraudulent transfers, and other avoidable transactions involving the debtor's property. Likewise, the trustee is to examine the debtor and appropriately challenge the debtor's claim of exemptions and right to a discharge of his debts.[51] Significantly, since the 2005 Amendments, case trustees may also seek to dismiss a Chapter 7 liquidation case due to "abuse."[52]

In the vast majority of consumer liquidation cases, in which no assets are available to distribute to creditors, trustees are compensated with a portion[53] of the debtor's filing fee.[54] When assets are available, the trustee's compensation is based on the size of the estate and the complexity of the trustee's duties in administering the estate.[55]

[47] Bankruptcy Code § 701(c).

[48] Bankruptcy Code § 1104; *see* § 19.03 Appointment of Trustee or Examiner, *infra*.

[49] In re Clemmons, 151 B.R. 860, 862 n.1 (Bankr. M.D. Tenn. 1993).

[50] Bankruptcy Code § 704(1); *see* § 17.05[B] Duties of the Trustee, *infra*.

[51] *See* § 17.09 Distribution of Estate Property, *infra*.

[52] *See* § 17.05 Role of a Chapter 7 Trustee, *infra*.

[53] Bankruptcy Code § 330(b)(1).

[54] 28 U.S.C.S. § 1930 (LexisNexis 2006).

[55] Bankruptcy Code § 330.

[2] Trustee in Chapter 11 Cases

There is no trustee in most Chapter 11 reorganization cases. Instead, the debtor's estate is administered by the debtor-in-possession, who has all of the same rights, powers, and duties of a trustee.[56] A trustee is appointed only for cause, which includes "fraud, dishonesty, incompetence, or gross mismanagement" of the debtor or its assets, or if the court determines that the appointment of a trustee is "in the interests of creditors."[57]

[B] Standing Trustees in Chapter 12 and 13 Cases

Rehabilitation cases under Chapters 12 and 13 utilize trustees in a way that is quite different from the way they are used in Chapter 7 cases. In rehabilitation cases, unlike liquidation proceedings, the debtor nearly always remains in possession and control of the estate's property. Most Chapter 12 family farmers remain in possession of and continue to operate their family farms.[58] Family fishermen keep possession of the boats, nets, and other gear used in the fishing operation and use it to operate the family fishing business. Similarly, Chapter 13 debtors remain in possession of their personal and business assets and use their earnings to fund payments to their creditors pursuant to a plan.[59] Because of the nature of these cases, which do not involve a liquidation and distribution of the estate's assets, there is no need for a trustee to administer the estate's assets.

Instead, debtors in these rehabilitation cases promulgate a plan that provides for the submission of regular payments to a trustee for distribution to creditors, from the debtor's future earnings.[60] The standing trustee for these cases is responsible for collecting and distributing these payments in accordance with the terms of the debtor's plan and to otherwise supervise the administration of the debtor's case. This includes reviewing the debtor's financial condition and his rehabilitation plan and objecting to confirmation of the plan, when appropriate. It might involve bringing actions to recover property that may be used to augment the debtor's estate. Moreover, the trustee has the right to object to claims filed by creditors, and if necessary, to seek dismissal or conversion of the debtor's case.

[C] Eligibility, Qualification, and Role of Standing and Case Trustees

To be eligible as either a standing trustee or a case trustee, an individual must be competent to perform the trustee's duties.[61] In a case under

56 Bankruptcy Code § 1107.

57 Bankruptcy Code § 1104(a); *see* § 19.03[D] Appointment of Trustee or Examiner, *infra*.

58 *See* § 20.03[A] Chapter 12 Debtor-in-Possession, *infra*.

59 *See* § 18.05[A] Role of a Chapter 13 Debtor, *infra*.

60 Bankruptcy Code § 1322(a)(1); *see* § 18.06[A] Submission of Sufficient Income to Fund the Plan, *infra*.

61 Bankruptcy Code § 321(a)(1).

Chapter 7, 12, or 13, the trustee must reside in or have an office in either the district in which the case is pending or a district adjacent to the district in which the case is pending.[62] A corporation can also serve as a trustee, though this is extraordinarily rare.[63] A person who has served as an examiner[64] in the case may not serve as trustee.[65] Finally, the United States Trustee may serve as a case trustee only "if necessary," such as where no one else is qualified or willing to serve.[66]

A case trustee must "qualify" to serve. To qualify, the person designated as trustee must acquire a sufficient bond,[67] must have no interests adverse to the interests of the estate or its creditors, and must be a "disinterested person."[68] Once appointed and qualified, the trustee is the representative of the debtor's estate.[69] The trustee thus has a fiduciary duty to act in the best interests of the estate. In the typical liquidation case, this means to obtain the maximum "dividend" for creditors.

[D] Examiners

In Chapter 11 cases, an examiner may be appointed as a less intrusive alternative to the appointment of a trustee.[70] When appointed, an examiner is normally charged with responsibility to investigate some or all of the debtor's financial affairs, and to report her findings to the court and to parties with an interest in the case, such as the members of a creditors' committee. An examiner might also be appointed to assist a debtor-in-possession to administer the estate or to fulfill other functions under more direct court supervision.

Although appointment of an examiner is normally within the sound discretion of the court, it is mandatory upon the request of a party in interest, or in a case involving more than $5 million in unsecured claims upon the request of the United States Trustee.[71]

As with other officials such as the trustee and professionals engaged by the trustee, debtor-in-possession, or a creditors' committee, an examiner must be a "disinterested person" within the meaning of § 101(14). Thus, the examiner may not be a creditor, an equity security holder, or an insider. In addition, he or she may not have served as a director, officer, or employee

---

[62] Bankruptcy Code § 321(a)(1).

[63] Bankruptcy Code § 321(a)(2).

[64] *See* § 19.03[D] Appointment of Trustee or Examiner, *infra*.

[65] Bankruptcy Code § 321(b).

[66] Bankruptcy Code § 321(c); *see* In re Tyrone F. Conner Corp., Inc., 140 B.R. 771 (Bankr. C.D. Cal. 1992).

[67] Bankruptcy Code § 322.

[68] *See* Bankruptcy Code § 101(14); *see generally* Chapter 21 Role of Professionals in Bankruptcy Proceedings, *infra*.

[69] Bankruptcy Code § 323(a).

[70] Bankruptcy Code § 1104(c).

[71] Bankruptcy Code § 1104(c)(2).

of the debtor within two years before the date of the petition. Likewise, the examiner may not have, either directly or indirectly, "an interest materially adverse to the interest of the estate or of any class of creditors or equity security holders."[72]

[E] The United States Trustee

The United States Trustee is another official that is involved in the bankruptcy system and may be directly involved in individual bankruptcy cases. Care must be taken to distinguish between a case or standing trustee on the one hand, and the office of the United States Trustee on the other. The former is assigned to serve in an administrative function in individual bankruptcy cases; the latter is an agency of the United States government and is part of the United States Department of Justice.

Prior to 1979, the bankruptcy courts had only a rudimentary administrative structure. Basic issues, such as the appointment and supervision of trustees and creditors' committees, were dealt with by the bankruptcy judge, sometimes rather haphazardly.[73] In this earlier era it was not uncommon for judges to wear several hats, sometimes serving as judicial officer in resolving disputes, sometimes dispensing patronage in appointing trustees, and sometimes dispensing ex parte wisdom and advice to attorneys and parties alike.[74] Although in the view of some, there is little evidence that these many roles led to outright corruption or systematic abuse, the inherent conflict in these functions was one reason for the subordinate status of bankruptcy judges and was one problem Congress was determined to address when the current Bankruptcy Code was adopted in 1978.

The congressional solution was to significantly limit the role of bankruptcy judges in case management, and to seek to limit their role to resolving disputes. At the same time, the office of the United States Trustee was created to take over the administrative functions that judges had performed.[75] Originally a pilot program for only a few districts, the United States Trustee program went nationwide under the 1986 Amendments to the Bankruptcy Code.[76] The United States Trustee for a geographic region

---

[72] Bankruptcy Code § 101(14).

[73] *See* Ted Janger, *Crystals and Mud in Bankruptcy Law: Judicial Competence and Statutory Design*, 43 Ariz. L. Rev. 559, 586–88 (2001); Harvey R. Miller, *The Changing Face of Chapter 11: A Reemergence of the Bankruptcy Judge as Producer, Director, and Sometimes Star of the Reorganization Passion Play,* 69 Am. Bankr. L.J. 431 (1995); Stephen A. Stripp, *An Analysis of the Role of the Bankruptcy Judge and the Use of Judicial Time*, 23 Seton Hall L. Rev. 1329 (1993).

[74] Harvey R. Miller, *The Changing Face of Chapter 11: A Reemergence of the Bankruptcy Judge as Producer, Director, and Sometimes Star of the Reorganization Passion Play*, 69 Am. Bankr. L.J. 431 (1995); Thomas E. Plank, *Why Bankruptcy Judges Need Not and Should Not Be Article III Judges*, 72 Am. Bankr. L.J. 567 (1998).

[75] 28 U.S.C. § 581 (2000).

[76] Michael J. Herbert, *Once More Unto the Breach, Dear Friends: The 1986 Reforms of the Reformed Bankruptcy Reform Act*, 16 Cap. U. L. Rev. 325 (1987). There is no United States Trustee in Alabama and North Carolina. There, "court administrators" perform the U.S. Trustee's functions.

is appointed by the United States Attorney General for a term of five years, subject to removal at any time, with or without cause.[77] The same act created the office of Assistant United States Trustee, who may be appointed when the public interest so requires and who serves at the pleasure of the Attorney General.[78]

The powers of the U.S. Trustee are broad. The U.S. Trustee is responsible for performing a wide variety of tasks related to bankruptcy cases. These duties include:

- appointing interim Chapter 7 trustees and establishing panels of trustees available to serve in individual bankruptcy cases;
- approving non-profit consumer counseling agencies to provide consumer counseling education programs to consumer debtors;[79]
- supervising the administration of bankruptcy cases and trustees;[80]
- monitoring and commenting on applications for attorney fees and other professional compensation;[81]
- interviewing small business debtors in chapter 11 cases;[82]
- moving to dismiss consumer Chapter 7 liquidation proceedings on the ground that the filing is a substantial abuse of the Bankruptcy Code;[83] and,
- making various reports to the Attorney General regarding administration of the bankruptcy system.[84]

The office of the United States Trustee is sometimes controversial.[85] The efficiency of having a tax-supported public official monitor cases that might otherwise be monitored by the creditors whose dollars are at stake has sometimes been questioned.[86] However, the Trustee's office has been expanded from an initial pilot program in a few districts to an almost nationwide system for governmental oversight of bankruptcy cases.[87]

---

[77] 28 U.S.C. § 581(b), (c) (2000).

[78] 28 U.S.C. § 582(a), (b) (2000).

[79] Bankruptcy Code § 111(b).

[80] 28 U.S.C.S. § 586(a)(3) (LexisNexis Supp. 2006).

[81] For a discussion of professional compensation under the Bankruptcy Code, see § 21.03 Professional Fees, *infra*.

[82] 28 U.S.C.S. § 586(a)(7) (LexisNexis Supp. 2006).

[83] *See* Bankruptcy Code § 707(b); *see* § 17.03[B] Dismissal of Consumer Cases Due to Abuse, *infra*.

[84] 28 U.S.C.S. § 586(a)(7) (LexisNexis Supp. 2006).

[85] Hon. Steven W. Rhodes, *Eight Statutory Causes of Delay and Expense in Chapter 11 Bankruptcy Cases*, 67 Am. Bankr. L.J. 287 (1993).

[86] *See* Thomas D. Buckle, *The Untapped Power of Bankruptcy's Wild Card: The United States Trustee*, 6 J. Bankr. L. & Prac. 249 (1997); Christopher W. Fros, *The Theory, Reality and Pragmatism of Corporate Governance in Bankruptcy Reorganizations*, 72 Am. Bankr. L.J. 103, 153 (1998).

[87] Bankruptcy cases in Alabama and North Carolina are not currently within the jurisdiction of the United States Trustee Program.

§ 4.06 Bankruptcy Courts and Bankruptcy Judges[88]

For most of the history of bankruptcy law in the United States, the bankruptcy system lacked its own independent court system. Its decision-makers were called "referees," rather than judges. While many of the referees were of outstanding ability, they were branded with second-class, if not third-class status. Today, the bankruptcy court is a largely autonomous adjunct of the federal district court.[89] It has its own judges, courtrooms, clerks, and dockets. Its pleadings, orders, and other documents are captioned with the designation "United States Bankruptcy Court." However, its jurisdiction is essentially derivative of the district court's jurisdiction,[90] and the district court may at any time withdraw part or all of any case from it.[91] Such withdrawals are rare, however, which reflects the practical reality that district court judges are often unfamiliar with bankruptcy and are overwhelmed with other litigation.[92]

While exercising considerable independence in nearly all bankruptcy cases, bankruptcy judges, unlike district judges, are not appointed by the President and do not have lifetime tenure. Rather, bankruptcy judges are appointed by the judges of the relevant federal Circuit Court of Appeals for terms of 14 years.[93] These appointments can be, and often are, renewed. Bankruptcy judges may be removed during the term by the circuit court judges.[94] By contrast, federal district judges, whose appointments are made pursuant to Article III of the Constitution, can only be removed by impeachment in the House of Representatives and conviction by the Senate.[95]

---

[88] Thomas E. Plank, *Why Bankruptcy Judges Need Not and Should Not Be Article III Judges*, 72 Am. Bankr. L.J. 567 (1998).

[89] *See* § 5.02[B] Bankruptcy Jurisdiction of Federal Courts, *infra*.

[90] 28 U.S.C. § 1334 (2000).

[91] 28 U.S.C. § 157(d) (2000).

[92] The relationship between district judges and bankruptcy judges is similar to that which one of your author's had with his immediate boss when they both served as church janitors. When questioned about why he never cleaned the bathrooms, the boss replied: "If I had wanted to do that, I wouldn't have hired you." Most federal district judges feel much the same way about becoming involved in bankruptcy matters.

[93] 28 U.S.C. § 152(a)(1) (2000). If a majority of the circuit judges cannot agree on an appointment, the bankruptcy judge is appointed by the chief judge of the circuit. *Id.* § 152(a)(3). In United States Territories, the district judges serve as bankruptcy judges, unless Congress authorizes the appointment of bankruptcy judges, in which case they are appointed by the Circuit Court within which the territorial district is located. *Id.* § 152(a)(4).

[94] The grounds for removal, however, are limited, and there are procedural protections:

> A bankruptcy judge may be removed during the term for which such bankruptcy judge is appointed, only for incompetence, misconduct, neglect of duty, or physical or mental disability and only by the judicial council of the circuit in which the judge's official duty station is located. Removal may not occur unless a majority of all the judges of such council concur in the order of removal.

28 U.S.C. § 152(e) (2000).

[95] Note, however, that bankruptcy judges are "judicial officers of the United States district court established under Article III of the Constitution." 28 U.S.C. § 152(a)(1) (2000).

§ 4.07 Lawyers and Other Professionals

Lawyers dominate bankruptcy proceedings. The trustee is usually a lawyer, and she is sometimes represented by another lawyer. Although pro se proceedings are permitted, debtors usually have a lawyer. Creditors' committees engage their own attorneys, paid for at the expense of the debtor's estate, and individual creditors are likely to be independently represented. In large cases, there are a great many lawyers, with correspondingly large fees; the largest business bankruptcies have fees in the tens of millions of dollars.

Other professionals may also be hired. These include accountants, actuaries, investment bankers, real estate brokers, and in rare cases, business consultants. Their fees too may be very high. Indeed, a perception exists that some cases, particularly some protracted Chapter 11 cases, serve mainly to provide lawyers with large fees at the expense of creditors.[96]

To avoid conflicts of interest that may result in harm to creditors, and in order to restrict fees that might otherwise impair the efficient administration of the debtor's estate, the retention and compensation of such professionals are regulated by the court.[97] Rules regarding the appointment and compensation of lawyers and other professionals are discussed elsewhere.[98]

---

[96] *See generally* Sol Stein, A Feast for Lawyers (1989); Lynn Lopucki, Courting Failure: How Competition for Big Cases Is Corrupting the Bankruptcy Courts (2005).

[97] Bankruptcy Code §§ 327, 328.

[98] *See* Chapter 21 Role of Professionals in Bankruptcy Cases, *infra*.

Chapter 5

Bankruptcy Procedure, Jurisdiction, and Venue

§ 5.01 Procedure in Bankruptcy Cases[1]

Bankruptcy is a body of both substantive and procedural law, with its own specialized court system. Bankruptcy courts have their own rules of procedure, jurisdiction, and venue. These rules are contained in the Federal Rules of Bankruptcy Procedure[2] and in various sections of the Federal Judicial Code.[3] The Federal Rules of Bankruptcy Procedure provide mechanisms for bankruptcy courts to handle the variety of matters necessary to the administration of bankruptcy cases. They also contain rules, modeled on the Federal Rules of Civil Procedure, that govern adversary litigation arising in bankruptcy cases.

Original and exclusive jurisdiction over bankruptcy cases is granted in the first instance to federal district courts.[4] However, each district court has exercised its statutory authority to refer bankruptcy cases to the bankruptcy court for the district.[5] District courts also have original jurisdiction over litigation that arises in connection with bankruptcy cases, but authority over these disputes is similarly referred to and routinely handled by bankruptcy courts.

As legislative courts, with judges who are neither appointed by the President nor confirmed by the Senate, bankruptcy courts are an adjunct to the federal district court and have limited constitutional powers.[6] Accordingly, the federal judicial code allocates responsibility for handling bankruptcy matters between bankruptcy courts and district courts. Although most matters relating to a bankruptcy case may be fully resolved in bankruptcy court, some must be litigated either in federal district court, or in rarer circumstances, in state court.

---

1 Stephen E. Snyder & Lawrence Ponoroff, Commercial Bankruptcy Litigation (1989); Thomas J. Salerno, Jordan A. Kroop, Bankruptcy Litigation and Practice: A Practitioner's Guide (3d ed. 2005); Michael Cook, Bankruptcy Litigation Manual (2004).

2 *See* 28 U.S.C. § 2075 (2000) (authorizing the Supreme Court to promulgate rules of bankruptcy procedure).

3 Provisions regarding the bankruptcy jurisdiction of federal district courts are at 28 U.S.C. § 1334 (2000). Authorization for bankruptcy courts to exercise this jurisdiction is contained in 28 U.S.C. § 157 (2000). Rules regarding venue of bankruptcy cases and attendant litigation are in 28 U.S.C. §§ 1408-1410, 1412.

4 28 U.S.C. § 1334 (2000); *see* § 5.02[C][1] Bankruptcy Jurisdiction of the District Court, *infra*.

5 28 U.S.C. § 157(a); *see* 5.02[C][2] Referral to the Bankruptcy Court, *infra*.

6 *See* 5.02[B] History of Bankruptcy Jurisdiction, *supra*.

In addition, the judicial code provides venue rules to determine the district in which a bankruptcy case may be filed and the district in which any litigation connected to a bankruptcy case may be pursued.[7]

Other broader procedural issues sometimes loom large in bankruptcy cases, such as the extent to which the parties may be entitled to a jury trial[8] or whether governmental parties are entitled to sovereign immunity.[9]

In considering procedural issues in bankruptcy, it is useful to distinguish between procedural rules that govern the administration of the bankruptcy case itself, and those that relate to the litigation of disputes that are ancillary to the bankruptcy case. Most disputes regarding administrative matters, such as objections to creditors' claims, motions for relief from the automatic stay, or motions seeking confirmation of a plan, are treated as "contested matters." These disputes are initiated through a motion rather than by a complaint.[10] Other matters, such as actions to recover money or property for the estate, to invalidate a lien, or regarding discharge of debts,[11] are normally handled through a lawsuit, referred to in bankruptcy cases as an "adversary proceeding."[12]

Appeals from bankruptcy court decisions are handled differently than appeals from other courts, with special "Bankruptcy Appellate Panels" hearing most appeals from decisions of bankruptcy court judges, before cases can be appealed further to the United States Circuit Courts of Appeals and on to the Supreme Court.[13]

[A] Rules of Bankruptcy Procedure[14]

Many of the procedural aspects of bankruptcy are contained in the Federal Rules of Bankruptcy Procedure and their accompanying Official Bankruptcy Forms. The Bankruptcy Rules were originally adopted in 1983 pursuant to the Supreme Court's authority to "prescribe by general rules, the forms of process, writs, pleadings, and motions, and the practice and procedure in cases under [the Bankruptcy Code]."[15] They have been amended many times. Indeed, as this book goes to press, amendments to reflect the changes made by the Bankruptcy Abuse Prevention and

---

[7] *See* § 5.03 Bankruptcy Venue, *infra*.

[8] *See* § 5.02[E] Jury Trials in Bankruptcy Court, *infra*.

[9] *See* § 5.05 Sovereign Immunity, *infra*.

[10] *See* Fed. R. Bankr. P. 9014.

[11] Fed. R. Bankr. P. 7001.

[12] *See* Fed. R. Bankr. P. 7001-7087.

[13] *See* § 5.01[C] Appellate Process in Bankruptcy Litigation, *infra*.

[14] Lawrence King, *The History and Development of the Bankruptcy Rules*, 70 Am. Bankr. L.J. 217 (1996); Kenneth N. Klee, *The Future of the Bankruptcy Rules*, 70 Am. Bankr. L.J. 277 (1996); James J. Barta, *The Impact of Technology on the Bankruptcy Rules*, 70 Am. Bankr. L.J. 287 (1996).

[15] 28 U.S.C.S. § 2075 (LexisNexis Supp. 2006). The rules are not permitted to "abridge, enlarge, or modify any substantive right." *Id.*

Consumer Protection Act of 2005 ("BAPCPA") are working their way through the rules enabling process.

These bankruptcy rules can be informally divided into three broad groups. The first group deals with administrative matters that arise in the course of various types of bankruptcy proceedings.[16] These include rules that specify the content of the debtor's petitions and schedules,[17] the appointment of various officers and professionals who will serve in bankruptcy cases,[18] claims and distributions to creditors,[19] the debtor's rights and duties,[20] bankruptcy courts and clerks,[21] and the collection and liquidation of estate assets.[22]

The second group of rules deals with adversary proceedings — litigation connected to a pending bankruptcy case.[23] These rules are modeled on the Federal Rules of Civil Procedure, which govern litigation in federal district courts. Many of the bankruptcy rules governing adversary proceedings merely incorporate the relevant district court rule by reference.[24] For example, Bankruptcy Rule 7005, which deals with "Service and Filing of Pleadings and Other Papers," simply provides: "Rule 5 Fed. R. Civ. P. applies in adversary proceedings."[25] Other adversary proceeding rules are quite different from those that apply in federal district court. Foremost among them is Bankruptcy Rule 7004, dealing with service of process. Among other variations from the Federal Rules of Civil Procedure, Bankruptcy Rule 7004(d) provides for nationwide service of process, permitting service of "the summons and complaint and all other process except a subpoena" to be made "anywhere in the United States."[26] This rule recognizes the close similarity between bankruptcy and statutory interpleader, where nationwide service is also authorized.[27]

The third group of rules deals with bankruptcy appeals[28] either to the district court or to the Bankruptcy Appellate Panel for the federal judicial circuit in which the bankruptcy court is located.[29]

---

[16] *See generally* Jennie D. Latta, *"What You Don't Know May Hurt You" — Time Limits under the Bankruptcy Code and Rules*, 28 U. Mem. L. Rev. 911 (1988).

[17] *E.g.*, Fed. R. Bankr. P. 1007.

[18] Fed. R. Bank. P. 2001-2020.

[19] Fed. R. Bankr. P. 3001-3022.

[20] Fed. R. Bank. P. 4001-4008.

[21] Fed. R. Bank. P. 5001-5011.

[22] Fed. R. Bankr. P. 6001-6010.

[23] Fed. R. Bankr. P. 7001-7087.

[24] *See generally* Christopher M. Klein, *Bankruptcy Rules Made Easy (2001): A Guide to the Federal Rules of Civil Procedure That Apply in Bankruptcy*, 75 Am. Bankr. L.J. 35 (2001).

[25] Fed. R. Bankr. P. 7005.

[26] Fed. R. Bankr. P. 4(d).

[27] *See generally* Jeffrey T. Ferriell, *The Perils of Nationwide Service of Process in a Bankruptcy Context,*, 48 Wash. & Lee L. Rev. 1199 (1991).

[28] Fed. R. Bankr. P. 8001-8020.

[29] 28 U.S.C.S. § 158 (LexisNexis Supp. 2006).

In addition, the Supreme Court has promulgated a set of official bankruptcy forms for such things as the petition, the schedules, proofs of claim, and the like.[30] However, as with all such forms, they do not have the force of law, and care must be taken to ensure that these forms comport with the requirements of the statute.

Individual federal judicial districts and even some divisions within those districts have their own set of local rules with which practicing lawyers and case trustees must be familiar. In some districts, the local rules deal with more than housekeeping matters.[31] For example, in many districts, local rules have been developed to deal with the problems of small Chapter 11 business cases. The proceeding for the rehabilitation of individuals with regular income that we now know as Chapter 13 began as little more than a local rule implemented during the Great Depression by a single bankruptcy referee in Birmingham, Alabama.[32]

Beyond these rules are innumerable local customs and traditions, sometimes dictated by the standard operating practices of local standing trustees.[33] Despite the constitutional mandate for a uniform law on bankruptcy, there are wide variations from district to district in the actual application of bankruptcy law.[34]

This book does not deal comprehensively with the Federal Rules of Bankruptcy Procedure, let alone with local rules, customs, or traditions. However, students of bankruptcy law should be aware from the outset that the academic view is a view from the top: that is, a view from the standpoint of statute and reported case law. Day-to-day bankruptcy practice down in the trenches is often significantly different.

[B] Trial Process in Bankruptcy Litigation

A bankruptcy case is a piece of litigation; indeed, bankruptcy is one of the most common forms of federal litigation.[35] However, disputes ancillary to a pending bankruptcy case may also arise. For example, even in a small consumer bankruptcy case, the trustee may object to the debtor's claim of exemptions,[36] or a creditor may seek to have a debt determined to be

---

[30] 28 U.S.C. § 2075 (2000).

[31] *See* Anne M. Burr, *Building Reform from the Bottom Up: Formulating Local Rules for Bankruptcy Court-Annexed Mediation*, 12 Ohio St. J. on Disp. Resol. 311 (1997).

[32] Timothy W. Dixon & David G. Epstein, *Where Did Chapter 13 Come From and Where Should it Go?*, 10 Am. Bankr. Inst. L. Rev. 741, 741 (2002).

[33] For example, Frank Pees, the Chapter 13 Standing Trustee in Columbus, Ohio, has long required Chapter 13 debtors to participate in a debtor education program as a condition of receiving a discharge. In 2005, this requirement was incorporated into the Bankruptcy Code.

[34] Jean Braucher, *Lawyers and Consumer Bankruptcy: One Code, Many Cultures*, 67 Am. Bankr. L.J. 501 (1993).

[35] In 2005, only about 330,000 federal civil and criminal cases were filed in federal district courts. *See* U.S. District Court — Judicial Caseload Profile, available at www.uscourts.gov/cgi-bin/cmsd2005.pl (last visited on Aug. 1, 2006). During this same time, over 2 million bankruptcy cases were filed.

[36] *See* § 12.02 Exemptions in Bankruptcy, *infra*.

non-dischargeable and thus excluded from the debtor's discharge.[37] In a reorganization case, there may be hundreds (if not thousands) of ancillary disputes, including actions to recover preferential transfers, to avoid liens, to liquidate claims against the debtor, or for relief from the automatic stay to permit a secured creditor to foreclose on its lien. If those disputes are not resolved between the parties by agreement, then they have to be tried.

Litigation that occurs within a bankruptcy case itself is conducted either as a "contested matter" or as an "adversary proceeding." Contested matters are usually brought to the court's attention through a motion.[38] Any necessary evidence can be introduced in a simple hearing or provided through documentation.

Adversary proceedings must be initiated by filing a complaint.[39] Adversary proceedings may be resolved through a simple evidentiary hearing, but sometimes they require a full-blown trial. With limited exceptions, the Federal Rules of Civil Procedure and the Federal Rules of Evidence apply. In a complex adversary proceeding, there may be extensive discovery and many witnesses. However, it is common for bankruptcy litigation to proceed more expeditiously than one might expect in a similar proceeding in another venue. Bankruptcy judges, sensitive to the risk of depleting an estate's assets, tend to be more restrictive than their federal district and state court counterparts in cases where one of the parties' solvency is not at stake. In other respects, the litigation process in bankruptcy court operates in much the same manner as in other courts, with pleadings,[40] discovery,[41] status conferences,[42] the opportunity for summary judgment,[43] and enforcement of any judgment obtained.[44] Jury trials, though rare, can occur.[45]

[C] Appellate Process in Bankruptcy Litigation[46]

Before 1994, the first level of appeal in bankruptcy litigation was to the district court, with subsequent appeals to the United States Circuit Courts of Appeal and then to the United States Supreme Court, usually by writ of certiorari. Today, the first appeal of a bankruptcy court's decision is to a three-judge "Bankruptcy Appellate Panel" or "BAP" for the circuit. However, the parties may still elect to submit the appeal to the district

---

[37] *See* § 13.03 Non-Dischargeable Debts, *infra*.

[38] Fed. R. Bankr. P. 9014.

[39] Fed. R. Bankr. P. 7003; Fed. R. Civ. P. 3.

[40] Fed. R. Bankr. P. 7003-7015.

[41] Fed R. Bankr. P. 7026-7037.

[42] Bankruptcy Code § 105(d).

[43] Fed. R. Bankr. P. 7056.

[44] Fed. R. Bankr. P. 7069.

[45] *See* § 5.02[E] Jury Trials in Bankruptcy Court, *infra*.

[46] Paul M. Baisier & David G. Epstein, *Resolving Still Unresolved Issues of Bankruptcy Law: A Fence or An Ambulance*, 69 Am. Bankr. L.J. 525 (1995); Lissa Lamkin Broome, *Bankruptcy Appeals: The Wheel Is Come Full Circle*, 69 Am. Bankr. L.J. 541 (1995).

court.[47] The Bankruptcy Appellate Panel to which the appeal is submitted must be comprised of three bankruptcy judges who are from a district other than the one in which the appeal originated.[48] This process assures that the judges who initially hear bankruptcy appeals already have considerable expertise.

As is generally true in appellate systems, appeals may ordinarily be taken only from final judgments, orders, and decrees.[49] Interlocutory orders or decrees may generally be appealed only with leave of court.[50] The principal exception to this is an order that reduces or expands the period during which a Chapter 11 debtor has the exclusive right to propose a plan of reorganization.[51]

In rare circumstances, a direct appeal may now also be made to the United States Circuit Court of Appeals, but only if the circuit court permits the usual procedure to be bypassed. This may be done only because of the absence of controlling authority regarding the issue, the public importance of the issue, the existence of conflicting decisions regarding the issue, or the likelihood that a direct appeal will materially advance the progress of the case or proceeding involved in the appeal.[52]

The final level of appellate review is to the United States Supreme Court, nearly always via a petition for a writ of certiorari. Historically, the Court has taken relatively few bankruptcy cases. But recent years have seen increased interest by the Court. The Bankruptcy Code has generated a large number of cases.[53] And, in the 2003-2004 term alone, the Court took six cases. The ambiguities created by the 2005 Amendments are likely to generate additional conflicts for the Court to resolve.

---

[47] 28 U.S.C.S. § 158(c) (LexisNexis Supp. 2006). The election to have the appeal heard by the district court must be made via "a statement of election contained in a separate writing filed within the [30 day] time [period] prescribed by 28 U.S.C. § 158(c)(1) (2000)." Fed. R. Bankr. P. 8001(e).

[48] 28 U.S.C. § 158(b)(5) (2000).

[49] 28 U.S.C. § 158(a)(1) (2000); *see* John P. Hennigan, Jr., *Toward Regularizing Appealability in Bankruptcy*, 12 Bank. Dev. J. 583 (1996); Charles J. Tabb, *Lender Preference Clauses and the Destruction of Appealability and Finality: Resolving a Chapter 11 Dilemma*, 50 Ohio St. L.J. 109 (1989).

[50] 28 U.S.C. § 158(a)(3) (2000); *see* Judy Beckner Sloan, *Appellate Jurisdiction of Interlocutory Appeals in Bankruptcy 28 U.S.C. § 158(d): A Case of Lapsus Calami.*, 40 Cath. U.L. Rev. 265 (1991).

[51] 28 U.S.C. § 158(a)(2) (2000).

[52] 28 U.S.C.S. § 157(d)(2) (LexisNexis Supp. 2006).

[53] Lee Dembart & Bruce A. Markell, *Alive at 25? A Short Review of the Supreme Court's Bankruptcy Jurisprudence, 1979-2004*, 78 Am. Bankr. L.J. 373 (2004); Robert M. Lawless, *Legisprudence Through a Bankruptcy Lens: A Study in the Supreme Court's Bankruptcy Cases*, 47 Syracuse L. Rev. 1 (1996); Robert M. Lawless & Dylan Lager Murray, *An Empirical Analysis of Bankruptcy Certiorari*, 62 Mo. L. Rev. 101 (1997); Charles Jordan Tabb & Robert M. Lawless, *Of Commas, Gerunds, and Conjunctions: The Bankruptcy Jurisprudence of the Rehnquist Court*, 42 Syracuse L. Rev. 823 (1991).

§ 5.02 Bankruptcy Jurisdiction of Federal Courts[54]

The subject matter jurisdiction of bankruptcy courts has long been one of the most vexing problems of bankruptcy law. For generations, lawyers, judges, and academics (not to mention bewildered law students) have complained about jurisdictional rules that are at best prolix and complicated.

[A] Article I Status of Bankruptcy Judges

Some serious questions about bankruptcy jurisdiction persist and have never been fully addressed. Most of these problems can be traced to Congress' unwillingness to grant life-tenure to bankruptcy judges.[55] The United States Constitution permits two kinds of federal judges: full Article III judges, who are appointed by the President and confirmed by the Senate for life, and more limited Article I or "legislative" judges, who serve either at will or, more commonly, for a term of years. Bankruptcy judges are Article I judges, appointed by the Judicial Council for each Circuit for fourteen year terms.[56]

As Article I judges, bankruptcy judges' powers are limited.[57] Article III district and circuit court judges are vested with authority to exercise the judicial power of the United States. This permits them to exercise far broader jurisdiction than Article I judges who sit on so-called Article I "legislative courts." This affects bankruptcy, because bankruptcy requires a broader exercise of jurisdiction than the Constitution affords to Article I judges. Someone must have those broad powers; otherwise, the bankruptcy system is unworkable. The conflict between the need for broad powers and the reluctance to grant them has led to a sometimes byzantine set of jurisdictional rules that may still suffer from some constitutional defects.[58]

---

[54] Ralph Brubaker, *On the Nature of Federal Bankruptcy Jurisdiction: A General Statutory and Constitutional Theory*, 41 Wm. & Mary L. Rev. 743 (2000); Ralph Brubaker, *One Hundred Years of Federal Bankruptcy Law and Still Clinging to an In Rem Model of Bankruptcy Jurisdiction*, 15 Bankr. Dev. J. 261 (1999).

[55] *Compare* Susan Block-Lieb, *The Costs of a Non-Article III Bankruptcy Court System*, 72 Am. Bank. L.J. 529 (1998), *with* Thomas E. Plank, *Why Bankruptcy Judges Need Not and Should Not Be Article III Judges*, 72 Am. Bankr. L.J. 567 (1998).

[56] 28 U.S.C. § 152 (2000).

[57] James E. Pfander, *Article I Tribunals, Article III Courts, and the Judicial Power of the United States,* 118 Harv. L. Rev. 643 (2004); *see also* Alan M. Ahern, *The Limited Scope of Implied Powers of a Bankruptcy Judge: A Statutory Court of Bankruptcy, Not a Court of Equity*, 79 Am. Bank. L.J. 1 (2005).

[58] Jeffrey T. Ferriell, *Constitutionality of the Bankruptcy Amendments and Federal Judgeship Act of 1984*, 63 Am. Bankr. L.J. 109 (1989).

[B] History of Bankruptcy Jurisdiction[59]

[1] The Bankruptcy Act

Under the Bankruptcy Act of 1898, bankruptcy jurisdiction was exercised in the name of the federal district courts whose judges had full Article III authority. In practice, bankruptcy referees working under the loose supervision of district courts made most routine decisions. The bankruptcy court's power depended to a large extent on the distinction between "summary" and "plenary" jurisdiction,[60] a distinction not entirely unlike the current division between "core" and "non-core" proceedings, discussed below.[61]

[2] The Bankruptcy Reform Act of 1978

The cumbersome distinction between summary and plenary jurisdiction was eliminated in 1978 when the current Bankruptcy Code replaced the Bankruptcy Act. Under the jurisdictional scheme contained in the 1978 Bankruptcy Reform Act, jurisdictional authority over all matters connected with a bankruptcy case was conferred on Article I bankruptcy courts. They were provided with direct jurisdiction over bankruptcy cases and over all civil proceedings connected to a bankruptcy case, whether they "arose under" the Bankruptcy Code, "arose in" a bankruptcy case, or were only "related to" a pending bankruptcy case. The district court's authority was largely limited to hearing appeals from bankruptcy judges' decisions.

[3] The *Marathon Pipeline* Decision[62]

Although the 1978 Bankruptcy Code expanded bankruptcy judges' authority, their constitutional status as Article I legislative judges remained the same as it had been under the Act. As a result, the broad jurisdictional grant included in the 1978 Bankruptcy Reform Act, that was once heralded as one of the great advances in bankruptcy law, survived only until 1982, when it was struck down by the Supreme Court in *Northern Pipeline Construction Co. v. Marathon Pipe Line Co.*[63]

The dispute in *Marathon Pipeline* arose out of a contract between Northern Pipeline Construction Company and Marathon Pipe Line Co. When

---

[59] *See* Ralph Brubaker, *One Hundred Years of Federal Bankruptcy Law and Still Clinging to an In Redm Model of Bankruptcy Jurisdiction*, 15 Bankr. Dev. J. 261 (1999); Jeffrey T. Ferriell, *The Constitutionality of the Bankruptcy Amendments and Federal Judgeship Act of 1984*, 63 Am. Bankr. L.J. 109, 113–21 (1989); Robert G. Skelton & Donald F. Harris, *Bankruptcy Jurisdiction and Jury Trials: The Constitutional Nightmare Continues*, 8 Bankr. Dev. J. 469, 473–76 (1991).

[60] *See* James E. Pfander, *Article I Tribunals, Article III Courts, and the Judicial Power of the United States*, 118 Harv. L. Rev. 643, 719–21 (2004).

[61] *See* Jeffrey T. Ferriell, *The Constitutionality of the Bankruptcy Amendments and Federal Judgeship Act of 1984*, 63 Am. Bankr. L.J. 109, 113–16 (1989).

[62] Geraldine Mund, *A Look Behind the Ruling: The Supreme Court and the Unconstitutionality of the Bankruptcy Act of 1978*, 78 Am. Bankr. L.J. 401 (2004); Martin H. Redish, *Legislative Courts, Administrative Agencies, and the* Northern Pipeline *Decision*, 1983 Duke L.J. 197.

[63] 458 U.S. 50 (1982), *judgment stayed*, 459 U.S. 813 (1982).

the action was filed, Northern Pipeline Construction was a Chapter 11 debtor-in-possession.[64] The action was not based on any provision of the Bankruptcy Code; it was a contract dispute based on state contract law. The defendant sought to dismiss the suit, alleging that the 1978 Reform Act unconstitutionally conferred jurisdiction over the matter to the bankruptcy court in violation of Article III of the Constitution.

The United States Supreme Court agreed with the defendant and struck down the statutory grant of jurisdiction as unconstitutional. By giving bankruptcy courts jurisdiction over disputes regarding private rights, that did not directly involve issues in the bankruptcy case, Congress had improperly granted a portion of the "judicial power" of the United States to an Article I court. The result was so unexpected and had such a potentially devastating effect on the nation's bankruptcy system that the Court took the unusual step of staying the effect of its decision for several months to give Congress the opportunity to enact corrective legislation.[65]

[4] The Emergency Rule

The Judicial Council of the United States responded to the crisis by immediately promulgating an Emergency Rule for adoption by district courts. The Rule divided jurisdiction between district courts and bankruptcy courts.[66] Although the Judicial Council's authority to implement this rule was in serious doubt, reluctance to bring the entire bankruptcy court system to a grinding halt discouraged challenges to the Rule's validity.[67] Congress found itself lacking the political will to enact legislation to resolve the problem, and bankruptcy courts operated under this Emergency Rule for nearly two years.

[5] The Bankruptcy Amendments and Federal Judgeship Act of 1984 (BAFJA)[68]

Congress finally acted in 1984, with the Bankruptcy Amendments and Federal Judgeship Act,[69] commonly known as "BAFJA." BAFJA's solution,

[64] *See* § 1.05[B][16] Debtor in Possession, *supra.*

[65] When Congress failed to act by the initial October 4, 1982 deadline, the Court extended the stay until midnight Christmas Eve, 1982. Bankruptcy attorneys involved in the case, one of whom was the author of the first edition of this book, initially thought that the first report they heard of the Court's decision was a joke. Michael J. Herbert, Understanding Bankruptcy 68 n.4 (1st ed. 1994).

[66] *See* Vern Countryman, *Scrambling to Define Bankruptcy Jurisdiction: The Chief Justice, the Judicial Conference, and the Legislative Process*, 22 Harv. J. on Legis. 1 (1985).

[67] *See generally* Vern Countryman, *Emergency Rule Compounds Emergency,* 57 Am. Bankr. L.J. 1 (1983); Jeffrey T. Ferriell, *Constitutionality of the Bankruptcy Amendments and Federal Judgeship Act of 1984*, 63 Am. Bankr. L.J. 109 (1989); Lawrence P. King, *The Unmaking of a Bankruptcy Court: Aftermath of* Northern Pipeline v. Marathon, 40 Wash. & Lee L. Rev. 99 (1983).

[68] Walter J Taggart, *The New Bankruptcy Court System*, 59 Am. Bank. L.J. 231 (1985).

[69] The Bankruptcy Amendments and Federal Judgeship Act of 1984, Pub. L. 98-353, 98 Stat. 341 (1984).

which was modeled on the Emergency Rule, is complicated, controversial, and perhaps constitutionally suspect. Its rules are reminiscent of the older arcane distinction between summary and plenary jurisdiction, but with added elements designed to buttress the constitutionality of the new regime. BAFJA's scheme, discussed below, remains in effect today.

[C] Bankruptcy Jurisdiction of Federal District Courts

The Bankruptcy Amendments and Federal Judgeship Act of 1984 circumvented *Marathon Pipeline* by assigning jurisdiction over all bankruptcy matters to district courts,[70] and permitting them to refer most bankruptcy matters to the bankruptcy courts.[71] This device is propped up by other provisions that circumscribe the power of bankruptcy judges to resolve some disputes and that permit the district court to withdraw any matter at any time from the bankruptcy court's docket. These mechanisms place bankruptcy courts under the technical supervision of the district court, even though district judges only rarely act to exercise their supervisory authority.[72]

[1] Bankruptcy Jurisdiction of the District Court

Bankruptcy jurisdiction is vested in federal district courts. The jurisdictional grant is divided into six categories:

- "cases under Title 11";[73]
- "civil proceedings arising under Title 11";[74]
- "civil proceedings . . . arising in . . . cases under Title 11";[75]
- "civil proceedings . . . related to cases under Title 11";[76]
- "property . . . of the debtor";[77] and
- "property of the estate."[78]

The first four categories are divided between the case itself and specific litigation that might occur in connection with a bankruptcy case. The final two categories give the court "in rem" jurisdiction over property involved in the case.

[70] 28 U.S.C. § 1334 (2000).

[71] 28 U.S.C. § 157(a) (2000).

[72] One notable exception is the general withdrawal of the reference by the District of Delaware. *See* Order of the United States Court for the District of Delaware (Jan. 23, 1997) (Farnan, C.J.) (withdrawing reference from Delaware bankruptcy courts); Leif Clark, *Crossing the Delaware*, Am. Bankr. Inst. J., March, 1997, at 34–35.

[73] 28 U.S.C. § 1334(a) (2000).

[74] 28 U.S.C. § 1334(b) (2000).

[75] 28 U.S.C. § 1334(b) (2000).

[76] 28 U.S.C. § 1334(b) (2000).

[77] 28 U.S.C. § 1334(e) (2000).

[78] 28 U.S.C. § 1334(e) (2000).

The first category gives district courts both "original and exclusive jurisdiction" over bankruptcy cases themselves. Accordingly, bankruptcy petitions may not be filed in state courts or in other federal courts.

The next three categories give the district court original (but not exclusive) jurisdiction over other civil litigation that is connected to a bankruptcy case. On the face of it, this means that civil proceedings involving the debtor may fall within the jurisdiction of a number of other courts. As a practical matter, however, the "automatic stay" of § 362 effectively prevents parties from bringing matters before other courts unless allowed to do so by the bankruptcy court where the case is pending.[79] Moreover, as explained below, most of the jurisdiction given to district courts is routinely exercised by bankruptcy courts, pursuant to referral by the district court.

[2] Referral to the Bankruptcy Court

With very few exceptions, district courts do not assume direct authority over bankruptcy cases or civil proceedings connected to bankruptcy cases. Instead, bankruptcy matters are routinely delegated to the bankruptcy court pursuant to a blanket order, entered in each district, generally referring nearly all matters within the district court's bankruptcy jurisdiction to the bankruptcy court.[80] Such a general order of reference moves bankruptcy cases from the life tenured Article III district court judges to their Article I subordinates in the bankruptcy court for the district.

The district court retains the power to withdraw the reference, in whole or in part, either on its own motion or the motion of any party.[81] However, the court's discretionary power to withdraw the reference is, as noted above, rarely exercised.[82]

Federal district court judges are occasionally required to withdraw the reference if the determination of a particular matter requires interpretation of a federal statute, other than the Bankruptcy Code, that regulates interstate commerce.[83] The relevant portion of the Judicial Code provides: "The district court shall, on timely motion of a party, so withdraw a proceeding if the court determines that resolution of the proceeding requires

[79] *See* Chapter 8, The Automatic Stay, *infra.*

[80] 28 U.S.C. § 157(a) provides: "Each district court may provide that any or all cases under title 11 and any or all proceedings arising under title 11 or arising in or related to a case under title 11 shall be referred to the bankruptcy judge for the district." All federal district courts took advantage of this language and entered a general order of reference as soon as possible after the ink used to sign the legislation granting them this authority was dry.

[81] 28 U.S.C. § 157(d) (2000).

[82] One dramatic example of withdrawal of the reference occurred in *In re A.H. Robbins, Inc.* which involved the reorganization of a firm with hundreds of thousands of potential product liability claims arising from a defective intrauterine birth control device, the Dalkon Shield. The district judge, who was a long-time personal acquaintance of Mr. Robbins, CEO of the debtor, withdrew the reference of the entire case. In re A.H. Robbins Co., Inc., 88 B.R. 742 (1988).

[83] 28 U.S.C. § 157(d) (2000); *see* Erich D. Anderson, Comment, *Closing the Escape Hatch in the Mandatory Withdrawal Provision of 28 U.S.C. § 157(d)*, 36 UCLA L. Rev. 417 (1988).

consideration of both [the Bankruptcy Code] and other laws of the United States regulating organizations or activities affecting interstate commerce."[84] This language has been applied to mandate withdrawal of the reference of actions involving federal antitrust,[85] securities fraud,[86] RICO,[87] and even tax disputes.[88] Despite the apparently clear import of the statutory language, most courts have ruled that withdrawal is mandatory if the dispute involves "substantial and material consideration" of federal law other than the Bankruptcy Code, even though the case may also require consideration of a Bankruptcy Code issue.[89]

Thus, either under the discretionary or mandatory withdrawal provisions, the district court retains nominal power over all aspects of a bankruptcy case despite the referral to the bankruptcy court. Nonetheless, it is almost always bankruptcy judges who exercise the district court's bankruptcy jurisdiction.[90]

[3] Authority of the Bankruptcy Court Over "Bankruptcy Cases" and "Core Proceedings"[91]

The Judicial Code provides: "Bankruptcy judges may *hear and determine* all cases under title 11 and all *core proceedings* arising under title 11, or arising in a case under title 11 . . . subject to [appellate review]."[92] Thus, the bankruptcy court has full authority over bankruptcy cases and all "core proceedings" that arise either under title 11 or in a case under title 11.[93] The court's authority over other disputes that are not "core proceedings" is, as explained in the next section, more limited.

Core proceedings[94] include most routine matters likely to occur in a bankruptcy case, specifically including those regarding:

1. administration of the estate;

---

[84] 28 U.S.C. § 157(d) (2000).

[85] *E.g.*, Michigan Milk Producers Ass'n v. Hunter, 46 B.R. 214 (N.D. Ohio 1985).

[86] Contemporary Lithographers, Inc. v. Hibbert (In re Contemporary Lithographers, Inc.), 127 B.R. 122 (N.D.N.C. 1991).

[87] In re Vicars Ins. Agency, Inc., 96 F.3d 949 (7th Cir. 1996).

[88] United States v. G. Holdings, Inc. (In re G. Holdings, Inc.), 295 B.R. 222 (D.N.J. 2003).

[89] *E.g.*, In re Vicars Ins. Agency, Inc., 96 F.3d 949 (7th Cir. 1996).

[90] Withdrawal seems most appropriate when a jury trial is required. *E.g.*, Lars, Inc. v. Taber Partners (In re Lars, Inc.), 290 B.R. 467 (D.P.R. 2003).

[91] Jeffrey T. Ferriell, *Core Proceedings in Bankruptcy Court*, 56 UMKC L. Rev. 47 (1987); Thomas S. Marrion, *Core Proceedings and the "New" Bankruptcy Jurisdiction*, 35 DePaul L. Rev. 675 (1986).

[92] 28 U.S.C. § 157(b)(1) (2000) (emphasis added).

[93] 28 U.S.C. § 157(b)(1) (2000); *see generally* Wood v. Wood (In re Wood), 825 F.2d 90 (5th Cir. 1987). It is entirely unclear what is supposed to happen in a matter that is not a "core proceeding" that "arises under" or "arises in" a bankruptcy case, or whether it is even theoretically possible for such a thing to exist.

[94] *See* 11 U.S.C. § 157(b) (2000).

2. allowance of claims;
3. counterclaims against persons who file claims against the estate;
4. turnover of estate property;
5. the use, sale, or lease of estate property;
6. the trustee's avoiding powers;
7. dischargeability of debts and objections to discharge;
8. the validity, extent, and priority of liens;
9. the automatic stay; and
10. confirmation of plans.

Roughly speaking, a core proceeding is one that fundamentally involves bankruptcy law and the management of the debtor's estate; other law may be involved, but only secondarily.

Explicitly excluded from the bankruptcy court's jurisdiction over "core proceedings" are "personal injury and wrongful death claims against the debtor's estate."[95] Absent the consent of the parties, such claims must be tried by the district court, unless it abstains and permits them to be heard by an appropriate state court. This provision is particularly important in cases involving mass tort claims, such as those involving producers of asbestos or other harmful consumer products which have caused injuries to a large number of people.[96]

[4] Limited Authority of the Bankruptcy Court Over Matters Merely Related to a Bankruptcy Case

Conspicuously missing from the list of matters fully delegated to the bankruptcy court as "core proceedings" are "civil proceedings *related to* a case under title 11," which are included within the reference to the bankruptcy court, but over which the bankruptcy court has less authority.[97]

A proceeding is related to a bankruptcy case if it "could conceivably have any effect on the estate being administered in bankruptcy."[98] Thus, the dispute need not involve a claim against either the debtor or the debtor's property. It is enough if the outcome of the matter "could alter the debtor's rights, liabilities, options, or freedom of action (either positively or negatively), and in any way impacts upon the handling and administration of the bankrupt estate."[99]

Examples of actions that are not core proceedings that are merely related to a bankruptcy case are those brought by the estate to collect pre-petition

[95] 28 U.S.C. § 157(c)(2)(B) (2000).

[96] *See* § 23.02 Mass Torts, *infra*.

[97] 11 U.S.C. § 157(c)(1) (2000) (emphasis added).

[98] Pacor, Inc. v. Higgins, 743 F.2d 984, 994 (3d Cir. 1984).

[99] Pacor, Inc. v. Higgins, 743 F.2d 984, 994 (3d Cir. 1984); *see also* Celotex Corp. v. Edwards, 514 U.S. 300, 308 n.6 (1994) (citing *Pacor* with approval).

accounts receivable,[100] the debtor's pre-petition personal injury claims against third-parties, and other actions based on private rights, similar to those involved in *Marathon Pipeline,* that arise completely under state law.

Cases which are merely "related to" a bankruptcy case or that are otherwise not within the definition of "core proceedings" may be *heard* by the bankruptcy court, but not *finally determined* without the participation of a district judge. Unless the parties consent to the bankruptcy court's entry of a final order, the bankruptcy judge is permitted to conduct any necessary evidentiary hearing and prepare a set of proposed findings of fact and conclusions of law for de novo review by the district court.[101] The district judge can either adopt or reject the bankruptcy judge's proposed ruling. In most cases, the district judge is likely to agree with the bankruptcy judge's recommended ruling.

Despite this limitation on the bankruptcy judge's authority, if no one makes a "timely and specific" objection to the bankruptcy judge's proposed ruling, the district judge may approve the bankruptcy judge's findings without reviewing them. Moreover, the parties may give their consent to the bankruptcy court's authority to finally resolve these matters.[102]

[5] Disputes Beyond the Court's Bankruptcy Jurisdiction

The district and bankruptcy court's limited authority over disputes that are "related to" a bankruptcy case raises a further issue regarding the outside limits of the court's jurisdiction. Disputes that are not related to a bankruptcy case are outside the court's bankruptcy jurisdiction. The usual test to determine whether a dispute is related to a bankruptcy case is whether "the outcome could alter the debtor's rights, liabilities, options, or freedom of action (either positively or negatively) and which in a way impacts upon the handling and administration of the bankruptcy estate."[103] The United States Supreme Court has ruled that this might include "suits between third parties if the outcome will have an effect on the bankruptcy estate."[104]

---

[100] Orion Pictures Corp. v. Showtime Networks, Inc. (In re Orion Pictures Corp.), 4 F.3d 1095, 1102 (2d Cir. 1993); *see generally* Jeffrey T. Ferriell, *Actions to Collect Accounts Receivable in Bankruptcy Court*, 26 Houston L. Rev. 603 (1989).

[101] Orion Pictures Corp. v. Showtime Networks, Inc. (In re Orion Pictures Corp.), 4 F.3d 1095, 1102, (2d Cir. 1993).

[102] 28 U.S.C. § 157(c)(2) (2000).

[103] Pacor v. Higgins (In re Pacor), 743 F.2d 987, 994 (1984).

[104] Celotex v. Edwards (In re Celotex), 514 U.S. 300, 307 n. 5 (1995); *see also* In re Dow Corning Corp., 86 F.3d 482 (1996).

[6] Jurisdiction over Jurisdictional Issues

As is generally true with matters of jurisdiction, the bankruptcy court has authority to make an initial determination regarding its own authority to handle the dispute. On the judge's own motion or on the motion of a party, the bankruptcy judge can determine whether a proceeding is a core proceeding.

[D] Abstention

Even when the district court has jurisdiction over a dispute, the bankruptcy or district court may elect to abstain from exercising its power over the action. If the court abstains, the matter will probably be resolved in state court. As with most matters within the district court's jurisdiction, abstention determinations are usually made by the bankruptcy court pursuant to the district court's referral of bankruptcy matters.

[1] Permissive Abstention[105]

The district court (and thus the bankruptcy court) is expressly authorized to permissively abstain from hearing civil proceedings that "arise under," "arise in," or are "related to" a bankruptcy case. The court is permitted to abstain whenever abstention is "in the interest of justice, or in the interest of comity with State courts, or [out of] respect for State law."[106] Of course, this authority does not extend to the court's jurisdiction over a bankruptcy case itself, over which the court has exclusive jurisdiction.

Permissive abstention is quite rare. However, it commonly occurs with respect to family law matters that might arise in the course of a bankruptcy case such as divorce, dissolution, custody, or support.[107] In *In re Fussell,*[108] the bankruptcy court even abstained from determining whether the debtor's post-divorce, pre-petition credit card obligations were in the nature of alimony, support, or maintenance, and thus non-dischargeable under the Bankruptcy Code, because of the strong connection between the bankruptcy dischargeability issue and questions of state law arising from the debtor's divorce decree. On the other hand, in *In re Causa,*[109] the court decided that it need not abstain from resolving questions of the "equitable distribution" of marital assets between the debtor and his spouse, even though these questions involved issues of domestic relations law that are normally relegated to state court.

Likewise, it might be appropriate for the court to abstain from resolving disputes "involving unsettled questions of state property law."[110]

---

[105] Andrew S. Atkin, Comment, *Permissive Withdrawal of Bankruptcy Proceedings under 28 U.S.C. Section 157(d)*, 11 Bankr. Dev. J. 447 (1995).

[106] 28 U.S.C. § 1334(c)(1) (2000).

[107] *See, e.g.*, In re Kriss, 217 B.R. 147 (Bankr. S.D.N.Y. 1998).

[108] 303 B.R. 539 (Bankr. S.D. Ga. 2003).

[109] 93 B.R. 409 (Bankr. E.D. Pa. 1988).

[110] *See* Thompson v. Magnolia Petroleum, 309 U.S. 478, 484 (1940); Orion Pictures Corp. v. Showtime Networks, Inc. (In re Orion Pictures Corp.), 4 F.3d 1095 (2d Cir. 1993).

Bankruptcy cases frequently involve questions of state property law, and if the underlying state property law is unclear, it makes sense for the dispute to be handled by an appropriate state tribunal. For example, in *Koken v. Reliance Group Holdings, Inc.*,[111] the court abstained from resolving a matter dealing partially with routine state contract and property law issues because it also required an intricate interpretation of the Pennsylvania Insurance Company Holding Act. And in *Allied Signal Recovery Trust v. Allied Signal, Inc.*,[112] the court determined abstention was appropriate in an action that, similar to the dispute in *Marathon Pipeline*, involved a debtor's cause of action based on state law but also involved related claims arising under the Bankruptcy Code.

[2] Mandatory Abstention

In limited circumstances, abstention is mandatory. The court is required to abstain when *all* of the following circumstances apply:

1. the proceeding is based on a state law claim or a state law cause of action;
2. the claim is merely "related to" a bankruptcy case;
3. there are no other grounds for federal jurisdiction;
4. an action has already been commenced in state court; and
5. the state court action can be timely adjudicated.[113]

Thus, mandatory abstention never applies to civil proceedings "arising under" the Bankruptcy Code or "arising in" a bankruptcy case. The dispute must be at the outside fringe of bankruptcy jurisdiction, similar to the dispute in *Marathon Pipeline*, where exercise of jurisdiction by the bankruptcy court was held unconstitutional.[114]

Further, for abstention to be mandatory, there must be no independent ground for the district court to assert federal jurisdiction. If the proceeding is based on a federal antitrust claim, abstention is not mandatory because the case falls within the court's federal question jurisdiction.[115] Similarly, if the parties are from different states and the amount in controversy is sufficient, abstention is not mandatory because the case is within the district court's diversity jurisdiction.[116] Of course, in these cases, the court may nevertheless abstain pursuant to its permissive abstention authority, or the district court may withdraw the reference and resolve the matter without the assistance of the bankruptcy court.

---

[111] Koken v. Reliance Group Holdings, Inc. (In re Reliance Group Holdings, Inc.), 273 B.R. 374, 384 (Bankr. E.D. Pa. 2002).

[112] 298 F.3d 263 (3d Cir. 2002).

[113] 28 U.S.C. § 1334(c) (2000).

[114] *See* § 5.02[B][3] The *Marathon Pipeline* Decision, *supra*.

[115] 28 U.S.C. § 1331 (2000). Here, the district court may be required to withdraw the reference of the matter to the bankruptcy court and handle the case itself. *See* § 5.02[C][2] Referral to the Bankruptcy Court, *supra*.

[116] 28 U.S.C. § 1332 (2000).

Finally, most courts have interpreted Judicial Code § 1334(c)(2) to mandate abstention only when a state court proceeding is underway.[117] Under this interpretation, abstention is not mandated where a state court proceeding could be commenced and would expeditiously resolve the dispute, but where a state action is not already pending. Likewise, abstention is not mandated simply because a state proceeding is already pending, if its disposition would significantly delay the liquidation or reorganization of the estate.[118]

There is one significant exception to the mandatory abstention rule: personal injury claims against the estate. Actions for "the liquidation or estimation of a contingent or unliquidated personal injury tort or wrongful death claims against the estate" are expressly excluded from the scope of core proceedings.[119] This exclusion might lead to cases that otherwise satisfy the elements for mandatory abstention, but these are explicitly excluded from the disputes from which the court must abstain.[120]

However, because they are excluded from the scope of core proceedings, the bankruptcy court may not hear and finally determine these claims on its own. Absent the consent of the parties, the most it can do is conduct a hearing and submit proposed findings to the district court for de novo review. Thus, if the debtor is in bankruptcy because it ruined the health of thousands of women to whom it sold a defective contraceptive device, the central issues of the case are not core proceedings[121] and may not be resolved by the bankruptcy court without the parties' consent. But, because abstention is not mandatory, they need not be sent to state courts for resolution.[122] Fortunately for the dockets of district judges, the matters may be heard by the bankruptcy court whose proposed findings may be submitted to the district court for review and final determination. In this regard, the bankruptcy courts function much like federal magistrates in other contexts.

A further venue provision states that personal injury tort and wrongful death claims are to be tried either in the district court in the district where bankruptcy case is pending or in the district court where the claim arose.[123]

---

117 *E.g.*, Walker v. Bryans (In re Walker), 224 B.R. 239 (Bankr. M.D. Ga. 1998); West Coast Video Enter. v. Owens (In re W. Coast Video Enter., Inc.), 145 B.R. 484 (Bankr. E.D. Pa. 1992).

118 28 U.S.C. § 1334(c)(2) (2000).

119 28 U.S.C. § 157(b)(2)(B) (2000).

120 28 U.S.C. § 157(b)(4) (2000).

121 *See* Georgene Vairo, *Mass Torts Bankruptcies: The Who, the Why and the How*, 78 Am. Bankr. L.J. 93 (2004).

122 These claims may still be the subject of voluntary abstention. The Code does not prohibit them from being tried in state court. Moreover, the rule does not apply to tort claims brought by the estate against someone else; it only applies to tort claims brought by a creditor against the estate. Thus, a personal injury claim by the estate may be subject to mandatory abstention. Although there is ambiguity in the wording of the relevant statutory provisions, it appears that § 157(b)(5), which requires personal injury cases to be tried in district court, applies only if the district court has not voluntarily abstained from hearing the proceeding.

123 28 U.S.C. § 157(b)(5) (2000).

Thus, the district court in which the bankruptcy is pending determines which court is likely to hear such cases.

[3] Appeal of Abstention Determinations

A district court's decision to abstain from a case is virtually unreviewable by a higher court. Judicial Code § 1334(d) specifies, "[a]ny decision to abstain or not to abstain made under [§ 1334(c)] . . . is not reviewable by appeal or otherwise by the court of appeals . . . or by the Supreme Court of the United States." Thus, a bankruptcy judge's decision regarding abstention is appealable to the district court or to the appropriate bankruptcy appellate panel, but not beyond.[124] The only exception to this broad rule permits appeal of a decision *not* to abstain under the mandatory abstention rule.[125] Despite the seemingly unequivocal language of § 1334(d) on this point, some courts have permitted limited review of all mandatory abstention decisions, at least for the purposes of ensuring that the statutory requirements for mandatory abstention have been met.[126]

[E] Jury Trials in Bankruptcy Litigation[127]

For many years, civil proceedings arising in the course of a bankruptcy case were regarded as equitable matters in which the parties had no right to a jury.[128] A few courts took the view that whether a right to a jury trial existed depended on whether the particular matter involved was legal or equitable, with a right to a jury attaching in proceedings that were derived from the common law rather than from equity.[129]

In *Granfinanciera, S.A. v. Nordberg*, the United States Supreme Court resolved these conflicting approaches and held that parties to a common law dispute were entitled to a jury trial, unless the right was waived. The Court said "a person who has not submitted a claim against a bankruptcy estate . . . [is entitled] to a jury trial when sued by the trustee in bankruptcy to recover an allegedly fraudulent monetary transfer."[130] The

[124] *See* § 5.01[C] Appellate Process in Bankruptcy Litigation, *supra*.

[125] 28 U.S.C. § 1334(d) (2000).

[126] *E.g.*, S.G. Phillips Constructors, Inc. v. City of Burlington (In re S.G. Phillips Constructors, Inc.), 45 F.3d 702 (2d Cir. 1995); *see also* Lindsey v. Dow Chem. Co. (In re Dow Corning Corp.), 113 F.3d 565, 569 (6th Cir. 1997) (permitting mandamus).

[127] S. Elizabeth Gibson, *Jury Trials in Bankruptcy: Obeying the Commands of Article III and the Seventh Amendment*, 72 Minn. L. Rev. 967 (1988); John C. McCoid, II, *Right to Jury Trial in Bankruptcy:* Granfinanciera, S.A. v. Nordberg, 65 Am. Bankr. L.J. 15, 28–37 (1991); G. Ray Warner, Katchen *Up in Bankruptcy: The New Jury Trial Right*, 63 Am. Bankr. L.J. 1 (1989); Symposium, *Jury Trials in Bankruptcy Courts*, 65 Am. Bankr. L.J. 1 (1991).

[128] Katchen v. Landy, 382 U.S. 323, 336–37 (1966) ("as the [summary] proceedings of bankruptcy courts are inherently proceedings in equity, there is no Seventh Amendment right to a jury trial."); *see* In re Global Int'l Airways Corp., 81 B.R. 541, 543–44 (W.D. Mo. 1988).

[129] American Universal Ins. Co. v. Pugh, 821 F.2d 1352 (9th Cir. 1987); *see* In re Global Int'l Airways Corp., 81 B.R. 541, 543–44 (W.D. Mo. 1988) (noting conflict in the authorities).

[130] Granfinanciera, S.A. v. Nordberg, 492 U.S. 33, 36 (1989).

Granfinanciera decision placed the question of the statutory authority of bankruptcy courts to conduct jury trials, and the constitutional sufficiency of those trials, squarely on the table.[131]

When *Granfinanciera* was decided, it was not clear that bankruptcy courts had statutory authority to conduct jury trials. Congress resolved this aspect of the problem in 1994 with legislation that specified:

> If the right to a jury trial applies in a proceeding that may be heard under this section by a bankruptcy judge, the bankruptcy judge may conduct the jury trial if specially designated to exercise such jurisdiction by the district court and with the express consent of all the parties.[132]

Because the bankruptcy judge may not resolve disputes in non-core proceedings, the bankruptcy court still lacks statutory authority to conduct a jury trial in such a case.[133]

The requirement of obtaining the parties' consent before the bankruptcy judge may preside over a jury trial would seem to put the constitutional issue aside most of the time. However, the theoretical question of a bankruptcy judge's constitutional authority to conduct jury trials in the absence of the parties' consent persists.

In many cases, a party who otherwise might prefer to make a jury demand will have waived its right to a jury. After *Granfinanciera*, the Supreme Court ruled that filing a claim against the estate amounts to a waiver of the right to a jury trial, not only with respect to the creditor's right to receive a distribution from the estate on account of its claim, but also with respect to any counterclaim the estate may have against the creditor that arises from the same circumstances as those that gave rise to the creditor's claim.[134] Whether filing a claim operates as a waiver of the right to a jury trial on causes of action arising from separate transactions between the parties remains open to debate.[135] Of course, a creditor who has not filed a proof of claim has not waived any right to a jury trial in an action brought against it by the estate.[136]

---

[131] S. Elizabeth Gibson, *Jury Trials and Core Proceedings: The Bankruptcy Judge's Uncertain Authority*, 65 Am. Bankr. L.J. 143 (1991); Ned W. Wasman, *Jury Trials After* Granfinanciera*: Three Proposals for Reform*, 52 Ohio St. L.J. 705 (1991).

There was also a practical problem. Unlike most other courtrooms, most bankruptcy courts were constructed without a jury box or a jury room.

[132] 28 U.S.C. § 157(e) (2000); *see* In re Vigh, 85 F.3d 630 (6th Cir. 1996).

[133] M. Sobel, Inc. v. Weinstein (In re Weinstein), 237 B.R. 567 (Bankr. E.D.N.Y. 1999) (bankruptcy court may not conduct jury trial in non-core proceeding).

[134] Langenkamp v. Culp, 498 U.S. 42 (1990), *reh'g denied*, 498 U.S. 1043 (1991).

[135] *See* Official Employment-Related Issues Comm. of Enron Corp. v. Lavorato (In re Enron Corp.), 319 B.R. 122 (Bankr. S.D. Tex. 2004).

[136] Heater v. Household Realty Corp. (In re Heater), 261 B.R. 145 (Bankr. W.D. Pa. 2001).

§ 5.03 Bankruptcy Venue[137]

The issue of bankruptcy venue arises in two settings. The first is where the bankruptcy case itself may be filed. The second is where litigation connected to the bankruptcy case may be filed.

[A] Venue of Bankruptcy Cases[138]

In most cases, a bankruptcy petition may be filed in any district where the debtor's "domicile, residence, principal place of business in the United States, or principal assets in the United States" are located during the 180 days immediately preceding the commencement of the case.[139] When an individual debtor has resided in multiple places during the 180 days immediately before filing her petition, venue is proper in the district in which the debtor was located "for a longer portion" of this 180 days.[140] In most cases, there is only one possible venue.

For example, if Ted lived in Columbus, Ohio, from January through April of 2007 before moving to Brooklyn, New York in May of that year, proper venue for a case he files in July, 2007, would be the Southern District of Ohio, where he resided for the bulk of the 180 days before filing his petition. If he wants to file his case close to his new home, he will have to wait until August, when he will have lived in New York for a majority of the 180 days prior to his petition.[141] The answer might be more complicated, however, if from January through April, he kept apartments in both cities, and commuted for work to New York three days each week.

For purposes of bankruptcy venue, a corporate debtor is regarded as being domiciled where it is incorporated. It may file either where it is incorporated, where its principal place of business in the United States is located, or where it owns significant assets.

Corporate debtors with affiliates in multiple districts have even greater flexibility with respect to venue. A debtor who is affiliated with another debtor[142] that is located in a different district may file in the district in which the affiliate's case is pending. Thus, a New York corporation that is owned by a parent corporation in California may file its petition in California, if that is where the parent's case is pending. Likewise, the

---

[137] Frank Kennedy, *The Bankruptcy Court Under the New Bankruptcy Law: Its Structure, Jurisdiction, Venue and Procedure*, 11 St. Mary's L.J. 251, (1979); Charles Seligson & Lawrence P. King, *Jurisdiction and Venue in Bankruptcy*, 36 J. Nat'l Ass'n Ref. in Bankr. 36 (1962).

[138] Lynn M. LoPucki & William C. Whitford, *Venue Choice and Forum Shopping in the Bankruptcy Reorganization of Large, Publicly Held Companies*, 1991 Wis. L. Rev. 11.

[139] 28 U.S.C. § 1408 (2000).

[140] 28 U.S.C. § 1408 (2000).

[141] Even then, he may find the New York court reluctant to permit him to take advantage of New York's more generous exemption statute. *See* In re Coplan, 156 B.R. 88 (Bankr. M.D. Fla. 1993) (homestead exemption of debtor who moved from Wisconsin to Florida before filing petition limited to value of homestead protected by Wisconsin exemption statute).

[142] Bankruptcy Code § 101(2) (2000) ("affiliate").

California parent may file its petition in the appropriate district in New York if the New York subsidiary's case is pending in New York. Corporate debtors with affiliates in many jurisdictions can take advantage of this "venue hook" to generate virtually unlimited choices of where to file.[143]

Similarly, general partners may file in the same district in which a case involving either their partners or their partnership is pending. Thus, Nancy, who resides in Las Vegas, Nevada, and is in partnership with Doug, who resides in San Diego, California, may file in either the District of Nevada or, if Doug already has a case pending in San Diego, in the Southern District of California.[144]

The familiar doctrine of forum non conveniens applies to bankruptcy in largely the same manner it applies to other types of cases. The court has the power to transfer a case to another district, even though it was filed in the proper district, if transfer is warranted "in the interest of justice or for the convenience of the parties."[145] In deciding whether to transfer venue of a bankruptcy case to another district, courts usually consider a variety of factors, including the location of the debtor and its assets, the location of the debtor's creditors, the location of witnesses whose testimony is necessary for administration of the estate, and the relative expense to the estate to handle the case where it was initially filed or to transfer it to another district.[146] Transfers under this rule are discretionary. On the other hand, if venue was improper in the first place, the court in which the case was filed has the authority to transfer it to a district where venue is proper.[147]

[B] Venue of Civil Proceedings in Bankruptcy Cases

Normally, civil proceedings connected to a bankruptcy case may be brought only in the district in which the bankruptcy case is pending.[148] This rule facilitates the efficient administration of the estate by permitting all litigation connected to the case to be conducted in one place under the supervision of a judge who is familiar with the debtor's circumstances.

Venue in another district is proper in only three limited situations. First, where the trustee brings an action as a "successor to the debtor or creditors under section[s] 541 or 544(b) [of the bankruptcy code] . . . venue is also proper in the district in which the proceeding might have been brought by the debtor or creditors who could have brought the action if the bankruptcy case had not been filed."[149] The most obvious example of this is a trustee's

---

[143] Lynn M. LoPucki & William C. Whitford, *Venue Choice and Forum Shopping in the Bankruptcy Reorganization of Large, Publicly Held Companies*, 1991 Wis. L. Rev. 11.

[144] 28 U.S.C. § 1408(2) (2000).

[145] 28 U.S.C. § 1412 (2000).

[146] *See* In re Commonwealth Oil Ref. Co., 596 F.2d 1239, 1247–48 (5th Cir. 1979); In re Enron Corp., 274 B.R. 327, 343 (Bankr. S.D.N.Y. 2002).

[147] 28 U.S.C. § 1477(a) (2000).

[148] 28 U.S.C. § 1409(a) (2000).

[149] 28 U.S.C. § 1409(c) (2000).

action to recover a fraudulent conveyance, brought under state law pursuant to § 544(b), asserting the right that one of the debtor's unsecured creditors would have had to recover the fraudulent transfer.[150]

Second, venue of actions brought to recover small amounts may only be brought in the "district in which the defendant resides." This rule applies to actions "to recover a money judgment or property worth less than $1,000"; to recover a "consumer debt of less than $15,000"; or to recover "a debt (excluding a consumer debt) against a noninsider of less than $10,000."[151] This rule protects defendants in what are essentially small claims actions from having to defend in a distant geographic forum

Third, actions initiated by the trustee that are based on claims arising "after commencement of [the] case from the operation of the business of the debtor" may be brought only in a district where venue would have been proper if the case was not pending.[152] Thus, the general federal venue statute applies to actions sought to be initiated by the trustee or the debtor in possession that are based on transactions that occur while the case is pending.[153] Actions against the estate that are based on such post-petition dealings may properly be brought where the case is pending or in the district where they might have been brought under otherwise applicable venue rules.[154]

As with venue of the underlying bankruptcy case, venue of civil proceedings connected to a bankruptcy case can be transferred to another district "in the interest of justice or for the convenience of the parties."[155]

§ 5.04 Nationwide Service of Process in Bankruptcy[156]

The broad "home court" venue rule, which permits most bankruptcy litigation to occur in the same district as the one in which the debtor's bankruptcy case is pending, is facilitated by Federal Rule of Bankruptcy Procedure 7004. Rule 7004 permits nationwide service of process in adversary litigation connected to a bankruptcy case. Rule 7004(d) provides: "The summons and complaint and all other process except a subpoena may be served anywhere in the United States."[157] This, of course, is quite different from the normal rule applicable to cases brought in federal court through the district court's federal question or diversity of citizenship jurisdiction, which requires that service on an out-of-state resident must be made

150 *See* § 14.03 Power to Use Rights of Actual Unsecured Creditors, *infra*.

151 28 U.S.C.S. § 1409(c) (LexisNexis Supp. 2006).

152 28 U.S.C. § 1409(D) (2000).

153 *See* 28 U.S.C. § 1391(c) (2000).

154 28 U.S.C. § 1409(e) (2000).

155 28 U.S.C. § 1412 (2000).

156 *See* Jeffrey T. Ferriell, *The Perils of Nationwide Service of Process in a Bankruptcy Context*, 48 Wash & Lee L. Rev. 1199 (1991).

157 Fed. R. Bankr. P. 7004(d).

through the long-arm statute of the state where the district court is located.[158]

Nationwide service of process permits the bankruptcy court to consolidate disputes between the debtor and anyone else located in the United States in a single forum. This is particularly useful in cases where the estate might have to collect property owned by or owed to the estate (sometimes as a result of the bankruptcy trustee's avoiding powers) or in simple collection cases to recover funds owed to the estate as a result of pre-bankruptcy transactions.

The power of nationwide service is magnified by the liberal venue rules that permit affiliated debtors to file their bankruptcy cases in the same district and by the broad "home court" venue rule that permits bankruptcy litigation to be commenced in the same district in which the debtor's bankruptcy case is pending. For example, assume that Titanic Industries, Inc. is a Delaware corporation with a wholly-owned subsidiary, Ismay, Inc., which is incorporated and doing business in New Mexico. If Titanic Industries files a Chapter 11 petition in Delaware, where venue for its case is proper, its subsidiary Ismay, Inc. could file its own Chapter 11 case in Delaware, even though Ismay, Inc. is incorporated in New Mexico and even though it neither conducts business nor owns assets outside that state. If Ismay, Inc. has a preference claim against one of its New Mexico creditors, it could bring that action in Delaware and serve process on the creditor in New Mexico, even though the creditor has no contact with the parent corporation or anyone else in Delaware.

Although it might seem that this application of nationwide service of process might raise procedural due process difficulties under *International Shoe Co. v. Washington*[159] and its progeny, courts have almost universally ruled that no such difficulties arise if the defendant has minimum contacts with the United States or any part of it.[160]

§ 5.05 Sovereign Immunity[161]

The Eleventh Amendment prohibits a citizen of one state from suing another state in federal court. Enacted as a response to the Supreme Court's decision in *Chisolm v. Georgia*,[162] its precise scope as a narrow or broad

[158] *See* Fed. R. Civ. P. 4(d).

[159] 326 U.S. 310 (1945).

[160] *See* Jeffrey T. Ferriell, *The Perils of Nationwide Service of Process in a Bankruptcy Context*, 48 Wash. & Lee L. Rev. 1199 (1991).

[161] Ralph Brubaker, *Of State Sovereign Immunity and Prospective Remedies: The Bankruptcy Discharge as Statutory* Ex Parte Young *Relief*, 76 Am. Bankr. L.J. 461 (2002); Leonard Gerson, *A Bankruptcy Exception to State Sovereign Immunity: Limiting the* Seminole Tribe *Doctrine*, 74 Am. Bankr. L.J. 1 (2000); Hon. Randolph J. Haines, *The Uniformity Power: Why Bankruptcy Is Different*, 77 Am. Bankr. L.J. 129 (2003); Ted Janger, *Strategies for Preserving the Bankruptcy Trustee's Avoidance Power Against States after* Seminole Tribe, 23 Ohio N.U. L. Rev. 1431 (1997); Richard Lieb, *State Sovereign Immunity: Bankruptcy Is Special*, 14 Am. Bankr. Inst. L. Rev. 201 (2006).

[162] Chisholm v. Georgia, 2 U.S. (2 Dall.) 419 (1793).

grant of sovereign immunity has been in flux for over a hundred years. Until 1996, Supreme Court decisions implied that a state's sovereign immunity could be abrogated by Congress, pursuant to the Commerce Clause, to allow a suit for money damages so long as that intention was "clearly stated."[163] However, in *Seminole Tribe v. Florida*,[164] the United States Supreme Court specifically held that Congress' legislative powers under the Commerce Clause do not generally empower Congress to abrogate the states' Eleventh Amendment sovereign immunity.[165] There was dicta in the *Seminole Tribe* opinion that suggested that the holding might also apply in bankruptcy cases. This raised a number of questions about the applicability of the Bankruptcy Code to states. Were states bound by the automatic stay or the discharge injunction? If a state received a preference prior to bankruptcy, could the trustee sue to recover it? The lower courts divided on these points, and the Supreme Court has recently spoken to both of these questions.

First, in *Tennessee Student Assistance Corporation v. Hood*, the Court held that a state student loan authority was subject to the discharge injunction, and moreover, that adjudicating the dischargeability of the claim did not submit the state to suit.[166] The Supreme Court reasoned that the power to grant a discharge emanated not from the power to sue or bind the state, but from the bankruptcy court's in rem jurisdiction over the bankruptcy estate. The Court likened the bankruptcy estate to a ship, and noted that in rem jurisdiction carried with it the power to adjudicate rights with regard to the property. This resolved the issue of the bankruptcy court's ability to use its injunctive power to preserve the estate (and by implication the status of the automatic stay), but it did no resolve the second question: Could property be recovered from a state through the use of the trustee's avoidance powers?

In *Central Virginia Community College v. Katz*,[167] the Supreme Court retreated from the *Seminole Tribe*[168] dicta and held that in ratifying the Bankruptcy Clause in Article I,[169] states ceded their sovereign immunity to the extent necessary to effectuate the purposes of that clause. Specifically, the *Katz* Court found that state sovereign immunity is not a defense to a trustee's action under Bankruptcy Code § 547 to recover a money judgment for preferential transfers made by the debtor to a state agency.[170]

---

163 United States v. Nordic Village, Inc., 503 U.S. 30 (1992); Hoffman v. Connecticut Dept. of Income Maintenance, 492 U.S. 96 (1989).

164 517 U.S. 44 (1996).

165 517 U.S. at 72–73. Because the Eleventh Amendment was passed after Article I was ratified, that Amendment creates a limitation on Congress' Article I powers. After *Seminole Tribe*, the Court reaffirmed its holding that Congress may not abrogate the states' Eleventh Amendment sovereign immunity based on powers enumerated in Article I. *See* Board of Trs. of Univ. of Ala. v. Garrett, 531 U.S. 356, 362 (2001).

166 Tennessee Student Assistance Corporation v. Hood, 541 U. S. 440 (2004).

167 126 S. Ct. 990 (2006).

168 517 U.S. at 72 n.16.

169 The Bankruptcy Clause authorizes Congress to enact "uniform Laws on the subject of Bankruptcies throughout the United States." U.S. Const. art. 1, § 8, cl. 4.

170 *See* Chapter 15 Avoidable Preferences, *infra*.

The precise issue before the Court in *Katz* was whether Congress effectively abrogated state sovereign immunity by enacting § 106(a), which provides that "sovereign immunity is abrogated as to a governmental unit . . . with respect to" specific sections of the Bankruptcy Code authorizing actions against creditors and others.[171] However, the Court did not decide whether Congress' enactment of § 106(a) — which made states susceptible to suits seeking a money judgment — was actually within the scope of its power to enact "Laws on the subject of Bankruptcies."[172] Instead, the Court reasoned that the Framers would have understood the Bankruptcy Clause to give Congress the power to authorize courts to avoid preferential transfers to state agencies and to recover the transferred property. If this was the understanding, then the states surrendered their sovereign immunity in agreeing to the Bankruptcy Clause at the Constitutional Convention.

Moreover, because the critical element of a bankruptcy proceeding is the court's exercise of jurisdiction over the debtor's property (i.e., in rem jurisdiction), the Court theorized that a proceeding to recover a money judgment for a preferential transfer is "ancillary" to bankruptcy courts' in rem jurisdiction. Thus, the Court declared that state sovereign immunity was relinquished under the Bankruptcy Clause with respect to bankruptcy courts' issuing "ancillary orders enforcing their in rem adjudications."[173]

Since the Court's ruling in *Katz*, the Eighth Circuit has stressed that the *Katz* exception for bankruptcy cases is narrow and, quoting language from *Katz*, indicated that the exception is based on the "unique history" of the Bankruptcy Clause and the "singular nature of bankruptcy courts' jurisdiction."[174] At the same time, however, the Court's ruling in *Katz* has been criticized as having the potential to be read too broadly: "[A]lthough its holding saved bankruptcy from the reach of the Eleventh Amendment, the Court neither specified what other bankruptcy proceedings will similarly overcome a sovereign immunity defense" — for example, if a state government seized property in violation of the automatic stay — "nor sufficiently explored the implications of its original intent analysis."[175] In addition, it has been argued that the *Katz* decision "cannot be reconciled with precedent."[176]

Where *Katz* will lead regarding the defense of state sovereign immunity in various bankruptcy proceedings remains to be seen. Some scholars have regarded *Katz* as slowing down if not stopping the development of the

---

[171] Bankruptcy Code § 106(a)(1).

[172] *Katz*, 126 S. Ct. at 1005.

[173] 126 S. Ct. at 1000.

[174] St. Charles County, Missouri v. Wisconsin, 447 F.3d 1055 (8th Cir. 2006).

[175] *State Sovereign Immunity — Bankruptcy*, 120 Harv. L. Rev. 125, 126 (2006); *see also* Richard Lieb, *State Sovereign Immunity: Bankruptcy Is Special*, 14 Am. Bankr. Inst. L. Rev. 201, 203 (2006) ("[*Katz*'s] 'ancillary order' theory is broad enough to preclude the states from asserting immunity as a defense to *any* proceeding grounded on a provision of the Bankruptcy Code or which affects property of the debtor's estate.") (emphasis added).

[176] Suzanna Sherry, *Logic Without Experience: The Problem of Federal Appellate Courts*, 82 Notre Dame L. Rev. 97, 114 (2006).

jurisprudence of sovereign immunity,[177] while others have pointed out that "*Katz* will likely face close scrutiny and resistance in the future."[178]

[177] Patrick McKinley Brennan, *Against Sovereignty: A Cautionary Note on the Normative Power of the Actual*, 82 Notre Dame L. Rev. 181, 188–89 (2006).

[178] *State Sovereign Immunity — Bankruptcy*, 120 Harv. L. Rev. 125, 134 (2006); *see* Richard Lieb, *State Sovereign Immunity: Bankruptcy Is Special*, 14 Am. Bankr. Inst. L. Rev. 201, 233 (2006) ("It is unclear just how far the Supreme Court intended to go in *Katz* . . . . It remains to be seen whether the lower courts will apply *Katz*, as logically required, to all ancillary bankruptcy proceedings, or will restrict it to avoidance proceedings brought pursuant to the Bankruptcy Code. It can be expected that they will reach conflicting results.").

Chapter 6

Commencement of the Case

§ 6.01 Commencement of Bankruptcy Cases[1]

[A] Voluntary Commencement

Bankruptcy cases are commenced by filing a petition in the proper form, with the proper fee, in the proper district.[2] Debtors unable to pay the filing fee in cash are permitted, upon application, to pay it in installments.[3] Until recently, debtors who were unable to pay the filing fee were not entitled to relief. However, the 2005 Amendments permit the court to waive the filing fee entirely for individual Chapter 7 debtors whose income is "less than 150 percent" of the poverty line established by the Federal Office of Management and Budget.[4] Thus, for the first time in the history of American bankruptcy law, the filing fee (at least) will not render debtors too poor to go bankrupt.[5]

Both voluntary and involuntary petitions are permitted. However, nearly all bankruptcy petitions are filed voluntarily by debtors willingly seeking relief under one of the various proceedings under the Bankruptcy Code.[6]

[B] Involuntary Commencement

Sometimes debtors are dragged into bankruptcy court involuntarily by one or more of their creditors. Involuntary petitions may be brought only

---

[1] Frank R. Kennedy, *The Commencement of a Case under the New Bankruptcy Code*, 36 Wash. & Lee L. Rev. 977 (1979).

[2] Bankruptcy Code § 301; *see* Fed. R. Bankr. P. 1002(a).

[3] 28 U.S.C. § 1930(a) (2000); Fed. R. Bankr. P. 1006.

[4] 28 U.S.C.S. § 1930(f) (LexisNexis Supp. 2006).

[5] The 2005 legislation was adopted in the wake of a pilot study implemented during the mid-1990s to evaluate the desirability of *in forma pauperis* bankruptcy petitions. *See* Karen Gross & Shari Rosenberg, *Reflecting on and beyond* United States v. Kras, 2 Am. Bankr. Inst. L. Rev. 57 (1994); Henry J. Sommer, *The Time Has Long Since Come*, 2 Am. Bankr. Inst. L. Rev. 93 (1994); *but see* Michael C. Markham & Bethann Scharrer, *An Unnecessary Privilege in Bankruptcy*, 2 Am. Bankr. Inst. L. Rev. 73 (1994). There are other costs associated with filing for bankruptcy, and some of those may have been increased by the 2005 amendments, so the overall effect of BAPCPA on the affordability of bankruptcy may be less than clear.

[6] *See* Susan Block-Lieb, *Why So Few Involuntary Petitions and Why the Number Is Not Too Small,* 57 Brook. L. Rev. 803, 804 & Appendix A at 863 (1991); David S. Kennedy et al., *The Involuntary Bankruptcy Process: A Study of the Relevant Statutory and Procedural Provisions and Related Matters*, 31 U. Mem. L. Rev. 1, 3 (2000) ("Of the 1,436,964 bankruptcy cases filed in the calendar year of 1998, only 847 were involuntary filings."); Lynn LoPucki, *A General Theory of the Dynamics of the State Remedies/Bankruptcy System,* 1972 Wis. L. Rev. 311.

under Chapter 7 or 11 and usually require the petitioning creditors to prove that the debtor is not payng its debts as they become due. An "order for relief" is entered against the debtor only if the creditor makes this showing, or if the debtor fails to defend the creditor's petition and thus acquiesces to the proceeding.[7] As explained below, some debtors, such as farmers and charitable corporations, are insulated from involuntary petitions, even though they are eligible for voluntarily relief.

[C] Eligibility for Relief

There are detailed eligibility requirements for both voluntary and involuntary petitions, which vary depending on whether the debtor seeks relief in a liquidation proceeding under Chapter 7 or in one of the three types of rehabilitation proceedings for private debtors under Chapter 11, 12 or 13. These eligibility requirements are a main topic of this chapter.

§ 6.02 Commencement of a Voluntary Case[8]

[A] Filing a Voluntary Petition

A voluntary bankruptcy case is commenced when the debtor files a petition with the bankruptcy court.[9] The form for the voluntary petition itself[10] is quite simple (though some of the other paperwork required to be filed with the petition is not).[11] The petition includes little more than the debtor's name and address; an indication of the debtor's status as an individual, a partnership, a corporation, or some other entity; a statement that the debtor has resided in the district in which the petition has been filed for at least 180 days;[12] a statement seeking an order for relief under the bankruptcy code; and an indication of the number of creditors the debtor has, the amount of its debts, and the value of its assets. However, a petitioning debtor is not required to explain the financial circumstances that precipitated the petition. Filing the voluntary petition with the clerk of the bankruptcy court constitutes an "order for relief" under the chapter for which the petition was filed.[13]

---

[7] Bankruptcy Code § 303(h); *see* § 6.03 Commencement of Involuntary Cases, *infra*.

[8] John C. McCoid, II, *The Origins of Voluntary Bankruptcy*, 5 Bankr. Dev. J. 361 (1988); Randal C. Picker, *Voluntary Petitions and the Creditors' Bargain*, 61 U. Cin L. Rev. 519 (1992).

[9] Bankruptcy Code § 301.

[10] *See* Official Bankruptcy Form 1.

[11] Bankruptcy Code § 521.

[12] This establishes the court's venue over the petition. *See* § 5.03[A] Venue of Bankruptcy Cases, *supra*.

[13] Bankruptcy Code § 301(b). Those familiar with practice under the Bankruptcy Act will recall that before 1979, the clerk's office would stamp a filed petition with "ADJUDICATED" instead of "FILED" as is the custom today. This reflected that the debtor had been voluntarily "adjudicated" to be a "bankrupt."

Filing a petition has numerous implications. It creates the debtor's estate and simultaneously transfers all of the property owned by the debtor when the petition was filed to that estate.[14] It also triggers the imposition of an automatic stay enjoining most types of proceedings and other actions by creditors against the debtor or the estate's property.[15] Further, it establishes the base point for various time periods, such as the preference period,[16] the fraudulent transfer period,[17] and the period of time in which both creditors and debtors may file various documents with the court.[18] For these and other reasons, the phrase "commencement of the case," referring to the filing of a petition, is one of the most important and frequently used phrases in the Bankruptcy Code.[19]

[B] Debtor's Eligibility for Voluntary Relief

[1] General Restrictions on Eligibility for Relief

Bankruptcy petitions under chapters 7, 11, 12, and 13 may be filed voluntarily by debtors with few restrictions other than the debtor's willingness to file. With limited exceptions, some kind of bankruptcy relief is available under the Bankruptcy Code to nearly every "person that resides or has a domicile, a place of business, or property in the United States, or a municipality."[20] "Person" is defined broadly to include individuals, partnerships, corporations, and other entities.[21] Even incompetent persons and minors are eligible for relief.[22]

[a] Connection to the United States

There is a general requirement, rarely litigated but applicable to all debtors, that the debtor must have some nexus with the United States. Individual and business entities must either reside in or have a domicile, a place of business, or property in the United States.[23] In addition, political

[14] Bankruptcy Code § 541(a)(1); *see* § 7.01 Creation of the Debtor's Estate, *infra.*

[15] Bankruptcy Code § 362; *see* Chapter 8, The Automatic Stay, *infra.*

[16] *See* § 15.02[E] Preference Period, *infra.*

[17] *See* Chapter 16, Fraudulent Transfers, *infra.*

[18] *E.g.,* Fed. R. Bankr. P. 1007(c) (fifteen days to file debtor's schedules and statement); Fed. R. Bank. P. 3002(c)(1) (proof of claim by governmental unit to be filed not later than 180 days after the date of the order for relief).

[19] In cases initiated via an involuntary petition, an "order for relief" will not be entered simultaneously with the commencement of the case. It will either be delayed until the debtor fails to contest the petition, until a trial is held on merits of the petition, or never entered if the petitioning creditors fail to prevail on those merits. Bankruptcy Code § 303(h); *see* § 6.03 Commencement of an Involuntary Case, *infra.*

[20] Bankruptcy Code § 109(a).

[21] Bankruptcy Code § 101(41).

[22] In re Murray, 199 B.R. 165 (Bankr. M.D. Tenn. 1996); *see* Elizabeth Warren, Essay, *Bankrupt Children,* 86 Minn. L. Rev. 1003 (2002).

[23] Bankruptcy Code § 109(a).

subdivisions, public agencies or instrumentalities[24] of one of the fifty states may be a debtor under Chapter 9.[25] However, there is no requirement that the debtor be a United States citizen.

[b] Abusive Repetitive Filings[26]

Debtors sometimes file repetitive petitions, usually in an effort to take advantage of the Bankruptcy Code's automatic stay,[27] even though their petitions are destined to be dismissed. Section 109(g) prevents individuals and "family farmers"[28] from deploying this tactic. A debtor is denied relief if it has been a debtor in a bankruptcy case during the 180 days immediately before its most recent petition was filed and if that case was dismissed, either due to the debtor's willful failure to abide by the bankruptcy court's orders or appear before the court to prosecute the case or in response to the debtor's request for dismissal following a creditor's request for relief from the automatic stay.[29]

For example, if Jack Dawkins is facing a real estate foreclosure action, he might file a voluntary Chapter 13 petition, even though he has no realistic hope of having a Chapter 13 plan confirmed. His petition invokes the automatic stay of § 362 and stops any pending state foreclosure proceeding. Under § 109(g)(2), if he voluntarily dismisses his Chapter 13 case after the mortgage holder files a motion for relief from the automatic stay, Jack is ineligible for bankruptcy relief until 180 days (approximately six months) after the date of his first petition. In most states, this time period is sufficient for the foreclosure proceeding to come to fruition.[30]

Several courts have regarded § 109(g) as discretionary.[31] However, the plain text of its language leaves little room for this conclusion. It unambiguously specifies that "no individual or family farmer may be a debtor" if the

---

[24] Bankruptcy Code § 101(40).

[25] Bankruptcy Code § 109(c). Municipal bankruptcies are highly specialized and generally beyond the scope of this book. Students interested in one of the largest municipal bankruptcies in the Nation's history may wish to consult Mark Baldassare, When Government Fails: The Orange County Bankruptcy (Univ. of Cal. Press 1998). The case was large enough to warrant its own directory on the Lexis database: BKRTCY/ORANGE.

[26] John Golmant & Tom Ulrich, *Bankruptcy Repeat Filings*, 14 Am. Bankr. Inst. L. Rev. 169 (2006); Katie Thein Kimlinger & William P. Wassweiler, *The Good Faith Fable of 11 U.S.C. § 707(a): How Bankruptcy Courts Have Invented a Good Faith Filing Requirement for Chapter 7 Debtors*, 13 Emory Bankr. Dev. J. 61 (1996); Lawrence Ponoroff & F. Stephen Knippenberg, *The Implied Good Faith Filing Requirement: Sentinel of an Evolving Bankruptcy Policy,* 85 Nw. U. L. Rev. 919 (1991); Ned W. Waxman, *Judicial Follies: Ignoring the Plain Meaning of Bankruptcy Code § 109(g)(2)*, 48 Ariz. L. Rev. 149 (2006).

[27] *See* Chapter 8, The Automatic Stay, *infra.*

[28] Bankruptcy Code § 101(18); *see* Chapter 20, Family Farmer and Family Fisherman Reorganization, *infra.*

[29] Bankruptcy Code § 109(g).

[30] *See* § 2.08[A] Real Estate Foreclosure, *supra.*

[31] *E.g.*, In re Hutchins, 303 B.R. 503 (Bankr. N.D. Ala. 2003); In re Beal, 347 B.R. 87 (E.D. Wis. 2006).

circumstances described in the remainder of the section exist.[32] Most courts have agreed that this is the only permissible result.[33]

In addition, §§ 362(c)(3) & (4) attempt to frustrate the efforts of repeat filers by terminating the automatic stay quickly, if the debtor has filed multiple petitions within a one year period. As explained in more detail elsewhere, § 362(c)(3) terminates the stay thirty days after the debtor's second petition within a year, unless the debtor demonstrates that the second petition was filed in good faith.[34] Section 362(c)(4) prevents the stay from going into effect at all in a third or subsequent case filed by a debtor within a one-year period.[35]

[c] Mandatory Credit Counseling[36]

The 2005 Amendments to the Bankruptcy Code impose a debtor education requirement for individual debtors seeking relief under any chapter of the Bankruptcy Code.[37] To be eligible to file a petition, an individual must receive either an individual or a group "briefing" which outlines "the opportunities for available credit counseling" and that includes providing the prospective debtor with assistance in "performing a related budget analysis."[38] The briefing may be conducted in person, over the telephone, or via the internet and must be provided by an "approved nonprofit budget and credit counseling agency."[39] Debtors' lawyers, who have a financial stake in the debtor's decision to file a bankruptcy petition, are not trusted to provide sufficient information to their clients in an objective manner. This briefing may be obtained any time "during the 180-day period *preceding* the date of filing of the petition,"[40] though there is some disagreement

---

[32] Ned W. Waxman, *Judicial Follies: Ignoring the Plain Meaning of Bankruptcy Code § 109(g)(2)*, 48 Ariz. L. Rev. 149 (2006).

[33] *E.g.*, In re Hackett, 233 F.3d 574 (5th Cir. 2000).

[34] Bankruptcy Code § 362(c)(3); *see* § 8.06[A][3]Automatic Termination — Prior Petition Within One Year, *infra*.

[35] Bankruptcy Code § 362(c)(4); *see* § 8.06[A][4] Automatic Termination — Multiple Prior Petitions Within One Year, *infra*.

[36] Gordon Bermant & Ed Flynn, *Planning for Change: Credit Counseling at the Threshold of Bankruptcy*, 20 Am. Bankr. Inst. L. Rev. 20 (2001); Jeffery A. Deller & Nicholas E. Meriwether, *Putting Order to the Madness: BAPCPA and the Contours of the New Prebankruptcy Credit Counseling Requirements,* 16 J. Bankr. L. & Prac. 1 (2007); Gary Neustadter, *A Consumer Bankruptcy Odyssey,* 39 Creighton L. Rev. 225, 234–58 (2006); Robin Miller, Annotation, *Validity, Construction, and Application of Credit Counseling Requirement Under Bankruptcy Abuse Prevention and Consumer Protection Act (BAPCPA), 11 U.S.C.A. § 109(h)*, 11 A.L.R. Fed. 2d 43 (2006).

[37] Bankruptcy Code § 109(h); *see* In re Piontek, 346 B.R. 126 (Bankr. W.D. Pa. 2006) (case of debtor's spouse dismissed due to failure of spouse to obtain briefing); In re Salazar, 339 B.R. 622 (Bankr. S.D. Tex. 2006) ("striking" petition of debtor who failed to obtain briefing); *see* Alan Eisler, *The BAPCPA's Chilling Effect on Debtor's Counsel*, 55 Am. U. L. Rev. 1333, 1339–41 (2006).

[38] Bankruptcy Code § 109(h).

[39] Bankruptcy Code § 109(h).

[40] Bankruptcy Code § 109(h)(1) (emphasis added).

among courts over whether the briefing may occur on the same day that the petition is filed or if it must be obtained at least one day before the petition.[41]

The pre-filing briefing may be excused if the debtor resides in a district where the United States Trustee's office has determined nonprofit counseling services are not reasonably available to the debtor;[42] if the debtor is unable to obtain the briefing due to "incapacity, disability, or active military service in a military combat zone";[43] if the debtor was unable to obtain the required briefing from a qualified credit counseling service within five days after his or her request;[44] or if the debtor faces "exigent circumstances that merit a waiver of the requirement."[45] Most courts rule that, absent one of these specified waivers, the bankruptcy court lacks discretion to refuse to dismiss the debtor's case.[46]

Whether required briefings will further reduce the number of petitions or provide debtors with more useful information than they already obtain from their attorneys remains uncertain. However, the consequences of a dismissal as the result of a failure to obtain pre-petition counseling may be considerable.

[d] Abstention

In rare circumstances, the court may abstain from a case, even though the debtor meets the technical eligibility requirements for relief § 109 imposes. Section 305 gives the court broad authority to abstain from entertaining a petition in "the interests of creditors and the debtor."[47]

The legislative history of § 305 outlines circumstances where abstention is appropriate, seeming to limit abstention to cases filed by a small number of creditors when most creditors oppose the bankruptcy, where a state insolvency proceeding or other out-of-court arrangement was already pending, and where dismissal of the case was otherwise in the best interests of the debtor and all creditors.[48] Some courts take a restrictive approach,

---

[41] *See* In re Cole, 347 B.R. 70 (Bankr. D. Tenn. 2006) (collecting cases); *see also* In re Dansby, 340 B.R. 564 (Bankr. D.S.C. 2006) (refusing to waive requirement for debtor who did not seek credit counseling at least five days before petition).

[42] Bankruptcy Code § 109(h)(2)(A).

[43] Bankruptcy Code § 109(h)(4).

[44] Bankruptcy Code § 109(h)(3)(A)(ii).

[45] Bankruptcy Code § 109(h)(3)(I); *see* Dixon v. LaBarge (In re Dixon), 338 B.R. 383 (B.A.P. 8th Cir. 2006) (foreclosure sale scheduled for day after petition was not an exigent circumstance); In re Petit-Louis, 338 B.R. 132 (Bankr. S.D. Fla. 2006) (debtor's language difficulties warrants waiver of pre-petition counseling requirement).

[46] *E.g.*, In re Hedquist, 342 B.R. 295, 297 (B.A.P. 8th Cir. 2006); In re Cleaver, 333 B.R. 430 (Bankr. S.D. Ohio 2005); *but see* In re Hess, 347 B.R. 489 (Bankr. D. Vt. 2006) (finding room for discretion in § 707(a)); *see also* In re Ginsburg, No. 06-42821-608, 2006 WL 3353810, *3 (Bankr. E.D.N.Y. Nov 13, 2006).

[47] Bankruptcy Code § 305(a)(1).

[48] *See* S. Rep. No. 95-989, at 35–36 (1978), *reprinted in* 1978 U.S.C.C.A.N. 5787, 5821–22; H.R. Rep. No. 95-595, at 325 (1977), *reprinted in* 1978 U.S.C.C.A.N. 5787, 6281.

and limit abstention to the specific circumstances mentioned in the legislative history.[49] Most courts take a more liberal stand, based on the express language of § 305, and permit abstention in a broader range of circumstances.[50] These cases have considered a wide variety of factors articulated in several ways, but boil down to the effect of abstention on the efficiency of the administration of the debtor's financial affairs,[51] the availability of an alternative mechanism or forum which will protect the interests of all of the parties,[52] and the purposes for which bankruptcy jurisdiction has been sought.[53] Under this multi-faceted approach, abstention is warranted in two-party "collection cases" where there is no need for collective creditor relief,[54] or in cases where a foreign debtor is technically eligible for relief because of the existence of negligible assets or business relationships in the United States, but where relief in a foreign country would be more appropriate because of the debtor's more prominent presence there.

[2] Eligibility for Relief Under Chapter 7 — Liquidation

Virtually any individual or business entity qualifies for voluntary liquidation under Chapter 7 of the Bankruptcy Code. The only exceptions are railroads, most domestic insurance companies, banks and similar financial institutions,[55] and municipalities.[56] Each exclusion reflects the availability of other avenues of relief for these types of debtors. For example, the FDIC maintains procedures to restructure insolvent banks, and state agencies provide mechanisms to handle the affairs of financially troubled insurance companies. Likewise, there is a special subchapter in Chapter 11 of the Bankruptcy Code for railroads,[57] and Chapter 9 of the Code deals with insolvent municipalities.[58]

---

[49] In re RAI Marketing Serv., Inc., 20 B.R. 943 (Bankr. D. Kan. 1982); *see* § 2.11 Compositions and Workouts, *supra*.

[50] *E.g.*, In re Spade, 258 B.R. 221, 231–33 (Bankr. D. Colo. 2001); In re Tarletz, 27 B.R. 787 (Bankr. D. Colo. 1983).

[51] *See* In re Fortran Printing, Inc., 297 B.R. 89 (Bankr. D. Ohio 2003) (considering, *inter alia*, the economy and efficiency of administration; the likelihood that the debtor and the creditors would be able to work out a less expensive out-of-court arrangement, which would better serve all interests in the case; and the effect on the debtor's business).

[52] In re Fortran Printing, Inc., 297 B.R. 89 (Bankr. D. Ohio 2003) (considering the availability of another forum to protect the interests of both parties; the pendency of a proceeding in state court; the availability of alternative means to achieve an equitable distribution of assets; and whether non-federal insolvency has proceeded so far that it would be costly and time consuming to start afresh with the federal bankruptcy process).

[53] *E.g.*, In re Fortran Printing, Inc., 297 B.R. 89 (Bankr. D. Ohio, 2003); In re Trina Associates, 128 B.R. 858, 867 (Bankr. E.D.N.Y. 1991).

[54] *E.g.*, In re Spade, 258 B.R. 221 (Bankr. D. Colo. 2001).

[55] Bankruptcy Code § 109(b)(1)-(3).

[56] This last exception arises from the fact that only a "person" may file under Chapter 7 (Bankruptcy Code § 109(b)) and, with one exception that is not relevant here, the term "person" does not include a governmental unit. Bankruptcy Code § 101(41).

[57] Bankruptcy Code §§ 1161-1174.

[58] Bankruptcy Code §§ 901-946. All of these specialized proceedings are beyond the scope of this book.

This broad eligibility rule must nevertheless be read in conjunction with the de facto limitation placed on the eligibility of consumer debtors for Chapter 7 relief under § 707(b), which requires the court to dismiss petitions that constitute an "abuse" of Chapter 7.[59] Whether a debtor's petition is abusive depends initially on whether the debtor's household income is above or below the state median income for similar sized households in the debtor's home state. If the debtor's household income is below this threshold, Chapter 7 relief is not presumed to be abusive. If the debtor's household income exceeds the state median, relief is denied if the debtor has sufficient disposable income to make meaningful payments to creditors under a Chapter 13 plan. Whether an above-the-median debtor's income is sufficient to make meaningful payments depends on a complex collection of facts and assumptions about the debtor's income and expenses, explained in detail in a later chapter.[60]

[3] Eligibility for Relief under Chapter 9 — Municipalities

Chapter 9 is available only for the reorganization of a municipality,[61] such as a city, county or other subdivision of state government.[62] States themselves are not eligible.

Initially, the debtor must be "specifically authorized" by state law to be a debtor in a bankruptcy proceeding.[63] In addition, unlike the requirements for relief under other chapters, the municipality must be "insolvent."[64] Further, it must "desire to affect a plan to adjust" its debts[65] and must either have obtained its creditors' consent to the filing, have failed to obtain creditor agreement after negotiating with them in good faith over the filing, have been unable to negotiate with its creditors, or reasonably believe that a creditor may attempt to obtain an avoidable preference.[66]

In connection with a municipality, insolvency means the debtor is either "(i) generally not paying its debts as they become due unless such debts are the subject of a bona fide dispute; or (ii) unable to pay its debts as they become due."[67] Thus, the legal test of insolvency that applies in other contexts under the Bankruptcy Code, which compares assets and liabilities, is not sufficient to permit Chapter 9 relief for a municipal entity. In the early 1990s, Bridgeport, Connecticut's Chapter 9 petition was dismissed

[59] Bankruptcy Code § 707(b).

[60] *See* § 17.03[B] Dismissal of Consumer Cases due to Abuse, *infra*.

[61] Bankruptcy Code § 109(c).

[62] Bankruptcy Code § 101(40).

[63] Bankruptcy Code § 109(c)(2); *e.g.*, In re County of Orange, 183 B.R. 594, 603 (Bankr. C.D. Cal. 1995).

[64] Bankruptcy Code § 109(c)(3).

[65] Bankruptcy Code § 109(c)(4).

[66] Bankruptcy Code § 109(c)(5). Broadly speaking, a preference is a payment that benefits one creditor at the expense of others. *See generally* Chapter 15, Avoidable Preferences, *infra*.

[67] Bankruptcy Code § 109(C).

when the court determined that the city, though struggling, was not insolvent under this definition when its petition was filed.[68]

[4] Eligibility for Relief Under Chapter 11 — Reorganization

Chapter 11's procedures permit reorganization of a wide variety of entities. The eligibility requirements for Chapter 11 are virtually the same as those for Chapter 7, with only two significant differences. First, a stockbroker or commodity broker is eligible for relief under Chapter 7 but not under Chapter 11.[69] Second, railroads, which are not eligible for liquidation under Chapter 7, are eligible for reorganization under Chapter 11.[70] However, railroad reorganizations are subject to a somewhat different set of rules within Chapter 11 than other debtors.[71]

For a number of years, it was uncertain whether Chapter 11 included an implicit "going concern" requirement that denied relief to debtors with no current business operations. The dispute was resolved in 1991, when the Supreme Court held that nothing in the Bankruptcy Code's plain language imposed such a requirement.[72] Accordingly, even individual consumer debtors are eligible to file a Chapter 11 petition; however, given its expense and complexity, consumers rarely find Chapter 11 relief desirable if the have the option to file in either Chapter 7 or 13.

[5] Eligibility for Relief Under Chapter 12 — Family Farmers and Family Fishermen[73]

Chapter 12 provides for the rehabilitation of family farmers and family fishermen through a court-approved repayment plan.[74] It is specially structured to deal with the uncertainties of income from farming operations. It contains the most complex eligibility requirements under the Code, most of which deal with the definitions of "family farmer" and "family fisherman." These definitions determine whether the debtor is eligible for the more liberal provisions of Chapter 12 or if it is instead compelled to seek relief under Chapters 11 or 13.

---

[68] In re City of Bridgeport, 129 B.R. 332, 334 (Bankr. D. Conn. 1991).

[69] Bankruptcy Code § 109(d).

[70] Bankruptcy Code § 109(d).

[71] Bankruptcy Code §§ 1161-1174; *see generally* § 19.15 Railroad Reorganizations, *infra.*

[72] Toibb v. Radloff, 501 U.S. 157 (1991); *see* Michael J. Herbert, *Consumer Chapter 11 Proceedings: Abuse or Alternative?*, 91 Com. L.J. 234 (1986).

[73] Linda King, *Chapter 12: Adjustment of Debts of a Family Farmer with Regular Income.* 29 S. Tex. L. Rev. 615 (1988); Susan A. Schneider, *The Family Farmer in Bankruptcy: Recent Developments in Chapter 12*, 3 Drake J. Agric. L. 161 (1998); Jonathan K. Van Patten, *Chapter 12 in the Courts*, 38 S.D. L. Rev. 52, 61–70 (1993); Ralph V. Seep, Annotation, *What Constitutes "Family Farmer" Entitled to Relief under Chapter 12 of Bankruptcy Code*, 101 A.L.R. Fed. 502 (1991).

[74] *See* Chapter 20, Family Farmer and Family Fisherman Reorganization under Chapter 12, *infra.*

Relief under Chapter 12 is available only to a "family farmer or family fisherman with regular income."[75] The reference to family fishermen was added in the 2005 Amendments to ensure that those engaged in commercial fishing operations were entitled to relief similar to that available to those involved in more traditional agricultural businesses.[76]

A family farmer with regular income is a "family farmer whose annual income is sufficiently stable and regular to enable such family farmer to make payments under a [Chapter 12 plan.]"[77] A family fisherman with regular income is similarly a "family fisherman whose annual income is sufficiently stable and regular to enable such family fisherman to make payments under a [Chapter 12 plan.]"[78]

[a] Stable and Regular Income

The requirement that the family farmer or family fisherman have income sufficiently stable and regular to make payments under a Chapter 12 plan possibly adds little meaning to these definitions. If the debtor's income is inadequate to fund a Chapter 12 plan, the proposed plan will not be confirmed in any event under Chapter 12's requirement that the proposed plan be feasible.[79] So long as the debtor qualifies as either a family farmer or a family fisherman, the plan need not be funded with revenue derived from the family farming or fishing business.[80] However, as will be seen, a significant portion of the debtor's income must be derived from farming or fishing for the debtor to qualify as a family farmer or a family fisherman.

To determine whether a debtor is eligible for relief under Chapter 12, the definitions of "family farmer," "farming operation," "family fisherman," and "commercial fishing operation" must be examined.

[b] Family Farmer

The definition of "family farmer" contains several elements that vary depending on whether the debtor is an "individual or individual and spouse"[81] or a "corporation or partnership."[82] Unlike Chapter 13, certain corporations and partnerships are eligible for relief under Chapter 12.

---

[75] Bankruptcy Code § 109(f).

[76] The expanded scope will alter the result in cases like *In re Watford,* 898 F.2d 1525, 1529 (11th Cir. Ga. 1990), where shell fishing was held not to be farming operation and thus the debtors were ineligible for Chapter 12 relief.

[77] Bankruptcy Code § 101(19).

[78] Bankruptcy Code § 101(19B).

[79] Bankruptcy Code § 1225(a)(6).

[80] *E.g.*, In re Mikkelsen Farms, Inc., 74 B.R. 280 (Bankr. D. Or. 1987).

[81] Bankruptcy Code § 101(18)(A).

[82] Bankruptcy Code § 101(18)(B).

[i] Farming Operation

Whether the debtor is an individual, an individual and spouse, a corporation, or a partnership, the debtor must be "engaged in a farming operation" when the case is commenced.[83] A "farming operation" includes but is not strictly limited to[84] "farming, tillage of the soil, dairy farming, ranching, production or raising of crops, poultry, or livestock, and production of poultry or livestock products in an unmanufactured state."[85] This definition has been interpreted to exclude merely renting farmland to others,[86] crop dusting, or harvesting manure from a third-party's farm,[87] but to encompass breeding dogs,[88] raising timber,[89] or running a feed lot.[90] The most important factor in determining whether a particular activity qualifies as a farming operation is whether the debtor's operation is exposed to the inherent risks of farming.[91]

[ii] Debt Limit for Family Farmers

In addition, the debtor's aggregate debts must not exceed $3,544,525.[92] Debtors engaged in farming operations with debts exceeding this threshold may reorganize under Chapter 11's more elaborate procedures or may simply liquidate under Chapter 7.

[iii] Source of Family Farmers' Debts

In addition, since the 2005 Amendments, at least 50% of the debtor's "aggregate noncontingent liquidated debts," measured as of the debtor's petition, must have arisen out of the debtor's farming operation.[93] To

---

83 Bankruptcy Code § 101(18)(A).

84 In re Watford, 898 F.2d 1525 (11th Cir. 1990).

85 Bankruptcy Code § 101(21).

86 In re Tim Wargo & Sons, Inc., 869 F.2d 1128 (8th Cir. 1989); *but see* In re Blanton Smith Corp., 7 B.R. 410 (Bankr. M.D. Tenn. 1980) (debtor who owned chickens that were tended by another was eligible for Chapter 12 relief).

87 Federal Land Bank of Columbia v. McNeal (In re McNeal), 848 F.2d 170 (11th Cir. 1988); *see also* In re Blackwelder Harvesting Co., 106 B.R. 301 (Bankr. M.D. Fla. 1989) (fruit picking service conducted for citrus growers).

88 In re Maike, 77 B.R. 832 (Bankr. D. Kan. 1987).

89 In re Sugar Pine Ranch, 100 B.R. 28 (Bankr. D. Or. 1989) (harvesting timber and replanting on a sustained yield basis).

90 In re Cattle Complex Corp., 54 B.R. 50 (Bankr. D.N.M. 1985) (for purposes of determining whether Chapter 11 debtor could be compelled to convert case to Chapter 7).

91 In re Osborne, 323 B.R. 489 (Bankr. D. Or. 2005).

92 Bankruptcy Code § 101(18)(A). Before the 2005 amendments, this amount was lower: only $1,500,000. As with most dollar amounts in the Bankruptcy Code, the $3,544,525 figure in § 101(18)(A) will be adjusted every three years by a factor reflecting the change in the United States Department of Labor's Consumer Price Index, and rounded to the nearest $25 amount that represents the change. Bankruptcy Code § 104(b).

93 Bankruptcy Code § 101(18)(A). Before the 2005 amendments, 80% of the debtor's aggregate debts must have arisen from the farming operation.

determine whether this 50% threshold is satisfied, "a debt for the [debtor's] principal residence" is not included unless that debt "arises out of a farming operation."[94]

[iv] Source of Family Farmers' Income

Moreover, if the debtor is an individual or an individual and spouse, 50% of the debtor's gross *income* must have been derived from the debtor's farm operations.[95] Debtors who have been too successful in finding other sources of income to support their failing farm finances must seek relief either under Chapter 11 or Chapter 13.[96]

[v] Corporate Family Farmers

If the debtor is a corporation or a partnership, additional requirements are imposed. First, a corporation or a partnership only qualifies as a "family farmer" if more than 50% of the stock or equity of the debtor is held by "one family, or by one family and the relatives of the members of such family," and if those family members and their relatives conduct the farming operations.[97] Moreover, if the debtor is a corporation, its stock must not be publicly traded.[98] Second, more than 80% of the debtor's assets must relate to the farming operation.[99] As with individual family farmers, the debtor's aggregate debts must be within the $3,544,525 threshold, and at least 50% of its total debt must arise from the farm.[100]

[c] Family Fisherman

The expansion of the scope of eligibility for relief under Chapter 12 to include "family fisherman" resolves most uncertainties regarding whether commercial fishing and aquacultural operations qualify debtors for Chapter 12 relief. The definition of a "family fisherman with regular annual income" is similar to the definition of a family farmer with regular income. So long

---

[94] Bankruptcy Code § 101(18)(A). In the case of a corporation or partnership, this exclusion is for a dwelling owned by the debtor and used as a principal residence by one of the debtor's shareholders or partners, however, consistent with the rule for individual debtors, the exclusion does not apply if the debt arises out of the farming operation. *Id.* § 101(18)(B)(ii).

[95] Bankruptcy Code § 101(18)(A). The debtor's income is based either on the taxable year immediately preceding the taxable year in which the petition was filed, or on "each of the 2d and 3d taxable years" preceding the year of the petition. *Id.* § 101(18)(A)(i)-(ii).

[96] *See also* In re Easton, 883 F.2d 630 (8th Cir. 1989) (rental income from farm land is not income from debtor's farming operation); *but see* In re Bircher, 241 B.R. 11 (Bankr. S.D. Iowa 1999) (capital gain from real estate that was previously used in farming operation included in farming operation's income).

[97] Bankruptcy Code § 101(18)(B). "Family" is not defined, but "relative" means an "individual related by affinity or consanguinity within the third degree as determined by the common law, or individual in a step or adoptive relationship within such third degree." Bankruptcy Code § 101(45).

[98] Bankruptcy Code § 101(18)(B)(iii).

[99] Bankruptcy Code § 101(18)(B)(i).

[100] Bankruptcy Code § 101(18)(B)(ii).

as the debtor is a "family fisherman" and has income sufficient to feasibly fund a Chapter 12 plan, relief is available. As with family farmers, the devil is in the details of who qualifies as a family fisherman.

[i] Commercial Fishing Operation

As with the definition of a family farmer, individuals, individuals and their spouses, corporations, and partnerships may all qualify for Chapter 12 relief as a family fisherman. Under this sub-category, the debtor must conduct a "commercial fishing operation."[101] A commercial fishing operation means either "the catching or harvesting of fish, shrimp, lobsters, urchins, seaweed, shellfish, or other aquatic species or products of such species" or "aquaculture activities consisting of raising for market any species or product [listed above]."[102]

[ii] Debt Limit for Family Fishermen

The debt limit for family fishermen is lower than that for family farmers at only $1,642,500, less than half of the limit imposed on family farmers. Thus, for otherwise-eligible debtors with debts between $1,642,500 and $3,544,525, the distinction between farming and fishing remains alive.[103]

[iii] Source of Family Fishermen's Debts

For prospective Chapter 12 debtors who are individuals, 80% or more of the debtor's "aggregate noncontingent, liquidated debts" must arise from the commercial fishing operation, excluding debt for a family residence that did not arise out of the fishing operation. Thus, if the debtor lives on his fishing boat, the debt on the boat is included to determine whether the 80% threshold has been met. For family farmers, only 50% of an individual's debt must have arisen from the debtor's farming operation, again making the distinction between agriculture and aquaculture important to a debtor's eligibility under Chapter 12.[104]

[iv] Corporate Family Fishermen

As with family farmers, provision is made for commercial fishing operations operated as a proprietorship, a partnership, or a corporation. If the debtor is an individual or an individual and spouse, the income received

---

[101] Bankruptcy Code § 101(19A).

[102] Bankruptcy Code § 101(7A).

[103] In re Watford, 898 F.2d 1525, 1529 (11th Cir. 1990) ("stone crabbing" not a farming operation). As with most dollar amounts in the Bankruptcy Code, the amount § 101(19A)(A)(i) will be adjusted every three years by a factor reflecting the change in the Department of Labor's Consumer Price Index, and rounded to the nearest $25 amount that represents the change. Bankruptcy Code § 104(b)(1).

[104] Prior to 2005, the debt threshold for family farmers was 80%. The 2005 legislation reduced the required percentage to 50%, and at the same time, it established an 80% threshold for family fishermen.

from the fishing operation must be more than 50% of the couple's gross income.[105] If the debtor is a corporation or a partnership, more than 50% of the stock or equity of the debtor must be held by "the family that conducts the commercial fishing operation, or by the family and the relatives of the members of such family [who] conduct . . . the . . . operation."[106] As with family farms, if the debtor is a corporation, its stock must not be publicly traded.[107] Further, more than 80% of the debtor's assets must relate to the fishing operation.[108] Likewise, as with individual family fishermen, the debtor's aggregate debts must be within the $1,642,500 threshold, and at least 80% of its total debt must arise from the fishing operation.[109]

[6] Eligibility for Relief Under Chapter 13 — Individuals with Regular Income

"Individuals with regular income" can obtain relief under Chapter 13 by submitting a plan to restructure their debts.[110] Eligibility for relief is also somewhat restricted, but with fewer details than those imposed for relief under Chapter 12.

[a] Individual or Individual and Spouse

A Chapter 13 debtor must be either an individual or an individual and spouse. Corporations, partnerships, and other artificial entities are not eligible. Further, an individual who is a stockbroker or commodity broker is ineligible and may seek relief only under Chapter 7.[111]

[b] Regular Income

The debtor must have income that "is sufficiently stable and regular to enable such individual to make payments under a [Chapter 13 plan]."[112] The source of the income does not matter.[113] Unlike old Chapter XIII, which required the debtor's income to be from wages or salaries, Chapter 13 permits the debtor to use income from such things as pensions, public assistance payments, self-employment, or investments. And, although income derived from the kindness of strangers may not be adequate, support payments and stable and predictable income from friends and family

---

[105] Bankruptcy Code § 101(19A)(A)(ii). Here, however, the debtor's income is based only on the taxable year immediately preceding the taxable year in which the petition was filed.

[106] Bankruptcy Code § 101(19A)(B)(i)(I)-(II).

[107] Bankruptcy Code § 101(19A)(B)(i)(III).

[108] Bankruptcy Code § 101(18)(B)(i).

[109] Bankruptcy Code § 101(18)(B)(ii).

[110] *See* Chapter 18, Rehabilitation of Individuals with Regular Income, *infra*.

[111] Bankruptcy Code § 101(30).

[112] Bankruptcy Code § 101(30).

[113] Under the Bankruptcy Act of 1898, in effect until 1979, former chapter XIII was available only to "wage earners."

is sufficient.[114] Likewise, reasonably predictable fluctuations in a debtor's income, such as those associated with seasonal employment, or a sole proprietorship in a seasonal business, do not necessarily preclude the debtor from Chapter 13 relief.

Prior to 2005, the typical Chapter 13 plan lasted three years, this translated into a requirement for reasonably predictable and steady income over that three-year period. Under BAPCPA, a Chapter 13 debtor whose income exceeds the state minimum must commit to a five-year plan. It is important to distinguish the regular income requirement, which is a threshold for eligibility from the feasibility standard for confirmation of a plan. The difference is that a party seeking to dismiss a debtor's case must show that the debtor does not have regular income. By contrast, under § 1325(a), the court must find that the debtor has sufficient income to make the payments provided for under the proposed plan.[115]

[c] Chapter 13 Debt Limits

The debtor (and, where applicable, the debtor's spouse) must have noncontingent, liquidated, unsecured debts less than $336,900, and noncontingent, liquidated, secured debts less than $1,010,650.[116] In a joint case involving a married couple, debts are aggregated to determine whether they exceed these thresholds. However, there is no requirement that both spouses file, nor any requirement that if they both file they must file jointly. These limits, which were once much lower,[117] were designed to restrict Chapter 13 to debtors with relatively modest debts. Even these limits, however, allow some Chapter 13 debtors to reorganize small businesses run as sole proprietorships without using the more cumbersome processes of Chapter 11.

[i] Contingent Debts

Debts are included in these calculations only if they are "noncontingent" and "liquidated."[118] Debts that are "contingent" and those that are

---

[114] In re Baird, 228 B.R. 324 (Bankr. M.D. Fla. 1999) (voluntary support from debtor's son); In re Murphy, 226 B.R. 601 (Bankr. M.D. Tenn. 1998) (income supplied by live-in companion of unmarried debtor).

[115] Bankruptcy Code § 1325(a)(6); *see* § 18.08[B] Feasibility, *infra*.

[116] Bankruptcy Code § 109(e). As with most dollar amounts in the Bankruptcy Code, the figures in § 109(e) will be adjusted every three years by a factor reflecting the increase in the Department of Labor's Consumer Price Index and rounded to the nearest $25 amount that represents the change. Bankruptcy Code § 104(b)(1).

[117] In the 1978 Bankruptcy Reform Act, the limits were $100,000 for unsecured debts and $350,000 for secured debts. Bankruptcy Reform Act of 1978, Pub. L. No. 95-958, 92 Stat. 2549, 2557. They were increased in 1994, the same time that the periodic escalation provision was added, to $250,000 and $750,000 respectively. Pub. L. No. 103-394 § 108, 108 Stat. 4106, 4112. The amounts were automatically escalated in 2001, 2004 and 2007 pursuant to Bankruptcy Code § 104(b). They were scheduled to be increased again on April 7, 2010 and 2013.

[118] Bankruptcy Code § 109(e).

unliquidated are excluded from the debt totals used to determine the debtor's eligibility. A debt is contingent if the debtor's liability is contingent on the occurrence or non-occurrence of an event that is uncertain to occur when the debtor's petition is filed.[119] The most common circumstance that makes a debt contingent is where the debtor is liable only as a guarantor, and the principal debtor is not in default when the guarantor's Chapter 13 petition is filed. For example, if Harlan Wolff has guaranteed a $340,000 note owed by Titanic Industries, Inc. to North Atlantic Finance Co., but Titanic Industries has not yet defaulted, Wolff's contingent liability on the note does not render him ineligible for Chapter 13 relief. However, if Titanic has already fallen into default at the time of Wolff's Chapter 13 petition, removing all contingencies on his liability, the amount of this unsecured debt alone place's Wolff beyond the $336,900 limit on unsecured debts for Chapter 13 debtors.[120] The mere fact that the creditor has not yet sued or obtained a judgment against the debtor whose legal responsibility for the debt is not contingent, does not make the debt contingent.[121]

[ii] Liquidated Debts

Whether a debt is liquidated depends on whether it is "subject to 'ready determination and precision in computation of the amount due.' "[122] The mere fact that a debt is disputed does not necessarily make it unliquidated. Courts use several different tests to establish whether a disputed debt is subject to ready determination and thus liquidated. Some courts treat disputed debts as liquidated if a precise computation can be accomplished after a simple hearing, but unliquidated if an extensive, contested evidentiary hearing is required.[123] Other courts treat disputed debts as liquidated if the process to establish the debt is "fixed, certain, or otherwise determined by a specific standard" regardless of the extent of the dispute or the amount of evidence necessary to determine the amount of the claim.[124]

Still other courts recognize that the nature of the dispute over liability might make the amount of the debt difficult to determine, and they refuse to exclude questions of liability from the test.[125] Under this method, disputed tort claims are far more likely to be unliquidated than disputed tax and contract claims. Debtors facing unresolved tort claims may find it best

---

[119] The fact that there was still a condition to be fulfilled after the petition date confirms that the debt in question was not noncontingent when the debtor entered Chapter 13, and, thus, the debt should not be considered in the § 109(e) eligibility analysis. *E.g.*, Mazzeo v. United States (In re Mazzeo), 131 F.3d 295 (2d Cir. 1997); In re Knight, 55 F.3d 231, 234 (7th Cir. 1995) (quoting S. Rep. No. 95-989 at 22 (1978), *reprinted in* 1978 U.S.C.C.A.N. 5787, 5809); *see also* H.R. Rep. No. 95-595 at 310 (1978), *reprinted in* 1978 U.S.C.C.A.N. 5963, 6267.

[120] *E.g.*, In re Winston, 309 B.R. 61 (Bankr. M.D. Fla. 2004).

[121] *E.g.*, In re Flaherty, 10 B.R. 118 (Bankr. N.D. Ill. 1981).

[122] *E.g.*, In re Slack, 187 F.3d 1070, 1073 (9th Cir. 1999); In re Huelbig, 299 B.R. 721, 723 (Bankr. D.R.I. 2004).

[123] Slack v. Wilshire Ins. Co. (In re Slack), 187 F.3d 1070, 1073–74 (9th Cir. 1999).

[124] In re Barcal, 213 B.R. 1008, 1014 (B.A.P. 8th Cir. 1997).

[125] Ho v. Dowell (In re Ho), 274 B.R. 867, 872–75 (B.A.P. 9th Cir. 2002).

to file a Chapter 13 petition before such claims are adjudicated in state court, rather than wait until after judgment, only to find that they are ineligible for Chapter 13 relief because of the size of the judgment.[126]

The debtor's eligibility is determined based on circumstances existing when the debtor's petition is filed. Thus, debts that become either noncontingent or liquidated while the debtor's case is pending do not impair the debtor's ability to continue his case, even if this places him beyond the § 109(e) debt limits.[127]

Of course, the debtor may not become eligible simply by contesting liability for a debt that would otherwise place him above the limit. As the foregoing discussion suggests, merely scheduling a debt as disputed will not lead a court to treat the debt as unliquidated if its amount can readily be determined.[128]

[iii] Secured Debts

The prevailing view uses the valuation test of Bankruptcy Code § 506(a) to determine the extent to which a debt is secured or unsecured.[129] Under that test, a "claim" is secured only to the extent of the value of the collateral.[130] Thus, if a debtor had a liquidated, noncontingent debt of $40,000, secured by collateral worth $25,000, only the $25,000 secured portion of the claim would count toward the secured credit limit. The remaining $15,000 unsecured portion of the claim would be added toward the limit on unsecured claims.

[C] Petition, Lists, Schedules, Statements, Certificates and Disclosures[131]

A debtor's petition must usually be accompanied by a number of other documents, as specified by the Bankruptcy Rules and their accompanying Official Forms. The main purpose of these other documents is to provide the court, the trustee, and creditors with information about the debtor's financial situation. These forms are designed to be easily completed and for the most part they are. Greater simplicity arises from the fact that there

---

126 Such debtors can still obtain relief in Chapter 11, which contains no debt limits. *See* Bankruptcy Code § 109(d).

127 In re Slack, 187 F.3d 1070, 1073 (9th Cir. 1999).

128 In re Pearson, 773 F.2d 751, 756 (6th Cir. 1985) (holding that the court will look only to the schedules to see if made in good faith and to determine if the debt meets the statutory limitations).

129 Scovis v. Henrichsen (In re Scovis), 249 F.3d 975 (9th Cir. 2001).

130 The modest difference between the language of § 506(a), which refers to secured "claims," and that in § 109(e), which refers to secured "debts," has not yielded a different result.

131 Henry E. Hildebrand, III & Keith M. Lundin, *Selected Changes Affecting Consumer Bankruptcy Practice in the Bankruptcy Abuse Prevention and Consumer Protection Act of 2005*, 59 Consumer Fin. L.Q. Rep. 370 (2005); Henry J. Sommer, *Trying to Make Sense Out of Nonsense: Representing Consumers Under the "Bankruptcy Abuse Prevention and Consumer Protection Act of 2005,"* 79 Am. Bankr. L.J. 191, 211 (2005).

is excellent software available from several sources to assist in translating raw information to completed forms.

Not surprisingly, corporate debtors must also submit a declaration by an officer or other authorized agent that the schedules are true and correct.[132] Individual debtors must sign a similar declaration.[133] Other documents may be required, depending on the type of bankruptcy. Generally speaking, these initial documents must be filed within fifteen days after the petition is filed.[134]

[1] Petition

The debtor's petition contains, among other information, the debtor's name and address; whether the debtor is an individual, partnership, corporation or other entity; the chapter under which the debtor seeks relief; the estimated number and amount of debts; the basis for proper venue in the district in which the petition is filed; and several other matters required by the Code or the Rules.[135]

[2] Schedules of Debts and Assets; Statement of Affairs

Along with their petition, debtors must file a list of their creditors[136] and Schedules A through J, providing detailed information concerning their property, debts, executory contracts, co-debtors, income, and expenses.[137] The required schedules consist of:

- Schedule A — All real property interests of the debtor, other than leasehold interests, and any encumbrances.
- Schedule B — All personal property, other than leases or executory contracts. Encumbrances on the property are not included on Schedule B.
- Schedule C — All property that the debtor claims as exempt.
- Schedules D through F — All secured, priority, and general unsecured claims.
- Schedule G — Executory contracts and unexpired leases.
- Schedule H — Co-debtors.
- Schedule I — Individual debtor's current income.

[132] *See* Official Bankruptcy Form 2.

[133] *See* Official Bankruptcy Form 1.

[134] Fed. R. Bankr. P. 1007.

[135] *See* Official Bankruptcy Form 1.

[136] Fed. R. Bankr. P. 1007(a). In a voluntary case, the list of creditors is not required if the schedule of liabilities is filed with the petition. Also note that in Chapter 11 and Chapter 9 proceedings, the debtor must supply a separate list of the twenty largest unsecured claims. Fed. R. Bankr. P. 1007(d).

[137] Bankruptcy Code § 521(1).

- Schedule J — Individual debtor's current living expenses.[138]
- A Statement of Financial Affairs, which provides information about the debtor's recent financial history.[139]

[3] Additional Documents for Individual Consumer Debtors[140]

Individual Chapter 7 debtors must provide a variety of other documents, designed to assist the trustee and creditors in evaluating the debtor's compliance with the Code's requirements and in detecting abuse. Many of these items are recent additions, added by BAPCPA. Some items must be filed with the court; others must be submitted to the trustee. This lengthy list of additional documents, some, but not all, of which may be waived by the court,[141] includes:

- a statement of the debtor's intention regarding his secured debts, indicating whether he expects to reaffirm the debts, redeem the collateral, avoid the lien, or surrender the collateral to the creditor;[142]
- a certification that the debtor has received an appropriate pre-bankruptcy credit briefing from an approved nonprofit budget-and-credit-counseling agency within 180 days prior to the debtor's petition;[143]
- a copy of any debt repayment plan developed through the debtor's credit counseling briefing;[144]
- a certificate from the debtor's attorney or "petition-preparer" indicating that the debtor has been given the notice required by § 342(b), briefly explaining Chapters 7, 11, 12, and 13 and the general purpose, benefits, and costs of proceeding under each of those chapters; describing "the types of services available from

[138] Fed R. Bankr. P. 1007(b)(1). *See also* Official Bankruptcy Form 6, which sets out the standardized form of the various schedules.

[139] *See* Official Bankruptcy Form 7.

[140] Henry J. Sommer, *Trying to Make Sense Out of Nonsense: Representing Consumers Under the "Bankruptcy Abuse Prevention and Consumer Protection Act of 2005,"* 79 Am. Bankr. L.J. 191, 211 (2005).

[141] *See* Bankruptcy Code § 521(a)(1)(B). In some jurisdictions, courts have exercised their authority to require some specified items, such as the debtor's pay stubs, to be submitted to the trustee rather than filed with the court. One might speculate that this was done at the request of the bankruptcy court clerk, who bears the burden of storing items that are filed with the court.

[142] Bankruptcy Code § 521(2)(A); Fed. R. Bankr. P. 1007(b)(2).

[143] Bankruptcy Code §§ 109(h), 521(b). Individual consumer debtors are also required to complete a "personal financial management course" from an appropriate credit counseling agency, prior to receiving a discharge. Bankruptcy Code §§ 111, 727(a)(11), 1328(g). Current Official Bankruptcy Form 1 includes a certification that this briefing has occurred as part of the debtor's petition.

[144] Bankruptcy Code § 521(b)(2).

credit counseling agencies";[145] alerting the debtor about the criminal penalties associated with concealing assets or making a false oath or statement in the case; and advising the debtor that the information supplied in connection with his petition is subject to review by the United States Attorney General;[146]

- if the debtor has an attorney, the written contract with the debtor and his attorney;[147]
- a copy of the debtor's most recent year's federal tax return;[148]
- upon request by the court, the trustee, or a creditor, a copy of any post-petition tax returns filed by the debtor while the case is pending;[149]
- copies of the debtor's pay stubs received by the debtor during the sixty days prior to his petition;[150]
- a statement of the debtor's "monthly net income, itemized to show how the amount is calculated";[151]
- in a Chapter 13 case, a statement disclosing any reasonably anticipated increase in the debtor's income or expenditures over the twelve months after the date of the debtor's petition;[152] and
- the record of any interest the debtor has in an education IRA or under a qualified state tuition program.[153]

Section 707(b)(4)(D), added in 2005, now provides that "[t]he signature of an attorney on the petition shall constitute a certification that the

---

[145] Bankruptcy Code §§ 521(a)(1)(B)(iii) & 342(b)(1); *see* Official Bankruptcy Form 1; Paul M. Black & Michael J. Herbert, *Bankcard's Revenge: A Critique of the 1984 Consumer Credit Amendments to the Bankruptcy Code*, 19 U. Rich. L. Rev. 845, 852–55 (1985).

[146] Bankruptcy Code §§ 521(a)(1)(B)(iii) & 342(b)(2). This latter section refers primarily to the Office of the United States Trustee, a branch of the United States Department of Justice, and also potentially to the Office of the United States Attorney for the district in which the petition was filed.

If the debtor is not represented by an attorney, and his petition is not signed by a "petition preparer" the debtor must supply a certificate that the necessary notice was "received and read by the debtor." Bankruptcy Code § 521(a)(1)(B)(iii)(II).

[147] Bankruptcy Code § 528(a)(1).

[148] Bankruptcy Code § 521(e)(2)(A)(i). In addition, the debtor must supply a copy of the return to any creditor who requests one. Chapter 13 debtors must also file copies of federal, state, and local tax returns with the appropriate tax authorities, or face dismissal. Bankruptcy Code § 1308.

[149] Bankruptcy Code § 521(f).

[150] Bankruptcy Code § 521(a)(1)(B)(iv); *see* In re Smith, No. 06-00249 B, 2006 WL 2946146 (Bankr. W.D.N.Y. Oct. 3, 2006). In some districts, this requirement is waived and replaced by a requirement that the debtor supply the necessary documents to the trustee.

[151] Bankruptcy Code § 521(a)(1)(B)(v). *See* Official Forms B22A (Chapter 7) and B22C (Chapter 13). These are the forms used in Chapter 7 cases to determine whether the debtor's Chapter 7 case is abusive. *See* § 707(b)(2)(C) & 18 U.S.C.S. § 2075 (2000) (that's right, it's part of the United States Criminal Code).

[152] Bankruptcy Code § 521(a)(1)(B)(vi).

[153] Bankruptcy Code § 521(c).

attorney has no knowledge after an inquiry that the information in the schedules filed with such petition is incorrect."[154] This language should be read in the context of a variety of other "attorney liability" provisions added in 2005, which seek to impose additional duties on attorneys who represent consumer debtors.[155] The principal question in interpreting § 707(b)(4)(D) is the extent of the "inquiry" necessary to avoid running afoul of any consequences of signing and thus certifying a set of inaccurate schedules.[156]

[D] Joint Petitions

As a practical matter, many individual bankruptcies are rooted in the mutual financial difficulties of a married couple. Because of this, the Code explicitly permits joint filing by spouses.[157] The key advantage to joint filing is lowered costs for both the court and the debtors. A joint case may make administration of the estate more efficient. At minimum, it at least limits the filing fee. In a joint case, only a single filing fee is required.

However, joint filing does not necessarily mean that the debtors' cases will be "consolidated" — handled as if they were a single case. Unless they are consolidated, each spouse's estate is separate.[158] Depending on the extent of the married couple's joint ownership of property and joint liability for their debts, the court may either leave both estates independent of each other, consolidate the estates in part, or consolidate them entirely.[159] For example, if the spouses held little property in joint ownership and had few obligations for which both were liable, the court would probably administer the case as two separate estates. However, most married debtors' assets and debts are considerably intermingled, making joint administration more sensible.

---

[154] Bankruptcy Code § 707(b)(4)(D).

[155] *See* § 6.02[F] Attorney's Obligations Regarding Debtor's Schedules; *see generally* Gary Neustadter, *2005: A Consumer Bankruptcy Odyssey,* 39 Creighton L. Rev. 225, 311–54 (2006); Henry J. Sommer, *Trying to Make Sense Out of Nonsense: Representing Consumers Under the "Bankruptcy Abuse Prevention and Consumer Protection Act of 2005,"* 79Am. Bankr. L.J. 191, 204–11 (2005); Catherine E. Vance & Corinne Cooper, *Nine Traps and One Slap: Attorney Liability Under the New Bankruptcy Law,* 79 Am. Bankr. L.J. 283 (2005); Ad Hoc Committee on Bankruptcy Court Structure, ABA Section of Business Law, *Attorney Liability Under Section 707(b)(4) of the Bankruptcy Abuse Prevention and Consumer Protection Act of 2005,* 61 Bus. Law. 697 (2006).

[156] Henry J. Sommer, *Trying to Make Sense Out of Nonsense: Representing Consumers Under the "Bankruptcy Abuse Prevention and Consumer Protection Act of 2005,"* 79 Am. Bankr. L.J. 191, 206 (2005).

[157] Bankruptcy Code § 302(a).

[158] In re Jorczak, 314 B.R. 474 (Bankr. D. Conn. 2004); Carpenter v. Fanaras (In re Fanaras), 263 B.R. 655 (Bankr. D. Mass. 2001).

[159] Bankruptcy Code § 302(b); *see generally* Reider v. FDIC (In re Reider), 31 F.3d 1102 (11th Cir. 1994).

[E] Filing Fees

Filing fees in bankruptcy cases range from $235 for a Chapter 13 case to $1,000 for a Chapter 11 case.[160] In addition, a $39 administrative fee is imposed for all cases and an additional $15 trustee's fee is charged in Chapter 7 cases.[161]

For many years, there was no such thing as a free bankruptcy case; the Bankruptcy Code made no provision for an *in forma pauperis* bankruptcy petition.[162] This changed in 2005 when Congress authorized bankruptcy courts to waive the filing fee for Chapter 7 debtors whose income is less than 150 percent of the poverty line.[163] Where the filing fee is not waived, it may be paid in installments with permission from the court (which is routinely granted).[164]

[F] Attorney's Obligations Regarding Debtors' Schedules[165]

The 2005 Amendments imposed new due diligence obligations on debtors' attorneys. They also subject debtors' attorneys to sanctions if they fail to meet these obligations. These obligations arise primarily in connection with the new means testing mechanisms to determine whether a debtor's Chapter 7 petition is an abuse of the opportunity for relief provided by liquidation cases.

New § 707(b)(4)(A) permits the court to use existing procedures under Bankruptcy Rule 9011 to order the debtor's attorney to "reimburse the trustee for all reasonable costs in prosecuting a [successful] motion" under § 707(b), seeking to have the debtor's case converted or dismissed due to abuse.[166] Similarly, new § 707(b)(4)(B) permits the court to assess an appropriate civil penalty and provide for payment of that penalty to the trustee if the attorney for the debtor violates Rule 9011 in some other manner.[167] Rule 9011 mirrors Federal Rule of Civil Procedure 11 by

---

160 28 U.S.C.S. § 1930(a) (LexisNexis Supp. 2006).

161 28 U.S.C.S. § 1930(b) (LexisNexis Supp. 2006).

162 *See* United States v. Kras, 409 U.S. 434 (1973) (denial of right to *in forma pauperis* bankruptcy petition not a deprivation of due process).

163 28 U.S.C.S. § 1930(f) (LexisNexis Supp.2006); In re Bradshaw, 349 B.R. 511, 515 (Bankr. E.D. Tenn. 2006) (court has discretion to grant or deny waiver to qualifying debtors); In re Nuttall, 334 B.R. 921 (Bankr. W.D. Mo. 2005) (granting waiver).

164 Fed. R. Bankr. P. 1006(b).

165 Alan Eisler, *The BAPCPA's Chilling Effect on Debtor's Counsel*, 55 Am. U. L. Rev. 1333, 1335–39 (2006); Gary Neustadter, *2005: A Consumer Bankruptcy Odyssey*, 39 Creighton L. Rev. 225, 342–44; Henry J. Sommer, *Trying to Make Sense Out of Nonsense: Representing Consumers Under the "Bankruptcy Abuse Prevention and Consumer Protection Act of 2005,"* 79 Am. Bankr. L.J. 191, 204 (2005); Catherine E. Vance & Corinne Cooper, *Nine Traps and One Slap: Attorney Liability under the New Bankruptcy Law*, Am. Bankr. L.J. 283, 286–88 (2005).

166 Bankruptcy Code § 707(b)(4)(A).

167 Bankruptcy Code § 707(b)(4)(B).

permitting the court to impose a civil penalty on attorneys who violate its provisions by advancing unwarranted positions.[168] Thus, § 707(b)(4)(A) and (B), by themselves, do not impose significant additional risks on debtors' attorneys than they already face as a result of their own misconduct.[169]

New § 707(b)(4)(C) is considerably more burdensome for consumer debtors' attorneys. It provides:

> The signature of an attorney on a petition, pleading, or written motion shall constitute a certification that the attorney has —
>
> (i) performed a reasonable investigation into the circumstances that gave rise to the petition, pleading, or written motion; and
>
> (ii) determined that the petition, pleading, or written motion —
>
> (I) is *well grounded in fact*; and
>
> (II) is warranted by existing law or a good faith argument for the extension, modification, or reversal of existing law and does not constitute an abuse under [§ 707(b)(1)].[170]

This requires attorneys to conduct a "reasonable investigation" into the accuracy of the information that is relayed to the attorney by his or her client and to make a "determination" that his or her client's positions are "well grounded in fact." This goes well beyond the traditional obligations imposed by Bankruptcy Rule 9011, which only require an attorney to certify that the factual assertions in the debtor's petition and schedules have "evidentiary support."[171] The Rule 9011 standard would likely be satisfied based on the debtor's statements to the debtor's attorney. The requirement of a reasonable investigation and a determination that the information filed with the court is "well grounded in fact" requires the debtor's attorney to go further and conduct an independent investigation of the accuracy of the information provided by the debtor. The attorney is likely required to seek independent verification of the nature and extent of the debtor's assets, their value, the number and amount of the debtor's obligations, the sources and amount of the debtor's income, and other aspects of the debtor's financial circumstances that are reflected by the debtor's petition and accompanying schedules. It also requires the debtor's attorney to verify that the debtor has not filed a bankruptcy petition during the past eight years. This does not quite make the debtor's attorney a guarantor of the accuracy of the information contained in these documents, but it may come dangerously close.

There are, of course, horror stories about the misconduct of dishonest or negligent lawyers whose firms create facts out of thin air in an effort to assist their clients.[172] But, the Code and professional conduct standards

---

[168] Fed. R. Bankr. P. 9011(b).

[169] Gary Neustadter, *2005: A Consumer Bankruptcy Odyssey*, 39 Creighton L. Rev. 225, 311–54 (2006).

[170] Bankruptcy Code § 707(b)(4)(C) (emphasis added).

[171] Fed. R. Bankr. P. 9011(b)(3).

[172] *E.g.*, In re Diaz, 348 B.R. 752 (Bankr. S.D. Tex. 2006) (attorney or members of his staff fabricated $800 monthly charitable contribution in completing client's schedules).

already prohibit this sort of dishonest conduct. Imposing additional requirements that require bankruptcy lawyers to investigate the accuracy of information provided by their clients is likely to drive up the costs of providing bankruptcy services to consumer debtors and thus increase the fees debtors' attorneys will inevitably charge to cover their additional expenses.[173] They also seem likely to drive away risk-averse bankruptcy practitioners, as well as those who only occasionally handle bankruptcy cases. Reducing the supply of consumer bankruptcy attorneys seems destined to have an inevitable effect on the price that will be charged by those who continue to provide these services.[174]

§ 6.03 Commencement of an Involuntary Case[175]

[A] Purpose of Involuntary Petitions

One of the great debates that surrounded the enactment of the 1898 Bankruptcy Act was over involuntary bankruptcy.[176] Representatives whose chief concerns were for the impecunious, especially farmers, wanted to make voluntary bankruptcy and its attendant discharge of debt available, but opposed involuntary bankruptcy, which they feared would be used by banks to force debtors into the clutches of the federal courts. The compromise that was enacted permitted creditors to bring involuntary bankruptcy cases against debtors, but only when the debtor was not just in some financial trouble, but also had engaged in conduct that either created special risks for creditors or was considered wrongful. Under the 1898 Act,

[173] The Congressional Budget Office estimated that attorney costs would increase between $150 and $500 per Chapter 7 cases as a result of the requirement that debtors' attorneys conduct a reasonable investigation of a debtor's financial affairs and that they compute the debtor's eligibility for Chapter 7 under the new means testing rules in § 707(b). Congressional Budget Office Cost Estimate, S. 256 Bankruptcy Abuse Prevention and Consumer Protection Act of 2005, 14 (2005), available at www.cbo.gov/ftpdocs/62xx/doc6266/s256hjud.pdf (last viewed on July 7, 2006).

[174] Gary Neustadter, *2005: A Consumer Bankruptcy Odyssey*, 39 Creighton L. Rev. 225, 347–53 (2006). In Columbus, Ohio, where one of your co-author's resides, local attorneys report that the price of a no frills Chapter 7 case rose $250-500 after the 2005 amendments went into effect. *Compare* In re Murray, 348 B.R. 917 (Bankr. M.D. Ga. 2006) (administrative order raising amount that Chapter 13 debtor's attorney could charge without a separate detailed fee application, from $1,500 to $2,500), *with* In re Grunau, No. 9:06-bk-20573-ALP, 2006 Bankr. LEXIS 2503 (Bankr. M.D. Fla. Oct. 4, 2006) (Paskay, J.) (ordering attorney to disgorge fees charged to Chapter 13 debtors above $2,000).

[175] Susan Block-Lieb, *Why Creditors File So Few Involuntary Petitions and Why the Number Is Not Too Small*, 57 Brook. L. Rev. 803 (1991); David S. Kennedy, James E. Bailey, III, & R. Spencer Clift, III, *The Involuntary Bankruptcy Process: A Study of the Relevant Statutory and Procedural Provisions and Related Matters* 31 U. Mem. L. Rev. 1 (2000); Lynn M. LoPucki, *A General Theory of the Dynamics of the State Remedies/Bankruptcy System*, 1982 Wis. L. Rev. 311, 352–62; John C. McCoid, II, *The Occasion for Involuntary Bankruptcy*, 61 Am. Bankr. L.J. 195 (1987).

[176] Charles Warren, Bankruptcy in United States History (1935); John C. McCoid, *The Occasion for Involuntary Bankruptcy*, 61 Am Bankr. L.J. 195, 196–212 (1987).

therefore, involuntary proceedings were predicated on an "act of bankruptcy," such as making a fraudulent transfer or a preferential payment.

The 1978 Bankruptcy Code abolished this concept almost entirely. There are no acts of bankruptcy. Instead, the key to involuntary bankruptcy is the debtor's general non-payment of its debts as they become due. However, other protections, some of which were also found in the Bankruptcy Act, remain intact in the form of general restrictions on the eligibility of some debtors to be "involuntary" debtors. In addition, except in cases with only a few creditors, three unsecured creditors must collaborate and join an involuntary petition. This prevents a single creditor from forcing a debtor into bankruptcy to gain leverage in single-creditor collection case.[177]

Today, involuntary bankruptcy provides creditors with the opportunity to force the debtor to deal with its creditors collectively, when the debtor's assets are at substantial risk of being dissipated while the debtor resists the separate collection efforts of individual creditors. It also permits creditors to take advantage of the Bankruptcy Code's preference and other avoiding powers that are not available in collective procedures, such as receiverships and assignments for the benefit of creditors under state law.[178]

It has long been noted that the number of involuntary bankruptcies is much lower than one might expect.[179] Indeed, there are now so few that the Administrative Office of the Courts no longer keeps separate records of them. Indeed, some scholars have suggested that the large percentage of unsuccessful Chapter 11 reorganizations indicates that a loosening of the standards to force debtors into bankruptcy might induce debtors to file voluntary petitions sooner, before their financial condition becomes so desperate that their prospects for reorganization are slim.[180]

[B] Chapters Under Which Involuntary Petitions Are Permitted

One key restriction on involuntary bankruptcy is the limitation of the chapters under which an involuntary petition can be filed. The Bankruptcy Code permits involuntary proceedings only if the case is filed under Chapter 7 or Chapter 11. No involuntary cases are allowed under Chapters 9, 12, or 13. In practice, nearly all involuntary proceedings are filed as Chapter 7 cases, though the debtor may later seek to convert the case to Chapter 11.

---

[177] *See* Brad E. Godshall & Peter M. Giluhy, *The Involuntary Bankruptcy Petition: The World's Worst Debt Collection Device?*, 53 Bus. Law. 1315 (1998).

[178] *See* § 2.10 State Insolvency Proceedings, *supra*.

[179] Susan Block-Lieb, *Why Creditors File So Few Involuntary Petitions and Why the Number Is Not Too Small*, 57 Brook. L. Rev. 803 (1991).

[180] *See* Lynn M. LoPucki, *A General Theory of the Dynamics of the State Remedies/Bankruptcy System*, 1982 Wis. L. Rev. 311.

Chapter 9 proceedings involve the bankruptcy of a municipality. Since these proceedings directly affect the sovereign powers of the state that created the municipality, they are only allowed if the state permits them. Chapter 13 cannot be commenced involuntarily because compelling individual debtors to submit a portion of their income to the repayment of their debts would come perilously close to indentured servitude[181] and because a Chapter 13 plan would be highly impractical to administer without the voluntary cooperation of the debtor.[182] Similarly, involuntary petitions are not allowed under Chapter 12 because that chapter is available only to family farmers and their aquacultural cousins, family fishermen, and there is a long tradition of prohibiting involuntary petitions against farmers. Note, however, that the policies militating against involuntary wage earner plans are not followed rigorously. Involuntary Chapter 11 proceedings are permitted, even though the debtor may be an individual. Prior to the 2005 Amendments, concern about this was minimal because a debtor was free to move to convert the case to a Chapter 7 liquidation case. However, where individuals with consumer debts whose income exceeds the state median are involved, converting to Chapter 7 may not be an option. As such, this concern may now be more pressing.

[C] Persons Against Whom an Involuntary Petition May Be Filed

Even when the filing is under Chapter 7 or Chapter 11, the debtor must be a person who is generally eligible for relief under that chapter and a person who may be forced into bankruptcy. Some debtors are eligible for voluntary relief under Chapters 7 or 11, but ineligible to be the subject of an involuntary petition.

Railroads may not file voluntarily under Chapter 7[183] and thus are not permitted to be forced into Chapter 7 involuntarily.[184] By contrast, all railroads may file voluntary Chapter 11 petitions, and thus be forced into Chapter 11 by petitioning creditors.[185]

Financial institutions and insurance companies are entirely excluded from bankruptcy proceedings because their insolvency is governed by state law or by other federal law. Consequently, they cannot be the debtor in an involuntary bankruptcy case.[186] The exceptions are stockbrokers or commodity brokers, who can be a voluntary or involuntary debtors in Chapter 7 but not in Chapter 11.[187]

[181] *See* U.S. Const. amend. XIII.

[182] *See* Paul M. Black & Michael J. Herbert, *Bankcard's Revenge: A Critique of the 1984 Consumer Credit Amendments to the Bankruptcy Code*, 19 U. Rich. L. Rev. 845, 850 n.22 (1985).

[183] Bankruptcy Code § 109(b)(1).

[184] Bankruptcy Code § 303(a).

[185] Bankruptcy Code §§ 109(d), 303(a).

[186] Bankruptcy Code §§ 109(b), (d); 303(a).

[187] Bankruptcy Code §§ 109(d), 303(a).

Farmers, family farmers, and non-profit corporations can never be put into involuntary bankruptcy.[188] The first two categories reflect the fact that, although this has been a predominantly urban nation since 1920 (and although suggestions that there are now more lawyers in this country than farmers is a gross exaggeration[189]) the great bankruptcy compromise of 1898 that protected farmers from being forced into bankruptcy remains intact. Indeed, the compromise was broadened by the Code; under the 1898 Act, farmer really meant farmer: an individual who worked the land.[190] Under the current law, the term includes any person that receives more than 80 percent of its gross income from farming operations,[191] and "person" includes individuals, partnerships and corporations.[192] Thus, the "farmer" sheltered by a kindly Congress from being crushed by creditors may well be a multi-million dollar limited partnership, run by accountants from air-conditioned offices. Family fishermen, engaged in commercial fishing operations, on the other hand, are not exempt, except to the extent they might also fit the broader definition of a "farmer."[193]

Section 303(a) further provides that an involuntary petition may not be filed against "a corporation that is not a moneyed, business, or commercial corporation."[194] This somewhat obscure language means that non-profit or charitable corporations cannot be the target of an involuntary petition.[195] Thus, most churches, colleges, foundations, and political campaigns cannot be forced into bankruptcy. Charities remain eligible to file a voluntary petition.

An involuntary petition must be against one debtor; there are no joint involuntary cases.[196] If there is a group of related debtors or a married couple who owe money to the same creditors, those creditors might file separate petitions against each of the debtors and seek to have the cases consolidated.[197] However, each of the petitions must comply with all of the requirements set out in the Code.

---

[188] Bankruptcy Code § 303(a).

[189] Some say that there are more employees of the Department of Agriculture than farms. The Department of Agriculture employs about 115,000. As of 2002 there were approximately 2.1 million farms in the United States, with 1.9 million of these farms operated by individuals or families. *See* www.nass.usda.gov/census/census02/volume1/us/st99_1_001_001.pdf (last visited on Jan. 3, 2007). At the same time there about 1 million lawyers.

[190] Bankruptcy Act of 1898 § 1(17), 30 Stat. 544, 545 ("Farmer shall mean an individual personally engaged in farming or tillage of the soil") (repealed 1979).

[191] Bankruptcy Code § 101(20).

[192] Bankruptcy Code § 101(41).

[193] Bankruptcy Code § 101(21).

[194] Bankruptcy Code § 303(a).

[195] *E.g.*, In re Memorial Medical Center, Inc., 337 B.R. 388 (Bankr. D.N.M. 2005).

[196] *E.g.*, In re Bowshier, 313 B.R. 232, 234 (Bankr. S.D. Ohio 2004).

[197] *See* § 23.05 Consolidation of Cases of Related Debtors, *infra*.

[D] Creditors Necessary to Join an Involuntary Petition[198]

In most cases, an involuntary petition must be joined by a minimum of three creditors. Each of these creditors must have a claim that is both non-contingent and not the subject of a bona fide dispute.[199] The petitioning creditors must have an aggregate of at least $13,475 in unsecured claims.[200] Thus, if the three petitioning creditors' claims are $4,400 each, the $13,200 aggregate is not enough to satisfy the $13,475 threshold. However, if one of the petitioning creditors holds a claim for $13,473 and each of the others is owed $1, the $13,475 minimum threshold is met and the involuntary petition may proceed.

Creditors with collateral for their claims may join the petition, but only the unsecured portion of their claims, if any, may count toward the $12,300 threshold. Thus, a creditor with a $10,000 claim, secured by collateral worth $7,000, counts only as $3,000 of the required jurisdictional amount.

Note that fully secured creditors rarely have a reason to force a debtor into bankruptcy. Their rights can be protected far more easily through a traditional state court foreclosure proceeding or, in the case of creditors with security interests on personal property under Article 9 of the U.C.C., via self-help.

An involuntary petition must ordinarily be joined by "three or more entities each of whom" must either be "a holder of a claim" against the debtor or an "indenture trustee representing" the holder of a claim. Those who do not hold a claim do not qualify to be one of the three petitioning creditors. "Claim" includes a broad variety of rights to legal and equitable remedies.[201]

The requirement of multiple petitioners, each of whom holds a claim, is a fundamental part of the compromise that opened the door to involuntary bankruptcy in the 1898 Act and continues in the current Code. Judge Friendly discussed this compromise in a famous case:

> [T]he entire process that resulted in the enactment of the Act of 1898 was a pitched battle between those who wanted to give the

198 David S. Kennedy, James E. Bailey III, & R. Spencer Clift, III, *The Involuntary Bankruptcy Process: A Study of the Relevant Statutory and Procedural Provisions and Related Matters*, 31 U. Mem. L. Rev. 1 (2000); Eric J. Taube, *Involuntary Bankruptcy: Who May Be a Petitioning Creditor*, 21 Hous. L. Rev. 339 (1984).

199 Lawrence Ponoroff, *The Limits of Good Faith Analyses: Unraveling and Redefining Bad Faith in Involuntary Bankruptcy Proceedings*, 71 Neb. L. Rev. 209 (1992).

200 Bankruptcy Code § 303(b)(1). Prior to the 1994 Amendments, this amount was only $5,000. In 1994 the amount was raised to $10,000. As with most dollar amounts in the Bankruptcy Code, the amount in § 303(b) has been adjusted every three years since 1994, by a factor reflecting the increase in the Department of Labor's Consumer Price Index and rounded to the nearest $25 amount that represents the change. Bankruptcy Code § 104(b)(1) (2006). The amount will continue to be increased, at three-year intervals, in accordance with any rise in the consumer price index. It is scheduled to be increased again in 2010 and 2013.

201 Bankruptcy Code § 101(5); *see* § 10.02[A] Definition of Claim, *infra*.

> creditor an effective remedy to assure equal distribution of a bankrupt's assets and those who were determined to protect the debtor from the harassment of ill-considered or oppressive involuntary petitions, including those by a single creditor interest. The requirement of three creditors was one of many provisions reflecting a compromise between the two opposing positions.[202]

In recognition that some debtors have only a few creditors, involuntary petitions may sometimes be brought by a single petitioning creditor. If the debtor has fewer than twelve creditors with non-contingent, undisputed claims,[203] then the petition may be filed by a single creditor with at least a $13,475 unsecured claim.[204] In determining the number of creditors, employees and insiders of the debtor are excluded, as are creditors who have received various types of avoidable transfers.[205] Thus, the actual number of creditors may exceed twelve and a single creditor may still be able to initiate an involuntary petition on its own.

A petitioning creditor may have obtained the claim via an assignment from a previous creditor.[206] However, a claim will not be counted toward the minimum amount necessary if it was transferred or split for the purpose of filing an involuntary petition.[207] For example, suppose Citizen's Bank wished to file an involuntary petition against Franklin Manufacturing, but was unable to persuade two other creditors to join in the petition. If Citizen's Bank split its claim into three parts, and assigned two parts to two of its subsidiaries and then joined with those entities in an involuntary petition, relief would still be denied because the three petitioners should count as one creditor rather than three.

The rule against multiplying creditors by splitting claims is designed to protect the policy underlying the three-creditor requirement. The rule protects most debtors from being put into bankruptcy by a single creditor whose motivations may include personal animus or simple refusal to deal reasonably with an unpaid debt. This policy, however, is not always rigorously followed. Closely affiliated creditors which have separate claims against the debtor have been counted as separate petitioners, as long as each claim arose separately and the parties were not simply alter-egos of one another.[208]

---

[202] In re Gibraltor Amusements, 291 F.2d 22, 28 (2d Cir.) (Friendly, J., dissenting), *cert. denied*, 368 U.S. 925 (1961).

[203] Following the 2005 amendments § 303(b)(1), it is clear that petitioning creditors are required to hold claims that were not the subject of dispute regardless of whether the dispute was over the debtor's liability or the amount of the creditor's claim.

[204] Bankruptcy Code § 303(b)(2).

[205] Bankruptcy Code § 303(b)(2); *see* In re DemirCo Group (North America), L.L.C., 343 B.R. 898 (Bankr. C.D. Ill. 2006) (former employees are not "employees" within meaning of § 303(b)(2) and are thus not excluded from calculation of the number of creditors).

[206] Fed. R. Bankr. P. 1003(a). A transferee of a claim must attach to the petition the documents that evidence the transfer.

[207] Fed. R. Bankr. P. 1003(a); In re McMeekin & Shoreman, 16 B.R. 805, 808–09 (Bankr. D. Mass. 1982).

[208] Subway Equip. Leasing Corp. v. Sims (In re Sims), 994 F.2d 210 (5th Cir. 1993); In re Gibraltor Amusements, 291 F.2d 22 (2d Cir.), *cert. denied*, 368 U.S. 925 (1961).

The claims of petitioning creditors must be both "not contingent" and "undisputed."[209] As explained earlier in this chapter,[210] a claim is contingent "when the debtor's duty to pay arises only upon the occurrence of a future event that was contemplated by the parties at the time of the contract's execution."[211] Thus, if one of three petitioning creditors' claims is based on the debtor's liability as a guarantor of the creditor's claim against another principal debtor and the principal debtor is not yet in default, the petitioning creditor's claim remains contingent. The creditor may not be one of the three petitioning creditors who are needed to join in the petition.

The petitioning creditors' claim also must not be "the subject of a bona fide dispute as to liability or amount."[212] Language excluding creditors with bona fide disputes was added in 1984.[213] The 2005 Amendments added language that made it clear that a bona fide dispute disqualified the creditor regardless of whether the dispute was over liability itself, or only over the size of the creditor's claim.[214]

There are some special additional rules for partnership debtors. First, an involuntary petition against a partnership may also be filed by "fewer than all of the general partners."[215] Petitions filed by all of the general partners are perfectly valid, but they are regarded as voluntary. Second, if all of the general partners are debtors in their own separate bankruptcy cases, an involuntary petition against the partnership itself may be filed either by a single general partner, by the trustee of any general partner, or by any creditor of the partnership.[216] There is no requirement that any set number of creditors file the petition, or that there be any particular amount of debt owed to the filing creditor.

There is also a special rule that deals with debtors who are already the subject of a foreign bankruptcy. An involuntary petition may be filed by a foreign representative of the estate in a foreign proceeding concerning the debtor.[217] For example, suppose InterGalactic Trading Corp., a

---

[209] Bankruptcy Code § 303(b).

[210] *See* § 6.02[B][6] Eligibility for Relief Under Chapter 13 — Individuals with Regular Income, *supra*.

[211] Chicago Title Ins. Co. v. Seko Invs., Inc. (In re Seko Invs., Inc.), 156 F.3d 1005, 1008 (9th Cir. 1998); In re All Media Properties, Inc, 5 B.R. 126, 133 (Bankr. S.D. Tex. 1980), *aff'd*, 646 F.2d 103 (5th Cir. 1981).

[212] Bankruptcy Code § 303(b)(1); *see* Lawrence Ponoroff, *Involuntary Bankruptcy and the Bona Fides of a Bona Fide Dispute*, 65 Ind. L.J. 315 (1989-1990).

[213] Bankruptcy Amendments and Federal Judgeship Act of 1984, Pub. L. No. 93-353 § 426(b)(1), 98 Stat 333, 378 (1984).

[214] Bankruptcy Abuse Prevention and Consumer Protection Act of 2005, Pub. L. No. 109-8, § 1234(a)(1)(A), 119 Stat. 23, 204.

[215] Bankruptcy Code § 303(b)(3)(A); *see* Karen Blaney, Note, *What Do You Mean My Partnership Has Been Petitioned into Bankruptcy?*, 19 Fordham Urb. L.J. 833 (1992).

[216] Bankruptcy Code § 303(b)(3)(B).

[217] Bankruptcy Code § 303(b)(4).

multinational company, is in receivership in Great Britain. If InterGalactic owns an office building, equipment, and inventory in New Jersey, the British receiver may file an involuntary bankruptcy petition against InterGalactic in the proper New Jersey district. The American bankruptcy case deals with the property in the U.S., while the British receivership administers the property located in Great Britain. Although the U.S. proceeding is technically separate from the British case and operates under U.S. rules, the British receiver has the opportunity to initiate the American proceeding to handle the New Jersey assets. The procedures for recognition of the foreign proceeding and the relief available to the foreign representative are governed by Chapter 15 which was added to the Bankruptcy Code in 2005.

[E] Grounds for Entry of "An Order for Relief"[218]

A small group of unpaid creditors are not entitled to force a debtor into bankruptcy simply because the debtor has defaulted on its obligations to them. This would give creditors far too much leverage over financially troubled debtors who find it difficult to pay some of their debts. Instead, before an order for relief against a debtor is entered, the petitioning creditors must demonstrate that the debtor's financial problems pose a threat to its creditors generally. Accordingly, an order for relief will be entered only if the debtor fails to resist the petition, the debtor is generally not paying its debts as they come due, or a custodian has already been appointed under state law to take control of substantially all of the debtor's assets.[219]

[1] Petition Not Controverted by the Debtor

As with any lawsuit in which the defendant does not answer, an order for relief is entered if the debtor does not oppose the petition within the time limits established by the Rules of Bankruptcy Procedure. Section 303(h) provides: "If the petition is not timely controverted, the court shall order relief against the debtor in an involuntary case under the chapter under which the petition was filed."

After an involuntary petition is filed, the bankruptcy court clerk's office issues a summons to be served on the debtor.[220] The Bankruptcy Rules provide the debtor twenty days after service to respond with any defenses or objections to the petition. If the debtor fails to reply, an order for relief is entered, much in the same way as a default judgment is entered in an ordinary civil suit.[221]

---

[218] John C. McCoid II, *The Occasion for Involuntary Bankruptcy*, 61 Am. Bankr. L.J. 195 (1987).

[219] Bankruptcy Code § 303(h).

[220] Fed. R. Bankr. P. 1010.

[221] Fed. R. Bankr. P. 1013(b).

If the debtor contests the petition, the creditors must prove that the grounds warranting relief asserted in their petition are true. This may require a trial to determine whether the statutory grounds to enter an order for relief exist. Or, where there is no dispute of material facts, an order for relief may be entered by summary judgment.[222]

[2] Debtor Generally Not Paying Debts as They Become Due

The primary basis for granting an involuntary petition is that the debtor is insolvent in the "equitable" sense because the debtor is generally not paying its debts as they become due.[223] Section 303(h)(1) provides:

> the court shall order relief against the debtor in an involuntary case under the chapter under which the petition was filed, only if (1) the debtor is not generally paying such debtor's debts as such debts become due unless such debts are the subject of a bona fide dispute as to liability or amount.[224]

The fact that the debtor is insolvent in the "legal" sense, because its balance sheet of assets and liabilities shows that its debts exceed the value of its assets, does not justify granting involuntary relief. Many businesses are insolvent in this legal sense but still remain able to pay their debts as they come due. Similarly, most law school and college students have debts in excess of their assets, but still manage to pay their monthly bills on time. Debtors who are able to make regular payments on their obligations may not be forced into bankruptcy simply because their overall debts exceed the total value of their assets. If a debtor's cash flow is adequate to remain current on its debts, an involuntary petition is not warranted.

Apart from this, the precise meaning of the statutory standard of § 303(h)(1) is ambiguous. The text is not clear regarding whether the standard is met by a debtor who has fallen behind on numerous small debts, but remains current with all of its larger obligations. Nor is the statutory language clear about whether the standard is satisfied by a debtor who is current on all of its smaller obligations, constituting a majority of its debts, but is in default on a few large debts that constitute a large proportion of its debt.[225]

A variety of factors have been articulated by courts in determining whether the standard has been met. Most focus on the size and number of debts that the debtor is not paying, the extent of the debtor's default on debts that have not been paid, and the state of the debtor's business and financial affairs generally.[226]

---

[222] In re Bishop, Baldwin, Rewald, Dillingham & Wong, Inc., 779 F.2d 471 (9th Cir. 1985).

[223] *See* Adams v. Richardson, 337 S.W.2d 911, 916 (Mo. 1960).

[224] *See* Adams v. Richardson, 337 S.W.2d 911, 916 (Mo. 1960).

[225] *E.g.*, Perez v. Feinberg, (In re Feinberg), 238 B.R. 781 (B.A.P. 8th Cir. 1999) (involuntary petition dismissed where debtor was in default on a single massive debt, but current on all other obligations).

[226] *E.g.*, In re ELRS Loss Mitigation, LLC, 325 B.R. 604 (Bankr. D. Okla. 2005).

Ordinarily, failing to pay a single creditor does not warrant relief, even though the size of the claim may be large in relation to the debtor's other obligations.[227] This general reluctance to approve a one-creditor involuntary bankruptcy reflects a broader concern about the appropriateness of bankruptcy to resolve disputes that involve only two parties.[228]

There is also a concern about the possibility of creditors improperly using the threat of an involuntary petition as a tool in negotiations.[229] Consequently, debts that are subject to a bona fide dispute are not counted when the court determines whether the debtor is generally failing to meet its obligations.[230] This prevents one party to a dispute from attempting to coerce the other party with threats of forced bankruptcy.

Whether a particular debt is the subject of a bona fide dispute depends on the same test that applies under § 303(b) to determine which creditors are eligible to join the petition.[231] The 2005 Amendments to both provisions make it clear that a dispute regarding either "liability or amount" reflects Congress' approval of a unified standard in both provisions.[232]

[3] Appointment of a "Custodian" of the Debtor's Property

Section 303(h)(2) provides a second, rarely used basis on which the court may grant a controverted petition. This section preserves a last vestige of the old "acts of bankruptcy" that predominated under the 1898 Act. Whether or not the debtor is equitably insolvent, the court must grant the petition if a "custodian," such as a receiver, trustee, or assignee for benefit of creditors, was appointed or took possession of the substantially all of the debtor's property within the 120 days before the petition was filed.[233] Thus, if a proceeding similar to a bankruptcy proceeding is pending in state court, creditors have the right to have the proceeding conducted instead under the Bankruptcy Code in a federal forum. This makes commencement of involuntarily bankruptcy proceedings somewhat similar to removal of a state insolvency proceeding from state court to federal court. The key difference is that both the procedure and the substance of the proceeding will be governed by federal law. This is consistent with the Bankruptcy Clause of the Constitution.[234]

---

[227] *E.g.*, Society of Lloyd's v. Harmsen (In re Harmsen), 320 B.R. 188 (B.A.P. 10th Cir. 2005); Perez v. Feinberg, (In re Feinberg), 238 B.R. 781 (B.A.P. 8th Cir. 1999).

[228] *See also* § 23.04 Single-Asset Real Estate Cases, *infra*.

[229] *See* Lawrence Ponoroff, *Involuntary Bankruptcy and the Bona Fides of a Bona Fide Dispute*, 65 Ind. L.J. 315 (1990).

[230] Bankruptcy Code § 303(h)(1).

[231] In re Busick, 65 B.R. 630 (N.D. Ind. 1986), *aff'd*, 831 F.2d 745 (7th Cir. 1987).

[232] Bankruptcy Abuse Prevention and Consumer Protection Act of 2005, Pub. L. No. 109-8, §§ 1234(a)(1), 1234(b), 119 Stat. 23, 203; H.R. Rep. No. 109-31 (Part I), at 148 (2005), *as reprinted in* 2005 U.S.C.C.A.N. 88, 206.

[233] Bankruptcy Code § 303(h)(2).

[234] U.S. Const. art. I, § 8, cl. 4.

On the other hand, if the state court proceeding involves less than substantially all of the debtor's assets,[235] which might occur in a conventional mortgage foreclosure proceeding, involuntary relief is not automatically warranted without an independent showing that the debtor is generally not paying its debts as they mature under § 303(h)(1).

[F] Dismissal of an Involuntary Petition

An involuntary petition may be dismissed without a determination of its merits on the motion of any petitioning creditor, with the consent of all of the petitioners and the debtor, or for lack of prosecution by the petitioning creditors.[236] Dismissal requires notice to "all creditors" and an opportunity for a hearing.[237] This notice gives other creditors, who may want the bankruptcy to go forward, an opportunity to join in the petition or otherwise intervene.

Otherwise, an involuntary petition is dismissed if the petitioning creditors fail to show that the debtor is not generally paying its debts as they become due or that a custodian has assumed control of the debtor's assets, as required for an order for relief under § 303(h).

[G] Penalties for Unsubstantiated Petitions

Creditors dare not file an involuntary petition in a cavalier manner. If the court dismisses an involuntary petition on its merits, the court may grant judgment against all of the petitioners for the debtor's costs and attorney's fees in contesting the petition.[238] Moreover, if the court determines that any petitioner acted in bad faith, the court may award additional damages against that petitioner, including any damages proximately caused by the bad faith filing, together with punitive damages.[239]

Courts have established a variety of tests of bad faith based on the petitioning creditor's subjective honesty in filing the petition, their motivations for filing the petition, whether a reasonable person would have filed the petition, whether the petition was an improper use of the bankruptcy code, and various combinations of these approaches.[240] Bad faith is most likely

---

[235] Bankruptcy Code § 303(h)(2).

[236] Bankruptcy Code § 303(j).

[237] Bankruptcy Code § 303(j).

[238] Bankruptcy Code § 303(i)(1). The wording of § 303(i) is somewhat ambiguous. It states that the court may grant judgment for costs "or" attorney's fees, suggesting that the court may be compelled to choose between awarding either the debtor's costs or the debtor's reasonable attorney fees. Nevertheless, it is reasonably clear that this means that the court may award one or the other, or neither, or both. It does not mean that the court may award only one or the other. *See* Kenneth N. Klee, *Legislative History of the New Bankruptcy Code*, 54 Am. Bankr. L.J. 275, 297 (1980); *see also* Bankruptcy Code § 102(5) (" 'or' is not exclusive").

[239] Bankruptcy Code § 303(i)(2); *see, e.g.*, In re John Richards Homes Bldg. Co., 291 B.R. 727 (Bankr. E.D. Mich. 2003) (compensatory damages, punitive damages, and attorney's fees totaling $6.4 million).

[240] *E.g.*, In re Cannon Express Corp., 280 B.R. 450 (Bankr. D. Ark. 2002); In re Landmark Distribs., Inc., 189 B.R. 290, 309 (Bankr. D.N.J. 1995).

to be inferred in circumstances where an involuntary petition is filed in disregard of facts that do not warrant relief,[241] or where a petitioning creditor is motivated by a desire to harm the debtor,[242] or to use the involuntary petition to obtain leverage in what otherwise is merely a two-party dispute.[243]

The consequences for the debtor of a meritless or bad faith petition can be substantial.[244] A teetering but not yet equitably insolvent debtor may fail as a result of bad publicity or expense caused by the involuntary petition. Ambiguity about the proper application of the "generally not paying" standard and the difficulty creditors might encounter before filing a petition in obtaining the facts relevant to the merits of their petition should lead creditors to be cautious about joining an involuntary petition precipitously.

[H] Transactions During the "Gap Period"

Unlike the circumstances when a debtor voluntarily files a bankruptcy petition, an involuntary petition does not immediately or even necessarily result in the entry of an order for relief. As explained earlier, the debtor has the opportunity to contest the petition; if it does, a hearing must be conducted to determine whether the debtor is not generally paying its debts as they come due. Consequently, the bankruptcy status of the debtor may remain in doubt for weeks or longer, while the involuntary petition is pending. This period of time between the petition and the entry of an order for relief is colloquially known as the "gap period" or the "involuntary gap."

During the involuntary gap, the debtor is likely to continue operating its business, buying and selling property, paying creditors, and incurring additional debts. Creditors who have not joined the petition may wish to continue efforts to collect claims owed by the debtor outside of bankruptcy court. Moreover, the petitioning creditors may become concerned that the debtor's continued operations will result in little more than a continued depletion of assets that will ultimately be available to pay their claims. A variety of provisions of the Bankruptcy Code deal with the problems created by the gap period.

---

[241] In re Cadillac by DeLorean & DeLorean Cadillac, Inc., 265 B.R. 574, 581–82 (Bankr. N.D. Ohio 2001).

[242] In re John Richards Homes Bldg. Co., 291 B.R. 727 (Bankr. E.D. Mich. 2003).

[243] *E.g.*, In re Cannon Express Corp., 280 B.R. 450 (Bankr. D. Ark. 2002).

[244] *E.g.*, In re John Richards Homes Bldg. Co., 439 F.3d 248 (6th Cir. 2006) ($2 million punitive damages); In re Salmon, 128 B.R. 313 (M.D. Fla. 1991) ($250,000 punitive damages).

[1] Control of the Estate During the Involuntary Gap

As with voluntary petitions, the filing of an involuntary petition results in the creation of a bankruptcy estate and the transfer of all of the debtor's property to that estate. According to Bankruptcy Code § 541(a), creation of this estate is triggered by the "commencement of a case."[245] However, unless the court orders otherwise, the debtor continues to manage its business and financial affairs and may continue to use, acquire, or dispose of property as if no case had been filed.[246]

Consistent with this rule, there is no automatic appointment of a trustee, even in an involuntary Chapter 7 case. Instead, the debtor remains in possession and control of the estate's assets. Where there is a risk that the debtor will dissipate the estate's assets while the involuntary petition is pending, the court may, after notice to the debtor and the opportunity for a hearing, appoint an interim trustee.[247] However, an interim trustee will be appointed only if "necessary to preserve the property of the estate or to prevent loss to the estate."[248]

[2] Effect of the Automatic Stay

As with a voluntary petition, the filing of an involuntary petition invokes the automatic stay of Bankruptcy Code § 362(a).[249] The stay restrains virtually every type of activity in which creditors might engage outside bankruptcy court to collect their claims. Thus, even creditors who do not join in the involuntary petition are stayed from further efforts to collect their claims while the court determines whether to act on the involuntary petition and enter an order for relief.

[3] Involuntary Gap Transfers of Estate Property

A debtor's transfer of its property after a petition has been filed depletes the debtor's estate and may harm the estate's creditors. As a consequence, Bankruptcy Code § 549 permits avoidance of post-petition transfers that are not authorized by the court or by a specific provision of the Bankruptcy Code, or that are authorized only under several narrow provisions, such as § 303(f), regarding certain transfers made during the gap period.[250] Transfers made in the ordinary course of business are protected, as are those made with the express approval of the court.[251] For purposes of this discussion, the most important exception to the trustee's avoiding power is for transfers of the estate's property during the involuntary gap to a transferee who gave value to the debtor in exchange for the property it

---

[245] Bankruptcy Code § 541(a).

[246] Bankruptcy Code § 303(f).

[247] Bankruptcy Code § 303(g).

[248] Bankruptcy Code § 303(g).

[249] Bankruptcy Code § 362(a); *see* Chapter 8, The Automatic Stay, *infra*.

[250] Bankruptcy Code § 549(a).

[251] Bankruptcy Code § 363.

received, so long as the transfer was something more than a payment for a pre-petition debt.[252] The transferee is protected, even if it knew about the pendency of the involuntary petition.

For example, if during the involuntary gap period, Titanic Industries manufactures and sells 500 deck chairs for the usual market price of $200 each, receiving a total price of $100,000, the buyer is permitted to keep the deck chairs, even if the buyer knew at the time that he received the goods that the bankruptcy case was pending.[253] Without this protection, Titanic's customers might be reluctant to deal with Titanic in fear that an order for relief would be granted and that the bankruptcy trustee would subsequently be able to recover the deck chairs or their value. Titanic's suppliers would be equally nervous that even cash transactions they entered into with the involuntary debtor would be overturned, leaving the supplier with nothing more than an unsecured claim against a financially troubled debtor. The reluctance of customers and suppliers to deal with the debtor would likely aggravate whatever financial difficulties the debtor was already facing, and drive otherwise financially viable debtors into liquidation.

Transfers that are nothing more than a payment of or security for a pre-petition debt are not protected. If an involuntary petition was filed against Titanic Industries on June 10, and on June 20 Titanic received a truckload of raw materials from one of its suppliers and gave the supplier a check in payment for those the materials, the transfer is protected. But, if the raw materials were delivered on May 20, and Titanic did not pay for them until June 15, after the petition had been filed against it, the payment would be subject to avoidance unless authorized by a specific provision of the Bankruptcy Code or by the court. Likewise, wages paid by the debtor during the gap period for work done by employees during the gap period may be retained by the employee.

Section 549 also provides limited protection to certain real estate transactions that are completed during the gap period. Protection is provided only to a "good faith purchaser without knowledge of the commencement of the case" who pays a "present fair equivalent value,"[254] but only if the transfer was recorded before notice of the bankruptcy case was recorded. Thus, a cautious purchaser, concerned about the possibility of the transferor's bankruptcy, will not part with value until it confirms that its deed or mortgage was recorded in the appropriate county recorder's office before notice of the debtor's bankruptcy case was recorded.

A purchaser who pays less than the fair equivalent value of the property may still have some protection. In the example given, suppose a gap-period buyer paid only $200,000 for property with a fair market value of $250,000.[255]

---

[252] Bankruptcy Code § 549(a), (b).

[253] Bankruptcy Code § 549(b).

[254] Bankruptcy Code § 549(c).

[255] Financially troubled debtors sometimes sell assets at a bargain basement price in order to obtain a quick infusion of cash.

The buyer is not permitted to keep the property because she has not paid fair equivalent value for it. However, she will be given a lien on the property for the $200,000 she paid and thus will have a secured claim in the debtor's bankruptcy case.

Moreover, § 549(c) does not protect buyers who purchase the property at a judicial foreclosure sale. Language protecting these buyers was removed from the Code in 1984,[256] and the definition of "purchaser" in § 101(43) is limited to a transferee in a "voluntary transfer."[257]

[4] Priority for Involuntary Gap Creditors

The final protection given to gap creditors is found in § 507. It gives certain post-petition gap creditors special priority, not only over other general unsecured creditors, but also over most other priority unsecured claims. Section 507(a) generally establishes priorities for a wide variety of unsecured claims, including those for the administrative expenses of the bankruptcy case, support claims, wages, and many taxes.[258] Section 507(a)(3) accords unsecured claims held by involuntary-gap creditors the third highest priority, behind support claims and claims for the administrative expenses of the bankruptcy case itself.[259] The priority is limited to claims arising in the ordinary course of the debtor's business or financial affairs after the commencement of an involuntary case but before the appointment of a trustee or the entry of an order for relief, whichever occurs first.[260]

Nevertheless, as a practical matter, priority may be of little help to these creditors. In many cases, more senior priority claims for the trustee's expenses in administering the bankruptcy case are left unpaid.[261] Thus, once creditors learn of an involuntary petition against a debtor, they are unlikely to be willing to deal with the debtor on anything but a cash basis. The risk of nonpayment, even with a third-priority claim, is simply too high.

This helps to explain why there are so many restrictions on involuntary petitions. The mere filing of an involuntary petition can have a devastating effect on a debtor's ability to obtain credit, even from suppliers who have extended credit in the ordinary course in the past. Thus, the mere fact that

---

[256] Pub. L. No. 98-353, § 464, 98 Stat. 333, 379 (1984).

[257] Bankruptcy Code § 101(43); 40235 Washington Street Corp. v. Lusardi, 329 F.3d 1076, 1081 (9th Cir. 2003).

[258] Bankruptcy Code § 507(a); *see* § 11.04[B] Priority Claims, *infra*.

[259] Bankruptcy Code § 507(a)(3). The relative priority between support claims and those for the administrative expenses associated with the bankruptcy case itself is complicated. *See* § 10.04[A][1] Support Claims, *infra*.

[260] Bankruptcy Code § 502(f).

[261] In a typical Chapter 7 case, there are no assets available to distribute to creditors. Such cases are colloquially referred to as "no asset" cases. *See* Michael J. Herbert & Dominic E. Pacitti, *Down and Out in Richmond, Virginia: The Distribution of Assets in Chapter 7 Bankruptcy Proceedings Closed During 1984-87*, 22 U. Rich L. Rev. 303 (1988). Note, however, that most involuntary cases involve businesses, and the chance for a distribution on priority claims is higher than in most consumer-debtor cases.

a petition has been filed may drive a basically sound company into insolvency.

Chapter 7

Property of the Estate

§ 7.01 Creation of the Debtor's Estate

Filing a bankruptcy petition results in the automatic creation of an "estate,"[1] much in the same way that a person's death results in the creation a decedent's estate. And, like a decedent's estate, a debtor's estate is, in many respects, regarded as a new legal entity separate and distinct from the debtor.

The bankruptcy estate becomes the owner of all of the property owned by the debtor when the petition was filed.[2] As will be seen, the estate may acquire additional assets by succeeding to certain property acquired by the debtor after the case commenced,[3] by avoiding transfers made by the debtor before the petition was filed,[4] or more simply, by engaging in revenue generating activities after the petition has been filed. In cases under Chapters 12 and 13, the estate also becomes the owner of the debtor's personal earnings while the case is pending.[5]

In voluntary Chapter 7 liquidation cases, an interim trustee is appointed shortly after commencement to act as the representative of the estate, to take control of the estate's property, and to conduct any of the estate's other financial affairs. Between the time the petition is filed and the time the interim trustee is appointed, the debtor usually remains in possession of the estate's property, but the debtor holds it in trust for the estate. Bankruptcy Code § 549 protects those who deal with the debtor in good faith and without knowledge that the property involved in any such deals belongs not to the debtor but to the estate. Once a trustee is in place, she has the right to take possession of property of the estate and may bring an action to compel the debtor or others to "turn over" any property of the estate that is in their possession or under their control.[6]

In reorganization cases, the debtor generally remains in possession of the property of the estate while the case is pending, though a trustee may be appointed in a Chapter 11 case if the debtor proves to be an unworthy steward of the estate's assets. In Chapter 12 and 13 cases, the debtor remains in possession of most of the estate's property but remits a portion of his income to a standing trustee who is responsible for distributing the

---

[1] Bankruptcy Code § 541(a).

[2] Bankruptcy Code § 541(a).

[3] Bankruptcy Code § 541(a)(5).

[4] Bankruptcy Code § 541(a)(3).

[5] *See* § 7.07 Expanded Estate in Reorganization Cases, *infra*.

[6] Bankruptcy Code § 542(a).

debtor's payments to creditors, according to the schedule specified by the debtor's plan.

§ 7.02 Property Included in the Estate[7]

Determining the scope of the estate is critical to the bankruptcy process. The scope of the estate defines what property is subject to both the court's jurisdiction and the trustee's control. Likewise, several prongs of the automatic stay that restrain creditors' actions while a case is pending are directed specifically at actions taken against property of the estate.[8]

Under the old Bankruptcy Act, the rules regarding property of the estate were complicated by the fact that exempt or fully encumbered property never became part of the estate. The Code's approach is different. Virtually everything goes into the estate. It is then divided between the debtor and creditors. Thus, exempt property begins as property of the estate, even though it is eventually handed back to the debtor. Likewise, the debtor's encumbered property is property of estate, even if it is certain to be abandoned into the hands of a secured creditor. This approach avoids preliminary squabbles over what is or is not part of the estate, leaving for later an orderly determination of who takes what from the pot.

The debtor's estate is comprised of the following property, regardless of where it is located or who possesses it, unless it is expressly excluded from the estate:[9]

- any interest in property held by the debtor when the case commenced;[10]
- community property interests of the debtor or the debtor's spouse, if those interests are under the management and control of the debtor, or if the property is liable under relevant state community property law for claims against the debtor;[11]
- property recovered by the trustee or a debtor-in-possession from third parties under various avoiding powers, such as the power to avoid preferences, to reverse setoffs, or to avoid security interests that were unperfected when the case commenced;[12]
- property interests preserved for the benefit of the estate under Bankruptcy Code §§ 510(c) or 551;[13]

---

[7] Thomas E. Plank, *The Outer Boundaries of the Bankruptcy Estate*, 47 Emory L.J. 1193 (1998).

[8] Bankruptcy Code § 362(a)(2)-(4); *see generally* § 8.02 Scope of the Automatic Stay, *infra.*

[9] Bankruptcy Code § 547(b); *see* § 7.04 Debtor's Property Excluded from the Estate, *infra.*

[10] Bankruptcy Code § 541(a)(1).

[11] Bankruptcy Code § 541(a)(2); *see* § 7.02[B] Community Property, *infra.*

[12] Bankruptcy Code § 541(a)(3); *see* § 7.02[C] Property Recovered from Third Parties, *infra.*

[13] Bankruptcy Code § 541(a)(4); *see* § 7.02[D] Property Preserved for the Benefit of the Estate, *supra.*

- certain property acquired by the debtor within 180 days after commencement of the case, such as property obtained by inheritance, as a result of a divorce decree, or as proceeds of a life insurance policy;[14]
- proceeds, products, offspring, rents and profits generated by property of the estate;[15] and
- property acquired by the estate itself after commencement.[16]

[A] Debtor's Interests in Property at Commencement of the Case

[1] Debtor's Property Included in the Estate

With limited exceptions, a debtor's estate acquires ownership of "all legal or equitable interests of the debtor in property as of the commencement of the case."[17] Thus, anything the debtor owned when the case began is property of the estate. This ordinarily includes any type of property interest, regardless of whether it is in real estate, goods, intellectual property, or other intangible personal property. It includes rights the debtor may have to sue someone. Bankruptcy trustees frequently include questions about any rights a debtor may have to sue someone among the few questions they ask consumer debtors in what otherwise may appear to be "no-asset" cases, with no property available for distribution to creditors.[18]

Nor does the nature of the debtor's interest affect whether it becomes property of the estate.[19] Whatever interest the debtor owns becomes estate property. Thus, if the debtor holds title to real estate in fee simple absolute, the estate acquires the property in fee simple absolute. If Mary, who owns a mere life estate in her ancestral home, becomes unable to pay her debts at age 97, the life estate is property of her bankruptcy estate. The same is true if the debtor's interest is a contingent remainder, an executory interest, an easement, or a mortgage; the debtor's estate acquires whatever limited rights the debtor held. The property might not be worth much to the creditors, but that does not prevent it from entering the estate.

---

[14] Bankruptcy Code § 541(a)(5); *see* § 7.02[E] Certain Post-Petition Property Acquired Within 180 Days of the Petition, *infra*.

[15] Bankruptcy Code § 541(a)(6); *see* § 7.02[F] Post-Petition Earnings, *infra*.

[16] Bankruptcy Code § 541(a)(7); *see* § 7.02[G] Post-Petition Property Acquired by the Estate, *infra*.

[17] Bankruptcy Code § 541(a)(1).

[18] *See* In re Upshur, 317 B.R. 446 (Bankr. D. Ga. 2004) (bankruptcy case re-opened to permit trustee to pursue previously undisclosed employment discrimination claim held by debtor when case was commenced); Anderson v. Acme Mkts., 287 B.R. 624 (D. Pa. 2002) (debtor lacked standing to bring discrimination claim that had accrued before bankruptcy petition was filed because it was property of the estate under the control of the case trustee).

[19] *See generally* George R. Pitts, *Rights to Future Payment as Property of the Estate Under Section 541 of the Bankruptcy Code*, 64 Am. Bankr. L.J. 61, 73–80 (1990) (regarding contingent future interests).

Jointly held property is treated in the same manner. A debtor's undivided interest in property held in joint tenancy or tenancy in common is part of his bankruptcy estate.[20] The extent of the estate's interest is identical to the interest held by the debtor under relevant state law. Thus, a bankrupt spouse's undivided joint interest in stock or other property held in joint tenancy with the debtor's spouse is property of the bankruptcy estate of the spouse who filed the bankruptcy petition.[21] The interest of the non-debtor spouse, on the other hand, is not part of the estate and is protected.[22] If Merl and Agnes own real estate as joint tenants and Merl alone files a bankruptcy petition, only Merl's undivided interest belongs to the estate. Depending on state law regarding the effect of a transfer of one joint tenant's interest in property, this may result in a severance of the joint property. In the common situation in which a husband and wife file a joint petition, their respective joint tenancy interests become part of their respective estates and will be "jointly administered."

Interests held in a tenancy by the entirety present particular problems in bankruptcy cases filed by only one spouse.[23] A tenancy by the entirety is an ancient form of ownership that rests upon the legal fiction that "husband and wife are but one person."[24] Many states have eliminated entireties property, but the estate is still valid in about twenty states.[25] Entireties property generally cannot be transferred by one spouse alone. In addition, entireties property is unavailable to satisfy debts owed by only one spouse.[26] This sometimes leads to a claim that entireties property is not a part of the estate of a bankruptcy case filed by only one spouse.[27] Whether this is true may turn on how a particular state defines entireties property. At least one court has held that entireties property, as defined under state law, comes into the estate.[28] As discussed in the next section, it is not one hundred percent clear whether a state might be able to define its entireties estate in such a way that it would be excluded from the estate in bankruptcy. While determining whether something is "estate property"

[20] One of your co-authors holds a 1/64 interest in several oil wells. They produce income of $200-400 per year. If he were to file a bankruptcy petition, these undivided interests would be part of his bankruptcy estate. His sister's 1/64 interest and his aunt's 1/32 interest would be unaffected.

[21] In re Becker, 136 B.R. 113 (D.N.J. 1992) (stock certificates); In re Fey, 91 B.R. 524 (E.D. Mo. 1988) (real estate).

[22] *E.g.*, In re Nicholson, 90 B.R. 64 (Bankr. W.D.N.Y. 1988).

[23] Benjamin C. Ackerly, *Tenants by the Entirety Property and the Bankruptcy Reform* Act, 21 Wm. & Mary L. Rev. 701 (1980); William G. Craig, Jr., *An Analysis of Estates by the Entirety in Bankruptcy*, 48 Am Bankr. L.J. 255 (1974); Lawrence Kalevitch, *Some Thoughts on Entireties in Bankruptcy*, 60 Am. Bankr .L.J. 141 (1986).

[24] Tyler v. United States, 281 U.S. 497, 503 (1930).

[25] 7 Richard R. Powell & Michael Allan Wolf, Powell on Real Property § 52.03[3] (2006).

[26] Thompson on Real Property § 33.07(e) (David A. Thompson ed. 1994).

[27] *E.g.*, In re Paeplow, 972 F.2d 730 (7th Cir. 1992).

[28] Chippenham Hosp. Inc. v. Bondurant, 716 F.2d 1057, 1058 (4th Cir. 1983) (dicta); *see* H.R. Rep. No. 95-595, at 368 (1977), *reprinted in* 1978 U.S.C.C.A.N. 5963, 6324; S. Rep. No. 95-989, at 82 (1978), *reprinted in* 1978 U.S.C.C.A.N. 5787, 5868.

is undoubtedly a question of federal law, the extent to which courts will disturb state definitions of property rights is an open question. Bankruptcy Code § 363(h) provides a mechanism for a bankruptcy trustee to administer entireties property by selling the estate's interest, together with the interest of the non-debtor spouse, after giving the non-debtor what amounts to a right of first refusal to buy the property at the proposed price.[29] Following a sale of the property, the non-debtor spouse is entitled to her share of the proceeds.

[2] Relationship Between Bankruptcy Law and State Property Law

Because property law is a creature of state law, there is an inherent connection (and tension) between state property law and the Bankruptcy Code's provisions on property acquired by the estate. Section 541(a)(1) specifies that the estate acquires all of the legal and equitable interests in property owned by the debtor when the case commences. State law necessarily determines the nature and extent of the debtor's legal and equitable interests when the petition is filed,[30] but federal bankruptcy law determines whether those interests are "property" and thus whether they are acquired by the debtor's estate.[31]

Whether a debtor's interests are "property" within the meaning of § 541(a)(1) depends on federal law, even though the nature and extent of the debtor's interest is a question of state law. This is true even though state law does not treat a debtor's interest as a "property right" for purposes of state property law. This fundamental principal was established in *Chicago Board of Trade v. Johnson*,[32] decided under the Bankruptcy Act. The debtor held a seat on the Chicago Board of Trade. Under Illinois law, the membership was not regarded as "property," even though memberships were generally transferable, and even though they had substantial economic value.[33] Nevertheless, the membership was "property" within the meaning of federal bankruptcy law, and thus the debtor's estate acquired the interests the debtor held in connection with his membership. Otherwise enforceable limitations on the debtor's membership, which could not be transferred under applicable state law because of the debtor's unpaid obligations to other members, remained effective.[34]

---

[29] Bankruptcy Code § 363(h); *e.g.*, In re Hunter, 970 F.2d 299 (7th Cir. 1992).

[30] Butner v. United States, 400 U.S. 48 (1979).

[31] Chicago Bd. of Trade v. Johnson, 264 U.S. 1 (1924). The Supreme Court recently made a similar point in a tax case, holding that even though Michigan's entireties law stated that one spouse had no property interest in property held by the entireties, a taxpayer had sufficient interest in entireties property for a tax lien to attach. United States v. Craft, 535 U.S. 274 (2002).

[32] 264 U.S. 1 (1924).

[33] The market value in 1924 when the case was decided was $10,500. This would be approximately $114,000 in 2005 dollars, adjusted for inflation. *See* S. Morgan Friedman, The Inflation Calculator, available at www.westegg.com/inflation (last visited Feb. 19, 2007).

[34] Chicago Bd. of Trade v. Johnson, 264 U.S. at 15.

This rule was solidified by *Butner v. United States.*[35] There, a mortgagee claimed the right to receive rent generated by the debtor's property after the petition was filed. The Court ruled that whether the creditor was entitled to receive the rents depended in the first instance on applicable state law. If state law creates a property interest in the creditor's favor, those rights are be respected in bankruptcy, unless "some federal interest requires a different treatment."[36] Thus, bankruptcy first looks to the extent of the parties' rights under state law. Bankruptcy invalidates the allocation of property rights under state law only if some specific provision of the Bankruptcy Code requires a reallocation of those rights. To do otherwise, the *Butner* Court indicated, would increase uncertainty, encourage forum shopping, and create the possibility of a windfall, merely because the parties' rights were being resolved in a bankruptcy proceeding instead of in state court.[37] Although *Chicago Board of Trade* and *Butner* were decided under the now-repealed Bankruptcy Act, the basic principle of the cases remains intact under the Bankruptcy Code.

[B] Community Property

Many states have a community property system for property acquired by married persons. Under general principles of community property law, most property acquired by a spouse is treated as "community property" and is both subject to the management and control of either spouse and liable for debts of either spouse.

Section 541(a)(2) of the Bankruptcy Code includes any interest of the debtor and the debtor's spouse in community property at the time the debtor's case commenced, if either the property is under the sole, equal, or joint management and control of the debtor, or if the property is "liable" for an allowable claim against the debtor or the debtor and the debtor's spouse. Property that is under the exclusive control of the non-debtor spouse or that is liable under applicable state law only for debts of the non-debtor spouse does not become property of the debtor's estate, even if it qualifies as community property.

Although the Bankruptcy Code has extensive rules to deal with property owned by married couples, it does nothing to consolidate the property rights of unmarried couples who have not structured their affairs in compliance with more traditional forms of joint ownership.[38]

---

[35] 440 U.S. 49 (1979).

[36] 440 U.S. at 55.

[37] 440 U.S. at 55.

[38] *See* Elizabeth Fella, Comment, *Playing Catch Up: Changing the Bankruptcy Code to Accommodate America's Growing Number of Non-Traditional Couples*, 37 Ariz. St. L.J. 681 (2005).

[C] Property Recovered under Avoiding Powers

Section 541(a)(3) includes in the debtor's estate any property recovered by the trustee from third parties pursuant to the trustee's array of avoiding powers.[39] For example, the debtor's estate includes property recovered as a fraudulent conveyance[40] or a preference.[41] Further, because a Chapter 11 debtor-in-possession enjoys all of the same rights, powers, and duties of a trustee,[42] § 541(a)(3) also operates to bring property recovered by a debtor-in-possession into a Chapter 11 debtor's estate. However, property that is subject to avoidance, but not yet recovered, is not property of the estate, and is not subject to the automatic stay.

[D] Property Preserved for the Benefit of the Estate

Section 541(a)(4) facilitates the operation of several other provisions of the Bankruptcy Code by including in the estate any property right that is preserved for the benefit of the estate or ordered to be transferred to the estate.[43] The most common application of this provision occurs in connection with the bankruptcy trustee's avoidance of what otherwise might be a senior lien on a debtor's property. Preservation of the lien for the benefit of the estate permits the trustee to enjoy the benefit of whatever priority the avoided lien may have had over other creditors who hold unavoidable liens on the same property.

For example, the trustee may be able to avoid a creditor's preferential security interest because it was granted to a creditor who was an "insider" within one year of the debtor's bankruptcy petition.[44] If not avoided, the insider's security interest might have been senior to another security interest that the trustee is unable to avoid. Preserving the avoided senior creditor's lien for the benefit of the estate, and transferring the preserved lien to the estate preserves value for the estate.

Assume, for example that North Atlantic Finance Co. has an avoidable senior mortgage on Titanic Industries' land, securing a $5 million dollar debt, and that White Star Bank has an unavoidable second mortgage on the land securing a $4 million debt. If the land is only worth $7 million,

---

[39] The scope of § 541(a)(3) is somewhat deceptive. The Code's language refers to property recovered under §§ 329(b), 363(n), 543, 550, 553, and 723. Bankruptcy Code § 550 is a broad provision, permitting the trustee to avoid transfers made by the debtor under an expanded number of other provisions, including § 544(a) (the strong-arm clause), § 544(b) (transfers avoidable by unsecured creditors under state law), § 545 (statutory liens), § 547 (preferences), 548 (fraudulent conveyances), § 549 (post-petition transfers), § 553 (setoffs), and § 724(a) (securing a fine or penalty). *See* Bankruptcy Code § 550. *See generally* Chapter 14, General Avoiding Powers; Limits on Avoiding Powers, *infra;* Chapter 15, Avoidable Preferences, *infra;* Chapter 16, Fraudulent Transfers, *infra.*

[40] *See* Chapter 16, Fraudulent Transfers, *infra.*

[41] *See* Chapter 15, Avoidable Preferences, *infra.*

[42] Bankruptcy Code § 1107; *see* § 4.02[B] Debtor-in-Possession, *supra.*

[43] Bankruptcy Code § 541(a)(4).

[44] *See* Bankruptcy Code § 547(b)(4)(B); Chapter 15, Avoidable Preferences, *infra.*

avoidance of North Atlantic's otherwise senior mortgage results in White Star Bank's junior lien being promoted to senior status. This would leave the estate to enjoy only $3 million of value in the land as a result of the equity created by the avoidance of North Atlantic's lien. Section 541(a)(4) preserves North Atlantic's lien, for the benefit of the estate. With this lien preserved, the estate recovers the first $5 million of the property's value and thus permits White Star Bank to recover only the $2 million it would have received from its collateral had North Atlantic's lien not been subject to avoidance. In effect, § 541(a)(4), working in conjunction with § 551, transfers North Atlantic's senior lien to the trustee for the benefit of the debtor's estate, and prevents junior lienholders from jumping ahead in priority as a result of the trustee's avoidance action.

[E] Certain Post-Petition Property Acquired Within 180 Days of the Petition[45]

Property acquired by a Chapter 7 debtor after his petition was filed does not generally become part of his bankruptcy estate. Instead, a liquidating debtor gives up the property he has when he files his petition, but is entitled to keep any property he receives afterwards. This is a key part of the Bankruptcy Code's "fresh start" policy.[46]

However, § 541(a)(5) brings some property interests into the estate, even though they are acquired by the debtor after his petition is filed. "Post-petition property" is brought into the estate in three distinct situations, but only if the property would have been part of the estate if the debtor had already owned it when the case began, and if the debtor either "acquires or becomes entitled to acquire [the property] within 180 days after" the date of the petition. These three situations are:

- the debtor acquired the property by "bequest, devise, or inheritance";[47]
- the debtor acquired the property through a spousal property settlement or divorce decree;[48] and
- the debtor acquired the property as a "beneficiary of a life insurance policy or a death benefit plan."[49]

All three situations involve windfalls to the debtor and might otherwise permit the debtor to time the filing of his bankruptcy petition in an attempt to prevent creditors from reaching valuable assets.

[45] Adam J. Hirsch, *Inheritance and Bankruptcy: The Meaning of the "Fresh Start,"* 45 Hastings L.J. 175 (1994); C.T. Foster, Annotation, *Construction and Application of Provision of Bankruptcy Act (§ 70, subd. (a)(8)) with Respect to Property Vesting in Bankrupt After Bankruptcy y Bequest, Devise, or Inheritance*, 11 A.L.R.2d 738 (1950).

[46] *See* § 1.01[B] Bankruptcy as a Debtors' Remedy: Fresh Start for Honest Debtors, *supra*.

[47] Bankruptcy Code § 541(a)(5)(A).

[48] Bankruptcy Code § 541(a)(5)(B).

[49] Bankruptcy Code § 541(a)(5)(C).

For example, suppose that Dora files a bankruptcy petition on July 1, 2007, and a week later, on July 8, inherits $1,000,000 from her mother. Although the property was received post-petition, it becomes part of Dora's bankruptcy estate and is available to pay Dora's creditors through the bankruptcy distribution process. If Dora is able to anticipate her mother's death by more than six months, she may be able to inherit her mother's fortune after discharging her debts, but few deaths can be planned with such precision.[50] Similarly, if Dora had been the beneficiary of her mother's $250,000 life insurance policy, the $250,000 Dora obtained the right to on July 8, when her mother expired, would be part of Dora's bankruptcy estate.

In both cases, the date Dora actually receives the payment from her mother's estate or the life insurance company, does not matter. The date of her mother's death is the critical date — this is the date Dora acquired the right to receive the property. Otherwise, it would be far too easy for debtors to avoid the effect of § 541(a)(5) by simply delaying receipt of the payments to which they are entitled.

Property the debtor receives as a result of a property settlement with her spouse is treated the same.[51] If the debtor acquires an interest in the property within 180 days of his petition, the property is included in his estate.

The usual reason given for these rules is that an impecunious debtor, foreseeing the imminence of any such events, might rush into bankruptcy to prevent the assets from becoming available to creditors.[52]

[F] Post-Petition Earnings

After the debtor's petition is filed, both the debtor and the estate may continue to generate income, which, depending on its source, may be included as property of the estate. The estate may generate income as a result of property being sold, invested, or otherwise producing a return. The simplest example is the interest earned on a bank account that became part of the estate when the debtor's petition was filed. Likewise, if the estate acquired rental property that was owned by the debtor when the petition was filed, the rent received from tenants is property received from property of the estate. Likewise, the debtor himself typically generates income by earning wages or income from other services after his petition has been filed.

---

[50] Having said this, however, as morally repugnant it is, it is not difficult to imagine an unscrupulous debtor filing a bankruptcy petition and then refusing to implement his mother's living will until the 180 period days has elapsed. Legal advice about the potential financial benefits of prolonging the life of a loved one in this situation would be difficult to provide.

[51] Bankruptcy Code § 541(a)(5)(B).

[52] *See* In re Woodson, 839 F.2d 610 (9th Cir. 1988) (debtor filed petition a few days before the death of his wife, whose life was insured for $1,000,000) (one of your co-authors represented Mr. Woodson in this matter).

[1] Proceeds, Products, Offspring, Rents and Profits from Property of the Estate Included

Section 541(a)(6) brings any "[p]roceeds, product, offspring, rents, or profits of or from property of the estate" into the estate. However, it sets a boundary between income that is attributable to property of the estate and income that is attributable to an individual debtor's post-petition labor.[53] Including the latter would impair a debtor's fresh start.

Money received when property of the estate is sold is "proceeds" from estate property and is included in the debtor's estate. Quite naturally, funds obtained by the trustee from a sale of estate property belongs to the estate. But, funds obtained by the debtor through any wrongful conversion of estate property also rightfully belongs to the estate.

If the debtor owns an office building, an apartment building, or a fleet of rental cars, any rent received from lessees of this property is considered "rents" that are likewise owned by the estate. If the estate includes livestock, offspring of the livestock are property of the estate, and milk produced by the estate's dairy cows or eggs or manure produced by the estate's chickens are examples of "products."

Any post-petition "proceeds" from a secured creditor's collateral, though unquestionably included among the estate's property, remain subject to a creditor's security interest, pursuant to U.C.C. § 9-315(2) and Bankruptcy Code § 546(c). However, under § 552(a), other collateral acquired by the estate after commencement that is covered by the terms of an after-acquired collateral clause in the creditor's security agreement (or "floating lien"), is not subject to a creditor's security interest, unless it is proceeds.[54] This distinction between "proceeds" and floating lien collateral, makes the definition and scope of proceeds particularly important in this context.

[2] Earnings from Individual Debtor's Post-Petition Services Excluded[55]

The "fresh start" policy of the Bankruptcy Code warrants a special rule with respect to an individual debtor's personal earnings that are attributable to services performed by the debtor after his case commenced. Section 541(a)(6) expressly excludes "earnings from services performed by an individual debtor after the commencement of the case" from the debtor's bankruptcy estate.[56]

---

[53] Bankruptcy Code § 541(a)(6).

[54] Bankruptcy Code § 552(a).

[55] Louis M. Phillips & Tanya Martinez Shively, *Ruminations on Property of the Estate — Does Anyone Know Why a Debtor's Postpetition Earnings, Generated by Her Own Earning Capacity, Are Not Property of the Bankruptcy Estate?*, 58 La. L. Rev. 623 (1998); George R. Pitts, *Rights to Future Payment as Property of the Estate Under Section 541 of the Bankruptcy Code*, 64 Am. Bankr. L.J. 61 (1990); James L. Rigelhaupt, Jr., Annotation, *Exception from Bankruptcy Estate, under 11 U.S.C.A. Sec. 541(a)(6), of Earnings from Services Performed by an Individual Debtor after Commencement of Case*, 76 A.L.R. Fed. 853 (1986).

[56] Bankruptcy Code § 541(a)(6).

In a simple case, this rule is easy to apply. If Ray files Chapter 7 bankruptcy petition at the end of the day on Friday, June 29, 2007, the earnings he receives for work performed the following week are not part of his estate. Paychecks received for work Ray performed after his petition, are not estate property. But a paycheck Ray receives on July 13, 2007, compensating him for services performed in the last two weeks of June (before he filed his petition) is property of his bankruptcy estate. Although the compensation is received post-petition, it is for services performed before the case commenced.

More difficult issues are presented when an individual debtor is entitled to payment for work performed partially before and partially after the petition. The court must allocate the payment between the pre-petition and the post-petition work. The former is property of the estate; the latter belongs to the debtor.[57] The issue is well illustrated by the decision in *Jess v. Carey (In re Jess),*[58] involving a debtor's right to a contingent fee payment that was partially attributable to work performed by the debtor, an attorney, before he filed his petition. The debtor naturally sought to exclude the entire fee from his estate, claiming that it was due only as a result of personal services he provided to his client after the date of his petition. The court rejected this contention and held that "the estate is entitled to recover the portion of the post-petition payments attributable to [his] pre-petition services."[59] The fact that the debtor's eventual receipt of the fee was contingent upon services provided after the petition did not mean that all of the fee was earned from services provided after the petition was filed.[60]

This result should make it clear that a debtor's rights to tax refunds[61] and accrued vacation pay,[62] derived from services provided by the debtor before his petition, are properly included in his bankruptcy estate. These rights, in the words of the Supreme Court's decision in *Segal v. Rochelle,*[63] are "sufficiently rooted in the pre-bankruptcy past and so little entangled with the bankrupts' ability to make an unencumbered fresh start that it should be regarded as 'property' . . . [of the estate]."[64]

The problem of determining which of the debtor's past earnings are included in his estate can be tricky if the earnings involve bonuses or

---

[57] *See* Rav v. Ryerson (In re Ryerson), 739 F.2d 1423 (9th Cir. 1984).

[58] 169 F.3d 1204 (1999).

[59] 169 F.3d at 1207 (1999).

[60] *See also* Turnver v. Avery, 947 F.2d 772 (5th Cir. 1991); In re Ballard, 238 B.R. 610 (Bankr. M.D. La. 1999).

[61] *E.g.,* In re Rash, 22 B.R. 323 (Bankr. D. Kan. 1982); *see* Kokoszka v. Belford, 417 U.S. 642 (1974).

[62] Matter of Nichols, 4 B.R. 711 (Bankr. D. Mich. 1980) (noting that the Supreme Court's Bankruptcy Act decision in *Lines v. Frederick*, 400 U.S. 18 (1970), which held that the estate did not include accrued, but unpaid, vacation pay of the bankrupt, was overruled by the enactment of § 541(a)(6); H.R. Rep. No. 95-595, 95 Cong., 1st Sess. 368 (1988), *reprinted in* 1978 U.S.C.C.A.N. 5787, 6324).

[63] 382 U.S. 375 (1966) (interpreting § 70a(5) of the former Bankruptcy Act).

[64] 382 U.S. at 380.

similar compensation related to or calculated on the basis of the debtor's performance over an extended period of time.[65] Assume, for example, that Jerrod is an assistant sales manager for Global Manufacturing and that Jerrod receives a base salary of $54,000 per year, plus a year-end performance bonus tied to his personal full-year sales results, combined with a year-end bonus representing a share of the firm's overall profits that is entirely within the discretion of his employer to award. If on September 1, 2007, Jerrod files a Chapter 7 bankruptcy petition and on December 31, 2007, is awarded a $10,000 personal results bonus based on his individual sales and a $5,000 discretionary bonus based on the firm's profits, there might be a dispute about how much of these bonuses should be swept into his estate. Jerrod may contend that all of the bonuses are attributable to the post-petition period, because his right to earn the bonus did not accrue until after the petition was filed. He might conclude that one-third of the bonuses are attributable to his post-petition work during the last four months of the year. He might even argue that the percentage should be higher, if most of his results or most of the company's profits were earned during those last four months. The trustee might claim all of the $5,000 profit-share bonus, arguing that Jerrod's sales took a real nose dive after he filed for bankruptcy.

The proper treatment of a debtor's rights to commissions attributable to post-petition renewals of accounts generated by the debtor before her petition was filed are similarly difficult to deal with. The difficulty is illustrated by *In re Wu,*[66] involving an insurance agent who sold insurance and annuity policies to State Mutual Life Assurance Co.'s customers over an extended period of time. After her petition was filed, State Mutual sent the debtor a check for $50,472.56, representing commissions due to the debtor for renewals of policies she had sold before her petition, but which had not been renewed by State Mutual's customers until after her petition. The issue was whether her right to receive these commissions was part of her estate. The court ruled that if the debtor's contract with State Mutual required her to remain employed by the insurer and to provide continued service with respect to the renewed policies in order to receive the renewal commissions,[67] the renewal commissions were not part of her estate. However, they would be included in the estate and available for distribution to her creditors if she were entitled to receive the renewal commissions even if her employment with the insurer had been terminated.[68] Thus, if her right to receive the commissions depended on her post-petition services, the commissions would be excluded from her estate, but if her right to receive them was not dependent on her post-petition services, they were "sufficiently rooted in the pre-bankruptcy past" to be included in her bankruptcy estate.

---

[65] *E.g.*, In re Palmer, 57 B.R. 332 (Bankr. W.D. Va. 1986).

[66] 173 B.R. 411 (B.A.P. 9th Cir. 1994).

[67] 173 B.R. at 414; *see also* In re Palmer, 57 B.R. 332, 334–35 (Bankr. W.D. Va.1986).

[68] In re Wu, 173 B.R. at 414; *see also* In re Braddy, 226 B.R. 479 (Bankr. N.D. Fla. 1998).

Many of the more difficult problems of this type involve better-paid executives and other highly-compensated employees[69] whose access to Chapter 7 was severely limited by the 2005 Amendments to the Bankruptcy Code. However, it may be that the issue will resurface in the guise of whether these debtors are eligible for Chapter 7 relief in the first place, at least where it is their year-end bonuses that place them beyond the threshold of eligibility under Chapter 7. While such earnings *would* be part of the debtor's Chapter 13 estate, it is not clear that they would be considered part of the debtor's "current monthly income" for the purposes of calculating the debtor's disposable income in either Chapter 13 or 11.

[G] Post-Petition Property Acquired by the Estate

As indicated earlier, in most respects, the Bankruptcy Code sharply distinguishes the estate and the debtor as distinct entities. A consequence of this is that property acquired post-petition by the estate, rather than by the debtor, is property of the estate. Section 547(a)(7) provides that "[a]ny interest in property that the estate acquires after commencement of the case" is property of the estate.[70]

This provision is essentially an extension of § 541(a)(6), discussed above. Section 547(a)(7) makes it clear that even if the property acquired by the estate is not "proceeds, product, offspring, rents, or profits" arising from property of the estate, if the property was acquired by the estate and not by the debtor, the property is part of the estate, not property of the debtor. For example, if Titanic Development Corp. designs computer software and continues to operate this business during its bankruptcy case, programs developed by the company might not qualify as "proceeds, product, offspring, rents, or profits," but they are unquestionably property acquired by the estate and thus part of the estate's property under § 547(a)(7).

§ 7.03 Effect of Restrictions on Transfer of Debtor's Property[71]

A debtor's property interests are sometimes saddled with limitations and restrictions. If enforced, these limits may prevent the debtor's assets from becoming property of his bankruptcy estate to the detriment of creditors and in possible violation of the Bankruptcy Code's "equal treatment"

---

[69] *See* § 17.03[B] Dismissal of Consumer Cases Due to Abuse, *infra*; *compare* Vogel v. Palmer (In re Palmer), 57 B.R. 332 (Bankr. W.D. Va. 1986) (post-petition bonus not property of the estate because employer had discretion not to award any bonus until after debtor's petition had been filed), *with* Towers v. Wu (In re Wu), 173 B.R. 411 (B.A.P. 9th Cir. 1994) (estate's right to post-petition insurance policy renewal commissions depended upon whether debtor's postpetition services were a prerequisite for right to renewal commissions, and if so, the extent to which commissions were attributable to postpetition as opposed to prepetition services).

[70] Bankruptcy Code § 541(a)(7).

[71] Marie Rolling-Tarbox, Note, *Powers of Appointment under the Bankruptcy Code: A Focus on General Testamentary Powers*, 72 Iowa L. Rev. 1041 (1987).

policy.[72] As will be seen, many of these restrictions are invalid in bankruptcy. Some, however, such as those that might appear in a valid spendthrift trust or an ERISA-qualified pension plan, are effective to keep these assets out of the debtor's estate and insulated from creditors' claims.

The common law rule *nemo dat qui non habet* (he who hath not, cannot give),[73] generally applies in bankruptcy as it does in other settings. The debtor's estate cannot acquire greater rights than the debtor owned when his petition was filed. Most limits inherent in a debtor's property rights remain intact in bankruptcy. If the debtor held a life estate, the bankruptcy estate acquires a life estate. Likewise, if the debtor held only a one-half undivided tenancy in common, the estate acquires the same undivided interest and nothing more. However, the Bankruptcy Code contains various provisions that invalidate attempts by debtors to gerrymander their ownership or contractual rights to avoid the effects of bankruptcy.

[A] Ipso-Facto Clauses Ineffective

Sometimes a debtor's property interest purportedly terminates upon the filing of a bankruptcy petition or upon the occurrence of some other event related to the debtor's financial condition. Restrictions of this type do not prevent the estate from acquiring whatever interest the debtor held. Section 541(c)(1)(B) provides:

> [A]n interest of the debtor in property becomes property of the estate under [§ 541(a)(1), (2), or (5)] notwithstanding any provision in an agreement, transfer instrument, or applicable nonbankruptcy law . . . (B) that is conditioned on the insolvency or financial condition of the debtor, on the commencement of a case under [the Bankruptcy Code], or on the appointment of or taking possession by a [bankruptcy] trustee . . . or a custodian before such commencement, and that effects or gives an option to effect a forfeiture, modification, or termination of the debtor's interest in property.[74]

Thus, so-called ipso-facto clauses in deeds and contracts that automatically terminate a debtor's property interest if the debtor files a bankruptcy petition, are ineffective.[75] For example, in *In re Robert L. Helms Construction & Development Co., Inc.*, the debtor entered into an option contract that contained a provision purporting to terminate the debtor's option if it filed a bankruptcy petition. Section 541(c) prevented it from operating as intended to stop the debtor's estate from acquiring the option.[76] Likewise, in *In re Mitchell* a security agreement contained language purporting

[72] *See* Whitaker v. Power Brake Supply (In re Olympia Holding Corp.), 188 B.R. 287 (M.D. Fla. 1994), *aff'd*, 68 F.3d 1304 (11th Cir. 1995); S. Rep. No. 95-989, at 83 (1977), *reprinted in* 1978 U.S.C.C.A.N. 5787, 5869.

[73] Black's Law Dictionary 1735 (8th ed. 2004).

[74] Bankruptcy Code § 541(c)(1)(B).

[75] Bankruptcy Code § 541(c)(1)(B).

[76] In re Robert L. Helms Constr. & Dev. Co., 139 F.3d 702 (9th Cir. 1998).

to terminate the debtor's ownership of the collateral upon the filing of a bankruptcy petition. This too, was ineffective. The collateral remained property of the estate and the automatic stay of § 362(a) prevented the creditor from repossessing the collateral.[77]

Permitting these types of provisions to operate as intended would allow the debtor to prefer particular creditors and would impair the effectiveness of bankruptcy as a means to resolve creditors' claims to the debtor's assets collectively and to permit debtors to obtain a fresh start by reorganizing with their property rights intact. Without § 541(c), the estate would not succeed to the debtor's valuable option in *Robert L. Helms Construction*. Likewise, if filing a bankruptcy petition deprived *Mitchell* of title to his property, the automatic stay would lose its bite. It would, in effect, slam the barn door after the animals were gone.

[B] Transfer Restrictions Ineffective

Creditors sometimes attempt to restrict a borrower's ability to transfer its property to another person. Such restraints are rarely effective under state law,[78] but when they are, they prevent a debtor's bankruptcy estate from succeeding to the debtor's property.[79] Giving effect to them might impair a financially troubled debtor's chances to reorganize by preventing the debtor's estate from acquiring the debtor's assets. Accordingly, Bankruptcy Code § 541(c)(1) makes "any provision in an agreement, transfer instrument, or applicable nonbankruptcy law that restricts or conditions transfer of such interest by the debtor" ineffective to prevent the estate from acquiring the debtor's property.[80] Thus, restraints on alienation that might be effective outside of bankruptcy do not prevent the debtor's bankruptcy estate from succeeding to the debtor's property.

For example, suppose that Doug owns property subject to a security interest held by Consumer Finance Co., and that their security agreement prohibits Doug from selling or otherwise transferring title to the collateral without the prior written permission of the finance company. Whether this provision is enforceable under state law does not matter because Bankruptcy Code § 541(c)(1)(A) makes the provision unenforceable. The collateral is part of Doug's bankruptcy estate, despite the provision in their security agreement and regardless of whether it is otherwise enforceable under state law.

This does not mean Consumer Finance Co. will lose its lien. In general, properly created liens survive bankruptcy. However, by ensuring that the encumbered property remains in the debtor's estate, the Bankruptcy Code preserves the trustee's ability to administer the property and to preserve

[77] In re Mitchell, 85 B.R. 564 (Bankr. D. Nev. 1988).

[78] *See, e.g.*, U.C.C. § 9-406(d) (2003).

[79] Whitaker v. Power Brake Supply (In re Olympia Holding Corp.), 188 B.R. 287 (M.D. Fla. 1994), *aff'd*, 68 F.3d 1304 (11th Cir. 1995).

[80] Bankruptcy Code § 541(c)(1)(A).

any equity for the benefit of the debtor's other creditors. It also ensures that the lien holder is restrained from attempting to enforce its security interest apart from the collective process of the bankruptcy case, without first obtaining relief from the automatic stay.

Franchise agreements frequently contain language prohibiting the franchisee from transferring the franchise to another person without the franchisor's consent. If enforced, this type of a transfer restriction prevents a debtor's fast food restaurant, auto dealership, or other franchise, from becoming property of the debtor's bankruptcy estate and impairs the franchisee's ability to reorganize. Section 541(c)(1)(A) makes these types of transfer restrictions ineffective and ensures that the debtor's estate owns and can operate the debtor's franchise.

Section 541(c)(1)(A) addresses only a very narrow issue: whether the transfer restriction prevents the *debtor's estate* from acquiring the property. In many cases, it may also be important to determine whether the restriction prevents the estate from transferring the property to a third person. This is a separate issue, dealt with by other provisions of the Bankruptcy Code.[81] But § 541(c)(1)(A) makes it clear that these restrictions generally do not, in the first instance, prevent the estate from acquiring whatever rights the debtor owned when it filed its petition.

[C] Restrictions on Transferability of Governmental Licenses Ineffective

Restrictions on the transferability of governmental licenses, such as liquor licenses, drivers licenses, and broadcast licenses, have sometimes led to the suggestion that the license was not property of the estate, either because under state law the license was not regarded as "property" or because the government's interest in regulating the activity for which the license was required effectively restrained the estate's ability to succeed to the debtor's rights.[82] True to the text of § 541(c)(1)(A), courts now generally regard liquor licenses[83] and FCC broadcast licenses[84] as property of the estate, regardless of any restriction imposed on the transferability of the license by the regulating authority.

For example, in *In re Barnes,* the court ruled that an Indiana liquor license was property of the estate even though it was not regarded as "property" under state law, and even though it was both nontransferable

---

[81] *See* § 10.05 Assignment of Executory Contracts, *infra*; *see also* § 9.03[E] Continuation of Liens and Other Interests; Sales Free and Clear, *infra.*

[82] *E.g.*, In re D.H. Overmyer Telecasting Co., 35 B.R. 400 (Bankr. N.D. Ohio 1983), *but see* Ramsay v. Dowden (In re Cent. Ark. Broad. Co., 68 F.3d 213, 215 (8th Cir. 1995) (expressing disagreement).

[83] *E.g.*, In re Barnes, 276 F.3d 927, 928–29 (7th Cir. 2002) (Posner, J.); In re Nejberger, 934 F.2d 1300 (3d Cir. 1991).

[84] *E.g.*, Ramsay v. Dowden (In re Cent. Ark. Broad. Co.), 68 F.3d 213, 214–15 (8th Cir. 1995); In re LAN Tamers, Inc., 329 F.3d 204 (1st Cir. 2003); In re Schmitz, 270 F.3d 1254, 1257 (9th Cir. 2001); *see* FCC v. NextWave Personal Communications, Inc., 537 U.S. 293 (2003).

without the state's consent and even though it was revocable by the state due to the licensee's misconduct.[85] In *In re Burgess,* even a license to operate a Nevada brothel was treated as property of the estate.[86]

Significantly, the Supreme Court's 2003 decision in *FCC v. NextWave Personal Communications, Inc.* assumed that an FCC spectrum license was an asset of the bankrupt debtor's estate, while holding that § 525, which generally prohibits the government from discriminating against bankrupt debtors,[87] prevented the FCC from terminating the debtor's license solely because the debtor had filed a bankruptcy petition.[88]

As with other restrictions on transfers of a debtor's property that do not prevent the property from becoming property of the debtor's estate, license restrictions may nevertheless prevent the debtor or the estate from transferring the license to a third party. Consider, for example, the absurdity of a rule that would permit a truck driver to transfer his or her commercial vehicle drivers' license or that would permit an attorney to transfer her license to practice law to someone else. The effectiveness of transfer restrictions to prevent the estate from transferring property to a third person is considered elsewhere in connection with rules governing the debtor's "use, sale, and lease" of estate property[89] and the debtor's ability to assign executory contracts that are part of the debtor's estate.[90]

§ 7.04 Property Excluded from the Debtor's Estate

Although the general approach of the Bankruptcy Code is to include everything in the estate, and then to remove certain property from the estate when it is distributed, abandoned, or exempted, there are a few exceptions. These exceptions are narrowly drawn and exclude very limited types of property. Most of the exceptions deal with interests arising from trusts or similar divisions of property into legal and equitable interests. Others, some of which were added by the 2005 Amendments, deal with various types of employment benefits, including pensions, as well as certain educational savings plans promoted by federal law.

[85] *E.g.*, In re Barnes, 276 F.3d 927, 928–29 (7th Cir. 2002) (Posner, J.); *see also* Ramsay v. Dowden (In re Cent. Ark. Broad. Co.), 68 F.3d 213 (8th Cir. 1995) (FCC broadcast license).

[86] 234 B.R. 793 (Bankr. D. Nev. 1999). One of your authors once represented a debtor who owned un-rated video tapes, copyrights to such movies, and the phone number to a phone-sex service. Persuading the trustee to sell these assets was difficult.

[87] *See* § 13.09[D][1] Governmental Discrimination, *infra.*

[88] 537 U.S. 293 (2003).

[89] *See* Chapter 9, Operating the Debtor, *infra.*

[90] *See* Chapter 11, Executory Contracts and Unexpired Leases, *infra.*

[A] Property Held by Debtor for Benefit of a Third Person

The first category of property that does not become part of a debtor's estate deals with powers of the debtor that may be exercised solely for the benefit of another person.[91] The most obvious example of this is a power of appointment under a trust that can only be exercised for the benefit of someone other than the debtor. For example, a trust might be created that empowers Terrel to assign the principal to one of his two nephews, Abdur or Basil, but not to himself. If Terrel goes into bankruptcy, his power to designate Abdur or Basil as recipients of the assets of the trust does not become part of Terrel's bankruptcy estate, and cannot be exercised by the trustee. The reason for this rule is to preserve the ability of the settlor of the trust — the person who created it — to determine both who will benefit and who will decide who benefits from the trust. Since Terrel's creditors cannot directly gain anything from Terrel's exercise of the power, the Code presumes there is no sound reason to subvert the settlor's intention by handing the power of appointment over to the trustee of Terrel's bankruptcy estate.

Of course, if the debtor is among those for whose benefit the power might be exercised, the power of appointment does become part of the estate, with the trustee empowered to exercise the debtor's power for the benefit of the debtor's estate. Thus, if the debtor has the power to designate himself as the beneficiary of a life insurance policy and withdraw the cash value of the policy, the policy is property of the estate.

[B] Expired Leases of Non-Residential Real Estate

The second exclusion from the debtor's estate is of broader significance. Section 541(b)(2) specifies that the estate does not acquire any interest of the debtor as lessee of nonresidential real property once the stated term of the lease expires.[92] If the lease expires before bankruptcy, the leasehold interest is never part of the estate; if it expires during the bankruptcy, the leasehold interest ceases to be part of the estate.[93]

For example, suppose that Dottie Lane, Inc. is the lessee of a warehouse, but that the lease expires on July 1, 2009, with no right of renewal. If the company files a bankruptcy petition on August 1, 2009, her previously expired lease would not be property of the estate. If it files its petition on June 1, 2009, with only one month remaining on the lease, the leasehold interest initially becomes part of the estate, but ceases to be property of the estate when the lease expires on July 1. This result is consistent with the general rule of § 541(a)(1), that the estate acquires whatever the debtor owned when its petition was filed. If only one month remains on the lease

[91] Bankruptcy Code § 541(b)(1).

[92] Bankruptcy Code § 541(b)(2).

[93] Erickson v. Polk, 921 F.2d 200 (8th Cir. 1990).

when the petition is filed, the estate succeeds only to what the debtor had at that time — one month.

The negative implication of § 541(b)(2) is that other types of leases might become property of the estate, despite having expired before the petition was filed. Thus, the language of § 541(b)(2) could easily be interpreted to imply that an expired lease of residential real estate or of an automobile or other personal property becomes property of the estate, notwithstanding its expiration before the lessee's bankruptcy petition.

A holdover tenant's right to possession under a residential property lease is part of the debtor's estate. In *In re Butler,* the debtor defaulted on the rent obligations on her month-to-month tenancy.[94] Her landlord obtained a judgment for unlawful detainer and, on the same day her Chapter 7 petition was filed, served the debtor with a notice to vacate the premises. The court ruled that the debtor's possessory interest in the premises was part of her estate. Accordingly, the automatic stay of § 362(a)(1)-(3), which prevents creditors from taking action against property of the estate, restrained the landlord from proceeding with the debtor's eviction, at least while the case was pending. At least conceptually, the tenant's month-to-month tenancy may not arise from the lease, but the tenant still has an interest that is part of the estate and subject to the automatic stay.

In reaching this conclusion, the court explained that "[t]he doctrine of expressio unius est exclusio alterius" was applicable and that Congress's creation of § 541(b)(2)'s express exception to § 541(a)(1) for "an expired lease of nonresidential property suggest[ed] that Congress intended possessory interests in residential property to be included in property of the estate."[95] The court went further and pointed out that Congress had considered and rejected proposed amendments to the Bankruptcy Code to treat expired leases of residential real estate in the same manner as expired non-residential leases under § 541(b)(2).[96]

The opinion in *In re Butler* emphasizes an important point: the landlord's right to evict the debtor is still governed by the automatic stay. Efforts to remove a holdover tenant from the premises by eviction violate the automatic stay, absent express approval of the bankruptcy court.[97] And, even though the Bankruptcy Code has been amended to provide an express exception to the stay to permit landlords to continue with evictions of residential tenants pursuant to a pre-petition judgment ordering their eviction,[98] prudent landlords seek the bankruptcy court's permission before permitting an eviction to continue after the case has been commenced.

Further, § 541(b)(2) applies only to leases that expire as scheduled according to the terms of the lease. It does not apply to leases that are

---

[94] In re Butler, 271 B.R. 867 (Bankr. C.D. Cal. 2002).

[95] 271 B.R. at 872 (Bankr. C.D. Cal. 2002).

[96] 271 B.R. at 872 (Bankr. C.D. Cal. 2002).

[97] *E.g.*, In re Sims, 213 B.R. 641 (Bankr. W.D. Pa. 1997).

[98] Bankruptcy Code § 362(b)(22); *see* § 8.03[A] Private Right Exceptions to the Stay, *infra*.

"terminated" by the landlord due to the tenant's breach.[99] If the landlord terminates the lease due to the tenant's default, § 541(b)(2) does not apply, and the lease becomes part of the tenant's bankruptcy estate when the tenant files a petition. The estate's authority to assume, reject, or assign the lease is governed by Bankruptcy Code § 365, dealing with "executory contracts and unexpired leases."[100]

[C] Debtor's Right to Participate in Educational Program; Accreditation

The third exclusion is of limited significance. The right of a debtor to participate in certain specified educational programs is not property of the estate. In addition, the debtor's accreditation or licensing as an educational institution is not property of the estate.[101] While § 541(b)(3) might provoke jokes about prominent colleges, such as Harvard, Yale, or Stanford being unable to use bankruptcy to sell their accreditation, it is far more important in the context of private elementary and secondary schools, where questions might be raised about the estate's ability to continue to operate. Not surprisingly, though, § 541(b)(3) has generated virtually no litigation.[102]

[D] Specific Oil Industry Rights

The fourth exclusion is also narrow and reflects the impact that lobbying groups for specific industries sometimes have on bankruptcy policy. Property of the estate does not include certain interests in liquid or gaseous hydrocarbons that had been transferred or are subject to an agreement to transfer them.[103] This exemption was designed to deal with specific problems created for the energy industry by the Bankruptcy Code's rules regarding the scope of a debtor's estate.

[E] Proceeds of Money Orders

The 1994 Amendments added a fifth exclusion from the estate for a debtor's interest in certain proceeds of a sale by the debtor of a money order.[104] These proceeds are excluded if the debtor sold the money order within fourteen days prior to the filing of the petition under an agreement that prohibited the commingling of the proceeds with other property of the debtor.[105]

---

[99] *See, e.g.*, In re Turner, 326 B.R. 563, 575 (Bankr. W.D. Pa. 2005); In re Morgan, 181 B.R. 579 (Bankr. N.D. Ala. 1994).

[100] Bankruptcy Code § 365(b); *see* § 10.04[C] Restrictions on Assumption, *infra*.

[101] Bankruptcy Code § 541(b)(3).

[102] *See* In re Betty Owen Sch., Inc., 195 B.R. 23 (Bankr. S.D.N.Y. 1996).

[103] Bankruptcy Code § 541(b)(4).

[104] Pub. L. No. 103-394, § 223, 108 Stat 4106, 4128 (1994).

[105] Bankruptcy Code § 541(b)(9) (2006) (previously codified at § 541(b)(5)). Note that it does not matter whether the proceeds were segregated from other funds or commingled. The key question is whether the agreement prohibited commingling.

[F] Spendthrift Trusts[106]

Section 541(c)(2) prevents many spendthrift trusts from becoming part of the debtor's estate. Its greatest significance is with respect to assets in debtors' pension funds. The statutory language provides: "A restriction on the transfer of a beneficial interest of the debtor in a trust that is enforceable under applicable nonbankruptcy law is enforceable in a case under [the Bankruptcy Code]."[107] This language effectively makes spendthrift trusts just as enforceable in bankruptcy as they are outside of bankruptcy.

[1] Meaning of "Spendthrift Trust"

The exclusion from the debtor's estate for certain spendthrift trusts is particularly important to consumer debtors. It deals with non-assignable beneficial interests held in trust. The non-assignability provision of the trust, if enforceable, prevents its beneficiary from spending the principal assets of the trust, and more importantly in this context, prevents the beneficiary's creditors from seizing those assets to satisfy the beneficiary's debts.

In any trust relationship, there are at least three roles, usually involving at least three persons. The "settlor" is the person who creates the trust by depositing money or property; the "trustee" administers the trust; and the "beneficiary" receives distributions from the trust.[108] The trustee holds legal title to the property placed in trust, with the beneficiary enjoying the equitable or "beneficial" interest in the property.[109] If a trust permits the beneficiary to assign the beneficial interest in the trust to a third party, the beneficiary's interest in the trust is property of the estate and will be distributed to its creditors.[110] However, spendthrift trusts prohibit the beneficiary from assigning the beneficial interest either as a gift, or to creditors who might seek to seize the beneficiary's property. In many circumstances, these restrictions are enforceable under non-bankruptcy law.

Where these restrictions on transfer of the beneficial interest are enforceable, creditors of the beneficiary cannot seize the corpus of the trust. No matter how much the beneficiary of such a trust owes, no matter how

---

[106] Robert B. Chapman, *A Matter of Trust, or Why "ERISA-Qualified" Is "Nonsense Upon Stilts": The Tax and Bankruptcy Treatment of Section 457 Deferred Compensation Plans as Exemplar*, 40 Willamette L. Rev. 1, 8 n.21 (2004); Patricia E. Dilley, *Hidden in Plain View: The Pension Shield Against Creditors*, 74 Ind. L.J. 355, 366 n.34 (1999); Anthony Michael Sabino, *A Final Battle at the Last Line of Defense — The Struggle to Keep ERISA-Qualified Pension Plans Outside the Reach of Creditors in Bankruptcy Cases*, 12 Am. Bankr. Inst. L. Rev. 501 (2004).

[107] Bankruptcy Code § 541(c)(2).

[108] Restatement (Third) of Trusts § 3 (2003).

[109] The trust corpus or "res" is the property that is administered. Restatement (Third) of Trusts § 40 (2003). It usually consists of various investment property, such as stocks, bonds, or other securities, but may be real estate, tangible personal property or anything else.

[110] Restatement (Third) of Trusts § 56 (2003).

delinquent he is on his debts, creditors may only latch on to trust property if and when funds in the trust are distributed to the beneficiary. Creditors may not reach the property while it is still held in trust.[111]

Trusts subject to transfer restrictions are often called "spendthrift trusts." This is because restrictions on transfer of beneficial interests in trusts have sometimes been used to ensure a continued income for the feckless offspring of the very rich. A wealthy parent or grandparent, dismayed by the inability of their potential heirs to avoid squandering money on snipe ranches and pearl mines, may set up a trust that pays out $5,000 per month for bare maintenance expenses and prohibits the transfer of the beneficiary's interest to anybody else.[112]

[2] Enforceability of Spendthrift Trusts in Bankruptcy

There is nothing in the Constitution that compels Congress to recognize spendthrift trusts in bankruptcy, and it is arguable that such recognition is unfair to those debtors whose ancestors had neither the wealth nor the wit to provide for their prodigal offspring.[113] However, § 541(c)(2) continues a long tradition of giving effect to this particular transfer restriction. Thus, if Bertie Wooster's rich aunt has had the good sense to restrict his ability to transfer his beneficial interest in the Wooster family trust, Bertie's future prosperity is secure from his creditors outside of bankruptcy, and the bankruptcy trustee should he file for bankruptcy.[114]

Because of the effect on creditors, courts usually closely examine the terms of a trust to determine whether it is a true spendthrift trust or merely a sham. For example, in *In re Herzig*, the trust permitted the debtor to terminate the trust and receive an immediate payment of all of its funds. This made its spendthrift trust provision invalid and enabled the bankruptcy trustee to acquire the trust property.[115] Similarly, in *Shurley v. Texas Commerce Bank-Austin, N.A. (In re Shurley)*, the Fifth Circuit ruled that a spendthrift trust that was partially self-settled, and thus invalid to the extent of the settlor's contribution to the trust, was part of the settlor's bankruptcy estate to the same extent it would have been invalid under governing state law.[116]

---

[111] Restatement (Third) of Trusts § 58 (2003); *see generally* George G. Bogert & George T. Bogert, The Law of Trusts and Trustees §§ 221, 223, 225–27 (Rev. 2d ed. 1992).

[112] Restatement (Third) of Trusts § 58 cmt. a (2003).

[113] Note, however, that recognition of spendthrift trusts is in line with one theory of bankruptcy, namely that it should be transparent to state property and creditor's rights law, neither broadening nor narrowing the substantive rights of creditors but only enforcing them more efficiently.

[114] *E.g.*, Ehrenberg v. Southern Cal. Permanente Med. Group (In re Moses), 167 F.3d 470, 473 (9th Cir. 1999); *see generally* Pelham G. Wodehouse, The World of Jeeves (1967).

[115] 167 B.R. 707 (Bankr. D. Mass. 1994); *see also* In re Gallagher, 101 B.R. 594, 601 (Bankr. W.D. Mo. 1989); *see generally* David B. Young, *The Pro Tanto Invalidity of Protective Trusts: Partial Self-Settlement and Beneficiary Control*, 78 Marq. L. Rev. 807 (1995).

[116] 115 F.3d 333 (5th Cir. 1997).

[3] Offshore Asset Protection Trusts[117]

Wily debtors, seeking to retain their assets and avoid financial responsibility for their debts (as well as tax on their income), have recently added a new quiver to their bows in the form of offshore "asset protection" trusts. These trusts, which operate under the laws of foreign countries, are intended to do little more than frustrate the efforts of American courts to recover assets placed in the trust by an uncooperative debtor.

Debtors wishing to use these asset protection trusts to shield their wealth from the claims of creditors must transfer their assets to a trust in a foreign jurisdiction that does not recognize or comply with judgments or other legal processes originating in the United States.[118] Courts where such trusts are established will not enforce an order from a state or federal court in the United States that compels turnover of the trust assets to a creditor who was defrauded under United States law or to a bankruptcy trustee representing the beneficiary's creditors.[119] The asset protection trust documents specify that upon the occurrence of an "event of duress," such as the issuance of a court order that would impair the trustee's ability to control the direction of the trust's assets, the debtor will be terminated as the trustee and control of the trust's assets is transferred to a foreign trustee who is beyond the jurisdiction of the United States.

American courts have reacted in predictable ways to these schemes. The debtor in *United States v. Brennan* was convicted of the federal crime of bankruptcy fraud for misrepresenting the extent of his assets and repatriating funds held in an offshore asset protection trust after his bankruptcy case was closed.[120] Other debtors who have used these devices have been held in contempt[121] and denied any discharge from their debts pursuant to Bankruptcy Code § 727.[122] Whether these debtors eventually recover their assets, after paying the price for their misconduct, is uncertain.

A number of states have sought to join the asset protection party by validating so-called "self-settled" trusts under state law, and treating them

---

[117] Karen E. Boxx, *Gray's Ghost — A Conversation About the Onshore Trust*, 85 Iowa L. Rev. 1195 (2000); Robert T. Danforth, *Rethinking the Law of Creditors' Rights in Trusts*, 53 Hastings L.J. 287 (2002); James T. Lorenzetti, *The Offshore Trust: A Contemporary Asset Protection Scheme*, 102 Com. L.J. 138, 143–44 (1997); Randall J. Gingiss, *Putting a Stop to "Asset Protection" Trusts*, 51 Baylor L. Rev. 987 (1999); Henry J. Lischer, Jr., *Domestic Asset Protection Trusts: Pallbearers to Liability?*, 35 Real Prop. Prob. & Tr. J. 479 (2000); Stewart E. Sterk, *Asset Protection Trusts: Trust Law's Race to the Bottom?*, 85 Cornell L. Rev. 1035 (2000).

[118] One may wonder how these debtors expect to recover their assets if they are converted by the unscrupulous trustees in violation of their fiduciary duties.

[119] FTC v. Affordable Media, LLC, 179 F.3d 1228, 1240 (9th Cir. 1999); *see* James T. Lorenzetti, *The Offshore Trust: A Contemporary Asset Protection Scheme*, 102 Com. L.J. 138, 143–44 (1997).

[120] 395 F.3d 59 (2d Cir. 2005).

[121] *E.g.*, In re Lawrence, 279 F.3d 1294 (11th Cir. 2002); FTC v. Affordable Media, 179 F.3d 1228 (9th Cir. 1999).

[122] *See* § 13.02 Denial of Discharge, *infra*.

as spendthrift (unreachable by creditors).[123] Even if state law validates a self-settled spendthrift trust, however, the 2005 Amendments explicitly permit the bankruptcy trustee to recover transfers to a self-settled trust made within the last ten years prior to the debtor' bankruptcy petition if the transfer was made with the intent to defraud an existing creditor.[124]

The 2005 Amendments to § 548 added language specifically directed at these and other self-settled trusts. Section 548(e)(1) now permits the trustee to avoid any:

> transfer of an interest of the debtor in property that was made on or within 10 years before the date of the filing of the petition if —
>
> (A) such transfer was made to a self-settled trust or similar device;
>
> (B) such transfer was by the debtor;
>
> (C) the debtor is a beneficiary of such trust or similar device; and
>
> (D) the debtor made such transfer with actual intent to hinder, delay, or defraud any entity to which the debtor was or became, on or after the date that such transfer was made, indebted.[125]

Section 548 has always provided that transfers made with the intent to hinder, defraud, or delay creditors are avoidable. The most important aspect of this new language is the portion that looks back ten years before the debtor's petition was filed, thus effectively expanding the scope of § 548 beyond the two-year period that applies to such transfers generally.[126]

[4] Employee Pension Plans[127]

The spendthrift trust provision has its most dramatic effect in connection with the type of pension funds that many middle-class Americans hold. It has long been clear that restrictions on the transfer of pension funds held in trust, if recognized or required by state law, fit within the exclusion. In its 1992 decision in *Patterson v. Shumate*,[128] the Supreme Court held that spendthrift trust restrictions imposed under ERISA[129] are equally effective.

---

123 For a discussion of these statutes, see Stewart E. Sterk, *Asset Protection Trusts: Trust Law's Race to the Bottom?*, 85 Cornell L. Rev. 1035, 1044 (2000).

124 Bankruptcy Code § 548(e).

125 Bankruptcy Code § 548(e)(1).

126 Bankruptcy Code § 548(a)(1). The trustee might also be able to avoid a fraudulent transfer under state fraudulent transfer law, through Bankruptcy Code § 544(b); *see* § 16.01[A] State Fraudulent Conveyance Law, *infra*.

127 Patricia E. Dilley, *Hidden in Plain View: The Pension Shield Against Creditors*, 74 Ind. L.J. 355, 387 (1999); Donna Litman, *Bankruptcy Status of "ERISA Qualified Pension Plans" — An Epilogue to* Patterson v. Shumate, 9 Am. Bankr. Inst. L. Rev. 637, 655 (2001); C. Scott Pryor, *Rock, Scissors, Paper: ERISA, the Bankruptcy Code and State Exemption Laws for Individual Retirement Accounts*, 77 Am. Bankr. L.J. 65 (2003); Ann K. Wooster, Annotation, *Retirement Funds Benefits or Refunds of Retirement Fund Contributions as "Property" of Bankruptcy Estate Under § 541 of Bankruptcy Code of 1978*, 174 A.L.R. Fed. 587 (2001).

128 504 U.S. 753 (1992).

129 "ERISA" is the Employee Retirement Income Security Act of 1974. Most of ERISA was

In doing so, the Court effectively further broadened the scope of § 541(c)(2) beyond what had traditionally been assumed. As a result of *Patterson*, funds in employees' ERISA-qualified pension plans are completely excluded from their bankruptcy estates and protected from their creditors' claims, regardless of the size of their pension fund.

The *Patterson* decision resolved a long dispute in the lower courts over whether the phrase "applicable nonbankruptcy law" in § 541(c)(2) referred to any law outside of the confines of the bankruptcy code or only to state law. The Court's analysis was uncomplicated. The debtor's pension plan contained an ERISA-mandated spendthrift clause, preventing alienation of the plan's funds.[130] It seemed evident to the Court that ERISA, appearing as it does outside of the Bankruptcy Code, was the type of "applicable nonbankruptcy law" to which § 541(c)(2) refers.[131] The Court held, "[a] debtor's interest in an ERISA-qualified pension plan may be excluded from the property of the bankruptcy estate pursuant to § 541(c)(2)."[132]

Unfortunately, the Court's cryptic phrase "ERISA-qualified" has left bankruptcy courts baffled about the scope of the exclusion.[133] The *Patterson* decision left open the possibility that the pension plan could still be invaded by the trustee if, due to some oversight, the pension plan failed to qualify for favorable tax treatment under ERISA. It also left open questions about the extent to which other pension plans, not governed by ERISA, qualified for the exclusion.

Most courts have applied one of several two- or three-pronged tests to determine if a debtor's pension is excluded by § 541(c)(2). One of these two-pronged tests asks whether the plan (1) is subject to title I of ERISA and (2) contains the necessary anti-alienation term prohibiting plan benefits from being assigned or alienated.[134] Another test modifies the second prong by requiring that the anti-alienation provision actually be enforceable

codified in Title 29 of the United States Code, but a significant part of it is contained in Title 26 (the Internal Revenue Code). A basic explanation of ERISA's provisions in relation to the exclusion of ERISA pension funds from the debtor's estate can be found in C. Scott Pryor, *Rock, Scissors, Paper: ERISA, the Bankruptcy Code and State Exemption Laws for Individual Retirement Accounts*, 77 Am. Bankr. L.J. 65, 71–74 (2003).

130 ERISA specifies that "[e]ach pension plan shall provide that benefits provided under the plan may not be assigned or alienated." ERISA § 206(d)(1), 29 U.S.C. § 1056(d)(1) (2000).

131 504 U.S. at 760; *see generally* Donna Litman, *Bankruptcy Status of "ERISA Qualified Pension Plans" — An Epilogue to* Patterson v. Shumate, 9 Am. Bankr. Inst. L. Rev. 637, 655 (2001).

132 504 U.S. at 765.

133 *E.g.*, In re Goldschein, 244 B.R. 595 (Bankr. M.D. Md. 2000); *see generally* Donna Litman, *Bankruptcy Status of "ERISA Qualified Pension Plans" — An Epilogue to* Patterson v. Shumate, 9 Am. Bankr. Inst. L. Rev. 637, 648–56 (2001).

134 *E.g.*, Traina v. Sewell (In re Sewell), 180 F.3d 707, 712 (5th Cir. 1999); In re Baker, 114 F.3d 636, 638–39 (7th Cir. 1997).

under ERISA.[135] Other courts have deployed a third requirement, insisting that the plan also be qualified under § 401 of the Internal Revenue Code.[136]

Benefits under a retirement plan that is not valid under ERISA should not be excluded from the debtor's estate under § 541(c)(2) even if the plan includes an anti-alienation or spendthrift provision and is thus otherwise "tax qualified" under the Internal Revenue Code.[137] But, in *Raymond B. Yates, M.D., P.C. Profit Sharing Plan v. Hendon*, the Supreme Court ruled that the owner of a business who also works as an employee of his business may qualify as a "participant" in an ERISA plan if the plan covers employees other than the business owner and his spouse. Thus, an employee who also serves as the employer is not disqualified from enjoying the benefits of participating in the firm's ERISA pension plan, including the right to have the employee's pension assets excluded from his or her bankruptcy estate.[138]

Language in the *Yates* decision, limiting its holding to situations were there are employees in addition to the debtor and his spouse, lends support to the holdings of some courts that the exclusion would not apply to funds in a profit-sharing plan whose sole participant was the debtor who served as the owner of the business and its only employee.[139]

Further consensus is hard to find. Courts using the two-pronged approach have taken the decidedly pro-debtor view that the debtor's pension funds are excluded under § 541(c)(2) and *Patterson* if the plan is generally regulated under ERISA and contains the necessary spendthrift trust language, even if the plan's administrators have not handled the plan or its funds in strict compliance with ERISA's requirements.[140] However, other courts have denied owner-employees the benefit of the exclusion where they have misused their control over the plan's assets in complete disregard of ERISA's restrictions, effectively using the plan as if it were a personal bank account.[141]

Debtors might have pension funds invested in a wide variety of pension plans and savings accounts, which, depending on their characteristics, may be included in their bankruptcy estate. Funds in a "Simplified Employee

---

135 *E.g.*, In re Hanes, 162 B.R. 733 (Bankr. E.D. Va. 1994).

136 *E.g.*, In re Hall, 151 B.R. 412, 419–20 (Bankr. W.D. Mich. 1993); *see generally* J. Gordon Christy & Sabrina Skeldon, Shumate *and Pension Benefits in Bankruptcy*, 2 J. Bankr. L. & Prac. 719, 722–23 (1992).

137 26 U.S.C. § 401(a)(13) (2000).

138 Raymond B. Yates, M.D., P.C. Profit Sharing Plan v. Hendon, 541 U.S. 1, 6 (2004).

139 *E.g.*, In re Sutton, 272 B.R. 802 (Bankr. M.D. Fla. 2002) (pension not excluded from estate because it did not comply with ERISA as a result of the debtor's status as sole employee and sole participant under the fund).

140 In re Baker, 114 F.3d 636 (7th Cir. 1997); In re Handel, 301 B.R. 421 (Bankr. S.D.N.Y. 2003).

141 In re Goldschein, 244 B.R. 595 (Bankr. D. Md. 2000); In re Harris, 188 B.R. 444, 449 (Bankr. M.D. Fla. 1995), *aff'd*, Harris v. Jensen, 116 F.3d 1492 (11th Cir. 1997), *cert. denied*, 522 U.S. 950 (1997).

Pension Plan" (SEP), a type of Individual Retirement Account (IRA),[142] which are neither required to be held in trust, nor required to be protected by an anti-alienation provision,[143] are not excluded from a debtor's estate by this provision.[144] In addition, funds in either a conventional IRA or a "Roth" IRA are excluded under this language.[145] However, particularly since the 2005 Amendments, these funds may be exempt from administration by the trustee under § 522.[146]

In 2005, Congress added language to § 541(b) excluding both amounts withheld by an employer from an employee's wages or received as contributions by the employee to one of several types of retirement funds or to health insurance plans.[147] Some pension funds provide for funding from both sources: the employer and the employee. This language supplements § 541(c)(2) and the *Patterson v. Shumate* decision by excluding amounts withheld by an employer or contributed by an employee, even if the funds have not yet been remitted by the employer to the employee's pension plan.

The new language resolves several issues that had been frequently litigated under *Patterson* and resolves most of the issues against inclusion of these types of assets in the debtor's estate. However, the amendment fails to address several related issues, including inclusion of amounts that may have been contributed by an employer without being withheld from the employee's wages, earnings acquired before the withheld or contributed amounts are remitted to the pension plan, and a debtor's right to receive payments under one of the enumerated plans.[148] Depending on the amounts involved, aggressive trustees might be expected to pursue employers to recover such funds that are not expressly excluded from the estate either under *Patterson* or under this new provision.

---

[142] C. Scott Pryor, *Rock, Scissors, Paper: ERISA, the Bankruptcy Code and State Exemption Laws for Individual Retirement Accounts*, 77 Am. Bankr. L.J. 65 (2003).

[143] 26 U.S.C. § 408(k) (2000).

[144] *E.g.*, In re Kellogg, 179 B.R. 379 (Bankr. D. Mass. 1995).

[145] *E.g.*, Velis v. Kardanis, 949 F.2d 78 (3d Cir. 1991). Individual retirement accounts fail to satisfy two criteria for ERISA qualification. IRAs are explicitly excluded from ERISA's scope. ERISA § 201(6), 29 U.S.C. § 1051(6) (2000). Likewise, IRAs are not qualified under Internal Revenue Code § 401. Moreover, even though an IRA might include an anti-alienation provision, nothing in ERISA, or any other provision of federal law, requires them to do so. C. Scott Pryor, *Rock, Scissors, Paper: ERISA, the Bankruptcy Code and State Exemption Laws for Individual Retirement Accounts*, 77 Am. Bankr. L.J. 65, 75–76 (2003).

[146] Margaret Howard, *Exemptions Under the 2005 Bankruptcy Amendments: A Tale of Opportunity Lost*, 79 Am. Bankr. L.J. 397 (2005).

[147] Bankruptcy Abuse Prevention and Consumer Protection Act of 2005, Pub. L. No. 109-8, § 323, 119 Stat 23, 97 (2005).

[148] Bankruptcy Code § 541(b)(7). This new language refers to both employer and employee payments to (1) employee benefit plans subject to Title 1 of ERISA; (2) government employee plans under I.R.C. § 414(d); (3) deferred compensation plans under I.R.C. § 457; (4) tax deferred annuities under I.R.C. § 403(b); and (5) health insurance plans regulated by state law.

[G] Debtor's Right as Trustee of Property

The final blanket exception excludes from the estate property in which the debtor holds only legal title and not an equitable interest.[149] All that the estate would acquire under § 541(a) is bare legal title; the real value of the property — the equitable interest — is not part of the estate in any event. Assume, for example, that the debtor is the trustee of Bertie Wooster's spendthrift trust. As trustee, he holds bare legal title. He is not entitled to take money out of the trust; to do so would not only violate his fiduciary duty but also create a non-dischargeable debt.[150] Thus, the property in the trust does not belong to the debtor, is not normally subject to the claims of his creditors, and is not a part of his bankruptcy estate.[151]

[H] Education IRAs & Tuition Credits

The Bankruptcy Abuse Prevention and Consumer Protection Act of 2005 added exclusions from a debtor's estate for certain federally protected education benefits.[152] Subject to certain limits, a debtor's contributions to "Coverdell" educational IRAs and for the purchase of state "tuition credits" are excluded from the debtor's estate.

New § 541(b)(5) excludes "funds placed in an education individual retirement account" more than one year before the debtor's petition, so long as the designated beneficiary of the account was a "child, stepchild, grandchild, or stepgrandchild of the debtor" in the taxable year for which the funds were placed in the account.[153] Thus, funds placed in an educational IRA for the benefit of the debtor's nieces or nephews, or for the benefit of his god-children are not protected. Likewise, funds contributed to an educational IRA for the benefit of the debtor's children in the last 365 days before his petition, remain part of his bankruptcy estate.

The exclusion does not apply if the funds were "pledged or promised to any entity in connection with any extension of credit" or if they represented an "excess contribution" to the fund within the meaning of the relevant portion of the Internal Revenue Code.[154] Moreover, there is also a $5,475 ceiling on the amount of funds that may be excluded with respect to contributions to any individual beneficiary's account made between two years and one year before the debtor's petition was filed.[155]

---

[149] Bankruptcy Code § 541(d).

[150] Bankruptcy Code § 523(a)(4).

[151] *See* Tort Claimants Committee v. Roman Catholic Archbishop of Portland in Oregon, Inc. (In Re Roman Catholic Archbishop of Portland in Or., Inc.), 345 B.R. 686 (D. Or. 2006).

[152] Bankruptcy Abuse Prevention and Consumer Protection Act of 2005, Pub. L. No. 109-8, § 225(a)(1)(C), 119 Stat. 23, 65 (2005).

[153] Bankruptcy Code § 541(b)(5).

[154] Bankruptcy Code § 541(b)(5)(B).

[155] Bankruptcy Code § 541(b)(5)(C). The current limit on total contributions to Coverdell IRAs for a single beneficiary is $2,000. Thus, it is unclear what effect the $5,475 per beneficiary limit will have with respect to contributions made between 720 and 365 days before the debtor's

The express language of the exclusion applies only to *"funds placed in* an educational individual retirement account," suggesting that earnings on the funds are not excluded from the debtor's estate. Whether courts will apply this language in such a strict fashion remains to be seen.

Similar protection has been added for "funds used to purchase a tuition credit or certificate or contributed to an account . . . under a qualified State tuition program."[156] These funds are subject to the same restrictions that apply to Coverdell educational IRAs, preventing debtors from taking steps to shield funds on the eve of their bankruptcy petitions or in excess of the amounts permitted to be contributed to these funds under the Internal Revenue Code.

[I] Pawned Goods

New § 541(b)(8) excludes from the estate tangible personal property that the debtor has pawned, as long as the debtor is not obligated to repay the loan made by the pawnshop or redeem the property from the shop to which it has been delivered.[157] The exclusion operates primarily for the benefit of licensed pawnshops who do not have to surrender pawned property, even though the debtor may still retain the right to redeem it under applicable state law. The property is part of the estate if the debtor has already exercised any right to redeem it[158] or if the transaction with the pawnshop is otherwise subject to avoidance under any of the trustee's avoiding powers.[159]

§ 7.05 Securitization

Asset securitization transactions, which involve trillions of dollars, raise difficult issues about property of a debtor's estate. Securitization deals are an alternative way for a business to use its accounts, chattel paper, and other receivables to generate immediate cash. The traditional way for a business to transform its receivables into cash is to sell them to a commercial factor, who is engaged in the business of buying receivables, or to use them as collateral for a loan. A securitization transaction combines the aspects of factoring (which involves the sale of receivables) with a secured

---

petition, unless it is meant to permit inclusion in the debtor's estate of funds contributed to a beneficiary's Coverdell IRA by individuals other than the debtor, such as parents, step-parents, grandparents, and step-grandparents.

Section 104(b) requires the $5,475 amount to be adjusted every three years by a factor reflecting the change in the United State's Department of Labor's Consumer Price Index, and rounded to the nearest $25 amount that represents the change. The next adjustment is scheduled to occur on April 1, 2010.

[156] Bankruptcy Code § 541(b)(6).

[157] Bankruptcy Code § 541(b)(8).

[158] Bankruptcy Code § 541(b)(8)(C).

[159] This latter result is made plain by language subjecting the exclusion to "subchapter III of chapter 5" of the Bankruptcy Code, where the trustee's various avoiding powers are located. Bankruptcy Code § 541(b)(8).

financing. These transactions have become immensely popular for a pair of reasons — liquidity enhancement and perceived advantageous treatment in bankruptcy. The first of these is efficiency enhancing, while the second, at least according to one of this book's authors, is more troubling.[160]

In a securitization transaction, the debtor (in this case known as an "originator") incorporates a company for the sole purpose of purchasing its accounts — a "Special Purpose Vehicle" or "SPV"[161] — and sells its receivables to the new company. The SPV then issues securities ("Asset Backed Securities" or "ABS"), backed by the stream of accounts purchased from the debtor, to outside investors. Assume, for example, that Titanic Industries regularly generates accounts receivables owed by its customers. This makes Titanic the "originator" of the accounts. Titanic would then sell the receivables to an SPV, "Ocean Receivables." Ocean Receivables would, in turn, obtain the cash necessary to pay for the receivables by selling bonds to investors. Collections from the receivables would then pay off the SPV's obligations to the bondholders. This form of financing often allows debtors to receive a more favorable interest rate than a conventional loan secured by the same assets.

The first reason for this price advantage is liquidity enhancement — the principle efficiency created by securitization transactions. Asset Backed Securities issued by the SPV can be issued in denominations, and with risk attributes that are attractive to capital markets participants such as mutual funds. This increases the number of investors who are available to purchase Titanic's debt and renders debt markets more competitive. A second key component of ABS transactions, and another reason that the interest rate may be better is the perception by the market that the receivables sold to the SPV will not, or indeed cannot be brought back into the originator's bankruptcy estate in the event that the originator goes bankrupt. In other words, the SPV is "bankruptcy remote." Unless the transaction is supported by an opinion of counsel that the transaction is structured in a way that protects the SPV's purchase of the receivables from the originator's bankruptcy, the bonds issued by the SPV will not receive an investment grade rating and will be difficult to sell. As such, the success of the entire transaction depends on whether the sale of the accounts can be insulated from recovery by the originator's bankruptcy in the event that the originator must seek bankruptcy protection from its creditors.

This, of course, is where the difficulty lies. In the originator's bankruptcy proceeding, the transaction is vulnerable to attack on three potential grounds: that it is a fraudulent transfer; that the transaction is "intended for security" and thus is not a "true sale"; or that the relationship between the originator and the SPV warrants piercing the SPV's corporate veil and

[160] Edward J. Janger, *The Death of Secured Lending*, 25 Cardozo L. Rev. 1759 (2004); Edward J. Janger, *Muddy Rules for Securitization Transactions*, 7 Fordham J. Corp. & Fin. L. 301 (2002).

[161] *See* Steven L. Schwarcz, *The Alchemy of Asset Securitization*, 1 Stan. J.L. Bus. & Fin. 133, 134 (1994).

therefore the originator and the debtor should be "substantively consolidated," thereby bringing its assets into the originator's bankruptcy estate.

The sale of receivables from the originator to the SPV might be a fraudulent transfer.[162] Depending on the originator's financial condition, if the price paid by the SPV to the originator was not a reasonably equivalent value for the transferred accounts (as may occur where the sale is "overcollateralized"), the entire transaction might be avoidable as a constructively fraudulent transfer.[163] Though less likely, the transaction might also be a fraudulent transfer if the circumstances surrounding the transaction indicate that it was merely a means to insulate the originator's assets from its creditors and thus "intended to hinder, delay, or defraud" the originator's creditors.[164]

A second avenue of attack to bring the "sale" of the receivables back into the originator's bankruptcy estate is to characterize the transaction as one that was "intended for security" and thus not a "true sale."[165] This is a particular risk if the terms of the sale obligate the originator to repurchase accounts that fall into default, or if the originator guaranties or warrants to the SPV that it will receive a particular rate of return on the purchased assets. Giving the buyer of accounts a "right of recourse" exposes the seller to the risk that the accounts may not be collectible. Placing this attribute of ownership back on the originator makes the transaction appear more like a loan from the SPV, secured by a floating lien in the originator's accounts.[166] This gives the SPV nothing more than a secured claim in the originator's bankruptcy and gives the originator's bankruptcy estate the right to any surplus value in the accounts. More importantly, if the assets of the SPV are considered property of the estate, then they would be considered "cash collateral" and could be used (with appropriate protections) to fund the debtor/originator's reorganization.[167] In the wake of a decision in the LTV bankruptcy that allowed securitized assets to be used as cash collateral, proponents of securitization transactions sought to avoid this risk by amending the Bankruptcy Code to prevent recharacterization of the transaction if the parties labeled it as a true sale.[168] This tactic was rejected, as a matter of federal law, leaving the substance of the transaction to control its characterization, rather than the label at the top of the page.

---

[162] Edward J. Janger, *Muddy Rules for Securitizations*, 7 Fordham J. Corp. & Fin. L. 301, 308-10 (2002); *see* § 16.03[B] Specific Transactions Involving Constructive Fraud, *infra*.

[163] Bankruptcy Code § 548(a)(1)(B); *see* Peter V. Pantaleo et al., *Rethinking the Role of Recourse in the Sale of Financial Assets*, 52 Bus. Law. 159, 185 (1996).

[164] Bankruptcy Code § 548(a)(1)(A).

[165] Stephen J. Lubben, *Beyond True Sales: Securitization and Chapter 11,* 1 N.Y.U. J. L. & Bus. 89 (2004); *see* In re LTV Steel, Inc., 274 B.R. 278 (Bankr. N.D. Ohio 2001).

[166] Thomas E. Plank, *The True Sale of Loans and the Role of Recourse*, 14 Geo. Mason U. L. Rev. 287 (1991).

[167] For an example of a case where this issue was litigated, *see* In re LTV Steel Co., Inc., No. 00-43866, 2001 Bankr. LEXIS 131 (Bankr. N.D. Ohio 2001).

[168] The proposed amendment is described in detail in Edward J. Janger, *Muddy Rules for Securitization Transactions*, 7 Fordham J. Corp. & Fin. L. 301 (2002).

Nonetheless, similar provisions have been enacted by a number of states. Whether these state statutes are effective to eliminate the doctrine of "true sale" as a matter of federal law has not yet been tested.[169]

Finally, depending on the intercorporate relationship between the originator and the SPV, the transaction might be collapsed and the accounts brought back into the originator's estate by piercing the corporate veil — or by its bankruptcy equivalent, "substantive consolidation" of the estates of the originator and the SPV.[170]

§ 7.06 Expanded Estate in Reorganization Cases

[A] Chapter 11 Cases

The basic provisions of § 541 apply in Chapter 11 reorganization cases the same as they do in Chapter 7 liquidation cases.[171] There are no special rules in Chapter 11 regarding the inclusion of post-petition property of the estate being included in the debtor's estate. However, in the typical Chapter 11 proceeding, the debtor's post-petition property is property of the estate under §§ 541(a)(6) and (7). Under those provisions, the estate includes "proceeds, product, offspring, rents, or profits of or from property of the estate," and "property acquired by the estate." This language encompasses most of what a Chapter 11 debtor normally receives after its case is commenced.

Significantly, however, and unlike Chapters 12 and 13, nothing in Chapter 11 brings earnings from an individual Chapter 11 debtor's post-petition services into his estate. Although Chapter 11 petitions by individuals who are not engaged in any business are rare, they are permitted, as the United States Supreme Court held in *Toibb v. Radloff*.[172] Thus, § 541(a)(6)'s exclusion of such earnings from the debtor's estate applies in Chapter 11 cases involving individual debtors.

Because a Chapter 11 debtor is likely to need these post-petition earnings to fund his plan, the primary significance of the exclusion of these assets from an individual debtor's chapter 11 estate is in connection with the scope of the automatic stay. For example, § 362(b)(2)(B) permits creditors to bring or maintain actions to collect amounts owed for a "domestic support obligation from property that is not property of the estate,"[173] without violating the automatic stay. A Chapter 11 debtor's spouse might be permitted to bring a wage garnishment action to collect a pre-petition

[169] For a discussion of these state statutes, see Edward J. Janger, *The Death of Secured Lending*, 25 Cardozo L. Rev. 1759 (2004).

[170] Steven L. Schwarcz, *Securitization Post-Enron*, 25 Cardozo L. Rev. 1539 (2004); Edward J. Janger, *Muddy Rules for Securitizations*, 7 Fordham J. Corp. & Fin. L. 301, 308–10 (2002).

[171] Bankruptcy Code § 103(a).

[172] 501 U.S. 157 (1991).

[173] Bankruptcy Code § 362(b)(2)(B).

support obligation from the debtor's post-petition earnings without running afoul of the automatic stay.[174]

[B] Chapter 12 Cases

Chapter 12 proceedings provide for the reorganization of family farmers and family fishermen.[175] These reorganization proceedings necessarily involve the debtor's post-petition earnings. Accordingly, the scope of property included in a Chapter 12 estate is broader than in a Chapter 7 liquidation case. Section 1207 brings into the estate not only the property included by § 541, but also any "property . . . that the debtor acquires after the commencement of the case"[176] and "earnings from services performed by the debtor after the commencement of the case."[177] This includes virtually every type of property that the debtor might acquire. Property acquired after the case is closed, dismissed, or converted to a Chapter 7 case is excluded from the Chapter 12 estate.[178] For example, income that the debtor earns from the operation of his farm or fishing operation while the case is pending belongs to the estate. Generally speaking, this would not be true in a Chapter 7 proceeding; under Chapter 7, only the income that is attributable to the property of the estate or received by the estate is included.

[C] Chapter 13 Cases

Chapter 13 of the Bankruptcy Code provides for the reorganization of individuals with regular income.[179] Like Chapters 11 and 12, Chapter 13 involves a reorganization; thus, it necessarily deals with property acquired by the debtor after his petition was filed. Indeed, the debtor's post-petition income is nearly always necessary to effectuate the plan of reorganization. Under Chapter 13, property of the estate includes everything included in a Chapter 7 estate;[180] any property that the debtor acquires after the commencement of the case but before the case is either closed, dismissed, or converted to Chapter 7, 11 or 12;[181] and all earnings from labor performed by the debtor after the commencement of the case but before the case is closed, dismissed, or converted to Chapter 7, 11, or 12.[182] Most importantly, the debtor's wages earned post-petition are property of the

[174] The Bankruptcy Abuse Prevention and Consumer Protection Act of 2005 added several related exceptions to the automatic stay, all dealing with various domestic relations and support obligations. Pub. L. No. 109-8, § 214, 119 Stat. 23, 54 (2005).

[175] *See* Chapter 20, Family Farmer and Family Fisherman Reorganization, *infra*.

[176] Bankruptcy Code § 1207(a)(1).

[177] Bankruptcy Code § 1207(a)(2).

[178] Bankruptcy Code § 1207(a).

[179] *See* Chapter 18, Rehabilitation of Individuals with Regular Income, *infra*.

[180] Bankruptcy Code § 1306(a).

[181] Bankruptcy Code § 1306(a)(1).

[182] Bankruptcy Code § 1306(a)(2).

Chapter 13 estate, even though they would not be included in his estate in a liquidation case under Chapter 7, where they are explicitly excluded by § 541(a)(6).

Chapter 8

The Automatic Stay

§ 8.01 Purpose of the Automatic Stay

The automatic stay is one of the most significant features of the Bankruptcy Code — as soon as a bankruptcy petition is filed, virtually all civil actions involving the debtor, the debtor's property, or property of the estate, and nearly all informal actions undertaken by creditors in their efforts to collect must stop dead in their tracks. Many individuals who file bankruptcy petitions do so to stop an imminent mortgage foreclosure sale, to put an end to a wage garnishment, or to stop the barrage of dunning letters and phone calls from their creditors' collection agencies. Businesses file to prevent creditors from levying on bank accounts, repossessing equipment and inventory, or terminating leases. The benefits of the automatic stay are thus a key incentive for debtors to file a bankruptcy petition.

The automatic stay serves the key purposes of bankruptcy: providing debtors with some breathing room and preventing the debtor's assets from being dissipated. When the case is completed, the automatic stay is replaced by the discharge injunction which implements the debtor's fresh start. One of the goals of bankruptcy is an orderly distribution of the debtor's property, through liquidation or reorganization, under bankruptcy court supervision. Stopping other efforts to collect the debtor's property facilitates this goal by freeing the trustee or debtor-in-possession from interference.[1]

Although this breathing space is important in any bankruptcy, it is particularly significant in Chapter 11 cases. It gives the debtor-in-possession an opportunity to negotiate with creditors and to propose a plan.[2] The automatic stay is also the focus of much bankruptcy litigation, particularly in Chapter 11, and especially between the debtor and its secured creditors.

As a general rule, creditors who have mortgages, security interests, or other liens on the debtor's property would rather get the property, sell it, and forget that the bankruptcy case was ever filed. Under some circumstances, these creditors can persuade the court to lift or modify the stay and permit them to foreclose their interests in the property. Requests to lift the stay are, for obvious reasons, usually resisted by the debtor, who may need to use the property as part of its efforts to reorganize.

The automatic stay rules craft a balance between a debtor's desire to keep its property and creditors' desires to seize it and foreclose. If the debtor has

---

[1] In re Winshall Settlor's Trust, 758 F.2d 1136, 1137 (6th Cir. 1985); Hillis Motors, Inc. v. Hawaii Auto. Dealers' Ass'n, 997 F.2d 581, 585 (9th Cir. 1993).

[2] *See* In re Lykes Bros. S.S. Co., Inc., 207 B.R. 282, 284 (Bankr. M.D. Fla. 1997).

no valuable interest in the property and does not need it to reorganize, the court must lift the stay and permit the creditor to foreclose, just as if the bankruptcy case had not been filed. Likewise, the court must release the creditor from the stay if the debtor cannot adequately protect the value of the creditor's interest in the property.

The stay itself is relatively uncontroversial; virtually all commentators, whatever their philosophy of bankruptcy, agree that a stay is necessary to make bankruptcy proceedings practical. There were initially a number of criticisms of the stay as applied, particularly of the apparent unwillingness of many courts to lift or modify the stay in protracted Chapter 11 reorganizations.[3] Refusal to lift the stay in hopeless proceedings results in unnecessary loss to creditors, especially undersecured creditors who are not entitled to interest on their claims during the period between filing a petition and confirmation of a plan. The automatic stay may also, by permitting the debtor to continue to operate its business, lead to the continued depletion of the debtor's assets and the useless accumulation of additional debts that will never be paid. It may even cause damage to other companies that are forced to deal with a competitor that does not have to pay its bills. These criticisms have led to adjustments of the stay in reorganization cases that seem destined to fail.[4]

In addition, some consumer debtors return to bankruptcy court time and time again, filing and dismissing one Chapter 13 bankruptcy case after another, even though they have no realistic hope of rehabilitating their financial circumstances, and are invoking the automatic stay only to forestall foreclosure of the mortgages on their homes.

While the automatic stay may adversely affect the substantive rights of creditors, the automatic stay is intended as a form of procedural protection to permit the debtor in a reorganization case to prepare and present a proposed plan, free from unauthorized creditor pressure. In liquidation proceedings, it permits the trustee to assemble and sell the debtor's assets in an efficient manner. The purpose of the automatic stay is not ultimately to determine the substantive rights of any party or to prevent parties from exercising their rights.[5] Instead, it channels determination of creditors' rights to the bankruptcy forum.

The rules regarding a creditor's right to obtain relief from the automatic stay are also important in the context of the rights of the trustee or the debtor-in-possession to use, sell, or lease property of the estate. Because much estate property is likely to be subject to outstanding liens, the same issues regarding the balance between the debtor's and the claimant's interest in estate property arise in determining the debtor's right to use or

---

[3] Thomas H. Jackson, The Logic and Limits of Bankruptcy Law 223 (1986); Douglas G. Baird, *The Uneasy Case for Corporate Reorganizations*, 15 J. Legal Stud. 127, 128 (1986).

[4] The Supreme Court's dicta in *United Savings Assn. v. Timbers of Inwood Forest*, 484 U.S. 365 (1988), was that the stay might be lifted if the debtor had no equity in the property and an effective reorganization was not "reasonably in prospect."

[5] In re Hughes-Bechtol, Inc., 117 B.R. 890, 905–06 (Bankr. S.D. Ohio 1990).

dispose of this property. Similar issues also arise in the context of the assumption of contractual and lease obligations by the trustee or debtor-in-possession. These issues are discussed in subsequent chapters dealing with the use, sale and lease of estate property.[6]

Further, the automatic stay of § 362(a) only restrains creditors' actions against the debtor, the debtor's property, and property of the estate. With very limited exceptions, third parties who have direct or secondary liability on the same obligations are unprotected by the statute. Even if the third party is an affiliate of the debtor, such as a co-principal, surety, or related company, the automatic stay generally does not apply.[7] Except in unusual circumstances, the creditor may pursue its rights against other obligors. Thus, if Harlan Wolff, Titanic Inc.'s president and controlling shareholder, has guaranteed a debt owed by Titanic Inc. to Bay Bank, the automatic stay does not prevent the bank from suing Wolff.

The first issue that must be addressed in connection with the automatic stay is its scope — the types of creditors' actions that it prevents. Related to this issue is the nature and extent of over two dozen specific exceptions to the stay. The Code also provides for several ancillary stays which apply in Chapters 12 and 13 to protect those who are jointly liable for the debtor's obligations, and courts periodically grant supplemental stays when they are necessary to facilitate a debtor's ability to focus on its efforts to reorganize. The grounds for the court to dispense with the automatic stay and permit secured creditors to continue their efforts to collect outside of bankruptcy court are a central issue in any reorganization case. As will be seen, a court's decision to grant a creditor relief from the automatic stay can herald the end of a debtor's hopes to reorganize. In addition, this chapter discusses the consequences for creditors who violate the stay.

§ 8.02 Scope of the Automatic Stay

Under § 362, the filing of the bankruptcy petition operates as a stay of nearly all judicial and administrative proceedings as well as most informal actions a creditor might take in an effort to collect.[8] Careful attention to the precise language of § 362(a) indicates that its subdivisions apply variously to different actions a creditor might take against the debtor,[9] against property of the estate,[10] and against property of the debtor.[11]

As the sections below demonstrate, the scope of the automatic stay is extremely broad. It extends to a wide variety of efforts creditors might take,

[6] *See* Chapter 9, Operating the Debtor, *infra*.

[7] *See* In re Sowers, 164 B.R. 256 (Bankr. E.D. Va. 1994) (action against debtor's employer for failure to honor pre-petition garnishment order not barred by the automatic stay, because it was not a disguised effort to collect).

[8] Bankruptcy Code § 362(a).

[9] Bankruptcy Code § 362(a)(1), (2), (6), (7).

[10] Bankruptcy Code § 362(a)(2), (3), (4), (5).

[11] Bankruptcy Code § 362(a)(5).

including lawsuits, repossessions, foreclosure sales, assessments, setoffs, etc. Still, as we will show in the next section, there are a few gaps between its various provisions. Morever, § 362(b) contains a wide array of explicit, narrow exceptions to the stay.[12]

[A] Judicial and Administrative Proceedings

The automatic stay blocks the commencement or continuation of any judicial or administrative action against the debtor that was or could have been commenced before the commencement of the case. It also bars judicial and administrative actions against the debtor to recover a pre-petition claim.[13]

For example, suppose that the debtor negligently injured Alice in an auto accident on July 7, 2007; also assume that the debtor entered into a contract with Belinda on August 1, 2007, but breached on October 30, 2007. If the debtor files a petition on January 1, 2008, cases that were pending or that could have been filed before that date are stayed. Accordingly, neither Alice nor Belinda are permitted to file suit against the debtor personally. They must pursue their claims in the debtor's bankruptcy case against the bankruptcy estate. If Alice or Belinda had brought suit against the debtor in December, 2007, before the debtor's bankruptcy petition, their suits must stop. Even if the pending litigation is in its final stages, the stay applies; the action is stayed and must not continue, even if the jury is already in deliberations.[14] Without getting relief from the court to permit these suits to continue, any action taken in the pending litigation is void.[15]

In a perhaps superfluous additional provision, the stay also specifically blocks the commencement or continuation of a proceeding before the United States Tax Court.[16]

[B] Enforcement of Judgments

The automatic stay also forbids actions to enforce judgments that were obtained before the bankruptcy case commenced against either the debtor or against property of the estate. Thus, if on March 14, 2007, Chelsea obtains a products liability judgment against Franklin Manufacturing Inc., and Franklin files a bankruptcy petition on April 1, 2007, Chelsea is stayed from taking any action to enforce her judgment against either the debtor or against property of the bankruptcy estate.[17]

Although § 362(a)(2) is not directed at creditors' efforts to enforce their pre-petition judgments against property of the debtor, § 541 is likely to

---

[12] Bankruptcy Code § 362(b); *see* § 8.03 Exceptions to the Automatic Stay, *supra*.

[13] Bankruptcy Code § 362(a)(1).

[14] Though in such a case, the court might grant relief from the stay to conclude the action. *See* § 8.06[B][2] For Cause — Other than for Lack of Adequate Protection, *infra*.

[15] *See* § 8.07[A] Actions in Violation of the Stay are Void, *infra*.

[16] Bankruptcy Code § 362(a)(8).

[17] Bankruptcy Code § 362(a)(2).

make virtually all of the debtor's property part of the estate and thus to protect it against these enforcement efforts.[18] Property that the debtor exempts will exit the estate, but it is protected by the debtor's § 522 exemptions.[19] Property that is subject to a pre-petition lien and is abandoned or otherwise returned to the debtor is protected from foreclosure by § 362(a)(5), discussed below. Thus, it is rare that there is much property of the debtor that can be seized while the bankruptcy case is pending, without express permission from the bankruptcy court.

Many debtors file their bankruptcy cases during, and because of, creditors' enforcement actions. The pressure of an enforcement action is one of the strongest motivations for a debtor to file, precisely because filing stops the enforcement proceeding. If the enforcement process is incomplete, the stay applies. For example, if the sheriff is in the midst of selling foreclosed property, but the sale has not been completed, the stay prevents the sale from going forward. If the sale is completed after the case is filed, the sale is void, even though no one associated with the sale knew that the case had been commenced and the stay imposed.

[C] Acts to Obtain Possession or Control of Estate Property

Section 362(a)(3) prohibits "any act to obtain possession of property of the estate, to obtain possession of property from the estate, or to exercise control over property of the estate."[20] This language extends the stay beyond any formal judicial or administrative proceeding. Most significantly, it prohibits self-help repossession, even though self-help is otherwise permitted by the U.C.C.[21]

Further, property that has been seized by a creditor but not yet sold before the debtor's bankruptcy petition is filed, remains property of the estate that must be turned over to the estate under § 542.[22] Thus, creditors who successfully repossess property before the petition is filed but have not yet sold it must return the property to the debtor upon learning of the debtor's bankruptcy petition.[23] Although this is the well-established rule, creditors sometimes persist in violating the stay by refusing to turn over estate property in their possession.[24]

---

[18] *See* Chapter 7, Property of the Estate, *supra.*

[19] *See* Chapter 12, Preserving Assets: Exemptions, Reaffirmation, and Redemption, *infra.*

[20] Bankruptcy Code § 362(a)(3).

[21] In re Holman, 92 B.R. 764 (Bankr. S.D. Ohio 1988).

[22] United States v. Whiting Pools, Inc., 462 U.S. 198 (1983).

[23] *E.g.*, In re Knaus, 889 F.2d 773 (8th Cir. 1989); Unified People's Fed. Credit Union v. Yates (In re Yates), 332 B.R. 1 (B.A.P. 10th Cir. 2005).

[24] Rutherford v. Auto Cash, Inc. (In re Rutherford), 329 B.R. 886 (Bankr. N.D. Ga. 2005); Metromedia Fiber Network Servs. v. Lexent, Inc. (In re Metromedia Fiber Network, Inc.), 290 B.R. 487 (Bankr. S.D.N.Y. 2003); Nissan Motor Acceptance Corp. v. Baker, 239 B.R. 484 (N.D. Tex. 1999).

Although § 523(a)(3) does not apply to property of the debtor, both exemption laws and the discharge stay of § 524(a)[25] prevent most efforts that creditors might take to seize property, such as a Chapter 7 debtor's post-petition earnings, that do not belong to the estate.

[D] Acts to Create, Perfect, or Enforce Liens

Section 362(a)(4) restrains any act to "create, perfect, or enforce" liens against estate property. Section 362(a)(5) does the same thing, but with respect to the debtor's property in connection with a lien that secures a pre-petition claim. Thus, creditors who have not recorded their mortgages, filed their financing statements, or filed other public documents necessary to perfect their liens are restrained from doing so after the debtor's petition is filed.

Although these provisions encompass purchase money security interests that might not yet have been perfected when the debtor's petition is filed, §§ 362(b)(3) and 546(b) permit creditors to take advantage of state statutory grace periods to perfect their interests. Thus a creditor who obtained a purchase money security interest on April 1, 2008, is permitted to file a financing statement perfecting its interest within twenty days of the time the debtor receives possession of the goods,[26] even if the debtor files a bankruptcy petition before the twenty days has expired.[27]

[E] Acts to Collect[28]

Section 362(a)(6) is the broadest prong of the automatic stay. It prohibits "*any* act to collect, assess, or recover a claim against the debtor that arose before the commencement of the case."[29] This restricts virtually every type of collection action a creditor might take. It prohibits creditors from sending letters and making phone calls in an effort to persuade the debtor to pay.[30] However, it is unlikely that, even if it found a technical violation of the stay, a court would impose any sanction on a creditor that inadvertently sent such a letter, e.g., because it forgot to instruct its computer not to do so, and stopped once informed about the stay.

Further, although creditors are permitted to discriminate against those who discharge their debts in bankruptcy, they are not allowed to condition their willingness to deal on the debtor's willingness to pay. In *In re Sechuan City, Inc.*,[31] the creditor (a hotel) violated the stay when it tried to coerce

[25] *See* § 13.09 Effect of Discharge, *infra.*

[26] *See* U.C.C. § 9-317(e) (2003).

[27] Bankruptcy Code § 362(b)(3); *see* § 8.03[A][2] Perfection of Certain Pre-Petition Property Interests, *infra.*

[28] Daniel Keating, *Offensive Uses of the Bankruptcy Stay*, 45 Vand. L. Rev. 71 (1992).

[29] Bankruptcy Code § 362(a)(6) (emphasis added).

[30] *E.g.*, In re Perviz, 302 B.R. 357 (Bankr. N.D. Ohio 2003) (debtor awarded $8,000 punitive damages); *see also* In re McHenry, 179 B.R. 165 (B.A.P. 9th Cir. 1995).

[31] In re Sechuan City, Inc., 96 B.R. 37, 40–42 (Bankr. E.D. Pa. 1989).

payment from the debtor (the restaurant in the hotel) by refusing to allow restaurant patrons to order from the hotel bar and by posting signs that encouraged hotel guests not to use the restaurant. Further, in *In re Sportfame of Ohio, Inc.*,[32] one of the debtor's suppliers was held in contempt when it refused to deal with the debtor, even for cash, with the sole purpose of trying to collect on its pre-petition debt. If it had simply refused, for any reason, to sell goods to the debtor or offered no explanation for its refusal to do business, it would not have been in contempt. But indicating its willingness to continue to deal with the debtor if the debtor repayed the pre-petition debt was an act to collect in violation of the stay. As a remedy, the court ordered the supplier to ship goods to the debtor, so long as the debtor paid cash on delivery.[33]

Courts draw a line between actions that indicate an effort to collect and those that merely inform the debtor of the obligation or of the creditor's refusal to do business.[34] For example, secured creditors are permitted to engage in a limited amount of contact with the debtor in connection with negotiations leading to a reaffirmation agreement that would permit the creditor to retain the collateral.[35] Unless creditors are permitted to communicate their willingness to allow the debtor to reaffirm these debts, reaffirmation agreements would be virtually impossible.

[F] Exercise of Right of Setoff

While § 553 preserves any rights that a creditor may have to set off their claims against the debtor against mutual debts owed by the creditor to the debtor, § 362(a)(7) prohibits creditors from exercising those setoff rights without court authorization. Rights of setoff frequently arise between debtors and the banks where they hold their accounts. For example, if Franklin Manufacturing borrows $750,000 from Peninsula Bank and has $600,000 on deposit with the bank, the bank may exercise its right of setoff against the account to satisfy $600,000 of the $750,000 debt. However, § 362(a)(7) restricts the bank's ability to actually set off after Franklin's case commences. Instead, the bank must make a motion to lift the stay in order to set off the debts.

On the other hand, banks are permitted to impose a "freeze" on the debtor's account to protect their interest in the debtor's funds. Although some courts held that such freezes were violations of the automatic stay, the Supreme Court, in *Citizens Bank of Maryland v. Strumpf*, held that these administrative freezes did not violate the automatic stay but merely preserved the status quo between the parties. The Court ruled that

---

[32] Sportfame of Ohio, Inc., v. Wilson Sporting Goods Co. (In re Sportfame of Ohio, Inc.), 40 B.R. 47 (Bankr. N.D. Ohio 1987).

[33] *See* Donald Wayne, Note, *Postbankruptcy Refusals to Deal with the Debtor and the Automatic Stay: A Fresh Approach*, 72 Wash. U. L.Q. 507 (1994).

[34] Morgan Guaranty Trust Co. v. American Sav. and Loan Assoc., 804 F.2d 1487, 1491 n.4 (9th Cir. 1986).

[35] *See* Jamo v. Katahdin Fed. Credit Union (In re Jamo), 283 F.3d 392 (1st Cir. 2002).

§§ 542(b) and 553(b), which also deal with setoff, manifested Congress' intent to preserve the status quo in this manner.[36] The *Strumpf* Court's language, focusing on the temporary nature of the freeze, suggests that creditors who impose a freeze on a debtor's account must promptly seek relief from the automatic stay to avoid committing a violation.[37]

The stay does not affect the creditor's rights in any other way. The creditor's right of setoff is included within the definition of a secured claim under § 506, and entitles the creditor to adequate protection for the value of its interest in the debtor's account. Moreover, the debtor is not permitted to withdraw the funds in its account without court permission, because this would be an unauthorized use of cash collateral in violation of § 363(c)(2).[38] The stay merely prevents the exercise of the creditor's rights while the case is pending.

[G] Tax Court Proceedings

Section 362(a)(8) restricts "the commencement or continuation of a proceeding before the United States Tax Court" concerning a corporate debtor's tax liability for any tax period determined by the bankruptcy court or concerning the tax liability of an individual debtor for a tax period that ended before the date of the order for relief.[39] Because § 362(a)(1) already enjoins the commencement or continuation of any judicial, administrative, or other action or proceeding against the debtor, this final portion of the automatic stay adds little additional protection for the debtor or the estate. Nevertheless, by staying all Tax Court proceedings against anyone regarding the debtor's tax liability, § 362(a)(8) protects the debtor against pressure from corporate officers who might be responsible for the corporation's taxes or for penalties associated with its failure to remit the corporation's withholding taxes to the government.

§ 8.03 Exceptions to the Automatic Stay

There are many limitations on the automatic stay. Some of these exceptions deal with the private rights of creditors; others deal with enforcement of the government's police and other regulatory powers. Some permit governmental entities to protect their financial interests. Most of the exceptions attempt to balance the interests of creditors in preserving the value of the debtor's estate and permitting an orderly administration of the debtor's assets with the interests of enforcing the government's police power.

---

[36] 516 U.S. 16 (1995). The Court also held that an administrative freeze did not violate § 362(a)(3)'s proscription against acts to obtain possession of estate property, because the debtor's bank account was nothing more than an obligation to pay the deposited funds to the debtor.

[37] *See* Gregory P. Johnson, *Following* Strumpf— *Will Allowance of an Administrative Freeze Begin the Erosion of the Automatic Stay?*, 5 J. Bankr. L. & Prac. 193 (1995).

[38] *See* § 9.03[B] Use of Cash Collateral, *infra*.

[39] Bankruptcy Code § 362(a)(8).

[A] Private Rights Excepted from the Stay

A few exceptions to the automatic stay protect the private rights of the debtor's creditors. Most of these exceptions facilitate the purposes of the automatic stay in preserving creditors' rights as if the bankruptcy case had never been filed, without depriving the estate of valuable assets. Other exceptions protect specific creditors, particularly those owed continuing support from the debtor.

[1] Family and Domestic Obligations

The first of the major private rights exceptions deals with a variety of family and domestic obligations. Significantly, the automatic stay does not apply to the commencement or continuation of actions to collect domestic support obligations.[40] The 2005 Amendments expanded this exception to permit "the withholding of income that is *property of the estate* or *property of the debtor* for payment of a domestic support obligation under a judicial or administrative order or a statute."[41] It also permits collection of any domestic support obligation from property, such as an individual Chapter 7 debtor's post-petition income,[42] regardless of whether it is property of the estate.[43] Thus, wage garnishment proceedings can continue, even in a Chapter 13 case, to withhold support from the debtor's post-petition earnings, which are property of a debtor's Chapter 13 estate,[44] even though the debtor's case is pending.

The Code also permits the commencement or continuation of actions:

- to establish paternity;
- to establish or modify domestic support obligations;
- concerning child custody or visitation rights;
- for dissolution of a marriage (but not including the division of estate property); and
- regarding domestic violence.[45]

These actions might be a distraction for the debtor, but they do not otherwise affect the administration of the bankruptcy case or impinge upon the bankruptcy court's authority over estate property. Moreover, the Code permits actions that are designed to facilitate recovery of support, such as suspending the debtor's driver's or other licenses, reporting the overdue support to a credit reporting agency, intercepting tax refunds, and enforcing medical obligations as specified by the Social Security Act.[46]

---

[40] *See* Bankruptcy Code § 101(14A).

[41] Bankruptcy Code § 362(a)(2)(C) (emphasis added).

[42] Bankruptcy Code § 541(a)(6); *see* § 7.02[F][2] Earnings from Individual Debtor's Post-Petition Services Excluded, *supra*.

[43] Bankruptcy Code § 362(b)(2)(B).

[44] Bankruptcy Code § 1306; *see* § 18.04 Property of the Chapter 13 Estate, *infra*.

[45] Bankruptcy Code § 362(b)(2)(A)(i)-(v).

[46] Bankruptcy Code § 362(b)(2)(D)-(G).

These provisions are largely consistent with other Code provisions regarding domestic support obligations, such as those making support debts non-dischargeable,[47] those giving them priority status,[48] and those authorizing dismissal of the debtor's Chapter 11, 12, or 13 case if they are not paid.[49]

[2] Perfection of Certain Pre-Petition Property Interests

The second major private rights exception gives limited relief to persons who acquire interests in the debtor's property just before bankruptcy, but who have not yet had time to perfect those interests. This provision primarily protects last-minute lienholders who extended credit during the final days before the debtor's petition. The exception is narrowly tailored to protect the interests of lienholders who would otherwise not be allowed the same amount of time to perfect as those who obtained their liens earlier.

The biggest impact of this exception is its protection of purchase money security interests acquired shortly before a bankruptcy case commences. If a purchase money security interest is created, the creditor has twenty days from the date the goods are delivered to perfect its liens and take priority over subsequent lien creditors and the trustee.[50] Section 362(b)(3) preserves this ability of purchase money lenders to file a financing statement to perfect their security interests, despite the automatic stay.[51]

For example, suppose Peninsula Bank and Franklin Manufacturing enter into a loan agreement on June 1. Pursuant to the agreement, Peninsula Bank loans Franklin $100,000 to enable it to purchase a new machine. The parties sign a security agreement giving Peninsula a security interest in the machine, which is delivered to Franklin on June 7. On June 20, before Peninsula files a financing statement to perfect its purchase money security interest, Franklin files a bankruptcy petition. Section 362(b)(3) permits Peninsula to take advantage of the U.C.C.'s twenty-day grace period and file its financing statement after Franklin's bankruptcy petition is filed. This, together with other limits on the trustee's avoiding powers, protects Peninsula's purchase money security interest from avoidance by the trustee.

Section 362(b)(3) also permits creditors with already perfected interests to take action, such as filing a continuation statement, to ensure that perfection of their interest does not lapse.[52] Thus, if the five-year effective period of a U.C.C. financing statement is scheduled to lapse after the debtor's petition is filed, the secured creditor may file a continuation statement

[47] Bankruptcy Code §§ 523(a)(5), 1141(d)(2), 1328(a)(2); *see generally* § 13.03[B][5][a] Domestic Support Obligations, *infra.*

[48] Bankruptcy Code § 507(a)(1); *see* § 10.04[A][1] Support Claims, *infra.*

[49] Bankruptcy Code §§ 1112(b)(4)(P), 1208(c)(10), 1307(c)(11).

[50] U.C.C. § 9-317(e) (2003).

[51] Bankruptcy Code § 362(b)(3).

[52] *See* U.C.C. § 9-515 (2003).

without violating the automatic stay.[53] Likewise, a creditor may file a new financing statement in a second state, in order to maintain the perfected status of a security interest already perfected under the law of one state.[54]

[3] Commercial Real Estate Leases

Section 362(a)(10) permits lessors of commercial real estate to retake possession of the land when the term of the lease expires either before the case commenced or while it is pending, without violating the automatic stay. For example, if the debtor occupies commercial real estate under a lease that expired on June 1, 2007, two months after it filed its bankruptcy petition, the lessor may retake possession of the premises, despite the automatic stay.

[4] Presentment of Negotiable Instruments

The last important private rights exception is rooted in the requirements of U.C.C. Article 3 for enforcement of negotiable instruments. The exception permits a creditor to satisfy the U.C.C.'s procedural requirements of presentment, notice of its dishonor, and in the rare circumstances where it is still necessary, protest, without violating the stay.[55]

The reason for this exception is somewhat complex. Under Article 3, the holder of a negotiable instrument cannot proceed against some of the parties to the instrument unless three things have happened. First, the holder must present the instrument by physically displaying the instrument and making a demand for payment from the person who is liable.[56] Second, the instrument must be dishonored.[57] Third, in many cases, the person whom the holder wishes to recover from must be given notice of the dishonor.[58] In some circumstances, presentment must be made and notice must be given within a short period of time; otherwise, the obligation of the person who was entitled to the notice is discharged.[59] In rare circumstances involving instruments issued in other countries, formal notice of dishonor must be given through the archaic mechanism of "protest."[60] All of this means that in some situations, a co-obligor could be discharged from its obligation because the stay prevented the creditor from presenting or giving the required notice. Because of this, the stay does not prevent

[53] H.R. Rep. 103-835, 21 (1994), *reprinted in* 1994 U.S.C.C.A.N. 3340, 3354; *see* In re Stetson & Assocs., Inc., 330 B.R. 613, 623 (Bankr. E.D. Tenn. 2005).

[54] *E.g.*, In re Halmar Distribs., Inc., 968 F.2d 121 (1st Cir. 1992) (refiling to continue perfection after debtor moved to a new state not in violation of the stay).

[55] Bankruptcy Code § 362(b)(11); *e.g.*, In re Blasco, 352 B.R. 888 (Bankr. D. Ala. 2006).

[56] U.C.C. § 3-501 (2003).

[57] U.C.C. § 3-502 (2003).

[58] Bankruptcy Code § 3-503(a) (2003).

[59] U.C.C. §§ 3-405(c), 3-414(d), 3-414(f), 3-415(c), 3-415(e) (2003).

[60] Protest was a formal mechanism to supply notice with respect to a draft drawn or payable outside the United States. The U.C.C. no longer requires it, though it may still be necessary under the law of some foreign countries. *See* U.C.C. § 3-505(b) (2003).

presentment, notice, or protest. However, if the debtor's bank actually paid the item, this *would* violate the automatic stay.

[5] Other Private Rights Exceptions to the Automatic Stay

There are a wide variety of additional exceptions to the automatic stay that apply only in narrow circumstances. Although they are important to the participants in the affected transactions, their scope is too narrow for discussion here. They deal with:

- various setoffs in certain securities and commodities contracts, repurchase agreements, swap agreements, and master netting agreements;[61]
- withholding of wages to repay loans from employer sponsored pension plans;[62]
- acts to enforce liens or security interests in real estate after relief from the stay was granted in an earlier case filed by the same debtor;[63]
- acts to enforce liens and security interests in real estate in a case filed by an ineligible debtor;[64]
- continuation of eviction proceedings where the landlord obtained a pre-petition judgment for possession of the premises;[65]
- actions to evict tenants due to illegal drug use on the premises;[66]
- certain post-petition mortgages recorded in connection with pre-petition real estate transfers;[67] and

---

[61] Bankruptcy Code § 362(b)(6), (7), (17), (27); Jeanne L. Schroeder, *Repo Madness: The Characterization of Repurchase Agreements Under the Bankruptcy Code and the UCC*, 46 Syracuse L. Rev. 99 (1996); Shmuel Vasser, *Derivatives in Bankruptcy*, 60 Bus. Law. 1507, 1530 (2005).

[62] Bankruptcy Code § 362(b)(19); Lisa A. Napoli, *The Not-So-Automatic Stay: Legislative Changes to the Automatic Stay in a Case Filed by or Against an Individual Debtor*, 79 Am. Bankr. L.J. 749, 752 (2005). This is consistent with § 1322(f), which prevents a Chapter 13 plan from modifying the terms of this type of pension fund loan and excludes amounts paid to the pension fund from the debtor's disposable income.

[63] Bankruptcy Code § 362(b)(20).

[64] Bankruptcy Code § 362(b)(21); Lisa A. Napoli, *The Not-So-Automatic Stay: Legislative Changes to the Automatic Stay in a Case Filed by or Against an Individual Debtor*, 79 Am. Bankr. L.J. 749, 753–55 (2005).

[65] Bankruptcy Code § 362(b)(22); Alan M. Ahart, *The Inefficacy of the New Eviction Exceptions to the Automatic Stay*, 80 Am. Bankr. L.J. 125 (2006).

[66] Bankruptcy Code § 362(b)(23); Alan M. Ahart, *The Inefficacy of the New Eviction Exceptions to the Automatic Stay*, 80 Am. Bankr. L.J. 125 (2006).

[67] Bankruptcy Code § 362(b)(24). Section 362(b)(24) puts to rest questions raised by the Nithth Circuit's subsequently withdrawn decision in *Thompson v. Margen (In re McConville)* regarding whether recording certain mortgages violated the automatic stay. *See* H.R. Rep. No. 109-31, 75-76 (2005), *reprinted in* 2005 U.S.C.C.A.N. 88, 142–44 (*addressing* Thompson v. Margen (In re McConville), 84 F.3d 340 (9th Cir. 1996), *withdrawn*, 110 F.3d 47 (9th Cir.), *cert. denied*, 522 U.S. 966 (1997)).

- self-regulatory proceedings by private securities organizations, such as stock and commodities exchanges.[68]

[B] Public Rights Exceptions to the Stay — Governmental Action Permitted

The vast majority of exceptions to the automatic stay permit various types of governmental action, usually related to the government's police or other regulatory powers.

[1] Criminal Proceedings

Not surprisingly, bankruptcy is not a haven for criminals. The automatic stay does not provide even temporary protection for those accused of criminal misconduct. Section 362(b)(1) provides that "[t]he filing of a [bankruptcy] petition . . . does not operate as a stay . . . of the commencement or continuation of a criminal action against the debtor."[69]

However, some criminal prosecutions border on "debt collection" either by government claimants or private parties, and bankruptcy courts are not insensitive to this point. For example, many states make issuing a check on insufficient funds a crime. Zealous prosecutors sometimes use these statutes to operate as little more than a very powerful collection agency for disgruntled local merchants, by bringing criminal actions against debtors who have violated these statutes, and subsequently dropping the charges if the debtor makes restitution to the merchant involved. Although such criminal prosecutions unquestionably do not violate the automatic stay, debtors sometimes seek extraordinary relief under § 105, which permits the bankruptcy court to issue injunctions as necessary in furtherance of the provisions of the Bankruptcy Code.[70]

The issue is complicated by the interplay of federalism and the general reluctance of federal courts, including bankruptcy courts, to interfere in state criminal matters. Because of these concerns, courts refuse to enjoin state criminal prosecutions unless they are brought in bad faith.[71] Courts sometimes deploy the more elaborate *Younger* abstention doctrine[72] to determine whether the court should abstain from interfering with state prosecutions. The test examines whether the debtor lacks an adequate remedy at law, whether the debtor will suffer great and immediate irreparable injury if the proceeding is not restrained, and whether continuation of the prosecution would impair any of the debtor's federally created rights, such as his right to a bankruptcy discharge.[73]

---

[68] Bankruptcy Code § 362(b)(25).

[69] Bankruptcy Code § 362(b)(1).

[70] Bankruptcy Code § 105(a); *see* § 8.05 Discretionary Stays, *infra*.

[71] *E.g.*, Barnette v. Evans, 673 F.2d 1250 (11th Cir. 1982).

[72] Younger v. Harris, 401 U.S. 37 (1971).

[73] Barnette v. Evans, 673 F.2d 1250, 1252 (11th Cir. 1982); Winkler v. Rickert (In re Winkler), 151 B.R. 807 (Bankr. N.D. Ohio 1992).

The critical issue is usually whether the prosecutor's "principal motivation" in pursuing the prosecution is to collect a debt or to vindicate the public good.[74] Prosecutors who use their offices primarily to collect debts owed to local merchants are likely to be enjoined. Not surprisingly, this test rarely results in an injunction against continuation of the prosecution, but some courts take a more inventive approach and enjoin the creditor from participating in the efforts to prosecute the debtor.[75]

[2] Regulatory Enforcement

Similarly, most branches of the stay are inapplicable to prevent the commencment or continuation of proceedings that "enforce [a] governmental unit's . . . police and regulatory power."[76] For example, an action to force a polluter to desist from contaminating air, water, or land is not stayed when the polluter files bankruptcy.[77] Similarly, the stay does not apply to proceedings to compel a debtor to comply with local zoning ordinances[78] or to impose sanctions against a disciplined attorney for participating in frivolous litigation.[79]

The police power exception deals only with government actions that are essential to protect "public interests" rather than the pecuniary interests of the government.[80] Many governments engage in a variety of commercial activities. Many cities operate water and electric departments with customers who have not paid their utility bills. Actions to collect those bills are stayed; the utility's pecuniary interest in being paid is not transformed into a police or regulatory power just because it happens to belong to a government. Similarly, state colleges charge tuition and collect rent from dormitory residents. Actions to recover unpaid charges are pecuniary in nature and do not fall within the police power exception to the stay. Exercise of a government power for the purpose of vindicating a private pecuniary right, rather than a general public interest, is subject to the stay. Accordingly, actions to enforce money judgments are normally stayed.

---

[74] Evans v. Bank of Eureka Springs (In re Evans), 245 B.R. 852, 856–57 (Bankr. W.D. Ark. 2000); *but see* Gruntz v. County of Los Angeles (In re Gruntz), 202 F.3d 1074 (9th Cir. 2000).

[75] *See* In re Caldwell, 5 B.R. 740 (Bankr. W.D. Va. 1980).

[76] Bankruptcy Code § 362(b)(4).

[77] *See* Penn Terra Ltd. v. Department of Envtl. Res., 733 F.2d 267 (3d Cir. 1984).

[78] Cournoyer v. Town of Lincoln, 790 F.2d 971 (1st Cir. 1986).

[79] In re Berg, 230 F.3d 1165 (9th Cir. 2000).

[80] Berg v. Good Samaritan Hosp., Inc. (In re Berg), 230 F.3d 1165 (9th Cir. 2000); Enron Corp. v. California (In re Enron Corp.), 314 B.R. 524 (Bankr. S.D.N.Y. 2004).

[3] Specific Governmental Pecuniary Interests

There are many narrow exceptions to the stay that protect governmental pecuniary interests. They include:

- certain foreclosure proceedings brought by the Department of Housing and Urban Development;[81]
- certain Department of Transportation ship mortgage foreclosure proceedings;[82]
- tax audit and assessment proceedings to administratively determine the debtor's tax liability;[83]
- proceedings regarding the accreditation, licensing, and eligibility of educational institutions to participate in guaranteed student loan programs;[84]
- creation and perfection of statutory liens securing certain ad valorem property taxes or special real estate taxes;[85]
- certain income tax refund setoffs;[86] and
- administrative exclusion of debtors from participating in certain federal health care programs, such as medicare.[87]

§ 8.04 Co-Debtor Stays in Chapters 12 and 13

In most bankruptcy proceedings, the automatic stay applies only to actions involving the debtor or the estate. Section 362 does not prevent a creditor from pursuing remedies against other persons or their property. Most significantly for a creditor, the stay does not affect its rights to go after co-obligors, such as co-signers or guarantors.

A different rule applies in Chapters 12 and 13. Both chapters impose a limited automatic stay against preventing creditors from pursuing certain co-debtors. For the co-debtor stay to apply, two conditions must be met: the debt involved must be a consumer debt; and the co-debtor must be an individual, not an organization such as a corporation or partnership.[88] In addition, if the co-obligor is a professional surety — someone who is in the business of providing financial guarantees — the stay does not apply, even if the co-debtor is an individual.[89]

---

[81] Bankruptcy Code § 362(b)(8).

[82] Bankruptcy Code § 362(b)(12), (13).

[83] Bankruptcy Code § 362(b)(9). But proceedings before the United States Tax Court are restrained.

[84] Bankruptcy Code § 362(b)(14), (15), (16).

[85] Bankruptcy Code § 362(b)(18).

[86] Bankruptcy Code § 362(b)(26).

[87] Bankruptcy Code § 362(b)(28).

[88] Bankruptcy Code §§ 1201(a), 1301(a).

[89] Bankruptcy Code §§ 1201(a), 1301(a).

The legislative history confirms what is obvious from the text; this limited stay is designed to protect co-obligors who incurred obligations because of a family relationship to or friendship with the debtor.[90] By doing so, the Code protects the debtor from the demands, both formal and informal, of the co-debtor. At least, that is the hope.

Although it is possible to imagine other situations in which the stay could apply, as a practical matter, it is usually limited to circumstances such as a parent, spouse, or friend co-signing a note. Congress was concerned that, because of the underlying relationship between these parties, the debtor would feel inordinate pressure to pay the obligation unless the co-debtor was protected, at least temporarily, by an automatic stay. Otherwise, the debtor's desire to pay his relatives and friends would disrupt the normal reorganization process. Congress may have been naive about the degree to which the stay actually relieves pressure on the debtor; after all, the stay does not discharge the co-debtor's obligation but merely delays the enforcement of that obligation. Thus, the stay may not in fact be sufficient to shield the debtor from pressure from the co-obligor.

These provisions are often colloquially referred to among bankruptcy professionals as the co-signer provisions. The term "co-signer" is somewhat misleading. It does not refer only to co-makers of an obligation; it encompasses all sureties. Indeed, although the word "co-signer" is used informally, the actual statutory text of §§ 1201 and 1301 refer to any person who is liable on the debt with the debtor.

There is only one statutory exception to the co-debtor stay. Rooted in the requirements of U.C.C. Article 3 for enforcement of a negotiable instrument,[91] the exception permits the creditor to present a negotiable instrument and to give notice of its dishonor.[92] This exception is exactly the same as the exception to the automatic stay regarding the debtor in § 362(b)(11).[93]

Because the co-debtor stay is designed to protect the Chapter 12 or Chapter 13 process, it does not apply in other situations. If the case is closed, dismissed, or converted to Chapter 7 or Chapter 11, the co-debtor stay terminates.[94] The stay may also be terminated by the court, as discussed in detail later in this chapter.[95]

---

[90] H.R. Rep. No. 95-595, 121–22 (1978), *reprinted in* 1978 U.S.C.C.A.N. 5963, 6081–82.

[91] *See* § 8.03[A][4] Presentment of Negotiable Instruments, *supra.*

[92] Presentment, dishonor, and notice are required only for suretyship agreements manifested in a negotiable instrument, usually a promissory note. *See generally* U.C.C. §§ 3-419, 3-412 to 3-415 (2003).

[93] *See* § 8.03[A][4] Presentment of Negotiable Instruments, *supra.*

[94] Bankruptcy Code §§ 1201(a)(2), 1301(a)(2).

[95] *See* § 8.06 Duration of the Automatic Stay; Termination, *infra.*

§ 8.05 Discretionary Stays[96]

The automatic stay is not the only power the court has to impose limits on creditor action. The court may impose other injunctions under § 105. Section 105 broadly empowers the court to "issue any order, process, or judgment that is necessary or appropriate to carry out the provisions of the [Bankruptcy Code]."[97] Courts sometimes use this language, which emulates the language of the All Writs Act,[98] to impose temporary stays on actions taken by creditors against persons other than the debtor.

The normal rules governing the availability of equitable relief apply with equal force to injunctions issued under § 105. Before issuing an injunction, the court must find:

- the plaintiff is likely to succeed on the merits;
- irreparable injury will result unless the injunction is issued;
- the balance of equities favors issuing the injunction; and
- the public interest is served by preserving the status quo until the merits of the controversy can fully be considered.[99]

Generally, discretionary injunctions are imposed only under circumstances where the bankruptcy case itself would be seriously disrupted if relief is not granted. Indeed, many courts recast the first two parts of the four part test slightly to focus on whether (1) a reorganization is reasonably in prospect, and (2) failing to grant the injunction will cause irreparable harm to the chance to reorganize.[100] For example, the debtor may be an indispensable party to litigation involving another. If the litigation goes forward, the non-debtor would be severely impaired in protecting its interests because of the absence of the debtor. The bankruptcy court has but two choices: lift the stay on actions against the debtor, which would protect the non-debtor but might disrupt the bankruptcy; or impose a stay on the proceedings against the non-debtor. Although neither choice is wholly attractive, a number of courts have held that the latter is better than the former in at least some cases. Similarly, it is sometimes true that a third-party action would inevitably distract the debtor's management from the case.

---

[96] Alan M. Ahart, *The Limited Scope of Implied Powers of a Bankruptcy Judge: A Statutory Court of Bankruptcy, Not a Court of Equity*, 79 Am. Bankr. L.J. 1 (2005); Daniel B. Bogart, *Resisting the Expansion of Bankruptcy Court Power Under Section 105 of the Bankruptcy Code: The All Writs Act and an Admonition from Chief Justice Marshall*, 35 Ariz. St. L.J. 793 (2003); Ralph Brubaker, *Nondebtor Releases and Injunctions in Chapter 11: Revisiting Jurisdictional Precepts and the Forgotten* Callaway v. Benton *Case*, 72 Am. Bankr. L.J. 1 (1998); Steve H. Nickles & David G. Epstien, *Another Way of Thinking About Section 105(a) and Other Sources of Supplemental Law Under the Bankruptcy Code*, 3 Chap. L. Rev. 7 (2000); Barry L. Zaretsky, *Co-Debtor Stays in Chapter 11 Bankruptcy*, 73 Cornell L. Rev. 213 (1988).

[97] Bankruptcy Code § 105(a).

[98] 28 U.S.C. § 1651(a) (2000).

[99] *See* A.H. Robbins Co. v. Piccinin (In re A.H. Robbins Co.), 788 F.2d 994 (4th Cir. 1986).

[100] In re Otero Mills, Inc., 25 B.R. 1018 (D.N.M. 1982); In re FTL, Inc., 152 B.R. 61 (Bankr. E.D. Va. 1993).

A good example of this occurred in the A.H. Robins reorganization, involving millions of claims against the manufacturer of a defective intrauterine contraceptive device, the Dalkon Shield. The manufacturer's insurer, Aetna, was involved in litigation related to the claims against the debtor. The court enjoined the actions against the insurer, despite the plaintiffs' promise to leave the Robins company alone as much as possible:

> Inevitably, Aetna must involve Robins in this litigation. Aetna's primary defence logically will be that Robins — not Aetna — is responsible for the injuries suffered by these plaintiffs . . . . Despite the plaintiffs' good intentions, Robins will inexorably be drawn into this litigation. Because this involvement will put a substantial burden on Robins, it will detract from the reorganization process.[101]

Discretionary injunctions are also frequently sought to protect insider guarantors such as controlling shareholders and directors of small corporate debtors, who provided personal guarantees for the corporation's debts. In these cases, the guarantors are usually intimately involved in the debtor's efforts to reorganize. Because of this, permitting a creditor to maintain an action from the guarantor might easily distract the guarantor from his responsibilities in connection with the debtor's reorganization.[102] In addition, permitting the creditor to pursue the guarantor's assets might jeopardize the debtor's efforts to reorganize by depriving the debtor of assets that the insider guarantor might contribute to the debtor's reorganization.

These and other factors sometimes lead courts to enjoin creditors from maintaining actions against insider guarantors. In *In re Otero Mills, Inc.*, the court granted an injunction that prohibited a creditor from enforcing a judgment against an insider guarantor where enforcement would have prevented the guarantor from using his personal assets to assist in the corporate debtor's reorganization.[103] And, in *In re FTL, Inc.*, the court awarded an injunction against continuation of a creditor's action against an insider guarantor where the insider's active involvement in the debtor's bankruptcy case was essential to the debtor's efforts to obtain new financing, which was to be secured by the guarantor's assets.[104]

However, bankruptcy courts are extremely sparing in their exercise of power over non-bankruptcy proceedings concerning non-debtors. Only in the absence of any alternative is a court likely to enter such a discretionary stay. Moreover, the court is not likely to make the stay broader or longer than is absolutely necessary.

A closely related issue is whether § 105 justifies entry of a permanent injunction, restraining creditors from pursuing a co-debtor. A permanent injunction effectively discharges the co-debtor from his liability. Here, the

---

[101] In re A.H. Robins Co., Inc., 828 F.2d 1023, 1026 (4th Cir. 1986); *see also* A.H. Robins Co. v. Piccinin, 788 F.2d 994 (4th Cir. 1986).

[102] *See* United States v. Seitles, 106 B.R. 36 (S.D.N.Y. 1989).

[103] In re Otero Mills, Inc., 25 B.R. 1018 (D.N.M. 1982).

[104] In re FTL, Inc., 152 B.R. 61 (Bankr. E.D. Va. 1993).

court's authority is more questionable, but courts still sometimes find that extraordinary circumstances justify a post-confirmation injunction.[105] In determining whether to grant a permanent injunction, courts frequently consider the following factors:

- whether there is identity of interest between the debtor and the non-debtor party;
- whether the non-debtor has contributed substantial assets to the debtor's reorganization;
- whether an injunction is essential to the debtor's reorganization;
- whether a substantial majority of creditors agree on the issuance of the injunction; and
- whether the debtor's Chapter 11 plan provides a mechanism for payment of all, or substantially all, of the claims or classes affected by the injunction.[106]

§ 8.06 Duration of the Automatic Stay; Termination

The automatic stay does not last forever. It ends when the bankruptcy case ends, though if the debtor receives a discharge, many features of the stay are continued through the discharge stay of § 524, at least as to discharged debt.[107] It might also end, at least with respect to specific estate assets, when the trustee abandons specific assets, or when a secured creditor seeks and obtains relief from the stay, and thus obtains permission to continue with state court foreclosure proceedings against the property. As explained below, disputes over whether creditors should be granted relief from the stay are a critical part of any reorganization proceeding.

[A] Automatic Termination of the Stay

The automatic stay is intended to serve only the limited purpose of giving the debtor-in-possession or trustee the opportunity to deal effectively with the property of the estate and the demands of creditors. Thus, the stay automatically terminates when that purpose is no longer served. The automatic stay terminates upon the occurrence of any of several specific events.

---

[105] *E.g.*, In re Master Mortgage Inv. Fund, Inc., 168 B.R. 930, 936 (Bankr. W.D. Mo. 1994).

[106] *See* In re Swallen's, Inc., 210 B.R. 123 (Bankr. S.D. Ohio 1997); In re Master Mortgage Inv. Fund, Inc., 168 B.R. 930 (Bankr. W.D. Mo. 1994).

[107] Bankruptcy Code § 524(c); *see* § 13.09[A] Discharge Injunction, *infra*.

[1] Property No Longer in the Estate

The stay of any act against property of the estate (but not the stay of an act against the debtor) terminates when the property is no longer part of the estate.[108] However, abandonment by the estate re-vests the property in the debtor, and § 362(a)(5) remains in effect with respect to the debtor's property.[109] Thus, when the trustee abandons property, the stay of § 362(a)(3) is terminated, but the stay of § 362(a)(5) against actions to "create, perfect, or enforce" any lien against the debtor's property that secures a pre-petition debt, remains in place.

[2] Conclusion of the Bankruptcy Case

The stay of all other actions, including actions against the debtor, terminates when the case is closed or dismissed or when a discharge is granted or denied.[110] For example, if a case is dismissed under § 707(b) due to abuse, the debtor and the debtor's property are no longer protected by the automatic stay.[111] Likewise, if the debtor's Chapter 11 reorganization case is dismissed due to the absence of a reasonable likelihood of rehabilitation or the debtor's inability to consummate its confirmed plan,[112] the stay ends and creditors are free to pursue the debtor through the customary mechanisms in state court.

The fact that the stay terminates upon closure of the case or the grant of a discharge does not necessarily mean that the debtor is once again vulnerable to its creditors. If a discharge is granted, the discharge injunction of § 524 takes over where the automatic stay leaves off with respect to discharged debts.[113] However, although discharge relieves the debtor of his personal liability, it does not remove creditors' liens on the debtor's assets. Thus, termination of the automatic stay upon completion of the case leaves secured creditors free to pursue their collateral. To retain their property, debtors must come to some accommodation with the creditor. This can be done through the bankruptcy proceeding itself — for example, through reaffirmation of the debt or confirmation of a reorganization plan — or outside the bankruptcy, through formal or informal agreement with the creditor.[114]

[3] Prior Petition Within One Year

The 2005 Amendments added two complicated provisions regarding automatic termination of the automatic stay, aimed at debtors who file repeated petitions in bad faith solely to take advantage of the stay, usually

---

[108] Bankruptcy Code § 362(c)(1).

[109] *E.g.*, In re Nicholson, 70 B.R. 398 (Bankr. D. Colo. 1987).

[110] Bankruptcy Code § 362(c)(2).

[111] *See* § 17.03[B] Dismissal of Consumer Cases Due to Abuse, *infra*.

[112] *See* Bankruptcy Code § 1112(b); § 19.05[B] Involuntary Conversion or Dismissal, *infra*.

[113] Bankruptcy Code § 524(c); *see* § 13.09[A] Discharge Injunction, *infra*.

[114] *See* Chapter 12 Preserving Assets: Exemptions, Reaffirmation, and Redemption, *infra*.

to stop a mortgage foreclosure. The first of these two provisions, discussed here, applies when the debtor filed one earlier Chapter 7, 11, or 13 case within a year of the case in question. The second, discussed immediately below,[115] applies when the debtor has filed more than one earlier Chapter 7, 11, or 13 case within a year of the case in question.

Section 362(c)(3) limits the duration of the automatic stay when the debtor has filed a previous petition within a year.[116] The automatic stay in the second case automatically terminates thirty days after the petition.[117] The automatic termination only applies in the case of an individual or joint debtor and does not apply if the second case is under Chapters 11, 12, or 13 and was filed after dismissal of the earlier Chapter 7 case due to abuse under § 707(b).[118]

The stay only terminates under § 362(c)(3) "with respect to any action taken with respect to a debt or property securing such debt or with respect to any lease."[119] Courts have construed this to mean that it does not terminate if creditors have not yet taken any action.[120] Thus, it applies only when creditors have sought to foreclose upon the debtor's property.[121] The language also specifies that the stay only terminates "with respect to the debtor."[122] This raises the question of whether the stay nevertheless continues with respect to estate property and terminates only with respect to property of the debtor. Most courts addressing the issue thus far have concluded that this means that the stay does not automatically terminate with respect to estate property.[123] It ends only with respect to the debtor's property. In the context of a Chapter 13 case, the estate is comprised of almost all of the assets that a debtor owned before filing his petition, and most of what he acquires after the petition. This has led some courts to reject the conclusion that the stay terminates only with respect to property of the debtor, but not with respect to property of the estate.[124] According to these courts, the majority approach would be contrary to Congress' purpose of discouraging opportunistic and abusive petitions.[125]

The stay can be extended if the later case was filed in good faith with respect to all creditors whose actions are stayed.[126] The burden of proof

---

115 Bankruptcy Code § 362(c)(4); *see* § 8.06[A][4] Multiple Prior Petitions Within One Year, *infra*.

116 *See* In re Pope, 351 B.R. 14 (Bankr. D.R.I. 2006).

117 Bankruptcy Code § 362(c)(3)(A).

118 Bankruptcy Code § 362(c)(3).

119 Bankruptcy Code § 362(c)(3)(A).

120 In re Paschal, 337 B.R. 274 (Bankr. E.D.N.C. 2006).

121 In re Brandon, 349 B.R. 130, 132 (Bankr. M.D.N.C. 2006).

122 Bankruptcy Code § 362(c)(3)(A).

123 *E.g.,* In re Brandon, 349 B.R. 130, 132 (Bankr. M.D.N.C. 2006).

124 *See* In re Jupiter, 344 B.R. 754 (Bankr. D.S.C. 2006); In re Jumpp, 344 B.R. 21 (Bankr. D. Mass. 2006).

125 *See* In re Jupiter, 344 B.R. at 761.

126 *See* In re Havner, 336 B.R. 98 (Bankr. M.D.N.C. 2006).

on the question of good faith is on the party seeking to have the stay continued — usually the debtor.[127] In several specified circumstances, there is a presumption of bad faith that may be rebutted only by clear and convincing evidence.[128] This presumption arises with respect to all creditors if:

- the debtor was a debtor in more than one previous case within the preceding year;[129]
- the debtor's previous case was dismissed within the past year after the debtor failed to file documents required by the court, provide adequate protection required by the court, or perform the terms of a plan confirmed by the court;[130] or
- the debtor's financial circumstances or personal affairs have not substantially changed since the debtor's most recent case was dismissed.[131]

The presumption also arises with respect to a single creditor if the debtor's previous case was dismissed while that creditor's motion for relief from the stay was still pending or had not yet been resolved.[132] This takes direct aim at debtors who file a petition to stop a creditor's foreclosure action, dismiss the case when the creditor's motion for relief from the stay seems likely to be granted, and then file a subsequent case when the creditor's subsequent foreclosure proceeding is close to fruition.

An exception to these presumptions is hidden in § 362(i). The presumption of bad faith does not arise if the debtor's earlier case is dismissed "due to the creation of a debt repayment plan."[133] This presumably refers to a debt repayment plan developed in connection with the consumer credit counseling that the Code now requires all individual debtors to obtain. However, one likely source of relief, a discretionary stay under § 105, may not be available, as it would fly in the face of § 362(c)(3).[134]

[4] Automatic Termination — Multiple Prior Petitions Within One Year

Section 362(c)(4) applies to debtors who are repeat offenders — those who have had two or more bankruptcy cases dismissed within the prior year. With respect to these debtors, the automatic stay does not go into effect

[127] *See* In re Kurtzahn, 337 B.R. 356 (Bankr. D. Minn. 2006); In re Baldassaro, 338 B.R. 178 (Bankr. D.N.H. 2006).

[128] Bankruptcy Code § 362(c)(3)(C)(i); In re Collins, 335 B.R. 646, 651 (Bankr. S.D. Tex. 2005); In re Baldassaro, 338 B.R. 178 (Bankr. D.N.H. 2006).

[129] Bankruptcy Code § 362(c)(3)(C)(i)(I).

[130] Bankruptcy Code § 362(c)(3)(C)(i)(II).

[131] Bankruptcy Code § 362(c)(3)(C)(i)(III).

[132] Bankruptcy Code § 362(c)(3)(C)(ii).

[133] Bankruptcy Code § 365(i).

[134] *See* In re Jumpp, 344 B.R. 21 (Bankr. D. Mass. 2006).

at all.[135] The limiting language that appears in § 362(c)(3), discussed above, limiting the effect of the stay's automatic termination does not appear in § 362(c)(4).

Assume, for example, that Charlie and Gail file a joint Chapter 13 petition in June, 2006, but subsequently dismiss it. In September, 2006, they file a Chapter 7 petition which is dismissed because of their failure to file the required schedules. If in January 2007 they file a third petition, the automatic stay does not take effect, ongoing actions are not restrained, and "upon request of a party in interest, the court *shall* promptly enter an order confirming that no stay is in effect."[136]

The debtor has the opportunity to invoke the stay, as to all or some creditors, by demonstrating to the court, after notice and a hearing, that the current case "is in good faith as to the creditors to be stayed."[137] But any stay obtained only goes into effect when the court enters its order — in other words, for debtors with multiple repeat petitions, the stay is not automatic at all. Moreover, in the hearing regarding the debtor's good faith, the debtor is burdened with the same presumption that the case was filed "not in good faith" in the circumstances where a similar assumption exists under § 362(c)(3), discussed above.[138]

[5] Individual Debtor's Failure to File Statement of Intention

Section 362(h), added in 2005, partially terminates the stay in cases involving individual debtors who fail to comply with the obligations imposed by § 521(a)(2).[139] Section 521(a)(2) requires individual debtors to file a "statement of intention with respect to the retention or surrender" of property subject to a security interest within thirty days of filing their petition.[140] Section 521(a)(6) further requires the debtor to enter into a reaffirmation agreement with the creditor holding the security interest, redeem the property pursuant to § 722, or turn the property over to the creditor within forty-five days of the "first meeting of creditors" under § 341.[141] Section 362(h) terminates the stay with respect to this property if the debtor does not file the statement of intention required by § 521(a)(2) or take the action required by § 521(a)(6). There is an exception to the automatic termination of the stay if the trustee demonstrates that the property involved is of "consequential value or benefit to the estate."[142]

---

135 Bankruptcy Code § 362(c)(4)(A)(i).

136 Bankruptcy Code § 362(c)(4)(A)(ii).

137 Bankruptcy Code § 362(c)(4)(B).

138 *See* § 8.06[A][3] Prior Petition within One Year, *supra.*

139 Bankruptcy Code § 362(h).

140 Bankruptcy Code § 521(a)(2); *see* § 12.08[D] Debtor's Statement of Intent, *infra.*

141 Bankruptcy Code § 521(a)(6).

142 Bankruptcy Code § 362(h)(2); *see* In re Record, 347 B.R. 450 (Bankr. M.D. Fla. 2006).

[B] Relief from Stay Upon Request of a Party[143]

Creditors may also obtain relief from the automatic stay upon application to the court. Secured creditors are those most likely to obtain this relief, which is most commonly granted to protect secured creditors from losses they may suffer if they are not permitted to foreclose on their collateral.

Consider, for example, a security interest held by Peninsula Bank in $100,000 worth of equipment owned by Franklin Manufacturing. When Franklin files its Chapter 11 bankruptcy petition and becomes a debtor-in-possession, Peninsula Bank is stayed from repossessing the equipment, even if Franklin is in default. Assume further that Franklin defaulted by permitting the insurance policy it carried on the equipment to lapse due to nonpayment of premiums. Without the automatic stay, Peninsula could have repossessed and sold the equipment. If a fire at Franklin Manufacturing's factory destroys the collateral, Peninsula is an unsecured creditor. In effect, the automatic stay has impaired Peninsula's secured status.

There are many less dramatic examples. Even properly maintained equipment depreciates in value over time. If the debtor fails to make regular payments, which undoubtedly include an interest component, the amount of the debt increases; this may result in unpaid debts that would never had been incurred if the creditor had been permitted to foreclose and sell the collateral. Moreover, as time passes and the debtor continues to use the collateral, it probably depreciates in value due to normal wear and tear. Shifts in market interest rates may mean that the lender is involuntarily locked into a transaction that is less profitable than a new one might be. Thus, the automatic stay may worsen the creditor's position each day that it remains in effect. The Bankruptcy Code's rules regarding "adequate protection" and "relief from the automatic stay" are designed to mitigate these harms.

Section 362(d) sets out the rules for relief from the stay. Its first two key provisions permit relief from the stay:

> (1) for cause, including the lack of adequate protection of an interest in property of such party in interest; or
>
> (2) with respect to a stay of an act against property . . . if —
>
> (A) the debtor does not have an equity in such property; and
>
> (B) such property is not necessary to an effective reorganization.

It provides two additional grounds for relief from the stay that apply, respectively, to single-asset real estate cases[144] and to creditors with mortgages or other enforceable liens on the debtor's real estate.[145]

---

[143] David Gray Carlson, *Junior Secured Creditors and the Automatic Stay,* 6 Am. Bankr. Inst. L. Rev. 249 (1998).

[144] Bankruptcy Code § 362(d)(3); *see* § 8.06[B][4] Single-Asset Real Estate Cases, *infra.*

[145] Bankruptcy Code § 362(c)(4); *see* § 8.06[B][5] Foreclosure in Cases Filed to Delay, Hinder, or Defraud Creditors, *infra.*

[1] For Cause: Lack of Adequate Protection

Most of the automatic stay litigation involves § 362(d)(1). It requires the court to grant relief from the stay "for cause, including the lack of adequate protection of an interest in property." Although the phrase "for cause" encompasses a number of other matters, nearly all of the disputes under § 362(d)(1) deal with adequate protection of a secured creditor's interest in the debtor's property.

In many Chapter 11 cases, secured creditors respond to the debtor's petition by asking the court for relief from the automatic stay to permit them to foreclose, insisting that their interest in the collateral is not adequately protected. Debtors respond that they have provided adequate protection to the creditor and that the court should keep the stay in place. If a secured creditor is granted relief from the stay and permitted to foreclose, the debtor has little chance of reorganizing. Without its land, equipment, or inventory, the debtor is likely to cease operations. Accordingly, debtors regard motions for relief from the stay as vital threats to the reorganization process. Adequate protection rules attempt to balance secured creditors' interests in preventing the deterioration of their secured status with debtors and unsecured creditors' interests in preserving the chance for a successful reorganization.

The concept of adequate protection is deeply rooted in the traditional respect given to property rights in bankruptcy. Although such respect may not be constitutionally required, it derives from the same concern for property rights that underlies the Fifth and Fourteenth Amendments.[146] The legislative history regarding adequate protection reflects its quasi-constitutional origin:

> The concept is derived from the 5th Amendment protection of property interests. It is not intended to be confined strictly to the Constitutional protection required, however. This section, and the concept of adequate protection, is based as much on policy grounds as on Constitutional grounds. Secured creditors should not be deprived of the benefit of their bargain. There may be situations in bankruptcy where giving a secured creditor an absolute right to his bargain may be impossible, or seriously detrimental to the bankruptcy laws. Thus, this section recognizes the availability of alternate means of protecting a secured creditor's interest. Though the creditor might not receive his bargain in kind, the purpose of the section is to insure that the secured creditor receives in value essentially what he bargained for.[147]

The earliest formulations of the doctrine long predate the Code.[148] Indeed, § 361, which deals with adequate protection, is essentially a mere

---

[146] Adequate protection is largely irrelevant where unsecured creditors are concerned. *See* In re Tellier, 125 B.R. 348 (Bankr. D.R.I. 1991).

[147] H.R. Rep. No. 95-595, at 339 (1977), *reprinted in* 1978 U.S.C.C.A.N. 5962, 6295.

[148] *See* In re Murel Holding Corp., 75 F.2d 941 (2d Cir. 1935).

codification of prior law. Some of its key language is taken directly from older cases. It refers to two specific methods of giving adequate protection, and sets a standard by which other methods are to be measured.

First, adequate protection may be given by making a payment or payments to the claimant.[149] Cash payments are one of the most common forms of adequate protection. For example, if the collateral is depreciating at a rate of $300 per month, the debtor might provide the secured creditor with adequate protection payments of $300 per month to compensate it for this loss in the value of its collateral. If the debtor does not have enough cash to make the required payments, and is otherwise unable to provide the creditor with adequate protection, the creditor is entitled to relief from the automatic stay and will likely foreclose. If continued use of the collateral is essential to the debtor's ability to remain in business, its inability to make the $300 monthly payments will end its effort to reorganize.

Section 361(2) permits the debtor to provide adequate protection by providing the claimant with an additional or replacement lien. Thus, instead of making cash payments to make up for the $300 monthly depreciation, the debtor might adequately protect a secured creditor by giving it a post-petition security interest on other property in which the debtor has some equity. This alternative is valuable to debtors that have tight cash flow but significant unencumbered assets. Because such debtors are rare, this is one of the least common methods of providing adequate protection.

Alternatively, depending on the value of the collateral, the presence of an "equity cushion" in the collateral might provide adequate protection. Alternative forms of adequate protection are sufficient if, in words borrowed from Judge Learned Hand in *In re Murel Holding Co.*,[150] they "result in the realization [by the creditor] of the indubitable equivalent" of the creditor's interest in the collateral.[151] *Murel Holding* provided more than a catchphrase. It supplied an attitude of skepticism toward anything but cash or other tangible property as a suitable equivalent for a creditor's property interest. The plan in *In re Murel Holding* substituted only a doubtfully secured and speculative promise of future payment for what otherwise would have been an immediate realization on a property interest. Hand found this inadequate and even suggested that permitting such a substitution might be unconstitutional. He explained:

> [W]e are to remember not only the underlying purposes of the section, but the constitutional limitations to which it must conform. It is plain that "adequate protection" must be completely compensatory; and that payment ten years hence is not generally the equivalent of payment now. Interest is indeed the common measure of the difference, but a creditor who fears the safety of his principal will

[149] Bankruptcy Code § 361(1).

[150] 75 F.2d 941 (2d Cir. 1935).

[151] Bankruptcy Code § 361(3).

> scarcely be content with that; he wishes to get his money or at least the property. We see no reason to suppose that the statute was intended to deprive him of that in the interest of junior holders, unless by a substitute of the most indubitable equivalence.[152]

The Code supplies little guidance about what constitutes an indubitable equivalent; the one thing we are told is that it is not sufficient to give the creditor an administrative priority claim.[153] The protection must be something more tangible and certain than that. The legislative history provides some suggestions but emphasizes flexibility:

> The [indubitable equivalent] method gives the parties and the courts flexibility by allowing such other relief as will result in the realization by the protected entity of the value of its interest in the property involved . . . . For example, another form of adequate protection might be the guarantee by a third party outside the judicial process of compensation for any loss incurred in the case. . . . . The paragraph also defines, more clearly than the others, the general concept of adequate protection, by requiring such relief as will result in the realization of value. It is the general category, and as such, is defined by the concept involved rather than any particular method of adequate protection.[154]

An equity cushion frequently satisfies the indubitable equivalent standard of § 361(3).[155] If the collateral is worth sufficiently more than the amount of the secured creditor's claim, the cushioning effect of this additional value supplies the creditor with adequate protection against a wide variety of risks, such as depreciation and the accumulation of interest on the creditor's fully secured claim.[156] For example, if the collateral for a creditor's $20,000 claim is worth $100,000, the $80,000 of equity protects the debtor against quite a bit of depreciation. Courts have routinely ruled that much smaller equity cushions are more than sufficient to protect a secured creditor from harm due to normal wear and tear or the accumulation of interest on the creditor's claim.

A cushion of 20% is usually enough. Thus, if the collateral is worth $24,000, the $4,000 cushion over the creditor's $20,000 claim is adequate. If the equity cushion drops to only 10%, or only $2,000 above the claim, additional protection is probably necessary.[157] However, these are not hard and fast rules; much depends on the nature of the collateral involved, the rate of dissipation of the cushion, and the degree of certainty about the

[152] 75 F.2d at 942.

[153] Bankruptcy Code § 361(3).

[154] H.R. Rep. No. 95-595, at 340 (1977), *reprinted in* 1978 U.S.C.C.A.N. 5962, 6296.

[155] *E.g.*, Prudential Ins. Co. v. Monnier (In re Monnier Bros.), 755 F.2d 1336 (8th Cir. 1985); Pistole v. Mellor (In re Mellor), 734 F.2d 1396 (9th Cir. 1984).

[156] *E.g.*, Bankers Life Ins. Co. v. Alyucan Interstate Corp. (In re Alyucan Interstate Corp.), 12 B.R. 803 (Bankr. D. Utah 1981).

[157] Matter of Mendoza, 111 F.3d 1264 (5th Cir. 1997); In re Kost, 102 B.R. 829, 831–32 (D. Wyo. 1989) (collecting cases).

value the court places on the collateral, because all these factors might expose the creditor to a greater or lesser degree of risk of becoming unsecured.

When adequate protection is based on an equity cushion, the creditor may again seek relief later in the case. As time passes, the cushion shrinks — interest accumulates and the value of the collateral declines. As the amount of the debt creeps close to the value of the collateral, the size of the cushion diminishes; the amount of the cushion might not be adequate to protect the creditors, even though it once was sufficient. This is an issue of particular significance in a protracted reorganization case.

On occasion, alas, courts err. They sometimes overestimate the value of the collateral or underestimate the rate by which its value will decline. When they do, there is no realistic way to provide the claimant with the true full equivalent of its claim. There is almost certainly little or nothing left in the estate. The Code does the best it can. It provides the claimant with a "super-priority" unsecured claim, prior to all other unsecured claims, including administrative claims.[158]

For example, assume North Atlantic Bank has a $5 million claim, secured by a mortgage on Titanic's land and building, and the court decides that the claim is adequately protected based on its valuation of the collateral at $6 million. As things turn out, when the collateral is finally liquidated, it yields only $4.8 million. North Atlantic has a super-priority unsecured claim for the $200,000 deficiency. Even with priority, however, it may not receive payment for the $200,000 priority claim. Whether it does depends on whether there is enough value in the estate to satisfy any claims. Moreover, the administrative expenses of a trustee appointed if the case is converted to Chapter 7 are entitled to an even higher priority.[159] These expenses may consume whatever minimal assets remain available for distribution to creditors.

Just as fundamental to adequate protection analysis as the form the protection must take is standing to insist on that protection. Not every claim must be protected. Unsecured claims are entitled to no protection, because they do not represent an interest in specific property.[160] Even secured claims may be entitled to only limited protection. This is particularly significant in reorganization proceedings. During the period between the petition and consummation of a confirmed plan, interest is added to fully secured claims. If the amount of the claim is less than the value of the property securing it, interest will accrue on the claim, but only to the extent of the surplus value.[161]

For example, if Peninsula Bank has a $45,000 claim, secured by collateral worth $50,000, up to $5,000 in interest may be added to the claim while

---

158 Bankruptcy Code § 507(b); *see* § 10.04[B][1] Claims for Inadequate "Adequate Protection," *infra*.

159 *See* § 10.04[B][3] Post-Conversion Liquidation Expenses, *infra*.

160 In re Tellier, 125 B.R. 348, 349 (Bankr. D. R.I. 1991).

161 Bankruptcy Code § 506(b); *see* § 10.03[B][3] Post-Petition Interest, *infra*.

the case is pending. By contrast, if the collateral were worth only $40,000, Peninsula Bank would hold a $40,000 secured claim and a $5,000 unsecured claim and would not be entitled to "pendency" interest on either claim.[162] If the collateral were worth exactly $45,000, the bank would hold a $45,000 secured claim but would have no right to add interest to its claim while the debtor attempted to forge a reorganization plan.[163]

Only the nominal value of the secured claim is entitled to adequate protection. An oversecured creditor is entitled to protection of the principal plus allowed interest. In the example above, in which the collateral is worth $50,000, the bank is entitled to adequate protection of up to $50,000 (if the collateral value later declines), depending on how much interest actually accrues on the $45,000 debt. The undersecured creditor or the exactly secured creditor is not so lucky. If the bank's secured claim is not entitled to interest, it is not entitled to obtain adequate protection for more than the original dollar value of its claim — in the last two examples above, $40,000 or $45,000, respectively.

This is true even though the real value of Peninsula's claim is diminishing. Because the stay prevents the bank from foreclosing, it incurs the opportunity cost of being unable to reinvest its funds. If Peninsula were permitted to foreclose, it would sell the collateral and invest the proceeds from the sale at whatever current rate of interest is available. If its collateral and thus its secured claim is $40,000, and the period between petition and confirmation lasts for one year, the stay causes Peninsula to lose the interest it could have otherwise earned during this time. In the 1980s, many commentators argued that this loss should be paid for — that Peninsula should be paid this interest as a price for keeping the stay in place.[164] Whatever the merits of this argument, the Supreme Court, relying on what it saw as the plain meaning of the Code, unequivocally rejected it in the *Timbers of Inwood Forest* case.[165] The undersecured creditor is entitled to nothing for its lost opportunity.[166] The Court clearly held that "adequate protection" does not include compensation for the time value of money. Therefore the "exactly secured" creditor — whose collateral equals but does not exceed the amount of the debt, and likewise the creditor who becomes exactly secured because of interest accrued during the pendency of the case — is not entitled to pendency interest as adequate protection.[167]

The point here is that adequate protection entitles the creditor to the property that it had at the outset of the case, and to receive only as much

[162] Bankruptcy Code § 502(b)(2).

[163] Bankruptcy Code § 506(b).

[164] *E.g.*, Douglas G. Baird & Thomas H. Jackson, *Corporate Reorganizations and the Treatment of Diverse Ownership Interests: A Comment on Adequate Protection of Secured Creditors in Bankruptcy*, 51 U. Chi. L. Rev. 97 (1984).

[165] United Sav. Ass'n of Tex. v. Timbers of Inwood Forest Assocs., Ltd., 484 U.S. 365 (1988).

[166] 484 U.S. at 382.

[167] David Gray Carlson, *Postpetition Interest under the Bankruptcy Code*, 43 U. Miami L. Rev. 577 (1987).

protection from bankruptcy as that collateral provides. To the extent that their collateral is insufficient to cover the delay occasioned by bankruptcy, then the remaining part of its claim is simply an unsecured claim for unmatured interest, and is disallowed under § 502(b). The policy justification for this is that bankruptcy is a common disaster, causing losses that ought to be shared in some reasonable way among those affected. Given the relatively good treatment afforded secured claimants, occasional opportunity costs represent little enough contribution from them for the greater good.

Most adequate protection issues are resolved through negotiation rather than through litigation. The most common reason for a secured creditor to seek relief from the stay is to force the debtor to negotiate reasonably. Because of the powerful position secured creditors have in most bankruptcies, the debtor is usually willing to come up with a reasonable method of providing protection, thereby avoiding both the cost and the risk of stay litigation. Given the relatively clear rules regarding what is normally required to pass muster before the court, the negotiated protection usually is identical to the protection a judge would order. The debtor commits to the maintenance of insurance and periodic payments equal to the depreciation of the property (plus, in some cases, the interest accruing on the debt). This does not mean that secured creditors are satisfied with what they can obtain, because most of the time they are not. But courts have developed fairly good guidelines as to what the debtor must give and what the creditor can get.

Finally, § 361's rules regarding adequate protection do not apply in cases involving a family farmer or a family fisherman brought under Chapter 12 of the Bankruptcy Code.[168] As explained elsewhere, Chapter 12 has a separate set of rules for what constitutes adequate protection.[169]

[2] For Cause — Other Than for Lack of Adequate Protection

Although most of the litigation concerning relief from the stay deals with lack of adequate protection for secured creditors, courts sometimes find other causes for granting relief from the automatic stay.

Courts are sometimes willing to grant relief from the stay when there is a more appropriate forum than the bankruptcy court to hear a matter that has some relationship to the debtor's bankruptcy case. This is especially true if the matter is only minimally or tangentially connected with the bankruptcy case. For example, domestic and probate cases are frequently permitted to continue. Similarly, ordinary civil suits might be permitted to continue to judgment where considerable work toward a judgment has already been completed, and where it is inefficient to require the action to be concluded in bankruptcy court.[170] The effect of a judgment

---

168 Bankruptcy Code § 361.

169 Bankruptcy Code § 361(b); *see* § 20.05[A] Adequate Protection in Chapter 12, *infra*.

170 *E.g.*, In re Robbins, 964 F.2d 345 (4th Cir. 1992); In re Haines, 309 B.R. 668 (Bankr. D. Mass. 2004).

against the debtor in such a suit, however, is simply to fix the amount of the creditor's claim. The resulting judgment is not entitled to special treatment or priority.

Proceedings against the debtor are also sometimes permitted to continue when an action must be maintained against the debtor in order to recover from the debtor's insurance carrier. As one court said, "[d]ebtors-defendants suffer little prejudice when they are sued by plaintiffs who seek nothing more than declarations of liability that can serve as a predicate for a recovery against insurers, sureties, or guarantors."[171]

The stay also might be terminated or even annulled if the debtor's petition was filed in bad faith.[172] In *In re Ironsides, Inc.*, the court explained: "[I]f there is not a potentially viable business in place worthy of protection and rehabilitation, the Chapter 11 effort has lost its raison d'etre."[173] Among the factors that lead to a finding that a petition was filed in bad faith are that:

- the debtor has one asset;
- the debtor engaged in improper conduct prior to the petition;
- the debtor has few unsecured creditors;
- the debtor's property has been scheduled for foreclosure;
- the debtor and one creditor have proceeded to a standstill in state court litigation, and the debtor has either lost or has been required to post a supersedeas bond that it cannot afford;
- the filing of the petition permits the debtor to evade court orders in another dispute;
- the debtor has no ongoing business; and
- the debtor has no possibility of successful reorganization.[174]

These same reasons might lead the court to dismiss or convert the case.[175] If the case is dismissed, the automatic stay terminates under § 362(c)(2)(B). If it is converted to Chapter 7, the stay remains in place, but a trustee is appointed and will likely sell or abandon the property involved.

[3] No Equity and Property Not Necessary for Reorganization

Relief from the stay is also granted if the debtor has no stake in the property and no use for it. Section 362(d)(2) authorizes relief from the stay "of an act against property . . . if — (a) the debtor does not have an equity

171 *E.g.*, In re Fernstrom Storage and Van Co., 938 F.2d 731, 735 (7th Cir. 1991).

172 Laguna Assocs., Ltd. v. Aetna Cas. & Sur. Co. (In re Laguna Assocs., Ltd.), 30 F.3d 734 (6th Cir. 1994).

173 In re Ironsides, Inc., 34 B.R. 337, 339 (Bankr. W.D. Ky. 1983).

174 *See* In re Charfoos, 979 F.2d 390, 393 (6th Cir. 1992).

175 *See* Trident Assocs. Ltd. v. Metropolitan Life Ins. Co. (In re Trident Assocs., Ltd.), 52 F.3d 127 (6th Cir. 1995).

in such property; *and* (b) such property is not necessary to an effective reorganization."[176] Both requirements must be met.

This basis for relief from the stay is significant primarily in reorganization proceedings under Chapters 11, 12, and 13. In Chapter 7 proceedings, where no reorganization is contemplated, the trustee ordinarily abandons property in which the debtor has no equity, making relief from the stay superfluous.

[a] No Equity in the Property

If the debtor has equity in the property, relief is unavailable under this exception, even if the property is to be liquidated. The debtor-in-possession may be in the best position to obtain a good price for it. An oversecured creditor with a lien on the property has little incentive to obtain the best price for the property; it is satisfied if the property is sold for enough to satisfy its senior lien.

Whether the debtor has equity in the property requires a comparison between the total of all liens against the property and the property's value.[177] Determining whether the debtor has any equity in the property thus requires a determination of the property's value. Whenever value must be determined, questions inevitably arise about the appropriate method of valuation to use. Consider, for example, equipment subject to a $100,000 security interest. If the liquidation value of the property of $95,000 is used, then the debtor has no equity. If the going concern value of the property (if it is left in place and sold as part of a sale of the entire premises in which it is installed) is $125,000, then the debtor has $25,000 of equity in the item. Similarly, if the property would cost $130,000 for the debtor to replace, its replacement value is $130,000 and again the debtor has equity in the property. Thus, whether the first prong of § 362(d)(2) is satisfied depends on whether the property is appraised at its liquidation, going concern or replacement value.

[b] Property Not Necessary for Effective Reorganization

In addition, for relief to be granted, the debtor must have no important use for the property. Even property in which the debtor has no equity can be vital to the operation of the debtor's business. If the property is needed for the debtor's reorganization, the automatic stay should remain in place unless a creditor with a lien on the property can establish other grounds, such as lack of adequate protection, to be permitted to foreclose. For example, Road Runner Transport, Co., a debtor-in-possession engaged in the trucking business, needs its tractor-trailers to continue in business and to have any chance of reorganization. Even if Navigator's Bank has a security interest in the vehicles that secure a debt well in excess of their

---

[176] Bankruptcy Code § 362(d)(2) (emphasis added).

[177] In re Indian Palm Assoc., 61 F.3d 197, 206–07 (3d Cir. 1995).

value, the stay should not be lifted. Of course, if Road Runner cannot adequately protect Navigator's interest in the tractor-trailers, relief should be granted under § 362(d)(1) for lack of adequate protection, as explained above.[178]

In effect, § 362(d)(2) protects two values that property has to a debtor and its creditors. It protects the value of the property as a financial asset that might be sold to generate cash. It also protects the debtor's possessory interest, the use value of the property to the debtor in its reorganization. Thus, both the liquidation value and the going concern value of the debtor's property are protected. Relief from the stay is granted under this test only if the property lacks value to the debtor in either sense.

Courts take a pro-debtor stance in interpreting § 362(b)(2), particularly with respect to whether the property is "necessary for reorganization." While it is clear that retention of the property must be more than merely convenient to the estate, there is no requirement that the property be absolutely indispensable.[179]

Implicit in the "necessary for effective reorganization" requirement is that there be some realistic possibility of reorganization. As the Supreme Court explained in *United Savings Association of Texas v. Timbers of Innwood Forest Associates:*

> Once the movant under Section 362(d)(2) establishes that he is an undersecured creditor, it is the burden of the *debtor* to establish that collateral at issue is "necessary to an effective reorganization." What this requires is not merely a showing that if there is conceivably to be an effective reorganization, this property will be needed for it; but that the property is essential for an effective reorganization *that is in prospect*. This means, as many lower courts, including the en banc court in this case, have properly said, that there must be a "reasonable possibility of a successful reorganization within a reasonable time."[180]

The usual textual justification for this reading of the rule is rooted in the fact that the statute refers to an "effective" reorganization.[181]

This is similar to a feasibility test. One of the points at which creditors may attack the entire reorganization is when they attempt to lift the stay. If the debtor has no equity in the property and there is no reasonable prospect for reorganization, the stay is lifted. In many cases, lifting the stay precipitates liquidation. The same issue arises when the debtor proposes the plan; one of the requirements for confirmation is that the plan be feasible.[182]

---

[178] *See* § 8.06[B][1] For Cause: Lack of Adequate Protection, *supra.*

[179] *E.g.*, In re Fields, 127 B.R. 150 (Bankr. W.D. Tex. 1991).

[180] United Sav. Ass'n of Tex. v. Timbers of Innwood Forest Assocs., Ltd., 484 U.S. 365, 375–76 (1988).

[181] *See* In re 8th Street Village Ltd., 94 B.R. 993, 996 (N.D. Ill. 1988).

[182] Bankruptcy Code § 1129(a)(11); *see* § 19.10[J] Feasibility of Plan, *infra.*

However, at the early stage of the case in which relief from the automatic stay is first likely to be sought, the feasibility test should be applied somewhat less rigorously than late in the case when the court is considering the details of the debtor's plan. Early in the case, the debtor might not yet have had the opportunity to determine why it is losing money, much less to evaluate its prospects for stemming the losses.

For example, assume that a creditor seeks to lift the stay under § 362(d)(2) only thirty days after the petition is filed, and that the court holds a hearing on the creditor's motion another thirty days later. This is only sixty days beyond the debtor's petition, and only half-way through the 120-day "exclusivity" period during which the debtor has the sole right to file a plan of reorganization.[183] In many cases, the debtor will simply not have had enough time to prepare and present a confirmable plan. The fact that it has not yet done so should not translate into an automatic lifting of the stay on the basis that there is no reasonable prospect for effective reorganization. While the debtor certainly must be able to present the court with more than "unsubstantiated hopes for a successful reorganization," it should not ordinarily be necessary to have an actual, finished plan in hand.[184]

In some circumstances, the debtor's situation is so obviously hopeless that lifting of the stay is appropriate, even at the very beginning of the proceeding. Debtors with irreversibly negative cash flow, no reasonable prospects for additional income or refinancing, and deteriorating property should be forced into liquidation at the earliest possible opportunity. Stay litigation provides the courts with a vehicle for doing this. Alternatively, a creditor might move to convert or dismiss the case.[185]

In addition, as time goes by and the proceeding drags on, the court's attitude toward feasibility is likely to change. If a debtor cannot show a strong prospect for reorganization six months or a year after the petition is filed, the court should move the case toward its almost inevitable close.

[4] Single-Asset Real Estate Cases

The Code supplies a special rule for relief from the stay to permit foreclosure or to take other action enforcing a lien in a single-asset real estate case. Single-asset real estate cases are those in which substantially all of the debtor's income is generated from leasing commercial real estate — usually an office building or an apartment building.[186] If the debtor operates a business out of the real estate, such as a hotel or a golf course,

---

[183] Bankruptcy Code § 1121(b); *see* § 19.08[B] Who May File a Plan; The Exclusivity Period, *infra*.

[184] In re Canal Place Ltd., 921 F.2d 569, 577 (5th Cir. 1991).

[185] Bankruptcy Code § 1112(b)(4); *see* § 19.05[B] Involuntary Conversion or Dismissal, *infra*.

[186] Bankruptcy Code § 101(51B); *see* In re Khemko, 181 B.R. 47 (Bankr. S.D. Ohio 1995) (boat marina); *see* Kenneth N. Klee, *One Size Fits Some: Single Asset Real Estate Bankruptcy*, 87 Cornell L. Rev. 1285 (2002).

from which substantial other revenues are generated, the Code's single-asset real estate rules do not apply.[187]

The rule requires the court to grant relief from the stay, unless within the later of (1) ninety days after the entry of an order for relief or a later date established by the court, or (2) thirty days after the court determines that the case is a single-asset real estate case, the debtor either: (i) files a reorganization plan that has a reasonable possibility of being confirmed within a reasonable time, or (ii) begins making regular monthly interest payments to the creditor. The amount of payments that must be made to stave off relief from the stay is "an amount equal to interest at the then applicable non-default contract rate of interest on the value of the creditor's interest in the real estate."[188]

Thus, if the debt is $12 million but the collateral is only worth $10 million, and the regular interest rate in the mortgage documents is 12% per year, interest must be paid at 12% on the $10 million value of the creditor's interest in the land, or $100,000 per month (12% per year on $10 million). This prevents the case from languishing, with no payments to the lender, while the debtor does nothing more than wait and hope that the local real estate market will improve. The source of the monthly payments may either be rents or other income generated from the property at any time, before, on, or after commencement of the case.[189]

[5] Foreclosure in Cases Filed to Delay, Hinder or Defraud Creditors

The 2005 Amendments added language that permits foreclosure of a real estate mortgage or other interest in real estate if the court finds that the debtor's petition was part of a "scheme to delay, hinder, and defraud creditors"[190] that involved either a transfer of ownership of the property to a third person without the creditor's consent or multiple bankruptcy filings affecting the same property.[191]

[6] Enforceability of Pre-Petition Waivers

Relief also might be terminated with respect to a particular creditor, based on a pre-petition waiver of the stay. For many years, the possibility that a contractual waiver of the automatic stay would be enforced was unthinkable.[192] However, courts have begun enforcing these pre-petition

---

[187] *See* Centofante v. CBJ Dev., Inc. (In re CBJ Dev., Inc.), 202 B.R. 467 (B.A.P. 9th Cir. 1996) (hotel); In re Larry Goodwin Golf, Inc., 219 B.R. 391 (Bankr. M.D.N.C. 1997) (golf course).

[188] Bankruptcy Code § 362(d)(3)(B)(ii).

[189] Bankruptcy Code § 362(d)(3)(B)(i).

[190] Bankruptcy Code § 362(d)(4).

[191] Bankruptcy Code § 362(d)(4); *see* In re Muhaimin, 343 B.R. 159 (Bankr. D. Md. 2006).

[192] Daniel B. Bogart, *Games Lawyers Play: Waivers of the Automatic Stay in Bankruptcy and the Single Asset Loan Workout*, 43 UCLA L. Rev. 1117 (1996); Michael Baxter, *Prepetition Waivers of the Automatic Stay: A Secure Lenders Guide*, 52 Bus. Law. 577 (1997); William J. Burnett, *Prepetition Waivers of the Automatic Stay: Automatic Enforcement Equals Automatic Trouble*, 5 J. Bankr. L. & Prac. 257 (1996).

agreements, particularly where the waiver was negotiated between the parties in the course of a settlement of a foreclosure action. Waivers are not usually self-executing but are frequently considered, together with other factors, in determining whether relief should be granted.[193] Courts that are willing to consider enforcing the waiver usually conduct an inquiry to evaluate "(1) the sophistication of the party making the waiver; (2) the consideration for the waiver, including the creditor's risk and the length of time the waiver covers; (3) whether other parties are affected including unsecured creditors and junior lienholders; and (4) the feasibility of the debtor's plan."[194]

[C] Form of Relief from the Stay

Although most lawyers think of stay litigation as an effort to lift the stay completely, and most cases deal with that issue, the court actually has considerable flexibility in crafting more limited remedies. The court may terminate, annul, modify, or place conditions on the continuation of the stay.[195]

At one extreme, the court may annul the stay *ab initio* and thereby validate prior actions that violated it. If the stay is annulled, it is as if it was never imposed. Annulment is rare. It is usually limited to situations in which the debtor's petition was filed in bad faith or where a creditor took action without knowledge that the petition had been filed.[196]

Alternatively, the court might modify the stay to permit future specific actions against the debtor or its property by a specific creditor. The most common illustration occurs when a creditor is permitted to commence or continue a state court foreclosure proceeding because the debtor is unable to supply it with adequate protection. Other creditors are still restrained.

The court also might deny relief but impose a condition on the continuation of the stay. For example, if the debtor fails to pay for casualty insurance on a creditor's collateral, the court may require the debtor to obtain and maintain adequate insurance in the future. An order of this type can be self-executing; in other words, the court may order that the stay automatically and immediately terminate if there is another lapse in the insurance coverage. This type of order avoids the need for further stay litigation. The court may also lift the stay for some purposes, but not for others. For example, the stay may be lifted to permit a state court to determine liability and assess damages but kept in place with regard to collection efforts.[197]

Relief may be given to one claimant, but not to another. For example, if two creditors have liens on the same property and only one requests

---

[193] *E.g.*, In re Desai, 282 B.R. 527 (Bankr. M.D. Ga. 2002).

[194] 282 B.R. at 532.

[195] Bankruptcy Code § 362(d).

[196] *E.g.*, Mutual Benefit Life Ins. Co. v. Pinetree, Ltd. (In re Pinetree, Ltd.), 876 F.2d 34 (5th Cir. 1989).

[197] *See* In re Revco D.S., Inc., 99 B.R. 768, 777 (N.D. Ohio 1989).

insurance as a condition of maintaining the stay, the court could order the debtor to maintain only enough insurance to protect the interest of the requesting creditor. This issue rarely arises, because in most cases there is only one creditor with a lien, or a least a significant lien, on any given piece of property.

[D] Procedure for Obtaining Relief from the Stay

Congress hoped to provide not only direct substantive protection to claimants' rights, but also procedural protection. Accordingly, it set out rules designed to expedite stay litigation. In the view of many, this effort has not been successful, and further tightening of the rules is a consistent demand of creditor groups.

Under § 362(e)(1), the court must take action upon a request for relief from the stay within thirty days after the request is made. If it does not do so, the stay terminates automatically.[198] Alas, what the Code gives, the Code also takes away. The court does not have to take any final action within that thirty-day period. Upon notice and an opportunity for a hearing, the court may — and often does — continue the stay, pending a final determination of the claimant's request.[199] The current version of § 362(e) requires the final hearing to be *concluded* within thirty days after the conclusion of the preliminary hearing. But the court is permitted to extend the stay with the consent of the parties or if the court finds that a specific additional time is required by compelling circumstances.[200]

In 2005, Congress added § 362(e)(2) as an exception to the thirty-day rule of § 362(e)(1). It applies only to Chapter 7, 11, and 13 cases "in which the debtor is an individual."[201] Section 362(e)(2) terminates the stay sixty days after a creditor moves for relief, unless the court enters a final decision before the end of the sixty days, the parties agree to an extension of the sixty days, or the court finds that there is "good cause" to extend the stay beyond the sixty days.[202] Thus, if the debtor is an individual, the court need not find compelling circumstances to continue the stay for more than sixty days beyond the time of the request for relief from the stay.

The Code also includes rarely used procedures for emergency ex parte relief from the stay. This is available only if two conditions are met. First, the action must be necessary to prevent irreparable damage to the claimant's property interest. Second, the damage must be imminent — if there is time for notice and a hearing, the court may not act without them.[203]

Finally, the Code codifies the basic rules regarding the burden of proof. The party requesting the relief carries the burden of proof as to the debtor's

198 Bankruptcy Code § 362(e)(1).

199 Bankruptcy Code § 362(e)(1).

200 Bankruptcy Code § 362(e)(1).

201 Bankruptcy Code § 362(e)(2).

202 Bankruptcy Code § 362(e)(2).

203 Bankruptcy Code § 362(f); Fed. R. Bankr. P. 4001(a)(2).

equity in the property.[204] Thus, if Peninsula seeks relief from the stay because Franklin Manufacturing has no equity in Peninsula's collateral and the property is not necessary for Franklin's effective reorganization, then Peninsula bears the burden of proof on the question of Franklin's lack of equity.

As to all other issues, the trustee or debtor-in-possession carries the burden of proof.[205] Thus, if Peninsula Bank proves that Franklin has no equity in the property, the debtor must prove that the property is necessary for reorganization; if it fails to do so, the stay is lifted.

Although not explicitly stated in the Code, it is reasonably clear that "burden of proof" means the burden of persuasion. The party that carries the burden of proof must not only put on evidence supporting its position, but also must convince the judge that its position is correct. The standard for carrying the burden of proof is the ordinary one in civil litigation — preponderance of the evidence.

§ 8.07 Enforcement of the Stay

[A] Actions in Violation of the Stay are Void[206]

Actions in violation of the automatic stay are regarded by most courts as entirely void, even if the person taking the action had no notice of the stay.[207] Even actions taken by the government, such as a foreclosure sale,[208] are without legal effect. The fact that the action taken may have been entirely innocent and in good faith is a defense against sanctions, but this does not protect the action itself.

[B] Damages for Violating the Stay[209]

Wilful violations of the stay are punishable under § 362(k) or as contempt under § 105.[210] Section 362(k)(1) provides: "[A]n individual injured by any

---

[204] Bankruptcy Code § 362(g)(1).

[205] Bankruptcy Code § 362(g)(2).

[206] Donna Renee Tobar, *The Need for a Uniform Void Ab Initio Standard for Violations of the Automatic Stay*, 24 Whittier L. Rev. 3 (2002); Timothy Arnold Barnes, Note, *Plain Meaning of the Automatic Stay in Bankruptcy: The Void/Voidable Distinction Revisited*, 57 Ohio St. L.J. 291 (1996).

[207] *See, e.g.*, Franklin Sav. Ass'n v. Office of Thrift Supervision, 31 F.3d 1020, 1022 (10th Cir. 1994); *but see* Jones v. Garcia (In re Jones), 63 F.3d 411, 412 (5th Cir. 1995) (not void, merely voidable).

[208] Anglemyer v. United States, 115 B.R. 510 (D. Md. 1990).

[209] Ann K. Wooster, Annotation, *What Constitutes "Willful Violation" of Automatic Stay Provisions of Bankruptcy Code (11 U.S.C.A. § 362(h)) Sufficient to Award Damages — Chapter 13 Cases*, 8 A.L.R. Fed. 2d 433 (2006); Ann K. Wooster, Annotation, *What Constitutes "Willful Violation" of Automatic Stay Provisions of Bankruptcy Code (11 U.S.C.A. § 362(h)) Sufficient To Award Damages — Chapter 11 and 12 Cases*, 2 A.L.R. Fed. 2d 459 (2005).

[210] Jove Eng'g, Inc. v. IRS, 92 F.3d 1539 (11th Cir. 1996).

wilful violation of a stay provided by this section, shall recover actual damages, including costs and attorneys' fees, and in appropriate circumstances, may recover punitive damages."[211]

Assume, for example, that Auto Finance Co. repossesses Ray's car, despite having received formal notice of his bankruptcy petition from the court, and that it refuses to return the car to Ray. Ray rented a car for $200 per week for six weeks so that he could commute to work and run family errands. Ray also had to pay his lawyer $300 to make a (successful) motion in the bankruptcy court to force Auto Finance to return the car and to establish damages for its violation of the stay. Ray is entitled to recover not only the car, but also the rental cost ($1200), plus his attorney's fees ($300); his monetary recovery is $1,500.

The court might also award him damages for any mental distress he suffered after the car was repossessed as an element of actual damages caused by the creditor's violation.[212] However, "[f]leeting or trivial anxiety or distress is not sufficient to support an award; instead, an individual must suffer significant emotional harm."[213] Thus, the debtor's mere embarrassment is not sufficient to justify an award of actual damages.[214]

Ray may also be able to recover punitive damages from the finance company. Courts are generally reluctant to grant punitive damages, because compensatory damages are usually sufficient both to recompense the debtor (or the estate) and to deter the creditor from future violations. Some courts have said that punitive damages are appropriate only if the creditor's conduct was not only willful, but also malicious or in bad faith.[215] However, if the creditor's action is sufficiently egregious — or, more precisely, if the judge views the creditor's action as sufficiently outrageous — punitive damages may be awarded. Under at least one case, if Ray's employer, after learning of the stay, continued to dock his paycheck to obtain payment on a pre-petition debt, punitive damages would be appropriate.[216]

Courts disagree over whether the reference to "an individual" prevents corporations, partnerships and other organizations from recovering under § 362(k).[217] Courts that give "individual" its normal meaning, impose damages under § 105(a).[218] It broadly permits the court to "issue any order, process, or judgment that is necessary or appropriate to carry out the provisions of this title."[219] Before the 1984 Amendments added specific language

---

[211] Bankruptcy Code § 362(k)(1).

[212] *E.g.*, Dawson v. Washington Mut. Bank (In re Dawson), 390 F.3d 1139, 1148 (9th Cir. 2004).

[213] Dawson, 390 F.3d at 1149.

[214] In re Kinsey, 349 B.R. 48, 53 (Bankr. D. Idaho 2006).

[215] *See* In re Crysen/Montenay Energy Co., 902 F.2d 1098, 1105 (2d Cir. 1990); In re Hooker Inv. Co., 116 B.R. 375 (Bankr. S.D.N.Y. 1990).

[216] *See* In re Everett, 127 B.R. 781, 784 (Bankr. E.D.N.C. 1991).

[217] *See* Spookyworld, Inc. v. Town of Berlin (In re Spookyworld, Inc.), 346 F.3d 1, 7 & 7n.3 (2003).

[218] 346 F.3d at 8.

[219] Bankruptcy Code § 105(a).

that authorizes damages for violations of the stay, courts routinely used § 105(a) to punish such violations by awarding damages and other relief.[220] In appropriate cases, punitive damages can be awarded. However, sanctions are inappropriate for an inadvertent violation or one taken without notice of the stay.

[C] Sovereign Immunity

Section 106 contains a broad abrogation of sovereign immunity with respect to actions brought against state governments under many provisions of the Bankruptcy Code. It provides in part: "Notwithstanding an assertion of sovereign immunity, sovereign immunity is abrogated as to a governmental unit to the extent set forth in this section, with respect to [many enumerated sections of the Bankruptcy Code including §§ 105 and 362]."[221] It expressly abrogates sovereign immunity with respect to "an order or judgment awarding a money recovery, but not including an award of punitive damages."[222] Moreover, § 106(b) provides:

> A governmental unit that has filed a proof of claim in the case is deemed to have waived sovereign immunity with respect to a claim against such governmental unit that is property of the estate and that arose out of the same transaction or occurrence out of which the claim of such governmental unit arose.[223]

Until 2006, Congress' power to abrogate sovereign immunity with respect to actions for damages against a state government was in serious question. In the years since the Supreme Court's 1996 decision in *Seminole Tribe v. Florida*,[224] § 106 was widely regarded as unconstitutional, at least with respect to actions to recover damages from state governments. In *Seminole Tribe*, the Court held that Congress lacked authority to abrogate state sovereign immunity to authorize suits by Indian tribes against states to enforce legislation that was enacted pursuant to the Indian Commerce Clause. *Seminole Tribe* did not involve § 362, § 105, or any other provision of the Bankruptcy Code, but its rationale, which was based on the limits imposed by the Eleventh Amendment on Congress' powers under Article I of the Constitution, seemed easily adaptable to Article I's Bankruptcy power. In the wake of *Seminole Tribe*, most courts held that § 106(a) was unconstitutional.[225]

There remained a question, however, of whether the automatic stay and discharge injunction implicated sovereign immunity at all. Since the

---

[220] *See* In re Crysen/Montenay Energy Co., 902 F.2d 1098, 1104 (2d Cir. 1990); In re A & J Auto Sales, Inc., 223 B.R. 839, 844–45 (D.N.H. 1998).

[221] Bankruptcy Code § 106(a).

[222] Bankruptcy Code § 106(a)(3).

[223] Bankruptcy Code § 106(b).

[224] 517 U.S. 44 (1996).

[225] *E.g.*, Georgia Higher Educ. Assistance Corp. v. Crow (In re Crow), 394 F.3d 918, 921 (11th Cir. 2004).

Supreme Court's decision in *Ex Parte Young*,[226] actions for an injunction brought against a state official acting in his or her official capacity were held not to be an "action" against the state itself. As such, enforcing the automatic stay against a state might not require an abrogation of sovereign immunity. The Supreme Court addressed this question in *Tennessee Student Assistance Corporation v. Hood*,[227] holding that sovereign immunity did not prevent a bankruptcy court from discharging a student loan issued by a state. The Court held that the bankruptcy court's *in rem* jurisdiction over the estate gave it the power to adjudicate the dischargeability of the state's claim. Finally, in 2006, in response to a split in the circuits regarding the issue, the Court overruled these earlier decisions, and in *Central Virginia Community College v. Katz* held that the Bankruptcy Clause authorized Congress to abrogate sovereign immunity in bankruptcy matters, and that states therefore are not immune from suit by a trustee to recover avoidable preferences.[228]

The Court explained:

> States agreed in the plan of the Convention not to assert any sovereign immunity defense they might have had in proceedings brought pursuant to "Laws on the subject of Bankruptcies." . . . The scope of this consent was limited; the jurisdiction exercised in bankruptcy proceedings was chiefly *in rem* — a narrow jurisdiction that does not implicate state sovereignty to nearly the same degree as other kinds of jurisdiction. But while the principal focus of the bankruptcy proceedings is and was always the *res*, some exercises of bankruptcy courts' powers — issuance of writs of habeas corpus included — unquestionably involved more than mere adjudication of rights in a *res*. In ratifying the Bankruptcy Clause, the States acquiesced in a subordination of whatever sovereign immunity they might otherwise have asserted in proceedings necessary to effectuate the *in rem* jurisdiction of the bankruptcy courts.[229]

Thus, to the extent enforcement of the stay is "necessary to effectuate" the court's *in rem* jurisdiction over estate property, there seems little doubt that under *Katz*, actions against states for violations of the stay are permitted.

---

[226] 209 U.S. 123 (1908).

[227] 541 U.S. 440 (2004).

[228] 126 S. Ct. 990 (2006); *see* Bankruptcy Code § 547; Chapter 15, Avoidable Preferences, *infra*.

[229] 126 S. Ct. at 1004–05.

Chapter 9

Operating the Debtor

§ 9.01 Responsibility for Operation of the Debtor

Reorganizing debtors are not static entities. Their financial affairs do not freeze when they file a bankruptcy petition. This is particularly true if the debtor operates a business. Businesses must obtain supplies, sell goods or services, pay their employees, use equipment, and obtain credit. Even a liquidating debtor might need to continue some of its operations to protect its assets from harm, or may wish to avoid selling assets in a hurry at fire sale prices. Thus, most debtors continue at least some of their operations while their bankruptcy case is pending. Debtors who hope to reorganize usually maintain most of their operations while they implement their strategy to resuscitate their failing business.

However, some or all of these actions may be opposed by creditors, especially those whose claims are fully secured. These creditors may believe that an immediate surrender of their collateral or a prompt liquidation would serve their interests better than a risky attempt to reorganize. At the same time, the debtor's efforts to continue its business operations may be supported by other creditors who have a great deal to lose if the debtor liquidates. These supportive creditors are likely to include suppliers whose only hope for payment depends on the success of the debtor's ongoing business. In addition, the debtor's owners and managers usually prefer reorganization, because only the debtor's success can save their jobs.

The Bankruptcy Code balances the interests of those who support the debtor's continued operation and those who oppose it. The fulcrum of this balance is "adequate protection," a concept that is explored more deeply in conjunction with the automatic stay of § 365 in the previous chapter.[1] The issue is the extent to which the Code should subject unwilling creditors to continued risks in an effort to reduce the harm to others.

Rules regarding a debtor's continued operation apply to all types of bankruptcy proceedings.[2] Even a Chapter 7 trustee may continue to operate the debtor for a time, if that is the most reasonable means to conduct its liquidation.[3] However, these rules are important primarily in reorganization proceedings, particularly those involving a business debtor under Chapter 11. This is because Chapter 11 cases nearly always involve a prolonged period of several months to several years between the commencement of the case and the consummation of a confirmed reorganization plan.

---

1 *See* § 8.06[B] Relief From the Stay Upon Request of a Party, *supra*.

2 Bankruptcy Code § 103(a).

3 Bankruptcy Code § 721; *see* § 17.05[B] Duties of the Trustee, *infra*.

§ 9.02 Supervisory Authority of the Court

At the core of the Code's rules about operating the debtor is the fact that the debtor is not quite the same person who filed the bankruptcy petition. When Franklin Manufacturing, Inc. files a bankruptcy petition, it is in many respects treated as a new legal entity: Franklin Manufacturing, Inc., Debtor-in-Possession.[4] This new role is accompanied by new responsibilities and new restrictions. The debtor-in-possession owns the same building and produces the same unreliable products that are shipped by the same disgruntled work force, and it has the same angry bankers trying to extract their collateral, but in many respects it is regarded as if it were an entirely new person.[5]

This has many implications, major and minor. Members of the debtor's management team frequently overlook the fact that they have new fiduciary duties to the debtor's creditors and that they are managing the debtor's business under court supervision. Managers are generally not used to, and often resent such outside oversight. Failure to accept these limitations on their power can create dangerous situations for the debtor (not to mention civil and even criminal liability for themselves). To take only one example: in one very large, well-publicized bankruptcy, the managers of the debtor-in-possession thought nothing of paying themselves huge bonuses without court permission. Those bonuses had to be returned and a trustee was nearly appointed.[6] Had the court decided that the managers acted fraudulently, rather than just foolishly, far more severe sanctions undoubtedly would have been applied.

§ 9.03 Use, Sale, or Lease of Estate Property

Section 363 authorizes the trustee or debtor-in-possession to use, sell, or lease property of the estate, subject to a complicated array of controls, depending on the nature of the property, the proposed use, and whether the property is subject to a creditor's lien. As will be seen, the debtor has considerable leeway to deal with property in the ordinary course. On the other hand, the debtor is subject to greater restrictions in dealing with

[4] For many years, the debtor-in-possession was regarded by most as a distinct legal entity. However, strict treatment of the debtor-in-possession as a new legal entity is inconsistent with several provisions of the Bankruptcy Code. *See* NLRB v. Bildisco & Bildisco, 465 U.S. 513, 528 (1984). As a result, many commentators have ceased treating the debtor-in-possession as an entirely new legal person. *E.g.*, Michael T. Andrew, *Executory Contracts in Bankruptcy: Understanding "Rejection,"* 59 U. Colo. L. Rev. 845, 855 n.51 (1988). Nevertheless, referring to the debtor-in-possession as a new entity is a useful device to remember that its discretion is limited in ways that did not apply before its petition was filed.

[5] *See generally* David Gray Carlson, *Voidable Preferences and Proceeds: A Reconceptualization*, 71 Am. Bankr. L.J. 517, 519–20 (1997) ("new entity" theory explains powers and new duties of debtor-in-possession better than other theories); Brett W. King, *Assuming and Assigning Executory Contracts: A History of Indeterminate "Applicable Law,"* 70 Am. Bankr. L.J. 95, 125 (1996) (regarding utility of "new entity" theory); Thomas E. Plank, *The Bankruptcy Trust as a Legal Person*, 35 Wake Forest L. Rev. 251 (2000).

[6] Ronald J. Bacigal, The Limits of Litigation: The Dalkon Sheild Controversy 64–71 (1990).

property outside the ordinary course of business or in dealing with property that is subject to a creditor's security interest.

[A] Use of Property in the Ordinary Course

Debtors[7] generally have authority to use estate property in the ordinary course of business without prior court approval.[8] This permits the debtor to continue to use its real estate and equipment as part of its ongoing operations and to continue to sell inventory to its customers. There is no requirement that there be any notice to others or any hearing.[9] There are special rules for co-owners[10] and for those claiming an interest arising from marital rights,[11] but even these do not give an absolute right to block the debtor's action. The reason for this is simple. The person responsible for the liquidation or reorganization of a business needs substantial leeway to make appropriate bargains for the disposition or acquisition of property. In this context, "appropriate" usually means "most profitable." Deference to the wishes of other claimants can impede profitable bargains. As is so often the case, the Code does not entirely ignore the interests of those claimants, but to some degree it subordinates them to the goal of achieving a reasonably quick, reasonably successful liquidation or reorganization. It is assumed that achievement of this goal produces benefits to creditors as a group, which outweigh any infringement on the interests of particular claimants. Thus, except with respect to "cash collateral"[12] and unless the court orders otherwise, the debtor "may enter into transactions, including the sale or lease of property of the estate, in the ordinary course of business . . . and may use property of the estate in the ordinary course of business."[13]

For example, if Franklin Manufacturing, debtor-in-possession, wishes to sell items it has manufactured to its customers, the company may continue to enter into the usual contracts to buy raw materials, employ factory workers, and sell completed items of its inventory, without any prior notice to creditors or approval from the court. Any other rule would seriously impair the ability of the business to operate, and the business would have no hope of successfully reorganizing.

[7] At this point, this chapter ceases to refer to the "trustee or debtor-in-possession" on every occasion. Instead, it will usually just refer to the "debtor" and trust the reader to understand that, unless the context otherwise requires, this refers either to the trustee or to the debtor-in-possession, depending on whether a trustee has been appointed. In most cases, a trustee will administers the estate in a Chapter 7 liquidation case. In other cases, the debtor-in-possession is usually responsible for the administration of the estate. Referring to both the trustee and the debtor-in-possession in these situations is cumbersome and detracts from the readability of the text.

[8] Bankruptcy Code § 363(c)(1).

[9] Bankruptcy Code § 363(c)(1).

[10] Bankruptcy Code § 363(h), (j).

[11] Bankruptcy Code § 363(i), (j).

[12] Bankruptcy Code § 363(a); *see* § 9.03[B] Use of Cash Collateral, *infra*.

[13] Bankruptcy Code § 363(c)(1).

On the other hand, the court has the authority to restrict the debtor's management of its business.[14] For example, if the court decides that Franklin's managers are entering into foolish or improper supply contracts, it might require Franklin to obtain prior court approval before entering into any future contracts. However, this is rarely done and is usually a preliminary step to displacing management altogether by appointing a trustee.

Whether a particular transaction is in the ordinary course depends on two tests: the horizontal dimension test and the vertical dimension test.[15] The horizontal dimension test considers "whether from an industry-wide perspective, the transaction is of the sort commonly undertaken by companies in that industry."[16] The vertical dimension test considers creditors' expectations and whether the economic risk of the transaction is different from those accepted by creditors that extended credit to the debtor pre-petition.[17]

A debtor's continued sale of inventory is likely to be in the ordinary course under both these tests. However, if the debtor's inventory is subject to a creditor's security interest, its sale might leave the creditor without adequate protection. This is particularly true given the effect of § 552(a), which prevents a creditor's pre-petition security interest from automatically attaching to any after-acquired inventory that was purchased by the debtor after its case commenced.[18] Section 363(d) protects secured creditors from dissipation of their collateral by preventing its sale, use, or lease in a way that would be inconsistent with any relief from the automatic stay provided to the creditor under § 362(d).[19] Creditors with security interests in the debtor's inventory who are fearful that the debtor will sell the collateral out from under them[20] and dissipate the proceeds are likely to seek relief from the automatic stay on the grounds that the debtor's continued sale of the inventory will leave it inadequately protected.[21] If inventory lenders are granted relief from the stay, and permitted to foreclose, the debtor's reorganization comes to an abrupt halt. To avoid this problem, many Chapter 11 debtors seek a court order, frequently on the first day of their

---

[14] Bankruptcy Code § 363(c)(1).

[15] *E.g.*, In re Roth Am., Inc., 975 F.2d 949, 952–54 (3d Cir. 1992); Vision Metals, Inc. v. SMS DEMAG, Inc. (In re Vision Metals, Inc.), 325 B.R. 138, 143–45 (Bankr. D. Del. 2005); *see* Benjamin Weintraub & Alan N. Resnick, *The Meaning of "Ordinary Course of Business" Under the Bankruptcy Code — Vertical and Horizontal Analysis*, 19 UCC L.J. 364 (1987).

[16] In re Roth Am., Inc., 975 F.2d 949, 953 (3d Cir. 1992); Vision Metals, Inc. v. SMS DEMAG, Inc. (In re Vision Metals, Inc.), 325 B.R. 138, 143–44 (Bankr. D. Del. 2005).

[17] In re Roth Am., Inc., 975 F.2d 949, 953 (3d Cir. 1992); Vision Metals, Inc. v. SMS DEMAG, Inc. (In re Vision Metals, Inc.), 325 B.R. 138, 144–45 (Bankr. D. Del. 2005); In re James A. Phillips, Inc., 29 B.R. 391, 394 (S.D.N.Y. 1983).

[18] Bankruptcy Code § 522(a).

[19] Bankruptcy Code § 363(d)(2).

[20] *See* U.C.C. § 9-320(a) (2003) (buyer in the ordinary course takes free from perfected security interest).

[21] Bankruptcy Code § 362(d)(1); *see* § 8.06[B][1] For Cause: Lack of Adequate Protection, *infra*.

case, that approves a post-petition financing agreement with their inventory lenders, arranges for post-petition financing, and grants the inventory lender a security interest in after-acquired inventory that is purchased to replace items that are to be sold in the ordinary course of business to the debtor's customers.[22]

[B] Use of Cash Collateral[23]

The most important restriction on a debtor's ability to use property in the ordinary course is with respect to "cash collateral." Cash collateral is cash and any cash equivalents in which someone other than the estate (such as a secured creditor) has an interest.[24] Section 363(c)(2) prohibits the debtor from using cash collateral without first obtaining either the consent of the creditor or authorization from the court. Neither the creditor nor the court are likely to approve unless the debtor provides the creditor with adequate protection against loss or dissipation of its interest.

This protection makes the definition of "cash collateral" important. It means "cash, negotiable instruments, documents of title, securities, deposit accounts, or other cash equivalents . . . and . . . proceeds, products, offspring, rents or profits of property" subject to a security interest.[25] It also includes "fees, charges, accounts or other payments for the use or occupancy of rooms and other public facilities in hotels, motels, or other lodging properties subject to a security interest [under § 552(b)]."[26] This definition creates some amusing if not particularly significant anomalies; for example, suppose Rural Finance Co. has a security interest in the debtor's dairy herd. Elsie the cow is not cash collateral, but the milk she produces and the calves she bears fit the definition.

Not only is the debtor prohibited from using cash collateral without court permission, but also the debtor must segregate and separately account for cash collateral, unless either the creditor consents to other treatment or the court relieves the debtor of this duty in an order permitting the use of cash collateral.[27] These provisions effectively place the burden on the debtor to raise the issue of adequate protection if it wishes to use cash to pay its employees, pay its utility bills, or purchase additional supplies or

---

22 Under state law, buyers in the ordinary course usually take free of the creditor's security interest. *See* U.C.C. § 9-320(a) (2003); *see generally* Bruce A. Henoch, Comment, *Postpetition Financing: Is There Life After Debt?*, 8 Bankr. Dev. J. 575 (1991).

23 Stephen A. Stripp, *Balancing of Interests in Orders Authorizing the Use of Cash Collateral in Chapter 11*, 21 Seton Hall L. Rev. 562 (1991); Benjamin Weintraub & Alan Resnick, *The Use of Cash Collateral in Reorganization Cases*, 15 UCC L.J. 168 (1982); Donald T. Polednak, Note, *Is the Secured Creditor Really "Secure"?: A Survey of Remedies and Sanctions for a Debtor's Unauthorized Use of Cash Collateral in Chapter 11 Bankruptcy*, 31 Washburn L.J. 344 (1992).

24 Bankruptcy Code § 363(a).

25 Bankruptcy Code § 363(a).

26 Bankruptcy Code § 363(a).

27 Bankruptcy Code § 363(d)(4).

equipment. In many cases, the court simultaneously hears the debtor's request to use cash collateral with a creditor's demand for adequate protection of its interest in the property.[28]

There are practical problems of timing. A reorganizing debtor frequently needs immediate access to cash collateral to continue the operation of its business. Thus, the court is required to made a decision "promptly."[29] The court may hold a preliminary hearing upon the debtor's request to use cash collateral and may give temporary permission — but only if there is a "reasonable likelihood" that the debtor will prevail at the final hearing.[30] Rule 4001(b) gives more detailed guidance for the conduct of hearings on use of cash collateral. The final hearing must be at least fifteen days after service of the debtor's motion for authorization. If the movant so requests, the court may conduct an earlier preliminary hearing. However, at the preliminary hearing, the court may only authorize the use of "that amount of cash collateral as is necessary to avoid immediate and irreparable harm to the estate pending a final hearing."[31] Obvious examples include an immediately due payroll or a vital shipment that is arriving C.O.D.

Even the rule, however, does not fully deal with the most difficult situation — one in which the need for cash collateral is so great and immediate that the ordinary forms of notice and a hearing are not available. It is generally assumed that, if the emergency is sufficiently grave, the notice may be nothing more than a telephone call to those creditors who can be reached; the hearing may be nothing more than a conference call. This hearing is likely to be conducted in connection with a variety of other "first-day motions" that are frequently necessary if the debtor is to survive.[32]

[C] Use, Sale, or Lease Outside the Ordinary Course[33]

In contrast to ordinary course of business transactions, non-ordinary course transactions are subject to prior court scrutiny. Section 363(b) requires any non-ordinary course use, sale, or lease of property to be preceded by notice and an opportunity for a hearing.[34] This provision deals with two rather different situations. The first is a liquidation case in which the trustee is not authorized to conduct the business of the debtor — the typical Chapter 7 case. The second is one in which the debtor-in-possession, or perhaps even a trustee, is authorized to conduct the debtor's business but wishes to enter into a transaction that is outside the ordinary scope of that business.

[28] Bankruptcy Code § 363(c)(3)

[29] Bankruptcy Code § 363(c)(3).

[30] Bankruptcy Code § 363(c)(3).

[31] Fed. R. Bankr. P. 4001(b)(2).

[32] *See* § 19.06[C] First-Day Orders, *infra.*

[33] Lee R. Bogdanoff, *Purchase and Sale of Assets in Reorganization*, 47 Bus. Law. 1367 (1992).

[34] Bankruptcy Code § 363(b)(1).

The former circumstance most commonly occurs in a Chapter 7 case in which the trustee has been authorized to conduct the debtor's business. In most Chapter 7 cases, the trustee simply liquidates the debtor's assets as quickly and efficiently as possible. But in other cases, it may be more fruitful for the trustee to continue to operate the debtor's business perhaps in anticipation of selling it as a going concern. In these cases, the trustee needs court authorization to continue the debtor's business operations.[35] In the course of operating the debtor's business, the trustee may determine that some of the debtors assets need to be jettisoned. If so, the trustee needs further court authorization to sell these assets outside the ordinary course.

The more common situation in which court authority is necessary involves a Chapter 11 debtor-in-possession that decides either that some of its real estate or equipment is unnecessary, or that an entire portion of the debtor's business cannot be operated at a profit. In either case, the debtor can seek court permission to sell the unproductive assets.

Section 363(c)(1) has been used to accomplish a sale of all or a substantial part of the debtor's assets in a single transaction.[36] This was done in *In re Adelphia Communications, Inc.*, involving the well-known cable-TV and Internet provider of the same name. The debtor sold substantially all of its assets to two of its competitors, Time-Warner Cable Co. and Comcast Corp., for $17 billion.[37] Such sales can effectively reorganize the debtor without complying with the normal process of preparing a disclosure statement and giving creditors the opportunity to vote on the plan. However, courts generally permit such sales if there is a sound business purpose for the transaction,[38] unless aspects of the sale restructure the priority and other rights of creditors.[39] Often, they will implement special procedures to safeguard, as much as possible, the interests that are protected through the plan process.

The sale in *In re Lionel Corp.* is frequently cited as an example.[40] Even though the company is known primarily for the toy train sets that many of us of a certain age played with in our childhood, Lionel's most valuable asset was 82% of the common stock of Dale Electronics, Inc., a manufacturer of electronic components. Lionel sought to sell its holdings in Dale to a suitor who was interested in acquiring the firm. The success of Lionel's

---

[35] Bankruptcy Code § 721.

[36] John J. Hurley, *Chapter 11 Alternative: Section 363 Sale of all of the Debtor's Assets Outside a Plan of Reorganization*, 58 Am. Bankr. L.J. 233 (1984); George W. Kuney, *Misinterpreting Bankruptcy Code Section 363(f) and Undermining the Chapter 11 Process*, 76 Am. Bankr. L.J. 235 (2002).

[37] *See Bankruptcy Court Backs Adelphia Sale*, N.Y. Times, June 28, 2006, at C7.

[38] *E.g.*, Committee of Equity Sec. Holders v. Lionel Corp. (In re Lionel Corp.), 722 F.2d 1063 (2d Cir. 1983).

[39] *See* Pension Benefit Guar. Corp. v. Braniff Airways, Inc. (In re Braniff Airways, Inc.), 700 F.2d 935 (5th Cir. 1983); *see also* Official Comm. of Unsecured Creditors v. Cajun Elec. Power Coop., Inc. (In re Cajun Elec. Power Coop., Inc.), 119 F.3d 349 (5th Cir. 1997).

[40] Committee of Equity Sec. Holders v. Lionel Corp. (In re Lionel Corp.), 722 F.2d 1063 (2d Cir. 1983).

reorganization plan was dependent on the sale of the Dale Electronics stock. Lionel could have submitted a reorganization plan calling for the Dale Electronics stock to be sold and waited for creditors to vote to approve the plan. However, this would have taken considerable time and the buyer of the stock might not have been willing to wait to see whether Lionel's creditors would vote to accept the plan in sufficient numbers to obtain court confirmation of the plan. Accordingly, Lionel simply sought court approval of the sale under § 363.

A Committee of Equity Security Holders was opposed. It believed that conducting the sale in this fashion deprived shareholders of the "safeguards of disclosure, solicitation and acceptance"[41] that proposing the sale as part of an overall reorganization plan would have provided. The court rejected the view advanced by the Committee of Equity Security Holders that this type of sale could be conducted only in an emergency. At the same time, however, the court also rejected any assertion that the bankruptcy court had "*carte blanche*" to approve sales of a substantial portion of a Chapter 11 debtor's assets.[42] The court indicated that the bankruptcy judge could approved a sale of a substantial portion of a debtor's assets if "from the evidence before him at the hearing [there was] a good business reason to grant [the] application [for the sale]."[43] In determining whether there was a good business reason for the proposed sale, the court should:

> consider all salient factors . . . [such as] the proportionate value of the asset to the estate as a whole, the amount of elapsed time since the filing, the likelihood that a plan of reorganization will be proposed and confirmed in the near future, the effect of the proposed disposition on future plans of reorganization, the proceeds to be obtained from the disposition vis-a-vis any appraisals of the property, which of the alternatives of use, sale or lease the proposal envisions and most importantly perhaps, whether the asset is increasing or decreasing in value.[44]

The "Lionel standard" has been widely followed.[45]

[D] Adequate Protection

Section 363(e) makes adequate protection an integral part of the rules regarding the debtor's use, sale, or lease of estate property. Upon request of a person who has an interest in estate property, the court must prohibit or condition its use, sale, or lease to the extent necessary to provide adequate protection.[46] This protects lienholders, lessors, lessees, and

[41] 722 F.2d at 1066.

[42] 722 F.2d at 1069 (emphasis in original).

[43] 722 F.2d at 1071.

[44] 722 F.2d at 1071.

[45] *E.g.*, Contrarian Funds, LLC v. Westpoint Stevens, Inc. (In re Westpoint Stevens, Inc.), 333 B.R. 30 (S.D.N.Y. 2005); Official Comm. of Subordinated Bondholders v. Integrated Res., Inc. (In re Integrated Res., Inc.), 147 B.R. 650 (S.D.N.Y. 1992).

[46] Bankruptcy Code § 363(e).

co-owners. Thus, if the debtor wished to sell a parcel of the estate's real estate, it would need to conduct the sale in a way that provided adequate protection for the mortgagee, any lessees, and any joint tenant who has an interest in the land.

The nature of the interest protected and the means of providing protection are largely the same as they are under § 362 with respect to the automatic stay.[47] In cases involving liens on estate property, the creditor seeking adequate protection usually seeks either some sort of protective relief as a condition to the debtor's proposed use of the property or permission for relief from the stay so that it can foreclose. The claimant with an interest in the property is entitled to have the value of that interest protected from diminution. This can be accomplished in a variety of ways, such as by giving the creditor an interest in the proceeds obtained from the sale of the property or an interest in substitute property, such as after-acquired inventory. In situations involving the debtor's proposed sale of estate property, the necessity of providing adequate protection is more urgent. This is particularly true in the case of sales of inventory, where buyers are likely to acquire their interest in the property free of the creditor's lien.[48] But even the debtor's continued use of a creditor's collateral leads to its loss of value through accelerated depreciation or possible casualty loss.

Section 363(d) coordinates with § 362's rules regarding terminating, limiting, or conditioning the automatic stay with rules on the use, sale, or lease of estate property. It prevents the debtor from using property in any manner that is inconsistent with relief granted from the stay.[49] For example, suppose that Perpetual Motors Acceptance Corporation has a security interest in some light trucks owned by Franklin Manufacturing Co. Shortly after Franklin files its bankruptcy petition, Perpetual Motors Acceptance obtains a court order that imposes certain conditions on continuation of the automatic stay. One of those conditions prohibits Franklin from using the trucks to haul more than the maximum load recommended by the manufacturer. Another condition prohibits Franklin from selling or leasing the trucks to anyone else without the creditor's consent or court permission. These conditions on the continuation of the automatic stay also act as restrictions on the debtor's use of the trucks. If Franklin fails to comply with these conditions, the court will likely provide Perpetual Motors with relief from the automatic stay. A serious misuse of the debtor's property may lead the court to appoint a trustee,[50] dismiss the case,[51] or refuse to confirm the debtor's plan.[52]

---

[47] *See* § 8.06[B] Relief From the Automatic Stay Upon Request of a Party, *supra.*

[48] U.C.C. § 9-320(a) (2003).

[49] Bankruptcy Code § 363(d).

[50] Bankruptcy Code § 1104; *see* § 19.03[D] Appointment of Trustee or Examiner, *infra.*

[51] Bankruptcy Code § 1112; *see* § 19.05[B][2] Failure to Comply with Code Requirements, *infra.*

[52] Bankruptcy Code § 1129(a)(2); *see* § 19.10[A] Compliance with the Bankruptcy Code, *infra.*

[E] Continuation of Liens and Other Interests; Sales Free and Clear

If property that is subject to a lien or other third-party interest is sold by the trustee or debtor-in-possession, one obvious question that arises is whether the buyer acquires ownership of the property free and clear of the other person's interest. Thus, if Franklin Manufacturing obtains court permission to sell some of the light trucks mentioned in the example immediately above, the issue is whether the buyer acquires them free and clear of Perpetual Motors' security interest or whether it must satisfy the secured creditor's lien to acquire clear title to the trucks. Sale of the property is subject to the rights of any other person, unless the requirements of § 363(f) regarding a sale "free and clear" of the other person's interests are satisfied.

[1] "Interests" that May be Removed by a Sale Free and Clear

Section 363(f) applies when the debtor wishes to sell estate property in which some person other than the estate also holds an interest. Most of the time, the "interest" § 363(f) refers to is some sort of a lien: a consensual lien, such as a mortgage or an Article 9 security interest;[53] a judicial lien, such as a judgment or execution lien;[54] or a statutory, common law, or equitable lien, such as a mechanics lien, a construction lien, or a tax lien.[55] In other circumstances, the other person's interest is that of a co-owner, such as a joint tenant or a tenant in common.

The more difficult question is what rights might a third party assert against the estate's property that is not the type of "interest" to which § 363(f) applies. One subject of debate is whether the trustee may sell the property free and clear of the interest of a lessee. Although it should be clear that a lessee's right to remain in possession of estate property is an interest, § 365(h)(1) expressly gives tenants the right to remain in possession after the debtor-in-possession or trustee has rejected the tenant's unexpired lease.[56] Courts have disagreed about how to resolve the apparent conflict between § 363(f), which permits such a sale free and clear of a tenant's rights, and § 365(h)(1), which permits the tenant to remain in possession.[57]

---

[53] *See* § 2.02 Consensual Liens and Other Interests, *supra*.

[54] *See* § 2.05 Judicial Liens, *supra*.

[55] *See* § 2.06 Statutory, Common Law, and Equitable Liens, *supra*.

[56] Bankruptcy Code § 365(h)(1); *see* § 11.04[A][2][b] Real Estate Leases, *infra*.

[57] *Compare* Precision Indus., Inc. v. Qualitech Steel SBQ, LLC (In re Qualitech Steel Corp.), 327 F.3d 537, 543–48 (7th Cir. 2003), *and* Hill v. MKBS Holdings, LLC (In re Hill), 307 B.R. 821 (Bankr. W.D. Pa. 2004) (permitting sale free and clear of lessee's interest), *with* In re Taylor, 198 B.R. 142 (Bankr. D.S.C. 1996), *and* In re Haskell L.P., 321 B.R. 1 (Bankr. D. Mass. 2005) (tenant may remain in possession); *see* Robert M. Zinman Fall, *Precision in Statutory Drafting: The* Qualitech *Quagmire and the Sad History of 365(h) of the Bankruptcy Code*, 38 J. Marshall L. Rev. 97 (2004); Michael St. Patrick Baxter, *Section 363 Sales Free and Clear of Interests: Why the Seventh Circuit Erred in* Precision Industries v. Qualitech Steel, 59 Bus. Law. 475 (2004).

Sometimes it is not clear whether the third-party's right qualifies as an "interest." In *Futuresource LLC v. Reuters Ltd.*, the court held that a business could be sold free and clear of a contractual obligation to provide intellectual property to a third party.[58] And in *EEOC v. Knox-Schillinger (In re Trans World Airlines, Inc.)*, the court permitted a sale of a debtor's assets free and clear of employment discrimination claims against the debtor, thus ensuring that the purchaser could not subsequently be held liable on a successor liability theory.[59] Cases such as these might instead be reasoned on a theory that the third party held no "interest" that made a sale free and clear necessary. Invoking § 363(f) might lead later courts to conclude that, like other situations where § 363(f) applies, the sale cannot be completed without providing the third party with adequate protection for its "interest," as § 363(e) usually requires.

[2] Circumstances Permitting Sale Free and Clear

The primary rules are set out in subsection (f), under which property may be sold free and clear of third party interests if one of five alternative conditions applies under § 363(f):

- nonbankruptcy law permits the property to be sold free and clear of the other party's interest;[60]
- the holder of the conflicting interest consents to the sale free and clear of its interest;[61]
- the conflicting interest is a lien, and the property will be sold for more than enough to satisfy all liens on the property;[62]
- the conflicting interest is the subject of a bona fide dispute;[63] or
- the holder of the interest could be compelled to accept a money satisfaction of the interest.[64]

[a] Nonbankruptcy Law Permits Property to be Sold Free and Clear

The most common circumstance in which applicable nonbankruptcy law permits property to be sold free and clear of a creditor's security interest is when the property is goods sold to a buyer in the ordinary course of business. In this situation, U.C.C. § 9-320(a) permits a buyer to obtain good title. Buyers usually qualify as buyers in the ordinary course of business if the seller, in this case the debtor, is in the business of selling goods of

[58] 312 F.3d 281 (7th Cir. 2002).

[59] 322 F.3d 283 (3d Cir. 2003).

[60] Bankruptcy Code § 363(f)(1).

[61] Bankruptcy Code § 363(f)(2).

[62] Bankruptcy Code § 363(f)(3).

[63] Bankruptcy Code § 363(f)(4).

[64] Bankruptcy Code § 363(f)(5).

the kind and the buyer has no knowledge that the sale to him violates the secured party's rights.[65]

[b] Creditor Consents to Sale Free and Clear

A secured creditor or another person with an interest in estate property may consent to the sale.[66] The other person may impose conditions on its consent. For example, a secured creditor may withhold consent unless the proceeds of the sale are remitted to the secured creditor, or unless its security interest attaches to those proceeds (probably making them cash collateral). In other words, the other party is likely to provide consent to a sale free and clear of its interest if the debtor voluntarily supplies adequate protection for the affected interest. Not surprisingly, however, consent need not be formal or express; it can be implied from notice of the proposed sale and failure to object.[67]

[c] Price Exceeds Aggregate of All Liens

The court may approve a sale of estate property free and clear of all interests if the interests in question are liens and the price received for the property "is greater than the aggregate value of all liens" on the property.[68] Assume, for example, that Titanic Corporation owns a parcel of real estate that it does not need for its reorganization, which is subject to two mortgages: a senior mortgage that secures a $1.5 million debt and a junior mortgage that secures a $300,000 debt. If the proposed price of the property is $2 million and thus exceeds the $1.8 million aggregate of both liens, the property may be sold free and clear of the liens. The mortgage lien creditors will, of course, either be paid out of or receive a lien on the proceeds of the sale.

Even though the language of § 363(f)(3) seems quite explicit that the sale price must exceed the aggregate amount of all liens on the property,[69] courts frequently permit a sale free and clear when the sale will generate less than enough to satisfy all liens.[70] Thus, the property still might be sold free and clear of these creditors' liens, even though the sale price was only $1.6 million. Courts reaching this conclusion apply the literal language of § 363(f), which refers to the "aggregate *value* of all liens"[71] rather than

---

[65] U.C.C. § 1-201(37) (2003).

[66] Bankruptcy Code § 363(f)(2).

[67] *E.g.*, In re Tabone, Inc., 175 B.R. 855, 858 (Bankr. D.N.J. 1994); *but see* In re Roberts, 249 B.R. 152, 154–57 (Bankr. W.D. Mich. 2000).

[68] Bankruptcy Code § 363(f)(3).

[69] *E.g.*, In re Riverside Inv. P'ship, 674 F.2d 634 (7th Cir. 1982).

[70] *See* In re Beker Indus. Corp., 63 B.R. 474, 477 (Bankr. S.D.N.Y. 1986) (interpreting "aggregate value of all liens" to refer to the economic value of the lien, rather than the face amount of the debt owed to the secured creditor); *see* George W. Kuney, *Misinterpreting Bankruptcy Code Section 363(f) and Undermining the Chapter 11 Process*, 76 Am. Bankr. L.J. 235, 244–45 (2002).

[71] *E.g.*, In re Collins, 180 B.R. 447, 450 (Bankr. E.D. Va. 1995); *see* Matsuda Capital, Inc. v. Netfax Dev., LLC (In re Netfax, Inc.), 335 B.R. 85 (D. Md. 2005).

the "aggregate amount of all debts secured by the affected property," as the language might have been phrased.[72]

[d] Lien Subject to a Bona Fide Dispute

Section 363(f)(4) permits a sale free and clear of a conflicting interest if the interest is the subject of a bona fide dispute. This facilitates the sale of estate property without the necessity of delaying the sale until after the dispute can be resolved.[73] For example, suppose Peninsula Bank has an undersecured lien on Franklin Manufacturing's equipment, but there is some dispute over whether the security agreement adequately describes the collateral. Because the lien is potentially avoidable under § 544(a), the collateral can be sold free and clear of what might turn out to be an invalid lien.

[e] Legal or Equitable Right to Compel Acceptance of Money Substitute

Section 363(f)(5) permits estate property to be sold free and clear of another party's interest in the property if the other party "could be compelled, in a legal or equitable proceeding, to accept a money satisfaction" of its interest.[74] Because of the breadth of circumstances in which a third party might be compelled to accept cash in lieu of its interest, this language has the potential to permit a sale free and clear in many situations. It is significant in this regard that § 363(f)(5) is not limited to situations where "nonbankruptcy law" would permit the other party to be compelled to accept a money substitute. Thus, the fact that a Chapter 11 plan that provides for a cash payment might be confirmed over the objection of the other party[75] makes § 363(f)(5) potentially broad enough to swallow up whatever other limits might be imposed by the remainder of § 363(f).[76] On the other hand, several courts have taken the position that § 363(f)(5) is inapplicable to liens and only applies to other interests, such as those held by co-owners of the estate's property and other similar interests.[77]

[3] Right to Adequate Protection

The fact that estate property can be sold free and clear of another party's interest, of course, does not mean that the other party can be completely

---

[72] *See* In re Heine, 141 B.R. 185, 189 (Bankr. D.S.D. 1992) (treating "value" as synonymous with "amount").

[73] *See* In re Clark, 266 B.R. 163, 171 (B.A.P. 9th Cir. 2001).

[74] Bankruptcy Code § 363(f)(5).

[75] *See* Hunt Energy Co. v. United States (In re Hunt Energy Co.), 48 B.R. 472 (Bankr. N.D. Ohio 1985).

[76] *See also* EEOC v. Knox-Schillinger (In re Trans World Airlines, Inc.), 322 F.3d 283, 290–91 (3d Cir. 2003) (permitting sale free and clear where Chapter 7 trustee could sell property free and clear in liquidation case).

[77] In re Beker Industries Corp., 63 B.R. 474 (Bankr. S.D.N.Y. 1986); In re Canonigo, 276 B.R. 257 (Bankr. N.D. Cal. 2002).

deprived of its rights. The other party is entitled to insist on adequate protection for the value of its interest in the property.[78] Buttressing this right is the prohibition against any sale, use, or lease of estate property that is inconsistent with any conditions placed on continuation of the automatic stay that a court imposed under § 363(d)(2).[79]

[4] Additional Special Protections for Joint Owners

[a] Protection of Dower and Curtesy Interests

There are a number of additional rules that deal with special situations. Section 363(g) makes it clear that regardless of any limitations imposed by § 363(f), estate property may be sold free and clear of any vested or contingent marital rights of dower or curtesy.[80] However, the affected spouse must be given a right of first refusal, to purchase the property for whatever price the proposed buyer has agreed to pay.[81] Moreover, if the property is sold to someone else, the non-debtor spouse must be paid whatever portion of the net proceeds of the sale that corresponds to his or her dower or curtesy interest.[82]

[b] Protection of Joint Tenants, Tenants in Common and Tenants by the Entirety

Section 363(h) provides additional protection for those who own interests with the debtor as tenants in common, joint tenants, or tenants by the entirety. It is designed to protect not only the joint owner's interest in the value of the property, but also the joint owner's interest in the property itself. To the extent feasible, the bankruptcy court is supposed to distribute the property in kind or to sell the debtor's interest in the whole rather than sell the entire property (including the co-owner's interest) and distribute to the co-owner its portion of the proceeds of sale.[83]

If it is feasible to split the property between the debtor and the co-owner(s), the court must do so. For example, suppose Nick is in bankruptcy, and he and his wife Nora are equal joint tenants of 100 virtually indistinguishable acres of farmland. Suppose further that these acres could readily be divided into two equal, compact halves, each half with adequate access, drainage, and water, and each half composed of equally tillable soil. Because partition in kind is practicable, the court may not sell the entire parcel in a single unit. If the parcel is partitioned, Nick's fifty acres will be sold and Nora's fifty acres will be left untouched.

---

78 Bankruptcy Code § 363(e).

79 Bankruptcy Code § 362(d)(2).

80 Bankruptcy Code § 363(g).

81 Bankruptcy Code § 363(i).

82 Bankruptcy Code § 363(j).

83 Bankruptcy Code § 363(h).

An alternative to partition is the sale of the debtor's undivided interest in the whole. Thus, the court might sell Nick's undivided interest and leave Nora's joint interest alone, so that the buyer becomes joint owner with Nora. If this form of sale would result in substantially the same amount for the estate as would a sale of the whole, then neither the trustee nor the debtor-in-possession may sell the property as a whole.

However, distribution in kind or sale of the debtor's interest alone is appropriate only where it would not impair the success of the bankruptcy proceeding. The court must sell the property as a whole, including the interest of the co-owner(s), if all four[84] of the following conditions are met:

- partition in kind between the estate and the co-owners is impracticable;[85]
- sale of the estate's undivided interest in the property would realize significantly less for the estate than sale of the property free of the co-owner(s) interest;[86]
- the benefit to the estate outweighs the detriment to the co-owner(s);[87] and
- the property is not used in the production, transmission, or distribution for sale of electric energy or of natural or synthetic gas for heat, light, or power.[88]

The constitutionality of selling the entire property, including the interest of a co-owner, has been challenged but upheld.[89]

[F] Ipso Facto Clauses

The Code generally limits the effect of so-called "ipso facto" clauses. These are provisions that place a borrower or lessee in default whenever it is in financial trouble or files a bankruptcy petition. Enforcement of these provisions would seriously impair the ability of the debtor to be liquidated or reorganize because they deprive the debtor of needed property. Moreover, if they were enforceable, nearly every commercial transaction in the country would be subject to a provision that permits the non-bankrupt party to escape the deal upon the filing of a bankruptcy petition.

Section 363(l) contains one of the Bankruptcy Code's provisions that impairs the effect of these contractual terms that might appear in a contract or lease agreement. It expressly provides that the debtor's ability to use, sell, or lease estate property is unaffected by any ipso facto clause that might otherwise apply. It also supercedes any conflicting legal rule that

---

[84] *See* In re Haley, 100 B.R. 13 (Bankr. N.D. Cal. 1989).

[85] Bankruptcy Code § 363(h)(1).

[86] Bankruptcy Code § 363(h)(2).

[87] Bankruptcy Code § 363(h)(3).

[88] Bankruptcy Code § 363(h)(4).

[89] In re Tsunis, 39 B.R. 977 (E.D.N.Y. 1983), *aff'd*, 733 F.2d 27 (2d Cir. 1984); *see* Thomas E. Plank, *The Constitutional Limits of Bankruptcy*, 63 Tenn. L. Rev. 487, 571–74 (1996).

would similarly impair the debtor's ability to use, sell, or lease estate property.[90]

[G] Rigged Sales[91]

A sale of estate assets that appears on its face to have been conducted properly may nevertheless be set aside by the trustee or the debtor-in-possession if the price was rigged — that is, controlled by an agreement among potential bidders at the sale.[92] Alternatively, the trustee or debtor-in-possession may enforce the sale but increase the price. It may "recover from a party to [the] agreement any amount by which the value of the property sold exceeds the price at which [the] sale was consummated."[93] This damage remedy may be recovered against anyone who was a party to the collusive sale, not just from the actual buyer.

A careful reading of § 363(n) reveals that it only applies to an agreement "among potential bidders."[94] Thus, it does not govern situations where the debtor enters into a conspiracy with a single buyer to control the price.[95]

Whichever alternative (avoidance or increased price) is chosen, costs, attorneys' fees, and expenses involved in the action to correct the rigged sale are also recoverable. Although the Code is not explicit on the point, it appears that these expenses may also be recovered from anyone who was involved in the bid rigging. In addition, the court has the discretion to award punitive damages against any of the bid-riggers who entered into the agreement "in willful disregard" of the applicable subsection of the Code.[96] It appears from the wording of § 363(n) that the requirement of "willful disregard" requires some knowledge or at least notice of the Code's prohibition on bid-rigging.

[H] Burdens of Proof Regarding Sales

Whenever there is a dispute over the right to use, sell, or lease property, § 363(p) regulates the burden of proof.[97] The debtor bears the burden of proof on the issue of adequate protection.[98] The party asserting an interest

---

[90] Bankruptcy Code § 363(l).

[91] C.R. Bowles & John Egan, *The Sale of the Century or a Fraud on Creditors?: The Fiduciary Duty of Trustees and Debtors in Possession Relating to the "Sale" of a Debtor's Assets in Bankruptcy*, 28 U. Mem. L. Rev. 781 (1998).

[92] Bankruptcy Code § 363(n); *see* Lone Star Indus., Inc. v. Compania Naviera Perez Compac (In re New York Trap Rock Corp.), 42 F.3d 747 (2d Cir. 1994).

[93] Bankruptcy Code § 363(n).

[94] Bankruptcy Code § 363(n).

[95] *E.g.*, Lone Star Indus., Inc. v. Compania Naviera Perez Companc (In re New York Trap Rock Corp.), 42 F.3d 747, 752–53 (2d Cir. 1994); C.R. Bowles & John Egan, *The Sale of the Century or a Fraud on Creditors?: The Fiduciary Duty of Trustees and Debtors in Possession Relating to the "Sale" of a Debtor's Assets in Bankruptcy*, 28 U. Mem. L. Rev. 781 (1998).

[96] Bankruptcy Code § 363(n).

[97] Bankruptcy Code § 363(p) (formerly at 11 U.S.C. § 363(o) (2000)).

[98] Bankruptcy Code § 363(p)(1).

in the property bears the burden of proof on the validity, priority, and extent of its interest.[99]

[I] Appeals from Orders Approving Sales of Estate Property

The Code imposes limits on the ability to effectively appeal a court's decision to permit sale or lease of estate property. To preserve rights against bona fide purchasers, the appellant must obtain a stay of the sale or lease pending the appeal.[100] Otherwise, reversal or modification of the decision does not affect the validity of the sale or lease if the buyer or lessee acquired the property in good faith.[101] For example, if the court has approved the non-ordinary course sale of Franklin Manufacturing's property to a bona fide purchaser free and clear of Peninsula Bank's security interest and the court is later reversed, the sale to the buyer is still valid and the bank can only seek redress, if any, against Franklin.

[J] Transfer of Customers' Personally Identifiable Information[102]

The 2005 Amendments amended § 363(b) to protect members of the public from inappropriate transfers of private information about the debtor's customers as part of a sale of a debtor's assets. It restricts the transfer of "personally identifiable information about individuals to persons that are not affiliated with the debtor."[103] Such information includes customers names, addresses, e-mail addresses, telephone numbers, and social security numbers.[104] The protection applies if the debtor, in connection with the sale of a product or provision of a service has previously disclosed to its customer an internal "privacy policy" that prohibits the transfer of these pieces of information about the debtor's customers. The information may not be transferred unless its sale or lease is consistent with the advertised policy or a "consumer privacy ombudsman" is appointed to represent and negotiate on behalf of the debtor's customers. Then, the court must give due consideration to the circumstances and conditions surrounding the sale, and find that the sale was not shown to violate any "applicable nonbankruptcy law" regarding the dissemination of such information.[105] The consumer

---

[99] Bankruptcy Code § 363(p)(2).

[100] *See* Fed. R. Bankr. P. 6004(g) (routinely staying orders approving the sale, use, or lease of estate property, other than those for cash collateral, for ten days).

[101] Bankruptcy Code § 363(m); *see, e.g.*, Hower v. Molding Systems Engineering Corp., 445 F.3d 935 (7th Cir. 2006) (effect of failure to obtain injunction); In re Abbots Dairies, Inc., 788 F.2d 14 (3d Cir. 1986) (regarding good faith).

[102] *See* Daniel J. Solove, *Privacy and Power: Computer Databases and Metaphors for Information Privacy*, 53 Stan. L. Rev. 1393 (2001); Xuan-Thao N. Nguyen, *Collateralizing Privacy*, 78 Tul. L. Rev. 553 (2004).

[103] Bankruptcy Code § 363(b)(1).

[104] Bankruptcy Code § 101(41A).

[105] Bankruptcy Code § 363(b)(1)(B).

privacy ombudsman must be appointed pursuant to new § 332.[106] This is similar to the mechanism used in §§ 333 and 352 to protect medical records of patients of bankrupt heath care providers.[107]

§ 9.04 Utility Service[108]

Section 366 sets out a series of special rules to deal with the debtor's utility services, such as electricity, water, natural gas, and telephone,[109] but not cable television[110] or internet services, which are not usually regarded as utilities. In most cases, these utility providers are government-run or government-regulated monopolies; it is usually impracticable or impossible for a debtor to obtain service from any alternate source.[111] Consequently, utilities are in an extraordinarily powerful position over a business debtor. A utility's refusal to deal with a debtor virtually forces the debtor to liquidate. For this reason, there are restrictions on a utility's ability to refuse or terminate service. In exchange, the utility is usually entitled to a special form of adequate protection — a deposit.[112]

Section 366(a) prohibits utilities from altering, refusing, or discontinuing service to the trustee, a debtor-in-possession, or the debtor merely because the debtor filed a bankruptcy case or because the debtor's pre-petition utility bills remain unpaid.[113] It also prohibits the utility from discriminating against them for any of these reasons — that is, it may not charge higher rates to the estate or, after the bankruptcy case is concluded, to the debtor. This is considerably more expansive than the automatic stay; the stay does not prohibit a creditor from refusing to deal, provided that refusal is not used to coerce payment of a pre-petition debt.[114] Under § 366(a), the utility's motives for refusing to deal with the debtor are irrelevant.

---

[106] Bankruptcy Code § 363(b)(1); *see* Bankruptcy Code § 332.

[107] *See* § 9.07 Health Care Providers, *infra*.

[108] Russell R. Johnson III, *Adequate Assurance of Payment for Utilities under 11 USC § 366(b): The Need for a Legislative Solution*, 4 J. Bankr. L. & Prac. 79 (1994); Richard Levin & Alesia Ranney-Marinelli, *The Creeping Repeal of Chapter 11: The Significant Business Provisions of the Bankruptcy Abuse Prevention and Consumer Protection Act of 2005*, 79 Am. Bankr. L.J. 603, 608–10 (2005); Veryl Victoria Miles, *Adequate Assurance of Payment under § 366 of the Bankruptcy Code: A Term for Interpretive Flexibility or Judicial Confusion*, 20 Akron L. Rev. 715 (1987); Bertrand Pan & Jennifer Taylor, *Sustaining Power: Applying 11 U.S.C. 366 in Chapter 11 Post-BAPCPA*, 22 Emory Bankr. Dev. J. 371 (2006); John F. Wagner, Jr, Annotation, *Debtor's Protection Under 11 U.S.C.A. § 366 Against Utility Service Cutoff*, 83 A.L.R. Fed. 207 (1987).

[109] One Stop Realtour Place, Inc. v. Allegiance Telecom, Inc. (In re One Stop Realtour Place, Inc.), 268 B.R. 430 (Bankr. D. Pa. 2001).

[110] *See* Darby v. Time Warner Cable, Inc. (In re Darby), 470 F.3d 573 (5th Cir. 2006) (cable television is not a utility governed by § 366).

[111] One Stop Realtour Place, Inc. v. Allegiance Telecom, Inc. (In re One Stop Realtour Place, Inc.), 268 B.R. 430 (Bankr. D. Pa. 2001).

[112] In re Steinebach, 303 B.R. 634 (Bankr. D. Ariz. 2004).

[113] Bankruptcy Code § 366(a).

[114] *See* § 8.02 Scope of the Automatic Stay, *supra*.

Utilities are entitled to adequate assurances that it will be paid for future goods or services that it provides to the reorganizing debtor.[115] They must be given "adequate assurance of payment [for post-petition services], in the form of a deposit or other security" within twenty days after the date of the order for relief.[116] The 2005 Amendments specify that assurance of payment may take the form of a cash deposit, a letter of credit, a certificate of deposit, a surety bond, a prepayment, or another form of security agreed upon between the parties.[117] The Code now makes it clear that giving the utility company an administrative expense priority is not enough.[118] Moreover, the utility does not need to ask for this protection; it is supposed to be offered voluntarily. If it is not, the utility may then alter, refuse, or discontinue service.[119]

However, some courts prevent the utility from demanding a deposit or other form of protection even if applicable state regulations permit the utility to do so.[120] Furthermore, the debtor's failure to provide adequate assurance of performance does not permit the utility to discriminate — it may cut off or reduce the debtor's service, but it may not charge extra. If the parties cannot come to an agreement regarding the assurance of payment, the court may, upon notice and an opportunity for a hearing, determine what is required. The nature and extent of the protection that may be required is subject to the court's discretion.[121]

Language added in the 2005 Amendments makes a Chapter 11 debtor's deadline for providing assurance of payment unclear.[122] Although § 366(b) suggests that the utility may refuse service to the debtor if the debtor does not provide assurance of payment within twenty days of the order for relief, new § 366(c)(2) permits a utility to "alter, refuse, or discontinue utility service, if during the thirty-day period beginning on the date of the filing of the petition, the utility does not receive . . . adequate assurance of payment."[123] In voluntary Chapter 11 cases, where the filing of a petition results in an immediate order for relief, it is unclear whether a utility may "alter, refuse, or discontinue" twenty days after the petition or not until

---

[115] Daniel Keating, *Offensive Uses of the Bankruptcy Stay*, 45 Vand. L. Rev. 71, 98 (1992); Stephanie A. Reday, Note, *Adequate Assurance Under Section 366:* In re Caldor, *a Step in the Right Direction*, 6 Am. Bankr. Inst. L. Rev. 235 (1998).

[116] Bankruptcy Code § 366(b); *see* Cheryl F. Anderson, Comment, *Providing Adequate Assurance for Utilities Under Section 366*, 9 Bankr. Dev. J. 199 (1992).

[117] Bankruptcy Code § 366(c)(1)(A); *but see* In re Astle, 338 B.R. 855 (Bankr. D. Idaho 2006) (new § 366(c) applies only in Chapter 11 cases).

[118] Bankruptcy Code § 366(c)(1)(B).

[119] Bankruptcy Code § 366(b); *see* In re Hanratty, 907 F.2d 1418 (3d Cir. 1990).

[120] *See, e.g.*, In re Coury, 22 B.R. 766, 768 (Bankr. W.D. Pa. 1982).

[121] Puget Sound Energy, Inc. v. Pacific Gas & Elec. Co. (In re Pac. Gas & Elec. Co.), 271 B.R. 626 (N.D. Cal. 2002).

[122] David G. Epstein, *BAPCPA and Commercial Credit: Who (Sic) Do You Trust*, 10 N.C. Banking Inst. 57, 77–78 (2006).

[123] Bankruptcy Code § 366(c)(2).

thirty days after the petition.[124] Moreover, § 363(c)(2) permits the utility to alter, refuse, or discontinue service unless the assurances supplied by the debtor are "satisfactory to the utility."[125] This appears to remove the court from the picture and place the adequacy of the assurances supplied by a Chapter 11 debtor solely in the hands of the utility.[126]

§ 9.05 Obtaining Credit[127]

Between the time a reorganization case is commenced and the debtor's plan is confirmed, most Chapter 11 debtors need additional credit. They are likely to require short-term credit, customarily supplied by utility providers and trade creditors, which is usually payable thirty days after it is extended. They are also likely to require continued financing to purchase inventory. Further, they may require long-term structural credit. A reorganizing debtor generally has to reorganize its entire financial structure, including its long-term institutional debt. For example, when Titanic Corporation reorganizes, it may need to pay existing mortgages by selling off some of its property to reduce and refinance the remainder of its debt with a lower monthly payment. It might wait to do this as part of its reorganization plan, or it might find it useful to restructure some of these debts while the case is pending.

[A] Unsecured Credit Acquired in the Ordinary Course

Section 364 governs a debtor's ability to obtain credit while the case is pending, prior to confirmation of a plan. It is structured much like § 363, which deals with use, sale, or lease of property.[128] It draws two key distinctions: (1) ordinary course debt vs. non-ordinary course debt; and (2) secured debt vs. unsecured debt. The degree of court control over the debtor's post-petition borrowing is at its nadir when the debt is ordinary course unsecured, and at its zenith when the debt is secured. The reason for this is that the risks to other creditors are generally greatest when the debtor is encumbering its assets. Secured creditors are paid first, and thus granting a security interest to one creditor increases the risk that others will eventually receive nothing. Therefore, the court should not permit the debtor to secure an obligation unless it is reasonably certain that the overall result of the transaction will benefit creditors generally.

---

[124] Richard Levin & Alesia Ranney-Marinelli, *The Creeping Repeal of Chapter 11: The Significant Business Provisions of the Bankruptcy Abuse Prevention and Consumer Protection Act of 2005*, 79 Am. Bankr. L.J 603, 608–09 (2005).

[125] Bankruptcy Code § 366(c)(2).

[126] David G. Epstein, *BAPCPA and Commercial Credit: Who (Sic) Do You Trust?*, 10 N.C. Banking Inst. 57, 78–79 (2006).

[127] Paul M. Baisier & David G. Epstein, *Postpetition Lending Under Section 364: Issues Regarding the Gap Period and Financing for Prepackaged Plans*, 27 Wake Forest L. Rev. 103 (1992); George G. Triantis, *A Theory of the Regulation of Debtor-in-Possession Financing*, 46 Vand. L. Rev. 901 (1993).

[128] *See* § 9.03 Use, Sale, or Lease of Estate Property, *supra*.

Under § 364(a), the debtor may usually obtain unsecured credit and incur unsecured debt in the ordinary course of business, without court approval.[129] No notice, hearing, or order is required for any particular transaction. Thus, management is permitted to allow the debtor's employees to show up for work the morning after its petition is filed, and those employees are permitted to turn the lights on when they arrive. Both transactions cause the debtor to incur a debt: to pay the employees' wages and to pay the electricity bill. Likewise, if the debtor customarily receives a delivery from one of its vendors every morning, incurring an obligation to pay at the end of the month for the items that are delivered, the debtor may permit these routine deliveries to continue. The resulting claims are allowed as an administrative expense and thus are accorded senior priority.[130]

The reason for this very loose rule is obvious; it would be pointlessly time-consuming and expensive for the debtor to run to court for every little credit transaction it engages in. In a single day, even a modest business might enter into a dozen small contracts with suppliers, each of which involves a brief extension of credit. Requiring approval of each would effectively kill the debtor who would be swimming in attorneys' fees. If the court is concerned that there is abuse of this power, it may enter an order imposing more stringent control over the debtor's routine transactions.

The test for whether a particular credit transaction is in the ordinary course is a two-stage test that is also applied in determining whether a use, sale, or lease of estate property is in the ordinary course.[131] The transaction is evaluated on the vertical and horizontal dimensions. The vertical test considers creditors' expectations and whether the economic risk of the transaction is different from those accepted by creditors that extended credit to the debtor pre-petition.[132] The horizontal dimension test, which some courts reject as unnecessary, considers "whether from an industry-wide perspective, the transaction is of the sort commonly undertaken by companies in that industry."[133] Some courts also apply a second test and require the loan transaction to be "actual, necessary costs and expenses of preserving the estate" as required by § 503(b)(1), to which § 363(a) explicitly refers.[134]

[129] Bankruptcy Code § 364(a).

[130] Bankruptcy Code § 364(a); *see* § 10.04[A][2] Administrative Expense Claims, *infra*.

[131] *E.g.*, In re Lodge America, 259 B.R. 728, 732 (D. Kan. 2001); In re Poff Constr., Inc., 141 B.R. 104 (W.D. Va. 1991).

[132] In re Roth Am., Inc., 975 F.2d 949, 953 (3d Cir. 1992); Vision Metals, Inc. v. SMS DEMAG, Inc. (In re Vision Metals, Inc.), 325 B.R. 138, 144–45 (Bankr. D. Del. 2005); In re James A. Phillips, Inc., 29 B.R. 391, 394 (S.D.N.Y. 1983).

[133] In re Roth Am., Inc., 975 F.2d 949, 953 (3d Cir. 1992); Vision Metals, Inc. v. SMS DEMAG, Inc. (In re Vision Metals, Inc.), 325 B.R. 138, 143–44 (Bankr. D. Del. 2005) (applying § 363(b)).

[134] *See, e.g.*, In re S. Soya Corp., 251 B.R. 302 (Bankr. D.S.C. 2001).

[B] Unsecured Credit Outside the Ordinary Course

If the proposed transaction involves a loan or other extension of credit outside the ordinary course, the transaction requires court approval[135] after notice and the opportunity for a hearing.[136] For example, if Franklin Manufacturing needs to obtain an unsecured $50,000 line of credit to help meet its payroll as it comes due, and Franklin has never had this type of credit facility in the past or such a line of credit is not customary in Franklin's industry, prior court approval is required. This is almost certainly a non-ordinary course transaction (at least, a cautious attorney for the lender will make that assumption) that requires notice and an opportunity to be heard.

[1] Administrative Expense Priority

With prior court approval, after whatever notice and hearing is appropriate, the creditor has an administrative priority claim under § 503(b).[137] However, if the debtor fails to obtain court authorization, or if there is a flaw in the notice provided to interested parties, the court may subsequently relegate the claim to general unsecured priority status.[138] Indeed, it is by no means clear that the debt is enforceable at all, as it did not arise prepetition, and was not authorized. On rare occasions, courts have retroactively validated the transaction and given the loan priority status.[139] However, creditors who provide credit outside the ordinary course, without obtaining prior court approval, do so at considerable risk.[140] Priority status entitles the creditor to full payment, in cash, on the effective date of a Chapter 11 plan[141] and entitles it to first crack at any equity remaining in the estate in a Chapter 7 liquidation. Creditors without priority usually recover a portion of their claims, but sometimes they receive nothing.

[2] Super-Priority

Unfortunately, simple administrative expense priority is no guarantee of payment. If a Chapter 11 debtor is unable to obtain confirmation of a plan and the case is converted to a liquidation case, the estate may be inadequate to make payments even to those with administrative expense priority. Accordingly, § 364(c)(1) permits the court to provide the creditor with a super-priority claim, with seniority over both routine administrative

[135] Bankruptcy Code § 364(b). This rule also applies to situations in which a trustee who is not authorized to conduct the debtor's business seeks to obtain credit.

[136] Bankruptcy Code § 102(1); *see* § 1.05[B][4] After Notice and a Hearing, *supra*.

[137] *See* § 10.04[A][2] Administrative Expense Claims, *infra*.

[138] *E.g.*, Credit Alliance Corp. v. Dunning-Ray Ins. Agency, Inc. (In re Blumer), 66 B.R. 109 (B.A.P. 9th Cir. 1986); *aff'd* 826 F.2d 1069 (9th Cir. 1987).

[139] In re American Cooler Co., 125 F.2d 496, 497 (2d Cir. 1942); In re Photo Promotion Associates, Inc., 881 F.2d 6, 9 (2d Cir. 1989).

[140] *See, e.g.*, In re Lehigh Valley Prof. Sports Clubs, Inc., 260 B.R. 745, 751 (Bankr. E.D. Pa. 2001) (refusing to supply nunc pro tunc approval of earlier loan).

[141] Bankruptcy Code § 1129(a)(A); *see* § 19.10[H] Full Payment of Priority Claims, *infra*.

expenses and the even higher super-priority claims of secured creditors whose "adequate protection" was inadequate to protect the full value of their interests in the estate's property.[142] This higher priority is available only upon a showing that the normal administrative priority is an insufficient inducement to obtain the extension of credit.[143]

[C] Secured Credit[144]

In many cases, the Code's provisions that authorize priority to unsecured credit extended outside the ordinary course are of little significance. Prospective creditors are simply reluctant to provide any unsecured credit to the debtor, even with an administrative or super-priority claim, for the simple reason that a bankrupt has great difficulty obtaining substantial unsecured credit. Those who are willing to extend credit at all to a reorganizing debtor usually want every possible personal guarantee and scrap of collateral that is available.

In recognition of this difficulty, the Code provides for debtors to acquire additional secured credit. Section 363(c)(2) permits the court to authorize credit that is secured by estate property and that is not encumbered by other liens, and § 362(c)(3) permits the court to authorize credit that is secured by a junior lien on previously encumbered property. If these steps are not sufficient to persuade a creditor to provide a loan, § 363(d) even permits the court to authorize credit that is secured by a lien that has senior priority over pre-existing liens (though the primed lienholders are, of course, still entitled to adequate protection).

[1] Granting a Lien on Unencumbered Equity

Section 364(c) permits the court to authorize a post-petition creditor to receive either a security interest on unencumbered estate property or a junior security interest on previously encumbered property.[145] Thus, if Franklin Manufacturing owns equipment that is not subject to any security interest, the court can authorize Franklin to borrow additional funds and give the new creditor a security interest on this unencumbered asset.[146] If Franklin has no unencumbered assets, a lender might be willing to extend credit in exchange for a junior lien on previously encumbered property. Thus, if Peninsula Bank holds a senior mortgage on Franklin's real estate, securing its $4.5 million claim, but the property is worth $7 million, another lender may be willing to loan up to another $2 million, and be reasonably confident that it is fully secured.

---

[142] *See generally* § 10.04[B][1] Claims for Inadequate "Adequate Protection," *infra*.

[143] Bankruptcy Code § 364(c)(1).

[144] David Gray Carlson, *Postpetition Security Interest under the Bankruptcy Code*, 48 Bus. Law. 483 (1993); Ralph C. McCullough, II, *Analysis of Bankruptcy Code § 364(d): When Will a Court Allow a Trustee to Obtain Post-Petition Financing by Granting a Superpriority Lien?*, 93 Com. L.J. 186 (1988).

[145] Bankruptcy Code § 364(c)(2), (3).

[146] Bankruptcy Code § 363(c)(2).

However, the court should be cautious about permitting the debtor's assets to be further encumbered in this fashion. If the extension of credit generates benefits above the cost of encumbering property, this step assists the estate in accomplishing its goal of successful reorganization. However, if the debtor's efforts are unsuccessful, despite the extension of new credit, the lien given to the creditor simply reduces the ultimate payout to existing creditors in a subsequent liquidation. As with grants of super-priority status, court approval for extensions of secured credit should not be granted unless the debtor is otherwise unable to obtain unsecured credit.[147]

[2] Granting an Equal or Priority Lien[148]

Sometimes it is impossible for debtors to obtain credit by giving the prospective creditor a lien on unencumbered equity. There may be no unencumbered assets and the creditor may refuse to accept a lien that is junior to a pre-existing creditor. The final and most drastic option is to permit the debtor to grant a lien that is equal with or senior to existing liens.[149] When an existing lien is subordinated in this way to a lien provided to a new post-petition creditor, the existing lien is said to have been "primed." This step presents one of the clearest conflicts between the Code's general policy of protecting existing property interests and the desire to find some means of to reorganize a debtor.

For example, suppose that Peninsula Bank has encumbered virtually all of Franklin Manufacturing's assets. Moreover, Peninsula refuses to extend more credit to Franklin and is seeking relief from the automatic stay to foreclose against all of its collateral and effectively terminate Franklin's efforts to reorganize. Sharque Investment Co., on the other hand, has offered to lend Franklin $2 million, but only if Sharque can obtain a first priority lien on Franklin's real estate and equipment (senior to Peninsula's pre-existing lien). No other potential lender is even willing to discuss the possibility of making a loan to Franklin. The debtor is out of cash and is unable to make its payroll unless it receives Sharque's loan. Failure to pay its employees will, of course, mean the certain end of Franklin's reorganization case, and will result in Franklin's converting its case to Chapter 7 or dismissing the case entirely and permitting Peninsula to foreclose.

If Franklin obtains the loan, it will likely be able to survive for at least six more months. By then, Franklin anticipates that market conditions will have improved and it will be possible to submit a suitable plan of reorganization that fully pays both Sharque and Peninsula and distributes a substantial dividend to pre-petition unsecured creditors. If market conditions do not turn around, Franklin may liquidate anyway, and its property will have continued to decline in value. This may deprive Peninsula of the

[147] Bankruptcy Code § 364(c)(1).

[148] James S. Rogers, *The Impairment of Secured Creditor's Rights in Reorganization: A Study of the Relationship Between the Fifth Amendment and the Bankruptcy Clause*, 96 Harv. L. Rev. 973 (1983).

[149] Bankruptcy Code § 364(d)(1).

value of its lien. In short, if Sharque provides the loan, Franklin has a chance to succeed but no guarantee; if Sharque does not make the loan, Franklin will be forced liquidate almost immediately.

Section 364(d) attempts to balance the interests posed by this situation by permitting but restricting the grant of equal or priority liens. As with other post-petition extensions of credit outside the ordinary course, granting a post-petition creditor a security interest with equal or senior priority to that of a pre-petition creditor requires court approval, after notice and a hearing.[150] At the hearing, the debtor must show first that the debtor cannot obtain the necessary credit in any way other than providing the creditor with the equal or senior lien it demands[151] and second that the interest of any existing lien holder is adequately protected.[152] The burden of proof that the requested priority should be approved is on the debtor.[153]

Authorization of the requested priority presents grave risks for pre-existing secured lenders. Suppose, for example, continuing with the above hypothetical, that the total value of Franklin' Manufacturing's real estate and equipment is $7 million, and that the amount of Peninsula Bank's pre-petition secured claims is $4.5 million, so even after Sharque's $2 million loan Peninsula is adequately protected by a $500,000 equity cushion. If the collateral is fully insured against casualty loss and Franklin has sufficient cash to make interest payments and cover any depreciation in the value of the collateral, both creditors are paid in full, even if Franklin's reorganization subsequently fails for other reasons. In this situation, Peninsula Bank is not harmed by granting Sharque Investment Co. a senior lien on Franklin's assets.

However, this result is based on the premise that the bankruptcy court correctly assessed the value of Franklin's property. If Franklin's real estate and equipment are only worth $5 million, granting Sharque a senior lien for its post-petition loan results in Peninsula holding an undersecured claim in any subsequent liquidation. With its new senior lien, Sharque receives the first $2 million derived from a sale of the collateral, leaving Peninsula with only $3 million for its $4.5 million debt. Section 507(b) provides Peninsula with an unsecured super-priority claim for its $1.5 million deficiency,[154] but even this is subordinate to whatever senior super-priority has been granted to someone else pursuant to § 363(c)(1),[155] as well as to the administrative expenses of any subsequent liquidating trustee in the Chapter 7 case.[156] Moreover, the debtor's assets are so heavily encumbered,

---

150 Bankruptcy Code § 364(d)(1).

151 Bankruptcy Code § 364(d)(1)(A).

152 Bankruptcy Code § 364(d)(1)(B).

153 Bankruptcy Code § 364(d)(2).

154 Bankruptcy Code § 507(b); *see* § 10.04[B][1] Claims for Inadequate "Adequate Protection," *infra.*

155 Bankruptcy Code § 363(c)(1); *see* § 10.04[B][2] Post-Petition Credit Claims, *infra.*

156 Bankruptcy Code § 726(b); *see* § 10.04[B][3] Post-Conversion Liquidation Expenses, *infra.*

that there may be no equity remaining to pay any unsecured claims, regardless of their right to priority treatment. Sharque's secured loan may have completely captured all of the priority to which Peninsula Bank had previously been entitled. Indeed, Pensinsula may prefer to extend the requested loan rather than allow Sharque to jump in front.

[3] Cross-Collateralization[157]

Among the more hotly contested debates with respect to post-petition credit is the enforceability of a security interest, authorized in connection with a post-petition loan, which secures both a post-petition and a pre-petition debt to the creditor who extended the loan. Suppose, for example, that at the time it files its bankruptcy petition, Franklin Manufacturing owes Peninsula Bank $35 million, secured by only $10 million of collateral, leaving Peninsula woefully undersecured. Assume further that Franklin needs an additional infusion of $3 million in cash to continue operating its business. Peninsula Bank is willing to loan Franklin the $3 million, but only if it receives a security interest in Franklin's other assets as collateral — not only for the $3 million post-petition loan, but also for the $25 million deficiency claim that was unsecured at the time of Franklin's petition.

Giving Peninsula a security interest for both its post-petition advance and its pre-petition unsecured claim is known as "cross-collateralization," or more specifically as "*Texlon* type cross-collateralization," after a famous Second Circuit case where the practice was first discussed.[158] The practice, though approved by some courts,[159] is controversial. Granting the lender a security interest for its pre-petition claim gives it a preference. If such a security interest were granted in the ninety days prior to the debtor's petition, it would undoubtedly be avoidable under § 547.[160] As with all preferences, it gives an advantage to a single creditor at the expense of others and thus frustrates bankruptcy's "equal treatment" policy.[161] On the other hand, the creditor's loan might make it possible for the debtor to reorganize successfully and to thus provide a substantially larger distribution to its unsecured creditors from the income it earns after its plan is confirmed.

The facts of the hypothetical described above outlines the circumstances in *Shapiro v. Saybrook Manufacturing Co.*[162] In *Saybrook*, the bankruptcy

---

[157] Jeff Bohm, *The Legal Justification for the Proper Use of Cross-Collateralization Clauses in Chapter 11 Bankruptcy Cases*, 59 Am. Bankr. L.J. 289 (1985); Charles J. Tabb, *A Critical Reappraisal of Cross-Collateralization in Bankruptcy*, 60 S. Cal. L. Rev. 109 (1987); Benjamin Weintraub & Alan Resnick, *Cross-Collateralization of Prepetition Indebtedness as an Inducement for Postpetition Financing: A Euphemism Comes of Age*, 14 UCC L.J. 86 (1981).

[158] In re Texlon Corp., 596 F.2d 1092 (2d Cir. 1979).

[159] *E.g.*, In re Keystone Camera Prods. Corp., 126 B.R. 177 (Bankr. D.N.J. 1991).

[160] *See* Chapter 15 Avoidable Preferences, *infra.*

[161] *See* § 1.01[C] Bankruptcy as a Creditor's Remedy — Equal Treatment of Creditors of the Same Class, *supra.*

[162] 963 F.2d 1490 (11th Cir. 1992).

court approved the post-petition loan, and several unsecured creditors appealed. The objecting creditors sought to stay the loan and security interest while their appeal was pending, but the bankruptcy court refused. The Court of Appeals refused to treat the dispute as moot and reversed the bankruptcy court's ruling that authorized the cross-collateralization aspects of the transaction. In reaching its decision, the court explained:

> [C]ross-collatereralization is inconsistent with bankruptcy law for two reasons. First, [it] is not authorized as a method of post-petition financing under section 364. Second, cross-collateralization is beyond the scope of the bankruptcy court's inherent equitable power because it is directly contrary to the fundamental priority scheme of the Bankruptcy Code.[163]

Thus, the creditor's lien was unenforceable, even though it made the loan in good faith, and even though the transaction had not been stayed by the court while the appeal was pending and the funds had already been distributed and spent. Not all courts take the same dim view of cross-collateralization as the *Saybrook* court. However, even courts that do approve such arrangements look closely to determine whether they are in the best interests of the creditors. For example, in the Franklin Bank example described above, the debtor agreed to grant security to $15,000,000 in return for a $3,000,000 loan. If the cross-collateralization were recharacterized as a loan initiation fee, the charge for making the loan would be a remarkable 500% of the principal amount. It is hard to believe that this would be a good deal under any circumstances. Moreover, it is difficult to believe that some other creditor might not be available to make the loan on more favorable terms. Where, by contrast, the value of the cross-collateralized assets or the amount of cross-collateralized debt could be recharacterized as a reasonable fee for initiating a risky loan, then the practice seems less objectionable.

As a practical matter, however, debtors frequently negotiate their post-petition financing facilities on the eve of the bankruptcy filing, and the post-petition lender is likely to be an existing secured creditor with a strong interest in ensuring that its deficiency gets paid. The debtor has little leverage at this moment, and no other creditors are in the room. As a result, many courts and creditors committees look closely at financing orders presented early in the case for signs of overreaching provisions. These issues are discussed in the next section.

[4] Emergency Loans[164]

The most difficult problems arise when the debtor is seeking emergency funding. In the early stages of a case, Chapter 11 debtors are frequently

[163] 963 F.2d at 1494–95 (citing Charles J. Tabb, *A Critical Reappraisal of Cross-Collateralization in Bankruptcy*, 60 S. Cal. L. Rev. 109 (1987)); *see also* Bland v. Farmworker Creditors, 308 B.R. 109 (S.D. Ga. 2003).

[164] Charles Jordan Tabb, *Emergency Preferential Orders in Bankruptcy Reorganizations*, 65 Am. Bankr. L.J. 75 (1991).

strapped for cash; yet they have immediate payroll obligations to meet, or need cash to pay for a shipment of vital supplies when they arrive, on a C.O.D basis. If the debtor does not obtain the financing necessary to meet these obligations, it may find it necessary to shut down its operations temporarily, or perhaps permanently.

In these emergency settings, providing interested parties with the necessary notice and the opportunity to be heard before the funds must be received may present an insurmountable pragmatic difficulty. Despite this, the exigence of the debtor's circumstances does not excuse the need for notice and a hearing. Further, even if the Code were amended to accommodate these emergency situations, constitutional due process requires some level of notice and the opportunity for a hearing, particularly where creditors' property interests are at stake.[165] Thus, some type of notice and some type of hearing must be supplied, even if it is only a telephone conference with the most significant creditors.

Failure to provide notice or an opportunity to be heard is a more serious problem for the creditor than are errors of judgment by the court. An attack on the adequacy of the notice and hearing is not protected by the rule that immunizes good faith transactions. Even though the creditor may have acted in good faith, that is not necessarily sufficient to preserve its rights under the credit agreement if the court failed to provide due process when issuing the order.[166]

[5] Compliance with Securities Laws

Another potential barrier to the debtor's obtaining necessary cash is the securities laws. Both federal and state law regulate the issuance of certain kinds of credit instruments. For example, a company issuing a bond that is to be publicly traded must generally comply with complex and burdensome state and federal "registration" laws that are designed to give information about the bond to the investing public.[167] These laws are not just expensive to comply with; they are also to some degree redundant in bankruptcy because the information disclosed in the registration process is generally available through the bankruptcy court, the creditors' committee, or (in a Chapter 11 case) the disclosure statement that must be made when soliciting approval of the plan.[168] There is, in consequence, a limited exemption from these laws under § 364(f). Unless the debtor is a securities underwriter,[169] § 364(f) preempts all state and federal registration laws

[165] *See* Credit Alliance Corp. v. Dunning-Ray Ins. Agency, Inc. (In re Blumer), 66 B.R. 109, 113–14 (B.A.P. 9th Cir. 1986), *aff'd*, 826 F.2d 1069 (9th Cir. 1987).

[166] *See, e.g.*, In re Ellingsen MacLean Oil Co., 65 B.R. 358, 361-63 (W.D. Mich. 1986), *aff'd*, 834 F.2d 599 (6th Cir. 1987), *cert. denied*, 488 U.S. 817 (1988).

[167] 1 Louis Loss & Joel Seligman, Securities Regulation ch. 2 (3d ed. 1989).

[168] *See* § 11.09[A][1] Court Approval of Disclosure Statement — Adequate Information, *infra*.

[169] An underwriter is a person who is distributing a security to others, rather than holding it for investment. See 2 Louis Loss & Joel Seligman, Securities Regulation 1108–10 (3d ed. 1989).

with regard to the offer or sale under § 364 "of a security that is not an *equity* security."[170] Thus, a debtor who wishes to raise cash by issuing a debt security (such as a bond or commercial paper), whether for its operations or to fund its reorganization plan, may do so without registering the security. Note, however, that this exemption does not include equity securities, such as common or preferred stock. Note too that it only exempts the debtor from compliance with registration laws. There are other securities laws — most notably, those that prohibit fraud in securities transactions — that continue to apply.

[D] Appeals of Orders Authorizing Post-Petition Credit[171]

Section 364(e) regarding appeals provides only limited protection against improvident extensions of credit. Interested parties may appeal a court's decision that approves an extension of credit on a priority, secured, or senior secured basis, but they must act promptly to obtain a stay, preventing the transaction from proceeding pending the appeal.[172] Absent a stay, any reversal or modification of the authorization or a grant of a priority or lien does not affect the validity of the debt, the priority, or the lien if the creditor extended credit in good faith.[173]

Section 363(e) goes a long way to protect creditors who provide post-petition loans in good faith reliance on the court's authorization of the loan. However, if the creditor knew that the debtor lacked statutory authority to make the loan, its reliance on the bankruptcy court's authorization may not suffice. As the court said in *In re EDC Holding Co.*:[174]

> We assume the statute was intended to protect not the lender who seeks to take advantage of a lapse in oversight by the bankruptcy judge but the lender who believes his priority is valid but cannot be certain that it is, because of objections that might be upheld on appeal. If the lender knows his priority is invalid but proceeds anyway in the hope that a stay will not be sought or if sought will not be granted, we cannot see how he can be thought to be acting in good faith.

For example, in *Shapiro v. Saybrook*, discussed above, the *Texlon* type cross-collateralization at issue was not protected by § 364(e) because the extension was deemed not "authorized" by the statute.[175]

---

[170] Bankruptcy Code § 364(f) (emphasis supplied). If the debtor wants to issue equity securities, it also gets an exemption pursuant to § 1145, but only for securities issued pursuant to a plan of reorganization.

[171] Charles Jordan Tabb, *Lender Preference Clauses and the Destruction of Appealability and Finality: Resolving a Chapter 11 Dilemma*, 50 Ohio St. L.J. 109 (1989).

[172] *See, e.g.*, In re Roberts Farms, Inc., 652 F.2d 793, 796–98 (9th Cir. 1981).

[173] Bankruptcy Code § 363(e).

[174] 676 F.2d 945, 948 (7th Cir. 1982).

[175] Shapiro v. Saybrook Manufacturing Company, 963 F.2d 1490, 1496 (6th Cir. 1992)

§ 9.06 Abandonment of Estate Property

Section 554 authorizes the trustee or debtor-in-possession to abandon estate property. Abandonment means exactly what it sounds like: the property is simply dropped from the estate and taken by either the debtor or another interest holder, such as a secured creditor. While this provision is primarily important in Chapter 7 liquidation cases, it applies across the board. The purpose of abandonment is to permit the trustee to shed property that is unduly difficult or expensive to retain or that is of such minimal value that it is not worth administering.

Section 554(a) permits the trustee or debtor-in-possession to abandon estate property "that is burdensome to the estate or that is of inconsequential value and benefit to the estate."[176] Similarly, § 554(b) permits any other party in interest to seek a court order to force the trustee to abandon burdensome or minimally valuable property.[177] In either case, there must be notice and an opportunity for a hearing.[178]

If, as is typically the case, no objection is made to the proposed abandonment after the notice is given, the court may dispense with a hearing; however, a hearing is required if there is an objection.[179]

The two substantive bases for abandonment are somewhat different. The first is that the property is burdensome; the second is that it is of inconsequential value and benefit. Although in many cases both bases are satisfied, the statute only requires one. The most common situation in which property is abandoned, arguably on both bases, is where property in a Chapter 7 liquidation case is subject to a lien that secures a debt that is greater than the value of the property. Thus, if Perpetual Motors Acceptance Corp. holds a perfected security interest in Ray's $7,000 car, securing an $8,000 debt, the trustee is likely to abandon the car if Ray files a bankruptcy petition. The same is true if the car is worth $9,000 and the debtor is entitled to a $1,000 exemption under the relevant state exemption statute. The debtor, who is undoubtedly in possession of the car, needs to redeem the car from the security interest under § 722, enter into a reaffirmation agreement with the creditor pursuant to § 524(c) (probably for the full amount of the debt), or surrender the vehicle to the creditor.[180]

In other settings, the property may be burdensome to the estate, even though there is some equity in the property. Equine enthusiasts of all types are familiar with the concept of being "horse poor." A horse-riding stable may own several horses, worth a total of $10,000 and subject to a security interest that secures a $9,500 debt. The debtor has some equity in the animals, but they cost $1,000 per month to maintain. If the stable is not earning more than $1,000 per month from the use of the horses, they are

---

176 Bankruptcy Code § 554(a).

177 Bankruptcy Code § 554(b); *see* Fed. R. Bankr. P. 6007(b).

178 Bankruptcy Code § 554(a), (b).

179 Fed. R. Bankr. P. 6007(a).

180 Bankruptcy Code § 521(a)(2)(A), (a)(6); *see* § 12.08 Retaining Collateral, *infra*.

a source of a continued loss and are burdensome to the estate and should be sold. Of course, if the horses are worth only $9,000 and cost more to maintain than the income they can produce, they are both burdensome to the estate and of inconsequential value. If they are burdensome to the estate, holding on to them is affirmatively harmful to other creditors because their maintenance depletes the estate of funds that could otherwise be distributed to satisfy creditors' claims. They should be abandoned under § 554(a).

The propriety of the abandonment may depend upon the nature of the proceeding or the point that the proceedings have reached when the issue arises. For example, while it is ordinarily appropriate in a liquidation to abandon property when there is no equity, this is not necessarily true in a reorganization setting. If the property is needed for an effective reorganization, then it does have value and benefit to the estate, even though the lien on it is in excess of the property's value and is "under water," as they say. Similarly, it may be inappropriate to abandon property at the beginning of the proceeding before the value of the property or its utility in producing income is determined. For this reason, it has long been established by the case law that the trustee may wait a reasonable time before deciding whether to abandon property.[181] In some cases, the trustee may have an affirmative duty to wait to abandon the property, especially if there is a reasonable possibility that the market price of the property will rise in the foreseeable future.

Under the Bankruptcy Act, it was often unclear whether abandonment had occurred, because it was not always necessary for the trustee to take any formal action to abandon. The Code appears to cure this problem (at least in a properly conducted proceeding) by requiring notice and opportunity for a hearing to effectuate abandonment. Subsections 554(c) and (d) also help to clarify the issue.

Subsection 554(c) specifies that, unless the court orders otherwise, all property that is scheduled but not otherwise administered by the time the case is closed is abandoned to the debtor.[182] This does not add a substantive basis for abandonment. It is always improper for the trustee to abandon property that is valuable and not burdensome. Rather, § 554(c) addresses the circumstance where property that could properly have been abandoned by the trustee has not been administered or formally abandoned.[183]

---

[181] Stanolind Oil & Gas Co. v. Logan, 92 F.2d 28 (5th Cir. 1937). Even astonishingly long periods of time may be permissible under rare circumstances. *See* In re Aldrich's Estate, 215 P.2d 724 (Cal. 1950) (twenty-five years); *cf.* Sparhawk v. Yerkes, 142 U.S. 1 (1891) (majority held that twelve years was too long; two Justices dissented, holding that the delay merely exhibited wise judgment).

[182] Bankruptcy Code § 554(c).

[183] Your authors are acquainted with a case in which the estate's principal assets were a collection of pornographic video tapes, copyrights on the works, and several telephone numbers used in the debtor's phone-sex business. The trustee was reluctant to sell the assets, despite the existence of a ready and willing buyer. The trustee was not interested in bringing a motion to abandon the assets, which had economic value to the estate. There is no end to the issues that bankruptcy lawyers sometimes must confront.

However, apart from this situation, formal abandonment is normally required. Section 554(d) makes this clear: "Unless the court orders otherwise, property of the estate that is not abandoned under this section and that is not administered in the case remains property of the estate."[184] This language applies primarily to property that was not scheduled, whether the failure to schedule was fraudulent or merely an honest error.[185] It remains a part of the estate, and, where appropriate, the case can be reopened to permit distribution of that property to the creditors.[186]

§ 9.07 Health Care Providers

The 2005 Amendments added special provisions that apply to all bankruptcy cases involving health care providers.[187] They apply to any "health care business" as that term is defined in § 101(27A).[188] These new provisions are designed to ensure the privacy of patient records, particularly in cases where the debtor may not have funds to ensure that patient's health care records are properly maintained. New § 351 requires the trustee to maintain these records for a year and to publish notice of their availability to patients and insurers in order to enable them to retrieve records to which they are entitled.[189] The trustee must then seek permission from any appropriate federal agency to take possession of these records and may (and indeed should) destroy them if no agency is willing to assume this responsibility.[190] This assures, at least, that patients' medical records are not thrown into the nearest dumpster.

The 2005 Amendments also require a bankruptcy trustee or debtor-in-possession to make a reasonable effort to transfer a closing health care provider's patients to a "an appropriate health care business."[191] This puts bankruptcy trustees in the business of finding new doctors for a failed health care provider's patients.

Accompanying these obligations is a provision that gives the trustee or any appropriate federal agency an administrative expense claim for the costs of storing and disposing of patients' records and for the costs associated with the transfer of patients to a new health care provider.[192] The Code also provides for the appointment of a patient care ombudsman, to be appointed under the usual rules in § 330 for hiring professionals. The

---

184 Bankruptcy Code § 554(d).

185 *See* § 6.02[C][2] Schedules of Debts and Assets; Statement of Affairs, *supra.*

186 In re Medley, 29 B.R. 84 (Bankr. M.D. Tenn. 1983).

187 *See* In re 7-Hills Radiology, Inc., 350 B.R. 902 (Bankr. D. Nev. 2006); In re Anne C. Banes, D.D.S., Inc., 355 B.R. 532 (M.D.N.C. 2006).

188 Bankruptcy Code § 101(27A); *See* In re Banes, No. 06-81341-7, 2006 Bankr. LEXIS 3194 (Bankr. M.D.N.C. Nov. 16, 2006); In re 7-Hills Radiology, Inc., 350 B.R. 902 (Bankr. D. Nev. 2006); In re Anne C. Banes, D.D.S., Inc., 355 B.R. 532 (M.D.N.C. 2006).

189 Bankruptcy Code § 351(1)(A).

190 Bankruptcy Code § 351(2).

191 Bankruptcy Code § 704(a).

192 Bankruptcy Code § 503(b).

patient care ombudsman is responsible for making regular reports to the court regarding the quality of patient care provided by the debtor.[193]

[193] Bankruptcy Code § 333(b).

Chapter 10
Claims and Interests

§ 10.01 Meaning of Claims and Interests; Priority

Parties other than the debtor who might assert a right to a distribution from the estate are divided into two basic categories: holders of "claims" and holders of equity "interests." "Claim" refers to the right to payment held by a creditor. It is a right based on either a debt owed by the debtor or a right to an equitable remedy against the debtor that gives rise to a right to payment.[1] "Interest," on the other hand, refers to an ownership interest in the debtor itself. In this context "interest" means an equitable ownership right in the debtor itself.[2] Such an equitable ownership interest in the debtor itself means a right to receive the residue of the debtor's estate after all creditors' claims have been satisfied. When used in this sense, the term is synonymous with "equity," and is sometimes called an "equity interest." Common examples are the rights of stockholders of a bankrupt corporation or the partnership interest of a general or limited partner in a partnership. When talking about "interests" or "equity interests," it is important to distinguish them from "security interests" which give rise to "secured claims" and represent an ownership interest in a particular asset of the debtor, or from "interest" when used to describe interest payable on a debt. The key attribute of an "equity interest" is that it does not represent an enforceable right to payment, but instead a right to a portion of the distribution of the debtor's property *after* all creditors' claims have been paid.

Claims are further divided into several additional categories. Claims might be "secured claims," "general unsecured claims" or "priority claims." A secured claim is a claim that is secured by collateral. In other words, it is a claim that is accompanied by an ownership interest in specific property of the debtor. By contrast, an unsecured claim is simply a debt, such as a contract or tort claim, owed by the debtor; the creditor has no interest in any particular property of the debtor that it may rely on if the debt is not paid. Unsecured claims are frequently also referred to simply as "general" claims. Priority claims are unsecured claims that are entitled to priority treatment, usually under § 507 of the Bankruptcy Code. Priority claims are entitled to different levels of statutory priority, with some priority claims having seniority over others.[3]

Sometimes, general unsecured claims are "subordinated." That is, their priority is lowered, so the claim is not paid until after both priority and

[1] Bankruptcy Code § 101(6).

[2] Bankruptcy Code § 101(5).

[3] *See* § 10.04[A] Priority Claims, *infra*.

general unsecured claims are satisfied. This might occur because the creditor has agreed to have its claim subordinated to the claims of other creditors, or because of some wrongdoing by the creditor that leads a court to subordinate its claim on equitable grounds.[4]

Interests in the debtor are also sometimes divided into several levels of priority. A corporation might have issued several different classes of stock, with one or more senior classes entitled to some sort of "liquidation preference." If the debtor is liquidated, such a preference entitles these stockholders to be paid ahead of those who hold only common stock.

In general, each category of claims and interests is entitled to full satisfaction before any junior category is entitled to anything. This makes priority critically important to creditors and owners. A creditor whose claim is junior to another creditor might receive nothing if the value of the assets in the debtor's estate is insufficient to satisfy the claims of more senior creditors in full. For example, unless the administrative expense claims (priority 2 claims) are paid in full, wage claims (priority 4) are paid nothing. Unless all priority claims are paid in full, general unsecured creditors receive nothing. Finally, unless the estate has sufficient assets to satisfy the claims of all creditors, shareholder's interests disappear: nothing is left for payment to holders of preferred or common stock.

For example, Titanic Industries might owe a total of $10,000,000 to a variety of creditors, including those with priority claims for the administrative expenses of handling the bankruptcy, former employees who are owed wage claims, tax authorities, and a variety of general non-priority trade creditors. If the debtor's estate is worth only $3,000,000, creditors with lower priority will likely receive nothing, while those higher on the priority ladder may be paid in full. If there are $1 million in priority administrative expenses and $2 million in priority wage and pension claims, nothing will be left to distribute to lower priority unsecured tax claims and non-priority general claims. In this situation, shareholders stand no chance of receiving anything from their ownership interests in the company.

In even a fairly simple business bankruptcy case, there might be claims and interests all entitled to different priority. Thus, it would not be unusual for claims and interests in such a case to consist of:

- Secured Claims
- Priority 2 Administrative Expenses[5]
- Priority 4 Priority Wage Claims
- Priority 5 Pension Claims
- Priority 8 Tax Claims (of several different stripes)

[4] *See* § 10.05 Subordinated Claims, *infra*.

[5] These might be further broken down, in order of priority, into super-super-priority claims under § 364(c)(1), super-priority claims under § 507(b), and priority administrative expense claims under § 503.

- General Unsecured Non-Priority Claims
- Subordinated Claims
- Interests based on Preferred Stock; and
- Interests based on Common Stock

Consumer cases are usually far less complicated, but can easily involve:

- Secured Claims
- Priority 1 Domestic Support Obligations
- Priority 2 Administrative Expenses
- Priority 8 Tax Claims
- General Unsecured Non-Priority Claims

Of course, in consumer cases, there are rarely enough assets to even begin to satisfy the most senior priority unsecured claims, making wrangling for inclusion in a class of priority claims superfluous.

The rule that claims and interests are paid according to a predetermined order that is established by the Bankruptcy Code is called the "absolute priority rule." Absolute priority governs the distribution of the estate's property under Chapters 7, 12, 13 and sometimes 11. As suggested, one distinguishing feature of Chapter 11 is that the absolute priority rule may be partially disregarded if enough claimants agree to do so.[6]

§ 10.02 Claims[7]

[A] Definition of Claim

The Bankruptcy Code defines "debt" as "liability on a claim,"[8] and in turn defines "claim" as:

> (A) right to payment, whether or not such right is reduced to judgment, liquidated, unliquidated, fixed, contingent, matured, unmatured, disputed, undisputed, legal, equitable, secured, or unsecured; or
>
> (B) right to an equitable remedy for breach of performance if such breach gives rise to a right to payment, whether or not such right to an equitable remedy is reduced to judgment, fixed, contingent, matured, unmatured, disputed, undisputed, secured, or unsecured.[9]

[6] *See* § 19.10 Confirmation of Chapter 11 Plans, *infra.*

[7] Timothy B. Matthews, *The Scope of Claims Under the Bankruptcy Code*, 57 Am. Bankr. L.J. 221 (1983); Menachem O. Zelmanovitz & Elana C. Jacobson, *The Reconsideration of Contingent and Disputed Claims Under Bankruptcy Code Section 502(j)*, 23 Seton Hall L. Rev. 1612 (1993).

[8] Bankruptcy Code § 101(12).

[9] Bankruptcy Code § 101(5).

The definition of "claim" is important for two reasons. First, most claims are entitled to receive a distribution from the debtor's estate. Moreover, in the bankruptcy hierarchy of distribution, claims get paid before equity interests. As noted above, this merely reflects a long-standing general rule that debt precedes equity. Indeed, this rule is virtually definitional, since equity is generally thought of as the residual claim against assets after debts are satisfied in full.

Second, because of the relationship between the definition of "claim" and the definition of "debt," creditors' claims are subject to discharge. If the creditor has a claim, the debtor's liability is a debt, and except with respect to several very specific exceptions,[10] debts are dischargeable.[11]

The Code has an exceptionally broad definition of the term claim. Virtually any kind of obligation owed or even potentially owed by the debtor to another is a claim. The term includes any "right to payment." The right to payment may be uncertain in amount ("unliquidated"). It may be uncertain as to ultimate liability ("contingent"). It may be disputed, and it may not even be due yet ("unmatured"). It may be secured or unsecured.[12] "Claim" also encompasses most equitable remedies by including any "right to an equitable remedy for breach of performance if such breach gives rise to a right to payment."[13]

The breadth of this definition is reflected in several key Supreme Court decisions. To the consternation of environmentalists everywhere, in *United States v. Kovacs*, the Court held that a debtor's obligation to remove hazardous waste was a claim and thus could be discharged in a Chapter 7 case.[14] In *Pennsylvania Department of Public Welfare v. Davenport*,[15] the Court departed from earlier dictum[16] and ruled that the debtor's obligation to provide restitution to the victim of his crime was a claim, even though the victim had no legal right to privately enforce the restitution order, based on the criminal judgment alone. And in *Johnson v. Home State Bank*,[17] the Court ruled that a creditor's purely "in rem" right to enforce a mortgage against the debtor's real estate was a claim, even though the debtor's personal liability had previously been discharged in a Chapter 7 bankruptcy case. In all of these cases, the Court has emphasized that Congress' intent

[10] *See* Bankruptcy Code § 523(a); § 13.03 Non-Dischargeable Debts, *infra*.

[11] *See* Ohio v. Kovacs, 469 U.S. 274 (1985) (debtor's environmental cleanup obligation was a claim and thus a debt included within the scope of the debtor's discharge); Pennsylvania Dep't of Pub. Welfare v. Davenport, 495 U.S. 552 (1990) (criminal restitution obligation was a claim and thus a dischargeable debt under now repealed provisions of Chapter 13).

[12] Bankruptcy Code § 101(5)(A).

[13] Bankruptcy Code § 101(5)(B).

[14] United States v. Kovacs, 469 U.S. 274 (1985) (state court judgment requiring the removal of hazardous waste); *see generally* Kathryn R. Heidt, *Environmental Obligations in Bankruptcy: A Fundamental Framework*, 44 Fla. L. Rev. 153 (1992).

[15] 495 U.S. 552, 562 (1990). Such claims are, however, non-dischargeable under Bankruptcy Code §§ 523(a)(13) and 1328(a)(3).

[16] *See* Kelly v. Robinson, 479 U.S. 36 (1986).

[17] 501 U.S. 78 (1991).

in framing the definition of a claim was to ensure that "all legal obligations of the debtor, no matter how remote or contingent, will be able to be dealt with in the bankruptcy. It permits the broadest possible relief in the bankruptcy court."[18]

It is common among lawyers and judges to speak of the holders of claims as "creditors," "unsecured creditors," "priority creditors," "secured creditors," and the like. However, the Bankruptcy Code does not speak in these terms. Instead, it deals not with debts and creditors but with "claims" and "holders of claims."[19] This seemingly nit-picking nomenclature clarifies that a creditor's status in the bankruptcy is based on its claim or claims, rather than on the underlying obligation owed by the debtor. For example, if collateral for a debt is inadequate to satisfy the debt in full, the creditor is treated as having two claims in bankruptcy: a secured claim to the extent of the value of the collateral, and an unsecured claim for the balance of the debt.[20] The creditor's rights in connection with each claim are quite independent of one another.

[B] Proof of Claim

Depending on the circumstances, creditors may have to file a proof of claim. A proof of claim is nothing more than a "written statement setting forth a creditor's claim."[21] Filing a proof of claim is no more trouble than completing the blanks on a simple form, indicating the name and address of the creditor, the basis and amount of the claim, whether the claim is secured or unsecured, and whether the claim is entitled to priority.[22] In cases under Chapters 7, 12, or 13, creditors must file a proof of claim to receive a distribution from the estate. As explained below, the procedure in Chapter 11 cases is somewhat different and, depending on the circumstances, creditors may not be required to file a proof of claim.

A proof of claim may be filed by a creditor or an indenture trustee acting on behalf of creditors.[23] An equity security holder is similarly entitled to file a proof of interest, reflecting its ownership interest in the debtor.[24] Moreover, the debtor, the trustee, or "an entity that is liable to [a] creditor with the debtor" may file a proof of claim on the creditor's behalf.[25]

However, in many Chapter 7 cases, there is no reason for creditors to file proof of their claims. Nearly all consumer liquidations are "no-asset"

[18] *See also* H.R. Rep. No. 95-595, at 309–10 (1977), *reprinted in* 1978 U.S.C.C.A.N. 5963, 6266–6267; S. Rep. No. 95-989, at 22 (1978), *reprinted in* 1978 U.S.C.C.A.N. 5787, 5808.

[19] Indeed, the term "creditor" is defined in the Bankruptcy Code in terms of claims: a creditor is an "entity" that has a claim. Bankruptcy Code § 101(10).

[20] *See* § 10.03 Secured Claims, *infra.*

[21] Fed. R. Bankr. P. 3001(a).

[22] Official Bankruptcy Form 10.

[23] Bankruptcy Code § 501(a).

[24] Bankruptcy Code § 501(a).

[25] Bankruptcy Code § 501(a).

cases in which the debtor's assets, if any, are exempt. With no anticipated distribution to creditors, there is no reason for creditors to submit claims, and no reason to require the bankruptcy court clerk's office to collect them. If the trustee determines that there are no assets to distribute to creditors, the bankruptcy court's notice to creditors advising them of the case will notify them there is no reason to file a proof of claim. In the unusual event that the trustee discovers assets not reflected in the debtor's schedules, the trustee will provide a further notice to the creditors, alerting them of the need to file proof of claims and establishing a deadline for these to be filed.[26]

In Chapter 11 reorganization cases, a proof of claim is deemed filed with respect to any claim listed in the debtor's schedules, unless the schedules indicate that the claim is "disputed, contingent, or unliquidated."[27] Of course, if the debtor fails to include a creditor's claim in its schedules, the creditor must file a proof of claim by the deadline established by the court. The same is true if the debtor's schedules indicate that the claim is disputed, contingent, or unliquidated. In addition, the creditor is permitted to file a proof of claim if the creditor believes that its claim is different from how it is reflected in the debtor's schedules.

On the other hand, if the Chapter 11 case is subsequently converted to a liquidation case, creditors must file a proof of claim, just as they would in any other case under Chapter 7. The fact that the case started out as an effort to reorganize the debtor does not excuse creditors from filing a proof of claim after the case is converted.[28]

The Bankruptcy Rules specify that, in a Chapter 7 or 13 case, a proof of claim must be filed no later than ninety days after the first date set for the § 341 "meeting of creditors."[29] Additional time is provided for claims held by governmental units; they have 180 days after the order for relief. The court has express statutory authority to extend the deadline for claims held by a governmental entity[30] and an "infant or incompetent person" or his or her representative.[31] Moreover, the 2005 Amendments established a special rule for Chapter 13 cases, treating a "claim of a governmental unit for a tax with respect to a return filed under [Bankruptcy Code] § 1308" as timely "if the claim is filed on or before . . . 60 days after the date on which [the] return was filed." Section 1308 is a new provision that requires Chapter 13 debtors to file any otherwise required federal, state, and local tax returns.[32]

---

[26] Official Bankruptcy Form 9 (for Chapter 7 Individual or Joint Debtor No Asset Case).

[27] Bankruptcy Code § 111(a); Fed. R. Bankr. P. 3003(b).

[28] Fed. R. Bank. P. 1019(3).

[29] Fed. R. Bankr. P. 3002(c). In Chapter 11 cases, the court sets the deadline for filing proofs of claim. Fed. R. Bankr. P. 3003.

[30] Bankruptcy Code § 502(b)(9); Fed. R. Bankr. P. 3002(c)(1).

[31] Fed. R. Bankr. P. 3002(c)(2).

[32] Bankruptcy Code § 1308. Requiring Chapter 13 debtors to file tax returns makes their failure to do so grounds, under § 1325(a)(9), to deny confirmation of their proposed Chapter 13 plan. Section 1325(a)(9) requires the court to confirm a plan only if "the debtor has filed applicable Federal, State, and local tax returns as required by section 1308."

[C] Allowance of Claims

The extremely broad definition of "claim" in § 101(5) is narrowed by § 502, which distinguishes between claims that are allowed and those that not. Claims that are allowed are entitled to receive a distribution from the debtor's estate. Disallowed claims receive no distribution.

Most claims are allowed perfunctorily. Claims are "deemed allowed" if a proof of claim is filed,[33] unless a party in interest, such as the debtor, the trustee, or another creditor, objects.[34] If there is an objection, the court, after notice and an opportunity for a hearing, determines the amount of the claim, if any, in "lawful currency of the United States as of the date of the filing of the petition."[35]

The allowable amount of a claim is that owed by the debtor "as of the date of the filing of the petition."[36] The effect of this rule is to accelerate any unmatured, contingent, or unliquidated claims.[37] Thus, even if the debtor is not in default at the time of the petition, the obligation is a claim for the full amount owed as if the claim had already matured. For example, if a debtor signed a promissory note, promising to pay $5,000 on June 1, 2010, but filed a bankruptcy petition before that date, on Oct. 15, 2007, the creditor's right to receive the $5,000 principal amount would be an allowed claim, even though it was not yet due. Any interest accumulated prior to the date of the petition would be included in the claim; however, as explained below, unmatured post-petition interest is not allowed.

[1] Contingent and Unliquidated Claims[38]

A creditor's right to receive payment is an allowed claim, even if the creditor's right is either contingent or unliquidated.[39] A claim is contingent if it does not become an obligation until the occurrence of a future event.[40] Sometimes the contingency is removed or the claim is liquidated before the bankruptcy proceeding is complete. For example, if Sam guaranteed a $1,000 debt owed by Dora but has not yet been called upon to pay the debt

[33] A proof of claim must ordinarily be filed for a claim to be allowed. Fed. R. Bankr. P. 3002(a). However, in a Chapter 11 or Chapter 9 case, if the claim is scheduled by the debtor, the filing of a proof of claim is permitted, but not required. Fed. R. Bank. P. 3003(c).

[34] Bankruptcy Code § 502(a).

[35] Bankruptcy Code § 502(b).

[36] Bankruptcy Code § 502(b).

[37] *E.g.*, In re Manville Forest Prods. Corp., 43 B.R. 293, 298 (Bankr. S.D.N.Y. 1984) ("It is a basic tenet of the Bankruptcy Code that bankruptcy operates as the acceleration of the principal amount of all claims against the debtor.").

[38] Benjamin Weintraub & Alan N. Resnick, *Treatment of Contingent and Unliquidated Claims Under the Bankruptcy Code*, 15 UCC L.J. 373 (1983).

[39] Bankruptcy Code § 101(5).

[40] *E.g.*, Mazzeo v. United States (In re Mazzeo), 131 F.3d 295 (2d Cir. 1997); In re Knight, 55 F.3d 231, 234 (7th Cir. 1995) (*quoting* S. Rep. No. 95-989 at 22 (1978), *reprinted in* 1978 U.S.C.C.A.N. 5787, 5809; *and* H.R. Rep. No. 95-595, at 310 (1978), *reprinted in* 1978 U.S.C.C.A.N. 5963, 6267).

when Dora's petition is filed, Sam's claim for reimbursement from Dora is contingent.[41] If, during the course of Dora's bankruptcy case, however, Sam is forced to pay the entire amount of Dora's debt to the creditor, the contingency is removed, rendering Sam's claim non-contingent.

Personal injury and other similar tort claims, on the other hand, are not usually regarded as contingent. Although liability may not have yet been determined, the facts upon which liability is predicated have already occurred. Of course, if the debtor has a defense, the estate enjoys the benefit of that defense and the claim is disallowed, and as such, these claims are frequently scheduled as "disputed."

Claims also might be unliquidated. A claim is unliquidated if the amount of liability depends on a future determination. If the amount of the claim is easily ascertainable, it is generally viewed as liquidated. Thus, it is liquidated if it is determinable by reference to an agreement, such as a promissory note or other contract that specifies a fixed liability, or through simple computation.[42] If its amount depends instead on a future exercise of discretion, not restricted by some specific criteria, the claim is unliquidated. Tort claims, for example, are frequently regarded as unliquidated, at least until the plaintiff obtains a judgment.

In no-asset cases, such as most Chapter 7 liquidation cases involving consumer debtors, it is not normally necessary to determine the amount of these claims. In fact, unless the estate is large enough that some distribution to creditors is anticipated, the notice sent to creditors in consumer liquidations usually advises creditors not to bother filing a proof of claim.[43] Unless there are some assets available to distribute to creditors, even the simple task of filling out a proof of claim form[44] is a waste of time.

On the other hand, if the estate has some assets, or if the case involves a reorganization of the debtor, the value and amount of contingent and unliquidated claims must be determined. Otherwise it is impossible to calculate the amount to be distributed to the holder of these claims from the debtor's estate. This is sometimes accomplished by lifting the automatic stay and permitting another court to conduct a trial to determine the extent of the debtor's liability. In other cases, this is not practical, either because of the time involved, or because there is no adequate way to measure the claim through normal litigation. In these circumstances, the bankruptcy court may estimate the amount of the claim at least for the purposes of creditors voting on a Chapter 11 plan of reorganization.[45]

---

[41] *E.g.*, Mazzeo v. United States (In re Mazzeo), 131 F.3d 295, 303 (2d Cir. 1997); In re Knight, 55 F.3d 231, 236 (7th Cir. 1995); *see also* S. Rep. No. 95-989 at 22 (1978), *reprinted in* 1978 U.S.C.C.A.N. 5787, 5809; H.R. Rep. No. 95-595 at 310 (1977), *reprinted in* 1978 U.S.C.C.A.N. 5963, 6267.

[42] *E.g.*, Mazzeo v. United States (In re Mazzeo), 131 F.3d 295, 304 (2d Cir. 1997); In re Knight, 55 F.3d 231, 235 (7th Cir. 1995).

[43] *See* Official Bankruptcy Form 9.

[44] *See* Official Bankruptcy Form 10.

[45] *See* § 10.02[E] Estimation of Claims, *infra*.

[2] Future Claims[46]

Cases involving business debtors who are liable to a large number of potential claimants raise issues about the allowability of claims by future claimants. Such cases might include victims of the debtor's defective product who have been injured but who have not yet traced the source of the injuries back to the debtor's product. They might also include those who have not yet detected their injuries. Thus, a construction worker exposed to asbestos fibers may not have yet developed symptoms of asbestosis when the manufacturer of the harmful fibers is undergoing reorganization. The problem might also arise with respect to claimants who do not use the defective product and suffer an injury until after the bankruptcy case has been closed, such as a person who is a passenger in a defectively manufactured automobile years after the manufacturer's case has been resolved.

To determine whether future claims are allowable against the debtor's estate, courts have adopted several approaches. One approach regards a claim as arising when the debtor's *conduct* that gave rise to the creditor's claim occurred, regardless of whether the creditor discovered his harm or had even been harmed when the bankruptcy case was pending. Thus, someone exposed to harmful asbestos fibers after the debtor's bankruptcy case is filed holds a claim if the debtor's manufacture and sale of the asbestos occurred before the bankruptcy case began.[47] This is the broadest of the three approaches.

A second approach depends on whether the claim is based on a relationship between the creditor and the debtor that arose before the debtor's bankruptcy case.[48] This test requires pre-bankruptcy conduct by the debtor, together with some sort of relationship between the creditor and the debtor that gave rise to the debtor's injury. If the creditor had no contact with the debtor or its defective product before the bankruptcy case commenced, the rights asserted by the creditor do not constitute a claim.[49]

The third and narrowest approach depends on whether the creditor's cause of action *accrued* under applicable nonbankruptcy law before the

---

[46] *See generally* Laura B. Bartell, *Due Process for the Unknown Future Claim in Bankruptcy — Is This Notice Really Necessary?*, 78 Am. Bankr. L.J. 339 (2004); *see also* Kathryn R. Heidt, *Products Liability, Mass Torts and Environmental Obligations in Bankruptcy: Suggestions for Reform*, 3 Am. Bankr. Inst. L. Rev. 117, 127 (1995); Ralph R. Mabey & Jamie Andra Gavrin, *Constitutional Limitations on the Discharge of Future Claims in Bankruptcy*, 44 S.C. L. Rev. 745, 752–53 (1993); Mark J. Roe, *Bankruptcy and Mass Tort*, 84 Colum. L. Rev. 846, 855–62 (1984); Frederick Tung, *Taking Future Claims Seriously: Future Claims and Successor Liability in Bankruptcy*, 49 Case W. Res. L. Rev. 435, 453, 457–58 (1999); J. Maxwell Tucker, *The Clash of Successor Liability Principles, Reorganization Law, and the Just Demand That Relief be Afforded Unknown and Unknowable Claimants*, 12 Bankr. Dev. J. 1, 55–56 (1995).

[47] *See, e.g.*, Grady v. A.H. Robins Co., 839 F.2d 198, 201 (4th Cir. 1988).

[48] *See, e.g.*, Epstein v. Official Comm. of Unsecured Creditors (In re Piper Aircraft Corp.), 58 F.3d 1573 (11th Cir. 1995).

[49] For the creditor to have an allowable claim, one branch of this test also requires the creditor's harm to have been fairly contemplated by the creditor prior to the bankruptcy. *E.g.*, In re Jensen, 995 F.2d 925, 929–31 (9th Cir. 1993).

debtor's petition was filed.[50] This frequently-criticized approach prevails only in the Third Circuit.[51]

[3] Debtor's Defenses

Claims are not allowable against the debtor's estate if they are unenforceable against the debtor or the debtor's property for any reason other than the fact that the claim remains contingent or unmatured.[52] This rule is reinforced by Bankruptcy Code § 558, which explicitly provides, "[t]he estate shall have the benefit of any defense available to the debtor as against any entity other than the estate, including statutes of limitation, statutes of frauds, usury, and other personal defenses."[53] Moreover, the debtor's "waiver of any such defense" does not bind the estate if the waiver occurred after the case commenced.[54] Thus, the estate enjoys the benefits of whatever defenses the debtor has based on any agreement between the parties or that were available under applicable law when the case commenced.[55]

[4] Interest on Claims[56]

If the debt was one on which interest accrued, either by contract or rule of law, the allowed claim includes any accrued pre-petition interest. This is limited to interest that accrued on the claim before the debtor's case commenced. However, post-petition interest, unmatured at the time the debtor's petition was filed, is not allowable on unsecured claims.[57]

Most of the time, it is easy to distinguish between principal and interest on a claim and to determine the amount of allowable pre-petition interest that accrued on the claim before the the debtor's petition. For example, if

---

[50] Matter of M. Frenville Co., Inc., 744 F.2d 332 (3d Cir. 1984).

[51] Laura B. Bartell, *Due Process for the Unknown Future Claim in Bankruptcy — Is This Notice Really Necessary?*, 78 Am. Bank. L.J. 339 (2004); Ralph R. Mabey & Annette W. Jarvis, In re Frenville: *A Critique by the National Bankruptcy Conference's Committee on Claims and Distributions*, 42 Bus. Law. 697 (1987); *but see* Gregory A. Bibler, *The Status of Unaccrued Tort Claims in Chapter 11 Bankruptcy Proceedings*, 61 Am Bankr. L.J. 145, 157–61 (1987).

[52] Bankruptcy Code § 502(b)(1).

[53] Bankruptcy Code § 558.

[54] Bankruptcy Code § 558.

[55] *E.g.*, In re Rolling Thunder Gas Gathering, Inc., 348 B.R. 803 (Bankr. D. Del. 2006) (lack of consideration).

[56] Walter J. Blum, *Treatment of Interest on Debtor Obligations in Reorganizations Under the Bankruptcy Code,* 50 U. Chi. L. Rev. 430 (1983); David G. Carlson, *Postpetition Interest Under the Bankruptcy Code*, 43 U. Miami L. Rev. 577 (1989); Chaim J. Fortgang, & Lawrence P. King, *The 1978 Bankruptcy Code: Some Wrong Policy Decisions*, 56 N.Y.U. L. Rev. 1148 (1981); John C. McCoid, II, *Pendency Interest in Bankruptcy*, 68 Am. Bankr. L.J. 1 (1994); Dean Pawlowic, *Entitlement to Interest under the Bankruptcy Code*, 12 Bankr. Dev. J. 149 (1995).

[57] Bankruptcy Code § 502(b)(2); *see, e.g.*, In re Tuttle, 291 F.3d 1238 (10th Cir. 2002); *see generally* Todd W. Ruskamp, Comment, *In the Interest of Fairness: Interest Payments in Bankruptcy*, 67 Neb. L. Rev. 646 (1988).

a promissory note provides for payment of a principal debt of $10,000 with 12% annual interest, it is a simple matter to calculate the amount of interest that has accumulated when the petition was filed. If the note was made on June 1, 2006, and the maker's bankruptcy petition was filed on December 1, 2006, six months of interest accumulated. At 12% per year (or 1% per month), simple interest of $600 ($100 per month) matured as of the date of the debtor's petition and is thus allowed as part of the creditor's claim.

However, if the stated principal amount of the note includes the interest that the parties anticipate will accumulate on the note before it is due, the amount of matured pre-petition interest needs to be calculated. Consider, for example, the claim of a creditor who makes a $10,000 loan, with the debtor agreeing to pay 12% annual interest for five years. Six thousand dollars of simple interest will accumulate over the life of the loan. The parties might prepare a promissory note calling for the debtor to pay $16,000 in equal monthly installments of $266.66, without any interest stated in the note, even though $6,000 of the $16,000 amount due is interest. If the maker of the note files a bankruptcy petition sometime during the five year amortization period of the note, the court must determine what portion of the $16,000 was interest that matured before the petition was filed. Under § 502(b)(2) the unmatured interest is not allowable as a claim against the debtor's estate.[58] Thus, the parties may not "front load" interest into the principal debt and thus avoid the limitation on the allowability of unmatured interest.[59]

There are two exceptions to the rule disallowing claims for post-petition interest. The first is of little consequence. In the unusual event that a Chapter 7 debtor turns out to be solvent, then post-petition interest is allowed on all claims, but only at the "legal rate" rather than at the agreed contract rate.[60] Because solvent Chapter 7 debtors are so rare, this rule has little practical significance.

The second exception is important. Section 506(b) allows post-petition interest to holders of over-secured claims.[61] A claim is over-secured if the value of the collateral securing the claim is greater than the amount of the claim. Thus, a $90,000 claim secured by real estate worth $100,000 is fully secured and entitled to recover post-petition interest up to the surplus value of the collateral — $10,000.

Partially secured claims do not qualify for this treatment. If the collateral for this creditor's $90,000 claim were worth only $70,000, the creditor would not be entitled to interest, even on the $70,000 that was secured. Undersecured creditors are not entitled to have post-petition interest added to their

---

[58] *E.g.*, In re Morris, 8 B.R. 924 (Bankr. N.D. Ohio 1981).

[59] *E.g.*, In re Auto Int'l Refrigeration, 275 B.R. 789 (Bankr. N.D. Tex. 2002); *see* In re Chateaugay Corp., 961 F.2d 378 (2d Cir. 1992) (regarding "original issue discount"); Craig Nemiroff, Note, *Original Issue Discount and the "LTV Risk" Reconsidered*, 105 Yale L.J. 2209 (1996).

[60] Bankruptcy Code § 726(a)(5).

[61] Bankruptcy Code § 506(b).

claims any more than creditors who are completely unsecured.[62] Furthermore, the Supreme Court made it clear in the *Timbers of Inwood Forest* case that adequate protection does not include a right to compensation for the delay in foreclosure caused by the automatic stay.[63]

Note, however, that the rule disallowing post-petition interest on claims applies only during the initial a part of a reorganization proceeding, before a plan is implemented. Interest does not accrue during the so-called "pendency period" of the case, from filing of the petition to implementation (or "consummation" as bankruptcy professionals say) of a plan. This may be anywhere from a few weeks to several years. The plan itself, however, must provide for paying interest on some claims. Secured creditors are entitled to interest on the secured portion of their claims, starting on the effective date of the plan of reorganization. Unsecured creditors are entitled to interest on the portion of their claim that represents what they would have received if the debtor had liquidated on the effective date of the plan. A fuller discussion of this aspect of reorganization is provided in the portions of this book dealing with reorganization cases under Bankruptcy Code Chapters 11, 12, and 13.[64]

[5] Fees and Expenses[65]

Most loan agreements and many other contracts expressly provide for the creditor to recover attorneys' fees and other costs incurred in efforts to collect the creditor's claim. Whether these expenses are allowable is subject to some dispute, depending in part on whether the costs and fees arose before or after the debtor's petition, whether the claim is fully secured, and on the inferences to be drawn from the language of §§ 502(b)(2) and 506(b).

[a] Pre-Petition Costs and Attorneys Fees[66]

It would seem as if the allowability of claims for pre-petition costs of collection and attorneys' fees should follow the general rule — that is, they should be disallowed if they would not have been recoverable under applicable non-bankruptcy law and allowed if they would have been recoverable against the debtor outside of bankruptcy. The general American rule is that attorneys' fees are not recoverable unless they are expressly

---

[62] United Sav. Ass'n v. Timbers of Inwood Forest, 484 U.S. 365, 372–73 (1988); Ford Motor Credit Co. v. Dobbins, 35 F.3d 860 (4th Cir. 1994).

[63] United Sav. Ass'n v. Timbers of Inwood Forest, 484 U.S. 365, 372–73 (1988).

[64] *See* § 18.08[E] Present Value, *infra*; § 19.10[F] Best Interests of Creditors, *infra*; § 20.08 Confirmation of Chapter 12 Plans, *infra*.

[65] David Gray Carlson, *Oversecured Creditors Under Bankruptcy Code Section 506(b): The Limits of Postpetition Interest, Attorneys' Fees, and Collection Expenses*, 7 Bankr. Dev. J. 381, 407–12 (1990).

[66] George Singer, *Section 506(b) and the Oversecured Creditor's Right to Recover Fees: A Matter of Right under "Federal" Law?*, 16 Am. Bankr. Inst. L. Rev. 1 (1997).

provided for by agreement or expressly recoverable under an applicable statute.[67]

Thus, the allowability of pre-petition collection costs and attorneys' fees depends initially on whether the creditor would have been entitled to recover these expenses and fees under relevant non-bankruptcy law.[68] This is consistent with § 502(b)(1), which subrogates the debtor's estate to whatever defenses the debtor might have raised outside of bankruptcy court.[69] If state or other applicable non-bankruptcy law denies the creditor the right to recover these costs and fees, they should not suddenly be available because the debtor has filed a bankruptcy petition.

Language in § 506(b) that limits the allowability of fully secured creditor's claims for post-petition collection costs and attorneys' fees to those that are "reasonable" has led some courts to impose a federal bankruptcy standard of reasonableness on any pre-petition fees, regardless of whether the fees would have been recoverable under applicable state law.[70] However, most courts have drawn a different conclusion, noting that § 502 is silent about any such limit on pre-petition claims for attorneys' fees[71] other than those the debtor owes to its own attorney.[72]

[b] Post-Petition Costs and Attorneys' Fees for Fully Secured Claims

Section 506(b) explicitly permits fully secured creditors to maintain a claim for both post-petition interest and "any reasonable fees, costs, or charges provided for under the agreement or State statute under which such claim arise."[73] Most courts hold that this language pre-empts state law rules dealing with the enforceability of agreements that provide for a creditor's recovery of these types of expenses, and that the "reasonableness" of the expenses under § 506(b) is the only standard by which the allowability of these expenses should be measured, at least to the extent of the value of the collateral.[74]

A creditor with an allowable $10,000 pre-petition claim, secured by property worth $12,000, is entitled to up to $2,000 in accumulated reasonable post-petition fees, costs, or charges — if those fees, costs and charges were either provided for in the parties' agreement or recoverable under an applicable *state* statute.[75] Thus, recovery of post-petition interest is

---

[67] *See generally*, *Symposium on Fee Shifting*, 71 Chi.-Kent L. Rev. 415–697 (1995).

[68] *E.g.*, Thrifty Oil Co. v. Bank of Am. Nat'l Trust and Sav. Ass'n, 322 F.3d 1039 (9th Cir. 2003); Blair v. Bank One, N.A., 307 B.R. 906 (N.D. Ill. 2004).

[69] Bankruptcy Code § 502(b)(1); *see* § 10.02[C][3] Debtor's Defenses, *supra*.

[70] Welzel v. Advocate Realty Inv., LLC (In re Welzel), 275 F.3d 1308 (11th Cir. 2001).

[71] *E.g.*, In re Nunez, 317 B.R. 666 (Bankr. E.D. Pa. 2004) (collecting cases).

[72] *See* § 10.02[D][4] Limits on Claims of Insiders, *infra*.

[73] Bankruptcy Code § 506(b).

[74] *E.g.*, Welzel v. Advocate Realty Inv., LLC (In re Welzel), 275 F.3d 1308, 1313–16 (11th Cir. 2001).

[75] United States v. Ron Pair Enters., Inc., 489 U.S. 235, 241 (1989).

unqualified, but recovery of fees, costs, and charges is allowed only if they are reasonable and if they were provided for either in a consensual agreement or an applicable state statute.[76]

Prior to the 2005 Amendments, § 506(b) referred only to reasonable fees, costs, and charges that are provided for in the parties' agreement. Language referring to an applicable state statute was added in 2005. The new language overrules decisions that denied fully secured creditors a claim for post-petition interest, costs, and fees where they were recoverable under a state statute, but not by an agreement between the parties.[77] This language permits fully secured state tax authorities to recover post-petition interest and costs if permitted to do so by state statute.[78] Significantly, there is no explanation for the conspicuous absence of a reference to amounts that may be recoverable under a *federal* statute. The principal impact of this absence is to deny post-petition interests, costs, & attorneys' fees to fully secured federal tax claims and to fully secured private claims under federal statutes that permit the recovery of such costs and fees.

[c] Post-Petition Costs and Attorneys' Fees for Unsecured and Partially Secured Claims[79]

The conspicuous absence of language in the Code allowing post-petition fees and costs for other kinds of claims, would seem to make it clear that creditors with partially secured or unsecured claims are not entitled to post-petition fees and expenses. However, some courts have drawn a contrary conclusion. The pre-Code decision *In re United Merchants and Manufacturers*[80] permitted an unsecured creditor to recover post-petition fees under statutory language identical to that in the current Code. Other courts have rejected this conclusion,[81] but the Supreme Court has not yet resolved the conflict.

[D] Limits on Allowance of Claims

The Code contains several specific provisions that limit the allowance of some specific claims.[82] These limitations address two potential problems.

---

[76] Rushton v. State Bank (In re Gledhill), 164 F.3d 1338, 1342 (10th Cir. 1999).

[77] *E.g.*, In re Nunez, 317 B.R. 666, 669 (Bankr. E.D. Pa. 2004).

[78] *See* Jo Ann C. Stevenson & Charles E. Consalus, *Taxing Authorities, Section 506(b) and the "Curious Comma"*, 61 Am. Bankr. L.J. 275 (1987) (discussing § 506(b) prior to the 2005 Amendments).

[79] James Gadsden, *Recovery of Attorney Fees as an Unsecured Claim*, 114 Banking L.J. 594 (1997); Liore Z. Alroy & J. Michael Mayerfeld, Note, *Contracted-For Post-Petition Attorneys' Fees and Collection Costs:* United Merchants *Revisited*, 1992 Colum. Bus. L. Rev. 309.

[80] 674 F.2d 134 (2d Cir. 1982).

[81] Pride Cos. L.P. v. Johnson (In re Pride Cos., L.P.), 285 B.R. 366, 370–73 (Bankr. N.D. Tex. 2002) (collecting cases).

[82] These limitations only apply if an objection is made. In the absence of an objection, a claim is equal to the amount stated in the proof of claim. Bankruptcy Code § 502(a).

First, some claims are so large that their allowance might deprive other claimants of a meaningful share in the meager proceeds of the estate. Second, some claims may be unusually large because the claim may include damages that were expected to accrue over a long period of time, and may not take into account mitigation that might occur after the claim was allowed; the claimant is allowed to ask for damages without regard to whether those damages could have been avoided.

[1] Claims for Rent[83]

The Bankruptcy Code imposes a cap on the claim of a lessor of real property for unpaid future rent. Because of the duration of some real estate leases, such claims might be overwhelming, particularly if they are not limited by state law imposing a duty on the lessor to mitigate its damages. More importantly, it is not likely that the property will remain unrented for the entire remaining term on the lease. For example, imagine a lease that, at the time of rejection, had fifteen years to run, at a rate of $50,000 per year. The unpaid rent on the lease would be $750,000. However, if the space was actually relet two years after the debtor vacated, the actual damages would be only $100,000. It is not practical for the trustee to wait until all of the various landlords have relet their space. Instead, the Code takes a standardized approach. A landlord's claim for breach of a real estate lease cannot exceed the sum of any past due rent plus the greater of one year's rent or 15% of the remaining rent on the lease, but in no event can the claim exceed three years' post-petition rent.[84]

Suppose that at the time of the bankruptcy that the debtor was a lessee under a long-term real estate lease that had twenty-five years remaining. If the lessor were able to make a claim for all of the unpaid future rent, the amount of the claim might reduce all the other claims to insignificant proportions. Thus, § 502(b)(6) limits the lessor's claim to whatever amounts the debtor already owed for past-due rent, plus rent due for three years of the twenty-five years remaining on the term of the lease.[85] If the remaining term had been only fifteen years, the landlord would be entitled to the past-due rent, plus rent due for 15% of the remaining fifteen years (twenty-seven months).

The landlord cannot avoid the impact of these limits by attempting to accelerate the tenant's obligation to pay rent. Section 502(b)(7) specifically addresses this possibility and provides that the amount of the allowable claim for "unpaid rent due under [the] lease [is to be calculated] without acceleration."[86]

---

[83] Thomas McIntyre Devaney, Comment, Klein Sleep *Decision: Section 502(b)(6) Lease Damages Cap as the Rule, Not the Exception*, 4 Am. Bankr. Inst. L. Rev. 557 (1996).

[84] Bankruptcy Code § 502(b)(6).

[85] Fifteen percent of the remaining twenty-five years is three years and nine months, which is greater than one year, but there is a three-year cap on the duration of the remaining term for which a claim may be allowed.

[86] Bankruptcy Code § 502(b)(6).

If the lessor has mitigated damages, the claim may be limited further, based on any defenses the debtor has under state property law.[87] However, the traditional common law rule did not require the lessor to seek a new tenant. Although most states have abandoned this archaic rule, § 502(b)(6) further limits the effect of this rule in jurisdictions where it has not been changed.[88]

[2] Limit on Claims for Salaries

Section 502(b)(7) imposes a limit on the allowability of claims by employees for damages resulting from termination of an employment contract.[89] Such claims are allowable only for wages owed to the employee for up to one year after the debtor's termination or the debtor's petition, whichever is earlier,[90] plus any past-due wages prior to that time.[91] Thus, an employee who is wrongfully terminated one month before the debtor's petition is filed, in the middle of a three-year employment contract, has a claim only for salary owed to her for work completed at the time of her termination, together with a claim for wages to which she was entitled for one year after she is let go, rather than wages for the entire contract.

Most employees are likely to be at-will employees with very limited claims for wages. Other employees, particularly highly-paid executives, may have long-term employment contracts that would result in sizeable claims without these limits. In addition, these employees, who may also have equity interests in the debtor, might otherwise be tempted to try to cause their employers to enter into long-term employment contracts immediately prior to bankruptcy in an effort to capture additional value from the business as a creditor. Thus, § 502(b)(8) effectively prevents an executive employee from obtaining a sizeable claim against the estate and possibly considerable voting rights over the debtor's plan by causing her employer to enter into a twenty-year employment contract with her immediately before bankruptcy. It should also be noted that all or a part of an employee's allowable wage claim may be entitled to priority under § 507(a)(4), discussed below.[92]

[3] Limits on Property Tax Claims

Property tax claims are allowable only to the extent of the value of the estate's interest in the property.[93] If real property worth $40,000 has been

---

[87] Bankruptcy Code §§ 502(b)(11) & 558.

[88] *E.g.*, Stonehedge v. Square Ltd. P'ship v. Movie Merchants, Inc., 715 A.2d 1082 (Pa. 1998); Christopher Vaeth. Annotation, *Landlord's Duty, on Tenant's Failure to Occupy, or Abandonment of, Premises, to Mitigate Damages by Accepting or Procuring Another Tenant*, 75 A.L.R.5th 1 (2000).

[89] Bankruptcy Code § 502(b)(7).

[90] Bankruptcy Code § 502(b)(7)(A).

[91] Bankruptcy Code § 502(b)(7)(B).

[92] *See* § 10.04[B][4] Wage Claims, *infra*.

[93] Bankruptcy Code § 502(b)(3).

assessed with real estate taxes of $50,000, only $40,000 of the claim is allowed. This limit effectively treats property taxes as non-recourse claims, collectable only against the property subject to the tax. As explained below, allowable property tax claims may be entitled to priority under § 508(a)(8)(B). However, the claim must be allowable to qualify for priority treatment.

[4] Limits on Claims of Insiders

Claims for services of insiders, such as close relatives and other affiliates of the debtor,[94] are allowable only to the extent the claim is for the reasonable value of the services supplied by the insider.[95] The same rule applies to claims held by the debtor's attorney.[96] Note that this limit is not related to the similar limit imposed by Bankruptcy Code § 329 with respect to services supplied by the debtor's attorney in connection with the case.

[5] Unmatured Support Claims

Past-due support is an allowable claim.[97] Moreover, in most cases, support is entitled to high priority under § 507(a)(1).[98] However, support payments not yet due when the debtor's petition is filed are generally not allowed. Section 502(b)(2) prevents allowance of unmatured and non-dischargeable domestic support obligations.[99] Rather than receiving a distribution from the debtor's estate, the child, former spouse, or other support claimant must rely on the fact that his or her claim is non-dischargeable. These creditors are relegated to whatever remedies they have in state court to recover post-petition support that the debtor fails to pay from his post-petition earnings. Moreover, because the automatic stay does not restrict a support claimant's ability to recover support from the debtor's earnings that are not included in the debtor's estate,[100] a support claimant might be able to pursue both her pre-petition and post-petition support claims in state court, while the debtor's bankruptcy case is pending.

Consider, for example, a Chapter 7 debtor who at the time of his petition owes $3,000 to his former spouse for an unpaid past-due domestic support obligation. After the case commences, the debtor further defaults on his duty to pay support at the rate of $1,000 per month. The $3,000 pre-petition support obligation is a fully allowable claim for which the receiving spouse is entitled to priority under § 507(a)(1).[101] Support beyond this amount that

---

[94] Bankruptcy Code § 101(31).

[95] Bankruptcy Code § 502(b)(4).

[96] Bankruptcy Code § 502(b)(4). Some lawyers may view this as a most regrettable provision.

[97] Bankruptcy Code § 502(a).

[98] Bankruptcy Code § 507(a)(1). The priority of past-due support obligations is somewhat complicated. *See generally* § 10.04[A][1] Support Claims, *infra*.

[99] Bankruptcy Code § 502(b)(5). For an explanation of the non-dischargeability of domestic support obligations, see§ 13.03[B][5][a] Domestic Support Obligations, *infra*.

[100] Bankruptcy Code § 362(b)(2)(B)-(C).

[101] *See* § 10.04[A][1] Support Claims, *infra*.

does not mature until after the debtor's petition is filed is neither allowable under § 502 nor entitled to priority under § 507. On the other hand, any portion of the past-due support that is not paid from the debtor's estate remains non-dischargeable.[102] Future support is similarly non-dischargeable. Thus, the receiving spouse will be able to recover these amounts from the debtor in the future. Moreover, because of the limited scope of the automatic stay, the receiving spouse is permitted to garnish the debtor's post-petition earnings to the extent permitted by state law, even while the debtor's bankruptcy case is pending.

[6] Disallowance of Late Claims

Section 502(b)(9) specifies the effect of a tardily filed proof of claim.[103] The claim of a creditor who fails to file a timely proof of claim is completely disallowed, except to the extent expressly permitted by either § 726(a)(1)-(3)[104] or by the Bankruptcy Rules.[105] The Code's language to this effect overruled a series of earlier cases[106] that permitted tardily filed priority claims to share in the distribution of the debtor's estate, despite the creditor's failure to file timely claim.[107] After the 1994 Amendments, late-filed claims are entitled to share in the distribution of a Chapter 7 estate, but these tardily filed claims are subordinated to claims of the same class that were timely filed.

[7] Unsecured Consumer Debts

In 2005, Congress added complicated language that permits the bankruptcy court to penalize recalcitrant creditors for failing to cooperate with the efforts of a credit counseling agency to restructure a consumer debtor's obligations. New § 502(k) permits the court to "reduce a claim . . . based in whole on an unsecured consumer debt"[108] by up to 20% of the claim if the creditor who asserts the claim "unreasonably refused to negotiate a reasonable alternative payment schedule proposed . . . by an approved nonprofit budget and credit counseling agency."[109] Congress' apparent belief that the threat of having their claims reduced by up to 20% if creditors unreasonably fail to renegotiate the terms of consumer debts overlooks the harsh reality that distributions to creditors in consumer liquidation cases are almost unheard of. Because distributions to unsecured creditors in Chapter 7 proceedings are so rare, § 502(k) may pose an empty threat to

[102] *See* § 13.03[B][5][a] Domestic Support Obligations, *infra.*

[103] Bankruptcy Code § 502(b)(9) (2000).

[104] *See* § 17.09 Distribution of Estate Property, *infra.*

[105] Bankruptcy Code § 502(b)(9).

[106] *E.g.,* United States v. Vecchio (In re Vecchio), 20 F.3d 555 (2d Cir. 1994); In re Hausladen, 146 B.R. 557 (Bankr. D. Minn. 1992).

[107] *See* Uwimana v. Government of Rwanda (In re Uwimana), 284 B.R. 218 (D. Md. 2002); Gregory G. Hesse, *Time Limitations for Objecting to Claims: Interplay Between Sections 502(d) and 546(a) of the Bankruptcy Code*, 26 St. Mary's L.J. 87 (1994).

[108] Bankruptcy Code § 101(8).

[109] Bankruptcy Code § 502(k)(1).

unsecured creditors such as credit card companies and health care providers. This limits the practical impact of § 502(k) to creditors' claims in cases under Chapter 13 and to creditors with secured claims.

There are several important limitations in § 502(k) that further impair its utility. First, it only applies if the proposed repayment plan is "made at least 60 days before the date of the filing of the petition."[110] Thus, it can only be invoked by a debtor who is willing to wait at least two months after her proposal is submitted to a creditor before filing her bankruptcy petition. Debtors who seek the assistance of a credit counseling agency in a last-ditch effort to avoid an impending bankruptcy will find § 502(k) unhelpful.

Second, the potential reduction in the amount of the claim only applies if the terms proposed on the debtor's behalf provide for payment of at least 60% of the debt "over a period not to exceed either the repayment period of the loan or a reasonable extension of that period." It is entirely unclear what a reasonable extension might be, particularly for the type of uninsured medical debts that many debtors owe, which are due immediately. How this rule might apply to credit card debts, which are payable over a period of seemingly unlimited years,[111] can only be surmised.

Third, the reduction can only be invoked by the debtor.[112] Other creditors who might have an incentive to pursue the motion lack standing. And debtors, the only ones with standing to bring the matter to the court's attention, have little incentive to do so. In a typical Chapter 7 case in which no assets are available to distribute to creditors, reducing the creditor's claim neither benefits the debtor nor harms the creditor. Even if there are assets to distribute in the Chapter 7 case, the reduction of the claim harms the creditor vis-a-vis other creditors, but does not free up assets for the debtor, or in any way change the nature of the debtor's fresh start.

In a Chapter 13 case, where the debtor submits her disposable income to satisfy creditors' claims, the debtor's only incentive to move to reduce the creditor's claim is the personal satisfaction the debtor may enjoy at the prospect of punishing the creditor's intransigent conduct. Given the strident new standards for the amount of income debtors must contribute toward

---

[110] Bankruptcy Code § 502(k)(1)(B)(i).

[111] The minimum payments required by many credit card companies are so low (typically around 4% of the principal balance, or $10, whichever is higher), it might take many years to fully amortize a credit card debt of several thousand dollars. A monthly 4% minimum payment on a $1000 credit card debt bearing interest at 18% per year, would require eighty-seven months (7.25 years) to fully amortize the debt. *See* http://www.bankrate.com/brm/calc/MinPayment.asp (last viewed on Sept. 1, 2006). If the debt were $3,000, payment of the debt would take 130 months. Until mid-2005, when the United States Office of Comptroller required banks to increase the minimum payments required to be made, a 2% minimum payment was the norm. At this level, the $1,000 debt would have taken 232 months (nearly twenty years) to pay in full. With interest accumulating at 1.5% per month ($15), the lion's share of the payment would be attributable to interest, with only .005% of the $1,000 balance ($5) being paid each month.

[112] Bankruptcy Code § 502(k)(1).

their Chapter 13 plans, it is unlikely that many debtors will be willing to contribute some of their limited remaining income to pay an attorney to pursue a motion under § 502(k).

Finally, the rare debtor who invokes § 502(k) in an effort to reduce the size of a creditor's claim is likely to find it difficult to prevail. The reduction only applies if the creditor "unreasonably refused to negotiate a reasonable alternative repayment schedule." Matters that must be litigated include whether the creditor's actions constituted a "refusal," whether any refusal was "unreasonable," and whether the alternative repayment schedule proposed by the debtor was "reasonable." The debtor has the burden of proof on the issue of whether the creditor's refusal to negotiate was unreasonable.[113] In addition, the reduction does not apply at all if any "part of the debt under the alternative repayment schedule is nondischargeable."[114] This last limitation could turn the debtor's motion into a full-blown dispute over the dischargeability of the debt, which may be an issue the debtor is likely to want to avoid putting on the table. Moreover, the statutory language is ambiguous concerning the meaning of "based in whole on an unsecured debt."

These impediments are likely to result in few motions pursuant to § 502(k), making its inclusion in the Code an empty threat.

[E] Estimation of Claims[115]

Taking the time to determine the amount of unliquidated or contingent claims through the usual mechanism of a full-blown trial could delay the administration of a debtor's estate. Likewise, it may be difficult for a court to calculate the amount of payment that may be appropriate compensation for the loss of a "right to an equitable remedy for breach of performance."[116] Consequently, in these circumstances, the bankruptcy court must sometimes estimate the amount of the creditor's claim.[117] The claim might be estimated merely for the purpose of voting on a plan of reorganization, or to finally determine the allowed amount of the claims for the purpose of distribution of the estate.

The court has wide discretion to use a variety of mechanisms to estimate claims.[118] It may not deviate from the legal rules governing the claim, but it is otherwise permitted to estimate the claim by whatever procedures are

---

[113] Bankruptcy Code § 502(k)(2)(A).

[114] Bankruptcy Code § 502(k)(1)(C).

[115] Francis E. Goodwyn, *Claims Estimation and the Use of the "Cleanup Trust" in Environmental Bankruptcy Cases*, 9 Am. Bankr. Inst. L. Rev. 769 (2001); See Barbara J. Houser, *Chapter 11 as a Mass Tort Solution*, 31 Loy. L.A. L. Rev. 451 (1998); David S. Salsburg & Jack F. Williams, *A Statistical Approach to Claims Estimation in Bankruptcy*, 32 Wake Forest L. Rev. 1119 (1997)..

[116] Bankruptcy Code § 502(c)(2).

[117] Bankruptcy Code § 502(c)(1).

[118] *See* In re Windsor Plumbing Supply Co., 170 B.R. 502 (Bankr. E.D.N.Y. 1994).

best suited to the circumstances.[119] Methods used by courts have "run the gamut from summary trials to full-blown evidentiary hearings to a mere review of pleadings, briefs, and a one-day hearing involving oral argument of counsel,"[120] to arbitration.[121]

The process of estimating unliquidated claims may be particularly important in bankruptcy cases involving mass tort claims.[122] In cases like *In re A.H. Robins, Inc.*,[123] which involved a defective and widely distributed intrauterine birth control device, and *In re Johns-Manville Corp.*,[124] which involved millions of asbestos claims, the court may be called upon to estimate not only the amount of pre-existing claims, but also to estimate the amount of claims held by victims who had no symptoms of their injuries at the time of the bankruptcy. These "future" claims present the court with two relatively unappetizing propositions. The court can treat the claims as arising pre-petition (because the conduct which gives rise to the claim occured pre-petition), and allow the claims to be discharged, even though the claimants don't yet know that their interests are implicated, or the court can deem the claims "post-petition." If the debtor liquidates, there is little difference, because once the assets are distributed, there will be nothing left to pay the future claimants. However, if the debtor reorganizes, one result leaves the future claimants with nothing. The other leaves them with a windfall, at least as compared to other tort claimants, in that they will get paid in full out of the reorganized debtor. The first approach encourages reorganization. The second makes it impossible for a reorganizing debtor to deal with possibly crushing tort liability in Chapter 11.

The courts are divided. Indeed, a court may appoint a guardian for future claimants to assure that these claimants are represented. In the Dalkon Shield case, the court appointed a representative for the future claimants, but allowed their claims to be discharged.[125] By contrast, in the *Piper Aircraft* case, the court held that the claims of creditors who had no relationship with the debtor at the time of the bankruptcy, and therefore

[119] In re Brints Cotton Mktg., Inc., 737 F.2d 1338 (5th Cir. 1984).

[120] In re Windsor Plumbing Supply Co., 170 B.R. 503, 520 (Bankr. E.D.N.Y. 1994).

[121] In re Seaman Furniture Co. of Union Square, Inc., 160 B.R. 40 (S.D.N.Y. 1993).

[122] Georgene Vairo, *Mass Torts Bankruptcies: The Who, The Why and The How*, 78 Am. Bankr. L.J. 93 (2004); *see* § 23.01 Mass Tort Claims, *infra*.

[123] *See* Grady v. A.H. Robins Co. (In re A.H. Robins Co.), 839 F.2d 198 (4th Cir.), *cert. dismissed*, 487 U.S. 1260 (1988); Georgene M. Vairo, Georgine, *The Dalkon Shield Claimants Trust, and the Rhetoric of Mass Tort Claims Resolution*, 31 Loy. L.A. L. Rev. 79, 154 (1997).

[124] In re Johns-Manville Corp., 57 B.R. 680 (Bankr. S.D.N.Y. 1986); *see generally* Alan Resnick, *Mass Torts: Bankruptcy as a Vehicle for Resolving Enterprise-Threatening Mass Tort Liability*, 148 U. Pa. L. Rev. 2045 (2000); *see also* National Bankr. Rev. Comm'n, Bankruptcy: The Next Twenty Years: National Bankruptcy Review Commission Final Report 316 (1997); Thomas A. Smith, *A Capital Markets Approach to Mass Tort Bankruptcy*, 104 Yale L.J. 367, 369 (1994).

[125] Grady v. A.H. Robins Co. (In re A.H. Robins Co.), 839 F.2d 198 (4th Cir.), *cert. dismissed*, 487 U.S. 1260 (1988).

no basis to know that they had a claim that was being discharged, could not be bound by the debtor's discharge.[126]

§ 10.03 Secured Claims[127]

The Bankruptcy Code distinguishes between secured claims and unsecured claims. Creditors with secured claims have senior priority over the estate's assets. Moreover, they are entitled to have their interests in the debtor's property adequately protected while the case is pending. Because of the primacy accorded to secured claims, drawing the distinction between secured claims, partially secured claims, and unsecured claims is a critical part of most bankruptcy cases.

[A] Creditors with Secured Claims

A secured claim is simply a claim that is coupled with some interest in the debtor's property. The mere fact that a debtor owes money to a creditor does not mean that the creditor has an interest in the debtor's specific assets.[128] Creditors have no interest in a debtor's property unless the creditor has acquired a lien[129] or other interest in the debtor's property to secure the debtor's obligation.

A creditor's claim is secured only if the creditor obtains an interest in the debtor's property to secure payment or performance of the creditor's claim. Creditors might acquire a secured claim in several ways. They might obtain a mortgage or security interest in the debtor's property by agreement with the debtor (consensual liens).[130] Alternatively, they might have obtained a judgment or execution lien on the debtor's property through judicial process (judicial liens).[131] In addition, some creditors are favored

---

[126] Epstein v. Official Comm. of Unsecured Creditors (In re Piper Aircraft Corp.), 58 F.3d 1573 (11th Cir. 1995). Where asbestos claims are involved, Bankruptcy Code § 524(g) and (h) allow future claims to be channeled against a trust fund.

[127] Lucian Arye Bebchuk & Jesse M. Fried, *The Uneasy Case for the Priority of Secured Claims in Bankruptcy*, 105 Yale L.J. 857 (1996); Steven L. Harris & Charles Mooney, Jr., *A Property-Based Theory of Security Interests: Taking Debtors' Choices Seriously*, 80 Va. L. Rev. 2021 (1994); Alan Schwartz, *The Continuing Puzzle of Secured Debt*, 37 Vand. L. Rev. 1051 (1984).

[128] The mother of one of your co-authors learned this, to her dismay, when her son refused to repossess a car she had sold to a co-worker on credit. The generally dutiful son was reluctant to take the car in the absence of evidence of a security agreement giving his mother the right to do so. *See* Ohio Rev. Code §§ 2913.02, 2319.03 (LexisNexis 2006) (theft & unauthorized use of a vehicle).

[129] The term "lien"' should be used with caution. It is sometimes used broadly, to refer to any property interest that gives rights in property to enforce an obligation, whether voluntary or involuntary. For example, Bankruptcy Code § 101(37) says that " 'lien' means charge against or interest in property to secure payment of a debt or performance of an obligation." At other times, "lien" refers only to involuntarily created rights, such as a statutory lien or a judicial lien.

[130] *See* § 2.02 Consensual Liens, *supra.*

[131] *See* § 2.05 Judicial Liens, *supra.*

with statutory or common law liens that arise by operation of law (primarily statutory liens).[132]

The Bankruptcy Code does not generally distinguish between these types of liens. Nor does the Bankruptcy Code generally distinguish between voluntary and involuntary liens: security interests and mortgages are treated in the same manner as judicial and statutory liens. With minor exceptions, all give rise to secured claims, and each of those claims has the priority given to it by the non-bankruptcy law that gave rise to the lien. What all of these lien claims have in common is that the holder does not have merely a claim for money; it also has a right to use specific property to satisfy the creditor's claim.

However, as will be seen, a claim is secured only to the extent of the value of the debtor's interest in the property that secures the claim. Thus, a creditor whose $100,000 claim is secured by property worth only $60,000 has a secured claim only up to the $60,000 value of the collateral. The remaining $40,000 of the creditor's claim is unsecured. This simple rule has numerous important consequences.

[B] Effect of Bankruptcy on Secured Claims[133]

Although secured claims are protected in many ways in bankruptcy,[134] they are not completely unaffected by the filing of a bankruptcy petition. At the very least, they are subject to the automatic stay that restrains creditors from taking a variety of actions against the debtor and her property while the bankruptcy case is pending.[135] In Chapter 7 liquidation cases, this may result in delaying a secured creditor from foreclosing until the bankruptcy case is nearly over. In some situations, the court may grant permission to the creditor to proceed with foreclosure while the case is pending. In reorganization proceedings under Chapters 11, 12 and 13, the debtor has the power to use the collateral during the case. The debtor may be able to adjust the terms of repayment of a secured creditor's claim, such as by extending the time for payment, altering the amount of monthly installments, lowering the rate of interest, or, depending on the value of the collateral with respect to some claims, reducing the amount of the secured debt. And, unless the collateral is worth more than enough to satisfy the secured creditor's claim fully and is thus "oversecured," bankruptcy will stop the accumulation of interest on the amount of the claim

---

[132] *See* § 2.06 Statutory, Common Law, and Equitable Liens, *supra*.

[133] Lawrence Ponoroff, & F. Stephen Knippenberg, *The Immovable Object Versus the Irresistible Force: Rethinking the Relationship Between Secured Credit and Bankruptcy Policy*, 95 Mich. L. Rev. 2234, 2307 (1997); James S. Rogers, *The Impairment of Secured Creditors' Rights in Reorganization: A Study of the Relationship Between the Fifth Amendment and the Bankruptcy Clause*, 96 Harv. L. Rev. 973 (1983).

[134] The Bankruptcy Code, like other Congressional statutes, is limited by the Takings Clause of the Fifth Amendment to the United States Constitution. Dewsnup v. Timm, 502 U.S. 410, 419 (1992); Louisville Joint Stock Land Bank v. Radford, 295 U.S. 555, 589 (1935).

[135] Bankruptcy Code § 362; *see* Chapter 8, The Automatic Stay, *supra*.

while the case is pending. Finally, the filing of a bankruptcy petition prevents a security interest or other lien from attaching to after-acquired collateral that the debtor or the estate acquires after the petition has been filed. These topics are discussed in the remainder of this section, in varying degrees of detail.

[1] Foreclosure Delayed or Restrained

The automatic stay of Bankruptcy Code § 362(a) has a dramatic and immediate effect on secured creditors' ability to enforce their claims. As explained in more detail elsewhere, the filing of a bankruptcy petition operates as an automatic injunction against a variety of creditors' efforts to collect, including "any act to obtain possession of . . . or to exercise control over property of the estate [or] to create, perfect, or enforce any lien against property of the estate."[136] This prevents secured creditors from repossessing what they view as "their" collateral. It also prevents them from selling collateral they have already repossessed or from permitting foreclosure sales they have scheduled to occur. It even requires them to return any property they have already repossessed to the trustee or to the debtor.[137]

In liquidation cases, the automatic stay only delays foreclosure. In many cases, where there is no non-exempt equity in the collateral, the trustee is likely to be willing to abandon the collateral and to permit the secured creditor to foreclose.[138] Or the court may grant the creditor relief from the automatic stay to permit the foreclosure to proceed.[139] For example, if collateral worth only $5,000 secures an allowed $7,000 claim, there will be no surplus value available following the sale of the collateral to distribute to other creditors. In most liquidation cases, where no reorganization is contemplated, none of the debtor's property is necessary for reorganization. Accordingly, secured creditors are nearly always entitled to relief from the automatic stay and permitted to proceed with their foreclosure against the collateral.[140]

In other liquidation cases, where the collateral is worth more than enough to satisfy a secured creditor, the property is likely to be sold by the bankruptcy trustee. Upon a sale of the collateral, the trustee distributes the proceeds of the sale to the secured creditor in an amount necessary to satisfy the secured creditor's claim and uses any surplus to satisfy any priority and non-priority unsecured claims. This may result in delayed payment to secured creditors who must wait for the trustee to dispose of the collateral.[141]

---

[136] Bankruptcy Code § 362(a)(3)-(4).

[137] In re Knaus, 889 F.2d 773 (8th Cir. 1989); Williams v. GMAC (In re Williams), 316 B.R. 534 (Bankr. E.D. Ark. 2004).

[138] *See* Bankruptcy Code § 554.

[139] Bankruptcy Code § 362(d)(2).

[140] *See* § 8.06[B] Relief From the Automatic Stay Upon Request of a Party, *supra.*

[141] Fortunately, fully secured creditors have allowable claims for post-petition interest, up to the value of their collateral. *See* § 10.02[C][4] Interest on Claims, *supra.*

In reorganization cases, secured creditors are unlikely to be permitted to foreclose, even if the debtor was in default when the debtor filed its petition. The debtor is allowed to use property of the estate during the course of the case, even if it is encumbered. As explained in detail elsewhere, the debtor's reorganization plan is likely to allow the debtor to retain its property and to restructure the debts it owes to secured and unsecured creditors alike. Payment may be extended over a longer period than called for in the debtor's contract with the secured creditor and both the interest rate and the amount of each installment payment might be reduced. Thus, a creditor with a $100,000 fully secured claim payable at 8% interest over a period of six years, might find its claim payable at only 6% interest with installments extended over ten years. In cases that involve partially secured claims, where the collateral is worth less than the amount of the outstanding debt, the reorganization plan may provide for a reduction of the amount of the secured portion of the creditor's claim.[142] Thus, if the creditor's $100,000 claim is secured by only $80,000 of collateral, the creditor will emerge from bankruptcy with collateral for only $80,000 if its claim, with payments extended over a longer period of time and at a reduced rate of interest. It's $20,000 unsecured claim will receive a distribution similar to that received by other unsecured creditors. In rarer cases, the debtor's reorganization plan substitutes alternative collateral or alters the seniority of a secured creditor's claim.[143] After the debtor's plan is confirmed by the court, the secured creditor's right to foreclose is governed by the provisions of the plan, rather than by whatever rights the creditor had before the bankruptcy case began.[144]

[2] Acceleration

As with all claims, the filing of a bankruptcy petition accelerates the due date of a secured creditor's claim, making the entire amount of the claim immediately due, despite the agreement between the parties that does not call for payment until some time in the future. Most loan agreements permit a creditor to accelerate the due date of a debtor's obligations upon the debtor's default. Regardless, bankruptcy accelerates the debtor's obligations, even if the parties' agreement does not provide for acceleration, and even though the creditor may not wish to assert its right to accelerate the debt.[145]

[3] Post-Petition Interest

As explained in more detail below,[146] filing a bankruptcy petition generally stops the accumulation of interest on unsecured and partially

---

[142] *See, e.g.*, Bankruptcy Code § 1123(b)(5) (generally permitting modifications of secured creditors' claims).

[143] *See* Bankruptcy Code § 364(d)(1); § 9.05[C] Secured Credit, *supra*.

[144] *See, e.g.*, Bankruptcy Code § 1327(a).

[145] *See, e.g.*, In re Allegheny Int'l, Inc., 100 B.R. 247 (Bankr. W.D. Pa. 1989).

[146] *See* § 10.03[C][3] Post-Petition Interest on Secured Claims, *infra*.

secured claims. If the claim is fully secured, interest continues to accumulate up to the amount of the value of the collateral. However, if the claim is only partially secured, filing a bankruptcy petition stops interest from accruing on the claim while the case is pending.

[4] After-Acquired Collateral

Some secured creditors' rights extend to property acquired by the debtor after the security agreement or mortgage is executed.[147] This is particularly true with respect to claims secured by inventory, accounts, chattel paper, and other receivables, where the creditor necessarily relies on the value of these after-acquired assets as collateral for the debt.[148] Some liens may extend much more broadly to after-acquired property. For example, an Article 9 security interest in a commercial transaction can encompass broad categories of collateral, both already owned and subsequently acquired by the debtor, if the parties so agree.[149] A business may grant a security interest in "all inventory, now owned or hereafter acquired." Under an after-acquired collateral clause of this type, the security interest immediately attaches to new inventory as soon as the debtor acquires it.

The attachment of a security interest, mortgage, or other lien to after-acquired collateral might have one of two possible effects. In most cases, it ensures that property subsequently acquired by the debtor serves as substitute collateral for the debtor's property that has been sold (in the case of inventory) or collected (in the case of accounts, chattel paper, and other types of receivables). For example, a creditor with a security interest in "existing and after-acquired inventory" may rely (sometimes desperately) on deliveries of new inventory the debtor receives to replace items that have been sold to customers.[150] Security interests in after-acquired collateral also might easily operate to expand the creditor's collateral, such as where the debtor expands its inventory or acquires new equipment, and thus provides the creditor with greater security than it previously enjoyed. In other situations, a creditor might depend on after-acquired collateral as a source of cash flow, such as where a mortgagor acquires a security interest in rents obtained from a mortgaged apartment building or office complex

[147] *See* U.C.C. § 9-204(a) (2003); *e.g.*, Stoumbos v. Kilimnik, 988 F.2d 949 (9th Cir. 1993) (absence of "after-acquired" collateral language did not prevent security interest from attaching to after-acquired inventory, but did preclude security interest from attaching to after-acquired equipment); United Okla. Bank v. Moss, 793 P.2d 1359 (Okla. 1990) (with appropriate language, mortgage could attach to after-acquired land).

[148] *See, e.g.*, In re Filtercorp, Inc., 163 F.3d 570 (9th Cir. 1998).

[149] There are many limitations on the ability to use after-acquired property clauses in consumer transactions. *See, e.g.*, U.C.C. § 9-204(2) (2003); Federal Trade Commission, Unfair Credit Practices Regulations, 16 C.F.R. § 444.2(a)(4) (2006).

[150] In most cases, these customers will acquire ownership of the items of inventory free and clear of the creditor's security interest, either because the secured party authorized the sale free of its interest, or because the buyers take free as buyers in the ordinary course of business. *See* U.C.C. §§ 9-315(a)(1) & 9-320(a) (2003).

to secure the debtor's obligation to make monthly payments on the mortgage.[151]

Another type of after-acquired property, familiar to those who have studied Article 9 of the Uniform Commercial Code on Secured Transactions, is "proceeds." Proceeds consist of money or other property obtained by the debtor when the encumbered property is sold or otherwise disposed of.[152] For example, suppose that Doug has given an Article 9 security interest in his car to Union Bank. If Doug sells his car to Boris for $2,000, that $2,000 is proceeds from the sale of the collateral and is automatically subject to the bank's security interest.[153]

Bankruptcy significantly curtails secured creditors' rights to after-acquired property. A pre-petition lien may encumber any property acquired up to the commencement of the case. However, unless the court orders otherwise, property acquired by the debtor after the commencement of the case is subject to the lien only if: (1) the property qualifies as "proceeds, products, offspring, rents, or profits of property that was subject to a security agreement"[154] prior to the commencement of the case; (2) the security interest covers proceeds;[155] and (3) the interest in proceeds is otherwise enforceable under the non-bankruptcy law applicable to the security agreement.[156]

The court may alter the scope of after-acquired property subject to the lien, but only after notice and an opportunity for a hearing, and only if it is appropriate "based on the equities of the case."[157] This frequently occurs in reorganization cases in which a reorganizing debtor finds it necessary to make a special court-approved deal with its secured creditors to permit the case to continue. It is quite appropriate, with court approval, for the debtor to enter into an agreement to give a secured creditor a lien on after-acquired post-petition property to secure a loan of additional funds[158] or

[151] At least in states following the "lien theory" of mortgages, any right to rents prior to foreclosure must be based on the contract between mortgagor and mortgagee; it is not an automatic incident of the mortgage itself. *See* Grant S. Nelson & Dale A. Whitman, Real Estate Finance Law § 4.23 (4th ed. 2001).

[152] U.C.C. § 9-102(a)(64)(A) (2003).

[153] U.C.C. § 9-306 (2003).

[154] In bankruptcy, the term "security agreement" extends to all consensual liens, not just to Article 9 security interests. Bankruptcy Code § 101(50). Thus, when it appears in the Bankruptcy Code, the term "security agreement" refers not only to contractual liens arising under Article 9 but also to real estate mortgages and deeds of trust. However, it excludes judicial liens, statutory liens, and common law liens.

[155] Article 9 does not require a security agreement to refer specifically to "proceeds" for the security interest to attach.

[156] Bankruptcy Code § 552(b)(1), (2). The 1994 Amendments slightly revised this section to encompass "the fees, charges, accounts, or other payments for the use or occupancy of rooms and other public facilities in hotels, motels, or other lodging properties."

[157] Bankruptcy Code § 552(b)(1), (2).

[158] *See* § 9.05 Obtaining Credit, *supra*.

to ensure that the creditor's rights in pre-petition collateral remains "adequately protected."[159]

[C] Allowance of Secured Claims[160]

Claims are allowed as secured claims only to the extent of the value of the collateral securing the claim. Creditors with a right of setoff are treated as having secured claims to the extent of their right of setoff. Bankruptcy Code § 506(a)(1) provides: "An allowed claim of a creditor secured by a lien on property in which the estate has an interest . . . is a secured claim to the extent of the value of such creditor's interest in . . . such property."[161] The extent of the secured claim depends on the value of the collateral. If the collateral is worth more than the amount of the debt, the claim is "fully secured." Thus, if Franklin Manufacturing owes $100,000 to Peninsula Bank and the debt is secured by a senior unavoidable lien on Franklin's equipment, Peninsula's claim is secured to the extent of the value of the collateral. If the equipment is worth $100,000, or more, Peninsula has an allowed secured claim for the full $100,000.

Section 506(a)(1) further provides that a creditor's claim is an "unsecured claim to the extent that the value of [the] creditor's interest . . . is less than the amount of [the] allowed claim." A claim that is greater than the value of the collateral is a "partially secured claim" and is accompanied by an unsecured claim for any deficiency in the value of the collateral. Thus, if Franklin's equipment is worth only $80,000, Peninsula's allowed secured claim is only $80,000. Peninsula also has an allowed unsecured claim for the remaining $20,000. When this bifurcation of an obligation occurs, the creditor has separate rights on each of its two claims.

A claim might also be bifurcated in this fashion due to the effect of a senior secured claim. Section 506(a)(1) limits a secured claim to the "extent of the value of such creditor's interest in the estate's interest in [the collateral]." Thus, a senior secured creditor's interest in the collateral might limit the secured status of a junior secured creditor's claim. For example, if Franklin's equipment is worth $200,000, Peninsula's $100,000 claim is only partially secured if there is another senior secured claim, securing a $130,000 debt, secured by the same equipment in which Peninsula holds its lien. The senior secured creditor holds a $130,000 fully secured claim and Peninsula holds both a $70,000 secured claim and a $30,000 unsecured claim.

---

[159] *See* § 8.06[B] Relief From the Automatic Stay Upon Request of a Party, *supra*.

[160] Jean Braucher, *Getting It for You Wholesale: Making Sense of Bankruptcy Valuation of Collateral After* Rash, 102 Dick. L. Rev. 763 (1997); Lucian Arye Bebchuk & Jesse M. Fried, *A New Approach to Valuing Secured Claims in Bankruptcy*, 114 Harv. L. Rev. 2386 (2001); David Grey Carlson, *Bifurcation of Undersecured Claims in Bankruptcy*, 70 Am. Bankr. L.J. 1 (1996); Margaret Howard, *Stripping Down Liens: Section 506(d) and the Theory of Bankruptcy,* 51 U. Chi. L. Rev. 97 (1984).

[161] Bankruptcy Code § 506(a)(1).

Of course, if a senior creditor's claim completely exhausts the value of the collateral, a junior secured creditor's claim might be completely "under water" and merely an unsecured claim. If Franklin's equipment is worth only $130,000 and is subject to a senior security interest that secures a $150,000 debt, then Peninsula's claim is completely unsecured.

[1] Valuation of Collateral[162]

Limiting secured claims to the value of the estate's interest in the collateral makes the method of determining the value of the collateral important. If, continuing with the above example, the court determines Franklin's equipment is worth $250,000, both creditors' claims are fully secured. If it were worth only $200,000, Peninsula's junior claim would be bifurcated. And if it is worth only $130,000, Peninsula's claim is wholly unsecured.

Section 506(a)(1) specifies that the value of the debtor's property is to be determined "in light of the purpose of the valuation and of the proposed disposition or use" of the property.[163] This language seems to favor use of liquidation value in circumstances where the collateral is to be liquidated, and replacement value or going concern value where the collateral continues to be used by the debtor, as it might in a reorganization proceeding.[164] However, some courts use a liquidation or foreclosure value standard to determine the amount of a secured creditor's allowed claim, even in cases where the debtor's reorganization plan contemplates the debtor's continued use of the collateral.[165] Other courts use the midpoint between the forced liquidation value and the replacement value.[166]

In *Associates Commercial Corp. v. Rash,*[167] the Supreme Court appeared to resolve this conflict by requiring use of the debtor's cost of replacing the collateral, at least in Chapter 13 cases where the debtor planned continued use of collateral. However, the Court's opinion in *Rash* re-introduced

---

[162] Jean Braucher, *Beneath the Surface of BAPCPA* Rash *and Ride-through Redux: The Terms for Holding on to Cars, Homes and Other Collateral under the 2005 Act*, 13 Am. Bankr. Inst. L. Rev. 457 (2005); Jean Braucher, *Getting It for You Wholesale: Making Sense of Bankruptcy Valuation of Collateral After* Rash, 102 Dick. L. Rev. 763 (1997); Lucian Arye Bebchuk & Jesse M. Fried, *A New Approach to Valuing Secured Claims in Bankruptcy*, 114 Harv. L. Rev. 2386 (2001); David Gray Carlson, *Secured Creditors and the Eely Character of Bankruptcy Valuations*, 41 Am U. L. Rev. 63 (1991); Lee Dembart & Bruce A. Markell, *Alive at 25? A Short Review of the Supreme Court's Bankruptcy Jurisprudence, 1979-2004*, 78 Am. Bankr. L.J. 373, 384 (2004); Robert M. Lawless & Stephen P. Ferris, *Economics and the Rhetoric of Valuation,* 5 J. Bankr. L. & Prac. 3 (1995); Chris Lenhart, *Toward a Midpoint Valuation Standard in Cram Down: Ointment for the* Rash *Decision,* 83 Cornell L. Rev. 1821 (1998); Kenneth L. Reich, *Continuing the Litigation of Collateral Valuation in Bankruptcy:* Associates Commercial Corp. v. Rash, 26 Pepperdine L. Rev. 655, 668 (1999).

[163] Bankruptcy Code § 506(a)(1).

[164] *E.g.*, In re Taffi, 96 F.3d 1190, 1191–92 (9th Cir. 1996).

[165] In re Rash, 90 F.3d 1036 (5th Cir. 1996), *reversed*, Associated Commercial Corp. v. Rash, 520 U.S. 953 (1997).

[166] In re Hoskins, 102 F.3d 311, 316 (7th Cir. 1996).

[167] 520 U.S. 953 (1997).

considerable uncertainty regarding the proper valuation method by recognizing that "[w]hether replacement value is the equivalent of retail value, wholesale value, or some other value will depend on the type of debtor and the nature of the property."[168] The Court also acknowledged that the value should not include enhancements to the value that might be attributable to improvements made to the collateral, such as warranties or reconditioning, that might affect the retail value of many used automobiles.[169]

Some courts resist *Rash*'s insistence on the use of replacement value by limiting the scope of the decision to its facts, which involved a determination of the amount of the allowed secured claim for purposes of confirming a Chapter 13 rehabilitation plan. For example, in *In re Weber*, a bankruptcy appellate panel approved using liquidation value to determine the size of a creditor's allowed secured claim to establish how much the debtor would be required to pay to accomplish a lump-sum redemption of the collateral under Bankruptcy Code § 722.[170] And, although some courts have applied *Rash* to determine the value of secured claims in Chapter 11 cases,[171] they have most frequently cited it for the proposition that valuation must be made in "light of the purpose of the valuation and of the proposed disposition or use of the property" rather than in direct support for use of the replacement cost of the collateral.[172] Despite *Rash*'s explicit rejection of the use of the midpoint between retail and wholesale value,[173] many courts continue to use exactly this standard.[174]

A related issue is whether the anticipated costs associated with any sale of collateral should be deducted from the value in calculating the amount of the creditor's secured claim. In *Brown & Co. Securities Corp. v. Balbus (In re Balbus)*,[175] the issue was whether the debtor was ineligible for relief under Chapter 13 because his unsecured debt exceeded the ceiling imposed by Bankruptcy Code § 109(e).[176] The court refused to permit the anticipated costs of the sale of a secured creditor's collateral to be deducted from the amount of a secured claim, thus keeping the size of the debtor's unsecured claims just barely within Chapter 13's limits.

---

168 520 U.S. at 965 n.6.

169 520 U.S. at 965 n.6; *see* Lucian Arye Bebchuk & Jesse M. Fried, *A New Approach to Valuing Secured Claims in Bankruptcy*, 114 Harv. L. Rev. 2386, 2397 n.41 (2001).

170 *See* § 12.08[A] Lump-Sum Redemption by Debtor, *supra.*

171 In re T-H New Orleans Ltd. P'ship, 116 F.3d 790, 799 (5th Cir. 1997).

172 In re LTV Steel Co., 285 B.R. 259 (Bankr. N.D. Ohio 2002); *see* Lucian Arye Bebchuk & Jesse M. Fried, *A New Approach to Valuing Secured Claims in Bankruptcy*, 114 Harv. L. Rev. 2386 (2001); Jean Braucher, *Getting It for You Wholesale: Making Sense of Bankruptcy Valuation of Collateral after* Rash, 102 Dick. L. Rev. 763, 764 (1998); Keith Sharfman, *Judicial Valuation Behavior: Some Evidence from Bankruptcy*, 32 Fla. St. U. L. Rev. 387 (2005).

173 Chris Lenhart, *Toward a Midpoint Valuation Standard in Cram Down: Ointment for the* Rash *Decision*, 83 Cornell L. Rev. 1821 (1998).

174 Lee Dembart & Bruce A. Markell, *Alive at 25? A Short Review of the Supreme Court's Bankruptcy Jurisprudence, 1979-2004*, 78 Am. Bankr. L.J. 373, 384 (2004).

175 933 F.2d 246 (4th Cir. 1991).

176 *See* § 6.02[B][6][c] Chapter 13 Debt Limits, *infra.*

In 2005 Congress amended § 506(a) by adding new subsection (2), which governs valuation of personal property in cases involving individual debtors under Chapters 7 and 13. In those cases "such value . . . shall be determined based on the replacement value of such property as of the date of the filing of the petition without deduction for costs of sale or marketing."[177] This codifies the result in *Rash*.[178] The language further provides, "with respect to property acquired for personal, family, or household purposes, replacement value [means] the price a retail merchant would charge for property of that kind considering the age and condition of the property at the time value is determined."[179]

This new language overrules decisions that base the amount of a creditor's secured claim on the liquidation value of an individual Chapter 7 or 13 debtor's property and that indicate that any advertising, sales, or other marketing costs incurred in selling the property should be deducted from the value used to determine the amount of the creditor's secured claim.[180] Moreover, with respect to consumer goods, it directs the court to use the retail price of used goods, despite the nearly complete absence of information regarding their retail value, except perhaps as reflected by online auction services and garage sales.[181] Otherwise, the only used consumer goods for which information is readily available are motor vehicles[182] and perhaps boats.

Broadly speaking, the value of the collateral is likely to be set higher in a reorganization than in a liquidation. Moreover, in business cases, most litigation over the value of collateral occurs in the context of adequate protection and the automatic stay, not the allowance of the claim itself. These rules, however, do not apply to Chapter 11 or 12 cases or to claims secured by interests in real estate.

[2] Enforceability of Lien or Setoff

A claim's secured status depends on the enforceability of the creditor's lien or right of setoff under both applicable non-bankruptcy law and the Bankruptcy Code. Not surprisingly, a lien that is unenforceable outside of bankruptcy enjoys no greater rights in bankruptcy. Likewise, if the secured

177 Bankruptcy Code § 506(a)(2).

178 *See* Scott F. Norberg, *Consumer Bankruptcy's New Clothes: An Empirical Study of Discharge and Debt Collection in Chapter 13*, 7 Am. Bankr. Inst. L. Rev. 415, 426 (1999); Jean Braucher, Rash *and Ride-through Redux: The Terms for Holding on to Cars, Homes, and Other Collateral Under the 2005 Act*, 13 Am. Bankr. Inst. L. Rev. 457, 465 (2005).

179 Bankruptcy Code § 506(a)(2).

180 Jean Braucher, Rash *and Ride-Through Redux: The Terms for Holding on to Cars, Homes, and Other Collateral Under the 2005 Act*, 13 Am. Bankr. Inst. L. Rev. 457, 465 (2005).

181 *See* Michael Korybut, *Online Auctions of Repossessed Collateral Under Article* 9, 31 Rutgers L.J. 29 (1999).

182 Richardo I. Kilpatrick, *Selected Creditor Issues Under the Bankruptcy Abuse Prevention and Consumer Protection Act of 2005*, 79 Am. Bankr. L.J. 817, 826 (2005); *see* http://www.cars.com (last visited July 11, 2006).

creditor's lien is avoidable via one of the bankruptcy trustee's numerous avoiding powers, the creditor's claim is relegated to unsecured status.

As long as the lien is otherwise enforceable, a secured claim can arise as a result of a consensual lien, a judicial lien, or a statutory lien.[183] A secured claim can also arise as the result of a creditor's right of setoff.[184] The nature or source of the lien does not matter.

[3] Post-Petition Interest on Secured Claims[185]

Most debt that is wholly or partially secured was originally incurred under an agreement that required the debtor to pay interest on the unpaid portion of the obligation. From the creditor's perspective, interest continues to accumulate on the debt after a bankruptcy petition is filed. However, whether the creditor is entitled to a claim for that post-petition interest depends on the value of the collateral in relation to the size of the claim.[186]

As explained above with respect to claims in general, unsecured creditors are not permitted to add post-petition interest to their claims. Although interest may accumulate on the debt, the creditor's claim for post-petition interest is not allowed as a claim against the debtor's estate, and an unsecured creditor receives no distribution for such interest in either a liquidation or a reorganization case. However, over-secured creditors are entitled to recover interest up to the value of the collateral securing their claims. Section 506(b) provides:

> To the extent that an allowed secured claim is secured by property the value of which . . . is greater than the amount of such claim, there shall be allowed to the holder of such claim, interest on such claim, and any reasonable fees, costs, or charges provided for under the agreement or State statute under which such claim arose.[187]

Thus, interest that continues to accumulate on the debt is added to the amount of the allowed secured claim, but only up to the value of the collateral for the debt. If a debt owed to Peninsula Bank is $100,000 and Franklin Manufacturing's equipment securing the debt is worth $120,000, Peninsula is allowed up to $20,000 in post-petition interest. Once the surplus has been exhausted, however, the creditor is not allowed either a secured or an unsecured claim for any further interest.

---

[183] United States v. Ron Pair Enters., Inc., 489 U.S. 235, 240 (1989); *see generally* Chapter 2, Basic Creditors' Collection Rights, *supra.*

[184] Boston Ins. Co. v. Nogg (In re Yale Express Sys., Inc.), 362 F.2d 111, 114 (2d Cir. 1966) (characterizing a right of setoff as the perfect kind of security); In re Bourne, 262 B.R. 745, 751 (Bankr. E.D. Tenn. 2001).

[185] Paul D. Bancroft, *Post Petition Interest on Tax Liens in Bankruptcy Proceedings*, 62 Am. Bankr. L.J. 327 (1988); John C. McCoid, II, *Pendency Interest in Bankruptcy*, 68 Am. Bankr. L.J. 1 (1994); Thomas H. Jackson & Robert E. Scott, *On the Nature of Bankruptcy: An Essay on Bankruptcy Sharing and the Creditors' Bargain*, 75 Va. L. Rev. 155 (1989); Dean Pawlowic, *Entitlement to Interest Under the Bankruptcy Code*, 12 Bankr. Dev. J. 149 (1995).

[186] United Sav. Ass'n. of Texas v. Timbers of Inwood Forest Assocs., Ltd., 484 U.S. 365 (1988).

[187] Bankruptcy Code § 506(b).

Correspondingly, if there were no surplus to begin with, the creditor would have no claim for post-petition interest. If Franklin Manufacturing's collateral were worth only $90,000, or even the full $100,000 amount of the debt, Peninsula would not have an allowed claim for interest that accumulates on the debt after Franklin's petition was filed.

Note that the secured claim may be increased not only by the interest that accrues on the loan, but also by "any reasonable fees, costs, or charges provided for under the agreement or State statute under which such claim arose."[188] This means post-petition late fees, attorneys' fees, collection costs, and the like may be added to the allowed secured claim but, as with post-petition interest, only up the value of the collateral.[189]

In reorganization cases, a careful distinction must be drawn between post-petition "pendency" interest and interest required to be paid under the terms of a confirmed reorganization plan. Interest is likely to be required under the latter, even if the secured creditor is not entitled to a claim for the former. "Pendency" interest refers to interest accumulating on a secured debt between the time the debtor's petition is filed and the time its reorganization plan is implemented. As explained immediately above, creditors have no claim for pendency interest beyond the value of the their collateral. However, Chapters 11, 12 and 13 all require post-confirmation interest to be paid on the amount of the "allowed secured claim" to compensate the creditor for deferral of payment of his claim under the terms of the confirmed plan of reorganization.[190]

Consider Peninsula Bank's security interest in Franklin Manufacturing's equipment. If the equipment is worth only $90,000 and the debt owed to Peninsula is $100,000, Peninsula does not have an allowed claim for any interest that accumulates on the debt between the time Franklin files its Chapter 11 case and the time Franklin's plan is confirmed, even though this may be a period of at least several months, perhaps several years. However, if Franklin's reorganization plan provides for deferred payment of Peninsula's $90,000 secured claim, the plan must provide for interest payments to Peninsula on this amount, commencing at the time when Franklin's plan is implemented.

The unavailability of pendency interest under the so-called *Timbers* rule[191] was attacked in the 1980s for providing many secured claims with less than full payment during the pendency period. Since the secured creditor loses the use of its property during that period, and it is not compensated for that lost use, the secured creditor does not in fact receive the full value of the property.[192] If, for example, Peninsula Bank has exactly

---

188 Bankruptcy Code § 506(b). The reference to fees, costs, and charges arising under a "State statute" was added in 2005.

189 *See* Rushton v. State Bank (In re Gledhill), 164 F.3d 1338, 1342 (10th Cir. 1999).

190 *See* § 19.11[B][1] Secured Claims, *infra*.

191 United Sav. Assoc. of Texas v. Timbers of Inwood Forest Assocs., Ltd., 484 U.S. 365 (1988).

192 Douglas Baird & Thomas Jackson, *Corporate Reorganization and the Treatment of Diverse Ownership Interests: A Comment on Adequate Protection of Secured Creditors in Bankruptcy*, 51 U. Chi. L. Rev. 97 (1984).

$100,000 of collateral available to secure its $100,000 claim, it is entitled to no pendency interest. This is in spite of the fact that, but for the automatic stay, Peninsula Bank could have seized and sold its collateral, and re-invested the proceeds. Although the bank eventually receives $100,000 through the bankruptcy proceeding, this is less than what it would have received outside of bankruptcy if it had foreclosed and reinvested. It may be considerably less if the proceeding is protracted, with a long pendency period between the time the petition is filed and the time a plan is ultimately confirmed.

In the view of some, this improperly forced a secured creditor, who was unlikely to benefit from the reorganization, to subsidize the reorganization for the benefit of unsecured creditors, who may get a better payout if the reorganization succeeds.[193] On the other hand, the no-interest rule was defended as recognizing that bankruptcy is a common disaster, like a shipwreck, in which the burden of loss should be shared among all stakeholders.[194] It is at least a crude means of helping to provide some payment on unsecured claims; virtually all or most debtors' non-exempt property already goes to pay secured claims,[195] and allowing interest on claims that are not oversecured simply exacerbates this problem. In any event, any doubt about the proper interpretation of the Code was resolved by the Supreme Court, when it ruled in 1988 that the plain language of the Code mandates the denial of any pendency interest on debts that are not oversecured.[196]

§ 10.04 Unsecured Claims[197]

Unsecured claims fall into two broad categories: priority claims and general claims. Among priority claims, there are a few super-priority claims that, when they exist, are entitled to be paid after secured claims, but before

---

[193] *E.g.*, Thomas H. Jackson, The Logic and Limits of Bankruptcy Law 189–90 (1986).

[194] *See* John C, McCoid II, *Pendency Interest in Bankruptcy*, 68 Am. Bankr. L.J. 1, 2 (1994). (Note that this is not Professor McCoid's own position.) The shipwreck model of bankruptcy dates back at least to the eighteenth century; Professor McCoid quotes a 1743 case, *Ex parte Bennet*: "[I]t is a dead fund, and in such a shipwreck, if there is salvage of part to each person, in this general loss, it is as much as can be expected." Ex parte Bennet, 26 Eng. Rep. 716, 717 (1743). *See also* Robert E. Scott, *A Relational Theory of Secured Financing*, 86 Colum. L. Rev. 901, 967–68 (1986); Robert E. Scott, *Through Bankruptcy with the Creditors' Bargain Heuristic*, 53 U. Chi. L. Rev. 690, 700–07 (1986).

[195] For a discussion regarding the percentage of a debtor's assets that are distributed on secured claims, see Michael J. Herbert & Dominic E. Pacitti, *Down and Out in Richmond, Virginia: The Distribution of Assets in Chapter 7 Bankruptcy Proceedings Closed During 1984-87*, 22 U. Rich. L. Rev. 303 (1988).

[196] United Sav. Assoc. of Texas v. Timbers of Inwood Forest Assocs., Ltd., 484 U.S. 365 (1988).

[197] James W. Bowers, *Wither What Hits the Fan?: Murphy's Law, Bankruptcy Theory, and the Elementary Economics of Loss Distribution*, 26 Ga. L. Rev. 27 (1991); Donald R. Korobkin, *Rehabilitating Values: A Jurisprudence of Bankruptcy*, 91 Colum. L. Rev. 717 (1991); Lynn M. LoPucki, *The Death of Liability*, 106 Yale L.J. 1 (1996).

other priority claims. These super-priority claims are explained below after claims entitled to ordinary priority.

Priority claims are unsecured claims that are singled out by the Bankruptcy Code for favorable treatment, primarily in § 507. These claims are entitled to be paid in full after secured claims are satisfied, but before holders of general unsecured claims receive anything. In liquidation cases, priority claims are paid only to the extent the estate has enough assets to pay unsecured creditors. If all of the estate's assets are consumed by secured claims and nothing is left to provide payment to creditors with unsecured claims, priority status means nothing. In reorganization cases, holders of priority claims are entitled to insist on full payment,[198] though they will nearly always agree to less favorable treatment if liquidation of the debtor would result in receiving even less. In Chapter 11 cases, some priority claims are entitled to payment in full immediately upon implementation of the debtor's plan.[199]

General unsecured claims are those held by most creditors whose claims are neither secured nor entitled to any special bankruptcy priority. In liquidation proceedings, which usually involve consumer debtors with no non-exempt assets, these claims rarely receive payment. In reorganization proceedings they may receive some payment, though nearly always less than 100% of the amount owed. Included among these claims are those of creditors whose security interests, mortgages, or other liens have been avoided by the bankruptcy trustee because they were unperfected, preferential, or otherwise,[200] and those of creditors whose collateral is inadequate to fully satisfy the entire claim.

[A] Priority Claims[201]

Section 507 establishes a group of claims entitled to priority status. Each claim in each priority class is entitled to payment in full before any payment is made on any claim in a lower priority class. When there is not enough to pay each claim in a particular class fully, all the claims in that class are paid pro rata, and no payment is made with regard to claims in a lower rung on the priority ladder. In business liquidation cases in particular, the difference between classification as a priority claim and a general claim can sometimes mean the difference between being paid in full or receiving nothing. Likewise, classification as a priority claim in a higher rung on the priority ladder (or a lower rung) can have the same importance.

---

198 Bankruptcy Code § 1129(a)(9); *see* § 19.08[G] Treatment of Priority Unsecured Claims, *infra*.

199 Bankruptcy Code § 1129(a)(9)(A).

200 *See generally* Chapters 14–16, *infra*.

201 Hanoch Dagan, *Restitution in Bankruptcy: Why All Involuntary Creditors Should Be Preferred*, 78 Am. Bankr. L.J. 247 (2004).

[1] Support Claims

In 2005, after considerable political wrangling, a new first priority was added for "domestic support obligations . . . owed to or recoverable by a spouse, former spouse, or child of the debtor, or such child's parent, legal guardian, or responsible relative."[202] A related second priority is accorded to the same sort of domestic support obligations that have previously been assigned to a governmental unit or otherwise owed to a governmental unit.[203] These new provisions promote support claims from seventh priority to first.

Despite this assurance of highest priority, new § 507(a)(1)(C) subordinates these domestic support claims to the administrative expenses of a bankruptcy trustee.[204] This provision recognizes the harsh reality that unless payment to the trustee is assured, no one will be willing to serve as trustee, and no one will incur the expenses necessary to liquidate the debtor's assets to pay the claims of other creditors.[205] Thus, despite the appearance of support claims in § 507(a)(1), administrative expenses of a Chapter 7, 11, 12, or 13 trustee really occupy the first priority position.[206]

Bumping support claims up from seventh priority to almost first is even less meaningful when considered in the broader context of the funds generally available to distribute to creditors. Approximately 96% of all consumer liquidation cases are "no-asset" cases, in which no assets are available to distribute to creditors, regardless of their priority. Thus, the priority potentially comes into play in only 4% of liquidation cases. Corporate debtors, of course, do not owe support. In a large percentage of these remaining liquidation cases, the trustee's administrative expenses are likely to exhaust the estate's assets. With no funds to distribute to spouses and children, their promotion from seventh priority is meaningful in only those rare consumer liquidation cases in which there are substantial assets available to distribute to creditors. In Chapter 12 and 13 cases, priority support claimants were already entitled to payment in full as a condition of confirming the debtor's rehabilitation plan, pursuant to their seventh position in former § 507(a)(7).

[2] Administrative Expense Claims

The expenses of administering the bankruptcy case itself are nearly always given the highest priority among unsecured claims and thus have the best chance of receiving payment. Section 507(a)(2) accords second priority to "administrative expenses allowed under section 503(b) of this title

---

[202] Bankruptcy Code § 507(a)(1)(A).

[203] Bankruptcy Code § 507(a)(1)(B). This priority does not apply if an assignment was voluntarily made to the governmental entity "for the purpose of collecting the debt."

[204] Bankruptcy Code § 507(a)(1)(C).

[205] Politicians who tried to insist on giving support claims priority over a trustee's administrative expenses ignored this practical reality.

[206] Samuel K. Crocker & Robert H. Waldschmidt, *Impact of the 2005 Bankruptcy Amendments on Chapter 7 Trustees*, 79 Am. Bankr. L.J. 333, 366 (2005).

and any fees and charges assessed against the estate under chapter 123 of title 28." Administrative expenses are those that arise from the expenses involved in the bankruptcy proceeding itself. Section 503 sets out the various administrative expenses.

The most obvious administrative expense claims are those derived from the "actual, necessary costs and expenses of preserving the estate."[207] The most important categories of these expenses are salaries paid to the debtor's employees for services rendered during the case;[208] taxes incurred by the estate;[209] and compensation to paid to the trustee, to any examiner appointed by the court, and to any other "professional person" engaged to render services to the estate, such as attorneys, accountants, investment bankers, appraisers, and real estate agents, pursuant to Bankruptcy Code § 330(a).[210]

While it might be thought that this latter category includes fees owed to the debtor's attorney for services rendered in connection with the "preservation of the estate," § 330 does not mention fees owed to an individual debtor's attorney in a Chapter 7 case. The exclusion of any provision for fees to a Chapter 7 debtor's attorney has been characterized as possibly a scrivener's error. Nevertheless, in *Lamie v. United States Trustee*, the Supreme Court felt constrained to take Congress at its word and denied the debtor's attorney a claim for fees in a Chapter 7 liquidation.[211] Section 330 specifically provides for recovery of attorneys' fees in cases under Chapters 12 and 13, and explicitly provides for their recovery in Chapter 11 cases where the debtor's attorney is appointed to represent the "debtor in possession."[212] However, after *Lamie*, Chapter 7 debtors' attorneys must plan to recover their fees in advance or run the risk of not being paid at all.

In consumer liquidation cases, attorneys' fees are normally paid in cash prior to the commencement of the case. This is usually also true in Chapter 13 cases, although the debtor's attorneys' fees are sometimes paid through distributions to creditors under the debtor's plan.[213] In Chapter 11 reorganization cases, the debtor's attorneys' fees can be considerable, running into the hundreds of thousands, and in large cases, millions of dollars.

---

207 Bankruptcy Code § 503(b)(1).

208 Bankruptcy Code § 503(b)(1)(A). This includes any wages and benefits awarded as back pay attributable to the debtor's pre-petition violation of state or federal law, regardless of when the debtor's violations took place or when the employee's services were rendered. Bankruptcy Code § 503(b)(1)(A)(ii).

209 Bankruptcy Code § 503(b)(1)(B)-(D) (this includes any fines, penalties, or reductions in credit relating to a post-petition tax).

210 Bankruptcy Code § 503(b)(2). The employment and compensation of such "professional persons" is subject to court approval in accordance with Bankruptcy Code § 330. *See* § 21.03 Fees for Professionals, *infra*.

211 540 U.S. 526 (2004).

212 Bankruptcy Code § 330(a); *see* In re Busetta-Silvia, 314 B.R. 218 (B.A.P. 10th Cir. 2004).

213 *See* In re San Miguel, 40 B.R. 481 (Bankr. D. Colo. 1984) (plan consisted primarily of payments to debtor's Chapter 13 attorney).

Administrative expense claims are sometimes paid for the actual, necessary expenses of creditors or their attorneys, but only if their efforts have made a substantial contribution to the administration of the case itself, such as by filing an involuntary petition or recovering property for the estate.[214] The creditor's contribution must have resulted in some definite tangible benefit to the estate that will accrue to the benefit of all creditors. Apart from this exception, creditors generally bear the cost of their own expenses and attorneys fees incurred in connection with their efforts to recover payment on their claims, even if they have generally been active participants in the case.[215]

[3] Involuntary Gap Creditors

Involuntary bankruptcy cases are initiated by creditors. Creditors seeking to force a debtor into bankruptcy usually must prove that the debtor is not generally paying its debts as they come due.[216] Unlike a voluntary case, in which an order for relief is entered at the same time the debtor's petition is filed, an order for relief is not entered in an involuntary case until the creditors prove facts that support this standard. As a result, there is usually a gap between the time the creditor's petition is filed and the time an order for relief is entered. Creditors whose claims arise in the ordinary course during this "involuntary gap" period are entitled to priority for their claims. Their claims are paid after other administrative expense claims but before other priority claims. This provides some measure of assurance to creditors who continue to provide credit to a debtor while an involuntary petition is pending.

[4] Wage Claims

Fourth priority is given to certain employees' wage claims. To qualify for priority treatment, an employee's claim must have been earned within 180 days before either the date the debtor (the employer) filed its petition or the date when the debtor ceased doring business, whichever occurred first.[217] The priority may not exceed $10,950 for each claimant.[218]

Consider, for example, the claim of an employee who is owed a total of $12,000 in unpaid wages earned during the last six months before the

---

214 Bankruptcy Code § 503(b)(3)-(4).

215 *E.g.,* In re The Columbia Gas Sys., 224 B.R. 540 (Bankr. D. Del. 1998) (creditors' fee applications denied); *see* Edward A. Stone, Comment, *Encouraging Creditor Participation: Integrating the Allowance of Administrative Expenses with the Common Fund Theory*, 15 Bankr. Dev. J. 223 (1999).

216 Bankruptcy Code § 303(h); *see* § 6.03[E] Grounds for Entry of "An Order for Relief," *supra.*

217 Bankruptcy Code § 507(a)(4). Before the 2005 Amendments, this time period was only 90 days.

218 Bankruptcy Code § 507(a)(4). Before the 2005 Amendments, the amount was only $4925 for each claimant. As with most other dollar figures in the Bankruptcy Code, this amount is adjusted every three years in accordance with increases in the Consumer Price Index. The next adjustments are scheduled for April 1, 2010, and 2013. *See* Bankruptcy Code § 104.

debtor's bankruptcy petition was filed, at the rate of $2,000 per month.[219] Only $10,950 of the claim is entitled to priority. The remaining $1,050 is a general unsecured claim. Even though the entire $12,000 was earned during the 180 days preceding the employer's bankruptcy petition, the total claim exceeds the $10,950 maximum.

This priority is intended to provide some protection for employees, because Congress assumes most employees have great need for, and little ability to obtain, protection against their employer's bankruptcy. If there are two employees, each owed $12,000, each employee is entitled to his own $10,950 priority claim.

Priority is usually accorded only to those who qualify as employees. It does not operate in favor of independent contractors. However, independent contractors who earn sales commissions from selling goods or services — but not real estate — are entitled to priority if the claimant earned at least 75% of his earnings from the debtor during the 12 months prior to the filing of the debtor's petition.[220] Thus, a sales agent who earned commissions by making sales for several merchants probably not qualify for the priority. Amounts not entitled to priority may still be allowable as general unsecured claims.

[5] Employee Benefit Plan Claims

Fifth priority is for contributions to employee benefit plans. Priority relates only to those contributions that arise from services rendered within the earlier of 180 days before the petition or 180 days before the debtor ceased doing business. The amount of priority for each employee benefit plan is capped — it may not exceed the number of employees covered by the plan, multiplied by $10,950, but minus the aggregate amount that was distributed to employees for priority wage claims under the fourth priority, and minus the amount paid by the estate on behalf of such employees under any other employee benefit plan.[221]

For example, suppose that during the 180–day period, thirty employees had earned the right to a $200,000 contribution to the Benefit Plan A, but the debtor failed to make the payment. Further assume that these thirty employees also held an aggregate of wage priority claims for $5,000 each (a total of $150,000), and that the employer made a $30,000 payment to Benefit Plan B on behalf of these same employees. Under these circumstances, Benefit Plan A has a priority claim in the amount of $148,500. This amount is based on thirty times the $10,950 threshold ($328,500) minus

---

[219] Such claims, of course, are rare. Few employees remain on the job for six months without compensation.

[220] Bankruptcy Code § 507(a)(4)(B).

[221] Bankruptcy Code § 507(a)(5). As with the priority for wage claims, before the 2005 Amendments, the amount was based on only $4925 multiplied by the number of members of the plan. As with other dollar figures in the Bankruptcy Code, this amount is adjusted every three years, in accordance with increases in the Consumer Price Index. The next adjustments are scheduled for April 1, 2010, and 2013. *See* Bankruptcy Code § 104.

the $150,000 in wage claims entitled to priority under § 507(a)(4), and also minus the $30,000 payment the employer made to Benefit Plan B ($328,500 – $150,000 – $30,000 = $148,500).

In 2006, the Supreme Court determined that an unsecured creditor's claim for unpaid workers' compensation liability insurance was not entitled to priority under this provision, because workers' compensation benefits were not intended as a substitute for wages.[222] Instead, the Court held that workers' compensation benefits (and thus the insurance premiums for those benefits) were substitutes for common law tort liability. As the court explained, tort claims, unlike claims for unpaid wages and other similar employee benefits, are not entitled to priority under § 507.

[6] Certain Claims of Farmers and Fisherman

The sixth priority addresses the special problems of farmers and fishermen who have delivered grain or fish to bankrupt grain elevators or fish storage facilities. Each is given a priority claim for its produce or proceeds. The priority is capped at $5,400.[223] No similar priority is provided to farmers who have claims for livestock that was delivered to a bankrupt meat packer or livestock dealer.[224]

[7] Consumer Deposits

The seventh priority gives limited protection to consumer buyers who have made a down payment or layaway deposit to a bankrupt seller. The payment may be for the purchase, lease, or rental of property or for the purchase of services. The property or services must have been intended for personal, family, or household use. The priority is capped at $2,425 per individual claimant.[225] The suggestion that payment in full is not a "deposit"[226] and thus does not fit within the plain meaning of the statutory language, has been repeatedly rejected by nearly every court that has considered the issue.[227]

---

[222] Howard Delivery Serv. Inc. v. Zurich American Ins. Co., 126 S. Ct. 2105, — U.S. — (2006).

[223] Bankruptcy Code § 507(a)(6). As with the priority for wage claims, before the 2005 Amendments, the amount was based on only $4925 multiplied by the number of members of the plan. As with other dollar figures in the Bankruptcy Code, this amount is adjusted every three years, in accordance with increases in the Consumer Price Index. Adjustments are scheduled for April 1, 2010, and 2013. *See* Bankruptcy Code § 104.

[224] *See* Bankruptcy Code § 557(a)(1) (defining grain for this purpose as "wheat, corn, flaxseed, grain sorghum, barley, oats, rye, soybeans, other dry edible beans, or rice"). Thus, sunflower seed farmers and hops farmers do not qualify either.

[225] Bankruptcy Code § 507(a)(7). As with other dollar figures in the Bankruptcy Code, this amount is set to be adjusted every three years, in accordance with increases in the Consumer Price Index. It was last adjusted in 2007. The next adjustments are scheduled for April 1, 2010, and 2013. *See* Bankruptcy Code § 104.

[226] Bonner v. Allman (In re Heritage Village Church & Missionary Fellowship, Inc.), 137 B.R. 888 (Bankr. D.S.C. 1991).

[227] *See* Salazar v. McDonald (In re Salazar), 430 F.3d 992 (9th Cir. 2005).

[8] Tax Claims[228]

The eighth and most complex of the priority provisions deals with various taxes, customs duties, and penalties.[229] Instead of dollar limits, most tax priorities have various time limits. Claims for past due income or gross receipts taxes are priority claims if they are for a tax "for a taxable year ending on or before the date of the filing of the petition for which a return, if required, is last due, including extensions, after three years before the date of the filing of the petition."[230] Thus, roughly speaking, unpaid income taxes for the debtor's previous three tax years enjoy priority treatment.[231] By contrast, the property tax priority includes one year's worth of back taxes.[232] Priorities are available for three years of income taxes, one year of property taxes, all withholding taxes, three years of employment taxes, three years of excise taxes, and one year of customs duties.[233]

Many tax claims are secured. An allowed secured tax claim has the same status as any other secured claim and has priority over all unsecured claims. Real estate property tax claims in particular are ordinarily secured by the debtor's interest in real estate subject to the tax. Federal tax claims may be secured as a result of the imposition and perfection of a federal tax lien under the Tax Lien Act.[234] If they are secured, tax claims are already senior to other claims. Consequently, § 507(a)(8) deals only with unsecured tax claims.

Claims for any tax penalties on a priority tax claim are also entitled to priority treatment, but only if the penalty is imposed as compensation for "actual pecuniary loss."[235] If other non-compensatory tax penalties were entitled to priority treatment, creditors with lower priority or general unsecured claims would be bearing the financial burden of the taxpayer's transgressions. If the purpose of the penalty is to compensate the taxing authority, the penalty is entitled to priority treatment; if its purpose is to punish the debtor, no priority is awarded.[236]

The priority includes income or gross receipts taxes "assessed within 240 days before the date of the filing the petition," with the 240-day period expressly excluding "any time" that an offer in compromise with respect

---

[228] Patrick M. Castleberry, *Individual Tax Claims in Chapter 7 and 13 Bankruptcies: Administrative Priorities and Dischargeability*, 47 Consumer Fin. L.Q. Rep. 433 (1993); Barbara K. Morgan, *Should the Sovereign Be Paid First? A Comparative International Analysis of the Priority for Tax Claims in Bankruptcy*, 74 Am. Bankr. L.J. 461 (2000).

[229] Bankruptcy Code § 507(a)(8).

[230] Bankruptcy Code § 507(a)(8)(A)(i).

[231] The precise operation of this language is explained in connection with the nondischargeability of income tax debts in Chapter 13. *See* § 13.03[B][1] Tax Debts, *infra*.

[232] Bankruptcy Code § 507(a)(8)(B).

[233] Bankruptcy Code § 507(a)(8).

[234] I.R.C. §§ 6321–6323.

[235] Bankruptcy Code § 507(a)(8)(G).

[236] *See generally* United States v. Reorganized CF & I Fabricators of Utah, Inc., 518 U.S. 213 (1996) (distinguishing between a tax and a penalty).

to the tax claim was pending.[237] This and other similar language effectively prevents taxpayers from using extended settlement negotiations with the IRS to demote the claim from priority to non-priority status.[238]

Another principal significance of the priority status of tax claims is that priority tax claims are non-dischargeable.[239] Thus, the debtor remains liable for any tax claim that is entitled to priority under § 507(a)(8) but remains unpaid due to the inadequacy of the estate. This makes § 507(a)(8) particularly important in many consumer bankruptcy cases involving unpaid and unsecured individual income taxes.

[9] Claims of Insured Depositary Institutions

The ninth priority, for claims of federally insured depositary institutions, had its genesis in the troubled financial world of the 1980s, when many federally insured financial institutions failed. It creates a priority claim for unkept commitments of the debtor to maintain the capital of an insured depository institution. This priority is uncapped.[240]

[10] Civil Liability for Driving While Intoxicated

In 2005, Congress added a tenth priority for claims "for death or personal injury resulting from the operation of a motor vehicle or vessel if such operation was unlawful because the debtor was intoxicated from using alcohol, a drug, or another substance."[241] This new priority will be practically meaningless in Chapter 7 liquidation cases that involve individual debtors, where few if any assets are available to distribute to creditors, regardless of their priority.[242] On the other hand, it will have a significant effect in Chapter 13 cases, where debtors may find it difficult to propose a plan calling for full payment of these claims as required by § 1322(a)(2).[243]

[B] Super-Priority Claims

Other provisions grant several other types of claims "super-priority" status of one type or another. These are complex provisions that have their greatest impact in cases where most of the debtor's value is almost consumed by secured creditors' claims. Using this limited remaining value to pay claims entitled to super-priority might easily deprive other priority creditors of any distribution.

---

237 Bankruptcy Code § 507(a)(8)(A)(ii)(I).

238 *See* Young v. United States, 535 U.S. 43 (2002).

239 Bankruptcy Code § 523(a)(1); *see* § 13.03[B][1][a] Priority Taxes, *infra.*

240 Bankruptcy Code § 507(a)(9).

241 Bankruptcy Code § 507(a)(10).

242 Liability for these debts is non-dischargeable. Bankruptcy Code § 523(a)(9). In 2005, the non-dischargeability provision in § 523 was amended to make it apply to liability for death or personal injury while operating either a "vessel" or an "aircraft," but only the reference to operation of a "vessel" made it into the priority provision of new § 507(a)(10).

243 *See* Bankruptcy Code § 1322(b)(2); § 18.06[B] Full Payment of Priority Claims, *infra.*

[1] Claims for Inadequate "Adequate Protection"

Just ahead of other § 503(b) administrative priority claims are claims held by secured creditors who were granted "adequate protection" that turned out to be inadequate. Secured creditors are sometimes provided with "adequate protection" for their claims pursuant to §§ 362, 363, and 364 to protect them from the harm that they otherwise would suffer due to the automatic stay or some other potential impairment of their rights in the debtor's property. This protection is sometimes in the form of a lien on additional or substitute collateral. If this protection turns out not to compensate them as anticipated, the secured creditor is entitled to super-priority status above all other § 507 priority claims. Assume, for example, that a creditor with a security interest in the debtor's equipment demands and receives adequate protection against the continued depreciation of its collateral in the form of a security interest in the debtor's accounts. If the equipment depreciates and the accounts turn out to have no value, the "protection" provided by the accounts was inadequate and the creditor will be compensated with a priority claim under § 507(b) for the loss caused by the depreciation of the equipment. This is consistent with the property rights and senior status of secured creditors, who are senior to all priority claims.

[2] Post-Petition Credit Claims

In addition, § 364(c)(1) permits the court to grant an even more senior super-priority administrative expense claim to a creditor who is willing to provide the estate with unsecured credit while the case is pending. This assures such post-petition creditors that their claims will be paid ahead of other post-petition claims and thus provides them with an added inducement to extend credit to a debtor that is reorganizing or that needs financing in order to accomplish an orderly liquidation. Thus, if an unsecured creditor were granted this priority for post-petition credit it extended to the debtor, its administrative expense claim for the amount of the loan would be paid ahead of all other § 507 priority claims and ahead of the super-priority claim of the secured creditor whose adequate protection turned out to be inadequate.

[3] Post-Conversion Liquidation Expenses

There is one final super-priority claim that is even more senior to the two super-priority claims already described, but it applies only in liquidation cases that have been converted from a case under Chapter 11, 12 or 13. Section 727(b) provides for payment of any § 503(b) administrative expenses incurred in the liquidation of the debtor after the case was converted ahead of all other the administrative claims, including those permitted by §§ 507(b) and 364(c)(1).[244] This priority is necessary to ensure the willingness of someone to wind up and liquidate the affairs of a debtor after its efforts to reorganize have failed.

[244] Bankruptcy Code § 726(b).

[C] General Unsecured Claims

General unsecured claims are those in the great residual pot into which claims not otherwise classified are placed. In consumer cases, these tend to consist of debts to retailers, health care providers, and credit card issuers.[245] In business cases, many general unsecured creditors are "trade creditors" who have delivered goods or services to the debtor in the ordinary course of their business, usually expecting payment in a month or two. In addition, it is not unusual for business debtors to owe unsecured debts to banks and other financial institutions. There may also be unsecured debt that is represented by investment securities. Long-term debt of this sort is generally represented by bonds; short-term debt is more often represented by commercial paper. Some or all of this type of unsecured debt may be publicly traded in the securities markets. Note, however, that bonds and commercial paper might be fully or partially secured.

Tort claimants, other than those secured by a non-avoidable judgment lien or an execution lien, are also nearly always general unsecured claims. Unlike those whose claims are based in contract, tort claimants have little or no opportunity to evaluate or to take precautions against the risk involved in dealing with the debtor.

In liquidation bankruptcy, general unsecured claims are likely to be paid little if anything.[246] By contrast, successful reorganizations may provide for substantial payment to claims of unsecured creditors. In rare cases, these claims might even be paid in full.

In liquidation, all general unsecured claims are treated equally; whatever assets remain after secured and priority claims are paid in full are divided among unsecured creditors pro rata. In reorganization, especially in Chapter 11 cases, general unsecured claims may be further subdivided by the plan into separate classes.[247] As long as the classifications are justified and the plan provides for payment of the liquidation value of each claim in each class, the plan may treat some classes more favorably than others.[248]

§ 10.05 Subordinated Claims

Claims are sometimes demoted in priority. This occurs as a result of a subordination agreement among creditors, due to equitable subordination, or as the result of a specific statutory subordination rule. When a creditor's claim is subordinated, it falls further behind in the line for a right to receive a distribution from the debtor's estate and thus runs the risk of receiving nothing, as if the claim had simply been disallowed. As a result, the mere

---

[245] *See* Teresa A. Sullivan, Elizabeth Warren & Jay Lawrence Westbrook, As We Forgive Our Debtors 275–76 (1989).

[246] See Dominic E. Pacitti & Michael J. Herbert, *Down and Out in Richmond, Virginia: The Distribution of Assets in Chapter 7 Bankruptcy Proceedings Closed During 1984-87*, 22 U. Rich. L. Rev. 303 (1988).

[247] *See* § 19.08[D] Classification of Claims, *infra.*

[248] Bankruptcy Code § 1122; *see* § 19.08[D] Classification of Claims, *infra.*

threat of subordination can have a dramatic impact on the negotiations that lead to the development of a reorganization plan. Section 510 partially codifies the rules regarding subordination.

[A] Contractual Subordination[249]

Sometimes creditors agree to subordinate their claims to the claims of other creditors. Section 510(a) states that "[a] subordination agreement is enforceable in a case under this title to the same extent that such agreement is enforceable under applicable nonbankruptcy law."[250] Thus, subordination agreements made between creditors are generally enforced in bankruptcy.[251]

A creditor may be willing to subordinate its claim if it is willing to accept additional risk for the opportunity for an additional reward, or in some cases, because the creditor wishes to make a quasi-equity investment. For example, the president of a closely held corporation may agree to subordinate any claim she has as a creditor of the corporation to another creditor as part of an effort to persuade the other creditor to loan money to her business. In addition, there is even a good deal of publicly traded subordinated debt, often referred to as debentures, which predictably offers a higher rate of interest than ordinary bonds to offset the higher risk of non-payment.

[B] Equitable Subordination[252]

Courts sometimes forcibly subordinate a creditor's claim due to the creditor's bad behavior. This is known as "equitable subordination."[253] When it applies, equitable subordination most commonly demotes a general unsecured claim to a position just below the claims of all other unsecured general creditors but immediately ahead of the interests of shareholders or other owners of "interests" in the debtor. Because this ordinarily results in the subordinated creditor receiving little or nothing, the possibility that

---

[249] David Gray Carlson, *A Theory of Contractual Debt Subordination and Lien Priority*, 38 Vand. L. Rev. 975 (1985); Kevin C. Dooley & Thomas G. Rock, *Subordination Agreements: Suggested Approaches to Key Issues*, 113 Banking L.J. 708 (1996).

[250] Bankruptcy Code § 510(a)(2000); *see* In re Sepco, 750 F.2d 51 (8th Cir. 1984); *but see* Bank of New England Corp. v. Branch (In re Bank of New England Corp.), 364 F.3d 355 (1st Cir. 2004).

[251] *E.g.*, In re Cliff's Ridge Skiing Corp., 123 B.R. 753 (Bankr. W.D. Mich. 1991).

[252] David Gray Carlson, *the Logical Structure of Fraudulent Transfers and Equitable Subordination*, 45 Wm. & Mary L. Rev. 157 (2003); Andrew DeNatale & Prudence B. Abram, *The Doctrine of Equitable Subordination as Applied to Nonmanagement Creditors*, 40 Bus. Law. 417 (1985); John J. Dvorske, Annotation, *Bankruptcy: Equitable Subordination, Under 11 U.S.C.A. § 510(c), of Insider Claims*, 2 A.L.R. Fed. 2d 119 (2005); Steven A. Karg, *A Bankruptcy Trap for the Unwary Creditor: Equitable Subordination Resulting from Excess Creditor Control*, 15 Seton Hall Legis. J. 434 (1991).

[253] Bankruptcy Code § 510(c). *See* Taylor v. Standard Gas & Elec. Co., 306 U.S. 307 (1939) ("Deep Rock doctrine" permitting subordination of debt below preferred stockholders' interests).

a claim might be subordinated is a powerful tool in negotiations over the terms of a plan.

Although it started as a court-created doctrine,[254] equitable subordination is now expressly authorized by the Bankruptcy Code. Section 510(c) provides: "[A]fter notice and a hearing, the court may (1) under principles of equitable subordination, subordinate for purposes of distribution all or part of an allowed claim to all or part of another allowed claim."[255]

As one might expect when the word "equitable" appears, there is no rigid test to apply the doctrine. The most widely used formulation sets out a three-part test:

- the claimant must have engaged in some type of inequitable conduct;
- the misconduct must have resulted in injury to the creditors of the bankrupt or conferred an unfair advantage on the claimant; and
- subordination must not be inconsistent with the provisions of the Bankruptcy Code.[256]

Although it is nearly impossible to catalog all of the actions that might be characterized as "inequitable conduct," the term unquestionably includes "(1) fraud, illegality, breach of fiduciary duties; (2) undercapitalization;[257] and (3) the claimant's use of the debtor corporation as a mere instrumentality or alter ego."[258] *Pepper v. Litton*,[259] decided before equitable subordination was codified, provides a good example of subordination of a claim due to an insider creditor's fraudulent behavior. In *Pepper*, a controlling shareholder permitted the corporation to confess a judgment against itself on an old unpaid wage claim that was held by the shareholder in such a way that, if permitted to stand, would have resulted in other unsecured creditors receiving nothing.

Undercapitalization refers to a situation where the debtor's capital structure is heavily leveraged by debt. Assume, for example, that Close Corp. is a small company with only five shareholders, funded with $100,000. On the books of the company, $1,000 of the initial capital is listed as common stock, and the remaining $99,000 is listed as loans made to the corporation by its five shareholders. This is a "highly leveraged" company

---

[254] Taylor v. Standard Gas & Elec. Co., 306 U.S. 307 (1938); Petter v. Litton, 308 U.S. 295 (1939); Sampsell v. Imperial Paper & Color Corp., 313 U.S. 215 (1941); Heiser v. Woodruff, 327 U.S. 726 (1946); Comstock v. Group of Institutional Investors, 335 U.S. 211 (1948).

[255] Bankruptcy Code § 510(c)(1).

[256] Benjamin v. Diamond (In re Mobile Steel Co.), 563 F.2d 692 (5th Cir. 1977).

[257] Jonathan A. Carson, *Pre-Petition Capital Contributions: The Road to Equitable Treatment in Bankruptcy*, 1999 Colum. Bus. L. Rev. 403 (1999).

[258] Matter of Herby's Foods, Inc., 2 F.3d 128, 131 (5th Cir. 1993); Fabricators, Inc. v. Technical Fabricators, Inc. (In re Fabricators, Inc.), 926 F.2d 1458, 1467 (5th Cir. 1991); Wilson v. Huffman (In re Missionary Baptist Found. of Am., Inc.), 712 F.2d 206, 209, 212 (5th Cir. 1983).

[259] 308 U.S. 295 (1939).

in which nearly all of its capital comes from loans. It is leveraged at a ratio of 99:1 — that is, 99% debt and only 1% equity. Assume further that under the loan agreement between the company and its shareholders, interest on the loan accrues at an annual "minimum" rate of 10%, but neither interest nor principal must be paid unless the company makes at least $20,000 in profits during a fiscal year. These terms make the loan seem as if it should be treated as a contribution of capital rather than as a loan. In other words, it represents an interest rather than a claim. If the company's liability to pay interest is forgiven in the event that the company earns less than $20,000 a year, this appearance is even more pronounced. And, if the "creditors" are entitled to a higher rate of "bonus" interest if the company turns a higher profit, the conclusion that this claim is really an ownership interest is hard to avoid. Such a loan, particularly when made by an insider, is highly vulnerable to being recast as equity and subordinated to the claims of outside creditors.[260]

Of greatest importance in this example is that the legal attributes of these types of debt are similar to those normally associated with a purchase of stock. If the company does poorly, the investors recover little or nothing on their investment. If the company does extraordinarily well, the "lenders" receive a larger return. The usual mark of debt is that the debtor is obligated to pay regardless of financial condition. and conversely, that if the debtor earns more than expected, it need only pay a fixed amount of interest or interest at a rate pegged to an unmanipulable external standard, such as a prime interest rate. Equity, on the other hand rises or falls with the success of the enterprise.[261]

Despite the frequent articulation of the statement that "undercapitalization" constitutes the type of inequitable conduct that justifies equitable subordination,[262] it now seems clear that undercapitalization by itself is not enough.[263] However, subordination is usually sought with respect to an insider's claim for repayment of a loan made to the thinly capitalized business. It is the combination of the undercapitalization with the insider's loan that justifies subordination.[264] The fact that insiders have used their dominant power over the debtor to improve their position at the expense of outside creditors, such as by raising their own salaries while not paying creditors, can also be sufficient.[265]

---

[260] *See* Fabricators, Inc. v. Technical Fabricators, Inc. (In re Fabricators, Inc.), 926 F.2d 1458, 1464 (5th Cir. 1991).

[261] *E.g.*, In re Carolee's Combine, Inc., 3 B.R. 324 (N.D. Ga. 1980).

[262] *E.g.*, Benjamin v. Diamond (In re Mobile Steel Corp.), 563 F.2d 692 (5th Cir. 1977); *see* Jonathan A. Carson, *Pre-Petition Capital Contributions: The Road to Equitable Treatment in Bankruptcy*, 1999 Colum. Bus. L Rev. 403 (1999); Markus C. Stadler, *Treatment of Shareholder Loans to Undercapitalized Corporations in Bankruptcy Proceedings*, 17 J.L. & Com. 1 (1997).

[263] Matter of Herby's Foods, Inc., 2 F.3d 128 (5th Cir. 1993); In re Fabricators, Inc., 926 F.2d 1458, 14659 (5th Cir. 1991); In re Phase I Molecular Toxicology, Inc., 287 B.R. 571 (Bankr. D.N.M. 2002).

[264] Matter of Herby's Foods, Inc., 2 F.3d 128, 132 (5th Cir. 1993).

[265] See In re Lemco Gypsum, Inc., 911 F.2d 1553 (11th Cir. 1990), *reh'g denied*, 930 F.2d 925 (11th Cir. 1991).

At one point it seemed as if creditors' claims might be vulnerable to subordination despite the absence of inequitable conduct by the creditor involved. However, in 1996, the Supreme Court unequivocally rejected subordination based simply on the nature of the creditor's claim, where the creditor had engaged in no wrongdoing. In *United States v. Noland*,[266] the Court prohibited the subordination of a federal tax penalty, which was entitled to an administrative expense priority, as part of the bankruptcy court's effort to more "equitably" distribute the debtor's estate. The Supreme Court held that absent inequitable conduct on the creditor's behalf, subordination amounts to little more than a judicial realignment of the priority scheme established by Congress. Later the same year, the Court reinforced its holding in *Noland* by reversing a bankruptcy court's order that subordinated a similar tax penalty, despite the absence of any misconduct on the part of the government. The Court indicated that subordination based on nothing more than the nature of the creditor's claim was similarly "outside the scope of any leeway under § 510(c) for judicial development of the equitable subordination doctrine."[267] As the Court held in *Noland*, bankruptcy courts are not permitted to engage in the type of "categorical reordering of priorities that takes place at the legislative level." To permit this type of subordination, the Court said, would be "beyond the scope of judicial authority."

[C] Statutory Subordination[268]

Subordination is also specifically required in several discreet situations. Section 510(b) requires subordination of claims "arising from rescission of a purchase or sale of a security of the debtor . . . or for reimbursement or contribution allowed . . . on account of such a claim."[269] This provision simply recognizes that the creditor's claim is based on an equitable ownership interest the creditor would have held, if not for the right to rescission, reimbursement, or contribution from the estate.

There are three other subordination provisions that apply only in liquidation cases. Section 724(b) provides for the subordination of certain tax claims. Section 726(a) subordinates claims that are filed late,[270] unless the delay occured through no fault of the creditor.[271] Finally, claims for noncompensatory fines, penalties, and punitive damages are subordinated below both secured and general unsecured claims.[272]

---

[266] 517 U.S. 535 (1996).

[267] United States v. Reorganized CF & I Fabricators of Utah, Inc., 518 U.S. 213, 229 (1996).

[268] Zach Christensen, Note, *The Fair Funds for Investors Provision of Sarbanes-Oxley: Is it Unfair to the Creditors of a Bankrupt Debtor?*, 2005 U. Ill. L. Rev. 339 (regarding potential conflict between Sarbanes-Oxley and Bankruptcy Code § 510(b)).

[269] Bankruptcy Code § 510(b).

[270] Bankruptcy Code § 726(a)(3).

[271] Bankruptcy Code § 726(a)(2)(C).

[272] Bankruptcy Code § 726(a)(4).

§ 10.06 Interests

[A] Meaning of Interests

The term "interest" has two primary meanings in the Code. When referring to specific property, the word refers to some form of co-ownership or lien. Thus, a secured creditor has an interest in property of the debtor or property of the estate. This type of interest is discussed throughout this book in the context of the treatment of liens and other divided property interests.

The other meaning refers to ownership interests in the debtor itself and thus obviously has meaning only if the debtor is a corporation, partnership, or entity other than an "individual." Interests of this type represent ownership not of particular property, but of the value of the entity above the amount of creditors' claims. This is the residual interest after all debt is paid. If the debtor is insolvent, there is no equity. The remainder of this section deals with this latter meaning of the term.

In liquidation proceedings, interests are nearly always ignored because there is hardly ever any residual value available to distribute to shareholders. Even in reorganization, interests in the debtor may be insignificant, because the debtor is still likely to be insolvent. However, in Chapter 11, it is possible for those who own interests to participate in the distribution under the plan, even if claims are not paid in full — so long as creditors agree. Moreover, Chapter 11 proceedings are more likely to involve a debtor whose going concern value exceeds its liquidation value or who is in bankruptcy not because of an excess of debts over equity, but as a result of inadequate cash flow. In addition, to the extent shareholders' active involvement in the debtor's business contributes to its financial success, creditors may be anxious to ensure that these interest holders have a stake in the future profitability of the firm and thus may be willing to agree to yield some amount to which they otherwise might be entitled to facilitate implementation of the debtor's plan.

[B] Allowance of Owners' Interests

The procedure for allowing an interest is virtually identical to the procedure for allowing a claim. Ordinarily, a proof of interest must be filed. If no objection is made, the interest is allowed. Any party in interest may object, including a creditor of a general partner in a partnership that is a debtor. As is true with claims, however, proof of interest need not be filed in Chapter 11 proceedings, so long as the interest is scheduled by the debtor.[273] Neither the Code nor the Bankruptcy Rules contain any detail concerning the adjudication of a contested interest. This is in contrast to the adjudication of contested claims. The reason for this lack of detail is undoubtedly that interests, which are almost always worthless, are rarely contested.

---

[273] Bankruptcy Code § 1111(a); Fed. R. Bankr. P. 3003(b)(1), (c)(2).

[C] Priority of Interests

Interests, like claims, might be entitled to different priority. These priorities, however, are not created by the Bankruptcy Code; rather, they are the result of the contract that created the interest. The most familiar example of a priority interest is stock with a liquidation preference. For example, assume Titanic Industries, Inc. issued a class of stock, Preferred Stock A, with a $100 liquidation preference. This means that, upon liquidation of the company, whether in bankruptcy or out, a payment of up to $100 per share is paid to the holders of this stock before anything is paid on common stock. Thus, once all debt of every kind is paid, whatever is left is first applied to this liquidation preference. If there is not enough to pay the full $100 for each share, whatever remains is distributed pro rata among the outstanding preferred shares. Of course, as a practical matter it is highly unlikely that liquidation will produce anything for preferred stock. But, if the $100 liquidation preference is fully paid, holders of common stock will receive something for their junior interests.

[D] Subordinated Interests

At the very, very bottom of the Bankruptcy Code's priority ladder are subordinated interests — interests that are even lower than typical common stock in a corporation. An interest may be subordinated in either of two ways. First, it may be subordinated by agreement. An agreement may have been entered into when the legal entity was created; it is certainly lawful to create a class of stock that is subordinated to common stock. A subordination agreement may also have been entered into after the stock was initially issued. The Bankruptcy Code makes subordination agreements enforceable to the extent they are enforceable under applicable non-bankruptcy law.[274]

Second, an interest may be equitably subordinated by the court. Although equitable subordination is usually thought of in the context of claims of creditors, the statutory provision that recognize equitable subordination applies to interest, as well. Section 510(c) states, in part, "after notice and [an opportunity for] a hearing, the court may under principles of equitable subordination, subordinate for purposes of distribution . . . all or part of an allowed interest to all or part of another allowed interest."[275] The considerations discussed with equitable subordination of claims also control for equitable subordination of an interest. However, given the fact that virtually all interests are worthless, the chance that anyone would bother to seek equitable subordination of an interest is only slightly more than zero.

---

[274] Bankruptcy Code § 510(a).

[275] Bankruptcy Code § 510(c)(1).

§ 10.07 Co-Ownership of Estate Property

[A] Joint Property

In a number of cases, the property rights of the estate co-exist with the property rights of another. The most obvious example occurs when the debtor is a joint tenant or a tenant in common of real estate.[276] The co-owner in that type of situation has neither a claim against the estate[277] nor an interest in the debtor. Moreover, the co-ownership right is normally not an interest in property of the estate, because, with a limited exception for community property, the co-owner's interest does not become property of the estate.[278]

Ideally, co-owners would be unaffected by the debtor's bankruptcy. However, this is sometimes impossible. On occasion, it is necessary either to partition the property and sell the debtor's portion or to sell property free and clear of all co-owner's interests.[279] If the latter is done, the co-owner who is not the debtor must be compensated for his interest in the jointly-owned asset.

[B] Leases

Leases, whether of real or personal property, have some of the features of liens. As students of Article 9 of the U.C.C. will recall, some personal property transactions that are called leases have the same economic effect as a credit sale of property subject to a security interest, and for that reason they are regarded as secured sales.[280] A true lease, however, is somewhat different, regardless of whether it is a lease of real or personal property. It is a form of divided ownership, but unlike a lien, the interest of the lessor exists for purposes other than insuring payment. At the end of the lease, the property is be returned to the lessor who, like any owner, may re-lease it, sell it, or use it. The assumption of both parties is that the lessor will get the property back, which is what differentiates it from a credit sale of the property. The lease also differs from other forms of joint ownership, such as joint tenancy, because in a lease, the interest of one of the "owners," the lessee, is limited in time and contingent upon the lessee making rent payments to the owner of the residual interest, the lessor.

---

[276] We do not discuss tenancies by the entirety at this point, because that form of ownership insulates both the rights of the debtor and the debtor's spouse if the debt incurred by the debtor was not a mutual debt.

[277] The term "claim" encompasses a right to payment and a right to an equitable remedy for breach of a duty. Bankruptcy Code § 101(5) (2006); *see* § 10.01 Meaning of Claims and Interests, *supra*. In a typical co-ownership case, neither of these exist.

[278] Bankruptcy Code § 541. The limited exception for community property is contained in Bankruptcy Code § 541(a)(2). *See* § 7.02[B] Community Property, *supra*.

[279] Bankruptcy Code § 363(f); *see* § 9.03 Use, Sale, or Lease of Estate Property, *supra*.

[280] *See* U.C.C. § 1-201(37) (2001); *See* William H. Lawrence, William H. Henning & R. Wilson Freyermuth, Understanding Secured Transactions 14 (3d ed. 2004).

Insofar as bankruptcy is concerned, the interest of a lessor of real or personal property is dealt with in a manner that recognizes its hybrid character. The lessor has a claim for rent. The lessor also has an interest in property of the estate; the debtor's leasehold is property of the estate, and the lessor has certain rights and obligation with regard to its ownership of the property. Finally, the lessor has a residual property interest that is not part of the estate. The lessor's right to possess the property at the end of the lease term is a right that never belonged to the debtor, and thus does not become part of the estate. The complexity of lease rights has generated difficult and complex rules, explained elsewhere.[281]

§ 10.08 Anomalous Rights

On occasion, it is extremely difficult to classify a particular right as a claim or an interest. As the discussion in the previous sections suggest, debt and equity are not two different species. They are simply shorthand ways of defining rights, and they exist on a continuum from the purest type of debt, a precisely defined right not in any way conditioned on the obligor's financial condition, to the purest form of equity, which is a variable right that wholly depends on the obligor's financial circumstances. A right to collect $10,000, whether or not the debtor can afford to pay, is unquestionably a claim. A right to participate in the obligor's profits, whatever they are, is unquestionably an interest. On the other hand, a right to collect $10,000, subject to a one-year postponement of the due date if the debtor is insolvent, a right to collect $10,000 which can at any time be converted into common stock, or common stock that can at any time be converted into debt at the rate of $100 per share tendered, falls somewhere in between these two guideposts.

As a general principle, the classification of anomalous rights is done functionally. If a particular right has the substance of equity, it is treated as equity.[282] However, this is sometimes entangled in the court's analysis of the propriety of the action that created the right. If it appears to the court that a particular right has odd features because it was used to cheat other claimants, the court will likely treat the right as one subordinate to those claimants.

§ 10.09 Setoff[283]

"Setoff" refers to the right to offset one mutual debt against another that is well-established in the law.[284] The most obvious example is a bank's right

---

[281] *See* Chapter 11 Executory Contracts and Unexpired Leases, *infra.*

[282] *See* § 10.05[B] Equitable Subordination, *supra.*

[283] Lawrence Kalevitch, *Setoff and Bankruptcy*, 41 Clev. St. L. Rev. 599 (1993).

[284] *See* § 2.07 Setoff of Mutual Debts, *supra*; John C. McCoid II, *Setoff: Why Bankruptcy Priority?*, 75 Va. L. Rev. 15 (1989); Michael Tigar, Comment, *Automatic Extinction of Cross Demands: Compensation From Rome to California*, 58 Cal. L. Rev. 224, 226–34 (1965); William H. Loyd, *The Development of Setoff*, 64 U. Pa. L. Rev. 541 (1916).

to set off a debt owed to it by one of its customers against funds the customer has on deposit with the bank.[285] Thus, if Franklin Manufacturing owes $50,000 to Peninsula Bank but also has $60,000 in an account at Peninsula Bank, the bank has a right to set off Franklin's $50,000 debt against the bank's obligation (represented by the deposit) to repay $60,000 to Franklin. The basic operation of the right of setoff and limitations on its use are explained in more detail elsewhere.[286]

The Bankruptcy Code treats a creditor's right of setoff as a secured claim. Section 506 provides:

> An allowed claim of a creditor . . . that is subject to setoff under section 553 of this title, is a secured claim . . . to the extent of the amount subject to setoff. . . and is an unsecured claim to the extent that . . . the amount so subject to setoff is less than the amount of such allowed claim.[287]

If Franklin only has $40,000 on deposit with Peninsula Bank, the bank has a secured claim as a result of its right of setoff for $40,000, and an unsecured claim for the $10,000 balance due from Franklin.

[A] Setoff Under Non-Bankruptcy Law

Whether a right of setoff exists depends on non-bankruptcy law.[288] Where a right of setoff exists, it is enforced in bankruptcy subject to some limitations. Section 553(a) specifies that the Bankruptcy Code "does not affect any right of a creditor to offset a mutual debt . . . that arose before the commencement of the case . . . except as otherwise provided" in §§ 553, 362, and 363.[289]

The most important limitation is one that usually emulates the operation of setoff under state law. Thus, the Bankruptcy Code does not create a right of setoff; it merely recognizes and (to some extent) limits any right of setoff that exists apart from bankruptcy law. As explained elsewhere, non-bankruptcy law usually only permits setoff of debts that are both "mutual" and "matured."[290]

Section 553 emulates the law of setoff in most states by permitting setoff only of "mutual debts." However, if state law were to permit setoff of debts in the absence of mutuality, § 553 would nevertheless require that the debts be mutual, as an independent limitation on the exercise of the right of setoff in bankruptcy. This requirement is explicit in § 553, which only permits

[285] *See, e.g.*, Citizens Bank of Md. v. Strumpf, 516 U.S. 16 (1995).

[286] *See* § 2.07 Setoff of Mutual Debts, *supra*.

[287] Bankruptcy Code § 506(a).

[288] *See* § 2.07 Setoff of Mutual Debts, *supra*.

[289] Bankruptcy Code § 553(a).

[290] *See* § 2.07[A] Creditor's Right of Setoff, *supra; e.g.*, In re Patterson, 967 F.2d 505 (11th Cir. 1992) (creditor's claim unmatured at time of debtor's bankruptcy).

setoff by a creditor of "a mutual debt owing by such creditor to the debtor."[291]

[B] Setoff Limited to Pre-Petition Claims

For a creditor to assert a right of setoff for its claim, the debt owed by the creditor to the debtor must be one "that arose before the commencement of the case."[292] Thus, a creditor's post-petition claim may not be set off against a prepetition debt owed by the creditor to the debtor. No provision is made for setoff of post-petition claims.

This limitation may require a determination of when the creditor's claim arose. Various tests have been used, in this and other contexts, to determine when a creditor's claim arose.[293] These include the "accrual" test, which depends on when liability accrued to the creditor under state law;[294] a "conduct" or "transactions" test, which depends on when the conduct that gave rise to the claim occurred;[295] the "relationship test," under which a claim cannot exist unless the parties had some pre-petition relationship that gave rise to the claim;[296] and a "foreseeability test," which depends on whether the debtor's liability arose from pre-petition conduct that made the creditor's claim foreseeable or "fairly contemplated" by the parties.

[C] No Setoff of Disallowed Claims

Not surprisingly, if the creditor's claim is disallowed, it may not provide the basis for a setoff.[297] This prevents a creditor who does not have a claim that is cognizable in bankruptcy from effectively reviving that claim in the form of a right of setoff.

The creation of a right of setoff on the eve of bankruptcy, like the transfer of a security interest or other lien to a creditor just before the debtor files a bankruptcy petition, can result in an inappropriate preference to a creditor at the expense of others. Section 553 imposes three limits on creditors' right of setoff that seek to avoid this result. It restricts a creditor's right of setoff if the right was acquired by the creditor during the last ninety days before bankruptcy and (1) results from transfer of a claim to the creditor,

[291] Bankruptcy Code § 553(a).

[292] Bankruptcy Code § 553(a).

[293] *See generally* In re Jensen, 127 B.R. 27 (B.A.P. 9th Cir. 1991).

[294] *E.g.*, Cooper-Jarrett, Inc. v. Central Transp. Inc., 726 F.2d 93 (3d Cir. 1984); *see also* Matter of M. Frenville Co., Inc., 744 F.2d 332, 337 (3d Cir. 1984), *cert. denied* 469 U.S. 1160 (1985); *but see* Lawrence Kalevitch, *Setoff and Bankruptcy*, 41 Clev. St. L. Rev. 599, 658 (1993) (noting criticism of the "accrual" test).

[295] *E.g.*, Braniff Airways, Inc. v. Exxon Co., 814 F.2d 1030 (5th Cir. 1987); *see generally* Grady v. A.H. Robins Co. (In re A.H. Robins Co.), 839 F.2d 198 (4th Cir.), *cert. dismissed sub nom.* Joynes v. A.H. Robins Co., 487 U.S. 1260 (1988).

[296] *E.g.*, In re Pettibone Corp., 90 B.R. 918 (Bankr. N.D. Ill. 1988).

[297] Bankruptcy Code § 553(a)(1). Note that the technical requirement is that the claim not be disallowed, rather than it be allowed. In re Davidovich, 901 F.2d 1533 (10th Cir. 1990).

(2) results from a claim created for the purpose of obtaining a right of setoff, or (3) improves the financial position of the creditor exercising the right of setoff.[298]

[1] Transfer of Claim

Section 553(a)(2) restricts the setoff of claims that the creditor has acquired through a transfer from another creditor.[299] Setoff is not permitted if the creditor's claim against the debtor was transferred to the creditor, by someone other than debtor, either after the debtor's petition was filed or during the ninety day period immediately before the petition was filed and while the debtor was insolvent.[300]

For example, suppose Franklin Manufacturing had $20,000 on deposit with Peninsula Bank while owing Industrial Supply Co. $15,000. State law would not ordinarily permit setoff in this situation, even if Industrial Supply Co. also owed a debt to the Bank. However, a right of setoff might be created if Industrial Supply were to assign its claim against Franklin to Peninsula Bank. After such an assignment, Peninsula would hold a $15,000 claim against Franklin and would be able to offset its claim against the $20,000 Franklin had on deposit with it. This might be an effective way for the Bank to collect the claim owed to it by Industrial Supply. If Franklin were insolvent at the time the Bank received the assignment that created the right of setoff, it would also effectively boost Industrial Supply's claim to a secured position, ensuring that it would be paid in full.

However, if the transfer of Industrial Supply's claim to Peninsula were within ninety days before Franklin's bankruptcy, and depending on the source of its claim, § 553(a)(2) would probably prevent Peninsula from exercising its right of setoff. Peninsula would still have a claim against Franklin, but could not assert a right of setoff or assert that its claim was secured as a result of its right of setoff.

This restriction discourages trafficking in setoff rights. It is problematic where a creditor with no setoff rights sells its claim to somebody who owed the debtor money. The claim may be worth almost nothing in the hands of the assigning creditor, but worth 100% in the hands of the creditor with setoff rights. This creates an opportunity for abuse. Imagine that Franklin Bank owes the debtor $100. Imagine further that Sam Supplier is owed $100 by the debtor. Sam may anticipate a distribution of $10 on his $100 claim from the estate. On the other hand, Franklin Bank might purchase

298 In 2005, these restrictions were removed with respect to setoff rights arising in a variety of narrow circumstances, most of which arise in connection with certain securities and commodities transactions, repurchase agreements, swap agreements, and master agreements that facilitate the operation of financial markets. Bankruptcy Abuse Prevention and Consumer Protection Act of 2005, Pub. L. No. 109-8, § 907, 119 Stat. 23 (2005).

299 Bankruptcy Code § 553(a)(2).

300 Bankruptcy Code § 553(a)(2). Note that for this purpose, the debtor is presumed to have been insolvent during the ninety days prior to bankruptcy. Bankruptcy Code § 553(c). This presumption may be rebutted by the creditor asserting the right of setoff.

the claim from Sam for $50 and then use the acquired setoff rights to settle its $100 obligation to the debtor. In some cases, however, the mere fact that a claim has been transferred from one creditor to another has no real impact on other creditors. Suppose, for example, that Industrial Supply had a right of setoff against Franklin Manufacturing as a result of other transactions between the parties, but that it transferred the claim for which it might have exercised its right of setoff to Peninsula Bank. Before the assignment to Peninsula, Industrial Supply had a right of setoff against Franklin. After the transfer, Peninsula enjoys the same right of setoff. The effect on other creditors is zero; both before and after the transfer, the offset reduces the assets available to other creditors by exactly the same amount.

[2] Intent to Create a Right of Setoff

Section 553(a)(3) operates similarly to § 553(a)(2), but deals with setoff of claims against debts owed by the debtor that are first created on the eve of the debtor's bankruptcy with the intent to create a right of setoff. The easiest illustration is where a debtor makes a deposit to its bank account, during the last ninety days before bankruptcy as part of an effort to supply the bank in which the deposit is made with collateral, in the form of a right of setoff, for what would otherwise be an unsecured claim against the debtor.

Assume, for example, that on June 1, Duarte owes $20,000 to Commerce Bank. If on July 1 Commerce Bank insists Duarte makes a $20,000 deposit to his account at the bank and maintain a $20,000 balance in the account as a condition of preserving the status of the loan in good standing, § 553(a)(3) will likely restrict the resulting right of setoff. Otherwise, the effect of the deposit would be to convert the Bank's unsecured $20,000 claim to a secured claim, which would violate the Bankruptcy Code's anti-preference policy. This provision fits squarely into the concerns underlying § 547, regarding avoidable preferences. In these circumstances, the right of setoff created by Duarte's deposit is really no different from the transfer of a security interest in Duarte's property during the last ninety days before his bankruptcy petition. It has the same effect as a security interest in Duarte's $20,000 automobile being transferred to the bank.

[3] Setoff Resulting in Improvement in Position

Section 553(b) permits the court to set aside a setoff that was exercised during the last ninety days before the debtor's bankruptcy petition was filed if the exercise of the right of setoff resulted in an improvement in the creditor's position in a manner similar to an avoidable preference. This provision operates similarly to § 547(c)(5)'s rules regarding the improvements in position that a creditor with a security interest in after-acquired inventory and receivables can obtain, unless avoidance is allowed. Because this deals more with one of the trustee's avoiding powers than with a creditor's claim, and because of its similarity to issues involving preferences created by secured creditors' "floating liens," it is dealt with elswhere with in connection with the trustee's power to avoid preferences under Bankruptcy Code § 547.[301]

---

[301] *See* § 15.06 Setoff Preferences, *infra*.

Chapter 11

Executory Contracts and Unexpired Leases

§ 11.01 Right to Assume or Reject; Assignment[1]

As a general matter, the Bankruptcy Code seeks to respect (or at least adequately protect) property rights, but discharges contractual claims against the debtor. This raises a fundamental conundrum for the debtor. Most contractual relationships are not a one way street. When the debtor and a non-debtor exchange executory promises, they do so with the expectation that they will both be better off once the promises are performed. This remains true even in bankruptcy. Sometimes the debtor is right, and completing performance is advantageous. Other times the debtor is wrong, and performance would be burdensome to the estate. Section 365 allows the debtor to make a choice whether to breach or perform its obligations under a contract. It has been the source of much confusion among judges and in Congress, which insists on increasing the complexity of the section. Thus, it is no surprise that the 2005 Amendments amended several of its key provisions.

Like many Code provisions, § 365 is designed to preserve value for the debtor's estate. It does this by providing the estate's representative (the trustee or a debtor-in-possession)[2] with several options in connection with the handling of certain types of contracts to which the debtor is a party. As will be seen, after filing its petition, a debtor has the right to treat executory contracts and unexpired leases in one of three basic ways. A debtor may:

- reject the contract (breach it);
- assume the contract and perform it according to its terms; or
- assume the contract and assign it to a third party to perform.

The purpose of permitting assumption or rejection of these contracts is to permit the trustee or debtor-in-possession to realize the value of transactions that are valuable to the estate and to treat the breach claims in burdensome transactions as pre-petition claims against the estate. Thus,

[1] Michael T. Andrew, *Exectutory Contracts in Bankruptcy: Understanding "Rejection,"* 59 U. Colo. L. Rev. 845, 889–94 (1988); Vern Countryman, *Executory Contracts in Bankruptcy*, 57 Minn. L. Rev. 439, 446 (1973); Jesse M. Fried, *Executory Contracts and Performance Decisions*, 46 Duke L.J. 517 (1996); Jessica L. Kotary & Nicole L. Inman, *Eliminating "Executory" from Section 365: The National Bankruptcy Review Commission's Panacea for an Ailing Statute*, 5 Am. Bankr. Inst. L. Rev. 513 (1997); Morris G. Shanker, *Bankruptcy Asset Theory and its Application to Executory Contracts*, 1992 Ann. Surv. Bankr. L. 97; Jay L. Westbrook, *A Functional Analysis of Executory Contracts*, 74 Minn. L. Rev. 227 (1989).

[2] Bankruptcy Code § 365.

the trustee or debtor-in-possession may make an inventory of the debtor's executory contracts and determine which ones it would be beneficial to adhere to and which ones it would be beneficial to reject.

At the most basic level, each of these alternatives is easy to understand. Consider, for example, a contract for the sale of goods between Franklin Manufacturing Co. and Industrial Supply Co. Franklin has agreed to purchase and Industrial has agreed to sell 12,000 yards of insulated copper wire, which will be delivered at a rate of 1,000 yards each month for $10 per yard. Sometime during the year, Franklin files a Chapter 11 petition and must decide how to handle this contract.

If the contract price is relatively high due to fluctuations in the market for copper wire, Franklin might wish to reject the contract under § 365(a). Franklin must seek the court's approval before rejection will be effective.[3] Because rejection is a breach of the contract, it will give rise to a claim for breach of contract. The conceptually tricky aspect of § 365 arises because this breach does not occur until after the petition has been filed. If the breach is treated as occurring post-petition, the non-debtor might be deemed to have a post-petition claim with administrative expense priority. By contrast, if the breach is treated as occurring pre-petition, the breach claim will be an unsecured claim, payable in bankruptcy dollars. The Code makes it clear that after rejection, Supply will have a general unsecured claim in Franklin's bankruptcy case.[4] The amount of the claim is calculated using ordinary, non-bankruptcy principles for calculating contract damages.

On the other hand, if Franklin still needs the copper wire and the contract price with Industrial Supply is favorable, it may wish to assume the contract, take delivery of the goods, and pay the contract price. Even if Franklin no longer needs the wire, if the contract price is low, Franklin may wish to go ahead with the sale and resell the wire to someone else. In either case, Franklin will seek to assume the contract and perform according to its terms.[5] Just as with the decision to reject, Franklin must obtain court approval to assume the contract. Once the decision to assume has been approved, all of the debtor's obligations under the contract are treated as post-petition obligations of the debtor and are entitled to administrative expense priority under §§ 503 and 507(a)(2) of the Code.[6] As such, Franklin's plan must provide for payment of the claim in full.[7]

Alternatively, Franklin may anticipate the sale of one of its manufacturing divisions as a going concern. If this were the division that expected to use the copper wire, Franklin may wish to assume the contract and assign the obligations and benefits to whomever buys this division from Franklin.

---

[3] Bankruptcy Code § 365(a).

[4] Bankruptcy Code § 365(g)(1).

[5] Bankruptcy Code § 365(a).

[6] Bankruptcy Code § 365(g)(2).

[7] Bankruptcy Code § 1129(a)(9)(A); *see* § 19.10[H] Full Payment of Priority Claims, *infra*.

To do so, Franklin must assume the contract and gain further court approval to assign it to the purchaser of this particular division of its business.

Regardless of what course of action the debtor wishes to pursue, the Bankruptcy Code imposes a variety of time limits and other legal restraints on the debtor's decision. The remainder of this chapter explains the meaning of "executory contract," examines the Code's restrictions on the debtor's various alternatives, and explores the consequences of each alternative the debtor might choose.

§ 11.02 "Executory Contract" and "Unexpired Lease" Defined

Section 365 permits the rejection of executory contracts and unexpired leases, not all contracts. Accordingly, the terms "executory contract" and "unexpired lease" must be defined. Most of the attention has been focused on the meaning of "executory contract."

[A] "Executory Contract" Defined[8]

For many years, courts have overwhelmingly used a definition originally suggested by Professor Vern Countryman in 1973: "A contract under which the obligation of both the bankrupt and the other party to the contract are so far unperformed that the failure of either to complete performance would constitute a material breach excusing performance of the other."[9] Thus, a contract is executory if *both parties* have material duties remaining to be performed.

Consider a simple contract for the sale of goods, involving a single delivery. Crash Construction Co. enters into a contract with Builder's Supply Inc. for the purchase and sale of 100 sheets of 3/8″ plywood for $1,000. If Crash pays the price in advance and is awaiting delivery from Builder's Supply when Crash files its bankruptcy petition, the contract is not executory, because Crash has substantially performed. Crash's right to receive the plywood is simply an asset of the estate.[10] Likewise, if Builder's Supply has already delivered the plywood, but Crash has not yet paid for it at the time of Crash's petition, Builder's Supply is the one who has substantially performed. The estate has already received whatever benefits it might derive from the contract and Builder's Supply simply has a

[8] Michael T. Andrew, *Exectutory Contracts in Bankruptcy: Understanding "Rejection,"* 59 U. Colo. L. Rev. 845, 889–94 (1988); Vern Countryman, *Executory Contracts in Bankruptcy*, 57 Minn. L. Rev. 439, 446 (1973); Morris G. Shanker, *Bankruptcy Asset Theory and its Application to Executory Contracts*, 1992 Ann. Surv. Bankr. L. 97; Jay L. Westbrook, *A Functional Analysis of Executory Contracts*, 74 Minn. L. Rev. 227 (1989).

[9] Vern Countryman, *Executory Contracts in Bankruptcy*, 57 Minn. L. Rev. 439, 446 (1973); *see* RCI Tech. Corp. v. Sunterra Corp. (In re Sunterra Corp.), 361 F.3d 257, 264 (4th Cir. 2004); Sharon Steel Corp. v. National Fuel Distrib. Corp., 872 F.2d 36, 39 (3d Cir. 1989).

[10] Bankruptcy Code § 541(a)(1).

general unsecured claim. Thus, the contract is not executory within the Countryman definition. Most courts agree that treating either one of these situations as invoking § 365 would expand the effect of the provision too broadly, "since it is the rare agreement that does not involve unperformed obligations on either side."[11]

On the other hand, if neither party has substantially performed, with Crash still owing payment and Builder's Supply still in possession of the plywood, the contract is executory and is subject to § 365. Crash or its bankruptcy trustee has the option to reject the contract, to assume and retain the contract, or to assume and assign the contract. Thus, if the contract involves both a set of rights (such as the right to receive the plywood) and a set of obligations (the duty to pay for the plywood), it is an executory contract.[12]

While the Countryman "material breach" test is useful in this and many other situations, several commentators[13] and a few courts[14] have pointed out that it would make more sense to apply a more functional test, based on the effect of treating a contract as executory, rather than the traditional test. This more functional test examines whether the debtor has remaining obligations to perform upon which the estate's right to receive the other party's performance depends. Unless there is some potential advantage to the estate from electing to assume or reject, the mechanisms of § 365 should play no role in connection with the contract. But, if the estate might gain a potential benefit from assumption, or avoid a significant detriment through rejection, § 365 applies and the estate may elect to assume or reject. This type of approach would make it unnecessary for courts to bend over backwards in an effort to find some remaining material obligation that would justify treating the contract as executory under the traditional Countryman test.

Installment land sale contracts are a good example of the difficulties encountered when applying the Countryman test. In a typical installment land sale contract, the buyer promises to make regular installment payments over a period of time. In return, the seller agrees to deliver good title upon completion of the buyer's payments.[15] Under the Countryman definition, this is an executory contract: the buyer has a material obligation to make the balance of the promised payments and the seller has a duty to deliver a deed. Yet, treating it as an executory contract makes it necessary for the buyer to assume the contract and pay the full price, even though

[11] Mitchell v. Streets (In re Streets & Beard Farm P'ship), 882 F.2d 233, 235 (7th Cir. 1989).

[12] *See* Thomas H. Jackson, The Logic and Limits of Bankruptcy Law 106-07 (1986).

[13] *See* Michael T. Andrew, *Execututory Contracts in Bankruptcy: Understanding "Rejection,"* 59 U. Colo. L. Rev. 845, 889–94 (1988); Morris G. Shanker, *Bankruptcy Asset Theory and its Application to Executory Contracts*, 1992 Ann. Surv. Bankr. L. 97; Jay L. Westbrook, *A Functional Analysis of Executory Contracts*, 74 Minn. L. Rev. 227 (1989).

[14] *E.g.*, In re Jolly, 574 F.2d 349 (6th Cir. 1978); In re Booth, 19 B.R. 53 (Bankr. D. Utah 1982).

[15] *See* § 2.02[A][1][c] Installment Land Contract, *supra*.

the value of the land may be lower than what the buyer agreed to pay. If the buyer instead had acquired immediate title to the land and granted the seller a mortgage on it to secure payment of the price, no one would have difficulty treating the transaction as giving rise to a secured claim. Subject to some exceptions, the buyer would be able to retain the property by paying the creditor only the amount of its allowed secured claim, rather than the full amount of the mortgage debt, and giving the creditor an allowed unsecured deficiency claim for the unpaid balance. Indeed, some courts will recharacterize such installment contracts as mortgages for just this reason.[16]

[B] "Unexpired Lease" Defined

Though it might seem easier to identify an unexpired lease, this is not always true. Here, the principal question is whether the transaction is a true lease or a disguised security agreement. The question is frequently considered in connection with leases of goods, but it has also presented itself in the context of a long-term lease of land.[17]

Courts nearly always examine the economic realities of the transaction to distinguish between a true lease and a security interest.[18] If the terms of the lease leave the lessor with no meaningful economic interest in the goods, it is a disguised security interest and should be handled by the Code's rules regarding secured claims. On the other hand, if at the end of the lease the lessor has an economically meaningful residual interest, it is a true lease and is subject to § 365. The most obvious example of a security interest disguised as a lease is one in which the "lessee" has a contractual obligation to make all of the payments provided for in the lease, without the right to early termination, and also has the right to buy the goods, at the end of the lease for a nominal price.[19] Likewise, if the duration of the lease is for the entire anticipated useful life of the goods, the transaction is really a secured sale, not a lease.[20] Any set of circumstances in which the economic reality of the transaction is the equivalent of a sale, where the lessor has no meaningful interest in the goods at the end of the leasehold period, is a disguised financing transaction and is not subject to § 365.[21]

---

[16] *E.g.*, In re Booth, 19 B.R. 53 (Bankr. D. Utah 1982); *see* Jay L. Westbrook, *A Functional Analysis of Executory Contracts*, 74 Minn. L. Rev. 227, 317–22 (1989); *see also* Thomas C. Homburger & Karl L. Marsche, *Recharacterization Revisited: A View of Recharacterization of Sale and Leaseback Transactions in Bankruptcy After Fifteen Years*, 41 Real Prop. Prob. & Tr. J. 123 (2006).

[17] *E.g.*, United Airlines, Inc. v. HSBC Bank USA, 416 F.3d 609 (7th Cir. 2005); In re PCH Associates, 804 F.2d 193, 198-200 (2d Cir. 1986).

[18] Margaret Howard, *Equipment Lessors and Secured Parties in Bankruptcy: An Argument for Coherence*, 48 Wash. & Lee L. Rev. 253 (1991).

[19] U.C.C. § 1-203(b)(2) (2003) (formerly U.C.C. § 1-201(37)).

[20] U.C.C. § 1-203(b)(1) (2003) (formerly U.C.C. § 1-201(37)).

[21] *See* Duke Energy Royal, LLC v. Pillowtex Corp. (In re Pillowtex, Inc.), 349 F.3d 711 (3d Cir. 2003).

§ 11.03 Procedure for Assumption or Rejection

Section 365 imposes restrictions on the trustee or debtor-in-possession's option to assume or reject an executory contract. Time limits on this decision vary somewhat, depending on the nature of the transaction and the type of bankruptcy proceeding involved. Moreover, debtors' desires are not controlling; the court must approve the decision to assume or reject. Finally, the Code imposes restrictions on the estate's treatment of executory contracts in any "limbo period" between commencement of the case and the decision to assume or reject. In Chapter 11 cases in particular, this may be an extended period of several months or even years.

[A] Timing of Assumption or Rejection[22]

In liquidation cases, the trustee has sixty days from the order for relief to assume executory contracts and unexpired leases. Afterwards, the contract or lease is "deemed rejected," unless the court has extended the sixty-day period.[23] However, the sixty-day limit does not apply to an unexpired lease of non-residential real estate. In reorganization cases under Chapters 11, 12, and 13, the determination may be deferred until confirmation of a plan, though the court may require it to be made earlier.[24]

Leases of non-residential real estate are treated differently. The 2005 Amendments require assumption or rejection of a commercial real estate lease within 120 days of the order for relief, or the date an order confirming a plan is entered, whichever is earlier.[25] This doubles the time limit that applied before BAPCPA. For cause, the court may extend the time period for an additional ninety days. Moreover, the extension must be granted before the initial 120 day period expires.[26] Any further extension requires the lessor's consent.[27] If these deadlines are not met, the lease is "deemed rejected."

This short time frame places considerable pressure on debtors to determine which premises are needed for their business plan. Debtors who are unsure whether to jettison certain locations may find it necessary to assume unexpired commercial real estate leases for property they may not require. Because subsequent rejection of an assumed lease gives the lessor an administrative priority expense claim, which must be paid in full in a

---

[22] Jennie D. Latta, *"What You Don't Know May Hurt You" — Time Limits Under the Bankruptcy Code and Rules*, 28 U. Mem. L. Rev. 911 (1998); Rosemary Williams, Annotation, *Time Limits on Assumption or Rejection of Executory Contract or Lease Under § 365 of Bankruptcy Code*, 137 A.L.R. Fed. 137 (1997).

[23] Bankruptcy Code § 365(d)(1).

[24] Bankruptcy Code § 365(d)(2).

[25] Bankruptcy Code § 365(d)(4)(A).

[26] Bankruptcy Code § 365(d)(4)(B)(I); In re DCT, Inc., 283 B.R. 442 (Bankr. E.D. Mich. 2002); *but see* In re Southwest Aircraft Servs., Inc., 831 F.2d 848, 851 (9th Cir. 1987) (finding statute ambiguous and permitting extension of the motion that was made before expiration of the statutory period).

[27] Bankruptcy Code § 365(d)(4)(B)(ii).

Chapter 11 plan, the time limits operate to give some lessors a considerable advantage over other creditors.

[B] Court Approval of Assumption or Rejection

Approval of the trustee or debtor-in-possession's motion to assume or reject an executory contract is not automatic. Most courts apply a "business judgment" standard to determine whether the debtor's application to assume or reject an executory contract or unexpired lease should be granted.[28] Under this standard, the scope of the court's review is narrow, and the debtor's management decision to seek assumption or rejection carries a presumption of reasonableness that is not normally disturbed absent a showing of bad faith or abuse of the debtor's discretion.[29]

[C] Performance Before Assumption or Rejection

The time period between a petition for assumption or rejection may be significant, particularly in Chapter 11 cases where many months may pass between commencement and confirmation of a plan, though the time is abbreviated with respect to commercial real estate leases. Sections 365(d)(3) and (d)(5) specify the estate's duties during the period before assumption or rejection.

[1] Commercial Real Estate Leases[30]

Section 365(d)(3) governs performance of nonresidential real estate leases. It requires the trustee or debtor-in-possession to "timely perform all the obligations of the debtor" until the lease is assumed or rejected.[31] During the first sixty days after the order for relief, the court may grant the estate a time extension for performance of the debtor's obligations, but the court is expressly forbidden from extending the debtor's obligations beyond this initial sixty-day period. This usually means that the trustee or debtor-in-possession must keep current on its rental payments during the 210-day maximum time period for assumption or rejection of a commercial real estate lease.[32] Moreover, the debtor's failure to pay the rent during this time may impair its ability to assume the lease.[33]

---

[28] *E.g.*, Orion Pictures Corp. v. Showtime Networks, Inc. (In re Orion Pictures Corp.), 4 F.3d 1095, 1099 (2d Cir. 1993); Richmond Leasing Co. v. Capital Bank, N.A., 762 F.2d 1303, 1309 (5th Cir. 1985).

[29] Phar-Mor, Inc. v. Strauss Bldg. Assocs., 204 B.R. 948, 951–52 (N.D. Ohio 1997); In re Lady Balt. Foods, Inc., No. 02-43428, 2004 Bankr. LEXIS 1413 (Bankr. D. Kan. Aug. 13, 2004).

[30] Jeffrey S. Battershall, *Commercial Leases and Section 365 of the Bankruptcy Code*, 64 Am. Bankr. L.J. 329 (1990); Joshua Fruchter, *To Bind or Not to Bind — Bankruptcy Code 365(d)(3): Statutory Minefield*, 68 Am. Bankr. L.J. 437 (1994).

[31] Bankruptcy Code § 365(d)(3).

[32] The debtor need not comply with "ipso facto" provisions that treat the debtor's financial condition as a default. Bankruptcy Code § 362(d)(3); *see* Bankruptcy Code § 362(b)(2).

[33] *See* In re Southwest Aircraft Servs., Inc., 831 F.2d 848, 853–54 (9th Cir. 1987) (failure

[2] Equipment Leases

Section 365(d)(5) provides somewhat different treatment of equipment leases. It applies only to personal property leased for business purposes. It requires the estate to "timely perform all of the obligations of the debtor" that first arise "from or after 60 days after the order for relief in a case under chapter 11."[34] The court has more flexibility with respect to permitting extensions or other deviations from timely full performance than it does with respect to commercial real estate leases. With respect to equipment leases, the court has authority based on the equities of the case to adjust the debtor's obligations before the lease is assumed or rejected. Section 365(d)(5) does not apply in cases under Chapters 7, 12, or 13; nor does it apply to leases of property used for personal, family, or household purposes.

[3] Other Executory Contracts[35]

Sections 365(d)(3) and (d)(5) leave several conspicuous gaps regarding the estate's duties, during what is informally referred to as the "limbo period" between commencement of the case and assumption or rejection of an executory contract or an unexpired lease. The Code is silent about the estate's duty to continue to make rental payments on leased equipment in cases under Chapter 7, 12, or 13, or on leased consumer goods in any proceeding. Likewise, it says nothing about executory contracts.

Cases decided under both the Act and the Code make it clear that these contracts are not enforceable against the estate until they have been assumed.[36] But the debtor must pay for the reasonable value of any occupancy or use of the property involved.[37] A special rule is carved out for goods or services supplied to the estate in connection with an unexpired lease — the estate must pay at the contract rate.[38]

---

to pay is a factor, but is not dispositive of debtor's ability to assume); Matter of Condominium Admin. Servs., Inc., 55 B.R. 792 (Bankr. M.D. Fla. 1985) (payment is a condition of assumption).

34 Bankruptcy Code § 365(d)(5) (formerly codified in 11 U.S.C. § 365(d)(10)).

35 Douglas W. Bordewieck, *The Postpetiton Pre-Rejection, Pre-Assumption Status of an Executory Contract*, 59 Am. Bankr. L.J. 197 (1985); Howard Buschman, *Benefits and Burdens: Postpetition Performance of Unassumed Executory Contracts*, 5 Bankr. Dev. J. 241 (1988).

36 NLRB v. Bildisco & Bildisco, 465 U.S. 513, 531 (1984); Philadelphia Co. v. Dipple, 312 U.S. 168 (1941), *aff'g* 111 F.2d 932 (3d Cir. 1940).

37 Philadelphia Co. v. Dipple, 312 U.S. 168 (1941), *aff'g* 111 F.2d 932 (3d Cir. 1940).

38 Bankruptcy Code § 365(b)(4).

§ 11.04 Rejection of Executory Contracts[39]

[A] Effect of Rejection

[1] Pre-Petition Claim

Rejection of an executory contract or unexpired lease is treated as a *pre-petition* breach.[40] Thus, the non-debtor party has a general unsecured claim for its damages. The claim is allowed or disallowed just as if the debtor had breached before the petition was filed.[41] Because the estate never became responsible for the contract or lease, the creditor's claim is not treated as an administrative expense. Instead, it is a general unsecured claim, allowed to the extent permitted by § 502.[42]

[2] Effect of Rejection on Non-Debtor's Rights

One key issue with respect to rejected executory contracts and leases is the effect of rejection on the rights of the other party. This issue arises in several different contexts. In each of these, it is important to remember that rejection operates as a breach, not as a rescission or termination of the contract. It does not act as an avoidance power and does not undo conveyances of property that have already occurred. As will be seen, when courts forget about this, they sometimes reach disastrous conclusions. Congress has reacted to several of these situations by enacting very specific provisions that correct the results of bad decisions.

[a] Land Sale Contracts and Timeshares

The Code directly addresses the buyer's rights when the seller rejects a land sale contract or a contract for the sale of a timeshare interest. These sales contracts are in part conveyances of property, and in part contractual obligations. Section 365(i) seeks to respect this distinction when the seller rejects the contract. If the buyer is already in possession when the seller rejects, the buyer may elect to treat the contract as terminated and file a claim against the estate or may remain in possession and offset her damages against amounts remaining due to the seller.[43] In other words, the rejection does not operate to undo the conveyance of the property to the buyer, but the buyer must still pay the purchase price (less any offset). If the buyer chooses to remain in possession and offset her damages, she has no further claim against the estate.[44] The trustee or debtor-in-possession

---

[39] Douglas Bordewieck & Vern Countryman, *The Rejection of Collective Bargaining Agreements by Chapter 11 Debtors*, 57 Am. Bankr. L.J. 293 (1983).

[40] Bankruptcy Code § 365(g)(1).

[41] Bankruptcy Code § 502(g).

[42] *See* § 10.02[C] Allowance of Claims, *supra*.

[43] Bankruptcy Code § 365(i).

[44] Bankruptcy Code § 365(i)(2)(A).

is required to deliver title to the buyer in accordance with the terms of the purchase contract.[45]

If the buyer treats the rejection as a termination of the contract, she has a lien on the property to the extent of her right to recover the portion of the purchase price that she paid before rejection.[46] Thus, her claim is secured, and the property interest that she had is respected.

[b] Real Estate Leases

Where the landlord rejects an unexpired real estate lease, the lessee's rights are similar to those of a buyer under a rejected land sale contract. Section 365(h) gives the lessee the same right it would have under applicable nonbankruptcy law to terminate the lease, vacate the premises, and file a claim against the estate to recover its damages.[47] Alternatively, assuming the term of the lease has already commenced, the lessee may remain in possession, retain whatever other rights it has under the lease (such as the right to sublet or assign the lease), and offset whatever damages it suffers as a result of the landlord's rejection against the rent remaining due.[48] These damages may be significant, particularly in connection with an office building or an apartment complex in which the bankrupt landlord is responsible for maintenance of common areas such as parking lots, lobbies, hallways, and elevators. Similar rights are accorded to purchasers of timeshare interests who have made a deposit but have not yet taken possession.[49]

The Code expressly provides that the landlord's rejection does not affect the rights of a tenant in a shopping center with respect to "radius, location, use, exclusivity, or tenant mix or balance."[50] This specific language may imply that similar rights of tenants in other real estate projects may not be entitled to similar protection.

[c] Intellectual Property Licenses[51]

Intellectual property licenses present issues similar to those involved in land sale contracts and unexpired real estate leases. When an intellectual property licensor files a bankruptcy petition, it may seek to reject contracts with its licensees. Again, § 365(n) follows the pattern described immediately above regarding the protections afforded to buyers under rejected land sale contracts and lessees under rejected real estate leases. It allows the licensor

---

45 Bankruptcy Code § 365(i)(2)(B).

46 Bankruptcy Code § 365(j).

47 Bankruptcy Code § 365(h)(1)(A)(i).

48 Bankruptcy Code § 365(h)(1)(B).

49 Bankruptcy Code § 365(h)(2).

50 Bankruptcy Code § 365(h)(1)(C).

51 Madlyn Gleich Primoff & Erica G. Weinberger, *E-Commerce and Dot-Com Bankruptcies: Assumption, Assignment and Rejection of Executory Contracts, Including Intellectual Property Agreements, and Related Issues Under Sections 365(c), 365(e) and 365(n) of the Bankruptcy Code*, 8 Am. Bankr. Inst. L. Rev. 307 (2000).

to walk away from any contractual obligations, but it does not allow the licensor to undo the conveyance of a property interest (the license) that has already occurred. When the licensor rejects, the licensee may, if warranted under otherwise governing nonbankruptcy law, treat the license as if it had been terminated.[52] Alternatively, it may retain its rights under the license.[53] However, unlike the rights of a lessee, an intellectual property licensee must make any future royalty payments as they come due and may neither set off any damages it suffers as a result of the rejection nor pursue any claim for damages as an administrative expense claim. Its only right to damages is as a general unsecured creditor.[54]

These provisions expressly preserve any rights the licensee has as the exclusive licensee of the intellectual property involved.[55] They also expressly preserve the licensee's rights to specifically enforce its rights as an exclusive licensee. They overrule decisions such as *In re Lubrizol*[56] and *In re Logical Software, Inc.*,[57] in which rejection terminated the license and stripped the licensee of its property rights.[58]

These rules only apply to trade secrets, patents, and copyrights. They do not apply to trademarks, which are not mentioned in the Code's definition of "intellectual property."[59]

[d] Personal Property Leases

The 2005 Amendments added new language, making it clear that if a lease of personal property is rejected, or not timely assumed, the leased property is no longer property of the estate.[60] Moreover, the automatic stay is automatically terminated, giving the lessor the right to recover possession of its property under applicable state law.[61]

---

[52] Bankruptcy Code § 365(n)(1)(A).

[53] Bankruptcy Code § 365(n)(1)(B).

[54] Bankruptcy Code § 365(g)(1).

[55] Bankruptcy Code § 365(n)(1)(B).

[56] Lubrizol Enter., Inc. v. Richmond Metal Furnishers (In re Lubrizol Enter., Inc.), 756 F.2d 1043, 1048 (4th Cir. 1985).

[57] In re Logical Software, Inc., 66 B.R. 683, 686 (Bankr. D. Mass. 1986), *rev'd,* and *remanded on other grounds*, Infosystems Tech. v. Logical Software, No. 87-0042, 1987 U.S. Dist. LEXIS 6285 (D. Mass. June 25, 1987).

[58] *See generally* Robert L. Tamietti, *Technology Licenses Under The Bankruptcy Code: A Licensee's Mine Field*, 62 Am. Bankr. L.J. 295 (1988); Michael T. Andrew, *Executory Contracts in Bankruptcy: Understanding Rejection*, 59 U. Colo. L. Rev. 845 (1988).

[59] Bankruptcy Code § 101(35A); *see* Xuan-Thao N. Nguyen, *Bankrupting Trademarks*, 37 U.C. Davis L. Rev. 1267 (2004).

[60] Bankruptcy Code § 365(p)(1).

[61] Bankruptcy Code § 365(p)(1).

[e] Covenants Not to Compete[62]

One related circumstance where Congress has not taken any action regards the enforceability of covenants not to compete against a debtor who has rejected the underlying contract (frequently a franchise agreement). For example, when the debtor in *In re Rovine*, a franchisee of a fast-food chain, rejected the franchise contract, the franchisor sought to enforce a covenant not to compete that had been included in the franchise contract. The court treated rejection as relieving the debtor of its responsibilities under the contract and thus depriving the hamburger chain of its ability to enjoin the debtor from violating the restrictive covenant.[63] The issue arises because, outside of bankruptcy, the covenant not to compete would be enforceable through specific performance, in addition to a claim for damages. Specifically enforceable contract rights straddle the conceptual line between property rights that are respected in bankruptcy, and contract rights that are discharged. Rejection of the contract converts the damage claim to a pre-petition claim. However, this raises the question of whether covenant can be specifically enforced, even though the underlying claim has been discharged. The definition of claim includes "equitable remedies for breach of performance" of a contractual obligation, so long as the equitable remedy gives rise to a right to payment. Courts have divided over where to put non-compete obligations in this regard.[64]

[3] Rejection after Assumption

If a debtor-in-possession assumes an executory contract under § 365(a), it assumes the contract with all of its burdens and responsibilities attached; damages for any breach that occurs post-assumption are treated as administrative expenses that are entitled to priority under §§ 503(b) and 507(a)(2).[65]

[B] Employee's Rights

In general, employment contracts are treated the same as other executory contracts. An employer has the right to reject any long-term employment contract with its employees. The employee has a pre-petition claim for damages. Allowance of an employee's claims is restricted by § 502(b)(7).[66] On the other hand, such claims are likely entitled to priority under § 507(a)(4).[67]

[62] Jeffrey C. Sharer, *Noncompetition Agreements in Bankruptcy: Covenants (Maybe) Not to Compete*, 62 U. Chi. L. Rev. 1549 (1995).

[63] In re Rovine, 6 B.R. 661 (Bankr. W.D. Tenn. 1980).

[64] *Compare* In re Rovine, 6 B.R. 661 (Bankr. W.D. Tenn. 1980), *with* Sir Speedy, Inc. v. Morse, 256 B.R. 657 (D. Mass. 2000), *and* Watman v. Groman (In re Watman), 331 B.R. 502 (D. Mass. 2005).

[65] Bankruptcy Code § 365(g)(2); Mason v. Official Comm. of Unsecured Creditors (In re FBI Distrib. Corp.), 330 F.3d 36, 42 (1st Cir. 2003).

[66] *See* § 10.02[D][2] Limit on Claims for Salaries, *supra*.

[67] *See* § 10.04[A][4] Wage Claims, *supra*.

Apart from these general rules, the Code contains detailed provisions regarding the rejection of collective bargaining contracts[68] and termination of employee's retirement benefits.[69] These provisions are discussed elsewhere.[70]

§ 11.05 Assumption of Executory Contracts

One of the estate's key alternatives is to assume executory contracts and leases entered into by the debtor. The principal effect of assumption is to bind the estate to the contract and give the non-debtor party the right to an administrative expense claim for any subsequent breach of the contract while the case is pending. The court generally defers to the trustee or debtor-in-possession's business judgment about whether to assume or reject. The Code imposes several restrictions on assumption of executory contracts.

[A] Effect of Assumption

It is well established that assumption is all or nothing. If the debtor assumes the contract or lease, the debtor assumes all the obligations under the contract or lease. The debtor cannot unilaterally choose the favorable terms and reject the unfavorable terms, although, of course, the other contracting party might agree to modification of the contract or lease. The obligations created by the assumption, if not met by the debtor, create administrative expenses with an administrative priority.[71] As noted above, rejection is deemed to be a breach of the contract or lease, creating a claim that ordinarily will be a general unsecured claim.[72]

[B] Cure of Defaults Required for Assumption

Debtors are frequently in default on their pre-petition contracts. This creates a barrier if the debtor-in-possession wants to assume the contract. In many cases, the debtor has defaulted. Assumption requires the cure of any existing default. Section 365(b)(1) prevents assumption of an executory contract or unexpired lease involving a pre-petition default unless the debtor:

- cures any pre-petition defaults;
- compensates the other party for damages it suffered as a result of these defaults; and
- provides adequate assurance of future performance.[73]

---

[68] Bankruptcy Code § 1113.

[69] Bankruptcy Code § 1114.

[70] *See* Chapter 23, Special Problems in Bankruptcy, *infra*.

[71] NLRB v. Bildisco & Bildisco, 465 U.S. 513, 531–32 (1984).

[72] Bankruptcy Code § 502(g).

[73] Bankruptcy Code § 365(b)(1).

For example, suppose that prior to the bankruptcy, Franklin Manufacturing was leasing its computer equipment from CompuWorld Corp. Franklin failed to make two $10,000 rental payments in the months before its Chapter 11 petition. In addition, the debtor let the insurance policy it was required to maintain on the equipment lapse. If Franklin wants to assume the lease, it must pay the past-due rent and reinstate the insurance policy (cure), pay CompuWorld interest on the missed payments (compensate), and provide CompuWorld adequate assurances that these and other defaults will not recur (assure).

If the debtor does not have the cash necessary to cure the pre-petition defaults and pay for the damages that the other party suffered immediately, the debtor may nevertheless assume the contract or lease if it is able to provide adequate assurance that it will "promptly cure" its defaults[74] and "promptly compensate"[75] the other party for its harm.

Providing adequate assurance of future performance may be difficult and is likely to require more than a simple promise. The debtor-in-possession might be required to place sufficient funds in escrow to cover future rent and insurance payments or to obtain a letter of credit or guarantee that will ensure payment of sums that come due. In addition, the Code contains special rules regarding adequate protection of future performance with respect to shopping center leases.[76]

[1] Cure of Nonmonetary Defaults

Many debtors' pre-petition defaults are monetary — the debtor missed a rental or other payment due under the contract. Other defaults arise from failure to perform a "nonmonetary obligation." Due to their very nature, some nonmonetary obligations are sometimes not susceptible to being cured. For example, a commercial real estate lease may require the debtor to maintain regular business hours from 9 a.m. to 6 p.m. six days per week. If, as a cost-savings effort, the debtor did not open until noon on Saturdays for several months before its petition was filed, its failure to have done this cannot be cured. The default is a historical fact that cannot be undone.[77]

The 2005 Amendments address the impossibility of curing defaults of nonmonetary obligations in unexpired real estate leases. The new language adjusts the obligation to cure a past default that was due to "any failure to perform nonmonetary obligations under an unexpired lease of real property, if it is impossible . . . to cure such default by performing nonmonetary acts at and after failure to operate in accordance with a nonresidential real

[74] Bankruptcy Code § 365(b)(1)(A).

[75] Bankruptcy Code § 365(b)(1)(B).

[76] Bankruptcy Code § 365(b)(3); *see* § 11.07 Shopping Center Leases, *infra*.

[77] *E.g.*, In re Claremont Acquisition Corp., 113 F.3d 1029, 1033–35 (9th Cir. 1997) (auto dealership ceased operations in violation of its franchise agreement); *see* James I. Stang, *Assumption of Contracts and Leases: The Obstacle of the Historical Default*, 24 Cal. Bankr. J. 39 (1998).

property lease."[78] Taking action to resume performance at the time of assumption and compensating the other party for any harm caused by the breach is sufficient.[79] This overrules earlier decisions that prevented assumption of unexpired leases because the pre-petition default could not be cured.

The new language does not apply to nonmonetary defaults of franchise agreements.[80] Nor does it apply to service contracts[81] or personal property leases.[82] It is unclear whether the new language applies to commercial real estate leases where the debtor's pre-petition breach was in connection with mishandling of goods it was required to purchase from the lessor, such as in *In re Deppe*, where a gas station breached its lease and supply contract with an oil refinery by mixing gasoline delivered by the refinery with fuel from another supplier.[83] Thus, the conflict in the circuits that led to the adoption of the new language may still need to be resolved.[84] The inclusion of language directly dealing with some nonmonetary defaults may signal Congress' intent to require the debtor to cure nonmonetary defaults in circumstances not explicitly addressed by the 2005 Amendments.[85]

[2] Cure of Ipso Facto Clauses Not Necessary

Some defaults do not have to be cured. If the default is under a so-called ipso facto clause, relating to the debtor's general financial condition, it need not be cured. These clauses purport to make the debtor's financial condition or filing of bankruptcy an act of default. Section 365(b)(2) exempts these types of default from the necessity of being cured.[86]

The same rules effectively apply with regard to the assignment of the contract or lease. To be assigned, the contract or lease must first be assumed properly.[87] This means that defaults, other than those under ipso facto clauses, must be cured. Moreover, whether or not there are defaults, the debtor must provide adequate assurance of future performance by the assignee of the lease or contract.[88]

---

[78] Bankruptcy Code § 365(b)(1)(A).

[79] Bankruptcy Code § 365(b)(1)(A).

[80] *E.g.*, In re Claremont Acquisitions, Inc., 113 F.3d 1029 (9th Cir. 1992).

[81] *E.g.*, Matter of GP Exp. Airlines, Inc., 200 B.R. 222 (Bankr. D. Neb. 1996).

[82] Richard Levin & Alesia Ranney-Marinelli, *The Creeping Repeal of Chapter 11: The Significant Business Provisions of the Bankruptcy Abuse Prevention and Consumer Protection Act of 2005*, 79 Am. Bankr. L.J. 603, 625–26 (2005).

[83] 110 B.R. 898 (Bankr. D. Minn. 1990).

[84] *Compare* In re Claremont Acquisitions, Inc., 113 F.3d 1029 (9th Cir. 1992) (duty to cure nonmonetary default prevents), *with* In re BankVest Capital Corp., 360 F.3d 291 (1st Cir. 2004) (cure of nonmonetary defaults unnecessary).

[85] *See* David G. Epstein & Lisa Normand, *"Real-world" and "Academic" Questions about "Nonmonetary Obligations" Under the 2005 Version of 365(b)*, 13 Am. Bankr. Inst. L. Rev. 617 (2005).

[86] Bankruptcy Code § 365(b)(2).

[87] Bankruptcy Code § 365(f)(2)(A).

[88] Bankruptcy Code § 365(f)(2)(B).

[C] Restrictions on Assumption

Some executory contracts and unexpired leases cannot be assumed. If assumption is impossible, a Chapter 11 debtor-in-possession is unable to take full advantage of the favorable terms of the contract as part of its reorganization effort. At a minimum, the debtor must renegotiate the terms of the contract; at worst, the debtor loses the deal entirely. Further, because assumption is necessary for any assignment of the contract to a third party, an unassumable contract cannot be sold by a Chapter 7 trustee to obtain valuable cash to make payments to the debtor's creditors. Likewise, a Chapter 11 debtor-in-possession is unable to assign the contract to obtain cash to fund its operations or make payments to creditors upon implementation of the plan.

[1] Pre-Petition Termination

To be assumed, the contract must remain in effect when the debtor's petition is filed. If the contract or lease has expired or has been terminated due to a pre-petition breach, it cannot be assumed. Thus, a three-year lease that expired a month before the debtor's petition was filed cannot be assumed. It is not an "unexpired" lease. Further, the lease may not be assumed if the lease has terminated and the debtor has been evicted before commencement due the debtor's default.[89] As one court explained: "[s]imply put, if a lease of nonresidential real property has been terminated under state law before the filing of a bankruptcy petition, there is nothing left for the trustee to assume."[90]

Most of the difficulty with respect to pre-petition termination deals with whether, under applicable law, the lease or contract has already terminated. First, not every breach gives the other party the right to terminate the contract. Second, lessors and other parties sometimes waive a breach, even though it was material and could have served as justification for termination. Third, the contract itself or governing law many give the debtor the right to cure a material breach. But, if the contract terminated before the debtor's case began, it cannot be assumed.[91]

[2] Termination Under an Ipso-Facto Clause

However, an ipso-facto clause that purports to terminate an executory contract or unexpired lease automatically, based on the debtor's financial condition, commencement of its bankruptcy case, or the appointment of a custodian of the debtor's property, are nearly always ineffective.[92] Thus, the parties may not impair the effect of § 365 through a contractual provision that purports to end the contract at the outset of the debtor's bankruptcy case. The same rule applies to a provision in "applicable law"

[89] Bankruptcy Code § 365(c)(3).

[90] In re Windmill Farms, Inc., 841 F.2d 1467, 1469 (9th Cir. 1988).

[91] Moody v. Amoco Oil Co., 734 F.2d 1200, 1212 (7th Cir. 1984).

[92] Bankruptcy Code § 365(d)(1).

that would automatically terminate a contract under these circumstances.[93] Thus, lobbying groups may not seek relief from § 365 by appealing to state courts or legislatures.

[3] Anti-Assignment Clauses

Many contracts contain provisions purporting to prohibit their assignment or delegation. These clauses are ineffective to prevent assumption of the contract by a bankruptcy trustee or a debtor-in-possession.[94] Thus, parties who are adverse to the risk of their long term contracts being assumed in a bankruptcy filed by their contracting partner may not sidestep the risk by negotiating for an anti-assignment clause in their contract. Rather, as explained immediately below, the contract must be unassignable under applicable law, without respect to whether it contains a contractual proscription against assignment, in order to prevent the contract from being assumed or assigned in bankruptcy.

[4] Non-Delegable Duties[95]

The Code prevents assumption of a contract if applicable non-bankruptcy law[96] excuses the other party from accepting performance from or rendering performance to a person other than the debtor.[97] This applies whether or not there is any contractual limitation on assignment or delegation.[98]

Thus, § 365(c)(1) implements the basic contract law principle that some duties cannot be delegated because they are fundamental to the underlying bargain. These duties are often misleadingly referred to as "personal services." This is not quite accurate. Many personal services can be delegated and some non-delegable duties are not personal services.[99] The real issue is whether performance by a particular person or organization is a fundamental part of the bargain. Personal services only come into it because it is easiest to find illustrations in certain types of personal service contracts. For example, if Paramount Film Studio enters into a contract to have Tom Cruise appear as the star of a new "Mission Impossible" movie, Cruise cannot file a Chapter 11 petition and assign the contract to Whoopi Goldberg. The identity and appearance of the actor and his acting skill are fundamental parts of the bargain.

---

[93] Bankruptcy Code § 365(e)(1).

[94] Bankruptcy Code § 365(e)(1).

[95] Daniel J. Bussel & Edward A. Friedlander, *The Limits on Assuming and Assigning Executory Contracts*, 74 Am. Bankr. L.J. 321 (2000); Michelle Morgan Harner, et al., *Debtors Beware: The Expanding Universe of Non-assumable/Non-assignable Contracts in Bankruptcy*, 13 Am. Bankr. Inst. L. Rev. 187 (2005).

[96] This encompasses all law applicable to the particular contract, whether state or federal.

[97] Bankruptcy Code § 365(c)(1)(A).

[98] *E.g.*, In re Pioneer Ford Sales, Inc., 729 F.2d 27 (1st Cir. 1984).

[99] *E.g.*, In re Pioneer Ford Sales, Inc., 729 F.2d 27, 29 (1st Cir. 1984) (Breyer, J.) (automobile franchise).

Even rarer than non-delegable duties are non-assignable benefits. There are now very few circumstances under which a party to a contract is prohibited from assigning the benefit of its bargain to another. Although Tom Cruise may not be able to delegate his duty to star in the film to Whoopi Goldberg, he would probably be permitted to assign his right to receive payment to the Screen Actor's Finance Company. Many of the few restrictions that still exist are nothing more than indirect ways of restricting improper delegations.

There are three distinct situations in which this issue arises with respect to assumption of executory contracts in a bankruptcy case: (1) performance of the contract by the debtor-in-possession; (2) performance of the contract by the trustee; and (3) performance of the contract by a third party. Technically speaking, the first two situations involve performance of the contract by the estate, following assumption of the contract, under the supervision of either the debtor-in-possession or the trustee. The third situation involves a two step process: assumption of the executory contract by the estate and assignment to a third party.

In dealing with these contracts, the precise text of the Code has proven quite elusive, leading to a serious division of authority with respect to the first of these three issues: whether a debtor-in-possession can assume and perform an otherwise non-delegable duty in a personal services contract.

The relevant language is in § 365(c):

> The trustee may not assume or assign any executory contract or unexpired lease of the debtor, whether or not such contract or lease prohibits or restricts assignment of rights or delegation of duties if:
>
> (1)(A) applicable law excuses a party, other than the debtor, to such contract or lease from accepting performance from or rendering performance to an entity other than the debtor or the debtor-in-possession, whether or not such contract or lease prohibits or restricts assignment of rights or delegation of duties; and
>
> (B) such party does not consent to such assumption.

In parsing this language, it is critical to remember that a debtor-in-possession has all of the same rights, powers, and duties of the trustee.[100] This justifies substituting the phrase "debtor-in-possession" for "trustee" in the first part of this language. With this adjustment, the statutory language, when stripped of superfluous phrases, seems to say:

> The [debtor-in-possession] may not assume . . . any executory contract . . . if applicable law excuses [the non-debtor] from accepting performance from or rendering performance to [anyone] other than the debtor or the debtor-in-possession.

In other words, it establishes a "hypothetical test"[101] that asks whether the debtor could assign the contract to a stranger. If the contract could be

[100] Bankruptcy Code § 1107.

[101] *See* In re Western Elec. Inc., 852 F.2d 79, 83 (3d Cir. 1988).

assigned to the stranger, it can be assumed by the estate. If it could not be assigned to a stranger, it cannot be assumed by the estate for performance either by a trustee or the debtor-in-possession. This at least is the conclusion drawn in cases such as *In re Catapult Entertainment, Inc.*[102] Other courts, such as in *Summit Investment* and *Development Corp. v. Leroux*,[103] have adopted an "actual test" that permits a debtor-in-possession to assume an executory contract, as long as the assumption does not actually require the other party to accept performance of the contract from a third party.[104] Cases taking the first approach would prevent Tom Cruise, as debtor-in-possession, from assuming and performing the movie deal he had entered into before filing his bankruptcy petition. Cases taking the second approach would prevent Cruise's bankruptcy trustee from assuming the contract[105] and would prevent Cruise assigning it to another actor.

[5] Contracts to Extend Credit and Issue Securities

In contracts to make a loan or otherwise extend credit, the identity (and credit score) of the borrower is a fundamental part of the bargain. Although one might question whether this logic entirely applies to modern mass-marketed credit cards, the Bankruptcy Code draws no distinction between them and other extensions of credit. It explicitly makes all contracts to "make a loan, or extend other debt financing or financial accommodations . . . or to issue a security of the debtor"[106] unassumable, regardless of how they are treated outside the Bankruptcy Code.

This limitation applies regardless of whether there is a limitation in the contract itself.[107] Moreover, because there is no provision in this subsection regarding consent, the prohibition applies regardless of the consent of the other party.[108] Of course, this does not prevent the lender and the debtor from entering into a new, post-petition credit agreement; that agreement, however, would nearly always require court approval.[109]

The limitation has been fairly narrowly construed. It applies only when the focus of the contract is an extension of credit. For example, many contracts for the sale of goods or services, and virtually all leases, involve

---

[102] 165 F.3d 747 (1999); *see also* RCI Tech. Corp. v. Sunterra Corp. (In re Sunterra Corp.), 361 F.3d 257 (4th Cir. 2004); City of Jamestown v. James Cable Partners (In re James Cable Partners), 27 F.3d 534 (11th Cir. 1994); In re W. Elec., Inc., 852 F.2d 79 (3d Cir. 1988).

[103] 69 F.3d 608 (1st Cir. 1995).

[104] In re Catapult Entmt. Inc., 165 F.3d 747 (9th Cir. 1999); *see generally* Daniel J. Bussel & Edward A. Friedlander, *The Limits on Assuming and Assigning Executory Contracts*, 74 Am. Bankr. L.J. 321 (2000).

[105] Whether the trustee could assume the contract and then assign it to Tom Cruise, is fun to consider, but it is difficult to imagine such a circumstance even occurring.

[106] Bankruptcy Code § 365(c)(2).

[107] Bankruptcy Code § 365(c).

[108] In re Sun Runner Marine, Inc., 945 F.2d 1089 (9th Cir. 1991).

[109] *See* § 9.05 Obtaining Credit, *supra*.

an extension of credit, because the buyer or lessee is not obligated to pay for the property or services immediately. The mere fact that a contract for sale of goods provides for thirty days' unsecured open account credit does not mean that the contract is non-assumable or non-assignable.

§ 11.06 Assignment of Executory Contracts and Unexpired Leases

If the estate may assume an executory contract or unexpired lease, a separate question arises over whether the contract may be assigned to a third party. Some contracts that may be assumed by the trustee or a debtor-in-possession may not be assigned to a stranger to the contract. Assumption by the estate and assignment to a third party are distinct events, and any effort to assign the contract must be evaluated independently from the question of whether the contract may be assumed.

[A] Effect of Assignment

Assignment of an executory contract or unexpired lease operates as a novation of the contract. Section 365(k) makes this clear: "Assignment . . . relieves the trustee and the estate from any liability for any breach of [the] contract or lease occurring after [its] assignment."[110] This, of course, is quite different from the usual treatment of delegated duties under the law of contracts, where a person who delegates a duty remains responsible for performance unless the other party to the original contract consents to her release.[111]

For example, if Franklin Manufacturing Inc. enters Chapter 11, assumes its long-term sales contract with Industrial Supply Co., and assigns the contract to Hocking Fabrications Corp., Franklin is off the hook with Industrial Supply. If Hocking Fabrications subsequently breaches, Industrial Supply's only recourse is to recover from Hocking Fabrications. It has no claim against Franklin.

This is also quite different from the consequence if Franklin breached the contract after assuming it, without an assignment to a third party. In that case, Industrial Supply would not only have a claim against Franklin, it would have a § 507(a)(2) priority administrative expense claim, entitled to payment in full in Franklin's reorganization plan.[112] The disparity of treatment between breach after assumption and breach after assignment suggests the wisdom of delaying assumption until it is clear whether the contract will be assigned to a third person.

---

[110] Bankruptcy Code § 365(k) .

[111] *See* Restatement (Second) of Contracts § 318(3) (1981); Jeffrey Ferriell & Michael Navin, Understanding Contracts 778 (2005).

[112] Bankruptcy Code § 365(g)(2).

[B] Restrictions on Assignment

The Code's language restricting assignments of executory contracts and unexpired leases is nearly incoherent. Section 365(f), which addresses assignments directly, must be read in conjunction with § 365(c) on assumptions. As explained below, the two sections do not fit well together.

[1] Assumption Required for Assignment

Not surprisingly, the estate can only assign contracts that it has assumed.[113] This means that the Code's restrictions on assumption of an executory contract operate as restrictions on any assignment of the contract. This includes the requirement of curing any defaults and compensating the other party for any damages it has suffered as a result of the debtor's breach. Thus, a contract remaining in default can neither be assumed nor assigned.

[2] Assurance of Future Performance by the Assignee

Assignment to a third party is possible only if the assignee provides "adequate assurance of future performance" of the contact or lease.[114] Adequate assurance of future performance by the assignee must be provided, even if there has been no default of the contract. Thus, the Bankruptcy Code treats proposals to assign an executory contract or unexpired lease as if the proposal to assign the contract constituted the type of "reasonable grounds for insecurity" which, under non-bankruptcy contract law, gives the other party the right to demand adequate assurances of performance.[115]

[3] Legal and Contractual Restrictions on Assignment

The law regarding the effect of legal and contractual restrictions on assignment of executory contracts and unexpired leases is a mess. The principle difficulty is in attempting to reconcile the conflicting language of § 365(c) with that of § 365(f).

Section 365(f)(1) permits the trustee or debtor-in-possession to assign an executory contract "notwithstanding a provision in [the contract], or in *applicable law* that prohibits . . . the assignment."[116] Read in isolation, this seems to take a very liberal approach to the assignability of executory contracts and unexpired leases. If applied without consulting other provisions of the Code, it completely abrogates state and other federal law that restricts the delegability of contractual duties.

---

113 Bankruptcy Code § 365(f)(2)(A).

114 Bankruptcy Code § 365(f)(2)(B).

115 *See* U.C.C. § 2-609 (2003).

116 Bankruptcy Code § 365(f)(1) (emphasis added).

However, § 365(f)(2)(A) makes it clear that a contract may not be assigned unless it is first assumed.[117] Section 365(c)(1), discussed above,[118] apparently prevents assumption if the contract could not be assigned to a third party under applicable law (indeed, this linguistic problem arises even if the debtor intends to perform the contract itself). Thus, what § 365(f)(2)(A) expressly permits, § 365(c)(1) seemingly explicitly prohibits.

Several courts have attempted to reconcile the provisions, without much success. In *In re Pioneeer Ford Sales, Inc.*, an auto dealership sought authority to assume and assign its Ford franchise to a Toyota dealer, over the Ford Motor Company's objection.[119] Under applicable Rhode Island law, auto dealers could not assign a franchise without the consent of the manufacturer.[120] The court reconciled the two provisions by indicating that § 365(c)(1)(A) applies to cases where nonbankruptcy law prohibits assignment, regardless of what the contract says, and that § 365(f)(1) applies to cases where state law prohibits assignment by specifically enforcing a contractual provision prohibiting assignment.[121] Unfortunately, as commentators[122] and several courts[123] have pointed out, this is not what the statute says.

Similar problems arise in connection with the enforceability of ipso facto clauses under § 365(e)(2). It contains language similar to that in § 365(f)(2) that seemingly impairs the effect of an ipso facto clause only if "applicable law excuses a party, other than the debtor . . . from accepting performance from or rendering performance to the trustee or to an assignee."[124] Courts applying this language, like those interpreting § 365(f)(2), usually preclude enforcement of the ipso facto clause against the debtor-in-possession, even if the other party could resist performance of the contract by a trustee or a third-party.[125]

[C] Appeals of Orders Permitting Assignment

Once the bankruptcy court has issued an order authorizing assignment of an executory contract or unexpired lease, the assignee may rely on the court's order and begin performance. This makes appeals of a court's order permitting assignment problematic. Accordingly, orders approving the

117 Bankruptcy Code § 365(f)(2)(A); *see* § 11.05[B][1] Assumption Required, *supra*.

118 *See* § 11.05[C][4] Non-Delegable Duties, *supra*.

119 *See* In re Pioneer Ford Sales, Inc., 729 F.2d 27 (1st Cir. 1984).

120 The manufacturer could not, however, unreasonably withhold its consent.

121 729 F.2d at 28–29.

122 Daniel J. Bussel & Edward A. Friedler, *The Limits on Assuming and Assigning Executory Contracts*, 74 Am. Bankr. L.J. 321, 336–37 (2000); Theresa J. Pulley Radwan, *Limitations on Assumption and Assignment of Executory Contracts by "Applicable Law,"* 31 N.M. L. Rev. 299 (2001).

123 In re Magness, 972 F.2d 689, 695 (6th Cir. 1992); Everex Sys. v. Cadtrak Corp. (In re CFLC, Inc)., 89 F.3d 673 (9th Cir. 1996).

124 Bankruptcy Code § 365(e)(2)(A)(i).

125 *E.g.*, In re Footstar, Inc., 337 B.R. 785 (Bankr. S.D.N.Y. 2005).

assignment of an executory contract or unexpired lease are stayed for ten days after they are entered.[126] This facilitates parties who oppose the assignment in seeking a longer stay while an appeal of the bankruptcy court's decision is pending.

§ 11.07 Shopping Center Leases

Shopping center leases are singled out for special treatment. The Code's special shopping center provisions are designed to protect the shopping center from particular hardships they may suffer if an important tenant goes bankrupt. Among the many goals of those who operate shopping centers is to have the right mix of stores. The classic shopping center has one or more "anchor" stores (usually large all-purpose retailers) and a variety of specialized shops. Certain kinds of stores may be prohibited entirely; for example, many shopping malls prohibit liquor stores and adult bookstores on the theory that these detract from the family atmosphere they are trying to create. Also, shopping center developers frequently promise particular stores that they will be the only store of their type in the center. For example, in order to induce Famous Pharmacy to locate in the shopping center, Colossal Developer may promise the Pharmacy that it will be the only pharmacy in the shopping center. If Sam's Sporting Goods goes bankrupt, and seeks to assign its lease to Discount Drug Stores, it will disturb the tenant mix and may create a violation in the lease agreement between Developer and Famous Pharmacy. Other considerations include common opening and closing times and avoidance of empty space. Nothing horrifies a mall manager more than the possibility of closed and shuttered shops.[127]

Under § 365(b)(3), the trustee or debtor-in-possession must provide the lessor with adequate assurance of a variety of matters:

- that there will be a sufficient source of rent and other consideration due under the lease;
- if the lease is assigned, that the financial condition and the operating performance of the assignee is similar to the financial condition and the operating performance that the debtor had when the debtor and the lessor entered into the lease;[128]
- that the percentage rent will not decline "substantially";[129]
- that the assumption or assignment of the lease is subject to all the provisions of the lease, particularly those that deal with "radius, location, use, or exclusivity";[130]

---

[126] Fed. R. Bankr. P. 6006(d).

[127] This is why vacant space, when it does exist, is usually hidden behind a facade.

[128] Bankruptcy Code § 365(b)(3)(A).

[129] Bankruptcy Code § 365(b)(3)(B).

[130] Bankruptcy Code § 365(b)(3)(C).

- that there will be no breach of any provision contained in any other lease relating to the shopping center, any financing agreement relating to the shopping center, or any master agreement relating to the shopping center;[131] and
- that assumption or assignment of the lease will not disrupt any tenant mix or balance in the shopping center.[132]

Note that these requirements are in addition to all of the other requirements imposed on an assuming or assigning trustee or debtor-in-possession, including the other requirements that relate generally to leases of real property.

[131] Bankruptcy Code § 365(b)(3)(C).

[132] Bankruptcy Code § 365(b)(3)(D).

Chapter 12

Preserving the Debtor's Assets

§ 12.01 Debtor's Retention of Estate Property

In a Chapter 7 liquidation case, debtors are supposed to give up their assets in exchange for being released from liability for their debts. However, debtors have never been required to give up all of their assets. Rather than leaving debtors without the shirts on their backs, the Bankruptcy Code permits Chapter 7 debtors to keep a limited amount of their property. Humanitarian concerns for the health and safety of these debtors, and for their families makes this necessary. Moreover, if debtors are to receive the "fresh start" that bankruptcy promises them, they need some critical items to make their way in the world. This policy also recognizes the practical reality that many personal items are frequently worth less than the cost of selling them.

A key question in bankruptcy, particularly from the debtor's perspective, is how much property she can protect from distribution to creditors in the bankruptcy process. The Bankruptcy Code provides several avenues for debtors to keep their assets. Some property is "exempt" under state law, or, where available, federal exemptions. This means that it is not subject to seizure by unsecured creditors and is not liquidated by the bankruptcy trustee.[1] Other property may not be exempt, but it may be encumbered beyond its market value. This property may sometimes be "redeemed" by the debtor from creditors' security interests.[2] Redemption permits the debtor to buy his property back from secured creditors for the amount the creditor would have received if the collateral had been liquidated.[3]

Reorganization provides debtors with other ways to keep their assets.[4] The most significant difference between liquidation under Chapter 7 of the Bankruptcy Code and reorganization under Chapters 11, 12, or 13 is that reorganization nearly always permits the debtor to retain more assets. But this privilege does not come for free. A reorganizing debtor is required to use post-petition income to pay creditors at least what they would have received if the debtor's non-exempt property had been liquidated.[5] Debtors who value their current assets more than their anticipated future income may find this an attractive alternative and seek relief under one of the

---

1 *See* § 1.05[B][20] Exemption, *supra.*

2 *See* § 12.08[A] Lump-Sum Redemption by Debtor, *infra.*

3 *See* § 12.08[A] Lump-Sum Redemption by Debtor, *infra.*

4 *See* Chapter 18 Rehabilitation of Individuals with Regular Income, *infra.*

5 *See* § 18.08[E][1] Best Interests of Creditors, *infra;* § 19.10[F] Best Interests of Creditors, *infra.*

Code's reorganization proceedings. Debtors who either value their future income more highly than their current property, or who determine that they will be able to use their exemption rights to protect much of their current property from liquidation, will seek bankruptcy protection in a Chapter 7 liquidation case. However, as will also be seen, Congress revised the Bankruptcy Code in 2005 to compel debtors with the prospects of significant future income to reorganize, even though they might prefer to liquidate.

There are also several quasi-reorganization strategies available to Chapter 7 debtors, which permit them to retain a larger quantity of their assets in exchange for some future payment to their creditors. Chapter 7 provides debtors with several mechanisms that may be used to restructure a few of their debts and to discharge others through liquidation. Redemption, mentioned above, is one such method. Another is to enter into a "reaffirmation" agreement with the creditor to repay all or most of the discharged debt from his future income in exchange for keeping possession of the collateral.[6] In the past, debtors have also been permitted to maintain an informal arrangement regarding property subject to a security interest or mortgage. There is anecdotal evidence that arrangements of this type may be used far more frequently than other more formal methods of protecting non-exempt property.[7] However, as will be seen, Congress' 2005 changes to the Bankruptcy Code placed additional restrictions on these less formal mechanisms.

§ 12.02 Exemptions in Bankruptcy

Section 522 of the Bankruptcy Code permits debtors to retain some of their property. Although exempt property is part of the debtor's estate, it is not available for administration by the trustee or for distribution to unsecured creditors. However, exemptions do not generally impair the rights of creditors with liens on the debtor's property.[8] Thus, creditors with a security interest or mortgage on otherwise exempt assets are normally entitled to enforce their rights against the debtor's assets despite the debtor's exemption rights.[9]

Exemptions are available only for an "individual debtor."[10] Corporations and partnerships enjoy no such rights. Thus, exemptions play a significant role in consumer liquidation cases under Chapter 7, nearly all of which are "no-asset" cases,[11] in which all of the debtor's assets are either exempt or

---

[6] *See* § 12.08[B] Reaffirmation to Retain Property, *infra.*

[7] *See* Marianne B. Culhane & Michaela M. White, *Debt After Discharge: An Empirical Study of Reaffirmation*, 73 Am. Bankr. Inst. L. Rev. 709 (1999).

[8] *See generally* Owen v. Owen, 500 U.S. 305, 308–09 (1991).

[9] *See* § 12.05[B] Liens on Exempt Property, *infra.*

[10] Bankruptcy Code § 522(b)(1).

[11] When a Chapter 7 case is filed, the clerk of the court initially determines, based on the schedules filed with the debtor's petition, whether a "dividend" will be available for creditors. If not, Bankruptcy Rule 2002(e) provides that the clerk informs creditors of this fact in the notice that is sent to them, formally advising them of the bankruptcy case and alerting them

subject to unavoidable security interests, leaving nothing available for distribution to unsecured creditors.[12]

Exemptions are also important in Chapter 13 rehabilitation cases. Although Chapter 13 debtors are generally permitted to keep their property regardless of whether it is exempt, exemption levels have an effect on the extent of payments necessary to meet the "best interests of creditors" test for confirmation of a Chapter 13 plan. The best interests test requires Chapter 13 debtors to pay creditors an amount that is equivalent to what the creditors would have received in a liquidation case.[13] More generous exemption rights reduce the amount necessary to satisfy this test. Less generous exemption rights require debtors, or at least those who have more assets, to pay a higher price for their Chapter 13 discharge.

[A] Exemption Policy

Exemptions have been an integral part of debtor-creditor and bankruptcy law for many years. The underlying policy for permitting debtors to keep some of their property is simple. It is generally accepted that, no matter how bad an individual's financial troubles, he should not be utterly deprived of the basic necessities of life. For this reason, creditors have long been prohibited from seizing such things as clothing, cooking and eating utensils, beds, linens, and other basic furnishings. Without these items, debtors are likely to become a burden on society in other ways. Moreover, sale of such items is unlikely to generate much value to pay to creditors, and the cost for the debtor to replace these necessities is likely to far exceed any marginal payment to creditors that might result from their seizure.

It is also generally true that items that are central to the debtor's identity, but (usually) of little monetary value, such as family Bibles and wedding rings, have been exempted. For many years, exemption laws remained static; many of them preserved in legal amber a picture of nineteenth century rural American life — exempting a cow, a couple of pigs, a spinning wheel, and the like. However, most states have now updated their exemption laws to reflect what are commonly regarded as the necessities of life in an urban industrial society. The most obvious example of this is the nearly universal inclusion of at least a portion of a debtor's equity in an automobile among the property that is exempt. Curiously, however, no

---

that they should not bother to file a proof of claim. If the trustee subsequently determines that assets are available for distribution, a revised notice is sent that advises creditors of the ninety day deadline to submit proof of claims. Fed. R. Bankr. P. 3002(c)(5).

[12] Seventy percent of bankruptcy cases in the United States are filed under Chapter 7. In ninety-eight percent of these cases, there are no assets available to distribute to creditors. *See* Jean Braucher, *Consumer Bankruptcy as Part of the Social Safety Net: Fresh Start or Treadmill?* 44 Santa Clara L. Rev. 1065, 1089 (2004); Rep. of the Nat'l. Bankr. Rev. Comm'n 137 (1997); Jean Braucher, *Options in Consumer Bankruptcy: An American Perspective*, 37 Osgoode Hall L.J. 155, 160–64 (1999).

[13] Bankruptcy Code § 1325(a)(4); *see* § 18.08[E][1] Best Interests of Creditors, *infra*.

special exemption has yet been carved out for personal computers, cellphones, MP3 players, or flat screen TVs.[14]

Even in bankruptcy, exemption laws have traditionally been the province of state governments. Although many state exemption statutes are quite similar to one another, a few state statutes stand out as notably pro-creditor or pro-debtor. Florida and Texas are often pointed out by critics as debtors' havens, permitting some debtors to exempt literally millions of dollars' worth of real estate.[15] However, in most states, exemptions are relatively modest, protecting only basic items, such as clothing, limited furniture, appliances, and limited equity in a car and a home.[16]

There has been much debate over whether exemption levels matter very much either as an incentive to borrow or to default and file bankruptcy. Theoretically, generous exemptions should encourage bankruptcy, because they permit a debtor to discharge debt "cheaply"; that is, without the surrender of much property. However, there is surprisingly little evidence to support that contention; to the contrary, the evidence indicates that exemption levels have little or no impact on the frequency of bankruptcy.[17] This does not mean that there are no bankruptcies in which the debtor exploits generous exemptions; it merely means that the number of such bankruptcies is so small as to be statistically invisible. Nevertheless, widely disseminated publicity about a even a few examples of abuse carries with it the potential to detract from public confidence in the system. Despite these concerns, the most recent round of revisions to the Bankruptcy Code left the most generous state exemption schemes largely intact,[18] though they did limit the ability of debtors to increase the value of their homesteads during the period prior to bankruptcy.

[14] Though exemptions for "a radio" might, in the right circumstances, be applied to these ubiquitous electronic devices.

[15] In Texas, debtors are permitted to exempt an "urban home" of land comprised of up to ten acres of contiguous real estate, together with any improvements that have been made to the land. Texas Prop. Code Ann. § 41.002(a) (Vernon 2000). Up to 200 acres of land, including a "rural home," may be exempted, though an unmarried adult is limited to a meager 100-acre ranch. Texas Prop. Code Ann. § 41.002(b). With respect to an "urban home," the Texas statute permits the exempted ten acres of homestead property to include a place to "exercise a calling or business" and thus does not limit the number of square feet of apartment or office space that might be part of the improvements to the urban home.

There is historical evidence that the Republic of Texas adopted America's first exemption statute as an inducement to settlers (immigrants?) from the United States. *See* Richard M. Hynes et al., *The Political Economy of Property Exemption Laws*, 47 J.L. & Econ. 19, 23 (2004) (citing Paul Goodman, *The Emergence of Homestead Exemptions in the United States: Accommodation and Resistance to the Market Revolution, 1840–1880*, 80 J. Am. Hist. 470, 477 (1993)). Thus it is possible that early Texas sought freedom, not from General Antonio López de Santa Anna, but from Chase Manhattan.

[16] *E.g.*, Ohio Rev. Code Ann. § 2329.66 (LexisNexis 2006 Supp.).

[17] Teresa Sullivan, Elizabeth Warren & Jay Lawrence Westbrook, As We Forgive Our Debtors: Bankruptcy and Consumer Credit in America 241–42 (1989).

[18] Margaret Howard, *Exemptions under the 2005 Bankruptcy Amendments: A Tale of Opportunity Lost*, 79 Am. Bankr. L.J. 397 (2005); Susan Jensen, *A Legislative History of the Bankruptcy Abuse Prevention and Consumer Protection Act of 2005*, 79 Am. Bankr. L.J. 485, 511–12 (2005).

[B] State or Federal Exemptions; Opt-Out[19]

Since the 1898 Act, federal bankruptcy law has largely left the level and extent of exemptions up to the states. The Bankruptcy Act permitted debtors to use the applicable state exemption statute to determine what they could retain in a bankruptcy case. This had the advantage of transparency to state law and thus limited forum shopping between state and federal courts. It had the disadvantage of limiting national uniformity, since exemptions differed so much from state to state. This non-uniformity has not, despite occasional challenges, posed any serious constitutional difficulties.[20] Unfortunately, it also had the effect of preserving exemption rules that were increasingly obsolete. Until recently, few states had amended their rules to account for the vast twentieth century migration of Americans from farms with mules to suburban tract houses with cars and garages.

In 1978, the drafters of the Bankruptcy Code were concerned that state exemption laws were too varied, too out of date, and too limited. There was some support for completely federalizing exemption law, but this turned out to be politically impossible. A compromise was reached that left ultimate control of debtors' exemption rights with state legislatures. The Bankruptcy Code now contains a set of federal exemptions and permits debtors to choose between the federal exemptions provided in the Bankruptcy Code or the exemptions authorized under state law. However, it also permits individual states to prohibit their residents from using the federal exemptions by "opting out" of the federal exemption scheme. Within a few years of implementation of this compromise, most states had opted out. Not surprisingly, the states that have not opted out are primarily those with more generous exemptions than those contained in what some had hoped would be a uniform schedule of federal exemptions. Thus, despite the Bankruptcy Code's list of exempt property, exemption law remains largely a state preserve.

In the opt-out states,[21] debtors may only use the state exemptions, plus a few related federal exemptions.[22] However, some courts have held that

---

[19] Judith Schenck Koffler, *The Bankruptcy Clause and Exemption Laws: A Reexamination of the Doctrine of Geographic Uniformity*, 58 N.Y.U. L. Rev. 22 (1983).

[20] In re Sullivan, 680 F.2d 1131 (7th Cir. 1982); *see* Erwin Chemerinsky, *Constitutional Issues Posed in the Bankruptcy Abuse Prevention and Consumer Protection Act of 2005*, 79 Am. Bankr. L.J. 571, 592–95 (2005).

[21] States that have opted out are: Alabama, Arizona, California, Colorado, Delaware, Florida, Georgia, Idaho, Illinois, Indiana, Iowa, Kansas, Kentucky, Louisiana, Maine, Maryland, Mississippi, Missouri, Montana, Nebraska, Nevada, New York, North Carolina, North Dakota, Ohio, Oklahoma, Oregon, South Carolina, South Dakota, Tennessee, Utah, Virginia, West Virginia and Wyoming.

[22] The federal exemptions that always apply are: civil service retirement benefits, 5 U.S.C. § 8346 (2000); Central Intelligence Agency retirement and disability payments, 50 U.S.C. § 2094 (2000); Congressional Medal of Honor winners special pensions, 38 U.S.C. § 3101 (2000); fishermen, seamen, and apprentices' wages, 46 U.S.C. § 11109 (2000); foreign service employees disability and retirement benefits, 22 U.S.C. § 4060 (2000); government employees' disability and death benefits, 5 U.S.C. § 8130 (2000); longshoremen's and harbor worker's death and disability benefits, 33 U.S.C. § 916 (2000); military survivors' benefits, 10 U.S.C. § 1450(i)

states may not adopt special exemption statutes for use in bankruptcy, that are not generally available to their residents. To attempt to do so would violate the Constitution's Supremacy Clause.[23] Nonetheless, a number of states have statutes that reduce the amount of the available exemptions if the debtor files for bankruptcy. For example, New York has an aggregate limit of $5000 dollars for personal property exemptions that only applies if the debtor files for bankruptcy.[24] In the states that have not opted out, each debtor may choose either the state or the federal exemptions. The choice is all or nothing; a debtor may not "mix and match" exemptions, choosing the most favorable state and the most favorable federal rules.[25] Moreover, if the case is a joint husband-and-wife bankruptcy, both must choose the same set of exemptions; if they cannot agree, then both are "deemed" to have chosen the federal exemptions.[26]

Opt-out affects only the list of exempt property. It does not affect other provisions of § 522. For example, even in an opt-out state, the Bankruptcy Code's rules permitting avoidance of certain liens on exempt property still apply.[27] In addition, married debtors are usually permitted to double the effective amount of state exemptions.

The federal exemptions have had an impact even in many of the opt-out states. During the 1980s, many states updated their exemption statutes, often using parts of the federal exemption scheme as a model.[28] Thus, although the goals of those who wanted to federalize the exemptions available to bankrupt debtors were not fully achieved, exemptions today are considerably more modern and at least somewhat more uniform than they were prior to the Code.[29]

(2000); military annuities, 10 U.S.C. § 1440 (2000); military pension benefits, 38 U.S.C. § 5301 (2000); railroad workers' pensions and annuities, 45 U.S.C. § 231m (2000); railroad workers' unemployment insurance benefits, 45 U.S.C. § 352(e) (2000); servicemembers' and veterans group life insurance benefits, 38 U.S.C. § 1970 (2000); student loans, grants, and work assistance payments, 20 U.S.C. § 1095a(d) (2000); social security payments, 42 U.S.C. § 407 (2000); veterans' benefits, 38 U.S.C. § 5301 (2000); and war hazard injury or death compensation payments, 42 U.S.C. § 1717 (2000).

[23] In re Wallace, 347 B.R. 626 (Bankr. W.D. Mich. 2006); In re Cross, 255 B.R. 25, 32–34 (Bankr. N.D. Ind. 2000).

[24] New York Debtor Creditor Law § 283(1).

[25] Bankruptcy Code § 522(b).

[26] Bankruptcy Code § 522(d). This provision was added in 1984 to curb the then-existing practice of "stacking" exemptions — that is, each spouse choosing a different set to get the largest overall number and value of exemptions. Stacking still might be possible for married debtors who do not file jointly and whose cases are not ordered to be jointly administered.

[27] *See* Bankruptcy Code § 522(f); *see* § 12.07[B] Avoiding Non-Purchase Money Security Interests, *infra*.

[28] *See, e.g.*, Ohio Rev. Code § 2329.66 (LexisNexis Supp. 2006).

[29] *See* James B. Haines, Jr., *Section 522's Opt-Out Clause: Debtors' Bankruptcy Exemptions in a Sorry State*, 1983 Ariz. St. L.J. 1, 11–15.

[C] Debtor's Domicile Controls Exemptions[30]

Because of variations in state exemption statutes, a determination must sometimes be made regarding which state's exemption statute governs the debtor's exemption rights. Section 522(b)(3) specifies that the "[s]tate or local law that is applicable on the date of the filing of the petition at the place in which the debtor's domicile has been located for the 730 days [2 years] immediately preceding the date of the filing of the petition" governs which state's exemption laws apply.[31] If the debtor has not been domiciled in the same place for the entire 730-day period prior to filing his petition, the exemption laws in the state where the debtor lived for more than half of the 180 day period *before* this 730-day period applies.[32] In the unusual circumstance in which this rule renders the debtor ineligible for any exemptions, the uniform federal exemption schedule applies.[33] Before the 2005 Amendments, the law of the debtor's domicile for only the 180 days prior to the debtor's petition determined which state's exemption statute controlled. Expansion of this period makes it particularly difficult for financially troubled debtors to change their state of domicile to a state with particularly generous exemption rights as part of an asset protection strategy prior to filing a bankruptcy petition.[34]

A debtor's domicile is generally regarded as actual residence coupled with present intent to remain.[35] A person's "residence" is considered as a less permanent place of abode.[36]

[D] Joint Debtors' Exemption Rights

Married couples who jointly own their exempt property and who are jointly liable for their debts frequently file joint bankruptcy petitions under § 302. Their cases are nearly always consolidated for the purposes of

---

30 Laura B. Bartel, *The Peripatetic Debtor: Choice of Law and Choice of Exemptions*, 22 Emory Bankr. Dev. J. 401 (2006).

31 Bankruptcy Code § 522(d)(3)(A).

32 Bankruptcy Code § 522(d)(3)(A).

33 Bankruptcy Code § 522(b)(3); *see* In re Jewell, 347 B.R. 120 (Bankr. W.D.N.Y. 2006).

34 This was a strategy sometimes employed by debtors, some of whom moved to Florida or Texas to take advantage of those states' unusually generous homestead exemption laws. The strategy was not always effective, as bankruptcy courts sometimes relied on their equitable powers to apply the exemption statute of the state of their previous domicile in complete frustration of their "pre-bankruptcy planning" strategy. In re Tanzi, 297 B.R. 607 (B.A.P. 9th Cir. 2003); In re Coplan, 156 B.R. 88 (Bankr. M.D. Fla. 1993); *but see* In re Adell, 321 B.R. 562 (Bankr. M.D. Fla. 2005); In re Young, 235 B.R. 666 (Bankr. M. D. Fla. 1999); *see generally* John M. Norwood & Marianne M. Jennings, *Before Declaring Bankruptcy, Move to Florida and Buy a House: The Ethics and Judicial Inconsistencies of Debtors' Conversions and Exemptions*, 28 Sw. U. L. Rev. 439 (1999).

35 *E.g.*, Morad v. Xifaras (In re Morad), 323 B.R. 818 (B.A.P. 1st Cir. 2005).

36 One of your co-authors temporarily resides each summer on the bucolic island of Martha's Vineyard, off the coast of Massachusetts, where he and his wife own real estate. He is domiciled elsewhere.

administration and are effectively treated as if they were only one bankruptcy case.[37]

This nearly always permits married debtors to double the amount of any limit on the amount of their available exemptions. Thus, if both spouses are liable for the same debts and jointly own their exempt property, each debtor is entitled to his or her own separate exemption. For example, under § 522(d)(2)'s motor vehicle exemption, each debtor is entitled to a separate exemption for $3,225 in equity in a motor vehicle, effectively making up to $6,450 of the couple's equity in a car, exempt.

This result applies because most exemption statutes are phrased in terms that permit an exemption to be claimed in "the debtor's interest in" the exempt category of property.[38] Section 522(d)(2), dealing with a debtor's exemption rights in a motor vehicle, supplies a good example. It exempts "[t]he debor's interest, not to exceed $3,225 in value, in one motor vehicle."[39] State exemption statutes nearly always contain equivalent language.[40]

If the state exemption statute only permits a married couple to assert one exemption, this result might not apply. Although Bankruptcy Code § 522(m) expressly provides that each individual debtor in a joint case may claim his or her own exemptions,[41] courts have reached different conclusions about its effect on some kinds of state exemption statutes. Some courts have held that if a married couple would be entitled to only one shared exemption in a state collection proceeding, that the same result will apply in bankruptcy.[42] Other courts apply § 522(m) to permit the debtors to double the amount of their exemption, as if the state exemption statute protected "each debtor's interest" in the property instead of their shared joint interests.[43]

However, the 1984 Amendments, compelling joint debtors in states that have not opted out to select either the federal exemptions or the applicable state exemptions, added language to § 522(m), making it expressly subject to this anti-stacking limitation. Thus, there is no conflict in the circuits regarding the statutory language as it now stands.

---

[37] Bankruptcy Code § 302; *see* § 6.02[D] Joint Petitions, *supra.*

[38] *E.g.*, Ohio Rev. Code Ann. § 2329.66 (LexisNexis Supp. 2006).

[39] Bankruptcy Code § 522(d)(2).

[40] *E.g.*, Ohio Rev. Code Ann. § 2329.66(A)(2) (LexisNexis Supp. 2006) ("*The person's interest*, not to exceed one thousand dollars, in one motor vehicle.") (emphasis supplied).

[41] Bankruptcy Code § 522(m).

[42] Stevens v. Pike County Bank (In re Stevens), 829 F.2d 693 (8th Cir. 1987); In re Talmadge, 832 F.2d 1120 (9th Cir. 1987); First Nat'l Bank v. Norris, 701 F.2d 902 (11th Cir. 1983).

[43] *See* John T. Mather Mem'l Hosp. v. Pearl, 723 F.2d 193 (2d Cir. 1983), Cheeseman v. Nachman (In re Cheeseman), 656 F.2d 60 (4th Cir. 1981).

[E] Exemption Planning[44]

Debtors with extensive non-exempt assets sometimes employ a variety of strategies in an effort to protect some of these assets. Some debtors liquidate non-exempt assets and use the proceeds to acquire property that fits within an exempt category. Other debtors try to change their state of domicile before filing their bankruptcy petitions, in an effort to take advantage of another state's more generous exemption statute. Such strategies are sometimes successful but are fraught with difficulty, including the risk that the debtor will be denied a discharge for having fraudulently transferred his property in an effort to "hinder, delay, or defraud, his creditors."[45] In 2005 Congress, amended the Bankruptcy Code to impose new restrictions on the most extreme examples of these strategies.

[1] Conversion of Assets to Exempt Status

Debtors with a surplus of non-exempt assets sometimes seek to protect their property by converting them into property covered by an exemption. For example, the debtor in *In re McCabe* bought a $10,000 Belgian Browning shotgun, not because of his interest in hunting or his dedication to the Second Amendment, but because he knew that Iowa's exemption for a "family gun" had no dollar limit.[46] While debtors might be tempted to load up on exempt household furnishings, wearing apparel, or even pets, the limited value of these items, combined with what is usually a ceiling on the exempt value of such assets, usually makes these exemptions less attractive havens for protecting non-exempt property.[47]

Exemptions for residential real estate, various retirement accounts, annuities, and life insurance, which sometimes contain a very high or an unlimited ceiling, are more attractive targets for debtors seeking to protect non-exempt cash.[48] Likewise, debtors with sizeable non-exempt

---

[44] A. Jay Cristol, William J. Cassidy & Alexandra Sarmiento Walden, *Exemption Planning: How Far May You Go?*, 48 S.C. L. Rev. 715 (1997); Theodore Eisenberg, *Bankruptcy Law in Perspective*, 28 U.C.L.A. L. Rev. 953, 995 (1981); Juliet M. Moringiello, *Distinguishing Hogs from Pigs: A Proposal for a Preference Approach to Pre-Bankruptcy Planning*, 6 Am. Bankr. Inst. L. Rev. 103 (1998); John M. Norwood & Marianne M. Jenning, *Before Declaring Bankruptcy, Move to Florida and Buy a House: The Ethics and Judicial Inconsistencies of Debtors' Conversions and Exemptions*, 28 Sw. U. L. Rev. 439 (1999); Lawrence Ponoroff & F. Stephen Knippenberg, *Debtors Who Convert Their Assets on the Eve of Bankruptcy: Villains or Victims of the Fresh Start*, 70 N.Y.U. L. Rev. 235 (1995); Alan N. Resnick, *Prudent Planning or Fraudulent Transfer? The Use of Nonexempt Assets to Purchase or Improve Exempt Property on the Eve of Bankruptcy*, 31 Rutgers L. Rev. 615 (1978).

[45] Bankruptcy Code § 727(a)(2); *see* § 13.02[B][2] Fraudulent Transfers; Destruction or Concealment of Property, *infra.*

[46] In re McCabe, 280 B.R. 841 (Bankr. N.D. Iowa 2002).

[47] *See, e.g.*, Ohio Rev. Code Ann. § 2329.66 (LexisNexis Supp. 2006).

[48] *E.g.*, In re Orso, 214 F.3d 637 (5th Cir. 2000) (annuities held not exempt); Hanson v. First Nat'l. Bank (In re Hanson), 848 F.2d 866 (8th Cir. 1988) (debtor converted about $34,000 of non-exempt property to $31,000 of exempt property, consisting of a $20,000 exempt life insurance policy and an $11,000 payment on the mortgage).

investments who live in a state with a virtually unlimited homestead exemption, sometimes liquidate their other investments and pay off as much of their mortgage as possible, in order to take full advantage of their home state's liberal homestead exemption statute.

The legislative history of § 522 expressly sanctioned these types of pre-bankruptcy conversions. The House and Senate Reports accompanying the 1978 Bankruptcy Code contained the same language:

> As under current law, the debtor will be permitted to convert non-exempt property into exempt property before filing a bankruptcy petition. The practice is not fraudulent as to creditors, and permits the debtor to make full use of the exemptions to which he is entitled under the law.[49]

Despite this apparent legislative approval, debtors who get carried away with these strategies sometimes find it necessary to meet creditors' objections. Creditors sometimes object directly to the debtor's claim of exemption. On other occasions, they use the far more devastating strategy of seeking denial of the debtor's discharge.

Successful objections to the debtor's claim of exemption lead only to the debtor's loss of the exemption and thus put the debtor and his creditors back into the position they would have been in if the debtor had not embarked on his plan to convert his assets to exempt status. Debtors who have converted assets into exempt forms have had some success in meeting creditors' objections to their claimed exemptions, as bankruptcy courts are usually constrained to adhere to the exemptions provided by state law in the debtor's domicile.[50] Absent a limitation on this type of behavior under the state exemption statute, bankruptcy courts are unable to restrain these tactics. However, creditors' objections sometimes result in limitations being imposed on the debtor's claim of exemption, particularly if the court finds that the debtor's actions were part of a scheme to defraud creditors.[51]

Debtors whose conversion of assets from non-exempt to exempt status was part of an effort to defraud creditors face more serious consequences. Section 727(a)(2) permits the court to deny the debtor a Chapter 7 discharge entirely if the debtor "with intent to hinder, delay, or defraud a creditor . . . has transferred, removed, destroyed, mutilated, or concealed" his property.[52] A debtor whose global discharge is denied gains no relief from his debts. The risk of denial of discharge makes exemption planning risky business for debtors whose creditors may feel cheated by the debtor's scheme.

---

[49] H.R. Rep. No. 95-595, 361 (1977), *reprinted in* 1978 U.S.C.C.A.N. 5963, 6317; S. Rep. No. 95-989, 76 (1978), *reprinted in* 1978 U.S.C.C.A.N. 5787, 5862.

[50] *E.g.*, First Tex. Sav. Assoc., Inc. v. Reed (In re Reed), 700 F.2d 986 (5th Cir. 1983).

[51] *E.g.*, In re Lacounte, 342 B.R. 908 (Bankr. D. Mont. 2005).

[52] Bankruptcy Code § 727(a)(2); *see* § 13.02[B][2] Fraudulent Transfers; Destruction or Concealment of Property, *infra*.

For example, the debtor in *In re Tveten* was denied a discharge after socking away over $700,000 in various life insurance and annuity contracts, which were fully exempt under his state exemption statute.[53] The debtor had moved otherwise non-exempt funds into these exempt resources in the last several months before filing his petition. In the notorious example of *In re Reed,* the debtor was denied a discharge after he held off his creditors' efforts to collect with a settlement agreement that held out the prospect of future payment and then liquidated nearly all of his assets, using the proceeds to build equity in his exempt home.[54]

Despite similar facts, other debtors have not been denied a discharge. During the fifteen days before filing their bankruptcy petition, the debtors in *In re Bowyer* used $24,000 in savings to reduce their mortgage, building exempt equity in their home in the process.[55] The debtor in *In re McCabe*, mentioned above, purchased a $10,000 "family gun" solely to take advantage of his state's liberal exemption statute.[56] Both of these debtors held on to their discharge.

The difficulty is in drawing the distinction between a debtor's intent to defraud his creditors in cases like *Tveten* and *Reed* and an honest effort to take full advantage of the reasonable expectations supplied by a state's exemption statute.[57] Most courts draw the distinction by inquiring whether there is "extrinsic evidence of fraud" beyond the conversion of assets to exempt status.[58] The debtor's conduct in *Reed*, enticing his creditors into a settlement agreement that he did not intend to perform to obtain time he needed to convert his assets, provides an obvious example of an overt act involving fraudulent intent. The exempt family gun in *McCabe* notwithstanding, some courts deny the debtor's discharge if the assets the debtor acquired prior to filing for bankruptcy seemed "unwise, uneconomical or unusual" for the debtor, apart from his attempt to protect his assets from bankruptcy.[59] These decisions make pre-bankruptcy planning a risky strategy. On the other hand, decisions like *In re Vangen*, permitting the debtor's conversion of $136,000 of nonexempt equity in her home into an exempt retirement fund, was regarded as part of an appropriate effort to ensure that she had funds available for her future retirement.[60]

---

[53] Norwest Bank Neb., N.A. v. Tveten (In re Tveten), 848 F.2d 871 (8th Cir. 1989). The debtor was facing over $19 million in liabilities as a result of a failed but highly leveraged real estate development project.

[54] First Tex. Sav. Assoc., Inc. v. Reed (In re Reed), 700 F.2d 986 (5th Cir. 1983).

[55] 932 F.2d 1100 (5th Cir. 1991) (en banc).

[56] 280 B.R. 841 (Bankr. N.D. Iowa 2002).

[57] Martin Marietta Materials Sw., Inc. v. Lee (In re Lee), 309 B.R. 468 (Bankr. W.D. Tex. 2004).

[58] In re Crater, 286 B.R. 756 (Bankr. D. Ariz. 2002).

[59] Jensen v. Dietz (In re Sholdan), 217 F.3d 1006, 1010 (8th Cir. 2000) (evidence of fraudulent intent where debtor's acquisition of assets represented a "radical departure from his previous lifestyle").

[60] In re Vangen, 334 B.R. 241 (Bankr. W.D. Wis. 2005).

Another risky approach that is deployed by some debtors is to transfer property into an offshore "asset protection trust."[61] These trusts are usually maintained in countries that have established themselves as debtors' havens.[62] The debtor transfers his assets to the trust naming himself as beneficiary of the trust. The duties of trustee are shared by the debtor and the offshore organization, frequently a bank or trust company. Under the terms of the trust, the debtor has complete control over the trust assets unless an "event of duress" occurs. An attempted garnishment by one of the debtor's creditors or a turnover order by a bankruptcy trustee qualifies as an event of duress. When such an event occurs, the debtor is automatically removed as trustee and loses his right to control disposition of the funds. The purpose, of course, is to frustrate the efforts of U.S. courts to seize the debtor's assets to satisfy the claims of creditors.

While these mechanisms have protected debtors' assets from the claims of creditors, they have occasionally led to contempt citations[63] and seem likely to result in bankruptcy courts denying debtors Chapter 7 discharges[64] or refusing to confirm their rehabilitation plans due to lack of good faith[65] or otherwise.[66] The further possibility of criminal sanction for bankruptcy fraud cannot be ignored.[67]

Alaska, Delaware and Nevada attempted to take advantage of the demand for "asset protection," by passing statutes that recognized self-settled asset protection trusts as spendthrift. The hope was that this would have the effect of excluding the assets in the trust account from the debtor's bankruptcy estate under § 541(c)(1). However, the 2005 Amendments to Bankruptcy Code § 548 added language specifically directed at both offshore and domestic asset protection trusts. Section 548(e)(1) now permits avoidance of:

---

[61] *See* § 7.04[F][3] Offshore Asset Protection Trusts, *supra*.

[62] *See* Elena Marty-Nelson, *Offshore Asset Protection Trusts: Having Your Cake and Eating it Too*, 47 Rutgers L. Rev. 11, 62 (1994) (indicating that "the Bahamas, Belize, Cayman Islands, Cook Islands, Cyprus, Gibralter, and the Turks and Caicos Islands" are popular offshore jurisdictions); *e.g.*, Marine Midland Bank v. Portnoy (In re Portnoy), 201 B.R. 685, 699 (Bankr. S.D.N.Y. 1996) (providing a history of debtor protection in the Channel Islands).

[63] FTC v. Affordable Media, 179 F.3d 1228 (9th Cir. 1999); *see also* In re Lawrence, 279 F.3d 1294 (11th Cir. 2002).

[64] *See* § 13.02 Denial of Discharge, *infra*.

[65] *See* § 18.08[C] Plan Proposed in Good Faith, *infra*.

[66] *See* § 18.08[E][1] Best Interests of Creditors, *infra*.

[67] Two federal criminal statutes govern bankruptcy fraud. Section 152 of the Federal Criminal Code prohibits knowing concealment of assets in connection with a bankruptcy case. If the law of the offshore jurisdiction, together with the terms of the trust instrument, deprives the settlor-debtor of power to control trust assets, and if the debtor discloses the trust's terms to the bankruptcy court, it might be difficult to find that the debtor had "knowingly and fraudulently conceal[ed] . . . property belonging to the estate of the debtor." 18 U.S.C. § 152 (2000). Section 157 criminalizes a debtor's filing of a bankruptcy petition "for the purpose of executing . . . a scheme" to defraud. 18 U.S.C. § 157 (2000). Under these provisions, debtors who disclose their asset protection trusts are unlikely to face prosecution by the United States.

> any transfer of an interest of the debtor in property that was made on or within 10 years before the date of the filing of the petition if —
>
> (A) such transfer was made to a self-settled trust or similar device;
>
> (B) such transfer was by the debtor;
>
> (C) the debtor is a beneficiary of such trust or similar device; and
>
> (D) the debtor made such transfer with actual intent to hinder, delay, or defraud any entity to which the debtor was or became, on or after the date that such transfer was made, indebted.[68]

Section 548 has always permitted the trustee to recover transfers made with the intent to hinder, defraud, or delay creditors.[69] The most important aspect of this new language is the preamble, which looks back ten years before the debtor's petition was filed, effectively expanding the scope of § 548 beyond the two-year period that applies to such transfers generally.[70]

[2] Federal Limits on Certain Exemptions[71]

[a] Limit on IRA Exemptions[72]

The Bankruptcy Code imposes only a few restrictions on a debtor's ability to assert the most generous state exemptions. Section 522(n), added in 2005, prevents a debtor from asserting an exemption in more than $1,095,000 in an Individual Retirement Account (IRA), but allows this ceiling to be raised by the court "if the interests of justice so require." Moreover, it only applies to IRAs funded by the debtor's contributions. Because of the annual limit on IRA contributions, it seems unlikely that many bankrupt debtors will accumulate enough funds in their IRAs for the limit to have any practical impact. Debtors with over $1,095,000 in an IRA are more likely to have accumulated such a large amount as a result of a rollover of their more traditional pension benefits into an IRA. IRA's funded by contributions from debtors' employers are not subject to the $1 million limit.[73]

---

[68] Bankruptcy Code § 548(e)(1)(A).

[69] *See generally* § 16.02 Actual Fraud: Intent to Hinder, Delay, or Defraud Creditors, *infra*.

[70] Bankruptcy Code § 548(a)(1). The trustee might also be able to avoid a fraudulent transfer under state fraudulent transfer law, through Bankruptcy Code § 544(b). *See* § 16.01[D] Sources of Fraudulent Transfer Law, *infra*.

[71] Juliet M. Moringiello, *Has Congress Slimmed down the Hogs?: A Look at the BAPCPA Approach to Pre-bankruptcy Planning*, 15 Widener L.J. 615 (2006).

[72] John Hennigan, Rousey *and the New Retirement Funds Exemption*, 13 Am. Bankr. Inst. L. Rev. 777, 796 (2005); Margaret Howard, *Exemptions Under the 2005 Bankruptcy Amendments: A Tale of Opportunity Lost*, 79 Am. Bankr. L.J. 397, 417 (2005).

[73] Margaret Howard, *Exemptions Under the 2005 Bankruptcy Amendments: A Tale of Opportunity Lost*, 79 Am. Bankr. L.J. 397, 417–18 (2005).

[b] Limit on Homestead Exemptions[74]

The 2005 Amendments to the Bankruptcy Code include language that sets limits on pre-bankruptcy transfers that might otherwise dramatically enhance a debtor's exemption rights. The new limits apply primarily to exemptions that would otherwise protect a debtor's residence, but also apply to burial plots.[75]

New Bankruptcy Code § 522(o) prevents debtors from claiming an exemption in an otherwise exempt residence or burial plot that the debtor acquired any time during the ten years before his petition via the conversion of non-exempt property "with the intent to hinder, delay, or defraud a creditor."[76] This overrules decisions such as *In re Reed,* where the court felt constrained to allow the exemption despite the debtor's apparent fraud, because nothing in the state exemption statute that applied to the debtor's case limited the exemption.[77]

In addition, new § 522(p) prohibits debtors from exempting interests in what would otherwise be an exempt interest in a residence or burial plot if the interest was acquired by the debtor during the 1215 days (three years and four months) before his bankruptcy petition and exceeds $136,875 in value.[78] Debtors who have changed residences during the 1215-day period are protected, at least to the extent that they simply reinvested equity from their original residence into a new home during that period.[79] Otherwise, this limit applies regardless of the debtor's intent.

This new language impairs debtors' efforts to take unfair advantage of several states' highly favorable homestead exemption laws.[80] However, a

[74] Samuel K. Crocker & Robert H. Waldschmidt, *Impact of the 2005 Bankruptcy Amendments on Chapter 7 Trustees*, 79 Am. Bankr. L.J. 333, 349–54 (2005); Margaret Howard, *Exemptions Under the 2005 Bankruptcy Amendments: A Tale of Opportunity Lost,* 79 Am. Bankr. L.J. 397, 399–408 (2005).

[75] New § 522(o)(3) and § 522(p)(1)(C) impose the same limits on exemptions for debtors' interests in a "burial plot," a somewhat more or less permanent place of either domicile or residence, depending on your perspective on other issues unrelated to bankruptcy law. Bankruptcy Code § 522(o)-(p).

[76] Bankruptcy Code § 522(o); *see* In re Maronde, 332 B.R. 593 (Bankr. D. Minn. 2005); In re Agnew, 355 B.R. 276 (Bankr. D. Kan. 2006).

[77] In re Reed, 12 B.R. 41 (Bankr. N.D. Tex. 1981).

[78] Bankruptcy Code § 522(p)(1). The limit applies to four types of property interests that are potentially exempt under applicable state law:

> (A) real or personal property that the debtor or a dependent of the debtor uses as a residence; (B) a cooperative that owns property that the debtor or a dependent of the debtor uses as a residence; (C) a burial plot for the debtor or a dependent of the debtor; or (D) real or personal property that the debtor or dependent of the debtor claims as a homestead.

[79] Bankruptcy Code § 522(p)(2)(B); In re Wayrynen, 332 B.R. 479 (Bankr. S.D. Fla. 2005).

[80] Florida, Iowa, Kansas, South Dakota, and Texas, have no cap on the value of a homestead that may be exempted by their residents. *E.g.*, Fla. Const. art. 10 § 4(a)(1) (West Supp. 2006)(1/2 acre in town; 160 acres in the country); Iowa Code Ann. § 561.2 (West 1992) (1/2 acre in town; 40 acres in the country); Kan. Stat. Ann. § 60-2301 (2005) (one acre in town; 160 acres in the country); S.D. Codified Laws Ann. § 43-31-4 (one acre in town; 160 acres in the country); Texas Prop. Code Ann. § 42.001(a) (Vernon 2000) (10 acres in town; 200 acres in the country).

few early bankruptcy court decisions interpreting § 522(p) have applied it narrowly. In *In re Mcnabb*,[81] the court ruled that § 522(p) only applies in states where the debtor retains a choice of his home state's exemptions or the uniform federal exemptions in the Bankruptcy Code. The court's ruling was based on language in § 522(p) that imposes the limit only when a debtor exempts a larger amount of property "as a result of *electing* under [Bankruptcy Code § 522(b)(3)(A)] to exempt property under State or local law."

In most states debtors do not "elect" their home state's exemption statute. As a result of their state legislature's decision to "opt-out" of the federal exemptions, they have no choice but to exempt property protected by their home state's exemption statute. Despite this suggestion, most courts impose the limitation on debtors in states that have opted-out of the uniform federal exemptions.[82]

In addition, courts have now ruled that the limit only applies to equity accumulated by the debtor as a result of transfers made by the debtor during the 1215-day period.[83] It does not apply to passive appreciation of the property that increases the debtor's equity beyond the dollar limit established by § 522(p).

A similar $136,875 limit is imposed on a debtor's exemption for residential real estate or a burial plot for debtors who have been convicted of certain bankruptcy crimes, securities fraud, fiduciary fraud, or criminal, intentional, wilful, or reckless misconduct resulting in personal injury or death.[84] This limit applies regardless of when the debtor acquired the exempt property.

Another new provision limits homestead exemptions claimed by debtors, like certain surviving Enron executives, who have been convicted of felonies or who owe debts as a result of violations of securities laws to $136,875.[85] Otherwise, the unlimited state homestead exemptions of states like Florida and Texas were left intact.[86]

§ 12.03 Types of Exemptions

A wide variety of exemptions are available under both the Bankruptcy Code and under applicable state law. Any effort to catalog them all would be beyond the scope of this book. Instead, we provide a general description of the most important categories of exempt property available under both Bankruptcy Code § 522(d) and many modern state exemption statutes.

---

[81] 326 B.R. 785 (Bankr. D. Ariz. 2005).

[82] In re Summers, 344 B.R. 108 (Bankr. D. Ariz. 2006) (collecting cases); In re Kaplan, 331 B.R. 483 (Bankr. S.D. Fla. 2005); In re Virissimo, 332 B.R. 201 (Bankr. D. Nev. 2005).

[83] In re Rasmussen, 349 B.R. 747 (Bankr. M.D. Fla. 2006); Wallace v. Rogers (In re Rogers), 354 B.R.792 (N.D. Tex. 2006).

[84] Bankruptcy Code § 522(q).

[85] Bankruptcy Code § 522(q); *see* In re Larson, 340 B.R. 444 (Bankr. D. Mass. 2006) (criminal conviction not required if debtor committed a "criminal act").

[86] Margaret Howard, *Exemptions Under the 2005 Bankruptcy Amendments: A Tale of Opportunity Lost*, 79 Am. Bankr. L.J. 397, 398–407 (2005).

[A] Residential Property — Homestead Exemptions

An exemption for property used as the debtor's residence is available in all states. In most jurisdictions, the exemption applies to either real or personal property used as a residence, avoiding questions about whether motor homes or interests in a "cooperative" are real or personal property.[87] In many states, the homestead exemption is extended to any "burial plot" owned by the debtor.[88]

Most states impose a dollar limit on the value of the debtor's interest that may be exempt, though the range of these limits is considerable, extending from only $5,000 in Ohio[89] and Tennesee,[90] to $75,000 in California,[91] $150,000 in Arizona,[92] and $500,000 in Massachusetts.[93] The Bankruptcy Code's residential property exemption stands at $20,200, but is slated, together with all other dollar limits on debtors' uniform federal exemption rights, to be increased in 2010 and every three years thereafter to reflect inflation as measured by the U.S. Department of Labor's Consumer Price Index.[94] Dollar limits on state exemptions are not subject to this periodic increase. In Texas and Florida, long regarded as debtors' havens, the limit is virtually nonexistent, with Texas domiciliaries enjoying protection for residential real estate and improvements in an urban area of up to ten contiguous acres, and in a rural area of up to either 100 or 200 acres, depending on whether the debtor is single or part of a "family." The Florida Constitution is far less generous, only permitting Florida residents to exempt up to one-half acre of an urban residence or 160 acres of a rural homestead, without regard to the debtor's marital status.[95]

Like other exemptions, the homestead exemption does not give the debtor any guarantee of keeping his home. Indeed, in most cases, it will not. The debtor must still deal with the mortgage debt, if any, and must also purchase any excess equity above the amount of the available exemption.

---

[87] The Bankruptcy Code's homestead exemption is illustrative. It exempts the debtor's interest in:

> real property or personal property that the debtor or a dependent of the debtor uses as a residence, in a cooperative that owns property that the debtor or a dependent of the debtor uses as a residence, or in a burial plot for the debtor or a dependent of the debtor.

Bankruptcy Code § 522(d)(1); *see also* Ohio Rev. Code Ann. § 2329.66(A)(1)(b) (LexisNexis Supp. 2006) ("the person's interest, not to exceed five thousand dollars, in one parcel or item of real or personal property that the person or a dependent of the person uses as a residence.").

[88] *See* Bankruptcy Code § 522(d)(1). There is no requirement that the debtor *reside* in his burial plot.

[89] Ohio Rev. Code Ann. § 2329.66(A)(1) (LexisNexis Supp. 2006).

[90] Tenn. Code Ann. § 26-2-301 (LexisNexis Supp. 2005).

[91] Cal. Civ. Proc. Code § 704.730(a)(3) (West Supp. 2006).

[92] Ariz. Rev. Stat. Ann. § 33-1101(A) (2000).

[93] Mass Gen. Laws. Ann. ch. 188 § 1 (West Supp. 2006).

[94] Bankruptcy Code § 104(b).

[95] *See* Peter Currin, *Florida's Homestead Exemption: Does This Chameleon Ever Die?*, 50 U. Fla. L. .Rev. 573 (1998).

That excess equity belongs to his bankruptcy estate and will be distributed, after sale of the debtor's home, to unsecured creditors.

For example, suppose the debtor's home is worth $100,000, but is subject to a $75,000 mortgage. This leaves $25,000 equity in the house. If the applicable exemption statute protects only $15,000 of that equity, an additional $10,000 of "non-exempt equity" remains. Following a sale of the home, the proceeds of the sale would be distributed first to satisfy the mortgage, second to fulfill the debtor's exemption rights, and third to distribute to other creditors.

In situations like this, the debtor must make some deal with both the mortgage holder and the trustee in order to hold on to her home. This could theoretically be accomplished through refinancing or via a combination of reaffirmation of the debt with the mortgagee and the sale of other exempt property to pay the trustee the amount of the non-exempt equity to which the estate is entitled. Anecdotal evidence indicates that trustees are generally willing to sell the excess equity to the debtor, so long as the debtor is willing to pay its full value. But if the excess is large, it may be impossible for the debtor to raise enough money to purchase it. As a result, these theoretical strategies can only rarely be implemented.

Debtors with excess equity in their homes are more likely to find it useful to file a Chapter 13 rehabilitation plan. However, the viability of this strategy depends on the debtor's financial ability to make the payments provided for in the plan. Debtors with inadequate income will run afoul of the requirement that their plans be "feasible."[96]

Likewise, if the house in the above example is only worth $80,000, the debtor may not enjoy the full extent of a $15,000 exemption, as all but $5,000 of the value of the property is consumed by the mortgage.[97] Debtors in this situation may be able, depending on the exemptions available in their jurisdiction, to apply some or all of the unused portion of their homestead exemption to protect other assets.[98]

[B] Wildcard Exemptions[99]

Some jurisdictions provide debtors with a so-called "wildcard" exemption, permitting the debtor to exempt a limited value of *any* property, without the necessity of limiting the exemption to a legislatively approved list of specific assets.[100] For example, § 522(d)(5) provides an exemption of $975 for the debtor's interest in "any property."[101] These types of statutes

---

[96] Bankruptcy Code § 1325(a)(6); *see* § 18.08[B] Feasibility, *infra.*

[97] *See* § 12.05[B] Liens on Exempt Property, *infra.*

[98] *See* § 12.03[B] Wildcard Exemptions, *infra.*

[99] Stephen F. Yunke, Comment, *The General Exemption of Section 522(d)(5) of the 1978 Bankruptcy Code*, 49 U. Chi. L. Rev. 564 (1982).

[100] *E.g.*, Tex. Prop. Code Ann. § 42.001(a) (Vernon 2000) ($60,000 for a family; $30,000 for a single adult).

[101] Bankruptcy Code § 522(d)(5).

provide a supplemental exemption in addition to the exemptions for a complicated list of specific types of property.[102] Thus, an avid bicyclist might use this provision to protect one or several of his bicycles, even though the exemption statute otherwise does not protect sporting goods or does not protect them to this extent.[103]

Under some state exemption statutes and under the Bankruptcy Code's uniform federal residential exemption, debtors are not required to use their homestead exemption to protect equity in a residence but may instead apply all or some of their unused homestead exemption to other non-exempt property.[104] When available, this type of provision enhances whatever wildcard exemption might otherwise be provided.

For debtors in states that have not opted out, Bankruptcy Code § 522(d)(5) operates in this fashion. It permits a debtor to use up to $10,125 of the unused portion of his homestead exemption to protect the debtor's interest "in any property."[105] This provides debtors with less than the full amount of equity protected by the homestead exemption, with some flexibility in the use of their exemption. Under § 522(d)(5), a debtor with only $10,000 equity in a home could use Bankruptcy Code § 522(d)(1) to exempt his $10,000 of equity and apply the remaining unused $8,450 to property not covered by other exempt categories. This amount might also be used to protect other property in which the debtor has too much equity, such as a car worth more than the amount protected by Bankruptcy Code § 522(d)(2).

These types of provisions also provide some measure of protection for renters. At the same time, however, it reflects the strong societal preference for home ownership, by giving renters only half of the exemption that is available to homeowners.

[C] Exemptions for Personal Property

Not surprisingly, exemption statutes commonly permit debtors to exempt a wide array of items of personal property of the type found in nearly all of our homes. These usually include household furnishings, wearing apparel, appliances, and other similar property used primarily for personal, family, or household purposes. There is usually a per-item limit on the value of these items and sometimes an aggregate limit on the total value of all similar items claimed as exempt.[106]

---

[102] *See also, e.g.*, Ohio Rev. Code Ann. § 6323.66(A) (LexisNexis Supp. 2006); Cal. Civ. Proc. Code §§ 704.010–704.200 (West Supp. 2006).

[103] Both of your authors have invested in bicycles with values exceeding this amount. One of your authors has invested in bicycles considerably beyond this amount.

[104] *See also, e.g.*, Ohio Rev. Code Ann. § 2329.66(A)(4) (LexisNexis Supp. 2006).

[105] Bankruptcy Code § 522(d)(5).

[106] Without an aggregate limit, debtors may be able to protect a treasure trove of smaller items. *E.g.*, In re Wahl, 14 B.R. 153 (Bankr. E.D. Wis. 1981) ($6,000 worth of silverware exempt under earlier version of § 522(d) limiting the debtor's exemption to $200 per item, without regard to the number of related items claimed).

[1] Exempt Categories

Bankruptcy Code § 522(d)(3) is a typical example of an exemption for various types of common household property. It protects

> [t]he debtor's interest, not to exceed $525 in value in any particular item or $10,775 in aggregate value, in household furnishings, household goods, wearing apparel, appliances, books, animals, crops, or musical instruments that are held primarily for the personal, family, or household use of the debtor or a dependent of the debtor.[107]

Given the low value of most household items, this exemption permits most debtors to keep virtually all of their clothes, furniture, and appliances.

Other exemption statutes draw more refined distinctions. For example, Ohio's exemption statute permits debtors to keep their interests in any number of items of "wearing apparel, bed, and bedding" so long as the value of each protected item does not exceed two hundred dollars but protects their interest in only "one cooking unit and one refrigerator or other food preservation unit . . . not to exceed three hundred dollars in each item."[108] Thus, debtors in Ohio are permitted to retain as many $195 leather jackets as they want, but may only keep either a refrigerator or a freezer, not both. Perusal of other states' exemption statutes reveal similar arcane distinctions.

Exemption statutes typically also protect the debtor's interest in a "motor vehicle,"[109] usually subject to some value limitation.[110] Here, however, there is wide disparity, with some jurisdictions protecting as much as $20,000 equity in a car[111] and some others protecting as little as $1,000.[112] As with other exemptions, the protection does not extend to value that is subject to an outstanding consensual security interest. Thus, debtors who wish to keep their automobiles, trucks, buses, and motor scooters must frequently enter into some sort of arrangement with their secured creditors to be able to retain the asset after their bankruptcy.

Exemptions are typically also provided, usually subject to both per-item and possibly aggregate value restrictions, for jewelry[113] and tools of a

107 Bankruptcy Code § 522(d)(3).

108 Ohio Rev. Code Ann. § 2329.66(A)(4) (LexisNexis Supp. 2006).

109 *E.g.*, Bankruptcy Code § 522(d)(2).

110 Bankruptcy Code § 522(d)(2) ($3,225).

111 Kan. Stat. Ann. § 60-2304(c) (2005). Married debtors in Texas can exempt a whopping $60,000 in a car, providing they claim no other personal property as exempt. Tex. Prop. Code. Ann. §§ 42.001(a), 42.002 (Vernon 2000).

112 Ohio Rev. Code Ann. § 2329.66(A)(2) (LexisNexis Supp. 2006). In most states the amount seems to be between $2000–3,000, with a few up in the $5,000 range. *See* John H. Williamson, The Attorney's Handbook on Consumer Bankruptcy and Chapter 13, Appendix III — Exempt Property (2005 ed.).

113 Bankruptcy Code § 522(d)(4) ($1,350 aggregate limit); *see also* Ohio Rev. Code Ann. § 6323(A)(4)(c) (LexisNexis Supp. 2006) ("not to exceed four hundred dollars in one item of jewelry and not to exceed two hundred dollars in every other item of jewelry" and also subject to aggregate limit imposed on most other items of furniture).

debtor's trade, business, or profession.[114] Nearly all jurisdictions[115] provide an unlimited exemption for health aids,[116] though some statutes require that they be both "professionally prescribed" and "medically necessary."[117]

Likewise, most exemption statutes protect the debtor's interest in a "burial plot,"[118] presumably to prevent creditors from frustrating debtors' efforts to be laid to rest in plots adjoining loved ones rather than to ensure that they are not relegated to a pauper's funeral. After 2005, these exempted interests are limited, together with interests in the debtor's homestead, to a ceiling of $136,875, to the extent the interest was acquired by the debtor within the 1215-day period before the filing of his bankruptcy petition.[119] Moreover, the entire exemption can be denied if the debtor acquired the interest in the burial plot within the ten-year period before his bankruptcy petition with the intent to "hinder, delay, or defraud a creditor."[120]

[2] Categorization Issues

The detail included in many exemption statutes inevitably leads to curious and sometimes amusing categorization issues. For example, the absence of a value limitation on the exemption for wearing apparel or household goods, combined with a meaningful limit on the exemption for jewelry, might lead to questions over whether a Rolex watch is more properly characterized as wearing apparel or jewelry.[121] Numerous cases have addressed the question of whether cameras qualify as the type of household goods[122] that are typically exempt either with or without a limit on their value. Similarly, aggressive trustees have sometimes raised

---

[114] *E.g.*, Bankruptcy Code § 522(d)(6) ($2,025 aggregate limit for "implements, professional books, or tools of the trade of the debtor or [his] dependent."); Ohio Rev. Code Ann. § 2329.66(A)(5) (LexisNexis Supp. 2006) ($750 "in all implements, professional books, or tools of the person's profession, trade, or business, including agriculture").

[115] Such an exemption is conspicuously missing from the exemption statutes in Delaware. One sometimes wonders what wheel-chair bound debtors do in states without such an exemption. Such items might be claimed as "furniture" or even "wearing apparel."

[116] Bankruptcy Code § 522(d)(9).

[117] Ohio Rev. Code Ann. § 2329.66(A)(7) (LexisNexis Supp. 2006) ("professionally prescribed *or* medically necessary health aids") (emphasis added).

[118] *E.g.*, Bankruptcy Code § 522(d)(1) (part of the homestead exemption); Ohio Rev. Code § 2329.66(A)(8) (LexisNexis Supp. 2006).

[119] *See* Bankruptcy Code § 522(p)(1)(C).

[120] Bankruptcy Code § 522(o).

[121] *Compare* In re Lynch, 139 B.R. 868 (Bankr. N.D. Ohio 1992) (separate exemption for jewelry prevents its characterization as household goods), *with* In re Stanhope, 76 B.R. 165, (Bankr. D. Mont. 1987) ($5,000 Rolex watch exempt as "wearing apparel" absent evidence that it had been purchased for investment purposes). One of your co-authors wears a geeky Timex watch that also keeps track of his appointments and stores important phone numbers — no one would confuse it with jewelry.

[122] *E.g.*, In re Whitney, 70 B.R. 443 (Bankr. D. Colo. 1989).

questions about whether ATVs[123] buses,[124] boats, motorcycles,[125] scooters, and airplanes[126] qualify for a "motor vehicle" or "automobile" exemption.

Due to the wide variety of terminology used in exemption statutes, it is difficult to draw any general conclusions about the proper characterization of individual items. However, courts are reluctant to permit items to be claimed as exempt under a general category when it also fits within a more specific class of exempt property. Thus, items regarded as jewelry do not ordinarily qualify as wearing apparel or household goods.[127] Likewise, debtors have had trouble having their motor vehicles alternatively characterized as "tools of the trade," even though they might be used by the debtor in his business or profession.[128]

The question of the proper characterization of property also arises in connection with § 522(f), which under some circumstances permits a debtor to avoid non-possessory, non-purchase money security interests in certain types of exempt property.[129]

[3] Regional Exemptions

There are, in addition, a number of exemptions that seem to reflect a different lifestyle than the ones imagined by most law students. For many years, and well into the last quarter of the twentieth century, many states' exemption statutes seemed to reflect a far more agrarian society than the one most Americans lives now enjoy.[130] A few of these persist. Thus, it is not unusual to find exemptions for certain quantities of firewood, chickens, church pews, and "horses, mules, or donkeys."[131] Other exemptions are hard to understand from any point of view. One state has an exemption for a debtor's leasehold interest in a piano.[132] At least one protects liquor licenses.[133]

---

[123] In re Moore, 251 B.R. 380 (Bankr. W.D. Mo. 2000) (ATV was a motor vehicle under state exemption statute even though it was used solely for recreational purposes).

[124] In re Johnson, 14 B.R. 14, (Bankr. W.D. Ky. 1981) ("'bus' and 'automobile' [are] species of the genus 'motor vehicle'").

[125] In re Drewes, 217 B.R. 978 (Bankr. D.N.H. 1998) (motorcycle not an "automobile").

[126] In re Wilbur, 25 B.R. 405 (Bankr. D. Me. 1982) (airplane not a motor vehicle).

[127] In re Lynch, 139 B.R. 868 (Bankr. N.D. Ohio 1992) (separate exemption for jewelry prevents its characterization as household goods).

[128] *Compare* In re Patterson, 825 F.2d 1140 (7th Cir. 1987) (farmer's tractor was not a tool of the trade under § 522(d)(6)), *with* Nazarene Fed. Credit Union v. McNutt (In re McNutt), 87 B.R. 84 (B.A.P. 9th Cir. 1988) (pickup truck a tool of the debtor's drywall hanging trade even though it was not specially equipped), *and* In re Giles, 340 B.R. 543 (Bankr. E.D. Pa. 2006) (milliner's auto, used to transport hats to various festivals, was a tool of the trade).

[129] *See* § 12.07[B] Avoiding Non-Purchase Money Security Interests, *infra.*

[130] *See* G. Stanley Joslin, *Debtors' Exemption Laws: Time for Modernization*, 34 Ind. L.J. 355 (1959); William T. Vukowich, *Debtors' Exemption Rights*, 62 Geo. L.J. 779 (1974).

[131] Tex. Prop. Code Ann. § 42.002(10)(A) (Vernon 2000).

[132] Del. Code Ann. tit. 10 § 4902 (LexisNexis 2004).

[133] Conn. Gen. Stat. § 30-14(a) (West Supp. 2006) (tools of the trade in other states?).

The adoption of the Bankruptcy Reform Act of 1978, with its effort to establish a set of uniform bankruptcy exemptions, and its provision authorizing states to opt-out of the uniform exemptions, led many states to revise their archaic exemption statutes in favor of new provisions that reflect life in the latter part of the twentieth century. One can only surmise how long it will be before these recently enacted statutes will become relics in need of further revision.[134] Indeed, without exemptions for laptop computers or cell phones, this may already have occurred.

[D] Wages and Other Financial Assets

A wide variety of financial assets are exempt in bankruptcy, either under § 522(d), or under state exemption statutes. Principal among these are wages, which are protected by the wage garnishment limits of the federal Consumer Credit Protection Act and sometimes more extensively by state exemption statutes. Certain other substitutes for wages, such as payments under life insurance policies,[135] payments due on account of the wrongful death of a person on whom the debtor was dependent,[136] spousal support,[137] and disability payments[138] are also commonly exempt. Both federal and state law also provide broad exemptions for a variety of types of retirement assets, which, after all, are nothing more than deferred wages. A mish-mash of provisions protect other forms of financial assets.

[1] Wage Exemptions

Wages are exempted primarily because of the Consumer Credit Protection Act.[139] It was enacted to make sure wage earners are able to receive at least enough of their take-home pay to enable them to meet their basic needs, and it was hoped at least to permit them to avoid being forced into bankruptcy.[140] In most cases, the Act exposes a maximum of only 25% of a person's "disposable earnings" to the claims of creditors.[141] Individuals whose weekly earnings are less than forty times the federal minimum wage

[134] No state provides a separate exemption for a personal computer. However, new Bankruptcy Code § 522(f)(4)(A) includes a personal computer among the items that are within the term "household goods" and thus potentially subject to lien avoidance by the debtor. *See* § 12.07 Avoiding Liens on Exempt Property, *infra*.

[135] *E.g.*, Bankruptcy Code § 522(d)(11)(B); Ohio Rev. Code Ann. § 2329.66(A)(6)(b) (LexisNexis Supp. 2006).

[136] *E.g.*, Bankruptcy Code § 522(d)(11)(B); Ohio Rev. Code Ann. § 2329.66(A)(12)(b) (LexisNexis Supp. 2006).

[137] *E.g.*, Bankruptcy Code § 522(d)(10)(D); Ohio Rev. Code Ann. § 2329.66(A)(11) (LexisNexis Supp. 2006).

[138] *E.g.*, Bankruptcy Code § 522(d)(10)(C); Ohio Rev. Code Ann. § 2329.66(A)(9)(f) (LexisNexis Supp. 2006).

[139] 15 U.S.C. § 1673(a)(1) (2000).

[140] *See* In re Kokoszka, 479 F.2d 990 (2d Cir. 1973), *aff'd sub. nom* Kokoszka v. Belford, 417 U.S. 642, *reh'g denied*, 419 U.S. 486 (1974).

[141] 15 U.S.C. § 1673(a)(1) (2000).

receive greater protection.[142] Not surprisingly, protection for earnings is less if the creditor seeking to recover those earnings is owed "support."[143]

This maximum percentage can only be garnished from a person's "disposable earnings." These are defined as "that part of earnings of any individual remaining after the deduction from those earnings of any amounts required by law to be withheld."[144] Amounts required to be withheld include deductions for social security, medicare, and income withholding taxes. Significantly, however, amounts required to be withheld do not include sums deducted from the debtor's earnings pursuant to an order of support for another creditor.[145]

Courts have generally been restrictive in determining what rights constitute earnings that are protected by these limits. For example, neither lump sum severance payments owed to a former employee[146] nor a debtor's tax refund owed by the government[147] have qualified for this protection. Further, although state exemption statutes may provide greater protection, the few decisions that exist have concluded that these federal restrictions do not apply to wages after they have been deposited into a bank account.[148]

Many states' wage exemption statutes adhere closely to the restrictions imposed by federal law and expose wages to garnishment to the full extent permitted by the Consumer Credit Protection Act.[149] Other states provide even greater protection than what the federal law requires. California, for example, exempts wages beyond the federal limits to the extent "necessary

---

[142] Section 303 of the Consumer Credit Protection Act always protects "thirty times the Federal minimum hour wage." 15 U.S.C. § 1673(a)(2) (2000). In late May, 2007, Congress increased the minimum wage, effective July 24, 2007, to $5.85 per hour. It will increase to $6.55 per hour in July 2008, and to $7.25 per hour in July 2009. The U.S. Troop Readiness, Veterans' Care, Katrina Recovery, and Iraq Accountability Appropriations Act, 2007, Pub. L. No. 110-28 § 8102(a), 121 Stat. 112, 188 (2007).

Thus, employees in sectors not governed by the minimum wage or who work less than forty hours may always protect $175.50 in wages per week from their creditors. Employees who earn more than the minimum wage and who work at least forty hours per week may protect more, with only 25% of their earnings subject to garnishment. For example, an employee who works forty hours, earning $8.00 per hour, may protect up to $240 from garnishment, without adjusting for the smaller of his total wages that constitute "disposable earnings."

The increase in the minimum wage that becomes effective in 2008 will protect a minimum of $196.50. When the minimum wage increases again in 2009, a minimum of $217.50 will be protected.

[143] A support claimant may recover anywhere from 50% to as much as 65% of a debtor's disposable earnings, depending on whether the debtor has other dependents and on whether the support claim involved, as so many of them are, is for past-due support. 15 U.S.C. § 1673(b) (2000).

[144] 15 U.S.C. § 1672(b) (2000).

[145] Marshall v. District Court for Forty-First-b Judicial Dist. of Mich., Mount Clemens Div., 444 F. Supp. 1110 (E.D. Mich. 1978).

[146] Aetna Cas. & Sur. Co. v. Rodco Autobody, 965 F. Supp. 104 (D. Mass. 1996).

[147] In re Trudeau, 237 B.R. 803 (B.A.P. 10th Cir. 1999).

[148] John O. Melby & Co. Bank v. Anderson, 276 N.W.2d 274 (Wis. 1979).

[149] *See* Ohio Rev. Code Ann. § 2329.66(A)(13) (LexisNexis Supp. 2006).

for the support of the judgment debtor or the judgment debtor's family,"[150] and Pennsylvania does not permit wage garnishment at all, except with respect to support and student loan claimants.[151]

Debtors in states that have opted out, as well as debtors in other, usually more generous states that have not opted out, who elect their home state's exemption statute receive the benefit of their own state's federally mandated restriction on wage garnishment. Debtors in states that have not opted out and who elect the uniform federal exemptions under § 522(d) appear to be out of luck, as that section contains no provision to exempt wages owed to the debtor from his bankruptcy estate.

[2] Wage Substitutes

Many exemption statutes contain provisions exempting a variety of wage substitutes. These commonly include payments under a life insurance policy due because of the death of a person on whom the debtor was dependent,[152] payments on account of the wrongful death of a person on whom the debtor was dependent,[153] spousal support,[154] disability payments,[155] awards for lost earnings,[156] unemployment, and social security benefits.[157]

Some such exemptions are specifically limited to the amount reasonably necessary for the support of the debtor and the debtor's dependents.[158] For example, the uniform federal exemptions protect support, wrongful death, and life insurance payments only "to the extent reasonably necessary for the support of the debtor and any dependent of the debtor,"[159] but they fully exempt veterans' benefits, unemployment benefits, and social security benefits.[160] State exemption statutes contain similar differences, reflecting an array of policies and political compromises.[161]

---

[150] Cal. Civ. Proc. Code § 706.051 (West 1987) (and those who have no dependents).

[151] 42 Pa. Cons. Stat. Ann. § 8127 (West Supp. 2006) (it also permits wage garnishment for "board of four weeks or less," and student loans).

[152] *E.g.*, Bankruptcy Code § 522(d)(11)(B); Ohio Rev. Code Ann. § 2329.66(A)(6)(b) (LexisNexis Supp. 2006).

[153] *E.g.*, Bankruptcy Code § 522(d)(11)(B); Ohio Rev. Code. Ann. § 2329.66(A)(12)(b) (LexisNexis Supp. 2006).

[154] *E.g.*, Bankruptcy Code § 522(d)(10)(D); Ohio Rev. Code Ann. § 2329.66(A)(11) (LexisNexis Supp. 2006).

[155] *E.g.*, Bankruptcy Code § 522(d)(10)(C); Ohio Rev. Code Ann. § 2329.66(A)(9)(f) (LexisNexis Supp. 2006).

[156] *E.g.*, Bankruptcy Code § 522(d)(11)(E); Ohio Rev. Code Ann. § 2329.66(A)(12)(d) (LexisNexis Supp. 2006) (for loss of future earnings).

[157] *E.g.*, Bankruptcy Code § 522(d)(10)(A); Ohio Rev. Code Ann. § 2329.66(A)(9)(c) (LexisNexis Supp. 2006).

[158] *E.g.*, Bankruptcy Code § 522(d)(10)(D).

[159] Bankruptcy Code § 522(d)(10)(D), (11)(B), (11)(C).

[160] Bankruptcy Code § 522(d)(10)(A).

[161] The Ohio statute, with which one of your authors is particularly familiar, fully exempts benefits from "life insurance," but protects payments for wrongful death claims only to the extent they are reasonably necessary for the support of the debtor and the debtor's dependents. *Compare* Ohio Rev. Code Ann. § 2329.66(A)(6)(b), *with* § 2329.66(A)(12)(b) (LexisNexis Supp. 2006).

[3] Retirement Funds[162]

Retirement assets are widely exempt. Many state exemption statutes protect a variety of traditional "defined benefit" pension plans,[163] more modern "defined contribution" plans,[164] and other modern tax-deferred retirement savings plans, such as the various types of IRAs, Keough Plans, SEPs, and so on from the claims of creditors. Not surprisingly, state exemption statutes are not always drafted to cover what seems like an ever-expanding type of retirement savings accounts and trust funds. The most obvious example of this has been Individual Retirement Accounts, which until recently have received considerably less protection than other retirement assets. Funds in an "ERISA qualified" pension plan are excluded entirely from a debtor's estate under the Supreme Court's ruling in *Patterson v. Shumate*,[165] which applied § 541(c)(2). As explained in more detail elsewhere, the 2005 Amendments extended this exclusion to a variety of tax deferred retirement, health, and educational savings accounts, including those under §§ 403(b), 414(d), 457, 529(b)(1), and 530(b)(1) of the Internal Revenue Code.[166]

In 2005, Congress also amended Bankruptcy Code § 522's treatment of retirement assets. These revisions ensure that a wide variety of retirement assets receive some protection, even for debtors in states that have opted out of the uniform federal exemptions. At the same time, they impose limits on the size of some of these exemptions.

New § 522(b)(3)(C) exempts "retirement funds to the extent that those funds are in a fund or account that is exempt from taxation under section 401, 403, 408, 408A, 414, 457, or 501(a) of the Internal Revenue Code."[167] This exemption applies regardless of whether the debtor's state has opted out of the uniform federal exemptions and regardless of whether a debtor in a state that has not opted out has elected his own state's exemptions

---

[162] John Hennigan, *Beneath the Surface of BAPCPA,* Rousey, *and the New Retirement Funds Exemption*, 13 Am. Bankr. Inst. L. Rev. 777 (2005); C. Scott Pryor, *Rock, Scissors, Papers: ERISA, the Bankruptcy Code and State Exemption Laws for Individual Retirement Accounts*, 77 Am. Bankr. L.J. 65 (2003).

[163] A defined benefit retirement plan specifies the amount of benefits the employee will receive upon his retirement. The amount is usually a percentage of the employee's highest salary, with the percentage dependent upon the total number of years of the employee's service to the employer. Defined benefit plans remain common for public employees but are now rare for those in the private sector.

[164] In a defined contribution plan, the employer contributes a specific amount (usually a percentage of the employee's salary) to the employee's pension fund. Employees also frequently contribute to the fund. The accumulated funds provide the basis for the employee's pension, which may be large or small depending on the sums contributed and their earnings performance while they accumulate.

[165] 504 U.S. 753 (1992).

[166] *See* § 7.04[F] Spendthrift Trusts, *supra.*

[167] Bankruptcy Code § 522(b)(3)(C); *see* Margaret Howard, *Exemptions under the 2005 Bankruptcy Amendments: A Tale of Opportunity Lost*, 79 Am. Bankr. L.J. 397, 413–18 (2005).

or those in § 522(d).[168] As a result, the following types of retirement funds are now completely exempt:

- Traditional employer-sponsored and defined-contribution pension, profit-sharing, and stock-bonus plans governed by I.R.C. § 401;
- Qualified annuity plans for employees of non-profit employers under I.R.C. § 503;
- Traditional Individual Retirement Accounts under I.R.C. § 408;
- "Roth" IRAs under I.R.C. § 408A;
- Retirement plans for certain controlled groups of employees under I.R.C. § 414;
- Deferred compensation plans maintained by certain eligible employers under I.R.C. § 457; and
- Retirement plans established and maintained by certain defined tax-exempt organizations under I.R.C. § 501(a).

While many of these retirement assets were already excluded from the debtor's estate under § 541(c)(2), the new language brings those that were not excluded, such as Individual IRAs and Roth IRAs, under a broad umbrella of protection. No longer will debtors whose retirement assets have been rolled over into an IRA need to decide whether to trade their security in retirement for a fresh start in bankruptcy during their working years.

This new exemption provision is combined with a new $1 million ceiling on the total value of assets in both Traditional IRAs and Roth IRAs that may be exempted under the new provision.[169] However, the $1 million limit does not apply to funds that have been deposited into the IRA as a "rollover" contribution from other traditional retirement funds that contain contributions from the debtor's employer. Also, it is anticipated that few debtors will have successfully accumulated over $1.095 million in IRA assets from accumulated $4,000 annual contributions. Even then, the limit may be increased by the court "if the interests of justice so require."[170]

[E] Tracing Exemptions into Non-Exempt Property

When a debtor has converted property that is protected by an exemption into a form that is not covered by an exemption, there is a question regarding whether the exemption may be traced from the property into its new form. Thus, a debtor in financial difficulty might sell his house and thus convert what otherwise would have been exempt equity in the home into cash or into a new Harley-Davidson motorcycle.

---

[168] This result is accomplished by the addition of identical language to the uniform federal exemptions in new § 522(d)(12).

[169] Bankruptcy Code § 522(n).

[170] Bankruptcy Code § 522(n).

Wages provide a key illustration. Seventy-five percent of a person's earnings are exempt from garnishment.[171] An initial question is whether the exemption applies when the debtor's wages are deposited into the debtor's bank account. Although the federal wage garnishment limits do not require the exemption to be traced into other forms of property, many state exemption statutes extend their own wage garnishment protections to wages that have been deposited into a bank account or other liquid asset readily available to meet the debtor's living expenses.

Extending the exemption further might easily lead to the conclusion that all of a debtor's property attributable to the debtor's wages should enjoy a 75% exemption. However, this has not been done.

Whether wages are exempt after being deposited into a debtor's bank account depends on the exemption statute the debtor relies on. Some states' exemption statutes expressly provide for tracing wages into other forms.[172] In some states where the exemption statute is not explicit, courts have ruled that the exemption continues notwithstanding the transfer of the wages to the debtor's bank account.[173] Other states' wage exemption statutes provide no such protection,[174] and the federal wage exemption limits do not require states to do so.

The question of tracing might also be applied to income substitutes such as workers' compensation benefits or personal injury awards. Decisions run in both directions, with some courts permitting the exemption to continue as long as the funds are contained in a segregated account,[175] and others permitting it to continue even if the funds have been commingled, as long as the amount of the award can be traced into the account using standard tracing methods.[176]

A dramatic example of the importance of the issue occurred in *Woodson v. Fireman's Fund Ins. Co. (In re Woodson)*. The court refused to trace the debtor's exemption in an unmatured whole life insurance policy on the life of his wife, into the $1 million proceeds the debtor received after his wife expired.[177] The court treated the proceeds of the policy as a separate asset,

---

[171] 15 U.S.C. § 1673 (2000); *see* § 2.12[A][4][a] Federal Restrictions on Wage Garnishment, *supra*.

[172] *See* Fla. Stat. Ann. § 222.11(3) (West 1998). Before the Florida statute was specifically amended to address this issue, wages placed into an account were not exempt. In re Ryzner, 208 B.R. 568, 569 (Bankr. M.D. Fla. 1997).

[173] Daugherty v. Central Trust Co., 504 N.E.2d 1100, 1103 (Ohio 1986).

[174] *E.g.*, In re Sinclair, 417 F.3d 527 (5th Cir. 2005) (applying the Louisiana exemption statute); In re Adcock, 264 B.R. 708 (D. Kan. 2000) (Kansas wage exemption statute). Nor does the federal Consumer Credit Protection Act require states to exempt wages after their deposit into an account. Usery v. First Nat'l Bank, 586 F.2d 107 (9th Cir.1978); *cf.* Kokoszka v. Belford, 417 U.S. 642, 651 (1974) (right to tax refund not exempt).

[175] *E.g.*, In re Nolen, 65 B.R. 1014 (Bankr. D.N.M. 1986).

[176] Matthews v. Lewis, 617 S.W.2d 43 (Ky. 1981).

[177] 839 F.2d 610 (9th Cir. 1988). In a previous life, one of your co-authors represented Mr. Woodson in his pursuit of this exemption.

brought into the estate under § 541(a)(5) and exempt only to the extent they were reasonably necessary for the support of the debtor and his remaining dependents.

[F] Exemption Protections for a Debtor's Dependents

The Bankruptcy Code contains several protections for debtors' dependents in connection with property that could be claimed as exempt. If the debtor does not submit a schedule of exempt property, the debtor's dependents are permitted to file the list or submit a claim of property as exempt from the estate on the debtor's behalf.[178] This provides a hedge against debtors who are either irresponsible in this regard, or who are perhaps estranged from their spouses or children and not interested in protecting property that may be in the their possession.[179] However, if the debtor files a schedule of exemptions, a dependent may not file a different or conflicting schedule,[180] unless the schedule filed by the debtor was supplied in bad faith.[181] In addition, § 522(e) makes a debtors' waiver of his exemptions or of his avoiding powers with respect to exempt property unenforceable.[182]

[G] Valuation of Exempt Property

Most consumer debtors' attorneys advise their clients to state the value of their assets based on what the client believes he would be able to recover from a sale of the asset at a garage sale. This usually comports with the definition of value in § 522(a)(2), which indicates that "value" means "fair market value" as of the date of the debtor's petition.[183] Fair market value is generally regarded as "[t]he amount at which property would change hands between a willing buyer and a willing seller, neither being under any compulsion to buy or sell and both having reasonable knowledge of the relevant facts."[184] Most courts have used "liquidation" value as the market value for the purpose of the debtor's exemption rights,[185] though this might vary according to differences in state exemption schemes.[186]

---

[178] Bankruptcy Code § 522(l).

[179] The debtor's spouse is specifically designated as one of the debtor's "dependents" even though he or she might not be financially dependent on the debtor in the ordinary sense. Bankruptcy Code § 522(a)(1). Bankruptcy Rule 4003(a) provides a mechanism permitting a dependent to claim the debtor's exemptions.

[180] *E.g.*, Kapila v. Morgan (In re Morgan), 286 B.R. 678 (Bankr. E.D. Wis. 2002).

[181] In re Crouch, 33 B.R. 271 (Bankr. E.D.N.C. 1983).

[182] *See generally* H.R. Rep. No. 95-595, 362 (1977), *reprinted in* 1978 U.S.C.C.A.N. 5963, 6318; S. Rep. No. 95-989, 76 (1978), *reprinted in* 1978 U.S.C.C.A.N. 5787, 5862.

[183] Bankruptcy Code § 522(a)(2).

[184] Black's Law Dictionary 537 (5th ed. 1979) (cited in In re Johnson, 165 B.R. 524 (Bankr. S.D. Ga. 1994).

[185] *E.g.*, In re Walsh, 5 Bankr. 239 (Bankr. D.D.C. 1980).

[186] *E.g.*, In re Belsome, 434 F.3d 774 (5th Cir. 2005) (applying Louisiana exemption statute which specifies use of National Automobile Dealers Association (NADA) valuations).

However, the Supreme Court's decision in *Associates Commercial Corp. v. Rash*, and the addition in 2005 of § 506(a)(2), may cast these decisions into doubt.[187] Both *Rash* and 506(a)(2) require the use of "replacement cost" to determine the allowed amount of a secured claim in a Chapter 13 case.[188]

Courts usually accept the debtor's valuation in the absence of persuasive evidence to the contrary. Where expert appraisal testimony is available regarding the market value of an asset, rebutting this presumption is not difficult.[189] Where there is no available market for the exempt property, the court is likely to accept the debtor's view, particularly with respect to unusual assets, such as a cause of action under the Truth in Lending Act or some other claim the debtor has against a third party.[190]

New requirements imposed on debtors' attorneys by § 707(b)(4)(C) undoubtedly influence how property values are determined. Section 707(b)(4)(C) provides that the debtor's attorney's signature on the debtor's petition certifies that the attorney has conducted a "reasonable investigation" into the underlying circumstances and that the documents submitted with the petition are "well grounded in fact."[191] Thus, debtors' attorneys are not permitted to rely on their client's representations about the value of the assets that are claimed as exempt.[192] They must conduct their own investigation.

§ 12.04 Tenancy by the Entireties

States that permit married couples to hold property as tenants by the entirety provide limited protection for property held in this manner. Further, although entireties property is usually associated with real estate, some states recognize the form of ownership for items of personal property.[193] Tenancy by the entirety is a form of joint ownership available only to married couples, which prevents transfer or encumbrance by the unilateral action of only one spouse. A deed or mortgage executed solely by the husband or the wife has no effect. Similarly, if a judgment is rendered on a debt incurred solely by the wife, no judicial lien arising from that

---

187 520 U.S. 953 (1997).

188 *E.g.*, In re Weber, 332 B.R. 432 (B.A.P. 10th Cir. 2005). In the context of redemption, this practice was legislatively overruled by the 2005 Amendments. The Code now specifies that the amount of the allowed secured claim, in the context of personal property owned by individual debtors, is to be based on the "price a retail merchant would charge for property of that kind considering the age and condition of the property at the time value is determined." Bankruptcy Code § 506(a)(2).

189 Matter of Salzer, 52 F.3d 708 (7th Cir. 1995).

190 In re Polis, 217 F.3d 899 (7th Cir. 2000).

191 Bankruptcy Code § 707(b)(4)(C).

192 *See* § 6.02[F] Attorney's Obligations Regarding Debtor's Schedules, *supra*; Gary Neustadter, *2005: A Consumer Bankruptcy Odyssey*, 39 Creighton L. Rev. 225, 338–53 (2006); Henry J. Sommer, *Trying to Make Sense Out of Nonsense: Representing Consumers Under the "Bankruptcy Abuse Prevention and Consumer Protection Act of 2005,"* 79 Am. Bankr. L.J. 191, 211 (2005).

193 *E.g.*, In re Caliri, 347 B.R. 788 (Bankr. M.D. Fla. 2006) (catamaran sailboat).

judgment can attach to the property. The property can be transferred or encumbered by both spouses acting jointly; it can also be subject to a judicial lien arising from a jointly incurred obligation.

For example, suppose Merl and Agnes own their home as tenants by the entireties. If Merl conveys a mortgage on the property to Red Rose Bank, the mortgage is unenforceable. If Agnes incurs an individual credit card debt to the bank, the bank is unable to obtain a judgment lien on their home to satisfy Agnes' individual debt. Only by acting jointly in incurring an obligation can Merl and Agnes subject their entireties property to any voluntary or involuntary lien.[194]

In the context of a bankruptcy case, this means only joint creditors have any rights to the debtors' home. If there are no joint creditors, the debtors may keep all of their entireties property, not just the amount protected by a homestead exemption. Thus, their mode of ownership acts as if it were an exemption, at least insofar as individual debts are concerned.

Despite this, most married couples have numerous joint debts. If both are liable on the family credit card, they can only protect their entireties property against the creditor's claim only to the extent of their ordinary homestead and wildcard exemptions.[195] Savvy creditors who provide credit to individual spouses in states that protect entireties property in this way frequently take care to obtain guarantees from their borrower's spouses to protect themselves from this limitation inherent in the tenancy by the entirety form of ownership.

§ 12.05 Loss of Exemptions

[A] Waiver of Exemptions

Under the old Bankruptcy Act and in many states today, the benefit of the exemption laws can be waived by agreement. However, under the Bankruptcy Code, such a waiver is ineffective. Section 522(e) makes any exemption waiver that is executed in favor of a creditor who holds an unsecured claim unenforceable.[196] Also unenforceable is any attempted waiver of the debtor's power to avoid certain liens on exempt property under § 522(f).[197]

The purpose for these provisions is consumer protection. Congress was concerned that many exemption waivers were made without full understanding of the consequences. This provision is also in line with other state and federal enactments that restrict or prohibit exemption waivers.[198]

---

[194] *See* 7 Richard R. Powell & Michael Allan Wolf, Powell on Real Property § 52.03[3] (2006).

[195] *See* 7 Richard R. Powell & Michael Allan Wolf, Powell on Real Property § 52.03[3] (2006).

[196] 11 U.S.C. § 522(e).

[197] 11 U.S.C. § 522(e).

[198] *See, e.g.*, Federal Trade Commission Unfair Credit Practices Regulations, 16 C.F.R. § 444.2(a)(2).

Of course, a debtor might effectively waive his exemptions by failing to assert them. In such a case, § 522(l) permits the debtor's dependents to file a schedule of exemptions on the debtor's behalf. Still, if no one files the list, the debtor's exemptions may be lost.[199]

[B] Liens on Exempt Property

Although waivers of exemptions are not enforceable, security interests are generally enforceable. Security interests impair a debtor's exemptions much in the same way that an exemption waiver would, if the waiver could be enforced.

Exemptions can only be claimed in "the debtor's interest" in property.[200] The debtor's interest is only his equity in the asset. The value of this equity is the value of the property above the amount necessary to satisfy any valid liens against the property, such as mortgages and security interests.

Consider, for example, a debtor who owns a home worth $100,000, but subject to a $90,000 mortgage. This leaves the debtor with only $10,000 in equity in the house. If the applicable exemption statute protects $15,000 of a debtor's interest in his residence, the debtor is unable to take advantage of more than $10,000 of the exemption. If the debtor had encumbered his home with a second mortgage, such as by using it as collateral for an "equity line" credit card, that secures a $12,000 debt, there would be no equity available for the debtor and his entire exemption in the house would be lost.

The same problem frequently occurs with respect to automobiles. If the debtor's car is worth $12,000 but is subject to a purchase money security interest that secures the unpaid $13,000, no equity exists and the debtor has no exemption in the car.

As will be discussed elsewhere in this chapter, some circumstances permit the debtor to avoid a non-purchase money security interest, at least to the extent that it impairs the debtor's exemption rights. A fair number of states have followed suit in their own exemption laws.[201]

Unless the debtor can avoid the security interest, he must either surrender the collateral to the secured party, enter into a reaffirmation agreement with the secured creditor, or more rarely, "redeem" the collateral from the lien by making a lump-sum payment to the creditor in the amount of the allowed secured claim.[202]

---

[199] This appears to be rather a remote contingency, however, since even if the debtor misses the deadline to list exemptions, amendments are rather freely allowed.

[200] *E.g.*, Ohio Rev. Code Ann. § 2329.66(A)(1) (LexisNexis Supp. 2006) (exempting "*the person's interest*, not to exceed five thousand dollars, in one parcel or item of real or personal property that the person or a dependent of the person uses as a residence.") (emphasis added).

[201] *See, e.g.*, Va. Code Ann. § 34-28 (LexisNexis 2005) (providing for the avoidance of non-purchase money liens on most types of exempt property).

[202] Bankruptcy Code § 521(a)(2); *see* § 12.08[D] Debtor's Statement of Intent, *infra*.

If the debtor has any non-exempt equity in the property, any deal with the secured creditor must include the trustee. The trustee wants to sell the property and distribute the surplus equity to the debtor's other creditors. For example, if a mortgage secures a debt of only $80,000, the debtor's $15,000 exemption would not be sufficient to protect all of a debtor's $20,000 equity in the home. The trustee desires to sell the house for its $100,000 value, distribute $80,000 to the mortgage holder on account of its lien, $15,000 to the debtor on account of his exemption, and the $5,000 balance to unsecured creditors. To save the house, the debtor needs to come up with an additional $5,000, possibly from the sale of other exempt assets or through an additional loan from the mortgage company or someone else. The debtor would thereby purchase the surplus equity from the trustee. As noted above, trustees are often willing to sell the excess to the debtor, so long as the debtor is willing and able to pay the full value of that excess. Alternatively, the trustee may simply wish to sell the property as the only way to determine the true amount of the surplus equity.

[C] Debtor Misconduct

A debtor may also be deprived of the benefit of his exemptions because of his fraud or other misconduct in the bankruptcy proceeding itself. The power of the court to strip the debtor of his exemptions may arise from any of several sources. First, and most obvious, exemptions created by state law are subject to state law restrictions (except where those restrictions are superseded by the Code). If the debtor's misconduct would deprive him of the exemption under state statutory or case law, the same result ordinarily applies in bankruptcy.[203]

Second, § 522(g) imposes a limit on exemptions claimed with respect to property recovered by the trustee from a third party.[204] The debtor may not exempt recovered property unless: (1) the transfer was involuntary and the debtor did not conceal the property; or (2) the debtor could have avoided the transfer himself under the rules in § 522(f) regarding avoidance of non-purchase-money security interests in household property, tools of the trade, and health aids.[205]

Thus, as a general rule, voluntarily transferred property recovered by the trustee under rules such as those for avoiding preferences or fraudulent transfers may not be exempted by the debtor. Section 522(g) does not require a showing of fraud or other specific misconduct; rather, it requires only a showing that the avoided transfer was made voluntarily. If the debtor voluntarily parted with possession of the property, the debtor effectively demonstrated that he did not need it to make his way in life.

Another potential problem arises if the debtor converted his non-exempt assets into an exempt category immediately prior to filing for bankruptcy.

---

[203] *E.g.*, In re Clemmer, 184 B.R. 935 (Bankr. E.D. Tenn. 1995).

[204] Bankruptcy Code § 522(g).

[205] *See* § 12.07 Avoiding Liens on Exempt Property, *infra*.

Although there is no general rule prohibiting debtors from converting their non-exempt assets into an exempt class, the Code now imposes some express limits on the practice, particularly with respect to residential property and burial plots. Section 522(o), enacted as part of the 2005 Amendments, prohibits debtors from asserting an exemption in residential real or personal property or a burial plot that was acquired with non-exempt property that the debtor disposed of during the ten-year period prior to his bankruptcy petition "with the intent to hinder, delay, or defraud a creditor."[206]

The very enactment of § 522(o) opens an avenue of support for the contention that other pre-bankruptcy conversions, not specifically prohibited by this new language, are to be permitted. Section 522(o) may be regarded as an exception to the normal rule that conversions of assets into exempt status are not prohibited.[207] Thus, although a debtor who used non-exempt assets to build exempt equity in his home with the intent to hinder his creditors would not be able to assert an otherwise available homestead exemption, a debtor who converted non-exempt assets to build up the value of an exempt life insurance policy or retirement plan might be able to assert the exemption, even though the conversion was accomplished with the same intent.[208]

§ 12.06 Procedures for Claiming and Objecting to Exemptions

As with most matters in bankruptcy, specific procedures are available for asserting and objecting to exemptions. Failure to follow these procedures may result in the debtor's losing valuable exemption rights, with a resulting windfall to creditors (and the trustee), or in a windfall to the debtor who may be able to retain property that should not have been exempt.

[A] What to File; Who May File; When to File

Exemptions are not automatically given to the debtor; the debtor must claim them. This is accomplished by filing a list of exempt property with the bankruptcy court.[209] The list of exemptions is ordinarily filed with the debtor's petition but may be filed within up to fifteen days after the petition, unless the court grants an extension.[210]

---

[206] Bankruptcy Code § 522(o).

[207] *But see* In re Crater, 286 B.R. 756 (Bankr. D. Ariz. 2002); *see also* In re Sholdan, 217 F.3d 1006 (8th Cir. 2000) (96 year-old living in assisted care facility converted all of his assets into a new home which far exceeded his housing needs).

[208] *See, e.g.*, First Tex. Sav. Ass'n, Inc. v. Reed (In re Reed), 700 F.2d 986 (5th Cir. 1983) (denial of discharge due to conversion of non-exempt property with intent to hinder, delay, and defraud creditors).

[209] Bankruptcy Code § 522(l); *see* Fed. Rule Bankr. P. 4003(a); Official Bankruptcy Form 6, Schedule C.

[210] Fed. R. Bankr. P. 1007(c).

Since exemptions are personal, they may generally be claimed only by the debtor. However, if the debtor fails to file the list (or "schedule" as it is usually called), a dependant of the debtor may do so.[211] If the debtor does not file, a dependant has thirty days from the time normally required for the debtor to file his schedules to file on the debtor's behalf.[212] This schedule may be examined by parties in interest who then may file objections.

[B] Objections to Exemptions

Objections to the debtor's exemptions must be filed within thirty days of the creditors' meeting or the filing of any amendment to the list of exempt property.[213] They may be filed by the case trustee or any creditor.[214] The burden of proving that an item of property is not exempt is on the objecting party.[215]

Trustees who fail to submit timely objections are unlikely to find sympathy with the court. In *Taylor v. Freeland & Kronz*, the Supreme Court ruled that the thirty-day period provided in § 522(l) is absolute, even if the debtor's claim of exemption is entirely specious.[216] In *Taylor,* the debtor's schedules asserted an exemption in the proceeds of the employment discrimination suit that was pending against her former employer. The trustee, believing that the claim against the employer was meritless and thus that it lacked any value, failed to object. When the debtor subsequently settled the claim for $110,000, the trustee objected to the exemption, asserting that the debtor had "no statutory basis" to claim the cause of action as exempt. The Court flatly rejected the trustee's objection, explaining, "[d]eadlines may lead to unwelcome results, but they prompt parties to act and they produce finality." In reaching this conclusion, the Court applied the plain language of Bankruptcy Rule 4003(b) in a straightforward manner, denying the trustee's assertion that the bankruptcy court's equitable powers permitted it to circumvent the thirty-day limit, even though the debtor's claimed exemption was both meritless and probably made in bad faith. Courts after *Taylor* have sometimes tried to mitigate its harsh outcome, either by distinguishing its facts,[217] or by construing debtors' exemption claims narrowly.[218]

---

[211] Bankruptcy Code § 522(l); Fed. Rule Bankr. P. 4003(a).

[212] Fed. R. Bankr. P. 4003(a).

[213] Fed. R. Bankr. P. 4003(b). The court may extend this if a request for extension is made before the thirty-day period expires.

[214] Fed. R. Bankr. P. 4003(b).

[215] Fed. R. Bankr. P. 4003(c).

[216] Taylor v. Freeland & Kronz, 503 U.S. 638 (1992).

[217] Dean v. Telegadis (In re Dean), 317 B.R. 482 (Bankr. W.D. Pa. 2004) (exempt property acquired after deadline for objections); In re Ruggles, 210 B.R. 57 (Bankr. D. Vt. 1997) (objection to good faith of Chapter 13 plan, based on flaws in debtor's asserted exemptions).

[218] *E.g.*, In re Clark, 266 B.R. 163 (B.A.P. 9th Cir. 2001) (initial claim regarded as ambiguous).

§ 12.07 Avoiding Liens on Exempt Property[219]

Although liens generally trump the debtor's exemption rights, the Bankruptcy Code carves out a few exceptions to this basic rule. Section 522(f) affects the validity of judgment liens and some security interests to the extent they interfere with exemptions. These rules are generally not subject to the states' power to opt out of the uniform federal exemptions. Thus, debtors in states that have opted out of the federal exemptions generally may invoke § 522(f) to avoid a lien that impairs their state exemptions.

This can be very important in some cases. For example, if state law creates a homestead exemption but prohibits a debtor from asserting it against a judgment lien-holder, the federal rule permitting avoidance of such liens when they impair exemptions prevails, and the exemption may be claimed.[220] Attempts by several states to restrict the effect of the bankruptcy rule avoiding some security interests on exempt property have been held unconstitutional as violations of the Supremacy Clause.[221] However, a few state limits on avoidance have since been expressly sanctioned by § 522.

[A] Avoiding Judgment Liens[222]

Section 522(f)(1) provides the debtor with a rather obvious protection for exempt property. It allows the debtor to avoid the "fixing" of most judicial liens to the extent the lien impairs an exemption to which the debtor otherwise would be entitled.[223] It applies to all exempt property.

However, § 522(f) does not destroy the lien entirely. Instead, it permits avoidance of the lien only to the extent the lien "impairs an exemption to which the debtor would have been entitled under [§ 522(b)]."[224] The lien remains enforceable to the extent that the property was not exempt.

Consider, for example, a debtor with a $100,000 home, subject to both a $40,000 mortgage and a $60,000 judgment lien, located in a jurisdiction that provides a $25,000 homestead exemption for residential real estate. Section 522(f)(1) permits avoidance of the judgment lien to the extent it impairs the debtor's $25,000 exemption. If the house is sold, the mortgage holder receives $40,000, the debtor receives $25,000, and the judgment lienholder receives the remaining $35,000. Thus, the lien is not completely

---

219 Robert H. Bowmar, *Avoidance of Judicial Liens That Impair Exemptions in Bankruptcy: The Workings of 11 U.S.C..§ 552(f)(1)*, 63 Am. Bankr. L.J. 375, 400 (1989); David Gray Carlson, *Security Interests on Exempt Property After the 1994 Amendments to the Bankruptcy Code*, 4 Am. Bankr. Inst. L. Rev. 57 (1996).

220 Owen v. Owen, 500 U.S. 305 (1991).

221 *E.g.*, In re Pelter, 64 B.R. 492 (Bankr. W.D. Okla. 1986); In re Vaughn, 67 B.R. 140 (Bankr. C.D. Ill. 1986); In re Strain, 16 B.R. 797 (Bankr. D. Idaho 1982).

222 Lawrence Ponoroff, *Exemption Impairing Liens under Bankruptcy Code Section 522(f): One Step Forward and One Step Back*, 70 U. Colo. L. Rev. 1 (1999).

223 Bankruptcy Code § 522(f)(1)(A).

224 Bankruptcy Code § 522(f)(1).

avoided, but is only set aside to the extent that it impairs the debtor's $25,000 homestead exemption.

The Supreme Court found it significant that this provision refers not to the lien itself but rather to the "fixing" of the lien. In *Farrey v. Sanderfoot*,[225] the Court held that this means the debtor's property interest must exist before the lien attaches to it. In *Sanderfoot*, the debtor's divorce decree granted him sole title to a home previously held in joint tenancy with his wife. His wife was simultaneously given a judgment lien against the property to secure his obligation to pay her for half of the value of the house. Because the interest was created simultaneously with the creation of his right to the property, it was treated not as a lien that had "fixed" ' to his property but as an encumbrance that the debtor took along with the real estate, "as if he had purchased an already encumbered [property]."[226]

Since *Sanderfoot*, most courts have ruled that judicial liens securing support obligations in divorce decrees are invulnerable to attack under § 522(f) where the debtor acquires a new interest in the property subject to the lien as a result of a realignment of marital property rights in the divorce decree. Using the analysis deployed by the *Sanderfoot* decision, § 522(f)(1)(A) could not apply because the debtor's property interest arose simultaneously with the creation of the lien.[227]

In 2005, Congress amended § 522(f)(1) by proscribing its use to avoid judicial liens that secure non-dischargeable "domestic support obligations."[228] This expands decisions following *Sanderfoot*, but only to the extent the judicial lien secures a support obligation. Judicial liens securing property settlement obligations or other debts remain subject to avoidance, unless under the *Sanderfoot* analysis, the lien is created simultaneously with a realignment of the debtor's property rights.

The *Sanderfoot* "fixing" approach is particularly troublesome with respect to the attachment of liens to after-acquired property in which the debtor did not acquire an interest in the property subject to the lien until after the lien was in place. Some courts have applied the *Sanderfoot* analysis to prevent use of § 522(f)(1)(A) in these settings. Others have distinguished *Sanderfoot* in these circumstances and permitted the lien to be avoided by limiting *Sanderfoot* to its precise facts, involving situations where the debtor's property interest and the lien were created simultaneously.

---

225 500 U.S. 291 (1991).

226 500 U.S. at 300.

227 *E.g.*, Estate of Catli, 999 F.2d 1405 (9th Cir. 1993); *see also* In re Parrish, 7 F.3d 76 (5th Cir. 1993), *cert. denied sub nom.* McVay v. Parrish, 511 U.S. 1006 (1994) (lien imposed on property previously owned by debtor alone remained subject to avoidance).

228 Bankruptcy Code § 522(f)(1)(A).

[B] Avoiding Non-Possessory, Non-Purchase Money Security Interests

Section 522(f)(1)(B) also permits the avoidance of some consensual security interests in certain items of the debtor's tangible personal property. The debtor may avoid the fixing of a non-possessory, non-purchase money security interest to the extent it impairs one of the debtor's exemptions in:

- household furnishings, household goods, clothing, appliances, books, animals, crops, musical instruments, or jewelry held primarily for the personal, family, or household use of the debtor or a dependent;
- implements, professional books, or tools of the debtor's trade or a dependent's trade; or
- professionally prescribed health aids for the debtor or a dependent of the debtor.[229]

This rule is narrow in several respects. First, it does not encompass all exempt property, only these few types. Second, it does not avoid all security interests, but only those that are both "non-possessory" and "non-purchase-money." Thus, it does not impair the possessory security interests of pawn shops. Third, it does not impair purchase money security interests — security interests of those who have sold the collateral to the debtor or provided credit to the debtor to enable him to acquire the goods.[230]

The primary impetus for the section 522(f) avoidance power was Congress' concern about the personal loan industry's practice of obtaining security interests in all of a debtor's household goods. These security interests had little to do with the value of those goods, which were for the most part scarcely worth selling. However, the creditor's right to repossess all of a debtor's household property gave the creditor considerable leverage over the debtor because of what was widely regarded as the "in terrorem" effect of the creditor's lien. A room full of used furniture, worn clothing, and an array of umatched and dented old pots and pans has little market value. But these items might be difficult for a bankrupt debtor to replace. Consumer creditors believed, with some justification, that a debtor faced with repossession of these goods would make extraordinary efforts to pay the debt, despite the minimal return the creditor would obtain upon their sale.[231]

It was thus not the value of the property lost but the pressure imposed by the possibility of repossession that concerned Congress. Significantly, however, § 522(f) does not impair the ability of a secured purchase money lender to seize its collateral, even if it is of the type described in § 522(f)(1)(B).

---

229 Bankruptcy Code § 522(f)(1)(B)(i)-(iii). Language added in 2005 supplies a detailed definition of "household goods." Bankruptcy Code § 522(f)(4).

230 *See* U.C.C. § 9-103 (2003).

231 *See* Michael J. Herbert, *Straining the Gnat: A Critique of the 1984 Federal Trade Commission Consumer Credit Regulations*, 38 S.C. L. Rev. 329, 352 (1987).

Permitting debtors to avoid purchase money loans would restrict the supply of credit available for the purchase of these items and might impair economic growth generally.

Section 522(f)(3) imposes an additional limit on the debtor's ability to avoid security interests on tools of the debtor's trade, farm animals, professional books, and crops. The statutory language is nearly incomprehensible, but seems to apply only if (1) the debtor is claiming exemptions under state law, (2) the state has "opted out" of the federal exemption scheme, and (3) state law either permits the debtor to claim exemptions without limitation and amount (subject to consensual liens) or prohibits avoidance of consensual liens on otherwise exempt property.[232] If these three conditions are met, the debtor may not use § 522(f) to avoid the fixing of a non-possessory, non-purchase money security interest in these limited types of property "to the extent that the value of [the property] exceeds $5,475."[233] Because no state permits debtors "to claim exemptions without limitation in amount," the literal language of § 522(f)(3) seems not to apply to any real-world situations. The text of the statute may have been intended to apply if the state permits the debtor to claim an exemption in an unlimited amount of tools of the debtor's trade, but the language of the statute does not say this.

Since the enactment of § 522(f), the enforceability of non-purchase money security interests in most household items has largely been dealt with by other bodies of law. Some states restrict the use of non-purchase money security interests in consumer transactions.[234] More significantly, in 1985 the Federal Trade Commission (FTC) promulgated a rule treating non-purchase money security interests in most types of household goods as an unfair trade practice.[235] Lenders have thus been prevented from obtaining non-purchase-money security interests in most of the types of collateral listed in § 522(f)(2), greatly diminishing its significance.

The FTC rule did not deprive § 522(f) of all of its effect. It still applies to types of property that are not protected by the Federal Trade Commission's rule, such as tools of the debtor's trade. Likewise, § 522(f) encompasses a wider range of creditors. For example, the FTC's rule applies only to professional consumer creditors, and not to other lenders.[236]

The potential conflict between § 522(f) and the constitutional prohibition on taking property without just compensation was resolved by the Supreme Court in *United States v. Security Industrial Bank.*[237] The Court ruled that

[232] Bankruptcy Code § 522(f)(3).

[233] Bankruptcy Code § 522(f)(3).

[234] Unif. Cons. Credit Code § 3.301 (1974).

[235] 16 C.F.R. §§ 444.1–444.5; *see* Michael J. Herbert, *Straining the Gnat: A Critique of the 1984 Federal Trade Commission Consumer Credit Regulations*, 38 S.C. L. Rev. 329, 352 (1987) (once described to its author by a supporter of the rule as "unduly negative and unnecessarily sarcastic"); Jean Braucher, *Defining Unfairness: Empathy and Economic Analysis at the Federal Trade Commission*, 68 B.U. L. Rev. 349 (1988).

[236] 16 C.F.R. §§ 444.2(a), 444.1(a).

[237] 459 U.S. 70 (1982).

although the retroactive application of § 522(f) might have been unconstitutional, Congress intended for it to apply only prospectively. This determination sidestepped the constitutional issue that had been brewing over its retroactive application to security interests created before adoption of the 1978 Bankruptcy Code.

§ 12.08 Retaining Collateral[238]

Debtors have several options to permit them to retain collateral covered by a security interest. In liquidation proceedings, § 722 permits debtors to "redeem" collateral by paying the secured creditor, in a lump sum, the amount of the "allowed secured claim" — either the amount of the debt or the value of the collateral, whichever is lower. Second, the debtor may enter into a "reaffirmation agreement" with the secured creditor holding the lien. Such agreements usually reinstate the debtor's personal liability to the creditor but permit the debtor to keep the collateral, so long as the debtor does not default on the terms of the reaffirmation agreement. Before the 2005 Amendments, debtors in some jurisdictions who were not in default on their obligations to their secured creditors had a third option of simply retaining the collateral and continuing to make payments according to the terms of their original agreement with the creditor. However, language added in 2005 seems to have eliminated this alternative (at least unless the creditor is willing to go along). Finally, debtors might keep their collateral pursuant to the terms of a confirmed reorganization plan under Chapters 11, 12, or 13.

As will be seen, debtors who implement none of these alternatives are required to surrender the collateral to the secured creditor. In addition, if the property is valuable enough, there may be non-exempt equity in the property that the trustee will wish to capture for distribution to unsecured creditors. If the collateral is worth too much, the debtor may be deprived of most, if not all of these choices.

[A] Lump-Sum Redemption by Debtor[239]

Under some circumstances, the debtor has the right to "redeem" property from a lien holder. Redemption simply means that the debtor may buy out the lien and thus become the owner of the property. Most states provide

[238] David Gray Carlson, *Redemption and Reinstatement in Chapter 7 Cases*, 4 Am. Bankr. Inst. L. Rev. 289 (1996); Scott B. Ehrlich, *The Fourth Option of Section 521(2)(A) — Reaffirmation Agreements and the Chapter 7 Consumer Debtor*, 53 Mercer L. Rev. 613 (2002); Margaret Howard, *Stripping Down Liens: Section 506(d) and the Theory of Bankruptcy*, 65 Am. Bankr. L.J. 373, 388 (1991); Lawrence Ponoroff & F. Stephen Knippenberg, *The Immovable Object Versus the Irresistible Force: Rethinking the Relationship Between Secured Credit and Bankruptcy Policy*, 95 Mich. L. Rev. 2234, 2239 (1997).

[239] Lucian Arye Bebchuk & Jesse M. Fried, *A New Approach to Valuing Secured Claims in Bankruptcy*, 114 Harv. L. Rev. 2386 (2001); David Gray Carlson, *Redemption and Reinstatement in Chapter 7 Cases*, 4 Am. Bankr. Inst. L. Rev. 289 (1996).

debtors with rights of redemption, some of which are discussed elsewhere.[240]

These rights are not disturbed by bankruptcy. However, the Code goes beyond the traditional recognition of state-created redemption rights. It includes an additional right of redemption, limited to individual Chapter 7 debtors who seek to retain encumbered but exempt or abandoned personal property.

The main problem with the typical state law redemption right is that to redeem, the debtor must pay the underlying obligation in full. Often, this is impossible. Insofar as personal property is concerned, the key provision is section 9-506 of the Uniform Commercial Code, which requires full payment for redemption.[241] By contrast, the Bankruptcy Code permits Chapter 7 debtors to redeem for the lesser of (i) the obligation owed or (ii) the value of the property redeemed.

Section 722 permits an individual debtor to redeem property from a lien if the property is "tangible personal property intended primarily for personal, family, or household use."[242] This right applies even if the debtor has previously waived his or her redemption rights. In addition, the property either must be exempt under § 522 or must have been abandoned by the trustee under § 554.[243] Other property is not subject to redemption because of the interest that unsecured creditors have in its liquidation and the distribution of the proceeds by the trustee. A further condition prohibits redemption if the debt secured by the property is non-dischargeable under § 523.[244]

The key benefit for the debtor is that full payment of the debt is unnecessary. The debtor only needs to pay the lien holder the amount of the allowed secured claim.[245] Because the secured claim cannot exceed the value of the collateral,[246] if the debt is more than the value of the collateral, the debtor must pay only the latter in order to redeem.

Assume, for example, that Doug owes Island Bank $10,000, representing the purchase price of a car financed by the bank. Assume further that the car is collateral for the debt but is only worth $7,000. Because the bank's lien is "under water," the trustee has no incentive to sell the car and will most likely be amenable to abandoning the estate's interest in it.[247] Even

---

[240] *See* § 2.08 Foreclosure Procedures, *supra*.

[241] U.C.C. § 9-623 (2003). In this context, full payment includes not only the principal and interest but also other contractual obligations, such as late fees and lawyer's fees. It also includes "the reasonable expenses and attorney's fees" incurred in enforcing the security interest and preparing the collateral for sale.

[242] Bankruptcy Code § 722.

[243] *See* § 9.06 Abandonment of Estate Property, *supra*.

[244] *See generally* § 13.03 Nondischargeable Debts, *infra*.

[245] Bankruptcy Code § 722.

[246] Bankruptcy Code § 506(b); *see* § 10.03[A] Creditors with Secured Claims, *supra*.

[247] Section 554 permits such abandonment when property can be shown to be burdensome

if the property has not been formally abandoned, redemption would probably be permitted, because the motor vehicle is probably subject to an available exemption, even though the exemption does not cover the entire value of the property.[248]

Under the Uniform Commercial Code, Doug would have to pay at least $10,000 to redeem the car from the bank's security interest. If the agreement provided for other costs, such as Island Bank's attorneys' fees and collection costs, Doug would also have to pay those expenses.[249] However, under § 722, Doug would have to pay only the amount of the allowed secured claim: $7,000. By cutting the potential cost of redemption, § 722 provides some help to those debtors who are trying to keep property — at least those who are trying to keep property that is worth less than the debt it secures.

The 2005 Amendments require the court to base the amount of the allowed secured claim on the "replacement value" of the collateral, rather than its liquidation value.[250] In many cases, however, the "price a retail merchant would charge" for property of the kind will be difficult to determine, given the general absence of a market for such goods.

Historically, the help provided by § 722 has been relatively meaningless. In the example given, it may be just as difficult for Doug to raise $7,000 as $10,000. In most cases, debtors are unable to find a source for either sum, unless well-heeled relatives or sub-prime lenders are willing to step in to provide the necessary cash. However, with the growth of sub-prime lending in recent years, a market has emerged for loans to allow Chapter 7 debtors to redeem their cars.[251]

Section 722 would be more meaningful if it permitted debtors to make an installment redemption by paying the amount of the allowed secured claim over an extended period of time. However, § 722 has consistently been interpreted to deny debtors the right to make installment payments to redeem the property,[252] and the 2005 Amendments added language removing any lingering doubt about the issue.[253] Consequently, many consumer debtors who wish to retain more property than § 522's exemption provisions allow must file for reorganization under Chapters 11, 12, or 13. A

to the estate or of inconsequential value and benefit to the estate. Bankruptcy Code § 554. Property that is covered by an unavailable lien securing a debt for more than the value of the collateral is of "inconsequential value and benefit to the estate." *See* § 9.06 Abandonment of Estate Property, *supra*.

[248] *See* In re Fitzgerald, 20 B.R. 27 (Bankr. N.D.N.Y. 1982).

[249] *See* U.C.C. § 9-623(b) (2003).

[250] Bankruptcy Code § 506(a)(2); *see* Jean Braucher, *Beneath the Surface of BAPCPA:* Rash *and Ride-through Redux: The Terms for Holding on to Cars, Homes and Other Collateral under the 2005 Act,* 13 Am. Bankr. Inst. L. Rev. 457 (2005).

[251] *See, e.g.,* http://www.freshstartloans.com/fslc/home.asp (last visited March 6, 2007).

[252] *See* In re Edwards, 901 F.2d 1383 (7th Cir. 1990); In re Bell, 700 F.2d 1053 (6th Cir. 1983); In re Horne, 132 B.R. 661 (Bankr. N.D. Ga. 1991).

[253] BAPCPA added the words "in full at the time of redemption." *See also* Fed. R. Bankr. P. 6008.

reorganization plan in one of these proceedings may be used to make payments over time, without the creditor's consent.[254]

Alternatively, as explained in the next section, debtors may be able to retain the property by entering into a reaffirmation agreement with the secured creditor, but these creditors are unlikely to be willing to make the agreement unless the debtor promises to pay the full amount of the outstanding debt, rather than just the amount of the allowed secured claim.

[B] Reaffirmation to Retain Property[255]

Debtors wishing to retain property subject to a security interest, but who are unable to obtain the cash necessary to redeem the collateral with a lump-sum payment under § 722, may be able to retain it by entering into a reaffirmation agreement with the creditor holding the security interest. A reaffirmation agreement would contain the debtor's renewed post-petition promise to repay the debt secured by the collateral, possibly with a revised payment schedule, in exchange for the creditor's agreement to refrain from exercising its right to repossess the collateral.[256]

Bankruptcy Code § 524(c) imposes limitations on the enforceability of reaffirmation agreements. To be enforceable, a reaffirmation agreement must:

- be in writing;[257]
- have been made before the debtor's discharge is granted;[258]
- be preceded by the debtor's receipt of several disclosure statements regarding the debtor's right not to enter into a reaffirmation agreement and about the consequences of making the agreement;[259]
- be filed with the court;[260]
- in a case in which an attorney represents the debtor in connection with the reaffirmation agreement, be accompanied by the attorney's affidavit, stating that the reaffirmation agreement was both

---

254 *See* § 18.07[B][2] Modifying Secured Claims, *infra.*

255 Marianne B. Culhane & Michaela M. White, *Debt after Discharge: An Empirical Study of Reaffirmation*, 73 Am. Bankr. L.J. 709 (1999).

256 A secured creditor's agreement not to repossess provides consideration for the debtor's renewed promise, but the debtor's promise does not need consideration to be enforceable under the common law of contracts. *See* Restatement (Second) of Contracts § 83 (1981) (making promises to repay debts discharged in bankruptcy enforceable without consideration).

257 Bankruptcy Code § 524(c)(3). Though not explicitly stated, the requirement that the agreement be filed with the court necessitates that it be in writing.

258 Bankruptcy Code § 524(c)(1).

259 Bankruptcy Code § 524(c)(2), (k); *see* David B. Wheeler & Douglas E. Wedge, *A Fully-Informed Decision: Reaffirmation, Disclosure, and the Bankruptcy Abuse Prevention and Consumer Protection Act of 2005*, 79 Am. Bankr. L.J. 789 (2005); Jean Braucher, *Counseling Consumer Debtors to Make Their Own Informed Choices — A Question of Professional Responsibility*, 5 Am. Bankr. Inst. L. Rev. 165 (1997).

260 Bankruptcy Code § 524(c)(3).

fully informed and voluntary, does not impose an undue hardship on the debtor or the debtor's dependents, and was made only after the attorney fully advised the debtor about the effect and consequences of the agreement;[261]

- in a case in which the debtor is not represented by an attorney in connection with the reaffirmation agreement, and the debt is not a consumer debt secured by real estate, must have been approved by the court as both not imposing an undue hardship and "in the best interest of the debtor";[262] and
- not have been rescinded by the debtor either before a discharge was granted or during the sixty days thereafter.[263]

Further, in the rare circumstance in which the court conducts a "discharge hearing," the court must as part of the hearing repeat the disclosures about the debtor's reaffirmation agreement that were to have been supplied to the debtor by the creditor.[264]

However, the most important limitation on reaffirmation agreements is that there must be an agreement. The debtor cannot unilaterally retain the collateral, but must obtain the secured party's assent to the terms of the reaffirmation agreement permitting him to do so. The practical impact of this limitation, which is inherent in the concept of reaffirmation, is that debtors will usually have to repay the entire debt owed to the secured party under the terms of the original agreement, and perhaps more.

For many years it has been unclear whether creditors' efforts to persuade a debtor to enter into a reaffirmation agreement are violations of the automatic stay. Section 362(a)(6) prohibits "*any act* to collect, assess, or recover a claim against the debtor that arose before the commencement of the case."[265] This seems to prohibit creditors from soliciting reaffirmation agreements while still permitting debtors to approach their lenders about reaffirming.

Courts have disagreed about the extent to which creditors can attempt to persuade a debtor to enter into a reaffirmation agreement without violating the automatic stay. Although § 362(a)(6) prohibits creditors from engaging in any act to collect a pre-petition debt, the text of § 524(c) is rife with references to the necessity for an "agreement," which implies the right of the creditor to hold out for terms it prefers. As the court said in *In re Turner*: "Implicit in the statute's repeated reference to an 'agreement' . . .

---

[261] Bankruptcy Code § 524(c)(3). It is completely unclear how debtors' attorneys are supposed to assess whether the agreement will impose an "undue hardship" on the debtor or the debtor's dependents. If "undue hardship" means the same thing as it does in the context of dischargeability of student loans under § 523(a)(8), then undue hardship will be found only in extreme situations. *See* § 13.03[B][8] Student Loans, *infra.*

[262] Bankruptcy Code § 524(c)(5); *e.g.*, In re Stillwell, 348 B.R. 578 (Bankr. N.D. Okla. 2006) (debtors' schedules reflected that their income inadequate to meet expenses).

[263] Bankruptcy Code § 524(c)(4).

[264] Bankruptcy Code § 524(c)(5), (d).

[265] Bankruptcy Code § 362(a)(6) (emphasis supplied); *see* § 8.02[E] Acts to Collect, *supra.*

is the requirement that the creditor as well as the debtor consent to the reaffirmation."[266] Agreements, like the proverbial Tango, require two participants. Prohibiting creditors from negotiating with debtors over the terms of a reaffirmation agreement would render much of § 524(c) superfluous.[267]

This does not permit the creditor to engage in "harassment or coercion."[268] However, secured creditors are permitted to invite the debtor to enter into a reaffirmation agreement and to inform the debtor about the consequences of either accepting or rejecting the creditor's proposed terms.[269] They are permitted, during the course of these negotiations to "make plain" their intent to foreclose on the collateral if the debtor does not agree to reaffirm the debt.[270]

Creditors also seem to be permitted to insist that the debtor agree to repay other debts owed to the them as a condition of being permitted to retain the collateral. This practice, though controversial, seems consistent with the principles of freedom of contract inherent in § 524(c) and has been permitted by a few courts.[271] It is in tension, however, with the automatic stay. Thus, if Robert owes $10,000 to Island Bank for the purchase price of his $7,000 pickup truck and also has an outstanding unpaid $6,000 balance on his Island Bank credit card, the bank might agree to permit him to keep the truck only if he agrees to repay the entire $16,000 owed on both debts combined.

[C] Retention without Redemption or Reaffirmation — "Ride-Through"[272]

Before the 2005 Amendments, debtors were sometimes able to deploy a fourth alternative strategy to retain property subject to a security interest.

---

[266] 156 F.3d 713, 718 (7th Cir. 1998).

[267] *See, e.g.*, In re Duke, 79 F.3d 43, 45 (7th Cir. 1996); Pertuso v. Ford Motor Credit Co., 233 F.3d 417, 423 (6th Cir. 2000).

[268] Pertuso v. Ford Motor Credit Co., 233 F.3d 417, 423 (6th Cir. 2000); Cox v. Zale Del. Inc., 239 F.3d 910 (7th Cir. 2001).

[269] Pertuso v. Ford Motor Credit Co., 233 F.3d 417, 423 (6th Cir. 2000).

[270] Jacqueline B. Stuart, *All or Nothing Reaffirmation: Can Secured and Unsecured Debts Be Linked?*, 58 Bus. Law. 1309, 1317 (2003).

[271] Jamo v. Katahdin Fed. Credit Union (In re Jamo), 283 F.3d 392 (1st Cir. 2002); In re Jacobs, 321 B.R. 451 (Bankr. N.D. Ohio 2004).

[272] Jean Braucher, *Beneath the Surface of BAPCPA,* Rash *and Ride-Through Redux: The Terms for Holding on to Cars, Homes and Other Collateral Under the 2005 Act*, 13 Am. Bankr. Inst. L. Rev. 457 (2005); Marianne Culhane & Michaela White, *But Can She Keep the Car? Some Thoughts on Collateral Retention in Consumer Chapter 7 Cases*, 7 Fordham. J. Corp. & Fin. L., 471, 477–78, 487–88 (2002); David Gray Carlson, *Redemption and Reinstatement in Chapter 7 Cases*, 4 Am. Bankr. Inst. L. Rev. 289 (1996); Scott B. Ehrlich, *The Fourth Option of Section 521(2)(A) — Reaffirmation Agreements and the Chapter 7 Consumer Debtor*, 53 Mercer L. Rev. 613 (2002); Henry J. Sommer, *Trying to Make Sense Out of Nonsense: Representing Consumers Under the "Bankruptcy Abuse Prevention and Consumer Protection Act of 2005*," 79 Am. Bankr. L.J. 191 (2005).

If the debtor were not in default on the underlying obligation to pay the secured debt, the creditor would not normally have the right to repossess or foreclose.[273] Rather than enter into a legally enforceable reaffirmation agreement, debtors who were not in default prior to bankruptcy might simply choose to continue making payments to the secured creditor according to the original terms of their agreement with the creditor, never committing a precipitating default that would permit the creditor to foreclose. The advantage of this, over entering into a reaffirmation agreement, was that the debtor's personal liability to repay the debt was discharged and he could cease making payments at any time, without being liable for the unpaid balance due. The creditor could foreclose on the collateral, but the debtor would not be liable for a deficiency. Indeed, the discharge stay of § 524(a) would prevent the creditor from even attempting to collect a deficiency.

This strategy was controversial. Prior to the BAPCPA, there was a split in the circuits over whether § 521(2) permitted it. Like current § 521(a)(2), former § 521(2)(A) required individual debtors to file a statement of intention regarding their plans for dealing with collateral securing a consumer debt. Debtors are required to file a statement that expresses whether they intend to surrender the collateral, redeem the collateral under § 722, or enter into a reaffirmation agreement with the secured creditor under § 524(c).[274] Former § 521(2)(C), which has since been renumbered and amended further, specified that nothing in the remainder of § 521(2) "shall alter the debtor's . . . rights" with respect to the collateral.[275] This language provided an avenue for debtors to claim that the statement of intent required to be filed by the debtor was purely procedural and that it did not create a substantive rule that required the debtor to surrender, redeem, or reaffirm. A majority of circuits addressing the issue agreed.[276]

Before the 2005 Amendments, debtors in these circuits who were not in default could retain possession of property subject to a security interest, even though the debt secured by the property had been discharged. As long as debtors continued to make payments, and to fulfill the other obligations in the terms of their original agreement with the secured creditor, they could keep the collateral.[277]

---

[273] *See, e.g.*, U.C.C. § 9-601 (2003) (making the secured party's rights to foreclose contingent upon "default.").

[274] *See* Bankruptcy Code § 521(a)(2)(A) (containing language identical to that in former § 521(2)(A)).

[275] Bankruptcy Code § 521(2)(C).

[276] *Compare* In re Price, 370 F.3d 362, 379 (3d Cir. 2004) (joining the Second, Fourth, Ninth, and Tenth Circuits in treating former § 521(2) as procedural, not substantive), *with* Bank of Boston v. Burr (In re Burr), 160 F.3d 843, 849 (1st Cir. 1998) (joining the Fifth, Seventh, and Tenth Circuits in regarding § 521(2) as substantive and prohibiting ride-through).

[277] *See* Oliver B. Pollak, *Reaffirmation and Retention in Bankruptcy: Conflict in the Circuits Over Protecting the Secured Creditor*, 111 Banking L.J. 302 (1994); Arnold B. Cohen, *Chapter 7 Debtors Who Are Current in Secured Debt Obligations May Retain Collateral Without Reaffirmation, or Use of Chapter 13*, 2 J. Bankr. L. & Prac. 323 (1993); Richard H. Nowka, *Validating a Debtor's Retention of Collateral by Continuing Performance: Removing the Obstructions of 11 USC § 521(2)(A) and Ipso Facto Clauses*, 6 J. Bankr. L. & Prac. 145 (1997); Ned W. Waxman, *Redemption or Reaffirmation: Debtor's Exclusive Means of Retaining Possession of Collateral in Chapter 7*, 56 U. Pitt. L. Rev. 187 (1994).

Though some doubt remains about the depth of its meaning, the text of amended § 521(a)(6) appears to have largely eliminated this option. The revised language now specifies:

> [I]n a case under chapter 7 . . . [an individual debtor may] not retain possession of personal property as to which a creditor has an allowed claim for the purchase price secured in whole or in part by an interest in such personal property unless the debtor, not later than 45 days after the first meeting of creditors under section 341(a) either —
>
> (A) enters into an agreement with the creditor pursuant to section 524(c) with respect to the claim secured by such property; or
>
> (B) redeems such property from the security interest pursuant to section 722.[278]

This language proscribes the debtor's ability to permit the security interest to ride through the bankruptcy, at least with respect to some security interests.[279] Thus, debtors who do not either surrender the collateral, redeem under § 722, or reaffirm under § 524(c) will find the creditor released from the automatic stay and free to repossess the collateral, even though the bankruptcy case is still pending.

However, the 2005 Amendments did not completely eliminate ride-through as an option. First, it applies only to individual debtors in Chapter 7 cases. Second, its prohibition applies only to personal property, not real estate.[280]

Naturally, debtors still have the option to retain the collateral if the secured creditor acquiesces.[281] In addition, the reference to "personal property as to which a creditor has an allowed claim for the purchase price" leaves open the possibility that § 521(a)(6) will be limited to creditors who were either the sellers of the collateral or whose claims arise from an assignment of the seller's rights. The plain language of the statute leaves it inapplicable to secured creditors who made loans to the debtor to enable him to pay the price in cash.[282]

---

[278] Bankruptcy Code § 521(a)(6).

[279] Bankruptcy Code § 362(h); In re Steinhaus, 349 B.R. 694, 702–03 (Bankr. D. Idaho 2006); In re Anderson, 348 B.R. 652, 657 (Bankr. D. Del. 2006).

[280] In re Bennet, No. 06-80241, 2006 WL 1540842 (Bankr. M.D.N.C. May 26, 2006); *see* Jean Braucher, *Beneath the Surface of BAPCPA,* Rash *and Ride-Through Redux: The Terms for Holding on to Cars, Homes and Other Collateral under the 2005 Act,* 13 Am. Bankr. Inst. L. Rev. 457, 479–81 (2005).

[281] Jean Braucher, *Beneath the Surface of BAPCPA,* Rash *and Ride-Through Redux: The Terms for Holding on to Cars, Homes and Other Collateral under the 2005 Act,* 13 Am. Bankr. Inst. L. Rev. 457, 475–77 (2005).

[282] The distinction between a secured seller and an enabling lender is reflected in U.C.C. § 9-103(b)(2) (2003) (defining "purchase money obligation"). Further, Bankruptcy Code § 547(c)(3) uses broader language to refer to all purchase money security interests, not just those retained by the seller. Bankruptcy Code § 547(c)(3).

[D] Debtor's Statement of Intent[283]

One of an individual debtor's duties is to file a notice, ordinarily within thirty days after filing his petition,[284] indicating his intent with respect to property that is subject to a security interest.[285] The statement of intent must indicate whether the debtor intends to surrender the collateral to the secured party, to redeem the property under § 722, or to enter into a reaffirmation agreement with the creditor holding the lien pursuant to § 524(c).[286]

Section 521(c) further specifies that the debtor "shall perform his intention with respect to such property" within thirty days after the "first date set for the meeting of creditors" under § 341, or "within such additional time as the court, for cause" may fix.[287]

As indicated above, the language of § 521(a)(2)(B) now seems to preclude a debtor who is not in default from simply maintaining his payments to the creditor and thus permitting the security interest to "ride-through" the bankruptcy case.

[E] Chapter 7 Lien-Stripping[288]

A fundamental axiom of bankruptcy law is that creditors' liens on a debtor's property pass through bankruptcy unaffected by the debtor's discharge.[289] This historic rule raises difficult questions with respect to the effect of bankruptcy on partially secured claims in which the value of the collateral at the time of bankruptcy is less than the debt the collateral secures.

In *Dewsnup v. Timm*, the Supreme Court held that a partially secured real estate mortgage in property that had been abandoned by the trustee, could not be avoided under § 506(d) so as to prevent the lien from securing post-bankruptcy improvements in the value of the collateral.[290] The Court's

---

283 Jean Braucher, *Beneath the Surface of BAPCPA, Rash and Ride-Through Redux: The Terms for Holding on to Cars, Homes and Other Collateral under the 2005 Act*, 13 Am. Bankr. Inst. L. Rev. 457 (2005).

284 If the "meeting of creditors" conducted pursuant to § 341 is held earlier than thirty days after the petition, the debtor must file his § 521(a)(2) statement of intent prior to that meeting. Bankruptcy Code § 521(a)(2)(A).

285 Bankruptcy Code § 521(a)(2); *see* Fed. R. Bankr. P. 1007(b)(2).

286 Bankruptcy Code § 521(a)(2).

287 Bankruptcy Code § 521(a)(2)(B). The language requires the court to make its decision whether to extend the time for performance during the initial thirty-day period after the date set for the § 341 meeting.

288 *See* David Gray Carlson, *Bifurcation of Undersecured Claims in Bankruptcy*, 70 Am. Bankr. L.J. 1 (1996); Margaret Howard, *Dewsnupping the Bankruptcy Code*, 1 J. Bankr. L. & Prac. 513 (1992); Jane Kaufman Winn, *Lien Stripping After Nobelman*, 27 Loy. L.A. L. Rev. 541 (1994).

289 Farrey v. Sanderfoot, 500 U.S. 291, 297 (1991) ("Ordinarily, liens and other secured interests survive bankruptcy"); Johnson v. Home State Bank, 501 U.S. 78 (1991); Dewsnup v. Timm, 502 U.S. 410, 417 (1992).

290 Dewsnup v. Timm, 502 U.S. 410, 417 (1992).

decision prevents Chapter 7 debtors from satisfying a partially secured claim by paying creditors the value that the collateral was worth at the time of bankruptcy. Thus, if land securing a $120,000 debt is worth only $40,000, and the trustee abandons the property without selling it, the debtors may not rescue the land from the creditor's mortgage by paying only the value of the collateral. The lien remains on the property to satisfy the full $120,000 debt, even though the debtor's in personam liability for the $120,000 debt is discharged.

To reach this result, the Court in *Dewsnup* read § 506(d) in a highly unorthodox manner. It provides: "To the extent that a lien secures a claim against the debtor that is not *an allowed secured claim*, such lien is void."[291] The conventional meaning of "allowed secured claim" is supplied by § 506(a)(1): "An allowed claim of a creditor secured by a lien on property in which the estate has an interest . . . is a secured claim to the extent of the value of such creditor's interest in the . . . property."[292] For other purposes, the creditor's allowed secured claim would be only $40,000 and § 506(d) would permit the lien to be avoided to the extent that it secured the $80,000 balance. In *Dewsnup* the Court read the word "secured" out of § 506(d) and refused to permit the debtor to avoid the lien.[293]

Whether *Dewsnup* permits a Chapter 7 debtor to use § 506(d) to "strip off" a completely unsecured and thus valueless junior lien from real property has left courts divided.[294] Most courts apply *Dewsnup* with equal vigor to liens that are wholly unsecured.[295] Thus, if the property were worth $80,000 and subject to both a senior $90,000 mortgage and a junior $30,000 mortgage, the junior mortgage could not be "stripped-off" under § 506(d). If, after bankruptcy, the property increased in value to $120,000, the creditor with the junior mortgage could still foreclose. To redeem her property from these creditors' claims, debtor would have to pay the entire $120,000 debt. Other courts rule that *Dewsnup* applies only to partially secured claims.[296] Whether a reconstituted Supreme Court will overrule *Dewsnup*'s interpretation of § 506(d) so as to permit lien stripping, or will instead adhere to stare decisis and apply *Dewsnup* to completely worthless liens, is uncertain.[297]

Dewsnup and its progeny apply only to Chapter 7 cases, and only to property that is not sold by the trustee as part of the Chapter 7 liquidation.

---

291 Bankruptcy Code § 506(d) (emphasis added).

292 Bankruptcy Code § 506(a)(1); *see* § 10.03[C] Allowance of Secured Claims, *supra*.

293 Margaret Howard, *Dewsnupping the Bankruptcy Code*, 1 J. Bankr. L. & Prac. 513, 516 (1992).

294 In re Talbert, 344 F.3d 555 (6th Cir. 2003).

295 In re Talbert, 344 F.3d 555 (6th Cir. 2003); Ryan v. Homecomings Financial Network, 253 F.3d 778 (4th Cir. 2001); Concannon v. Imperial Capital Bank (In re Concannon), 339 B.R. 90 (B.A.P. 9th Cir. 2006).

296 *E.g.*, Howard v. National Westminister Bank, U.S.A. (In re Howard), 184 B.R. 644 (Bankr. E.D.N.Y. 1995).

297 Dewsnup v. Timm, 502 U.S. 410, 421–31 (1992) (Scalia, J., dissenting).

Chapters 11, 12, and 13 all contain provisions expressly permitting the sort of strip-down and strip-off that *Dewsnup* precludes.[298]

[298] *See* Bankruptcy Code §§ 1129(b)(2)(A), 1225(a)(5), & 1325(a)(5).

Chapter 13

Discharge

§ 13.01 The Nature of Discharge[1]

The main goal of nearly all debtors is to obtain a discharge of their debts.[2] Discharge is the feature that distinguishes bankruptcy from state insolvency proceedings. Discharge prohibits creditors from taking action to collect most pre-petition debts.[3] Further, discharge provides debtors with a valid legal defense in any action brought by creditors in an effort to collect. This is the essence of the debtor's "fresh start." Some debtors may feel a moral responsibility to pay their discharged debts, but they have no legal obligation to do so.[4]

The Bankruptcy Code contains a number of discharge rules. Both the availability and the scope of discharge depend on the type of bankruptcy proceeding involved, and in some cases, on whether the debtor is a natural person or an organization. Further, discharge may be denied entirely because of the debtor's misconduct.[5] Under new rules promulgated in 2005, debtors may be precluded from obtaining a discharge in a liquidation case if they are deemed able to pay a substantial portion of their debts.[6]

In addition, even if the debtor is generally entitled to a discharge, individual debts may be "nondischargeable" and thus excluded from the scope of

---

[1] Barry Adler, Ben Polak & Alan Schwartz, *Regulating Consumer Bankruptcy: A Theoretical Inquiry*, 29 J. Legal Stud. 585 (2000); Douglas Boshkoff, *Limited, Conditional, and Suspended Discharges in Anglo-American Bankruptcy Proceedings*, 131 U. Pa. L. Rev. 69 (1982); John M. Czarnetzky, *The Individual and Failure: A Theory of the Bankruptcy Discharge*, 32 Ariz. St. L.J. 393 (2000); Vern Countryman, *Bankruptcy and the Individual Debtor — And a Modest Proposal to Return to the Seventeenth Century*, 32 Cath. U. L. Rev. 809 (1983); Adam Feibelman, *Defining the Social Insurance Function of Consumer Bankruptcy,* 13 A.B.I. L. Rev. 129 (2005); Margaret Howard, *A Theory of Discharge in Consumer Bankruptcy*, 48 Ohio St. L.J. 1047 (1987); Thomas Jackson, *The Fresh-Start Policy in Bankruptcy Law*, 98 Harv. L. Rev. 1393 (1985); John E. Matejkovic & Keith Rucinski, *Bankruptcy "Reform": the 21st Century's Debtors' Prison*, 12 Am. Bankr. Inst. L. Rev. 473 (2004); Charles Jordan Tabb, *The Historical Evolution of the Bankruptcy Discharge*, 65 Am. Bankr. L.J. 325 (1991).

[2] It is not the only goal, however. Some debtors file in order to delay imminent foreclosure on their house. Others use bankruptcy to utilize the bankruptcy court's ability to sell assets free and clear of liens. Indeed, it should be noted that corporate debtors that liquidate do not receive a discharge at all.

[3] Bankruptcy Code § 524(a)(2); *see* § 13.09 Effect of Discharge, *supra*.

[4] Conscientious students may remember from their course in contract law that this moral obligation supplies the consideration necessary to make any renewed promise to pay a discharged debt (in the form of a reaffirmation agreement) enforceable. However, the Bankruptcy Code provides further restrictions on these agreements, discussed elsewhere. *See* § 12.08[B] Reaffirmation to Retain Property, *supra*.

[5] Bankruptcy Code § 727.

[6] *See* § 17.03[B][2] Presumptive Abuse — Means Testing, *infra*.

the debtor's discharge. Moreover, some debts are dischargeable in one bankruptcy chapter but not in others. Still other debts may or may not be dischargeable depending on the debtor's financial circumstances.

Discharge is an individual benefit given to the debtor who files the bankruptcy case. If other persons are liable for the debtor's obligations, they remain liable during and after the bankruptcy case. For example, if Mark and Amy are jointly liable on a debt incurred while they were married, and Amy files a bankruptcy petition after their divorce, Amy's discharge has no effect on Mark's liability for the debt. If Mark wants relief, he will have to file his own bankruptcy case. Similarly, if Betty, the owner of all of the stock of Metcalf, Inc., has signed a promissory note as an accommodation party,[7] guaranteeing repayment of a loan made to her corporation, a bankruptcy discharge of Metcalf, Inc. does not relieve Betty from her personal responsibility for the debt.

A final preliminary point bears emphasis. A bankruptcy discharge affects debts, not liens. Courts frequently reiterate the rule that liens survive discharge.[8] Although discharge prevents a creditor from obtaining payment from the debtor personally, it does not restrain a creditor from enforcing any rights it had in the debtor's property, such as a consensual, judicial, or statutory lien. In precise legal terms, discharge provides debtors with relief from their in personam liability but does not affect creditors' in rem rights against a debtor's property.

For example, suppose that Carrie owes $12,000 to Friendly Finance Co. and that the debt is secured by a security interest in Carrie's carpenter's tools, which are worth only $9,000. In Carrie's bankruptcy case, Friendly Finance has a $9,000 secured claim and a $3,000 unsecured claim.[9] Because Carrie had no equity in her tools that can be distributed to her other creditors, the bankruptcy trustee is unlikely to sell them. Instead, the trustee will likely abandon the estate's interest in the tools and permit Friendly Finance to enforce its lien against them.[10]

Thus, after Carrie's discharge, Friendly Finance retains its property interest in the tools and retains its right to sell them to satisfy its claim. But any amount of Carrie's debt that is not satisfied from the sale of the tools has been discharged, and Friendly Finance is not entitled to recover the deficiency from Carrie personally.

As will be seen, the discharge provisions of the Bankruptcy Code have been the battleground for much of the debate over bankruptcy policy.[11] In

---

[7] *See* U.C.C. § 3-419 (2003).

[8] H.R. Rep. No. 95-595, 361 (1977), *reprinted in* 1978 U.S.C.C.A.N. 5963, 6317; S. Rep. No. 95-989, 76 (1978), *reprinted* in 1978 U.S.C.C.A.N. 5787, 5862; *see* Dewsnup v. Timm, 502 U.S. 410, 420 (1992); Farrey v. Sanderfoot, 500 U.S. 291, 297 (1991); Long v. Bullard, 117 U.S. 617 (1886).

[9] Bankruptcy Code § 506.

[10] *See* Bankruptcy Code § 554. Under § 554, the trustee has the right to abandon property that is "burdensome" to the estate. *See* § 9.06 Abandonment of Estate Property, *supra.*

[11] *See generally* Susan Block-Lieb & Edward J. Janger, *The Myth of the Rational Borrower:*

many critics' view, discharge is too easy and too cheap. According to them, discharge is granted without sufficient inquiry into the debtor's ability to pay and thus provides debtors with an incentive to resort to bankruptcy unnecessarily and wastefully.[12] They contend that these inefficiencies burden the entire economy, especially for those whose economic situations force them to seek high-risk credit. Discharge risk may make such credit unavailable or very expensive.

In the view of those who defend the Code, the discharge rules have engendered little abuse, especially by consumers.[13] These scholars contend that, except in rare cases, discharge merely confirms what is all too palpably the case — the debtor cannot pay, or at least cannot pay without enduring undue hardship or imposing unconscionable difficulties on her dependents. According to them, bankruptcy discharge merely imposes an official end to an already fruitless collection effort. Any serious attempt to impose a higher cost on discharge will be either futile or cruel.

In 2005, this ongoing debate culminated in adoption of the "Bankruptcy Abuse Prevention and Consumer Protection Act."[14] This overhaul of the Bankruptcy Code, which went into effect in October, 2005, imposed new restrictions on the availability of a Chapter 7 bankruptcy discharge, based primarily on what was determined to be an ability of debtors to pay a substantial portion of their debts.

Behaviorism, Rationality and the Misguided "Reform" of Bankruptcy Law, 84 Tex. L. Rev. 1481 (2006); Charles Jordan Tabb, *The Historical Evolution of the Bankruptcy Discharge*, 65 Am. Bankr. L.J. 325 (1991); John M. Czarnetzky, *The Individual and Failure: A Theory of the Bankruptcy Discharge*, 32 Ariz. St. L.J. 393 (2000).

[12] *See* Gordon Bermant & Ed Flynn, *Consumer Filings in a Complex Economy*, 18 J. Am. Bankr. Inst. J. 22 (Dec./Jan. 2000). The best elaboration of this argument is found in the Purdue Study, which argued that $1,100,000,000 of debt was unnecessarily discharged each year. Credit Research Center, Krannert School of Management, Purdue University Monograph No. 23, Consumer Bankruptcy Study, vol. 1 at 88–91 (1982).

The methodology used by the Purdue Study, which was funded by members of the consumer credit industry, has been criticized. *See, e.g.*, Teresa A. Sullivan, Elizabeth Warren & Jay Lawrence Westbrook, *Limiting Access to Bankruptcy Discharge: An Analysis of the Creditors' Data*, 1983 Wis. L. Rev. 1091 (1983) (indicating that the Purdue Study's methodology suffered from a selection bias); Elizabeth Warren, *Reducing Bankruptcy Protection for Consumers: A Response*, 72 Geo. L.J. 1333, 1338–39 (1984) (arguing that the Purdue Study lacked crucial expertise, was improperly designed, gathered data poorly, mis-analyzed the data, and drew erroneous and biased conclusions).

[13] Teresa A. Sullivan, Elizabeth Warren & Jay Lawrence Westbrook, As We Forgive Our Debtors: Bankruptcy and Consumer Credit in America 219–24 (1989).

[14] Bankruptcy Abuse Prevention and Consumer Protection Act of 2005, Pub. L. No. 109–8, 119 Stat 23 (2005); *see generally* Susan Jensen, *A Legislative History of the Bankruptcy Abuse Prevention and Consumer Protection Act of 2005*, 79 Am. Bankr. L.J. 485 (2005).

§ 13.02 Denial of Discharge[15]

Discharge from their obligations is the principal remedy debtors seek in liquidation cases, nearly all of which involve individual debtors. If the debtor is ineligible for a discharge, she will not obtain the "fresh start" that bankruptcy provides. When discharge is denied, it is usually because of the debtor's own wrongdoing, either in connection with the bankruptcy case itself or in dealing with creditors generally before seeking relief through bankruptcy. Further, in order to deny debtors who might be tempted to incur obligations that they know they will not have to pay, relief is denied to debtors who seek relief too frequently. Relief is also now denied, under a different set of rules, to those who are deemed capable of making meaningful payments to their creditors.

[A] Consequences of Denial of Discharge

Under some circumstances, a debtor may be denied a discharge entirely. Denial of discharge means that the debtor is not relieved of responsibility for her debts. Instead, she remains saddled with whatever obligations she owed at the beginning of the case, reduced only by whatever amount was paid to her creditors through liquidation of her assets.

Without a discharge, a debtor does not enjoy the benefits of the discharge injunction of § 524. Instead, creditors are permitted to engage in any of the collection activities they had been permitted to deploy in state court before the bankruptcy case began.[16] These include informal collection efforts to persuade the debtor to pay voluntarily, initiation or continuation of actions to obtain a judgment against the debtor in court, and enforcement of any judgment that they have already obtained.

Denial of discharge does not mean that the debtor's assets are unaffected by the bankruptcy case. The debtor's property is still assembled and sold by the trustee, with the proceeds distributed to creditors. The debtor thus loses her non-exempt assets. In precise statutory jargon, the trustee still fulfills its duties to "collect and reduce to money the property of the estate"[17] and to distribute the money collected according to the priorities established by the Code.[18] Thus, the debtor is deprived of any non-exempt equity she has in her property and does not receive the "fresh start" that a bankruptcy discharge would otherwise provide.[19]

Denial of discharge is mostly commonly an issue in Chapter 7 liquidation cases. Discharge is most often denied because of some sort of misconduct by the debtor, usually in connection with the bankruptcy case itself.

---

[15] William Houston Brown, *Taking Exception to a Debtor's Discharge: The 2005 Bankruptcy Amendments Make it Easier*, 79 Am. Bankr. L.J. 419 (2005).

[16] *See* Chapter 2, Creditors' Collection Rights, *supra*.

[17] Bankruptcy Code § 704(1).

[18] *See* Bankruptcy Code § 726.

[19] *See* Local Loan v. Hunt, 292 U.S. 234 (1934).

It should also be remembered that dismissal of a Chapter 7 case at the outset due to "abuse" under § 707(b) has the same effect as a denial of discharge: the debtor obtains no relief from her debts and creditors remain free to pursue the debtor in state court. However, denial of discharge is different from dismissal, in that the debtor's assets are administered by the trustee even though discharge is denied; if a case is dismissed, the trustee does not collect, sell, or distribute the debtor's assets.

In reorganization proceedings, the issue of discharge is dealt with in the context of the confirmation of a plan; any misconduct by the debtor in connection with the case is punished by the court's refusal to confirm a plan. Since discharge in these types of proceedings cannot occur unless a plan is confirmed,[20] denial of confirmation in a reorganization case has roughly the same effect as denial of discharge in a liquidation case. This section deals with the denial of discharge under these various types of proceedings, but focuses primarily on denial of discharge in liquidation cases under Chapter 7.

[B] Denial of Discharge in Chapter 7[21]

As indicated above, the reasons for denying discharge are nearly always rooted in the debtor's misconduct. The most common basis for denying debtors a discharge is because of their fraudulent transfer or concealment of assets or their failure to provide the information necessary for the administration of their bankruptcy case. Debtors are also denied a discharge if they have obtained another discharge in a case commenced within eight years of the time of a subsequent petition.

The right to challenge the debtor's eligibility for a discharge is extended to all "parties in interest."[22] This includes the trustee, creditors, and the office of the United States Trustee. Further, on request of any party in interest, the court may order the trustee to examine the debtor's actions and conduct to determine whether there is a basis for denying discharge.[23]

[1] Eligibility for Chapter 7 Discharge — Individual Debtors

Individuals are eligible for a Chapter 7 discharge,[24] even if they are

[20] In Chapter 11 cases, discharge occurs upon confirmation of a plan. Bankruptcy Code § 1141(d). In Chapter 12 and 13 cases, discharge occurs upon the debtor's completion of the terms of a previously confirmed plan. Bankruptcy Code §§ 1228(a), 1328(a).

[21] William Houston Brown, *Taking Exception to a Debtor's Discharge: The 2005 Bankruptcy Act Makes it Easier*, 79 Am. Bankr. L.J. 419 (2005).

[22] Bankruptcy Code § 727(c)(1).

[23] Bankruptcy Code § 727(c)(2). One of your authors once observed a bankruptcy judge angrily departing from the bench in order to make an immediate call to the trustee to suggest that he make such a motion in the belief that one of your author's clients had concealed assets from the court. Ouch!

[24] Bankruptcy Code § 727(a)(1).

deceased.[25] Other entities, such as corporations and partnerships, are not eligible for a Chapter 7 discharge and must seek relief, if at all, under Chapter 11.[26] While this may seem odd, when these other entities are deprived of all of their assets, they are likely to dissolve. Denying them the right to a discharge prevents trafficking in corporate shells and bankrupt partnerships.[27]

The 2005 Amendments impose further restrictions on which debtors are eligible for discharge by restricting their ability to file a bankruptcy petition in the first place. As explained elsewhere, Chapter 7 liquidation cases of debtors whose incomes are high enough to enable them to make what Congress has determined are meaningful payments to their creditors are either dismissed or converted to Chapter 13.[28]

[2] Fraudulent Transfers; Destruction or Concealment of Property

Debtors who hide their property from their creditors are not the type of "honest debtors" who are entitled to relief. Consequently, § 727(a)(2) denies a discharge of debtors who "with intent to hinder, delay, or defraud a creditor [or the trustee have] transferred, removed, destroyed, mutilated, or concealed" their property either within one year before the date of their bankruptcy petition or after it was filed.[29] Section 727(a)(2) is based on the premise that debtors who intentionally seeks to deny creditors access to their property should not be entitled to enjoy the benefits of Chapter 7.

The relationship between § 727(a)(2) and fraudulent conveyance law is clear. Both § 4 of the Uniform Fraudulent Transfer Act and § 548(a)(1)(A) of the Bankruptcy Code permit intentionally fraudulent transfers of the debtor's property to be avoided.[30] Section 727(a)(2) compounds the consequences of such improper behavior by denying the debtor a discharge.

The fact that the transferred property is ultimately recovered by the bankruptcy trustee and used to pay creditors' claims does not preserve the debtor's discharge. Thus, the fact that creditors suffered no harm as a result of the debtor's misconduct is not a defense.[31] The debtor's intentional misconduct is enough. If this were not the case, debtors might have too great an incentive to attempt to engage in this type of bad behavior.[32]

---

[25] H.R. Rep. 95-595, 384 (1977), *reprinted in* 1978 U.S.C.C.A.N. 5963, 6340; S. Rep. No. 95-989, 98 (1978), *reprinted in* 1978 U.S.C.C.A.N. 5787, 5885.

[26] Bankruptcy Code § 727(a)(1).

[27] H.R. Rep. 95-595, 384 (1977), *reprinted in* 1978 U.S.C.C.A.N. 5963, 6340; S. Rep. No. 95-989, 98 (1978), *reprinted in* 1978 U.S.C.C.A.N. 5787, 5885.

[28] *See* § 17.03[B][2] Presumptive Abuse — Means Testing, *infra.*

[29] Bankruptcy Code § 727(a)(2).

[30] *See* Chapter 16, Fraudulent Transfers, *infra.*

[31] *E.g.*, In re Smiley, 864 F.2d 562, 569 (7th Cir. 1989).

[32] The debtor's misconduct might also constitute a federal crime punishable by up to five years in prison. 18 U.S.C. § 152(1) (2000); *see generally* Tamara Ogier & Jack F. Williams, *Bankruptcy Crimes and Bankruptcy Practice*, 6 Am. Bankr. Inst. L. Rev. 317 (1998).

In many cases, there will be no direct evidence of the debtor's fraudulent intent. However, as under fraudulent conveyance law generally, circumstantial evidence, or "badges of fraud," are used to infer the requisite intent. The commonly recurring circumstances that reflect the intent to defraud creditors have not changed much since *Twyne's Case* in 1601.[33] They still include the inadequacy of consideration, the existence of a family or other close relationship between the parties, the debtor's retention of the possession of the property, the financial circumstances of the debtor before and after the transfer, and the proximity in time between the transfer and the initiation of creditors' efforts to collect.[34]

However, transfers of property that are only constructively fraudulent because of the inadequacy of the consideration received for the transfer, do not warrant denial of discharge,[35] even though the transfer might be recoverable as a fraudulent transfer. Thus, a debtor who sells her property at a steep discount in an effort to raise cash to pay her creditors or meet her current living expenses will not be denied a discharge.[36] Because the debtor's intent was benign, she still qualifies for relief from her debts.

The text of § 727(a)(2) denies the debtor a discharge only on account of transfers occurring within one year before the date of her bankruptcy petition. However, transfers made more than one year before the case was filed might still result in a denial of discharge under the "continued concealment" doctrine. It treats transfers of property as continuing up through the time of the petition if the debtor retains a secret ownership interest in the transferred property within the year prior to filing.[37] Thus, a debtor who arranges to re-acquire the transferred property may be denied a discharge, even though she initially transferred her property more than a year before filing her bankruptcy petition.

A debtor's conversion of non-exempt property into an exempt form might also constitute grounds for denial of discharge.[38] For example, in *In re Reed*, the debtor sold many of his nonexempt assets and used the proceeds to make mortgage payments on his otherwise fully exempt residence. Because this was done with the actual intent to place his assets beyond the reach of his creditors, Reed's discharge was denied.[39] Despite this result, cases

---

[33] 76 Eng. Rep. 809 (Star Chamber 1601).

[34] *See* Unif. Fraudulent Transfer Act § 4(b) (1984); *see e.g.*, Village of San Jose v. McWilliams, 284 F.3d 785, 791 (7th Cir. 2002); Martin v. Bajgar (In re Bajgar), 104 F.3d 495 (1st Cir. 1995) (transfer to spouse in exchange for love and affection); *see also* 16.02[A] Actual Fraud, *infra*.

[35] *See* Unif. Fraudulent Trans. Act § 5(a) (1984)

[36] Commerce Bank & Trust Co. v. Burgess (In re Burgess), 955 F.2d 134 (1st Cir. 1992) (debtor used assets meet its payroll).

[37] *E.g.*, Keeney v. Smith (In re Keeney), 227 F.3d 679 (6th Cir. 2000).

[38] *E.g.*, Ford v. Poston, 773 F.2d 52 (4th Cir. 1985) (transfer of property held in joint tenancy by husband and wife to themselves in "tenancy by the entireties" accompanied by extrinsic evidence of intent to defraud creditors warranted denial of discharge).

[39] First Tex. Sav. Ass'n, Inc. v. Reed (In re Reed), 700 F.2d 986 (5th Cir. 1983); *see also* Norwest Bank Neb. v. Tveten (In re Tveten), 848 F.2d 871, 874 (8th Cir. 1988); *see generally* Lawrence Ponoroff & F. Stephen Knippenberg, *Debtors Who Convert Their Assets on the Eve*

like *Reed* have usually been limited to situations where the debtor committed some act extrinsic to the conversion that hindered, delayed, or defrauded his creditors. Reed, for example, had entered into an agreement with his creditors that delayed their collection efforts in a way that facilitated his efforts to place his assets beyond his creditors' reach.[40]

The debtor in *In re Tveten* also ran afoul of § 727(a)(2).[41] Dr. Tveten sought bankruptcy protection, not, as one might imagine in the case of a physician, as a result of medical malpractice liability, but as a result of the collapse of a highly leveraged $19 million investment scheme. In an effort to protect his assets from his creditors, Dr. Tveten participated in seventeen separate transfers, which resulted in the conversion of nearly $700,000 worth of non-exempt assets into exempt life insurance policies and annuities. The court regarded this systematic conversion of non-exempt assets into exempt categories as an attempt to obtain not just a "fresh start" but a "head start." Although his assets were exempt under state law, denial of his discharge meant that he would not be able to reconvert them back into non-exempt status without running the risk that they would become exposed to the claims of his creditors in the years after his bankruptcy.

Other debtors whose conversions of non-exempt assets into exempt categories have been less dramatic usually receive more generous treatment. Courts generally require some extrinsic evidence of fraudulent intent other than the mere conversion of nonexempt assets into an exempt class.[42]

[3] Failure to Maintain Records[43]

A debtor may also be denied a discharge for failure to keep or preserve books from which her financial situation may be ascertained, unless the failure is justified under all the circumstances of the case.[44] Thus, the court must first determine whether the debtor's records were sufficient, and, if not, the court must evaluate the debtor's justification for failing to maintain them.[45]

Even though some debtors destroy their financial records or fail to create them in the first place as part of a dishonest scheme, most are simply

of Bankruptcy: Villains or Victims of the Fresh Start?, 70 N.Y.U. L. Rev. 235 (1995); Theodore Eisenberg, *Bankruptcy Law in Perspective*, 28 UCLA L. Rev. 953, 992–96 (1981); Alan N. Resnick, *Prudent Planning or Fraudulent Transfer? The Use of Non-Exempt Assets to Purchase or Improve Exempt Property on the Eve of Bankruptcy*, 31 Rutgers L. Rev. 615 (1978).

40 *See also* Grover v. Jackson, 472 F.2d 589 (9th Cir. 1973); In re Adlman, 541 F.2d 999 (2d Cir. 1976); Love v. Menick, 341 F.2d 680 (9th Cir. 1965); Forsberg v. Secured State Bank of Canova, 15 F.2d 499 (8th Cir. 1926); In re Johnson, 80 B.R. 953 (Bankr. D. Minn. 1987).

41 Norwest Bank Neb. v. Tveten (In re Tveten), 848 F.2d 871 (8th Cir. 1988).

42 Gill v. Stern (In re Stern), 345 F.3d 1036 (9th Cir. 2003). On the question of whether the debtor will be denied the exemption, see § 12.02[E] Exemption Planning, *supra*.

43 *See* David S. Kennedy & James E. Bailey, III, *Gambling and the Bankruptcy Discharge: An Historical Exegesis and Case Survey*, 11 Bankr. Dev. J. 49 (1994).

44 Bankruptcy Code § 727(a)(3).

45 Floret, L.L.C. v. Sendecky (In re Sendecky), 283 B.R. 760, 764 (B.A.P. 8th Cir. 2002).

careless.[46] The adverse impact of the absence of these records on the estate's creditors is likely to be the same regardless of the debtor's motivation. Without adequate financial records, the trustee might find it difficult to locate assets of the estate, to determine whether pre-bankruptcy transfers of estate property are recoverable, or to evaluate the allowability of creditors' claims. As one court explained, "[t]he purpose of this provision is to ensure that the trustee and creditors receive sufficient information to trace a debtor's financial history for a reasonable period past to present."[47] Accordingly, intent is not an element of this ground for denial of discharge; the standard imposed is one of reasonableness.[48]

In determining the adequacy the debtor's records, courts consider the complexity of the debtor's business, the customary business practices for record keeping in that type of business, the degree of accuracy of any existing books, and sometimes even the debtor's courtroom demeanor.[49] According to the leading case decided under the old Bankruptcy Act, "[t]he law is not unqualified in imposing a requirement to keep books or records, and it does not require that if they are kept they shall be kept in any special form . . . . It is a question in each instance of reasonableness in the particular circumstances."[50] The obligation of some debtors to keep records may be satisfied by something pretty sketchy, especially if minimal records are normal in the debtor's line of work. Courts in general require very little of ordinary wage earners whose financial activities are not complex.[51]

Although debtors without records have the opportunity to provide a reason for the lack of sufficient records, debtors who present unsubstantiated or fanciful claims about the loss of their records receive the same treatment as elementary school students who claim that their homework was eaten by by the family dog. Debtors who claim that their records were stolen, despite their obvious lack of market value,[52] or who assert, as one debtor claimed, that they were inadvertently removed from the garage by the garbage man,[53] have little success in justifying their failure to produce adequate records.

---

[46] *E.g.*, Ledbetter v. Zaidan (In re Zaidan), 86 B.R. 296 (Bankr. S.D. Fla. 1988).

[47] United States v. Trogdon (In re Trogdon), 111 B.R. 655, 658 (Bankr. N.D. Ohio 1990).

[48] Wolfe v. Wolfe (In re Wolfe), 232 B.R. 741, 745 (B.A.P. 8th Cir. 1999); Riley v. Riley (In re Riley), 305 B.R. 873 (Bankr. W.D. Mo. 2004).

[49] Floret, L.L.C. v. Sendecky (In re Sendecky), 283 B.R. 760, 764 (B.A.P. 8th Cir. 2002).

[50] In re Underhill, 82 F.2d 258, 259–60 (2d Cir. 1936).

[51] In re Weismann, 1 F. Supp. 723 (S.D.N.Y. 1932); Simcich v. Haugen (In re Haugen), 9 B.R. 4 (Bankr. S.D. Fla. 1980) (laborer who worked about eight days a month should not be denied a discharge for failing to retain the passbook from a closed savings account that contained nominal sums); *see also* Buckeye Retirement Properties of Indiana, Inc. v. Tauber (In re Tauber), 349 B.R. 540 (Bankr. N.D. Ind. 2006) (lack of records of $35,000 in gambling losses did not warrant denial of discharge).

[52] Vetri v. Meadowbrook Mall Co., 174 B.R. 143 (M.D. Fla. 1994).

[53] In re Harron, 31 B.R. 466 (Bankr. D. Conn. 1983).

[4] Misconduct in the Debtor's Bankruptcy Proceeding

Sections 727(a)(4)-(6) deny the debtor a discharge due to the debtor's misconduct in her own bankruptcy proceeding. This misconduct might consist of perjury, bribery, withholding records, failure to account for missing assets, refusal to obey court orders, and the like.[54]

Debtors who knowingly and fraudulently misrepresent their financial affairs,[55] either on the schedules they file in connection with their petition[56] when examined by the trustee at the § 341 meeting of creditors,[57] or in an examination of the debtor conducted pursuant to Bankruptcy Rule 2004,[58] are intentionally impeding the orderly administration of their estate and should not receive the benefit of a discharge.

For example, the debtor in *In re Weiner* was denied a discharge because he had intentionally and seriously undervalued his assets on the schedules filed with his petition.[59] His discharge was denied because his misrepresentation was both material and was made with the intent to defraud his creditors.[60] Likewise, debtors who knowingly and fraudulently either present a false claim,[61] commit or attempt bribery,[62] or withhold otherwise available financial records in their own bankruptcy case[63] may be denied a discharge.

Not surprisingly, debtors who fail to provide a satisfactory explanation for the loss of their assets are also denied a discharge.[64] Debtors have sometimes attempted to explain the loss of their assets by claiming that they "lost it all" at a casino or in a poker game.[65] In *In re McNamara*, the debtor claimed to have lost over $130,000 in a poker game, but was suspiciously unable to describe any of the details of the game. Other evidence suggested that he had simply hidden his assets in an offshore account. The court explained, "[a] person who loses $130,000 in a poker game would be expected to have some recollection of the details of the event which could be corroborated, or at least a credible explanation for why he did not."[66] Likewise, the debtor in *In re Shahid* was denied a discharge

[54] Bankruptcy Code § 727(a)(4)-(6).

[55] Bankruptcy Code § 727(a)(4)(A).

[56] *See* Fed. R. Bankr. P. 1007(a).

[57] *See* Bankruptcy Code § 341; Fed. R. Bankr. P. 2003; *e.g.*, Korte v. IRS (In re Korte), 262 B.R. 464 (B.A.P. 8th Cir. 2001).

[58] *See* Fed. R. Bankr. P. 2004.

[59] Weiner v. Perry, Settles & Lawson, Inc. (In re Weiner), 208 B.R. 69 (B.A.P. 9th Cir. 1997).

[60] *See also* Korte v. IRS (In re Korte), 262 B.R. 464, 474 (B.A.P. 8th Cir. 2001).

[61] Bankruptcy Code § 727(a)(4)(B).

[62] Bankruptcy Code § 727(a)(4)(C).

[63] Bankruptcy Code § 727(a)(4)(D).

[64] Bankruptcy Code § 727(a)(5); David S. Kennedy & James E. Bailey, *Gambling and the Bankruptcy Discharge: An Historical Exegesis and Case Survey*, 11 Bankr. Dev. J. 49 (1994).

[65] *E.g.*, In re Wilbur, 211 B.R. 98 (Bankr. M.D. Fla. 1997).

[66] In re McNamara, 310 B.R. 664 (Bankr. D. Conn. 2004).

when his explanation for the loss of $25,000 received as a loan from a bank was simply that he had "spent it" with no further elaboration on what expenditures he had incurred.[67]

Debtors who fail to cooperate with the bankruptcy court's orders understandably receive the same treatment. Section 727(a)(6) provides that a Chapter 7 discharge may be denied if the debtor has refused "to obey any lawful order of the court."[68] However, discharge is not denied if there is a sufficient justification for the debtor's refusal. Moreover, a debtor cannot be forced to surrender her right against self-incrimination.[69] However, if she refuses to answer questions about her financial affairs after being granted immunity from prosecution, discharge is denied.[70]

[5] Misconduct in Prior or Concurrent Bankruptcy Proceedings.

Discharge can be denied not only because of misconduct in the debtor's current case but also because of her misconduct in an earlier case involving either the debtor herself or a closely related person.[71] Thus, the debtor cannot escape the consequences of her misconduct simply by filing another case. If, during the year before the debtor's petition, the debtor has made a fraudulent transfer, concealed or destroyed records, lied in conjunction with a case, committed perjury, or committed any of the acts specified in section 727(a)(2)-(6), discharge may be denied. Discharge may also be denied if, during the case, the debtor has done any of these things in another case that concerns an "insider" of the debtor.[72]

Cases where this has been an issue frequently involve cases of spouses or sometimes corporations with which the debtor is affiliated. Debtors who fail to cooperate in cases filed by their spouses may be unable to obtain their own Chapter 7 discharge. Likewise, an officer, director or other insider of a corporation who acts improperly in the corporation's bankruptcy may subsequently be denied a Chapter 7 discharge in her own individual bankruptcy case.

[6] Repeat Filings — The 8-year Bar[73]

There is a time limit on how frequently a debtor can obtain a Chapter 7 discharge. Otherwise, it would be too easy for debtors to run up their debts, enjoy the benefits of their profligate spending, and discharge their

---

[67] In re Shahid, 334 B.R. 698 (Bankr. N.D. Fla. 2005).

[68] Bankruptcy Code § 727(a)(6)(A).

[69] Bankruptcy Code § 727(a)(6)(B).

[70] Bankruptcy Code § 727(a)(6)(B).

[71] Bankruptcy Code § 727(a)(7).

[72] "Insiders" are close affiliates of the debtor, such as relatives or related legal entities. *See* Bankruptcy Code § 101(31).

[73] Saul Schwartz, *The Effect of Bankruptcy Counseling on Future Creditworthiness*, 77 Am. Bankr. L.J. 257, 267 (2003).

obligations whenever their creditors started to close in.[74] For many years, debtors were prohibited from obtaining a Chapter 7 discharge within six years of the filing of any earlier Chapter 7 or Chapter 11 case in which a discharge was supplied.[75] In 2005, the bar following a Chapter 7 or Chapter 11 discharge was extended to eight years.[76] The period remains at six years following a prior discharge in an earlier Chapter 12 or 13 case.

The rules discussed here only apply to the availability of a discharge in a Chapter 7 liquidation case after a discharge in an earlier liquidation or reorganization case. Rules regarding the availability of a discharge in Chapters 11, 12, or 13, after a discharge in an earlier proceeding are explained elsewhere.[77]

[a] Prior Chapter 7 or 11 Discharge

A debtor who receives a discharge in either Chapter 7 or Chapter 11 is barred from a subsequent Chapter 7 discharge for eight years.[78] The eight-year period is measured from the filing of the petition in the first case to the filing of the petition in the second case. The time period runs from filing date to filing date, not from the dates of discharge. Thus, if Debbie filed a Chapter 7 petition on June 30, 2006, and received a discharge, she cannot obtain another Chapter 7 discharge in any proceeding filed before July 1, 2014.

This "eight-year bar" partially explains why individuals who have discharged their debts sometimes find it surprisingly easy to obtain credit: lenders know that they will not be able to discharge their debts again for another eight years. Note that the bar does not prohibit a debtor from submitting a premature petition; it only prohibits discharge in the second case.

[b] Prior Chapter 12 or 13 Discharge

The time bar is more flexible if the earlier discharge was obtained in a Chapter 12 or a Chapter 13 case. When the earlier discharge has been pursuant to a completed Chapter 12 or Chapter 13 plan,[79] the bar is only six years in duration. Thus, if Debbie filed a Chapter 13 case on June 30, 2006 and received a Chapter 13 discharge upon the completion of her Chapter 13 case three years later, she would be eligible for a Chapter 7 discharge in a case filed on July 1, 2012 or thereafter. This is true even if her prior

[74] Although one might imagine that debtors who have received a bankruptcy discharge would find it impossible to obtain credit, this has not proven to be true. *See* Saul Schwartz, *The Effect of Bankruptcy Counseling on Future Creditworthiness*, 77 Am Bankr. L.J. 257 (2003).

[75] Bankruptcy Code § 727(a)(8).

[76] Bankruptcy Abuse Prevention and Consumer Protection Act of 2005, Pub. L. No. 109-8, § 312, 119 Stat. 23, 87.

[77] *See* § 13.05 Chapter 13 Discharge; § 13.06 Chapter 11 Discharge, *infra*.

[78] Bankruptcy Code § 727(a)(8).

[79] Under Chapters 12 and 13, discharge is ordinarily granted only if the debtor has fully performed the terms of her plan. *See generally* § 13.05 Chapter 13 Discharge, *infra*.

Chapter 13 plan provided only for negligible payments to her creditors. Thus, debtors gain a two-year advantage by filing under Chapter 13 rather than Chapter 7, even if the payments made to their creditors under the Chapter 13 plan are modest.

Further, the bar does not apply at all if the debtor's earlier Chapter 12 or 13 discharge was granted after completing a plan that provided for payment of 100% of her allowed unsecured claims.[80] This makes sense: debtors who have paid their creditors in full should remain eligible for a subsequent discharge if their financial circumstances again turn sour.

Whether a debtor's prior Chapter 12 or 13 case resulted in 100% payment, there is some question about whether the plan payments must be equal to the *value* of the claims or simply to their *amount*. In other words, the question is whether 100% payment is required to include an interest component on the amount of the unsecured claims to compensate the creditor for the delay in receiving payment. The Code says that the payments must equal "the allowed unsecured claims," not "the value" of the amount of the allowed unsecured claims.[81] The plain meaning of this language, at least in "bankruptcy-speak," is that the plan need not provide for payment of interest on the amount of the creditors' claims in order to avoid the six-year bar.

For example, if a debtor's allowed unsecured claims in her earlier Chapter 13 cases were $10,000, and the debtor paid a total of $10,000, the requirement appears to have been satisfied, even though the payment was made over a three-to-five-year period. Obviously, payments of $10,000 over a period of time have an actual value of something less than $10,000.

Even if the debtor's prior Chapter 12 or 13 plan did not provide for 100% payment, the six-year bar of § 727(a)(9) does not apply if the earlier plan provided for payment of at least 70% of her unsecured claims and if "the plan was proposed by the debtor in good faith and was the debtor's best effort."[82] "Best effort" is a rather open-ended standard. The legislative history to § 727(a)(9) indicates that in determining whether the debtor's plan represented his or her best effort, the court should:

> balance the debtor's assets, including family income, health insurance, retirement benefits, and other wealth, a sum which is generally determinable, against the foreseeable necessary living expenses of the debtor and the debtor's dependents, which unfortunately is rarely quantifiable. In determining the expenses of the debtor and the debtor's dependents, the court should consider the stability of the debtor's employment, if any, the age of the debtor, the number of the debtor's dependents and their ages, the condition of equipment and tools necessary to the debtor's employment or to the operation of his business, and other foreseeable expenses that the debtor

[80] Bankruptcy Code § 727(a)(9)(A).

[81] Bankruptcy Code § 727(a)(9)(A).

[82] Bankruptcy Code § 727(a)(9)(B).

will be required to pay during the period of the plan, other than payments to be made to creditors under the plan.[83]

Significantly, it is not unusual for debtors to include language in their Chapter 12 and 13 plans specifying that the payments provided for in their plans constitute their "best effort." This is done in an effort to preclude creditors in any Chapter 7 discharge hearing in a subsequent case, from contending otherwise.

[7] Waiver of Discharge

Debtors also are denied a discharge if they have made an effective waiver of their right to one.[84] To be effective, a waiver of the right to a discharge must be in writing, be executed by the debtor after the order for relief (in a voluntary case, after the filing of the petition), and be approved by the court. Not surprisingly, discharge waivers are rare. They are to be expected generally only as a result of a settlement agreement in a denial of discharge proceeding.

Waiver of discharge is completely different from reaffirmation of individual debts. The enforceability of reaffirmation agreements is governed by § 524(c).[85]

[8] Failure to Complete Credit Counseling Course[86]

One of the key features of the 2005 Amendments is the requirement that individual debtors "complete an instruction course concerning personal financial management."[87] Debtors who fail to complete a "credit counseling" course with an approved "non-profit budget and credit counseling agenc-[y]"[88] are ineligible for a Chapter 7 discharge.[89] This instructional course

---

[83] 124 Cong. Rec. H11,908 (Sept. 28, 1978) (statement of Rep. Edward); 124 Cong. Rec. S17415 (Sept. 28, 1978) (statement of Senator DeConcini).

[84] Bankruptcy Code § 727(a)(10).

[85] Bankruptcy Code § 524(c); *see* § 12.08[B] Reaffirmation to Retain Property, *supra.*

[86] Susan Block-Lieb et al., *The Coalition for Consumer Bankruptcy Debtor Education: A Report on Its Pilot Program*, 21 Bankr. Dev. J. 233 (2005); Jean Braucher, *An Empirical Study of Debtor Education in Bankruptcy: Impact of Chapter 13 Completion Not Shown*, 9 Am. Bankr. Inst. L. Rev. 557 (2001); A. Michele Dickerson, *Can Shame, Guilt, or Stigma Be Taught? Why Credit-Focused Debtor Education May Not Work*, 32 Loy. L.A. L. Rev. 945 (1999); Gary Neustadter, *A Consumer Bankruptcy Odyssey*, 39 Creighton L. Rev. 225, 258–70 (2006); Saul Schwartz, *The Effect of Bankruptcy Counseling on Future Creditworthiness*, 77 Am. Bankr. L.J. 257 (2003); Robin Miller, Annotation, *Validity, Construction, and Application of Credit Counseling Requirement Under Bankruptcy Abuse Prevention and Consumer Protection Act (BAPCPA), 11 U.S.C.A. § 109(h)*, 11 A.L.R. Fed. 2d 43 (2006).

[87] Bankruptcy Code § 727(a)(11). Debtors must also participate in a credit counseling "briefing" prior to filing their petition. *See* Bankruptcy Code § 521(b)(1); *see generally* § 6.02[B][1][c] Mandatory Credit Counseling Briefing, *supra.*

[88] Bankruptcy Code § 111(a)(1).

[89] Completion of a credit counseling program is also required in order to obtain relief under Chapter 13. Bankruptcy Code § 1328(g); *see* § 13.05[A] Debtors Eligible for Chapter 13 Discharge, *infra.*

in personal financial management is different from the less complicated credit-counseling briefing that individual debtors must obtain to file a petition.[90]

Both § 727(a)(11) and § 1328(g) provide for a waiver of this requirement based on either the debtor's personal circumstances or on the unavailability of approved courses in the debtor's geographic region.[91] Among the circumstances that justify a waiver are "incapacity, disability, or active military duty in a combat zone."[92] Thus, in *In re Hall*, an 81-year-old debtor who was hearing impaired, confined to a scooter for mobility, and suffering from other ailments including prostate cancer, was excused from completing an instructional course in personal financial management after he had made a reasonable effort to do so.[93]

Such credit counseling programs are not free, and the debtor's dire financial circumstances do not provide the basis for a waiver. The necessity of completing a credit counseling program adds to the cost of obtaining a bankruptcy discharge.

Many are skeptical about the long-term benefits of these mandatory credit counseling programs, while there is some empirical evidence that voluntary programs are beneficial.[94] Whether these benefits exist where the debtors are compelled to take the course remains to be seen.

[9] Criminal Convictions

New § 727(a)(12) also permits the court to deny the debtor a discharge if "there is reasonable cause to believe that . . . the debtor may be found guilty of a felony" in a pending criminal proceeding in which the debtor is charged with a bankruptcy crime, securities fraud, RICO, or a crime involving wilful or reckless misconduct that resulted in personal injury or death[95] and where the debtor sought a homestead exemption otherwise available under a state exemption statute, in excess of $136,875. Thus,

---

[90] Bankruptcy Code § 109(h); *see* § 6.02[B][1][c] Mandatory Credit Counseling Briefing, *supra*.

[91] Bankruptcy Code §§ 727(a)(11), 1328(g).

[92] Bankruptcy Code § 109(h)(4).

[93] In re Hall, 347 B.R. 532 (Bankr. N.D. W. Va. 2006); *see also* In re Tulper, 345 B.R. 322, 326 (Bankr. D. Colo. 2006).

[94] *See* Susan Block-Lieb, Karen Gross & Richard L. Wiener, *Lessons from the Trenches: Debtor Education in Theory and Practice*, 7 Fordham J. Corp. & Fin. L. 503 (2002); Susan Block-Lieb, Corinne Baron-Donovan, Karen Gross & Richard Wiener, *The Coalition for Consumer Bankruptcy Debtor Education: A Report on its Pilot Program*, 21 Bankr. Dev. J. 233 (2004); Karen Gross & Susan Block-Lieb, *Beneath the Surface of BAPCPA: Empty Mandate or Opportunity for Innovation? Pre-petition Credit Counseling and Post-petition Financial Management*, 13 Am. Bankr. Inst. L. Rev. 549 (2005); Richard L. Stehl, *The Failings of the Consumer Credit Counseling and Debtor Education Requirements of the Proposed Consumer Bankruptcy Reform Legislation of 1998*, 7 Am. Bankr. Inst. L. Rev. 133 (1999); Richard L. Wiener, Susan Block-Lieb, Karen Gross & Corinne Baron-Donovan, *Debtor Education, Financial Literacy, and Pending Bankruptcy Legislation*, 23 Behav. Sci. & L. 347 (2005).

[95] *See* Bankruptcy Code § 522(q).

executives of large corporations who are found guilty of criminal activity in connection with the management of their financially troubled employers will find relief from their own personal financial difficulties unavailable. However, because of the working of §§ 727(a)(12) and 522(q)(1), denial of discharge under § 727(a)(12) applies only to debtors who elect to exempt property under the applicable state exemption statute.[96] Moreover, it may not apply to debtors in states that have opted out, as these debtors have not "elected" to exempt property under state or local law.[97]

[10] Failure to Supply Tax Returns

Although not formally listed as grounds for denial of a discharge, a debtor's failure to provide the trustee with her most recent year's federal tax return will result in dismissal of the debtor's case, effectively denying her a discharge.[98] An exception is made only for debtors who are able to demonstrate that their failure to comply "is due to circumstances beyond their control."[99]

[C] Denial of Discharge in Chapter 11

Most Chapter 11 cases involve corporations or partnerships. In these Chapter 11 cases, the debtor nearly always receives a discharge upon confirmation of its Chapter 11 plan.[100] Without confirmation of a plan that will continue the operations of the business, there is no discharge. Some debtors choose to liquidate in Chapter 11. In such cases, even where a plan is confirmed, the debtor does not receive a discharge.

This does not mean that important issues such as misconduct by the debtor are irrelevant. Rather, it means they arise in the context of the court's determination of whether to confirm a plan, rather than in a separate discharge proceeding. Thus, by refusing to confirm the debtor's plan, the court can effectively deny discharge for one or more of the same reasons that it would directly rule on discharge in a Chapter 7 case.

Nor is there any limitation on frequency of Chapter 11 discharges. Unlike Chapter 7 discharges, which are available only once every eight years, Chapter 11 discharges are available anytime, provided that a plan can be confirmed. However, because it is difficult (though not impossible) to obtain confirmation of a Chapter 11 plan without the consent of a majority of the debtor's creditors,[101] their reluctance to vote in favor of a debtor's plan is the most imposing barrier to a Chapter 11 discharge. This, and the other

---

96 In re Jacobs, 342 B.R. 114 (Bankr. D.D.C. 2006).

97 *See* Bankruptcy Code § 522(q)(1).

98 Bankruptcy Code § 521(e)(2)(A)(i).

99 Bankruptcy Code § 521(e)(2)(B).

100 Bankruptcy Code § 1141(d).

101 *See generally* § 19.09 Acceptance of Plan by Holders of Claims and Interests: Disclosure and Voting, *infra*.

requirements for confirmation under Chapter 11 are discussed elsewhere.[102]

The principle exception to the general availability of a Chapter 11 discharge is § 1141(d)(3). It precludes discharge in the same circumstances as those in which a Chapter 7 discharge would be denied if the plan provides for nothing more than the debtor's liquidation. A liquidating plan might result in the Chapter 11 case being virtually indistinguishable from a Chapter 7 proceeding. Accordingly, Chapter 7's rules for denial of discharge apply to Chapter 11 cases in which "(1) the plan provides for the liquidation of all, or substantially all, the property of the estate, (2) the debtor does not engage in business after consummation of the plan, and (3) discharge would have been denied under section 727(a) if the case had been brought under chapter 7."[103]

Finally, as in Chapter 7, a Chapter 11 discharge can be waived. To be effective, the waiver must be in writing; it must be executed by the debtor after the order for relief (i.e., in a voluntary case, after the filing of the petition), and it must be approved by the court.[104]

Although individuals only rarely seek relief in Chapter 11, those who do will not receive their discharge until they complete all of the payments provided for in their plan.[105] Other Chapter 11 debtors receive their discharge upon confirmation of their plan.[106]

[D] Denial of Discharge in Chapters 12 and 13

Ordinarily, a discharge is granted under Chapters 12 and 13 only upon completion of the payments to creditors provided for in the plan. As is true in Chapter 11, the court must confirm the plan, and it is nearly always in the process of confirmation that issues related to the debtor's misconduct arise. Confirmation can be denied, even if the plan otherwise complies with the financial requirements of Chapters 12 and 13, if the plan has not been proposed in "good faith."[107] The court may refuse confirmation — and thus effectively preclude discharge — for many of the same reasons that it would directly rule on discharge in a Chapter 7 case.

Before 2005, there was no general time bar for discharge in either a Chapter 12 or 13 proceeding. A debtor could receive a discharge under Chapter 12 or 13 despite having received an earlier discharge under any chapter.

---

[102] *See* § 19.10 Confirmation of Chapter 11 Plans, *infra.*

[103] Bankruptcy Code § 1141(d)(3).

[104] Bankruptcy Code § 1141(d)(4).

[105] Bankruptcy Code § 1141(d)(5)(A).

[106] Bankruptcy Code § 1141(d)(1)(A).

[107] Bankruptcy Code §§ 1225(a)(3), 1325(a)(3); *see generally* Robert Bein, *Subjectivity, Good Faith and the Expanded Chapter 13 Discharge*, 70 Mo. L. Rev. 655 (2005); § 18.08[C] Plan Proposed in Good Faith, *infra.*

The 2005 Amendments to the Bankruptcy Code changed this in Chapter 13 cases. A debtor is ineligible for a discharge in a Chapter 13 case if she received a discharge in an earlier Chapter 7, 11, or 12 case that was filed within four years before the date of the order for relief[108] in the later Chapter 13 proceeding.[109] For example, if Gail obtains a Chapter 7 discharge in a case filed on October 1, 2006, she is not be eligible for a Chapter 13 discharge in a case filed before October 2, 2010. And, because a Chapter 13 discharge is not usually granted until completion of the debtor's plan, the earliest Gail will be able to receive a Chapter 13 discharge is in the fall of 2013, and possibly not until 2015 if she is required to submit a five year plan.

This change prevents debtors from filing sequential Chapter 7 and 13 cases in a strategy that had become known as "chapter 20." Previously, it might have been possible for debtors to discharge their personal liability in Chapter 7 and immediately file a Chapter 13 case. The subsequent Chapter 13 case would be used to restructure the debtor's secured debts, or perhaps to cure and reinstate a home mortgage that was vulnerable to foreclosure due to the debtor's default. In 1991, the United States Supreme Court ruled that the debts discharged in the earlier Chapter 7 case were still "claims" (as that term is defined in Bankruptcy Code), in the subsequent Chapter 13 case, and could thus be dealt with in the debtor's Chapter 13 plan.[110] Although the definition of "claim" has not been changed, new § 1328(f)(2)'s restrictions on the debtor's ability to obtain a subsequent Chapter 13 discharge in a case filed on the immediate heels of an earlier Chapter 7 discharge impairs use of this strategy.

The 2005 Amendments also restrict debtors' eligibility for successive Chapter 13 discharges. New § 1328(f)(2) prohibits a debtor from obtaining a discharge in a Chapter 13 case if the debtor received a Chapter 13 discharge in a case filed within two years before the date of the order for relief in the later case.[111] The way this language is written, it will rarely, if ever, prevent a debtor from obtaining a discharge. Most Chapter 13 plans take a minimum of three years to complete. Although it is possible for a debtor to receive a discharge sooner, by completing a 100% payment plan in less than three years, or by obtaining a hardship discharge, these circumstances are rare. It is even more rare for a debtor to obtain a Chapter 13 discharge and file a second Chapter 13 case within two years of the time of the first petition. Nevertheless, the plain language of § 1328(f)(2) indicates that its two-year period runs from the dates the petitions are filed.[112]

---

[108] Ordinarily the date of the "order for relief" is the same as the date the debtor's Chapter 13 petition was filed. However, it might be later if the order for relief in the Chapter 13 case is entered following the conversion of a case filed by the same debtor under Chapter 7, 11, or 12. *See generally* § 18.03[B] Conversion and Dismissal of Chapter 13 Cases, *infra.*

[109] Bankruptcy Code § 1328(f)(1); *see* In re Lewis, 339 B.R. 814 (Bankr. S.D. Ga. 2006); In re Sours, 350 B.R. 261 (Bankr. E.D. Va. 2006) (earlier Chapter 13 cases converted to Chapter 7).

[110] Johnson v. Home State Bank, 501 U.S. 78 (1991).

[111] Bankruptcy Code § 1328(f)(2).

[112] *See* In re West, No. 4:06-BK-11215E, 2006 Bankr. LEXIS 2562 (Bankr. E.D. Ark., Oct. 10, 2006).

There is no similar provision restricting the availability of a Chapter 12 discharge. Chapter 12 debtors are denied a discharge only if they have been involved in certain types of criminal activity.[113]

A Chapter 12 or a Chapter 13 discharge can be waived. The waiver must be in writing, it must be executed by the debtor after the order for relief (i.e., after the filing of the petition), and it must be approved by the court.[114] Cases involving waivers of discharge are few and far between.

§ 13.03 Nondischargeable Debts[115]

[A] Meaning of Nondischargeability

A debtor who is granted a global discharge may not be relieved from all of her debts. Section 523 lists a number of debts that are not included within the scope of a debtor's discharge. Debts are nondischargeable usually because of the debtor's misconduct or because permitting their discharge would result in the debtor receiving an unfair benefit or a creditor bearing an unfair burden. Further, some grounds for nondischargeability reflect broader public policies about individual responsibility and preserving perceptions about the integrity of the bankruptcy system.

Whether these nondischargeable debts will ever actually be paid is, of course, speculative. What little data there are suggests that nondischargeable debts are seldom recovered, either because the debtor rarely acquires enough money to pay them or because the cost of monitoring the debtor to determine whether the debtor has the ability to pay is burdensome to creditors.

There is a long tradition of interpreting the exceptions to discharge narrowly. Many cases have held that, to be nondischargeable, the debt must fit clearly within one of the exceptions. On the other hand, Congress has over time expanded the categories of nondischargeable debts, further limiting the scope of a debtor's fresh start.

Whether a particular debt is nondischargeable depends on the chapter under which the debtor has filed. As part of its effort to make Chapter 13 more attractive to consumer debtors than Chapter 7, Congress historically has provided a broader discharge in Chapter 13 cases than in Chapter 7 cases. Thus, some of the obligations discussed in this section may be discharged upon completion of a Chapter 13 plan. For some debtors, this broader discharge, though narrowed considerably by the 2005 Amendments, is one of the main attractions of Chapter 13.

---

113 Bankruptcy Code § 1228(f).

114 Bankruptcy Code §§ 1228(a), 1328(a).

115 William Houston Brown, *Taking Exception to a Debtor's Discharge: The 2005 Bankruptcy Act Makes it Easier*, 79 Am. Bankr. L.J. 419 (2005); George H. Singer, *Section 523 of the Bankruptcy Code: The Fundamentals of Nondischargeability in Consumer Bankruptcy*, 71 Am. Bankr. L.J. 325 (1997).

Section 523(a) now contains nearly two dozen categories of nondischargeable debts.[116] The major ones that consumer debtors are likely to owe are family obligations, student loans, tax debts, and debts for various types of intentional torts, including fraud. Other less commonly occurring categories abound.

[B] Types of Nondischargeable Debts[117]

[1] Tax Debts

As Justice Holmes said, "taxes are the price we pay for civilization." Therefore, not surprisingly, many tax debts to federal, state, and local governments are nondischargeable. This section explains the most important categories of nondischargeable tax debts under § 523(a)(1) of the Bankruptcy Code.

[a] Priority Taxes[118]

As discussed elsewhere, some unsecured claims are entitled to priority. Some claims are, after all, more equal than others.[119] Among those claims that are entitled to priority are a wide variety of tax claims.[120] But priority does not guarantee payment. Many debtors' estates are inadequate to pay even those debts that are entitled to priority. Accordingly, § 523(a)(1) makes any tax claim that is entitled to priority under § 507(a)(3) or § 507(a)(8) nondischargeable. Any tax claim that would have been entitled to priority under § 507, but which was not paid by funds in the debtor's bankruptcy estate, is not discharged. Thus, if priority tax claims are not paid through the administration of the debtor's estate, the government is entitled to recover the unpaid taxes from the debtor after her bankruptcy case is closed.

[i] Income Taxes

Foremost among the nondischargeable tax debts that individual debtors are likely to be concerned about are those for income taxes. Income tax debts are nondischargeable if the tax was due "for a taxable year ending on or

116 Twenty-one to be precise. *See* Bankruptcy Code § 523(a)(1)-(19) (including §§ (14A) and (14B), lest it appear that your authors cannot count).

117 William Houston Brown, *Taking Exception to a Debtor's Discharge: the 2005 Bankruptcy Amendments Make it Easier*, 79 Am. Bankr. L.J. 419 (2005); Margaret Howard, *Theory of Discharge in Consumer Bankruptcy*, 48 Ohio St. L.J. 1047 (1987); George H. Singer, *Section 523 of the Bankruptcy Code: The Fundamentals of Nondischargeability in Consumer Bankruptcy,* 71 Am. Bankr. L.J. 325 (1997).

118 William H. Brown & Daniel A. Hawtof, *Tolling the Three-year Period for Discharge of Income Taxes: Is There Plain Meaning in 11 U.S.C. § 507(a)(8)(A)(i)?*, 18 Miss. C. L. Rev. 483 (1998); Stephen W. Sather, Patricia L. Barsalou & Richard Litwin, *Borrowing from the Taxpayer: State and Local Tax Claims in Bankruptcy*, 4 Am. Bankr. Inst. L. Rev. 201 (1996).

119 George Orwell, Animal Farm: A Fairy Story (1945).

120 Bankruptcy Code § 507(a)(8); *see* § 10.04[A][8] Tax Claims, *supra*.

before the date of the filing of the [bankruptcy] petition for which a return . . . is last due, including extensions, after three years before the date of the filing of the petition."[121] This is the dreaded "after three years before" language that sometimes causes law students (and lawyers) so much trouble. However, when considered in the context of several simple examples, the language is not so difficult to fathom.[122]

Consider a debtor who filed her bankruptcy petition on March 20, 2007, and who owes unpaid income tax obligations for the past several years, extending through the 2003 tax year. If she owes income tax for 2006, the debt is entitled to priority under § 507 and is thus nondischargeable under § 523. The first part of § 507(a)(8)(A)(i) asks whether the tax owed is for a taxable year that ended before the date of the filing of the debtor's bankruptcy petition. Our debtor's bankruptcy petition was filed on March 20, 2007. Absent unusual circumstances, her 2006 taxable year ended at midnight on December 31, 2006, and thus her income tax liability for 2006 was for a taxable year that ended before her bankruptcy petition was filed.

Further, still following the text of § 507(A)(8)(A)(i), we must determine whether the deadline for any required return for the debtor's 2006 taxes was "after three years before" the date her petition was filed. The deadline for filing a federal tax return is usually April 15 of the year following the end of the tax year involved, so the normal deadline for the filing of this debtor's 2006 return would be April 15, 2007. Thus, the question is whether April 15, 2007, is sometime after "three years before" the date she filed her bankruptcy petition. The point in time three years before her bankruptcy petition was March 20, 2004. Put another way: Is April 15, 2007, *after* March 20, 2004? On our calendars it is. Because the debtor's 2006 tax year ended before her bankruptcy petition was filed, and because her 2006 return was due sometime after three years before her bankruptcy petition, the taxes she owes for the 2006 tax year are nondischargeable. The debtor's only hope is that there will be enough funds in her bankruptcy estate to ensure that this debt will be paid from funds she was going to lose to her creditors in the bankruptcy case anyway.

If the debtor still owes taxes for 2005, the result is the same. Her 2005 tax year ended before her bankruptcy petition was filed, and her 2005 return was due on April 15, 2006, which is *after* March 20, 2004. Thus, any unpaid income taxes she still owes for 2005 are nondischargeable.

Any taxes she still owes for 2004 will suffer the same fate because her 2004 return was due on April 15, 2005, which is still sometime *after* March 20, 2004. Worse yet, any taxes she owes from back in 2003 are also nondischargeable. Her 2003 tax return was due after three years before the date

[121] Bankruptcy Code § 508(a)(8)(A).

[122] In understanding the detailed operation of this rule, it is helpful to remember that the general statute of limitations for unpaid federal income taxes is three years. In a broad sense, income tax debts that are beyond this statute of limitations are dischargeable, while those that are still within the statute of limitations are nondischargeable. The text of § 507 closely follows the rules in the Internal Revenue Code regarding this statute of limitations for unpaid income taxes.

of her bankruptcy petition. The bankruptcy petition was March 20, 2007. Three years before that date was March 20, 2004, and her 2003 tax return was due twenty-five days *after* that date, on April 15, 2004.

Note that this debtor could have obtained a discharge of her 2003 taxes by waiting a month, until after April 15, 2007, to file her bankruptcy petition. Then, the April 15, 2004 due date for her 2003 return would have been *before* three years before his bankruptcy petition, and her 2003 tax debt, at least, would not fit the language of § 507(a)(8)(A)(i). Taxes due for 2004, 2005, and 2006 would still be nondischargeable.

If this debtor had sought an automatic extension for the due date for her 2003 return, until July 15, 2004, then she would have to wait until July 16, 2007, to file her bankruptcy petition to ensure that any 2003 income taxes still owed would be dischargeable. The problem with waiting, of course, is that the IRS (and other creditors) might in the meantime succeed in garnishing her wages, seizing her property, or simply obtaining a tax lien to secure the debt.

Although these examples refer to federal income tax obligations, neither § 507 nor § 523 are limited to taxes owed to the federal government. Income tax obligations owed to state and local authorities are nondischargeable under the same set of rules. In addition, other portions of § 507 prevent taxpayers from entering into settlement negotiations with tax collectors in an effort to obtain a delay that might result in another year's tax liabilities becoming dischargeable by falling outside the three year period.[123]

[ii] Property Taxes

A debtor's real estate and personal property taxes are entitled to priority under § 507 and are thus nondischargeable under § 523(a)(1) if the tax was "assessed before the commencement of the case and last payable without penalty *after one year before the date of the filing of the petition.*"[124] This language provides for a similar reach-back period to that applicable to income taxes, but it is for property taxes that were assessed less than one year before the date of the debtor's petition.

A debtor who filed her petition on March 20, 2007, would find that all of her property tax debts that were assessed before she filed her bankruptcy petition but that were payable without the imposition of a penalty sometime after March 20, 2006, are nondischargeable. The dischargeability of her debts depends on when any property taxes she owes were assessed and when, under applicable tax law, they were payable without the imposition of a penalty. If her 2005 real estate taxes were assessed on December 31, 2005, and could have been paid without the imposition of a penalty anytime after March 20, 2006, then they are nondischargeable. If the deadline for payment of her 2005 taxes, without the imposition of a penalty, was before March 20, 2006, the property tax is dischargeable.

[123] Bankruptcy Code § 507(a)(8)(A)(ii).

[124] Bankruptcy Code § 507(a)(8)(B).

Discharge of the debtor's tax liability does not affect the enforceability of any otherwise enforceable tax lien that has been imposed on her property. Thus, although the debtor might obtain a discharge of her personal liability for an earlier year's unpaid property tax, her property might remain subject to a lien for the unpaid tax.

[iii] Other Nondischargeable Priority Taxes

Section 507 also accords priority to taxes "required to be collected or withheld"; thus trust fund taxes, such as income and social security taxes withheld from employees' paychecks[125] and sales taxes collected from customers[126] are nondischargeable. The employer's share of social security taxes and federal unemployment taxes are entitled to a similar priority, also making them nondischargeable.[127] Significantly, this category includes the personal liability of a "responsible officer" for the employee's share of income and social security taxes that were withheld from an employee's pay but not remitted to the IRS.[128]

Finally, excise taxes and customs duties, entitled to priority under § 507(a)(8)(E) and (F) are also nondischargeable.

[iv] Tax Penalties

Section 507(a)(8)(G) provides that tax penalties that are related to a priority tax claim are also entitled to priority and thus are similarly nondischargeable, so long as the penalty imposed is "in compensation for actual pecuniary loss."[129] But this language must be read in conjunction with § 523(a)(7), which generally makes debts for a non-compensatory "fine, penalty, or forfeiture payable to and for the benefit of a governmental unit" nondischargeable. Exceptions to this rule leave tax penalties dischargeable if the penalty relates to an otherwise dischargeable tax or if the penalty was "imposed with respect to a transaction or event that occurred [more than] three years before the date of the filing of the petition."[130]

[v] Involuntary Gap Period Taxes

Taxes arising during the gap between the time an involuntary bankruptcy petition is filed and the time an order for relief is entered are entitled to priority under Bankruptcy Code § 507(a)(2) and are thus nondischargeable under § 523(a)(1)(A). In involuntary cases, an order for relief is entered, requiring the debtor's estate to be administered only if the petitioning creditors demonstrate that relief is warranted. Taxes accumulating between the

---

[125] *E.g.*, Billingsley v. United States (In re Billingsley), 146 B.R. 775 (Bankr. S.D. Ill. 1992).

[126] *E.g.*, Western Sur. Co. v. Waite (In re Waite), 698 F.2d 1177 (11th Cir. 1983) (taxes on liquor sales).

[127] Bankruptcy Code § 507(a)(8)(D); *e.g.*, In re Reichert, 138 B.R. 522 (Bankr. W.D. Mich. 1992) (federal unemployment tax).

[128] I.R.C. § 6672 (2000); *see* United States v. Sotelo, 436 U.S. 268 (1978).

[129] Bankruptcy Code § 507(a)(8)(G).

[130] Bankruptcy Code § 523(a)(7)(B).

filing of the creditors' petition and the entry of an order for relief are entitled to priority. If not paid as a result of the administration of the case, they are nondischargeable.

For example, if an involuntary petition is filed against a debtor on January 10, 2006, but the court does not enter an order for relief against the debtor until April 20 of that year, the debtor is likely to incur taxes during the interim. Any taxes that become due during this "involuntary gap" period are nondischargeable.[131]

[b] Taxes Owed on Unfiled or Late Filed Return

Debtors who file their tax returns late should not be surprised to learn that unpaid taxes associated with these returns cannot be discharged in bankruptcy.[132] If the debtor never filed a return, the tax owed is nondischargeable, regardless of how long ago the tax was incurred or when the return for the tax was due.[133] If a debtor failed to file a return for 1970, her 1970 tax debt is nondischargeable in a bankruptcy case commenced in 2007.

Debtors will find it difficult to evade the effect of § 523(a)(1)(B) by filing any overdue returns on the eve of bankruptcy. Section 523(a)(1)(B)(ii) makes taxes nondischargeable if the late return was filed "after two years before the date of the filing of the [bankruptcy] petition." Thus, to avoid these particular consequences of having failed to file a tax return, a debtor must file her return more than two years before the filing of her bankruptcy petition. Further, the "after two years before" language makes it clear that delaying the return until after the date of the petition achieves nothing. A return filed after the date the bankruptcy petition is still filed sometime *after* the point in time two years before the petition. If the petition is filed on March 20, 2007, a tax return filed on March 30, 2007, is "after" March 20, 2005.

[c] Fraudulent Tax Returns

Debtors who attempt to evade their taxes by filing fraudulent returns or by otherwise willfully attempting to evade tax liabilities receive similar treatment. A tax "with respect to which the debtor made a fraudulent return or willfully attempted in any manner to evade or defeat such tax" is nondischargeable.[134] The date the tax or return was due or filed is irrelevant.

[d] Debts Incurred to Pay Nondischargeable Taxes

Sections 523(a)(14) and 523(a)(14A) make debts incurred to pay a nondischargeable tax owed either to the United States or to any other

[131] *See* § 10.04[A][3] Involuntary Gap Creditors, *supra*.

[132] Bankruptcy Code § 523(a)(1)(B).

[133] In re Bergstrom, 949 F.2d 341 (10th Cir. 1991).

[134] Bankruptcy Code § 523(a)(1)(C).

governmental unit nondischargeable.[135] Thus, a debtor may not evade the effect of § 523(a)(1) by borrowing the funds necessary to repay her tax debts and then seeking a discharge of the loan. The creditor need not prove that the debtor borrowed the funds as part of a fraudulent scheme to attempt to discharge an otherwise nondischargeable debt. However, in order to support a finding of nondischargeability, the lender must trace the amount of the borrowed funds to the repayment of the nondischargeable tax debt.

[2] Debts Fraudulently Incurred[136]

Section 523(a)(2) makes debts incurred through various types of fraud nondischargeable.[137] Debtors who dishonestly obtain money, property, or services, or who obtain an extension, renewal, or refinancing of existing credit remain liable for these debts after their bankruptcy case has been concluded. This result implements the broad general policy of the Bankruptcy Code of providing a fresh start to "honest debtors." Those who have behaved dishonorably in their dealings with their creditors are not entitled to be relieved from debts owed to creditors they have defrauded.

Section 523(a)(2) divides this basis for nondischargeability into two main categories. The broadest of these makes debts incurred through "false pretenses, a false representation, or actual fraud," nondischargeable.[138] Debts incurred through the use of a false financial statement are dealt with separately.[139]

[a] Actual Fraud

To have a debt determined to be nondischargeable due to actual fraud, other than through the use of a false financial statement, a creditor must establish:

- the debtor made false representations to the creditor;[140]

---

[135] Bankruptcy Code § 523(a)(14)-(14A).

[136] Margaret Howard, *Shifting Risk and Fixing Blame: The Vexing Problem of Credit Card Obligations in Bankruptcy*, 75 Am. Bankr. L.J. 63, 143 (2001); Richard H. Gibson, *Credit Card Dischargeability: Two Cheers for the Common Law and Some Modest Proposals for Legislative Reform*, 74 Am. Bankr. L.J. 129 (2000); David F. Snow, *The Dischargeability of Credit Card Debt: New Developments and the Need for a New Direction*, 72 Am. Bankr. L.J. 63 (1998); Lawrence M. Ausubel, *Credit Card Defaults, Credit Card Profits, and Bankruptcy*, 71 Am. Bankr. L.J. 249 (1997); Barry L. Zaretsky, *The Fraud Exception to Discharge Under the New Bankruptcy Code*, 53 Am. Bankr. L.J. 253 (1979); *see also* Elizabeth Lea Black, Annotation, *Credit Card Debt as Nondischargeable under Bankruptcy Code Provision Concerning Nondischargeability of Individual Debt Obtained Through False Pretenses, False Representation, or Actual Fraud, Other than Statement Respecting Debtor's or Insider's Financial Condition*, 158 A.L.R. Fed. 189 (1999).

[137] Bankruptcy Code § 523(a)(2).

[138] Bankruptcy Code § 523(a)(2)(A).

[139] Bankruptcy Code § 523(a)(2)(B).

[140] *But see* In re McClellan v. Cantrell, 217 F.3d 890 (7th Cir. 2000) (fraudulent conveyance constituted actual fraud, despite lack of misrepresentation).

- the debtor knew the representations were false;
- the debtor made the representations with the intent of deceiving the creditor;
- the creditor relied on the representations; and
- the creditor sustained a loss as a result of the debtor's misrepresentations.[141]

The most troublesome issues have been proof of the debtor's intent and the extent of the creditor's reliance on the debtor's representations.

Many cases involve charges to credit cards. A debtor's use of a credit card is often treated as an implied representation to the credit card company that the cardholder intends to pay the charges incurred.[142] The debtor's representation of her intent to pay occurs not at the time the credit card was initially obtained, but at the time she incurred the charges in question.

A debtor who intended to pay, but who was unable to pay at the time her debts were incurred, might also run afoul of § 523(a)(2)(A). Recently, however, courts have begun to reject the contention that use of a credit card implies the debtor's representation that she is in fact able to pay for the goods or services acquired with the use of the card.[143] The standard should be the debtor's intent to repay rather than her ability to repay, even though her knowledge of any inability to pay may be a relevant factor in the inquiry concerning into the debtor's intent. Thus, the debtor's inability to pay for transactions charged to her account is evidence of fraud, but it is not dispositive.

Most courts employ a wide variety of factors to evaluate the debtor's intent to repay charges to her credit card. These factors frequently include the time between use of the card and the debtor's bankruptcy; whether the debtor consulted an attorney about bankruptcy before incurring the charges; the number of charges; the amount of the charges; the debtor's financial condition when the card was used; whether any credit limit was exceeded; whether multiple charges were made on the same day; whether the debtor was employed; the debtor's employment prospects; the debtor's financial sophistication; whether the debtor's buying habits changed suddenly; and whether the card was used to purchase luxuries or necessities.[144]

The level of the creditor's reliance necessary to make the debt nondischargeable has been the subject of some debate. Although courts at one time

[141] McCrory v. Spigel (In re Spigel), 260 F.3d 27, 32 (1st Cir. 2001); American Express Travel Related Serv. Co. v. Hahemi, 104 F.3d 1122 (9th Cir. 1996).

[142] AT & T Universal Card Servs. v. Mercer (In re Mercer), 246 F.3d 391, 404 (5th Cir. 2001).

[143] *See* In re Mercer, 246 F.3d 391 (5th Cir. 2001).

[144] *See* Citibank S.D., N.A. v. Dougherty (In re Dougherty), 84 B.R. 653, 657 (B.A.P. 9th Cir. 1988). Other courts have rejected their use as not reflective of the statutory subjective standard in § 523(a)(2)(A). *E.g.*, American Express Travel Related Servs. Co., Inc. v. Christensen (In re Christensen), 193 B.R. 863, 866 (N.D. Ill. 1996) (multi-factor "objective" test inconsistent with common-law "subjective" standard).

required "reasonable" reliance on the a debtor's intentionally false representation, the United States Supreme Court ruled in *Field v. Mans* that this standard was too stringent.[145] Instead, "justifiable" reliance is regarded as sufficient.[146] The precise point of demarcation between "reasonable" reliance and mere "justifiable" reliance remains unclear. Cases interpreting *Field* have indicated that an issuer of a credit card company justifiably relies on a debtor's representation of intent to pay as long as the account is not in default and any initial investigations into the debtor's credit report "did not raise red flags that would make reliance unjustifiable."[147] Thus, although creditors have no affirmative duty to investigate the truth of the debtor's representations, the creditor cannot purport to rely on "preposterous representations or close his eyes to avoid discovery of the truth."[148]

At least one court has held that credit card charges are dischargeable, despite the debtor's misrepresentation of their intent to repay, if the creditor fails to conduct a sufficient inquiry into the debtor's financial circumstances.[149] And, in *In re Curtis,* a college-educated investor was held not to have justifiably relied on the debtor's promise of a 2,000% return on a risk-free investment of $100,000, making the debtor's obligation to return the funds dischargeable despite the debtor's obviously fraudulent intent.[150]

It may be thought that a debtor who has passed a bad check in payment for goods or services runs afoul of § 523(a)(2)(A). However, the mere fact that a check has been dishonored due to insufficient funds is not, standing alone, sufficient to constitute fraud. Issuance of the check is a "promise" as required by § 523(a)(2)(A).[151] But the fact that a check is dishonored due to insufficient funds does not necessarily reflect any fraudulent intent on the part of the debtor when she issued the check. The check might have been written on insufficient funds because of a the drawer's mistake about the balance in her account.[152] Or the debtor might have intended to make a subsequent deposit of funds sufficient to cover the item. If so, the debtor lacks the necessary fraudulent intent necessary for the debt to be declared nondischargeable under § 523(a)(2)(A).

---

[145] Field v. Mans, 516 U.S. 59, 75 (1995).

[146] *See* Lentz v. Spadoni (In re Spadoni), 316 F.3d 56 (1st Cir. 2003).

[147] In re Anastas, 94 F.3d 1280, 1296 (9th Cir. 1996).

[148] In re Hashemi, 104 F.3d 1122, 1126 (9th Cir. 1996); In re Mercer, 246 F.3d 391, 421 (5th Cir. 2001).

[149] In re Ellingsworth, 212 B.R. 326 (Bankr. W.D. Mo. 1997); *but see* Bankruptcy Abuse Prevention and Consumer Protection Act of 2005, Pub. L. No. 109-8, § 1229, 119 Stat. 23, 200 (sense of Congress provision casting doubt on *Ellingsworth*).

[150] In re Curtis, 345 B.R. 870 (Bankr. N.D. Ill. 2006).

[151] Goldberg Sec., Inc. v. Scarlata (In re Scarlata), 979 F.2d 521 (7th Cir. 1992); Bednarsz v. Stanislaw Brzakala (In re Brzakala), 305 B.R. 705, 710 (Bankr. N.D. Ill. 2004). The drawer of a check issues an "order." U.C.C. § 3-104 (2003).

[152] As students of the law of commercial paper know, the account might even have been drawn down because of checks containing a forgery of the drawer's signature, which, because they were not properly payable from the drawer's account, should not have been paid. *See* U.C.C. § 4-401 (2003).

However, a debtor who issues a bad check with the intent not to pay its amount commits garden variety fraud by misrepresenting her intent to perform the obligation for which the check was issued.[153] Thus, obligations incurred in check-kiting or other similarly dishonest schemes are nondischargeable.[154] Likewise, obligations incurred on the eve of bankruptcy, after the debtor has already formed the intent to file a bankruptcy proceeding, are nondischargeable due to fraud.

[b] Luxury Goods or Services

Section 523(a)(2)(C)(i)(I) establishes a rebuttable presumption of fraud for consumer debts owed to a single creditor for "luxury goods or services" and aggregating more than $550 "within 90 days before the order for relief."[155] The rule seems to be based on the premise that debtors who incur such charges do so without the intent to repay their debts.

The most difficult question has been determining what types of purchases qualify as "luxury goods or services." Luxury goods or services do not include those which are "reasonably *necessary* for the support or maintenance of a debtor or a dependent of the debtor."[156] Note, however, that this does not exempt charges that were reasonably necessary for support or maintenance from a claim that they are nondischargeable. It merely exempts them from the burden of the presumption that they were incurred through fraud.

Cases interpreting § 523(a)(2)(C) have examined the circumstances surrounding the purchase to determine whether the item should be classified as a luxury item. In particular, courts have inquired into whether the items purchased served any significant family function and whether the transaction evidenced some fiscal irresponsibility. Purchases that are "extravagant, indulgent, or nonessential under the circumstances are considered luxury goods."[157] In *Carroll & Sain v. Vernon*, legal services necessary to obtain a divorce were not regarded as a luxury and thus did not raise this evidentiary presumption in the creditor's favor.[158] In *In re Allen,* where most of the debtor's charges were made at gas stations, grocery stores, department stores such as Wal-Mart, Sears, and J.C. Penney, a pharmacy, and several restaurants, the court was unwilling, without further information about the

---

[153] *E.g.*, In re Mercer, 246 F.3d 391 (5th Cir. 2001) (listing factors used to determine absence of intent to perform).

[154] *See* In re Eashai, 87 F.3d 1082 (9th Cir. 1996).

[155] Bankruptcy Code § 523(a)(2)(C)(i)(I). Prior to the 2005 Amendments, this provision applied to consumer debts to a single creditor for luxury goods or services incurred during the last 60 days before the debtor's petition aggregating more than $1,000. Expansion of the time period in which the charges were incurred and reducing the dollar threshold, expanded this category of nondischargeability.

[156] Bankruptcy Code § 523(a)(2)(C)(ii)(II) (emphasis supplied). This language has recently changed. Prior to 2005 "luxury goods or services" were those not "reasonably *acquired*" for support or maintenance.

[157] In re McDonald, 129 B.R. 279 (Bankr. M.D. Fla. 1991).

[158] 192 B.R. 165 (Bankr. N.D. Ill. 1996).

nature of the transactions, to regard the transactions as involving purchases of luxury goods or services. Without more specific information about the items purchased (a hamburger and fries or filet mignon?), a mere listing of the merchant's name and the amount of the charge was not sufficient to raise the presumption.[159] However, in *In re Simpson*,[160] the court had little difficulty in concluding that charges for over $200,000 in gambling losses in the period immediately before the debtor's bankruptcy petition were "luxury goods or services" and thus presumably nondischargeable, even though it remains a question whether gambling losses constitute "consumer debts."[161]

Decisions like the one in *In re Olwan*,[162] and *In re Woodman*,[163] regarding a debtor's pre-petition purchase of tobacco products, raises the question of how the 2005 change to § 523(a)(2)(C) regarding what is regarded as "luxury goods and services" will be applied. Before BAPCPA, luxury goods and services excluded purchases that were "reasonably acquired" for the maintenance or support of the debtor and the debtor's dependents. BAPCPA narrowed the exclusion to only those goods or services that are "reasonably necessary" for the maintenance or support of the debtor. This language matches that used for determining disposable income under Chapter 13 (and the means test), and may bring the standard for what does not qualify as luxury goods or services *in pari materia* with the standard for the kinds of expenses that are not to be deducted in determining a debtor's disposable income in determining amounts that must be devoted to payments under a Chapter 13 plan. In making this decision in a Chapter 13 case, the *Woodman* court remarked:

> If smoking is "bad" and therefore not "reasonably necessary," could not similar arguments be made in favor of ruling that any Chapter 13 debtor's expense, however minimal, for alcohol (even one can of beer), lottery tickets (a single one), cosmetics, sugared breakfast cereal, candy bars, or even, say, scented soap is never reasonably necessary, as well? Could not the same be said as to automobiles that seat more than (or fewer than), say, four adults, or achieve less than twenty-three-point-five miles-per-gallon?

Applying § 523(a)(2)(C)'s presumption regarding luxury goods and services inherently involves moral judgments that may not be well-suited to judicial determination.

---

[159] 296 B.R. 849 (Bankr. N.D. Ala. 2003); *see also* In re Zeman, 347 B.R. 28 (Bankr. W.D. Tex. 2006) (judge suggested that creditor's lack of proof that receipts from fast-food restaurants, discount retailers, grocery store, movie theater, and beauty salon were for luxury goods and services was nothing more than a "shake-down" tactic that might warrant Rule 9011 sanctions).

[160] 319 B.R. 256 (Bankr. M.D. Fla. 2003).

[161] Richard I. Aaron, *Collection of Gambling Debts and the Bankruptcy Reform Act of 2005*, 9 Gaming L. Rev. 299 (2005).

[162] 312 B.R. 476 (Bankr. E.D.N.Y. 2004).

[163] 287 B.R. 589 (Bankr. D. Maine 2003).

The presumption applies only to "consumer debts," which are defined as those incurred "by an individual primarily for a personal, family, or household purposes."[164] Debts incurred for a business purpose, however extravagant or frivolous they may be, do not fit within the presumption.

[c] Cash Advances

A similar presumption of nondischargeability due to fraud applies to "cash advances aggregating more than $825 that are extensions of consumer credit under an open end credit plan obtained by an individual debtor on or within 70 days before the order for relief."[165] Here, the purpose of the cash advance does not matter.

Debtors on the verge of bankruptcy are presumed to have made such withdrawals without the intent to repay, even if the charges are incurred for food, clothing, or shelter. Thus, debtors who use their credit cards to purchase "reasonably necessary" items are not faced with the presumption of § 523(a)(2)(C)(i)(I), but those who withdraw cash to make the same type of purchases need to rebut the presumption of § 523(a)(2)(C)(i)(II).

The presumption of course can be rebutted. However, courts have reached different conclusions about the effect of the presumption.[166] Some courts adhere to Federal Rule of Evidence 301 and treat the presumption as doing nothing more than shifting the burden of going forward with evidence regarding the debtor's fraud and leaving the ultimate burden of proof on the creditor.[167] Other courts have treated the presumption of placing the burden of proving that the debt is dischargeable "squarely on the shoulders of the debtor."[168]

The presumptions of § 523(a)(2)(C) can be overcome by evidence that the debtor experienced a sudden change in circumstances or that the debtor did not contemplate filing a bankruptcy petition until after the transaction took place.[169] In *In re Davis*, the debtor successfully rebutted the presumption by demonstrating that she had commenced payments on charges for luxury items according to the terms of her contract with the creditor before filing bankruptcy.[170] In *In re Leaird*, the debtor rebutted the presumption by explaining that he had purchased the luxury goods on an impulse and did not form the intent to file for bankruptcy until after the purchases had been made.[171] Finally, in *In re Manning*, the debtor successfully rebutted the presumption that his repeated transfers of balances from one credit card

164 Bankruptcy Code § 101(8).

165 Bankruptcy Code § 523(a)(2)(C)(i)(II). Before BAPCPA, the thresholds were $1,225 advanced within sixty days of the debtor's petition.

166 In re Manning, 280 B.R. 171 (Bankr. S.D. Ohio 2002).

167 *E.g.*, Sears, Roebuck & Co. v. Green (In re Green), 296 B.R. 173 (Bankr. C.D. Ill. 2003).

168 *E.g.*, Novus Servs., Inc. v. Cron (In re Cron), 241 B.R. 1, 8 (Bankr. S.D. Iowa 1999).

169 Sears, Roebuck & Co. v. Green (In re Green), 296 B.R. 173 (Bankr. C.D. Ill. 2003).

170 56 B.R. 120 (Bankr. D. Mont. 1985).

171 106 B.R. 177 (Bankr. D. Wis. 1989).

account to another account that offered a lower introductory rate was not a fraudulent credit card kite, but was part of his attempt to keep afloat financially until obligations imposed by the divorce court had ended.[172] In all of these cases, facts demonstrating the circumstances of the charges that were consistent with the debtor's intent to repay were sufficient to rebut the presumption of fraud.

[d] False Financial Statements

Section 523(a)(2)(B) carves out a separate rule for debtors who use a false financial statement to incur or restructure a debt. Loan application forms usually seek information concerning a debtor's obligations, assets, and income. A debtor's exaggeration of her assets or income or an omission of her debts could easily lead to a claim that the debt owed to the creditor who relied on the information from the debtor is nondischargeable.

On the other hand, loan and credit card application forms usually provide only a few lines for the debtor to list all of her debts. Moreover, loan applicants are sometimes advised by the creditor's loan officer to list only their most important debts on these applications.[173] In addition, creditors nearly always obtain credit reports to gain a fuller picture of their borrower's ability to pay. These factors make it difficult for a creditor to successfully pursue a complaint that debt is nondischargeable under § 523(a)(2)(B).

In order to have a debt declared nondischargeable because of an inaccurate financial statement, a creditor must show that (1) the statement is in writing;[174] (2) it is materially false; (3) it is a statement regarding the financial condition of the debtor or an insider; (4) the creditor to whom the debt is owed reasonably relied on the statement; and (5) the debtor supplied the statement with the intent to deceive the creditor.[175]

[i] Written Statement

Section 523(a)(2)(B) requires that the debtor's statement about her financial condition be "in writing." The debtor's oral representations about her financial condition may not be used to have a debt ruled nondischargeable.

[ii] Materially False

Misinformation about a debtor's substantial debts, assets, or income is likely to be regarded as material, as these matters have a "natural tendency to influence" a creditor's decision about whether to advance a loan.[176]

---

[172] National City Bank v. Manning (In re Manning), 280 B.R. 171 (Bankr. S.D. Ohio 2002).

[173] H.R. Rep. No. 95-595, 130–131 (1977), *reprinted in* 1978 U.S.C.C.A.N 5787, 6091.

[174] *See* In re Gulevsky, 362 F.3d 961 (7th Cir. 2004).

[175] Bankruptcy Code § 523(a)(2)(B); *see* Insurance Co. of N. Am. v. Cohn (In re Cohn), 54 F.3d 1108 (3d Cir. 1995); In re Bogstad, 779 F.2d 370 (7th Cir. 1985).

[176] United States v. Keefer, 799 F.2d 1115, 1127 (6th Cir. 1986); *cf.* Kungys v. United States, 485 U.S. 759, 771 (1988).

Likewise, inaccurate information on a financial statement is material if it "influences a creditor's decision to extend credit [or] if it is so substantial that a reasonable person would have relied upon it, even if the creditor did not in fact rely upon it in the case at hand."[177]

[iii] Debtor or Insider's Financial Condition

Section 523(a)(2)(B) applies only to a debtor's inaccurate statements regarding his financial condition or regarding the financial condition of an "insider" of the debtor. Such statements usually consist of a schedule of assets, liabilities, and income that reflects a debtor's net worth,[178] cash flow, or both.

The reference to the debtor's "insiders"[179] is most likely to be important with respect to representations about the financial condition of the debtor's spouse[180] or of a partnership or corporation for which the debtor is a general partner, officer, or director.

False representations regarding other matters are dealt with in § 523(a)(2)(A), nondischargeability due to fraud, discussed above.[181]

[iv] Creditor's Reasonable Reliance

Whether a creditor has "reasonably relied" on the debtor's false financial statement depends on a variety of factors. Courts examine the extent to which the creditor acted in compliance with its normal business practices, as well as the extent to which it followed the standards or customs of others in the creditor's industry in evaluating the debtor's credit worthiness.[182] Quite naturally, a creditor who has obtained a credit report with accurate information about the debtor's credit history or other financial condition is unable to claim that it "reasonably relied" on conflicting inaccurate information in a financial statement supplied by the debtor.[183]

A few courts have held that a creditor who fails to take simple steps to verify the accuracy of a debtor's financial statement assumes the risk that it contains inaccurate information; this preserves the dischargeability of the debt despite the debtor's factual misrepresentations.[184] However, this

[177] Insurance Co. of N. Am. v. Cohn (In re Cohn), 54 F.3d 1108 (3d Cir. 1995).

[178] *See, e.g.*, In re Batie, 995 F.2d 85, 90 (6th Cir. 1993).

[179] "Insider" is defined in Bankruptcy Code § 101(31).

[180] In re Batie, 995 F.2d 85, 90 (6th Cir. 1993).

[181] *See* § 13.03[B][2][a] Actual Fraud, *supra*.

[182] Insurance Co. of Am. v. Cohn (In re Cohn), 54 F.3d 1108, 1114, 1117 (3d Cir. 1995).

[183] Under § 523(a)(2)(B), the statutory standard is "reasonable" reliance. In *Field v. Mans*, the Supreme Court interpreted § 523(a)(2)(A) to impose a lesser standard of "justifiable" reliance.

516 U.S. 59 (1995). Thus, the standard for the level of a creditor's reliance that is necessary to have a debt determined nondischargeable under § 523(a)(2) varies slightly depending on whether the debt is claimed to be nondischargeable due to the fraudulent use of a false financial statement or due to some other type of fraudulent misrepresentation.

[184] In re Ward, 857 F.2d 1082 (6th Cir. 1988).

assumption of the risk approach has been rejected in cases involving credit cards, where courts have held that each use of the card involves an independent promise to pay for the charges incurred.[185] A creditor who disbelieves the information contained on the debtor's financial statement cannot claim to have relied on it.[186]

The reliance standard of § 523(a)(2)(B) is different from that under § 523(a)(2)(A), where the Supreme Court has ruled that only "justifiable reliance" need be shown.[187] The "reasonable reliance" standard of § 523(a)(2)(B) is harder to satisfy, though quantifying the difference between "justifiable" and "reasonable" reliance is difficult.

[v] Intent to Deceive

Finally, the debtor must have supplied the false financial statement with the intent to deceive the creditor. The debtor's intent to deceive can be established either through a showing of her subjective intent to trick the creditor or through evidence exhibiting the debtor's reckless disregard for the truth or falsity of information in her financial statement.[188]

[e] Securities Fraud

Section 523(a)(19) makes debts incurred through securities fraud nondischargeable, regardless of whether the liability was incurred as a result of a violation of Federal securities laws or regulations, state securities laws or regulations, or "common law fraud, deceit, or manipulation in connection with purchase or sale of any security."[189] To fit within the scope of this category of nondischargeable debts, the liability must be based on a judgment, settlement agreement, court order, or administrative decree.[190] Thus, § 523(a)(19) merely gives preclusive effect to a prior judgment or settlement and makes the liability imposed on the debtor as a result of that judgment or settlement nondischargeable.[191]

[3] Unscheduled Debts

Debts not listed on the schedule of debts filed in conjunction with the debtor's bankruptcy petition may be excluded from the scope of the debtor's discharge. The purpose of § 523(a)(3) is to ensure that creditors will have time to file a proof of claim in the case. Thus, a debt is nondischargeable

---

185 *E.g.*, In re Burdge, 198 B.R. 773 (B.A.P. 9th Cir. 1996).

186 Shaw Steel, Inc. v. Morris, 240 B.R. 553 (N.D. Ill. 1999), *aff'd*, 223 F.3d 548 (7th Cir. 2000).

187 Field v. Mans, 516 U.S. 59 (1995).

188 Insurance Co. of N. Am. v. Cohn (In re Cohn), 54 F.3d 1108, 1119 (3d Cir. 1995); In re Batie, 995 F.2d 85 (6th Cir. 1993).

189 Bankruptcy Code § 523(a)(19)(A).

190 Bankruptcy Code § 523(a)(19)(B).

191 *E.g.*, Frost v. Civiello (In re Civiello), 348 B.R. 459 (Bankr. N.D. Ohio 2006).

if the debtor has not scheduled it in time for the creditor to file a "timely . . . proof of claim."[192]

In no-asset cases, where the notice sent to creditors about the bankruptcy case advises them that there is no need to file a claim, the deadline to file a proof of claim is never imposed, and thus the debtor's failure to schedule a debt does not make it nondischargeable. In cases where there are no assets to distribute to creditors, the right to file a proof of claim is meaningless. In such cases, a creditor omitted from the debtor's schedules is not harmed by the debtor's failure.[193]

In the case of debts that are dischargeable under § 523(a)(2), (4), (6), or (15), the debt must be scheduled in time for the creditor to permit both a "timely filing of a proof of claim and [a] timely request for a determination of dischargeability."[194] Because the bankruptcy court has exclusive jurisdiction to determine the dischargeability of such debts, they must be scheduled by the debtor in time for creditors to bring their right to have the debt determined nondischargeable under these provisions. Some courts have read § 523(a)(3)(B) expansively, including debts for which the creditor had only a colorable claim for nondischargeability under these provisions.[195]

However, the debtor's failure to schedule the debt does not result in nondischargeability if the creditor had "notice or actual knowledge of the [bankruptcy] case in time" to meet the deadline in question. Thus, even if the debtor failed to schedule a debt, if the creditor learns of the bankruptcy through other means, the unscheduled debt remains dischargeable.

[4] Fraud or Defalcation in a Fiduciary Capacity; Embezzlement; Larceny[196]

Section 523(a)(4) specifies that a debt for "fraud or defalcation while acting in a fiduciary capacity, embezzlement, or larceny" is nondischargeable.[197] Debts incurred through most other types of fraud are, of course, made nondischargeable by § 523(a)(2).[198]

The references to fraud, embezzlement, and larceny in § 523(a)(4), as well as nondischargeability under § 523(a)(2) of all debts fraudulently incurred, raises the question of whether "defalcation" refers to a lower standard of

---

[192] Bankruptcy Code § 523(a)(3).

[193] Judd v. Wolfe (In re Judd), 78 F.3d 110 (3d Cir. 1996); Horizon Aviation of Va., Inc. v. Alexander, 296 B.R. 380 (E.D. Va. 2003); *see also* In re Madaj, 149 F.3d 467 (6th Cir. 1998).

[194] Bankruptcy Code § 523(a)(3)(B).

[195] *See, e.g.*, Haga v. National Union Fire Ins. Co. (In re Haga), 131 B.R. 320, 327 (Bankr. W.D. Tex. 1991).

[196] Peter M. Reinhardt & William G. Horlbeck, *Defalcation While Acting in a Fiduciary Capacity: What Does it Mean?*, 24 Colo. Law. 1773 (1995); Jennifer Liotta, Comment, *ERISA Fiduciaries in Bankruptcy: Preserving Individual Liability for Defalcation and Fraud Debts under 11 U.S.C. § 523(a)(4)*, 22 Emory Bankr. Dev. J. 725 (2006).

[197] Bankruptcy Code § 523(a)(4).

[198] *See* § 13.03[B][2] Debts Fraudulently Incurred, *supra*.

misconduct.[199] Courts have interpreted § 523(a)(4) in three different ways.[200] Some courts permit § 523(a)(4) to apply to any kind of loss by a fiduciary in breach of her fiduciary obligation, even if it was by mistake or otherwise innocent.[201] Some courts apply it only when the fiduciary's conduct was at least negligent.[202] Other courts limit it to reckless or even more serious defalcations.[203]

Some years ago, the Supreme Court ruled that the exception for fiduciary capacity under the former Bankruptcy Act applied only to express trusts and not to equitable trusts created by the debtor's conduct.[204] Thus, it does not apply to breaches of duties by mere agents whose responsibilities rise to the level of a fiduciary obligation,[205] such as that one owed by a trustee to the beneficiaries of a trust[206] or by an attorney to her client.[207]

In addition, § 523(a)(11) and (12) provide special rules for certain types of debts owed to federal depositary institutions. Section 523(a)(11) makes such debts nondischargeable if they are for a judgment, order, or consent decree "arising from any act of fraud or defalcation while acting in a fiduciary capacity committed with respect to any depositary institution or insured credit union."[208] Section 523(a)(12) applies more specifically to any "malicious or reckless failure to fulfill any commitment . . . to a Federal depositary institutions [sic] regulatory agency to maintain the capital of an insured depositary institution."[209]

---

[199] *See* Central Hanover Bank & Trust Co. v. Herbst, 93 F.2d 510 (2d Cir. 1937) (Hand, J.).

[200] Putanen v. Baylis (In re Baylis), 313 F.3d 9, 18 (1st Cir. 2002).

[201] *E.g.*, Republic of Rwanda v. Uwimana (In re Uwimana), 274 F.3d 806 (4th Cir. 2001); Commonwealth Land Title Co. v. Blaszak (In re Blaszak), 397 F.3d 386 (6th Cir. 2005); Mountbatten Sur. Co. v. McCormick (In re McCormick), 283 B.R. 680 (Bankr. W.D. Pa. 2002).

[202] Antlers Roof-Truss & Builders Supply v. Storie (In re Storie), 216 B.R. 283 (B.A.P. 10th Cir. 1997).

[203] *E.g.*, Schwager v. Fallas (In re Schwager), 121 F.3d 177 (5th Cir. 1997); Rutanen v. Baylis (In re Baylis), 313 F.3d 9, 20 (1st Cir. 2002).

[204] Davis v. Aetna Acceptance Co., 293 U.S. 328, 333 (1934) (interpreting former Bankruptcy Act § 17(a)(4)); Peerless Ins. v. Swanson (In re Swanson), 231 B.R. 145, 148 (Bankr. D.N.H. 1999).

[205] Angelle v. Reed (In re Angelle), 610 F.2d 1335 (5th Cir. 1980); Quaif v. Johnson, 4 F.3d 950 (11th Cir. 1993) (insurance agent).

[206] *See generally* Fowler Bros. v. Young (In re Young), 91 F.3d 1367 (10th Cir. 1996).

[207] *E.g.*, Ball v. McDowell (In re McDowell), 162 B.R. 136 (N.D. Ohio 1993).

[208] Bankruptcy Code § 523(a)(11).

[209] Bankruptcy Code § 523(a)(12).

[5] Family Obligations[210]

The Bankruptcy Code historically has drawn a sharp distinction between support obligations, which have never been dischargeable, and debts owed to a former spouse as a result of a property settlement or for some other reason.[211] For many years, the latter were dischargeable but the former were not. In 1994, Congress expanded the nondischargeability of family obligations by making the dischargeability of domestic obligations, other than those for support, dependent on the application of two alternative tests that address either the debtor's ability to pay or the relative hardship on the debtor and the creditor if the debt were discharged.[212] In 2005, these tests were removed, making nearly all support and property settlement obligations nondischargeable. This reflects a general expansion, over a period of time, of the classes of nondischargeable debts.

[a] Domestic Support Obligations

Section 523(a)(5) contains the traditional rule that any debt "for a domestic support obligation" is nondischargeable.[213] Domestic support obligations are defined broadly to include nearly every imaginable type of support obligation[214] owed to the debtor's spouse, a former spouse, the debtor's child, a parent or guardian of the debtor's child, or to even a governmental unit.[215] The support obligation qualifies for nondischargeability if it was established in any one of a wide variety of ways, including a separation agreement, a divorce decree, a property settlement agreement, a court order, or an order of any other governmental unit.[216] But the obligation is not a domestic support obligation if it has been "assigned to a non-governmental entity," unless the obligation was assigned voluntarily by the creditor for the purpose of collecting the debt.[217]

---

[210] Peter C. Alexander, *Building "A Doll's House": A Feminist Analysis of Marital Debt Dischargeability in Bankruptcy*, 48 Vill. L. Rev. 381 (2003); James H. Gold, *The Dischargeability of Divorce Obligations Under the Bankruptcy Code: Five Faulty Premises in the Application of Section 523(a)(5)*, 39 Case W. Res. L. Rev. 455 (1989); Veryl Victoria Miles, *The Nondischargeability of Divorce-Based Debts in Bankruptcy: A Legislative Response to the Hardened Heart*, 60 Alb. L. Rev. 1171 (1997); Sheryl L. Scheible, *Bankruptcy and the Modification of Support: Fresh Start, Head Start, or False Start?*, 69 N.C. L. Rev. 577 (1991); Jana B. Singer, *Divorce Obligations and Bankruptcy Discharge: Rethinking the Support/Property Distinction*, 30 Harv. J. on Legis. 43 (1993); Catherine E. Vance, *Till Debt Do Us Part: Irreconcilable Differences in the Unhappy Union of Bankruptcy and Divorce*, 45 Buff. L. Rev. 369 (1997).

[211] *E.g.*, In re Farelli, 347 B.R. 501 (Bankr. W.D. Pa. 2006).

[212] *See* Pub. L. No. 103-394, § 304(e), 108 Stat 4106, 4133 (repealed) (formerly codified at 11 U.S.C. § 523(a)(15)(A), (B) (2000).

[213] Bankruptcy Code § 523(a)(5).

[214] Section 101(14A)(B) includes any debt that is "in the nature of alimony, maintenance, or support (including assistance provided by a governmental unit . . .) whether such debt is expressly so designated." Bankruptcy Code § 101(14A)(B).

[215] Bankruptcy Code § 101(14A)(A).

[216] Bankruptcy Code § 101(14A)(C).

[217] Bankruptcy Code § 101(14A)(D).

[b] Other Obligations to a Spouse, Former Spouse, or Child

Section 523(a)(5) deals with support obligations. But divorcing spouses also frequently owe property settlement and other obligations to one other. For example, if one spouse keeps the marital home, he or she will likely be obligated to pay the other for his or her joint ownership in the property. In addition, divorce and separation agreements frequently provide for one spouse to pay specific marital debts and hold the other spouse "harmless" for the obligation. Creditors, of course, are not bound by these agreements and may seek recovery from either spouse, regardless of the agreement between the divorcing couple. After the 2005 Amendments, these obligations are completely nondischargeable, without regard to the debtor's ability to pay or to the relative impact on the other spouse. Thus, the traditional distinction between support and property settlement, no longer needs to be made.

[6] Wilful and Malicious Injury

Section 523(a)(6) makes any debt for a "wilful and malicious injury" to a person or property nondischargeable. This makes liability for traditional intentional torts, such as assault, battery,[218] intentional infliction of emotional distress,[219] invasion of privacy,[220] and trespass nondischargeable.[221] It also embraces more modern causes of action, such as intentional sexual harassment,[222] copyright infringement,[223] and intentional illegal discrimination of all types.[224]

[a] Recklessness

However, liability for reckless or negligent conduct does not fall within the ambit of § 523(a)(6). In the 1998 decision *Kawaauhau v. Geiger*, the Supreme Court reviewed the history of § 523(a)(6) and rejected language in a much older case that had suggested that liability for any voluntary

[218] *E.g.*, In re Chapman, 46 B.R. 90 (Bankr. N.D. Ohio 1980); In re Brown, 263 B.R. 832 (Bankr. S.D. Ohio 2000) (homicide); In re Love, 47 B.R. 349 (Bankr. W.D. Mo. 2006) (child molestation).

[219] In re Elder, 262 B.R. 799 (C.D. Cal. 2001) (stalking); In re Cunningham, 59 B.R. 743 (Bankr. N.D. Ill. 1986); *but see* In re Lopez, 292 B.R. 570 (E. D. Mich. 2003) (limiting collateral estoppel effect of state court judgment where state law permits liability based on reckless or negligent conduct).

[220] Mazurczyk v. O'Neil (In re O'Neil), 268 B.R. 1 (Bankr. D. Mass. 2001).

[221] In re Bundick, 303 B.R. 90 (Bankr. E.D. Va. 2003).

[222] *See* Jones v. Svreck (In re Jones), 300 B.R. 133 (B.A.P. 1st Cir. 2003); In re Busch 311 B.R. 657 (Bankr. N.D.N.Y. 2004) (distinguishing hostile environment claims); Andy Gaunce, Note, *Rethinking* In re Busch*: Bankruptcy Discharge of Sexual Harassment Judgments under Section 523(a)(6)*, 56 S.C. L. Rev. 645 (2005).

[223] In re Albarran, 347 B.R. 369 (B.A.P. 9th Cir. 2006).

[224] Speaking of all types, see Jeffries v. Sullivan (In re Sullivan), 337 B.R. 210 (Bankr. W.D. Mo. 2005), where, to make a long story short, the debtor willfully rammed the creditor's vehicle with her own.

act which resulted in an injury fell within its ambit.[225] The older case, *Tinker v. Colwell*, ruled that liability for the largely archaic tort of "criminal conversation" (with the plaintiff's spouse) was nondischargeable because it was an inherently malicious act that had been done intentionally.[226] *Geiger* resolved the issue and made it clear that § 523(a)(6) applies only to "intentional torts" where "the actor intend[ed] the consequences of an act, not simply the act itself."[227]

Thus, neither negligent nor reckless conduct are enough to make a debt nondischargeable.[228] Liability for medical or other professional malpractice, based on simple negligence, is not a wilful and malicious injury and is thus fully dischargeable.[229] Likewise, liability for many traditional intentional torts, which might be based on a finding of recklessness, might not satisfy the scienter standard required by *Geiger*. Courts interpreting *Geiger* have sometimes required the bankruptcy court to inquire into the debtor's subjective motive to inflict injury while other courts have been satisfied that the necessary finding of wilful and malicious intent can be found if harm from the debtor's intentional conduct was substantially certain to occur.[230]

[b] Conversion of Secured Creditor's Collateral[231]

Hoping to rely on the expansive language of *Tinker v. Colwell*, secured creditors sometimes claim that the debtor's sale of their collateral is a conversion that is nondischargeable under § 523(a)(6).[232] Earlier cases support this result.[233] Courts now largely resist these claims and limit them to circumstances where the debtor both knew of the creditor's security interest and knew that her intentional conduct would cause financial harm to the secured party. Debtors who attempt to conceal their sales of the creditor's collateral are likely to run afoul of § 523(a)(6). After *Geiger*,

---

225 Kawaauhau v. Geiger, 523 U.S. 57 (1998).

226 Tinker v. Colwell, 193 U.S. 473 (1904) (applying § 14(a)(6) of the Bankruptcy Act).

227 193 U.S. at 63 (quoting the Restatement (Second) of Torts § 8A, comment a (1964)).

228 193 U.S. at 64.

229 Kawaauhau v. Geiger, 523 U.S. 57 (1998); James L. Rigelhaupt, Jr., Annotation, *When Does Medical Practitioner's Treatment of Patient Constitute "Willful and Malicious Injury" So as to Make Practitioner's Debt Arising from Such Treatment Nondischargeable Under Section 523(a)(6) of Bankruptcy Act*, 77 A.L.R. Fed. 918 (1986).

230 *Compare* Carillo v. Su (In re Su), 290 F.3d 1140, 1142 (9th Cir. 2002), *and* Markwitz v. Campbell (In re Markowitz), 190 F.3d 455, 464 (6th Cir. 1999) (subjective intent), *with* Raspanti v. Keaty (In re Keaty), 397 F.3d 264 (5th Cir. 2005), *and* Miller v. J.D. Abrams, Inc. (In re Miller), 156 F.3d 598 (5th Cir. 1998).

231 Charles J. Tabb, *The Scope of the Fresh Start in Bankruptcy: Collateral Conversions and the Dischargeability Debate*, 59 Geo. Wash. L. Rev. 56 (1990); Annotation, *Conversion as Wilful and Malicious Injury to Property Within Provision of Bankruptcy Act Preventing Discharge from Liability for Such Injury*, 98 A.L.R. 1454 (1935).

232 *E.g.*, In re Burns, 276 B.R. 441 (Bankr. N.D. Miss. 2000).

233 *See* McIntyre v. Kavanaugh, 242 U.S. 138 (1916); Davis v. Aetna Acceptance Co., 293 U.S. 328 (1934) (dealer's sale of inventory out of trust); *see also* C.I.T. Fin. Serv. v. Posta (In re Posta), 866 F.2d 364 (10th Cir. 1989).

creditors should be required to show that the debtor's sale of the collateral was accomplished with the intent to cause the creditor some harm.[234]

[7] Governmental Fines, Penalties, or Forfeitures

[a] Non-Compensatory Fines and Penalties

It will surprise no one to learn that criminal fines and other penalties owed to a governmental unit are nondischargeable. Section 523(a)(7) excludes debts that are "for a fine, penalty, or forfeiture payable to and for the benefit of a governmental unit" from the scope of a debtor's discharge so long as the obligation is "not compensation for actual pecuniary loss."[235] Obligations to pay restitution to a victim of the debtor's crimes, entered as a condition of the debtor's probation or parole, are similarly nondischargeable.[236] However, non-compensatory tax penalties are dischargeable if they either relate to an otherwise dischargeable tax[237] or were imposed in connection with a "transaction or event that occurred [more than] three years before the date of [the debtor's bankruptcy] petition."[238]

[b] Federal Election Law Fines

In 2005, language was added to make debts "incurred to pay fines or penalties imposed under federal election law" nondischargeable.[239] Thus, a debtor who borrows money in order to pay his or her federal election law penalties cannot escape the penalty by using bankruptcy to discharge the debt to the creditor who provided financing for the debtor to pay her fine.[240] The narrow language of new § 523(a)(14B) implies that debts incurred to pay other fines or penalties, including election law penalties imposed under state law, remain dischargeable.

[c] Federal Criminal Restitution Orders

Federal criminal restitution obligations, imposed under the United States Criminal Code, are nondischargeable.[241] Unlike § 1328(a)(3), which only

---

[234] *Compare* In re Crump, 247 B.R. 1 (Bankr. W.D. Ky. 2000) (debtor's sale of collateral and disposition of proceeds in effort to keep business afloat was not intended to harm creditor), *and* In re Tomlinson, 220 B.R. 134 (Bankr. M.D. Fla. 1998) (sale of inventory and use of proceeds with intent to save business was not done with intent to harm secured creditor), *with* The Magic Lamp, Inc. v. LeBanc (In re LeBlanc), 346 B.R. 706 (Bankr. M.D. La. 2006) (debtor disposed of collateral and converted proceeds with knowledge of harmful effect on secured creditor).

[235] Bankruptcy Code § 523(a)(7).

[236] Kelly v. Robinson, 479 U.S. 36 (1986); *see* Colton v. Verola (In re Verola), 446 F.3d 1206 (11th Cir. 2006).

[237] *E.g.*, In re Roberts, 906 F.2d 1440 (10th Cir. 1990).

[238] Bankruptcy Code § 523(a)(7).

[239] Bankruptcy Code § 523(a)(14B).

[240] This language is similar to that contained in § 523(a)(14) & (14A) regarding debts incurred to pay otherwise nondischargeable tax debts.

[241] Bankruptcy Code § 523(a)(13).

applies to Chapter 13 cases,[242] it does not make state-imposed criminal restitution orders nondischargeable.

[8] Student Loans[243]

Section 523(a)(8) makes a wide variety of student loans nondischargeable "unless excepting the debt from discharge would impose an undue hardship on the debtor and the debtor's dependents."[244] The language of the statute presents two different issues: first, whether the debt falls within the category of student obligations deemed nondischargeable by the statutory language; and second, whether the debtor suffers from an undue hardship that might nevertheless permit the debt to be discharged.

[a] Types of Nondischargeable Student Loans

Section 523(a)(8) applies to virtually every imaginable type of student loan. Foremost among them are educational loans made directly or guaranteed by a federal, state, or local government unit.[245] Section 523(a)(8) also applies to loans made under a program "funded in whole or in part by a governmental unit or nonprofit institution."[246] Thus, if the source of even part of a loan provided to a student is either a governmental agency or a nonprofit organization, such as the college itself, a fraternal organization, or other charitable entity, the entire loan is nondischargeable.

It also applies to any "obligation to repay funds received as an educational benefit, scholarship, or stipend." If a student accepted a scholarship or fellowship that was subject to the condition that the student engage in some sort of public or community service job after graduation, she would find her obligation to repay the amount of the scholarship nondischargeable if she failed to fulfill the terms of the program.

Finally, § 523(a)(8) now makes any educational loan that qualifies for tax deductible interest payments nondischargeable.[247] Deductible interest represents a smaller but nevertheless discernable federal subsidy that gives the government a stake in ensuring that these loans are repaid.

Curiously, however, unpaid tuition bills are fully dischargeable. Thus, a student who borrows funds to pay her tuition is likely to find that the

---

[242] *See* § 13.05[C] Scope of Chapter 13 Discharge, *infra*.

[243] Thad Collins, *Forging Middle Ground: Revision of Student Loan Debts in Bankruptcy as an Impetus to Amend 11 U.S.C. § 523(a)(8)*, 75 Iowa L. Rev. 733 (1990); Darell Dunham & Ronald A. Buch, *Educational Debts Under the Bankruptcy Code*, 22 Mem. St. U. L. Rev. 679 (1992); Roger Roots, *The Student Loan Debt Crisis: A Lesson in Unintended Consequences*, 29 Sw. U. L. Rev. 501 (2000); Kurt Wiese, Note, *Discharging Student Loans in Bankruptcy: The Bankruptcy Court Tests of "Undue Hardship,"* 26 Ariz. L. Rev. 445 (1984); Jeffrey L. Zackerman, Note, *Discharging Student Loans in Bankruptcy: The Need for a Uniform "Undue Hardship" Test*, 65 U. Cin. L. Rev. 691 (1997).

[244] Bankruptcy Code § 523(a)(8).

[245] Bankruptcy Code § 523(a)(8)(A)(i).

[246] Bankruptcy Code § 523(a)(8)(A)(i).

[247] Bankruptcy Code § 523(a)(8)(B).

debt is nondischargeable, but a student who simply fails to pay her tuition is able to obtain relief from her debt.[248] Colleges that wish to preserve their ability to collect unpaid tuition bills will refuse to permit students to register for classes without a formal loan agreement containing the student's express promise to repay the extension of credit provided by the college. Obtaining a promissory note or other acknowledgment of liability for the unpaid tuition bill, after it is overdue, is not enough.[249]

Separate rules outside the Bankruptcy Code govern the dischargeability of certain health educational loan programs, such as those under the Health Education Assistance Loan Act[250] and the National Health Service Corp Scholarship Program.[251] These benefits are nondischargeable under a stricter standard, depending on whether more than five years have expired since the first payment became due and whether requiring repayment would be "unconscionable."[252]

[b] Undue Hardship[253]

Obligations to repay educational loans and benefits are nevertheless dischargeable if excluding the debt from discharge "will impose an undue hardship on the debtor and the debtor's dependents."[254] Whether a particular debtor's situation presents a case of undue hardship has been subject to several tests, but none of them are easy to satisfy.

Most courts employ the three-part test adopted by the court in *Brunner v. New York State Higher Education Services Corp.*,[255] which permits discharge of a student loan due to undue hardship if: (1) the debtor cannot maintain, based on current income and expenses a "minimal" standard of living for himself and his dependents if she is forced to repay the debt; (2) additional circumstances exist indicating that the debtor's circumstances are likely to persist for a significant portion of the repayment period for the loan; and (3) the debtor has made a good faith effort to repay the loan.[256]

---

[248] *E.g.*, In re Chambers, 348 F.3d 650 (7th Cir. 2003).

[249] In re Renshaw, 222 F.3d 82 (2d Cir. 2000) (student's formal acknowledgment of obligation to pay overdue tuition did not transform the unpaid tuition debt into an educational loan).

[250] 42 U.S.C. § 292f(g) (2000).

[251] 42 U.S.C. § 254o(c)(3) (2000).

[252] 42 U.S.C. § 292f(g) (2000).

[253] Andrew M. Campbell, Annotation, *Bankruptcy Discharge of Student Loan on Ground of Undue Hardship Under § 523(a)(8)(B) of Bankruptcy Code of 1978 — Discharge of Student Loans*, 144 A.L.R. Fed. 1 (1998); Richard Fossey, *The Certainty of Hopelessness: Are Courts Too Harsh Toward Bankrupt Student Loan Debtors?*, 26 J.L. & Educ. 29 (1997); Rafael I. Pardo & Michelle R. Lacey, *Undue Hardship in the Bankruptcy Courts: An Empirical Assessment of the Discharge of Educational Debt*, 74 U. Cin. L. Rev. 405 (2005); Robert F. Salvin, *Student Loans, Bankruptcy, and the Fresh Start Policy: Must Debtors Be Impoverished to Discharge Educational Loans?*, 71 Tul. L. Rev. 139 (1996).

[254] Bankruptcy Code § 523(a)(8).

[255] 831 F.2d 395 (2d Cir. 1987).

[256] 831 F.2d at 396; *see* In re Tirch, 409 F.3d 677 (6th Cir. 2005); Educarion Credit Mgmt. Corp. v. Mason (In re Mason), 464 F.3d 878, 881–85 (9th Cir. 2006).

For example, in *Educational Credit Management Corp. v. Mason (In re Mason)*,[257] the debtor had completed eight years in the military, an undergraduate degree in philosophy, and had completed law school, despite having suffered from a learning disability since the third grade. Deprived of the special testing accommodations he received while in law school, he was unsuccessful on the bar exam and earned no more than $1,200 per month as a part-time laborer. His average monthly expenses were about $1,300, without taking payments on the nearly $200,000 in educational debts he owed into consideration. Thus, his standard of living was minimal. Further, his life-long learning disability impaired his prospects for earning enough income to repay his student loans in the future. However, the court found that several factors supported the conclusion that he had not demonstrated a good faith effort to repay his student loans. He had apparently abandoned plans to retake the bar exam and was unwilling to look for a second part-time job to supplement the income he earned from the part-time employment he held. Moreover he had failed to attempt to renegotiate the terms of his student loans or to vigorously seek to take advantage of the Income Contingent Repayment Plan, a federal program that reduces debtors' payments based on their ability to pay.[258] Under these circumstances, a full discharge due to undue hardship was not warranted.[259]

Two circuits take a more flexible approach based on the "totality of the circumstances" with "special attention" to the debtor's reasonably reliable present and future financial resources, the reasonable and necessary living expenses of the debtor and his dependents, and "any other circumstances unique to the particular bankruptcy case." In applying the first two factors, the court should evaluate the extent to which the debtor has "done everything possible to minimize expenses and maximize income."[260] In applying this totality of the circumstances test, some courts have looked to a laundry list of specific factors:

- the debtor's total incapacity now and in the future to pay his debtors for reasons outside of his control;
- whether the debtor has made a good-faith effort to negotiate a deferment or forbearance of payment;
- whether the debtor's hardship will be long-term;
- whether the debtor has already made payments on the loan;
- whether the debtor suffers from a permanent or long-term disability;

[257] 464 F.3d 878 (9th Cir. 2006).

[258] *See* 34 C.F.R. § 685.209(c)(4)(iv) (2005); *see also* In re Bender, 338 B.R. 62 (Bankr. W.D. Mo. 2006) (assistant public defender who failed to participate in ICRP program ineligible for discharge of student loans).

[259] The court nevertheless provided the debtor with a "partial" hardship discharge. *See* § 13.03[B][8][c] Partial Discharge of Student Loans, *infra*.

[260] In re Long, 322 F.3d 549 (8th Cir. 2003); Hornsby v. Tennessee Student Assistance Corp., 144 F.3d 433 (6th Cir. 1998).

- the ability of the debtor to obtain gainful employment in the area in which he studied;
- whether the debtor has made a good faith effort to maximize his income and minimize his expenses;
- whether the dominant purpose of the bankruptcy petition was to discharge the debtor's student loans; and
- the ratio of the student loan to the debtor's total obligations.

It is impossible to ignore the overlapping nature of several of these factors, which do not appear to be markedly different from the smaller number of factors taken into account by the *Brunner* test.

Debtors who could adjust their standard of living have little chance of meeting the undue hardship standard. *In re Salyer* supplies a good example. The birth of the debtors' triplets seven months before their petition, all of whom suffered from disabilities, led them to have monthly expenses that exceeded their income by $500. However, their expenditure of $146 per month for digital cable television and internet access, $87 per month for unlimited long distance telephone service, and $146 per month for cellular phones, combined with discretionary spending for movie rentals and fast food, persuaded the court that they "could reduce their monthly expenses without foregoing a comfortable quality of life and afford to make some, if not all, of their student loan payments."[261]

The tests for "undue hardship" are not easy to satisfy. Debtors who are successful nearly always find themselves faced with a combination of unappealing circumstances, leaving them with what seem to be insurmountable odds of scratching out even a modest living, even if their student loans are discharged.[262] Most debtors would gladly choose to repay their student loans rather than deal with the difficult circumstances necessary to discharge them under the undue hardship test of § 523(a)(8).

[c] Partial Discharge of Student Loans[263]

The straightforward text of § 523(a)(8) seems to make student loans either completely nondischargeable or completely dischargeable, depending

---

[261] In re Salyer, 348 B.R. 66 (Bankr. M.D. La. 2006); *see also* In re Gharavi, 335 B.R. 492 (Bankr. D. Mass. 2006) (debtor's smoking expense of $175 per month is reasonable).

[262] *E.g.*, In re D'Ettore, 106 B.R. 715 (Bankr. M.D. Fla. 1989) (debtor supporting a minor child while earning $12,500 per year and living with her father did not face undue hardship where her frugal living expenses resulted in a $118 monthly surplus); Naylor v. Higher Educ. Student Assist. Auth. (In re Naylor), 348 B.R. 680 (Bankr. W.D. Pa. 2006) (debtor was seventy-one years old, retired, and partially disabled, supporting himself and his wife on social security benefits).

[263] Frank T. Bayuk, *The Superiority of Partial Discharge for Student Loans Under 11 U.S.C. § 523(a)(8): Ensuring a Meaningful Existence for the Undue Hardship Exception*, 31 Fla. St. U. L. Rev. 1091, 1119 (2004); Brendan Hennessy, Comment, *The Partial Discharge of Student Loans: Breaking Apart the All or Nothing Interpretation of 11 U.S.C. § 523(a)(8)*, 77 Temp. L. Rev. 71 (2004); *see also* Kevin C. Driscoll Jr., Note, *Eradicating the "Discharge by Declaration" for Student Loan Debt in Chapter 13*, 2000 U. Ill. L. Rev. 1311 (2000).

on whether excepting the debt from discharge would impose an undue hardship. Despite this "all or nothing" language, some courts have relied on Bankruptcy Code § 105 to grant a partial discharge of a student loan "to the extent" that excluding it from the debtor's discharge would impose an undue hardship.[264] Other courts have rejected this interpretation as unsupported by the plain language of § 523(a)(8).[265]

[9] Liability for Personal Injuries while Driving Drunk

Debts owed for simple negligence are generally fully dischargeable. However, liability for personal injury and wrongful death "caused by the debtor's operation of a motor vehicle, vessel, or aircraft if such operation was unlawful because the debtor was intoxicated from using alcohol, a drug, or another substance" is nondischargeable.[266] Liability for property damage on the other hand is not nondischargeable under this provision; it applies only to liability for "death or personal injury." Nondischargeability also depends on whether the debtor's operation of the vehicle was unlawful under applicable local law "because the debtor was intoxicated."[267] If the debtor's operation of the vehicle was unlawful for some other reason, the debt remains dischargeable.

[10] Debts Excluded from Discharge in Prior Bankruptcies

Not surprisingly, debts that were not discharged in an earlier bankruptcy involving the same debtor, either because they were unlisted in the debtor's earlier case or because the debtor waived her discharge or was denied a discharge under § 727(a)(2)-(7), may not be discharged through the simple expedient of filing a subsequent bankruptcy case. But, denial of discharge in the earlier case due to the eight-year bar of § 727(a)(8) or the six-year bar of § 727(a)(9) does not make debts scheduled in that earlier case nondischargeable in a later case filed after the time barrier to a discharge has passed. Likewise, if discharge was denied only because the debtor failed to complete a credit counseling program, as now required by § 727(a)(10), debts scheduled in the earlier case can be discharged in a subsequent case if the debtor participates in the necessary education program.

---

[264] *See* Education Credit Mgmt. Corp v. Mason (In re Mason), 464 F.3d 878 (9th Cir. 2006); Alderete v. Education Credit Mgmt. Corp. (In re Alderete), 412 F.3d 1200 (10th Cir. 2005); Miller v. Pennsylvania Higher Educ. Assistance Agency (In re Miller), 377 F.3d 616 (6th Cir. 2004).

[265] *E.g.*, Salinas v. United Student Aid Funds, Inc. (In re Salinas), 258 B.R. 913 (Bankr. W.D. Wis. 2001).

[266] Bankruptcy Code § 523(a)(9).

[267] *See* In re Hart, 347 B.R. 635 (Bankr. W.D. Mich. 2006) (operation unlawful due to impairment even though the debtor was not criminally charged).

[11] Other Nondischargeable Debts

A variety of other obligations are nondischargeable under the ever-growing list of debts excluded from the scope of a Chapter 7 discharge. Among these are:

- condominium or cooperative fees that become due "after the order for relief";[268]
- certain court imposed fees on state and federal prisoners in connection with civil actions they might pursue while incarcerated;[269] and
- debts owed to pension funds for loans permitted under certain provisions of ERISA.[270]

[C] Procedure for Determining Nondischargeability; Exclusive Jurisdiction

[1] Jurisdiction over Dischargeability

In most cases, the dischargeability of a debt can be determined either in bankruptcy court or state court. However, bankruptcy courts have exclusive jurisdiction to determine the nondischargeability of debts under § 523(a)(2), (4), or (6). Thus, actions to determine the dischargeability of a debt incurred through fraud, fiduciary fraud, embezzlement, larceny, or for wilful and malicious injuries must be brought in bankruptcy court while the bankruptcy case is pending.

[2] Adversary Proceeding to Determine Dischargeability

Bankruptcy court actions to determine the dischargeability of a debt are "adversary proceedings" governed by Part VII of the Rules of Bankruptcy Procedure.[271] These rules are similar in most every respect to the Federal Rules of Civil Procedure.

Under Bankruptcy Rule 4007, either the debtor or a creditor may initiate an action to determine the dischargeability by filing a complaint.[272] The debtor may seek to have any question about a debt's dischargeability resolved in bankruptcy court rather than in what might be viewed as a less friendly state forum.

Most dischargeability complaints can be filed any time while the bankruptcy case is pending.[273] However, complaints to determine the

---

[268] Bankruptcy Code § 523(a)(16).

[269] Bankruptcy Code § 523(a)(17).

[270] Bankruptcy Code § 523(a)(17).

[271] *See* Fed. R. Bankr. P. 4007(e), 7001(6).

[272] Fed. R. Bankr. P. 4007(a).

[273] Fed. R. Bankr. P. 4007(b).

nondischargeability of a debt under § 523(a)(2), (4), or (6) must be filed "no later than 60 days after the first date set" for the § 341(a) meeting of creditors.[274] To prevent creditors from being unfairly surprised by this short time frame, Bankruptcy Rule 4007 requires the standard notice that is sent to all creditors regarding the debtors bankruptcy case to include information about this time limit.[275] The court has authority to extend the limit "for cause" upon the motion of the debtor, a creditor, or any other party in interest.

[D] Collateral Estoppel Effect of Prior State Court Decisions[276]

If a creditor has obtained a pre-bankruptcy judgment against the debtor regarding a debt that might be nondischargeable, the prior judgment may have some collateral estoppel effect on a subsequent bankruptcy court dispute of the dischargeability of the debt. If the creditor has previously established that the debt was incurred through fraud or that it involved some wilful and malicious personal injury, the creditor may attempt to set up the prior judgment to prevent the debtor from relitigating those issues in the creditor's dischargeability action. Alternatively, if the creditor previously alleged, but failed to prove elements of some basis for determining the nondischargeability of the debt, the debtor may attempt to use the earlier judgment to preclude the creditor from renewing its assertion that the element can be satisfied.

In *Grogan v. Garner*, the Supreme Court has held that collateral estoppel, or "issue preclusion," applies in dischargeability actions with the same force and effect that it applies in other matters.[277] The full faith and credit statute, which generally requires federal courts to give full faith and credit to judgments of state courts,[278] normally requires bankruptcy courts to give a prior state court judgment the same collateral estoppel effect that it would be given by a court of the state that issued the judgment. Thus, a bankruptcy court should apply state collateral estoppel principles, unless Congress has established an exception to the full faith and credit statute that permits a federal court to deviate from the preclusive effect that would

---

[274] Fed. R. Bankr. P. 4007(c).

[275] Fed. R. Bankr. P. 4007(c).

[276] G. Harvey Boswell & Abigail Gerlach, *Coming and Going: The Revolving Jurisdictional Door of the Bankruptcy Court*, 28 U. Mem. L. Rev. 885 (1998); Bernice B. Donald & Kenneth J. Cooper, *Collateral Estoppel in Section 523(c) Dischargeability Proceedings: When Is a Default Judgment Actually Litigated?*, 12 Bankr. Dev. J. 321 (1996); Tisha Morris Federico, *Dischargeability Proceedings and Prepetition Default Judgments: Does the Bankruptcy Code Implicitly Repeal the Full Faith and Credit Requirement of 28 U.S.C. 1738?*, 71 Am. Bankr. L.J. 563 (1997); Jeffrey T. Ferriell, *The Preclusive Effect of State Court Judgments in Bankruptcy, Part I*, 58 Am. Bankr. L.J. 349 (1984), and *Part II*, 59 Am. Bankr. L.J. 55 (1985); Christopher Klein, Lawrence Ponoroff, & Sarah Borrey, *Principles of Preclusion and Estoppel in Bankruptcy Cases*, 79 Am. Bankr. L.J. 839 (2005).

[277] Grogan v. Garner, 498 U.S. 279 (1991).

[278] 28 U.S.C. § 1738 (2000).

be given to the judgment by the state whose courts issued the judgment.[279] However, where the elements of issue preclusion have not been satisfied, such as where the underlying issue was not actually litigated, the matter can still usually be resolved in bankruptcy court.

In *Archer v. Warner*, the Supreme Court reinforced this position by holding that a settlement agreement entered into between parties to an underlying claim, does not preclude the bankruptcy court from determining whether the debt is nondischargeable, even if the earlier settlement agreement by its terms substituted the settlement agreement for the underlying debt.[280] Thus, debtors who enter into settlement agreements involving claims that might be nondischargeable cannot use their settlement agreement to eliminate the risk that their debt will later be held nondischargeable.

§ 13.04 Chapter 7 Discharge

Because most bankruptcies are filed, and still more are closed, under Chapter 7, eligibility for discharge and the scope of discharge are primarily issues that arise under Chapter 7. Moreover, because there are usually no assets to distribute to creditors in Chapter 7 cases, discharge is the only real function of most Chapter 7 cases.[281]

[A] Debtors Eligibile for Chapter 7 Discharge

In order to be eligible for a Chapter 7 discharge, debtors must be eligible for some kind of Chapter 7 relief. As explained elsewhere in more detail, Chapter 7 is generally available to individuals, corporations, partnerships, trusts, non-profit organizations, and unincorporated associations. However, railroads, insurance companies, and banks or other financial institutions are ineligible for Chapter 7 relief.[282]

Although a wide variety of other types of entities are eligible to file a petition under Chapter 7, natural persons — human beings — are the only ones eligible for a Chapter 7 discharge.[283] Organizations, such as corporations, partnerships, trusts, and other business entities may not receive a Chapter 7 discharge. This rule prevents "shell" corporations from obtaining tax advantages that might otherwise be available to a company that has

---

[279] Meindl v. Genesys Pac. Techs., Inc. (In re Genesys Data Techs., Inc.), 245 F.3d 312 (4th Cir. 2001); *cf.* Migra v. Warren City Sch. Dist. Bd. of Educ., 465 U.S. 75 (1984); *see generally* Jeffrey T. Ferriell, *The Preclusive Effect of State Court Judgments in Bankruptcy, Part I*, 58 Am. Bankr. L.J. 349 (1984), and *Part II*, 59 Am. Bankr. L.J. 55 (1985).

[280] 538 U.S. 314 (2003).

[281] *See* Michael J. Herbert & Domenic E. Pacitti, *Down and Out in Richmond, Virginia: The Distribution of Assets in Chapter 7 Bankruptcy Proceedings Closed During 1984-87*, 22 U. Rich. L. Rev. 303, 311 (1988) (92.3% of Chapter 7 cases are no-asset cases).

[282] Bankruptcy Code § 109(b); *see* § 6.02[B][2] Eligibility for Relief in Chapter 7 — Liquidation, *supra*.

[283] Bankruptcy Code § 727(a)(1).

discharged its debts in liquidation. State and federal tax laws sometimes permit a profitable company to acquire and use the net operating loss of a defunct firm, thus enabling the acquiring company to reduce its taxes. Drafters of the Bankruptcy Code disapproved of this practice and consequently imposed a price on companies who might seek to deploy this strategy. A profitable company may acquire a company that has been in Chapter 7 and, if the Internal Revenue Code permits, may use its net operating losses to defray its income. However, to obtain the tax benefits, the acquiring entity must merge with the shell, the acquiring entity thereby becomes liable for the shell's remaining debts because those debts have not been discharged.

As a result of this rule, few business entities seek relief under Chapter 7. When these types of debtors find themselves in a Chapter 7 case, it is usually because they have failed in their attempt to successfully reorganize under Chapter 11. Indeed, while it is permissible to liquidate in Chapter 11, corporations that liquidate in Chapter 11 do not receive a discharge either.[284]

As is true throughout the Code, any particular debtor may be denied discharge because of various types of misconduct. Denial of discharge due to various types of misconduct is discussed earlier in this chapter.[285]

[B] Timing of Discharge

A Chapter 7 discharge is supposed to be granted promptly. Under Bankruptcy Rule 4004, once the time is set for filing objections to discharge and motions to dismiss for substantial abuse, the court is to grant the discharge "forthwith" after expiration of whatever time has been fixed.[286] The discharge need not be granted if there is a pending objection to discharge[287] or to dismiss the case entirely due to abuse.[288] Moreover, the court may sua sponte delay entry of the order of discharge for thirty days, and if there is a motion made within that thirty day period, to a further date certain.[289]

[C] Scope of Debtor's Chapter 7 Discharge

The full list of nondischargeable debts set out in Bankruptcy Code § 523 is discussed earlier in this chapter.[290] This means that under some circumstances, Chapter 7 will be a poor choice for the debtor. For example, if the debtor owes large recent tax obligations, or has committed fraud or

[284] *See* § 19.05 Conversion and Dismissal of Chapter 11 Cases, *infra*.

[285] *See* § 13.02[B] Denial of Discharge in Chapter 7, *supra*.

[286] Fed. R. Bankr. P. 4004(c).

[287] *See* § 13.02[B] Denial of Discharge in Chapter 7, *supra*.

[288] *See* § 17.03[B] Dismissal of Consumer Cases due to Abuse, *supra*.

[289] Fed. R. Bankr. P. 4004(c)(2).

[290] *See* § 13.03 Nondischargeable Debts, *supra*.

some other intentional tort, it may be better for the debtor to file under Chapter 13 and obtain its more expansive discharge.

Apart from § 523 debts, a Chapter 7 discharge extends to all debts that arose before the order for relief.[291] In voluntary cases, this means all dischargeable pre-petition debts. As a general rule, post-petition debts are not discharged. This is part and parcel of the structure of Chapter 7, which is designed to deal almost exclusively with pre-petition debts and pre-petition assets. Some post-petition debts are encompassed in the discharge, but only if some specific provision of the Code treats them "as if" they were incurred pre-petition. These include claims of involuntary gap creditors, who extended credit after an involuntary petition but before the order for relief; the claims of those from whom property was recovered by the trustee; and claims arising from the rejection of executory contracts and unexpired leases.[292]

§ 13.05 Chapter 13 Discharge

A discharge in Chapter 13 cases is broader than the narrower discharge available in Chapter 7 liquidation cases. But a discharge in Chapter 13 is only available for individuals — living, breathing, human beings.[293] A Chapter 13 discharge is normally granted only upon completion of the debtor's Chapter 13 repayment plan, usually at least three years after her petition has been filed, and for debtors with too much anticipated income, not until five years after the petition has been filed.

[A] Debtors Eligible for Chapter 13 Discharge

[1] Individual Debtors

Chapter 13 is available only to individual debtors.[294] Corporations, partnerships, and other organizations who seek relief in a reorganization proceeding must file under either Chapter 11, or if they qualify as a "family farmer," under Chapter 12. Consequently, there is no need for any additional limitation on those eligible for discharge. Since corporations, partnerships, and other business organizations cannot use Chapter 13, there are no concerns about the sale of shell companies emerging from it.

[2] Debtor's Misconduct Affecting Chapter 13 Discharge

Chapter 13 debtors who have engaged in misconduct in connection with their case may have difficulty obtaining confirmation of their plans.[295]

---

[291] Bankruptcy Code § 727(b).

[292] Bankruptcy Code §§ 502, 727(b).

[293] A deceased person who had completed the terms of her Chapter 13 plan can receive a Chapter 13 discharge.

[294] Bankruptcy Code § 109(e).

[295] *See* § 18.08[C] Good Faith, *infra*.

Because Chapter 13 debtors are generally only eligible for a discharge upon completion of the terms of their confirmed Chapter 13 plan,[296] misconduct that results in denial of confirmation prevents the debtor from satisfying the requirements for a Chapter 13 discharge.

[3] Effect of Prior Discharge on Subsequent Chapter 13 Discharge

In addition, § 1328(f) prevents a debtor from receiving a discharge if the debtor has received a previous Chapter 7, 11, or 12 discharge in a bankruptcy case filed within four years before the date of the debtor's pending Chapter 13 case.[297] This new provision must be read in conjunction with the rules in Chapter 13 regarding the duration of a Chapter 13 plan, which will usually be either three or five years. Assume, for example, that Lisa obtained a Chapter 7 discharge in a case filed on October 10, 2007. She would thus not be eligible to receive a subsequent Chapter 13 discharge until October 11, 2011.[298] However, because any Chapter 13 plan she files will provide for payments extending for a minimum of three years, it is unlikely that she will be affected by this new provision unless she files her Chapter 13 case earlier than October 11, 2008. This four-year bar impairs her ability to obtain a Chapter 13 "hardship discharge," under § 1328(b) before October 11, 2011, even if she has otherwise satisfied the requirements of Bankruptcy Code § 1328(b).[299]

The four-year bar impairs much of the utility of what had become known as "Chapter 20." This maneuver consisted of obtaining a Chapter 7 discharge and immediately filing a subsequent Chapter 13 case. The terms of the Chapter 13 plan would provide for making payments to their secured creditors, whose debts had been discharged in the earlier Chapter 7 case, but whose security interests and mortgages would otherwise have permitted them to foreclose upon their collateral.[300]

The four-year bar restricts this strategy, but does not eliminate it. Section 1328(f)(1) does not prevent a debtor from filing a Chapter 13 case immediately after receiving a Chapter 7 discharge, it merely prevents the debtor from obtaining a Chapter 13 discharge in fewer than four years after the earlier discharge. Debtors can still use "Chapter 20" to impose the automatic stay while they make payments to their secured creditors under the terms of the plan. And if their plan lasts for a minimum of four years, they can obtain a discharge in the subsequent Chapter 13 case.

---

[296] *See* § 13.02[D] Denial of Discharge Under Chapters 12 and 13, *supra.*

[297] Bankruptcy Code § 1328(f)(1). The statutory language refers to the "date of the order for relief under this chapter," but because Chapter 13 cases are always voluntary, the date of the debtor's petition is always the date of the order for relief.

[298] *E.g.*, McDow v. Ratzlaff (In re Ratzlaff), 349 B.R. 443 (Bankr. D.S.C. 2006); Lewis v. Lewis (In re Lewis), 339 B.R. 814 (Bankr. S.D. Ga. 2006).

[299] *See* § 13.05[C][2] Chapter 13 Hardship Discharge, *infra.*

[300] *See* Johnson v. Home State Bank, 501 U.S. 78 (1991) (discharged secured debts from previous Chapter 7 case are "claims" in subsequent Chapter 13 case, thus permitting "Chapter 20").

Section 1328(f) also now prevents debtors from obtaining a Chapter 13 discharge if they have received a previous Chapter 13 discharge "in a case filed under Chapter 13 during the 2-year period" before the date of the their previous petition. Because Chapter 13 plans must usually last for a minimum of three years,[301] it is unlikely that many debtors will file a second Chapter 13 case within two years of filing a Chapter 13 case in which they received a discharge. It is still possible for a debtor to receive a hardship discharge without completing the terms of her earlier plan,[302] or the terms of plan providing for 100% payment to her creditors in fewer than two years. However, these are the only circumstances in which the two-year bar of § 1328(f)(2) applies.[303]

[B] Timing of Chapter 13 Discharge

Ordinarily, a Chapter 13 discharge is granted only upon completion of the debtor's repayment plan. The court is to grant the discharge "as soon as practicable" after the debtor makes the last plan payment.[304] In most cases this means that the debtor will not receive a discharge until either three or five years after her case has been filed. An earlier discharge may be requested under some circumstances, involving "hardship" as explained later in this chapter.[305]

[C] Scope of Chapter 13 Discharge[306]

The scope of discharge under Chapter 13 depends on whether the debtor successfully completes her plan. Successful completion, either of the original plan or a modified plan, entitles the debtor to a broader discharge than is available under other chapters. Debtors who do not complete their plans may, under some circumstances, obtain a narrower hardship discharge.

In general, the discharge encompasses only those debts that were provided for under the plan and those that were disallowed under Bankruptcy Code § 502. It also permits discharge of a few post-petition debts that involve either taxes or consumer obligations arising from property or services necessary for the debtor's performance under the plan.[307]

---

[301] Debtors who have sufficient income to pay their creditors in full in a shorter period may obtain confirmation of a shorter plan. Bankruptcy Code § 1325(b)(1)(A).

[302] *See* Bankruptcy Code § 1328(b); § 13.05[C][2] Chapter 13 Hardship Discharge, *infra.*

[303] There is a distinct possibility that Congress intended this two-year period to run from the time of the earlier Chapter 13 discharge. However, the plain meaning of § 1328(f)(2) refers to "a case *filed* under chapter 13 . . . during the 2-year period preceding the date of the [order for relief]."

[304] Bankruptcy Code § 1328(a).

[305] *See* § 13.05[C][2] Chapter 13 Hardship Discharge, *infra.*

[306] Scott F. Norberg, *Consumer Bankruptcy's New Clothes: An Empirical Study of Discharge and Debt Collection in Chapter 13*, 7 Am. Bankr. Inst. L. Rev. 415 (1999).

[307] *See* Bankruptcy Code § 1305(a).

[1] Full-Compliance Chapter 13 Discharge[308]

As discussed in depth in a subsequent chapter, the core of the Chapter 13 proceeding is the debtor's repayment plan. Chapter 13 plans usually provide for repayment of some or in rarer cases all of the debtor's obligations over either a three or five year period.[309] As one of the incentives given to debtors to choose Chapter 13 over Chapter 7, Congress provided a broader discharge for those who complete their Chapter 13 plans. Under § 1328, all plan obligations and all disallowed obligations are discharged, except for:

- "long term" debts — claims on which the last payment is due after the due date of the final payment under the plan;[310]
- tax debts entitled to priority under § 507(a)(8)(C) or nondischargeable under § 523(a)(1)(B) or (C);[311]
- debts fraudulently incurred under § 523(a)(2);[312]
- unscheduled debts under § 523(a)(3);[313]
- debts for fiduciary fraud, embezzlement, or larceny under § 523(a)(4);[314]
- domestic support obligations under § 523(a)(5), as defined in § 101(a)(14A);[315]
- student loans under § 523(a)(8);[316]
- debts for wrongful death or personal injury while driving drunk under § 523(a)(9);[317]
- criminal restitution orders or fines;[318] and
- restitution or damages awarded in a civil action against the debtor for personal injuries or death suffered as a result of wilful or malicious injuries inflicted by the debtor.[319]

This means of course that some debtors may gain considerably from a Chapter 13 filing, instead of seeking relief under Chapter 7. The most

---

308 Farris E. Ain, Comment, *Never Judge a Bankruptcy Plan by its Cover: The Discharge of Student Loans Through Provisions in a Chapter 13 Plan*, 32 Sw. U. L. Rev. 703 (2003).

309 *See* Chapter 18, Rehabilitation of Individuals with Regular Income under Chapter 13, *infra*.

310 Bankruptcy Code §§ 1328(a)(1), 1322(a)(5).

311 *See* § 13.03[B][1] Tax Debts, *supra*.

312 *See* § 13.03[B][2] Debts Fraudulently Incurred, *supra*.

313 *See* § 13.03[B][3] Unscheduled Debts, *supra*.

314 *See* § 13.03[B][4] Fraud or Defalcation in a Fiduciary Capacity; Embezzlement, Larceny, *supra*.

315 *See* § 13.03[B][5][a] Domestic Support Obligations, *supra*.

316 *See* § 13.03[B][8] Student Loans, *supra*.

317 *See* § 13.03[B][9] Liability for Personal Injuries Caused by Drunk Driving, *supra*.

318 Bankruptcy Code § 1328(a)(3).

319 Bankruptcy Code § 1328(a)(4).

important categories of debts that are nondischargeable in Chapter 7 but that can be discharged in Chapter 13 are those owed to a former spouse for something other than support,[320] liability for property damage due to intentional torts,[321] and debts incurred to repay otherwise nondischargeable non-priority tax debts.[322]

It might appear from § 1328(a)(2) as if debts for most income, property, and other tax debts are dischargeable in Chapter 13. Although § 1328 leaves most tax debts fully dischargeable, what § 1328 giveth, § 1322 taketh away. Section 1322(a)(2) requires Chapter 13 plans to "provide for full payment . . . of all claims entitled to priority under section 507." Most income, property, excise, and other tax debts are among those entitled to § 507 priority treatment.[323] This, combined with delaying the debtor's discharge until she has completed the terms of her plan, effectively makes § 507(a)(8) tax obligations dischargeable only after they have been fully paid.

Congress itself has shown considerable ambivalence about the breadth of the Chapter 13 discharge. The scope of the Chapter 13 regular discharge has gradually narrowed since it was implemented in 1978. The 2005 Amendments dramatically reduced the scope of the Chapter 13 discharge by, among other things, excepting debts fraudulently incurred, and, at the same time, expanding the presumption of fraud in § 523(a)(2)(C).

Nothing could better illustrate the difficulties presented by any effort to strike a reasonable balance between competing interests in bankruptcy. Congress at first sought to draw debtors into Chapter 13 by offering a generous discharge; then, seemingly appalled by the fact that people actually took advantage of that offer, it gradually made Chapter 13's discharge more and more restrictive.

[2] Chapter 13 Hardship Discharge

Many Chapter 13 debtors find that they are unable to complete the terms of their rehabilitation plans. Consider the difficulty of living within a strict budget for three to five years. Few of us manage more than a week on such a strict regimen, even without the intervention of unforseen adverse circumstances.

Debtors in this situation may modify their plan, and if the modified plan is confirmed and completed, the debtor is still eligible for a full Chapter 13 discharge.[324] However, depending on the circumstances that make completion of the original plan difficult, modification may be impractical.[325]

---

[320] *See* Bankruptcy Code § 523(a)(15); § 13.03[B][5][b] Other Marital Obligations, *supra*.

[321] *See* Bankruptcy Code § 523(a)(6); § 13.03[B][6] Wilful & Malicious Injury, *supra*.

[322] *See* Bankruptcy Code § 523(a)(14), (14A); § 13.03[B][1] Tax Debts, *supra*. Note, however, that such debts may be nondischargeable due to fraud, under §§ 1328(a)(2) and 523(a)(2), if the debt was incurred in anticipation of discharging the debt in a subsequent Chapter 13 bankruptcy proceeding.

[323] Bankruptcy Code § 507(a)(8); *see* § 13.03[B][1][a] Priority Taxes, *supra*.

[324] *See* Bankruptcy Code § 1329; § 18.10 Modification of Chapter 13 Plan, *infra*.

[325] *See* In re Bond, 36 B.R. 49 (Bankr. E.D.N.C. 1984) (Chapter 13 debtor's death made completion or modification impossible).

The debtor may fall ill, lose her job, or need to resign to care for a sick child. If neither modification nor completion seems possible, a Chapter 13 debtor might choose to convert the case and obtain a Chapter 7 discharge or to request the court to grant a Chapter 13 hardship discharge. Either way, the debtor's discharge is the same. The principal difference is that by seeking a hardship discharge, the debtor avoids the loss of any further property beyond what she had already contributed to the payment of her debts through her plan.

[a] Grounds for Hardship Discharge

A hardship discharge is not always available. Section 1328(b) permits the court to grant a hardship discharge only if:

- the debtor's failure to complete the plan payments is due to circumstances for which the debtor should not justly be held accountable;
- the creditors have received at least the Chapter 7 liquidation value of their unsecured claims; and
- modification of the plan is not practicable.[326]

In determining whether the debtor's failure to complete the plan is as a result of circumstances for which the debtor should not justly be held accountable, courts frequently decide that disruptions in the debtor's income stream due to previously unforeseeable circumstances that make performance of the plan impossible, such as a permanent disruption of the debtor's income or an unanticipated increase in the debtor's expenses, qualifies.

Although courts have sometimes indicated that the debtor need not show that she was facing "catastrophic circumstances" to obtain a hardship discharge, courts have sometimes denied a hardship discharge in situations many of us would regard as catastrophic. For example, in *In re Easley*, married debtors were denied a hardship discharge where the husband's position with his employer was completely eliminated, because the husband remained healthy, they lived in an area where the rate of unemployment was generally low, and there was no evidence that the wife, who had not been looking for work, was unable to work outside the home.[327]

Among the factors courts frequently consider in making this determination are (1) whether the debtor has presented substantial evidence that she had the ability and intent to perform the plan when it was confirmed; (2) whether the debtor materially performed the plan up to the time of the event that impaired her ability to perform; (3) whether the disrupting event was foreseeable at the time the plan was confirmed; (4) whether the intervening circumstances that impair the debtor's ability to continue performing are reasonably expected to continue; (5) whether the debtor had direct

[326] Bankruptcy Code § 1328(b).

[327] 240 B.R. 563 (Bankr. W.D. Mo. 1999).

or indirect control of the intervening circumstances; and (6) whether the intervening events were a sufficient and proximate cause of the debtor's inability to continue performance under the terms of the plan.[328]

Consistent with the basic bargain struck in a Chapter 13 case, a hardship discharge is available only if the payments made to unsecured creditors, at the time the hardship discharge is sought, is the equivalent of what they would have received if the debtor had liquidated in Chapter 7. Thus, the value of payments made to unsecured creditors under the plan must be discounted to their present value, and then compared with what unsecured creditors would have received if the debtor had simply liquidated. This makes sense, as unsecured creditors would be seriously prejudiced by a hardship discharge if they have not received payments compensating them for at least what they would have received if the debtor had liquidated.

For example, if the debtor owned $10,000 in non-exempt equity that would have been distributed to unsecured creditors if the debtor had liquidated, the *value* of payments made under the plan must equal that same amount. If a total of exactly $10,000 has been distributed to unsecured creditors through two years of payments under the plan, a hardship discharge cannot be granted. Payments totaling $10,000, spread out over two years does not have the same value as the $10,000 the unsecured creditors would have received all at once if the debtor had liquidated her estate. A hardship discharge can be granted if the payments distributed under the plan exceed $10,000 by a sufficient amount to compensate her creditors for the delay in receiving the liquidation value of her estate.

Finally, in order to grant the debtor a hardship discharge, the court must determine that modification of the debtor's plan is not feasible. In most cases, the same circumstances that make continued payments under the plan impossible makes modification impractical. If the debtor has lost her job or suffered some injury, making continued employment impossible, it is unlikely that she can fund any plan. Still, before a hardship discharge is granted, the debtor's circumstances should be evaluated to determine if a plan, which is feasible and meets the financial standards imposed by §§ 1325 and 1329 for confirmation, can be proposed.

[b] Scope of a Hardship Discharge

Unfortunately, the scope of a Chapter 13 hardship discharge is no broader than a discharge in a Chapter 7 liquidation case, and in some respects, it is narrower. Section 1328(c)(2) provides that a hardship discharge "discharges the debtor from all unsecured debts provided for by the plan or disallowed under section 502 . . . except any debt . . . of a kind specified in section 523(a)."[329] Thus, a Chapter 13 hardship discharge is subject to the same limits as those imposed by § 727 on a Chapter 7 discharge. Also excluded from the hardship discharge are any long-term debts, which would

[328] Bandilli v. Boyajian (In re Bandilli), 231 B.R. 836 (B.A.P. 1st Cir. 1999).

[329] Bankruptcy Code § 1328(c).

ordinarily extend beyond the terms of the debtor's plan within the meaning of § 1322(b)(5).[330]

The principal advantage of obtaining a hardship discharge is that it permits the debtor to retain her non-exempt assets. The alternative, converting the case to Chapter 7, would result in the appointment of a trustee who would administer any non-exempt assets that the debtor owns. Thus, although a hardship discharge does not provide the debtor with an expanded discharge, it at least permits the debtor to retain her property.

§ 13.06 Chapter 11 Discharge

[A] Persons Eligible for Chapter 11 Discharge

Chapter 11 is broadly available to nearly every type of person eligible for relief generally under the Bankruptcy Code.[331] Railroads, which are ineligible for relief under Chapter 7, may reorganize under Chapter 11. Stockbrokers and commodity brokers, however, are ineligible for reorganization and must seek relief, if at all, under Chapter 7.[332]

[1] Corporations, Partnerships and other Organizations

Most Chapter 11 cases involve corporations or partnerships. In these cases, the debtor receives a discharge upon confirmation of its Chapter 11 plan.[333] If no plan is confirmed, the debtor does not receive a discharge, and the case will most likely be dismissed or converted to Chapter 7. Thus, the ability to obtain confirmation is the principal barrier to obtaining a Chapter 11 discharge.

This does not mean that important issues such as misconduct by the debtor are irrelevant in a Chapter 11 case. Instead, it means they arise in the context of the court's determination of whether to confirm a plan, rather than in a separate adversary proceeding to determine whether to grant or deny a discharge. Thus, by refusing to confirm the debtor's plan, the court can effectively deny discharge for one or more of the same reasons that it would directly rule on denial of discharge in a Chapter 7 liquidation case.

Chapter 11 contains nothing like the eight-year bar of § 727 that prevents debtors from obtaining successive Chapter 7 discharges.[334] Debtors may receive a Chapter 11 discharge as frequently as they are able to obtain confirmation of a Chapter 11 plan.

---

[330] Bankruptcy Code § 1328(c)(1).

[331] *See* § 6.02[B] Debtor's Eligibility for Voluntary Relief, *supra*.

[332] Bankruptcy Code § 109(d).

[333] Bankruptcy Code § 1141(d).

[334] *See* § 13.02[B][6] Repeat Filings — The Eight-Year Bar, *supra*.

However, it is difficult to obtain confirmation of a Chapter 11 plan without the consent of a majority of the debtor's creditors. In Chapter 11, creditors have the right to vote to approve or reject the debtor's plan.[335] A Chapter 11 debtor's past misconduct may lead creditors to refuse to vote in favor of the debtor's plan, making confirmation difficult or impossible. Likewise, creditors who have voted to "accept" a plan in a recent Chapter 11 case may be reluctant to give the debtor a second chance to reorganize and may effectively deny a corporate debtor a second successive Chapter 11 discharge simply by refusing to vote in favor of the second plan.[336]

As noted above, there is one circumstance in which a Chapter 11 debtor may be denied a discharge even though it has obtained confirmation of a plan. If the debtor's Chapter 11 plan provides for liquidation rather than reorganization, the debtor may not receive a discharge. Section 1141(d)(3) prevents discharge if: (1) the plan provides for the liquidation of all, or substantially all of the property of the estate; (2) the debtor does not engage in business after consummation of the plan; and (3) discharge would have been denied under § 727(a) if the case had been brought under Chapter 7.[337]

Finally, as in Chapter 7, a Chapter 11 discharge can be waived. There are procedural requirements that must be met. To be effective, the waiver must be in writing; it must be executed by the debtor after the order for relief (i.e., in a voluntary case, after the filing of the petition); and it must be approved by the court.[338]

[2] Discharge of Individual Debtors in Chapter 11

Although Chapter 11 is generally regarded as suitable primarily for corporations, partnerships, and other organizations, individual debtors are also eligible for Chapter 11 relief.[339] Indeed, individuals who are ineligible for Chapter 7 because they cannot satisfy the means test, and who do not satisfy the Chapter 13 debt limits must file in Chapter 11. However, a Chapter 11 discharge relieves individuals debtors only from their dischargeable debts.[340] Debts excluded from the scope of discharge by § 523 are not within the discharge available in Chapter 11.[341] However, for a Chapter 11 plan to provide the debtor with effective relief, the debtor's plan will normally provide for the payment of nondischargeable debts. Otherwise the plan may not be feasible, as required by § 1129(a)(11), and cannot be confirmed.[342]

---

[335] *See generally* § 19.09 Acceptance of Plan by Holders of Claims and Interests: Voting, *infra.*

[336] *See* § 19.10 Confirmation of Chapter 11 Plans, *infra.*

[337] Bankruptcy Code § 1141(d)(3).

[338] Bankruptcy Code § 1141(d)(4).

[339] Toibb v. Radloff, 501 U.S. 157 (1991).

[340] Bankruptcy Code § 1141(d)(2).

[341] *See* § 13.03 Nondischargeable Debts, *supra.*

[342] *See* § 19.10[J] Feasibility of Plan, *infra.*

[B] Timing of Chapter 11 Discharge

Unlike under Chapters 12 and 13, a Chapter 11 discharge is normally granted as soon as the plan becomes effective. Indeed, it is the fact of confirmation itself that ordinarily discharges the debtor. As noted earlier, the only exception to this is in cases involving individual debtors who are not normally eligible for discharge until their plans are fully performed. Mere confirmation of a Chapter 11 plan does not provide an individual debtor with a discharge. Unlike other entities, individual debtors must wait to receive their discharge until "the court grants a discharge on completion of all payments under the plan."[343]

A discharge may be granted earlier if the payments made to unsecured creditors under the plan are the equivalent of what the creditors would have received in a Chapter 7 liquidation case and modification of the plan is not practicable.[344] This emulates the rules applicable in cases under Chapters 12 and 13 where the debtor finds herself unable to complete a confirmed plan after making payments that would at least provide her unsecured creditors with the amount they would have received if the debtor had simply liquidated.

[C] Scope of Chapter 11 Discharge

The scope of a Chapter 11 discharge is simple. The obligations under the Chapter 11 plan substitute for the debtor's pre-confirmation obligations. Insofar as corporations and other artificial entities are concerned, virtually all existing debt is discharged, and the sole remaining obligations are those undertaken in the plan.[345]

The situation of an individual Chapter 11 debtor is more complicated. She remains obligated on all the debts listed in § 523 as nondischargeable, the same as she would have been if she had obtained relief under Chapter 7. Thus, individual Chapter 11 debtors remain liable for family obligations, debts incurred through fraud, willful and malicious injuries, student loans, and other debts specified in § 523, even though their plans have been confirmed, and even though they have received a Chapter 11 discharge.

§ 13.07 Chapter 12 Discharge

[A] Persons Eligible for Chapter 12 Discharge

The Chapter 12 discharge is available to anyone who may be a Chapter 12 debtor. Eligibility for Chapter 12 is limited to family farmers and family fishermen and thus can include some closely held family corporations and

---

[343] Bankruptcy Code § 1141(d)(5)(A).

[344] Bankruptcy Code § 1141(d)(5)(B).

[345] Bankruptcy Code § 1141(d)(1)(A).

partnerships.[346] Otherwise, discharge is available to any eligible debtor whose Chapter 12 plan is confirmed and completed.

[B] Timing of Chapter 12 Discharge

Ordinarily, a Chapter 12 discharge is granted only upon completion of the plan of reorganization. The court is to grant the discharge "as soon as practicable" after the debtor makes the last plan payment (other than certain payments permitted on long-term debt).[347] An earlier hardship discharge may be requested under circumstances similar to those in which a hardship discharge may be granted in cases under Chapter 13.[348] A hardship discharge may be granted if the debtor's failure to complete the plan is excusable, if creditors have received at least the liquidation value of their claims, and if modification of the plan is not practicable. In this respect, Chapter 12 is similar to Chapter 13.

[C] Scope of Chapter 12 Discharge

A Chapter 12 discharge encompasses those debts that were provided for under the plan, administrative expenses, and claims that were disallowed under § 502.[349] Unlike a Chapter 13 discharge, a Chapter 12 discharge does not encompass otherwise nondischargeable debts. The Chapter 12 debtor thus remains obligated, even after the discharge is granted, on the full list of § 523 debts.[350] In addition, the Chapter 12 debtor remains obligated on long-term debts that extend beyond the completion of the plan.[351]

§ 13.08 Revocation of Discharge

Under very limited circumstances, a discharge previously granted may be revoked. Revocation always involves serious misconduct by the debtor. In addition, revocation may only be requested within a relatively short time after the discharge was granted. Even when the debtor has committed a seriously wrongful act, the need for finality and closure militates for an early statute of repose. Because this need for finality is considered to be greater in a reorganization proceeding than in a liquidation proceeding, the requirements for revoking confirmation under Chapters 11, 12 and 13 are even more restrictive than the requirements under Chapter 7.

[346] *See* § 6.02[B][5] Eligibility for Relief in Chapter 12 — Family Farmers and Family Fishermen, *supra.*

[347] Bankruptcy Code § 1228(a).

[348] Bankruptcy Code § 1228(b); *see* § 13.05[C][2] Chapter 13 Hardship Discharge, *supra.*

[349] Bankruptcy Code § 1228(a) (2006).

[350] *See* § 13.03 Nondischargeable Debts, *supra.*

[351] Bankruptcy Code § 1228(a)(1).

[A] Revocation of Chapter 7 Discharge

A Chapter 7 discharge may be revoked only in five circumstances:

- the discharge was obtained by fraud;[352]
- the debtor fails to report its acquisition of estate property or fails to surrender the property to the trustee;[353]
- the debtor refuses to obey any lawful order of the court;[354]
- the debtor fails to satisfactorily explain any discovered misstatement;[355] or
- the debtor fails to provide records in connection with a Justice Department audit of the debtor's case.[356]

The court may not revoke the discharge without notice and an opportunity for a hearing.[357] Actions to revoke a Chapter 7 discharge are adversary proceedings conducted under Part VII of the Federal Rules of Bankruptcy Procedure.[358]

There are tight time limitations placed on invoking any of these grounds. Fraud may be raised only within one year after the discharge is granted.[359] Failure to report or surrender property and misconduct may only be raised within one year after the discharge is granted or within one year after the case is closed, whichever is later.[360] However, there is no time limit on the court's ability to revoke the debtor's discharge due to the debtor's failure to cooperate with an audit of the debtor's case conducted by the United States Department of Justice.[361]

[B] Revocation of Chapter 11 Discharge

Under Chapter 11, confirmation is nearly always the point at which the debtor obtains a discharge. Because of this, revocation of the discharge is dealt with in conjunction with revocation of confirmation. Confirmation may be revoked if it was procured by fraud, but only if revocation is sought

352 Bankruptcy Code § 727(d)(1).

353 Bankruptcy Code § 727(d)(2).

354 Bankruptcy Code § 727(d)(3), (a)(6).

355 Bankruptcy Code § 727(d)(4).

356 Bankruptcy Code § 727(d)(4).

357 Bankruptcy Code § 727(d).

358 Fed. R. Bankr. P. 7001(4).

359 Bankruptcy Code § 727(e)(1).

360 Bankruptcy Code § 727(e)(2).

361 This appears to have been an oversight. The 2005 Amendments added a mechanism that permits the United States Trustee's office to conduct audits of bankruptcy cases. 28 U.S.C.S. § 586(f) (2006). At the same time, Congress added § 727(d)(4), permitting the court to revoke a debtor's discharge if the debtor fails to provide a satisfactory explanation of any misstatement discovered in the course of such an audit or to provide information requested during such an audit. However, no corresponding amendment was made to § 727(e), which imposes a time limit for discharge revocations prompted by such an audit.

within 180 days after the order confirming the plan was entered.[362] If the confirmation is revoked, the court must, among other things, revoke the debtor's discharge.[363]

[C] Revocation of Chapter 12 and 13 Discharge

Chapters 12 and 13 have identical revocation provisions. Note that unlike Chapter 11, Chapters 12 and 13 separate confirmation from discharge; thus, revocation of an order of confirmation is unrelated to an order revoking the debtor's discharge. It is virtually impossible for a discharge to be granted during the time in which the confirmation could still be revoked.

Following completion of a plan, any party in interest may move for revocation of the discharge. The motion must be made within one year after the discharge was granted. The discharge may be revoked if — and only if — the discharge was obtained by fraud, and the moving party did not know of the fraud until after the discharge was granted.[364] Prior to any revocation of the discharge, the court must provide notice and an opportunity for a hearing.[365]

§ 13.09 Effect of Discharge

Discharge has a number of direct and indirect effects on the debtor and the debtor's obligations. The discharge voids any judgment based on the debtor's personal liability for a discharged debt.[366] It operates as an injunction against any action to collect, recover, or offset any discharged debt as a personal liability of the debtor.[367] Taken together, these two rules provide the debtor with considerable relief from her pre-petition debts: judgments against her are void and thus cannot be enforced, and creditors are enjoined from "any action" to collect a discharged debt from the debtor. In addition, the Bankruptcy Code prohibits certain types of discrimination against debtors by creditors, governmental agencies, and employers.

[A] Discharge Injunction

Discharge prevents creditors from efforts to collect the discharged debt. The prohibition against any action to collect a discharged debt is broad. Section 524(a)(2) enjoins "the commencement or continuation of an action, the employment of process, or *an act*, to collect, recover or offset any [discharged] debt as a personal liability of the debtor."[368] This not only

[362] Bankruptcy Code § 1144.

[363] Bankruptcy Code § 1144(2).

[364] Bankruptcy Code §§ 1228(d), 1328(e).

[365] Bankruptcy Code §§ 1228(d), 1328(e).

[366] Bankruptcy Code § 524(a)(1).

[367] Bankruptcy Code § 524(a)(2).

[368] Bankruptcy Code § 524(a)(2) (emphasis supplied).

prevents creditors from suing debtors on discharged debts, but also prevents them from resuming the barrage of phone calls, dunning letters, or other efforts aimed at persuading the debtor to pay.[369] Creditors' efforts to shame the debtor into paying, such as by posting signs publicizing the debtor's failure to pay or parking a car outside the debtor's place of business containing a sign publishing a "public service announcement" about the debtor's failure to pay also likely violate the stay.[370] Colleges have occasionally violated the discharge stay by refusing to issue transcripts to students who discharged unpaid tuition bills.[371] Creditors who do nothing more than refuse to do business with the debtor violate the stay only if the creditor expresses a willingness to resume business with the debtor upon repayment of the discharged debt.[372] However, a creditor's failure to have a discharged debt removed from the debtor's credit report, is not an act to collect that violates § 524(a).[373] Creditors whose claims against the debtor have been discharged can refuse to provide future service to the debtor, but they may not condition future service on repayment of the discharged debt or actively seek repayment through other means.

Despite these rules, § 524(j) now permits home mortgage lenders to act in the ordinary course to obtain monthly payments due from the debtor, rather than pursuing their in rem rights to foreclose the mortgage and have the property sold.[374] There is no similar provision permitting creditors with a security interest in personal property, such as an automobiles or furniture, to send even routine reminders to the debtor, seeking resumption of payments, as an alternative to foreclosure.

In addition, special rules deal with the effect of the discharge on a debtor's community property.[375]

Although § 524 enjoins creditors from efforts to collect, it does not provide a private right of action for debtors who are injured by a creditor's violation of the injunction.[376] Nevertheless, the bankruptcy court can use its civil contempt power under § 105 to award damages to the debtor for harm it suffers as a result of a debtor's wilful violation of § 524.[377] However, courts

---

[369] *See, e.g.*, In re Latanowich, 207 B.R. 326 (Bankr. D. Mass. 1997) (Sears, Roebuck & Co.'s deliberate efforts to persuade debtor to enter into a reaffirmation agreement without complying with the requirements of § 524(c)).

[370] *E.g.*, In re Crudup, 287 B.R. 358 (Bankr. E.D.N.C. 2002) (creditor's First Amendment rights not impaired by prohibition against signs posted in effort to collect); In re Andrus, 189 B.R. 413 (N.D. Ill. 1995).

[371] In re Parraway, 50 B.R. 316 (W.D. Mich. 1984). Similar actions taken while a case is pending violate the automatic stay. *E.g.*, In re Lanford, 10 Bankr. 132 (Bankr. D. Minn. 1981).

[372] Olson v. McFarland Clinic, P.C. (In re Olson), 38 B.R. 515 (Bankr. N.D. Iowa 1984).

[373] Irby v. Fashion Bug (In re Irby), 337 B.R. 293 (Bankr. N.D. Ohio 2005).

[374] Bankruptcy Code § 524(j). This is consistent with rule that provides creditors' liens on the debtor's property to survive.

[375] Bankruptcy Code § 524(a)(3), (b), (e).

[376] *See* Walls v. Wells Fargo Bank, 276 F.3d 502, 509 (9th Cir. 2002).

[377] *See* Walls v. Wells Fargo Bank, 276 F.3d 502, 509 (9th Cir. 2002); Bessette v. Avco Fin. Servs., Inc., 230 F.3d 439, 444–45 (1st Cir. 2000).

have split over whether this extends to damages for emotional distress the debtor may suffer as a result of the creditor's actions.[378]

[B] Enforcement of Liens Permitted

The discharge stay applies only to actions aimed at collecting from the debtor personally. Unavoided liens on the debtor's property survive ("ride through") and can be enforced in an in rem action, such as one to foreclose a real estate mortgage or to obtain possession of personal property in order to have it sold, despite discharge of the debtor's in personam responsibility for the debt.[379]

Thus, if Julie and Richard default on their mortgage payments and discharge the debt in a Chapter 7 bankruptcy case, the mortgagee, Empire Bank, is permitted to foreclose upon the debtors' home. Likewise, if New Motors Acceptance Corporation holds a security interest in the debtors' car, it is allowed to repossess or replevy the car after the case is closed.[380]

Creditors with real estate mortgages are now expressly permitted to communicate with the debtor in the ordinary course of business to obtain monthly or other "periodic payments" associated with the creditor's mortgage.[381] Before the 2005 Amendments, creditors with security interests in personal property were given some modest leeway in advising the debtor of its right to repossess the collateral if payments were not resumed. In *Garske v. Arcadia Financial, Ltd. (In re Garske)*, the court permitted a secured creditor's phone calls to the debtor advising the debtor of its right to repossess and requesting the debtor to pay in order to avoid repossession.[382] As the court explained: "because [the] Debtor must pay . . . to retain the Vehicle, contact between them is unavoidable."[383] Whether this leeway for creditors with security interests in personal property will survive the enactment of § 524(j), which is limited to creditors who retain "a security interest in real property that is the principal residence of the debtor," remains to be seen. Even if decisions like *Garske* continue to be followed, creditors who barrage the debtor with requests and demands for repayment, that go beyond the type of contact necessary to facilitate the debtor's intent to retain the collateral, still run afoul of § 524(a)(2).[384]

---

378 *See* In re Feldmeier, 335 B.R. 807 (Bankr. D. Or. 2005).

379 *See* Long v. Bullard, 117 U.S. 617 (1886).

380 *See* § 2.08 Foreclosure Proceedings, *supra*.

381 Bankruptcy Code § 524(j).

382 287 B.R. 537 (B.A.P. 9th Cir. 2002).

383 287 B.R at 544.

384 *E.g.*, Mooney v. Green Tree Serv., LLC (In re Mooney), 340 B.R. 351 (Bankr. E.D. Tex. 2006).

[C] Recovery from Co-Debtors

The discharge stay of § 524(a)(2) does not prohibit creditors from pursuing others who may be liable, such as guarantors and insurers.[385] Section 524(g) imposes a limited exception to this rule by prohibiting actions against insurers who otherwise might be liable for claims against the debtor arising from asbestos injuries.[386]

The co-debtor stays that apply in Chapters 12 and 13 expire upon conclusion of the case and thus do not prevent creditors from pursuing these third parties in the event that the entire debt is not repaid through the debtor's completed plan. In Chapter 11 cases, it is not unusual for the plan to include language purporting to discharge any such guarantors. Whether these provisions should be permitted remains open to dispute.[387]

[D] Discrimination Against Debtors

The Bankruptcy Code also contains several limited prohibitions against certain types of discrimination against bankrupt debtors. These apply primarily to discriminatory treatment by governmental bodies and employers. Creditors, on the other hand, are usually free to discriminate against debtors, so long as they do not discriminate in an effort to recover payment of a discharged debt.

[1] Governmental Discrimination

With a few narrow exceptions, governmental units are prohibited from discriminating against debtors with regard to licenses, permits, charters, franchises, or employment.[388] Thus, a debtor's drivers' license may not be suspended or revoked due to the debtor's failure to pay a dishcarged debt arising from an auto accident.[389] Business debtors who discharge their debts in reorganization may not have their business or other licenses revoked due to their discharge.[390]

The express language of § 525(a) prohibits such discrimination "solely because" of the debtor's discharge.[391] Any suggestion that discrimination is permitted if the government has some underlying motive associated with

---

385 *E.g.*, Green v. Welsh, 956 F.2d 30 (2d Cir. 1992); In re Castle, 289 B.R. 882 (Bankr. E.D. Tenn. 2003).

386 Bankruptcy Code § 524(g).

387 *Compare* Republic Supply Co. v. Shoaf, 815 F.2d 1046 (5th Cir. 1987) (treating such a provision as res judicata with respect to the guarantor's liability), *with* Gillman v. Continental Airlines (In re Continental Airlines), 203 F.3d 203 (3d Cir. 2000) (sustaining objections to provisions of the debtor's plan providing for discharge of guarantors), *and* Class Five Nev. Claimants v. Dow Corning Corp. (In re Dow Corning Corp.), 280 F.3d 648 (6th Cir. 2002) (permitting such provisions in unusual circumstances based on several complex factors).

388 Bankruptcy Code § 525(a).

389 *See* Perez v. Campbell, 402 U.S. 637 (1971).

390 FCC v. NextWave Personal Commc'ns, Inc., 537 U.S. 293 (2003).

391 Bankruptcy Code § 525(a).

its refusal to grant or renew the debtor's license, was dispelled by the Supreme Court's decision in *Federal Communications Commission v. NextWave Personal Communications, Inc.*[392] In *NextWave*, the court explained that interpreting the "solely because" language to permit discrimination in order to implement whatever underlying motive the government had to discriminate against the debtor "would deprive § 525 of all force."[393] It ruled that "section 525 means nothing more or less than that the failure to pay a dischargeable debt must alone be the proximate cause of the cancellation — the act or event that triggers the agency's decision to cancel, whatever the agency's ultimate motive in pulling the trigger may be."[394] Discrimination is permitted only if there is some other reason, apart from discharge of the debt, that is the "proximate cause" of the government's action.[395]

One potential impact of the *NextWave* decision is that it may prevent state supreme courts from denying licenses to practice law to those whose only moral defect is the irresponsibility reflected by the decision to discharge their debts in bankruptcy. Unless there is some other aspect of the aspiring lawyer's background that reflects dishonesty, moral turpitude, or irresponsible behavior, denying a license to practice law to those who have invoked the Bankruptcy Code violates § 525(a).

The key question is whether the government is applying a test that is facially neutral — a test that applies equally to all. For example, a reasonably based rule that every person who wishes to obtain a business license must either have a minimum level of unencumbered assets or obtain a minimum level of insurance is normally permissible, even though this would disqualify a disproportionate number of former bankrupts. To put it in language familiar to civil rights attorneys, § 525(a) does not include a disparate impact test.

Most courts have been more flexible in their interpretation of the matters encompassed by the anti-discrimination prohibition. The language "license, permit, charter, franchise, or other similar grant" has been read to encompass a wide variety of government benefits. Obvious things, such as business licenses and drivers' licenses are covered; also certain entitlements, such as the right to remain in public housing and thus receive an indirect subsidy from the government, have been held to be protected.[396] On the other hand, if the government benefit involves an extension of credit, courts are likely to find that the government is not prohibited from discriminating, because that form of discrimination is not prohibited by § 525.

---

[392] 537 U.S. 293 (2003).

[393] 537 U.S. at 301–02.

[394] 537 U.S. at 301–02.

[395] 537 U.S. at 301–02.

[396] *E.g.*, In re Sudler, 71 B.R. 780 (Bankr. E.D. Pa. 1987).

[2] Employment Discrimination

Section 525(b) imposes a more limited prohibition on discrimination by private parties. Private employers may not terminate or otherwise discriminate against former bankrupts merely because of the bankruptcy, the debtor's pre-discharge insolvency, or the fact that discharged debts are unpaid.[397] There remains very little reported litigation applying this prohibition. What little there is suggests that the employer's duty is no greater than that of a governmental entity. The employer may not discriminate per se against the former bankrupt.

[3] Credit Discrimination

Creditors are, of course, generally permitted to discriminate against debtors who have previously discharged their debts. This discrimination takes many forms, including denials of credit, increased interest charges, smaller debt limits, and more onerous default provisions.

The only exception to this general rule, permitting credit discrimination, is with respect to student loans. Both governmental units and private lenders are prohibited from denying a student loan to a previously bankrupt debtor.[398] The prohibition applies to the grant of a loan, a loan guarantee, or loan insurance.[399] This provision was apparently added in the belief that refusal of student loans to former bankrupts would, by restricting their access to further education, unduly increase the possibility of future financial trouble. Although the precise language does not seem to prohibit governmental entities or private lenders from charging higher interest rates to those who have discharged their debts in bankruptcy, most student loan programs carry a set rate of interest that does not vary from one borrower to the next.

---

397 Bankruptcy Code § 525(b).

398 Bankruptcy Code § 525(c).

399 Bankruptcy Code § 525(c).

Chapter 14

General Avoiding Powers; Limitations on Avoiding Powers

§ 14.01 Avoidance of Transfers

In this and subsequent chapters, we explore the so-called avoiding powers of the trustee and the debtor-in-possession. The trustee has authority to set aside various transactions that deplete the debtor's estate in ways that advantage one creditor at the expense of the creditor body generally. In some cases, the unfairness to creditors is obvious, such as a transfer of assets by an insolvent debtor for no consideration — a fraudulent conveyance. Debtors who are unable to pay their creditors are not permitted to give away their few remaining assets. In other circumstances, the rationale for permitting the trustee to avoid the transfer is less obvious. Some transactions are avoidable only in bankruptcy. Others are borrowed directly from state law. Most depend on state law to some extent, but a few rely exclusively on federal bankruptcy law.

This chapter discusses a number of general avoiding powers that, while important, do not require extensive discussion. There are many other avoiding powers discussed in detail elsewhere in this book. These include preferences,[1] fraudulent transfers,[2] and certain non-possessory, non-purchase money security interests in exempt property.[3]

There are also limitations on the trustee's avoidance powers. Some of these limitations are specific to the particular avoiding power; others of broader application are discussed in this chapter.

In Chapter 7 cases, avoidance powers are exercised primarily by the trustee. In Chapter 11[4] and Chapter 12[5] cases, they are exercised by the debtor-in-possession, unless a trustee is appointed to take over administration of the case. There is some confusion about who exercises the avoidance rights in a Chapter 13 case, because the Chapter 13 debtor-in-possession is not explicitly given the broad powers that are provided to the debtor-in-possession in Chapters 11 and 12. The courts are divided over whether the Chapter 13 debtor-in-possession may avoid transactions; many have held that only the Chapter 13 trustee may exercise the avoidance powers.[6] The

[1] *See* Chapter 15, Preferences, *infra.*

[2] *See* Chapter 16, Fraudulent Transfers, *infra.*

[3] *See* § 12.07 Avoiding Liens on Exempt Property, *supra.*

[4] Bankruptcy Code § 1107(a).

[5] Bankruptcy Code § 1203; *e.g.*, Hoeger v. Teigen (In re Teigen), 123 B.R. 887, 888 (Bankr. D. Mont. 1991).

[6] *See, e.g.*, Wood v. Mize (In re Wood), 301 B.R. 558, 561–63 (Bankr. W.D. Mo. 2003) (collecting cases).

remainder of this chapter refers to the avoiding powers of the trustee with the understanding that in most situations a debtor-in-possession has the same right to invoke the avoiding power as the trustee.[7]

§ 14.02 Strong-Arm

Section 544(a), long known as the "strong-arm clause," is the trustee's most important avoiding power. This section primarily affects transfers that were incomplete on the date of the bankruptcy. It gives the trustee the status of a person whose rights as a lien creditor or bona fide purchaser of real estate, whose interest becomes effective against third parties at the moment of the bankruptcy petition. This means that any transfer of the debtor's property that is not yet effective against third parties can be avoided by the trustee. As explained in more detail below, this gives the trustee the power to avoid unperfected security interests in personal property and unrecorded or improperly recorded sales and mortgages of real estate. Because a Chapter 11 debtor-in-possession enjoys all of the same rights, powers, and duties of a trustee, the debtor-in-possession can avoid transfers as the representative of the estate, even though the transfer would have been effective against the debtor under applicable state law.

[A] Trustee as Hypothetical Judicial Lien Creditor[8]

Section 544(a)(1) gives the trustee the status of a hypothetical judicial lien holder. More specifically, it gives the trustee the rights of a person who obtained, as of the commencement of the case, "a judicial lien on all property on which a creditor on a simple contract could have obtained . . . a judicial lien."[9] This status arises whether or not there actually is such a creditor. Section 544(a)(1) treats the trustee as a "hypothetical lien creditor." The trustee is sometimes said to "stand in the shoes" of a lien creditor.[10]

The single most significant impact of this rule is on unperfected Article 9 security interests (including sales of accounts and chattel paper), though these are by no means the only interests that it affects. As noted elsewhere, an Article 9 security interest usually must be perfected to achieve priority over a judicial lien creditor.[11] Thus, an unperfected security interest is subject to the rights of and cannot be asserted against the trustee.[12] As one court explained:

---

[7] *E.g.*, Gandy v. Gandy (In re Gandy), 299 F.3d 489, 497 (5th Cir. 2002).

[8] David Gray Carlson, *The Trustee's Strong Arm Power Under the Bankruptcy Code*, 43 S.C. L. Rev. 841 (1992); C. Scott Pryor, *How Revised Article 9 Will Turn the Trustee's Strong-Arm into a Weak Finger: A Potpourri of Cases*, 9 Am. Bankr. Inst. L. Rev. 229 (2001).

[9] Bankruptcy Code § 544(a)(1).

[10] *E.g.*, In re Halabi, 184 F.3d 1335, 1337 (11th Cir. 1999).

[11] U.C.C. § 9-317(a)(2) (2003); *see* § 2.02[B][1][d] Priority Rules Under U.C.C. Article 9, *supra*.

[12] Most cases regarding the perfection or lack of perfection of an Article 9 security interest arise in the context of bankruptcy.

> The Trustee stands in the shoes of a hypothetical lien creditor whose lien arose on the day the bankruptcy petition was filed. With this "strong-arm" power, she may avoid and recapture for the debtor's estate any junior claim. Thus, the security interest of a creditor who has not perfected is defeated by the Trustee's section 544 power and relegated to the status of an unsecured debt.[13]

On the other hand, if the security interest is perfected at the moment the debtor's bankruptcy was filed, it is unassailable under § 544(a),[14] though it may be vulnerable under one of the trustee's other avoidance powers.

Section 544(a) achieves these results indirectly. It does not expressly provide that the trustee can avoid unperfected security interests. Instead, it operates via the interplay between § 544(a)(1) and state law.[15] Section 544(a)(1) gives the trustee whatever priority rights a lien creditor would enjoy under applicable state law. Section 544(a) treats the trustee as if it were a creditor who had obtained a judicial lien on all of the debtor's property at the precise moment the debtor's bankruptcy petition was filed.[16] Because a creditor who acquired a judicial lien on the debtor's property would take priority over an unperfected security interest, the trustee enjoys the same power.[17] As one court explained: "[a]lthough the rights of the trustee as a lien creditor are governed by federal law, our determination of whether [the creditor] possesses a perfected security interest which has priority over the trustee as a lien creditor is controlled by . . . state law."[18]

Section 544(a)'s reliance on state law means that the trustee's rights depend on whatever limits state law imposes on the rights of judicial lien creditors. If under state law a secured creditor would prevail against a lien creditor, the secured creditor similarly prevails against the trustee's rights under § 544(a). The most basic example of this is the effect of the relationship between § 544(a) and U.C.C. § 9-317. Section 9-317(b)(2) specifies that a "security interest . . . is subordinate to the rights of . . . a person that becomes a lien creditor before . . . the security interest . . . is perfected."[19] Section 544(a) gives the trustee the rights of a hypothetical lien creditor who acquired its lien at the moment the bankruptcy petition was filed.

---

[13] Wind Power Sys., Inc. v. Cannon Fin. Group, Inc. (In re Wind Power Sys., Inc.), 841 F.2d 288, 292 (9th Cir. 1988).

[14] Aerocon Eng'g, Inc. v. Silicon Valley Bank (In re World Auxiliary Power Co.), 303 F.3d 1120 (9th Cir. 2002).

[15] *E.g.*, LMS Holding Co. v. Core-Mark Mid-Continent, 50 F.3d 1520 (10th Cir. 1995); *see* C. Scott Pryor, *How Revised Article 9 Will Turn the Trustee's Strong-arm Into a Weak Finger: A Potpourri of Cases,* 9 Am. Bankr. Inst. L. Rev. 229 (2001).

[16] It is as if the Bankruptcy Code were the trustee's "fairy godmother" who tapped the trustee on the head with her magic wand and said: "Congratulations — you are now a lien creditor with a judicial lien on all of the debtor's property."

[17] To continue the fairy godmother analogy, she might also tell the trustee: "Go out and avoid uperfected security interests, wherever you can find them."

[18] Pearson v. Salina Coffee House, Inc., 831 F.2d 1531, 1432–33 (10th Cir. 1987).

[19] U.C.C. § 9-317(b)(2) (2003).

Thus, the trustee's power to avoid a security interest under § 544(a) depends on whether the security interest was perfected at the moment the debtor's bankruptcy petition was filed, when the trustee acquired its rights as a lien creditor.

Assume, for example, that on January 1, Merchant's Bank loans Franklin Manufacturing $100,000 and obtained and immediately perfected a security interest in Franklin Manufacturing's equipment. Later, on August 1, Franklin Manufacturing filed a bankruptcy petition. Section 544(a) treats the trustee as a lien creditor who acquired its lien on August 1. Because the bank's security interest was perfected back in January, before Franklin's bankruptcy petition was filed, the trustee may not use § 544(a) to set aside the bank's security interest.

If, on the other hand, Merchant's Bank failed to perfect its security interest in January and remained unperfected on August 1 when Franklin filed its petition, the trustee could use its status as a lien creditor to avoid the bank's security interest.[20] On the other hand, if in July the bank realized that it was still unperfected and rushed to the Secretary of State's filing office to file a financing statement and become perfected, its interest would be protected from attack under § 544(a). Unfortunately, a security interest that is perfected late might be vulnerable to attack by the trustee as a voidable preference.[21]

Section 544(a) also permits the trustee to avoid security interests whose perfection lapsed before the debtor's bankruptcy petition. Thus, if Merchant's Bank perfected by filing on January 30, 2004, but failed to file a continuation statement by January 30, 2009, its perfection would have lapsed. If Franklin initiates a bankruptcy proceeding after January 30, 2009, before the bank has re-perfected, the bank's security interest will fall to the trustee's power under § 544(a).

Article 9's twenty-day grace period for purchase money security interests provides a wrinkle in the application of § 544(a) that illustrates how it is completely dependent upon the state law scheme for allocation of priority between a security interest and a lien creditor. Under Article 9, a creditor with a purchase money security interest can achieve priority over a judicial lien creditor who acquires its lien between the time the security interest attaches and the time it is perfected, if the purchase money lender perfects within twenty days of the time the debtor receives possession of the collateral.[22]

Thus, if Industrial Supply Co. sells goods to Titanic, Inc. on credit, but Industrial Supply retains a security interest in the goods sold, then Industrial Supply achieves priority over any subsequent creditor who obtains a judicial lien on the goods, provided Industrial perfects its security interest within twenty days of when Titanic received possession. So, if

---

[20] *E.g.*, LMS Holding Co. v. Core-Mark Mid-Continent, 50 F.3d 1520 (10th Cir. 1995).

[21] *See* Chapter 15, *infra*.

[22] U.C.C. § 9-317(e) (2003).

Industrial Supply delivered the goods to Titanic on July 10, and North Atlantic Bank obtained a judicial lien on them on June 17, but Industrial Supply perfected by June 30, then Industrial Supply has priority. Likewise, if Titanic, Inc. filed a bankruptcy petition on June 17, and Industrial Supply perfected on June 28, the trustee's rights under § 544(a)(1) as a hypothetical lien creditor do not permit the trustee to avoid Industrial Supply's security interest.[23]

[B] Trustee as Creditor Whose Attempted Execution Is Returned Unsatisfied

Section 544(a)(2) endows the trustee with the rights of a hypothetical creditor that extends credit to the debtor when the case is commenced and simultaneously obtains an attempted writ of execution against the debtor's property that is returned unsatisfied.[24] This aspect of the trustee's strong-arm power is relatively insignificant. It gives the trustee whatever rights would be accorded by state law to a creditor who had exhausted its legal remedies.[25]

One of the most important rights § 544(a)(2) gives to the trustee is to compel what is known as "marshaling of assets" for the benefit of the estate.[26] The equitable doctrine of marshaling applies where there is a common debtor of senior and junior creditors and the senior creditor alone has the right to resort to both the common fund and a separate fund. Assume, for example, that State Bank has a senior mortgage on two parcels of land: Brambleburst and Xanadu, securing a $3 million debt, and Jamaica Bank has a junior mortgage on Xanadu alone, securing a $2 million debt. Further assume that Brambleburst and Xanadu are worth $3 million each. Without marshaling, State Bank might foreclose first upon Xanadu, exhausting its value and leaving Jamaica Bank completely unsecured. Jamaica Bank could use marshaling to compel State Bank to foreclose upon Brambleburst first. This would result in full payment to State Bank and leave Xanadu subject to foreclosure by Jamaica.

Some state laws give judgment creditors whose efforts to execute against the debtor's property through the customary legal mechanism, a writ of execution, are unsuccessful, the right to compel other creditors to marshal assets in this fashion. By anointing the trustee as such a judgment creditor, § 544(a)(2) gives the trustee a right similar to that of Jamaica Bank to force State Bank to marshal its assets.[27]

---

[23] Section 362(b)(3) provides an express exception to the automatic stay to cover this situation, and § 546(b) makes it clear that the trustee's rights are subject to the purchase money secured creditor's rights under U.C.C. § 9-317(e). *See* § 8.03[A][2] Perfection of Certain Pre-Petition Security Interests, *supra*.

[24] Bankruptcy Code § 544(a)(2).

[25] Whenever a "writ" is involved, the remedy is "legal" rather than "equitable."

[26] *See, e.g.*, Committee of Unsecured Creditors v. Lozinski (In re High Strength Steel, Inc.), 269 B.R. 560 (Bankr. D. Del. 2001).

[27] *E.g.*, Committee of Unsecured Creditors v. Lozinski (In re High Strength Steel, Inc.), 269 B.R. 560 (Bankr. D. Del. 2001) (Pennsylvania marshaling rules); In re Wilmot Mining Co., 167 B.R. 806, 811 (Bankr. W.D. Pa. 1994) (Ohio marshaling rules).

[C] Trustee as Bona Fide Purchaser of Real Estate

Section 544(a)(3) gives the trustee the rights of a hypothetical bona fide purchaser of real estate (other than fixtures) who acquires its rights at the moment the debtor's bankruptcy petition is filed.[28] Its most significant impact is with respect to unrecorded mortgages, leases, and deeds. If under applicable state law, a bona fide purchaser would prevail over these interests, then the trustee similarly prevails.

As with the trustee's power as a hypothetical lien creditor, § 544(a)(3) does not depend on whether there actually is a bona fide purchaser of the debtor's real estate or whether anyone has been injured by the failure to record the mortgage, lease, or deed. For example, suppose Dora executed a deed, transferring Blackacre to Bette on April 1, 2007. The deed was never recorded, and under state law, bona fide purchasers without notice take free of rights created by unrecorded deeds. If Dora files a bankruptcy petition on April 10, 2007, the trustee, as a hypothetical bona fide purchaser, can avoid the transfer to Bette. This pulls Blackacre back into the estate.

State law limits the ability of bona fide purchasers to avoid unrecorded deeds. If the bona fide purchaser has or should have notice of the buyer's rights, the bona fide purchaser usually takes subject to those rights. For example, it is generally true that if the buyer is in possession of the property, a bona fide purchaser cannot avoid the purchase even though the buyer failed to record her deed. In the example above, if Bette had been in possession of Blackacre, her rights would probably have been superior to those of an actual bona fide purchaser, even though her deed was unrecorded.[29]

However, this type of limitation does not necessarily affect the rights of the trustee under § 544(a)(3). The bankruptcy question is not whether all bona fide purchasers take free of the purchaser's interest, but whether *any* bona fide purchaser takes free.[30] Thus, if under governing state law there is any type of bona fide purchaser who takes free of an unrecorded interest, the unrecorded interest is avoidable by the trustee. This is clear from the statutory language of § 544(a)(3): "The trustee shall have, as of the commencement of the case, *and without regard to any knowledge of the trustee or of any creditor* the rights and powers of . . . (3) a bona fide purchaser of real property."

If under state law Bette's possession protected her interest against any bona fide purchasers, regardless of whether they had knowledge or notice of her occupancy of the land, then Bette's interest prevails over the trustee.[31] However, if Bette's possession protected her interest only against

[28] Bankruptcy Code § 544(a)(3).

[29] *See* Richard R. Powell & Michael Allan Wolf, Powell on Real Property § 82.01 (2007).

[30] *See* In re Hojnoski, 335 B.R. 282 (Bankr. W.D.N.Y. 2006).

[31] Thacker v. United Cos. Lending Corp., 256 B.R. 724, 729 (W.D. Ky. 2000).

those bona fide purchasers who knew or should have known that she was in possession, then her interest is avoidable by the trustee.

The biggest impact of § 544(a)(3) is with respect to unrecorded or improperly executed mortgages. It can have a devastating effect. In *In re Huffman*, mortgages were avoided by the trustee because they had not been witnessed by two persons, as required by governing Ohio law. Because Ohio law made a recorded but defectively executed mortgage ineffective against a bona fide purchaser for value, the creditors' mortgages were avoided by the trustee.[32]

In Chapter 11 reorganization cases, § 544(a)(3) permits the debtor-in-possession to avoid mortgages on estate property, even though the mortgage was supplied by the debtor before it filed its bankruptcy petition.[33] This is true even though the debtor-in-possession obviously has notice that the mortgage exists. This is because the debtor-in-possession's right to invoke § 544(a)(3) is the same as the right of a trustee to utilize its provisions and because a trustee would be able to avoid an unrecorded mortgage if *any* bona fide purchaser could avoid it. Thus, if Titanic Corporation grants a mortgage on its land to Pacific Bank and Pacific Bank fails to record it by the time Titanic files its Chapter 11 petition, Titanic Corporation, acting as debtor-in-possession, can avoid Pacific Bank's mortgage.

This ability to set aside unrecorded mortgages, together with the ability to set aside unperfected security interests under § 544(a)(1), provides some debtors with a powerful inducement to file a Chapter 11 petition. These debtors can avoid unrecorded or defectively recorded liens and thereby acquire exempt equity in their property that may not have been available outside of bankruptcy court.

§ 14.03 Power to Use Rights of Actual Unsecured Creditors

Section 544(b) gives the trustee the power to avoid transactions that are avoidable by actual general unsecured creditors under non-bankruptcy law.[34] Unlike § 544(a), § 544(b) does not create a set of hypothetical rights. Rather, it merely permits the trustee to enforce rights that the actual unsecured creditors of the debtor already have.[35] Thus, for the trustee to take advantage of § 544(b), she must find an actual unsecured creditor who has standing to avoid the transaction in question. In effect, § 544(b) subrogates the trustee to any actual creditors who might have avoided the

[32] Kovacs v. First Union Home Equity Bank (In re Huffman), 408 F.3d 290 (6th Cir. 2005); *see also* Field v. ABN AMRO Mortg. Group, Inc. (In re Wheeler), No. 04-1386, 2005 Bankr. LEXIS 2912 (Bankr. D. Ohio, July 21, 2005).

[33] Cox v. Griffin (In re Griffin), 319 B.R. 609, 612 (B.A.P. 8th Cir. 2005), *aff'd* 178 Fed. App'x 595 (8th Cir. 2006).

[34] Bankruptcy Code § 544(b).

[35] Specifically, it gives the trustee the rights of those creditors who have claims that are allowed under § 502 or that are disallowed only because of § 502(e) (disallows claims for reimbursement or contribution). Bankruptcy Code § 544(b).

transfer if the bankruptcy had not occurred. The trustee's claim under 544(b) is not, however, limited by the size of the debt owed to the creditor whose rights she asserts.[36] The transfer can, therefore, be avoided entirely, with the proceeds distributed to all creditors — even those who would not have enjoyed the benefits of avoiding the transfer if no bankruptcy case had been filed.[37]

Thus, while the avoidance power is derivative of the power held by a real creditor, it is exercised for the benefit of all the creditors. The effect can be dramatic. Consider, for example, a $30,000 transfer that could have been avoided, under applicable state law, only by a single creditor who was owed $100. Outside bankruptcy, this one creditor could have recovered the $100 from the person who received the avoidable $30,000 transfer. The trustee's recovery is not so limited. Section 544(b) permits the trustee to avoid the entire $30,000 transfer. This result, derived from the classic case *Moore v. Bay*,[38] is controversial, but legislative efforts to supercede the decision have repeatedly failed.[39]

Section 544(b)'s biggest impact is with respect to fraudulent conveyances. Although § 548 gives the trustee her own fraudulent transfer avoiding power, § 544(b) gives the trustee whatever additional fraudulent transfer avoiding powers that creditors generally have under state law. Because the statute of limitations under most state fraudulent conveyance statutes is three years, § 544(b) effectively expands the reach-back period of the trustee in connection with pre-petition fraudulent conveyances.

Section 544(b) is not limited to fraudulent transfers. It can be used to deploy any state or federal statute or doctrine that permits an unsecured creditor to attack a pre-bankruptcy transfer of the debtor's property. It has been used to avoid unrecorded mortgages, intercorporate guarantees,[40] illegal commissions,[41] and before the widespread repeal of U.C.C. Article 6, on bulk transfers.[42]

[36] *E.g.*, Stalnaker v. DLC, Ltd. (In re DLC, Ltd.), 295 B.R. 593, 606 (B.A.P. 8th Cir. 2003).

[37] *See* Coleman v. Community Trust Bank (In re Coleman), 426 F.3d 719, 726–27 (4th Cir. 2005).

[38] *See* Moore v. Bay (In re Estate of Sassard & Kimball), 284 U.S. 4 (1931).

[39] Douglas J. Whaley, *The Dangerous Doctrine of* Moore v. Bay, 82 Tex. L. Rev. 73 (2003).

[40] Scott F. Norberg, Comment, *Avoidability of Intercorporate Guarantees under §§ 548(a)(2) and 544(b) of the Bankruptcy Code*, 64 N.C. L. Rev. 1099 (1986).

[41] *E.g.*, Terlecky v. Abels, 260 B.R 446 (S.D. Ohio 2001).

[42] *E.g.*, In re Villa Roel, Inc., 57 B.R. 835 (Bankr. D. Colo. 1985). Article 6 required notice to be given to the unsecured creditors whenever substantially all of assets of an "inventoried" business were sold. Creditors who were not notified could set aside the sale. *See* Steven L. Harris, *Article 6: The Process and the Product — An Introduction,* 41 Ala. L. Rev. 549 (1990); Fred H. Miller, *The Scope of Uniform Commercial Code Article 6: A Tale of Two Proposals,* 41 Ala. L. Rev. 587 (1990); Benjamin Weintraub & Harris Levin, *Bulk Sales Law and Adequate Protection of Creditors*, 65 Harv. L. Rev. 418 (1952).

§ 14.04 Avoidance of Statutory Liens[43]

Liens on the debtor's property that are created by statute are usually enforceable in bankruptcy and give the lien holder a secured claim. However, some exceptions exist. Section 545 permits the trustee to avoid "the fixing of a statutory lien" on certain "property of the debtor."[44]

A statutory lien is a lien that arises "solely by force of a statute on specified circumstances or conditions." It also includes liens "of distress for rent," whether or not that lien arises from a statute. But consensual liens, like security interests and mortgages, and judicial liens, such as those obtained through legal or equitable proceedings, are excluded.[45]

Avoidable statutory liens fall into three groups:

- those that first become effective based on the debtor's financial condition;
- those that are not perfected or enforceable when the debtor's bankruptcy case commences; and
- those that are for rent.

The Code properly treats statutory liens that do not become effective unless the debtor faces adverse financial circumstances as nothing more than state legislative efforts to circumvent the bankruptcy distribution system. If these statutory liens were permitted to stand, state legislatures would be able to give secured status to favored creditors who otherwise would be limited to unsecured status.[46] Thus, the trustee can avoid a statutory lien that "first becomes effective against the debtor": (1) when a bankruptcy or other insolvency proceeding is commenced,[47] when a custodian is appointed to take possession of the debtor's property,[48] when the debtor becomes insolvent or fails to maintain some other financial condition,[49] or when the debtor's property is levied upon by some other creditor.[50] Thus, if a state medical association were to persuade the legislature to pass legislation that gives health care providers a statutory lien on a debtor's home in the event that the debtor ceases to make payments to health care providers when they come due, the lien would be avoidable as

[43] Thomas H. Jackson, *Statutory Liens and Constructive Trusts in Bankruptcy: Undoing the Confusion*, 61 Am. Bankr. L.J. 287 (1987); John McCoid II, *Statutory Liens in Bankruptcy*, 68 Am. Bankr. L.J. 269 (1994); Gene S. Schneyer, *Statutory Liens Under the New Bankruptcy Code — Some Problems Remain*, 55 Am. Bankr. L.J. 1 (1981).

[44] Bankruptcy Code § 545.

[45] Bankruptcy Code § 101(53); *see* In re A & R Wholesale Distrib., Inc., 232 B.R. 616, 618 (Bankr. D.N.J. 1999).

[46] *Cf.*, John A.E. Pottow, *Greed and Pride in International Bankruptcy: The Problems of and Proposed Solutions to "Local Interests,"* 104 Mich. L. Rev. 1899 (2006).

[47] Bankruptcy Code § 545(1)(A), (B).

[48] Bankruptcy Code § 545(1)(C).

[49] Bankruptcy Code § 545(1)(D), (E).

[50] Bankruptcy Code § 545(1)(F).

a lien that "first becomes effective against the debtor . . . when the debtor's financial condition fails to meet a specific standard."[51]

The second group of avoided statutory liens are those that are not "perfected or enforceable" when the debtor's case is commenced against a hypothetical bona fide purchaser that purchases the property subject to the lien at that time.[52] This overlaps to a large extent with § 544(a)'s strong-arm clause. As is true with the strong-arm clause of § 544(a), there is no requirement that there be an actual bona fide purchaser of the encumbered property. Rather, the trustee is treated as if she were a bona fide purchaser with respect to any statutory liens on the debtor's property.

The third group of avoided liens is for rent and distress for rent.[53] Most states provide landlords with a lien on their tenants' property as security for rent. These liens need not be statutory to be vulnerable to avoidance. Because these liens would disrupt the priority rules of the Bankruptcy Code, they are avoidable by the trustee. However, consensual landlord liens, such as a security interest granted by the terms of the lease agreement between the parties, are not avoidable under § 545.

§ 14.05 Post-Petition Transfers of Estate Property[54]

As explained elsewhere, when a debtor files a bankruptcy petition, all of her property is instantaneously transferred to her bankruptcy estate.[55] Nevertheless, the debtor still has possession of most if not all of her property and might transfer it without proper authority.

[A] Unauthorized Transactions[56]

The trustee may avoid any transfer of property of the estate that occurs after the commencement of the case and is not authorized either by the Bankruptcy Code or by the court.[57] For example, if the debtor uses estate property (her bank account) to pay some of her creditors, without proper authority to make these payments, the court can compel the creditors who received the payments to return the funds.

Limited protection against avoidance is provided for post-petition real estate transactions. A transferee of real estate may keep the real estate transfer if: (1) the transferee is a good faith purchaser; (2) the transferee

[51] Bankruptcy Code § 545(1)(E).

[52] Bankruptcy Code § 545(2).

[53] Bankruptcy Code § 545(3), (4).

[54] David Gray Carlson, *Bankruptcy's Acephalous Moment: Postpetition Transfers under the Bankruptcy Code*, 21 Bankr. Dev. J. 113 (2004); Darrell W. Dunham, *Postpetition Transfers in Bankruptcy*, 39 U. Miami L. Rev. 1 (1984).

[55] Bankruptcy Code § 541(a)(1); *see* § 7.02 Property Included in the Estate, *supra*.

[56] William J. Rochelle, III & Gwen L. Feder, *Unauthorized Sales of a Debtor's Property: The Rights of a Purchaser Under § 549 of the Bankruptcy Code*, 57 Am. Bankr. L.J. 23 (1983).

[57] Bankruptcy Code § 549(a)(1), (2)(B).

had no knowledge that the bankruptcy case had commenced; (3) the transferee paid a fair equivalent value for the property; and (4) the transferee's interest was recorded before notice of the bankruptcy case was recorded.[58] If the transferee meets all of the requirements except the requirement that fair equivalent value be paid, the transferee has a lien on the property for whatever present value it paid.[59]

Avoidable post-petition transfers must be avoided within the applicable time limit. An action or proceeding must be commenced before the earlier of two years after the date of the transfer, or the time the case is closed or dismissed.[60]

[B] Involuntary Gap Transfers

In an involuntary case, there can be a gap between the filing of the petition and the court's determination as to whether an order for relief should be entered.[61] Transfers of property by the estate may occur during this period. The treatment of those transfers, which are given somewhat more protection than other post-petition transfers, is discussed elsewhere.[62]

§ 14.06 Preservation of Avoided Transfers for the Benefit of the Estate[63]

Section 551 provides that any transfer avoided under §§ 522 (Exempt Property), 544 (Strong-Arm Clause), 545 (Statutory Liens), 547 (Preferences) 548 (Fraudulent Transfers), 549 (Post-Petition Transfers), or 724(a) (Liens Securing Noncompensatory Damages), and any lien that is void under § 506(d) (Undersecured Creditors), is preserved for the benefit of the estate with respect to property of the estate.[64]

Preservation of an avoided transfer is beneficial to the estate when the property involved is subject to a junior lien that would otherwise move up in priority to take the place of the avoided senior lien.[65] Assume, for

---

[58] Bankruptcy Code § 549(c).

[59] Bankruptcy Code § 549(c). For a somewhat more detailed discussion of this provision in the context of the protection of those transferees during the "involuntary gap" period between the filing of an involuntary petition and the entry of an order for relief, see § 6.03[H][2] Involuntary Gap Transfers of Estate Property, *supra*.

[60] Bankruptcy Code § 549(d).

[61] Bankruptcy Code § 303; *see* § 6.03[E] Grounds for Entry of "An Order for Relief," *supra*.

[62] *See* § 6.03[H][3] Involuntary Gap Transfers of Estate Property, *supra*.

[63] John C. Chobot, *Preserving Liens Avoided in Bankruptcy — Limitations and Applications*, 62 Am. Bankr. L.J. 149 (1988); John C. McCoid, II, *Preservation of Avoided Transfers and Liens*, 77 Va. L. Rev. 1091 (1991).

[64] Bankruptcy Code § 551.

[65] According to the legislative history, the purpose of § 551 is to prevent "junior lienors from improving their position at the expense of the estate when a senior lien is avoided." H.R. Rep. 95-595, 376 (1977), *reprinted in* 1978 U.S.C.C.A.N. 5963, 6332; S. Rep. No. 95-989, 91 (1978), *reprinted in* 1978 U.S.C.C.A.N. 5787, 5877.

example, that Franklin Manufacturing's land is encumbered by two liens: a senior mortgage for $4.5 million held by First National Bank and a junior judgment lien that secures a $6 million judgment in favor of Industrial Supply Co., one of Franklin's suppliers. Franklin's land and building are now worth only $5 million. Assume further that First National's senior mortgage is not recorded, but that First National's mortgage is senior to Security Bank's mortgage under the applicable state recording statute because Industrial Supply had prior notice of the earlier First National Bank mortgage.

Because of its failure to record, First National's mortgage is avoidable under § 544(a). Without § 551, avoidance of First National's mortgage moves Industrial Supply's judgment lien into the senior position. Because the land is worth less than the amount of Industrial Supply's lien, avoiding First National's mortgage brings no additional value into the estate to be distributed to creditors. Section 551 prevents this from happening. It preserves First National's mortgage "for the benefit of the estate" and keeps Industrial Supply in the junior position it would have held had the bankruptcy not been filed. In effect, the bankruptcy trustee takes over First National's senior position. When the land and building are sold for $5 million, the trustee receives the first $4.5 million and Industrial Supply receives only $500,000.

Section § 551 effectively subrogates the trustee to the rights of the person whose rights she avoids. As is true with other subrogation rights, it puts the trustee in exactly the same position as the holder of the avoided transfer or the void lien, neither better nor worse. Section 551 represents a decision by Congress that the benefit of the avoidance should go to the unsecured creditors, and not to the holder of the junior interest in the property involved.

§ 14.07 Recovery of Avoided Transfers

The trustee's avoidance powers are not self-executing. If property has been transferred, and that transfer is avoidable, there has to be a mechanism for getting the property back. Even a court judgment ruling that a transfer is avoidable requires further action to recover the property involved, unless the transferee surrenders it. Section 550 contains rules that govern the actual recovery of avoidable transfers. If a transfer is avoided under §§ 544 (Strong-Arm Clause), 545 (Statutory Liens), 547 (Preferences), 548 (Fraudulent Transfers), 549 (Post-Petition Transfers), 553(b) (Set-off Preferences), or 724(a) (liens securing noncompensatory damages), the trustee may recover the property transferred, or if the court so orders, the value of the property.[66]

Section 550 only comes into play if there has been a transfer of ownership. Avoidance of a lien does not usually require any action beyond entry of a declaratory judgment. In most cases, the previously encumbered property

[66] Bankruptcy Code § 550(a).

is in the custody of the trustee or the debtor in possession and there is no way for the creditor to exercise any power over the property. However, if tangible property has been physically transferred, or if money has been credited to the transferee's account, then the property must be physically recaptured or the transfer reversed on the books of the banks involved.

[A] Recovery of the Property or Its Value

The ability of the trustee to recover either the property transferred or its value is particularly significant when the avoidable transfer was something other than a cash payment. Although court approval is required to obtain the value of the property (money), rather than the property itself, courts routinely grant such permission. Particularly in a liquidation case, the trustee often prefers money rather than the property itself, which the trustee would then have to turn around and sell. Moreover, the property may have been damaged or destroyed after the transfer; or it may have simply depreciated in value over time. It is well established that the value the trustee can recover is the value it had when it was transferred, not the value at the time of recovery.[67] If the value of the property has increased since it was transferred, however, some courts permit recovery of the higher value and give the transferee a lien on the property for the amount of any expenses the transferee incurred in making improvements.[68]

[B] Recovery from Transferees

In most cases, the property, or its value, may be recovered either from the initial transferee or entity for whose benefit the transfer was made, or any immediate or mediate transferee of the initial transferee.[69] This means that the trustee can pursue a recovery not only from the person who received the transfer from the debtor, but also from anyone who was the beneficiary of the transfer and any subsequent transferee. For example, suppose that shortly before filing bankruptcy, Vicki fraudulently transferred her car to her husband, Doug. Doug then transferred the car to his cousin, Sam. In Vicki's bankruptcy case, the trustee can recover the value of the car from Doug (the trustee cannot recover the car itself *from Doug* because he no longer has it), or the trustee can recover either the car or its value from Sam. Of course, the trustee is entitled to only one recovery; if the trustee recovers the value of the car from Doug, the trustee cannot also recover from Sam.[70]

---

[67] *E.g.*, Drewes v. FM Da-Sota Elevator Co. (In re Da-Sota Elevator Co.), 939 F.2d 654 (8th Cir. 1991).

[68] *E.g.*, Feltman v. Warmus (In re American Way Serv. Corp.), 229 B.R. 496, 531 (Bankr. S.D. Fla. 1999).

[69] Bankruptcy Code § 550(a)(1), (2).

[70] Bankruptcy Code § 550(d) provides: "The trustee is entitled to only a single satisfaction under sub-section (a) of this section."

§ 14.08 General Limitations on Avoiding Powers

There are a number of limitations on the avoiding powers of the trustee. Some of these are discussed in the context of the specific avoiding power — for example, the exceptions to the preference avoidance rules under § 547. Others are of such narrow applicability that they are beyond the scope of this book.[71]

[A] Statute of Limitations

There are a number of time-based limitations on the trustee's avoidance powers. Some of these relate to the filing of the petition; for example, most preferential transfers that occur more than ninety before the petition are unavoidable.[72] Others relate to non-bankruptcy statutes of limitation. For example, when the trustee seeks to use § 544(b) to avoid a transfer that an unsecured creditor could have avoided outside of bankruptcy, the trustee is limited by whatever time limits the underlying state law avoidance power imposes.[73] In addition, § 546 sets time limits for the avoidance of transfers under §§ 544 (Strong-Arm Clause), 545 (Statutory Liens), 547 (Preferences), 548 (Fraudulent Transfers) and 553 (Setoff). Section 550(f) imposes a further statute of limitations on actions to recover property or the value of property that have been the subject of an avoidable transfer. Thus § 546(a) imposes a limit on when an action to declare that the transfer is *avoidable* must be filed; § 550(f) imposes a limit on when an action to implement its avoidance by *recovering the property or its value* must be filed.

In most cases, an avoidance action must be commenced within two years after the entry of the order for relief or the closing or dismissal of the case, whichever is earlier. However, if a trustee is first appointed or elected in the case more than one year but less than two years after the entry of the order for relief, then the avoidance action must be commenced by the earlier of one year after appointment or election of the trustee or the closing or dismissal of the case.[74] This is designed to give a trustee who is appointed late in the day a reasonable opportunity to investigate avoidable transfers. This might easily occur in Chapter 11 cases in which the debtor-in-possession manages the estate for a period of time before its gross mismanagement or fraud leads the court to appoint a trustee. Rather than force the trustee to hastily investigate transfers that might be avoided, the limitations period is extended beyond the normal two-year limit to give the trustee a minimum of one year to bring an appropriate action.

---

[71] *See* Bankruptcy Code § 546(e)-(g). These provisions limit avoidance of margin payments and transfers under swap agreements.

[72] *See* § 15.02[E] Preference Period, *infra.*

[73] *See* § 14.03 Power to Exercise Rights of Actual Unsecured Creditors, *supra.*

[74] Bankruptcy Code § 546(a).

Section 549 (Post-Petition Transfers) has its own limitations period. An action to avoid a post-petition transfer must be commenced by the earlier of two years after the transfer or the closing or dismissal of the case.[75]

Section 550, which deals with the recovery of property or its value after its transfer is avoided, imposes a different limit. An action to recover the property transferred, or its value, must be commenced by the earlier of one year after the transfer was avoided or the time the case is closed or dismissed.[76]

For example, suppose Titanic Industries filed its voluntary Chapter 11 petition on May 1, 2006, resulting in an immediate order for relief, and wants to bring an action to avoid a payment that it made to one of its suppliers as an avoidable preference. Under § 546(a), Titanic, as debtor-in-possession, must bring an action to avoid the transfer by May 2, 2008, "2 years after the entry of the order for relief."[77] If a trustee is appointed, the trustee has until one year after her appointment to bring the action, even if that delays its filing until after May 2, 2008.[78] But in no event may the avoidance action be brought, by either Titanic as debtor-in-possession or a trustee, after the case is closed or dismissed.[79]

Further assume that Titanic files the avoidance action on April 30, 2008, and that on June 1, 2008, obtains a judgment avoiding the transfer. Section 550(f)(1) requires any action to recover the avoided transfer be brought within one year of the June 1, 2008, judgment.

[B] Effect of Non-Bankruptcy Law Grace Periods

The right of the trustee to avoid a transfer under §§ 544 (Strong-Arm Clause), 545 (Statutory Liens), and 549 (Post-Petition Transfers) is subject to any "generally applicable law" that permits perfection of an interest in property to be effective against an entity that acquired rights in the property before perfection.[80] This protects two-step transactions that are incomplete at the time of bankruptcy, such as security interests and mortgages.[81]

A simple example of this is contained in Article 9 of the Uniform Commercial Code. Article 9 security interests are two-step transactions; the first step is attachment, which grants the security interest to the secured party, and the second step is perfection, usually accomplished by the filing of a financing statement in the office of the secretary of state. Perfection protects the transfer against subsequent third parties, such as other

---

[75] Bankruptcy Code § 549(d).

[76] Bankruptcy Code § 550(e).

[77] Bankruptcy Code § 546(a)(1)(A).

[78] Bankruptcy Code § 546(a)(1)(B).

[79] Bankruptcy Code § 546(a)(2).

[80] Bankruptcy Code § 546(b). This limitation does not apply to other avoiding powers, such as those involving preferences or fraudulent transfers.

[81] *See* § 2.02 Consensual Liens, *supra*.

secured parties and those who acquire a judicial lien on the property.[82] Generally, an interest in the property that arises between attachment and perfection has priority over the security interest. However, there are exceptions. The most important of these relates to "purchase money security interests" (PMSI), which are created in conjunction with the debtor's acquisition of the property used as collateral. Article 9 supplies a twenty-day period during which the PMSI may be perfected and remain effective against interests that arose during the grace period.[83]

Section 546(b) protects these two-step transfers from avoidance by the trustee when the petition is filed during whatever grace period other law, such as the U.C.C., provides. Its purpose "is to protect, in spite of the surprise intervention of a bankruptcy petition, those whom State law protects by allowing them to perfect their liens or interests as of an effective date that is earlier than the date of the perfection."[84]

For example, if on March 10, Industrial Supply delivers equipment to Franklin Manufacturing, that is subject to Industrial Supply's purchase money security interest, and Franklin files a Chapter 11 petition on March 17, before Industrial Supply has filed a financing statement to perfect its security interest, the security interest might be avoidable under the strong-arm clause of § 544(a). Outside of bankruptcy, Industrial Supply enjoys a twenty-day grace period beginning on March 10, the day Franklin received possession of the collateral, to file its financing statement and perfect the security interest. Section 546(b) preserves Industrial Supply's right to file within the twenty-day period and prevents the trustee from avoiding Industrial's security interest. Section 362(b)(2) facilitates the operation of § 546(b) by creating an exception to the automatic stay for creditors whose conduct merely takes advantage of the type of generally applicable law to which § 546(b) refers.[85]

[C] Seller's Reclamation Rights

Unpaid sellers sometimes enjoy the right to reclaim goods from a buyer who has not paid for them. However, the Bankruptcy Code imposes limits on this right of reclamation, and, other creditors may achieve priority over the seller's right to reclaim, even if the Bankruptcy Code's limits do not apply.

[1] Seller's Right to Reclaim under U.C.C. Article 2

Under U.C.C. § 2-702(2), an unpaid seller may reclaim goods that it delivered to a buyer on credit, if the buyer was insolvent at the time the goods were delivered.[86] Section 2-702 gives sellers the right to reclaim goods sold

[82] *See* § 2.02[B] Security Interests in Personal Property, *supra*.

[83] *See* U.C.C. § 9-317(d) (2003).

[84] S. Rep. No. 95-989, at 86 (1978), *reprinted in* 1978 U.S.C.C.A.N. 5787, 5872.

[85] Bankruptcy Code § 362(b)(2); *see* § 8.03 Exceptions to the Automatic Stay, *supra*.

[86] U.C.C. § 2-702(2) (2002).

on credit to an insolvent buyer, but only if the seller demands return of the goods within ten days of the buyer's receipt. In some instances, the ten-day limit is expanded to an unlimited time.[87]

In addition, U.C.C. § 2-507(2) gives unpaid sellers a similar right to reclaim the goods in cash transactions in which the buyer's mode of payment fails. Section 2-507(2) is not limited to situations where the seller can prove that the buyer was insolvent, and does not impose a time limit on the seller's right to reclaim the goods.[88]

[2] Enforcement of Reclamation Rights in Bankruptcy

Before 2005, the Bankruptcy Code permitted the bankruptcy court to implement a seller's right to reclaim either by ordering the debtor to return the goods, by giving the unpaid seller a lien on the goods to secure the seller's claim for payment, or by granting the seller an administrative priority claim for the payment owed.[89] In 2005, these statutory alternatives were eliminated from the Code. Their elimination makes enforcement of a seller's reclamation rights uncertain.

At a minimum, it seems that the seller's reclamation rights should be treated similarly to the rights of a secured creditor and thus entitled to adequate protection under § 362(d)(1). In a Chapter 11, 12, or 13 reorganization plan, the reclaiming creditor should be treated as if it held a secured claim on the goods involved, with the right to return of the goods or repayment of their value.

[3] Bankruptcy Limits on Right to Reclaim

The Bankruptcy Code imposes limits on a seller's right to reclaim delivered goods that do not appear in Article 2. Here, it must be emphasized that § 546(c) does not give sellers a right of reclamation. It merely recognizes reclamation rights created by non-bankruptcy law, such as the U.C.C. As one court explained:

> [The] Bankruptcy Code does not create any right of reclamation for sellers of goods to insolvent buyers. It merely recognizes such a right to a limited extent in a bankruptcy case, if any such right exists under either common law or statute other than the Bankruptcy Code. Thus, section 546(c) requires as [a] premise that the reclaiming seller have an independent right of reclamation under applicable nonbankruptcy law. Section 546(c) then narrows those nonbankruptcy reclamation rights by imposing additional procedural and substantive requirements before such rights will be recognized in a bankruptcy case.[90]

---

[87] U.C.C. § 2-702(2) (2002). NCCUSL's revisions to U.C.C. § 2-702, that have not yet been adopted in any state, remove both ten-day and three-month limits in favor of a requirement that the seller demand reclamation within a "reasonable time." U.C.C. § 2-702 (2003).

[88] U.C.C. § 2-507, cmt. 3 (2002); *see* § 2.06[E] Seller's Right of Reclamation, *supra*.

[89] Former 11 U.S.C. § 546(c)(2) (2000) (repealed 2005).

[90] In re Video King of Ill., Inc., 100 B.R. 1008, 1013 (Bankr. N.D. Ill. 1989).

First, the seller's demand for return of the goods must be made in writing. Although sensible sellers will make a written demand, the Bankruptcy Code makes this a necessity.

Second, the Code permits reclamation only with respect to goods delivered to the debtor within forty-five days before the debtor's bankruptcy petition.[91] Thus, if Century Slate Co. delivers slate shingles to Ron's Roofing on June 1, and Ron files his bankruptcy petition on July 20, Century is unable to reclaim them, even if it held a right of reclamation under the U.C.C.

Third, the seller's written demand for return of the goods must be made no later than forty-five days after the buyer received the goods, or, if this forty-five day period expires after the buyer's bankruptcy petition, no later than twenty days after the petition.[92]

In short, for the seller's right of reclamation to be good in bankruptcy, the seller must comply with all the requirements of both the U.C.C. and of the Bankruptcy Code. Compliance with the U.C.C. is required because it establishes the seller's right to reclaim the goods in the first place. Compliance with the Bankruptcy Code is required because it imposes limits on whatever right of reclamation exists when the buyer has gone into bankruptcy.

[4] Reclamation Rights Subordinate to Competing Secured Creditor

A seller's right of reclamation is also limited to the right of a competing secured creditor who may have a floating lien on after-acquired property of the type involved in the sale.[93] Such a purchaser encompasses creditors whose security interest attaches to the goods when the buyer acquires rights in them pursuant to the terms of the security agreement between the parties. Thus, the seller's right of reclamation may end up subordinate to the competing claims of a senior secured creditor. Loss of priority in this manner does not seem to impair the seller's right to an administrative expense priority under § 503(b)(9).

[5] Administrative Expense Priority

A seller who fails to comply with the Bankruptcy Code's time limits for asserting its right of reclamation is provided with one more chance for relief. Sections 546(c)(2) and 503(b)(9) give a seller who does not comply with § 546(c)(1)'s time limits an administrative priority expense for the "value of any goods received by the debtor within twenty days before [the petition] in which the goods have been sold to the debtor in the ordinary course of such debtor's business."[94]

---

[91] Bankruptcy Code § 546(c)(1).

[92] Bankruptcy Code § 546(c)(1)(A)-(B).

[93] *E.g.*, Genesee Merchants Bank & Trust Co. v. Tucker Motor Sales, 372 N.W.2d 546 (Mich. Ct. App. 1985); *see* § 2.06[E] Seller's Right of Reclamation, *supra*.

[94] Bankruptcy Code § 503(b)(9).

This language is broader than § 546(c)(1) in that it protect sellers regardless of whether they enjoy a right to reclamation under state law. However, in other respects, it is more limited than § 546(c), because it only applies to goods sold to business debtors and to goods sold in the ordinary course of the debtor's business operations. It provides no protection to those who sell to consumers. Moreover, the priority is for the "value" of the goods, which may or may not be the same as the agreed contract price.

[D] Protection for Good Faith Transferees

Immediate transferees from the debtor generally enjoy little protection and must return the property or its value to the estate, though in some cases they have the right to a lien for the amount they paid in good faith for the transferred property or for improvements they have made since acquiring the property. Remote transferees, who acquired the property from the initial transferee, enjoy greater protection.

[1] Remote Transferees

Some protection against avoidance is given to remote good faith transferees. The rule is similar to the rules regarding holders in due course of negotiable instruments and good faith purchasers of investment securities. The trustee may not recover from a subsequent transferee if the transferee "takes for value, including satisfaction or securing of present or antecedent debt, in good faith, and without knowledge of the voidability of the transfer avoided."[95] Moreover, any transferee of the property after a protected remote transferee who takes the property in "good faith" is also protected from liability.[96]

Assume, for example, that shortly before he filed his bankruptcy case, Charlie fraudulently transferred his car to his sister Gail. Gail sold the car for its fair market value to Reliable Motors, who had no knowledge of Charlie's fraudulent transfer of the car to Gail. Reliable Motors then sold the car to Bonita, who purchased it in good faith.

In Charlie's bankruptcy case, the trustee can recover the value of the car from Gail, as the "initial transferee of the transfer."[97] However, the trustee cannot recover the value of the car from Reliable Motors, nor can it recover either the car or the value of the car from Bonita. As a transferee for value, in good faith, and without knowledge of the voidability of the transaction, Reliable Motors meets all the requirements for protection under § 550(b)(1). Bonita is similarly protected.

[2] Amounts Paid by a Transferee

Several provisions of the Code protect good faith transferees for the amount they paid for property transferred to them by the debtor. The Code's

---

[95] Bankruptcy Code § 550(b)(1).

[96] Bankruptcy Code § 550(b)(2)

[97] Bankruptcy Code § 550(a)(1).

protections are generally supplied by the portion of the Code that makes the transfer avoidable in the first place.

With respect to fraudulent transfers, § 548(c) protects good faith transferees by giving them a lien on the transferred property "to the extent that [the] transferee gave value to the debtor in exchange for the transfer."[98] Thus, if Gail (from the example above) acted in good faith in buying the car from Charlie, she has a lien on the recovered property to the extent of her payment. Section 549 provides similar protection for good faith purchasers of property transferred by the debtor after commencement of the case.[99]

No similar protection is supplied to transferees of property under §§ 544 (Strong-Arm Clause), 545 (Statutory Liens), or 547 (Preferences). However, these transferees have a claim against the estate for the amount of the transferred property; this restores them to the position they would have been in if the transfer had not been made.

[3] Improvements by a Transferee

Additional protection is given to transferees who make improvements to the transferred property. A good faith transferee from whom the trustee may recover has a lien on the property recovered to secure the lesser of (a) the cost to the transferee of any improvement made after the transfer, less the amount of any profit realized by or accruing to the transferee from the property, or (b) any increase in the value of the property as a result of the improvement.[100]

For example, assume that before his bankruptcy, Jerry transferred a parcel of real estate to Chu in satisfaction of a $150,000 debt he owed to Chu. Although the transfer was a preference, Chu acted in good faith with no knowledge that Jerry was preparing to file a bankruptcy petition. After taking possession of the property, Chu spent $50,000 renovating the kitchen. His efforts increased the value of the land by $40,000. When the trustee recovers the property, Chu is entitled to a lien on the property for the amount by which his improvements increased the value of the land — $40,000. If his work had increased the value to $60,000, Jerry would be entitled to a lien for the full $50,000 he spent, but because he was willing to spend $50,000 to improve the value by only $40,000, the Code limits his lien to the expenses incurred or the enhancement in value achieved, whichever is lower.

The lien exists only if improvements are made on the property, and only if those improvements increase the value of the property. If the property increases in value on its own, and not because of any improvements made by the transferee, the transferee has no lien at all. The term "improvement" encompasses physical additions or changes to the property, repairs to the

[98] Bankruptcy Code § 548(c).

[99] Bankruptcy Code § 549(c).

[100] Bankruptcy Code § 550(d)(1).

property, payment of tax on the property, payment of any debt secured by a lien that is superior to or equal to the rights of the trustee, and preservation of the property.[101]

No similar protection is provided to transferees who act in bad faith. Thus, if Chu, in the above example, had knowingly assisted in Jerry's fraudulent conveyance of his land, and subsequently paid to have the land improved, he would not be entitled to a lien for the amount of his improvements.

[101] Bankruptcy Code § 550(d)(2).

Chapter 15

Preferences

§ 15.01 Preference Policies

This chapter deals with the power of the trustee (or debtor-in-possession)[1] to avoid certain pre-petition transactions as "preferences." The preference power, contained in § 547 of the Bankruptcy Code, allows the trustee-in-bankruptcy (TIB) to recover certain payments made by the debtor to creditors on the eve of the bankruptcy filing. The purpose of the preference power is to prevent a race by creditors to dismember the debtor, and to reverse the consequences of such a race when it occurs.[2]

Broadly speaking, a preference occurs whenever a debtor favors one creditor over another in paying out its limited resources. For example, if Donna owes $1000 to Chuck and $500 to Carla, but has only $500 in available assets, Donna may decide to pay the entire $500 to Carla shortly before filing for bankruptcy. Such a payment "prefers" Carla to Chuck. Such preferences are legal under state law, but the Bankruptcy Code takes the view that, when the debtor is insolvent, similarly situated creditors should be treated equally. In bankruptcy, therefore, many such preferences may be avoided (returned to the estate).[3]

In the above example, if the payment to Carla is a preference as that term is defined under the Bankruptcy Code, and is not subject to any defense, Carla will have to return the $500 payment to the bankruptcy estate. In return, Carla will receive a $500 claim against the estate.[4] Unfortunately for Carla, her $500 claim will share with other claims against the estate, and she is likely therefore to receive far less than $500. The difference between the $500 returned by Carla to the estate, and the estate's payment to Carla on account of her claim is the gain to the estate.

Many justifications for preference law have been put forward. The two most widely cited are "preservation of the estate" and "equality of

---

1 Section 547 speaks in terms of the ability of the trustee to avoid preferences. However, in a Chapter 11 case, the debtor usually remains in possession of the property of the estate and controls the reorganization process. Consequently, the debtor manages the estate as the "debtor-in-possession" and has all of the same rights, powers, and duties of a trustee, including the right to deploy the trustee's avoiding powers. Bankruptcy Code § 1107(a); *see* § 4.02[B] Debtor-in-Possession, *supra*.

2 Vern Countryman, *The Concept of a Voidable Preference in Bankruptcy*, 38 Vand. L. Rev. 713 (1985); Thomas H. Jackson, *Avoiding Powers in Bankruptcy*, 36 Stan. L. Rev. 725 (1984); Charles J. Tabb, *Beneath the Surface of BAPCPA: The Brave New World of Bankruptcy Preferences*, 13 Am. Bankr. Inst. L. Rev. 425 (2005).

3 Bankruptcy Code § 550.

4 Bankruptcy Code § 502(h).

distribution."[5] The former justification is based on the not-unreasonable assumption that creditors as a whole are likely to receive a greater payout if the debtor's assets remain intact until bankruptcy.[6] If they do, the trustee can conduct an orderly liquidation or the debtor-in-possession will have a greater chance of reorganizing. Orderly liquidation tends to produce more money than piecemeal dismemberment; reorganizations are likely to produce more money than any form of liquidation. In theory, preference law, by forcing the return of property transferred to creditors, preserves the estate. If creditors must return what they have obtained from the debtor by individual actions, they have no incentive to pick off the debtor's assets one by one; thus, the debtor's assets will remain intact to be administered as a whole through the bankruptcy proceeding. The most sophisticated version of this theory is rooted in the "creditor's bargain" theory of bankruptcy law. This view assumes that creditors would generally prefer to receive equal treatment in a larger asset pool than unequal treatment in a smaller one, even though they might sometimes benefit from taking a disproportionate share of the smaller pool.[7]

The second traditional rationale is that preference law protects the Bankruptcy Code's policy of equal distribution among creditors by forcing those who have received unequal distributions to return the excess they received.[8] A more subtle version of this rationale recognizes that distributions under the Bankruptcy Code do not treat all unsecured creditors equally. Instead, it is probably more accurate to say that the preference rules help effectuate the system of distribution mandated by Congress in the Bankruptcy Code. Bankruptcy is the last opportunity for most creditors to obtain any payment from the debtor, and it is virtually certain that there will not be enough in the estate to go around. Given these facts, Congress has established a set of priorities that identify those debts it thinks should be given the best chance of payment. Congress has ranked debts in order of perceived importance and has further mandated pro rata payment of claims within each rank, so that each creditor in the rank bears only a proportionate share of the loss. Preferences disturb this statutory distribution system by allowing the preferred creditor to obtain more than the Code would give it. Preferences are thus avoided to increase the number and amount of claims, and the value of the assets, dealt with under the Code's

[5] *E.g.*, In re Bullion Reserve of N. Am., 836 F.2d 1214, 1217 (9th Cir. 1988); Vern Countryman, *The Concept of a Voidable Preference in Bankruptcy*, 38 Vand. L. Rev. 713, 748, 778 (1985).

[6] *See* § 1.01[B] Bankruptcy as a Debtors' Remedy: Fresh Start for Honest Debtors, *supra.*

[7] *See generally* Bruce R. Krause, Note, *Preferential Transfers and the Value of The Insolvent Firm*, 87 Yale L.J. 1449, 1450 (1978); Thomas H. Jackson, The Logic and Limits of Bankruptcy Law 124 (1986); John McCoid, *Bankruptcy, Preferences, and Efficiency: An Expression of Doubt*, 67 Va. L. Rev. 249 (1981); Lawrence Ponoroff, *Evil Intentions and an Irresolute Endorsement for Scientific Rationalism: Bankruptcy Preferences One More Time*, 1993 Wis. L. Rev. 1439; Robert Weisberg, *Commercial Morality, The Merchant Character, and the History of the Voidable Preference*, 39 Stan. L. Rev. 3 (1986).

[8] *See* § 1.01[C] Bankruptcy as a Creditor's Remedy; Equal Treatment of Creditors of the Same Class, *supra.*

system. In short, a creditor who "ought to have" received $10,000, but who in fact received $20,000 because of a preference must pay back the preference and be given instead the $10,000 that Congress says it deserved.[9]

§ 15.02 Preferences Defined

The Code's primary preference provision is § 547. "Preferences" are defined in § 547(b), which sets out six elements. A preference is a transfer (i) of property, (ii) to or for the benefit of a creditor, (iii) on account of an antecedent debt, (iv) made while the debtor was insolvent, (v) made during the preference period (usually the ninety days before the bankruptcy, but one full year for insiders of the debtor), (vi) that enables the creditor to receive more than it would get in a Chapter 7 liquidation of the debtor.[10] Each of these six elements requires careful analysis of the statute and the very extensive case law.

[A] Transfer of Property; Date of Transfer

A preference involves "any transfer of an interest of the debtor in property." It is important to recognize that the property need not be in the form of money. It may be in the form of tangible property, intangible property, or in the form of a security interest in the debtor's property.[11] The transfer may also be voluntary or involuntary.[12] For example, a voluntary payment of a debt may be a preference; but so may the involuntary imposition of a judicial lien[13] or a tax lien on the debtor's property.[14] The transfer may be of all rights in the property or only a partial interest in the property. For example, the grant of a security interest in the property, which gives the secured party only limited rights, is a transfer that may be a preference.[15]

It is often important to determine the date on which the transfer occurs. The date may determine whether the transfer was within the preference period,[16] whether it was a payment of an antecedent (preexisting) debt,[17]

---

[9] See generally Charles Jordan Tabb, *Rethinking Preferences*, 43 S.C. L. Rev. 981 (1992); Vern Countryman, *The Concept of a Voidable Preference in Bankruptcy*, 38 Vand. L. Rev. 713 (1985).

[10] Bankruptcy Code § 547(b).

[11] Bankruptcy Code § 101(54)(B).

[12] Bankruptcy Code § 101(54)(D).

[13] *See* § 2.05 Judicial Liens, *supra*.

[14] *See* § 2.06 Statutory, Common Law, and Equitable Liens, *supra*.

[15] *See* Irving A. Breitowitz, *Article 9 Security Interests as Voidable Preferences*, 4 Cardozo L. Rev. 357 (1982); David Gray Carlson, *Security Interests in the Crucible of Voidable Preference Law*, 1995 U. Ill. L. Rev. 211; Vern Countryman, *The Concept of a Voidable Preference in Bankruptcy*, 38 Vand. L. Rev. 713 (1985); Thomas M. Ward & Jay A. Shulman, *In Defense of the Bankruptcy Code's Radical Integration of the Preference Rules Affecting Commercial Financing*, 61 Wash U. L.Q. 1 (1983).

[16] *See* § 15.02[E] Preference Period, *infra*.

[17] *See* § 15.02[C] Antecedent Debt, *infra*.

or whether the debtor was insolvent at the time the transfer occurred.[18] It may also determine whether an exception to the avoidance rule applies.[19]

Most of the difficulty regarding the date of transfer involves two-step transfers.[20] The first step makes the transaction effective between the original parties to the transaction. A second step is required to establish the transferee's rights against third parties. For example, a conveyance of real property generally requires both the execution of a deed and the recording of the deed.[21] Step one — execution — makes the transaction effective between the seller and the buyer. Step two — recording — is required to establish the buyer's rights against certain third parties, such as subsequent bona fide purchasers of the realty.

Similarly, an Article 9 secured transaction often requires two steps.[22] Step one is attachment, which establishes the rights and obligations of the debtor and the secured party.[23] Step two is an additional act to perfect the security interest, which establishes the secured party's rights in the collateral as against other claimants to the same collateral, such as the holder of a subsequent judgment lien the property.[24] Similar rules apply to other personal property security transactions, such as preferred ship mortgages.[25] At which point — step one or step two — is the transfer made for preference purposes?

This issue is addressed by § 547(e). It sets out rules to determine the time at which a transfer is complete. These rules deal with transfers of both real property and personal property, and with one-step and two-step transfers.

Section 547(e)(2) sets out the basic rules for determining when a transfer is made. It distinguishes between the time at which the transfer is effective between the parties and the time at which it is "perfected." There are four situations dealt with by the rules. The first two deal with situations in which the transfer was perfected prior to the commencement of the bankruptcy case; the second two with situations in which perfection occurred after the commencement of the case.

First, if the transfer is perfected at the time it becomes effective between the parties, or within thirty days thereafter, the transfer occurs on the date it becomes effective. For example, suppose the debt was incurred on January 1, 2006 and that transfer became effective between debtor and creditor on the same day, January 1, 2006, but was not perfected until January 15, 2006. The transfer is deemed to have occurred on January 1.

[18] *See* § 15.02[D] Insolvent at Time of Transfer, *infra*.

[19] *See* § 15.03 Exceptions to Avoidance of Preferences, *infra*.

[20] *See* § 2.02[A][2] Two Step Process: Agreement and Recordation, *supra*.

[21] *See, e.g.*, In re Lewis W. Shurtleff, Inc., 778 F.2d 1416 (9th Cir. 1985); In re Freedlander, Inc., 107 Bankr. 88 (Bankr. E.D. Va. 1989).

[22] *See* § 2.02[B][1] Uniform Commercial Code Article 9, *supra*.

[23] U.C.C. § 9-203 (2003).

[24] U.C.C. §§ 9-317 to -339 (2003).

[25] In re Gottschalk, 46 B.R. 49 (Bankr. M.D. Fla. 1985).

Since this is simultaneous with the incurring of the debt, the transfer is not a preference because it is not on account of an antecedent debt.[26]

Second, if the transfer is perfected more than thirty days after the time it becomes effective, the transfer occurs on the date it was perfected. If the debt was incurred and the transfer became effective on January 1, but was not perfected until February 15, the transfer is deemed to have occurred on February 15. This is important: because attachment occurred 45 days before the transfer, the transfer is now on account of an antecedent or preexisting debt.[27]

Third, if the transfer was not perfected by the later of the date of commencement of the case or thirty days after the transfer became effective, the transfer occurs immediately before the date of the filing of the petition.[28] For example, suppose that the transfer became effective on January 1, the bankruptcy was filed on January 7, and the transfer was perfected on February 15. The transfer is deemed to have occurred immediately before January 7 (which apparently means that it is deemed to have occurred on January 6).[29]

Fourth, if the transfer was not perfected on the date of commencement of the case, but was perfected within thirty days after it became effective, the transfer occurs on the date it became effective. If the transfer became effective on January 1, the bankruptcy was filed on January 5, and the transfer was perfected on January 7, the transfer is deemed to have occurred on January 1.[30]

The key problems are determining what is necessary to make the transfer effective between the parties and what is necessary to perfect the transfer. The Code does not deal with the first issue, which is consequently left to non-bankruptcy law. Nor does the Code state what acts are necessary to perfect the transfer; this too is a question resolved outside the Code.[31] However, the Code does define what legal status constitutes perfection. In other words, the Code does not tell you how to perfect (this is determined by relevant non-Code law) but it does tell you what legal result your actions must have for the transfer to be perfected under § 547.

If the property transferred is realty (other than fixtures), the transfer is perfected only when a bona fide purchaser (BFP) of that property from the debtor cannot acquire an interest that is superior to the right of the transferee.[32] This does not mean that there is such a purchaser, nor does

---

[26] Bankruptcy Code § 547(e)(2)(A).

[27] Bankruptcy Code § 547(e)(2)(B).

[28] In most cases, if the transfer was not perfected at the time the petition is filed, it is avoidable under § 544(a). *See* § 14.02 Strong-Arm Clause, *supra*.

[29] Bankruptcy Code § 547(e)(2)(C).

[30] Bankruptcy Code § 547(e)(2)(A), (C).

[31] Webb v. General Motors Acceptance Corp. (In re Hesser), 984 F.2d 345, 348 (10th Cir. 1993); Grover v. Gulino (In re Gulino), 779 F.2d 546, 550 (9th Cir. 1985).

[32] Bankruptcy Code § 547(e)(1)(A).

it make the trustee a bona fide purchaser.[33] Neither does it mean that every bona fide purchaser would have a superior interest. For example, it is generally true that a bona fide purchaser who has notice of an existing interest takes subject to it. This is irrelevant in determining the date of perfection under § 547(e); the question is not whether a BFP would have a superior right but rather whether a BFP *could* have a superior right. Broadly speaking, a BFP can obtain rights superior to those of the holder of an unrecorded interest in the realty.[34] Thus, as a general principle, an interest in realty is not perfected until it is properly noted in the real estate records.[35]

For example, suppose that on August 1 Alice executes and delivers to Bette a mortgage on her home. Under relevant state law, a BFP without notice does not take subject to an unrecorded mortgage. Bette records the mortgage on August 8. The transfer became effective between Alice and Bette on August 1 and was perfected on August 8; because this was within the 30 day grace period given by § 547(e)(2)(A), the transfer is deemed to have occurred on August 1. If Bette had not recorded until September 12, the transfer would be deemed to have occurred on September 12.

With regard to personal property and fixtures, the rule is somewhat different. A transfer is perfected when a creditor on a simple contract cannot acquire a judicial lien that is superior to the interest of the transferee.[36] There does not have to be such a creditor; nor must all such creditors have rights superior to the transferee. All that is required is that a creditor of that type could obtain a lien that has priority over the rights of the transferee.

This rule is of primary importance with regard to security interests under Article 9 of the Uniform Commercial Code; indeed the Bankruptcy Code rule was designed to mesh with the related U.C.C. rules.[37] Most but not all security interests in personalty and fixtures are governed by Article 9. Like the Bankruptcy Code, Article 9 uses the word "perfection" to describe the status and priority of security interests. Article 9 security interests may either be perfected or unperfected. Under Article 9, a judicial lien generally has priority over a security interest that is not perfected under the Article 9 perfection rules.[38] By contrast, a security interest that is perfected under Article 9 has priority over a subsequent judicial lien.[39]

---

[33] *E.g.*, Grover v. Gulino (In re Gulino), 779 F.2d 546, 551 (9th Cir. 1985).

[34] *See, e.g.*, Midlantic Nat'l Bank v. Bridge (In re Bridge), 18 F.3d 195 (3d Cir. 1994); In re Lewis W. Shurtleff, Inc., 778 F.2d 1416 (9th Cir. 1985).

[35] This remains a matter of state law, however; if in the relevant state a BFP takes subject to an unrecorded deed, then the transfer is complete when the deed is executed and delivered. Webb v. General Motors Acceptance Corp. (In re Hesser), 984 F.2d 345, 348 (10th Cir. 1993).

[36] Bankruptcy Code § 547(e)(1)(B).

[37] *See* § 2.02[B][1][d] Priority Rules under U.C.C. Article 9, *supra*.

[38] U.C.C. § 9-317 (2003).

[39] This is not directly stated in the U.C.C., but derives from U.C.C. § 9-201, which states that the security interest is effective against third parties except as otherwise stated in Article 9. Note that a perfected security interest can be subordinate to a judicial lien with regard to certain advances of credit made to the debtor after the lien attaches. U.C.C. § 9-323 (2003).

This means that, for all practical purposes, perfection under Article 9 is also perfection under the Bankruptcy Code. Except with regard to purchase money security interests in consumer goods, and possessory security interests, Article 9 perfection generally requires that a public record of the security interest be made.[40] For most transactions, this record is a document called a financing statement.[41] Except for real estate related collateral, the financing statement is filed "centrally" in the state capital, usually with the office of the state's secretary of state. For fixtures or other real estate related collateral, "local" filing may be required at the county courthouse or register of deeds.[42] There are other forms of recording for other types of property. For example, if the property is a titled motor vehicle, the record is a notation on the certificate of title.[43]

Suppose that on June 1 Paul lends money to Danuta, and Danuta executes a security agreement giving Paul rights in her business equipment as collateral. Paul files the necessary financing statement on June 5. The transaction became effective between the parties on June 1, and was perfected on June 5. The transfer is deemed to have occurred on June 1, since perfection was within the thirty day grace period.

A final aspect of the date of transfer rules is of special significance to certain types of Article 9 security interests. For § 547 purposes, no transfer can occur until the debtor has rights in the property transferred.[44] Under Article 9, the debtor and secured party may agree that the security interest will attach to "after-acquired property," that is, property that the debtor does not have at the time the security agreement is entered into.[45] When the debtor does acquire the property, the security interest will automatically attach without any further action by the parties.[46]

If a proper financing statement has been filed, that security interest will also be perfected.[47] These rules are carried over into § 547; the transfer of the after-acquired property from the debtor to the secured party will not occur until the debtor acquires rights in it. For example, if on January 1, Franklin Manufacturing and Peninsula Bank enter into a security agreement that covers all of Franklin's inventory, including after-acquired inventory, and Franklin acquires new inventory on June 1, the transfer of the security interest in the new inventory occurs on June 1, not January 1. This has considerable significance in connection with the extent to which floating liens are treated as preferences.[48]

---

[40] U.C.C. § 9-310 (2003).

[41] U.C.C. § 9-310(a) (2003). The proper form for an Article 9 financing statement is set out in U.C.C. § 9-502 (2003).

[42] U.C.C. § 9-501 (2003).

[43] U.C.C. § 9-311(a)(3) (2003).

[44] Bankruptcy Code § 547(e)(3).

[45] U.C.C. § 9-204(a), (b) (2003).

[46] U.C.C. § 9-204 cmt. 2 (2003)

[47] U.C.C. § 9-502 cmt. 2 (2003).

[48] Bankruptcy Code § 547(c)(5); *see* § 15.03[E] Floating Liens, *infra*.

[B] To or For the Benefit of a Creditor

The preference may either be direct or indirect; that is, the property may either be transferred *to* a creditor (direct preference) or *for the benefit* of a creditor (indirect preference).[49] In most cases, this element is self-evident. However, it has created problems in one situation: the treatment of indirect preferences that benefit creditors who are also "insiders" (close affiliates) of the debtor.[50]

[C] Antecedent Debt

A preference is a transfer made regarding an antecedent, or preexisting, debt — an obligation of the debtor that arose before the transfer was made.[51] A contemporaneous exchange is not a preference (although if inadequate value is received by the debtor, it may be a fraudulent transfer).[52] For example, if Doug pays $18,000 in cash to buy a new car during the preference period, his transfer of cash to the seller is not a preference. The antecedent debt requirement derives from the notion that preference law deals with transfers that deplete the estate — more precisely, transfers that reduce the amount available for distribution under the Code's rules. The exchange of one asset for another — of $18,000 cash for an $18,000 car — does not diminish the amount available to creditors.[53]

The antecedent debt requirement is met if there is any appreciable time lag between the creation of the obligation and the transfer. Even a gap of a day or less is sufficient.[54] Thus, if Doug buys the car on Monday, but does not pay for it until Tuesday, his payment may be an avoidable preference.

The strict reading of antecedent debt creates a number of practical problems, because it is often impossible for an exchange to be absolutely contemporaneous. To take the example given above, Doug is much more likely to pay for his new car by giving the dealer a check than $18,000 in cash; yet payment by check is not technically a contemporaneous transfer.[55] These problems have been ameliorated in part by the thirty-day grace period given by § 547(e) for two-step transfers and in part by various exceptions to the avoidance rules set out in § 547(c). For example, suppose that a debt was incurred on January 1, and was secured by a mortgage

[49] Bankruptcy Code § 547(b)(1).

[50] *See* § 15.04 Indirect Preferences, *infra*.

[51] Bankruptcy Code § 547(b)(2).

[52] Bankruptcy Code § 548(a)(1)(B); *see* Chapter 16 Fraudulent Transfers, *infra*.

[53] Bankruptcy Code § 547(b)(2).

[54] For an extreme example, see National City Bank of New York v. Hotchkiss, 231 U.S. 50 (1913) (holding that a lapse of several hours between making loan and obtaining collateral meant that transfer of collateral was on an antecedent debt).

[55] See H.R. Rep. No. 95-595, 373 (1977) ("Strictly speaking [a payment by check] may be a credit transaction because the seller does not receive payment until the check is cleared through the debtor's bank.").

executed and delivered the same day. The mortgage was not filed until January 20. There is no antecedent debt problem because the mortgage transfer was perfected within thirty days of the date it became effective between the parties; thus, the transfer is deemed to have occurred on January 1, contemporaneously with the creation of the obligation.[56] Similarly, § 547(c)(1) ordinarily protects payments by check where completion of the payment may take several days.[57]

[D] Insolvent at the Time of Transfer

For the transfer to be avoidable the debtor must be insolvent at the time of the transfer.[58] When a solvent debtor pays one creditor before another, or does anything else with his or her money, there is no real harm. There will still be enough assets available for all creditors to be paid in full. Insolvency occurs for preference purposes when a debtor's assets are worth less than the amount of its debts. This is the so called "balance sheet" test. It reflects the fact that, once a debtor is insolvent, the creditors are competing for a limited fund of assets, and their claims will not be paid in full.[59] There may be difficulties in valuing assets and debts, so the issue of insolvency can present considerable evidentiary problems. The trustee is aided by a statutory presumption that the debtor was insolvent during the ninety days immediately preceding the filing of the petition.[60] This presumption shifts only the burden of going forward with the evidence, not the burden of persuasion; if the transferee adduces any significant evidence that the debtor was solvent at the time of the transfer, the presumption is rebutted.[61] If there is no evidence either way, however, the trustee has carried its burden of proving insolvency by virtue of the presumption.

[E] Preference Period

Section 547 does not avoid all transfers that prefer one creditor over another. Only those proximate to filing are avoided. Under the current version of the Code, the preference period generally extends back only ninety days, unless the creditor is an insider, in which case the preference period extends one year prior to the filing.[62]

Thus, if Deng pays Clara the $10,000 he owes her on January 1, but does not file bankruptcy until May 1, Clara has not received a preference. But, if Clara is an insider, she has received a preference. The longer preference

---

[56] Bankruptcy Code § 547(e)(2)(A).

[57] See § 15.03[A] Substantially Contemporaneous Exchange for New Value, *infra*.

[58] Bankruptcy Code § 547(b)(3).

[59] Bankruptcy Code § 101(32).

[60] Bankruptcy Code § 547(f).

[61] In re Taxman Clothing Co., 905 F.2d 166, 168 (7th Cir. 1990); In re Koubourlis, 869 F.2d 1319, 1322 (9th Cir. 1989); WJM, Inc. v. Massachusetts Dept. of Pub. Welfare, 840 F.2d 996 (1st Cir. 1988); Clay v. Traders Bank, 708 F.2d 1347 (8th Cir. 1983).

[62] Bankruptcy Code § 547(b)(4)(A), (B).

period for insiders is based on the plausible theory that insiders have special knowledge of the debtor's financial state, special ability to coerce payment from the debtor, and often some level of control over whether and when to file bankruptcy. They thus have a great advantage over other creditors based on their relationships to the debtor; some of this advantage is taken away by subjecting them to greater preference risk.

"Insider" is defined in § 101(31). If the debtor is an individual, "insider" includes certain of the debtor's relatives, the debtor's business partners, and business entities of which the debtor is a general partner, officer, director, or control person.[63] If the debtor is a business organization, "insider" includes persons who are partners, officers, directors, or control persons, as well as business affiliates (such as subsidiary or parent corporations).[64]

Finally, it is important to keep in mind the significance of the thirty day grace period for two-step transfers. If the second step occurred during the preference period, but within thirty days of the first step, the transfer is deemed to have occurred when the first step was taken. If that was outside the preference period, there is no preference.

[F] Improvement in Position

The final requirement focuses on whether the transfer allows the transferee to obtain more than it would under the Code's basic distributional structure. That structure, which is rigidly enforced in Chapter 7 (liquidation) bankruptcy, becomes the yardstick by which the transferee's position is measured.[65] The law compares the actual, post-transfer position of the creditor with the position it would have been in if there had been no transfer and the claim had been dealt with under Chapter 7. (Note that treatment in a hypothetical Chapter 7 is always the base line for improvement in position, even if the actual bankruptcy is under one of the other chapters). If the creditor, as a result of the transfer, is in a better position than it would have been in under Chapter 7, the requirement is met.[66]

For example, suppose that Clara holds a general unsecured claim in the amount of $500. During the preference period, Clara received a $100 payment on that claim, reducing it to $400. Suppose further that Clara would have received 6% of her $500 claim ($30) if her debtor had gone into Chapter 7 and no transfer had been made. The transfer has enabled her to receive more than the $30 she would have got in the hypothetical Chapter 7. She has already received $100 and still has a $400 claim against the debtor. If her debtor is in an actual Chapter 7 proceeding, Clara will still

---

[63] Bankruptcy Code § 101(31)(A).

[64] The relevant definition of "insider" appears at Bankruptcy Code § 101(31)(b)-(c), (e)-(f); the definition of "affiliate" is at Bankruptcy Code § 101(2).

[65] *See* § 10.01 Meaning of Claims and Interests, *supra*.

[66] Bankruptcy Code § 547(b)(5); Rafael I. Pardo, *On Proof of Preferential Effect*, 55 Ala. L. Rev. 281 (2003).

receive about 6% on her remaining claim ($24 on her $400 claim); thus, the transfer has enabled her to receive $124 instead of $30. Her position has thus been improved by the transfer. Even if Clara had received only a $30 transfer during the preference period, she still would have improved her position; she would have not only the $30 she would have received in Chapter 7, but also her remaining $470 claim, worth about $28.20 in the bankruptcy.

The requirement that the transfer enable the creditor to better its position is nearly always met if the debt is unsecured and the debtor is insolvent. Almost by definition, any payment on an unsecured debt by an insolvent debtor betters the creditor's position, because there will not be enough money to pay all the creditors in full.

The only significant exception is payment on a priority unsecured debt. If there would have been enough money in a Chapter 7 proceeding to pay in full all debts with the same priority, then there is no preference. For example, suppose that during the preference period the debtor paid $500 in back wages to its employees. Suppose further that these wages would have been entitled to priority under the rules of § 507(a)(4)[67] and that in a hypothetical Chapter 7 liquidation of the debtor, there would have been enough money to pay all of the priority wage claims. There is no preference, because the claim would have been paid in full anyway.

By contrast with payments on unsecured claims, payments on fully secured claims are usually protected against preference avoidance precisely because of the betterment in position rule. Broadly speaking, secured claims have the highest priority in the bankruptcy distribution structure. In Chapter 7 (and indeed in every Chapter), secured claims must almost always be paid in full.[68] Thus, payments on fully secured claims during the preference period do not improve the creditor's position and are not preferences.[69]

However, it is important to note a limitation on the protection of secured claims. If an obligation is only partially secured, the Bankruptcy Code treats that obligation as generating two claims: a secured claim and an unsecured claim.[70] The secured claim is equal to the value of the collateral. The unsecured claim is equal to the excess of the obligation over the value of the collateral. If $80,000 of collateral secured $100,000 of debt, the creditor has an $80,000 secured claim and a $20,000 unsecured claim.

This creates a preference problem for payments on an undersecured obligation. To the extent the payment is credited to the unsecured claim, there is a betterment in position; to the extent the payment is credited to the secured claim, there is no betterment in position. Generally, courts have

---

[67] Bankruptcy Code § 507(a)(4); *see* § 11.04[A][4] Wage Claims, *supra*.

[68] *See* § 11.03 Secured Claims, *supra*.

[69] *E.g.*, In re Smith's Home Furnishings, Inc., 265 F.3d 959, 964 (9th Cir. 2001).

[70] Bankruptcy Code § 506(a). For a fuller discussion of the Bankruptcy Code's treatment of undersecured obligations, see § 10.03 Secured Claims, *supra*.

treated payments on undersecured obligations as applying first to the unsecured claim. In the example given ($80,000 collateral and $100,000 debt), if $15,000 in payments were made during the preference period, all of the payments would be subject to avoidance.[71] If $30,000 in payments were made, only the first $20,000 would be subject to avoidance; the remainder would be payments on the secured claim, payments that did not better the creditor's position.

§ 15.03 Exceptions to Avoidance

Not all transfers that meet the requirements of § 547(b) are actually avoided. Sometimes the trustee/DIP will not bother to attempt recovery of the preference because the amount is too small to warrant the costs of recovery. Of greater significance for the lawyer, however, are the statutory exceptions set out in § 547(c). That subsection immunizes certain transactions from avoidance even though those transaction meet all of the requirements for avoidance in § 547(b).

The overarching goal of most of the exceptions is to seek to distinguish "ordinary" repayment of debt, from payments that constitute part of the race of diligence — the race of creditors to dismember an insolvent debtor. As such, the so-called "contemporaneous exchange," "ordinary course," "purchase money," "subsequent advance" and "floating lien" exceptions all seek to distinguish transfers where the creditor is simply "doing business" with an insolvent debtor from those where the creditor (or the debtor) is engaging in "opt out" behavior — seeking to give a particular creditor a better distribution than the Code would otherwise allow. Finally, several of the exceptions can overlap; some parts of a transaction may fit into one exception while other parts fit into another exception. Also note that the § 547(c) exceptions only affect the trustee's power to avoid a transfer under § 547. If the transfer runs afoul of another avoidance power, such as the power to avoid fraudulent transfers, § 547(c) will not preserve it.

[A] Substantially Contemporaneous Exchange for New Value

The first exception protects transfers to the extent they were intended by the debtor and the creditor to be a contemporaneous exchange for new value and were in fact substantially contemporaneous.[72] Most of the litigation has concerned two issues. What is the scope of this exception? What is a substantially contemporaneous exchange?

---

[71] In re El Paso Refinery, 171 F.3d 249 (5th Cir. 1999). If the creditor were to release an equivalent value of collateral, the payment on the unsecured portion of the debt would not be avoidable. Michael A. Bloom, Richard D. Gorelick & Heather A. MacKenzie, *Exceptions to Bankruptcy Preferences: Countryman Updated*, 47 Bus. Law. 529 (1992); Vern Countryman, *The Concept of a Voidable Preference in Bankruptcy*, 38 Vand. L. Rev. 713, 744 (1985); *see also* Bankruptcy Code § 547(c)(1).

[72] Bankruptcy Code § 547(c)(1).

The legislative history of § 547(c)(1) indicates that Congress had in mind the technical preference problem created when the debtor pays by check. A payment by check is not complete until the check is paid by the bank on which it is drawn. Suppose Diaz purchases widgets on January 1, and gives Shiraz a check to pay for those widgets at the same time. The check clears Diaz' bank on January 4. Technically, the payment was made on January 4, and was consequently on account of an antecedent debt. However, according to the legislative history, this is normally a transaction intended to be contemporaneous and is, provided that the check clears, substantially contemporaneous; thus, even if it fits within § 547(b), it is not avoidable.[73]

What if the check was post-dated to January 15? In that case, the parties would not have intended a contemporaneous transfer, but rather a credit transaction in which payment was delayed for 14 days. It would thus not fall under the exception. Similarly, if the seller failed to deposit the check within a reasonable period of time, it would not be a substantially contemporaneous exchange.[74] Finally, if the check bounces, it is not a substantially contemporaneous exchange, even if the check clears when it is submitted a second time.[75] There is nothing in the language of § 547(c)(1) that limits the exception to payments by check, and it has certainly been used to protect things other than check payments.[76]

The other major interpretive difficulty is created by the phrase "substantially contemporaneous." The legislative history suggests that a time lapse of thirty days or more between the debt and the payment might still be substantially contemporaneous.[77] The courts have not always been so generous.[78] Probably the best rule of thumb is that a transfer is substantially contemporaneous if the time lag is caused by the normal processing of documents necessary to complete the transfer.

---

[73] H.R. Rep. No. 95-595, 373 (1977); S. Rep. No. 95-989, 88 (1978).

[74] Michael J. Herbert, *The Trustee versus the Trade Creditor: A Critique of Section 547(c)(1), (2) & (4) of the Bankruptcy Code*, 17 U. Rich. L. Rev. 667, 673 n.23 (1983).

[75] Goger v. Cudahy Foods Co. (In re Standard Food Servs., Inc.), 723 F.2d 820 (11th Cir. 1984).

[76] *See, e.g.*, Drabkin v. A.I. Credit Corp., 800 F.2d 1153 (D.C. Cir. 1986) (holding that release of security interest can constitute substantially contemporaneous exchange for new value under § 547(c)(1) exception).

[77] Michael J. Herbert, *The Trustee versus the Trade Creditor: A Critique of Section 547(c)(1), (2) & (4) of the Bankruptcy Code*, 17 U. Rich. L. Rev. 667, 673 n.23 (1983).

[78] *See* In re JWJ Contr., Co., 371 F.3d 1079 (9th Cir. 2004) (eighteen days too long); In re Maracle, 159 Fed. Appx. 692 (6th Cir. 2005) (fourty-two days too long); In re Coco, 67 B.R. 365 (S.D.N.Y. 1986) (seven days not too long; thirty-four days too long); In re Arctic Air Conditioning, Inc., 35 B.R. 107 (Bankr. E.D. Tenn. 1983) (thirty days too long); *cf.* In re Quade, 108 B.R.. 681 (Bankr. N.D. Iowa 1989) (six days not too long).

[B] Ordinary Course of Business Transfers

The second exception is for certain transactions that are in the ordinary course of business for the debtor and the transferee. Specifically, a transfer is not avoidable to the extent that it meets the following requirements:[79]

- The debt was incurred in the ordinary course of business or financial affairs of the debtor and the transferee; and either
- The transfer was made in the ordinary course of business or financial affairs of the debtor and the transferee; or[80]
- The transfer was made according to ordinary business terms.[81]

The history of this defense has been one of consistent and successive liberalization. Prior to 1994, the defense only applied to debt that was incurred within forty-five days of the date on which it was paid. The 1984 amendments eliminated the forty-five day limit, but courts were divided over whether the defense was limited to short term trade debt. Until 1991, it was unclear whether this exception could apply to payments on long term indebtedness. Courts were split between the plain language of the text on the one hand and policy arguments, linked to the legislative history and the purpose of preference law, on the other.[82] In *Union Bank v. Wolas*[83] the Supreme Court ruled in favor of the plain language of the statutory text and held that payments of long term debt could be protected by the ordinary course exception. This rule has, to say the least been controversial; in the view of some, it profoundly undercuts the whole purpose of preference law.[84] After the *Wolas* case, a question remained open as to whether long term debt incurred outside the ordinary course of business (such as debt incurred as part of a leveraged buyout transaction) could be "incurred" in the "ordinary course."

Finally, prior to the 2005 Amendments, courts debated whether "ordinary course" refers to general practice in the industry (objective) or to prior conduct between the parties (subjective) or both. For example, suppose debtor is a buyer of widgets who has consistently paid its supplier thirty

[79] Before 2005, there were three requirements, (1) that the debt be incurred in the ordinary course, (2) that the debt be paid in the ordinary course, and (3) that the transfer be made according to ordinary business terms. Prior to the 1984 Amendments, there was a fourth requirement that the transfer be made within forty-five days after the debt was incurred. Howard N. Gorney, *The Ordinary Course Defense to a Preference Payment: A Trade Creditor's Impossible Dream*, 21 Emory Bankr. Dev. J. 183 (2004).

[80] Bankruptcy Code § 547(c)(2)(A).

[81] Bankruptcy Code § 547(c)(2)(B).

[82] A. Ari Afilalo, *The Impact of* Union Bank v. Wolas *on the Ordinary Course of Business Defense to A Trustee's Avoiding Powers*, 72 B.U. L. Rev. 625 (1992). For an extended critique of the issue, see Lissa L. Broome, *Payments on Long-Term Debt as Voidable Preferences: The Impact of the 1984 Bankruptcy Amendments*, 1987 Duke L.J. 78; *see also* Michael J. Herbert, *The Trustee versus the Trade Creditor II: The 1984 Amendment to Section 547(c)(2) of the Bankruptcy Code*, 2 Bankr. Dev. J. 201 (1985).

[83] 502 U.S. 151 (1991).

[84] *See* Charles Jordan Tabb, *Rethinking Preferences*, 43 S.C. L. Rev. 981 (1992).

days late, even though most widget buyers pay on time. Is this "ordinary course" or not?[85] The 2005 Amendments make it clear that either will do.[86] Even quite long time lags between the due date of the obligation and its payment may be excused, if this truly reflects an established practice between the parties.[87] Sporadic and irregular payments may indeed be ordinary course if they are consistent with the parties' mode of dealing.[88] Also of great significance are the actions of the creditor. If the creditor put pressure on the debtor to make payments, most courts say the payments are not in ordinary course.[89]

[C] Grace Period for Late Perfection of Purchase Money Interests

Section 547(c)(3) protects from preference avoidance certain purchase money security interests that were not perfected in a timely fashion.[90] This exception is exceedingly narrow in scope and has been almost indistinguishable from the grace period for perfection provided by § 547(e). It applies only to certain security interests that are given to enable the debtor to acquire the property that is used to secure the debt, and that are in fact so used. A typical example is a security interest in a car given to secure a loan made to acquire the car. Further, to qualify for protection under this exception, the security interest must be perfected within thirty days after the debtor receives possession of the property.

In most cases in which the § 547(c)(3) exception applies, the § 547(e)(2)(B) grace period also applies, and there is thus no preference in the first place.[91] However, the grace period given under the two provisions differs in three respects, two slight and one significant. The grace period under § 547(e)(2)(B) runs from the time the transfer is effective between the parties (attachment) to the time it is perfected; the § 547(c)(3) grace period runs from the time of debtor's possession until the time it is perfected. In

[85] *See* In re Ajayem Lumber Corp, 145 B.R. 813 (S.D.N.Y. 1992) (delay of thirty-four days within range of parties' prior practice and industry norm); In re Steel Improvement Co., 79 B.R. 681 (Bankr. E.D. Mich. 1987); *cf.* In re Xonics Imaging, Inc., 837 F.2d 763 (7th Cir. 1988) (transferee must show a pattern of late payments for such payments to constitute ordinary course transfers).

[86] In re National Gas Distributors, LLC, 346 B.R. 394 (Bankr. E.D.N.C. 2006).

[87] In re Gardiner Matthews Plantation Co., 118 B.R. 384 (Bankr. S.C. 1989) (payments protected under ordinary course of business exception even though time lag between delivery and payment ranged from 108 to 191 days).

[88] In re National Office Products, Inc., 119 B.R. 896 (D.R.I. 1990).

[89] Xtra, Inc. v. Seawinds, Ltd. (In re Seawinds), 888 F.2d 640 (9th Cir. 1989); Marathon Oil Co. v. Flatau (In re Craig Oil), 785 F.2d 1563 (11th Cir. 1986) (whenever the debtor's "normal" payments are the result of unusual collection activity by the creditor, the exception does not apply).

[90] Bankruptcy Code § 547(c)(3). Note that this provision applies to interests in both real estate and personalty; the term "security interest" is defined as any "lien created by agreement." Bankruptcy Code § 101(51).

[91] *See* § 15.02[A] Transfer of Debtor's Property; Date of Transfer, *supra*.

addition, the § 547(e)(2)(B) grace period merely establishes the date of the transfer, while the § 547(c)(3) exception protects the transfer regardless of its date. This is occasionally important if the debt was incurred prior to the date that the debtor obtained possession.

Suppose that on January 1, the debtor enters into a contract to purchase a farm tractor and incurs an obligation to pay for it. The purchase is on credit; the seller retains a security interest in the tractor to secure payment of the price. The tractor is delivered on January 5, and the financing statement is filed on January 7. Under § 547(e)(2)(b), the transfer of the security interest in the tractor occurred on January 5, because under Article 9, the transfer became effective between the parties on January 5 when the debtor acquired rights in the collateral, and was perfected within thirty days thereafter. This, however, does not cure the creditor's preference problem; the obligation was incurred on January 1, so the transfer of the security interest on January 5 was a transfer on account of an antecedent debt. However, the transfer is protected from avoidance under § 547(c)(3). The extension of credit enabled the debtor to acquire the tractor and was perfected within thirty days after the debtor received possession of the tractor. The exception in effect excuses the delay between the creation of the debt and the transfer of the security interest.

Prior to the 2005 Amendments, the grace period under § 547(e) was ten days, and the grace period under 547(c)(1) was twenty days. This difference periodically created complicated problems. The 2005 Amendments fixed this problem by extending both periods to thirty days. It should be noted that Article 9 of the U.C.C. has a twenty day grace period for the perfection of purchase money security interests.[92]

[D] Advance of New Value Subsequent to Preference

Section 547(c)(4) provides what amounts to a setoff of post-preference advances of credit against previous preferences.[93] The theory underlying the subsequent advance exception is that the transferee has "replenished" the estate by adding new value to it, and indeed that the preferential payment may in fact have been the reason that the transferee was willing to extend new credit.[94] To qualify, the advance must:

- either be unsecured, or secured by an avoidable security interest; and
- either be not paid by the debtor, or paid by the debtor, but the payment itself is avoidable.[95]

[92] U.C.C. § 9-324 (2003).

[93] Bankruptcy Code § 547(c)(4).

[94] Richard B. Levin, *An Introduction to the Trustee's Avoiding Powers*, 53 Am. Bankr. L.J. 173, 187 (1979).

[95] Bankruptcy Code § 547(c)(4). According to at least some courts, if the debt is paid by someone other than the debtor, and the payment has no effect on the debtor's property, the fact that the debt was paid does not preclude the application of this exception. In re Formed Tubes, Inc., 46 B.R. 645 (Bankr. E.D. Mich. 1985).

For example, suppose that Pushkin received a $3000 preference on January 1 and made a subsequent $2000 advance of credit to DuBois on February 1. If the February 1 advance was unsecured, and was not subsequently repaid by the debtor, the amount of the preference is reduced to $1000. If the February 1 advance was fully secured by collateral, and that security interest is not itself avoidable, then the preference is not reduced at all. If the February 1 advance was repaid, but $500 of that repayment is avoided by the trustee, then the preference is reduced to $2500.

The key thing to keep in mind about this exception is that the preference and the advance of credit must occur in a particular order: the advance must follow the preference.[96] For example, suppose that during the preference period the following transactions occurred:

January 1 Advance of $5000 by Pushkin to DuBois

February 1 Preference of $3500 paid by DuBois to Pushkin

February 15 Advance of $4000 by Pushkin to DuBois

February 20 Preference of $5500 paid by DuBois to Pushkin

The January 1 advance of new value may not be set off against either of the preferences, because it occurred before both of them. The February 15 advance of new value may be set off only against the prior preference, the February 1 preference. Thus, Pushkin still has a preference liability of $5,500. This is true even though the total of the two advances equals the total of the two preferences. The "subsequent advance rule" is sometimes erroneously referred to as the "net result rule," but the preceding example demonstrates that this is a mischaracterization. Section 547(c)(4) does not net out all transactions during the preference period but merely permits later advances of new value to reduce earlier preferences.[97]

[E] Floating Liens

Section 547(c)(5) creates an exception for certain Article 9 floating liens.[98] A floating lien is created when a security agreement creates a security interest in "after acquired property." Under such a security agreement, property floats into the creditor's lien when the debtor acquires it, and floats out again, when the debtor sells it. As such, the creditor has a security interest in a pool of collateral rather than specific items of collateral. For example, Peninsula Bank might have a security interest in all of Franklin

[96] In re Wingspread Corp., 120 B.R. 8 (Bankr. S.D.N.Y. 1990); In re Excel Enterprises, Inc., 83 B.R. 427 (Bankr. W.D. La. 1988).

[97] It is generally assumed that the non-statutory, pre-Code net result rule does not survive the enactment of the Code. In re Fulgham Constr. Corp., 706 F.2d 171 (6th Cir. 1983). Indeed, according to one authority, the net result rule should not have been applied after 1903, when an amendment to the Bankruptcy Act made it obsolete. Michael J. Herbert, *The Trustee versus the Trade Creditor: A Critique of Section 547(c)(1), (2) & (4) of the Bankruptcy Code*, 17 U. Rich. L. Rev. 667, 674–75 & n.29 (1983).

[98] U.C.C. § 2-204 (2003).

Manufacturing Co.'s existing and after-acquired inventory and accounts receivable. As Franklin Manufacturing sells its inventory, it generates accounts receivable; as it collects its receivables it obtains cash; it uses the cash to pay Peninsula Bank, which then advances it more money to buy more inventory. The collateral is an ever-changing pool of inventory and receivables on which the security interest floats.

Prior to the 1970s, floating liens were subject to substantial preference risk, because each time the debtor obtained new collateral for the pool, a new transfer of property to the secured creditor was made. A series of cases largely eliminated the risk, holding that the transfer occurred at the time the creditor filed its financing statement.[99] The 1978 Bankruptcy Code took a different approach, taking the view that the transfer occurred when property floated into the floating lien, but adding a defense under § 547(c)(5) to provide limited protection to the most common forms of the floating liens.

The floating lien exception applies to perfected security interests in inventory, receivables, and their proceeds.[100] It does not apply to floating liens on other types of collateral; but floating liens on things other than inventory or receivables are rare. Section 547(c)(5) applies what is commonly referred to as a "two point net improvement" test. A preference occurs for § 547(b) purposes when property floats into the lien of an undersecured creditor. However, that transfer is insulated from avoidance if it does not result in an improvement of the creditor's position during the ninety day preference period. To the extent that the obligation secured by the floating lien is less undersecured (the lienholder's deficiency is smaller) on the date of the petition than it was at the beginning of the preference period (or on the date the lender first gave new value, if that date was later than the beginning of the preference period) there is a preference to the extent of that reduction in deficiency.[101]

For example, on July 1 Merchant's Bank had a security interest in the Reliable Motors' inventory. The obligation secured was $100,000; the inventory was worth $80,000; since Merchant's Bank was an outsider, the preference period was ninety days. Ninety days later, on September 30, Reliable Motors filed its petition. At that time, the obligation secured was $60,000 and the inventory was worth $55,000. Merchant's Bank was $20,000 undersecured at the beginning of the preference period and $5,000 undersecured at the time of filing the petition. Merchant's Bank must repay $15,000 to the estate.

[99] *See* Dubay v. Williams, 417 F.2d 1277 (9th Cir. 1969); Grain Merchants of Ind., Inc. v. Union Bank & Sav. Co., 408 F.2d 209 (7th Cir. 1969); In re Gibson Products of Arizona, 543 F.2d 652 (9th Cir. 1976); Richard F. Duncan, *Preferential Transfers, The Floating Lien, and Section 547(c)(5) of the Bankruptcy Reform Act of 1978*, 36 Ark. L. Rev. 1 (1982); Jeffrey T. Ferriell, Note, *Bankruptcy — Voidable Preferences — Uniform Commercial Code Section 9-306(4)(d) Operates as a Voidable Preference*, In re Gibson Products of Arizona, 17 Santa Clara L. Rev. 967 (1977) (the beginning of a lifelong interest in bankruptcy law).

[100] Bankruptcy Code § 547(c)(5).

[101] Bankruptcy Code § 547(c)(5)(A).

There are several things to note about this exception. First, it is a true net result rule; the court does not look at the individual transactions that occurred during the preference period, but only the net result.[102] In the example given, there may have been a dozen or more payments by Reliable Motors and advances of credit by Merchant's Bank; these are all ignored. The court merely takes snapshots at the beginning and the end of the ninety day or (in the case of an insider) one year period.

Second, the key to the provision is the value of the collateral on the two snapshot dates. As elsewhere under the Code, valuation can be a tricky business. It might make sense to use wholesale value, retail value, liquidation value, or going concern value. The cases indicate that value should be pegged to the actual situation of the debtor.[103] Thus, if the debtor is a wholesaler in liquidation, a liquidation wholesale value is appropriate. If, by contrast, the debtor is a retailer with a reasonable chance of reorganization, a going concern retail value would normally be appropriate.

Third, it is reasonably clear that if the creditor was fully secured or oversecured at the beginning of the preference period, it does not matter at all what the creditor's position was at the end.[104] The exception, by its terms, preserves the lien to the extent it does not reduce a deficiency. If there is no deficiency to start with, there is no avoidance. Thus, a fully secured creditor who becomes even more secured apparently retains all of its collateral.[105]

Fourth, the rule deals with increases of value that relate to transfers made during the preference period. An increase in value due solely to an increase in market price does not raise a preference issue, let alone the application of the floating lien exception because there has been no transfer.[106] For example, if Finance Bank has a floating lien on an inventory of 100 $20 U.S. "Double Eagle" gold coins, and the market value of those 100 coins rises from $675 each to $750 each during the preference period, that $7,500 increase in value is not a preference. No new property was acquired; no transfer occurred; thus neither § 547(b) nor § 547(c)(5) apply. It is clear, however, that if any measurable part of the increase in value was due to new property incorporated into the inventory, there has been a transfer and thus may be a preference. For example, suppose the inventory became more valuable because it was completed by the addition of parts that were not previously inventory. The necessary transfer would

---

[102] *See* Matter of Missionary Baptist Foundation of America, Inc., 796 F.2d 752, 760 & n.11 (5th Cir. 1987) (two-point test); In re Parker Steel Co., 149 B.R. 834, 848 (Bankr. N.D. Ohio 1992) (intervening fluctuations are ignored).

[103] In re Ebbler Furniture and Appliances, Inc., 804 F.2d 87 (7th Cir. 1986); In re Lackow Brothers, Inc., 752 F.2d 1529 (11th Cir. 1985).

[104] In re Southwest Equip. Rental, Inc., 137 B.R. 263 (Bankr. E.D. Tenn. 1992).

[105] This appears to be so even though there is a potential betterment in position; the more oversecured a creditor is, the more interest it can potentially obtain on the debt during the pendency period.

[106] *See, e.g.*, In re Nivens, 22 B.R. 287 (Bankr. N.D. Tex. 1982).

occur; if the other requirements of § § 547(b) and (c)(5) were met, the transfer would be voidable.[107]

[F] Statutory Liens

The sixth exception protects statutory liens, such as mechanic's liens and repair liens, that are not avoidable under § 545.[108] As discussed elsewhere, there are a variety of liens created by state and federal laws that give the lienholder the right to claim property as security for an unpaid obligation.[109] If the lien is triggered by the obligor's insolvency or bankruptcy, is unprotected from bona fide purchasers of the property, or is related to a rental obligation, the lien is avoided.[110] The § 547(c)(6) exception applies to those liens that are *not* avoidable under § 545 and protects them from avoidance under § 547.

A simple illustration: On February 1, Darcy takes her car to Garibaldi for repairs. The repairs are performed that day, giving rise to Darcy's obligation to pay Garibaldi, and Garibaldi gives Darcy an itemized bill. Under local state law, Garibaldi is given a lien on the car if Darcy does not pay within three days of being given an itemized bill, and this lien is good against a bona fide purchaser.[111] Darcy fails to pay, so the lien "fixes" on February 4. A few days later, Darcy goes into bankruptcy. Since the lien attached to the car several days after the debt was incurred, there was a transfer on an antecedent debt and most likely a § 547(b) preference. However, since Garibaldi's lien is not avoidable under § 545, it is not avoidable under § 547 either.

[G] Alimony, Maintenance, Support

To the extent that a preference is a payment of a "domestic support" obligation, it is not avoidable. The term domestic support obligation is defined in § 101(14A) of the Bankruptcy Code.[112] The debt must be owed to a "spouse, former spouse, child of the debtor . . . or a governmental unit." The debt must be embodied in a separation agreement, divorce decree, property settlement agreement, court order, or other administrative order, and must be in the nature of alimony, maintenance or support, regardless of whether it was designated as such. This definition is similar to that contained in former § 547(c)(7) except for the addition of payments of child support to a governmental unit.

---

[107] It is less clear whether this is true if the increase in value was due to the debtor's labor rather than the addition of new property. The increase in value due to labor is not an increase that merely relates to market fluctuation; however, it is not a transfer of property, either.

[108] Bankruptcy Code § 547(c)(6); John C. McCoid, II, *Statutory Liens in Bankruptcy*, 68 Am. Bankr. L.J. 269 (1994); *see* § 14.04 Avoidance of Statutory Liens, *supra*.

[109] *See* § 2.06 Statutory, Common Law, and Equitable Liens, *supra*.

[110] Bankruptcy Code § 545.

[111] *See* § 2.06[B] Repair Liens, *supra*

[112] *See* § 13.03[B][5][a] Domestic Support Obligations, *supra*.

[H] Small Preferences[113]

Section 547(c)(8) provides a limited exception for relatively small payments made by debtors. If the debtor is an individual whose debts are primarily consumer debts, then § 547(c)(8) applies to transfers aggregating less than $600 to a particular creditor. If the debtor's debts are not primarily consumer debts, then § 547(c)(9) applies to protect transfers aggregating less than $5,475.[114] The usual reason given for this exception is that such small transfers have little effect on the actual distribution of the estate and are often unduly expensive to recover.

There is considerable ambiguity in the wording of the exception. Two difficulties stand out. First, if there is a transfer of more than $600 (or $5,475 for a non-consumer debtor), does the exception permit the transferee to keep $599.99 or must the entire transfer be returned? The very limited case law suggests that the latter reading is correct.[115] Second, the statute oddly links the phrases "aggregate value" and "such transfer." Does the aggregate value language mean that we aggregate the value of all transfers made to the same creditor on the same debt to determine whether we are within the $600 limit — or does the phrase "such transfer" mean that we aggregate only the amounts of property transferred at the same time? For example, suppose that a consumer debtor paid $500 on the first of each month on the same unsecured debt during the preference period. If the three payments are aggregated, the $600 ceiling is breached and the entire $1500 must be repaid. If each is viewed separately, all three are within the ceiling and are protected. The very few cases that are squarely on point have supported the view that payments to the same creditor within the preference period are to be aggregated; if together they equal $600 or more, all are avoidable.[116]

While it might be better policy to aggregate all of the payments, the statutory language seems clear that only payments made at the same time as part of the same transfer should be aggregated. If this is the correct reading, then, in the example given, all three payments should be protected. By contrast, if the debtor had made two of the $500 payments at the same time (for example, by simultaneously giving the creditor $500 in cash and a security interest in $500 of collateral) they should be aggregated.

[I] Payments Sanctioned by Credit Counseling Agency

The 2005 Amendments added an exception to the trustee's preference power, but hid it apart from other exceptions, in new § 547(h). The trustee

---

113 Paul Giorgianni, Note, *The Small Preference Exception of Bankruptcy Code Section 547(c)(7)*, 55 Ohio St. L.J. 675 (1994).

114 Bankruptcy Code § 547(c)(9).

115 Harr v. Paradigm Mgmt. Co. (In re Harr), 1997 Bankr. LEXIS 1164 (4th Cir. 1997); In re Via, 107 B.R. 91 (Bankr. W.D. Va. 1989); In re Vickery, 63 B.R. 222 (Bankr. E.D. Tenn. 1986).

116 Electric City Merchandise Co. v. Hailes (In re Hailes), 77 F.3d 873 (5th Cir. 1996); Maus v. Joint Twp. Dist. Mem'l Hosp. (In re Maus), 282 B.R. 836 (Bankr. N.D. Ohio 2002).

may not avoid a transfer if it was made "as part of an alternative repayment schedule between the debtor and any creditor of the debtor created by an approved nonprofit budget and credit counseling agency."[117] This new exception may lead savvy creditors to encourage debtors to seek credit counseling and to enter into an approved repayment schedule as a means of attempting to insulate payments they receive from recovery by the trustee.

[J] Substitution of Creditors[118]

A final exception to the preference rules appears nowhere in the Code. Rather, it has been carved out by case law, both pre-Code and post-Code. It is, or at least arguably is present in the policies underlying § 547. Whether it would find favor with the present Supreme Court, with its insistence on the statutory text, is uncertain.

This exception relates to what are often referred to as "earmarked" loans — that is, loans earmarked for the repayment of an existing loan. Suppose that Danuta owes State Bank $100,000. Danuta refinances this loan by borrowing $100,000 from Sam with the specific purpose, agreed to by both parties, of repaying the loan to State Bank; and the funds are applied to that debt. However, the repayment is made within the preference period, and all of the other requirements of § 547(b) appear to be met.

On the face of it, the bank has received a preference. However, a long line of cases has ruled otherwise. The rationale is that there has been no diminution of the estate — the financial situation of Danuta, and the liquidation shares of its creditors, are exactly the same as they were before the transaction. All that has changed is the identity of one of those creditors: Sam is now a creditor, State Bank is not. The courts have generally tried to fit this rationale into the structure of the preference rule by saying that the proceeds of the second loan never really became part of the debtor's assets; thus, there was no transfer by the debtor. Since a transfer by the debtor is an element of a preference, there is no preference.[119]

The reasoning is somewhat disingenuous. The rule applies not only where the payment is made directly by the new creditor to the old but also where the payment is made through the borrower. In the former situation, it is at least plausible to argue that the borrower never "owned" the money newly lent; in the latter it is not. However, in the latter situation there must be a specific agreement that the new loan be for repayment of the old; where the payment is made directly, no such specific agreement is required.[120]

---

[117] Bankruptcy Code § 547(h).

[118] David Gray Carlson & William H. Widen, *The Earmarking Defense to Voidable Preference Liability: A Reconceptualization*, 73 Am. Bankr. L.J. 591, 648 (1999).

[119] *See, e.g.*, Grubb v. General Contract Purchase Corp., 18 F. Supp. 680 (S.D.N.Y. 1937), *aff'd*, 94 F.2d 70 (2d Cir. 1938); In re Sun Railings, Inc., 5 B.R. 538 (Bankr. S.D. Fla. 1980).

[120] In re Bohlen Enterprises, Ltd., 859 F.2d 561 (8th Cir. 1988).

§ 15.04 Indirect Preferences

Preferences can either be direct or indirect — either "to" a creditor or "for the benefit" of a creditor.[121] A series of cases utilized this rule to create a somewhat strange result when an insider received an indirect benefit during the preference period. The 1994 Amendments overturned the cases discussed, but did not entirely eliminate indirect preferences. To understand this issue, it is first necessary to examine a bit of suretyship law and how it interacts with bankruptcy law.

Suppose that Harlan Wolf, the president of Titanic Industries guarantees an obligation of Titanic to North Atlantic Finance Co. The president, as a guarantor (a form of surety), owes a contingent obligation to North Atlantic (if Titanic fails to pay, the president must). In addition, as a surety, the president has a right of reimbursement against Titanic — if he has to pay any of the debt Titanic owes to North Atlantic, he is entitled to recover an equal amount from Titanic. Thus, the president has a contingent claim against Titanic for any money paid to North Atlantic under the guarantee. The contingent claim against Atlantic makes Wolf a creditor of Titanic, at least for bankruptcy purposes.[122] And, since every payment made by Titanic reduces Wolf's possible obligation to North Atlantic, Wolf indirectly benefits from those payments. Thus, each payment by Titanic on the loan is a payment that is both directly to one of its creditors (North Atlantic) and is indirectly for the benefit of another (Harlan Wolf). Finally, Wolf, as president of Titanic Corporation, is an insider of the company.[123]

This created a problem for lenders, because a number of cases have held that this dual benefit means that the payments to the lender (North Atlantic Finance Company) fall under the one year insider preference period rather than the normal ninety day preference period. In syllogistic form:

- Titanic's president is an insider creditor of Titanic.
- Titanic's payments to North Atlantic are for the benefit of Titanic's president.
- Therefore, Titanic's payments to North Atlantic are for the benefit of an insider creditor.
- The preference period for a payment that is for the benefit of an insider creditor is one year.
- Therefore, the preference period for Titanic's payments to North Atlantic is one year.
- Therefore, *North Atlantic* has to disgorge the payments it received during the year prior to bankruptcy.[124]

---

[121] Bankruptcy Code § 547(b)(1).

[122] Bankruptcy Code §§ 101(5), (10).

[123] *See* Bankruptcy Code § 101(31)(B)(ii).

[124] This syllogism encapsulates the core of the leading case, *Levit v. Ingersoll Rand Financial Corp. (In re Deprizio)*, 874 F.2d 1186 (7th Cir. 1989).

This was true even though the payments were made to North Atlantic, an outsider, rather than to the president.

This approach was criticized for various reasons. In the view of some, it represented an excessive reliance on a literal reading of several complex statutory texts, thereby reaching an end result that Congress surely never had in mind. Others complained that it unduly increased the risk to creditors by reducing the value of suretyship rights.[125] A few commentators were supportive, although even they tended to suggest that a more sophisticated analysis was in order.[126]

In 1994, Congress specifically overturned the case that applied § 547 in this way, although in a slightly unusual fashion. Rather than address this issue in § 547, Congress amended § 550, which deals with the actual recovery of avoided transfers. Under the new provision, if a transfer is made between ninety days and one year before the filing of the petition, and is avoided under § 547(b), and was for the benefit of a creditor who was an insider at the time of the transfer, the trustee may not recover from a transferee that is not an insider.[127] The reason for putting this provision in § 550 is that Congress intended to protect the third party creditor who received the payment, not the insider who benefited from it. Thus, in the example given, the payment made by Titanic to North Atlantic Finance Co. can be recovered from Titanic's president (the insider creditor) but not from North Atlantic Finance Co. (the outsider creditor). In essence, the new provision puts the outside creditor who obtains an insider guarantee in exactly the same position as the outside creditor who does not obtain such a guarantee. Either is at risk for payments made during the ninety-day period; neither is at risk for payments made during the ninety-one day to one-year period. However, the basic principle, that an indirect beneficiary may be forced to disgorge a preference, remains largely intact. The insider guarantor (in our example, Titanic's president, Harlan Wolf) who indirectly benefitted from the debtor's preferential transfers (in our example, the payments made by Titanic Corporation) may still be forced to disgorge the benefit it received to the estate.

The 2005 Amendments added language to facilitate these earlier revisions. New § 547(i) specifies that if the trustee avoids a preference made between ninety days and one year before the debtor's petition, "to an entity that is not an insider" the transfer is considered to be avoided "only with respect to the creditor that is an insider."[128]

---

[125] *See* Donald W. Baker, *Repayments of Loans Guaranteed by Insiders as Avoidable Preferences in Bankruptcy:* Deprizio *and Its Aftermath*, 23 U.C.C. L.J. 115 (1990); Robert F. Higgins & David E. Peterson, *Is There a One-Year Preference Period for Non-Insiders?*, 64 Am. Bankr. L.J. 383 (1990).

[126] Jay Lawrence Westbrook, *Two Thoughts About Insider Preferences*, 76 Minn. L. Rev. 73 (1991).

[127] Bankruptcy Code § 550(c).

[128] Bankruptcy Code § 547(i).

§ 15.05 Procedural Issues; The Effect of Avoidance

Preference law is not self-executing; the trustee or debtor-in-possession must take action to recover the transfer. This is normally done by adversary proceeding (a trial) in the bankruptcy court.[129] If the creditor has submitted itself to the jurisdiction of the bankruptcy court (as, for example, by filing a proof of claim), there is no right to a jury trial.[130] The trustee carries the burden of persuasion as to all elements of the preference; however, there is a rebuttable presumption that the debtor was insolvent during the nintey days prior to the filing of the petition.[131] The creditor carries the burden of persuasion as to the applicability of any exception to the avoidance rules.[132]

Occasionally a trustee or debtor-in-possession has refused or neglected to pursue a preference. Sometimes this decision is legitimate — for example, it might be unduly expensive to the estate to attempt recovery of a small preference or a preference made to a person not subject to service of process in the United States. Other times, however, the failure to recover a preference is based on neglect or even bad faith — for example, a debtor-in-possession might be reluctant to recover insider preferences made to its managers. This is clearly a breach of the fiduciary duty owed to the creditors. Less clear is the appropriate remedy. Some cases have held that a Chapter 11 creditors' committee has the implicit right to pursue a preference if the trustee or debtor-in-possession improperly fails to do so,[133] and it is not unusual for creditors' committees to pursue preference actions on behalf of the estate, where the debtor has declined to do so, and the court approves. An individual creditor, however, has no such right. It may be possible to have the DIP replaced with a trustee, or have the trustee replaced; it might also be possible to obtain an order from the court under § 105 to force the trustee to take appropriate action.[134]

The effect of avoidance varies with the nature of the transfer. If the transfer was merely of a lien on property still in possession of the debtor, the lien simply ceases to exist and the creditor is left with a general unsecured claim. If the transfer was of money or other property physically transferred to the creditor, the trustee may recover the property or (if the court so orders) the value of the property.[135] The trustee ordinarily seeks recovery against the preferee. However, the trustee may often recover from a subsequent transferee.[136] Subsequent transferees are given some

[129] In re McCombs Properties, VI, Ltd., 88 B.R. 261 (Bankr. C.D. Cal. 1988); In re Magic Circle Energy Corp., 64 B.R. 269 (Bankr. W.D. Okl. 1986).

[130] Langencamp v. Culp, 498 U.S. 42 (1990).

[131] Bankruptcy Code § 547(f), (g).

[132] Bankruptcy Code § 547(g).

[133] In re Cybergenics Corp, 330 F.3d 548 (3d Cir. 2003) (en banc); In re STN Enterprises, 779 F.2d 901 (2d Cir. 1985).

[134] Bankruptcy Code § 105(a) permits the court to enter any "necessary or appropriate" orders.

[135] Bankruptcy Code § 550(a).

[136] Bankruptcy Code § 550(a)(2).

protection by bona fide purchaser rules, which are discussed elsewhere.[137] Similarly, creditors who have improved property that is subsequently recovered by the estate are provided with some protection for the value of their improvements. The creditor who is forced to return property is given a general unsecured claim equal to the value of the property.[138] This may create practical problems for a Chapter 11 debtor if the resulting claim is large, because the preferee is likely to be a particularly hostile creditor, unwilling to cooperate in the formulation or confirmation of the plan.

§ 15.06 Setoff Preferences

Not all preference rules are contained in § 547. Section 553(b) contains a preference provision that in key respects resembles the net result rule applied to floating liens in the § 547(c)(5) exception. The § 553 provision permits the trustee to recover certain pre-petition setoffs as preferences.[139]

With certain limited exceptions, a setoff exercised within ninety days prior to the filing of the petition can be avoided to the extent there was a reduction in the insufficiency. "Insufficiency" means the amount by which the debt owed by the offsetting creditor to the debtor was larger than the debt owed by the debtor to the offsetting creditor.[140] The amount of the insufficiency is measured at two points — (1) the date of the setoff and (2) the later of (a) ninety days before the filing of the petition and (b) the first date during that ninety days on which there was an insufficiency.[141]

Suppose that on June 1, which is ninety days before the filing of the petition, Debussy owes Chopin $10,000 and Chopin owes Debussy $12,000. On August 15, Debussy owes Chopin $11,000 and Chopin owes Debussy $11,500. On August 15, Chopin offsets the two obligations, leaving a net obligation of $500 owed by Chopin to Debussy. At the beginning of the ninety-day period, the insufficiency was $2000 ($12,000 -$10,000). At the time the debts were offset, the insufficiency was $500 ($11,500 -$11,000). Thus, a setoff preference of $1,500 occurred, and that amount may be recovered.

Note that the setoff preference rule is much simpler than the § 547 preference rules. There are no elaborate requirements; most notably, there is no requirement that the debtor be insolvent. Similarly, there are no exceptions to the rule. One troubling question, however, about § 553 is whether it applies when the insufficiency has been reduced during the 90 days prior to bankruptcy, but the creditor does not set off.

Two other quasi-preference rules appear in §§ 553(a)(2) and (3). These are structured as provisions dealing with the basic right of setoff, rather

---

137 *See* § 14.08[D] Protection of Good Faith Transferees, *infra*.

138 Bankruptcy Code § 502(h).

139 For a general discussion of setoff, see § 2.06 Setoff, *supra*.

140 Bankruptcy Code § 553(b)(2).

141 Bankruptcy Code § 553(b)(1).

than as provisions avoiding setoffs already made. For this reason, they are discussed in the general material on setoffs.[142]

[142] *See* § 11.09 Right of Setoff, *supra*.

Chapter 16

Fraudulent Transfers

§ 16.01 Purposes and Sources of Fraudulent Conveyance Law[1]

[A] Fraudulent Conveyances

Among the avoidance powers given to the bankruptcy trustee or a debtor-in-possession is the power to avoid fraudulent transfers. Fraudulent transfers are those that are made either with the intent to defraud creditors, or made by a person who is insolvent (by one of several measures) for grossly inadequate consideration. Many classic fraudulent transfers fit both categories. The most obvious example is a person who, on the eve of suffering a $10,000,000 judgment, transfers all her assets to a trusted relative for $1. There are, however, many far less obvious examples that even savvy bankers fail to detect before it is too late.

There is a strong policy, both inside and outside bankruptcy, of preventing debtors from harming their creditors by dissipating their assets in this fashion. Debtors who dispose of their assets, either in an effort to hide them from creditors, or for far less than they are worth, deprive their creditors of assets from which the creditors might seek payment.

Many reasons have been advanced for avoiding fraudulent transfers. Some of these are simple moral statements — one should not seek to avoid liability on a contract or for a wrong by secreting assets. Others focus on creditors' expectations. The most commonly stated reason is that the debtor is violating an implied term of the agreement, and even implicitly misrepresenting its intentions regarding its assets. Despite this, even non-consensual creditors have claims under fraudulent conveyance law.

[B] Fraudulent Obligations

Parallel to the fraudulent transfer is the fraudulent obligation, which is also prohibited. By making themselves appear more indebted than they really are, debtors sometimes dissuade legitimate creditors from attempting to collect. This is particularly true if the debtor's obligations appear to be secured, making the debtor appear to have few unencumbered assets. For example, Charlie might execute a promissory note to pay his cousin Gail

[1] Robert Charles Clark, *The Duties of the Corporate Debtor to Its Creditors*, 90 Harv. L. Rev. 505 (1977); Michael L. Cook, *Fraudulent Transfer Liability Under the Bankruptcy Code*, 17 Hous. L. Rev. 263 (1980); James McLaughlin, *Application of the Uniform Fraudulent Conveyance Act*, 46 Harv. L. Rev. 404 (1933).

$100,000 and give Gail a mortgage on his $100,000 home, even though Charlie has borrowed no money from Gail and owes her no debt. When other creditors conduct a title search, they find Gail's recorded mortgage. This might make Charlie appear judgment proof and induce his creditors to avoid pursuing collection as vigorously as they otherwise might. Thus, the motivation to create fraudulent obligations is much the same as the motivation to make a fraudulent transfer; the difference is that the former involves the creation of a claim while the latter involves the transfer of property.

[C] Fraudulent Transfers Distinct from Preferences

Fraudulent transfers differ in significant ways from preferences, although some transactions might be avoidable under both powers. Both deplete the debtor's estate in ways that are unfair to creditors. However, preferences involve payments by the debtor of legitimate claims that undercut the equality of distribution inherent in the bankruptcy priority scheme. As such, it applies whether or not the transaction was wholly bona fide.[2] Fraudulent transfer doctrine, on the other hand, is frequently concerned with the actual or presumed motivation underlying the transaction. Many preferences are received by creditors who are not even aware of the fact that the payments are preferential, and who did nothing to cause the preference to be made. By contrast, in many cases, the beneficiary of a fraudulent transfer or obligation had at least some notice that the transaction was flawed.

[D] Sources of Fraudulent Transfer Law[3]

Fraudulent conveyance law is traced historically to the Statute of Elizabeth, enacted in 1570.[4] The text of the Statute of Elizabeth is startlingly similar to modern fraudulent conveyance law. For example, the language regarding transactions made with the "intent to hinder, delay, or defraud creditors" appears in both the Statute of Elizabeth and the modern Uniform Fraudulent Transfer Act that was promulgated over 400 years later.

Today, fraudulent transfer law is manifested in both state law and in the Bankruptcy Code. The Uniform Fraudulent Transfer Act (UFTA),[5] promulgated in 1984, applies in forty-three states, and its predecessor, the Uniform Fraudulent Conveyance Act (UFCA), developed in 1918,[6] still

---

[2] *See generally* Lawrence Ponoroff, *Evil Intentions and an Irresolute Endorsement for Scientific Realism: Bankruptcy Preferences One More Time*, 1993 Wis. L. Rev. 1439.

[3] Frank R. Kennedy, *Reception of the Uniform Fraudulent Transfer Act*, 43 S.C. L. Rev. 655 (1992).

[4] An Act Against Fraudulent Deeds, Alienations, 13 Eliz., ch. 5 (1570) (Eng.), *repealed by* The Law of Property Act, 15 Geo. 5, ch. 20, § 172 (1925).

[5] *See* Michael L. Cook & Richard E. Mendales, *The Uniform Fraudulent Transfer Act: An Introductory Critique*, 62 Am. Bankr. L.J. 87 (1988).

[6] *See* James McLaughlin, *Application of the Uniform Fraudulent Conveyance Act*, 46 Harv. L. Rev. 404 (1933).

applies in many of the remaining states. In bankruptcy cases, the trustee may invoke state fraudulent conveyance law through § 544(b), which permits the trustee to avoid any transfer that an actual unsecured creditor could have avoided outside of bankruptcy.[7] In addition, § 548 gives the trustee his own fraudulent transfer avoiding power that is not dependent on either state law or upon the standing of any individual creditor to avoid the transfer.

The UFTA and § 548 both authorize avoidance of two types of transfers: (1) transfers that the debtor made with the "actual intent" to defraud his creditors; and (2) transfers based on "constructive fraud" because of their effect on creditors, without regard to the debtor's intent. A key difference between § 548 and the UFTA, that will be discussed later in this chapter, is that state statutes of limitations reach further back in time than § 548, making it a more effective tool for the bankruptcy trustee than § 548 to recover property transferred long before the debtor filed his bankruptcy petition.

§ 16.02 Actual Fraud: Intent to Hinder, Delay, or Defraud Creditors

A debtor's actual intent to "hinder, delay, or defraud" creditors has formed the basis of fraudulent conveyance law since 1570. It is codified today in Bankruptcy Code § 548(a)(1)(A) and UFTA § 4(a)(1). Section 548(a)(1)(A) permits the bankruptcy trustee to avoid

> any transfer of an interest of the debtor in property . . . that was made within two years before the date of the filing of the petition, if the debtor voluntarily or involuntarily (A) made such transfer . . . with actual intent to hinder, delay, or defraud any entity to which the debtor was or became . . . indebted.[8]

UFTA § 4(a)(1) similarly provides:

> [a] transfer made by a debtor is fraudulent as to a creditor, whether the creditor's claim arose before or after the transfer . . . if the debtor made the transfer . . . (1) with the actual intent to hinder, delay, or defraud any creditor of the debtor.[9]

Both provisions make a transfer avoidable because of the debtor's fraudulent intent, and both make them avoidable regardless of whether the transfer occurred before or after the debtor became indebted.

Likewise, both apply equally to voluntary and involuntary transfers, although it is unusual for an involuntary transfer to be made with actual fraudulent intent.[10] The predicate intent to establish actual fraud can be

[7] *See* § 14.03 Power to Use Rights of Actual Unsecured Creditors, *supra.*

[8] Bankruptcy Code § 548(a)(1)(A).

[9] UFTA § 4(a)(1).

[10] *Compare* Bankruptcy Code § 548(a)(1), *with* UFTA § 1(12) (defining transfer).

difficult to prove. Indeed, it is very rare for a debtor to be so foolish as to declare openly an intention to injure his creditors. For this reason, intent must ordinarily be inferred from the circumstances surrounding the transaction. Since *Twyne's Case* in 1602,[11] intent has usually been proven through circumstantial evidence that demonstrates the strong likelihood of the debtor's deceitful intent. These traditional "badges of fraud" are now codified in UFTA § 4(b) to include, among others, whether:

- the transfer or obligation was to an insider;[12]
- the debtor retained possession or control of the property transferred after the transfer;[13]
- the transfer or obligation was disclosed or concealed;[14]
- before the transfer was made or obligation was incurred, the debtor had been sued or threatened with suit;[15]
- the transfer was of substantially all of the debtor's assets;[16]
- the debtor absconded after making the transfer;[17]
- the debtor removed or concealed assets;[18]
- the value of the consideration received by the debtor was reasonably equivalent to the value of the asset transferred or the amount of the obligation incurred;[19]
- the debtor was insolvent or became insolvent shortly after the transfer was made or the obligation was incurred;[20]
- the transfer occurred shortly before or shortly after a substantial debt was incurred;[21] and

---

[11] 76 Eng. Rep. 809 (Star Chamber 1601); *see* Michael L. Cook, *Fraudulent Transfer Liability Under the Bankruptcy Code*, 17 Hous. L. Rev. 263, 270–71 (1980).

[12] UFTA § 4(b)(1); *see* McWilliams v. Edmonson, 162 F.2d 454 (5th Cir. 1947) (sister); Levy v. Bukes, 65 F. Supp. 494 (W.D. Pa. 1946) (spouse).

"Insider" ' as used in the UFTA has much the same definition as it has under the Bankruptcy Code. It encompasses close relatives and close business affiliates. *See* UFTA § 1(7).

[13] UFTA § 4(b)(2); *e.g.*, In re Nemeroff, 74 B.R. 30 (E.D. La. 1987). Under modern secured transactions law, the fact that a debtor remains in physical possession of property that is subject to a security interest is not a fraudulent transfer (nor does it create a badge of fraud), provided that the security interest has properly been perfected by the filing of a financing statement or other notice-giving device. Prior to the later development of laws that provided for public notice in the late nineteenth century, however, such security interests were often struck down as fraudulent transfers.

[14] UFTA § 4(b)(3).

[15] UFTA § 4(b)(4).

[16] UFTA § 4(b)(5).

[17] UFTA § 4(b)(6). The modern extension of long-arm jurisdiction, permitting the service of process across state lines, has reduced the significance of this badge of fraud.

[18] UFTA § 4(b)(7).

[19] UFTA § 4(b)(8).

[20] UFTA § 4(b)(9).

[21] UFTA § 4(a)(10).

- the debtor transferred the essential assets of the business to a lienor who transferred the assets to an insider of the debtor.[22]

This is by no means an exhaustive list of the "badges of fraud" that courts have used to detect the debtor's fraudulent intent. Rather, they are those that were sufficiently common for specific inclusion in the UFTA.

Transfers to family members, whom the debtor might more confidently trust to return the transferred property at a later date, are particularly suspect. Contrary to what is sometimes said, however, it is not per se fraudulent to make a transfer to a spouse, sibling, or parent. However, it is strong evidence of fraudulent intent, especially if the consideration for the transfer is inadequate.[23] Indeed, none of the badges of fraud is dispositive. They are only guidelines, creating inferences that the trier of fact may or may not draw in any particular case.

The "actual intent" branch of fraudulent conveyance law has greatly diminished in significance over the years. This is primarily due to the development of the rules regarding "constructive fraud" involving transfers by a person who was insolvent when the transfer was made. There are very few cases covered by the actual intent rules that are not also covered by the insolvent transferor rules; and the latter ground is usually easier to prove.

§ 16.03 Constructive Fraud

The second major branch of fraudulent conveyance law deals with situations in which the transfer or obligation was in exchange for unreasonably small consideration and was made by a person who is unable to pay his debts. This branch is based on the effect that the transfer has on creditors rather than on the debtor's intent, which is irrelevant.

Although intentional fraud and constructive fraud are distinct, there is often a degree of confusion about the difference between them. This is in part because of our long-established habit of referring to the second branch as constructive fraud, and because many of the same facts that might be used to establish the debtor's fraudulent intent are also used to establish the avoidability of the transfer regardless of his intent. For example, both insolvency and inadequacy of consideration are elements of constructive fraud and are also among the traditional badges of actual fraud.

[A] Elements of Constructive Fraud

Constructive fraud involves two elements. The first is that the debtor received, in exchange for the transfer or the obligation, less than "a reasonably equivalent value."[24] The second, stated broadly, is that the debtor, one way or another, was insolvent or otherwise at inappropriate

[22] UFTA § 4(b)(11).

[23] *See* Chichester v. Golden, 204 F. Supp. 634 (S.D. Cal. 1962).

[24] Bankruptcy Code § 548(a)(1)(B)(i); UFTA §§ 4(a)(2), 5(a).

risk of being unable to pay its debts. As explained more fully below, the second element may be satisfied in a variety of distinct ways, some of which are stated somewhat differently in the UFTA and § 548.

[1] No Reasonably Equivalent Value

Both the UFTA and § 548 make the debtor's receipt of less than a "reasonably equivalent value"[25] a key element of constructive fraud. But neither statute supplies a definition of reasonably equivalent value. Both statutes indicate that "value means property, or satisfaction or securing of a present or antecedent debt . . . but does not include an unperformed promise to furnish support to the debtor or to a relative of the debtor."[26] This is to prevent a debtor from shielding a transfer by claiming that the transferor has made an unperformed promise to take care of him — for example, if Charlie transfers all of his property to his sister Sue in exchange for Sue's promise to take care of him for the rest of his life, value has not been given.

If the transfer was for reasonably equivalent value, the debtor's financial circumstances do not matter. After all, the creditors will not be harmed. The classic cases, in which property is transferred to a relative for no consideration (love and affection) or for nominal consideration (a pepper-corn), are easy.[27] More difficult are those in which the transferee is getting a good deal but not an incredible one. For example, Reliable Motors might attempt to resolve its financial difficulty by selling cars to customers at slightly below cost, in order to raise cash quickly. These sales at $50 over the factory invoice price are for a price that is hundreds of dollars below that of its competitors. Sales below cost are not a good long-term strategy, but they might resolve a temporary cash-flow problem for Reliable. If the strategy fails and Reliable files a bankruptcy petition, the debtor's bankruptcy trustee might try to undo the sales, arguing that the purchase price was abnormally low and that Reliable thus made little or no profit. The buyers, in turn, might argue that in context the price was reasonable. Reliable was trying to clear old model cars off its lot to make room for newer cars, and the value paid by its customers was reasonable given Reliable's efforts to pay down debts to its inventory lender and reduce its interest payments. On these facts, the buyers will probably prevail.

It is clear that reasonably equivalent value does not mean dollar for dollar equivalence.[28] Whether sufficient value was received depends on the "totality of the circumstances" (a rather unhelpful phrase).[29]

---

[25] Bankruptcy Code § 548(a)(2)(A); UFTA §§ 4(a)(2), 5(a).

[26] Bankruptcy Code § 548(d)(2)(A); *see* UFTA § 3(a) (1984). Section 548 contains language that does not appear in the UFTA regarding value in securities transactions, repurchase transactions, swap agreements, and master netting agreements. Bankruptcy Code § 548(d)(2)(B)-(E).

[27] Williams v. Marlar (In re Marlar), 267 F.3d 749 (8th Cir. 2001) (700 acres exchanged for $10 and "love and affection").

[28] *See* In re Fairchild Aircraft Corp., 6 F.3d 1119 (5th Cir. 1993).

[29] In re Besing, 981 F.2d 1488, 1495–96 (5th Cir. 1993).

There are many reasons why a sale at a bargain price should not necessarily be avoided. It may be difficult to determine what the "real" value of the property was when it was sold. Indeed, economists tell us that there is no "real" value except the price a willing buyer will exchange with a willing seller. Financially troubled debtors often have to sell at low prices because they need immediate cash to continue operating, and their buyers are taking the added risk that the seller will be unable to pay for claims that warranty terms or other parts of the bargain were breached. There is also the obvious problem of determining what the value was at the time of the transaction, because subsequent events may, in hindsight, alter the perception of the deal.[30]

These problems are particularly acute if the value is not entirely tangible. It is fairly easy to determine the value of fungible goods that are regularly sold in an established market. It is far more difficult to determine the value of an investment in an uncertain business venture. For example, *In re Fairchild Aircraft Corp.*[31] involved payments made by Fairchild for aviation fuel purchased by its affiliate, Air Kentucky. Air Kentucky was a struggling commuter airline that Fairchild hoped to prop up so that it could purchase Fairchild planes. The court held that the indirect benefits that Fairchild reasonably hoped it would gain were value in determining whether its fuel payments were for reasonably equivalent value.[32]

One plausible justification for the acceptance of indeterminate values as reasonably equivalent value is the hands-off approach that courts have long taken toward business decisions. In the corporate law arena, this is called the business judgment rule — which broadly means that boards of directors are free to take actions that have a legitimate business justification, and are not palpably absurd or adverse to shareholder interests. If courts were too narrow in their review of intangible sources of value, then fraudulent transfer law would significantly inhibit business decision making. That is generally assumed to be undesirable, usually on the basis that courts lack the experience necessary to make business judgments.

[2] Debtor Unable to Pay Its Debts

The second element of constructive fraud is stated in several alternative ways, all of which point to the debtor's actual or potential inability to pay his creditors. Debtors who remain able to pay their debts are free to squander their assets. However, those who are already unable to pay their debts, or who are at substantial risk of being unable to pay, must not exchange their assets for less than they are reasonably worth.

Section 548 and the UFTA express these elements in slightly different ways. Thus, if the debtor did not receive reasonably equivalent value in exchange for its property, the transfer is fraudulent if:

---

[30] It is well accepted that the reasonable equivalence of the value is to be determined as of the time the value is given. In re Morris Commc'ns NC, Inc., 914 F.2d 458 (4th Cir. 1990).

[31] 6 F.3d 1119 (5th Cir. 1993).

[32] 6 F.3d at 1126.

- the debtor was insolvent when the transfer was made;[33]
- the debtor became insolvent as a result of the transfer;[34]
- the debtor was engaged in a business or transaction for which its remaining property was an unreasonably small capital;[35]
- the debtor was about to engage in a business or transaction for which its remaining property was an unreasonably small capital;[36]
- the debtor intended to incur debts that would be beyond its ability to pay as they came due;[37] or
- the debtor believed that it would incur debts that would be beyond its ability to pay as they came due.[38]

The transfer involved may be either voluntary or involuntary.

In the context of these provisions, "insolvent" refers to balance-sheet insolvency; that is, fewer assets than debts.[39] For example, if the fair value of the debtor's property is $500,000, and the total of its debts is $750,000, the debtor is insolvent. In calculating the debtor's solvency, the Bankruptcy Code excludes exempt assets.[40]

The intent of the transferor is generally irrelevant. It matters only with respect to transfers made by a person who intended to incur debts beyond his ability to pay. Even then, the intent does not relate to the transfer; rather, it relates to the transferor's future financial activity. Thus, the person challenging the transfer on this basis does not have to prove, directly or by inference, that the transferor meant to cheat creditors. In addition, evidence of the debtor's good intentions is admissible.

The 2005 Amendments added language to § 548 regarding transfers to insider employees. It makes plain that transfers and obligations to an insider, made under an employment contract and not in the ordinary course of business, are avoidable fraudulent transfers if the debtor received less than a reasonably equivalent value in exchange.[41] This new language is designed to enhance the level of scrutiny of payments made or obligations incurred to insider employees under "golden parachute" employment contracts. It is significant because it makes these contracts avoidable

---

[33] Bankruptcy Code § 548(a)(1)(B)(ii)(I); UFTA § 5(a) (1984).

[34] Bankruptcy Code § 548(a)(1)(B)(ii)(I); UFTA § 5(a) (1984).

[35] Bankruptcy Code § 548(a)(1)(B)(ii)(II); UFTA § 4(a)(2)(i); *see* Bruce A. Markell, *Toward True and Plain Dealing: A Theory of Fraudulent Transfers Involving Unreasonably Small Capital*, 21 Ind. L. Rev. 469 (1988).

[36] Bankruptcy Code § 548(a)(1)(B)(ii)(II); UFTA § 4(a)(2)(i).

[37] Bankruptcy Code § 548(a)(1)(B)(ii)(III); UFTA § 4(a)(2)(ii) (1984).

[38] Bankruptcy Code § 548(a)(1)(B)(ii)(III); UFTA § 4(a)(2)(ii) (1984).

[39] Bankruptcy Code § 101(32); UFTA § 2(a).

[40] Bankruptcy Code § 101(32)(A)(ii).

[41] Bankruptcy Code § 548(a)(1)(B)(IV).

regardless of whether the employer was insolvent when the transfer was made or the obligation was incurred.[42]

[B] Specific Transactions Involving Constructive Fraud

Bankruptcy trustees rarely have any difficulty avoiding gifts made by an insolvent person on the eve of bankruptcy.[43] Even when fraudulent intent cannot be shown, the constructive fraud provisions in the UFTA and § 548 make recovery of these transfers fairly easy. The most difficult factual issue is proving the necessary element of the debtor's financial condition when the transfer was made.

Other transactions that may be recoverable as fraudulent transfers do not so obviously fit within the Code's fraudulent transfer rubric. Among these are pre-petition mortgage and security interest foreclosure sales, where inadequate value is received for the encumbered collateral; intercorporate guarantees; asset securitization transactions; transfers by a partnership to its general partners; and leveraged buy-outs. As explained below, fraudulent transfer law is frequently applied to all of these transactions, with often uncertain results.

[1] Pre-Petition Foreclosure Sales[44]

Foreclosure sales are usually concluded at bargain-basement prices. The winning bid is frequently far less than the supposed value of the property. This is frequently because of the customary practice of foreclosing creditors buying the property involved in their own foreclosure sale by bidding the amount of the debt involved in the foreclosure. This, together with other factors that make buying property at foreclosure a risky proposition for other prospective bidders, keep foreclosure sale prices low.[45]

It was traditionally assumed that fraudulent transfer law did not apply to a properly conducted foreclosure sale. This tradition is reflected in the

---

[42] *See* Steve H. Nickles, *Behavioral Effect of New Bankruptcy Law on Management and Lawyers: Collage of Recent Statutes and Cases Discouraging Chapter 11 Bankruptcy*, 59 Ark. L. Rev. 329, 349–60 (2006).

[43] Detecting the transfer is usually the hard part, particularly if the transfer was made many months before the debtor's petition was filed. One of your authors recalls attending a § 341 meeting, with one of his first clients, and observing a meeting involving different debtors (a physician and his spouse), who had given each of their three adult daughters sets of valuable silverware as Christmas presents several months before filing their joint petition. If they had not listed these assets on a loan application several years earlier, with a lender who carefully compared the assets listed on the loan application with those provided to the bankruptcy court in the schedules filed with the debtor's petition, the transactions would never have been discovered.

[44] Marie T. Reilly, *A Search for Reason in "Reasonably Equivalent Value" After* BFP v. Resolution Trust Corp., 13 Am. Bankr. Inst. L. Rev. 261 (2005).

[45] *See* § 2.08 Foreclosure Procedures, *supra*; *see generally* Robert M. Washburn, *The Judicial and Legislative Response to Price Inadequacy in Mortgage Foreclosure Sales*, 53 S. Cal. L. Rev. 843 (1980); Debra Pogrund Stark, *Facing the Facts: An Empirical Study of the Fairness and Efficiency of Foreclosures and a Proposal for Reform*, 30 U. Mich. J.L. Ref. 639 (1997).

UFTA, which expressly provides that a buyer gives reasonably equivalent value for property if the buyer acquired the property in a "regularly conducted, non-collusive foreclosure sale."[46] Thus, under state law, the focus is on the propriety of the sale procedure, rather than on any disparity between the foreclosure sale price and the fair market value.

However, § 548 is silent on the topic. In 1980, the Fifth Circuit Court of Appeals in *Durett v. Washington National Insurance Co.*, held that a properly conducted foreclosure sale could be a fraudulent conveyance because of the inadequacy of the price obtained at the sale.[47] The analysis was simple: the debtor was insolvent and the property had been transferred for less than a reasonably equivalent value. The decision sent shock-waves through the banking industry and resulted in a storm of law review articles, continuing legal education programs, and academic presentations.[48]

Fourteen years later, the Supreme Court resolved the issue in *BFP v. Resolution Trust Corp.*[49] The Court held that the traditional assumption was consistent with the plain language of § 548 and that the consideration received from a non-collusive real estate mortgage foreclosure sale, conducted in conformance with applicable state law, conclusively satisfies the reasonably equivalent value standard of § 548. Thus, if Peninsula Bank forecloses its mortgage on Franklin Manufacturing's land and building, and buys the property for $1.5 million (the amount of the outstanding mortgage debt), the purchase is not a fraudulent transfer even though the fair market value of the property is $ 2.5 million, provided the foreclosure sale was conducted in compliance with governing state law and that there was no collusive bidding involved in the sale. However, foreclosure sales that do not conform to the established procedures remain vulnerable to attack as fraudulent conveyances. Also, since *BFP* is an interpretation of § 548, it is important to check the state laws that might apply under § 544(b) to see if they diverge from the UFTA in this regard.

Despite the Court's decision in *BFP v. Resolution Trust*, courts have not always agreed about other forced sales.[50] Where the opportunity for competitive bidding exists, the Court's rationale has held sway, and the sale is not subject to attack.[51] However, where there has been neither a public sale nor competitive bidding, the transaction remains vulnerable to attack.[52]

---

[46] UFTA § 3(b).

[47] 621 F.2d 201 (5th Cir. 1980).

[48] Durrett v. Washington Nat'l Ins. Co., 621 F.2d 201 (5th Cir. 1980); *see* Helen J. Durham, *A Decade of Division Among the Circuits: Application of Section 548(a)(2) of the Bankruptcy Code to Foreclosure Sales*, 19 Mem. St. U. L. Rev. 381 (1989).

[49] 511 U.S. 531 (1994).

[50] Marie T. Reilly, *A Search for Reason in "Reasonably Equivalent Value" After* BFP v. Resolution Trust Corp., 13 Am. Bankr. Inst. L. Rev. 261 (2005).

[51] *E.g.*, T.R. Stone Co. v. Harper (Matter of T.F. Stone Co.), 72 F.3d 466 (5th Cir. 1995) (tax sale).

[52] *E.g.*, In re Murphy, 331 B.R. 107 (Bankr. S.D.N.Y. 2005); In re Sherman, 223 B.R. 555 (B.A.P. 10th Cir. 1998).

[2] Intercorporate Guarantees[53]

Most of the foregoing discussion has focused on fraudulent "transfers." However, both § 548 and the UFTA permit avoidance of a fraudulent "obligation."[54] The most obvious example of a fraudulent obligation occurs when a debtor creates documents, making it appear as if he owes money to someone to whom he is not indebted. These obligations, incurred with the intent to hinder, delay, and defraud creditors, are avoidable due to actual fraud. More problematic are intercorporate guarantees, such as ones that might be made by a corporation in exchange for a loan to a different company that is under the control of the same shareholders,[55] or a guarantee by a company in exchange for a loan to the company's shareholders.[56]

These obligations are arguably fraudulent because the surety receives no benefit for its promise. Whatever benefit was involved in the transaction is delivered to the principal debtor, not the surety. For example, if Harlan Wolff, the president of Titanic Industries, guarantees a loan to Titanic from Manufacturer's Bank, Wolff receives no direct benefit from the transfer. If Wolff was insolvent when he provided the guarantee, it might be fraudulent as to Wolff's other creditors. Likewise, if Wolff pays Manufacturer's Bank in fulfillment of his obligation as a guarantor, the payment might be a fraudulent transfer because it deprives Wolff's other creditors of funds that would otherwise be available to pay their claims, and, as with the guarantee itself, Wolff received no direct benefit from the Bank for making the guarantee.

Assume further that Wolff is also the sole stockholder of Olympic, Inc., and that the two companies are involved in related businesses.[57] When the economic vitality of the companies begins to falter and Olympic is in need of cash, Olympic borrows additional funds from Manufacturer's Bank, with Titanic guaranteeing the debt owed by Olympic and supplying the bank with a security interest in Titanic's assets. To the extent Olympic's economic survival is essential to keep Titanic afloat,[58] Titanic receives a real benefit in exchange for its guarantee.

Whether such guarantees are fraudulent depends on the circumstances. The issues are whether the guarantors received any benefit in exchange for their guarantees, and if they did, whether the benefit obtained was a

[53] Scott F. Norberg, Comment, *Avoidability of Intercorporate Guarantees Under Sections 548(a)(2) and 544(b) of the Bankruptcy Code*, 64 N.C. L. Rev. 1099 (1986); Jack F. Williams, *The Fallacies of Contemporary Fraudulent Transfer Models as Applied to Intercorporate Guaranties: Fraudulent Transfer Law as a Fuzzy System*, 15 Cardozo L. Rev. 1403 (1994).

[54] Bankruptcy Code § 548(a)(1); UFTA §§ 4(a), 5 (1984).

[55] *See* Rubin v. Manufacturers Hanover Trust, 661 F.2d 979 (2d Cir. 1981).

[56] *See* Rubin v. Manufacturers Hanover Trust, 661 F.2d 979 (2d Cir. 1981).

[57] Frontier Bank v. Brown (In re N. Merch., Inc.), 371 F.3d 1056 (9th Cir. 2004).

[58] I'm sorry, after this many examples involving this name, I couldn't resist. "Olympic" was the Titanic's sister ship.

reasonably equivalent value for their guarantees.[59] In many cases, the guarantor receives an indirect benefit that provides reasonably equivalent value for the obligation.[60] In *In re Jeffrey Bigelow Design Group, Inc.*, the corporate debtor's shareholders obtained a $1 million line of credit from First American Bank, accompanied by a guarantee from the debtor.[61] The corporation simultaneously executed a promissory note for $1 million payable to the shareholders. Funds drawn on the line of credit were paid to the debtor, and when the debtor made payments to First American for amounts that had been drawn, the debtor's obligation to the shareholders was reduced. In holding that the payments the debtor made on the shareholder's debt to the bank was not a fraudulent conveyance, the Fourth Circuit explained:

> [T]he proper focus is on the net effect of the transfers on the debtor's estate, the funds available to the unsecured creditors. As long as the unsecured creditors are no worse off because the debtor, and consequently the estate, has received an amount reasonably equivalent to what it paid, no fraudulent transfer has occurred . . . . It seems apparent that the transfers have not resulted in the depletion of the bankruptcy estate, [but rather] served simply as repayment for money received.[62]

In *Bigelow Design Group*, the indirect benefit to the corporate guarantor was clear and tangible. In cases where the benefit to the debtor is more obscure, the transfer may be fraudulent. Lenders must be wary of such guarantees and take steps to ensure that they can establish both the fact and the amount of any indirect benefit supplied to the guarantor, lest they lose the advantage of obtaining the guarantee in the very circumstances for which it was sought.

[3] Distributions to Shareholders[63]

Corporate dividends by an insolvent company are vulnerable to attack both as fraudulent transfers and as violations of state corporate law. The same is true for redemptions of shareholders' stock.[64] If the company is insolvent and thus unable to pay its debts, it has no business distributing its remaining assets to its shareholders and thus depriving creditors of

---

[59] *See* In re Xonics Photochemical, Inc., 841 F.2d 198 (7th Cir. 1988) (Posner, J.).

[60] *See* Frontier Bank v. Brown (In re N. Merch., Inc.), 371 F.3d 1056 (9th Cir. 2004) (corporation's secured guarantee given in exchange for loan to shareholders not a fraudulent conveyance because of indirect benefit to the corporation).

[61] Harman v. First Am. Bank (In re Jeffrey Bigelow Design Group, Inc.), 956 F.2d 479, 481 (4th Cir. 1992).

[62] 956 F.2d at 484–85.

[63] Norwood P. Beveridge, Jr., *Does a Corporation's Board of Directors Owe a Fiduciary Duty to Its Creditors?*, 25 St. Mary's L.J. 589 (1994); Jonathan P. Lipson, *Directors' Duties to Creditors: Power Imbalance and the Financially Distressed Corporation*, 50 UCLA L. Rev. 1189 (2003).

[64] Robinson v. Wangemann, 75 F.2d 756 (5th Cir. 1935).

assets needed to pay the company's debts.[65] Payments to shareholders violate creditors' priority rights.

State corporations statutes frequently proscribe such distributions and make them recoverable. The Model Business Corporation Act, as well as state statutes patterned after it, prohibits a corporation from making a distribution to shareholders if after the distribution the corporation would be insolvent, either in the "legal" balance sheet sense or in the "equitable" sense of being unable to pay its debts as they mature.[66] The estate succeeds to the corporation's right to recover these transactions, and under § 544(b), the trustee can set aside any transfer that an unsecured creditor could have avoided under applicable state law. Alternatively, the transfers are vulnerable to avoidance under § 548.

[4] Charitable Contributions[67]

If made by a person who is unable to satisfy his debts, contributions to a church, college, or other charitable organization look very much like fraudulent conveyances. The debtor is insolvent and whatever benefits the debtor receives from the contribution are highly intangible. And, whatever one may think of the social benefits associated with charitable contributions, they are rarely of any value to a debtor's creditors.

Section 548(a)(2) directly addresses charitable contributions. It provides:

> A transfer of a charitable contribution to a qualified religious or charitable entity or organization shall not be considered to be a [constructively fraudulent transfer] under § 548(b)(1)(B) in any case in which —
>
> (A) the amount of that contribution does not exceed 15% of the *gross* annual income of the debtor for the year in which the transfer of the contribution is made; or
>
> (B) the contribution made by a debtor exceeded the percentage of the amount of gross annual income specified in subparagraph (A) if the transfer was consistent with the practices of the debtor in making charitable contributions.[68]

Thus, for a debtor with gross annual income of $100,000 per year, a charitable contribution up to $15,000 is not fraudulent under § 548(a)(2)(B), though it may still be recoverable if the contribution was made with the actual intent to hinder, delay, or defraud creditors under § 548(a)(1)(A). And

---

65 *See* Wood v. National City Bank, 24 F.2d 661 (2d Cir. 1928) (Hand, J.).

66 Model Bus. Corp. Act. § 6.40 (1984).

67 Daniel Keating, *Bankruptcy, Tithing, and the Pocket-Picking Paradigm of Free Exercise*, 1996 U. Ill. L. Rev. 1041; Kenneth N. Klee, *Tithing and Bankruptcy*, 75 Am. Bankr. L.J. 157 (2001); Goria Jean Liddell, Pearson Liddell, Jr. & Stephen K. Lacewel, *Charitable Contributions in Bankruptcy: An Empirical Analysis*, 39 Am. Bus. L.J. 99 (2001); Todd J. Zywicki, *Rewrite the Bankruptcy Laws, Not the Scriptures: Protecting a Bankruptcy Debtor's Right to Tithe*, 1998 Wis. L. Rev. 1223.

68 Bankruptcy Code § 548(a)(2) (emphasis added).

a charitable contribution of even more than 15% might be protected from attack if the contribution was consistent with the debtor's history of making charitable contributions.

This might at first appear to be a limit on the total percentage of charitable contributions a debtor makes, but it is not. Despite the language of § 548(a)(2)(B), the 15% threshold applies to the aggregate of transfers made to the same charity throughout the taxable year, not to each separate transfer that the debtor made at various times throughout the year. Thus, if a debtor who earns $100,000 per year makes two $10,000 contributions to the same charity, $5,000 of the transfers are recoverable by the trustee. Any other result would permit the debtor to transfer all of his income to a single charity.[69]

The Religious Liberty and Charitable Donation Protection Act added this language to the Code in response to the Supreme Court's 1997 decision in *City of Boerne v. Flores.*[70] *City of Boerne* struck down as unconstitutional the Religious Freedom Restoration Act of 1993, which, among many other things, sought to protect contributions to religious organizations from attack as fraudulent transfers.[71]

The new language prevents the trustee from recovering charitable donations, within these limits, as fraudulent conveyances, unless the trustee can establish that the donation was made with fraudulent intent. Section 544(b) was also amended to prevent the trustee from mounting a similar attack through state fraudulent conveyance law.[72] On the other hand, nothing in these changes prevents the trustee from avoiding a fraudulent "obligation" — a charitable pledge to make a contribution to a charity.

Likewise, charitable contributions might still be recoverable by creditors under state law outside of bankruptcy, even though they are largely invulnerable, within the limits outlined above, to attack once the debtor has filed its petition. As explained elsewhere, Chapter 13 contains similar language that permits debtors to deduct charitable contributions, up to 15% of their gross income, from the income they must submit to the trustee for distribution to creditors under their plan.[73] Likewise, Chapter 7's new

[69] The Universal Church v. Geltzer, 463 F.2d 218 (2d Cir. 2006); *but see* In re Zohdi, 234 B.R. 371, 370 n. 20 (Bankr. M.D. La. 1999).

[70] 521 U.S. 507 (1997).

[71] The same day, the Court granted certiorari and remanded *Christians v. Crystal Evangelical Free Church* to the Eighth Circuit for reconsideration in light of its decision in *City of Boerne.* 521 U.S. 1114 (1997). On remand, the Eighth Circuit held that the fraudulent conveyance provisions of RFRA were severable from its other unconstitutional provisions, and that Congress had the power under Article I of the Constitution to revise portions of the Bankruptcy Code regarding the avoidability of fraudulent conveyances in bankruptcy. Christians v. Crystal Evangelical Free Church, 41 F.3d 854 (8th Cir. 1998).

[72] Bankruptcy Code § 544(b)(2) (expressly pre-empting state fraudulent conveyance law to this extent).

[73] Bankruptcy Code § 1325(b)(2)(A)(ii); *see* § 18.08[E][2] Debtor's Projected Disposable Income, *infra.*

means testing rules, used to determine whether a debtor's petition should be dismissed due to abuse, permit deduction of up to 15% of the debtor's gross income in calculating the amount of the debtor's disposable income.[74]

[5] Leveraged Buy-Outs[75]

During the 1980s, the so-called leveraged buy-out (LBO) became a popular tool to change control of publicly held corporations. The typical LBO involves a group of investors, who buy out the interests of the stockholders using borrowed money ("leverage"). The company that is purchased is an obligor (often the only obligor) on the loan. In effect, the buyers use the credit worthiness of the company they are acquiring to buy out the equity interests of the shareholders, and then use the operating income of the target to pay off the loan. LBOs can be used for many purposes, including the spin-off of an unwanted division or subsidiary. However, the most publicized LBOs have involved taking a company private. This means that the end result of the LBO is the conversion of a corporation with many stockholders, an actively traded stock, and lots of shareholder equity, to a corporation with few stockholders and stock that is rarely if ever traded. In place of most of the shareholder equity is a massive debt.

For example, suppose Franklin Manufacturing is a widely-held company whose major stockholders and leading managers are Adams, Brown, and Crim. The three of them borrow money from Peninsula Bank and use the funds to purchase all of the other stock of Franklin. After obtaining control, they cause Franklin to guarantee payment of the debt they owe and grant the bank a security interest in all of Franklin's assets. Subsequently, Franklin, not Adams, Brown, or Crim, makes payments on the debt to Peninsula when they fall due. When Franklin ends up bankrupt, its other creditors (and any trustee who is appointed) complain that Franklin's guarantee, security interest, and payments are all fraudulent transfers or obligations. Their rationale is simple: the secured guarantee rendered Franklin insolvent and it received nothing in exchange for its transfers. If Franklin was insolvent when the transfer was made, became insolvent as a result of the transfer, had inadequate capital, or lacked ability to pay its debts, the basic requirements of § 548 and the UFTA appear to be met.

Various aspects of the transaction are vulnerable to attack. The guarantee itself might be a fraudulent obligation; the transfer of the security interest in Franklin's assets might be a fraudulent transfer; or the stream

---

[74] Bankruptcy Code § 707(b)(1); *see* § 17.03[B][2][b][iv] Deduction of Charitable Contributions, *infra*.

[75] Douglas G. Baird & Thomas H. Jackson, *Fraudulent Conveyance Law and Its Proper Domain*, 38 Vand. L. Rev. 829, 850–54 (1985); Richard M. Cieri, et al., *An Introduction to Legal and Practical Considerations in the Restructuring of Troubled Leveraged Buyouts*, 43 Bus. Law. 333 (1989); Robert A. Fogelson, *Toward a Rational Treatment of Fraudulent Conveyance Cases Involving Leveraged Buyouts*, 68 N.Y.U. L. Rev. 552 (1993); Emily L. Sherwin, *Creditors' Rights Against Participants in a Leveraged Buyout*, 72 Minn. L. Rev. 449 (1988); Kathryn V. Smyser, *Going Private and Going Under: Leveraged Buyouts and the Fraudulent Conveyance Problem*, 63 Ind. L.J. 781, 784–85 (1988).

of Franklin's payments to Peninsula might be fraudulent transfers. Depending upon whether the company met the other requirements for avoidance, they may be able to attack all or any of these steps in the LBO.

It should be clear that Franklin did not receive any direct benefit from the transaction. All of the money the bank provided was paid to Franklin's former stockholders. Franklin did, however, arguably receive indirect benefits: Adams, Brown, and Crim presumably may be especially hard-working managers now that they own the entire company, and that ownership interest is only valuable if the company can meet its debt obligations. The problem, almost insurmountable, is to convince a skeptical bankruptcy court, once the company has filed for bankruptcy, that the value of the managers' sweat equity is real, let alone reasonably equivalent.

The transaction might take one of several other forms too numerous to fully describe here.[76] Those who structure LBOs work tirelessly to avoid the provisions of § 548 and the UFTA. To a large degree, these efforts, at least insofar as they apply to reasonably equivalent value, have been unsuccessful. It is very difficult to convince a court that new or rejuvenated management constitutes a measurable, reasonably equivalent value.[77] The exact structure of the transaction makes little difference.[78] In some cases, the structure of the transaction may affect who is liable, because of the protections given by § 548 and other fraudulent transfer laws to bona fide purchasers. More important as a defense to fraudulent conveyance attack is ensuring that when the transaction is complete, the leveraged entity is not left insolvent or with unreasonably small capital.[79]

Similarly, a good faith transferee may escape liability. Courts have protected transfers made to former shareholders who were not insiders and who had no reason to believe that the debtor was insolvent or that the transaction would create any financial difficulty for it.[80] Some courts have also held that payments to shareholders constitute "settlement payments" protected by § 546 unless fraudulent intent can be proven.

---

[76] David G. Carlson, *Leveraged Buyouts in Bankruptcy*, 20 Ga. L. Rev. 73, 80–83 (1985).

[77] *See, e.g.*, Moody v. Security Pac. Bus. Credit, Inc., 127 B.R. 958 (W.D. Pa. 1991); Credit Managers Ass'n v. Federal Co., 629 F. Supp. 175 (C.D. Cal. 1985).

[78] Keven J. Liss, *Fraudulent Conveyance Law and Leveraged Buyouts*, 87 Colum. L. Rev. 1491, 1499 (1987).

[79] *E.g.*, Committee of Unsecured Creditors v. ASEA Brown, 313 B.R. 219, 230 (N.D. Ohio 2004).

[80] *E.g.*, Kupetz v. Wolf, 845 F.2d 842 (9th Cir. 1988); Zahn v. Yucaipa Capital Fund, 218 B.R. 656 (D.R.I. 1998); *but see* Bay Plastics, Inc. v. BT Commercial Corp. (In re Bay Plastics, Inc.), 187 B.R. 315 (Bankr. C.D. Cal. 1995) (no protection for shareholders who did not pay value "to the debtor"); *see* Michael L. Cook, Brad J. Axelrod & Geoffrey S. Frankel, *The Judicially Created "Innocent Shareholder Defense" to Constructive Fraudulent Transfer Liability in Failed Leveraged Buyouts*, 43 S.C. L. Rev. 777 (1992).

[6] Asset Securitization Transactions[81]

Securitization transactions have emerged over the last ten to fifteen years as a big business, involving several trillion dollars in transactions outstanding at any one time. They serve as a substitute for traditional sales of accounts or accounts receivable financing, but they provide significant advantages for their sponsors, who use them to obtain capital more cheaply than they otherwise might.

In a securitization transaction, the debtor incorporates a company to purchase its accounts, and issues securities in the company backed by the stream of accounts purchased from the debtor. For example, Franklin Manufacturing, as the "originator" of the accounts, might transfer them to a second corporation, known in the business as a "special purpose vehicle" (SPV),[82] which was formed for the express purpose of purchasing the accounts. After purchasing the accounts for the originator, the SPV sells securities backed by the accounts (ABS). The ABS produce the stream of revenue used to pay dividends to investors. Securitization transactions are regarded as superior to traditional methods of lending secured by a debtor's accounts receivable and sales of such accounts because it is less risky than these traditional mechanisms, and because it increases the pool of potential investors by carving the originator's debt into small, easily transferable chunks.[83]

However, the transaction is attractive to investors who might be expected to purchase the securities only if it can be insulated from any bankruptcy proceeding that the originator might file. Unless this can be accomplished, the securities will not be sufficiently attractive to investors to be successful. Thus, the success of the entire transaction depends on whether the sale of the accounts can be insulated from recovery by the originator's bankruptcy in the event that the originator must seek bankruptcy protection from its creditors.

Securitization transactions are vulnerable to attack on several fronts, including avoidance as a fraudulent transfer.[84] Depending on the originator's financial condition, if the price paid by the SPV to the originator was not a reasonably equivalent value for the transferred accounts, the entire transaction might be avoidable as a constructively fraudulent transfer.[85]

---

[81] Rhett G. Campbell, *Financial Markets Contracts and BAPCPA*, 79 Am. Bankr. L.J. 697 (2005); Edward J. Janger, *Muddy Rules for Securitizations*, 7 Fordham J. Corp. & Fin. L. 301 (2002); Peter J. Lahny, *Asset Securitization: A Discussion of the Traditional Bankruptcy Attacks and an Analysis of the Next Potential Attack, Substantive Consolidation*, 9 Am. Bankr. Inst. L. Rev. 815 (2001).

[82] *See* Steven L. Schwarcz, *The Alchemy of Asset Securitization*, 1 Stan. J.L. Bus. & Fin. 133, 134 (1994).

[83] *See, e.g.*, Gregory R. Salathé, Note, *Reducing Health Care Costs Through Hospital Accounts Receivable Securitization*, 80 Va. L. Rev. 549 (1994).

[84] Edward J. Janger, *"The Death of Secured Lending,"* 25 Cardozo L. Rev. 1759 (2004); Edward J. Janger, *Muddy Rules for Securitizations*, 7 Fordham J. Corp. & Fin. L. 301, 308–10 (2002); *see* § 7.05 Securitization, *supra.*

[85] Bankruptcy Code § 548(a)(1)(B).

Though less likely, the transaction might also be a fraudulent transfer if the circumstances surrounding the transaction indicate that it was merely a means to insulate the originator's assets from its creditors and thus "intended to hinder, delay, or defraud" the originator's creditors.[86]

One of the difficulties that makes the transaction susceptible to attack as a fraudulent transfer is that investors in the SPV are likely to want the value of the underlying receivables to be high enough to assure them a meaningful return. This is sometimes called "overcollateralization." This pushes the sale price lower in relation to the value of the underlying receivables, and thus increases the likelihood that a court might later conclude that the amount paid by the SPV was not a reasonably equivalent exchange for the receivables.[87]

As explained elsewhere, the securitization transaction might also be attacked as "intended for security" and thus not a "true sale" of the originator's receivables, or, if corporate formalities have not been fully observed, through an effort to pierce the corporate veil of the SPV and bring its assets into the originator's bankruptcy estate.[88]

§ 16.04 Transfers to General Partners

Section 548(b) contains a special fraudulent transaction provision that applies only to bankrupt partnerships. The trustee may avoid any transfer of property or any obligation incurred within two years of the debtor's petition if the partnership was insolvent or the partnership became insolvent as a result of the transfer or obligation.[89] This rule is far more absolute than any of the other grounds for avoidance: fraudulent intent is immaterial, and the transfer is avoidable even if the exchange was for a reasonably equivalent value.

In understanding this rule, it is important to stress that it only applies when the partnership, together with its general partners, has fewer assets than liabilities. A partnership is only insolvent when its assets, together with the excess of each partner's own properties over the partner's own debts, is less than the total debts of the partnership.[90] This is because general partners are answerable for the debts of a partnership; thus, the excess of the partners' assets over the partners' personal debts are for all practical purposes assets of the partnership and are available to the partnership's creditors. Therefore, to determine whether the partnership is insolvent, the financial condition of the partnership and all of its general partners must be determined.

---

[86] Bankruptcy Code § 548(a)(1)(A).

[87] *See generally* Steven L. Schwarcz & Adam Ford, Structured Finance, A Guide to the Principles of Asset Securitization § 4:7 (3d ed. 2002); Jeffrey E. Bjork, *Seeking Predictability in Bankruptcy: An Alternative to Judicial Recharacterization in Structured Financing*, 14 Bankr. Dev. J. 119 (1997).

[88] *See* § 7.05 Securitization, *supra*.

[89] Bankruptcy Code § 548(b); *see also* UFTA § 8 (1984).

[90] Bankruptcy Code § 101(32)(B).

For example, assume Arsenio and Bernice are partners. Their partnership owns $50,000 in assets and has $70,000 in debts. Arsenio and Bernice each own $10,000 in nonpartnership property and each has $4,000 of nonpartnership debts. Arsenio's "excess" is $6,000; Bernice's excess is $6,000. The sum of Arsenio's excess plus Bernice's excess plus the partnership's property is $62,000 — $8,000 less than the partnership's debts. Thus, the partnership is insolvent. Any transfer of property by the partnership to Bernice is fraudulent. Even if Bernice were to pay the partnership $5,000 for $5,000 worth of the partnership's property, the situation would be the same. In either case, the creditors of the partnership would be able to reach only a total of $62,000, regardless of whether the assets are held by Arsenio, Bernice, or their partnership. Thus, Bernice's purchase, although for a reasonably equivalent value, would be avoidable.

§ 16.05 Reach-Back Periods for Fraudulent Transfer

Both § 548 and state fraudulent transfer law limit the reach-back period for fraudulent transfers. Transfers made and obligations incurred many years before the bankruptcy petition are not recoverable even though the debtor may have been insolvent when they were made. However, the limit under§ 548 is shorter than it is under most state laws. As explained below, state law generally has a much longer reach-back period, in some states going back ten years. This is tempered by restrictions on which creditors have standing to recover the fraudulent conveyance. These limits are important, because the trustee must find an actual unsecured creditor who could have avoided the transfer, in order to recover it under state fraudulent conveyance law through § 544(b).

[A] Bankruptcy Code's Fraudulent Transfer Recovery Period

Section 548 permits recovery of fraudulent transfers that occurred within two years before the debtor's petition.[91] Before the 2005 Amendments, the reach-back period was only one year. Thus, BAPCPA dramatically expanded the recoverability of fraudulent transfers.

This two-year limit must be considered in light of other portions of § 548 that specify the time when transfers are deemed to have been made. Section 548(d)(1) states that a transfer occurs when the transfer "is so perfected that a bona fide purchaser . . . against whom applicable law permits such transfer to be perfected cannot acquire an interest . . . that is superior to [that of] the transferee."[92] This provision deals with the same two-step transfer problem discussed in other contexts, such as avoidable preferences[93] and the strong-arm clause of § 544(a).[94]

---

[91] Bankruptcy Code § 548(a)(1), (b).

[92] Bankruptcy Code § 548(d)(1).

[93] *See* § 15.02[A] Transfer of Debtor's Property; Time of Transfer, *supra*.

[94] *See* § 14.02 Strong-Arm Clause, *supra*.

Some transfers require more than one step to become valid against third parties. For example, execution of a deed or mortgage on realty does not make the conveyance good against all third parties; recordation is required. In particular, a bona fide purchaser can take free of the interest represented by the unrecorded deed or mortgage. Until recordation occurs, therefore, the transaction has not occurred for § 548 purposes.

For example, suppose that on February 1, 2007, Vera executes a deed in favor of Park. The deed is not recorded until August 15, 2007, and Vera files her bankruptcy petition on July 1, 2009. The transfer from Vera to Park occurred on August 15, 2007; it is thus within the two-year period before her bankruptcy petition. If at the time of the transfer Vera was insolvent, and if the price paid was grossly inadequate, the trustee may avoid the transfer. If the deed had been recorded on March 1, 2007, the transfer would have occurred on that date and the transaction would not be avoidable under § 548, although it might still be under state law, which the trustee might also be able to use. If the deed had never been recorded, the transfer would have occurred "immediately before the date of the filing of the petition,"[95] which presumably means on June 30, 2009.

[B] State Law Fraudulent Transfer Recovery Period

The trustee's power to avoid a fraudulent transfer is not limited to § 548. Pursuant to § 544(b), a fraudulent transfer or fraudulent obligation may also be avoided if it is avoidable under relevant state law by someone who is actually a creditor in the bankruptcy proceeding.[96] Most states have a longer fraudulent transfer reach-back period than the two years in § 548. This makes state fraudulent transfer law especially important, despite other limitations imposed by § 544(b).

The UFTA generally uses a four-year statute of limitations.[97] Because the trustee's right to use state fraudulent conveyance law depends on the rights of actual unsecured creditors, this effectively imposes a four-year reach-back period that prevents the trustee from recovering transfers that were made more than four years before the debtor's bankruptcy petition. For cases involving actual fraud under UFTA § 4(a)(1), the period is extended until "one year after the transfer or obligation was or could reasonably have been discovered by the claimant" whose rights the trustee asserts.[98] Some states impose longer periods,[99] though a few are shorter.[100]

[95] Bankruptcy Code § 548(d)(1).

[96] Bankruptcy Code § 544(b) gives the trustee the power to "avoid any transfer of an interest of the debtor in property or any obligation incurred by the debtor that is voidable under applicable law by a creditor holding an unsecured claim that is allowable." *See generally* § 14.03 Power to Use Rights of Actual Unsecured Creditors, *supra*.

[97] UFTA § 9(a), (b).

[98] UFTA § 9(a) (1984).

[99] *E.g.*, Ala. Code § 8-9A-9 (2001) (ten-year statute of limitations for transfers of real property and a six-year statute for transfers of personal property in Alabama); N.Y. Debt. & Cred. Law § 273 (2001) (six years in New York).

[100] *See* Pa. Cons. Stat. § 12-5109 (2001) (two years).

The UFTA contains rules, similar to those in § 548(d), that determine when a transfer occurred. With respect to transfers of real estate, the transfer is deemed to have been made when it was "so far perfected that a good-faith purchaser of the asset from the debtor . . . cannot acquire an interest in the asset that is superior to the interest of the transferee."[101] In most cases, this means that the transfer is made when recorded. With respect to personal property and fixtures, the transfer is made when it is sufficiently perfected to prevent a subsequent judicial lien creditor from acquiring a superior interest.[102]

However, in other respects state fraudulent transfer law is narrower than § 548. The trustee may only use state fraudulent transfer law if it can find an actual unsecured creditor with standing to set the transfer aside. UFTA § 4(a) permits a person who was a creditor before or after the transfer to set it aside,[103] but § 5(a), regarding transfers by an insolvent debtor for less than a reasonably equivalent value, only gives standing to those who were creditors before the transfer was made.[104] In addition, the creditor whose rights the trustee asserts must have an allowable claim in the bankruptcy case. Thus, if Franklin Manufacturing made a transfer two years before its petition, that could have been set aside by its existing creditors, but Franklin then paid those creditors, state fraudulent transfer law is of no avail to the trustee. The rights of the trustee under § 544(b) are entirely derivative of those of an actual creditor — if there is no actual creditor who has standing to avoid the transaction under state fraudulent conveyance law, the trustee has no standing either.

This standing problem does not arise under § 548, which draws no distinction between types of creditors and in any event does not require that there be any actual creditor who is affected by the transfer. Section 548 conveys standing to the trustee if the transaction is avoidable under its provisions.

§ 16.06 Liabilities of and Protections for Bona Fide Purchasers[105]

As discussed more fully elsewhere,[106] the trustee may usually recover an avoidable transfer from either the immediate recipient of the transferred property or from subsequent transferees. However, if a remote transferee is a bona fide purchaser, the trustee may not recover the property. Moreover, as a general rule, those who make valuable improvements to the transferred property are given a lien on the property — in effect, a secured claim for the improvements made. Finally, the trustee has the option to recover the value of the property rather than the property itself.

---

[101] UFTA § 6(1)(i).

[102] UFTA § 6(1)(ii).

[103] UFTA § 4(a) (1984).

[104] UFTA § 5 (1984).

[105] Michael L. Cook, *Fraudulent Transfer Liability Under the Bankruptcy Code*, 17 Hous. L. Rev. 263 (1980).

[106] *See* § 14.08[D] Protection for Good Faith Transferees, *supra*.

Section 548(c) also provides some protection to the immediate transferee. The protection is given only if three conditions are met. First, the transfer must not be avoidable under §§ 544, 545, or 547. Second, the transferee must have given value. Third, the value must have been given in good faith. If these conditions are met, the transferee is given a lien on the transferred property for the amount of the value given. In some cases, the transferee may even be permitted to retain the transferred property.[107]

Actions brought under state fraudulent conveyance law through § 544(b) are subject to whatever protections are accorded by the state law that authorizes the transaction to be avoided. The UFTA generally exposes the immediate transferee[108] and any subsequent transferee to liability but protects subsequent transferees who acted in good faith and acquired the property from a subsequent transferee for value.[109] The UFTA extends full protection to good faith transferees who supplied a reasonably equivalent value from liability due to an intentionally fraudulent transfer.[110] However, immediate transferees are usually aware of the debtor's fraudulent intent.

In addition, the UFTA provides good faith transferees with a lien on the property that was the subject of the avoided transfer. However, unlike § 548, it gives them no protection for the value of improvements they might have made after the transfer.

107 Bankruptcy Code § 548(c).

108 UFTA § 8(b)(1).

109 UFTA § 8(b)(2).

110 UFTA § 8(a).

Chapter 17

Liquidation Under Chapter 7

§ 17.01 Debtor Liquidation[1]

Chapter 7 proceedings are usually referred to as "straight" bankruptcy or "liquidation" bankruptcy cases. In theory, debtors in a Chapter 7 liquidation proceeding give up all of their property in exchange for relief, in the form of a discharge, from their debts.[2] In reorganization proceedings under Chapters 11, 12 and 13, on the other hand, debtors usually keep their property and make payments to creditors from their future income, pursuant to a court-approved plan. Theoretically, liquidation makes sense when creditors will receive more from an immediate sale of the debtor's assets than they would from the receipt of installment payments made by the debtor over a period of time.

The reality is quite different, particularly in cases involving consumer debtors. Nearly all consumer debtors have few, if any assets available to distribute to creditors. In these "no-asset" consumer bankruptcy cases, the debtors' assets are either exempt or completely encumbered by security interests and mortgages. Debtors receive an immediate discharge, retain their exempt property, and usually end up either surrendering any assets that are subject to a security interest, or more likely, entering into a reaffirmation agreement with their secured creditors. This permits the debtor to keep her property in return for renewing her obligation to repay the debt. In this respect, some Chapter 7 liquidation cases are similar to cases under Chapter 13, but with no recovery for unsecured creditors, such as credit card issuers and health care providers.

Business cases are different, at least where there are some unencumbered assets.[3] But few businesses that intend to continue their operations seek bankruptcy protection under Chapter 7. The prospect of the immediate appointment of a trustee, responsible for taking over the day-to-day operation of the debtor's business, discourages most corporate managers from seeking this type of relief. Nevertheless, some businesses end up in Chapter 7 when their efforts to reorganize in Chapter 11 fail.

Although liquidation of the debtor is primarily the function of Chapter 7, liquidation may also occur under other chapters. A Chapter 11 plan may

---

[1] Scott Fay, Erik Hurst & Michelle J. White, *The Household Bankruptcy Decision*, 92 Amer. Econ. Rev. 706, 706 (2002); Michelle J. White, *Why It Pays to File for Bankruptcy: A Critical Look at the Incentives Under U.S. Personal Bankruptcy Law and a Proposal for Change*, 65 U. Chi. L. Rev. 685 (1998).

[2] *See* Chapter 13, Discharge, *supra*.

[3] Lynn M. LoPucki, *The Death of Liability*, 106 Yale L.J. 1 (1996); *but see* Steven L. Schwarcz, *The Inherent Irrationality of Judgment Proofing*, 52 Stan. L. Rev. 1 (1999).

provide for partial or even complete liquidation of the debtor.[4] Moreover, Chapter 7 does not necessarily result in an immediate "fire sale" of all of the debtor's assets. When appropriate, the Chapter 7 trustee may opt for an extended, orderly liquidation and may even continue to run the debtor's business for a time, anticipating selling the enterprise as a going concern.

Despite the reluctance of businesses to seek Chapter 7 relief, most bankruptcies are filed under Chapter 7, and an even greater number are closed in it.[5] Moreover, the result reached in a Chapter 7 liquidation case provides the baseline for the minimum recovery that creditors must receive in reorganization cases under Chapters 11, 12, and 13. Thus, Chapter 7 is the touchstone for all other types of bankruptcy proceedings.

There are, however, many important respects in which Chapter 7 is distinctive. For example, the role of the Chapter 7 trustee is quite different from that of the Chapter 12 or Chapter 13 trustee. A number of the most important of these distinctive provisions are discussed in this Chapter.

This chapter addresses the liquidation process under Chapter 7. Perhaps most importantly, it will explain the financial "means test" adopted in 2005, which sets the standard for whether a Chapter 7 liquidation case involving a consumer debtor must be dismissed, due to "abuse."[6] This new standard determines whether individual debtors will receive relief under Chapter 7 or whether they will be compelled either to seek relief under Chapters 11, 12 or 13 (primarily 13), or to deal with creditors' demands outside of bankruptcy.

§ 17.02 Commencement of a Chapter 7 Liquidation Case

Details regarding the commencement of a Chapter 7 liquidation case are covered elsewhere.[7] Most entities, individuals, corporations, partnerships, and unincorporated associations are all eligible for relief under Chapter 7 if they reside in the United States, have a domicile in the United States, have a place of business in the United States, or own property in the United States.[8] Among these debtors, only railroads, insurance companies, and financial institutions are prohibited from seeking relief in Chapter 7.[9]

Like other bankruptcy proceedings, Chapter 7 cases are commenced with the filing of a petition[10] that contains the debtor's representation that she

---

[4] *See* Bankruptcy Code § 1123(b)(4).

[5] In 2005, 2,078,415 bankruptcy cases were filed. Of these, nearly 1.7 million were Chapter 7 cases. Only 6800 were filed under Chapter 11. Of the 1.7 million Chapter 7 cases, only 39,000 involved what were primarily business debts. The remainder involved primarily consumer debtors. www.uscourts.gov/bnkrpctystats/statistics.htm (last visited on Oct. 7, 2006).

[6] *See* § 17.03[B] Dismissal of Consumer Cases Due to Abuse, *infra.*

[7] *See* Chapter 6, Commencement the Case, *infra.*

[8] Bankruptcy Code § 109(a); *see* § 6.02[B][1][a] Connection to the United States, *supra.*

[9] Bankruptcy Code § 109(b); *see* § 6.02[B][2] Eligibility for Relief Under Chapter 7 — Liquidation, *supra.*

[10] Bankruptcy Code § 301(a).

is eligible for relief, and that she has resided in the district in which the petition is filed for the preceding 180 days or that venue is proper for some other reason, such as that an affiliate has a case pending in the same district.[11]

Voluntary Chapter 7 petitions are usually accompanied by a list of creditors; schedules of assets, liabilities, income and expenditures; and other documents that enable creditors and the trustee to verify the accuracy of the information contained in the petition.[12] Among these documents are copies of a debtor's pay stubs, an itemized statement of monthly income, and a statement disclosing any reasonably anticipated income or expenditures for the twelve-month period following filing of the petition.[13] If the debtor is an individual debtor whose debts are primarily consumer debts, the debtor must include a certificate verifying that the debtor received a notification, either from her attorney, a bankruptcy petition preparer, or the court, briefly describing "chapters 7, 11, 12, and 13 and the general purpose, benefits, and costs of proceeding under each of those chapters [and] the types of services available from credit counseling agencies."[14] These debtors must also supply a certificate verifying that they have received a statement alerting them that "a person who knowingly and fraudulently conceals assets or makes a false oath or statement under penalty of perjury in connection with [the bankruptcy case is] subject to fine, imprisonment or both" and that "all information supplied by a debtor . . . is subject to examination by the Attorney General."[15]

All individual debtors (not just those with primarily consumer debts) must also submit a certificate from an approved nonprofit budget and credit counseling agency, verifying that the debtor has participated in a consumer credit counseling "briefing" sometime within the 180 days immediately preceding her petition,[16] and a copy of any "debt repayment plan" that was developed in the course of this briefing.[17] The briefing must be provided by a non-profit credit counseling provider approved by the United States Trustee.[18] The necessity of this credit counseling briefing may be waived by the court if the debtor is unable to complete the briefing due to "disability or active military duty in a military combat zone."[19]

---

[11] 28 U.S.C. § 1408 (2000); Official Bankruptcy Form 1.

[12] Bankruptcy Code § 521(a); *see* Fed. R. Bankr. P. 1007(a).

[13] Bankruptcy Code § 521(a)(1)(B)(iv)-(vi).

[14] Bankruptcy Code §§ 521(a)(1)(B)(iii), 342(b)(1).

[15] Bankruptcy Code §§ 521(a)(1)(B)(iii), 342(b)(2).

[16] Bankruptcy Code § 521(b)(1).

[17] Bankruptcy Code § 521(b)(2); *see generally* Karen Gross & Susan Block-Lieb, *Empty Mandate or Opportunity for Innovation? Pre-petition Credit Counseling and Postpetition Financial Management Education*, 13 Am. Bankr. Inst. L. Rev. 549 (2005).

[18] Bankruptcy Code § 109(h)(1). A list of approved non-profit credit counseling agencies is maintained on the United States Trustee's website: www.usdoj.gov/ust/eo/bapcpa/ccde/cc_approved.htm (last visited March 10, 2007).

[19] Bankruptcy Code § 109(h)(4).

Once filed, a voluntary petition operates as the entry of an order for relief for the debtor.[20] As explained elsewhere, it invokes the automatic stay of § 362.[21]

§ 17.03 Dismissal and Conversion of a Chapter 7 Case

The successful filing of a petition and the entry of an order for relief does not guarantee that a debtor will ultimately obtain relief in Chapter 7. Liquidation cases can be dismissed by the court for a variety of reasons, including due to "abuse" under the new financial means test incorporated into the Bankruptcy Code in 2005 as a key component of the Bankruptcy Abuse Prevention and Consumer Protection Act (BAPCPA). In rare cases the court might "abstain" from the case.[22]

[A] Dismissal For Cause

Section 707(a) permits a Chapter 7 case to be dismissed for cause[23] and specifies three straightforward and non-controversial bases for dismissing a case. Neither the listed bases nor any other unspecified grounds commonly occur. The three non-exclusive bases are: "unreasonable delay by the debtor that is prejudicial to creditors,"[24] "nonpayment of any [required] fees or charges,"[25] and "failure of the debtor in a voluntary case to file . . . the information required by [Bankruptcy § 521(a)(1)] within fifteen days" of the time of the debtor's petition.[26] Unlike the other bases for dismissal under § 707(a), only the United States Trustee may move for dismissal because of a failure to meet this fifteen-day deadline.

There are some procedural requirements for dismissal. Not surprisingly, the customarily loose rules regarding notice and the opportunity to be heard do not apply when the question is dismissal.[27] There must be a strict twenty days' notice to the debtor, the trustee, and all creditors.[28] In addition,

---

[20] Bankruptcy Code § 301(b). Indeed, the practice for many years was for the bankruptcy court's clerk's office to stamp "ADJUDICATED" on the filed petition, instead of the more innocuous "FILED."

[21] *See* Chapter 8, The Automatic Stay, *supra.*

[22] Bankruptcy Code § 707(b); *see* § 17.03[B] Dismissal of Consumer Cases Due to Abuse, *infra.*

[23] Bankruptcy Code § 707(a); *see* In re Simmons, 200 F.3d 738, 743 (11th Cir. 2000).

[24] Bankruptcy Code § 707(a)(1).

[25] Bankruptcy Code § 707(a)(2). In most cases, this will be the debtor's filing fee, which can be paid in installments and can sometimes now be waived. *See* § 6.02[E] Filing Fees, *supra.*

[26] Bankruptcy Code § 707(a)(3); *see* In re Fawson, 338 B.R. 505 (Bankr. D. Utah 2006). This information consists primarily of the debtor's schedules of assets, liabilities, income, and expenditures, with the required accompanying documents to verify the accuracy of the debtor's income. *See* Bankruptcy Code § 521(a)(1). The statutory reference in § 707(a)(3) is to a non-existing provision, "paragraph (1) of section 521" but undoubtedly was meant to refer to § 521*(a)*(1).

[27] *See* § 1.05[B][4] After Notice and a Hearing, *supra.*

[28] Fed. R. Bankr. P. 2002(a).

unlike many matters before a bankruptcy court, there must be an actual hearing on the motion to dismiss.[29]

[B] Dismissal of Consumer Cases Due to Abuse[30]

Chapter 7 cases of individual debtors whose debts are "primarily consumer debts" can also be dismissed due to "abuse." After the 2005 adoption of BAPCPA, the principal means to detect abuse is the presumptive "means test" of § 707(b)(2).[31] It requires a complex and somewhat artificial calculation of the amount of income that is presumably available to the debtor after meeting her basic living expenses and making payments to secured and priority creditors. Chapter 7 cases filed by debtors who have the financial ability or "means" to make what Congress has determined are meaningful payments to their unsecured creditors are required to be dismissed. As will be seen, the means test applies only to debtors whose annual income places them above the median for debtors in their home state. Those whose family income is below their states' median remain generally eligible for Chapter 7 relief. However, even debtors whose income is too low to meet the means test of presumptive abuse may be vulnerable to having their Chapter 7 cases dismissed if the court determines that their financial situation or other circumstances would otherwise constitute "abuse" within a separate discretionary standard.

[1] Consumer Debts

Dismissal for abuse applies only to an "individual debtor . . . whose debts are primarily consumer debts."[32] Consumer debts are those "incurred by an individual primarily for a personal, family, or household purpose."[33] Thus, Chapter 7 cases of individuals in financial difficulty due to small business failure are not vulnerable to dismissal due to abuse, regardless of their anticipated future ability to pay the debts that their business has incurred.

Cases decided under former § 707(b), permitting dismissal of Chapter 7 cases of the same types of debtors due to the former standard of "substantial

---

[29] Bankruptcy Code § 707(a).

[30] Jean Braucher, *Means Testing Consumer Bankruptcy: The Problem of Means*, 7 Fordham J. Corp. & Fin. L. 407 (2002); Marianne B. Culhane & Michaela M. White, *Taking the New Consumer Bankruptcy Model for a Test Drive: Means-Testing Real Chapter 7 Debtors*, 7 Am Bankr. Inst. L. Rev. 27 (1998); Gary Neustadter, *2005: A Consumer Bankruptcy Odyssey*, 39 Creighton L. Rev. 225 (2006); Henry Sommer, *Trying to Make Sense Out of Nonsense: Representing Consumers Under the Bankruptcy Abuse Prevention and Consumer Protection Act of 2005*, 79 Am Bankr. L.J. 191 (2005); Eugene W. Wedoff, *Means Testing in the New 707(b)*, 79 Am. Bankr. L.J. 231 (2005).

[31] Susan Jensen, *A Legislative History of the Bankruptcy Abuse Prevention and Consumer Protection Act of 2005*, 79 Am. Bankr. L.J. 485 (2005); Jack F. Williams, *Distrust: The Rhetoric and Reality of Means-Testing*, 7 Am. Bankr. Inst. L. Rev. 105 (1999).

[32] Bankruptcy Code § 707(b)(1).

[33] Bankruptcy Code § 101(8).

abuse," indicate that debts incurred in pursuit of a profit are not consumer debts,[34] even though the profit might have been sought in order to support the debtor's family. Though student loans might at first blush seem like consumer debts, they are regarded as part of the start-up expenses for a business or profession, at least to the extent that they are incurred for tuition and books. The portion that is for living expenses and support of the debtor's dependents are consumer debts.[35] Debts incurred as part of a marital settlement or in making improvements to the debtor's home are consumer debts.[36] Liability for negligence seems not to be a consumer debt, because "volition" is a necessary element of incurring a debt for personal, family, or household "purposes."[37]

Whether debts are "primarily" consumer debts or not depends on whether more than a majority of the *amount* of the debtor's obligations are consumer debts,[38] without regard to whether the debt is secured or unsecured.[39] The sheer number of debts should not matter. Thus, a debtor who owes ten $1000 consumer debts but owes $100,000 to a business creditor is not subject to dismissal for abuse. The amount of her $10,000 in consumer debts pales in comparison to the $100,000 business debt.

[2] Presumptive Abuse — Means Testing[40]

The financial means test of § 707(b)(2) provides a rigid, and in some places, incoherent set of presumptive standards to determine whether a Chapter 7 case is subject to dismissal for "abuse." Debtors whose cases are dismissed need to seek relief under Chapter 13 or go it alone with their creditors, perhaps with the assistance of a credit counseling agency. The

[34] *E.g.*, Citizens Nat'l Bank v. Burns (In re Burns), 894 F.2d 361, 363 (10th Cir. 1990).

[35] In re Stewart, 175 F.3d 796, 806 (10th Cir. 1999); In re Gentri, 185 B.R. 368 (Bankr. M.D. Fla. 1995).

[36] In re Gentri, 185 B.R. 368 (Bankr. M.D. Fla. 1995).

[37] *E.g.*, In re Marshalek, 158 B.R. 704 (Bankr. N.D. Ohio, 1993).

[38] *E.g.*, In re Miller, 335 B.R. 335 (Bankr. E.D. Pa. 2005) (discussing cases); In re Kelly, 841 F.2d 908, 913 (9th Cir. 1988) (relying on dictionary definition of "primarily").

[39] *See* In re Kelly, 841 F.2d 908, 912–13 (9th Cir. 1988) (legislative history of § 101(7) expresses intent that home mortgage debts not be treated as consumer debts); In re Price, 353 F.3d 1135, 1139 (9th Cir. 2004).

[40] Jean Braucher, *Increasing Uniformity in Consumer Bankruptcy: Means Testing as a Distraction and the National Bankruptcy Review Commission's Proposals as a Starting Point*, 6 Am. Bankr. Inst. L. Rev. 1, 11 (1998); Marianne B. Culhane & Michaela M. White, *Catching Can-Pay Debtors: Is the Means Test the Only Way?*, 13 Am. Bankr. Inst. L. Rev. 665 (2005); Marianne B. Culhane & Michaela M. White, *Taking the New Consumer Bankruptcy Model for a Test Drive: Means-Testing Real Chapter 7 Debtors*, 7 Am. Bankr. Inst. L. Rev. 27 (1999); Gary Klein, *Means Tested Bankruptcy: What Would It Mean?*, 28 U. Mem. L. Rev. 711, 736 (1998); Charles Jordan Tabb, *The Death of Consumer Bankruptcy in the United States?*, 18 Bankr. Dev. J. 1 (2001); Eugene W. Wedoff, *Means Testing in the New 707(b)*, 79 Am. Bankr. L.J. 231, 235 (2005).

test is complex and in places difficult to fathom. It is also highly controversial.[41]

The means test calculation begins by comparing the debtor's income with the median income of debtors with the same size household in the debtor's home state. If the debtor's income is equal to or below the state median, the debtor's case cannot be dismissed under the means test of § 707(b)(2), though it is still vulnerable to dismissal under the court's discretionary standard for abuse in § 707(b)(1). Despite this theoretical vulnerability, few debtors with incomes below their state's median are likely to find their cases dismissed under the discretionary standard.

Debtors whose income is above the state median must make a complicated calculation of a combination of presumed and actual living expenses to determine the amount of their surplus income. Many of the expenses that are to be deducted from income do not depend on the debtor's actual living expenses but on a set of expense guidelines used by the IRS as the basis for negotiation when establishing repayment schedules with delinquent taxpayers. Other expenses, such as payments to secured creditors, health insurance premiums, childcare costs, and others, are based on a debtor's actual expenses.

After making this calculation, many debtors find that they have no surplus income. Others must compare the amount of this surplus income with another set of complex standards which are designed to determine whether they have enough income to make what Congress has determined are meaningful payments to their unsecured creditors. Chapter 7 cases of debtors with too much surplus income are subject to dismissal due to abuse. Cases of debtors with insufficient surplus income are not subject to dismissal under the means test but are still theoretically subject to dismissal under the discretionary abuse standard, but only on the motion of either the United States Trustee or the court itself.[42]

What a mess!![43]

---

[41] *Compare* Judge Edith H. Jones & Todd J. Zwicki, *It's Time for Means-Testing*, 1999 B.Y.U. L. Rev. 177 (1999), *and* Eric A. Posner, *Should Debtors Be Forced Into Chapter 13?* 32 Loy. L.A. L. Rev. 965 (1999), *with* Jean Braucher, *Increasing Uniformity in Consumer Bankruptcy: Means Testing as a Distraction and the National Bankruptcy Review Commission's Proposals as a Starting Point*, 6 Am. Bankr. Inst. L. Rev. 1 (1998), *and* Elizabeth Warren, *The Bankruptcy Crisis*, 73 Ind. L.J. 1079, 1101 (1998).

[42] Bankruptcy Code § 707(b)(1).

[43] Some basic bankruptcy courses go no further than this in exploring the means test of § 707(b). Bankruptcy practitioners, students taking an intensive course in consumer bankruptcy practice, clinic students, and those taking a course in "General Practice" must delve further into the statute and the accompanying official forms.

[a] Current Monthly Income[44]

The first step in applying the means test involves determining the debtor's "current monthly income." The Code defines this precisely as "the average monthly income from all sources that the debtor receives . . . during the 6-month period ending [in most cases] on the last day of the calendar month immediately preceding the date of commencement of the [debtor's] case."[45]

The statutory language does not indicate whether this includes income before or after any required federal, state, or local withholding tax, or whether it includes an employer's contribution to the debtor's retirement account or employer payments for health insurance that are not deducted from the cash the debtor would otherwise receive.[46] Income includes court-ordered payments received by the debtor as well as "any amount paid by [anyone] on a regular basis for the household expenses of the debtor or the debtor's dependents." This presumably includes voluntary contributions to the debtor's household by a family member, a companion, or a friend, if they are made on a "regular basis."[47] Current monthly income includes retirement income, unemployment compensation, disability payments, interest and dividends, and any royalties received as well as rental or business income that the debtor might receive.[48]

---

[44] Gary Neustadter, *2005: A Consumer Bankruptcy Odyssey*, 39 Creighton L. Rev. 225, 285–300 (2006); Eugene W. Wedoff, *Means Testing in the New 707(b),* 79 Am. Bankr. L.J. 231, 276–84 (2005).

[45] Bankruptcy Code § 101(10A)(A)(i). The language goes on to indicate that if the debtor does not file a schedule of current income as required by § 521(a)(1)(B)(ii), then current income is based on income received by the debtor during the six months immediately preceding whatever date that the court ends up making its determination of the debtor's current income. Thus, if the debtor fails to file the finishes schedule, the court must conduct a hearing to determine the amount of the debtor's income and make a finding of fact. Basing the income determination on income received by the debtor during the six months immediately before the court's decision makes it necessary for the court to have information that is accurate right up to the day of its decision. Alternatively, the court may dismiss the case under § 707(a)(3).

[46] The stipulation in § 101(10A) that "current monthly income" includes income "without regard to whether such income is taxable income" suggests that these amounts might be included. On the other hand, the official forms used in conducting the means test calculations indicate that "gross wages, salary, tips, bonuses, overtime, and commissions" should be included, indicating that no deduction should be made for withholding taxes, and that employer contributions to retirement plans are not included. Amounts deducted from the employee's gross salary to be contributed to retirement, health insurance premiums, or other benefits, however, should be counted as "income," according to the formulas contained in these forms.

[47] *See* In re Quarterman, 342 B.R. 647 (Bankr. M.D. Fla. 2006).

[48] The official forms indicate that only net profits from a business, farm, or rental property need to be included. This makes good sense, but is not fully compatible with the statutory language of § 101(10A), which indicates that "income from all sources that the debtor *receives*" shall be included. The statutory language does not provide for deducting expenses associated with the production of this income. Curiously, although the forms indicate that all "dividend" income must be included, it does not mention deducting expenses associated with the production of this dividend income, such as investment advisor fees, accounting fees, or even tax preparation expenses. These and other expenses might be deducted later, in making the calculations necessary to determine whether the debtor has enough surplus income for his or her petition to constitute an "abuse."

On the other hand, "current monthly income" specifically excludes social security benefits, even apparently for those individuals whose social security benefits, combined with their retirement income, would place them well above the state median income among households in their state.[49] Consider an example involving two married couples who live next door to one another in a small Ohio town: Fred and Wilma and Barney and Betty. Fred and Wilma both work, and together earn $60,000 per year, before taxes. Barney and Betty, on the other hand, are retired. They receive a combined total of $75,000 in dividend and retirement income from their defined contribution retirement funds and IRAs, including the $40,000 they receive in social security benefits. Exclusion of their social security benefits from their "current monthly income" places them below their $46,376 state median for a two-person Ohio household even though they have considerably more income than their working neighbors, Fred and Wilma.

There might easily be another retired couple in the neighborhood, Nick and Nora, who worked their entire careers in state government, where they made no social security contributions and accordingly live on income from their § 403(b) defined-contribution pension fund and their generous state defined-benefit pension plans from which they receive exactly the same $60,000 annual income amount as their neighbors, Fred and Wilma. Like Fred and Wilma, they are subject to means testing under § 707(b), even though their income is below that of Barney and Betty, merely because of the source of their funds. These are just two examples of the inequities that are likely to result from the means testing calculations required by BAPCPA.

"Current monthly income" is then based on the "average monthly income" received from the included sources, making it necessary to divide the total income for the applicable six-month period by six.[50] Section 707(b)(7) then specifies that the amount of the debtor's current monthly income should be multiplied by twelve and compared with the "median family income" of the debtor for the same sized "household"[51] as determined with reference to available United States Census data for households in the state in which the debtor resides.[52]

---

[49] To prevent what might otherwise have been a political disaster, current monthly income also excludes payments to victims of war crimes, crimes against humanity, and international and domestic terrorism under several federal statutes. Payments received under state crime victim statutes, on account of more mundane crimes such as rape, robbery, and murder, appear to be included in income.

[50] "Average" presumably is to be taken to refer to the "plain meaning" of "average," the "arithmetic mean" or "[t]he number obtained by dividing the sum of a set of quantities by the number of quantities in the set." The American Heritage Dictionary of the English Language (1969).

[51] Bankruptcy Code § 707(b)(7).

[52] "Median family income" is defined in Bankruptcy Code § 101(39A). Tables containing information necessary for this calculation are available on the websites of the United States Trustee and the Bureau of the Census. Compare the figures at the United States Trustee's website, www.usdoj.gov/ust/eo/bapcpa/20061001/bci_data/median_income_table.htm (last

Use of the six-month period immediately before the debtor's petition again leads to dramatically different results for otherwise similarly situated debtors, depending on the financial circumstances they were facing in the six months before the filing of their petition. Debtors who received a bonus in the preceding six months may find their cases vulnerable to dismissal under the means test, while debtors who anticipate receipt of a bonus in the near future may be protected.[53] Debtors who have been working extraordinary hours in an effort to deal with their financial situations may similarly find their cases vulnerable to dismissal, while those who have been working only part time may remain eligible for relief.[54] Likewise, debtors with seasonal or erratic income may have an easier time avoiding dismissal for abuse, even though their annual income is greater than other debtors with identical annual income. Debtors who are relying on support from unemployed spouses, whose support payments will rapidly decline in the short-term future, may be vulnerable to dismissal, while debtors with spouses who have only recently started making support payments are protected. Whether the discretionary abuse standard of Bankruptcy Code § 707(b)(1) and the escape hatch for debtors facing "special circumstances" under § 707(b)(2)(B) will prove elastic enough to deal with these and other variations remains to be seen.

If the debtor's annual income is below the applicable median income figure, there is no presumption of abuse. If the debtor's annual income is above the applicable state median household income, further calculations of the debtor's expenses must be made to determine if the debtor's surplus of income in excess of expenses is high enough for the debtor's effort to use Chapter 7 to constitute an abuse. Further, debtors whose income is below the state median remain vulnerable to dismissal under the discretionary abuse standard of revised Bankruptcy Code § 707(b)(1).[55]

Consider, for example, a debtor living in Ohio, who was receiving disability payments of $1,500 a month for three of the months immediately

---

viewed March 10, 2007) with those supplied by the Census Bureau, www.census.gov/hhes/www/income/statemedfaminc.html (last viewed March 10, 2007).

With respect to the statutory formula, those who have been paying close attention will note that the same figure for annual income can be reached in a more direct fashion: by multiplying the six-month income figure on which current monthly income is based by 2. In algebraic format, the Bankruptcy Code's calculation is: $((mi1+mi2+mi3+mi4+mi5+mi6)/6) \times 12$, where mi1 is monthly income in the month immediately preceding the debtor's petition, mi2 is monthly income in the month before the month represented by mi1, and so forth. The same figure can be arrived by using the formula: $(mi1+mi2+mi3+mi4+mi5+mi6) \times 2$.

[53] Debtors whose circumstances seem likely to radically change in the months immediately after their bankruptcy petition seem to be those most vulnerable to having their Chapter 7 cases dismissed under the discretionary abuse standard of § 707(b)(1). Significantly, § 521(a)(1)(B)(vi) requires debtors to include "a statement disclosing any reasonably anticipated increase in income or expenditures during the 12-month period following the date of the filing of the petition" as a supplement to their petition. Bankruptcy Code § 521(a)(1)(B)(vi).

[54] *See* In re Barraza, 3 B.R. 724 (Bankr. N.D. Tex. 2006) (debtor's past income based on 80-hour work weeks). One of your co-author's parents worked 80 hours per week for many years, due not to financial necessity but to an overdeveloped work ethic. It is not a pretty sight.

[55] *See* § 17.03[B][3] Abuse under the Discretionary Standard, *infra*.

preceding her bankruptcy petition and earning pre-tax wages of $6,000 per month for the other three months. Her total income immediately before filing was $22,500, with an average "currently monthly income" of $3,750 ($22,500). If this figure, $3,750, multiplied by 12 is below her state's median annual income for debtors in the same sized household, her case is not vulnerable to dismissal due to presumed abuse under the means test. According to figures released by the Census Bureau and the United States Trustee's office for cases filed after October 1, 2006, Ohioans in a single household have a median annual income of $38,502. Ohioans living in larger households have median incomes starting at $46,376. Thus, if the debtor lives alone, her annual income is above the state median and further calculations would be necessary to determine whether she presents a case of presumed abuse. If she is a single mother with custody of a child, her income is below the $46,376 median for two person Ohio households, and her case would not be presumed to constitute abuse.

[b] Expenses[56]

Debtors whose current monthly income is above the applicable state median[57] must calculate their presumed and actual living expenses to determine whether they have sufficient surplus income to make presumably meaningful payments to creditors. Portions of the expense calculation are based on the debtor's actual living expenses. However, a large part of the calculation, for items such as food, clothing, housing, and transportation, is based on presumptive expenses derived from Internal Revenue Service Guidelines for use by IRS agents in developing payment plans for delinquent taxpayers.[58]

As will be seen, these calculations are complicated.[59] Technical amendments to § 707(b) may be necessary to correct certain inequities in the calculations which appear to have been enacted by mistake.

[i] Expenses in IRS Financial Analysis Handbook

Rather than deduct the debtor's actual expenses for food, clothing, housing, utilities, transportation, and other basic living expenses, the Code

---

[56] Gary Neustadter, *2005: A Consumer Bankruptcy Odyssey*, 39 Creighton L. Rev. 225, 285–300 (2006); Eugene W. Wedoff, *Means Testing in the New 707(b)*, 79 Am. Bankr. L.J. 231, 251–77 (2005).

[57] Debtors whose income is below the applicable household median are not required to complete the portion of the official forms that are designed to calculate the debtor's presumed and actual expenses. Official Bankruptcy Form B22A, Line 15. However, Bankruptcy Code § 707(b) seems to require that the calculation be completed, despite the form's dispensation from the requirement.

[58] Links to these standards are available at the web site of the Executive Office of the United States Trustee: www.usdoj.gov/ust/eo/bapcpa/meanstesting.htm (last visited March 10, 2007).

[59] Comparing the precise language of § 707(b) with Official Bankruptcy Form 22A is likely to be of great assistance for those seeking to plow the depths of the Chapter 7 means testing calculation. Those doing so should be on the lookout for discrepancies between the statutory language and the official forms. Examining the relevant portions of IRS' Revenue Manual is also helpful in this regard.

specifies that amounts for these expenses are to be based on a set of presumed expenses. Section 707(b)(2)(A)(i) specifies:

> the debtor's monthly expenses shall be the debtor's applicable monthly expense amounts specified under the National Standards and Local Standards, and the debtor's actual monthly expenses for the categories specified as Other Necessary Expenses issued by the Internal Revenue Service for the area in which the debtor resides . . . in effect on the date of the order for relief.[60]

As explained by the House Report accompanying the BAPCPA, this language is a reference to portions of the Financial Analysis Handbook which was prepared by the Internal Revenue Service for use by IRS agents in their dealings with delinquent taxpayers. The Handbook contains a schedule of living expenses for agents to use in preparing repayment plans for these taxpayers.[61] The standards in the IRS Handbook contain expense schedules for

- "housing and utilities," including utilities and either rent or mortgage payments;[62]
- "allowable living expense" for food, clothing, housekeeping supplies, personal care and other miscellaneous items;[63]
- the "cost of ownership" of up to two motor vehicles;[64] and
- motor vehicle operating expenses.[65]

Debtors are able to deduct the amounts specified in the IRS standards, regardless of whether their actual expenses are lower and regardless of whether they even have these expenses. The only exception to this is with respect to automobile ownership expenses. Although there is some disagreement about this, most courts rule that debtors who do not own or lease a

---

[60] Bankruptcy Code § 707(b)(2)(A)(ii)(I).

[61] H.R. Rep. No. 109-31, pt. 1, at 13–14 (2005), *reprinted in* 2005 U.S.C.C.A.N. 88, 99–100. This manual is available on the IRS website, at www.irs.gov/irm/ and through online search engines, such as Lexis (in source "Internal Revenue Manual or IRM") and Westlaw (in library "RIA-IRM"). Eugene W. Wedoff, *Means Testing in the New 707(b)*, 79 Am. Bankr. L.J. 231, 253 n.50 (2005).

[62] *See* Official Bankruptcy Form 22, Lines 20A and 20B. A link to the local standards for these amounts is available online: www.usdoj.gov/ust/eo/bapcpa/meanstesting.htm (last visited March 10, 2007).

[63] *See* Official Bankruptcy Form 22, Line 19. A link to the local standards for these amounts is available online: www.usdoj.gov/ust/eo/bapcpa/meanstesting.htm (last visited March 10, 2007).

[64] *See* Official Bankruptcy Form 22, Line 23–24. These national standards monthly are $471 for the first car and $322 for the second car. A link to the local standards for these amounts is available online: www.usdoj.gov/ust/eo/bapcpa/20061001/bci_data/IRS_Trans_Exp_Stds_MW.htm (last visited March 10, 2007).

[65] *See* Official Bankruptcy Form 22, Line 22. A link the local standards for these amounts is available online: www.usdoj.gov/ust/eo/bapcpa/meanstesting.htm (last visited March 10, 2007).

motor vehicle may not deduct the amounts specified in the guidelines for the cost of ownership.[66]

Debtors are expressly permitted to adjust the amounts slated for food and clothing upward by 5%, as specified in the IRS's guidelines, if "reasonable and necessary."[67] Moreover, § 707(b)(2)(A)(ii)(V) permits debtors to deduct as monthly expenses "an allowance for housing and utilities" in excess of the amount permitted by the IRS's guidelines "based on the actual expenses for home energy costs if the debtor provides documentation of such actual expenses and demonstrates that [they] are reasonable and necessary."[68]

In addition, the IRS standards for "Other Necessary Expenses"[69] permit debtors to deduct their actual expenses for a variety of other items:

- income, social security, and medicare taxes;[70]
- mandatory payroll deductions for items such as mandatory retirement contributions, union dues, and uniform expenses;[71]
- term life insurance on the life of the debtor (but not her dependents);[72]
- court ordered payments of any kind, such as future spousal or child support;[73]
- education expenses that are required for a physically or mentally challenged dependent child for whom no public education providing similar services is available;[74]
- actual childcare expenses;[75]
- actual health care expenses;[76] and

---

[66] In re Barraza, 346 B.R. 724 (Bankr. N.D. Tex. 2006) (no ownership expense deduction for 18-year old pickup truck); In re Hardacre, 338 B.R. 718 (Bankr. N.D. Tex. 2006); *contra* Eugene W. Wedoff, *Means Testing in the New 707(b)*, 79 Am. Bankr. L.J. 231, 256–58 (2005). Significantly, the Internal Revenue Manual specifies: "If the taxpayer has no car payment, or no car, question how the taxpayer travels to and from work, grocer, medical care, etc. The taxpayer is only allowed the operating cost or the cost of transportation." Internal Revenue Manual, Financial Analysis Handbook § 5.15.1.7.

[67] Bankruptcy Code § 707(b)(2)(A)(ii)(I); *see* Official Bankruptcy Form 22, Line 39.

[68] *See* Official Bankruptcy Form 22, Line 37. One wonders the extent to which inquiries will be made about the thermostat settings in debtors' homes.

[69] Internal Revenue Service, Internal Revenue Manual, Collecting Process, § 5.15.1.10, www.irs.gov/irm/part5/ch15s01.html (last visited March 10, 2007).

[70] *See* Official Bankruptcy Form 22, Line 25.

[71] *See* Official Bankruptcy Form 22, Line 26.

[72] *See* Official Bankruptcy Form 22, Line 27. The statute does not authorize deductions for whole life insurance premiums or for term insurance on the lives of the debtor's dependents.

[73] *See* Official Bankruptcy Form 22, Line 28.

[74] *See* Official Bankruptcy Form 22, Line 29.

[75] *See* Official Bankruptcy Form 22, Line 30.

[76] *See* Official Bankruptcy Form 22, Line 31.

- cell phone, pager, call waiting, caller ID, special long distance, and internet connection expenses, but only if these are "necessary for the health and welfare" of the debtor or her dependents.[77]

Notably, although the IRS Standards provide for deduction of payments to certain other unsecured creditors, § 707(b)(2)(A)(ii) expressly prohibits deductions for "any payments for debts."

[ii] Other Statutory Living Expenses

In addition to these expenses specifically provided for in the IRS Guidelines, debtors may deduct specific items expressly mentioned in § 707(b)(2)(A). These include:

- reasonably necessary health and disability insurance premiums and health savings account contributions;[78]
- various types of expenses for disabled children and the care of elderly or otherwise infirm dependents;[79]
- reasonably necessary expenses incurred to maintain the safety of the debtor and her family under the federal "Family Violence Prevention and Services Act";[80]
- actual public or private or school expenses for dependent children under eighteen, up to $1500 if they are "reasonable and necessary" and "not already accounted for" in the IRS Standards;[81]
- the actual administrative expenses of administering a Chapter 13 plan in the debtor's federal judicial district as determined by schedules published by the Executive Office of the United States Trustee.[82]

[iii] Payments to Secured and Priority Creditors

The Code also expressly permits the debtor to deduct payments to secured and priority creditors.[83] The provision permitting the deduction of payments owed to secured creditors introduces several ambiguities into the calculation, primarily in connection with payments to secured creditors that might overlap with amounts separately slated in the IRS Standards for

---

[77] *See* Official Bankruptcy Form 22, Line 32. The IRS Guidelines indicate that these expenses are to be deducted only if they are necessary for the health and welfare of the taxpayer or her family, or for the production of income. *See* In re Lara, 347 B.R. 198 (Bankr. N.D. Tex. 2006).

[78] Bankruptcy Code § 707(b)(2)(A)(ii)(I); *see* Official Bankruptcy Form 22, Line 34.

[79] Bankruptcy Code § 707(b)(2)(A)(ii)(II); *see* Official Bankruptcy Form 22, Line 35.

[80] Bankruptcy Code § 707(b)(2)(A)(ii)(I); *see* Official Bankruptcy Form 22, Line 35.

[81] Bankruptcy Code § 707(b)(2)(A)(ii)(IV); *see* Official Bankruptcy Form 22, Line 38.

[82] Bankruptcy Code § 707(b)(2)(A)(ii)(III); *see* Official Bankruptcy Form 22, Line 45. Deduction of this amount, which would not be distributed to creditors in a Chapter 13 case in any event, is compatible with the "best interests" test of creditors in Chapter 13. *See* § 18.08[E][1] Best Interests of Creditors, *infra*.

[83] Bankruptcy Code § 707(b)(2)(A)(iii).

deduction of housing and transportation expenses, but also in relation to the types of secured debts that qualify for these deductions.

Section 707(b)(2)(A)(i) permits the debtor to deduct her "average monthly payments owed on account of secured debts."[84] The amount that can be deducted includes the sixty-month average of

> amounts scheduled as contractually due to secured creditors in each month of the 60 months following the date of the petition . . . [plus] any additional payments to secured creditors necessary for the debtor, in filing a plan under chapter 13 . . . to maintain possession of the debtor's primary residence, motor vehicle, or other property necessary for the support of the debtor and the debtor's dependents, that serves as collateral for secured debts.[85]

This language contemplates totaling the amount due to secured creditors in the sixty months after the date of the debtor's petition together with all arrearages that would be required to be paid to a more limited class of secured creditors and dividing the total by sixty. This yields a monthly amount that will be deducted from the debtor's income in determining the amount of any surplus the debtor has available to make payments to creditors in a Chapter 13 plan or otherwise.

Using the average of the amounts required to be paid over sixty months could lead to anomalies. Consider, for example, a debtor who is contractually obligated to make monthly auto payments of $500 per month for an additional thirty-six months. The total of these payments is $18,000. However, the sixty-month average is only $300.

A debtor who owes arrearages to a secured creditor can add the total of the arrearages to the amount used as the basis for the average. Thus, if the debtor described above is three months behind in her $500 monthly payments, she may add the $1500 in arrearages to bring the total to be averaged to $19,500, for a monthly average over a sixty-month period to $325.[86]

The language of § 707(b)(2)(A)(iii)(I), which pertains to the amount of future payments that can be deducted, makes no distinction between debts secured by collateral that is reasonably necessary for the support of the

[84] Bankruptcy Code § 707(b)(2)(A)(iii); *see* Official Bankruptcy Form 22, Line 42.

[85] Bankruptcy Code § 707(b)(2)(A)(iii)(I)-(II); *see* Official Bankruptcy Form 22, Line 43.

[86] The arrearages that can be included in the total include "payments to secured creditors, necessary for the debtor, in filing a plan under Chapter 13 . . . to maintain possession of the [collateral]." Bankruptcy Code § 707(b)(2)(A)(iii)(II). Under Chapter 13, the amounts necessary for the debtor to pay to retain possession of the collateral would be an amount necessary to provide "adequate protection" to the creditor under the standard for relief from the automatic stay in § 362(d)(2). Bankruptcy Code § 1325(a)(5)(B)(iii)(II). In addition, the payments must at least have a value equal to the amount of the creditor's "allowed secured claim." Bankruptcy Code § 1325(a)(5)(B)(ii). Further, in some cases, particularly those involving motor vehicles, a chapter 13 debtor may be required to pay the entire debt. Bankruptcy Code § 1325(a). *See generally* § 18.08[F] Treatment of Secured Claims — Chapter 13 Secured Creditor Cramdown, *infra.*

debtor and her dependents and debts secured by assets that it might seem frivolous, irresponsible, or dare we say, "abusive" for the debtor to attempt to retain. It appears that the amount includes payments owed to any secured creditor, regardless of the type of collateral involved or whether the collateral for the debt is property that is reasonably necessary for the debtor's support.[87] Thus, payments owed to a creditor with a security interest in the debtor's private airplane, recreational vehicle, racing bicycle,[88] or vacation home seem to be slated for deduction simply because of the creditor's secured status.[89]

This is made clear by the somewhat different language of § 707(b)(2)(A)(iii)(II) regarding the deduction of amounts owed for arrearages. This language permits the debtor to deduct arrearages only if their payment is necessary "to maintain possession of the debtor's primary residence, motor vehicle, or other property necessary for the support of the debtor and the debtor's dependents, that serves as collateral for secured debts."[90]

It is also somewhat unclear whether the phrase "amounts scheduled as contractually due to secured creditors" refers only to principal and interest payments or if it includes any casualty insurance or tax payments that the debtor is contractually required, under the terms of the mortgage or security agreement, to pay either directly to the secured creditor or to the appropriate insurance carrier or governmental entity. Most mortgages require the debtor to make these payments; many require them to be paid directly to the creditor, who will disburse the payments, when they are due, to the insurance company or tax authority involved.[91]

Even more unclear is whether the debtor is permitted to deduct both the amount of payments contractually required to be made to secured creditors for debts secured by residential real estate and motor vehicles, *plus* the full

[87] *Cf.* In re Thompson, 350 B.R. 770 (Bankr. N.D. Ohio 2006) (payments on loan secured by 401(k) account).

[88] Have you priced high-quality racing bikes, lately? One of your authors used to drive to bicycle rides with a bicycle on top of his car that was worth more than the car underneath. Then he bought a nicer car.

[89] This conclusion is reinforced by the limitation contained in language in the second category of secured creditor payments that can be deducted, for arrearages that would have to be paid in a Chapter 13 case to permit the debtor to retain possession of "the debtor's primary residence, motor vehicle, or other property necessary for the support of the debtor and the debtor's dependents." Bankruptcy Code § 707(b)(2)(A)(iii)(II).

[90] Bankruptcy Code § 707(b)(2)(A)(iii)(II). Even here, the phrasing is unclear. It seems as if the phrase "debtor's primary" does not modify "motor vehicle," even though that might be a fair conclusion to draw. The language seems limited to only one "motor vehicle" and no provision is made for a motor vehicle owned by the debtor's dependents. Even more unclear is whether the payments are only to be deducted if the motor vehicle that serves as collateral for the loan must be "necessary for the support of the debtor and the debtor's dependents."

[91] Official Bankruptcy Form 22A, Line 42 indicates that the debtor should deduct amounts for taxes and insurance that are required "by the mortgage." This presumably was meant to include similar amounts owed under the terms of a security agreement covering personal property.

amount of the IRS's schedule of housing and transportation expenses permitted to be separately deducted by § 707(b)(2)(A)(ii)(I). Permitting deduction of both home mortgage payments and the housing expense in the IRS's scheduled "National and Local Standards" seems to permit debtors who own their homes to deduct their housing expenses twice. The same may be true for the debtor's car.

On this point, the statutory language passed by Congress and signed by the President could not be more clear. Section 707(b)(2)(A)(i) provides that "the court shall presume abuse" based on "the debtor's current monthly income reduced by the amounts determined under clauses (ii), (iii) *and* (iv)."[92] The National and Local Standards, which include the IRS's housing allowance, is included in § 707(b)(2)(A)(ii), and amounts to be paid to secured creditors appears in § 707(b)(2)(A)(iii). Thus, the plain language of the statute permits debtors to deduct both the amount of the IRS's housing and transportation allowances and the amount of the debtor's home and auto payments.

This, of course, is extraordinarily unfair to renters, who may not count their housing expenses twice. It is likewise unfair to those who lease their cars, who are not able to deduct their auto ownership expenses twice. Moreover, it has a disparate impact on debtors whose secured assets are not reasonably necessary for their support.

Early decisions addressing this apparent inequity have refused to permit debtors to deduct their housing expenses twice in this fashion. In *In re Hardacre,* the court rejected the debtor's contention that the plain meaning § 707(b)(2)(A)(ii)(I) required the court to permit the debtor to deduct both his mortgage payment and the IRS guidelines housing expenses. It ruled, quite to the contrary, that the plain meaning of another part of this section compelled otherwise. Section 707(b)(2)(A)(ii)(I) also provides: "Notwithstanding any other provision of this clause, the monthly expenses of the debtor shall not include any payment for debts." This, the court ruled, prevented the debtor from doubling up on this deduction.[93]

The statute makes no provision for the deduction of automobile lease payments, beyond the statutory amount allowable for the "costs of ownership." Debtors who lease their automobiles are treated in a manner similar to those who rent their homes: they can deduct only the amount specified in the IRS Standards, regardless of the amount of their actual rental payments. This may lead to a new round of decisions regarding the difficult distinction between a lease and a security interest.[94]

A related question is whether the debtor must owe car payments to be permitted to deduct amounts for the costs of ownership specified in the IRS guidelines. Courts do not agree on this point, with some holding that the debtor must have a car payment in order to claim the ownership

---

[92] Bankruptcy Code § 707(b)(2)(A)(i).

[93] 338 B.R. 718, 724–28 (Bankr. N.D. Tex. 2006).

[94] *See* § 2.03[B] Personal Property Leases, *supra.*

deduction[95] and other courts permitting a debtor to deduct this amount even if he owns his car free and clear from any lien.[96]

Another anomaly is that the strict statutory language appears to permit the debtor to deduct the amount of payments due to secured creditors, regardless of whether the debtor intends to reaffirm these debts. The first few cases to address the issue have disagreed, with some courts holding that the plain meaning of § 707(b)(2)(A)(iii) required deduction of payments that are contractually due to the creditor, even if the debtor intends to surrender the collateral,[97] and other courts reaching the opposite conclusion after finding that the statutory language was ambiguous.[98]

[iv] Deduction of Charitable Contributions

Although a debtor's charitable contributions are not listed as a permissible deduction, § 707(b)(1) specifies: "In making a determination whether to dismiss a case under this section, the court may not take into consideration whether a debtor has made, or continues to make, charitable contributions . . . to any qualified religious or charitable organization."[99] The statute specifies no limit to the amount that can be deducted. The only restriction specified by the statute is that the contributions must be ones that the debtor "continues to make," though the mechanism for policing this requirement is unclear.[100] Although this provision is extraordinarily generous, it seems unlikely that many debtors will seek to evade the consequences of the means test by making large contributions to their favorite charities. Debtors who perceive the opportunity for receiving something in exchange for their contributions, on the other hand, may seek to use this provision in ways that neither creditors nor bankruptcy trustees would approve of.

[v] Expenses Not Deducted From Income

Some debtors have other significant expenses that are not deducted from their income for the purposes of determining whether the debtor falls under the presumptive abuse standard. Most significant among these are expenses for non-dischargeable, non-priority payments to unsecured creditors that the debtor is required to pay. The most significant of these are unsecured property settlement payments, student loans, debts incurred through fraud,

---

[95] *See* In re Hardacre, 338 B.R. 718 (Bankr. N.D. Tex. 2006); In re Barraza, 346 B.R. 724 (Bankr. N.D. Tex. 2006); In re McGuire, 342 B.R. 608 (Bankr. W.D. Mo. 2006); In re Carlin, 348 B.R. 795 (Bankr. D. Or. 2006).

[96] In re Fowler, 349 B.R. 414 (Bankr. D. Del. 2006); In re Grunert, 353 B.R. 591 (Bankr. D. Wis. 2006); In re Haley, 354 B.R. 340 (Bankr. D.N.H. 2006); In re Hartwick, 352 B.R. 867 (Bankr. D. Minn. 2006).

[97] In re Walker, 2006 Bankr. LEXIS 845 (Bankr. N.D. Ga. May 1, 2006); In re Oliver, No. 06-30076RLD13, 2006 WL 2086691 (Bankr. D. Or. June 29, 2006).

[98] In re Skaggs, 349 B.R. 594 (Bankr. E.D. Mo. 2006).

[99] Bankruptcy Code § 707(b)(1).

[100] *See* Eugene W. Wedoff, *Means Testing in the New 707(b)*, 79 Am. Bankr. L.J. 231, 271–72 (2005).

drunk-driving, or wilful and malicious injuries, and any non-priority, non-dischargeable tax obligations. It remains to be seen whether debtors facing these liabilities will find it possible to circumvent the presumptive abuse standard under the "special circumstances" escape hatch of § 707(b)(2)(B).

[c] Excess Surplus Income

After deducting these expenses from current monthly income, the debtor must compare the amount of her surplus or "monthly disposable income" with the standards in § 707(b)(2)(A)(i). Abuse is presumed and the petition will likely be dismissed if the debtor's current monthly income, when multiplied by sixty (months) is enough to repay what Congress has determined is a meaningful amount to unsecured creditors. If the surplus is more than $10,000 (or $166.67 per month), abuse is presumed. If the surplus is less than $6000 ($100 per month), abuse is not presumed. If the surplus is between $6000 ($100 per month), and $10,000 ($166.66 per month), an additional calculation must be made.

For debtors with a five-year surplus of between $6000 and $10,000, the amount of the surplus must be compared with the amount of the debtor's non-priority unsecured claims. Abuse is presumed if the surplus is more than 25% of the debtor's non-priority allowed unsecured claims. If the surplus is less than 25% of these claims, abuse is not presumed, but the court may still find abuse under the discretionary standard.

For example, the petition of a debtor with $32,000 of unsecured claims and more than $8000 in total surplus income ($133.33 per month) would be subject to dismissal for abuse. A debtor with slightly less surplus income, such as only $130 per month, or slightly more non-priority debt, such as $32,100, would not be subject to dismissal due to presumed abuse. Debtors on the margin of these thresholds might be able to avoid dismissal due to abuse simply by delaying the filing of their petition while interest accumulates on their unsecured debts. Other debtors might be able to avoid dismissal by cutting back slightly on their overtime or by turning the thermostat back up to seventy-two degrees, making additional contributions to a health savings account, enrolling their child in an after-school "pay to play" sports or music program, or increasing their charitable contributions.

[d] Special Circumstances

Debtors whose cases are vulnerable to dismissal might still escape dismissal by demonstrating "special circumstances" under § 707(b)(2)(B) to rebut the presumption of abuse. Section 707(b)(2)(B)(i) provides that a "serious medical condition or a call to order to active duty in the Armed Forces" might qualify as the type of special circumstances that warrant rebuttal of the presumption, but even then, only to the extent they "justify additional expenses or adjustments of current monthly income for which where is no reasonable alternative."[101]

---

[101] Bankruptcy Code § 707(b)(2)(B)(i).

The Code's language makes it clear that rebuttal of the presumption is discouraged. Debtors seeking to rebut the presumption must provide "documentation" for any adjustments to their expenses or income and supply a "detailed explanation" of the special circumstances that make the adjustment necessary.[102] Morever, debtors are required to "attest under oath" regarding the accuracy of the already documented information they supply.[103] Even with testimony under oath and documentary evidence, the presumption can be rebutted only if the debtor's surplus income, after further deductions for additional expenses or reduced earnings, fall under the established thresholds for detecting abuse.[104]

Early decisions interpreting § 707(b)(2)(B)(i) suggest that courts might take a flexible approach to the types of circumstances that might qualify as "special," provided that the debtors are able to document their extraordinary expenditures. In *In re Batzkiel*, the court decided that the debtors' unusually high operating expenses for their automobile, caused by their significant commuting distances and the rising price of gasoline since the establishment of the IRS's local standards for operating a motor vehicle, justified providing the debtor with an additional allowance for these expenses.[105] There, the debtors were able to carefully document the miles they commuted to work each month, the price of gasoline, the costs of regular oil changes, and new tires every other year. On the other hand, in *In re Renicker*, the court would not consider whether the debtor's claim of special circumstances was valid, where they failed to provide documentation for their claim regarding their rental and gasoline expenses.[106]

A question that undoubtedly will continue to arise is whether the debtor's inability to make substantial payment to her unsecured creditors in a Chapter 13 plan is sufficient to rebut the presumption of abuse established by § 707(b). Early indications indicate that this is not sufficient evidence of special circumstances to avoid dismissal due to abuse.[107]

[e] Safe Harbor

Section 707(b) provides several safe harbor provisions, establishing various levels of protection for debtors, depending on their status and income.

[i] Disabled Veterans

Section 707(b)(2)(D) protects certain disabled veterans from dismissal due to presumptive abuse. This safe harbor applies "if the debtor is a disabled

---

[102] Bankruptcy Code § 707(b)(2)(B)(ii).

[103] Bankruptcy Code § 707(b)(2)(B)(ii). The debtor's attorney might be subject to sanction under § 707(b)(4)(C) if her pleadings in support of rebuttal are not "well grounded in fact."

[104] Bankruptcy Code § 707(b)(2)(B)(iv).

[105] In re Batzkiel, 349 B.R. 581 (Bankr. N.D. Iowa 2006).

[106] In re Renicker, 342 B.R. 304, 310 (Bankr. W.D. Mo. 2006); *see also* In re Demonica, 345 B.R. 895, 903–04 (Bankr. N.D. Ill. 2006).

[107] In re Johns, 342 B.R. 626 (Bankr. E.D. Okla. 2006).

veteran"[108] whose indebtedness was incurred "primarily during a period during which [the veteran] was (i) on active duty . . . or (ii) performing a homeland defense activity." The exemption does not apply to disabled veterans whose debts were incurred before or after performing these duties. And, of course, even disabled veterans are subject to having their cases dismissed under the discretionary abuse standard in § 707(b)(1).

[ii] Debtors with Income Below the State Median

Debtors whose household income is below the state median are invulnerable to dismissal under the presumptive standard[109] but remain subject to dismissal under the discretionary standard of § 707(b)(3), discussed below.[110] However, § 707(b)(6) provides at least a protected (if not entirely safe) harbor for these debtors by permitting a dismissal for abuse motion to be made only by "the judge or United States trustee."[111] This is similar to the situation that existed for all debtors before the 2005 Amendments, which protected debtors from motions to dismiss that might be made to harass debtors who lacked the resources to defend a dismissal motion.[112]

[3] Abuse under the Discretionary Standard[113]

Debtors whose cases are not subject to dismissal under the presumptive standard might still be vulnerable to dismissal under a discretionary abuse standard that is virtually identical to the standard that existed before the 2005 Amendments.[114] In exercising its discretion, the court is directed to "consider (A) whether the debtor filed the petition in bad faith; or (B) the totality of the circumstances . . . of the debtor's financial situation."[115]

The discretionary standard is most likely to apply to debtors whose current or anticipated income is considerably higher than their presumed income under the "current monthly income" standard of § 101(10A).[116] Because this standard is based on debtors' actual income for the six months prior to filing their petitions, debtors whose income rose around the time their petitions were filed may not be ensnared by the presumptive test, even

---

108 The debtor must satisfy the definition of a disabled veteran in 38 U.S.C. § 3741(1) (2000).

109 Bankruptcy Code § 707(b)(7).

110 In re Paret, 347 B.R. 12 (Bankr. D. Del. 2006); Eugene Wedoff, *Means Testing in the New 707(b)*, 79 Am. Bankr. L.J. 231 (2005).

111 Bankruptcy Code § 707(b)(6).

112 *See* § 17.03[B][3][a] Substantial Abuse Before 2005, *infra*.

113 Wayne R. Wells, Janell M. Kurtz & Robert J. Calhoun, *The Implementation of Bankruptcy Code Section 707(b): The Law and the Reality*, 39 Clev. St. L. Rev. 15 (1991); Teresa A. Sullivan, Elizabeth Warren & Jay Lawrence Westbrook, *The Persistence of Local Legal Culture: Twenty Years of Evidence from the Federal Bankruptcy Courts*, 17 Harv. J.L. & Pub. Pol'y 801 (1994).

114 In re Pennington, 348 B.R. 647 (Bankr. D. Del. 2006); In re Pak, 343 B.R. 239, 244 (Bankr. N.D. Cal. 2006).

115 Bankruptcy Code § 707(b)(3).

116 Bankruptcy Code § 101(10A); *see* § 17.03[B][2][a] Current Monthly Income, *supra*.

though they are actually able to make meaningful payments to creditors from their current or anticipated income.

For example, a young doctor, earning $60,000 in the final year of her surgical residency program might not have sufficient income, depending on the size of her family and the extent of payments she owes to secured creditors, to fall into the presumptive abuse standard of § 707(b). Upon completion of her residency, however, she is likely to earn in excess of $200,000. If she files a Chapter 7 shortly after she starts earning income at this level, her total financial circumstances might be closely examined to determine if her case should be dismissed under the discretionary standard for abuse.[117]

Prior to the adoption of BAPCPA, the standard for discretionary dismissal was "substantial abuse." Courts interpreting revised § 707(b)(3) will no doubt look to the earlier cases to interpret the new language. Certainly circumstances that would have constituted "substantial abuse" under the old standard would also constitute "abuse" under the new standard. Whether there are situations that will constitute "abuse" that would not have constituted "substantial abuse" remains to be seen.

[a] Substantial Abuse Before 2005

Chapter 7 cases have been subject to discretionary dismissal due to "substantial abuse" since 1984. There is a difference in terminology between former § 707(b) and the current law. Current § 707(b) permits dismissal due to "abuse" under either the presumptive standard explained above or under the discretionary standard described below. Former § 707(b) permitted dismissal due to "substantial abuse" and was entirely discretionary, with no presumptive standard one way or the other. Moreover, former § 707(b) did not even contain the meager guidance supplied by current § 707(b)(3), which directs the court to consider whether the petition was abusive due either to bad faith or based on the totality of the debtor's financial circumstances.

Under the substantial abuse standard, only the court itself or the United States Trustee had standing to raise the question.[118] A motion to dismiss could not be made by the case trustee or by a creditor. The statute even specified that the issue could not be brought before the court at the "request or suggestion" of other parties.

In applying the "substantial abuse" standard, courts applied two separate tests in a variety of ways. Many courts examined whether the debtor had income that made her "able to pay" her debts. Her ability to pay was usually measured by evaluating the amount of disposable income that the debtor

---

[117] *See, e.g.*, In re Stewart, 175 F.3d 796 (10th Cir. 1999).

[118] *See* Michael J. Herbert, *Once More Unto the Breach, Dear Friends: The 1986 Reforms of the Reformed Bankruptcy Reform Act*, 16 Cap. U. L. Rev. 325, 331 (1987).

could have used to make payments under a a hypothetical Chapter 13 plan.[119]

Most courts rejected this ability to pay test in favor of a considerably more flexible "totality of the circumstances" test, which required a careful inquiry into the circumstances each debtor faced.[120] These courts agreed that the debtor's ability to pay was relevant but also considered other factors, including (1) whether the debtor's financial difficulty was precipitated by unanticipated illness, calamity, disability, or unemployment; (2) whether the debtor made consumer purchases shortly before his bankruptcy that far exceeded what he could repay; (3) whether the debtor's household budget was extravagant; (4) whether the schedules and statements of financial affairs accurately depicted the debtor's financial condition; and (5) whether the debtor filed his petition in good faith.

[b] Discretionary Dismissal for Abuse under BAPCPA[121]

The discretionary standard for dismissal due to abuse indicates that if the presumption of abuse does not arise, or if it is rebutted based on the debtor's presumed expenses, a finding of abuse is still warranted after considering "whether the debtor filed the petition in bad faith" or "the totality of the circumstances of the debtor's financial situation."[122] As indicated earlier, notwithstanding the change in statutory language, it is anticipated that whether a debtor presents a case of discretionary "abuse" under § 707(b)(3) is likely to depend on the same types of circumstances that courts relied on before the 2005 Amendments to detect "substantial abuse."[123]

[i] Bad Faith

Circumstances that might indicate that a Chapter 7 petition was filed in bad faith include serial filings designed primarily to take advantage of the automatic stay and thus forestall foreclosure, the debtor's concealment of assets, and intentional credit card abuse. It might also be used to restrict debtors' efforts to manipulate exemption rights unfairly.[124]

---

119 *See, e.g.*, In re Koch, 109 F.3d 1285, 1288 (8th Cir. 1997); In re Kelly, 841 F.2d 908 (9th Cir. 1988); *see* Carl Felsenfeld, *Denial of Discharge for Substantial Abuse: Refining — Not Changing — Bankruptcy Law*, 67 Fordham L. Rev. 1369 (1999).

120 *See* In re Price, 353 F.3d 1135, 1139 (9th Cir. 2004); In re Lamana, 153 F.3d 1 (1st Cir. 1998); In re Kornfield, 164 F.3d 778 (2d Cir. 1999); In re Green, 934 F.2d 568, 572 (4th Cir. 1991); In re Krohn, 886 F.2d 123, 126 (6th Cir. 1989); In re Ontiveros, 198 B.R. 284 (7th Cir. 1996); In re Stewart, 175 F.3d at 796 (10th Cir. 1999); In re White, 49 B.R. 869 (Bankr. W.D.N.C. 1985).

121 Eugene R. Wedoff, *Judicial Discretion to Find Abuse under § 707(b)(3)*, 71 Mo. L. Rev. 1035 (2006).

122 Bankruptcy Code § 707(b)(3).

123 Eugene Wedoff, *Means Testing in the New 707(b)*, 79 Am. Bankr. L.J. 231, 236 n.8 (2005).

124 Marianne B. Culhane & Michaela M. White, *Catching Can-Pay Debtors: Is the Means Test the Only Way?*, 13 Am. Bankr. Inst. L. Rev. 665, 696–98 (2005); *Final Report of the Bankruptcy Foreclosure Scam Task Force*, 32 Loy. L.A. L. Rev. 1063 (1999).

[ii] Totality of the Circumstances

The Code's direction that courts should consider the totality of the circumstances of the debtor's financial situation seems to codify the numerous pre-BAPCPA decisions that adopted a totality of the circumstances approach to determine whether the debtor's Chapter 7 filing constituted a "substantial abuse." The debtor's ability to pay would be one factor, but would not be dispositive.

Here it is useful to remember that the means-test standard for presumptive abuse depends on a calculation of the debtor's past income which may not accurately reflect the debtor's current or anticipated circumstances. Thus, a debtor whose "current monthly income," based on the six months before her petition,[125] might be considerably lower than her current or anticipated actual income. Such a debtor might not trigger the presumption of abuse under § 707(b)(2) but might warrant dismissal under the more discretionary standard of § 707(b)(1). On the other hand, it might be argued that the means test tells the court how to calculate current monthly income, and therefore the circumstances justifying dismissal must be things other than the debtor's income.

Likewise, a debtor's presumed living expenses, calculated by using the statutorily mandated IRS living expense tables, might be lower than her actual living expenses. Even more likely is the possibility that the debtor's payments to secured creditors reflect an ability to "live large" by making payments on secured debts, while at the same time using Chapter 7 to discharge debts to unsecured creditors whom the debtor could pay if she surrendered some of her collateral. It is not difficult to imagine a debtor living in an extravagant home filled with plush furnishings, with several luxury vehicles parked in the garage, using her substantial income to make payments to the secured creditors who financed her purchases, while attempting to discharge unsecured debts incurred for sumptuous dinners at expensive restaurants and elaborate vacations at resorts usually frequented only by the rich and famous. The discretionary test for abuse would seem to be well suited to prevent these debtors from taking advantage of Chapter 7's discharge provisions.[126]

Despite this, some scholars suggest that permitting a debtor's ability to pay to be considered under the discretionary test renders the presumptive test of § 707(b)(2) superfluous.[127]

The few decisions to address this issue reject this suggestion, at least for debtors whose "current monthly income" was below the applicable state median.[128] The close similarity between language in pre-2005 "totality of

[125] *See* § 17.03[B][2][a] Current Monthly Income, *supra*.

[126] Eugene Wedoff, *Means Testing in the New 707(b)*, 79 Am. Bankr. L.J. 231, 278–79 (2005).

[127] See Marianne B. Culhane & Michaela M. White, *Catching Can-Pay Debtors:Is the Means Test the Only Way?,* 13 Am. Bankr. Inst. L.Rev. 665, 677–82 (2005).

[128] In re Pak, 343 B.R. 239 (Bankr. N.D. Cal. 2006); In re Paret, 347 B.R. 12 (Bankr. D. Del. 2006); In re Richie, 353 B.R. 569 (Bankr. E.D. Wis. 2006).

the circumstances" cases and the express language of § 707(b)(3)(B) seems to cut in favor of this interpretation.[129] On the other hand, the "circumstances" now include the presence in the statute of § 707(b)(2).

The precise language of § 707(b)(3)(B) also directs the court to consider "whether the debtor seeks to reject a personal services contract and the financial need for such rejection as sought by the debtor."[130] This parenthetical was aimed at a relatively small (but highly visible) number of debtors in the sports and entertainment industries who have sometimes attempted to use Chapter 7 primarily to renegotiate their recording contract, or make a better deal with another team or another recording label.[131]

[4] Attorney Sanctions[132]

Section 707(b)(4) now permits bankruptcy trustees to seek reimbursement from debtor's attorneys for the trustee's reasonable costs in prosecuting a motion for dismissal under either the presumptive or the discretionary abuse standard of § 707(b), if the "action of the attorney for the debtor in filing a case under [Chapter 7] violated Bankruptcy Rule 9011." In addition, if the attorney's actions have violated Rule 9011, the court may assess civil penalties against the debtor's attorney, possibly awarding them to either the case trustee or the United State Trustee.[133]

Debtors' attorneys must remain mindful, in determining whether to file Chapter 7 cases on behalf of their clients, that their signatures on a petition, a pleading, or a motion "constitute a certification that the attorney has (i) performed a reasonable investigation into the circumstances that gave rise to the [pleading]" and (ii) determined that the pleading is both *"well* grounded in fact"[134] and "warranted by existing law or a good faith argument for the extension, modification, or reversal of existing law and does not constitute an abuse."[135]

---

[129] *See* Eugene Wedoff, *Judicial Discretion to Find Abuse under § 707(b)(3)*, 71 Mo. L. Rev. 1035 (2006).

[130] Bankruptcy Code § 707(b)(3)(B).

[131] *See* H.R. Rep. 105-794, 123 (1998) (accompanying a much earlier version of what became BAPCPA); *see, e.g.*, In re Carrere, 64 B.R. 156 (Bankr. C.D. Cal. 1986) (dismissing Chapter 7 case of an "A Team" actress who sought bankruptcy relief in an effort to switch TV networks).

[132] Walter W. Miller, Jr., *The Proposed "Bankruptcy Abuse Prevention and Consumer Protection Act of 2002"*, 22 Ann. Rev. Banking & Fin. L. 301 329–30 (2003); Henry J. Sommer, *Trying to Make Sense Out of Nonsense: Representing Consumers Under the "Bankruptcy Abuse Prevention and Consumer Protection Act of 2005"*, 79 Am. Bankr. L.J. 191, 204 (2005).

[133] Bankruptcy Code § 707(b)(4)(B).

[134] Bankruptcy Code § 707(b)(4)(C) (emphasis added). This goes well beyond the language of Rule 9011, which only requires the attorney certify that "to the best of the [her] knowledge, information and belief, formed after an inquiry reasonable under the circumstances . . . the allegations and other factual contentions have *evidentiary support* or . . . are likely to have evidentiary support after a reasonable opportunity for further investigation or discovery." Fed. R. Bank. P. 9011(b)(3) (emphasis added).

[135] Bankruptcy Code § 707(b)(4)(C).

While attorneys already have a professional obligation to have "evidentiary support" for their factual contentions,[136] the more rigorous language of § 707(b)(4)(C) regarding a certification that the petition is "well grounded in fact," combined with congressional encouragement to the United States Trustee's office to vigorously enforce these new provisions, seems destined both to weed out attorneys who lack a thorough familiarity with the law and to discourage attorneys from pursuing aggressive positions on behalf of their clients, particularly with respect to the standards for presumptive abuse.

[C] Conversion of Chapter 7 Cases

Debtors have the right to convert their Chapter 7 cases to Chapters 11, 12, or 13 at any time. This right is limited by the requirement that the debtor be eligible for the chapter selected and that the case was not previously converted from one of those chapters to Chapter 7.[137] Any purported waiver of the right to convert is unenforceable.[138] Despite the unqualified language of § 706, which appears to impose no further limits on the debtor's right to convert, the court may prevent a debtor from converting a case if the debtor has acted in bad faith.[139]

Other parties in interest may also seek to have the case converted,[140] except conversion to Chapters 12 or 13 is not permitted without the debtor's consent.[141] This is in line with the wholly voluntary nature of proceedings under those chapters. In fact, motions to convert a case *from* Chapter 7 to another chapter are rare and most commonly occur in the context of involuntary corporate or partnership Chapter 7 cases that are converted, at the request of the debtor, to Chapter 11.

§ 17.04 Role of a Chapter 7 Trustee

In Chapter 7 cases, a trustee is appointed or (more rarely) elected and provided with broad administrative responsibility over the case. The trustee is generally responsible for collecting the property of the estate, selling it, and distributing its proceeds to creditors according to whatever priority rights they have under state law and the Bankruptcy Code. Trustees are usually appointed from a panel of those who have qualified, in each federal judicial district, to serve as trustees in bankruptcy cases.

The trustee is sometimes referred to as the "case trustee" or "TIB" as a means of distinguishing this trustee from the United State Trustee or "UST." The United States Trustee is a federal administrative agency, operating

[136] Fed. R. Bankr. P. 9011(b)(3).

[137] Bankruptcy Code § 706(a).

[138] Bankruptcy Code § 706(a).

[139] Marrama v. Citizens Bank (In re Marrama), 127 S. Ct. 1105 (2007).

[140] Bankruptcy Code § 706(b).

[141] Bankruptcy Code § 707(c).

as part of the United States Department of Justice, to establish rules and procedures governing bankruptcy cases and to supervise case trustees who serve in individual cases. The United States Trustee selects and supervises panel trustees, but does not ordinarily exercise any responsibility over individual Chapter 7 cases.

[A] Selection of a Trustee

The Chapter 7 trustee may be elected by creditors, though in practice this rarely happens. If creditors want to elect a trustee, virtually every creditor who holds an allowable, undisputed, fixed, liquidated, unsecured claim may vote.[142] Creditors who have interests that are materially adverse to creditors generally, and creditors who are also insiders of the debtor, are not eligible to vote.[143] The concern is that they might not vote for the person who is best able to vindicate the rights of creditors. The limitation to those with unsecured claims is based on a similar concern: the fundamental role of the trustee is to protect the interests of unsecured creditors. Although the trustee is involved with secured claims, as a practical matter that function is a minor one because the collateral is usually just abandoned to the secured party.

An election must be requested by creditors who are eligible to vote. The requesting creditors must hold at least twenty percent (in amount) of the claims that may vote.[144] The election is held at the creditors' § 341 meeting.[145] At least twenty percent (in amount) of the eligible claims must vote; the trustee candidate wins upon a majority of the votes cast by the creditors. The vote is based on the amount of creditors' claims, not simply the number of creditors.[146]

Despite these rules, in all but a handful of cases, the case trustee is simply appointed by the United States Trustee. The United States Trustee is obligated to appoint a "disinterested" member of the panel of private trustees to serve as interim trustee "promptly after the order for relief."[147] If another person is elected trustee, then the interim trustee is displaced by the elected trustee.[148] However, when no trustee is elected, the interim trustee becomes the trustee.[149]

[B] Duties of the Trustee

The duties of a Chapter 7 trustee are extensive; much more so than those of a Chapter 12 or Chapter 13 trustee. The reason is that the Chapter 7

142 Bankruptcy Code § 702(a).

143 Bankruptcy Code § 702(a)(2), (3).

144 Bankruptcy Code § 702(b).

145 *See* § 4.02[A] Debtor, *supra*.

146 Bankruptcy Code § 702(c).

147 Bankruptcy Code § 701(a)(1).

148 Bankruptcy Code § 701(b).

149 Bankruptcy Code § 702(d).

trustee administers the estate, while the Chapter 12 trustee (usually) and the Chapter 13 trustee (always) merely supervise the debtor-in-possession and distribute payments made under the debtor's plan. In most Chapter 7 cases, the debtor does practically nothing after the petition and schedules are filed.

One of the primary duties of a Chapter 7 trustee is to collect the property of the estate, reduce it to cash and close the estate expeditiously.[150] Of course some property will be exempt; other property will be surrendered to secured creditors. Liquidation of the estate should occur promptly, but if the case is complicated, or if an orderly liquidation will better the position of creditors,[151] the trustee may and should take the time necessary. However, there appear to be more problems of undue delay than of unseemly haste. At least in the 1980s, there were problems in some districts with getting even simple Chapter 7 cases closed promptly.[152]

The trustee is also accountable for all property received.[153] This is a part of the trustee's fiduciary duty to the estate. The trustee is personally liable for property misappropriated or just mislaid. It is also part of the reason why the trustee must post a bond, securing proper performance of duties.[154]

The trustee is also responsible for ensuring that the debtor performs her stated intentions with respect to property subject to a security interest as required by § 521(a)(2)(A).[155] Under § 521, an individual consumer debtor must file a statement of intention with regard to retention, surrender, exemption, and redemption of property subject to a security interest.[156] Section 521(a)(6) gives the debtor forty-five days to act on her stated intention by either entering into a reaffirmation agreement with the secured creditor pursuant to § 524(c),[157] redeeming the property with a lump-sum payment to the secured creditor pursuant to § 722,[158] or surrendering the collateral to the creditor.

The trustee is also required broadly to "investigate the financial affairs of the debtor."[159] In most cases, this investigation is slight and may consist of little more than reviewing the schedules and statements accompanying the debtor's petition and questioning the debtor at the § 341 meeting. In complex cases, it may be quite extensive and may involve hiring professionals, such as accountants hired to audit the debtor's books.

---

[150] Bankruptcy Code § 704(a)(1).

[151] *See* Bankruptcy Code § 721.

[152] Michael J. Herbert & Domenic E. Pacitti, *Down and Out in Richmond, Virginia: The Distribution of Assets in Chapter 7 Bankruptcy Proceedings Closed During 1984–87*, 22 U. Rich. L. Rev. 303, 317–18 (1988).

[153] Bankruptcy Code § 704(a)(2).

[154] Bankruptcy Code § 322.

[155] Bankruptcy Code § 704(a)(3).

[156] *See* § 12.08[D] Debtor's Statement of Intent, *supra*.

[157] *See* § 12.08[B] Reaffirmation to Retain Property, *supra*.

[158] *See* § 12.08[A] Lump-Sum Redemption by Debtor, *supra*.

[159] Bankruptcy Code § 704(a)(4).

"If a purpose would be served," the trustee is required to examine the proofs of claim and object to the allowance of any improper claim.[160] The opening passage of this provision recognizes the fact that in most Chapter 7 cases, there is no reason to examine proofs of claim. In no-asset cases, where there will be no assets distributed to unsecured creditors, there is no reason to evaluate the credibility of their claims.[161] In most such cases, proof of claim forms are not even submitted. In complicated cases, with assets to distribute to unsecured creditors, examining the extent and validity claims may constitute a large part of the trustee's role.

The estate enjoys the benefit of any defenses that would have been available to the debtor, and creditors with valid claims have a substantial interest in the trustee not permitting the estate to be distributed to those whose claims are invalid. Thus, in complicated cases with numerous claims, the trustee may have to defend against claims based largely on non-bankruptcy principles that would have provided the debtor with a defense had the bankruptcy proceeding not been filed.

The case trustee is also required, "if advisable," to oppose the debtor's discharge.[162] The available grounds to deny the debtor a Chapter 7 discharge are specified in § 727(a).[163] The trustee does not, on the other hand, have a financial stake in pursuing grounds for having individual debts determined to be non-dischargeable.[164]

Unless the court orders otherwise, the trustee is also required to supply to any party in interest any information requested about the estate and the estate's administration.[165] Thus, the case trustee is one of the primary conduits of information concerning the case to creditors.

In rare cases, the trustee might also have responsibility for operating the business of a Chapter 7 debtor. However, the typical Chapter 7 case involves a speedy liquidation of the debtor's meager assets. This, however, is not always required or desirable. If the debtor operated a business, the trustee may, depending on the situation, continue to operate the business for a time, generally for the purpose of winding up profitable contracts. This is governed by § 721, which states: "the court may authorize the trustee to operate the business of the debtor for a limited period, if such operation is in the best interest of the estate and consistent with the orderly liquidation of the estate."[166] Whether the trustee does so is largely a matter of business judgment.

Unlike Chapter 11, Chapter 7 requires that the trustee to obtain court authorization to continue the debtor's business. Note that operation of the

---

160 Bankruptcy Code § 704(a)(5).

161 In no-asset cases, creditors are directed not to file proofs of claims. *See* Official Bankruptcy Form B9A, for use in "No Asset Case."

162 Bankruptcy Code § 704(a)(6).

163 Bankruptcy Code § 707(a); *see* § 13.02 Denial of Discharge, *supra.*

164 *See* § 13.03 Non-Dischargeable Debts, *supra.*

165 Bankruptcy Code § 704(a)(7).

166 Bankruptcy Code § 721.

business is not an end in itself; it is simply a means of liquidation. The trustee is not to rehabilitate the business, but only to facilitate the sale of its assets. The court may permit operation of the business only if it is in the best interest of the estate. Moreover, the authorization may only be for a "limited period."[167]

If the trustee has been authorized to operate the debtor's business, she is required to supply the court, the United States Trustee's office, and any relevant governmental tax authority, with periodic reports and summaries of the operation of the business. These reports and summaries must include a statement of receipts and disbursements, as well as any other information that the U.S. Trustee or the court requires.[168] At the end of the case the trustee is also required to "[m]ake a final report and file a final account of the administration of the estate with both the court and the United States trustee."[169]

The 2005 Amendments to the Bankruptcy Code added several very specific duties related to very narrow and specific circumstances that may or may not be relevant to every case. These duties include:

- providing the notice required by § 704(c) to holders of claims for domestic support obligations;[170]
- performing the debtor's duties of any ERISA employee benefit plan previously administered by the debtor;[171] and
- "us[ing] all reasonable and best efforts" to transfer patients of debtor who operates a health care business to a new health care provider.[172]

§ 17.05 United States Trustee

The United States Trustees are government officials, supervised by the United States Attorney General who are charged with responsibility for a variety of matters related to bankruptcy cases. There are twenty-one separate U.S. Trustees, covering the entire country. Most U.S. Trustees operate in more than one federal judicial district, with many of the twenty-one U.S. Trustee regions cutting across state lines.[173]

These government employees' responsibilities include establishing and supervising panels of private trustees who are eligible to serve as case trustees in Chapter 7 and 11 bankruptcy cases.[174] The U.S. Trustee

[167] Bankruptcy Code § 721.

[168] Bankruptcy Code § 704(a)(8).

[169] Bankruptcy Code § 704(a)(9).

[170] Bankruptcy Code § 704(a)(1), (c).

[171] Bankruptcy Code § 704(a)(12).

[172] Bankruptcy Code § 704(a)(12).

[173] 28 U.S.C. § 581 (2000); *see* www.usdoj.gov/ust/eo/ust_org/judicial_districts.htm (last visited March 11, 2007).

[174] 28 U.S.C. § 586(a)(1) (2000).

actually serves as case trustee only if it must do so because of the unavailability of an eligible private trustee willing to serve in a particular case.[175] They also exercise discretion to supervise the administration of cases "whenever the United States trustee considers it to be appropriate."[176] In Chapter 7 cases, the United States Trustee's office is responsible for reviewing materials filed by individual debtors and determining whether their cases would be "presumed to be an abuse under § 707(b)."[177] The trustee's office must file its report regarding abuse within ten days after the date of the § 341 meeting.

In cases where the debtor's case should be presumed to be an abuse under the presumptive test set out in § 707(b)(2), the United States Trustee has a further duty to either file a motion to dismiss the debtor's case or file a statement explaining why a motion to dismiss is not appropriate.[178]

The United States Trustee has additional responsibilities in connection with "small business cases" where there has been a historic concern about the lack of creditor involvement.[179] In these cases, the United States Trustee conducts interviews with the debtor, investigates its viability, and monitors the debtor's activities to evaluate the likelihood that it will be able to have a plan confirmed.[180]

The United States Trustee's office also conducts research and disseminates information about bankruptcy cases. Its website collects data necessary to apply § 707(b)'s means test for presumptive abuse of Chapter 7.[181] It also approves and monitors the activities of non-profit credit counseling agencies from whom consumer debtors must obtain credit counseling briefings and training programs.

§ 17.06 Creditors' Committees

Creditors' committees can be appointed in Chapter 7 and 11 cases. Creditors' committees are extraordinarily rare in Chapter 7 cases, however, and are usually only active in larger Chapter 11 proceedings.

In Chapter 7 cases, creditors may elect a creditors' committee at a § 341 meeting; every creditor who has the right to vote on a trustee has the right to vote for a creditors' committee. The committee must be composed of not fewer than three and not more than eleven creditors; each of the creditors

175 28 U.S.C. § 586(a)(2) (2000).

176 28 U.S.C. § 586(a)(3) (2000).

177 Bankruptcy Code § 704(b)(1)(A).

178 Bankruptcy Code § 704(b)(2).

179 These cases involve debtors engaged in commercial or business operations with not more than $2,000,000 in secured and unsecured debts in which there is either no committee of unsecured creditors or in which the committee "is not sufficiently active and representative to provide effective oversight of the debtor." Bankruptcy Code § 101(51D).

180 28 U.S.C. § 586(a)(7) (2000).

181 *See* www.usdoj.gov/ust/eo/bapcpa/meanstesting.htm (last visited March 11, 2007).

must hold an allowed unsecured claim entitled to distribution in the proceeding.[182]

The powers of the Chapter 7 creditors' committee are rather circumscribed. The committee may consult with the trustee and the United States Trustee regarding the administration of the estate. It may make recommendations about the trustee's performance (*i.e.*, it may complain about the trustee's performance). It may also submit either to the court or to the U.S. Trustee any question "affecting the administration of the estate."[183] In sum, any such the committee acts in purely an advisory capacity; it is expected to do so in the interests of all creditors, and not merely in the interests of its members.[184]

The key function of a creditors' committee in a Chapter 7 case is to keep an eye on the case and make noise. Its chief right is to be heard by the court. It has a right to be heard on any matter materially affecting the liquidation. This would certainly include the proposed sale of property, the trustee's method of dealing with claims, and the discharge. The committee may take positions contrary to those of the trustee, and in some circumstances, the committee may even have the right to appeal decisions of the bankruptcy court.[185]

§ 17.07 Partnership Liquidation

Partnership liquidations are somewhat more complicated than other cases because of the hybrid nature of partnerships. Partnerships have most of the attributes of a legal entity. Partnerships can own property in their own name, can enter into contracts, and can sue or be sued. In these respects, partnerships are like corporations. However, unlike the shareholders of a corporation, general partners of a partnership are personally liable for all of the partnership's debts. But, their liability is only secondary; a creditor of the partnership cannot reach the assets of a general partner unless and until the assets of the partnership have been exhausted.

This same basic pattern is preserved in bankruptcy. One of the provisions that reflects this is § 723, which deals with the rights of the partnership's bankruptcy trustee against its general partners. The trustee of the partnership, as representative of the partnership's creditors, is given the right to do what the creditors themselves would do outside of bankruptcy — to recover unpaid claims from the individual partners.

There are two somewhat different situations dealt with in § 723. The first deals with an action by the trustee against a general partner who is not in bankruptcy. The second deals with a claim by the trustee against a general partner who is a debtor in her own separate bankruptcy proceeding.

182 Bankruptcy Code § 705(a).

183 Bankruptcy Code § 705(b).

184 In re Kenney Co., 136 F. 451 (D. Ind. 1905).

185 SEC v. U.S. Realty & Improvement Co., 310 U.S. 434 (1940).

If none of the individual partners is involved in a bankruptcy proceeding, the partnership's bankruptcy trustee has a claim against each partner to the extent that, under applicable non-bankruptcy law, the general partner is personally liable for the partnership's debts. Assume, for example, that Sam Spade and Miles Archer are general partners in the firm of Spade & Archer, and that the Spade & Archer partnership has filed a Chapter 7 bankruptcy case.[186] However, neither Sam Spade nor Miles Archer has filed any form of bankruptcy. The total assets of their partnership are $150,000. Its total obligations are $500,000. All of these obligations are allowed unsecured claims in the partnership bankruptcy.

Because the property of the estate is insufficient to pay all of the allowed claims, and because under state law both Sam Spade and Miles Archer are personally liable for the unpaid claims, the trustee of Spade & Archer has a claim against each partner to the extent that, under applicable non-bankruptcy law, the general partner is personally liable. Normally, this personal liability would be for the entire amount of the deficiency ($350,000).[187] The trustee may recover from either Sam Spade or Miles Archer or both; of course, the total recovery from both of them cannot exceed $350,000. One implication of this, assuming that at least one of the partners has sufficient assets, is that creditors of the partnership will be paid in full.

Of course, in many cases, the financial failure of a partnership also means the financial failure of the individual partners. It is thus quite common for one or more of the general partners to be in bankruptcy as well. Assume that, in the hypothetical given, Sam Spade is not in bankruptcy, but Miles Archer is. To the extent practicable, the trustee is required to seek recovery of the deficiency from a general partner who is *not* in bankruptcy.[188]

Thus, the trustee is normally required to seek recovery of the $350,000 deficiency first from the non-bankrupt partner; in this case, Sam Spade. If the trustee is unable to recover the entire deficiency from the non-bankrupt partner, the trustee can pursue a claim in the bankrupt partner's bankruptcy proceeding. In this example, if the partnership's bankruptcy trustee is unable to recover the full $350,000 deficiency from Sam Spade, the trustee has a claim in Miles Archer's bankruptcy case for the remainder.

There is an obvious problem created when the trustee pursues the bankrupt partner. This partner is already in bankruptcy and has other creditors, not related to the failed partnership, who have not been paid. These other creditors would prefer not to share with the creditors of the partnership.

For example, what happens if Sam Spade is not in bankruptcy, but instead is in Patagonia where the partnership trustee cannot find either him or his assets? His partner, Miles Archer, did not escape to South America,

---

[186] Partnerships are eligible to file a petition under Chapters 7 and 11. *See* Bankruptcy Code §§ 109, 101(41). In the right circumstances, they might be eligible to file under Chapter 12 as a "family farmer" or a "family fisherman." *See* Bankruptcy Code §§ 101(18)(B), 101(19A)(B).

[187] Bankruptcy Code § 723(a).

[188] Bankruptcy Code § 723(b).

but instead, filed his own Chapter 7 bankruptcy proceeding and turned his assets over to his estate for administration by his own Chapter 7 trustee. Assume that his individual assets are worth $100,000, and that there are $200,000 of allowed unsecured claims against him, all of them unrelated to the failed partnership.

Archer's personal creditors receive a fifty percent distribution if the claims of his partnership creditors are not considered. However, if the $350,000 of unpaid claims from the Spade & Archer partnership bankruptcy are allowed in Miles Archer's estate, then there is a total of $550,000 in claims against Archer, with only $100,000 in assets to be used to satisfy them. Creditors receive only about 18%. With a very limited exception, all of the claims against the partnership are bundled together into the trustee's claim against the partner.[189]

§ 17.08 Distribution of Estate Property

Although assets are rarely available to provide creditors in a Chapter 7 case with any distribution, there is a fairly elaborate set of rules for those cases where such a "dividend" is available.[190] Secured claims are dealt with only indirectly, because encumbered property is either abandoned by the trustee to the lien holder, or, if the property is worth more than the lien, the property is sold and the lien holder is paid from the proceeds of the sale.[191]

The primary rule for the distribution of property with regard to unsecured claims is § 726(a). That section sets out six categories that are to be paid in order.

First payment goes to allowed priority claims in order of their priority.[192] Thus, claims entitled to priority under § 507 are paid first, in strict compliance with the levels of priority set out in that section.[193] If the available assets of the estate are sufficient only to pay the administrative claims provided for in § 507(a)(2), claims entitled to priority in § 507(a)(3) receive nothing.

Priority claimants must file a timely proof of claim, or if tardy, file it before the earlier of ten days before the mailing of the trustee's summary report or the date of the trustee's final distribution.[194] This category

[189] Bankruptcy Code § 723(c). If this produces a surplus in the partnership bankruptcy, the surplus would be returned to Archer's estate. *See* Bankruptcy Code § 723(d).

[190] The colloquial reference to payments made to unsecured creditors as a "dividend" informally recognizes that when a debtor is insolvent, creditors are the ones who, as a practical matter, are entitled to the benefits of ownership.

[191] *Cf.* Bankruptcy Code § 725 (requiring the trustee, before final distribution of the property of the estate, and after notice and an opportunity for a hearing, to dispose of any property in which an entity other than the estate has an interest, such as a lien).

[192] Bankruptcy Code § 726(a)(1).

[193] *See generally* § 10.04[A] Priority Claims, *supra*.

[194] Bankruptcy Code § 726(a)(1).

includes claims entitled to super-priority treatment, which are ahead of other § 507(a) priority claims.[195]

Second in line for payment are the allowed general unsecured claims, other than certain claims that were filed late and certain claims for fines, penalties, and punitive damages. To be included in this group, the claimant must have filed a timely proof of claim, or, if the proof of claim was late, the delay was excusable.[196]

The third group consists of those claims that, although they were filed late and the late filing was not excused, have still been allowed.[197] Thus, a creditor who files late does not necessarily lose its right to receive a distribution from the estate, but the likelihood that funds will be available is considerably diminished.

The fourth group consists of those allowed claims, whether secured or unsecured, that represent any fine, penalty, or forfeiture; or represent multiple, exemplary, or punitive damages arising before the earlier of the order for relief or the appointment of a trustee, to the extent the fine, penalty, forfeiture, or damages do not represent compensation for actual pecuniary loss suffered by the holder of such claim.[198] For example, if a claimant has obtained a judgment for both compensatory damages and punitive damages arising out of a battery committed by the debtor, the compensatory damages would be paid under § 726(a)(2) and the punitive damages would fall in this fourth category. These non-compensatory fines and penalties are paid fourth, even if they otherwise constitute the type of claim entitled to priority under § 507. Any other treatment would impose punishment intended for the debtor on its creditors.

Fifth in line to receive payment are claims for post-petition interest on claims in the first four categories, charged at the legal rate from the date of the filing of the petition to the date of payment.[199] As explained elsewhere, interest does not otherwise accrue on unsecured claims,[200] and accrues on secured claims only to the extent that the value of the collateral exceeds the amount of the debt.[201] However, in the very, very rare cases in which there is property left in the estate after other claims have been paid, a further payment of interest on those claims will also be provided. Note that this further payment is at the "legal rate," which means the rate set by statute, not the rate established by the parties' contract.

Finally, if after the payment of all the claims and interest on the claims, there is still money in the estate, this surplus is paid to the debtor.[202] The

[195] *See* § 10.04[B] Super-Priority Claims, *supra.*

[196] Bankruptcy Code § 726(a)(2).

[197] Bankruptcy Code § 726(a)(3).

[198] Bankruptcy Code § 726(a)(4).

[199] Bankruptcy Code § 726(a)(5).

[200] *See* § 10.02[C][3] Interest on Claims, *supra.*

[201] *See* § 10.03[D] Post-Petition Interest on Secured Claims, *supra.*

[202] Bankruptcy Code § 726(a)(6).

availability of funds to distribute to the debtor means that the debtor was not insolvent. This is virtually unheard of.

§ 17.09 Liquidation Treatment of Certain Liens

Section 724 supplies a variety of rules that permit the avoidance and subordination of certain liens. Appearing, as they do in Chapter 7, these rules do not apply in reorganization cases under Chapter 11, 12, or 13.[203] However, they do affect the dynamics of plan negotiation, since they give these lien claimants a stronger interest in confirmation of a reorganization plan than those secured claimants who will receive the value of their collateral regardless of whether the debtor liquidates.

[A] Subordination of Liens Securing Non-Compensatory Penalties

Section 724(a) permits the trustee to avoid a lien that secures a claim for a noncompensatory "fine, penalty, forfeiture" or for an award of "exemplary or punitive damages."[204] This avoidance effectively subordinates the claims secured by such liens and prevents them from reducing distributions to other competing creditors who had nothing to do with the debtor's wrongdoing that led to the punitive claim. These claims are further subordinated by § 726(a)(4) and not paid until after all other priority and unsecured claims.[205]

[B] Subordination of Secured Tax Claims.

Section 724(b) provides a complicated mechanism that subordinates other unavoidable *secured* tax claims to unsecured priority non-tax claims.[206] Property subject to an unavoidable tax lien is distributed first to any creditor with a senior lien on the property.[207] Any excess value would then normally be distributed to the holder of the tax lien in question, but § 724(b)(2) instead calls for this value to next be distributed to holders of most non-tax § 507(a) priority claims.[208] If there is any excess value that would have been distributed to the tax lien, after these unsecured priority claims are satisfied, it is distributed to the holder of the subordinated tax lien.[209]

A simple example illustrates how this first part of the rule operates. Assume Empire Bank holds a senior mortgage on Titanic Corporation's land

---

[203] *See* Bankruptcy Code § 103.

[204] Bankruptcy Code §§ 724(a), 726(a)(4).

[205] *See* § 17.08 Distribution of Estate Property, *supra*.

[206] Bankruptcy Code § 724(b).

[207] Bankruptcy Code § 724(b)(1).

[208] Bankruptcy Code § 724(b)(2). Non-wage administrative expenses incurred while the case was in Chapter 11, before it was converted to Chapter 7, are excluded from this distribution.

[209] Bankruptcy Code § 724(b)(3).

and buildings, securing a $10 million claim. Humboldt County holds an unavoidable but junior real estate tax lien, securing an unpaid $1 million tax debt on the same property. Subordinate to the tax lien is Atlantic Finance Co.'s second $3 million mortgage on the property. Assume further that there are $700,000 in unsecured priority claims.

When the property is sold, Empire Bank's senior mortgage is paid first. The next $1 million of value received from the property is distributed to the $700,000 in unsecured § 507(a)(1)-(7) priority claims; then, up to the $300,000 balance of the $1 million tax lien is paid to the holder of the subordinated tax lien.[210] This treatment subordinates the tax lien to unsecured priority claims, but preserves the priority of Atlantic Finance Co.'s junior mortgage. Atlantic Finance Co.'s mortgage will be be paid next.[211]

Atlantic Finance Co. is not harmed by promoting the unsecured priority claims because it is in any event subordinated to $11 million worth of claims — those of Empire Bank and Humboldt County. Atlantic Finance will likely be indifferent as to who receives this $11 million and to whether the amount of Humboldt County's $1 million tax claim is paid to Humboldt County or to other claimants.

The distribution of $700,000 of Humboldt County's $1 million tax claim to holders of § 507(a) priority claims leaves $700,000 of Humboldt County's tax claim unpaid. If the property is worth more than the $14 million necessary to pay all three secured claims, the balance is distributed to the holder the subordinated tax lien and then to the estate, which distributes it in accordance with § 726(a), described in the immediately preceding section.[212]

Section 724 also provides for treating *any* statutory lien as a tax lien if the priority of the tax lien is determined in the same manner as a Federal Income Tax Lien under the provisions of the Federal Tax Lien Act.[213] To simplify matters somewhat, § 724(e) now provides for the equitable marshaling of assets in a manner that avoids the necessity of subordinating the tax lien if unencumbered assets could be used to satisfy the § 507 priority claims that are promoted through the operation of § 724(b).[214]

§ 17.10 Special Liquidations

Chapter 7 contains several sets of rules that apply only to liquidations of particular types of debtors: stockbrokers, commodity brokers, and clearing banks (banks whose only business is to facilitate transfers of funds between banks). Sections 741–753 govern stockholder liquidations. Sections 761–767 apply to liquidations of commodity brokers. Sections 781–784

[210] This amount is distributed according to whatever priority would otherwise apply under § 507. Bankruptcy Code § 724(c).

[211] Bankruptcy Code § 724(b)(4).

[212] *See* § 17.08 Distribution of Estate Property, *supra*.

[213] Bankruptcy Code § 724(d).

[214] Bankruptcy Code § 724(e).

apply to clearing bank liquidations. All of these provisions are highly specialized and unlikely to be encountered except in the most sophisticated bankruptcy practice. They are beyond the scope of this book.

Chapter 18

Rehabilitation of Individuals with Regular Income

§ 18.01 Goals of Rehabilitation of Individuals with Regular Income[1]

Chapter 13 provides individual debtors with an alternative to liquidation. In Chapter 7 liquidation cases, debtors trade their non-exempt property for a discharge.[2] In Chapter 13 rehabilitation cases, debtors instead use their future income to, in effect, repurchase their non-exempt property from their creditors. Debtors pay this future income to a trustee for three to five years and the trustee distributes it to creditors according to the terms of the debtor's court approved payment plan. Debtors receive a discharge only after they complete the terms of that plan.

Chapter 13 is the descendent of former Chapter XIII of the old Bankruptcy Act. These "Wage Earner Plans" gave wage-earning individuals an opportunity to obtain the advantages of reorganization bankruptcy.[3] When drafting the Bankruptcy Code in 1978, Congress decided to broaden the old chapter and make it more attractive in hope that more debtors would use it instead of Chapter 7.[4] Relief under Chapter 13 is no longer limited to wage earners.[5] Since 1978, it has been available to all individuals with regular income sufficient to fund an appropriate plan.[6] This requirement means only that the debtor must have some source of income that is sufficiently regular to make it possible to fund a plan.[7]

Chapter 13 debtors obtain several advantages that not available to those who seek relief under Chapter 7: (1) the ability to retain their property by using future income to make payments to creditors; (2) a somewhat broader

---

[1] Donald Boren, *An Analysis of Changes in the Use of Chapter 13 Since the Enactment of the Bankruptcy Reform Act of 1978*, 23 Am. Bus. L.J. 451 (1985); William C. Whitford, *Has the Time Come to Repeal Chapter 13?*, 65 Ind. L.J. 85 (1989).

[2] *See* § 17.01 Debtor Liquidation, *supra.*

[3] *See generally* Harry H. Haden, *Chapter XIII Wage Earner Plans — Forgotten Man Bankruptcy*, 55 Ky. L.J. 564 (1967).

[4] Timothy W. Dixon & David G. Epstein, *Where Did Chapter 13 Come from and Where Should it Go?*, 10 Am. Bankr. Inst. L. Rev. 741 (2002).

[5] Under old Chapter XIII, only "wage earners" were eligible for relief. Those who were self-employed or sole proprietors of a small business were ineligible. To be eligible, one was required to be an employee.

[6] Bankruptcy Code § 109(e).

[7] Bankruptcy Code § 101(30); *see* § 6.02[B][6] Eligibility for Relief in Chapter 13, Individuals with Regular Income, *supra.*

discharge;[8] and a slightly expanded automatic stay that prevents creditors from seeking recovery from individual co-debtors while the case is pending.[9] Since the automatic stay remains in effect for three to five years, the debtor's payments under the plan are likely to be the sole source of payment for most creditors.

§ 18.02 Eligibility for Relief under Chapter 13

Chapter 13 is available only to individual debtors.[10] Corporations, partnerships, unincorporated associations, and other organizations must reorganize, if at all, under Chapter 11, or, if they qualify, as "family farmers" or "family fishermen" under Chapter 12.[11] The only exception to this is for joint cases filed by individuals who are married to one anther and who may seek relief under Chapter 13.[12]

In addition, Chapter 13 debtors must have income that "is sufficiently stable and regular to enable such individual to make payments under a [Chapter 13 plan]."[13] The source of the income does not matter.[14] Income from odd jobs and collecting junk qualifies.[15] So does income from government benefits,[16] and maybe even regular contributions from family members.[17] Debtors who operate a business as a sole proprietor are eligible for Chapter 13 relief, so long as their obligations do not exceed Chapter 13's debt limits.

As explained in greater detail in an earlier chapter,[18] the debtor (and where applicable, the debtor's spouse) must have non-contingent,

---

[8] Since its inception in 1978, the scope of a Chapter 13 discharge has gradually narrowed. The 2005 Amendments limited debtors' access to Chapter 7, forcing some to seek relief in Chapter 13, by making Chapter 7 unavailable. *See* § 17.03[B][2] Presumptive Abuse — Means Testing, *supra.*

[9] Bankruptcy Code § 1301; *see* § 8.04 Automatic Co-Debtor Stay in Chapters 12 and 13, *supra.*

[10] Bankruptcy Code § 109(e).

[11] Bankruptcy Code § 109(f). In some circumstances, a corporation may qualify as either a family farmer or a family fisherman. Bankruptcy Code §§ 19, 19(A); *see* § 6.02[B][5] Eligibility for Relief in Chapter 12, Family Farmers & Family Fishermen, *supra.*

[12] Bankruptcy Code § 101(30).

[13] Bankruptcy Code § 101(30); *see* James Lockhart, Annotation, *Who is "Individual with Regular Income" Eligible to Be Chapter 13 Debtor under §§ 101(30) and 109(e) of Bankruptcy Code of 1978*, 161 A.L.R. Fed. 127 (2000).

[14] Under the Bankruptcy Act, in effect until 1979, former Chapter XIII was available only to "wage earners."

[15] Matter of Cole, 3 B.R. 346 (Bankr. S.D. W. Va. 1980).

[16] Bibb County Dep't of Family & Children Services v. Hope (In re Hammond), 729 F.2d 1391, 1393 (11th Cir. 1984) (AFDC payments).

[17] *See, e.g.*, Rowe v. Connors (In re Rowe), 110 B.R. 712, 717–18 (Bankr. E.D. Pa. 1990) (determining that payments from son were stable and regular);*but see* In re Cregut, 69 B.R. 21, 22–23 (Bankr. D. Ariz. 1986) (characterizing monthly payments from father to son as gifts, not income).

[18] *See* § 6.02[B][6][c] Chapter 13 Debt Limits, *supra.*

liquidated, unsecured debts of less than $336,900, and non-contingent, liquidated, secured debts of less than $1,010,650.[19] In a joint case involving a married couple, the debts are aggregated to determine whether they exceed these thresholds. These limits restrict Chapter 13 to relatively small proceedings.

§ 18.03 Filing, Conversion, and Dismissal in Chapter 13

[A] Filing Chapter 13 Cases

A Chapter 13 bankruptcy may be filed by either an individual or an individual and his or her spouse.[20] As of late spring 2006, the filing fee was $235,[21] plus a $39 "administrative fee,"[22] making a grand total of $274.[23] As with Chapter 7 petitions, the filing fee may be paid in installments,[24] but unlike Chapter 7,[25] no provision is made for an in forma pauperis Chapter 13 petition.[26]

In most cases, the debtor files his plan together with his petition. The plan, in any event, must be filed within fifteen days after the petition.[27] Moreover, payments must commence within thirty days of the time of the "order for relief" or the "filing of the plan" whichever is earlier.[28] Thus, payments nearly always commence before the plan is confirmed.

Chapter 13 debtors must also file a variety of other documents, including schedules of the debtor's assets and liabilities, a statement of the debtor's current income and current expenditures, a statement of his financial affairs, a statement that the debtor has received certain notices about the differences between Chapter 7, 11, 12, and 13 and about the consequences of submitting falsified schedules, a detailed statement concerning the debtor's monthly net income, and a statement disclosing any future increase

[19] Bankruptcy Code § 109(e). As with most other dollar amounts in the Bankruptcy Code, the figures in § 109(e) are adjusted every three years by a factor based on the increase in the Department of Labor's Consumer Price Index and rounded to the nearest $25 amount that represents the change. Bankruptcy Code § 104(b)(1). The most recent increase was April 1, 2007. The amounts are scheduled to be adjusted again in 2010, and 2013.

[20] Bankruptcy Code §§ 109(e), 302.

[21] 28 U.S.C.S. § 1930(a)(1)(B) (LexisNexis Supp. 2006).

[22] 28 U.S.C.S. § 1930(b) (LexisNexis Supp. 2006).

[23] *See* 28 U.S.C.S. § 1930 (LexisNexis Supp. 2006).

[24] Fed. R. Bankr. P. 1006(b).

[25] *See* 28 U.S.C.S. § 1390(f) (LexisNexis Supp. 2006) (permitting waiver of the Chapter 7 filing fee for debtors whose income is less than 150% of the poverty line).

[26] Karen Gross, *In Forma Pauperis in Bankruptcy: Reflecting On and Beyond* United States v. Kras, 2 Am. Bankr. Inst. L. Rev. 57 (1994).

[27] Fed. R. Bankr. P. 3015(b).

[28] Bankruptcy Code § 1326(a)(1). Involuntary Chapter 13 petitions are not permitted. Bankruptcy Code § 303. Thus, the order for relief nearly always coincides with the filing of the petition, except in cases involving conversion from another chapter.

in income or expenditures that the debtor reasonably anticipates.[29] Chapter 13 debtors, like Chapter 7 debtors, are required to submit a certificate that they have received a credit counseling briefing from an approved nonprofit budget and credit counseling agency, along with a copy of any repayment plan developed in the course of that briefing.[30]

[B] Conversion or Dismissal of Chapter 13 Cases

The Code does not permit involuntary Chapter 13 cases. Although debtors with too much disposable income can be precluded from filing a case under Chapter 7, they cannot be forced to seek relief under Chapter 13. Compelling debtors to submit a portion of their income would be both impractical and would smack of involuntary servitude.[31] As a result, Chapter 13 cases may always be dismissed voluntarily at the debtor's request.[32] They may also be converted voluntarily to Chapter 7, at any time, regardless of any waiver of this right that the debtor may have supplied.[33]

Chapter 13 cases may also be converted or dismissed "on request of a party in interest or the United States Trustee . . . for cause."[34] Good cause covers a wide range of territory, including failure to comply with any of the requirements of Chapter 13, failure to file a timely plan, denial of confirmation, and "material default" of a term of a confirmed plan.[35] The 2005 Amendments also permit conversion or dismissal if the debtor fails to pay any post-petition "domestic support obligation," regardless of whether such payments are provided for in the debtor's plan or are simply part of the debtor's budgeted expenses.[36] The case may also be converted or dismissed if the debtor fails to "file a [post-petition] tax return" as required by § 1308.[37]

The only source of real dispute in interpreting the grounds for conversion or dismissal involves whether a debtor's default is "material." If the default was due to circumstances that were beyond the debtor's control or unexpected and the debtor's performance can easily be resumed, a default may

[29] Bankruptcy Code § 521(a); *see* § 6.02[C] Petition and Schedules; Statement of Debtor's Affairs, *supra.*

[30] Bankruptcy Code § 521(b).

[31] *See* H.R. Rep. No 95-595, at 322 (1977), *reprinted in* 1978 U.S.C.C.A.N, 5963, 6278.

[32] Bankruptcy Code § 1307(b); *e.g.*, Barbieri v. RAJ Acquisition Corp. (In re Barbieri), 199 F.3d 616 (2d Cir. 1999).

[33] Bankruptcy Code § 1307(a).

[34] Bankruptcy Code § 1307(c).

[35] Bankruptcy Code § 1307(c); *see* In re Simmons, 346 B.R. 552 (Bankr. N.D. Ga. 2006) (debtor voluntarily converted Chapter 7 case to Chapter 13, but failed to file a plan after a year).

[36] Bankruptcy Code § 1307(c)(11).

[37] Bankruptcy Code § 1307(e). This new language presumably overrules cases such as *Howard v. Lexington Investments, Inc.*, 284 F.3d 320 (1st Cir. 2002) (failure to file tax returns timely was not necessarily a "material" default).

not be material.[38] But, if the debtor's default was due to his own neglect, or circumstances within the debtor's control make it impossible for him to complete payments under the plan, the default is material and the case is vulnerable to being dismissed.

§ 18.04 Property of the Chapter 13 Estate

The scope of estate property is broader in Chapter 13 than in Chapter 7. The Chapter 13 estate is comprised of all property specified in § 541, together with any income of the debtor, from personal services or otherwise, earned while the case is pending.[39] This is congruent with the basic approach of Chapter 13 which contemplates the payment of a portion of the debtor's post-petition earnings to creditors. Chapter 13 plans are required to provide for "the submission of . . . future earnings or future income of the debtor to the supervision and control of the trustee as is necessary for the execution of the plan."[40] Chapter 13 plans ordinarily provide for the debtor to submit a portion of his post-petition earnings to the control of the trustee, who distributes these earnings to creditors with allowed claims. Therefore, a debtor's post-petition wages, which would not have been included in his Chapter 7 estate, are part of his Chapter 13 case, if they were earned as a result of services performed after his petition was filed, and thus are protected from seizure by creditors by the automatic stay.[41]

Unlike Chapter 7, where the trustee takes control of non-exempt estate property, Chapter 13 permits the debtor to remain in possession of all of the estate's property, except as provided otherwise in the debtor's plan.[42] Ordinarily, the debtor's plan requires the debtor to submit whatever portion of his earnings to the trustee that are necessary for execution of the plan.[43] The plan may also provide for the surrender of specific assets to secured creditors, or for the liquidation of property the debtor does not need to provide further payments to creditors with unsecured claims.

Chapter 13 is available to business debtors with regular income, provided they conduct their business as individual proprietors, rather than as corporations, partnerships, or other legal entities, and provided they fit within Chapter 13's debt limits.[44] Chapter 13 debtors who are engaged in

---

[38] In re Durben, 70 B.R. 14 (Bankr. S.D. Ohio 1986) (no material default where debtor's payments were temporarily disrupted by debtor diverting funds to repair secured creditor's collateral).

[39] Bankruptcy Code § 1306(a).

[40] Bankruptcy Code § 1322(a)(1); *see also* Fed. R. Bankr. P. 3013.

[41] Bankruptcy Code § 362(a)(3); *see* § 8.02[C] Acts to Obtain Possession or Control of Estate Property, *supra*.

[42] Bankruptcy Code § 1306(b).

[43] Bankruptcy Code § 1322(a).

[44] Robert Lawless & Elizabeth Warren, *The Myth of the Disappearing Business Bankruptcy*, 93 Cal. L. Rev. 743, 773 tbl.2 (estimating that 19.7 % of Chapter 13 bankruptcies are filed by those starting or operating a small business).

a business are empowered to operate the business in the ordinary course and may, consistent with the debtor's status as a "debtor in possession," incur credit and sell, use, or lease property in the ordinary course,[45] subject to the usual limitations on the operation of a business imposed by §§ 363 and 364.[46] Moreover, the court may impose additional limitations and conditions as it deems appropriate.[47]

§ 18.05 Parties in Chapter 13 Cases

The parties in Chapter 13 are much the same as those in Chapter 7, but the debtor and the trustee's roles are diffeent. Instead of liquidating the debtor's assets, the Chapter 13 trustee collects and distributes the debtor's payments under the plan. Instead of receiving an immediate discharge, the debtor must continue funding the plan out of income, receiving a discharge only after payments are complete. Also, unlike Chapters 7 and 11, which provide for the formation of "creditors' committees," Chapter 13 deploys no such device.

[A] Role of a Chapter 13 Debtor

All Chapter 13 estates remain under the control and possession of the debtor. The debtor has the same rights and obligations of debtors in other types of cases. In addition, the Chapter 13 debtor has many of the rights that a trustee would have regarding the use, sale, and lease of property.[48]

As a practical matter, the typical Chapter 13 debtor does virtually nothing except pay his lawyer and submit payments to the trustee to fund the plan. The estate is usually small and only rarely involves a business to manage; the debtor simply continues to go to work and collect a paycheck. Even where the debtor does operate a business, the Chapter 13 trustee would not involve him or herself in its operation. Few Chapter 13 cases involve any litigation, and what litigation exists focuses mainly on whether the plan complies with Chapter 13's mandatory provisions.

The 2005 Amendments impose a few additional continuing duties on the debtor, such as the duty to supply the court or the trustee with copies of the debtor's income tax returns,[49] the duty to pay any post-petition domestic support obligations,[50] and, perhaps not surprisingly, the duty to report any increase in income to the trustee.[51]

---

[45] Bankruptcy Code § 1304(b).

[46] *See generally* Chapter 9, Operating the Debtor, *supra.*

[47] Bankruptcy Code § 1304(b).

[48] Bankruptcy Code § 1303.

[49] Bankruptcy Code § 1307(c)(11).

[50] Bankruptcy Code § 1307(c)(11).

[51] *See* Bankruptcy Code § 521(f)(4).

[B] Role of Standing Chapter 13 Trustee

A Chapter 13 trustee has a different role than a trustee in a Chapter 7 case. There is no case trustee in Chapter 13; in most districts, however, a standing trustee is appointed to supervise all cases in the district.[52]

The standing trustee's duties are primarily to supervise the debtor;[53] to appear and be heard on questions of valuation, confirmation, and modification;[54] to ensure that the debtor commences payments in a timely fashion;[55] and to disburse payments made under the plan.[56]

There is evidence that the accepted practices of the standing trustee influences the number of Chapter 13 cases filed and the structure of debtors' plans. The right of the trustee to object to confirmation places the standing trustee in a particularly powerful position with respect to the structure and content of Chapter 13 plans. Litigation is expensive, and debtors are likely to go along with the requirements imposed by a standing trustee in order to avoid such a challenge. Indeed, debtors' attorneys may shy away from presenting alternatives that might involve a potential challenge.

Differences in the degree of such influence, and the influence of the judges who handle Chapter 13 cases, creates considerable differences in the operation of Chapter 13 from district to district, and even within districts within the same state. Supporters of active standing trustees, however, insist that their work not only benefits creditors by increasing the amount of debt collected, but also benefits debtors by restoring their pride and self-esteem.[57]

[C] The United States Trustee in Chapter 13

The United States Trustee has no formal role in individual Chapter 13 cases. Its responsibility is limited, as it is in most other consumer cases, to appoint and supervise the standing trustees who administer Chapter 13 cases in their region, and if necessary, because of the unwillingness of a private trustee to serve, to act as the trustee in an individual case. The United States Trustee also might be required to take action, where necessary, to prevent fraud and abuse by parties connected to bankruptcy cases, such as the occasional dishonest trustee. The United States Trustee also monitors awards of professional fees to standing Chapter 13 trustees, their attorneys, and other professionals engaged pursuant to §§ 327 and 330.

---

52 Bankruptcy Code § 1302(a). The Executive Office of the United States Trustee maintains a list of standing Chapter 13 trustees. *See* http://www.usdoj.gov/ust/eo/private_trustee/locator/13.htm (last visited Nov. 8, 2006).

53 Bankruptcy Code § 1302(b)(1).

54 Bankruptcy Code § 1302(b)(2).

55 Bankruptcy Code § 1302(b)(5).

56 Bankruptcy Code § 1326(c).

57 Jean Braucher, *Lawyers and Consumer Bankruptcy: One Code, Many Cultures*, 67 Am. Bankr. L.J. 501, 557–58 (1993).

[D] Creditors in Chapter 13 Cases

Some secured creditors play an active role in Chapter 13 cases; others do little more than cash the monthly checks they receive from the debtor or the trustee. As explained more fully below, debtors cannot use Chapter 13 to modify residential real estate mortgages.[58] Mortgage lenders therefore have little reason to be involved in most cases, except perhaps with respect to efforts to dismiss the case or to obtain relief from the automatic stay. Other secured creditors are likely to play an active role with respect to the valuation of their collateral for the purposes of determining the amount of their allowed secured claim. However, portions of the 2005 Amendments, which require full payment of many purchase money obligations, make this role less significant than it previously had been.[59]

Unsecured creditors play a minimal role in most Chapter 13 cases. Most of the time, the standing Chapter 13 trustee can be counted on to make any necessary challenges to confirmation of the debtor's plan. Also, under the 2005 Amendments, the means test often serves to determine the amount that debtors must pay to their unsecured creditors. This provides creditors with little incentive to become active in individual cases, apart perhaps from financing the occasional test case. They are most likely to have a wider impact on the trustee's behavior by pressing their complaints with the local offices of the United States Trustee.

§ 18.06 The Chapter 13 Plan — Required Provisions

At the core of Chapter 13 is the debtor's plan. Unlike the Chapter 11 plan, the Chapter 13 plan is usually formulated without creditor participation. The debtor is the only one with the right to submit a plan, and creditors do not vote on whether to "accept" the plan.[60] As a result, unsecured creditors especially are given no direct or even indirect role in the promulgation of the plan. Consequently, the contents of the plan are almost entirely set by the statutory (and judicial) requirements for confirmation.[61] Indeed, it is routine for debtors to file their plan with their petition.[62] Broadly speaking, these requirements adhere to the absolute priority rule that no junior class of creditors may receive a distribution unless all senior classes have been paid in full.[63] They also establish the standard by which the adequacy of the proposed payments is to be measured by the court.

---

[58] *See* § 18.07[B][2][a] Residential Real Estate Mortgages, *infra.*

[59] *See* § 18.08[F][6] Certain Purchase Money Security Interests, *infra.*

[60] *See* § 19.09 Acceptance of Plan by Holders of Claims and Interests; Disclosure and Voting, *infra.*

[61] The standing Chapter 13 trustee may have a great deal of influence over what goes into the plan. *See* Jean Braucher, *Lawyers and Consumer Bankruptcy: One Code, Many Cultures*, 67 Am. Bankr. L.J. 501, 556–61 (1993).

[62] If the plan is not filed with the petition, it must normally be filed within fifteen days after the petition, although the court can extend this time "for cause shown and on notice as the court may direct." Fed. R. Bankr. P. 3015(b).

[63] *See* § 19.11[B] Fair and Equitable — The Absolute Priority Rule, *infra.*

There are only three mandatory provisions of a plan spelled out in § 1322(a). However, these mandatory provisions must be read in light of § 1325's requirements for confirmation, which have a significant influence on how the mandated provisions are drafted.

[A] Submission of Sufficient Income to Fund the Plan

The basic structure of Chapter 13 contemplates that the debtor will pay his or her surplus income (after deductions for living expenses) into the plan.[64] Notice that § 1322(a)(1) does not specify exactly what portion of the debtor's income must be submitted to the trustee, it only mandates that it be "sufficient . . . to fund the plan." The amount necessary to fund the plan depends on the other terms of the plan, which are determined by the requirements for confirmation imposed by § 1325.

[B] Full Payment of Priority Claims

[1] Priority Claims in Chapter 13

Section 1322(a)(2) requires all Chapter 13 plans to "provide for the *full payment* . . . of all claims entitled to priority under section 507 . . . unless the holder of a particular claim agrees to a different treatment."[65] This, together with § 1325(a)(1)'s requirement that the plan comply with all of the provisions of Chapter 13[66] makes paying priority claims in full a requirement for confirmation.

Unless they operate a business, few Chapter 13 debtors are likely to have priority claims, other than those for administrative expenses (such as the trustee's fees and bankruptcy attorney fees),[67] unpaid tax claims,[68] and unpaid support claims.[69]

Note that full payment does not require the sum distributed to priority claims to have the same "value" as the amount of the claim. Section 1322(a)(2) requires only the "amount" of § 507 priority claims to be paid in full. Thus, if a debtor owes a $3,000 unsecured pre-petition priority debt to the IRS, the debtor's plan can be confirmed if it provides for a $3,000 payment to the IRS without any interest. If the claim were instead a secured claim, § 1325(a)(5) would require the creditor to pay the present value of the creditor's allowed secured claim.[70] Similarly, under § 1325(a)(4),

---

[64] Bankruptcy Code § 1322(a)(1).

[65] Bankruptcy Code § 322(a)(2).

[66] Bankruptcy Code § 1325(a)(1).

[67] *See* In re San Miguel, 40 B.R. 481 (Bankr. D. Colo. 1984) (plan provided for payments of only $1.00 each to unsecured creditors, but it provided for payment in full to debtor's attorney for § 507(a)(2) administrative priority claim).

[68] Bankruptcy Code § 507(a)(8).

[69] Bankruptcy Code § 507(a)(1).

[70] Bankruptcy Code § 1325(a)(5); *see* § 18.08[F][4] Cramdown of Chapter 13 Plan over Secured Creditor's Objection, *infra*.

the distribution to unsecured creditors must be at least the present value of any distribution they would have received in a Chapter 7 liquidation.

[2] Domestic Support Obligations

Sections 1322(a)(2) and 507(a)(1) require the debtor's plan to provide for payment in full of any domestic support obligations.[71] However, § 1322(a)(2) must be read together with § 1322(a)(4). The latter permits a Chapter 13 plan to provide for less than full payment of some domestic support obligations if the plan requires the debtor to continue making payments of all of his projected disposable income for five years.[72] In a five-year plan, domestic support obligations that have previously been assigned to a governmental agency or unit need not be paid in full.[73] Thus, a plan may provide for less than payment in full of past-due domestic support claims that have already been assigned to a governmental unit, but only if the debtor submits a five-year plan. But, the plan must provide for full payment of domestic support obligations that have not yet been assigned to a governmental agency.

These are not the only rules that seek to ensure that debtors pay support claims. The debtor's plan cannot be confirmed if the debtor has fallen further into default on payment of his or her domestic support obligations since his petition was filed.[74] In addition, the debtor's failure to make timely payment of any domestic support obligation that comes due any time after the date of the petition is grounds for dismissal of the case.[75] Moreover, unpaid portions of domestic support obligations are nondischargeable in Chapter 13, even under the hardship discharge provisions.[76] Thus, the Code contains several avenues for requiring payment of support and the debtor remains liable for any past due support that is not fully paid at the conclusion of the debtor's case.[77]

Property settlement obligations to a spouse, former spouse, or child are not entitled to priority and thus need not be paid in full. Such debts remain fully dischargeable in Chapter 13; this preserves the traditional distinction between support on the one hand and property settlements and other marital obligations on the other.[78]

---

[71] Bankruptcy Code § 1322(a)(2); *see* In re Reid, No. 06-50147, 2006 WL 2077572 (Bankr. M.D.N.C. July 19, 2006) (domestic support obligations must be paid in full but need not be paid before other claims).

[72] Bankruptcy Code § 1322(b)(4).

[73] Bankruptcy Code § 507(a)(1)(B); *see* § 10.04[A][1] Support Claims, *supra*.

[74] Bankruptcy Code § 1325(a)(8).

[75] Bankruptcy Code § 1307(c)(11).

[76] Bankruptcy Code § 1328(a)(2).

[77] § 13.05[C] Scope of Debtor's Chapter 13 Discharge, *supra*.

[78] In Chapter 7 cases, both support and property settlement obligations are nondischargeable. *See* § 13.03[B][5] Family Obligations, *supra*.

§ 18.07 Chapter 13 Plan — Permissive Provisions

Section 1322(b) specifies a variety of optional provisions that may or may not be included in a Chapter 13 plan. Many of these optional provisions are routinely used, such as those that provide for the modification of secured and unsecured claims. The most important passages in § 1322(b) are those that impose limitations on these otherwise permissive terms. In addition, the range of latitude permitted by § 1322(b) must be read in conjunction with the standards for plan confirmation imposed by § 1325, which in many cases further restricts what the plan may provide.

[A] Classification of Claims[79]

Chapter 13 debtors have limited ability to classify general unsecured claims.[80] "Classification" refers to the division of creditors into separate groups for the purpose of different treatment under the plan. The most obvious example would be a plan that provides for paying one class 100% of the amount of their allowed claims, while paying members of a separate class less, perhaps only 60%. Claims might also be segregated into separate classes for the purpose of paying members of one class earlier in the life span of the plan. This is sometimes done as a hedge against the risk that the plan will fail. If this happens, the debtor may find it useful to have fully paid debts that are nondischargeable in Chapter 7. Or the debtor may have other reasons to be more concerned that one group of creditors, such as family members, co-workers, or in the case of a debtor engaged in business, key suppliers, receive more than others or receive payment sooner.[81]

Section 1322(b)(1) permits a plan to separate claims of unsecured creditors into separate classes as long as the classification scheme comports with the requirements of § 1122, which applies in Chapter 11 cases, and as long as the classification does not "discriminate unfairly" against any class. Because there is little creditor participation in Chapter 13 cases, particularly because creditors do not vote on the plan, the general view is that it is unfair to give the debtor substantial power to distinguish between types of general unsecured claims. Unfair discrimination is not the clearest standard imaginable. All classifications discriminate; the question is under what circumstances is the proposed discrimination unfair.

The Code singles out one type of permissible discrimination. If a debt is a consumer debt[82] on which an individual other than the debtor is liable

---

[79] Stefan A. Riesenfeld, *Classification of Claims and Interest in Chapter 11 and 13 Cases*, 75 Cal. L. Rev. 391 (1987); Stephen L. Sepinuk, *Rethinking Unfair Discrimination in Chapter 13*, 74 Am. Bankr. L.J. 341 (2000); Kevin D. Hart, Annotation, *Payments to Partially Secured Creditors Outside Chapter 13 Plan as Unfair Discriminatory Treatment of Class of Unsecured Claims under Bankruptcy Code § 1322(b)(1) of Bankruptcy Code of 1978*, 50 A.L.R. Fed. 694 (1980).

[80] Bankruptcy Code § 1122(b)(1).

[81] In re Wolff, 22 B.R. 510 (B.A.P. 9th Cir. 1982) (classification favoring existing insurance carrier and materials supplier not justified).

[82] Bankruptcy Code § 101(8); *see generally* In re Westberry, 215 F.3d 589 (6th Cir. 2000).

with the debtor, the plan may separately classify that debt and give it more favorable treatment than debts owed to other creditors.[83] This is little more than a bow to reality. In many cases, a consumer's co-debtor is a family member or friend, and many debtors, feeling a strong moral obligation to protect the co-debtor, try to pay the debt outside of the plan. This endangers the viability of the plan, since those extra payments come out of whatever income the debtor has left after making payments required by the plan. Because of this risk to the plan and the fact that many debtors try to find some way to pay the debt regardless, Congress has legitimized a degree of disparate treatment under the plan itself.[84]

Despite this, the fact that the plan may treat co-signed consumer debts differently than other debts does not mean that any degree of discrimination is permitted. The Code still prohibits "unfair discrimination" in favor of such claims.[85]

The test of unfair discrimination that has flourished, under a variety of names,[86] considers four, and sometimes five factors:

1. Is there a reasonable basis for the discrimination?
2. Can the debtor fulfill the plan without the discrimination?
3. Is the discrimination in good faith?
4. Are other creditors receiving meaningful payment?
5. Is there a direct relationship between the degree of the discrimination and the rationale for the discrimination?

Some courts simply inquire as to whether the classification scheme is "reasonable,"[87] but as others have pointed out, there is little reason to believe that this different articulation results in a markedly different approach to the question.[88]

In applying these tests, courts are skeptical of plans that provide different treatment to creditors based on the nondischargeability of claims in the favored class,[89] though separate classifications of nondischargeable support claims are treated with more favor.[90] Likewise, courts do not usually

---

[83] Bankruptcy Code § 101(8).

[84] The Senate Committee report, prepared at the time this amendment was made, explained: "If, as a practical matter, the debtor is going to pay the codebtor claim, he should be permitted to separately classify it in Chapter 13." S. Rep. 98-65, at 18 (1983).

[85] In re Whitelock, 122 B.R. 582 (Bankr. D. Utah 1990).

[86] *See* Stephen L. Sepinuk, *Rethinking Unfair Discrimination in Chapter 13*, 74 Am. Bankr. L.J. 341, 354–55 (2000).

[87] *E.g.*, In re Alicea, 199 B.R. 862, 866 (Bankr. D.N.J. 1996).

[88] *See* Stephen L. Sepinuk, *Rethinking Unfair Discrimination in Chapter 13*, 74 Am. Bankr. L.J. 341, 355 (2000).

[89] *E.g.*, In re Groves, 39 F.3d 212 (8th Cir. 1994) (denying confirmation of a plan that favored nondischargeable educational loans over other unsecured debts); *see* Seth J. Gerson, Note, *Separate Classification of Student Loans in Chapter 13*, 73 Wash. U. L.Q. 269 (1995).

[90] *See* In re Crawford, 324 F.3d 539 (7th Cir. 2003); In re Bentley, 250 B.R. 475, 478 (Bankr. D.R.I. 2000). Such claims are entitled to priority under § 507(a)(1) and thus must be paid in full.

approve classification schemes that favor the debtor's friends and relatives at the expense of creditors with whom the debtor is less well acquainted.

On the other hand, it makes sense to permit the debtor to favor one creditor over another where the favorable treatment seems likely somehow to enhance the debtor's income and result in better treatment for other creditors generally. Restitution payments to the victims of the debtor's crimes, necessary to keep the debtor out of jail, and which are, in any event, nondischargeable, are an obvious example. Likewise, discriminatory treatment should be permitted when the debtor would otherwise lose some financial advantage that can be gained only by paying the creditor in full, such as where a debtor engaged in business would have to shift to an otherwise more expensive supplier or to move to a more expensive location.[91]

Finally, any discrimination between claims or types of claims must be done through separate classifications.[92] A debtor may not place differently treated claims in the same class; rather, each claim in any class must be treated the same.[93]

[B] Modification of Rights of Creditors

One of Chapter 13's most important provisions permits a plan to "modify the rights of holders of secured claim . . . or holders of unsecured claims."[94] The simplest modification is an extension of the time for payment of a creditor's claim.[95] For example, a creditor who is legally entitled to immediate payment might find that the plan provides for extending payment for up to five years. For creditors whose own financial success depends on the flow of regular payments from their customers, this kind of extension is not only disappointing, but it also can have a devastating effect on the creditor's own financial circumstances.

Worse, the debtor's plan might reduce the total amount that will be paid to the creditor. For example, the plan might provide for payment of only 20% or less of the creditor's claim. Note, however, that the debtor's ability to do this is subject to specific restrictions in the language of § 1322(b)(2) itself and elsewhere in Chapter 13.

The plan might also reduce, or in the case of unsecured creditors, eliminate interest payments to the creditor. Creditors who expected to earn a profit on the interest they receive from their borrowers, quite naturally view this negatively. But, the Code unquestionably permits it.

---

[91] *See* Stephen L. Sepinuk, *Rethinking Unfair Discrimination in Chapter 13*, 74 Am. Bankr. L.J. 341, 372–73 (2000).

[92] An example of how this is accomplished in the text of a plan is illustrated by the sample plan online at: http://vls.law.vill.edu/prof/cohen/cletranscripts/Sample-1-ch13plan.htm (last visited Nov. 8, 2006).

[93] Bankruptcy Code § 1322(a)(3).

[94] Bankruptcy Code § 1322(b)(2).

[95] *See* § 2.11 Compositions and Workouts, *supra*.

Finally, the plan might implement all three of these strategies: reduce the amount that will be paid; reduce the interest rate; and extend the period over which payments will be made, disappointing the creditor's expectations on several fronts.

[1] Modifying Unsecured Claims

Debtors are given wide leeway to modify the rights of creditors that hold unsecured claims. As mentioned above, payments may be extended or reduced. However, § 1325 imposes indirect restraints on this latitude by requiring that the payments made to unsecured creditors are worth at least what they would have received if the debtor had liquidated.[96] Further, if a creditor objects, § 1325(b) requires the debtor to submit all of his "projected disposable income" for payments to unsecured creditors for a minimum of three years.[97] Another indirect limit is imposed by § 1322(a)(2), discussed above, which requires full payment of all priority claims.[98]

Remember that unsecured claims include the unsecured portion of any partially secured claim. Thus, a creditor who is owed $3,000, secured by a lien on the debtor's $2,000 garden tractor, hold two claims: a secured claim of $2,000 and an unsecured claim of $1,000.[99]

The unsecured claim can be dealt with in any number of ways. Depending on the circumstances, the plan may provide for payments of very little or even nothing with respect to this unsecured claim. This, of course, is one of the reasons creditors usually try to take steps to ensure that the value of their collateral is sufficient to satisfy the entire amount the debtor owes.

Whether the debtor is able to avoid paying anything to holders of unsecured claims depends, as will be explained below, on two factors: first, the amount of non-exempt equity owned by the debtor's estate that would have been distributed to unsecured creditors in a Chapter 7 case;[100] and second, the amount of disposable income available to the debtor to pay his creditors.[101]

[2] Modifying Secured Claims

Chapter 13 also permits the plan to modify secured claims.[102] A secured creditor's claim might be modified by changing the amount and duration of monthly payments or by extending or accelerating the amortization

[96] Bankruptcy Code § 1325(a)(4); *see* § 18.08[E][1] Best Interests of Creditors, *infra*.

[97] Bankruptcy Code § 1325(b).

[98] Bankruptcy Code § 1322(a)(2); *see* § 18.06[B] Full Payment of Priority Claims, *supra*.

[99] If the creditor holds a purchase money security interest in the tractor, securing a debt incurred within one year before the debtor's petition, the paragraph hanging at the end of § 1325(a)(9) prevents the debtor from bifurcating the claim. *See* § 18.08[F][6] Certain Purchase Money Security Interests, *infra*.

[100] *See* § 18.08[E][1] Best Interests of Creditors, *infra*.

[101] *See* § 18.08[E][2] Debtor's Projected Disposable Income, *infra*.

[102] Bankruptcy Code § 1325(a)(4).

schedule of the secured debt. Thus, payments to a creditor with a security interest in the debtor's garden tractor might be spread out over the entire three to five years of the debtor's plan, even though the contract between the debtor and the secured creditor calls for full amortization of the debt within the next six months.

A secured claim might also be modified by changing the rate of interest to be paid to the creditor on the unpaid balance of its secured claim. The contract might require the debtor to pay 18% interest; the plan might reduce this to a much lower rate. Creditors who have agreed to reduce the price of goods they have sold to the debtor, in exchange for the higher interest rate they hope to recover on the debtor's installment payments will find this result quite dissatisfying. Nevertheless, the plan can be confirmed as long as the interest rate is sufficient to ensure that the value of the payments made to the creditor over the life of the plan are worth as much as the amount of the allowed secured claim.

In *Till v. SCS Credit Corp.,*[103] the Supreme Court sought to determine the appropriate cram down interest rate for a loan secured by a Chapter 13 debtor's truck. A plurality of the Court concluded that the appropriate rate of interest was the prime rate (which they described as a "risk free" rate of interest) plus 1–3% to adjust for the extra risk involved in making a loan to a Chapter 13 debtor. Thus, even though the parties' contract calls for interest to accumulate at 16%, if the prime rate is 6%, an appropriate cramdown rate would be 7–9%. Justice Thomas concurred, stating that there was no need to adjust the rate to account for risk and that a lower rate was appropriate.[104] Therefore, the highest rate appropriate would appear to be the one endorsed by the plurality.

The *Till* decision has been criticized on a number of fronts. First, the prime rate (as set by various banks) is not a risk free rate. It is the rate that banks state that they charge for unsecured loans to their best business customers. Secured loans (even loans to consumers) often bear rates of interest below prime. The risk-free rate is usually associated with the rate charged on United States Treasury bills. This too is generally lower than the prime rate. Second, and on the other hand, Chapter 13 debtors are much riskier than other debtors, so the 1–3% adjustment may also be too small.

In addition to the power to modify the interest rate, the Chapter 13 debtor also has the power to "strip down" a lien to an undersecured creditor. This means that the payments to a secured creditor need only be worth the value of the creditor's allowed secured claim. If the claim is only partially secured, because the collateral is worth less than the debt it secures, the stream of payments only need to be worth the present value of this lower amount. Thus, if the garden tractor in which the security interest is held is worth $800 but the debt secured by the item is $1,000, the payments made under the plan must only be worth the value of the lower amount, $800.

---

[103] Till v. SCS Credit Corp. 541 U.S. 465 (2004).

[104] Till v. SCS Credit Corp. 541 U.S. 465 (2004) (Thomas, J., concurring); *see* § 18.08[F][4][b] Payments Equivalent to Amount of Secured Claim, *infra*.

The Code imposes restrictions on the types of secured claims that can be modified or "stripped down" in this fashion. These restrictions apply to residential mortgages and some purchase money security interests in automobiles and other personal property, as explained below.

[a] Residential Real Estate Mortgages

Apart from general rules regarding cramdown, the most important restriction on a debtor's ability to modify the rights of secured creditors is contained in § 1322(b)(2). It prevents debtors from modifying the rights of holders of a mortgage on the debtor's residential real estate.[105] In other words, a debtor may not use Chapter 13 to modify his home mortgage.

The precise language, of course, is a bit more complicated. Section 1322(b)(2) permits the plan to "modify the rights of holders of secure claims, *other than a claim secured only by a security interest in real property that is the debtor's principal residence*"[106] Thus the creditor's claim cannot be modified if:

- the collateral for the debt is the debtor's principal residence;
- the collateral is real property; and
- there is no other collateral for the creditor's claim.[107]

This means that the creditor's partially secured claim cannot be "stripped-down" to the value of the collateral.[108]

However, if the residence is personal property, not real estate, such as a motor home, the claim can be modified. Further, if the creditor obtained a security interest in additional collateral, such as the debtor's car, his furniture, or more likely "any and all appliances, machinery, furniture and equipment (whether fixtures or not)," the creditor's claim may be modified.[109] The same is true if the collateral is a multi-unit dwelling and the debtor resides in only one of the units.[110] However, a security interest in fixtures, or income derived from the collateral does not permit the creditor's claim to be modified.[111]

---

[105] Bankruptcy Code § 1322(b)(2).

[106] Bankruptcy Code § 1322(b)(2) (emphasis added).

[107] Pigs get fat; hogs get slaughtered! *Cf.* Juliet M. Moringiello, *Has Congress Slimmed Down the Hogs?: A Look at the BAPCPA Approach to Pre-Bankruptcy Planning*, 15 Widener L.J. 615 (2006); Lynn M. LoPucki & Walter O. Weyrauch, *A Theory of Legal Strategy*, 49 Duke L.J. 1405, 1455 (2000).

[108] Nobleman v. American Sav. Bank, 508 U.S. 324 (1993).

[109] In re Johns, 37 F.3d 1021 (3d Cir. 1994).

[110] *E.g.*, In re Scarborough, 461 F.3d 406 (3d Cir. 2006) (creditor's mortgage on multi-unit dwelling was not secured only by the debtor's residence).

[111] *See* Allied Credit Corp. v. Davis (In re Davis), 989 F.2d 208 (6th Cir. 1993) (hereditaments and appurtenances, rents, royalties, profits and fixtures); In re Washington, 967 F.2d 173 (5th Cir. 1992) (credit life and disability insurance); In re Halperin, 170 B.R. 500 (Bankr. D. Conn. 1994) (rents, royalties, oil and gas rights, profits, stocks and fixtures).

If the secured creditor's claim cannot be modified, the plan must provide for payments to be made according to the terms of the contract with the creditor.

If the debtor is already in default on his obligations, he is nevertheless able to "cure and reinstate" the mortgage pursuant to § 1322(c)(1). This is an explicit exception to the no modification of home mortgages rule of § 1322(b)(2)[112] and permits cure and reinstatement any time prior to a foreclosure sale of the mortgaged property. Thus, the plan might call for the debtor to resume making regular monthly installment payments at the contract rate and make additional payments to the creditor for any payments he missed before filing his Chapter 13 petition. However, once the property has been sold at a foreclosure sale, cure and reinstatement are no longer permitted.

This ability to "cure and reinstate" a home mortgage is a key provision of Chapter 13 that induces many debtors to seek bankruptcy protection in the first place. Unburdened by the requirement of making payments to other creditors, debtors sometimes find that they are able to resume their monthly mortgage payments and keep their homes.

A key exception to the rule prohibiting modification of residential real estate mortgages applies when the last payment on the mortgage is due before the end of the debtor's plan.[113] This might occur if the debtor filed its Chapter 13 case sometime in the last few years of his residential mortgage, but it is more likely to arise when there is a balloon payment due sometime within three to five years after the debtor's Chapter 13 petition. In this situation, the secured creditor's claim can be modified within the restraints otherwise imposed by § 1325(a)(5) regarding cramdown of secured claims and within the restraints imposed by the five-year limit on the duration of a Chapter 13 plan.[114]

[b] Certain Purchase Money Loans

The right to modify the rights of secured claims is further restrained by language added by the 2005 Amendments and attached to the end of § 1325(a).[115] This new language, which has already led to some difficult interpretive problems, was apparently intended to prevent the bifurcation and stripdown of partially secured claims in some motor vehicles and other goods subject to purchase money security interests. This new restriction applies to purchase money security interests that are secured either by motor vehicles acquired within 910 days before the debtor's petition or by

---

[112] Bankruptcy Code § 1322(c); In re Cain, 423 F.3d 617 (6th Cir. 2005).

[113] Bankruptcy Code § 1322(c)(2); *e.g.*, In re Sturgill, 337 B.R. 599 (Bankr. W.D. Ky. 2006) (short-term debt secured by lien on debtor's residence could be modified).

[114] *See* Timothy B. McCaffrey, Jr., Comment, *Cramdown Under the New 1332(c)(2) from* Dewsnup*to* Nobelman *to the Bankruptcy Reform Act of 1994: Did Congress Intend to Change "Pre-amendment" Law When it Enacted 1322(c)(2)?*, 30 Loy. L.A. L. Rev. 841 (1997).

[115] Referring to it this way always seems like "the artist previously known as Prince."

other personal property acquired within one year before the debtor's petition.[116]

[C] Cure and Waiver of Defaults; Reinstatement

The debtor's pre-petition default on a debt involving installment payments nearly always results in the acceleration of the debt, making it payable in full immediately. The debtor's Chapter 13 plan can provide for the reversal of this acceleration. Section 1322(b)(3) permits the plan to provide for the cure and waiver of any default.[117] Likewise, § 1322(b)(5) permits the plan to cure defaults and reinstate the payment schedule on long-term debts for which the last payment is due after the plan is scheduled to be completed.[118] This ability has its biggest impact on secured claims that the debtor is otherwise prevented from modifying. Since the secured lender's contract provides for acceleration, de-acceleration requires a modification to the contract. Without the ability to de-accelerate the debt, it will certainly be impossible for the debtor to pay the full amount of the loan immediately.

[1] Amount Necessary to Cure Defaults

The amount necessary to effectuate a cure is determined in accordance with § 1322(e). It provides: "Notwithstanding [§§ 1322(b)(2), 506(b) and 1325(a)(5)], if it is proposed in a plan to cure a default, the amount necessary to cure the default, shall be determined in accordance with the underlying agreement and applicable non-bankruptcy law."[119] This language was adopted to overrule the Supreme Court's decision in *Rake v. Wade*[120] holding that interest was required to be paid on mortgage arrearages by debtors who were curing defaults on their mortgages even if such interest on defaulted interest payments was not recoverable under the parties' agreement or under applicable state law. In effect, *Rake v. Wade* required Chapter 13 debtors to pay interest they had not agreed to pay or, if they had agreed to interest on interest, that would have been unrecoverable outside of bankruptcy. The purpose of § 1322(e) was to limit secured parties to the terms of the original deal they had struck with the debtor and prevent them from recovering interest on capitalized interest that *Rake v. Wade* required.[121] After § 1322(e), Chapter 13 cure payments need not include interest on the interest component of the arrearages the debtor is curing unless such interest would have been recoverable outside of bankruptcy.[122]

---

[116] The hanging paragraph appearing immediately after Bankruptcy Code § 1325(a)(9); *see* § 18.08[F][6] Certain Purchase Money Security Interests, *infra*.

[117] Bankruptcy Code § 1322(b)(3).

[118] Bankruptcy Code § 1322(b)(5).

[119] Bankruptcy Code § 1322(e).

[120] 508 U.S. 464 (1993).

[121] *See* H.R. Rep. No. 103-835, at 55 (1994), *reprinted in* 1994 U.S.C.C.A.N. 3340, 3364.

[122] *See, e.g.*, In re Hoover, 254 B.R. 492 (Bankr. N.D. Okla. 2000); In re Lake, 245 B.R. 282 (Bankr. N.D. Ohio 2000).

The same analysis applies to attorney fees, collection costs, and other charges. The debtor need not pay these charges in order to cure unless the charges are both recoverable under the terms of the parties' agreement, and recoverable under applicable non-bankruptcy law.[123]

[2] Cure Payments Through the Trustee

Debtors are sometimes permitted to continue to make their regular monthly mortgage payments directly to the mortgagee, rather than making them indirectly through the plan via the Chapter 13 trustee.[124] Any arrearages necessary to effectuate the cure, on the other hand, are paid through the trustee.

[3] Reasonable Time for Cure

The debtor's cure of arrearages must be accomplished within a reasonable time.[125] What qualifies as a reasonable time varies on a case-by-case basis within the discretion of the court.[126]

The only hard and fast limit is the three to five year duration of the debtor's plan.[127] But courts have approved cure periods ranging from six months to the maximum sixty-month plan duration allowed by § 1322(d).[128]

The ability to cure and reinstate long-term debts should be read in conjunction with § 1328(a)(1), which exempts these long-term debts from the scope of a Chapter 13 discharge.[129] Thus, the debtor remains liable for the unpaid portion of the de-accelerated debt after his Chapter 13 plan has been fully performed and he receives a Chapter 13 discharge. At this point, the debtor is obligated simply to continue making payments under the terms of his long-term debt as if the Chapter 13 case had never occurred.

The ability to cure defaults and reinstate also applies to student loans and other long-term non-dischargeable unsecured debts with an amortization period that extends beyond the duration of the plan.[130]

---

[123] *E.g.*, In re Evans, 336 B.R. 749 (Bankr. S.D. Ohio 2006).

[124] *See* In re Lopez, 350 B.R. 868 (Bankr. C.D. Cal. 2006).

[125] *E.g.*, United Cal. Sav. Bank v. Martin (In re Martin), 156 B.R. 47 (B.A.P. 9th Cir. 1993); Steinacher v. Rojas (In re Steinacher), 283 B.R. 768 (B.A.P. 9th Cir. 2002).

[126] *See* Steinacher v. Rojas (In re Steinacher), 283 B.R. 768 (B.A.P. 9th Cir. 2002).

[127] United Cal. Sav. Bank v. Martin (In re Martin), 156 B.R. 47, 50 (B.A.P. 9th Cir. 1993).

[128] *See, e.g.*, In re Ford, 221 B.R. 749, 754 (Bankr. W.D. Tenn. 1988) (six months); In re Chavez, 117 B.R. 730, 733 (Bankr. S.D. Fla. 1990) (thirty-six months); In re Anderson, 73 B.R. 993, 996 (Bankr. W.D. Okla. 1987) (seventeen months); In re East, 172 B.R. 861, 867 (Bankr. S.D. Tex. 1994) (fifty-two months); In re Cole, 122 B.R. 943, 951–52 (Bankr. E.D. Pa. 1992) (sixty months).

[129] Bankruptcy Code § 1328(a)(1); *see* § 13.05 Chapter 13 Discharge, *supra*.

[130] *See* Labib-Kiyarash v. McDonald (In re Labib-Kiyarash), 271 B.R. 189 (B.A.P. 9th Cir. 2001).

[D] Concurrent or Sequential Payment of Claims

Section 1322(b)(4) gives the debtor considerable leeway with respect to the sequence of payments made under the plan, permitting it to provide for payments to creditors to be made concurrently or sequentially.[131] Because cramdown requirements make it necessary to pay interest to holders of secured claims, the debtor may find it beneficial to pay these claims in the early months of a plan and save payments to unsecured creditors for later.

Moreover, § 1325(a)(5)(B)(iii)(II) now explicitly requires payments under the plan to be sufficient to provide adequate protection to secured creditors. In many cases, this makes it necessary for the plan to provide for payments to holders of secured claims in the early months of the plan.

Likewise, because of the risk of default on the terms of the plan and either conversion or dismissal of the debtor's case, it may be beneficial for the plan to provide for early payment to creditors that hold non-dischargeable claims. If unanticipated circumstances prevent the debtor from fully performing the plan for its entire duration, this may lead to full payment of claims held by creditors whose claims cannot be discharged either in Chapter 7 or in a hardship discharge in Chapter 13. Of course, a plan filed with the intent of such a conversion would be in bad faith and should not be confirmed.

Section 1326(b) limits some of this leeway by requiring certain administrative priority expenses to be paid simultaneously with "each payment" made to creditors under the plan. Some courts have ruled that this permits only partial payment of these claims, which consist primarily of the standing trustee's fees. Other courts have ruled that the plain meaning of § 1326(b) is that these administrative expense priority claims must be paid in full as the plan progresses.[132]

[E] Payment of Post-Petition Claims

Chapter 13 also permits a plan to provide for the payment of post-petition claims, allowed with the approval of the court pursuant to § 1305.[133] Under that section, creditors with certain post-petition claims, such as for taxes or consumer debts for property or services necessary for the debtor's performance under the plan, may file proofs of claim and receive payments under the plan.[134] Section 1322(b)(6) facilitates plan provisions that call for the payment of such claims.

---

[131] Bankruptcy Code § 1322(b)(4).

[132] *E.g.*, In re DeSardi, 340 B.R. 790, 808–09 (Bankr. S.D. Tex. 2006); *see* Richardo Kilpatrick, *Selected Creditor Issues Under the Bankruptcy Abuse Prevention and Consumer Protection Act of 2005*, 79 Am. Bankr. L.J. 817, 836 (2005).

[133] Bankruptcy Code § 1322(b)(6).

[134] Bankruptcy Code § 1305.

[F] Assumption, Rejection or Assignment of Executory Contracts

Few Chapter 13 consumer debtors are parties to many executory contracts. But debtors who rent their homes or who drive leased automobiles are likely to want to assume their unexpired leases. Section 1325(b)(7) permits the plan to provide for the assumption, rejection, or even assignment of any such executory contract or unexpired lease pursuant to the requirements of § 365, which governs these matters generally.[135] That section's restrictions on assumption of leases of *non-residential* real estate obviously do not apply to debtors who wish to assume the lease of their living quarters. But it impairs the ability of some Chapter 13 sole proprietorship business debtors from assuming leases on their business premises.

This provision might also apply to certain "rent-to-own" transactions, unless they are more properly characterized as secured sales and thus not subject to § 365.[136] However, if the transaction is not an unexpired lease but a secured sale, it might be subject to the cramdown restrictions now imposed by the paragraph hanging at the end of § 1325(a).[137]

[G] Payment of Claims from Estate Property or Property of the Debtor

Though it is largely implied from the overall structure of Chapter 13, § 1322(b)(8) expressly permits the plan to provide for "the payment of all or part of a claim . . . from property of the estate or property of the debtor."[138] This is usually done through the debtor's post-petition income submitted to the trustee under § 1322(a)(1). However, payments to creditors might also be made through the liquidation of other property that belongs either to the estate or to the debtor.[139] Thus, although one of the chief advantages of Chapter 13 is that it permits debtors to keep their property, debtors might choose to sell property in order to provide the funding necessary to fulfill the terms of the plan. Less frequently, a plan might simply provide for the delivery of property to a creditor in lieu of a cash payment.[140]

---

[135] Bankruptcy Code § 1322(b)(7); *see* Chapter 10, Executory Contracts and Unexpired Leases, *supra*.

[136] *See* In re Smith, 262 B.R. 365 (Bankr. E.D. Va. 2000).

[137] *See* § 18.08[F][6] Certain Purchase Money Security Interests, *infra*.

[138] Bankruptcy Code § 1322(b)(8).

[139] *E.g.*, In re Lapin, 302 B.R. 184 (Bankr. S.D. Tex. 2003) (IRA liquidated to make payments to creditors under the plan).

[140] The only restriction on this is in § 1322(b)(2), which requires priority claims to be paid in cash. Bankruptcy Code § 1322(b)(2).

[H] Vesting of Property of Estate in the Debtor or Another Entity

A Chapter 13 plan might also provide for estate property to vest either in the debtor or in another entity.[141] This works in conjunction with § 1327(b), which automatically vests property of the estate in the debtor upon confirmation, unless the plan or a court order specifies otherwise. Delaying vesting of the property back in the debtor until the plan is fully performed and a discharge is granted may be useful to preserve the effect of the automatic stay with respect to estate property while the case is pending.[142]

[I] Payment of Interest on Nondischargeable Debts

Although post-petition interest on unsecured claims is generally not allowable,[143] § 1322(b)(10), added in 2005, permits the plan to "provide for the payment of interest accruing after the date of the filing of the petition on unsecured claims that are nondischargeable under section 1328(a)."[144] However, this is permissible only if the debtor has "disposable income available to pay such interest after making provision for full payment of all allowed claims."[145] In other words, the plan can provide for the payment of post-petition interest on nondischargeable claims only if it provides for the payment of other allowed claims in full.

This new provision facilitates debtors' efforts to complete their Chapter 13 plans free of any otherwise non-dischargeable debts. Without the ability to make plan payments to creditors whose right to recover post-petition interest would not be discharged, the debtor would be liable for this interest upon conclusion of his plan. The rule preventing debtors from paying such post-petition interest unless they are able to make full payment to all other creditors is consistent with decisions that refuse to permit Chapter 13 plans from discriminating between dischargeable and non-dischargeable debts.[146]

---

[141] Bankruptcy Code § 1322(b)(9).

[142] *See* Telfair v. First Union Mortgage Corp., 216 F.3d 1333 (11th Cir. 2000), *cert. denied*, 531 U.S. 1073 (2001) (no automatic stay protection for property revested in the debtor).

[143] Bankruptcy Code § 502(b)(2).

[144] Bankruptcy Code § 1322(b)(10).

[145] Bankruptcy Code § 1322(b)(10). Section 1322(b)(10)'s reference to "disposable income," which is based on the debtor's past income, rather than on the *projected* disposable income that must be paid to unsecured creditors under the plan, could well lead to a quirky interpretive problem. As of mid-2006, several bankruptcy courts had already ruled that "disposable income," defined in § 1325(b)(2), and "projected disposable income," required to be paid to unsecured creditors under a plan, are not synonymous. *E.g.*, In re Kibbe, 342 B.R. 411 (Bankr. D.N.H. 2006).

[146] *See* Bankruptcy Code § 1322(b)(1); § 18.07[A] Classification of Claims, *supra*.

[J] Other Consistent Provisions

Section 1322(b)(11) permits the inclusion of any other provision, as long as it does not directly conflict with some other provision of the Bankruptcy Code.[147] When considered together with § 1325(a)(3), which permits confirmation only if the plan has not been proposed by any means forbidden by law,[148] § 1322(b)(11) permits the inclusion of any provision that is not incompatible with any other aspect of federal or non-preempted state law.

§ 18.08 Confirmation of Chapter 13 Plans

A Chapter 13 plan can be confirmed only if it meets the standards of Bankruptcy Code § 1325. The court is required to confirm a Chapter 13 plan only if:

- the plan complies with the rest of Chapter 13 and the Bankruptcy Code;
- the debtor has paid the necessary filing fee and any other fees imposed on Chapter 13 debtors;
- the debtor's petition and the plan itself has been proposed in good faith and not by any means otherwise forbidden by law;
- the plan is in the best interests of creditors in that it pays them at least what they would have received had the debtor liquidated under Chapter 7;
- it provides for secured creditors to receive the value of their collateral (and sometimes more);
- the plan is financially feasible;
- the debtor is current on his support obligations; and
- the debtor has filed any required Federal, State, and local income tax returns.

The requirements that the debtor pay any fees associated with the bankruptcy case and that he file his tax returns are easily understood. Some of the other requirements are more complicated.

[A] General Requirements for Confirmation

[1] Compliance with the Bankruptcy Code

To be confirmed, the debtor's plan must comply "with the provisions of [Chapter 13] and with the other applicable provisions of [the Bankruptcy Code]" in general.[149] The requirement that the plan comply with the other provisions of Chapter 13 might lead to objections based on the plan's failure

[147] Bankruptcy Code § 1322(b)(11).

[148] Bankruptcy Code § 1325(a)(3).

[149] Bankruptcy Code § 1325(a)(1).

to comply with the mandatory provisions of § 1322(a), such as the requirement that priority claims be paid in full. Or the plan might be objectionable because it contains a provision prohibited by § 1322(b) or is for an improper duration.[150]

The requirement that the plan comply with the requirements of other applicable provisions of the Bankruptcy Code brings all of the provisions of Chapters 1, 3 and 5 of the Code into play as the basis for potential objections to confirmation.[151]

[2] Filing Tax Returns[152]

The requirement that the debtor comply with both the requirements of Chapter 13 and the Bankruptcy Code generally, together with the language of § 1308, prevents confirmation of the debtor's plan if the debtor has not filed tax returns due to be filed for the four tax years prior to the petition.[153] Failure to file any subsequent returns is grounds for dismissal of the case.[154]

[3] Payment of Fees and Charges

Section 1325(a)(2) makes confirmation depend upon the debtor's payment of the fees imposed by the relevant provision of the Judicial Code, primarily the $235 filing fee of 28 U.S.C. § 1930(a)(1)(B) and the $39 "administrative fee" of 28 U.S.C. § 1930(b).[155] These fees can be paid by installment[156] and in some districts are permitted to be paid through the plan.

[B] Feasibility

Section 1325(a)(6) requires that "the debtor will be able to make all payments under the plan and to comply with the plan."[157] Thus, it must be feasible for the debtor to perform the plan according to its terms. If the debtor lacks sufficient income to fund the plan and to meet both his living expenses and those of his dependents, the plan cannot be confirmed. Likewise, if the debtor's ability to fund the plan depends upon his receipt of a lump-sum payment from someone who may not supply it, feasibility of the plan is too speculative, and the plan should not be confirmed.[158] But

[150] *See* Bankruptcy Code § 1322(d).

[151] *See* Bankruptcy Code § 103.

[152] Carl M. Jenks, *The Bankruptcy Abuse Prevention and Consumer Protection Act of 2005: Summary of Tax Provisions*, 79 Am. Bankr. L.J. 893, 907–09 (2005).

[153] *See* Bankruptcy Code § 1308.

[154] Bankruptcy Code § 1307(e).

[155] 28 U.S.C.S. § 1930 (LexisNexis Supp. 2006).

[156] 28 U.S.C.S. § 1930 (LexisNexis Supp. 2006).

[157] Bankruptcy Code § 1325(a)(6).

[158] *E.g.*, First Nat'l Bank v. Fantasia (In re Fantasia), 211 B.R. 420 (B.A.P. 1st Cir. 1997); *but see* In re Schwalb, 347 B.R. 726 (Bankr. D. Nev. 2006) (plan to be funded by voluntary contributions from the debtor's father who had demonstrated willingness and capacity to pay).

if the source of the lump-sum is credible, the mere fact that the plan calls for such a payment does not prevent confirmation.[159]

In most cases, determining the feasibility of a plan is easy. If the total of the amount of payments required to be paid under the plan combined with the debtor's actual anticipated other expenses exceed the debtor's income, the plan is not feasible. If the debtor's projected income is sufficient, the plan is usually feasible.

The amount required to be paid under the plan, based on presumptive calculations of the debtor's projected disposable income, may exceed the actual amount available to the debtor after paying his actual (as opposed to his presumed) living expenses. To the extent that the debtor's presumed expenses, based on the allowable figures in the IRS's standards, are unrealistically low, the debtor's plan may not be feasible, unless the debtor makes significant changes in his living arrangements. On the other hand, because disposable income is calculated after deducting contractually required payments to secured creditors, the debtor might end up with more than enough income to fund the plan by surrendering some of his collateral to the secured party.[160]

In Chapter 13 cases involving debtors engaged in a business, the feasibility of the debtor's plan is more difficult to evaluate. Feasibility depends on the accuracy of the debtor's projected business income and operating expenses. Both of these items are likely to be more difficult to evaluate than a wage-earning debtor's projections about his future salary or his monthly living expenses.[161] Even a wage-earning debtor, whose ability to fund the plan depends on the availability of overtime hours at his place of employment, might face the same sort of difficulty.

[C] Good Faith

Section 1325(a)(3) requires that "the plan has been proposed in good faith and not by any means forbidden by law."[162] In addition, § 1325(a)(7) requires that "the action of the debtor in filing the petition was in good faith."[163] Thus, if either the debtor's plan or his petition was not in good faith, confirmation should be denied.

---

[159] Chelsea State Bank v. Wagner (In re Wagner), 259 B.R. 694 (B.A.P. 8th Cir. 2001) (plan was feasible where debtor's father indicated willingness to provide assistance in making lump-sum payment).

[160] One might wonder whether a creditor's acceptance of such a surrender, if not provided for in the plan, would violate the automatic stay, and if anyone would have the incentive to assert the violation. If a tree falls in the forest . . . .

[161] *E.g.*, In re Torelli, 338 B.R. 390 (Bankr. E.D. Ark. 2006).

[162] Bankruptcy Code § 1325(a)(3).

[163] Bankruptcy Code § 1325(a)(7).

[1] Good Faith Plan

Whether a plan is submitted in good faith involves consideration of a wide range of circumstances, including the amount of proposed payments, the amount of surplus income available to the debtor, the debtor's ability to earn income, the anticipated duration of plan, the accuracy of the plan's statements, the extent of preferential treatment between classes of creditors, the extent to which secured claims are modified, the types of debt to be discharged under the plan, whether any discharged debt is nondischargeable in Chapter 7, the presence or absence of special circumstances such as medical expenses, the frequency with which the debtor has sought bankruptcy relief, the motivation and sincerity of the debtor, and the burden that the plan's administration places on the trustee.[164]

Some courts have relied on the requirement of good faith to require Chapter 13 plans to provide something more than a negligible payment to claims of unsecured creditors.[165] The 1994 addition of § 1325(b), which establishes minimum financial standards for the amounts that must be paid to unsecured creditors, did not lay to rest the issue of how much debtors should pay into the plan, because the court might conclude that the debtor could make lifestyle adjustments in order to make additional payments to his creditors.[166]

The technical details involved in calculating the amount of a debtor's disposable income, which are mandated by the 2005 Amendments, are likely to limit further the significance of many of these factors. However, they are likely to resurface in connection with payments made to secured creditors, particularly if the collateral for these debts are regarded as luxury items or otherwise not reasonably necessary for the support of the debtor and his dependents.

For those who have filed and dismissed an earlier petition, the question may arise whether the court's denial of an extension of the automatic stay under § 362(c)(3), due to lack of good faith,[167] prevents subsequent confirmation of the debtor's plan for the same reason. A finding that the debtor lacks good faith, made in connection with a motion for extension of the stay, might estop the debtor from obtaining confirmation. However, in *In re Tomasini*, the court ruled that the standard of good faith under § 362(c)(3) is different from the standard for good faith under § 1325(a)(7) and thus the court could confirm the debtor's plan despite its earlier ruling regarding the debtor's lack of good faith.[168]

---

[164] *E.g.*, In re Doersam, 849 F.2d 237 (6th Cir. 1988); *see* Bradley M. Elbein, *The Hole in the Code: Good Faith and Morality in Chapter 13*, 34 San Diego L. Rev. 439 (1997); Diane M. Allen, Annotation, *Effect, on "Good Faith" Requirement of Sec. 1325(a)(3) of Bankruptcy Code of 1978 for Confirmation of Chapter 13 Plan, of Debtor's Offer of Less than Full Repayment to Unsecured Creditors*, 73 A.L.R. Fed. 10 (1985).

[165] *E.g.*, In re Iacovoni, 2 B.R. 256 (Bankr. D. Utah 1980).

[166] *E.g.*, In re Leone, 292 B.R. 243 (Bankr. W.D. Pa. 2003).

[167] Bankruptcy Code § 362(c)(3); *see* § 8.06[A][3] Prior Petition Within One Year, *supra*.

[168] In re Tomasini, 339 B.R. 773 (Bankr. D. Utah 2006).

[2] No Legally Forbidden Means

The requirement that the plan not be proposed by any means forbidden by any other law adds little to the requirement that the plan be submitted in good faith. It makes it clear that the plan must comply with legal requirements outside the Bankruptcy Code that are not superceded by the Code.

[3] Petition Filed in Good Faith

The requirement that the debtor's action in filing the petition must be in good faith was added in 2005. The inclusion of this element in § 1325 indicates that a bad faith petition should be grounds for denying confirmation rather than grounds for dismissal of the debtor's case entirely.[169] On the other hand, if a bad faith petition is grounds to deny any plan the debtor might file, the case would seem to be destined for dismissal in any event under § 1325(c)(5), regarding dismissal due to "denial of confirmation."[170]

[D] Duration of the Plan

For many years, the customary duration of a Chapter 13 plan was three years, though the court could permit it to be extended for as long as five years. These three-and five-year time limits were imposed because of a concern that some plans under old Chapter XIII extended far longer and amounted to virtual peonage for the debtor.[171]

Under the 2005 Amendments, the required duration of a plan depends on the "applicable commitment period."[172] Debtors with "current monthly income" that is equal to or higher than their home state's median income for households of similar size, are required to submit plans that call for a five-year commitment period.[173] Debtors with current monthly income that is lower than their home state's median income may submit plans that last for a shorter period, usually three years.

"Current monthly income" is a defined term.[174] It is based, as with the Chapter 7 means test, on amounts that the debtor earned during the six months before filing his petition.[175] This might mean that the applicable

---

[169] *E.g.*, Alt v. United States (In re Alt), 305 F.3d 413 (6th Cir. 2002) (bad faith petition by debtor who had intentionally failed to schedule tax debt warranted dismissal).

[170] In re Hall, 346 B.R. 420 (Bankr. W.D. Ky. 2006); *see* § 18.03[B] Conversion and Dismissal of Chapter 13 Cases, *supra*.

[171] Discussing the unlimited time period for Chapter XIII plans, the House Report on the Bankruptcy Code remarked: "Extensions on plans, new cases, and newly incurred debts put some debtors under court supervised repayment plans for seven to ten years. This has become the closest thing there is to indentured servitude." H.R. Rep. No. 95-595, at 117 (1977), *reprinted in* 1978 U.S.C.C.A.N. 5963, 6078.

[172] Bankruptcy Code § 1425(b)(1)(B), (b)(4); *see* In re Davis, 348 B.R. 449 (Bankr. E.D. Mich. 2006).

[173] Bankruptcy Code § 1325(b)(4)(A)(ii).

[174] Bankruptcy Code § 101(10A).

[175] *See* § 17.03[B][2][a] Current Monthly Income, *supra*.

commitment period for a particular debtor might be only three years, even though the debtor's anticipated future income is above the state median. For example, in *In re Beasley*, the debtor's current monthly income, calculated according to the formula specified by § 101(10A) was below the applicable state median.[176] His projected income on the other hand, which would have been available to fund his plan, was above the state median. The court was constrained by the plain meaning of § 1322(d) and confirmed the debtor's three-year plan over the trustee's objection that the applicable commitment period should have been five years.[177]

Courts are in disagreement over whether the "applicable commitment period" of § 1325(b)(1)(B) establishes merely a financial standard or whether it also imposes a temporal requirement for the duration of the debtor's plan.[178] A few courts have ruled that it only sets a monetary standard for the amount a debtor's plan must submit to the trustee for payment to creditors.[179] Under this approach, a debtor whose projected disposable income is a negative number might obtain confirmation of a plan calling for payments over less than the three-or five-year period that applies to the debtor's situation, or a debtor who anticipates greater income might choose to accelerate the payment schedule and pay off the required amount in a shorter period.

Other courts treat the applicable commitment period as establishing not just a financial requirement, but also imposing a temporal standard on the duration of the debtor's plan.[180] Under this approach, the debtor's plan must last for the full three-or five-year term, depending on whether the debtor's income is under or over the applicable household median income threshold imposed by § 1325(b)(4)(A).

Consider the situation in *In re Fuger*.[181] The debtors' household income was above his home state's median household income. Thus the applicable commitment period was five years. Nevertheless, the income and expenditures reflected on their Official Form B22 indicated that their disposable income was a negative sum. This was probably due to payments they were contractually obligated to make to secured creditors. The plan provided for payment of only $500 to unsecured creditors and permitted him to pay creditors early thus possibly reducing the duration of the plan to less than a full five years. The court held that this was permissible, because the plan did provide for payment of "all of the debtor's projected disposable income

176 342 B.R. 280 (Bankr. C.D. Ill. 2006); *see also* In re Dew, 344 B.R. 655 (Bankr. N.D. Ala. 2006).

177 In re Beasley, 342 B.R. at 284.

178 *See* Alane A. Becket & Thomas A. Lee, III, *Applicable Time Commitment: Time or Money?*, Amer. Bank. Inst. J., March 2006, at 16.

179 In re Fuger, 347 B.R. 94 (Bankr. D. Utah 2006).

180 In re Davis, 348 B.R. 449 (Bankr. E.D. Mich. 2006); In re Schanuth, 342 B.R. 601 (Bankr. W.D. Mo. 2006) (Venters, J.); In re McGuire, 342 B.R. 608 (Bankr. W.D. Mo. 2006) (Federman, J.).

181 In re Fuger, 347 B.R. 94 (Bankr. D. Utah 2006).

to be received in the [five-year] applicable commitment period" to unsecured creditors. Because the debtor had zero projected disposable income during that time, the plan could provide for payment of that sum in considerably less than five years. The court explained that the clear meaning of the statutory language and the legislative history of the 2005 Amendments supported this conclusion.

Courts that have found § 1325(b)(1)(B) to establish a temporal requirement have relied on the use of the word "period" which strongly implies a specific duration. They also regard the *Fuger* court's conclusion as incompatible with § 1325(b)(1)(A). It permits the debtor to submit less than all of his projected disposable income if unsecured creditors will nevertheless be paid in full. Permitting the debtor's plan to last less than the full duration of the applicable commitment period in other circumstances would, according to these courts, render § 1325(b)(1)(A) meaningless.[182]

If § 1325(b)(1)(B) establishes a temporal requirement, debtors with household income below their state's median are required to submit only a three-year plan. Nevertheless, the debtors might still find it desirable to seek court approval of a longer plan, up to a maximum of five years.[183] They may do so with the approval of the court.[184]

Cases decided before the 2005 Amendments indicated that an extension beyond the presumptive three-year period was justified by the debtor's inability to pay priority or secured debts fully in such a short time.[185] Likewise, extension beyond three years might be justified to enable the debtor to cure a default and reinstate a loan that the debtor might not be able to cure within three years.[186] Extending the duration of a plan beyond three years might also enhance the feasibility of the debtor's plan, by reducing the amount of monthly payments to be submitted to the trustee.[187] Moreover, some debtors who own substantial non-exempt assets will be unable to satisfy the "best interests" test in only three years, and will need the additional time to ensure that their unsecured creditors receive at least the equivalent of what they would have obtained in a liquidation case.[188] The debtor's simple desire to repay a larger portion of his debts might also justify extension to a maximum of five years, particularly if it enables the debtor to repay creditors in full.[189] However, the debtor cannot be compelled to extend his plan for this reason alone.[190]

---

[182] In re Schanuth, 342 B.R. 601, 607–08 (Bankr. W.D. Mo. 2006); In re Davis, 348 B.R. 449, 455 (Bankr. E.D. Mich. 2006).

[183] Bankruptcy Code § 1322(d)(2).

[184] Bankruptcy Code § 1322(d)(2). To appreciate how long a time period this is, recall the last time you prepared a household budget and resolved to live within its limits.

[185] *E.g.*, In re Norris, 175 B.R. 515 (Bankr. M.D. Fla. 1994).

[186] *See* In re Pierce, 82 B.R. 874, 881 (Bankr. S.D. Ohio 1987).

[187] In re Capodanno, 94 B.R. 62 (Bankr. E.D. Pa. 1988).

[188] Bankruptcy Code § 1325(a)(4); *see* § 18.08[E][1] Best Interests of Creditors, *infra.*

[189] In re Robertson, 84 B.R. 109 (Bankr. S.D. Ohio 1988).

[190] *See* In re Greer, 60 B.R. 547 (Bankr. C.D. Cal. 1986); In re Festa, 65 B.R. 85 (Bankr.

[E] Payments to Creditors with Unsecured Claims

Chapter 13 contains two requirements with respect to payments that must be made to unsecured creditors that hold general non-priority claims. First, the plan must be in the "best interests of creditors" in that it must ensure that unsecured creditors receive at least the same value they would have received if the debtor had liquidated under Chapter 7. Second, unless unsecured creditors are being paid in full, the plan must provide for the debtor to pay all of his "projected disposable income" to "unsecured creditors" for the duration of his three-or five-year plan. As will be seen, this second requirement has been linked to the "disposable income" calculation in the new "means testing" standards of the 2005 Amendments. The calculation itself is both complex and the subject of interpretive disputes — its interface with Chapter 13 adds its own set of complexities.

[1] Best Interests of Creditors

The "best interests of creditors" test[191] ensures that creditors receive no less from the debtor in a Chapter 13 case than they would have received if the debtor had liquidated in Chapter 7. This makes perfect sense. Chapter 13 would be of little benefit to creditors if they could be compelled both to both wait for payment *and* to receive less than they would have received if the debtor had simply liquidated.

Thus, § 1324(a)(4) requires that:

> the value, as of the effective date of the plan, of property to be distributed under the plan on account of each allowed unsecured claim is not less than the amount that would be paid on such claim if the estate of the debtor were liquidated under chapter 7 . . . on such date.[192]

Application of the best interest test requires a detailed liquidation analysis of the debtor's situation. Usually this involves comparing the value of payments to be made to unsecured creditors under the plan with the amount of non-exempt equity in the estate. If the present value of the payments to be made under the plan is less than the non-exempt equity, the best interests test is not satisfied.

[a] Liquidation Value of Debtor's Non-Exempt Equity

Consider a simple example involving a debtor with only a few assets: a home worth $100,000, a car worth $15,000, and various items of clothing

S.D. Ohio 1986); *but see* In re Walsh, 224 B.R. 231 (Bankr. M.D. Ga. 1998) (three-year plan inadequate with respect to debtor seeking to use Chapter 13 to retain a non-essential automobile while making negligible payments to unsecured creditors).

[191] The phrase "best interests of creditors" is derived from the same test employed under the Bankruptcy Act. Bankruptcy Act §§ 651, 652(a) (repealed 1978). The traditional phrase appears nowhere in the Bankruptcy Code but remains in wide use to refer to § 1325(a)(4). *E.g.*, In re Van Der Heide, 164 F.3d 1183 (8th Cir. 1999).

[192] Bankruptcy Code § 1325(a)(4).

and household furnishings, worth 3,000.[193] The home is subject to a $70,000 mortgage and is eligible for a $20,000 homestead exemption, leaving $10,000 of non-exempt equity. The car is subject to a $12,000 security interest and is eligible for a $2,000 exemption, leaving $1,000 of non-exempt equity. The debtor owns his clothing and furnishings outright and they are entirely exempt. The amount of secured creditors' claims and the amount of the debtor's exemptions must be deducted from the value of these assets, because in a liquidation, these sums would not be available for distribution to unsecured creditors.[194] Thus, the debtor's estate is comprised of $11,000 that would be available for distribution to unsecured creditors in a liquidation case. To paraphrase § 1324(a)(4): the present value of plan payments to unsecured creditors must not be less than the $11,000 that these creditors would receive in a liquidation case. If the present value of the total that will be distributed to unsecured creditors is less than the $11,000 they would have received in liquidation, the plan is not in the best interests of all creditors.

[b] Valuation of Debtor's Assets in Best Interests Analysis

This analysis presumes that it is easy to determine the value of the debtor's assets. The value of the debtor's clothes and furniture is probably not worth fighting over, unless the debtor owns some unusually valuable items. Because the best interests test is based on the amount unsecured creditors would receive in liquidation, it is appropriate to use the liquidation value of the debtor's assets in determining their value.

Before the 2005 Amendments, bankruptcy courts rejected suggestions that the replacement value standard of *Associates Commercial Corp. v. Rash,*[195] which is used to determine the value of secured creditors's claims,[196] should be used in determining whether the best interests test has been met.[197] Further, because real estate agents and auctioneers expect to be paid for their efforts, the administrative costs that would be incurred to realize this value should be deducted from their estimated worth.[198]

---

[193] Until you have been to an estate sale, it is difficult to realize how economically worthless most of these items are. At the estate sale following the death of his mother, one of your co-authors watched most of the 360 lots of household items that had surrounded him during his childhood walk out the door with strangers for a total of approximately $15,000. Eight unusually valuable items (a set of silverware and some antiques) brought about $5,000 of this amount. The average price for the remaining items was about $28, with many items selling for $5 or less. After the auctioneer's percentage was paid, the sale netted about $10,000. Everyone agreed that it was one of the best estate sales they had seen.

[194] *E.g.,* In re Ruggles, 210 B.R. 57, 59–60 (Bankr. D. Vt. 1997).

[195] 520 U.S. 953 (1997).

[196] *See* § 18.08[F][4][c] Valuation of the Collateral, *infra.*

[197] In re Delbrugge, 347 B.R. 536 (Bankr. W.D. Va. 2006).

[198] In re Delbrugge, 347 B.R. 536 (Bankr. N.D. W. Va. 2006); In re Dixon, 140 B.R. 945 (Bankr. W.D.N.Y. 1992);*see also* In re Young, 153 B.R. 886, 888 (Bankr. D. Neb. 1993) (deducting capital gains tax).

However, new § 506(a)(2) now requires use of the property's replacement value.[199]

Section 1325(a)(4) refers to payments made to "each creditor." Thus, the best interests test applies to each unsecured creditor, rather than to unsecured creditors as a class. But, if the class of unsecured creditors is receiving less than the amount than it would receive in liquidation, the plan fails the best interests test as to at least one of these creditors, even if it satisfies the test as to some others.[200]

The fact that a creditors' claim would not be discharged in a Chapter 7 liquidation case is not part of the determination of whether the plan is in the best interests of an unsecured creditor, even if the creditor's claim is subject to discharge in Chapter 13. The best interests test depends on a calculation of what an unsecured creditor would receive from the liquidation of the debtor's estate in a Chapter 7 case, not what the creditor might ultimately recover from the debtor as a result of the non-dischargeability of the debt. However, some courts have relied on the non-dischargeability of a creditor's claim in Chapter 7 as the basis for determining that a plan providing for nominal payments to unsecured creditors was not in good faith.[201]

[c] Present Value

The key word in § 1325(a)(4) is *value*. The value of whatever payments the creditor receives must be worth at least the amount the creditor would have received if the debtor had liquidated. Because payments under a plan are made over several years, the payments made must be more than the nominal amount that the creditor would have received if the debtor had liquidated.

Consider a simple example in which an unsecured creditor, owed $1,000, would have received the proverbial 10¢ on the dollar, or a total of $100, if the debtor had elected to liquidate under Chapter 7. A plan that provided for payment of a total of $100 in monthly cash payments of approximately $1.66 per month over a 5-year period would result in the creditor's receiving something that was *worth* less than the $100 the creditor would have received if the debtor had simply liquidated. To compensate the creditor for

---

199 In re Steakley, No. 06-31181, — B.R. — , 2007 Bankr. LEXIS 496 (Bankr. E.D. Tenn. Jan. 26, 2007); In re De Anda-Ramirez, Nos. KS-06-086, 06-20892-13, — B.R. — , 2007 Bankr. LEXIS 168 (10th Cir. BAP January 29, 2007); *see* In re McElroy, 339 B.R. 185, 189 n.2 (Bankr. C.D. Ill. 2006) (acknowledging that § 506(a)(2) would require use of replacement cost in cases filed after effective date of the 2005 Amendments).

200 In many cases it is inappropriate to treat creditors with non-priority unsecured claims differently from one another, but this is sometimes done. *See* § 18.07[A] Classification of Claims, *supra*.

201 *Compare* Davis v. Mather (In re Davis), 239 B.R. 573 (B.A.P. 10th Cir. 1999) (nominal payment plan not in good faith), *with* In re Smith, 286 F.3d 461 (7th Cir. 2002) (nominal payment to creditors with claims that are nondischargeable in Chapter 7 not dispositive of issue of lack of good faith); *see generally* § 18.08[C] Good Faith, *infra*.

the delay in receiving payment, the Chapter 13 plan must provide for interest on the $100 that the creditor would have received in liquidation.[202]

This creates a difficulty in determining the appropriate rate of interest that must be paid to ensure that the creditor receives the "present value" of what it would have received in liquidation as compensation for the delay in receiving payment. In many Chapter 13 cases, the requirement of § 1325(b) — that the debtor submit all of its disposable income for payments under the plan — eclipses the significance of the best interests tests. In many Chapter 7 cases, unsecured creditors receive nothing. Even where they receive a distribution, the debtor's payment of all of his disposable income for three to five years frequently results in payments that are more than sufficient to give unsecured creditors the same value as what they would have received in liquidation.

In the rare Chapter 13 case where this is not true, the interest rate necessary to satisfy the best interests test is probably based on the standard established by the Supreme Court's 2004 decision in *Till v. SCS Credit Corp.*[203] There, the Court addressed the method used to determine the appropriate rate of interest that must be paid to holders of secured claims under § 1325(a)(5).[204] It required use of the prime interest rate together with an upward adjustment of 1–3% to reflect the creditor's risk of non-payment.

However, a few courts have rejected the use of the *Till* standard with respect to the best interests test of § 1325(a)(4). These courts continue to require the use of whatever method for picking the appropriate rate of interest that they deployed before *Till.*[205] Before *Till,* some courts used a "coerced loan" approach based on market rates available to other lenders for similar loans while others used various "formula" approaches that, like *Till,* started from some form of "risk free" rate and then added a risk adjustment.

---

[202] As one court put it: "[The] Debtor would gladly pay his creditors Tuesday for a hamburger today. However, the Code recognizes that a hamburger eaten today is worth more than payment for it on Tuesday due to the time value of money and, in the view of some courts, the risk of nonpayment." In re Cook, 322 B.R. 336, 339 (Bankr. N.D. Ohio 2005). Students unfamiliar with the combined effects of inflation and risk sometimes fail to comprehend this logic. To drive the point home, one of your authors sometimes suggests that the student loan him $1000 and that the student be repaid in 100 equal monthly payments of $10 each until the $1,000 is fully repaid. At this stage of the discussion, everyone gets the point.

[203] *Cf.* Till v. SCS Credit Corp., 541 U.S. 465 (2004) (present value for secured claims under § 1325(a)(5)).

[204] *See, e.g.,* In re Bivens, 317 B.R. 755 (Bankr. N.D. Ill. 2004); Carmen H. Lonstein & Steven A. Domanowski, *Payment of Post-petition Interest to Unsecured Creditors: Federal Judgment Rate Versus Contract Rate,* 12 Am. Bankr. Inst. L. Rev. 421 (2004).

[205] In re Cook, 322 B.R. 336, 345 (Bankr. N.D. Ohio 2005) (coerced loan approach based on current market interest rates for loans in similar situations). *Cf.* In re American HomePatient, Inc., 420 F.3d 559 (6th Cir. 2005) (applying § 1129(a)(5)); *see* generally § 18.08[F][4][b] Payments Equivalent to Amount of Secured Claim, *infra.*

[d] No-Asset Cases

In many cases, the best interest test has little practical impact. If the debtor's non-exempt equity that would have been distributed to his creditors in Chapter 7 is zero, or would be consumed by the administrative expenses of liquidating the estate, the best interests test is easily satisfied. Even if there were assets available for distribution to creditors in a Chapter 13 debtor's liquidation, the second requirement — that the debtor contribute all of his "projected disposable income" for three to five years — usually requires more to be paid to unsecured creditors than the amount made necessary by the best interests test.

[2] Debtor's Projected Disposable Income

Unless the plan provides for full payment to unsecured creditors, together with interest to compensate them for the delay,[206] the plan must provide for payment of "all of the debtor's projected disposable income [during the three-to five-year plan] . . . to unsecured creditors."[207] Depending on how much of the debtor's projected income is "disposable," this could easily require significantly higher payments to unsecured creditors than what would otherwise be required by the best interests test. The key to determining how much this second standard requires is the meaning of "projected disposable income."

Despite its importance, the Code supplies no definition of "*projected* disposable income," though it does provide a definition of "disposable income." The debtor's disposable income is to be calculated in two alternative ways, depending on whether the debtor's household income is above or below the applicable state median as calculated by the Census Bureau.

[a] Disposable Income for Debtors with Income Above the State Median

The Code's definition of "disposable income" refers to "current monthly income received by the debtor" with a few exclusions, minus amounts "reasonably necessary to be expended" for (1) maintenance and support of the debtor and his dependents, (2) for a limited amount of charitable contributions,[208] and, (3) if the debtor is engaged in a business, for the "continuation, preservation, and operation" of the debtor's business.[209]

[206] Bankruptcy Code § 1325(b)(1)(A). The statutory language refers to the "*value* of property to be distributed under the plan" thus requiring interest on the amount of the claim to ensure that creditors receive the equivalent of full payment of their claims.

[207] Bankruptcy Code § 1325(b)(1)(B).

[208] The code specifies that up to 15% of the debtor's "gross income" may be deducted as an amount "reasonably necessary to be expended . . . for charitable contributions" It remains to be seen whether somewhat less than 15% might be considered reasonably necessary. *See generally* Carol Koenig, *To Tithe or Not to Tithe: The Constitutionality of Tithing in a Chapter 13 Bankruptcy Budget*, 32 Santa Clara L. Rev. 1231 (1992); Anne Mclaughlin, Note, *Tithing in a Chapter 13 Plan: The Requirement of Reasonableness under the Religious Liberty and Charitable Donation Protection Act*, 47 B.C. L. Rev. 375 (2006).

[209] Bankruptcy Code § 1325(b)(2).

However, § 1325(b)(3) directs that amounts reasonably necessary to be expended by the debtor under § 1325(b)(2) are to be determined in accordance with § 707(b)(2)(A) and (B).[210] This raises the question of whether categories of expenses referred to in § 1325(b)(2), such as charitable contributions, but not covered by the means testing calculations of § 707(b)(2)(A) or (B), may be deducted in determining the debtor's disposable income. The first few courts to address the issue have ruled that § 1325(b)(3) restricts the types of expenses that may be deducted in determining disposable income, rather than simply specifying the amounts that may be deducted for items covered by both § 1325(b)(2) and § 707(b)(2)(A) and (B).[211]

[i] Income

The calculation of disposable income starts with "current monthly income," defined in § 101(10A). As explained in more detail in connection with Chapter 7's means testing provisions, current monthly income is based on nearly all of the debtor's actual income during the six month period before his petition, excluding only social security benefits and certain war crimes and terrorism victims' benefits.[212] However, unlike the standards for means testing, Chapter 13's definition of disposable income expressly excludes "child support, foster care payments, or disability payments" for dependent children, at least to the extent these income items are "reasonably necessary to be expended" for the child.[213]

[ii] "Means Testing" Expenses for Maintenance or Support

If the debtor's household income is greater than the state median income for similarly sized households, Chapter 7's rules for means testing are used to determine the amounts that are to be deducted from the debtor's income in calculating the debtor's disposable income. As explained in more detail in connection with means testing under Chapter 7,[214] this includes sums specified by the IRS to be deducted from the debtor's income for basic living expenses and various insurance payments,[215] limited children's school

---

210 Bankruptcy Code § 1325(b)(3); *see* In re Fuller, 346 B.R. 472 (Bankr. S.D. Ill. 2006).

211 In re Fuller, 346 B.R. 472 (Bankr. S.D. Ill. 2006).

212 Bankruptcy Code § 101(10A); *see* § 17.03[B][2][a] Current Monthly Income, *supra*.

213 Bankruptcy Code § 1325(b)(2). This exclusion creates an interpretive issue concerning whether the dependent child should be included or excluded in the size of the debtor's household for the purposes of determining the extent of expenditures to be deducted from income in calculating the amount of income that is disposable. Official Bankruptcy Form B22C does not provide for deduction of these items of income.

214 *See* § 17.03[B][2][b] Expenses, *supra*.

215 Bankruptcy Code § 707(b)(2)(A)(ii).

expenses,[216] sums contractually required to be paid to secured creditors,[217] amounts necessary to satisfy priority claims,[218] and other amounts.[219]

Deduction of amounts contractually required to be paid to secured creditors injects several difficult interpretive questions into the calculation. The Code specifies that two amounts are to be deducted in calculating the debtor's disposable income:

> (I) amounts scheduled as contractually due to secured creditors in each month of the 60 months following the date of the petition; and (II) any additional payments to secured creditors necessary for the debtor, in filing a plan under chapter 13 of this title, to maintain possession of the debtor's primary residence, motor vehicle, or other property necessary for the support of the debtor and the debtor's dependents, that serves as collateral for secured debts.[220]

According to this language, read in conjunction with § 1325(b)(3), the amount of payments "scheduled as contractually due" are to be deducted in calculating the amount of the debtor's disposable income, even though retaining the collateral might be frivolous.[221] Further, it contemplates deducting the amount contractually scheduled to be paid without regard to the debtor's intent to retain possession of the collateral.[222] Deducting amounts scheduled to be paid for collateral not reasonably necessary for the debtor's support effectively overrules pre-BAPCPA decisions like *In re Hedges*[223] and *In re Brooks*,[224] in which debtors were not permitted to deduct payments for debts that were secured by luxury items in determining the amount of their disposable income. The question becomes far more difficult when dealing with items such as children's musical instruments or sports equipment, which might not be considered luxury goods but which are not necessary for their support.[225]

In addition, the IRS standards on which means testing is based, provide a deduction for housing and transportation expenses. The Code seems to

---

216 Bankruptcy Code § 707(b)(2)(A)(ii)(IV).

217 Bankruptcy Code § 707(b)(2)(A)(iii).

218 Bankruptcy Code § 707(b)(2)(A)(iv).

219 Bankruptcy Code § 707(b)(2)(A)-(B). Among the other amounts to be deducted, as explained in more detail in connection with means testing, are amounts reasonably necessary to protect the debtor and his family from family violence, sums reasonably necessary for the care and support of an elderly, chronically ill, or disabled member of the debtor's household or family, and housing and utility expenses in excess of what is permitted by the IRS schedules. Bankruptcy Code § 707(b)(2)(A)(ii)(I), (II) & (V).

220 Bankruptcy Code § 707(b)(2)(A)(iii).

221 Eugene Wedoff, *Means Testing in the New 707(b)*, 79 Am. Bankr. L.J. 231, 274 (2005).

222 *See* Official Bankruptcy Form B22C, Line 47. This form instructs debtors to deduct the amount of the average monthly payment "for each of your debts that is secured by an interest in property that you own."

223 68 B.R. 18 (Bankr. E.D. Va. 1986) (boat).

224 241 B.R. 184 (Bankr. S.D. Ohio 1999) (recreational vehicle).

225 *See* In re King, 308 B.R. 522 (Bankr. D. Kan. 2004) (adult college student child's auto payments not deducted from income in calculating disposable earnings).

permit deducting these expenses from the debtor's income *and* deducting amounts contractually required to be paid to secured creditors, even though they represent some of the same housing and transportation expenses included in the IRS standards. As explained in connection with Chapter 7 means testing, this results in deducting these expenses twice in determining the debtor's projected monthly income.

Likewise, §§ 1325(b)(3) and 707(b)(2)(A)(iii)(I) require the deduction of amounts "scheduled as contractually due," even though the debtor's plan might provide for a cramdown of the creditor's claim and reduce the amount of payments that will be made to these creditors.[226] Thus, the calculation to determine the debtor's disposable income might deduct the payments that are contractually owed to the creditor even though the debtor's plan does not provide for paying this full amount to the creditor.

On the other hand, debtors who purchase luxury items in anticipation of filing a Chapter 13 petition and diverting income to pay for these unnecessary items may be found to have acted in bad faith in violation of § 1325(a)(3).[227] Further, there is some authority that the debtor's effort to retain collateral which is not reasonably necessary for the maintenance and support of the debtor and his dependents constitutes bad faith, even if the asset was not acquired in an attempt to shelter income by retaining unnecessary property during the plan.[228]

The text of § 1325(b)(3) is bound to create difficulties, particularly for courts who heed the Supreme Court's nearly constant drum-beat about using the "plain meaning" of statutory language. For example, it is completely unclear how the administrative expenses of Chapter 13 cases should be handled. The reference to § 707(b)(2)(A), in § 1325(b)(3), seemingly requires deduction of the hypothetical administrative expenses of a Chapter 13 case from the debtor's income in determining the amount of income available for payment into the plan, even though those payments will again be deducted, pursuant to § 1322(a)(2), as amounts required to be paid to the trustee under the plan as part of the 100% payment of administrative expense claims.

Moreover, deducting from income actual payments that are contractually required to be made to secured creditors, regardless of whether retention of the collateral that secures such debt is appropriate for a debtor in financial difficulty, might easily result in a dramatically lowering of the debtor's "disposable income" while the debtor maintains an otherwise extravagant lifestyle, rich with encumbered but luxurious assets.

226 Bankruptcy Code § 1325(a)(5)(B); *see* § 18.08[F] Treatment of Secured Claims — Chapter 13 Secured Creditor Cramdown, *infra*.

227 *See* In re Young, 237 F.3d 1168 (10th Cir. 2001) (affirming finding that purchase of luxury auto was in bad faith).

228 In re Walsh, 224 B.R. 231 (Bankr. M.D. Ga. 1998) (additional car used to transport debtor's grandchildren).

[iii] Charitable Contributions[229]

In calculating disposable income, debtors appear to be permitted to deduct "amounts reasonably necessary to be expended . . . (ii) for charitable contributions" up to to 15% of their "gross income"[230] This could be a hefty sum. However, it is not clear whether large (or even small) charitable contributions are "reasonably necessary" as they must be in order to be deducted from the debtor's "current monthly income" to determine his "disposable income." Moreover, debtors whose household income is above the state median are directed to calculate their disposable income "in accordance with [§ 707(b)(2)(A) and (B)]."[231] Sections 707(b)(2)(A) and (B) make no provision for deducting charitable contributions from a debtor's income for purposes of the Chapter 7 means test.[232] Thus, the text of § 1325(b)(3) prevents debtors with income above the state median from deducting any charitable contributions they wish to make from their disposable income.[233]

[iv] Business Expenses of Debtors Engaged in Business

Sole proprietors are eligible for Chapter 13 relief as long as their debts do not exceed Chapter 13's limits.[234] Individual Chapter 13 debtors engaged in business will naturally need to spend a good portion of their income to keep the business running. Accordingly, § 1325(b)(2)(B) permits these debtors to deduct "expenditures necessary for the continuation, preservation, and operation" of their business in calculating their disposable income.[235] This could include expenses for the purchase and maintenance of office equipment, inventory expenses, employees' salaries, and other continuing expenses necessary to keep the doors of the debtor's business open.

[b] Disposable Income for Debtors with Income Below the State Median

The income of debtors with household income below the applicable state median is calculated in the same manner as it is for those with household income above the median, but without resort to Chapter 7's means testing rules to determine the "amounts reasonably necessary to be expended" for

---

229 Anne Mclaughlin, Note, *Tithing in a Chapter 13 Plan: The Requirement of Reasonableness under the Religious Liberty and Charitable Donation Protection Act*, 47 B.C. L. Rev. 375 (2006); Todd J. Zywicki, *Rewrite the Bankruptcy Laws, Not the Scriptures: Protecting a Bankruptcy Debtor's Right to Tithe*, 1998 Wis. L. Rev. 1223 (1998).

230 Bankruptcy Code § 1325(b)(2)(A)(ii).

231 Bankruptcy Code § 1325(b)(3).

232 *See* In re Fuller, 346 B.R. 472 (Bankr. S.D. Ill. 2006).

233 In re Diagostino, 347 B.R. 116 (Bankr. N.D.N.Y. 2006); In re Tranmer, — B.R. — , No. 06-60353-13, 2006 Bankr. LEXIS 3150 (Bankr. D. Mont. Nov 16, 2006).

234 *See* § 6.02[B][6][c] Chapter 13 Debt Limits, *supra.*

235 Bankruptcy Code § 1325(b)(2)(B).

the debtor's maintenance and support. Instead, the amount of expenses that should be deducted from the debtor' income to determine "disposable income" is largely discretionary, as it was before the 2005 Amendments.

Such amounts might be higher or lower than amounts specified in § 707(b) and the IRS Guidelines which are stipulated to be used by those with household income above the state median. This also might mean that the court will have greater discretion in determining whether payments to secured creditors are not reasonably necessary for the debtor's maintenance or support. The means testing rules in Chapter 7 provide for the deduction of all payments to secured creditors, without regard to whether the collateral that secures their claims is reasonably necessary for the debtor's support. For debtors below the state median, a further inquiry into the debtor's retention of the collateral may be appropriate.

[c] "Projected" Disposable Income

Section 1325(b)(2) requires Chapter 13 debtors to pay all of their "projected disposable income" to their unsecured creditors. However, despite the complex definition of "disposable income" explained above, the Code contains no definition of "projected disposable income." While it might be presumed that "disposable income" and "projected disposable income" were intended to be derived from the same formula, courts are not in agreement that this is the case.[236]

Several bankruptcy courts have concluded that the addition of the word "projected" in § 1325(b)(1) requires the court to consider not only debtors' past income and expenses, but also their predicted future income.[237] Debtors' projected income controls, regardless of whether it is higher or lower than the debtor's past income.[238] This result was reached even though calculations conducted pursuant to Official Bankruptcy Forms are based solely on the debtor's past income.[239] As one court explained: "Had Congress intended 'projected disposable income' to be synonymous with section 1325(b)(2)'s 'disposable income' Congress could have deleted the word 'projected' from section 1325(b)(1)(B) or defined 'projected gross income,' rather than only 'disposable income,' in section 1325(b)(2)."[240]

---

[236] *See* In re Rotunda, 349 B.R. 324, 327 (Bankr. D.N.Y. 2006).

[237] *See* In re Edmunds, 350 B.R. 636 (Bankr. D.S.C. 2006); In re Demonica, 345 B.R. 895 (Bankr. N.D. Ill. 2006); In re Kibbe, 342 B.R. 411 (Bankr. D.N.H. 2006); In re Jass, 340 B.R. 411 (Bankr. D. Utah 2006); In re Hardacre, 338 B.R. 718 (Bankr. N.D. Tex. 2006); In re Fuller, 346 B.R. 472 (Bankr. S.D. Ill. 2006).

[238] *E.g.*, In re Grady, 343 B.R. 747 (Bankr. N.D. Ga. 2006) (projected income lower than past income due to spouse's development of heart condition that prevented her from working).

[239] Official Bankruptcy Form B22C makes precisely this assumption, and bases the amount a Chapter 13 debtor must pay into his plan solely on the debtor's "current monthly income" as determined under § 101(10A). *See* Official Bankruptcy Form B22C, Line 1 ("All figures *must* reflect average monthly income for the six calendar months prior to filing the bankruptcy case.") (emphasis added).

[240] In re Kibbe, 342 B.R. 411 (Bankr. D.N.H. 2006).

Other courts disagree.[241] These decisions regard "disposable income" as a defined term based on the calculations mandated by § 1325(b)(2) and that the projection is to be based exclusively on the debtor's disposable income as that term is defined. This interpretation permits debtors who, as a result of improvements in their financial circumstances, seem capable of making payments to unsecured creditors to obtain confirmation of a plan that pays these creditors nothing. However, courts taking this approach regard this as a problem that Congress created and is for Congress to correct. As one court explained: "[E]ven if this law is producing unintended results, it is the job of Congress to amend the statute."[242] Quoting the United States Supreme Court's decision in *Lamie v. United States Trustee*,[243] the court said: " 'It is beyond our province to rescue Congress from its drafting errors, and to provide for what we might think . . . is the preferred result.' "[244]

[d] Payment to "Unsecured Creditors"

The text of § 1325(b)(1)(B) requires the plan to call for distribution of all of the debtor's projected disposable income during the three-or five-year mandatory duration of the plan to "unsecured creditors."[245] The precise meaning of this poorly articulated rule remains obscure. First, the remainder of the Bankruptcy Code refers not to "creditors" or to "unsecured creditors" but to "holders of allowed claims" and "holders of allowed unsecured claims." If Congress intended the debtor's projected disposable income to be distributed to holders of "allowed unsecured claims," it should have used this term, which has an established meaning. It is unlikely that Congress intended for payments to holders of disallowed claims to be included; however, the Code's use of the term "unsecured creditors" leaves the door open for that possible interpretation.

The phrase "unsecured creditors" also creates some uncertainty as to whether payments to holders of unsecured priority claims should be considered as part of this calculation. The deduction of amounts to be paid to holders of "all priority claims"[246] from the debtor's "disposable income"[247] suggests that amounts paid under the plan to these unsecured creditors should not be included when calculating whether § 1325(b)(1)(B)'s standard has been satisfied, but the plain meaning of the phrase "unsecured creditors" indicates otherwise.

Consider, for example, a debtor with "projected disposable income," after deducting the amounts specified in § 707(b)(2)(A) and (B), of $30,000 over the five-year period of his plan. Assume further that this $30,000 figure

[241] In re Guzman, 345 B.R. 640 (Bankr. E.D. Wis., 2006); In re Alexander, 344 B.R. 742 (Bankr. E.D.N.C. 2006); In re Barr, 341 B.R. 181 (Bankr. M.D.N.C. 2006).

[242] In re Alexander, 344 B.R. 742, 748 (Bankr. D.N.C. 2006).

[243] 540 U.S. 526, 533 (2004).

[244] In re Alexander, 344 B.R. 742, 748 (Bankr. D.N.C. 2006).

[245] Bankruptcy Code § 1325(b)(1)(b).

[246] Bankruptcy Code § 707(b)(2)(A)(iv).

[247] Bankruptcy Code § 1325(b)(2)(A)(i), (b)(3).

was reached after deducting amounts necessary to pay the debtor's ex-spouse's unsecured § 507(a)(1) priority claim for past due support, as specified by the means test formula of § 707(b)(2)(A)(iv). Amounts to be paid under the plan to the debtor's ex-spouse on account of this priority claims would reduce the amount that would have to be distributed to other unsecured creditors. This would, in effect, result in the deduction of the amount to be paid for the priority support claim twice, in undoubted contravention of Congress' intent, but consistent with what otherwise might easily be viewed as the "plain meaning" of the Code's language. Perhaps significantly, the Official Bankruptcy Forms call for the deduction of payments to holders of priority claims in calculating the amount of a debtor's "disposable income."[248]

[F] Treatment of Secured Claims — Chapter 13 Secured Creditor Cramdown

Chapter 13 permits debtors to handle secured claims in a wide variety of ways, depending on the debtor's desires and abilities and on certain aspects of the creditor's claim. Debtors may sometimes wish simply to surrender the collateral to the creditor. A few debtors may be successful in persuading a secured creditor to "accept" less than what the creditor is entitled to demand. Chapter 13 facilitates both of these alternatives, but it also provides for the cramdown of most secured claims, permitting the debtor to retain the collateral and make payments to the secured creditor on terms the creditor might not prefer. For debtors who seek Chapter 13 relief in order to maintain possession of property subject to secured creditors' claims, cramdown is the most common treatment of secured claims. As will be seen, its precise form varies, depending on the nature of the collateral and the creditor's claim.

[1] Surrender of the Collateral to the Creditor

Section 1325(a)(5)(C) permits a plan to be confirmed over the objection of a secured creditor if "the debtor surrenders the property securing such claim to [the creditor]."[249] Surrender is preferred by debtors who lack enough income to satisfy the claim and by debtors who do not desire to retain possession of the collateral.

Before the 2005 Amendments, debtors who attempted to retain luxury items sometimes found that surrender of the collateral was the only way to obtain confirmation of their plans. The 2005 Amendments, which *require* amounts owed to secured creditors to be deducted from income that otherwise would be available to distribute to unsecured creditors, may change this result. However, the newly promulgated Official Bankruptcy Forms,[250]

---

[248] *See* Official Bankruptcy Form B22C, Line 49.

[249] Bankruptcy Code § 1325(a)(5)(C).

[250] Official Bankruptcy Form B22C, Line 47, specifies that debtors should deduct amounts for the average monthly payment "for each of your debtors that is secured by an interest in property that you own."

inertia,[251] and debtors' attorneys' reluctance to risk the imposition of sanctions all may lead to continuation of the past practice.

[2] Secured Creditor Acceptance of Plan

Alternatively, § 1325(a)(5)(A) permits a debtor's plan to be confirmed, regardless of what payments it requires to be submitted to a secured creditor, as long as the creditor "has accepted the plan."[252] Although a few of the debtor's family members might agree to accept less than they are otherwise legally entitled to demand, acceptance of a Chapter 13 plan by a secured creditor is so rare that there is no routine procedural mechanism to seek acceptances from secured creditors.[253]

[3] Cure and Reinstatement[254]

As explained earlier, plans sometimes provide for the debtor to cure any pre-petition defaults on obligations to holders of secured claims and reinstate the stream of scheduled payments as if there had been no default.[255] In cases involving mortgages on residential real estate, this "de-acceleration" may be the only adjustment of the secured creditor's rights that is permitted.[256]

In *In re Taddeo*, one of the early decisions in which the right to cure was recognized, the debtors had fallen into default on their home mortgage.[257] When the creditor brought an action to foreclose on the mortgage, the Taddeos tendered full payment of all of their arrearages, but the creditor refused to accept the debtors' proposed cure. The Taddeos responded by filing a Chapter 13 petition. They filed a plan proposing to pay the arrearages in several equal monthly installments and simultaneously to resume making regular monthly principal and interest payments according to the amortization schedule required by the mortgage agreement. The court held that § 1322(b)(2)'s proscription against modifying home mortgages did not prevent the debtors from utilizing § 1322(b)(3) or (b)(5) to cure their default and thus negate the effect of the creditor's acceleration of the

---

[251] "Lex I: Corpus omne perseverare in statu suo quiescendi vel movendi uniformiter in directum, nisi quatenus a viribus impressis cogitur statum illum mutare." Sir Isaac Newton, Philosophiae Naturalis Principia Mathematica (1687) (translation: Every object in a state of uniform motion tends to remain in that state of motion unless an external force is applied to it). It is the most powerful force in the universe.

[252] Bankruptcy Code § 1325(a)(5)(A).

[253] This is in sharp distinction to what occurs in Chapter 11, where acceptances are solicited from all creditors pursuant to Bankruptcy Code § 1125. *See* § 19.09 Acceptance of Plan by Holders of Claims and Interests; Disclosure and Voting, *supra*.

[254] *See* David Gray Carlson, *Car Wars: Valuation Standards in Chapter 13 Bankruptcy Cases*, 13 Bankr. Dev. J. 1, 2 (1996).

[255] *See* § 18.07[C] Cure and Waiver of Defaults; Reinstatement, *supra*.

[256] Bankruptcy Code § 1322(b)(2); *see* § 18.07[C] Cure and Waiver of Defaults; Reinstatement, *supra*.

[257] 685 F.2d 24 (2d Cir. 1982).

mortgage debt. In effect, such a cure and reinstatement was not a modification of the secured creditor's rights, or if it was a modification, it was one expressly permitted by § 1322(b)(5).

Payments made to cure the debtor's arrearages must be made over a reasonable time and are customarily through the standing trustee. Regular monthly mortgage payments, on the other hand, are usually made directly to the creditor, without the involvement of the trustee. This has the advantage of saving the administrative expenses that would normally accompany the trustee's distribution of plan funds.

The right to cure defaults and reinstate a mortgage does not last forever. Permitting debtors to restore the status quo after their home has been sold at foreclosure would have a deleterious effect on the willingness of buyers to purchase property at such sales. Accordingly, the right to de-accelerate a residential mortgage does not apply if the property has already been sold at a foreclosure sale that has been conducted in compliance with whatever nonbankruptcy law applies to the sale.[258]

[4] Cramdown of Chapter 13 Plan over Secured Creditor's Objection[259]

In many cases, Chapter 13 permits debtors to confirm a plan over the objection of a secured creditor who is dissatisfied with its treatment under the plan. The plan can be confirmed as long as it: (1) permits the creditor to retain its lien on the collateral; (2) provides for making payments to the creditor that are the equivalent of the amount of the allowed secured claim; and (3) ensures that the stream of payments on claims secured by personal property are sufficient to "adequately protect" the creditor for the duration of the plan.[260]

[a] Retention of the Creditor's Lien

The requirement that the secured claim holder retain its lien ensures that the creditor will not be left with an unsecured claim against the debtor if the plan fails. Section 1325(a)(5)(B)(i) requires that the creditor retain its lien until the underlying debt is fully paid or is discharged in Chapter 13. A Chapter 13 discharge is normally only obtained when the debtor fully performs the terms of his plan.[261] Permitting the creditor to retain its lien for the full underlying debt preserves the creditor's secured status in the event that the debtor does not perform the terms of his plan fully and dismisses or converts the case without receiving a Chapter 13 discharge.

Consider a creditor with a security interest in the debtor's $2,000 garden tractor, securing a $3,000 debt. A creditor in this situation has a $2,000

---

[258] Bankruptcy Code § 1322(c)(1).

[259] Michael Elson, Note, *Say "Ahhh!": A New Approach for Determining the Cram Down Interest Rate After* Till v. SCS Credit, 27 Cardozo L. Rev. 1921 (2006).

[260] Bankruptcy Code § 1325(a)(5)(B)(i)-(iii).

[261] Bankruptcy Code § 1328(a); *see* § 13.05[C][1] Discharge upon Completion of Plan, *supra*.

secured claim and a $1,000 unsecured claim. The plan might provide for regular monthly installment payments to the creditor, in an amount sufficient to amortize the $2,000 secured portion of the claim. It might also provide for payments in addition to those distributed to other unsecured creditors in partial satisfaction of the $1,000 unsecured deficiency claim. If, after one year of payments, the secured claim is whittled down to around $1,700, with nothing yet paid with respect to the unsecured portion of the claim, and the debtor defaults, the creditor still has its lien securing the entire $2,700 balance. This provides the creditor with some measure of protection from the risk that the court had undervalued the collateral at $2,000; it also provides the creditor with the ability to repossess the collateral after dismissal of the case unless the debtor pays the full $2,700 remaining due. Lest there be any doubt about this result, § 1325(a)(5)(B)(i)(II) specifies that "if the [Chapter 13] case . . . is dismissed or converted without completion of the plan, such lien shall also be retained by such holder to the extent recognized by applicable nonbankruptcy law."[262]

This will have a huge effect on partially secured claims dealt with by plans that fail after a substantial portion (or even all) of the secured portion of the debt is paid. Consider the result in the same situation if the plan fails after four and a half years of payments, with the secured portion of the claim having been paid after four years, but with a $500 balance due on the unsecured portion of the underlying debt. Even though the secured claim has been fully paid under the plan, § 1325(a)(5)(B)(i)(II) means the creditor's lien will survive as security for the unpaid $500 of the underlying debt, as recognized by applicable non-bankruptcy law. This overrules cases decided before the 2005 Amendments that eliminated the creditor's lien once the amount of the secured portion of the claim was paid.[263]

[b] Payments Equivalent to Amount of Secured Claim

The most important aspect of secured creditor cramdown, not only in Chapter 13, but also under Chapters 11 and 12, is the requirement that the "value, as of the effective date of the plan, of property to be distributed under the plan on account of such claim is not less than the allowed amount of such claim."[264] The key component of this passage, as it is in connection with the best interests test of § 1325(a)(4), is "value." For a stream of payments to have the same value as the amount of the creditor's claim, the payments must include an interest component to compensate the creditor for the delay in receiving payment.

After more than twenty-five years of debate in the lower courts, the Supreme Court in 2004 ruled that the rate of interest required to be paid to secured creditors in Chapter 13 is the prime rate as augmented by an

---

262 Bankruptcy Code § 1325(a)(5)(B)(i)(II).

263 *E.g.*, In re Rheaume, 296 B.R. 313 (Bankr. D. Vt. 2003).

264 Bankruptcy Code § 1325(a)(5)(B)(ii).

amount necessary to reflect the risk of the debtor's default.[265] However, the plurality nature of the Supreme Court's opinion in *Till v. SCS Credit Corp.* leaves some doubt as to the lasting effect of the Court's decision.[266]

In addition, the *Till* Court provided guidance about the factors that should affect the amount over the prime rate that should be required. It indicated that bankruptcy courts should consider: (1) the probability that the plan will fail, (2) the rate at which the collateral will depreciate, (3) the general liquidity of the market for the collateral, and (4) the administrative expenses of enforcement.[267] The Court further cautioned that the

> requirement obligates the court to select a rate high enough to compensate the creditor for its risk but not so high as to doom the plan. If the court determines that the likelihood of default is so high as to necessitate an "eye-popping" interest rate, . . . the plan probably should not be confirmed [presumably on the ground that performance is not feasible within the meaning of § 1325(a)(6)].[268]

Cases decided since *Till v. SCS Credit Corp.* indicate that lower courts will follow the Court's "formula approach" setting the rate of interest at 1% to 3% above the prime rate.[269] Moreover, most courts have ruled that *Till* retains its vitality after the 2005 Amendments, and have rejected creditors' arguments for requiring the debtor to pay a higher contract rate of interest, even if the collateral is subject to the new hanging paragraph added at the end of § 1325(a) with respect to purchase money security interests in many motor vehicles.[270] However, the extent to which *Till* applies to secured creditor cramdown in Chapters 11 and 12, and the rate of interest due to unsecured creditors under a plan, remain up in the air.[271]

[c] Valuation of the Collateral

Another key component of the determination of whether the payments made to a secured creditor are the equivalent of the amount of the secured claim is the determination of the actual amount of the secured claim. Under § 506,[272] if the collateral is worth more than the debt, the secured claim is the full allowed amount of the debt. This rarely occurs in Chapter 13

---

[265] Till v. SCS Credit Corp., 541 U.S. 456 (2004).

[266] James D. Walker Jr. & Amber Nickell, *Bankruptcy*, 55 Mercer L. Rev. 1101, 1127–28 (2004); Carmen H. Lonstein & Steven A. Domanowski, *Payment of Post-petition Interest to Unsecured Creditors: Federal Judgment Rate Versus Contract Rate*, 12 Am. Bankr. Inst. L. Rev. 421 (2004).

[267] *See also* Michael Elson, Note, *Say "Ahhh!": A New Approach for Determining the Cram Down Interest Rate After* Till v. SCS Credit, 27 Cardozo L. Rev. 1921 (2006).

[268] 541 U.S. at 480–81.

[269] *E.g.*, In re Cantwell, 336 B.R. 688 (Bankr. D.N.J. 2006) (1% above prime); In re Nowlin, 321 B.R. 678, 685 (Bankr. E.D. Pa. 2005) (3.5–4% above prime).

[270] *E.g.*, In re Soards, 344 B.R. 829, 831–32 (Bankr. W.D. Ky. 2006).

[271] *E.g.*, In re Deep River Warehouse, Inc., No. 04-52749, 2005 Bankr. LEXIS 1793 (Bankr. M.D.N.C. Sept. 22, 2005).

[272] Bankruptcy Code § 506; *see* § 11.03 Secured Claims, *supra*.

cases, except with regard to claims secured by the debtor's home, which are not usually subject to cramdown in any event.[273] In cases involving security interests in the debtor's personal property, the collateral is usually worth less than the amount of the secured debt, making the value of the collateral the amount of the allowed secured claim.[274] This makes valuation of the collateral critical to the debtor's plan.

In determining the value of the personal property, courts are now directed to use its "replacement value . . . as of the date of the filing of the petition without deduction for costs of sale or marketing."[275] This language, added to § 506 as part of the 2005 Amendments, codifies most of the Supreme Court's 1997 decision in *Associates Commercial Corp. v. Rash.*[276] However, like *Rash*, it leaves the precise method for determining the property's replacement value up in the air, particularly in cases where it may be difficult to identify an appropriate secondary market for the property.[277]

Of course, valuation does not matter with respect to mortgages on residential real estate or security interests subject to § 1325(a)'s hanging paragraph. These claims may not be bifurcated.

[d] Equal Monthly Installment Payments

In most cases, secured creditors' claims are satisfied with regular monthly installment payments. Language added in 2005 specifies that if "periodic payments" are to be distributed to the holder of a secured claim, the payments must be made in equal monthly amounts.[278] Thus, unless the creditor agrees otherwise and thus "accepts" the plan, the plan may not provide for only annual or quarterly payments. In addition, the payments must be in equal amounts.[279] This could prove to be a problem for debtors whose income is sporadic or seasonal. It undoubtedly prevents use of "balloon payments" near the end of a plan included with the anticipation that the debtor will be able to refinance the debt.[280]

The requirement of equal monthly payments also may conflict with the customary practice in some districts that permits debtors to cure arrearages on their home mortgages before commencing payments to other secured lenders. This may make it necessary for debtors to extend the period during which these arrearages will be cured.

It also might be difficult to reconcile the equal monthly payments requirement with the requirement of § 1325(a)(5)(b)(iii)(II) that the payments ensure that the creditor is adequately protected.[281] If the collateral

[273] *See* § 18.08[F][5] Real Estate Mortgages, *supra.*

[274] *See* § 11.03[C] Bifurcation of Secured Claims, *supra.*

[275] Bankruptcy Code § 506(a)(2).

[276] 520 U.S. 953 (1997).

[277] E-Bay?

[278] Bankruptcy Code § 1325(a)(5)(B)(iii)(I).

[279] In re DeSardi, 340 B.R. 790, 804–05 (Bankr. S.D. Tex. 2006).

[280] In re Lemieux, 347 B.R. 460 (Bankr. D. Mass. 2006).

[281] *See* § 18.08[F][4][e] Adequate Protection, *infra.*

depreciates at an uneven rate over the life of the plan, this may require the debtor to make unequal payments as the rate of depreciation changes. Considering both requirements together may make it necessary for equal payments to be made at a rate that keeps up with the steepest portion of the anticipated depreciation rate for the collateral. Alternatively, the court might permit adequate protection payments pursuant to §§ 362(d) and 1325(a)(5)(B)(iii)(II) as separate and distinct from the equal monthly installment payments made under § 1325(a)(5)(B)(iii)(I).[282]

[e] Adequate Protection

As suggested above, the 2005 Amendments added language that requires payments made on claims secured by personal property to "adequately protect" the creditor's interest in the collateral throughout the duration of the plan.[283] In most cases, this requires debtors to commence payments to secured creditors from the outset of the plan.[284] It also might necessitate payments to secured creditors at an accelerated rate, particularly if the collateral threatens to decline speedily in value.[285] In cases where the debtor lacks sufficient income to pay the claim at a fast enough rate, it may prevent confirmation of the plan.

In addition, § 1326(a)(4) now requires a debtor who retains possession of personal property that is subject to a purchase money security interest or a lease, to provide "reasonable evidence of the maintenance of any required insurance coverage" on the property and to "continue to do so for as long as the debtor retains possession of such property." The requirement of adequate protection to keep the automatic stay in effect, probably requires no less.[286]

[5] Residential Real Estate Mortgages

Claims secured solely by residential real estate cannot be modified in Chapter 13.[287] As explained above, the debtor can cure any pre-petition default and thus de-accelerate the debt and resume regular monthly payments, but otherwise the debtor is required to perform the terms of his residential mortgage in accordance with the terms of the contract.

Most residential purchase money mortgages are fully secured, but the same rules apply regardless of whether the mortgage secures a purchase money debt, a construction loan, a home equity line, or otherwise. And they apply regardless of whether the debt is fully or only partially secured. Thus,

---

282 In re DeSardi, 340 B.R. 790, 805–10 (Bankr. S.D. Tex. 2006).

283 Bankruptcy Code § 1325(a)(5)(B)(iii)(II).

284 Richardo Kilpatrick, *Selected Creditor Issues Under the Bankruptcy Abuse Prevention and Consumer Protection Act of 2005*, 79 Am. Bankr. L.J. 817, 836 (2005).

285 *See* In re White, 352 B.R. 633 (Bankr. D. La. 2006).

286 Bankruptcy Code § 362(d)(1); *see* § 8.06[B][1] Relief for Cause — Lack of Adequate Protection, *supra.*

287 Bankruptcy Code § 1322(b)(2).

if the debtor owns a $100,000 home subject to a $70,000 senior mortgage and a $40,000 junior mortgage, both debts must be paid in full according to the terms of the respective agreements between the debtor and the creditors.[288] On the other hand, if the collateral is completely consumed by senior secured claims, a junior secured creditor's claim is regarded as not being secured.[289] Accordingly, in the above example, a third mortgage securing a $5,000 debt would be regarded as completely unsecured and subject to modification, the same as any other unsecured claim.

This different treatment could lead to dramatic results, depending on the value of the collateral. Consider what would happen in the above example if the property were worth $100,100. The $5,000 third mortgage would only be marginally secured — to the extent of $100. The debtor's plan would have to pay the entire $5,000 debt and would have to pay it according to the terms of the parties' agreement. Under these circumstances, the debtor, or perhaps unsecured creditors, would have some incentive to make sure that the house looked as bad as possible on the day it was scheduled to be appraised.

Section 1322(b)(2) only prevents modification if the only collateral for the debt is "real property that is the debtor's principal residence."[290] If the terms of the agreement add other collateral, not inextricably associated with the land,[291] the creditor's secured claim may be modified.[292] Likewise, if the collateral is a mobile home that does not qualify as real estate, or if the premises are not the debtor's principal residence, the claim is subject to the same rules as other secured claims and may be modified consistent with § 1325(a)(5)'s usual secured creditor cramdown rules.

[6] Certain Purchase Money Security Interests

In 2005, Congress imposed additional limits on debtors' ability to modify secured creditors' claims. This was accomplished through what has been described as a hanging paragraph appearing at the end of § 1325(a), between § 1325(a)(9) and the beginning of § 1325(b).[293] The new language provides:

---

[288] Nobleman v. American Sav. Bank, 508 U.S. 324 (1993).

[289] *E.g.*, McDonald v. Master Fin. Inc. (In re McDonald), 205 F.3d 606 (3d Cir.), *cert. denied*, 531 U.S. 822 (2000); Lane v. Western Interstate Bancorp (In re Lane), 280 F.3d 663 (6th Cir. 2002).

[290] Bankruptcy Code § 1322(b)(2).

[291] In re Davis, 989 F.2d 208 (6th Cir. 1992); *see* David Gray Carlson, *Rake's Progress: Cure and Reinstatement of Secured Claims in Bankruptcy Reorganization*, 13 Bankr. Dev. J. 273 (1997); David J. Jesulaitis, Comment, *Lien Stripping After* Nobelman v. American Savings Bank*: What Is "Additional Collateral"?*, 32 Hous. L. Rev. 201 (1995); James H. Longino, Note, *Nobelman v. American Savings Bank: Bankruptcy, Bifurcation, and Residential Mortgages — Lender Beware*, 47 Ark. L. Rev. 907, 936 (1994).

[292] *See* Daniel C. Fleming & Marianne McConnell, *The Treatment of Residential Mortgages in Chapter 13 After* Nobleman, 2 Am. Bankr. Inst. L. Rev. 147 (1994).

[293] *See* In re Carver, 338 B.R. 521, 523 (Bankr. S.D. Ga. 2006); In re Payne, 347 B.R. 278 (Bankr. S.D. Ohio 2006); In re Phillips, No. 06-71604-SCS, — B.R. — , 28 n. 7, 2007 Bankr.

> For purposes of paragraph (5) section 506 shall not apply to a claim described in that paragraph if the creditor has a purchase money security interest securing the debt that is the subject of the claim, the debt was incurred within the 910-day [sic] preceding the date of the filing of the petition, and the collateral for that debt consists of a motor vehicle . . . acquired for the personal use of the debtor, or if the collateral for that debt consists of any other thing of value, if the debt was incurred during the 1-year period preceding that filing.

This was apparently intended to prevent debtors from using § 506(a)(1) to "strip-down" or bifurcate a partially secured claim into two separate claims. Normally § 506 requires bifurcation of a partially secured claim. A $20,000 auto loan secured by a vehicle worth only $16,000 normally would be bifurcated into a $16,000 secured claim and a $4,000 unsecured claim. In Chapter 13, the debtor's plan could modify the secured creditor's claim and satisfy the cramdown standards of § 1325(a)(5)(B) by calling for payments to satisfy the $16,000 secured claim, at an appropriate rate of interest to ensure that the creditor received the full "value" of the amount of its secured claim. The $4,000 unsecured claim would be thrown in with other unsecured claims and would share in whatever distribution the plan provided to holders of those general unsecured claims.

The apparent effect of this hanging paragraph, as many have referred to it,[294] is to require the debtor to treat the claim as if it were fully rather than only partially secured. As a fully secured claim § 1325(a)(5)(B)(ii) could only be satisfied by a plan that provided for payment of the full $20,000 of the claim, with interest to be paid on the entire $20,000 debt.[295] Most courts applying the hanging paragraph have applied it in this fashion.[296]

[a] Creditors Deprived of Secured Claim

Some commentators and at least one court have suggested that the hanging paragraph of § 1325(a) should be given its "plain meaning," which they contend would turn the creditor's claim into a completely *unsecured*

LEXIS 791 (Bankr. E.D. Va. 2006). The new language is sometimes hard to locate. In some publications, it appears as if it were an additional lengthy sentence made a part of § 1329(a)(9). In other publications, it is set apart as an unnumbered additional paragraph between § 1329(a) and 1329(b). Congress' failure to provide it with its own designated home in the Bankruptcy Code is a testament to the poor drafting that typifies the legislation that many bankruptcy professionals now refer to as "BAPCRAP." *Cf.* David C. Farmer, *Bankruptcy Reform: Like a BAPCPA Out of Hell?*, 10 Haw. B.J. 6 (2006).

[294] *See* In re Carver, 338 B.R. 521, 523 (Bankr. S.D. Ga. 2006).

[295] Though this is not yet entirely clear, new § 1325(a)(5)(B)(iii)(II), which requires the stream of payments to be sufficient to ensure that the creditor is adequately protected, seems to be satisfied if the amortization rate of the debtor's payments keeps up with the depreciation rate of the $16,000 value of the collateral.

[296] In re Brown, 339 B.R. 818 (Bankr. S.D. Ga. 2006); In re Johnson, 337 B.R. 269 (Bankr. M.D.N.C. 2006); In re Robinson, 338 B.R. 70 (Bankr. W.D. Mo. 2006); In re Wright, 338 B.R. 917 (Bankr. M.D. Ala. 2006).

claim.[297] In *In re Carver*, the court ruled that the literal language of the amendment specifies that § 506 "shall not apply" and that if § 506 does not apply there is nothing else to support treating the creditor's claim as secured. The court explained:

> Without application of § 506(a), a claim is merely an allowed claim; it cannot be a secured claim. With that understanding of § 506, the hanging paragraph must be read to provide that for purposes of § 1325(a)(5), a 910 [day] claim is not a secured claim and therefore not subject to the treatment provided in that paragraph.[298]

A few courts have agreed with *Carver*'s reasoning and result,[299] but most have rejected it.[300] As one court explained:

> [it was] unlikely that Congress would create a new, undefined type of claim, and then furnish no guidance as to how such a claim should be handled. Rather, this Court turns to basic principles of Code interpretation and finds that a 910-paragraph claim is an allowed secured claim and may be treated under § 1325(a)(5).

Another well-known judge drew the same conclusion but explained the difficulty in construing the hanging paragraph with a reference to Alice in Wonderland, declaring that: "making practical sense of this provision, like trying to make sense of much of BAPCPA, requires bankruptcy judges to adopt the approach of the White Queen, and believe in 'as many as six impossible things before breakfast.'"[301]

[b] Purchase Money Security Interests

The hanging paragraph only applies to certain purchase money security interests. A purchase money security interest is one that is retained by the seller of the collateral to secure the debtor's obligation to pay the price of the goods, or for value given by the secured creditor to enable the debtor to acquire rights in the collateral.[302] The security interest does not qualify for purchase money status to the extent that it secures other sums loaned to the debtor, such as those for an extended warranty or for insurance.[303]

---

[297] Timothy D. Moratzka, *The "Hanging Paragraph" and Cramdown: Bankruptcy Code §§ 1325(a) and 506 After BAPCPA*, 25-4 Am. Bankr. Inst. J. 18 (May 2006).

[298] In re Carver, 338 B.R. 521, 524 (Bankr. S.D. Ga. 2006); *see also* In re Green, 348 B.R. 601, (Bankr. M.D. Ga. 2006) (the *Carver* judge elaborating on the analysis in his earlier decision in *Carver*).

[299] In re Taranto, 344 B.R. 857 (Bankr. N.D. Ohio 2006); In re Wampler, 345 B.R. 730 (Bankr. D. Kan. 2006).

[300] *See* In re Turner, 349 B.R. 437 (Bankr. D.S.C. 2006) (collecting cases); In re McCormick, — B.R. — , No. 06-23358-SVK, Bankr. LEXIS 3377 (Bankr. E.D. Wis. Dec. 5, 2006).

[301] In re Trejos, 352 B.R. 249 (Bankr. D. Nev. 2006) (Markell, J.) (quoting Lewis Carroll, Alice's Adventures in Wonderland & Through the Looking Glass, ch.5, at 157 (Bantam Classic ed. 1981) (1865 & 1871)).

[302] U.C.C. § 9-103(a)(2) (2003).

[303] *See* In re White, 352 B.R. 633 (Bankr. D. La. 2006).

Whether refinancing of a purchase money loan results in its transformation is likely to be governed by cases addressing the same problem in connection with § 522(f).[304]

Nothing in the hanging paragraph refers to leases. Thus a debtor who wishes to keep a leased motor vehicle must assume the unexpired lease. In this respect, the hanging paragraph results in purchase money security interests in motor vehicles being treated similarly to leases, except that cram-down of a security interest requires the debtor to pay interest at the cramdown rate rather than at the rate provided in the contract that must be paid when the debtor assumes an unexpired lease.

[c] Motor Vehicles Financed Within 910 Days of Petition

The biggest impact of this provision is with respect to purchase money security interests in recently purchased motor vehicles.[305] With respect to purchase money security interests in motor vehicles, it applies only if the debt was "incurred within the 910-day [period] preceding the date of the filing of the petition." Nine-hundred and ten days is approximately two and a half years. With many auto finance deals now lasting for five and sometimes six years, the hanging paragraph will affect auto purchase loans only for the first half or so of their duration.

The 910-day limit will have a dramatic effect when the debtor is able to delay filing his Chapter 13 petition until after expiration of the time period. If the debtor bought the car within the 910 days immediately before his petition, he must pay the full debt. If the debtor bought the car more than 910 days before his petition, he must only pay what it would cost him to purchase a similar car on a used auto lot.[306]

Even where the debtor may not bifurcate the claim, he is nevertheless permitted to modify the claim in other ways, such as by extending the time over which the claim is paid or adjusting the interest rate payable on the claim in accordance with the Supreme Court's decisions in *Associates Commercial Corporation v. Rash*[307] and *Till v. SCS Credit Corp.*[308] The

[304] *E.g.*, In re Horn, 338 B.R. 110 (Bankr. M.D. Ala. 2006) (applying state law definition of purchase money security interest); Christopher Harry, Comment, *To Be (Transformed), or Not to Be: The Transformation Versus Dual-Status Rules for Purchase-Money Security Interests Under Kansas' Former and Revised Article 9*, 50 U. Kan. L. Rev. 1095, 1122 (2002); Keith G. Meyer, *A Primer on Purchase Money Security Interests Under Revised Article 9 of the Uniform Commercial Code*, 50 U. Kan. L. Rev. 143, 156 (2001); *see generally* § 12.07[B] Non-Purchase Money Security Interests, *supra*.

[305] For the purpose of the hanging paragraph, "motor vehicle" is defined in accordance with 49 U.S.C. § 30102 (2000). This definition applies broadly to any "vehicle driven or drawn by mechanical power and manufactured primarily for use on public streets, roads, and highways, but does not include a vehicle operated only on a rail line." Non-motorized bicycles don't count.

[306] Section 506(a)(1) specifies that the amount of the allowed secured claim will be based on the replacement value of the collateral. *See* § 10.03[C] Allowance of Secured Claims, *supra*.

[307] 520 U.S. 953 (1997); *see* § 10.03[C][1] Valuation of Collateral, *supra*.

[308] 541 U.S. 465 (2004).

hanging paragraph at the end of § 1325(a) did nothing to affect this aspect of Chapter 13 cramdown.[309]

[d] Post-Petition Interest

Courts disagree about whether and the extent to which creditors are entitled to post-petition interest on 910-day claims.[310] Courts that read the hanging paragraph literally, as eliminating the creditor's secured claim, naturally conclude that the creditor is not entitled to post-petition interest.[311] A few courts recognize that the hanging paragraph preserves the creditor's secured claim, but limit the creditor's interest rate to one that protects only the value of the secured claim as determined under § 506.[312] Other courts require debtors to pay the prime-plus rate of interest required by *Till* on the entire amount of the unbifurcated claim.[313]

[e] Debtor's Personal Use

With respect to motor vehicles, the hanging paragraph only applies if the collateral was "acquired for the personal use of the debtor." This presumably means that autos acquired for a business purpose are not subject to the rule. One court has ruled that an auto used by the debtor to commute to work was acquired for a business purpose and not for personal use. Accordingly the hanging paragraph did not apply and the debtor was free to strip-down the secured creditor's lien.[314] The normal way of expressing this is to refer to the collateral as "consumer goods,"[315] to refer to the debt secured by the collateral as a "consumer debt,"[316] or to make the language applicable only to motor vehicles purchased for "personal, family, or household purposes." The absence of these customary terms means the section might not apply to goods purchased for use by someone else in the debtor's family, such as the debtor's spouse or child.[317] On the other hand, it might mean that it applies to motor vehicles purchased for a business purpose, so long as the debtor personally is the one who is expected to drive the car.

---

[309] *See* In re Wright, 338 B.R. 917 (Bankr. M.D. Ala. 2006); In re Vagi, No. 06-40033, 2006 Bankr. LEXIS 2406 (Bankr. N.D. Ohio Sept. 26, 2006).

[310] *See* In re Green, 348 B.R. 601 (Bankr. M.D. Ga. 2006) (collecting cases).

[311] In re Green, 348 B.R. 601 (Bankr. M.D. Ga. 2006); In re Wampler, 345 B.R. 730 (Bankr. D. Kan. 2006).

[312] In re Carver, 338 B.R. 521 (Bankr. S.D. Ga. 2006); *see* Robin Miller, Annotation, *Effect of "Hanging" or "Anti-Cramdown" Paragraph Added to 11 U.S.C.A. § 1326(a) by Bankruptcy Abuse Prevention and Consumer Protection Act (BAPCPA)*, 19 A.L.R. Fed. 2d 157 (2007).

[313] *E.g.*, In re Brill, 350 B.R. 853 (Bankr. D. Wis. 2006) (collecting cases); *see* David Grey Carlson, *Cars and Homes in Chapter 13 after the 2005 Amendments to the Bankruptcy Code*, 14 Am. Bankr. Inst. L. Rev. 301, 340 (2006).

[314] In re Johnson, 350 B.R. 712 (Bankr. W.D. La. 2006).

[315] *Cf.* U.C.C. § 9-102 (2003).

[316] Bankruptcy Code § 101(8).

[317] In re Jackson, 338 B.R. 923 (Bankr. M.D. Ga. 2006).

[f] Effect of Debtor's Surrender of Collateral

Rather than attempt to retain the collateral, a Chapter 13 debtor might propose to cramdown the plan over the objection of a secured creditor by surrendering the collateral to the creditor.[318] Courts have also disagreed about whether the debtor's surrender of the collateral to the secured creditor fully satisfies the creditor's claim.[319] Most courts have taken the hanging paragraph at face value in this regard and ruled that the debtor's surrender of the collateral eliminates the creditor's deficiency claim.[320] According to these courts, making § 506 inapplicable to these claims, the hanging paragraph prevents bifurcation of the creditor's claim into a secured and an unsecured portion. Thus, surrender of the collateral to the creditor satisfies any deficiency claim that the creditor otherwise might have had.[321] Courts that disagree rely on the likely intent of Congress, rather than the plain meaning of the statute.[322]

[g] Personal Property Other than Motor Vehicles

With respect to a purchase money security interest in other collateral, referred to in the hanging paragraph as "any other thing of value," the language only applies if the "debt was incurred during the 1-year period preceding [the debtor's petition]." Thus, with respect to collateral other than a motor vehicle, it does not matter whether the collateral was acquired for the personal use of the debtor, and thus applies to consumer goods, business equipment, and presumably even inventory owned by a Chapter 13 debtor. Of course, the rising use of unsecured credit cards for consumer purchases makes this provision somewhat less important than it otherwise might be, except with respect to big-ticket consumer items such as furniture and appliances, and even then only if the goods are purchased pursuant to a retail installment purchase contract or other purchase money loan.

[7] Direct Payments "Outside the Plan"[323]

There is a strong presumption that payments to creditors will be made through the Chapter 13 trustee.[324] However, payments to secured creditors

---

[318] Bankruptcy Code § 1325(a)(5)(C); *see* § 18.08[F][1] Surrender of the Collateral to the Creditor, *supra.*

[319] *Compare* In re Ezell, 338 B.R. 330 (Bankr. E.D. Tenn. 2006) (surrender satisfies creditor's claim) *with* In re Duke, 345 B.R. 806 (Bankr. W.D. Ky. 2006) (surrender does not satisfy secured creditor's claim). As of December 8, 2006, the issue was pending before the Sixth Circuit Court of Appeals in *In re Long*, No. 06-30651, 2006 WL 2090246 (Bankr. E.D. Tenn. Mar. 13, 2006).

[320] *E.g.*, In re Payne, 347 B.R. 278 (Bankr. S.D. Ohio 2006) (Preston, J.).

[321] In re Ezell, 338 B.R. 330 (Bankr. E.D. Tenn. 2006); In re Sparks, 346 B.R. 767, 773 (Bankr. S.D. Ohio 2006) (Aug, J.); In re Pool, 351 B.R. 747, 752 (Bankr. D. Or. 2006).

[322] Dupaco Comm. Credit Union v. Zehrung (In re Zehrung), 351 B.R. 675, 678 (W.D. Wis. 2006); In re Duke, 345 B.R. 806, 808 (Bankr. W.D. Ky. 2006).

[323] Michaela M. White, *Direct Payment Plans*, 29 Creighton L. Rev. 583 (1996).

[324] *See, e.g.*, In re Perez, 339 B.R. 385, 389 (Bankr. S.D. Tex. 2006).

might also be made outside the plan. The plain language of § 1326(c) is that the plan or the order confirming the plan can "otherwise provide" for payments to creditors under the plan.[325] This language has been uniformly interpreted as authorizing bankruptcy courts to permit debtors to make payments directly to secured creditors.[326] Thus, debtors who are not seeking to use Chapter 13 to adjust the rights of a secured creditor through its cramdown provisions or to discharge a portion of the debt are permitted to pay secured creditors directly on their own, independent of the services of (and free of the commission charged by) the Chapter 13 trustee.[327] Early indications are that this practice continues to be viable after the enactment of the 2005 Amendments.[328]

[F] Hearing on Confirmation of Plan

The court is required to hold a hearing on confirmation of the debtor's proposed plan. This hearing is normally required to be held in a window between the twentieth and the forty-fifth day after the § 341 meeting of creditors, but the court may order the hearing held earlier if no one objects and the court determines that an earlier hearing is in the best interest of creditors.[329] Twenty-five days advance notice of the hearing is required to be given to these parties.[330] Any party in interest may object to the confirmation.[331]

§ 18.09 Effect of Confirmation of Chapter 13 Plan

[A] General Effect of Chapter 13 Plan Confirmation

Confirmation of the Chapter 13 plan binds the debtor and every creditor, whether or not the creditor has been provided for by the plan and whether or not the creditor has accepted, objected to, or rejected the plan.[332] Confirmation also vests all property of the estate in the debtor, unless the order of confirmation provides otherwise.[333] Creditors with security interests in estate property are permitted to insist that the debtor's plan provides for retention of the creditor's lien.

---

[325] Bankruptcy Code § 1326(c).

[326] *E.g.*, In re Aberegg, 961 F.2d 1307, 1309 (7th Cir. 1992); In re Foster, 670 F.2d 478, 486 (5th Cir. 1982).

[327] In re Case, 11 B.R. 843, 846 (Bankr. D. Utah 1981) (R. Maybe, J.); *see, e.g.*, In re Aberegg, 961 F.2d 1307 (7th Cir. 1992).

[328] In re Clay, 339 B.R. 784, 788 (Bankr. D. Utah 2006); In re Vigil, 344 B.R. 624, 633–34 (Bankr. D.N.M. 2006).

[329] Bankruptcy Code § 1324(b).

[330] Fed. R. Bankr. P. 2002(b).

[331] Bankruptcy Code § 1324(a).

[332] Bankruptcy Code § 1327(a). Creditors neither accept nor reject a Chapter 13 plan, because they have no vote on it.

[333] Bankruptcy Code § 1327(b). Property vests free and clear in the debtor unless otherwise provided in the plan or the confirmation order. Bankruptcy Code § 1327(c).

Confirmation does not discharge a Chapter 13 debtor.[334] Chapter 13 debtors are discharged only upon completion of their plan or upon the grant of a hardship discharge. However, because the case remains pending until the terms of the plan are completed or until the case is dismissed or converted, the automatic stay of § 362 remains in effect.

Confirmation is res judicata with respect to all matters that were or could have been litigated in connection with the confirmation process.[335] The addition of § 1325(a)(5)(B)(iii)(II), which prevents confirmation unless payments to secured creditors provide adequate protection for the creditor's interest in the collateral, removes any doubt that might have existed about whether confirmation precludes secured creditors from subsequently seeking relief from the automatic stay, due to a lack of adequate protection, provided of course that the debtor complies with the terms of the plan.

[B] Payments Before Confirmation[336]

The commencement of payment is ordinarily pegged to the filing of the plan, not its confirmation. Unless the court orders otherwise, payments must begin within thirty days after the plan is filed.[337] Plans are usually filed with the debtor's petition.

These pre-confirmation payments are held by the trustee until the plan is either confirmed or not confirmed. If the plan is confirmed, the trustee distributes payments in accordance with the plan. If the plan is not confirmed, the trustee returns the payments, minus any allowed administrative expenses, to the debtor.[338] After 2005, however, the trustee is permitted to disburse payments to creditors that have "become due," even though the plan has not yet been confirmed.[339] Payments on any unpaid administrative priority debt and of any unpaid portion of the standing trustee's fee must occur prior to or at the same time as each payment to creditors under the plan.[340] Although nothing in the Code requires this, it is generally contemplated that the debtor's payments and the trustee's disbursements occur on a monthly basis.[341]

---

[334] The same is true in Chapter 11 cases involving "individuals." Bankruptcy Code § 1141(d)(2). Otherwise, confirmation of a Chapter 11 plan provides the debtor with a discharge. Bankruptcy Code § 1141(d)(1)(A); *see* § 19.13[A] Effect of Confirmation, *infra*.

[335] *E.g.*, In re Harvey, 213 F.3d 318 (7th Cir. 2000).

[336] Henry E. Hildebrand, III, *Impact of the Bankruptcy Abuse Prevention and Consumer Protection Act of 2005 on Chapter 13 Trustees*, 79 Am. Bankr. L.J. 373, 379 (2005).

[337] Bankruptcy Code § 1326(a)(1).

[338] Bankruptcy Code § 1326(a)(2).

[339] Bankruptcy Code § 1326(a)(2).

[340] Bankruptcy Code § 1326(b).

[341] Further, § 1325(a)(5)(B)(iii)(I) requires payments on account of secured claims to be "distributed" in equal monthly amounts. This language does not require the debtor to make payments to the trustee in equal monthly amounts. It refers instead to the amounts to be distributed to the secured creditor.

In addition to any payments provided for in the plan, the debtor must now make "adequate protection" payments to creditors who hold claims secured by purchase money security interests secured by personal property, before the plan is confirmed.[342] The debtor is also required to make lease payments on leases of personal property that become due after the order for relief.[343] The Code presumes that these payments are to be made directly to the creditor rather than to the trustee, but gives the court discretion to order otherwise.[344] Payments made directly to these creditors reduce the amount that must be paid under the plan.

§ 18.10 Modification of Chapter 13 Plans

[A] Pre-Confirmation Modification of Chapter 13 Plans

The debtor has the right to modify the plan at any time prior to confirmation. The modified plan must comply with all of the mandatory requirements of § 1322.[345] After the debtor submits a modified plan, it becomes "the plan" for the purposes of other provisions of the Code.[346] Any secured creditor who accepted or rejected the original plan is deemed to have accepted or rejected the modified plan, unless (1) the modification changes the creditor's rights, and (2) the creditor changes its previous acceptance or rejection.[347] Since unsecured creditors do not vote on a Chapter 13 plan, their view of the modified plan is irrelevant.

[B] Post-Confirmation Modification of Chapter 13 Plans

The rules regarding modification of a plan after it has been confirmed depart somewhat from the notion that Chapter 13 cases must be entirely voluntary. A Chapter 13 case cannot be commenced by a creditor.[348] Nor may a creditor file an initial plan.[349] Nevertheless, unsecured creditors or the standing trustee may propose modifications of the debtor's plan after it has been confirmed.[350] To this rather limited extent, a Chapter 13 debtor may be forced into a plan he does not want, or more precisely, he may be forced to chose between accepting an unwanted plan, converting his case to Chapter 7, or dismissing his case altogether.[351]

---

[342] Bankruptcy Code § 1326(a)(1)(C).

[343] Bankruptcy Code § 1326(a)(1)(B).

[344] In re Brown, 348 B.R. 583 (Bankr. N.D. Ga. 2006); In re Beaver, 337 B.R. 281, 284 n.2 (Bankr. E.D.N.C. 2006).

[345] Bankruptcy Code § 1323(a); *see* § 18.06 The Chapter 13 Plan — Required Provisions, *supra*.

[346] Bankruptcy Code § 1323(b).

[347] Bankruptcy Code § 1323(c).

[348] Bankruptcy Code § 303(a).

[349] Bankruptcy Code § 1321.

[350] Bankruptcy Code § 1329(a).

[351] The debtor always has the right to convert to Chapter 7 and nearly always has the right to dismiss the case voluntarily. Bankruptcy Code § 1307(a), (b).

A modification may be proposed by the debtor, an unsecured creditor, or the trustee at any time after confirmation but before completion of payments. The modification may (i) increase or decrease payments, (ii) extend or reduce the time for payments, (iii) alter the distribution to a creditor, to the extent necessary to take account of payments made outside the plan, or (iv) reduce the amounts to be paid under the plan by the amount of "the actual amount expended by the debtor to purchase health insurance for the debtor and any of the debtor's dependents who do not otherwise enjoy health insurance coverage."[352]

The plan must comply with the usual requirements for confirmation in "[s]ections 1322(a), 1322(b), 1323(c) . . . and 1325(a)."[353] However, in applying the best interests test and cram-down requirements, the court does not re-evaluate the debtor's financial position. Instead, these tests depend on the amount and value of the debtor's assets when the case was initially filed.[354] However, the rate of interest necessary to satisfy these tests can be re-evaluated, even though the rate of interest required to be paid to satisfy the best interests test and secured creditor cram-down requirements necessarily took into account the possibility that the rate of inflation or the debtor's risk of non-payment might change. Likewise, parties may not use the modification hearing to raise issues that could have been raised at the original confirmation hearing.[355]

Curiously, the statutory language of § 1329(b) does not expressly require the modified plan to comply with the "projected disposable income" requirement of § 1325(b). This seems odd, given that increases in the debtor's income seem to be the most likely circumstance that would give rise to an effort by a creditor or the trustee to modify the debtor's plan. Courts addressing the conspicuous absence in § 1329(b) of any reference to the disposable income test, have divided over its significance, with most courts ruling that the debtor's disposable income is just as relevant to a modified plan as it is to the original plan.[356] Debtors' efforts to sidestep the projected disposable income requirement are likely to be met with "bad faith" objections under § 1325(a)(3), which requires the plan to be proposed in "good faith."

---

352 Bankruptcy Code § 1329(a)(4). The expenses for the coverage must be "reasonable and necessary" and must not be "materially larger" than any expenses previously paid by the debtor or than the amount that would be incurred by an otherwise similarly situated debtor. *Id.* It is entirely unclear what the debtor is supposed to do if he cannot otherwise obtain health insurance.

353 Bankruptcy Code § 1329(b)(1).

354 Forbes v. Forbes (In re Forbes), 215 B.R. 183 (B.A.P. 8th Cir. 1997).

355 In re Stage, 79 B.R. 487 (Bankr. S.D. Cal. 1987). However, in *Rowley v. Yarnall*, 22 F.3d 190 (8th Cir. 1994), creditors of a Chapter 12 debtor successfully contended that the plan failed to meet the disposable income test through an objection to the debtors' motion for discharge.

356 *Compare* Forbes v. Forbes (In re Forbes), 215 B.R. 183 (B.A.P. 8th Cir. 1997) (favoring consideration of changes to disposable income), *with* In re Sunahara, 326 B.R. 768 (B.A.P. 9th Cir. 2005) ("Section 1329(b) expressly applies certain specific Code sections to plan modifications but does not apply § 1325(b). Period.").

As with pre-confirmation modifications, any secured creditor who accepted or rejected the original plan is deemed to have accepted or rejected the modified plan unless (i) the modification changes the creditor's rights, and (ii) the creditor changes its previous acceptance or rejection.[357] Since unsecured creditors do not vote on the plan, their view of the modified plan is irrelevant. The modified plan becomes "the plan," unless it is disapproved after notice and an opportunity for a hearing.[358]

§ 18.11 Revocation of Confirmation of Chapter 13 Plans

The rules regarding revocation of an order of confirmation must inevitably balance the interest of fairness to creditors with the interest of finality to others. Thus, the timing and the substantive basis for revocation are both limited. Upon request of a party in interest, and after notice and an opportunity for a hearing, the court may revoke confirmation if it was procured by fraud. The request must be made within 180 days after the date the order of confirmation was entered.[359] If the order of confirmation is revoked, the court may either convert or dismiss the case under § 1307, or if the debtor submits a modified plan, the court may confirm the modification.[360] If the court confirms the modification, the case proceeds under the new plan.

§ 18.12 Chapter 20

Before the 2005 Amendments, debtors sometimes sought to gain greater leverage over their home mortgage holders by filing a Chapter 7 case and a Chapter 13 case in succession. Before 2005, Chapter 13 did not require a four-year wait between discharges. Thus, it was possible to obtain, in quick succession, a Chapter 7 discharge and a Chapter 13 discharge. These serial cases were nicknamed "Chapter 20" (7 plus 13).

The primary advantage of chapter 20 is that it greatly reduced the difficulty of dealing with an undersecured home mortgage. The Chapter 7 discharge eliminated the unsecured portion of the mortgage debt. A Chapter 13 plan cannot alter the mortgage debt, but the mortgage debt would have been reduced by the Chapter 7 discharge. Although the use of Chapter 20 has been attacked, the Supreme Court, in *Johnson v. Home State Bank*, broadly validated its use while noting that in particular cases, the Chapter 13 plan might be refused confirmation on the grounds of bad faith.[361]

---

[357] Bankruptcy Code § 1323(c).

[358] Bankruptcy Code § 1329(b)(2).

[359] Bankruptcy Code § 1330(a); *but see* In re Thomas, 337 B.R. 879 (Bankr. S.D. Tex. 2006) (invoking § 105(a) to permit revocation of confirmation more than 180 days after confirmation due to debtor's fraud).

[360] Bankruptcy Code § 1330(b).

[361] 501 U.S. 78 (1991); *see* Lex A. Coleman, *Individual Consumer "Chapter 20" Cases After* Johnson*: An Introduction to Non-Business Serial Filings Under Chapter 7 and Chapter 13 of the Bankruptcy Code*, 9 Bankr. Dev. J. 357 (1992).

At a minimum, although the plan may not have to deal with the entire amount of the mortgage debt, the lien is not discharged until the entire amount of the mortgage debt is paid. Thus, even if the mortgage debt is undersecured, the amount secured by the lien cannot be reduced either in Chapter 7 or under the home mortgage provisions of Chapter 13. Consequently, it does not appear that a Chapter 20 can eliminate a mortgage for anything less than full payment of the underlying debt.

There are other possible reasons for filing a Chapter 20. The discharge of unsecured debt in Chapter 7 can make it possible for a debtor to fit within the debt limitations of Chapter 13. Indeed, this was the case in *Johnson v. Home State Bank.*[362]

The 2005 Amendments eliminated most but not all of the incentives to file sequential Chapter 7 and 13 cases. A debtor is no longer able to obtain a Chapter 13 discharge "if the debtor has received a discharge in a case filed under chapter 7, 11, or 12 . . . during the 4-year period preceding the date of the order for relief under this chapter."[363] However, this does not explicitly prevent debtors from filing a Chapter 13 petition, immediately on the heels of a Chapter 7 discharge, intending to invoke the automatic stay while making payments under a Chapter 13 plan. If this tactic is attempted, it is bound to be attacked on the grounds that the second petition was not filed in "good faith."[364]

---

[362] 501 U.S. at 80. Note that these caps have since been raised to $336,900 and $1,010,650 and are slated for periodic adjustment every three years. As with most other dollar amounts in the Bankruptcy Code, these amounts are adjusted every three years by a factor reflecting the increase in the Department of Labor's Consumer Price Index and rounded to the nearest $25 amount that represents the change. Bankruptcy Code § 104(b)(1) (2006). The last such adjustment was on April 1, 2007. The next adjustments will occur in 2010 and 2013.

[363] Bankruptcy Code § 1329(f)(1).

[364] Bankruptcy Code § 1325(a)(7).

Chapter 19

Reorganization Under Chapter 11

§ 19.01 Development of Chapter 11[1]

Bankruptcy reorganization seeks to enable financially troubled businesses to capture and preserve their "going concern value." In doing so, reorganization benefits everyone involved with the business. Creditors obtain a greater distribution for their claims, employees keep their jobs, suppliers keep their customers, and the owners may even preserve some of their investments.[2]

The earliest attempts to reorganize businesses through insolvency law generally involved railroads that collapsed with depressing frequency in the nineteenth century.[3] Bankruptcy law moved into the railroad reorganization arena with old § 77 and into corporate reorganization with former § 77B.[4] Reorganization was embraced more broadly in 1938 by the Chandler Act, which provided four chapters (X through XIII) that provided reorganization procedures for nearly every type of debtor.

Chapter 11 of the Bankruptcy Code is the successor to Chapters X and XI of the Bankruptcy Act.[5] Those were the business reorganization chapters, each theoretically designed for a different type of reorganization.

Under the former Act, considerable confusion and difficulty was created by the fact that the two primary business reorganization proceedings, in old Chapters X and XI, had substantially different requirements and procedures. Most notably, in Chapter X, which was designed for large companies with publicly traded stocks and bonds, existing management was replaced and the Securities and Exchange Commission (SEC) played a major role. By contrast, in Chapter XI, which was designed for smaller, closely held companies, existing management generally stayed in place and the

---

[1] Daniel J. Bussel, *Coalition-Building Through Bankruptcy Creditors' Committees*, 43 UCLA L. Rev. 1547, 1552–58 (1996); Douglas G. Baird & Robert K. Rasmussen, *Control Rights, Priority Rights and The Conceptual Foundations of Corporate Reorganizations*, 87 Va. L. Rev. 921, 925–36 (2001).

[2] *See* United States v. Whiting Pools, Inc., 462 U.S. 198, 203 (1983).

[3] David A. Skeel, Jr., Debt's Dominion: A History of Bankruptcy Law in America 48–70 (2001); Stephen J. Lubben, *Railroad Receiverships and Modern Bankruptcy Theory*, 89 Cornell L. Rev. 1420 (2004); Edward S. Adams, *Governance in Chapter 11 Reorganizations: Reducing Costs, Improving Results*, 73 B.U. L. Rev. 581, 584–86 (1993); Douglas G. Baird & Thomas H. Jackson, *Bargaining After the Fall and the Contours of the Absolute Priority Rule*, 55 U. Chi. L. Rev. 738, 739–40 (1988).

[4] *See* William L. Cary, *Liquidation of Corporations in Bankruptcy Reorganization*, 60 Harv. L. Rev. 173, 174 (1946).

[5] Chapter 13 is the successor to old Chapter XIII.

SEC was not involved. The rationale for these differences was that a Chapter X reorganization involved the interests of the investing public (and thus needed the scrutiny of their watchdog, the SEC); while a Chapter XI case only involved a few owners who did not need any government protection of their interests. In practice, however, the distinction often led to protracted struggles over chapter choice that exhausted the estate's scarce resources.[6]

Consequently, in 1978, Congress devised Chapter 11 as a "one size fits all" reorganization proceeding. Even in its original version, it imposed a few special rules for railroad reorganizations, and now includes special provisions for "small business" debtors, and "single asset real estate cases."[7] Chapter 11 draws on old Chapter XI in the dominant role it gives to the existing management of the debtor, or "debtor-in-possession." In most Chapter 11 cases, it is the debtor-in-possesion or DIP who nearly always controls the estate throughout the proceeding. Similarly, the SEC, which had so prominent a role under old Chapter X is reduced to the level of a "party in interest" in Chapter 11, but without the right to appeal the court's decisions.[8]

Although used most often by businesses, a Chapter 11 debtor need not have any business activities.[9] After years of conflict in the lower courts, the Supreme Court in 1991 flatly stated that Chapter 11 is available even to purely individual debtors.[10] Indeed, now that the 2005 Amendments deny high income debtors access to Chapter 7, Chapter 11 may be the only option for debtors who do not satisfy the Chapter 13 debt limits.

Chapter 11 itself has been the subject of serious criticism. In the view of some commentators, Congress went too far in giving control of the Chapter 11 debtor to the debtor-in-possession, and indeed of the whole Chapter 11 process to the debtor's pre-bankruptcy management.[11] In the view of still others, more value might be preserved through a swift and cheap auction of the debtor.[12]

---

[6] *See generally* SEC v. American Trailer Rentals Co., 379 U.S. 594 (1965). Note that Chapter XII, which was hardly ever used, was not implicated in this struggle between the two primary reorganization chapters.

[7] *See* § 23.04 "Single Asset" Real Estate Cases, *infra*.

[8] *See* § 19.06 Role of the Securities and Exchange Commission in Public Company Reorganizations, *infra*.

[9] *See* Toibb v. Radloff, 501 U.S. 157 (1991) (unemployed lawyer as Chapter 11 debtor).

[10] Toibb v. Radloff, 501 U.S. 157 (1991). The Court relied primarily on the plain meaning of Bankruptcy Code § 109(e), not to mention the careful explication of the statute and the underlying policy set out in Michael J. Herbert, *Consumer Chapter 11 Proceedings: Abuse or Alternative?*, 91 Com. L.J. 234 (1986).

[11] Lynn M. LoPucki, *The Debtor in Full Control — Systems Failure Under Chapter 11 of the Bankruptcy Code,* pts. 1 & 2, 57 Am. Bankr. L.J. 99, 247 (1983).

[12] Michael Bradley & Michael Rosenzweig, *The Untenable Case for Chapter 11*, 101 Yale L.J. 1043, & 1045 n.11 (1992); *but see* Elizabeth Warren, *The Untenable Case for Repeal of Chapter 11*, 102 Yale L.J. 437 (1992); Donald R. Korobkin, *The Unwarranted Case Against Corporate Reorganization: A Reply to Bradley and Rosenzweig*, 78 Iowa L. Rev. 669 (1993).

§ 19.02 Goals of Reorganization[13]

The main difference between liquidation and reorganization is that in liquidation, assets are sold piecemeal to provide payment to creditors.[14] In reorganization, the debtor continues to operate its business, and the income from operations is used to repay creditors. This distinction is not absolute. Most reorganizations involve a sale of at least some of the debtor's assets. To understand the goal of Chapter 11, it is necessary to understand the concept of "going concern" value. Consider a business debtor that owns a building, ten machines, 100,000 unassembled parts, two computers, a room full of office equipment, six trucks, and three forklifts, and that employs fifty skilled production workers and seven competent managers. If sold piecemeal, those assets might yield $4,000,000 to distribute to the creditors. On the other hand, if the business continues to operate, it might produce $1,000,000 a year in income after the costs of running the business have been paid. The question is whether the income from operations is worth more than the proceeds of liquidation.

In many cases, a manufacturing company, with its equipment, supplies, and personnel already functioning as a combined unit, will be more valuable than the separate items that go into it. The workers have experience working with the machines and with each other. The company has name recognition, customers, and suppliers willing to do business with it. This is the going concern value that Chapter 11 seeks to preserve. In the example above, the present value of a cash flow of $1,000,000/year is greater than $4,000,000 now.

Of course, this model is not always descriptive of a financially troubled company. Sometimes a company is simply burning through cash. If the firm produces low quality items that nobody wants, the firm's assets might be more valuable if sold off. Nonetheless, it might make sense to sell the factory as a going concern.

§ 19.03 Roles of the Participants

There are several participants in Chapter 11 reorganizations. These include:

---

[13] John D. Ayer, *The Role of Finance Theory in Shaping Bankruptcy Policy*, 3 Am. Bankr. Inst. L. Rev. 53 (1995); Douglas G. Baird, *The Untenable Case for Corporate Reorganizations*, 15 J. Legal Stud. 127 (1985); Douglas G. Baird & Robert K. Rasmussen, *The End of Bankruptcy*, 55 Stan. L. Rev. 751 (2002); Lucian Arye Bebchuk, *A New Approach to Corporate Reorganizations*, 101 Harv. L. Rev. 775 (1988); Randolph J. Haines, *The Unwarranted Attack on New Value*, 72 Am. Bankr. L.J. 387 (1998); Robert M. Lawless & Elizabeth Warren, *The Myth of the Disappearing Business Bankruptcy*, 93 Cal. L. Rev. 743 (2005); Lynn Lopucki, *Stange Visions in a Strange World: A Reply to Professors Bradley and Rosenzweig*, 91 Mich. L. Rev. 79 (1992); Bruce A. Markell, *Owners, Auctions, and Absolute Priority in Bankruptcy Reorganizations*, 44 Stan. L. Rev. 69, 84–85 (1991); Michael Bradley & Michael Rosenzweig, *The Untenable Case for Chapter 11*, 101 Yale L.J. 1043 (1992); Alan Schwartz, *A Normative Theory of Business Bankruptcy*, 91 Va. L. Rev. 1199 (2005); Elizabeth Warren, *The Untenable Case for Repeal of Chapter 11*, 102 Yale L.J. 437 (1992).

[14] *See* Chapter 17, Liquidation Under Chapter 7, *supra*.

- the debtor and its existing management;
- creditors, who may participate on their own behalf, but who are also represented by a creditors' committee;
- owners of the debtor, such as shareholders and partners, who, if the court permits, may also be represented by an equity security holders' committee;
- the United States Trustee.

In some cases, the court may appoint a trustee or examiner to manage or investigate the debtor's financial affairs, and, if the debtor is a publicly held company, the United States Securities Exchange Commission also has standing to appear in the case.

[A] Role of Existing Management[15]

A unique innovation of Chapter 11 in the U.S. is that the debtor's business remains under the operation and control of incumbent management, as the "debtor-in-possession" of the estate.[16] In other words, the same people who operated the business before bankruptcy remain in control throughout the bankruptcy case.[17]

Continued control of the estate by existing management is authorized by § 1107. It gives the debtor-in-possession the same rights, powers, and duties as a trustee.[18] Most important is the power to "operate the debtor's business."[19]

This raises some obvious concerns: if the debtor is financially troubled because its management is incompetent, then retention of that management seems foolish. On the other hand, replacement of existing management imposes potentially crippling costs on the debtor. New management must learn about the business and must do so at a time when the demands of both operation and reorganization allow precious little time for on-the-job training. In addition, the appointment of new management sacrifices existing relations between and among suppliers, customers, and employees. More importantly, as a practical matter, the fact that the Bankruptcy Code allows existing management will stay in place is not by any stretch of the imagination a guaranty that they will.

In many cases, key creditor constituencies have lost faith in existing management prior to filing for bankruptcy and installed managers with

---

[15] *See* Edward S. Adams, *Governance in Chapter 11 Reorganizations: Reducing Costs, Improving Results*, 73 B.U. L. Rev. 581, 584–86 (1993); Thomas G. Kelch, *The Phantom Fiduciary: The Debtor in Possession in Chapter 11*, 38 Wayne L. Rev. 1323 (1992); Lynn M. LoPucki, *The Debtor in Full Control — Systems Failure Under Chapter 11 of the Bankruptcy Code*, pts.1 & 2, 57 Am. Bankr. L.J. 99, 247 (1983).

[16] Bankruptcy Code § 1101(1); *see also* § 4.02 Debtors and Debtors-in-Possession, *supra*.

[17] Bankruptcy Code § 1107(a); *see* § 4.02[B] Debtor-in-Possession, *supra*.

[18] Bankruptcy Code § 1107(a).

[19] Bankruptcy Code § 1108.

whom they are comfortable, or in many cases, turnaround managers who have particular skills with managing reorganizations. If this transition does not happen prior to bankruptcy, it very often happens shortly afterwards. Unlike old Chapter X and many bankruptcy statutes outside the U.S., the Code does not mandate replacement of management or addition of a trustee. Instead, it is handled on a case by case basis by the court and the key creditor constituencies.

Even though there is not usually a trustee appointed, the officers and managers of the debtor cannot function in precisely the same way that they did prior to bankruptcy. The managers are now responsible principally to the creditors not the owners. Their ability to act outside the ordinary course of business is constrained, because they must obtain court permission to do so. This opportunity for a hearing gives creditors a chance to object, and exposes these important decisions to considerable scrutiny.

[B] Role of Creditors and Creditors' Committees[20]

The role of individual creditors in a reorganization may be large or small, mostly depending on the relative size of the creditor and whether its claims are fully secured, partially secured, or unsecured. Secured creditors whose claims are secured by collateral that the debtor needs to keep in order to operate its business are likely to play a significant role in the reorganization process. The debtor needs to provide adequate protection against a decline in value of the creditor's interest in the debtor's property while the case is pending[21] and is required to promulgate a plan that fully compensates the creditor for its allowed secured claim.[22]

The level of participation of an unsecured creditor is likely to depend on the relative size of its claim. Chapter 11 plans cannot be confirmed consensually without the approval of creditors holding two-thirds of the amount of unsecured claims.[23] Thus, creditors with larger unsecured claims may have considerable influence in negotiations that lead to a plan of reorganization. Creditors with more than one third of the debt in a particular class may even have what amounts to a veto power over the plan. Large creditors whose claims are not quite large enough to block the plan entirely are still likely to have a big impact on the votes of smaller creditors who will follow the leadership of those with more at stake in the case.

---

[20] Daniel J. Bussel, *Coalition-Building Through Bankruptcy Creditors' Committees*, 43 UCLA L. Rev. 1547 (1996); Andrew DeNatale, *The Creditors' Committee Under the Bankruptcy Code — A Primer*, 55 Am. Bankr. L.J. 43 (1981); Kenneth N. Klee & K. John Shaffer, *Creditors' Committees Under Chapter 11 of the Bankruptcy Code*, 44 S.C. L. Rev. 995 (1993); Lynn M. LoPucki, *The Debtor in Full Control — Systems Failure Under Chapter 11 of the Bankruptcy Code?*, pts. 1 & 2, 57 Am. Bankr. L.J. 99, 247 (1983); Churchill Rodgers, *Rights and Duties of the Committee in Bondholders' Reorganizations*, 42 Harv. L. Rev. 899 (1929); Greg M. Zipes & Lisa L. Lambert, *Creditors' Committee Formation Dynamics: Issues in the Real World*, 77 Am. Bank. L.J. 229 (2003).

[21] *See* § 8.06[B] Relief from the Stay Upon Request of a Party, *supra*.

[22] *See* § 19.08[H] Treatment of Secured Claims, *infra*.

[23] *See* § 19.09[B] Voting by Classes of Claims and Interests, *infra*.

Except for "small business" cases,[24] the United States Trustee will appoint an official creditors' committee. In some cases, there may be more than one such committee.[25] The basic function of a creditors' committee is to act as advisor to and watchdog over the debtor, and to negotiate and appear on behalf of the creditors. Ideally, the committee scrutinizes the debtor's actions, makes recommendations concerning such matters as appointment of a trustee or examiner, and serves as the creditors' representative in negotiating the plan. Unfortunately, committees do not function equally well in all cases. In cases where there is not likely to be a large distribution to creditors, the committee may not be active, and in small Chapter 11 proceedings, it is sometimes impossible to assemble a creditors' committee.[26] When this happens, the United States Trustee is left to fulfill the supervisory and advisory role of a committee.

The 2005 Amendments added language requiring creditors' committees to provide access to information about the debtor to creditors who are not members of the committee.[27] Wide dissemination of information available to members of the committee carries with it the risk of the inappropriate dissemination of trade secrets and other private information about the debtor's customers and employees. Courts have begun to address these issues with appropriate protective orders.[28]

The United States Trustee is charged with responsibility for appointing a creditors' committee.[29] Members of the committee must hold unsecured claims and should be representative of the various types of unsecured creditors.[30] Ordinarily, the committee starts with the holders of the seven largest unsecured claims who are willing to serve.[31]

This in itself can create problems. There are some Chapter 11 cases in which there are fewer than seven unsecured creditors. There are many in which only one or two unsecured claims are large enough to make it worth the creditors' while to serve on the committee. The U.S. Trustee has no power of conscription; only those who are "willing to serve" are to be appointed.[32]

There are also frequent conflict of interest problems.[33] Not uncommonly, a major unsecured creditor also holds a large secured claim. For example,

---

[24] *See* § 19.17 Small Business Debtors, *infra.*

[25] *See also* § 4.04[B] Creditors' Committees, *supra.*

[26] In an effort to encourage participation on creditors' committees, the court is permitted to reimburse committee members' out-of-pocket expenses from the estate. Bankruptcy Code § 503(b)(3)(F).

[27] Bankruptcy Code § 1102(b)(3).

[28] *E.g.*, In re Refco, Inc., 336 B.R. 187 (Bankr. S.D.N.Y. 2006); *see* Deborah L. Thorne, *Creditors' Committees: The Fallout from BAPCPA Changes to 1102*, Am. Bankr. Inst. J., April 2006, at 20.

[29] Bankruptcy Code § 1102.

[30] Bankruptcy Code § 1102(a)(1).

[31] Bankruptcy Code § 1102(b)(1).

[32] Bankruptcy Code § 1102(b)(1).

[33] Carl A. Eklund & Lynn W. Roberts, *Bankruptcy Ethics: Article: The Problem with Credi-*

a creditor owed $650,000 that is secured by $500,000 worth of collateral may well be the one of the largest unsecured creditors because of its $150,000 unsecured claim. Yet there is a serious question about the propriety of a creditor with a large secured claim sitting on the creditors' committee. Because of its secured status, the creditor may well favor the immediate liquidation of the debtor. That, however, may not be in the best interests of unsecured creditors, whose only hope for substantial payment is a successful reorganization. It is generally accepted that the members of the creditors' committee owe a fiduciary duty to unsecured creditors;[34] the undersecured creditor's conflict of interest may prevent it from fulfilling that duty. Yet if that creditor is excluded, the likelihood that the committee will even exist, let alone do anything, is greatly reduced. For this and other reasons, partially secured creditors are not automatically disqualified from serving on the creditors' committee.[35]

Nor is this the only circumstance that might result in a creditor's having a conflict of interest that might disqualify it from serving on the committee. Creditors have sometimes been disqualified because of their status as shareholders, officers, directors, competitors, customers, employees, or insiders.[36] However, these creditors are not automatically disqualified; whether they are permitted to serve depends not only on the creditor's status, but also on any conduct that demonstrates that it will not act in the best interests its constituents.[37]

Creditors' committees are sometimes comprised of those who belonged to a pre-petition creditors' committee.[38] In cases where the debtor has engaged in extensive negotiations with a creditors' committee before filing its petition, permitting the existing committee to continue to function is likely an efficient way to facilitate the development of a reorganization plan. However, the United States Trustee may not appoint any such pre-petition committee as the creditors' committee unless it was "fairly chosen and is representative of the different kinds of claims to be represented."[39]

---

tors' Committees in Chapter 11: How to Manage the Inherent Conflicts Without Loss of Function, 5 Am. Bankr. Inst. L. Rev. 129 (1997); Greg M. Zipes & Lisa L. Lambert, *Creditors' Committee Formation Dynamics: Issues in the Real World*, 77 Am. Bankr. L.J. 229 (2003).

[34] In the words of one case, a member of a creditors' committee must be "honest, loyal, trustworthy and without conflicting interests, and with undivided loyalty and allegiance to their constituents . . . . Conflicts of interest on the part of representative persons or committees are thus not [to] be tolerated." Johns-Manville Sales Corp. v. Doan (In re Johns-Manville Corp.), 26 B.R. 919, 925 (Bankr. S.D.N.Y. 1983).

[35] *Compare* In re Walat Farms, Inc., 64 B.R. 65 (Bankr. E.D. Mich. 1986) (partially secured creditor not per se disqualified), *with* In re Glendale Woods Aparptments., Ltd., 25 B.R. 414 (Bankr. D. Md. 1982) (partially secured creditor should not serve because of its potential conflict of interest).

[36] Kenneth N. Klee & K. John Shaffer, *Creditors' Committees Under Chapter 11 of the Bankruptcy Code*, 44 S.C. L. Rev. 995, 1012–21 (1993).

[37] Kenneth N. Klee & K. John Shaffer, *Creditors' Committees Under Chapter 11 of the Bankruptcy Code*, 44 S.C. L. Rev. 995, 1013 (1993).

[38] Bankruptcy Code § 1102(b)(1).

[39] Bankruptcy Code § 1103(b)(1).

Sometimes additional creditors' committees are appointed. Upon the request of a party in interest, the court may order the United States Trustee to appoint one or more special creditors' committees, if this is necessary to assure adequate protection of some group of creditors.[40] For example, in some of the mass tort bankruptcies, the tort victims have been given a separate creditors' committee to represent their special interests.[41]

[C] Role of Owners[42]

Owners of the debtor's business — in the Code's parlance, "interest holders" — have little formal function *as such* in the Chapter 11 reorganization process. Interest holders include stockholders, partners, and in the case of an individual sole proprietorship, the debtor. They have the right to be heard in matters that affect them.[43] They have the right to vote on a plan of reorganization.[44] However, some reorganization plans give interest holders nothing. If so, they are deemed to have rejected the plan and there is no need for them to vote.[45]

However, except in cases involving larger publicly-held corporations, the owners of the business are also likely to be its managers. As managers, they have an important role to play in the day-to-day affairs of the debtor-in-possession. But as owners, they are largely irrelevant unless they are able to convince the creditors to permit them to retain a stake in the debtor after it is reorganized.

In a medium-to-large reorganization, where the company's stock is publicly traded, the existing equity holders are sometimes displaced wholly or in part as owners by creditors. Indeed, where creditors are not being paid in full, it is difficult to see why old equity should receive any distribution at all on account of its ownership interest. Nonetheless, creditors are often willing to consent to a small distribution to old equity to obtain their cooperation. For example, a plan might provide that the reorganized company would be owned 98% by pre-petition creditors (who would in effect be trading part of their debt for equity in the new company) and 2% by pre-petition stockholders.

In rare cases, there is a committee, similar in structure and purpose to a creditors' committee, to represent the interest holders. Upon the request of a party in interest, the court may order the U.S. Trustee to appoint a

[40] Bankruptcy Code § 1102(a)(2).

[41] *See* Ronald J. Bacigal, The Limits of Litigation: The Dalkon Shield Controversy 59–61 (1990). In the *A.H. Robbins* case, which involved a defective intrauterine birth control device, the first tort claimants' committee disintegrated and was replaced by a second committee.

[42] Douglas G. Baird, Robert K. Rasmussen & Christopher W. Frost, Essay, *Control Rights, Priority Rights, and the Conceptual Foundations of Corporate Reorganizations*, 87 Va. L. Rev. 921 (2001); Christopher W. Frost, *The Theory, Reality and Pragmatism of Corporate Governance in Bankruptcy Reorganizations*, 72 Am. Bank. L.J. 103 (1998).

[43] Bankruptcy Code § 1109(b).

[44] Bankruptcy Code § 1126(a).

[45] Bankruptcy Code § 1126(g).

committee of equity security holders.[46] This is done only if necessary to assure adequate representation of the equity holders, because they are particularly numerous, and there is some chance that they might receive a distribution.[47] Normally, this committee again consists of the seven largest holders of the debtor's equity securities.[48]

There is some uncertainty about the degree to which equity holders can exercise power over the management of the debtor. Outside of bankruptcy, the function of corporate management is to create the maximum return for shareholders on their investment. All of this changes in bankruptcy.

The function of the debtor-in-possession (or, more precisely, those persons who are actually managing the debtor-in-possession) is to act on behalf of the entire bankruptcy estate.[49] This creates a diffuse and sometimes contradictory set of fiduciary duties to all stakeholders in the reorganizing entity.[50] As a practical matter, the debtor-in-possession's efforts normally are aimed at producing a maximum return for creditors, because in nearly all Chapter 11 cases the entity is hopelessly insolvent and the equity interests are completely under water.

One of the specific questions that has arisen in a few cases is whether the shareholders of a Chapter 11 debtor still retain their state law right to replace the board of trustees. Generally speaking, the courts have allowed shareholders to elect a board, provided this will not interfere with the bankruptcy proceeding.[51] However, the ability to elect a board is rather hollow. The board cannot unilaterally exercise its most important power — that is, to replace the management — at least before confirmation of the plan.[52]

[D] Appointment of Trustee or Examiner[53]

In most Chapter 11 reorganization cases, no trustee is appointed to take over the management of the debtor's affairs. As explained above, replacing current management with a trustee involves considerable expense. It generally occurs only when both the creditors and the court have lost faith in the ability of incumbent management to turn the business around and

[46] Bankruptcy Code § 1102(a)(2).

[47] Bankruptcy Code § 1102(a)(2).

[48] Bankruptcy Code § 1102(b)(2).

[49] *See* Official Committee of Unsecured Creditors v. Chinery (In re Cybergenics Corp.), 226 F.3d 237, 243 (3d Cir. 2000); In re Pacific Forest Indus., Inc., 95 B.R. 740 (Bankr. C.D. Cal. 1989).

[50] Raymond T. Nimmer & Richard B. Feinberg, *Chapter 11 Business Governance: Fiduciary Duties, Business Judgment, Trustees and Exclusivity*, 6 Bankr. Dev. J. 1 (1989).

[51] In re Johns Manville Corp., 801 F.2d 60 (2d Cir. 1986); Saxon Indus. Inc. v. NKFW Partners (In re Saxon Indus., Inc.), 39 B.R. 49 (Bankr. S.D.N.Y. 1984).

[52] In re Lifeguard Indus., 37 B.R. 3 (Bankr. S.D. Ohio 1983).

[53] Richard Levin & Alesia Ranney-Marinelli, *The Creeping Repeal of Chapter 11: The Significant Business Provisions of the Bankruptcy Abuse Prevention and Consumer Protection Act of 2005*, 79 Am. Bankr. L.J. 603, 618–20 (2005).

no practical alternative exists. Management may be so incompetent or corrupt that the impact of replacing them, however bad, is preferable to keeping them in place. In such cases, the court is empowered to displace current management by appointing a trustee.[54]

Any time after commencement of the case and before confirmation of a plan, any party in interest (or the United States Trustee) may request appointment of a trustee to displace management.[55] The Code specifies that after notice and an opportunity for a hearing, the court "shall order the appointment of a trustee" if either of two alternative statutory grounds is established: "for cause, including fraud, dishonesty, incompetence or gross mismanagement of the affairs of the debtor by current management," or "if such appointment is in the interests of creditors, any equity security holders, and other interests of the estate."[56] The mere fact that the debtor's business has been losing money and has found it necessary to file a bankruptcy petition is not, by itself, a sufficient justification for the appointment of a trustee. Likewise, the mere fact that current management has made bad decisions or has been guilty of some mismanagement is not enough to warrant the appointment of a trustee.[57] Quite to the contrary, Chapter 11 contemplates a strong presumption that the debtor should remain in control of the estate and thus imposes a burden on the moving party to demonstrate, by clear and convincing evidence, that appointment of a trustee is necessary.[58]

The duties of a Chapter 11 trustee are nominally the same as those of a Chapter 7 trustee.[59] In practice, though, there are differences.[60] Chief among these are that the Chapter 11 trustee has a somewhat broader duty to investigate the debtor, and he must make a written report on the results of his investigation.[61] Moreover, if it is still possible to go forward in Chapter 11, the trustee is to prepare and file a reorganization plan; if Chapter 11 is not feasible, the trustee is to recommend either a conversion of the case to another chapter or dismissal.[62]

The trustee may be discharged and the debtor-in-possession restored, but this is even rarer than the initial displacement of the debtor-in-possession. At any time prior to confirmation and upon the request of a party in interest

[54] *See* In re Bonneville Pac. Corp., 196 B.R. 868 (Bankr. D. Utah 1996) (requiring disgorgement of fees paid to attorneys who represented the debtor-in-possession, due to mismanagement of the debtor's affairs).

[55] Bankruptcy Code § 1104(a).

[56] Bankruptcy Code § 1104(a)(1)-(2).

[57] *See* In re Adelphia Commc'n Corp., 342 B.R. 122 (S.D.N.Y. 2006).

[58] Official Comm. of Asbestos Claimants v. G-I Holdings, Inc. (In re G-I Holdings, Inc.), 385 F.3d 313, 317–18 (4th Cir. 2004); In re Sharon Steel Corp., 871 F.2d 1217, 1225 (3d Cir. 1989); *see also* In re Adelphia Commc'n Corp., 336 B.R. 610 (Bankr. S.D.N.Y. 2006).

[59] Bankruptcy Code § 704; *see* § 4.05[A] Case Trustees, *supra*.

[60] Bankruptcy Code § 1106(a).

[61] Bankruptcy Code § 1106(a)(3), (4).

[62] Bankruptcy Code § 1106(a)(5).

(or the United States Trustee), the court may terminate the trustee's appointment and restore the debtor to possession and management of the property and business.[63] Note, however, that this does not necessarily mean that the pre-trustee management is restored; the debtor-in-possession may well be managed by somebody else.

The court has a less drastic alternative to appointment of a trustee that is more commonly exercised: appointment of an examiner.[64] Upon the motion of a party in interest (including the United States Trustee), the court "shall" appoint an examiner to investigate the debtor if doing so is in the interests of creditors, equity security holders, and others with an interest in the estate,[65] or if the debtor's fixed, unliquidated, unsecured debts (excluding those for goods, services, or taxes, and those owed to an insider) exceed $5 million.[66] Note that the court's discretion is considerably more restrained; if the debtor exceeds the $5 million threshold and a motion is made, the court must make the appointment.[67] Appointment of an examiner in these cases is not mandatory unless someone asks to have one appointed. This requirement is one of the last formal vestiges of the old distinction drawn in the Bankruptcy Act between "big" reorganizations (Chapter X) and little ones.

In cases where appointment is not mandatory, the courts exercise considerable discretion, just as they do with appointment of trustees. Appointment of an examiner is far less disruptive to the debtor than the appointment of a trustee; thus, the considerations that underlie the reluctance to appoint the latter do not apply in full force when someone seeks appointment of the former. However, appointment of an examiner should not be routine. Examiners can be expensive and can slow down the proceeding. Moreover, much of what the examiner does can be done by the creditors' committee — assuming it has the resources and the debtor is cooperative.

An examiner's job is implicit in the title: to investigate "fraud, dishonesty, incompetence, misconduct, mismanagement or irregularity . . . by current or former management of the debtor."[68] The examiner is then to report to the court and the creditors' committee regarding its investigation.[69] The

---

[63] Bankruptcy Code § 1105.

[64] Bankruptcy Code § 1104(c); *see* Paula Hunt, Note, *Bankruptcy Examiners Under Section 1104(b): Appointment and Role in Complex Chapter 11 Reorganizations of Failed LBOs*, 70 Wash. U. L.Q. 821 (1992).

[65] Bankruptcy Code § 1104(c)(1).

[66] Bankruptcy Code § 1104(c)(2).

[67] Morgenstern v. Revco. D.S., Inc. (In re Revco D.S., Inc.), 898 F.2d 498 (6th Cir. 1990) (plain language of the Code requires appointment of examiner if unsecured debt exceeds $5,000,000 and U.S. Trustee so moves); *but see* In re Rutenberg, 158 B.R. 230, 233 (Bankr. N.D. Fla. 1993) (examiner not mandatory where appointment would delay administration of the case).

[68] Bankruptcy Code §§ 1104(c), 1106(a)(3).

[69] Bankruptcy Code § 1106(a)(4).

report may include recommendations for further action, such as the appointment of a trustee, or, in the case of misconduct by the debtor's counsel, disallowance of fees.[70] Recently, examiners are sometimes appointed and given "enhanced powers" such as to pursue lawsuits against third parties[71] (whom members of the debtor's management team may not want to offend) or to otherwise supervise the debtor's affairs.[72]

[E] Role of the Securities and Exchange Commission

Under the Bankruptcy Act, the Securities and Exchange Commission (SEC) played a crucial role in Chapter X proceedings.[73] Moreover, because of the uncertain line between Chapter X and Chapter XI, the SEC also had considerable influence in large Chapter XI proceedings as well (even though it had no formal role).[74]

The SEC's role is considerably diminished compared to what it was under the Bankruptcy Act. Under § 1109(a), it may raise, appear, and be heard on any issue in a Chapter 11 case.[75] It may not, however, appeal from any judgment, order, or decree entered by the court.[76] In practice, the SEC has virtually disappeared from the bankruptcy courts.[77]

[F] Role of the United States Trustee

Some of the vacuum left by the SEC has been occupied by the United States Trustee, an agency of the United States government, operating as part of the United States Department of Justice, with responsibility for supervising some aspects of bankruptcy cases.

In Chapter 11 cases, the United States Trustee plays a role in convening meetings of creditors and equity security holders,[78] appointing official creditors' committees and equity interest holders' committees,[79] monitoring and commenting on applications for attorneys' fees and other professionals' compensation,[80] and monitoring cases that involve small business

---

[70] *See* In re The Leslie Fay Co., 175 B.R. 525 (Bankr. S.D.N.Y. 1994).

[71] *See, e.g.*, In re Apex Oil Co., 111 B.R. 235 (Bankr. D. Mo. 1990).

[72] *E.g.*, In re Boileau, 736 F.2d 503 (9th Cir. 1984); Schuster v. Dragone, 266 B.R. 268 (D. Conn. 2001).

[73] David A. Skeel, Jr., Debt's Dominion: A History of Bankruptcy Law in America 160–66 (2001).

[74] The SEC often engaged in negotiations with borderline Chapter X or Chapter XI debtors to determine the conditions under which the debtor would be, in effect, allowed by the SEC to use the latter chapter.

[75] Bankruptcy Code § 1109(a).

[76] Bankruptcy Code § 1109(a).

[77] James J. White, *Death and Resurrection of Secured Credit*, 12 Am. Bankr. Inst. L. Rev. 139, 188 (2004).

[78] *See* Bankruptcy Code § 341(a), (b).

[79] Bankruptcy Code § 1102.

[80] For a discussion of professional compensation under the Bankruptcy Code, see § 21.03 Fees for Professionals, *infra*.

debtors.[81] The United States Trustee has standing to seek appointment of a trustee or an examiner,[82] but is unlikely to take this action if there is an active creditors' committee in the case. Likewise, the United States Trustee may seek to have a Chapter 11 case converted or dismissed if there are no active creditors and if the case does not seem to be making sufficient progress toward promulgation of a plan.[83]

§ 19.04 Property of a Chapter 11 Estate[84]

The property of a debtor's Chapter 11 estate is mostly determined by § 541. Thus, it includes all property interests of the debtor when the petition was filed,[85] plus any proceeds, products, offspring, rents, or profits earned from property of the estate.[86] Unlike a typical Chapter 7 liquidation case where the debtor's business has already ceased operations or is quickly wound up by the trustee, Chapter 11 debtors usually continue their business operations in much the same fashion as they had before the case began. Accordingly, these proceeds, products, rents, and profits are likely to be considerable. Section 541 also contemplates that the estate will acquire new property rights after commencement of the estate, and that these new assets naturally belong to the estate.

The 2005 Amendments added a special provision, like those already appearing in Chapters 12 and 13, that bring the post-petition earnings of an individual Chapter 11 debtor into the estate.[87] In a Chapter 11 case of an individual, as in Chapter 13 cases and many Chapter 12 cases, the debtor's post-petition operations are likely to be funded primarily through the debtor's personal earnings. Without this provision, an individual's post-petition personal earnings would be excluded from his estate.[88] Though even with it, individual debtors who wanted to confirm plans still used those earnings to make payments. More importantly, the 2005 Amendments carried over the "disposable income" and "commitment period" requirements from Chapter 13, so Chapter 11 now effectively requires an individual Chapter 11 debtor to submit all of his disposable income to payments under the plan, for five years.[89]

---

[81] 28 U.S.C.S. § 586(a)(7) (LexisNexis Supp. 2006).

[82] Bankruptcy Code § 1104(a).

[83] Bankruptcy Code § 1112(e).

[84] Robert J. Keach, *Dead Man Filing Redux: Is the New Individual Chapter Eleven Unconstitutional?*, 13 Am. Bankr. Inst. L. Rev. 483 (2005).

[85] Bankruptcy Code § 541(a)(1).

[86] Bankruptcy Code § 541(a)(6).

[87] Bankruptcy Code § 1115; *see* Robert J. Keach, *Dead Man Filing Redux: Is the New Individual Chapter Eleven Unconstitutional?*, 13 Am. Bankr. Inst. L. Rev. 483 (2005).

[88] Bankruptcy Code § 541(a)(6); *see* § 7.02[F][2] Earnings from Individual Debtor's Post-Petition Services Excluded, *supra*.

[89] Bankruptcy Code § 1129(a)(15)(B); *see* James Nash, *18th Congressional District Race, Bankruptcy May Haunt Padget*, Columbus Dispatch, Sept. 29, 2006, at D1 (if elected, congressional candidate's salary as member of Congress would be submitted to bankruptcy court to fund candidate's Chapter 11 plan, filed in wake of small town hardware store collapse).

A Chapter 11 debtor's ability to use, sell, or lease estate property is governed primarily by § 363.[90] As explained elsewhere, it imposes restrictions on the debtor's use of any cash collateral[91] and on the debtor's use of any estate property outside the ordinary course of business.[92] However, the power to use and sell collateral in the ordinary course is perhaps the single greatest innovation in Chapter 11, and allows the business to continue operating without interruption, notwithstanding bankruptcy.

§ 19.05 Conversion and Dismissal of Chapter 11 Cases

Chapter 11 debtors sometimes realize that their hopes for successful reorganization are unrealistic. In these cases, the debtor may voluntarily seek to convert the case to Chapter 7 or to dismiss the case and permit the state law collection process to run its course. In other circumstances, the debtor may be unwilling to accept the inevitability of its financial demise, and may resist creditors' efforts to end the reorganization process. Section 1112 provides for both voluntary and involuntary conversion or dismissal.

"Conversion" refers to transferring the case from one chapter of the Bankruptcy Code to another. In the context of a Chapter 11 reorganization case it involves converting the case from Chapter 11 to Chapter 7. In Chapter 7, a trustee is appointed to take over administration of the debtor's estate, and liquidation is the most likely outcome.

Not surprisingly, the case may be converted to Chapter 7 only if the debtor is otherwise eligible for Chapter 7 relief. Because railroads and some financial institutions are eligible for relief under Chapter 11, but are not eligible for relief under Chapter 7,[93] their cases cannot be converted.

Alternatively, the case might be dismissed. If this occurs, the case is terminated. Termination of the case dissolves the automatic stay and thus permits creditors to initiate or continue their efforts to collect from the debtor. Unless the debtor has recovered from its financial difficulties or is able to enter into an out-of-court settlement with its creditors, dismissal is likely to lead to piecemeal liquidation of the debtor's assets.

[A] Voluntary Conversion or Dismissal

The language of § 1112, which says that "[t]he debtor may convert a case under this chapter," appears to give a Chapter 11 debtor a nearly absolute right to give up on its efforts to reorganize and convert the case to Chapter 7. However, courts usually read § 1112(a) on voluntary conversion or dismissal together with § 1112(b) regarding involuntary conversion and

[90] *See* § 9.03 Use, Sale, or Lease of Estate Property, *supra.*

[91] *See* § 9.03[B] Use of Cash Collateral, *supra.*

[92] *See* § 9.03[C] Use, Sale, or Lease Outside the Ordinary Course, *supra.*

[93] *See* Bankruptcy Code § 109.

dismissal and dismiss the case, rather than convert it, where involuntary dismissal rather than conversion is otherwise warranted.[94]

As specified in § 1112(a), the debtor also lacks the right to convert the case if (i) the debtor is not a debtor-in-possession (that is, if a trustee has been appointed to administer the estate and the business); (ii) the case began as an involuntary Chapter 11 case; or (iii) the case was converted to Chapter 11 on the motion of someone other than the debtor.[95]

[B] Involuntary Conversion or Dismissal

A debtor's case can be converted or dismissed involuntarily at the request of any party in interest.[96] Section 1112(b)(4) supplies a long, but non-exclusive list of circumstances that require the court to convert or dismiss a case, unless the court finds that there are "unusual circumstances specifically identified by the court that establish that" conversion or dismissal "is not in the best interests of creditors and the estate."[97] Although the items contained in laundry list of circumstances warranting conversion or dismissal are conjoined by the word "and"[98] no one would plausibly contend that all sixteen specified circumstances must exist to warrant conversion or dismissal.[99] The debtor or other party who resists conversion or dismissal must also demonstrate "that there is a reasonable likelihood that a plan will be confirmed within the time frames established [elsewhere in the Code],"[100] and if the grounds for granting the motion are not among the items specifically listed in § 1112(b)(4), that the act or omission involved both was reasonably justified and will be cured within a reasonable time.[101]

The 2005 Amendments added language that ensures that motions for conversion or dismissal will be heard and determined quickly. New § 1112(b)(3) requires the court to "commence the hearing on a motion [to convert or dismiss] not later than 30 days after the filing of the motion." It further requires the court to "decide the motion not later than 15 days after the commencement of [the] hearing, unless the movant expressly consents to a continuance for a specific period of time or compelling circumstances prevent the court from meeting the [specified] time limits."[102]

---

[94] Monroe Bank & Trust v. Pinnock, 349 B.R. 493 (E.D. Mich. 2006); In re Adler, 329 B.R. 406 (Bankr. S.D.N.Y. 2005).

[95] Bankruptcy Code § 1112(a)(1)-(3).

[96] Bankruptcy Code § 1112(b)(1). Language in former § 1112(b), that explicitly permitted the United States Trustee or a bankruptcy administrator to bring the motion, has been removed. However, because § 307 explicitly permits the United States Trustee to "appear and be heard on any issue," the language in former § 1112(b) that refers to these parties may have been considered superfluous.

[97] Bankruptcy Code § 1112(b)(1).

[98] Bankruptcy Code § 1112(b)(4)(O).

[99] In re TCR of Denver, Inc., 338 B.R. 494 (Bankr. D. Colo. 2006) ("and" means "or").

[100] Bankruptcy Code § 1112(b)(2)(A).

[101] Bankruptcy Code § 1112(b)(2)(B).

[102] Bankruptcy Code § 1112(b)(3).

The specific statutory grounds for conversion or dismissal fall into several broad categories. The most important grounds are those based on the unlikelihood that the debtor will be able to reorganize, usually due to devastating financial circumstances that make the debtor's hopes for successful reorganization unrealistic. Other grounds for conversion or dismissal are based on the debtor's inability or unwillingness to comply with technical requirements imposed on Chapter 11 debtors. The debtor's bad faith in filing the petition, not surprisingly, also provides grounds for conversion or dismissal.

Since a Chapter 11 discharge is normally granted when the plan is confirmed,[103] conversion or dismissal prevents the debtor from obtaining a discharge. However, many of the grounds for conversion or dismissal might also justify appointment of a trustee.[104] In determining whether to convert or dismiss the case, the court is first required to determine whether appointment of a trustee or examiner would be in the best interests of creditors and the estate.[105]

[1] Inability to Reorganize

Cases involving debtors who are financially incapable of reorganizing should be converted or dismissed. The Bankruptcy Code identifies several specific circumstances that indicate a debtor's inability to reorganize successfully. These circumstances nearly always reflect terminal flaws in the debtor's business plan or the debtor's practical inability to effectuate its financial strategies.

Thus, conversion or dismissal is usually warranted if there has been a "substantial or continuing loss to or diminution of the estate," combined with "the absence of a reasonable likelihood of rehabilitation."[106] In other words, if the debtor continues to lose money while the case is pending and cannot even sustain its current operations, there is no reason to believe that it will be able to earn enough money to begin making payments to its creditors.

Consider, for example, an auto repair shop, with rent, utilities, and salaries of $6,000 per month that is earning only $5,500 in monthly revenue. The debtor is losing $500 each month it remains in business, without taking into account its obligations to creditors. It has no hope of reorganizing, and because liquidation is both inevitable and imminent, the court is likely to convert it to Chapter 7. In the blunt words of an old § 77B case, "however honest in its efforts the debtor may be, and however sincere its motives, the District Court is not bound to clog its docket with visionary or impracticable schemes for resuscitation."[107]

---

[103] Bankruptcy Code § 1141(d).

[104] Bankruptcy Code § 1104(a)(1); *see* § 19.03[D] Appointment of Trustee or Examiner, *supra.*

[105] Bankruptcy Code § 1104(a)(3).

[106] Bankruptcy Code § 1112(b)(4)(A).

[107] Tennessee Publ'g Co. v. American Nat'l Bank, 299 U.S. 18, 22 (1936).

However, a creditor's motion to convert the case during the early stages of the case, when the debtor has not had sufficient time to resolve its underlying business problems, is unlikely to be successful. Chapter 11 debtors are likely to have been losing money in the months leading up to their decision to reorganize, and there is nothing in Chapter 11 that automatically alters the debtor's ongoing business operations.

However, the debtor's failure to propose a plan or obtain confirmation of a plan within the time limits imposed by the Code is a powerful indicator that the debtor is unlikely to reorganize, and should be liquidated. Accordingly, the Bankruptcy Code specifies that the case should either be converted or be dismissed if, within the time limits imposed by the court, the debtor fails to file a plan, fails to file a disclosure statement regarding a plan that has already been submitted, or fails to obtain confirmation of a plan.[108]

In most cases, debtors have an exclusive right to file a plan for 120 days and a minimum of 180 days to have it confirmed.[109] These deadlines can be extended by the court for an outside maximum of eighteen and twenty months, respectively.[110] The court's refusal to extend the deadlines indicates the court's belief that the debtor's prospects for reorganization are slim, and it is likely to prompt a creditor to seek conversion or dismissal. But during the exclusive period, courts generally give the debtor the benefit of the doubt.

"Gross mismanagement of the estate" is a basis for conversion or dismissal.[111] Mismanagement of the debtor, however severe, prior to the initiation of the case, is not sufficient; the mismanagement complained of must have been that of *the estate*. Moreover, mere negligence in the management of the estate does not constitute grounds for conversion or dismissal. The mismanagement must have been gross. Alternatively, gross mismanagement of the estate might warrant appointment of a trustee or an examiner, particularly if the debtor's prospects for reorganization would improve significantly with the substitution of new management.[112]

The Code also provides for dismissal or conversion due to circumstances that may develop after a plan is confirmed. These circumstances include revocation of confirmation under § 1144,[113] the debtor's inability to effectuate substantial consummation of a confirmed plan,[114] the debtor's material

[108] Bankruptcy Code § 1112(b)(4)(J); *see* In re Woodbrook Assocs., 19 F.3d 312 (7th Cir. 1994).

[109] Bankruptcy Code § 1121(c).

[110] Bankruptcy Code § 1121(d).

[111] Bankruptcy Code § 1112(b)(4)(B).

[112] Bankruptcy Code § 1104(a)(1); *see* § 19.03[D] Appointment of Trustee or Examiner, *supra*.

[113] Bankruptcy Code § 1112(b)(4)(L); *see* § 19.13[B] Revocation of Confirmation, *supra*.

[114] Bankruptcy Code § 1112(b)(4)(M); *see* § 19.13[C] Implementation of the Plan, *supra*.

default with respect to the terms of a confirmed plan,[115] or termination of a confirmed plan due to the failure of a condition specified in the plan.[116]

"Substantial consummation" is defined by the Code. It means (i) transfer of all or substantially all the property that the plan proposes be transferred; and (ii) the debtor or it's successor's assumption of the business or of the management of all or substantially all the property dealt with by the plan; and (iii) commencement of distributions under the plan.[117] It is important to distinguish "substantial consummation" from confirmation. A plan may be confirmed, but the debtor may nonetheless be unable to accomplish what the plan provides. If the debtor is unable to accomplish these essential tasks, the plan has not been substantially consummated. In plain terms, the debtor's inability to perform the plan is a basis for conversion or dismissal.[118]

[2] Failure to Comply with Code Requirements

The Bankruptcy Code imposes an array of duties on a Chapter 11 debtor. Failure to comply with these obligations might constitute grounds for dismissal or conversion. Section 1112(b)(4) identifies several such failures that provide grounds for dismissal or conversion unless the debtor demonstrates that the failure was due to unusual circumstances, not customarily encountered in a Chapter 11 reorganization, that establish that conversion or dismissal is not in the best interests of creditors and the estate, despite the debtor's defalcation. Most of these specific grounds reflect the debtor's inability to maintain viable ongoing business operations. Others are designed to ensure the integrity of the reorganization process.

The 2005 Amendments also added "failure to maintain appropriate insurance that poses a risk to the estate or to the public" to the list of explicit grounds for conversion or dismissal.[119] A debtor's failure to maintain casualty insurance on a secured creditor's collateral is likely, as explained elsewhere, to lead to relief from the automatic stay, which would permit the secured creditor to foreclose immediately.[120] Section 1112(b)(4)(C) goes beyond this and contemplates casualty insurance on all of the estate's property, regardless of whether it is covered by a creditor's lien.

The reference to risks posed to "the public" requires the debtor to maintain liability insurance. At a minimum, this seems to require the debtor to maintain liability coverage for motor vehicles that it operates and coverage for injuries that the debtor's customers might suffer as a result of unsafe

[115] Bankruptcy Code § 1112(b)(4)(N).

[116] Bankruptcy Code § 1112(b)(4)(O).

[117] Bankruptcy Code § 1101(2).

[118] The plan can be modified either before or after its confirmation. If the modified plan is confirmed, it becomes the plan that must be substantially consummated. *See* § 19.12 Modification of Chapter 11 Plans, *supra*.

[119] Bankruptcy Code § 1112(b)(4)(C).

[120] *See* § 8.06[B] Relief from the Stay Upon Request of a Party, *supra*.

conditions on the debtor's premises. Depending on the debtor's business, it might also require the debtor to maintain insurance to protect those who might be injured or adversely affected by the debtor's business activities. Thus, a hospital would be required to carry malpractice coverage, and a manufacturer might be required to carry insurance to protect it from product liability claims. Debtors who are unable to provide coverage that is equivalent to that which is carried by other similar businesses who are not in financial difficulty will probably be forced to liquidate.

Section 1112(b)(4)(D) specifies that conversion or dismissal is warranted by the debtor's "unauthorized use of cash collateral [that is] substantially harmful to one or more creditors." This new language must be read in conjunction with § 363(c)(2), which prohibits a debtor from using collateral that consists of cash or cash equivalents (cash collateral) without prior court approval.[121] Chapter 11 debtors who use funds in a bank account that is subject to a creditor's security interest, without obtaining prior approval of the court are vulnerable to having their cases converted or dismissed if the debtor's use of the collateral was "substantially harmful" either to the creditor who held the security interest or to other creditors. However, if the debtor's business remains viable, despite the debtor's misconduct, appointment of a trustee is more likely to be in the best interests of creditors and the estate.

Not surprisingly, the debtor's "failure to comply with an order of the court" can have a devastating effect on the viability of a case. The broad language of § 1112(b)(4)(E) requires conversion or dismissal upon the request of a party in interest, for any violation of a court order unless, due to unusual circumstances, conversion or dismissal is not in the best interests of creditors.[122] Cases decided before 2005, when this language was added to § 1112(b), permitted the court to convert or dismiss a case for failure to comply with the court's orders, but most of the decisions granting a motion to convert or dismiss involved a debtor's willful failure to comply.[123] Under the amended language, negligent or even inadvertent failures require the court to grant a party's motion, unless the debtor explains the unusual circumstances that warrant continuation of the case, despite the debtor's inability or unwillingness to comply with the court's orders.

Language has been added to § 1112(b)(4) that requires dismissal or conversion due the debtor's "failure to satisfy timely any filing or reporting requirement established by this title or by any [applicable] rule."[124] Chapter 11, the Federal Rules of Bankruptcy Procedure, and commonly

[121] Bankruptcy Code § 363(c)(2); *see* § 9.03[B] Use of "Cash Collateral," *supra*.

[122] Bankruptcy Code § 1112(b)(1).

[123] Babakitis v. Robino (In re Robino), 243 B.R. 472, 485–86 (Bankr. N.D. Ala. 1999); Matter of Berryhill, 127 B.R. 427 (Bankr. N.D. Ind. 1991); *see also* Hall v. Vance, 887 F.2d 1041, 1045 (10th Cir. 1989) (denying motion to convert and noting likelihood that pro se debtor's failure to comply was due to his unfamiliarity with Chapter 11, rather than willful attempt to defy a court order).

[124] Bankruptcy Code § 1112(b)(4)(F).

applicable local rules require Chapter 11 debtors to regularly submit a variety of reports, including regular monthly reports concerning the financial operations of their business. Like all of the paperwork associated with operating a business in Chapter 11, preparing these reports is not free. Debtors without the funds necessary to prepare these reports are vulnerable to having their cases dismissed under this provision.[125]

Language added in 2005 makes the debtor's failure to attend the § 341 meeting of creditors convened after the filing of a Chapter 11 petition, or failure to attend an examination of the debtor ordered pursuant to Bankruptcy Rule 2004, cause for conversion or dismissal of the debtor's case. There are few justifications a debtor might provide, other than an accident or unanticipated illness, that would justify the debtor's failure to appear for these scheduled events. Whether courts will order conversion or dismissal when the debtor's failure was due to inadvertence or neglect, in cases where conversion would likely reduce the distribution to creditors, remains to be seen. However, the tough new language of § 1112(b)(1), which compels conversion or dismissal "absent unusual circumstances . . . that establish that the requested conversion or dismissal is not in the best interests of creditors" indicates that courts should be less tolerant than in the past.[126] On the other hand, it seems unlikely that few debtors who are earnestly seeking the benefits of Chapter 11 will miss either the § 341 meeting or a Rule 2004 examination for frivolous reasons.

The 2005 Amendments make the debtor's "failure timely to provide information or attend meetings reasonably requested by the United States Trustee" grounds for conversion or dismissal.[127] The United States Trustee (or a bankruptcy administrator, in districts where the U.S. Trustee's office is not operating) has authority to seek information from debtors concerning their operations. It also has authority to require the debtor to attend meetings concerning the progress of the case. Section 1112(b)(4)(H) gives teeth to these powers by making the debtor's failure to comply with these demands grounds for dismissing or converting the debtor's case.

New § 1112(b)(4)(I) specifies that the debtor's failure to pay any taxes "owed after the date of the order for relief or to file tax returns due after the date of the order for relief" warrants conversion or dismissal of the debtor's case.[128] This language reinforces decisions reached before the 2005 Amendments that permit the court to dismiss or convert the debtor's case on account of these failures[129] by making conversion or dismissal

[125] *E.g.*, In re Robino, 243 B.R. 472, 485–86 (Bankr. N.D. Ala. 1999).

[126] Bankruptcy Code § 1112(b)(1).

[127] Bankruptcy Code § 1112(b)(4)(H).

[128] Bankruptcy Code § 1112(b)(4)(I).

[129] *E.g.*, Berryhill v. United States (In re Berryhill), 189 B.R. 463, 466 (N.D. Ill. 1995); *see* Craig A. Gargotta, *Post-Petition Tax Compliance Under the Bankruptcy Code: Can the IRS Enforce Tax Collection After Bankruptcy is Filed?*, 11 Am. Bankr. Inst. L. Rev. 113, 126 (2003) (regarding conversion of Chapter 13 cases).

mandatory, unless the debtor explains the unusual circumstances that establish why dismissal is not in the bests interests of creditors and the estate.[130]

Finally, new § 1112(b)(4)(P) now specifies that the debtor's failure to pay any "domestic support obligation that first becomes payable after the date of the filing of the petition" is grounds for conversion or dismissal.[131] This added language only applies to the few Chapter 11 cases filed by individual debtors, as corporations and partnerships do not have domestic support obligations.[132]

[3] Bad Faith Filing[133]

In addition to the statutory grounds contained in § 1112, a Chapter 11 case may be dismissed on the grounds that it was filed in bad faith.[134] However, the precise parameters of this judicially created rule are both uncertain and controversial. Courts do not agree whether good faith should be measured by a subjective test that focuses on the debtor's intent[135] or an objective test that focuses on the debtor's practical ability to reorganize.[136]

Dismissal due to bad faith issues often arise in the context of proceedings that deviate from the traditional pattern of Chapter 11. For example, good faith challenges have been made to the use of bankruptcy as a means of dealing with products liability litigation.[137] The most important and common use of "bad faith" filing has been single asset real estate cases.[138] These cases involve debtors with only one substantial asset, usually an apartment or office building. They usually also have only one substantial creditor — the bank that loaned the money to purchase or build the

---

130 Bankruptcy Code § 1112(b)(1).

131 Bankruptcy Code § 1112(b)(4)(P).

132 Bankruptcy Code § 101(14A).

133 Ali M.M. Mojdehi & Janet Dean Gertz, *The Implicit "Good Faith" Requirement in Chapter 11 Liquidations: A Rule in Search of a Rationale?*, 14 Am. Bankr. Inst. L. Rev. 143 (2006); Janet Flaccus, *Have Eight Circuits Shorted? Good Faith and Chapter 11 Bankruptcy Petitions*, 67 Am. Bankr. L.J. 401 (1993); Lawrence Ponoroff & F. Stephen Knippenberg, *The Implied Good Faith Filing Requirement: Sentinel of an Evolving Policy*, 85 Nw. U. L. Rev. 919 (1991).

134 Little Creek Dev. Co. v. Commonwealth Mortgage Corp. (In re Little Creek Dev. Co.), 779 F.2d 1068, 1071 (5th Cir. 1986); In re Victory Constr. Co., Inc., 9 B.R. 549, 551–58 (Bankr. C.D. Cal. 1981).

135 *See* In re Phoenix Piccadilly, Ltd., 849 F.2d 1393 (11th Cir. 1988).

136 *See* Carolin Corp. v. Miller, 886 F.2d 693 (4th Cir. 1989).

137 *See* In re Johns-Manville, 36 B.R.. 727 (Bankr. S.D.N.Y. 1984), *appeal denied*, 39 B.R. 234 (S.D.N.Y. 1984); Sandrea Friedman, Note, Manville: *Good Faith Reorganizations or "Insulated Bankruptcy,"* 12 Hofstra L. Rev. 21 (1983); Jonathan C. Lipson, *Fighting Fiction with Fiction — The New Federalism in (A Tobacco Company) Bankruptcy*, 78 Wash. U. L.Q. 1271 (2000).

138 Brian S. Katz, *Single Asset Real Estate Cases and the Good Faith Requirement: Why Reluctance to Ask Whether a Case Belongs in Bankruptcy May Lead to the Incorrect Result*, 9 Bankr. Dev. J. 77 (1992).

building.[139] The problem here is that Chapter 11 really has nothing to offer these debtors. It is being used simply as a tool to delay the creditor's inevitable foreclosure on the property. An apartment or office building, once constructed and leased, has no real going concern value. It has a rent roll that produces a cash flow that has a present value. This cash flow is either sufficient to pay the mortgage (in which case the debtor has equity in the property, and bankruptcy is not necessary), or it is not, in which case the mortgage lender has a right to foreclose. There are no particular obstacles to negotiation that Chapter 11 can overcome, and courts are concerned that they are merely being used as a tool to add cost and delay.

Similarly, petitions that have been filed by solvent debtors, usually as part of an effort to obtain negotiating leverage in their dispute with a single creditor, are also likely to be dismissed as having been filed in bad faith.[140] This is consistent with the view of bankruptcy in general and Chapter 11 in particular as a mechanism for preventing coordination problems among creditors from causing an inefficient liquidation, rather than as a procedure for resolving a debtor's dispute with a single creditor.

§ 19.06 Post-Petition Operation of the Debtor's Business

Authorization for the debtor-in-possession to operate the business is automatic and may only be revoked upon the request of a party in interest after notice and an opportunity for a hearing.[141] However, this constitutes authority to operate in the ordinary course of business only; court permission must be obtained for non-ordinary course transactions (and for incurring secured debt).[142]

Because of the ongoing nature of a Chapter 11 case and the continued operation of the debtor's business, a number of the familiar provisions of the Code operate differently in that Chapter. For example, the automatic stay is of much longer duration in a Chapter 11 case than in a Chapter 7 case. As a result, the creditor's loss of its repossession rights are more significant. Moreover, during the pendency of the stay, the debtor may continue to use the creditor's collateral, and the collateral may therefore decline in value. There are also a few rules that apply to very narrow issues that arise only in some Chapter 11 cases and an entire subchapter that deals with railroad reorganizations. In addition, Chapter 11 contains specific provisions for rejecting collective bargaining agreements[143] and paying employees' retirement benefits. Finally, there are a few special rules regarding security interests and leaseholds in ships and airplanes.[144]

---

139 *See* § 23.04 Single-Asset Real Estate Cases, *supra*.

140 *See* In re SGL Carbon Corp., 200 F.3d 154 (3d Cir. 1999).

141 Bankruptcy Code § 1108.

142 *See* Chapter 9, Operating the Debtor, *supra*.

143 *See* § 23.03 Employees' Rights, *infra*.

144 Bankruptcy Code § 1110.

[A] Sale and Use of Estate Property

[1] Sale and Use of Property in the Ordinary Course

The debtor's power to use and sell estate property in the ordinary course of business permits the debtor to continue to use its real estate and equipment as part of its ongoing operations and to continue to sell inventory to its customers. Despite this general authority, continued use of any creditor's collateral, particularly sale of inventory, is likely to raise issues of adequate protection under § 362(d)(1). Unless the debtor is able to maintain casualty insurance on the collateral, compensate the creditor for the depreciating value of the collateral, and provide the creditor with a security interest in new items of inventory purchased to replace what the debtor sells, secured creditors will seek relief from the automatic stay due to a lack of adequate protection.[145]

[2] Use of Cash Collateral

The principal exception to the debtor's ability to use estate property in the ordinary course without prior court approval is with respect to cash collateral. "Cash collateral" is "cash negotiable instruments, documents of title, securities, deposit accounts or other cash equivalents . . . in which the estate and an entity other than the estate have an interest."[146] Cash collateral most commonly arises as proceeds of other property, such as inventory or accounts, in which a creditor holds a security interest. Section 363(c)(2) prohibits a debtor from using cash collateral without first obtaining the consent of the creditor with an interest in the cash collateral or permission from the court.[147] Thus, if the debtor's cash and bank accounts are subject to a creditor's security interest, the debtor usually needs court permission to use the cash in any way. The court must not grant the debtor permission to use cash collateral unless the creditor's security interest is adequately protected.[148] These restrictions impair the ability of most Chapter 11 debtors to continue their business operations for more than a few weeks without seeking court approval to use funds in their bank accounts and other cash equivalents. In many cases, debtors seek court approval to use their cash collateral on the first day of the case.[149]

---

[145] Bankruptcy Code § 362(d)(1); *see* § 8.06[B][1] For Cause — Lack of Adequate Protection for Secured Creditors, *supra*.

[146] Bankruptcy Code § 363(a); *see* § 1.05[B][8] Cash Collateral, *supra*.

[147] Bankruptcy Code § 363(c)(2); *see* § 9.03[B] Use of Cash Collateral, *supra*.

[148] *See* Bankruptcy Code § 363(d)(2); § 9.03[D] Adequate Protection, *supra*.

[149] *See* § 19.06[C] First-Day Orders, *infra*.

[3] Sale or Use Outside the Ordinary Course

A Chapter 11 debtor needs prior court approval to use, sell, or lease estate property outside the ordinary course of business,[150] regardless of whether a creditor holds a security interest in the affected property. Thus, Chapter 11 debtors whose strategies for resolving their business difficulties include reducing the size of their business and selling or leasing surplus land or equipment must obtain prior court approval. Court approval is usually granted if the proposed sale or use satisfies the business judgment test and is otherwise in the best interests of the estate.

In some cases, the debtor may seek to sell substantially all of the assets of the estate in one or a series of transactions, leaving the estate with nothing but a large bank account. This is what was done in *In re Adelphia Communications, Inc.*, involving the well-known cable-TV and internet provider of the same name. The debtor sold substantially all of its assets to two of its competitors, Time-Warner Cable Co. and Comcast Corp., for $17 billion.[151] Such sales can effectively reorganize the debtor without complying with the normal process of preparing a disclosure statement and giving creditors the opportunity to vote on the plan. Courts permit such sales if there is a sound business purpose for the transaction,[152] unless aspects of the sale restructure the priority and other rights of creditors.[153] Courts are generally sensitive to the "sub rosa" plan concerns, and will take steps to make sure that interested creditors receive notice and have an opportunity to object. A number of courts have adopted local rules to govern such asset sales.

When the debtor's assets are encumbered by liens of secured creditors, any sale outside the ordinary course will likely leave the buyer "subject to" the secured creditors' rights, unless the debtor obtains approval for the sale of the assets free and clear of existing liens. The Bankruptcy Code authorizes such a sale, provided the secured creditor consents.[154] Secured creditors are likely to supply their consent if the terms of the sale ensure that the creditor will receive at least as much as it would have obtained if it had been permitted to foreclose. If the sale price exceeds the aggregate amount of all liens encumbering the property, creditors have no reason to object and their consent is not required.[155]

---

[150] Bankruptcy Code § 363(b)(1); *see* § 9.03[C] Use of Property Outside the Ordinary Course, *supra.*

[151] *See Bankruptcy Court Backs Adelphia Sale*, N.Y. Times, June 28, 2006, at C7.

[152] *E.g.*, Committee of Equity Sec. Holders v. Lionel Corp. (In re Lionel Corp.), 722 F.2d 1063 (2d Cir. 1983).

[153] *See* Pension Benefit Guar. Corp. v. Braniff Airways, Inc. (In re Braniff Airways, Inc.), 700 F.2d 935 (5th Cir. 1983); *see also* Committee of Unsecured Creditors v. Cajun Elec. Power, Coop., Inc. (In re Cajun Elec. Power Coop., Inc.), 119 F.3d 349 (5th Cir. 1997).

[154] Bankruptcy Code § 363(f)(2).

[155] Bankruptcy Code § 363(f)(3).

[B] Post-Petition Financing

Few Chapter 11 debtors are capable of continuing in business without obtaining some additional financing. Even turning the lights on every morning and permitting employees who expect to be paid to show up for work involves an extension of credit by the local electricity provider and by the debtor's employees. Most debtors require additional infusions of cash to finance adjustments that they must make to restore their profitability.

Accordingly, the Bankruptcy Code permits the debtor to "obtain unsecured credit and incur unsecured debt in the ordinary course of business" without prior court approval.[156] Creditors' claims to be paid for such advances are entitled to administrative expense priority under § 503(b)(1).[157]

Chapter 11 debtors may also be permitted to incur unsecured debts outside the ordinary course if they obtain prior court approval, after notice and a hearing.[158] Creditors who provide such extensions of credit are also entitled to payment as an administrative expense priority under § 503(b)(1). This priority, combined with Chapter 11's requirement that the debtor's plan provide for full payment of all priority claims, provides post-petition creditors with a substantial assurance of eventual payment.

However, many prospective lenders will not be confident of the debtor's ability to propose, confirm, and consummate a reorganization plan. Thus, the debtor may not be able to find lenders who are willing to provide further extensions of credit on an unsecured basis. Accordingly, § 363(c) also permits the court to permit the debtor to obtain funding and permits the court to grant the post-petition creditor either a super-priority claim or a security interest in the debtor's assets.[159] Moreover, if existing secured creditors can be adequately protected, the court may authorize the debtor to provide a new lender with a senior lien on already encumbered assets.[160]

[C] First-Day Orders[161]

Chapter 11 debtors usually find it necessary to obtain immediate court approval of a variety of matters necessary to continue to operate the debtor's business and to get the debtor's reorganization process off the ground.[162] As a result, debtors frequently file a long list of motions along with their petition. These "first-day" motions frequently regard:

---

156 Bankruptcy Code § 364(a); *see* § 9.05[A] Unsecured Credit Acquired in the Ordinary Course, *supra*.

157 Bankruptcy Code § 364(a).

158 Bankruptcy Code § 364(b); *see* § 9.05[B] Unsecured Credit Outside the Ordinary Course, *supra*.

159 Bankruptcy Code § 363(c); *see* § 9.05[C] Secured Credit, *supra*.

160 Bankruptcy Code § 363(d); *see* § 9.05[C] Secured Credit, *supra*.

161 Debra Grassgreen, First-Day Motions Manual: A Practical Guide to the Critical First Days of a Bankruptcy Case (2003).

162 *See* Official Comm. of Unsecured Creditors Metalsource Corp. v. U.S. Metalsource Corp. (In re U.S. Metalsource Corp.), 163 B.R. 260, 266–68 (Bankr. W.D. Pa. 1993).

- employment and compensation of bankruptcy professionals, such as attorneys, accountants, and investment bankers;[163]
- joint administration of cases involving related debtors;
- extension of deadlines for filing the debtor's schedules and its statement of financial affairs;
- extension of deadlines for giving utilities adequate assurance of future performance;[164]
- continuation of the debtor's cash-management operations and permission for the use of cash collateral;
- continued payment of employees and continued contributions to employee benefit programs;
- permission to pay pre-petition debts to "critical vendors," without whose cooperation the debtor's business would fail;[165]
- permission to incur post-petition debt;[166]
- assumption or rejection of executory contracts and unexpired leases;[167]
- adjustment of investment and deposit guidelines;[168] and
- where necessary, authority to operate in a foreign country.[169]

The most controversial of these first-day motions are those that permit payment of pre-petition claims, such as the "critical vendor" motion. The court's authority to authorize payment of pre-petition creditors is not specified in the Code. Some courts, however, have derived such a power from § 105 (or in one instance[170] the debtor's power to use and sell collateral and operate the business under § 363) and the judicially developed "doctrine of necessity." Section 105 permits the court to "issue any order, process, or judgment that is necessary or appropriate to carry out the provisions of [the Bankruptcy Code]."[171]

The doctrine of necessity developed in the context of railroad reorganizations of the nineteenth century, which was based partially on the necessity of permitting payments to preserve the debtor's prospects for reorganization and partially on the public's interest in maintaining the nation's

[163] *See* Chapter 21, Role of Professionals in Bankruptcy Cases, *infra*.

[164] *See* Bankruptcy Code § 366.

[165] *See generally* In re Kmart Corp., 359 F.3d 866 (7th Cir. 2004).

[166] *E.g.*, In re The Colad Group, Inc., 324 B.R. 208 (Bankr. W.D.N.Y. 2005); In re Ames Dep't Stores, Inc., 115 B.R. 34, 36 (Bankr. S.D.N.Y. 1990).

[167] Bankruptcy Code § 365; *see* Chapter 10, Executory Contracts and Unexpired Leases, *supra*.

[168] Bankruptcy Code § 345.

[169] *See* Bankruptcy Code § 1505.

[170] *See* In re Kmart Corp., 369 F.3d 866 (7th Cir. 2004).

[171] Bankruptcy Code § 105.

transportation system.[172] The doctrine has gradually expanded to cover a wide range of payments to vendors whose refusal to deal with the debtor would impede the debtor's continued operations.[173]

It has also become quite controversial, in that these critical vendors are receiving, in effect, a "post-petition" preference. They will be paid in full, while other creditors may receive cents on the dollar. Where the prepetition arearage is small, this may not be a big problem, but where it is large, it might be better for the debtor to seek to do business with another supplier. For example, if, in return for a shipment of $1,000 in goods, the debtor must make good on prepetition debts of $20,000 or $30,000, the cost is disproportionate to the benefit. Since the Seventh Circuit's decision in *K-mart*,[174] these critical vendor motions have been scrutinized more closely.

§ 19.07 Treatment of Claims and Interests in Chapter 11

The status of the various claims and interests in Chapter 11 is generally the same as it is in other chapters of the Bankruptcy Code. Allowed claims and interests are divided into secured claims, priority unsecured claims, general unsecured claims, subordinated unsecured claims, and equity interests.[175] Disallowed claims are entitled to nothing and have no opportunity to vote on the debtor's plan.

[A] Priority of Claims and Interests

The priority scheme applicable in Chapter 7 liquidation cases applies with equal force in Chapter 11.[176] Secured claims are entitled to be paid the value of the collateral before other claims receiving anything. Priority claims are entitled to payment in full, with some priority claims entitled to be paid in cash as soon as the plan is implemented.[177] General unsecured claims, such as those held by trade creditors, holders of commercial paper issued by the debtor, bond-holders, and partially secured creditors with deficiency claims, are paid next. As explained elsewhere, these claims are sometimes separated into separate classes for purposes of voting on the

---

[172] *See* Miltenberger v. Logansport Ry., 106 U.S. 286 (1882) (authorizing payment of pre-receivership claims to prevent creditor from terminating delivery of supplies); In re Boston & Maine Corp., 634 F.2d 1359, 1370 (1st Cir. 1980).

[173] *E.g.*, In re Ionosphere Clubs, Inc., 98 B.R. 174 (Bankr. S.D.N.Y. 1989); In re Eagle-Picher Industries, Inc., 124 B.R. 1021, 1023 (Bankr. S.D. Ohio 1991); Russell A. Eisenberg & Frances F. Gecker, *The Doctrine of Necessity and Its Parameters*, 73 Marquette L. Rev. 1 (1989); Charles J. Tabb, *Emergency Preferential Orders in Bankruptcy Reorganizations*, 65 Am. Bankr. L.J. 75 (1991). The propriety of such payments and the legal reasoning supporting such payments has recently been criticized as lacking statutory support. *See, e.g.*, In re Kmart Corp., 359 F.3d 866, 871–74 (7th Cir. 2004); In re Coserv, LLC, 273 B.R. 487, 493–95 (Bankr. N.D. Tex. 2002).

[174] In re Kmart Corp., 369 F.3d 866 (7th Cir. 2004).

[175] *See generally* § 10.01 Meaning of Claims and Interests; Priority, *supra*.

[176] *See generally* § 10.01 Meaning of Claims and Interests; Priority, *supra*.

[177] Bankruptcy Code § 1129(a)(9); *see* § 9.08[G] Treatment of Priority Unsecured Claims, *infra*.

plan, and different classes receive different treatment under the plan. Subordinated claims are paid next, if the debtor has sufficient value to provide them with any distribution. Finally, if the debtor was not insolvent, equity interest holders are entitled to receive something.

Many Chapter 11 plans alter this strict hierarchy to some extent. Chapter 11 debtors have a broad right to classify general unsecured claims and to pay differing percentages to each class. If all classes of creditors accept the plan by the required majorities, the plan need not adhere to the "absolute priority rule"; in other words, a lower-ranked class may get a distribution even though a higher rank is not paid in full. This is based on the assumption that the plan produces a going-concern surplus, which need not be divided as rigidly as the basic liquidation value. In other words, so long as the claimants are paid as much as they would have received in a liquidation case, the allocation of the surplus can be negotiated. In particular, if creditors believe that the going concern value of the debtor's business will be enhanced through the continued participation of existing managers who also hold stock in the debtor, these creditors may be willing to permit stockholders to retain some or all of their shares in the debtor as an inducement for them to participate. If unsecured creditors are unwilling to consent, shareholders may not receive a distribution on account of their prepetition ownership interest.

[B] Proof of Claims and Interests

Although it is probably better practice to file a proof of claim or interest in Chapter 11, it is not always necessary. If the claim (or interest) is scheduled by the debtor, a proof of claim is "deemed" to have been filed, unless the debtor's schedules indicated that the claim or interest is disputed, contingent or unliquidated.[178] As is true throughout the Code, the filing of the proof of claim or interest establishes the claim or interest (the claim or interest is "allowed) unless the proof is disputed.[179]

[C] Chapter 11 Treatment of Partially Secured Claims

Under § 506(a), undersecured obligations are divided into two claims: a secured claim for the value of the collateral and an unsecured claim for the balance.[180] This is true in Chaper 11, even where the secured creditors' claim is "non-recourse" — or to put it another way, even where the undersecured creditor would not have a claim for a deficiency against the debtor under applicable non-bankruptcy law. For example, some secured creditors whose collateral consists of real estate, may not have the right to recover any deficiency because their loan agreement expressly waives the right to a deficiency. Others may have lost their right to a deficiency because of some state law "anti-deficiency" rule. Section 1111(b) grants

[178] Bankruptcy Code § 1111(a).

[179] *See* § 10.02[B] Proof of Claim, *supra.*

[180] *See* § 10.03[C] Allowance of Secured Claims, *supra.*

recourse to these partially secured creditors, unless the creditor elects to waive it. Gaining an understanding of how this election works and the circumstances in which creditors might find it useful to make the election is a difficult hurdle for those seeking to understand the law of business bankruptcies under Chapter 11.

Section 1111(b) actually contains two related sets of rules. The first involves the treatment of non-recourse debt. The second involves the treatment of partially secured debtors, regardless of whether they involve recourse or non-recourse debts.

[1] Treatment of Non-Recourse Claims

Non-recourse debt is debt that is enforceable only against the property securing the debt. For example, suppose Triangle Development Co. borrows $10 million from Canal Bank secured by Triangle's new office building. Under the loan agreement, the secured debt is "non-recourse." In other words, Triangle has no personal liability for the debt. Under their agreement, if Triangle defaults, Canal Bank may foreclose on the building and sell it. However, whether or not the foreclosure sale yields enough to cover the debt, Canal Bank cannot pursue Triangle or recover the balance from any of Triangle's other assets.

Under § 1111(b), however, non-recourse creditors, such as Canal Bank, are treated as if they were recourse creditors. In other words, they have a claim against the debtor for the unsecured portion of the debt, even though their loan agreement gives them no such rights. The practical significance of this is that the undersecured, non-recourse creditor has an unsecured claim for the amount of the deficiency. In the example given, if Triangle's office building was worth only $8 million, Canal Bank is given an $8 million secured claim and a $2 million unsecured claim, even though Canal Bank does not have any right outside of Chapter 11 to seize Triangle's other assets.[181]

There are two exceptions to this rule. The first applies if the creditor elects somewhat different treatment under § 1111(b)(2) — the "1111(b) election." If the creditor makes the § 1111(b) election, it gives up its unsecured claim in exchange for a lien that secures the entire amount of its debt. If Canal Bank makes this election, it has a secured claim for the full $10 million and retains a lien on the office building for the entire $10 million debt. In doing so, it gives up its right to share in whatever distribution is made to unsecured creditors,[182] but it must receive a distribution on its secured claim of at least the nominal amount of its secured debt. The second exception applies if the debtor sells the collateral under § 363[183] or pursuant to the debtor's reorganization plan. If the debtor disposes of the collateral, the creditor is entitled only to what it is entitled

[181] Bankruptcy Code § 1111(b)(1)(A).

[182] *See* § 19.07[C][2] The 1111(b) Election, *infra*.

[183] *See* § 9.03[C] Use of Property Outside the Ordinary Course, *supra*.

to pursuant to the sale, and does not have a claim for any deficiency that may result.[184] Thus, if the building actually sells for only $8.3 million (net of sale costs), that is all Canal Bank recovers. The theory behind this latter exception is that the creditor is receiving exactly what it bargained for when it made a non-recourse loan — the proceeds from the sale of the encumbered property.

[2] The 1111(b) Election

The remainder of § 1111(b) deals with all undersecured claims, whether or not the claimant has recourse against the debtor. The underlying purpose of the § 1111(b) election is to protect secured creditors from the risk that debtors will use a temporary decline in the value of their collateral to obtain a bargain price. Although the election is available to all secured creditors, it has its greatest significance cases involving debtors whose principal asset and primary source of income is a building — a "single-asset real estate" case.

Under § 1111(b), a secured claim is treated as a recourse claim, even though no recourse would be available under state law.[185] Suppose that Ridge Bank has a claim for $15 million, secured by property valued in the bankruptcy at only $12 million. Regardless of whether Ridge Bank's claim is a recourse claim or a non-recourse claim, it is treated as a recourse claim. As a result, Ridge will have a $12 million allowed secured claim and a deficiency claim (created by § 1111(b)) of $3 million.

On the other hand, Ridge may choose to make the "1111(b) election." Under that election, Ridge will waive its deficiency claim, and in return for waiving the deficiency, the claim will be treated as a fully secured claim. In other words, if Ridge Bank has a $15 million claim, secured by $12 million in assets, and Ridge Bank validly makes the § 1111(b) election, then the bank has a $15 million secured claim. This is in contrast to the normal treatment of Ridge Bank's claim; ordinarily, it would have an $12 million secured claim and a $3 million unsecured claim.[186]

However, unlike most secured claims, while Ridge Bank's claim must be paid in full, it need not receive the present value of its allowed secured claim; only the nominal value of the collateral must actually be paid.[187]

There are two circumstances where a creditor may not make the 1111(b) election. First, if the claimant's interest in the property is of inconsequential value, the election may not be made.[188] For example, if Ridge Bank's

---

[184] Bankruptcy Code § 1111(b)(1)(A)(ii).

[185] Technically, the provision states that the election must be made by the class of which the claim is a part, and that the election must be by at least two-thirds in amount and more than half in number of the creditors in the class. Bankruptcy Code § 1111(b)(1)(A)(i). However, as a general rule, each secured claim is in its own class, and thus this election is ordinarily made by individual creditors.

[186] *See* § 10.03[C] Allowance of Secured Claims, *supra*.

[187] *See* § 19.08[H][4] Treatment of the § 1111(b) Election, *supra*.

[188] Bankruptcy Code § 1111(b)(1)(B)(i).

interest in the collateral were only worth $10, it could not make the 1111(b) election. Second, if the property is sold under § 363 or is to be sold under the plan, the election cannot be made.[189]

The effect of the election reveals its purpose. It prevents lien stripping.[190] Suppose, for example, that the property involved in the example above is worth $12 million only because of a temporary slump in the local real estate market. There is reason to believe that it will soon be worth more than $12 million.[191] In the normal circumstance, where Ridge Bank's claim is bifurcated between a secured and an unsecured claim, the debtor can effectively strip the lien from the property by paying the $12 million secured claim in full and only a portion of the $3 million unsecured claim, according to the treatment accorded to unsecured claims generally. Later, when the market recovers, the debtor captures the increase in value. Allowing Ridge Bank to elect to have a $15 million secured claim prevents the debtor from obtaining this advantage.

§ 19.08 Contents of a Chapter 11 Plan

As is true with any reorganization proceeding, the goal of Chapter 11 is the confirmation and successful completion of a plan of reorganization. The Chapter 11 plan is the fruit of a process of negotiation among the debtor, creditors, and (in some cases) equity interest holders. Nearly all creditors vote on the plan — it is difficult to get the plan confirmed unless the required majorities of creditors approve.

In Chapter 11, creditors vote under a modified form of majority rule. If the requisite majority is obtained, then all creditors are bound. Only in limited circumstances may the plan be "crammed-down" — i.e., confirmed over the objection of a class of creditors.

Chapter 11 plans are likely to involve considerably more property and debt than even a large Chapter 12 or 13 proceeding, therefore their financial structure is likely to be more complex, with multiple layers of claims and interests, entitled to different priority. This, in and of itself, makes the Chapter 11 plan process more complex than in other chapters. However, additional layers of complexity are added by the facts (1) that the debtor has greater flexibility in formulating a plan; and (2) the plan confirmation process gives creditors a vote, and hence more voice in the plan negotiation process. The usual justification for this greater flexibility is precisely the fact that the Chapter 11 creditors do have a much greater degree of input.

As noted elsewhere, Chapter 13 debtors usually file their plans simultaneously with their petition. By contrast, Chapter 11 debtors commonly

---

[189] Bankruptcy Code § 1111(b)(1)(B)(ii).

[190] *See* § 19.08[H][3] Chapter 11 Lien Stripping, *supra*.

[191] As the depression-era comedian and social commentator Will Rogers famously said: "Buy land, buy land. They ain't making any more of the stuff." (Rogers was similar in many respects to Jon Stewart of Comedy Central's "Daily Show").

delay filing a plan for several months or, if the court permits, even years.[192] A plan is developed only after the debtor has an opportunity to adjust its business operations to correct whatever circumstances led it into financial difficulty in the first place, and has had an opportunity to negotiate with its creditors about how to reorganize its financial structure.

[A] Process of Negotiating the Plan's Terms

In some cases, a plan is partially or fully negotiated even before the Chapter 11 petition is filed. Often a bankruptcy is filed after prepetitition attempts to negotiate a workout have failed. The principal advantages offered by bankruptcy are (1) the control that Chapter 11 gives to the debtor over the process; (2) the automatic stay, that gives the debtor some breathing room; and (3) the power to bind holdouts to the plan, so long as the plan is supported by a sufficient number of creditors and otherwise meets the requirements of the Code.

[B] Who May File a Plan; The Exclusivity Period[193]

The debtor may file a plan either with the petition or at any other time during the case.[194] Except, however, in so called "prepackaged" cases, Chapter 11 plans are rarely filed until after the case begins. This is because Chapter 11, unlike Chapter 13, envisions negotiations with creditors over the plan, and the process of negotiation takes time.

In most cases, for 120 days after the order for relief, the debtor has the exclusive right to file a plan.[195] If the debtor files a plan during this initial 120-day period, others are prohibited from filing a competing plan until 180 days after the order for relief. This gives the debtor two months to complete the confirmation process by disseminating a disclosure statement and obtaining a sufficient number of acceptances to have the plan confirmed. This "exclusive period" is designed to give the debtor time to negotiate and draft a plan.

The 120/180 day time limits may be extended at the discretion of the court. For many years, the Code provided for unlimited extensions of the 120- and 180-day periods, as long as the court thought the case was moving

---

[192] Despite this, some debtors are able to file a so-called pre-packaged plan with their petition. These are usually plans that have been worked out in advance but that require Chapter 11's voting procedures to enforce the plan on a minority of dissenting creditors. For a fuller discussion of pre-packaged plans, and the various considerations that have made them especially popular, see Marc S. Kirschner, et al., *Prepackaged Bankruptcy Plans: The Deleveraging Tool of the'90s in the Wake of OID and Tax Concerns*, 21 Seton Hall L. Rev. 643 (1991).

[193] Novica Petrovski, *The Bankruptcy Code, Section 1121: Exclusivity Reloaded*, 11 Am. Bankr. Inst. L. Rev. 451 (2003).

[194] Bankruptcy Code § 1121(a).

[195] Bankruptcy Code § 1121(b).

forward.[196] Extensions beyond the 120-and 180-day periods were commonly granted.[197]

In 2005, in response to creditors' complaints, Congress added language prohibiting the 120-day period from being extended beyond "18 months after the date of the order for relief"[198] and prohibiting the 180-day period from being extended beyond "20 months after the date of the order for relief."[199] Creditors hope this new limitation will prevent debtors from using Chapter 11 to delay the inevitable liquidation of debtors who have no realistic hope of reorganizing. On the other hand, it may force debtors to propose plans prematurely, before their managers have had sufficient time to adjust their operations to return to profitability. Worse yet, because there is a known and firm end date to the debtor's period of control over the case, the debtor may be tempted to present a plan that is overly optimistic in order to get it approved. This may in turn lead to a round of refilings, or requests for modification or dismissal as the debtors are unable to comply with the plan's requirements.

After expiration of either of these two periods, or after the appointment of a trustee, "any party in interest . . . may file a plan."[200] Plans submitted by creditors frequently call for the debtor's liquidation and for eliminating the interests of existing stockholders.

[C] Mandatory and Optional Chapter 11 Plan Provisions

[1] Mandatory Plan Provisions

Section 1123(a) contains a number of mandatory provisions — topics that must be addressed in the plan. However, as a practical matter, the Code's standards for confirmation have a further significant impact on what must be included in most plans.

[a] Designation of Classes of Claims and Interests

All Chapter 11 plans are required to "designate . . . classes of claims . . . and classes of interests."[201] Thus, Chapter 11 plans divide creditors' claims into separate classes. Chapter 11 plans always divide claims based on their priority, and frequently on other characteristics, such as the underlying transaction that gave rise to the claim, the maturity of the claim, and the size of the claims. The plan's classification scheme must comply with

[196] Bankruptcy Code § 1121(d)(1).

[197] *See* Eric W. Lam, *Of Exclusivity and For Cause: 11 U.S.C. § 1121(d) Re-examined*, 36 Drake L. Rev. 533 (1986-1987).

[198] Bankruptcy Code § 1121(d)(2)(A).

[199] Bankruptcy Code § 1121(d)(2)(B). Somewhat different rules apply in cases involving "small business debtors," with less than $2,000,000 in debts. *See* Bankruptcy Code § 1121(e).

[200] Bankruptcy Code § 1121(c).

[201] Bankruptcy Code § 1123(a)(1).

§ 1122,[202] in that "a plan may place a claim or an interest in a particular class only if such claim or interest is substantially similar to the other claims or interests of such class."[203] In other words, the plan may not lump together claims of creditors whose legal rights are substantially different from one another.[204] A separate question, and one on which the Code gives no guidance, is the question of when similarly situated creditors may be classified separately.

[b] Specification of Unimpaired Classes

The plan must also specify whether a class is "impaired" or "unimpaired" by the plan.[205] Whether a particular class is impaired is governed by § 1124.[206] A creditor is unimpaired if its legal and equitable rights are not altered by the plan. Creditors in classes that are not impaired by the terms of the plan are deemed to have accepted the plan and thus do not have the right to vote on the terms of the plan.[207]

[c] Specification of Treatment of Impaired Claims and Interests

Most Chapter 11 plans impair one or all classes of claims and interests. The plan is required to specify how any impaired class of claims or interests is treated by the plan.[208] As explained in more detail later in this chapter, the range of treatment of impaired classes of claims is considerable and may extend from cash payment in full on the day the plan is first implemented, to nothing. Classes of equity interest holders in particular, may receive nothing.

[d] Equal Treatment of Claims and Interests Within a Class

A Chapter 11 plan must provide "the same treatment for each claim or interest of a particular class."[209] In other words, every creditor included in a class must be treated the same as every other creditor in the same class. And, every equity interest holder in a class must be treated the same as every other interest holder in that class. If the debtor wishes to treat one group of creditors differently from others, they must be classified separately. Because creditors vote to approve or reject the plan in classes, this prevents creditors from receiving more favorable treatment by ganging

---

[202] Bankruptcy Code § 1123(a)(1).

[203] Bankruptcy Code § 1122(a).

[204] *See* § 10.07[D] Classification of Claims, *infra*.

[205] Bankruptcy Code § 1123(a)(2).

[206] *See* § 19.08[E] Impairment of Claims, *infra*.

[207] Bankruptcy Code § 1126(f).

[208] Bankruptcy Code § 1123(a)(3).

[209] Bankruptcy Code § 1123(a)(4).

up on creditors who are receiving less during the voting process.[210] However, separate classification can also provide a mechanism for creating an accepting class, which may be necessary if the plan is going to be approved by cram-down.

[e] Adequate Means for Implementing the Plan

The plan must provide adequate means for its implementation.[211] In a simple plan, the means may include nothing more than necessary adjustments to debt, such as curing defaults and de-accelerating debt,[212] reducing the amount of unsecured claims, and extending the maturity of secured claims.[213] In other cases, the reorganization is more profound, and includes the partial liquidation of the debtor and the merger of the remainder of its business with another, healthy company.[214] A corporate debtor may also have to rewrite its charter as part of its restructuring; and many larger debtors have to issue securities as part of the plan, or to raise additional capital. New stock or bonds may be issued as part of the plan distribution or to new investors.[215] Section 1123 gives a partial list of the types of things that may be needed to make the plan work; it includes all of the matters just mentioned.

[f] Protecting Shareholders' Voting Rights

If the debtor is a corporation, the plan must provide for the debtor's corporate charter to include certain provisions relating to the appropriate distribution of voting power among classes of voting securities.[216] In addition, the plan must "contain only provisions that are consistent with the interests of creditors and equity security holders and with public policy with respect to the manner of selection of any officer, director, or trustee."[217] These requirements ensure that the plan allocates voting power among various stakeholders according to their relative priority.[218] It is particularly important when creditors receive stock in the reorganized

---

[210] *See* § 19.08[D][3] Identical Treatment of Claims in the Same Class, *infra.*

[211] Bankruptcy Code § 1123(a)(5).

[212] Bankruptcy Code § 1123(a)(5)(G). Defaults on obligations owed to creditors with secured claims can sometimes be cured, leaving the creditor unimpaired under § 1124. Creditors in classes that are unimpaired are deemed to have accepted the plan and do not vote. *See* § 19.08[E] Impairment of Claims, *infra.*

[213] Bankruptcy Code § 1123(a)(5)(F).

[214] Bankruptcy Code § 1123(a)(5)(C).

[215] Bankruptcy Code § 1123(a)(5)(J). That's right! Existing stockholders may be eliminated. If so, new stock is issued to others — buyers of the debtor, or sometimes to its creditors.

[216] Bankruptcy Code § 1123(a)(5)(J).

[217] Bankruptcy Code § 1323(a)(7).

[218] *See* Acequia, Inc. v. Clinton (In re Acequia), 787 F.2d 1352, 1361–62 (9th Cir. 1986); *see also* In re Machne Menachem, Inc., 304 B.R. 140 (Bankr. M.D. Pa. 2003).

debtor that they obtain a voice in the management of the debtor that is commensurate with their stake in the success of the company.[219]

[g] Provide for Payment of an Individual Debtor's Personal Earnings

The 2005 Amendments added language essentially requiring the plan of any individual debtor to "provide for the payment to creditors . . . of all or such portion of earnings from personal services performed by the debtor after the commencement of the case or other future income of the debtor as is necessary for the execution of the plan."[220] This language makes it clear that an individual debtor who must file under Chapter 11, because he is ineligible for relief under either Chapter 7 (because of the "abuse" test), or under Chapter 13 (because of its debt limits), must submit a portion of his future income to creditors in his Chapter 11 plan. Indeed, § 1129(a)(15) requires most individual debtors to submit all of their projected disposable income for five years.[221] This is consistent with the projected disposable income test of § 1325(b)(1)(B) for debtors who seek relief under Chapter 13.[222]

[2] Optional Plan Provisions

Many plans go far beyond the requirements of the statute to include other provisions that may facilitate reorganization. Section 1123(b) gives blanket authorization for a variety of these provisions. The plan may:

- impair, or leave unimpaired, any class of secured claims, unsecured claims, or interests;[223]
- provide for the assumption, rejection, or assignment of any executory contract or unexpired lease of the debtor, unless it has previously been rejected;[224]
- provide for the settlement or adjustment of any claim or interest that belongs to the debtor or the estate; or in the alternative, provide for the retention and enforcement by the debtor, the trustee (if any), or a representative of the estate of any claim or interest that belongs to the debtor or the estate;[225]

---

219 Myron N. Krotinger, *Management and Allocation of Voting Power in Corporate Reorganizations*, 41 Colum. L. Rev. 646, 649, 664 (1941); Alfred N. Heuston, *Corporate Reorganization under the Chandler Act*, 38 Colum. L. Rev. 1199, 1213–14 (1938).

220 Bankruptcy Code § 1123(a)(8).

221 Bankruptcy Code § 1129(a)(15)(B).

222 *See* § 18.08[E][2] Debtor's Projected Disposable Income, *supra*.

223 Bankruptcy Code § 1123(b)(1); *see* § 19.08[E] Impairment of Claims, *infra*.

224 Bankruptcy Code § 1123(b)(2); *see* Chapter 11, Executory Contracts and Unexpired Leases, *supra*.

225 Bankruptcy Code § 1123(b)(3). For example, if the estate has a claim for damages against a third party, this may be compromised or otherwise dealt with in the plan.

- provide for the sale of all or substantially all of the property of the estate and distribution of the proceeds of the sale among holders of claims or interests;[226]
- modify the rights of holders of secured and unsecured claims;[227]
- include any other "appropriate provision not inconsistent with the applicable provision of this title."[228]

The last of these provisions is the most important. It permits the plan to include almost anything that does not contradict the Code or frustrate its purposes.

[D] Classification of Claims[229]

As indicated above, § 1123(a)(2) requires a Chapter 11 plan to designate classes of claims and classes of interests.[230] "Classification" of claims and interests means that the debtor subdivides creditors and interest holders into narrower categories, usually based on differences in their legal rights, but frequently also based on their business relationships to the debtor. For example, the Code treats all general unsecured debts alike. Under Chapter 7, all are paid pro-rata if anything is left over from the secured and priority claims.

Chapter 11 debtors have a broad right to classify claims, provided the creditors approve the plan and that each claim is paid at least its liquidation value. The Code itself says remarkably little about classification.

---

[226] Bankruptcy Code § 1123(b)(4). This is the provision that permits a "liquidation plan," under which Chapter 11 becomes a substitute for Chapter 7.

[227] Bankruptcy Code § 1123(b)(5). There is an important exception to this provision. As in Chapter 13, the plan may not modify the rights of a holder of a claim secured only by a security interest in real property that is the debtor's principal residence. *See* § 18.07[b][2][a] Residential Real Estate Mortgages, *supra*. This exception is likely to apply only in the rare Chapter 11 case that involves an individual debtor. It was included to dissuade such debtors from seeking Chapter 11 relief as a means of evading the similar limitation in § 1322(b)(2).

[228] Bankruptcy Code § 1123(b)(6).

[229] John C. Anderson, *Classification of Claims and Interests in Reorganization Cases Under the New Bankruptcy Code*, 58 Am. Bankr. L.J. 99 (1984); William Blair, *Classification of Unsecured Claims in Chapter 11 Reorganization*, 58 Am. Bankr. L.J. 197 (1984); David Gray Carlson, *The Classification Veto in Single-Asset Cases: Bankruptcy Code Section 1129(a)(10)*, 44 S.C. L. Rev. 565 (1993); Henry J. Friendly, *Some Comments on the Corporate Reorganizations Act*, 48 Harv. L. Rev. 39, 70–74 (1934); Bruce A. Markell, *Clueless on Classification: Toward Removing Artificial Limits on Chapter 11 Claim Classification*, 11 Bankr. Dev. J. 1 (1995); Meter E. Meltzer, *Disenfranchising the Dissenting Creditor Through Artificial Classification or Artificial Impairment*, 66 Am. Bankr. L.J. 281 (1992); Scott F. Norberg, *Classification of Claims Under Chapter 11 of the Bankruptcy Code: The Fallacy of Interest Based Classification*, 69 Am. Bankr. L.J. 119, 120 (1995); Stefan A. Riesenfeld, *Classification of Claims and Interests in Chapter 11 and 13 Cases*, 75 Cal. L. Rev. 391 (1987); Linda J. Rusch, *Gerrymandering the Classification Issue in Chapter Eleven Reorganizations*, 63 U. Colo. L. Rev. 163 (1992); Charles F. Vihon, *Classification of Unsecured Claims: Squaring a Circle?*, 55 Am. Bankr. L.J. 143 (1981).

[230] Bankruptcy Code § 1123(a)(1).

[1] Substantial Similarity of Claims in the Same Class

Since all claims or interests within a class to be substantially similar to each other,[231] secured claims cannot be placed in the same class as unsecured claims, priority claims cannot be placed in the same class as general unsecured claims,[232] and interests of shareholders who own preferred stock cannot be placed in the same class of as interests of shareholders who own common stock.

The rule prohibiting the grouping together claims that are materially different from one another usually means that there is only one creditor in each class of secured claims. The rights of a creditor with a senior mortgage on the debtor's land is not substantially similar to the rights of a creditor with a senior security interest in the debtor's equipment.[233] Quite to the contrary — their rights are markedly different from one another because they have property interests in different assets. Likewise, the rights of a creditor with a senior mortgage on the debtor's land are materially different from the rights of a creditor with a junior mortgage on the same land — they have different priority. Thus, in most Chapter 11 cases, there is only one creditor in each class of secured claims.[234] This means that this one creditor must vote in favor of the plan for that class to "accept" the plan by the requisite majority.[235]

The principal exception to this common pattern occurs when multiple creditors join together to contribute to a "participation" loan and share the same seniority in the same collateral.[236] Thus, if Ridge Bank, Peninsula Bank, and Valley Bank each loaned Franklin Manufacturing $1 million as part of a $3 million participation loan for which they share a senior mortgage in Franklin's land and building, it is appropriate to place all three creditors in the same class.

In determining whether claims are substantially similar, the focus is on the nature of the claim rather than on the identity of the claim holder.[237] This depends primarily on the relative rights and priority of the claims outside of bankruptcy.[238] This does not mean that all claims in the same

---

[231] Bankruptcy Code § 1122(a).

[232] John C. Anderson, *Classification of Claims and Interests in Reorganization Cases Under the New Bankruptcy Code*, 58 Am. Bankr. L.J. 99, 117 (1984).

[233] Brady v. Andrew (In re Comm. W. Fin. Corp.), 761 F.2d 1329, 1338 (9th Cir. 1985).

[234] Mokava Corp. v. Dolan, 147 F.2d 340 (2d Cir. 1945); In re Commercial W. Fin. Corp., 761 F.2d 1329 (9th Cir. 1985).

[235] *See* Bankruptcy Code § 1126(c); § 19.09[B] Voting by Classes of Claims and Interests, *infra*.

[236] *E.g.*, In re Keck, Mahin & Cate, 241 B.R. 583, 589–90 (Bankr. N.D. Ill. 1999); *see generally* W. Crews Lott, Larry A. Makel & Walter E. Evans, *Structuring Multiple Lender Transactions*, 112 Banking L.J. 734 (1995).

[237] In re Martin's Point, Ltd., 12 B.R. 721 (Bankr. N.D. Ga. 1981); *see* J.P. Morgan & Co. v. Missouri Pac. R.R., 85 F.2d 351 (8th Cir.), *cert. denied*, 299 U.S. 604 (1936).

[238] Bruce A. Markell, *Clueless on Classification: Toward Removing Artificial Limits on Chapter 11 Claim Classification*, 11 Bankr. Dev. J. 1, 27 (1995).

class must be identical. For example, it is possible to lump together claims arising from accounts payable with claims arising from unsecured operating loans. These claims might have different due dates, but they are both unsecured and entitled to no special priority. Moreover, both claims probably have the same stake in the proceeding and have similar goals in connection with the debtor's reorganization.

On the other hand, tort claimants and contract claimants may have very different interests at stake in the debtor's reorganization. Suppose, for example, that Titanic Corporation has both personal injury claimants and contract claimants, all of whom have general unsecured claims. The contract claimants have ongoing commercial relations with Titanic, and may be willing to accept a relatively protracted payout because they expect to recoup some of their losses by entering into new, profitable contracts with the debtor after it reorganizes. By contrast, the personal injury claimants are likely to want to receive as much as possible immediately. The contract claimants' primary benefit from reorganization is the new business it will generate in the future; the tort claimants' only benefit from reorganization is a quick, maximum payout of the prior debt. Moreover, the suppliers may have more leverage with the debtor who may need their cooperation in order to continue to operate the business. Therefore, it could be argued that these groups are not sufficiently similar. If the tort claims can easily be outvoted by the contract claims, the tort claimants' interests may not be adequately taken into account in formulating the plan.

[2] Separate Classification of Similar Claims

The Bankruptcy Code is conspicuously silent about the separate classification of substantially similar claims. Claims that are materially different cannot be lumped together, but the Code does not expressly prohibit the *separation* of substantially similar claims into different classes. Indeed, this is the essence of classification. The debtor often seeks to separate apparently similar claims, for reasons that are sometimes clearly bona fide and at other times dubious.

[a] Small Claims Classified for Administrative Convenience

One basis for separate classification of similar claims is explicitly recognized in the Code. Section 1122(b) provides: "A plan may designate a separate class of claims consisting of every unsecured claim that is less than or reduced to an amount that the court approves as reasonable and necessary for administrative convenience."[239] It is common for the plan to include a class of small claims that will be paid in full as soon as the plan is consummated. This has the advantage of avoiding making small payments to these creditors over a longer period of time.

239 Bankruptcy Code § 1122(b).

The plan in *Troy Savings Bank v. Travelers Motor Inn, Inc.*[240] provides a good example. It established a separate class for all claims under $250 and provided for members of the class to receive a lump sum payment immediately upon confirmation of the plan. Without this separate designation, payments to these small creditors would have been spread out over five years. With quarterly payments of no more than $5 to each creditor with a claim of less than $250, the administrative cost of making payments to these creditors would probably be greater than the total of what they would receive.[241]

[b] Segregation of Substantially Similar Claims

Some separate classification of substantially similar claims is permitted, but the limits of such classifications are ill-defined. While classification frequently makes sense to accommodate the different interests that various creditors have in the debtor's reorganization, some classification schemes are the bankruptcy equivalent of political gerrymandering — defining the classes in order to assure confirmation of the plan and/or to provide favorable treatment to preferred constituencies.

The leading decision regarding separate classification of general unsecured claims, other than for administrative convenience, is *Teamsters National Freight Industry Negotiating Committee v. U.S. Truck Co. (In re U.S. Truck Co).*[242] The plan in *U.S. Truck Co.* segregated claims of several unsecured creditors based on the circumstances that gave rise to their claims. In particular, it segregated the unsecured claims of employees based on the debtor's rejection of its collective bargaining agreement with the Teamsters union from most other general unsecured claims above $200.[243] The class of claims of the Teamsters rejected the plan that was being confirmed ("crammed down") over its objection. The class of general unsecured claims had accepted the plan. A special creditors' committee representing the Teamsters objected to confirmation, contending that these two classes had been improperly segregated from one another, and that if they had been combined, the plan could not have been confirmed. By segregating the Teamsters' claim from the claim of other general unsecured creditors and obtaining the class of general unsecured creditors' acceptance of the plan, the debtor was able to satisfy the cramdown requirement that at least

240 215 B.R. 485, 489–90 (N.D.N.Y. 1997).

241 *See also* In re Jartran, Inc., 44 B.R. 331, 397 (Bankr. N.D. Ill. 1984). Plans usually also provide for creditors with larger claims to elect to reduce their claims to whatever dollar threshold is imposed on this class. Thus, a creditor with a $300 claim could elect to reduce its claim to $250 and receive $250 in immediate cash, rather than receive only a few dollars a year for several years.

242 800 F.2d 581 (1986).

243 There were two other classes of unsecured claims. A class of unsecured claims of less than $200, separately classified for administrative convenience pursuant to § 1122(b), and the unsecured deficiency claim of the bank that also held a secured claim on the debtor's land. *U.S. Truck*, 800 F.2d at 584.

one class of impaired claims accept the plan.[244] If the class was improperly constituted, this confirmation requirement would not have been met.

In reviewing the legislative history of § 1122 and pre-Code cases that Congress intended to incorporate into the Code's language, the court found "one common theme." "[L]ower courts were given broad discretion to determine proper classification according to the factual circumstances of each individual case."[245] The court also found that these earlier decisions had permitted and indeed required separate classification of claims where the interests of the creditors holding these claims "differ[ed] substantially from those of other impaired creditors."[246] Because creditors who represented employees had both a different stake in the future viability of the reorganized debtor and alternative means to protect its interests, segregating their claims into a separate class was justified.[247]

This same rationale has been used to justify the separate classification of trade claims held by the debtor's suppliers, because their continued cooperation with the debtor is essential to the success of the debtor's continued business and thus to the success of its reorganization. Other courts have been less persuaded, particularly when the segregated class of trade creditors is receiving no better treatment than another class that has rejected the plan.[248] Such identical treatment belies the assertion that the classification scheme was proposed as a means to ensure the cooperation of members of the segregated class and indicates that it was designed instead to artificially separate creditors into separate classes simply to obtain an affirmative vote on the plan of reorganization.

Courts are in agreement that such gerrymandering is inappropriate. As the court in *In re Greystone III Joint Venture* put it, " 'one clear rule' has emerged from the otherwise muddled § 1122 caselaw: 'thou shalt not classify similar claims differently in order to gerrymander an affirmative vote on a reorganization plan.' "[249] But beyond that, there is little clarity. Some courts follow the *U.S. Truck* approach and are fairly permissive, while other courts say that if claims are similar enough to be classified together, then they must be so classified.[250]

---

244 Bankruptcy Code § 1129(a)(10). *See* § 19.10[G] Acceptance by One Impaired Class, *infra*. Note that if all impaired classes accept the plan, the plan is consensual and there is no "cramdown."

245 800 F.2d at 586.

246 800 F.2d at 588.

247 To the extent that separate classification is being used to satisfy the requirement for cramdown that one impaired class accept the plan, the *U.S. Truck* court stated that the question was whether there was a substantial impaired creditor constituency that favored the plan.

248 In re Coram Healthcare, Corp., 315 B.R. 321, 349 (Bankr. D. Del. 2004) (collecting cases).

249 In re Greystone III Joint Venture, 948 F.2d F.2d 134, 139 (5th Cir. 1991), *cert denied*, 113 S. Ct. 72 (1992); *see also* In re Bryson Properties, XVIII, 961 F.2d 496 (4th Cir.), *cert. denied*, 506 U.S. 866 (1992).

250 In re Bloomingdale Partners, 170 B.R. 984 (Bankr. N.D. Ill. 1994).

[c] Classification in Single-Asset Real Estate Cases[251]

The gerrymandering issue frequently arises in cramdown cases that involve debtors whose principle asset is a single parcel of real estate, usually an office building or an apartment complex. These "single-asset real estate" cases commonly involve the same problem that existed in *U.S. Truck Co.*, the necessity of having at least one impaired class of claims accept the debtor's plan in order to "cram down" a dissenting class.

Single-asset real estate cases frequently involve a large unsecured deficiency claim held by a lender who holds a partially secured mortgage on the debtor's land. Since such real estate loans are often made on a non-recourse basis, the deficiency claim may exist solely as a result of § 1111(b)'s creation of "artificial recourse." Such creditors are usually opposed to reorganization and prefer the immediate sale of the real estate and payment of the secured portion of the debt that would result. Including this creditor's claim in a single general class of claims of unsecured creditors would probably lead to the class' rejection of the debtor's plan.

Many courts preclude debtors from segregating unsecured deficiency claims of mortgagees into a class separate from the claims of other unsecured creditors.[252] Some courts take the same view when the claim would have been a non-recourse claim, but for the effect of § 1111(b), which gives holders of non-recourse claims the right to a deficiency that they would not have had outside of bankruptcy.[253] However, a few courts take the complete opposite view and require segregation of recourse claims created by § 1111(b)(1)(A) into a separate class.[254] These courts take the view that claims that would not be entitled to a deficiency outside of bankruptcy are significantly different from the claims of other unsecured creditors and thus are not permitted to be included in the same class with other general unsecured claims.[255]

---

[251] David Gray Carlson, *Artificial Impairment and the Single Asset Chapter 11 Case*, 23 Cap. U. L. Rev. 339 (1994).

[252] *E.g.*, In re Greystone III Joint Venture, 948 F.2d F.2d 134, 139 (5th Cir. 1991), *cert denied*, 506 U.S. 821 (1992) (separate classification prohibited due to debtor's improper gerrymandering motive); *see also* In re Bloomingdale Partners, 170 B.R. 984 (N.D. Ill. 1994) (separate classification prohibited due to similarity of claims, irrespective of debtor's motive); *see generally* In re JRV Indus., Inc., 342 B.R. 635 (Bankr. M.D. Fla. 2006) (collecting cases).

[253] *E.g.*, Boston Post Rd. Ltd. v. FDIC (In re Boston Post Rd. Ltd.), 21 F.3d 477, 483 (2d Cir. 1994), *cert. denied*, 513 U.S. 1109 (1995); *see* § 19.07[C][1] Treatment of Non-recourse Claims, *supra*.

[254] In re D & W Realty Corp., 156 B.R. 140, 144 (Bankr. S.D.N.Y. 1993); Beal Bank SSB v. Waters Edge Ltd., 248 B.R. 668, 691 (D. Mass. 2000); *see generally* In re SM 104, Ltd., 160 B.R. 202, 218–19 (Bankr. S.D. Fla. 1993).

[255] *E.g.*, Matter of Woodbrook Assoc., 19 F.3d 314 (7th Cir. 1994); In re SM 104, Ltd., 160 B.R. 202, 218–19 (Bankr. S.D. Fla. 1993).

[3] Identical Treatment of Claims in the Same Class

Although a plan can provide unequal treatment between classes, it must provide equal treatment within a class. Every claim or interest in a particular class must receive the same treatment, unless the holder of a particular claim or interest agrees to receive less.[256] This prevents a plan from lumping together creditors who get favorable treatment with those who get unfavorable treatment in the hope that the former will vote "yes" in a sufficient majority to override the "no" votes of the latter.

[E] Impairment of Claims[257]

Every class of claims and interests is either impaired or unimpaired by the debtor's reorganization plan. This distinction plays a crucial role, because impaired classes vote; unimpaired classes are deemed to have accepted the plan and have no right to vote. The Code's definition of impairment is written from the practical standpoint that classes of claims or interests are nearly always impaired; thus, § 1124 provides, with one minor exclusion, that a class of claims or interests is impaired *unless* the plan either:

- leaves the legal, equitable, and contractual rights of the holder of claim or interest holder unaltered,[258] or
- cures the debtor's defaults, de-accelerates the obligation, compensates the holder of the claim or interest for damages, and does not otherwise alter the legal, equitable, or contractual rights of the holder.[259]

Although § 1124 speaks in terms of the impairment of classes of both claims and interests, its biggest practical impact is with respect to claims. Few Chapter 11 plans leave equity interest holders unimpaired.

[1] Rights Unaltered by the Plan

A class of claims is unimpaired if the plan preserves the legal, equitable, and contractual rights of the claims. Thus, to be unimpaired the plan must provide for satisfaction of the claims in the class according to whatever rights they held outside of bankruptcy, unaffected by the provisions of the plan.

---

[256] Bankruptcy Code § 1123(a)(4).

[257] David Gray Carlson, *Artificial Impairment and the Single Asset Chapter 11 Case*, 23 Cap. U. L. Rev. 339 (1994).

[258] Bankruptcy Code § 1124(1).

[259] Bankruptcy Code § 1124(2).

Prior to 1994, § 1124(3) provided a third method for leaving a class of claims unimpaired: paying members of the class in full, in cash, immediately upon consummation of the plan. It was eliminated to ensure that unsecured creditors of solvent debtors could obtain post-petition interest for claims treated in this fashion. *See* Linda Rusch, *Unintended Consequences of Unthinking Tinkering: The 1994 Amendments and the Chapter 11 Process*, 69 Am. Bankr. L.J. 349, 373–77 (1995).

Assume, for example, that Titanic Corp. is legally obligated to make regular monthly payments on a fully secured mortgage debt, and that the debtor has never missed a single payment or otherwise defaulted on any of the mortgage's terms. The claim is unimpaired if the plan provides for all payments to be made to the creditor in full when they fall due and for the debtor to otherwise fulfill all the terms of the mortgage contract.[260] However, their claims are impaired, even if they are to be paid in full, if the plan calls for the claims to be paid over a different time than that provided for under the contract, or at a reduced rate of interest.[261] This makes sense because creditors who have a right to immediate payment but who will only receive payment over time may lack confidence in the debtor's ability to make the payments called for in the plan.[262]

Note that claims remain unimpaired, even though they may be affected by statutory provisions of the Bankruptcy Code, provided the terms of the plan itself do not alter the creditor or interest holder's rights. For example, § 502(b)(6) imposes a statutory limit on claims of landlords due to termination of a lease.[263] Enforcement of this mandatory Code provision does not alter the landlord's "legal, equitable, and contractual rights *to which such claim . . . entitles the holder of [the] claim*"[264] and thus does not impair the creditor's claim within the meaning of § 1124.[265] The distinction is between provisions of the plan that alter the creditor's rights and provisions of the Code that alter the creditor's rights. Alterations derived from the plan impair the creditor's claim; alterations derived from the Code define but do not alter the creditor's claim.[266]

[2] Defaults Cured and Rights Reinstated; De-Acceleration

A plan also leaves a class of claims unimpaired if it alters the claim of the creditor *only* by curing any of the debtor's defaults and reinstating the creditor's legal, equitable, and contractual rights to their status prior to the debtor's default.[267] The plan must not only cure any of the debtor's defaults,[268] but also must reinstate the maturity of the claim[269] and "compensate the holder of such claim . . . for any damages incurred as a

[260] *E.g.*, In re Atlanta-Stewart Partners, 193 B.R. 79, 82 (Bankr. N.D. Ga. 1996) (regarding the deletion of former § 1124(3)).

[261] In re G.L. Bryan Inv. Inc., 340 B.R. 386 (Bankr. D. Colo. 2006).

[262] *See also* In re Valley View Shopping Center, 260 B.R. 10, 32–33 (Bankr. D. Kan. 2001) (payments to be deferred for 90 days).

[263] *See* § 10.02[D][1] Claims for Rent, *supra*.

[264] Bankruptcy Code § 1124(1) (emphasis added).

[265] *E.g.*, Solow v. PPI Enters., Inc. (In re PPI Enters., Inc.), 324 F.3d 197 (3d Cir. 2003).

[266] In re Monclova Care Ctr., Inc., 254 B.R. 167 (Bankr. N.D. Ohio 2000).

[267] Bankruptcy Code § 1124(2).

[268] Bankruptcy Code § 1124(2)(A).

[269] Bankruptcy Code § 1124(2)(B).

result of any reasonable reliance by such holder on such contractual provision or applicable law."[270]

For example, assume Titanic Corp owes a fully secured $1 million debt to North Atlantic Finance Co., which calls for regularly monthly payments of $10,000 per month, and permits North Atlantic to accelerate the debt, making the $1 million balance immediately due upon the debtor's default. Before bankruptcy, Titanic missed a payment and North Atlantic exercised its right to accelerate the debt. The plan calls for Titanic to make the missed payment, pay North Atlantic any penalties and interest due on the missed payment, and resume regular monthly installment payments according to the schedule specified in the original loan agreement. This plan provision cures the debtor's default, reinstates the maturity of the debtor's obligations, and, by requiring interest and penalty payments, compensates the creditor for the debtor's default. Thus, North Atlantic's claim is unimpaired and the creditor is not entitled to vote on the debtor's plan.

Certain technical defaults need not be cured. For example, § 365(b)(2) specifies that "ipso-facto clauses" in the debtor's contracts that make the commencement of a bankruptcy case or other circumstances related to the debtor's financial condition a default, need not be cured.[271] Section 1124(2) leaves creditors' claims unimpaired even though the plan does not provide for cure of these types of defaults.

[F] Treatment of General Unsecured Claims

The Bankruptcy Code allows broad flexibility with respect to the treatment of classes of unsecured claims. Unless the plan leaves their claims unaffected and thus unimpaired, unsecured creditors have the right to reject the plan. Therefore, the key protections accorded to unsecured creditors are those that prevent discrimination, ensure that no creditor is harmed by the reorganization, and protect the voting process by insuring adequate disclosure and fair voting procedures.

Section 1123 does not contain all of the mandatory provisions of the plan. The plan must also be formulated with an eye to the requirements for confirmation which indirectly impose a number of other requirements. The key other provisions are those relating to the treatment of claims and interests. As discussed earlier, the plan must set out all classes of unsecured debt, specify whether the class is impaired or unimpaired, state the treatment of each class under the plan, and provide for equal treatment of all claims within a class.[272]

The Code adds a further requirement that applies to all claims and interests, most importantly with respect to unsecured claims: the plan must be

---

[270] Bankruptcy Code § 1124(2)(C).

[271] Bankruptcy Code § 365(b)(2); *see* § 11.04[B] Cure of Defaults Required for Assumption, *supra*.

[272] Bankruptcy Code § 1123(a)(1)-(4); *see generally* § 19.07[D] Classification of Claims, *supra*.

in the best interests of creditors.[273] More precisely, any creditor who does not accept the plan must "receive or retain . . . property of a value, as of the effective date of the plan, that is not less than the amount [it] would . . . receive or retain if the debtor were liquidated under Chapter 7 . . . on such date."[274] This implements creditors' most basic entitlement in bankruptcy: their right to the liquidation value of their claims. Because Chapter 11 plans normally provide for payments over a period of time, the payments proposed must exceed the present value of the amount that would be paid if the debtor was liquidated as of the time the plan is implemented. The present value of what the creditor receives under the plan must be worth at least what the creditor would get if the debtor were liquidated in Chapter 7.[275]

[G] Treatment of Priority Unsecured Claims

Priority claims are treated very favorably in Chapter 11. Section 1129(a)(9) divides priority claims into three groups. The first group[276] consists of priority 2 (administrative)[277] and priority 3 (involuntary gap) claims.[278] The second group[279] consists of priority 1 (alimony, maintenance, support),[280] priority 4 (wages),[281] priority 5 (employee benefits),[282] priority 6 (grain elevators and fish processing facilities),[283] and priority 7 (consumer deposits)[284] claims. The third group contains priority 8 (tax) claims.[285] There is no special treatment required for priority 9 (bank bailout) claims[286] or priority 10 (drunk driving liability) claims.[287]

The first group (priorities 2 and 3) are given the most favored status in the plan. These claims, including super-priority administrative claims, are entitled to immediate full payment in cash on the effective date of the

[273] Bankruptcy Code § 1129(a)(7)(A)(ii). Despite its familiar name, this test applies to both claims and interests — interests are also entitled to liquidation value. However, in virtually every case, the Chapter 7 value of an owner's equity interest is zero, so the "best interest of interest holders" test is virtually insignificant. *See* § 19.10[F] Best Interests of Creditors, *infra.*

[274] Bankruptcy Code § 1129(a)(7)(A). This rule is subject to an exception if the creditor has made the § 1111(b) election. Bankruptcy Code § 1129(a)(7)(B); *see* § 19.07[H][4] Treatment of the § 1111(b) Election, *supra.*

[275] *See* § 19.10[F] Plan in Best Interests of Creditors, *supra.*

[276] Bankruptcy Code § 1129(a)(9)(A).

[277] *See* § 10.04[A][2] Administrative Expense Claims, *supra.*

[278] *See* § 10.04[A][3] Involuntary Gap Creditors, *supra.*

[279] Bankruptcy Code § 1129(a)(9)(B).

[280] *See* § 10.04[A][1] Support Claims, *supra.*

[281] *See* § 10.04[A][4] Wage Claims, *supra.*

[282] *See* § 10.04[A][5] Employee Benefit Plan Claims, *supra.*

[283] *See* § 10.04[A][6] Certain Claims of Farmers and Fishermen, *supra.*

[284] *See* § 10.04[A][7] Consumer Deposits, *supra.*

[285] *See* § 10.04[A][8] Tax Claims, *supra.*

[286] *See* § 10.04[A][9] Claims of Insured Depositary Institutions, *supra.*

[287] *See* § 10.04[A][10] Civil Liability for Driving While Intoxicated, *supra.*

plan.[288] The only exception is if the holder of a claim agrees to less favorable treatment.[289] The class itself, however, cannot bind any particular claimant; the right to full, immediate payment is specific to each claim. Thus, even if the statutory majority of claims entitled to priority 2 or 3 accepts a plan that calls for less favorable treatment, the plan cannot be confirmed. This requirement may cripple a debtor's efforts to gain court confirmation of its plan (unless the debtor has a considerable amount of cash set aside to make these payments).[290]

The second group (priorities 1 and 4 through 7) are given slightly less favorable treatment. Each claim in the class is entitled to payment in full, but the class can vote to accept deferred payments, spread out over time.[291] If the class rejects the plan, each member of the class must be treated in the same manner as claims in the first group: full payment, in cash, on the effective date of the plan.[292] Thus, each class of these claims can vote to permit the debtor to defer payments to members of the class. However, each member of the class remains entitled to receive payment in full.

Note that this is different from claims in the first group, where each claimant has the right to demand payment immediately, regardless of how the class votes. In the second group, the class may vote to accept deferred payment in full, and this vote binds dissenters. Any individual holder of a claim may agree to accept less than full payment, but this binds no one else.

The third group (priority 8 tax claims) is given still less favorable treatment. Each claim remains entitled to payment in full, but neither individual claims nor the class is entitled to insist on immediate cash payment.

Finally, deferred payments to creditors in the second and third groups, when reduced to their present value, must equal the allowed amount of each claim on the effective date of the plan.[293] Any deferred payments must be made over no more than five years after the date of the order for relief.[294]

The 2005 Amendments added language that protects holders of secured tax claims that would have been entitled to priority treatment if they had been unsecured. These claims may no longer be treated less favorably than unsecured priority tax claims.[295] Without this new language, payments of

---

[288] Bankruptcy Code § 1129(a)(9)(A).

[289] Bankruptcy Code § 1129(a)(9)(A).

[290] The plan must also be feasible. *See* § 19.10[J] Feasibility of Plan, *supra*. Unless the debtor has the means to implement the plan, it cannot be confirmed.

[291] Bankruptcy Code § 1129(a)(9)(B)(i).

[292] Bankruptcy Code § 1129(a)(9)(B)(ii).

[293] Bankruptcy Code § 1129(a)(9)(C)(i).

[294] Bankruptcy Code § 1129(a)(9)(C)(ii). Note that this may be considerably less than five years from the effective date of the plan. Any individual claimant may accept a different treatment, but this does not bind other creditors.

[295] Bankruptcy Code § 1129(a)(9)(D).

secured tax claims that would have been entitled to priority if they were not secured, could have been paid over a longer period than if they had been unsecured. The 2005 Amendments also added language that requires priority 8 tax claims to be treated at least as well as non-priority unsecured claims paid under the plan.[296]

[H] Treatment of Secured Claims[297]

As is true throughout bankruptcy, Chapter 11 treats secured claims very favorably. Although the Code permits considerable changes in the rights of secured creditors, the value of most secured claims remains intact throughout the proceeding and after the plan is confirmed. The holder of a secured claim is thus generally in a relatively powerful position. Many plans founder on the requirement that the secured claims be paid the full value of their claim.

In considering the Code's treatment of secured claims, it is useful to remember that most of the time each secured claim is in its own class. This is partly for the sake of convenience, partly because secured claimants generally want to negotiate individual deals with the debtor, but primarily because it is unusual for a secured claim to be sufficiently similar to other secured claims to warrant combining them in the same class.

[1] Mandatory Treatment of Secured Claims

The key mandatory provision regarding impaired secured claims is contained in § 1129's requirements for confirmation. Specifically, the best interests of creditors test requires that each claimant receive over the course of the plan the present value of the liquidation value of its claim.[298] In other words, the value of the payment stream under the plan must have a present value equal to the lesser of the amount of the debt or the value of the collateral securing the debt on the plan's effective date.

Moreover, a secured creditor cannot be bound, without its consent, to a plan that does not provide it the minimum to which it would be entitled in a non-consensual plan — a "cramdown." As explained in more detail in connection with secured creditor cramdown, secured creditors are again entitled to deferred cash payments under the plan that are worth as much as their allowed secured claim.[299] In other words, the plan must provide for interest to be paid to the secured creditor on the amount of its secured claim to compensate the creditor for any delay in receiving payment.

For example, if the debt is undersecured and the property securing the debt is worth $100,000, the payments under the plan must have a present

[296] Bankruptcy Code § 1129(a)(9)(C)(iii).

[297] Darrell G. Waas, *Letting the Lender Have It: Satisfaction of Secured Claims by Abandoning a Portion of the Collateral*, 62 Am. Bankr. L.J. 97 (1988).

[298] Bankruptcy Code § 1129(a)(7)(A). Any individual creditor may agree to accept less, but this virtually never happens.

[299] Bankruptcy Code § 1129(b)(2)(A)(i)(II).

value of $100,000. Just as with the best interests of creditors test, this means that the payments must total more than $100,000. How much more depends on the length of the payout period and the estimated interest rates for that period. In effect, this means that even if the debt is undersecured, the debtor must pay interest on it.

In addition, the holder of a secured claim must retain the lien on its collateral for the full amount of its secured claim.[300] Otherwise, holders of secured claims would be vulnerable to becoming unsecured creditors in any subsequent bankruptcy proceeding filed by the debtor after failing to fully perform the terms of its confirmed plan.

Alternatively, secured creditors are entitled to a lien on any proceeds derived from the sale of their collateral free and clear of their lien,[301] or anything else that permits the secured creditor to realize the "indubitable equivalent" of its claim.[302]

[2] Optional Treatment of Secured Claims

As is true with unsecured debt, so long as the debtor does not resort to cramdown, the Code expressly permits the inclusion of "any other appropriate provision not inconsistent with the applicable provisions of this title."[303] Because there is usually only one creditor in each class of secured claims, acceptance of the proposed provisions depends on the consent of that one creditor. This makes negotiations over the terms of the plan with respect to a secured creditor more akin to the negotiations between any two parties to a business deal.

Except with respect to residential mortgages, claims of secured creditors can be modified by extending the due date, reducing the monthly payments, or adjusting the interest rate, and, unless the creditor makes the § 1111(b) election, stripping the lien down to the value of the collateral.[304] The plan might call for sale of the debtor's assets[305] free and clear of any lien, with creditor's liens transferred to the proceeds obtained from the sale.[306] What the debtor may offer to its secured creditors is limited almost solely by the imagination, provided they agree to the proposed treatment,[307] or even without their consent, if they receive the "indubitable equivalent" of the value of their secured claims.[308]

---

[300] Bankruptcy Code § 1129(b)(2)(A)(i)(I).

[301] Bankruptcy Code § 1129(b)(2)(A)(ii).

[302] Bankruptcy Code § 1129(b)(2)(A)(iii).

[303] Bankruptcy Code § 1123(b)(6).

[304] Bankruptcy Code § 1123(a)(5).

[305] Bankruptcy Code § 1123(b)(4).

[306] Bankruptcy Code § 1129(b)(2)(A)(ii).

[307] Bankruptcy Code § 1129(a)(8)(A).

[308] Bankruptcy Code § 1129(b)(2)(A)(iii).

[3] Chapter 11 Lien Stripping

Lien stripping refers to reducing the amount of a partially secured claim to the value of the collateral. Thus, a $10 million debt, secured by a mortgage on land worth only $8 million, is bifurcated into two claims: an $8 million secured claim and a $2 million unsecured claim. The creditor's lien is thus "stripped" away from the undersecured portion of the debt.

Lien stripping is not permitted for mortgages on real estate that is the debtor's principal residence.[309] This rule parallels a similar rule in Chapter 13.[310] Because only individuals have a principal residence, it does not apply to most Chapter 11 cases, which usually involve corporations and partnerships. However, there is nothing in Chapter 11 similar to the hanging paragraph at the end of § 1325(a)(9), which prevents lien stripping with respect to purchase money security interests in motor vehicles or other personal property.[311] Chapter 11 debtors are free to strip purchase money security interests away from personal property, without limitation.

[4] Treatment of the § 1111(b) Election[312]

As noted earlier, partially secured creditors usually may elect to have their claims treated as non-recourse secured claims for the entire nominal amount of the debt, rather than as recourse claims that are bifurcated into secured claims and unsecured claims.[313] If a creditor is owed $5 million, secured by property worth only $3 million, the creditor has the option to be treated in the "normal" way — to have a secured claim for $3 million and an unsecured claim for $2 million or to make the § 1111(b)(2) election and have a secured claim for $5 million but no deficiency claim.

On the face of it, the election is very attractive and provides strong protection against lien stripping. However, most of the time this apparent appeal is illusory. Section 1129(a)(7)(B) eliminates much of the benefit of § 1111(b)(2). This provision sets out the mandatory treatment of an 1111(b)(2) claim. It provides that the holder of a § 1111(b)(2) claim must receive or retain under the plan "property of a value, as of the effective date of the plan, that is not less than the value of such holder's interest in the estate's interest in the property that secures such claim."[314] This means that the best interests of creditors test[315] does not require payment of the present value of the entire claim, but only payment of the present value

309 Bankruptcy Code § 1123(b)(5).

310 Bankruptcy Code § 11322(b)(2); *see* § 18.07[B][2][a] Residential Real Estate Mortgages, *supra.*

311 *See* Bankruptcy Code § 1325(a)(9); § 18.07[B][2][b] Certain Purchase Money Loans, *supra.*

312 Steven R. Haydon et al., *The 1111(b)(2) Election: A Primer*, 13 Bank. Dev. J. 99 (1996).

313 Bankruptcy Code § 1111(b)(1); *see* § 19.07[C][1] Treatment of Non-Recourse Claims, *supra.*

314 Bankruptcy Code § 1129(a)(7)(B).

315 *See* § 19.10[F] Best Interests of Creditors, *infra.*

of the collateral. Thus, in the example given, the best interest of creditors test is met if the sum of all payments made equals at least $5 million and has a present value of at least $3 million. This treatment can be enforced by cramdown, as § 1129(b)(2)(A)(i)(II) requires payment of only the nominal amount of the allowed secured claim.

Thus, if any meaningful payment is provided to creditors with unsecured claims, a secured creditor who makes the § 1111(b) election may be worse off than it would have been if it had elected to have its claim treated in the usual fashion. If the creditor does *not* make the election, it would still be entitled to payments with a present value of $3 million and would also receive payments worth at least the liquidation value of the $2 million unsecured deficiency claim.

This does not always mean that making the § 1111(b) election is a bad idea. For example, it may not be possible for the debtor to extend the plan for such a long period of time that it will meet both the requirement of paying the nominal amount of the claim and the actual value of the collateral. The property also might be sold during the life of the plan for more than it is presently worth; and, under at least some circumstances, the § 1111(b) creditor will then be able to collect the full amount of its claim from the sale proceeds. Such a sale might occur in a subsequent liquidation, if, for example, the debtor's reorganization fails within several years after the plan has been implemented. However, given the plan confirmation standards, the protection provided by § 1111(b) is so uncertain that the election is only rarely made. The most common setting in which it might be utilized is in a single-asset real estate case where unsecured claims are to receive very little or where the affected creditor has little confidence in the debtor's ability to succeed following reorganization.

[I] Executory Contracts and Unexpired Leases in Chapter 11

As explained elsewhere, a Chapter 11 trustee or debtor-in-possession has the authority to assume, reject, or assign any executory contract or unexpired lease of the debtor.[316] The estate's treatment of these unperformed contracts plays a key role in many Chapter 11 reorganization cases. Section 365 might apply to permit the debtor to reject, assume, or assign a wide variety of executory contracts and unexpired leases, including:

- real estate leases of its retail outlets, factories, or storage facililties;
- equipment leases;
- franchise agreements; and
- employment contracts, including collective bargaining agreements.[317]

---

[316] *See* Chapter 11, Executory Contracts and Unexpired Leases, *supra.*

[317] Rejection of collective bargaining agreements is conducted pursuant to § 1113. *See* § 23.03 Employees' Rights, *infra.*

The Code expressly permits the debtor's plan to provide for the assumption, rejection, or assignment of any executory contract or unexpired lease that has not previously been rejected under § 365.[318] Section 365 specifies that, although the court may require a Chapter 11 debtor to make an earlier decision, the debtor otherwise has until confirmation of its plan to determine how to handle these contracts.[319] Normally, debtors desire to defer their decision until after they have had sufficient time to evaluate their business operations to determine which contracts they want to retain and which make more sense to either reject or assign.

§ 19.09 Acceptance of the Plan — Disclosure and Voting

Chapter 11's core is the agreement between the debtor and its creditors on a plan of reorganization. Creditors express their agreement by participating in negotiations leading to the promulgation of the debtor's plan and by voting to accept it. Creditors vote in classes. But, rather than the traditional "one person, one vote" approach that prevails in politics, Chapter 11 plan voting proceeds on a dual "one creditor, one vote," and a "one dollar, one vote" regime. More than half of a debtor's creditors must vote for the plan, and at least two-thirds of the dollar value of claims against the debtor must approve the plan.[320] Thus, most confirmed Chapter 11 plans implement the collective wisdom of the debtor's creditors.

Their agreement is meant to be an informed one. The debtor, who is in control of most of the information about its financial position and its prospects for future success, must provide that information to creditors and equity interest holders who are to vote on its plan. Moreover, this information must be presented in a way that enables the voter to make a reasoned decision, and it must be provided in a timely manner. This scheme, although simpler in structure, is a substitue for (and serves the same function as) the disclosure laws which govern issuers of publicly traded stocks and bonds.

[A] Consensual Chapter 11 Plans

As suggested above, most Chapter 11 plans are confirmed with the acceptance of creditors. For a plan to be regarded as consensual, every impaired class of creditors and interest holders must vote to "accept" the plan. There still might be dissenters. Some classes of creditors, whose claims are not impaired, are deemed to accept the plan and do not have the right to vote, even though they are dissatisfied with the debtor's prospects for success.[321] Other dissenting creditors may belong to a class that has accepted the plan. Even though there are dissenters, the plan is

[318] Bankruptcy Code § 1129(b)(2).

[319] Bankruptcy Code § 365(d)(2).

[320] Bankruptcy Code § 1126(c).

[321] Bankruptcy Code § 1126(f).

regarded as a consensual plan if each class entitled to vote has accepted it by the requisite number and amount. If so, the plan is not subject to the requirements for a "cramdown."

[B] Disclosure and Solicitation of Ballots

[1] Court Approval of Disclosure Statement; Adequate Information[322]

Section 1125 deals with the process of providing information to the creditors and owners of the debtor about a proposed reorganization plan. It prohibits anyone from soliciting the acceptance or rejection of a plan unless it has simultaneously or previously given the person solicited both a copy of the plan or a summary of the plan and a written disclosure statement approved by the court.[323] The disclosure statement provides creditors and owners with the information they need to make an informed judgment about accepting or rejecting a reorganization plan.

The disclosure statement may be approved by the court only after there has been both notice and an opportunity for a hearing.[324] The court may approve the disclosure statement only if the court determines that it contains "adequate information."[325]

"Adequate information" means information that is sufficient to enable a hypothetical "reasonable investor typical of holders of claims or interests of the relevant class" to make an informed judgment about the proposed plan.[326] It should be as detailed as practicable given the "nature and history of the debtor and the condition of the debtor's books and records . . . [but it does not have to] include information about other proposed or possible plan[s]."[327] Thus, a small proprietorship with sketchy books may have a lesser burden in preparing its disclosure statement than a large, publicly-traded corporation, both because the issues are less complex and because the records are less complete.

[2] Contents of Disclosure Statement

Note that the adequacy of the information is not measured against some absolute standard. Rather, it is measured from the perspective of the "typical investor," who is defined as an investor who has (1) a claim or

---

322 Glenn W. Merrick, *The Chapter 11 Disclosure Statement in a Strategic Environment*, 44 Bus. Law. 103 (1988); Nicholas S. Gatto, Note, *Disclosure in Chapter 11 Reorganizations: The Pursuit of Consistency and Clarity*, 70 Cornell L. Rev. 733 (1985); Note, *Disclosure of Adequate Information in a Chapter 11 Reorganization*, 94 Harv. L. Rev. 1808 (1981).

323 Bankruptcy Code § 1125(b). This may not be necessary in a case involving a "small business." Bankruptcy Code § 1125(f); *see* § 19.14 Small Business Debtors, *infra*.

324 Bankruptcy Code § 1125(b); *see* Fed. R. Bankr. P. 3017(a).

325 Bankruptcy Code § 1125(b).

326 Bankruptcy Code § 1125(a)(1).

327 Bankruptcy Code § 1125(a)(1).

interest of the relevant class; (2) the same type of relationship with the debtor as holders of claims or interests of that class generally have; and (3) the same ability to gather information about the debtor as holders of claims or interests, of that class generally have.[328] The latter two requirements make it clear that information that would be adequate for, say, an insider, would not necessarily be adequate information if most persons who held claims or interests of the same class were not insiders. The debtor does not have to send the same disclosure statement to everybody. Different classes may receive different disclosure statements; however, everyone within a particular class must receive the same disclosure statement.[329]

One frequently cited decision provides a detailed list of the items courts frequently require to be included in a disclosure statement:

1. the circumstances that gave rise to the filing of the bankruptcy petition;

2. a complete description of the available assets and their value;

3. the anticipated future of the debtor;

4. the source of the information provided in the disclosure statement;

5. a disclaimer, which typically indicates that no statements or information concerning the debtor or its assets or securities are authorized, other than those set forth in the disclosure statement;

6. the condition and performance of the debtor while in Chapter 11;

7. information regarding claims against the estate;

8. a liquidation analysis setting forth the estimated return that creditors would receive under Chapter 7;

9. the accounting and valuation methods used to produce the financial information in the disclosure statement;

10. information regarding the future management of the debtor, including the amount of compensation to be paid to any insiders, directors, or officers of the debtor;

11. a summary of the plan of reorganization;

12. an estimate of all administrative expenses, including attorneys' fees and accountants' fees;

13. the collectibility of any accounts receivable;

14. any financial information, valuations, or pro forma projections that would be relevant to creditors' determinations of whether to accept or reject the plan;

15. information relevant to the risks being taken by the creditors and interest holders;

[328] Bankruptcy Code § 1125(a)(2).

[329] Bankruptcy Code § 1125(c).

16. the actual or projected value that can be obtained from avoidable transfers;

17. the existence, likelihood, and possible success of non-bankruptcy litigation;

18. the tax consequences of the plan; and

19. the relationship of the debtor with affiliates.[330]

The 2005 Amendments added language that specifically requires "a discussion of the potential material Federal tax consequences of the plan to the debtor, any sucessor to the debtor, and a hypothetical investor typical of holders of claims or interests in the case."[331] The 2005 Amendments tempered the requirements for a disclosure statement, by specifying that in determining whether to approve a disclosure statement the court should consider the complexity of the case, the benefit to creditors and others of requiring additional information, and the costs of providing additional information.[332]

Creditors who wish to oppose the plan can raise many of the issues that are raised at other points in the proceeding at the hearing on the disclosure statement. These include the adequacy of protection, feasibility, good faith, and so on. Indeed, while lack of feasibility, for example, is technically an objection to confirmation, a court is much more likely to be receptive to feasibility arguments at the hearing on disclosure, because at that point the debtor may still have sufficient time to demonstrate whether it has the financial means to implement the plan, or to amend it.

[3] Soliciting Rejection of a Plan[333]

In some cases, dissenting creditors take a proactive approach to resist confirmation and actively solicit other creditors to reject a proposed plan. The rules for soliciting votes also apply to efforts to solicit rejections.[334] Thus, those opposed to a plan may not solicit rejections until after the disclosure statement has been approved by the court and transmitted to interested parties.[335]

Despite this, those soliciting rejections need not distribute their own disclosure statement. Moreover, they need not obtain prior court approval

---

330 In re Scioto Valley Mortg. Co., 88 B.R. 168 (Bankr. S.D. Ohio 1988).

331 Bankruptcy Code § 1125(a)(1).

332 Bankruptcy Code § 1125(a)(1).

333 Douglas E. Deutsch, *Ensuring Proper Bankruptcy Solicitation: Evaluating Bankruptcy Law, the First Amendment, the Code of Ethics, and Securities Law in Bankruptcy Solicitation Cases*, 11 Am. Bankr. Inst. L. Rev. 213 (2003); Paul R. Glassman, *Solicitation of Plan Rejections under the Bankruptcy Code*, 62 Am. Bankr. L.J. 261 (1988); Claude D. Montgomery, et al., *Solicitation Under Section 1125 of the Bankruptcy Code:* Century Glove *and the First Amendment*, 23 Seton Hall L. Rev. 1570 (1993).

334 Bankruptcy Code § 1125(b).

335 Bankruptcy Code § 1126(e) (providing for disqualification of votes solicited before a disclosure statement is disseminated).

of all of the information they supply to creditors as part of their effort to persuade them to vote against a plan. In *Century Glove, Inc. v. First American Bank*, the court sanctioned the actions of a group of dissenting creditors who had encouraged rejection of the plan by several key unsecured creditors and circulated a draft alternative plan.[336] None of the circulated materials had been approved by the court, and they were not accompanied by a separate disclosure statement. In reversing the bankruptcy court's disqualification of the rejections of the plan by several creditors who had received these materials, the court of appeals read § 1125 narrowly to permit such communications, provided a disclosure statement containing "adequate information" had previously been made.[337] Subsequent decisions have taken a similar approach.[338] However, a creditors' efforts to solicit acceptances of its alternate plan, without prior approval and dissemination of a separate disclosure statement about the substitute plan, are not permitted.

[4] Exemption from Registration with the Securities Exchange Commission

In some Chapter 11 plans, the debtor issues "securities" as a means to distribute the plan proceeds. For example, the debtor might propose to issue voting stock to the holders of unsecured claims; say, one share for every $100 of claim, or the debtor might issue some form of publicly traded debt security. This creates some potential problems with the securities laws. The issuance of stocks, bonds, and other securities is regulated by a number of state and federal laws; among the requirements is "registration" of the security with state and federal authorities. Compliance with the registration requirement is often time-consuming and expensive; imposing them on a Chapter 11 debtor would create yet another barrier to effective reorganization.[339] The function of registration overlaps with that of the disclosure statement.

Because of this, the Bankruptcy Code provides a broad exemption from securities laws for most debtors who are issuing plan-related securities. Assuming the debtor is not an "underwriter,"[340] any securities it issues that are entirely or primarily in exchange for a claim or an interest are entirely

---

336 860 F.2d 94 (3d Cir. 1988).

337 860 F.2d at 100; *but see* In re Apex Oil Co., 111 B.R. 245 (Bankr. E.D. Mo. 1990).

338 *E.g.*, In re Trans Max Technologies, Inc., 349 B.R. 80 (Bankr. D. Nev. 2006); *but see* In re Clamp-All Corp., 233 B.R. 198 (Bankr. D. Mass. 1999) (prohibiting distribution of materials that solicit rejections before approval and dissemination of proponent's disclosure statement); *see generally* John F. Wagner Jr., Annotation, *What Constitutes Improper Solicitation of Acceptance or Rejection of Reorganization Plan Under 11 U.S.C.A. Sec. 1125(b)*, 100 A.L.R. Fed. 226 (1990).

339 *See generally* Louis Loss & Joel Seligman, Securities Regulation (Rev'd 3d ed. 2004).

340 Broadly speaking, an underwriter is a person who is distributing a security to others, rather than holding it for investment. *See* 2 Louis Loss & Joel Seligman, Securities Regulation 1138.44-1138.70 (3d rev'd ed. 2004).

exempt from federal, state, and local laws that require registration.[341] This exemption only applies to securities exchanged for existing debt or equity; it does not apply to securities issued to raise funds to finance the plan, although the narrower registration exemption in § 364(f) can be used for that purpose.[342] Likewise, the exemption only relates to the registration requirements. There are other securities laws — most notably, those that prohibit fraud in securities transactions — that still apply.[343] Chapter 11 provides no safe-harbor against claims of securities fraud. Indeed, fraud committed in connection with promulgation of a disclosure statement would raise problems beyond violations of the securities laws.

[5] Disclosure in Small Business Cases

Disclosure may be considerably simplified in cases involving "small business debtors." These are business debtors with less than $2 million in claims, held by creditors other than insiders.[344] These debtors' financial circumstances usually are not complex. Accordingly, the court has the authority to determine that the plan itself provides adequate information and thus that a separate disclosure statement is not necessary.[345] Alternatively, the court may approve a disclosure statement that is submitted on standardized disclosure statement forms approved by the Supreme Court, pursuant to its authority to adopt Bankruptcy Rules, or by local rule.[346] Further, the court may conditionally approve a disclosure statement and defer final approval of its adequacy until the hearing on plan confirmation.[347]

[6] Pre-Petition Solicitation

Debtors who have attempted to deploy an out-of-court workout or composition in an unsuccessful effort to avoid bankruptcy may have solicited acceptances before filing their bankruptcy petition. Such a debtor may seek to use Chapter 11 to obtain confirmation of the proposed out-of-court settlement. However, solicitations of acceptances or rejections of the debtor's plan prior to the filing of the petition are subject to the securities laws.[348]

---

[341] Bankruptcy Code § 1145(a)(1).

[342] See § 9.05 Obtaining Credit, *supra*.

[343] *See generally* Thomas Lee Hazen, The Law of Securities Regulation 560–698 (2002).

[344] Bankruptcy Code § 101(51D). The definition excludes single-asset real estate debtors regardless of the amount of their debt.

[345] Bankruptcy Code § 1125(f)(1).

[346] Bankruptcy Code § 1125(f)(2); *see* 28 U.S.C. § 2075.

[347] Bankruptcy Code § 1125(f)(3).

[348] Bankruptcy Code § 1126(b)(1).

[C] Voting by Classes of Claims and Interests[349]

Ordinarily, confirmation of the plan requires the approval of each impaired class of creditors and equity security holders.[350] Voting is primarily by claim, not by claimant, and is conducted by each class of claim and interest holders. Normally, every allowed claim has a vote; however, if a claim is held by an entity whose vote was in bad faith, or whose vote was solicited or procured in bad faith, the vote of that claim can be disqualified, or "designated," and does not count.[351]

Some classes of claims or interests do not vote. A class and all of the members of a class whose claims are unimpaired are deemed to have accepted the plan and do not vote.[352] Likewise, claims on which nothing will be paid do not vote; a class of claims that receives nothing is deemed to have rejected the plan.[353]

[1] Voting by Classes of Claims

Approval does not require a unanimous vote. Instead, it requires a dual majority. The first is a simple majority of more than half of the number of claims.[354] The second is a super-majority of at least two-thirds of the amount of the claims.[355]

In each case, whether the requisite majority is reached depends on the number and amount of claims in the class, not just the number or amount of the claims that actually vote. Abstentions do not count.

Both requisite majorities must be reached. For example, suppose a class consists of thirty claims, totaling $180,000. If sixteen claims totaling $120,000 vote to approve the plan, the class has approved the plan. More than half (16 of 30) of the claim holders have voted for the plan and two-thirds ($120,000 of $180,000) of the amount of the claims have voted in its favor. If fewer than sixteen claim holders accept the plan, the class has rejected it. Even if fifteen claim holders (exactly 50% in number) totaling $179,999.85 (not quite 100%) accept the plan, the class has rejected it, because both majorities must be achieved. Similarly, if twenty-nine claims totaling $119,999.99 vote in favor, the class rejects the plan. This is due to the size of the one remaining claim, which was more than one-third of the total amount of claims in the class.

This dual majority requirement prevents a plan from being accepted by a few large creditors over the objections of many small creditors or accepted

---

[349] David Arthur Skeel, Jr., *The Nature and Effect of Corporate Voting in Chapter 11 Reorganization Cases*, 78 Va. L. Rev. 461 (1992).

[350] *See* § 10.01 Meaning of Claims and Interests, *supra*.

[351] Bankruptcy Code § 1126(c), (e).

[352] Bankruptcy Code § 1126(f). Though they can still object to the plan on the grounds that it is not feasible.

[353] Bankruptcy Code § 1126(g).

[354] Bankruptcy Code § 1126(c).

[355] Bankruptcy Code § 1126(c).

by many small creditors over the objections of a few large creditors. The latter probably has more practical significance; in many Chapter 11 cases, a single creditor can block the plan if it holds more than one-third of the debt in a class.[356]

[2] Voting by Classes of Interests

Equity interest holders are subject to a somewhat different rule. A class of interests accepts a plan if two-thirds in the amount of the allowed interests in the class accept the plan.[357]

[D] Disqualification of Votes[358]

Acceptances or rejections that are submitted in bad faith are disqualified.[359] This should not be confused with a requirement that creditors vote in accordance with the best interests of the debtor or that they have a fiduciary duty to other creditors.[360] Rather, creditors are entitled to vote in accordance with their own self-interest.[361]

The questionable good faith of votes in favor of or against the plan (usually against it), usually arises in one of several contexts, all of which involve some ulterior motive on the part of the claimant casting the vote. A creditor's efforts to destroy the debtor's business out of malice or ill will toward the debtor, though rarely the source of a vote in contravention of the claimant's financial interests, is in bad faith.[362] Votes against the debtor's plan as part of an effort to assume control of the debtor,[363] or to put the debtor out of business in order to gain a competitive advantage are also regarded as cast in bad faith.[364]

However, the most common circumstance in which the good faith of a rejection is called into question involves creditors who have purchased claims that were held by another creditor in an effort to obtain more influence over the debtor's plan than they otherwise would have enjoyed.[365] Creditors

[356] *E.g.*, In re Eitemiller, 149 B.R. 626 (Bankr. D. Idaho 1993).

[357] Bankruptcy Code § 1126(d).

[358] Chaim J. Fortgang & Thomas Moers Mayer, *Developments in Trading Claims: Participations and Disputed Claims*, 15 Cardozo L. Rev. 733 (1993).

[359] Bankruptcy Code § 1126(e); *see generally* 255 Park Plaza Assocs. Ltd. v. Connecticut Gen. Life Ins. Co. (In re 255 Park Plaza Assocs. Ltd.), 100 F.3d 1214, 1219 (6th Cir. 1996).

[360] *E.g.*, In re Federal Support Co., 859 F.2d 17, 19–20 (4th Cir. 1988).

[361] *See, e.g.*, In re Figter, Ltd., 118 F.3d 635 (9th Cir. 1997).

[362] *E.g.*, In re MacLeod Co., 63 B.R. 654, 655–56 (Bankr. S.D. Ohio 1986).

[363] *E.g.*, In re Allegheny Int'l, Inc., 118 B.R. 282, 290 (Bankr. W.D. Pa. 1990).

[364] In re Landing Assocs. Ltd., 157 B.R. 791, 807–08 (Bankr. W.D. Tex. 1993).

[365] Andrew Africk, Comment, *Trading Claims in Chapter 11: How Much Influence Can Be Purchased in Good Faith under Section 1126?*, 139 U. Pa. L. Rev. 1393 (1991); Frederick Tung, *Confirmation and Claims Trading*, 90 Nw. U. L. Rev. 1684 (1996); David Arthur Skeel, Jr., *The Nature and Effect of Corporate Voting in Chapter 11 Reorganization Cases.*, 78 Va. L. Rev. 461 (1992).

opposed to a plan might try to block confirmation simply by purchasing claims of other creditors in a sufficient number or amount to prevent the debtor from obtaining sufficient acceptances to satisfy § 1126(c). When this occurred in *In re Allegheny International, Inc.*,[366] the court disqualified the votes of an undersecured creditor who paid a premium to several unsecured creditors in order to acquire a sufficient amount in claims to have an effective veto over the plan. Without the huge voting block of this one creditor, the class of unsecured claims voted to accept the plan, and it was confirmed.

Other courts have been more tolerant of this tactic. In *Figter Ltd. v. Teachers Ins. & Annuity Association (In re Figter Ltd.)*,[367] a fully secured creditor was dissatisfied with the debtor's plan to convert its collateral, an apartment complex, into condominium units. It purchased twenty-one of the thirty-four unsecured claims in the class of general unsecured creditors, paying the creditors the face value of their claims in full.[368] It then submitted rejections for all twenty-one claims. This prevented consensual confirmation of the plan.

The debtor raised two arguments in an effort to resist the creditor's strategy. First, it asserted that the claims purchased by this one creditor should be consolidated and treated as a single claim. Because of the small size of the twenty-one claims in comparison to the other unsecured claims, consolidation of the transferred claims would have resulted in acceptance of the plan by the requisite simple majority in the number of claims and at least two-thirds in amount of the claims in the class. However, the court reminded the debtor that § 1126(c) "speaks in terms of the number of claims, not the number of creditors, that actually vote for or against the plan."[369] Thus, because each of the purchased claims arose from different transactions, it was improper to regard them as a single claim, even though they were all held by the same creditor.

Figter's main argument was that the creditor's acquisition of the twenty-one claims and its rejection of the plan was in bad faith. The court found otherwise. The court ruled that a creditor whose purchase of additional claims was implemented for the purpose of "protecting his own existing claim does not demonstrate bad faith or an ulterior motive."[370] Instead, the creditor was quite naturally concerned that if the plan were implemented, it would be left with a complex bundle of mortgages on nearly 200 different condominium units, instead of a single mortgage on a single apartment building. Thus, the purchase of other creditors' claims was part of its "enlightened self interest," even though it frustrated the debtor's hopes.[371]

---

366 118 B.R. 282 (Bankr. W.D. Pa. 1990).

367 118 F.3d 635 (9th Cir. 1997).

368 Notice of transfer of claims is required to be filed. Fed. R. Bankr. P. 3001(e)(2).

369 118 F.3d at 640.

370 118 F.3d at 639.

371 118 F.3d at 639.

[E] Pre-Packaged Plans[372]

Sometimes Chapter 11 proceedings are presented to the court as "pre-packaged" — that is, the plan has been negotiated and acceptances have been obtained before the case is filed.[373] Section 1126 facilitates such pre-packaged cases by obviating the need for a second disclosure or a second vote. When its requirements are met, holders of claims or interests who either accepted or rejected the plan prior to the commencement of the case are "deemed" to have accepted or rejected the plan. Such pre-packaged plans are used to facilitate quick confirmation where resort to bankruptcy court is necessary to deal with a small group of recalcitrant dissenters, or to obtain other legal benefits available only in bankruptcy.

For a pre-packaged plan (or a "pre-pack") to pass muster under Chapter 11, one of two requirements must have been satisfied. First, the plan can be confirmed if the solicitation of creditors' acceptances or rejections was compliant with any applicable nonbankruptcy law, rule, or regulation.[374] In other words, if the debtor adhered to any state law requirements that govern efforts to obtain approval from creditors of a plan of reorganization, the bankruptcy court regards those procedures as sufficient. Alternatively, if no applicable state law, rule, or regulation applies, the plan can be confirmed if disclosures made to claim and interest holders provided the type of adequate information that is necessary in a Chapter 11 disclosure statement.[375]

In addition, § 1125(g) now authorizes the debtor to continue soliciting those whose acceptances were solicited before the case was commenced, provided that the creditor or equity security holder "was solicited before commencement of the case in a manner complying with applicable nonbankruptcy law."[376] Before the 2005 Amendments, continued efforts to solicit acceptances had to cease until the disclosure statement received court approval. After the 2005 Amendments, pre-petition solicitation may continue so long as the original pre-petition efforts to solicit acceptances (or rejections) complied with the state and federal securities laws that govern the solicitation process outside of bankruptcy court.[377]

In addition, of course, all of the other requirements for confirmation must be satisfied. The debtor cannot use pre-petition acceptances to deprive

[372] Ronald Barliant, et al., *From Free-Fall to Free-For-All: The Rise of Pre-Packaged Asbestos Bankruptcies*, 12 Am. Bankr. Inst. L. Rev. 441 (2004); Mark D. Plevin, et al., *Pre-Packaged Asbestos Bankruptcies: A Flawed Solution*, 44 S. Tex. L. Rev. 883 (2003).

[373] *See* Douglas G. Baird & Robert K. Rasmussen, *Beyond Recidivism*, 54 Buff. L. Rev. 343, 347–48 (2006); Melissa B. Jacoby, *Fast, Cheap, and Creditor-Controlled: Is Corporate Reorganization Failing?*, 54 Buff. L. Rev. 401 (2006).

[374] Bankruptcy Code § 1126(b)(1).

[375] Bankruptcy Code § 1126(b)(2).

[376] Bankruptcy Code § 1125(g).

[377] Richard Levin & Alesia Ranney-Marinelli, *The Creeping Repeal of Chapter 11: The Significant Business Provisions of the Bankruptcy Abuse Prevention and Consumer Protection Act of 2005*, 79 Am. Bankr. L.J. 603, 630–31 (2005).

dissenters of their right to insist that the plan was filed in good faith, that the distribution to creditors satisfies the best interests of creditors test, or that the plan conforms to other requirements of the Bankruptcy Code. But, the proponent of the plan need not obtain court approval of a new disclosure statement, disseminate new copies of the plan and disclosure statement, or require creditors to resubmit their ballots, indicating their approval or disapproval of the debtor's plan.

§ 19.10 Confirmation of Chapter 11 Plans

Confirmation of the plan is the court action that puts the plan into effect. Confirmation may occur only after notice and an actual hearing — not merely the opportunity for a hearing.[378] Confirmation may be granted only if § 1129's long list of statutory requirements are met. However, § 1129 should not be read in isolation; other provisions, particularly § 1121 through § 1126, play a major role in whether a plan is confirmed.

[A] Compliance with the Bankruptcy Code[379]

Section 1129(a)(1) permits confirmation only if "the plan complies with the applicable provisions of [the Bankruptcy Code]." This brings the remainder of the Bankruptcy Code into play in determining whether the plan can be confirmed. For example, this means that the plan must classify and treat claims consistently with § 1123(a)(1)-(4) and § 1122.[380] Likewise, the plan may not call for modification of claims secured by an individual debtor's residence in violation of § 1123(b)(5). Nor may it violate provisions of the Code outside of Chapter 11, such as those that deal with compensation of professionals.[381]

In addition, the "proponent of the plan" must comply with the provisions of the Bankruptcy Code.[382] This creates a potential minefield for Chapter 11 debtors who are in jeopardy of being unable to obtain confirmation as a result of any possible violation of the Code's provisions.[383] Courts have mitigated this potential in two ways. First, despite the clear language of § 1129(a)(2) that requires the proponent of the plan to comply "with the applicable provisions of this *title*,"[384] courts have sometimes held that it only mandates compliance with the reorganization provisions of the

---

[378] Bankruptcy Code § 1128(a).

[379] Harley J. Goldstein & Craig A. Sloan, *Spending Other People's Money: Creditors' Remedies for the Misuse of Cash Collateral in Bankruptcy*, 7 U. Miami Bus. L. Rev. 243, 264–66 (1999).

[380] *See* § 19.08[D] Classification of Claims, *supra*.

[381] *E.g.*, In re Beyond.com Corp., 289 B.R. 138, 143 (Bankr. N.D. Cal. 2003).

[382] Bankruptcy Code § 1129(a)(2).

[383] *See, e.g.*, Matter of Cothran, 45 B.R. 836, 838 (S.D. Ga. 1984) (misuse of cash collateral); In re Wermelskirchen, 163 B.R. 793 (Bankr. N.D. Ohio 1994) (failure to schedule all creditors).

[384] Bankruptcy Code § 1129(a)(2) (emphasis supplied).

Code.[385] Other courts have permitted it to be used only for serious deviations from the Code's requirements, thus effectively creating a de minimis exception to the requirement that the proponent comply with all of the Code's provisions. Thus, if the proponent's misbehavior had no material effect on creditors, or on the plan, confirmation is still permitted.[386] Debtors who violate the Code in some serious fashion may still find it impossible to obtain confirmation because of their defalcation.[387]

[B] Plan Proposed in Good Faith[388]

Section 1129(a)(3) specifies that the plan must have been "proposed in good faith and not by any means prohibited by law."[389] Lack of good faith might also lead to dismissal of the case under § 1112.[390] Good faith has a wide array of potential meanings. In this context, it most commonly deals with whether the plan's goals are consistent with Chapter 11's purposes.[391] Good faith has been a particular stumbling block in single-asset real estate cases, where the debtor's purposes may simply be to delay the inevitable foreclosure, rather than to restructure its finances consistently with the purposes of Chapter 11.[392]

The requirement that the plan be proposed by any means not forbidden by law casts a wide net. It encompasses violations not only of bankruptcy law, but also of other applicable federal, state, and local law.[393] Thus, if the plan calls for a legally prohibited source of funding, a legally proscribed organizational structure, or illegal business activities, it cannot be confirmed.

[C] Court Approval of Previous Payments

For the plan to be confirmed, the court must have approved payments made by the proponent, the debtor, and certain other parties, if those payments are for services, costs, or expenses incident to the plan or to the

[385] *E.g.*, In re Landing Assocs., Ltd., 157 B.R. 791, 811 (Bankr. W.D. Tex. 1993); *but see* In re Briscoe Enters., Ltd. II, 138 B.R. 795, 809 (N.D. Tex. 1992) (taking the draconian view that § 1129(a)(2) might prevent confirmation even if code violations were cured or were approved by the court nunc pro tunc).

[386] *E.g.*, In re Greate Bay Hotel & Casino, Inc., 251 B.R. 213 (Bankr. D.N.J. 2000).

[387] *E.g.*, Cothran v. United States (In re Cothran), 45 B.R. 836, 838 (S.D. Ga. 1984).

[388] Ali M.M. Mojdehi & Janet Dean Gertz, *The Implicit "Good Faith" Requirement in Chapter 11 Liquidations: A Rule in Search of a Rationale?*, 14 Am. Bankr. Inst. L. Rev. 143 (2006).

[389] Bankruptcy Code § 1129(a)(3).

[390] *See* § 19.05[B][3] Bad Faith Filing, *supra*; *e.g.*, In re SGL Carbon Corp., 200 F.3d 154 (3d Cir. 1999).

[391] In re Madison Hotel Assocs., 749 F.2d 410, 424–25 (7th Cir. 1984).

[392] Brian S. Katz, *Single-asset Real Estate Cases and the Good Faith Requirement: Why Reluctance to Ask Whether a Case Belongs in Bankruptcy May Lead to the Incorrect Result*, 9 Bankr. Dev. J. 77 (1992).

[393] In re Koelbl, 751 F.2d 137, 139 (2d Cir. 1984).

case.[394] This is a part of the broader issue of court control of the costs of administration, which is more fully discussed elsewhere,[395] and overlaps to some extent with the requirement discussed above, that the plan comply with other applicable provisions of the Code.

[D] Disclosure of Identity of Insiders and Affiliates of Debtor

The proponent of the plan must disclose the identity and affiliations of individuals who will be directors, officers or voting trustees of the reorganized debtor; any affiliate of the debtor who is participating with the debtor in a joint plan of reorganization; or of any successor to the debtor under the plan.[396] Moreover, the appointment or retention of directors, officers, or any voting trustee must be consistent with the interests of creditors, equity security holders, and any applicable public policy.[397] In addition, the proponent of the plan must disclose the identity of any insider who will be retained or employed by the reorganized debtor and the nature of that insider's compensation.[398] These requirements ensure that the identity and affiliations of those who manage the debtor are fully disclosed to those who vote on the plan. These matters can be expected to be dealt with in disclosure statements that are distributed in connection with the plan.

[E] Regulatory Approval

Debtors engaged in an industry that is subject to rate regulation and whose plan provides for a change in rates must have their proposed new rates approved by the appropriate governmental agency.[399] An electric utility company is a good example of the type of debtor who must comply with this provision. This helps to ensure that aspects of the debtor's plan that depend on changes in the debtor's revenue are realistic.

[F] Best Interests of Creditors

Section 1129(a)(7) requires that each holder of an impaired claim or interest has either "accepted the plan"[400] or:

> will receive or retain under the plan on account of such claim or interest property of a value, as of the effective date of the plan, that is not less than the amount that such holder would so receive or

[394] Bankruptcy Code § 1129(a)(4).

[395] *See generally* Chapter 9, Operating the Debtor, *supra*; Chapter 21, Professionals in Bankruptcy Cases, *infra*.

[396] Bankruptcy Code § 1129(a)(5)(A)(i).

[397] Bankruptcy Code § 1129(a)(5)(A)(ii).

[398] Bankruptcy Code § 1129(a)(5)(B).

[399] Bankruptcy Code § 1129(a)(6).

[400] Bankruptcy Code § 1129(a)(7)(A)(i).

> retain if the debtor were liquidated under chapter 7 of this title on such date.[401]

This statutory language has long been referred to as "the best interests of creditors" test.[402] The "property" that creditors receive usually consists of cash payments, though it may be any type of property, such as stock in the reorganized company, or even tangible property such as inventory or equipment.[403]

The best interests of creditors test only applies to claims and interests that belong to an impaired class. Under the test, each affected creditor is entitled to receive payments that, when reduced to their present value, equal at least the Chapter 7 liquidation value of the affected claim or interest. It is easy to understand a requirement that creditors receive at least as much in reorganization as they would in liquidation, but the requirement is more complex than it first appears. The key component of the statutory language is its requirement that creditors receive payments that are equivalent to the *value* of what they would receive in liquidation. Because Chapter 11 plans nearly always call for payments to creditors to be distributed over a period of time, the amount of these payments must be discounted to reflect their "present value" on the effective date of the plan. In simple terms, $10 paid out one dollar at a time, over a ten-year period is worth less than $10 received today.

For example, if in a liquidation of Titanic Corp., $100,000 would be distributed to general unsecured creditors who have claims aggregating $1,000,000, each creditor would be paid 10% of its claim. In Titanic Corp.'s liquidation, a creditor with a $300,000 claim would receive $30,000. A plan that provides for payments to unsecured creditors at the rate of $20,000 per year for five years for a total of $100,000 would result in the creditor's receiving $6,000 a year for a five-year total of $30,000. This does not satisfy the best interests of creditors test. This is because five annual $6,000 payments spread out over five years, totaling $30,000, is worth less than $30,000 paid immediately. For the plan to be confirmed, the stream of future payments must include an interest component to compensate creditors for the delay.

Every creditor has the right to receive the liquidation value of its claim. This is clear from the language of § 1129(a)(7) that refers to "each holder of a claim." Thus, each creditor has the right to insist that the plan provides it with the liquidation value of its claim, even if the creditor's class has accepted the plan. This protects dissenting members of a class that has voted to accept the plan.

Of course, a class of creditors rarely accepts a plan that gives its members less than this statutory minimum. Thus, it is unusual for a plan to be

---

[401] Bankruptcy Code § 1129(a)(7)(A)(ii).

[402] Bankruptcy Code § 1129(a)(7).

[403] One of your authors is acquainted with a San Francisco Bay Area bankruptcy lawyer who received several very nice tennis racquets as compensation for his pre-petition services to a sporting goods store.

accepted by the requisite majority and still fail the best interests of creditors test. The best interests test is more commonly invoked with respect to a plan that is being "crammed down" without the approval of a class of creditors.

Nevertheless, because it protects dissenting members of a class that has accepted the plan, it may still play a role in cases where dissenting members of the class have a more accurate assessment of the debtor's liquidation value than those who voted to accept the plan. Moreover, the fact that dissenters might object, and thus force the court to determine the debtor's liquidation value, gives these creditors bargaining leverage that they might use to induce the debtor to pay more to the members of the class than it otherwise might.

The best interests test requires the court to make two factual determinations.[404] First, it must determine how much the creditor would have received if the debtor had liquidated. This requires a a calculation of the debtor's liquidation value and a determination of how that value would be distributed in a Chapter 7 liquidation proceeding. The process of making this determination is difficult, expensive, and like any other valuation proceeding, inexact. And, because the debtor's business might be sold as a going concern in a Chapter 7 case, the court may find it necessary to calculate the value of the debtor's business as a going concern. This value depends on the future earnings of the debtor, and not the book value or the appraised value of the debtor's individual assets.[405] However, most of the time, the liquidation value is based on appraisals of what the debtor would be worth if liquidated in piecemeal fashion.[406]

In addition, the court must determine what discount or interest rate to use in determining whether the stream of future payments are equivalent to the liquidation value creditors would have received in a Chapter 7 case. The appropriate interest rate was a subject of much debate. In 2004, the United States Supreme Court decided *Till v. SCS Credit Corp.*,[407] and perhaps confused the matter further.

Till was a Chapter 13 case regarding the appropriate discount rate to use in determining whether amounts paid to a secured creditor were equivalent to the present value of its secured claim as required by § 1325(a)(5). The Court's plurality decision required use of a formula based on the prime rate of interest, adjusted upward to reflect risks facing the creditor in the circumstances of the case. It is still unclear whether this formula approach applies to the best interests test of § 1129(a)(7). A few courts have rejected its use under Chapter 13's best interests test, reasoning that *Till* was merely a plurality decision, and applies only to the facts

404 For a discussion of the best interest test as it applies to Chapter 13 plans, see § 18.08[E][1] Best Interests of Creditors, *supra*.

405 *See* Consolidated Rock Prods. Co. v. DuBois, 312 U.S. 510 (1941).

406 *E.g.*, In re Lason, Inc., 300 B.R. 227, 233 (Bankr. D. Del. 2003).

407 541 U.S. 465 (2004) (present value for secured claims under § 1325(a)(5)).

of the case before it, which involved secured creditor cramdown under Chapter 13.[408] As a result, in Chapter 11, a number of different approaches are still used.

Section 1129(a)(7) also imposes requirements for treatment of those secured creditors who have made the § 1111(b) election to have their claims treated as non-recourse claims. As explained in more detail elsewhere, it requires payments under the plan to have a present value equivalent to the value of collateral. Thus, if the creditor held a $500,000 claim, secured by $300,000 of collateral, the plan would have to provide for payment of $500,000 to the creditor, with a discounted present value of at least $300,000. This would seem to be implicit in § 1129(a)(7), but, since a creditor who has made the election has an allowed secured claim equal to the amount of the debt, § 1129(a)(7)(B) (mirrored in § 1129(b)(2)(A)(i)(II)) specifies that the payments made on account of that claim need only have a present value equal to the value of the collateral (not the amount of the debt).

[G] Acceptance by Impaired Classes

Section 1129(a)(8) seems to require each class of claims or interests to accept the plan by the required statutory majority or be unimpaired by the plan.[409] The language of § 1129(a)(8) appears to make this requirement mandatory, but it is not. Section 1129(b), dealing with Chapter 11 cramdown (when read in conjunction with § 1129(a)(10)), permits confirmation even though a class of impaired claims has rejected the plan so long as at least one impaired class votes to accept the plan and certain other requirements are met.

Note that § 1129(a)(8) does not require every impaired claim or interest to accept the plan; it requires only that each *class* of impaired claims or interests accept. Thus, the plan may be confirmed over the objection of a dissenting group of creditors who are outvoted by creditors with substantially similar claims included in the same class. This is one of the significant advantages of Chapter 11 over informal workouts and state insolvency proceedings.

[H] Full Payment of Priority Claims

As explained elsewhere, to be confirmed, a Chapter 11 plan must provide for full payment of most priority claims.[410] Administrative expenses

[408] In re Cook, 322 B.R. 336, 345 (Bankr. N.D. Ohio 2005) (coerced loan approach based on current market interest rates for loans in similar situations). *Cf.* In re American HomePatient, Inc., 420 F.3d 559 (6th Cir. 2005) (applying § 1129(a)(5)); *see generally* § 18.09[F][4][b] Payments Equivalent to Amount of Secured Claim, *supra*.

[409] Bankruptcy Code § 1129(a)(8); *see* § 19.09[B] Voting by Classes of Claims and Interests, *supra*, regarding the necessary voting majorities.

[410] Bankruptcy Code § 1129(a)(9); *see* § 19.08[G] Treatment of Priority Unsecured Claims, *supra*.

associated with the bankruptcy case itself and § 502(f) involuntary gap period claims must be paid in full, in cash, on the effective date of the plan.[411] Most other priority claims must be paid in full, and in cash, but they may be paid over time if the class of affected claims has accepted the plan.[412] Otherwise, they must be paid in full immediately, with administrative claims, on the plan's effective date.[413] Priority tax claims must be paid in full, but may be paid over a maximum of five years after the order for relief[414] and not more slowly than any non-priority claim.[415] Other priority claims, such as those owed to the FDIC or for personal injury or death in a drunk driving incident, are not entitled to any special treatment other than that required by the absolute priority rule. A class of these claims can prevent confirmation if any class of general unsecured claims receives anything under the terms of the plan.[416]

[I] Acceptance by One Impaired Class

A Chapter 11 plan must be accepted by at least one impaired class.[417] Most Chapter 11 plans are confirmed with acceptances from all classes. However, a consensual plan may not be possible. If so, the proponent of the plan may seek to have it confirmed over the objection of a class of claims or interests. If no class of impaired claims has accepted the plan, it cannot be confirmed. This is a key aspect of Chapter 11 cramdown. Note that, unlike other aspects of the requirements for confirmation, this rule applies only with respect to classes of claims; it does not apply to classes of interests — acceptance by a class of interests does not satisfy the requirement.

Moreover, in determining that at least one impaired class of claims has accepted, the votes of insiders are not counted.[418] Thus, if the only class that accepts the plan contains five claims, with two of them held by insiders,[419] two of the three non-insiders must have accepted the plan. Otherwise, the requirement that more than half of the claims in the class has accepted the plan is not met.

[J] Feasibility of Plan

The plan must be feasible — there must be a realistic chance for it to be successfully implemented. However, like "best interests," the term

[411] Bankruptcy Code § 1129(a)(9)(A).

[412] Bankruptcy Code § 1129(a)(9)(B)(i).

[413] Bankruptcy Code § 1129(a)(9)(B)(ii).

[414] Bankruptcy Code § 1129(a)(9)(C). This may be considerably less than five years from the time of confirmation.

[415] Bankruptcy Code § 1129(a)(9)(C)(iii). The one exception is for small claims that are segregated into a separate class for administrative convenience under § 1122(b). These are usually paid in cash on the effective date of the plan.

[416] *See* § 19.11 Confirmation over Objection of Impaired Class; Cramdown, *infra*.

[417] Bankruptcy Code § 1129(a)(10).

[418] Bankruptcy Code § 1129(a)(10).

[419] Bankruptcy Code § 101(31).

"feasibility" appears nowhere in the code. Instead, § 1129(a)(11) specifies: "Confirmation of the plan is not likely to be followed by the liquidation, or the need for further financial reorganization, of the debtor, or any successor to the debtor under the plan, unless such liquidation or reorganization is proposed in the plan."

The goal of this requirement is to curb repeated proceedings. Debtors are expected to solve their financial problems permanently. However, courts have sometimes characterized the standards for determining whether a plan is feasible as "not rigorous."[420] Confirmed plans do not always succeed, and cases sometimes find themselves back in bankruptcy after their plan has been confirmed.[421] Moreover, if the statutory majority of creditors have voted for the plan, it is perhaps only rarely appropriate for the judge to second-guess them on its prospects for success.

Despite this drawback, the feasibility requirement gives dissenting creditors who doubt the viability of the debtor's business plan, an avenue for attack. The feasibility requirement requires the court to determine whether the plan "offers a reasonable probability of success."[422] As one court explained: "Guaranteed success in the stiff winds of commerce without the protections of the Code is not the standard under [§ 1129(a)(11)] . . . . All that is required is that there be a reasonable assurance of commercial viability."[423]

The complexities and uncertainties of modern business make it far more difficult to evaluate the feasibility of a Chapter 11 plan than to make the same determination with respect to a Chapter 13 plan, where feasibility is also required. In evaluating whether the debtor has a reasonable probability of success, courts frequently examine:

> (1) the adequacy of the debtor's capital structure; (2) the earning power of its business; (3) economic conditions; (4) the ability of the debtor's management; (5) the probability of the continuation of the same management; and (6) any other related matters which determine the prospects of a sufficiently successful operation to enable performance of the provisions of the plan.[424]

Projecting a business debtor's income and estimating its operating expenses may require sophisticated calculations. This might make it difficult, but not impossible to obtain confirmation of a plan calling for a "balloon" payment sometime in the future.[425]

---

[420] In re Greate Bay Hotel & Casino, Inc., 251 B.R. 213, 226 (Bankr. D.N.J. 2000); In re Orfa Corp., 129 B.R. 404, 410 (Bankr. E.D. Pa. 1991).

[421] *Compare* Lynn Lopucki, Courting Failure (2005), *with* Kenneth Ayotte & David Skeel, *An Efficiency-Based Explanation for Current Corporate Reorganization Practice*, 73 U. Chi. L. Rev. 425 (2006).

[422] In re Monnier Bros., 755 F.2d 1336, 1341 (8th Cir. 1985).

[423] In re Prudential Energy Co., 58 B.R. 857, 862 (Bankr. S.D.N.Y. 1986).

[424] In re Temple Zion, 125 B.R. 910, 915 (Bankr. E.D. Pa. 1991).

[425] *E.g.*, In re Chapin Revenue Cycle Management, Inc., 343 B.R. 722 (Bankr. M.D. Fla. 2006).

[K] Payment of Bankruptcy Fees

For a plan to be confirmed, all court-imposed bankruptcy fees, such as quarterly fees payable to the United States Trustee and those permitted to be imposed by the Judicial Conference of the United States, must either have been paid or scheduled to be paid by the effective date of the plan.[426]

[L] Continuation of Retirement Benefits

Section 1114 contains detailed provisions for determining the amount of retirement benefits a Chapter 11 debtor must pay to retired employees and their spouses.[427] Section 1129(a)(13) mandates that Chapter 11 plans must provide for the debtor to continue to pay whatever meager retirement benefits § 1114 requires.[428]

[M] Individual Chapter 11 Debtors

The 2005 Amendments added two requirements that are aimed at individual Chapter 11 debtors. Chapter 11's procedures and requirements are too expensive to be useful for all but a few individuals. However, the Supreme Court's 1991 decision in *Toibb v. Radloff* made it clear that individuals are entitled to Chapter 11 relief regardless of whether or not they are engaged in a business.[429] The 2005 Amendments ensure that individual debtors do not seek to take advantage of Chapter 11 to evade new requirements imposed on Chapter 13 debtors.

First, § 109(h) requires all individual debtors to obtain a financial counseling and planning briefing within 180 days prior to filing their petition.[430] This is necessary regardless of whether the debtor's obligations are primarily business debts or consumer debts. However, Chapter 11 debtors do not need to complete the subsequent financial management course required for individuals in Chapter 7 or Chapter 13.

Second, § 1129(a)(14) prevents confirmation unless the debtor has paid any post-petition domestic support obligations owed under a "judicial or administrative order, or by statute." Thus, individual debtors who expect to obtain Chapter 11 relief must maintain any child or spousal support payments that become due after the debtor's petition. This requirement should be read in conjunction with § 1129(a)(9)(B), which requires Chapter 11 debtors to pay any past-due priority support obligations in full, either

---

426 Bankruptcy Code § 1129(a)(12).

427 Bankruptcy Code § 1114; *see* Daniel Keating, *Bankruptcy Code § 1114: Congress' Empty Response to the Retiree Plight*, 67 Am. Bankr. L.J. 17 (1993); Susan J. Stabile, *Protecting Retiree Medical Benefits in Bankruptcy: The Scope of § 1114 of the Bankruptcy Code*, 14 Cardozo L. Rev. 1911 (1993).

428 *See* Amy Lassiter, Note, *Mayday, Mayday!: How the Current Bankruptcy Code Fails to Protect the Pensions of Employees*, 93 Ky. L.J. 939 (2005).

429 501 U.S. 157 (1991); *see* Michael J. Herbert, *Consumer Chapter 11 Proceedings: Abuse or Alternative?*, 91 Com. L.J. 234 (1986).

430 Bankruptcy Code § 109(h)(1).

on the effective date of the plan, or, with acceptance by the affected class of creditors, in deferred cash payments.

Third, § 1129(a)(15) requires most individual debtors to submit all of their projected disposable income for five years.[431] This is consistent with the projected disposable income test of § 1325(b)(1)(B) for debtors who seek relief under Chapter 13.[432]

[N] Transfer of Property by Non-Profit Organization

New § 1129(a)(16) prevents non-profit trusts and corporations from using bankruptcy to sidestep restrictions that many states impose on property owned by these organizations. It specifies that "[a]ll transfers of property of the plan shall be made in accordance with any applicable provisions of nonbankruptcy law that govern the transfer of property by a corporation or trust that is not a moneyed, business, or commercial corporation or trust."[433] It is expected that this provision will be enforced by State Attorney General's offices, as they are commonly responsible for enforcing state laws on the transfer of property by non-profits entities.[434]

§ 19.11 Confirmation over Objection of an Impaired Class; Cramdown[435]

Ideally, a Chapter 11 plan will be approved by the requisite dual majority of creditors in each class. However, even where one or more of the classes rejects the plan, the debtor may still seek confirmation. Confirmation over the objection of a class of creditors is graphically known as "cramdown" (as in crammed down the objecting creditors' throats).[436]

There are three key requirements for confirmation over the objection of a class of creditors. First, as described above, in the discussion of *U.S. Truck*, the plan must be accepted by at least one class of impaired claims.[437] Second, the plan must be "fair and equitable" with respect to each dissenting class.[438] The test for whether a plan is fair and equitable is somewhat different with respect to classes of secured claims, classes of unsecured claims, and classes of interests,[439] but it essentially requires adherence to

---

431 Bankruptcy Code § 1129(a)(15)(B).

432 *See* § 18.08[E][2] Debtor's Projected Disposable Income, *supra*.

433 Bankruptcy Code § 1129(a)(16).

434 Pub. L. No. 109-8, § 1221(d) (2005).

435 Kenneth N. Klee, *All You Ever Wanted to Know About Cram Down Under the New Bankruptcy Code*, 53 Am. Bankr. L.J. 133 (1979).

436 Dissenting creditors in a class that has accepted the plan also have the plan "crammed down" their throats. Section 1129(b) comes into play, however, only when a class as a whole rejects the plan.

437 Bankruptcy Code § 1129(a)(10).

438 Bankruptcy Code § 1129(b)(1).

439 Bankruptcy Code § 1129(b)(2)(A)-(C).

the "absolute priority rule." The absolute priority rule prevents a debtor from distributing anything to a junior class over the objection of a senior class, unless the senior class is paid in full. Third, the plan must not "discriminate unfairly."[440]

[A] Acceptance by One Impaired Class

One limitation on cramdown already discussed is the requirement that at least one impaired class of creditors accept the plan.[441] Thus, confirmation over the objection of all classes is not possible. This means that at least one impaired creditor constituency must support the plan. And, since the votes of insiders do not count,[442] the existing owners cannot confirm a plan over the dissent of all other claimants.

The requirement that one class accept has been one of the barriers to confirmation in single-asset real estate cases. In those proceedings, there is usually only one significant creditor, a financial institution, who would prefer to foreclose upon its collateral and terminate the debtor's business. Debtors in this situation have tried to work around this requirement by cobbling together a class of small claims that are technically impaired, but to such a slight degree that they are virtually certain to vote to accept the plan. As explained elsewhere, courts have generally disfavored this type of gerrymandering.[443] Nonetheless, where there is a legitimate justification for separate classification, such as a "non-creditor" interest, as in *U.S. Truck*, where the national union was thought to be particularly concerned about its position in other cases, rather than its interest as a creditor in the particular case, separate classification has been permitted.[444] Courts are divided over how strong such a justification must be.[445]

[B] Fair and Equitable — The Absolute Priority Rule[446]

A Chapter 11 plan may not be confirmed if a class of claims or interests has rejected the plan unless the plan is "fair and equitable" with respect

---

[440] Bankruptcy Code § 1129(b)(1).

[441] Bankruptcy Code § 1129(a)(10).

[442] Bankruptcy Code § 1129(a)(10). For the definition of insider, see Bankruptcy Code § 101(31).

[443] *See* § 19.08[D][2][c] Classification in Single-Asset Real Estate Cases, *supra*.

[444] In re U.S. Truck Co., Inc., 800 F.2d 581 (1986).

[445] In re Bloomingdale Partners, 170 B.R. 984 (Bankr. N.D. Ill. 1994).

[446] John D. Ayer, *Rethinking Absolute Priority After* Ahlers, 87 Mich. L. Rev. 963 (1989); Douglas G. Baird & Thomas H. Jackson, *Bargaining After the Fall and the Countours of the Absolute Priority Rule*, 55 U. Chi. L. Rev. 739 (1988); Lynn M. LoPucki & William C. Whitford, *Bargaining over Equity's Share in the Bankruptcy Reorganizaton of Large Publicly Held Companies*, 139 U. Pa. L. Rev. 125 (1990); Bruce Marckel, *Owners, Auctions, and Absolute Priority in Bankrukptcy Reorganization*, 44 Stan. L. Rev. 69 (1991); Raymond T. Nimmer, *Negotiated Bankruptcy Reorganization Plans: Absolute Priority and New Value Contributions*, 36 Emory L.J. 1009 (1987); Elizabeth Warren, *A Theory of Absolute Priority*, 1990 Ann. Surv. Am. L. 9.

to that class.[447] For the plan to be fair and equitable, it must conform to the "absolute priority rule." Stated briefly, for unsecured claims, no junior class may receive any distribution unless all senior classes are paid in full, and for secured claims, the creditor must retain a lien stripped down to the value of the collateral, and receive payments with a present value equal to the value of the collateral as of the effective date of the plan.

The absolute priority rule and the phrase "fair and equitable" long predate the Code. They are derived from early twentieth century railroad equity receivership cases, in which the rule was developed,[448] and from § 77B of the Bankruptcy Act, which codified the phrase "fair and equitable" to refer to the absolute priority rule.[449] Broadly speaking, it means that the plan must follow absolute, rather than relative priorities. As explained elsewhere, priority rights undcr the Bankruptcy Code range downward from secured claims, through priority and general unsecured claims to equity interests, with the residual rights of owners at the bottom.[450]

In Chapter 7 liquidation cases, this list is followed strictly; each rank is paid in full before the next rank is paid anything. When the money runs out, the last rank for which there is any money is paid pro rata.[451] Chapter 11 usually permits the debtor to follow relative priority — each rank is entitled to its liquidation value,[452] but the surplus realized through the reorganization's capture of going concern value may be distributed in almost any manner to which the debtor and creditors agree. However, if they cannot agree, the Code reimposes strict rank ordering. To put it another way, Chapter 11 permits relative priority in the distribution of the plan payments only if enough of the creditors are satisfied with that form of distribution; the debtor cannot impose relative priority on them.

The absolute priority rule may make it impossible for the owners to participate in the reorganized entity. Equity comes last. Only in the rarest Chapter 11 cases are all debts paid; and under the absolute priority rule, only if all debts are paid may equity receive anything. Thus, it is very hard for the existing owners to retain any portion of the residual value of the company on account of their prepetition ownership interest. The most difficult and interesting issues in Chapter 11 derive from owners' efforts to retain a stake in the reorganized company without obtaining creditors' consent.[453]

Despite (or perhaps because of) the rule's historic antecedents, the drafters of the Code provided a detailed definition of "fair and equitable," with distinct but nevertheless compatible formulations for secured claims,

---

[447] Bankruptcy Code § 1129(b)(1).

[448] Northern Pac. Ry. Co. v. Boyd, 228 U.S. 482 (1913); Kansas City Terminal Ry. Co. v. Central Union Trust Co., 271 U.S. 445 (1926).

[449] *See* Case v. Los Angeles Lumber Prods. Co., 308 U.S. 106 (1939).

[450] *See* § 10.01 Meaning of Claims and Interests, *supra.*

[451] *See* § 17.08 Distribution of Estate Property, *supra.*

[452] Bankruptcy Code § 1129(a)(7)(A)(ii); *see* § 19.10[F] Best Interests of Creditors, *supra.*

[453] *See* § 19.11[C] New Value Exception to Absolute Priority Rule, *infra.*

unsecured claims, and equity interests. The first two formulations are of greatest significance, because when the rule is applied, there is rarely any value remaining to distribute to equity after unsecured claims have been satisfied.

[1] Secured Claims

The absolute priority rule is particularly important with respect to secured claims, even in cases involving a consensual plan. This is because secured creditors, particularly fully secured creditors, are unlikely to accept a plan that provides them with less than they would be entitled to if the plan were confirmed over their objection in a cramdown.[454] Fully secured creditors usually have nothing to lose by forcing the debtor to liquidate; and in most cases, that is what they would prefer. Consequently, although they frequently agree to debtors' plans, they rarely accept a plan that provides them with less than they could obtain if they forced a cramdown of the plan. In considering the application of the absolute priority rule to classes of secured claims, it is useful to remember that in most cases each class is comprised of a single creditor.

With respect to a class of secured claims, the plan must provide one of the three alternative treatments: (1) permit the creditor to retain a lien in the amount of its allowed secured claim and provide it with payment of its allowed secured claim;[455] (2) sell the collateral and transfer the creditor's lien to the proceeds from the sale;[456] or (3) use some other method to provide the secured creditor with the "indubitable equivalent" of its claim.[457]

[a] Lien Retention and Full Payment[458]

The most common method of satisfying the absolute priority rule with respect to a secured creditor's claim is to permit the creditor to retain a lien for the amount of the creditor's allowed secured claim[459] and make payments to the creditor in satisfaction of the claim. In other respects, the creditor's claim may be modified, such as by changing the monthly payment, extending the payment period, or reducing the interest rate.

Permitting the creditor to retain its lien gives the creditor the right to foreclose if the debtor defaults on the payments called for by the plan. Moreover, it ensures that it will have a secured claim in any subsequent liquidation case that results from the failure of the debtor's plan to succeed.

---

[454] Charles D. Booth, *The Cramdown on Secured Creditors: An Impetus Toward Settlement*, 60 Am. Bankr. L.J. 69 (1986).

[455] Bankruptcy Code § 1129(b)(2)(A)(i).

[456] Bankruptcy Code § 1129(b)(2)(A)(ii).

[457] Bankruptcy Code § 1129(b)(2)(A)(iii).

[458] Patrick Halligan, *Cramdown Interest, Contract Damages, and Classical Economic Theory*, 11 Am. Bankr. Inst. L. Rev. 131 (2003).

[459] Bankruptcy Code § 1129(b)(2)(B)(i)(I).

However, unless the creditor elects otherwise under § 1111(b), its lien applies only to the secured portion of its claim as of the effective date of the plan; it does not protect the unsecured deficiency claim of a partially secured creditor.

For example, if Titanic Corp. owes North Atlantic Finance Co. $100,000, secured by equipment worth only $70,000, then North Atlantic has a $70,000 secured claim and a $30,000 unsecured claim. Titanic's plan is fair and equitable with respect to North Atlantic's secured claim if it provides for North Atlantic to retain a lien that secures a $70,000 claim. The $30,000 unsecured claim is handled separately and has nothing to do with how § 1129(b)(2)(A) applies to the $70,000 secured claim. If the collateral were worth $100,000 or more, it would be fully secured, and the plan would have to provide for North Atlantic to retain a lien on the equipment to satisfy the full $100,000 debt.

If the collateral for Titanic's debt to North Atlantic were real estate worth $4 million, securing a claim for $5 million, it might make sense for North Atlantic to make the § 1111(b) election.[460] If it did so, North Atlantic's claim would be secured for the full $5 million and the lien it would retain would secure the entire $5 million debt. If Titanic subsequently defaulted, North Atlantic could enforce its lien against the collateral for up to $5 million. Obviously, this is not worth much if the value of the collateral was still only $4 million, but if the value of the property increased, say to $6 million, the 1111(b) election would permit the creditor to capture any increase in value of the collateral that occurred before the plan failed.

As noted above, the plan may modify the secured creditor's claim in other ways. It may alter the duration and frequency of payments, the amount of each payment, and the interest rate applicable to the claims. However, the interest rate must ensure that the creditor receives the *value* of its secured claim. Section 1129 requires any "deferred cash payments . . . of a value, as of the effective date of the plan, of at least the value of [the creditor's] interest in the estate's interest in [the collateral]."[461] To compensate a secured creditor for the delay, any deferred cash payments must include interest on the amount of the allowed secured claim.[462] This is similar to the approach followed with regard to secured claims in Chapter 13. However, as noted elsewhere, it is unclear whether courts are required to follow the same "formula" approach used in *Till* in Chapter 11 cases.[463]

---

[460] As explained in more detail elsewhere, whether making the election would be an advantage for a secured creditor in this position, would depend on several other factors, including the plan's treatment of unsecured claims, the likelihood that the real estate would increase in value, the amortization period of the payments to be made to the secured creditor, and the likelihood that the debtor would default on the terms of the plan. *See* § 19.08[H][4] Treatment of the § 1111(b) Election, *supra*.

[461] Bankruptcy Code § 1129(b)(2)(A)(i)(II).

[462] Bankruptcy Code § 1129(b)(2)(A)(i)(II).

[463] *See* § 18.08[F][4] Cramdown of Chapter 13 Plan over Secured Creditor's Objection, *supra*.

Applying these rules requires the court to make two determinations: the value of the collateral; and the interest rate necessary to provide the creditor with the present value of its secured claim.[464]

Courts have used a variety of approaches to calculate the appropriate rate of interest.[465] Courts have been known to use any of four different methods.[466] Some courts take a "coerced loan" approach and require the rate of return to correspond to the rate that would be charged or obtained by the creditor making a loan to a third party with similar terms, duration, collateral, and risk.[467] Other courts use a presumptive contract rate method, adjusting the negotiated contract rate between the parties upward or downward to reflect circumstances in the case that have changed since the original loan was made.[468] A third approach, the "costs of funds" method, depends on the cost that the creditor would incur to obtain the cash equivalent of the collateral; in other words, the interest rate the creditor would pay on a loan of an amount equal to the value of the collateral.[469] Fourth, some courts use a formula approach, based on a benchmark "risk free" interest rate, with adjustments based on factors affecting the circumstances faced by the parties.[470] For example, the Second Circuit in *In re Valenti*, adopted a formula based on the rate for United States Treasury securities plus a risk adjustment of 1–3%.[471]

The "formula" approach was adopted by the Supreme Court in *Till v. SCS Credit Corp.*[472] for use in Chapter 13 cramdown cases. However, instead of using the treasury bill rate, as in *Valenti*, it used the so-called "prime rate" as the putative risk free rate.[473] As a result of the Court's decision in *Till,* lower courts have insisted on interest rates of 1% to 3% above prime in Chapter 13 cases.[474] A number of courts have rejected the formula method

---

[464] In re Valenti, 105 F.3d 55 (2d Cir. 1997)

[465] *See, e.g.*, Till v. SCS Credit Corp., 541 U.S. 465, 472 (2004); In re Bryson Properties, 961 F.2d 496, 500 (4th Cir. 1992); In re Memphis Bank & Trust Co., 692 F.2d 427, 431 (6th Cir. 1982).

[466] Patrick Halligan, *Cramdown Interest, Contract Damages, and Classical Economic Theory*, 11 Am. Bankr. Inst. L. Rev. 131, 134–37 (2003).

[467] Bank of Montreal v. Official Comm. of Unsecured Creditors (In re Am. HomePatient, Inc.), 420 F.3d 559 (6th Cir. 2005); Wade v. Bradford, 39 F.3d 1126 (10th Cir. 1994); In re Byrd Foods, Inc., 253 B.R. 196, 200 (Bankr. E.D. Va. 2000).

[468] In re Monnier Bros., 755 F.2d 1336, 1339 (8th Cir. 1985).

[469] In re Till, 301 F.3d 583, 592 (7th Cir. 2002), *reversed, sub. nom*, Till v. SCS Credit Corp., 541 U.S. 456 (2004); In re Valenti, 105 F.3d 55, 59–60 (2d Cir. 1997).

[470] In re Fowler, 903 F.2d 694 (9th Cir. 1990); United States v Doud, 869 F.2d 1144 (8th Cir. 1989).

[471] In re Valenti, 105 F.3d 55 (2d Cir. 1997).

[472] 541 U.S. 456 (2004).

[473] *See* § 18.08[F][4][b] Payments Equivalent to Amount of Secured Claim, *supra*; Michael Elson, Note, *Say "Ahhh!": A New Approach for Determining the Cram Down Interest Rate After* Till v. SCS Credit, 27 Cardozo L. Rev. 1921 (2006).

[474] In re Cantwell, 336 B.R. 688 (Bankr. D.N.J. 2006) (1%).

as inappropriate for use in Chapter 11 cases.[475] As a consequence, the applicability of *Till*'s formula method outside the context of Chapter 13 cramdown remains uncertain.[476]

The second key component in applying the fair and equitable standard in this manner is to determine the value of the creditor's interest in the debtor's property. The value of the creditor's interest depends initially on the value of the collateral. For example, if North Atlantic Finance Company is owed $100,000, secured by senior security interest in $120,000 of Titanic's equipment, the value of the creditor's interest in the collateral is $100,000. But, if the equipment is only worth $70,000, North Atlantic's interest is worth only $70,000.

The value of the creditor's interest is affected by the existence of a senior lien on the collateral. If, for example, North Atlantic's security interest is subordinate to the senior security interest held by Pacific Bank, which has a claim for $50,000, and the equipment is worth only $70,000, North Atlantic's interest in the collateral is worth only $20,000, even though it is owed $100,000. This $20,000 is the value available to North Atlantic after Pacific's senior claim is satisfied.

Moreover, as explained in more detail elsewhere, courts use different methods to determine the value of the collateral.[477] Section 506(a)(1) specifies that the value of the debtor's property is to be determined "in light of the purpose of the valuation and of the proposed disposition or use" of the property.[478] This language suggests using the collateral's liquidation value in circumstances where the collateral is to be liquidated, and replacement value in situations like those where the creditor will retain its lien and receive deferred payments from the creditor.[479] However, some courts use a liquidation or foreclosure value standard to determine the amount of a secured creditor's allowed claim, even in cases where the debtor's reorganization plan contemplates the debtor's continued use of the collateral.[480] Other courts use the midpoint between the forced liquidation value and the replacement value.[481]

In Chapter 13 cases, the Supreme Court's decision in *Associates Commercial Corp. v. Rash*[482] requires use of the cost to the debtor of replacing the collateral as the method of determining the amount of the secured creditor's

[475] Bank of Montreal v. Official Comm. of Unsecured Creditors (In re Am. HomePatient, Inc.), 420 F.3d 559 (6th Cir. 2005) (characterizing *Till*'s approach as catastrophic in Chapter 11 cases).

[476] *E.g.*, In re Deep River Warehouse, Inc., 2005 Bankr. LEXIS 1793 (Bankr. M.D.N.C. Sept. 22, 2005) (refusing to apply *Till* in Chapter 11).

[477] *See* § 10.03[C][1] Valuation of Collateral, *supra*.

[478] Bankruptcy Code § 506(a)(1).

[479] *E.g.*, In re Taffi, 96 F.3d 1190, 1191–92 (9th Cir. 1996).

[480] In re Rash, 90 F.3d 1036 (5th Cir. 1996), *rev'd, sub nom.*, Associates Commercial Corp. v. Rash, 520 U.S. 953 (1997).

[481] In re Hoskins, 102 F.3d 311, 316 (7th Cir. 1996).

[482] 520 U.S. 953 (1997).

allowed secured claim. The 2005 Amendments codified some aspects of *Rash* and require using replacement cost in Chapter 7 or 13 cases involving individual debtors.[483] Many courts regard *Rash* as binding in Chapter 11 cases, but the replacement cost method has not yet been seriously challenged in the context of a Chapter 11 cramdown.[484] The addition of § 506(a)(2), specifying use of replacement cost in Chapter 7 and 13 cases of individual debtors, leads to a negative implication that courts are free to use other methods of valuing the collateral in cases under other Chapters. Moreover, the context of *Rash*, which involved a truck tractor, made use of replacement cost a more pragmatic method, because of the wider availability of market prices for similar items.[485] Determining the replacement cost of manufacturing equipment might be more difficult.

[b] Sale of Property and Attachment of Lien to Proceeds

Debtors who do not need to use the creditor's collateral as part of their ongoing business operations might propose a sale of the collateral, with the creditor's lien to attach to the proceeds derived from the sale. A plan proposing this treatment is fair and equitable.[486] This treatment amounts to little more than a foreclosure sale, albeit with the debtor in control of the manner of the sale. In many cases, property the debtor does not need will have been sold in a similar manner, pursuant to § 363, before the debtor's plan was proposed.[487]

[c] Creditor Receives the "Indubitable Equivalent" of Its Claims

The third alternative is open-ended. A plan is fair and equitable if it provides "for the realization by such [secured claim] holders of the indubitable equivalent of [their] claims."[488] The "indubitable equivalent" standard is derived from Judge Learned Hand's opinion in the decision, *In re Murel Holding Co.*[489] The indubitable equivalent standard is also widely used in connection with methods for providing secured creditors with adequate protection, described in § 361, to forestall them from obtaining relief from the automatic stay.[490] Alternative treatments that might satisfy this standard might take many forms, but undoubtedly include surrender of all

---

483 Bankruptcy Code § 506(a)(2).

484 *E.g.*, In re T-H New Orleans Ltd., 116 F.3d 790, 799 (5th Cir. 1997); In re Mulvania, 214 B.R. 1 (B.A.P. 9th Cir. 1997).

485 *See, e.g.*, www.trucker.com/search/basic_trucks.asp (last viewed March 27, 2007).

486 Bankruptcy Code § 1129(b)(2)(A)(ii).

487 Bankruptcy Code § 363(f); *see* § 9.03[C] Sale or Use of Property Outside the Ordinary Course, *supra*.

488 Bankruptcy Code § 1129(b)(2)(A)(iii).

489 75 F.2d 941 (2d Cir. 1935).

490 *See* § 8.06[B][1] For Cause — Lack of Adequate Protection for Secured Creditors, *supra*.

of the collateral to the creditor[491] or transfer of the creditor's lien to other property with the same or higher value.[492] However, surrender of only some of the collateral to the creditor, in what has sometimes been called a "dirt-for-debt" plan, which usually involves real estate, is questionable. Substitution of collateral is also questionable where the new collateral is property of a different type which is more difficult to value or which is subject to different types of market forces than the original collateral.

[2] Unsecured Claims

The absolute priority rule has its biggest impact on the reorganization process with respect to a class of unsecured creditors. Even when a plan is not "crammed down," negotiations over the terms of the plan are usually conducted against the backdrop of the absolute priority rule.

The rule can be satisfied in one of two ways. First, a plan that provides for "each holder of a claim [to receive] property of a value as of the effective date of the plan, equal to the allowed amount of [its] claim" is fair and equitable.[493] In other words, a plan is fair and equitable if it provides for payment to unsecured creditors that amount to 100% of the value they are owed. Alternatively, the plan can be confirmed over the objection of a class of unsecured claims only if junior claims receive nothing.[494]

[a] Payment in Full

Satisfying the absolute priority rule by paying creditors in full requires paying them not only the full amount of their claims, but the full value of the amount of their claims. As with other situations where full *value* must be paid, this means that if payment is deferred, the payments must include interest to compensate the creditor for any delay.[495]

Paying holders of unsecured claims the entire value of their claims might be accomplished in several ways. First, many plans designate a class of creditors with small claims, segregated from claims of larger creditors for administrative convenience pursuant to § 1122(b). These claims are usually paid in full, in cash, on the effective date of the plan. This undoubtedly satisfies § 1129(b), but cramdown is rarely necessary with respect to a class treated in this manner. Given the opportunity to receive cash, creditors usually vote to accept the plan.

Claims of unsecured creditors might also be fully satisfied by distributing stock in the reorganized company to members of the class. This gives

---

491 124 Cong. Rec. 32,407 (1978) (statement of Rep. Edwards); *cf.* Bankruptcy Code § 1325(a)(5)(C).

492 124 Cong. Rec. 32,407 (1978) (statement of Rep. Edwards).

493 Bankruptcy Code § 1129(b)(2)(B).

494 Bankruptcy Code § 1129(b)(2)(B)(ii).

495 *E.g.*, Liberty Nat'l Enters. v. Ambanc La Mesa Ltd. (In re Ambanc La Mesa Ltd.), 115 F.3d. 650, 653–64 (9th Cir. 1997) (plan failed to provide interest payments to unsecured claims of dissenting class of creditors).

creditors an equity position in the reorganized debtor. Creditors who prefer cash can sell their stock, if there is a market for it. Nevertheless, this method of providing unsecured claim holders with payment in full is fraught with difficulty, primarily because it may require a difficult and expensive valuation of the business as a going concern to determine if the stock they are receiving is really the equivalent of the full value of their claims.

The plan might also simply provide for deferred cash payments to holders of unsecured claims in full satisfaction of their claims. This satisfies the absolute priority rule only with respect to debtors who are solvent as a going concern. Otherwise, such a plan is not feasible.

[b] Eliminating Junior Claims and Interests

Although providing full payment to a class of unsecured creditors is a legally sufficient way to satisfy the absolute priority rule, it is rarely feasible. Debtors rarely have sufficient capital to provide unsecured creditors with the full value of their claims. If their consent cannot be obtained, the only other way to confirm a plan is to propose a plan that provides nothing to those with claims or interests that are junior to those of unsecured creditors. They key statutory language is in § 1129(b)(2)(B)(ii): A plan is fair and equitable "[w]ith respect to a class of unsecured claims . . . [if] the holder of any claim or interest that is junior to the claims of such class will not receive or retain under the plan on account of such junior claim or interest any property."[496] Thus, if the plan is to be confirmed over the objection of a dissenting class of unsecured creditors who are not to be paid in full, those junior to the members of the class may not receive anything on account of their prepetition ownership interest in the debtor. In plain terms, shareholders lose their stock.

This aspect of the absolute priority rule makes the negotiations leading to the development of a plan tantamount to what someone once described as a game of financial "chicken."[497] The debtor's shareholders, who may also be its directors, officers, and employees, hope to give unsecured creditors as little as possible of the remaining value of the reorganized company. They hope that the company will return to profitability and that they will resume receiving dividends on their capital investment. They also hope to keep their jobs, but they might find it easier to find new jobs than to recover their capital. Creditors would like to receive payment for money they have loaned or for goods or services they have provided to the debtor. Those who are vendors also prefer the debtor to remain in business. In addition, more often than not, creditors and debtors alike realize that the going concern value of the debtor's business is greater than the value its

[496] Bankruptcy Code § 1129(b)(2)(B)(ii).

[497] *See* John D. Ayer, *Bankruptcy as an Essentially Contested Concept: The Case of the One-Asset Case*, 44 S.C. L. Rev. 863, 896 n.129 (1993); Daniel B. Bogart, *Games Lawyers Play: Waivers of the Automatic Stay in Bankruptcy and the Single Asset Loan Workout*, 43 UCLA L. Rev. 1117, 1201 (1996); J. Bradley Johnston, *The Bankruptcy Bargain*, 65 Am. Bankr. L.J. 213, 302 (1991).

assets would produce in a piecemeal liquidation sale. At liquidation, unsecured creditors receive little or nothing; shareholders almost inevitably lose all of their investments, and if they are employed as members of the debtor's management team, they lose their jobs. The debtor threatens to liquidate, hoping to persuade creditors to accept whatever payment the debtor is offering in the plan. Creditors threaten to reject the plan, and force the debtor to deprive its existing stockholders of any interest in the company as a means of encouraging the debtor to pay more. It is as if the debtor were standing on the ledge outside the window on the thirtieth floor, threatening to jump, with the creditors hovering all around, threatening to push.

Plans calling for the elimination of existing shareholders are sometimes filed by unsecured creditors. They might propose a redistribution of the shares of the company to creditors, or a sale of the debtor (or its assets) as a going concern and a distribution of the cash obtained from the sale to creditors according to their established priorities. Such a plan might easily satisfy the absolute priority rule.

The principal difficulty with applying the absolute priority rule is that it nearly always requires a valuation of the business as a going concern. This is particularly true where members of a dissenting class of unsecured creditors receive stock in full satisfaction of their claims and shareholders are to retain an interest in the reorganized company without contributing any new value on account of their interest. Without determining the value of the reorganized debtor as a going concern, it is impossible to know whether this treatment of unsecured creditors amounts to full satisfaction of their claims and thus whether the full-payment branch of the fair and equitable standard has been satisfied.[498] Determining the going concern value of the debtor is expensive itself and may deprive the debtor of the going concern value upon which the plan depends.

There is one final uncodified but inherent feature of the absolute priority rule: no class senior to a dissenting class may receive *more* than its full present value under the plan.[499] This, of course, makes sense. If a senior class of creditors is receiving payment of more than full value of its claim, the junior class is being deprived of some residual value of the debtor on a dollar-for-dollar basis.[500]

The 2005 Amendments added language to the end of § 1129(b)(2)(B)(ii) that applies only to those Chapter 11 cases that involve individual debtors.[501] It creates a modest exception to the absolute priority rule, but only

---

[498] Bankruptcy Code § 1129(b)(2)(B)(i).

[499] *See* Omer Tene, *Revisiting the Creditors' Bargain: The Entitlement to the Going-concern Surplus in Corporate Bankruptcy Reorganizations*, 19 Bankr. Dev. J. 287, 397 (2003).

[500] Kenneth Klee, *Cram Down II*, 64 Am. Bankr. L.J. 229, 231–32 (1990); Kenneth Klee, *All You Ever Wanted to Know About Cram Down Under the New Bankruptcy Code*, 53 Am. Bankr. L.J. 133, 144–56 (1979).

[501] Robert J. Keach, *Dead Man Filing Redux: Is the New Individual Chapter Eleven Unconstitutional?*, 13 Am. Bankr. Inst. L. Rev. 483 (2005).

with respect to earnings the debtor will earn from his post-petition personal services.[502] Thus, individual Chapter 11 debtors may retain the value of their personal services even though their unsecured creditors are not paid in full. In other words, Chapter 11 does not force individual debtors into indentured servitude. Despite this, the plan must still provide for the debtor to continue to make payments for post-petition support obligations.

[3] Equity Interests

Cramming a plan down over the objection of a class of interest holders is more common. If the debtor is insolvent, stockholders' interests are worthless. A plan can be confirmed over their objection in one of two ways. First, it be confirmed if the plan permits interest holders to receive or retain property equal to the "value of their interest."[503] Worthless interests are satisfied in full if they receive nothing.

Here, the principal difficulty is in determining whether the debtor is insolvent. Making this determination requires a difficult and expensive valuation of the debtor's business. In many cases, it may be cheaper to give stockholders something as a way to avoid this expense. A class of preferred stock must be paid any "fixed liquidation preference" or "fixed redemption price,"[504] even if the debtor is insolvent. However, this difficulty can be avoided if no interest junior to the affected class receives anything. A plan that gives nothing to holders of common stock is fair and equitable with respect to preferred shareholders, even if they are not paid their liquidation preference.[505]

[C] New Value Exception to Absolute Priority Rule[506]

One of the most contentious issues regarding Chapter 11 cramdown is whether there is a new value exception to the absolute priority rule. More precisely, the question is whether shareholders may retain an interest in

[502] Bankruptcy Code § 1129(b)(2)(B)(ii); *see* Bankruptcy Code § 1115(a)(2).

[503] Bankruptcy Code § 1129(b)(2)(C)(i).

[504] Bankruptcy Code § 1129(b)(2)(C)(i).

[505] *E.g.*, Northwest Village Ltd. v. Franke (In re Westpointe), 241 F.3d 1005, 1007 (8th Cir. 2001).

[506] John D. Ayer, *Rethinking Absolute Priority After* Ahlers, 87 Mich. L. Rev. 963 (1989); Robert M. Zinman, *New Value and the Commission: How Bizarre!*, 5 Am. Bankr. Inst. L. Rev. 477 (1997); Nicholas L. Georgakopoulos, *New Value, Fresh Start*, 3 Stan. J. L. Bus. & Fin. 125 (1997); Michelle Craig, *The New Value Exception: A Plea for Modification or Elimination*, 11 Bankr. Dev. J. 781 (1995); Julie L. Friedberg, *Wanted Dead or Alive: The New Value Exception to the Absolute Priority Rule*, 66 Temp. L. Rev. 893 (1993); Elizabeth Warren, *A Theory of Absolute Priority*, 1991 Ann. Surv. Am. L. 9 (1992); Lynn M. LoPucki & William C. Whitford, *Bargaining over Equity's Share in the Bankruptcy Reorganization of Large, Publicly Held Companies*, 139 U. Pa. L. Rev. 125 (1990); Kenneth N. Klee, *Cram Down II*, 64 Am. Bankr. L.J. 229 (1990); Douglas G. Baird & Thomas H. Jackson, *Bargaining After the Fall and the Contours of the Absolute Priority Rule*, 55 U. Chi. L. Rev. 738 (1988); Raymond T. Nimmer, *Negotiated Bankruptcy Reorganization Plans: Absolute Priority and New Value Contributions*, 36 Emory L.J. 1009 (1987).

the reorganized debtor over the objection of an impaired class of unsecured creditors by contributing "new value" to the debtor as part of the reorganization plan.[507]

Consider the following example, which illustrates the issue.[508] City Bank has a senior mortgage on BroadHigh, Inc.'s office building, the only asset that the debtor owns.[509] The debt is $90 million, but the collateral is worth only $50 million. This leaves the Bank with a $40 million unsecured deficiency claim. There are, in addition, $100,000 in claims of unsecured trade creditors who supply cleaning, security, and maintenance services to the debtor. The debtor's plan proposes to pay City Bank's $50 million secured claim in full by extending payments for ten years beyond the original term. It proposes to pay only 15% of the Bank's $40 million unsecured claim. Under the debtor's proposal, shareholders of BroadHigh, Inc., retain their stock and will make an additional $4 million capital contribution to the corporation. Not surprisingly, the bank prefers to immediately foreclose. As a result, it rejects the plan and objects to its confirmation.[510]

At first glance, the absolute priority rule appears to support the Bank's objection. The class of unsecured creditors is impaired and has rejected the plan. Thus, the plan can only be confirmed if it can be crammed down. However, the Bank is receiving only 15% of the value of its unsecured claim and thus § 1129(b)(2)(B)(i), which permits cramdown if the plan pays members of the dissenting class the full value of their claim, is not satisfied. Further, in apparent violation of § 1129(b)(2)(B)(ii), shareholders, who are junior in priority to the Bank retain an interest in the reorganized company. Thus, the plan does not have the necessary consent of every class, and it is not fair and equitable.

On the other hand, one might view the interest held by the old shareholders at the end of the case as purchased through the $4 million contribution. Nothing would have prohibited an outside investor from purchasing the reorganized debtor for $4 million. The only question would have been whether the price was fair. The new value exception is based on the idea that the old shareholders might be permitted to buy the company back from the creditors for a fair price. Whether this is allowed has been an issue since

---

[507] *See* Bank of Am. Nat'l Trust & Sav. Ass'n v. 203 N. Lasalle St. P'ship, 526 U.S. 434, 437 (1999).

[508] *See* David R. Perlmutter, *Navigating a Proposed "New Value" Plan Through the Cross-Currents of the Confirmation Process: An Arduous Journey for the Debtor of a Single-Asset Real Estate Case*, 17 Whittier L. Rev. 427 (1996).

[509] This example illustrates the most common situation in which the new value exception is invoked, a single-asset real estate case. *See* David Gray Carlson & Jack F. Williams, *The Truth About the New Value Exception to Bankruptcy's Absolute Priority Rule*, 21 Cardozo L. Rev. 1303, 1305 n.10 (2000).

[510] With a few adjustments to supply round numbers, these were the basic facts facing the Supreme Court in its *203 North Lasalle Partnership* decision. Bank of Am. Nat'l Trust & Sav. Ass'n. v. 203 N. Lasalle St. P'ship, 526 U.S. 434, 437–41 (1999).

the development of the absolute priority rule in the early twentieth century.[511]

The Supreme Court has failed to address the issue directly, though it has discussed it in dictum on numerous occasions.[512] Its most recent references to the new value exception were in *Norwest Bank Worthington v. Ahlers*[513] and *Bank of America v. 203 North LaSalle Street Partnership.*[514] In *Ahlers*, the Court ruled that, assuming a "new value exception" existed, "sweat equity" was not sufficient to satisfy the exception. The Court did not directly determine whether other, more concrete value would have been sufficient.[515] In *LaSalle*,[516] the Court again assumed for the sake of argument that the new value exception existed, but held that if it did exist, shareholders could not retain an interest without permitting others to compete for the opportunity to obtain a share in the reorganized firm. Again, however, the Court explicitly reserved judgment on whether the exception itself exists.[517]

Thus, although the Court has suggested that under the right circumstances shareholders might avoid elimination of their interests by contributing new value to the enterprise,[518] the Court has never found a case where the right circumstances were present. Lower court decisions after *Ahlers* and *LaSalle* have not settled the issue,[519] but most courts and commentators regard *LaSalle* as implicitly recognizing the general validity

[511] *See* Case v. Los Angeles Lumber Co., 308 U.S. 106 (1939) (shareholders' proposal to contribute their managerial skill and stature in the community was rejected as insufficient new value). *See, e.g.,* Bonner Mall P'ship v. U.S. Bancorp Mortgage. Co. (In re Bonner Mall P'ship), 2 F.3d 899, 910–16 (9th Cir. 1993) (approving the new value exception); In re Coltex Loop Cent. Three Partners, L.P., 138 F.3d 39, 44–45 (2d Cir. 1998) (doubting its validity); Unruh v. Rushville State Bank, 987 F.2d 1506, 1510 (10th Cir. 1993) (skirting the issue); *see* Elizabeth Warren, *A Theory of Absolute Priority*, 1991 Ann. Surv. Am. L. 9 (1992); John D. Ayer, *Rethinking Absolute Priority After* Ahlers, 87 Mich. L. Rev. 963 (1989).

[512] The Court dismissed *U.S. Bancorp Mortgage Co. v. Bonner Mall P'ship*, 513 U.S. 18 (1994), after granting certiorari, ruling that the dispute was moot due to a settlement agreement among the parties over the proposed reorganization.

[513] 485 U.S. 197 (1988).

[514] 526 U.S. 434 (1999).

[515] 485 U.S. 197 (1988).

[516] 526 U.S. 434 (1999).

[517] 526 U.S. at 545; *see* Anthony L. Miscioscia, Jr., *The Bankruptcy Code and the New Value Doctrine: An Examination into History, Illusions, and the Need for Competitive Bidding*, 79 Va. L. Rev. 917 (1993).

[518] Lee Dembart & Bruce A. Markell, *Alive at 25? A Short Review of the Supreme Court's Bankruptcy Jurisprudence, 1979-2004*, 78 Am. Bank. L.J. 373, 381 (2004).

[519] Barry E. Adler & George G. Triantis, *The Aftermath of* North Lasalle Street, 70 U. Cin. L. Rev. 1225 (2002); Paul B. Lewis, 203 N. Lasalle *Five Years Later: Answers to the Open Questions*, 38 J. Marshall L. Rev. 61 (2004); Nicholas L. Georgakopoulos, *New Value After* LaSalle, 20 Bankr. Dev. J. 1 (2003); Bruce A. Markell, LaSalle *and the Little Guy: Some Initial Musings on the Ultimate Impact of* Bank of America, NT & SA v. 203 North LaSalle Street Partnership, 16 Bankr. Dev. J. 345 (2000); Omer Tene, *Revisiting the Creditors' Bargain: The Entitlement to the Going-Concern Surplus in Corporate Bankruptcy Reorganizations*, 19 Bankr. Dev. J. 287 (2003).

of the a new value exception to the absolute priority rule, on the one hand, but requiring that the equity be exposed to the market to at least some degree, either by holding an auction, shopping the company, or at least lifting the exclusive period.[520]

It is not clear, actually, that the "new value" exception is actually an exception. Indeed, it may be implicit in the absolute priority rule itself. Old equity may not receive a distribution "on account of" its old equity interest. On the other hand, if the debtor has residual value after claims of creditors are paid, it seems reasonable to permit shareholders to purchase it. Moreover, shareholders who participate in management might be in a better position to operate the business successfully. On the other hand, creditors may be concerned that shareholders might be taking unfair advantage of their better information about the debtor's prospects to purchase any residual value at a bargain-basement price. This risk may be acute when the market for prospective buyers of the debtor's residual value is limited. The Court's decision in *LaSalle* prevents shareholders from contributing new value without providing other potential contributors with an opportunity to invest in the debtor, but it does not explain the mechanisms that might be used to encourage other bidders if the opportunity were made available.

[D] Unfair Discrimination[521]

Section 1129(b)'s cramdown rules also prohibit "unfair discrimination" in a non-consensual plan.[522] Remember that § 1122(a) prohibits a plan from combining dissimilar claims in a single class, but is silent about segregating similar claims into separate classes.[523] Section 1129(b)'s prohibition against unfair discrimination prevents different treatment of similar classes without good justification.

The one justification for discrimination among classes of similar claims that is expressly sanctioned by the Code concerns small claims that are treated favorably for administrative convenience.[524] Debtors sometimes segregate similar claims into different classes to isolate dissenting creditors into a class with other creditors who are likely to vote in favor of the plan

---

520 *See, e.g.*, In re Davis, 262 B.R. 791, 799 n.9 (Bankr. D. Ariz. 2001); *see* Paul B. Lewis, 203 N. Lasalle *Five Years Later: Answers to the Open Questions*, 38 J. Marshall L. Rev. 61, 83 (2004).

521 Bruce A. Markell, *A New Perspective on Unfair Discrimination in Chapter 11*, 72 Am. Bankr. L.J. 227 (1998); Denise R. Polivy, *Unfair Discrimination in Chapter 11: Comprehensive Compilation of Current Case Law*, 72 Am. Bankr. L.J. 191 (1998); Stephen L. Sepinuck, *Rethinking Unfair Discrimination in Chapter 13*, 74 Am. Bankr. L.J. 341 (2000); *but cf.* G. Eric Brunstad, Jr. & Mike Sigal, *Competitive Choice Theory and the Unresolved Doctrines of Classification and Unfair Discrimination in Business Reorganization Under the Bankruptcy Code*, 55 Bus. Law. 1 (1999).

522 Bankruptcy Code § 1129(b)(1).

523 *See* § 19.08[D] Classification of Claims, *supra*.

524 Bankruptcy Code § 1122(b); *see* § 19.08[D][2][a] Small Claims Classified for Administrative Convenience, *supra*.

to gain acceptance of the plan by the requisite majorities. As explained in more detail elsewhere, § 1122(a) does not permit this type of gerrymandering, even in an otherwise consensual plan.[525] It is also not permitted where the purpose of the gerrymander is to obtain the one accepting class required by § 1129(a)(10).

Other reasons for treating similar claims differently are subject to greater controversy. The test most commonly used to determine whether separate treatment of a class of creditors is unfair considers several factors: (1) whether the discrimination has a reasonable basis; (2) whether the debtor can carry out a plan without the discrimination; (3) whether the discrimination is proposed in good faith; and (4) whether the degree of discrimination is directly related to the basis or rationale for the discrimination.[526] For example, a plan that treats the deficiency claim of the main secured creditor vastly differently from other long-term unsecured claims usually fails this test. Treating key suppliers differently from other creditors, however, usually passes the test (for reasons similar to courts' willingness to recognize the doctrine of necessity at the beginning of the case).

[E] Valuation of the Debtor[527]

Confirming a plan via cramdown nearly always makes it necessary to determine the debtor's value as a going concern.[528] Evaluations of the debtor's prospects are also a key component of the evaluation of a plan's feasibility. If the debtor cannot generate enough value to make the payments called for in the plan, the plan should not be confirmed. As the Supreme Court said in *Consolidated Rock Products Co. v. Du Bois*,[529] "whether or not the earnings may reasonably be expected to meet the interest and dividend requirements of new securities is a sine qua non to a determination of the integrity and practicability of the new capital structure. It is also essential for satisfaction of the absolute priority rule."[530] While creditors will usually make their own judgment about the debtor's value as a going concern in deciding whether to vote in favor of a plan, this is not nearly as complicated as bringing the matter to the bankruptcy court and asking it to make a decision.

Accountants use three basic methods to evaluate an enterprise's reorganization value: the "discounted cash flow" method, the market comparison"

---

525 *See* § 19.08[D][2][b] Segregation of Substantially Similar Claims, *supra*.

526 Amfac Distrib. Corp. v. Wolff (In re Wolff), 22 B.R. 510, 512 (9th Cir. B.A.P. 1982); Mickelson v. Leser (In re Leser), 939 F.2d 669, 672 (8th Cir. 1991).

527 Kerry O'Rourke, *Valuation Uncertainty in Chapter 11 Reorganizations*, 2005 Colum. Bus. L. Rev. 403.

528 Kenneth N. Klee, *All You Ever Wanted to Know About Cram Down Under the New Bankruptcy Code*, 53 Am. Bankr. L.J. 133 (1979).

529 312 U.S. 510 (1941).

530 312 U.S. at 525 (1941); *see* Douglas G. Baird & Donald S. Bernstein, *Absolute Priority, Valuation Uncertainty, and the Reorganization Bargain*, 115 Yale L.J. 1930 (2006).

method, and the "comparable transaction" method.[531] The discounted cash flow approach is the one most commonly used in bankruptcy settings. It involves several steps but primarily bases the value of the enterprise on the discounted present value of a debtor's projected cash flows. The market comparison approach determines the debtor's value by examining the market value of other similar firms and making an appropriate comparison to the debtor's situation. The comparable transaction approach is similar, but examines actual market transactions that involve the sale of enterprises similar to the debtor.[532]

§ 19.12 Modification of Chapter 11 Plans

Many Chapter 11 plans prove unacceptable to creditors. Other plans are confirmed, but turn out to have been too ambitious. In the former case, the debtor may seek to amend the plan prior to the confirmation hearing. In the latter, the debtor must seek post-confirmation modification. Not surprisingly, the rules regarding amendment before confirmation are considerably more liberal than they are for modification afterwards. Before confirmation, amendments are made routinely as the debtor adjusts its formal proposal to conform to the results of ongoing negotiations with creditors. Thus, it is not unusual for debtors to file a third, fourth, or fifth amended plan of reorganization. Matters become a bit more complicated after creditors have voted on a plan, and they become considerably more complicated if the debtor wishes to modify a plan after it has been confirmed.

In either event, the modified plan must conform to the usual requirements for confirmation,[533] and appropriate disclosures nearly always need to be made before creditors vote to accept or reject the modified plan.[534]

[A] Pre-Confirmation Modification of Chapter 11 Plan

Before confirmation, the proponent of a plan may modify it at any time.[535] Others who wish to propose a modification need to submit their own plan.[536] The modified plan must still conform to the requirements of §§ 1122 and 1123. Once the modification is filed with the court, the modified plan becomes "the plan."[537]

---

531 *See* In re Exide Technologies, 303 B.R. 48 (Bankr. D. Del. 2003); Bank of Montreal v. Official Comm. of Unsecured Creditors (In re Am. HomePatient, Inc.), 298 B.R. 152, 174 (Bankr. M.D. Tenn. 2003).

532 *See* Peter V. Pantaleo & Barry W. Ridings, *Reorganization Value*, 51 Bus. Law. 419, 421–36 (1996); Bradford Cornell, Corporate Valuation 243–46 (1993); *see, e.g.*, In re Exide Technologies, 303 B.R. 48, 62–63 (Bankr. D. Del. 2003).

533 Bankruptcy Code § 1127(f)(1).

534 Bankruptcy Code § 1127(f)(2).

535 Bankruptcy Code § 1127(a).

536 *See* § 19.08[B] Who May File a Plan; The Exclusivity Period, *supra*.

537 Bankruptcy Code § 1127(a).

If the plan needs to be modified after a disclosure statement has been approved and disseminated, and after votes have been solicited, the proponent must take additional steps to modify the plan. The proponent of the modification must comply with the disclosure and solicitation requirements of § 1125.[538] This means that further disclosures will need to be made to any creditor or interest holder whose rights are affected by the modification to the plan. These disclosures need to be approved by the court before they can be used to solicit acceptances.[539]

Bankruptcy Rule 3019 addresses the treatment of modifications that are proposed after the original plan has been accepted but before it has been confirmed. It requires the court to give notice, to conduct a hearing,[540] and to determine whether the proposed modification adversely changes the treatment of any creditor or equity security holder who has not formally accepted the modification. If the court finds that the change was not materially adverse to a creditor who accepted the plan, those creditors may not change their votes.[541] If the plan materially affects some creditors who have previously accepted the plan, a new round of disclosure and voting must take place. But if the modification has no adverse affect on creditors who have already accepted the plan, there is no reason to require approval and dissemination of a new disclosure statement.[542]

[B] Post-Confirmation Modification of Chapter 11 Plan

After confirmation, a proposal to modify the plan may be made by only by a reorganized debtor or the proponent of the confirmed plan.[543] In most cases, where the proponent of the original plan was the debtor, this will be the same person.

Any proposal to modify a confirmed plan must be submitted before the plan has been substantially consummated.[544] If, once the plan has been implemented, the debtor determines that a further adjustment of its finances is necessary, it must either enter into an out-of-court workout with its creditors or file a new petition. Substantial consummation means:

(a) transfer of all or substantially all of the property proposed by the plan to be transferred;

[538] Bankruptcy Code § 1127(c); *see* § 19.09[A] Consensual Chapter 11 Plans, *supra*.

[539] Bankruptcy Code § 1127(c).

[540] Notice must be given to the trustee (if one has been appointed), to any official committees, and to anyone else designated by the court, such as creditors whose rights are affected by the modification. Fed. R. Bankr. P. 3019.

[541] Fed. R. Bankr. P. 3019; *see* Enron v. The New Power Co. (In re The New Power Co.), 438 F.2d 1113 (11th Cir. 2006) (modification that extended examiner's powers to post-modification period was not materially adverse to creditor).

[542] In re Mount Vernon Plaza Cmty. Urban Redevelopment Corp. I, 79 B.R. 305 (Bankr. S.D. Ohio 1987); *see also* In Enron Corp. v. The New Power Co. (In re The New Power Co.), 438 F.3d 1113, 1117–18 (11th Cir. 2006).

[543] Bankruptcy Code § 1127(b).

[544] Bankruptcy Code § 1127(b).

(b) assumption by the debtor, or by the successor to the debtor, of the management of all or substantially all of the property dealt with by the plan; and

(c) commencement of distribution under the plan.[545]

Moreover, even if the plan has not yet been substantially consummated, the modification can be confirmed only if the circumstances warrant modification.[546] But, because most modifications are proposed to surmount unanticipated difficulties in implementing a plan, this requirement is rarely difficult to satisfy. Because post-confirmation modifications usually reduce payments to creditors, those affected by the modification are more likely to change their votes than those whose rights are enhanced by a pre-confirmation modification.

The 2005 Amendments added new language, applicable only to Chapter 11 debtors who are individuals, that permits modification after a plan has been substantially consummated.[547] The new language brings Chapter 11's modification rules in cases of individuals in conformity with the provisions for modifying Chapter 13 plans.[548] In these cases, the plan may be modified upon the request of the debtor, the trustee, the United States Trustee, or the holder of any unsecured claim. Modifications may increase or reduce the amount of payments made to any class, extend or reduce the duration of the plan, or alter the amount of the distribution to any individual creditor to account for payments that the creditor is receiving under the terms of any other plan involving a related debtor.[549]

§ 19.13 Post-Conformation Issues[550]

Confirmation of the plan is not the end of the case. Issues sometimes arise over the effect of confirmation. Moreover, the plan still must be implemented by distributing any property or securities called for by the plan, and payments must be commenced. In rare circumstances, involving fraud in the confirmation process, confirmation may be revoked. And the plan may provide for the bankruptcy court to retain jurisdiction over the case to consider these or other issues that may arise.

[A] Effect of Confirmation

With very limited exceptions, the confirmation of the plan binds the debtor, its creditors, and its owners to the terms of the plan.[551] This is true

[545] Bankruptcy Code § 1101(2).

[546] Bankruptcy Code § 1127(b).

[547] Bankruptcy Code § 1127(e).

[548] *See* § 18.10[B] Post-Confirmation Modification of Chapter 13 Plan, *supra*.

[549] Bankruptcy Code § 1127(e)(1)-(3).

[550] Frank R. Kennedy & Gerald K. Smith, *Chapter 11 Issues: Postconfirmation Issues: The Effects of Confirmation and Postconfirmation Proceedings*, 44 S.C. L. Rev. 621 (1993).

[551] Bankruptcy Code § 1141(a).

whether or not the creditor or owner accepted the plan. This is the single greatest difference between the Chapter 11 plan and the common law composition. In addition, unless otherwise provided, confirmation re-vests the property of the estate in the debtor.[552] In effect, confirmation re-establishes the original entity and extinguishes the estate.

At least as important is the fact that confirmation is the point at which the discharge is granted.[553] In this respect, Chapter 11 differs from Chapters 12 and 13, under which discharge is normally granted only when the plan is completed. With limited exceptions, all of the claims and interests that existed prior to confirmation cease to exist[554] and are replaced by the obligations and rights created by the plan. In this respect, confirmation is roughly equivalent to a novation, in which the new obligation contained in the plan is a complete substitute for the discharged obligation that existed before. It is the debtor's fresh start: a new financial structure of both debt and equity.

However, there are a few limited exceptions to this fresh start. An individual Chapter 11 debtor, unlike the successful Chapter 13 debtor, is subject to the full list of debts made non-dischargeable by § 523.[555] Thus, confirmation does not discharge an individual from those debts.[556] Moreover, a liquidating debtor who would be denied discharge in Chapter 7 is not entitled to any discharge.[557]

[B] Revocation of Confirmation

As is true in the other reorganization chapters, an order confirming the plan may be revoked only in very limited circumstances. Upon the request of a party in interest, made within 180 days of the entry of the confirmation order, the court, after notice and an opportunity for a hearing, may revoke the order "if and *only if*" it was procured by fraud.[558] The order revoking confirmation must contain provisions to protect any entity that acquired rights in good faith reliance on the confirmation.[559] It must also revoke the debtor's discharge.[560] The very limited time period and fraud as the only basis for revocation are imposed because of the need for finality in the proceeding is so great. The debtor must be able to resume its normal

---

552 Bankruptcy Code § 1141(b).

553 Bankruptcy Code § 1141(d).

554 Bankruptcy Code § 1141(d)(1)(A), (B). Note that claims are extinguished whether or not a proof of claim was filed or deemed filed; whether or not it was allowed; and whether or not the claimant voted to accept the plan. Bankruptcy Code § 1141(d)(1)(A). By contrast, interests are terminated only if the rights of holders of those interests are provided for by the plan. Bankruptcy Code § 1141(d)(1)(B).

555 *See* § 13.03 Non-Dischargeable Debts, *supra*.

556 Bankruptcy Code § 1141(d)(2).

557 Bankruptcy Code § 1141(d)(3); *see* § 12.02[C] Denial of Discharge in Chapter 11, *supra*.

558 Bankruptcy Code § 1144 (emphasis added).

559 Bankruptcy Code § 1144(1).

560 Bankruptcy Code § 1144(2).

business and financial affairs; those with whom it is dealing must have assurance that their transactions are valid.

[C] Implementation of the Plan

Chapter 11 differs from Chapters 12 and 13 in that the implementation of the plan is largely in the hands of the debtor. There is no standing trustee assigned to collect payments from the debtor and transmit them to creditors. Although the court retains the power to issue any orders necessary to implement the plan,[561] it is the debtor and any entity organized for this purpose, who puts the plan's provisions into action.[562] Thus, for example, payments due under the plan are paid directly by the debtor, or in some cases they are paid from a separate trust or similar entity created by the plan for this purpose.

[D] Bankruptcy Court Jurisdiction After Confirmation[563]

Most plans contain some provision for the court to retain jurisdiction over the case while the plan is implemented. However, the propriety and extent of the court's continued jurisdiction remains a contentious issue.

There is no doubt about the court's authority to issue appropriate orders in the time immediately after confirmation until the "effective date" of the plan, when its provisions become effective and it begins to be implemented. Section 1142 expressly authorizes the court to:

> direct the debtor and any other necessary party to execute or deliver or to join in the execution or delivery of any instrument required to effect a transfer of property dealt with by a confirmed plan, and to perform any other act, including the satisfaction of any lien, that is necessary for the consummation of the plan.[564]

Thus, the court has the authority to compel parties to sign or deliver any deeds, bills of sale, contracts, negotiable instruments, or other documents that may be necessary to implement the plan's provisions.

However, the parameters of the court's jurisdiction are established by the relevant provisions of the United States Judicial Code, primarily 28 U.S.C. § 1334, not by § 1142, much less by language in a plan that purports to

---

[561] Bankruptcy Code § 1142(b).

[562] Bankruptcy Code § 1142(a).

[563] Daniel B. Bogart, *Unexpected Gifts of Chapter 11: The Breach of a Director's Duty of Loyalty Following Plan Confirmation and the Postconfirmation Jurisdiction of Bankruptcy Courts*, 72 Am. Bankr. L.J. 303 (1998); Darrell Dunham, *Bankruptcy Court Jurisdiction*, 67 UMKC L. Rev. 229, 267–71 (1998); Benjamin Weintraub & Michael J. Crames, *Defining Consummation, Effective Date of Plan of Reorganization and Retention of Postconfirmation Jurisdiction: Suggested Amendments to Bankruptcy Code and Bankruptcy Rules*, 64 Am. Bankr. L.J. 245 (1990).

[564] Bankruptcy Code § 1142(b).

grant the court continuing jurisdiction over the case. Once the plan has been substantially consummated, issues sometimes arise over whether the court retains jurisdictional authority over its implementation. In some cases, particularly those involving trust funds establish to pay claims to hundreds and perhaps thousands of injured claimants, courts have retained broad jurisdiction over the case for many years.[565]

Despite these cases, bankruptcy courts generally adhere to the oft-quoted passage in *North American Car Corp. v. Peerless Weighing & Vending Machine. Corp.*:

> We have had occasion before to deplore the tendency of District Courts to keep reorganized concerns in tutelage indefinitely by orders purporting to retain jurisdiction for a variety of purposes, extending from complete supervision of the new business to modifications of detail in the reorganization. Since the purpose of reorganization clearly is to rehabilitate the business and start it off on a new and to-be-hoped-for more successful career, it should be the objective of courts to cast off as quickly as possible all leading strings which may limit and hamper its activities and throw doubt upon its responsibility. It is not consonant with the purposes of the Act, or feasible as a judicial function, for the courts to assume to supervise a business somewhat indefinitely.[566]

Bankruptcy courts have generally avoided becoming enmeshed in matters that have nothing to do with the provisions of the Bankruptcy Code, such as missed payments, foreclosure suits, or other disputes that are routinely handled by other courts.[567] Where issues of state law predominate and the dispute has nothing to do with the administration of the bankruptcy case, bankruptcy courts decline to assume jurisdiction.[568]

---

[565] *See, e.g.*, Official Dalkon Shield Claimants' Comm. v. Mabey (In re A.H. Robins Co.), 880 F.2d 769 (4th Cir. 1989).

[566] 143 F.2d 938, 940 (2d Cir. 1944).

[567] *E.g.*, Bank of La. v. Craig's Stores of Tex., Inc. (In re Craig's Stores of Tex., Inc.), 266 F.3d 388 (5th Cir. 2002) (post-consummation action over alleged breach of an executory contract assumed under the plan); *see* Zahn Assocs. v. Leeds Bldg. Prods., Inc. (In re Leeds Bldg. Prods., Inc.), 160 B.R. 689 (Bankr. N.D. Ga. 1993) (missed payment).

[568] Guccione v. Bell, No. 06 Civ. 492 (SHS), 2006 U.S. Dist. LEXIS 49526 (S.D.N.Y. July 20, 2006) (action by former officer of magazine publishing business — you know which one — alleging breach of contract, fraud, unjust enrichment, promissory estoppel, failure to pay severance, breach of fiduciary duty, and conspiracy to defraud).

§ 19.14 Small Business Debtors[569]

Because of its elaborate and expensive procedures, Chapter 11 has sometimes been of little benefit to small businesses. This was one of the reasons Congress permitted small sole proprietorships to seek relief under Chapter 13. It was also one of the factors that led to the 1986 adoption of Chapter 12 for family farmers and its 2005 expansion to apply to family fishermen. Pressure is occasionally exerted to enact a separate new small business reorganization chapter. While Congress has largely resisted this pressure, in 1994 it added a few provisions to Chapter 11 to deal with small business reorganizations. These provisions were revised and expanded by the 2005 Amendments.

[A] Small Business Debtor Defined

The term "small business debtor" is defined narrowly. It means any person engaged in commercial or business activities whose aggregate, noncontingent liquidated debts (both secured and unsecured) do not exceed $2 million on the date of the debtor's petition.[570] However, this definition excludes debtors whose primary business activity is owning or operating real estate. Thus, small single-asset real estate cases do not fall within the special procedures for small business debtors.

Before the 2005 Amendments, debtors could elect to have the Bankruptcy Code's small business provisions applied to their case. The 2005 Amendments removed this "election" and applies the small business debtor provisions to all debtors who fit the definition.[571] However, as will be seen, some of the small business provisions apply only upon court approval of an appropriate motion.

[B] Expedited and Simplified Procedures for Small Business Debtors

The procedures for small business cases are simpler than for other cases. For example, a creditors' committee is not required, though the Code still presumes that there will be a creditors' committee, unless the court approves a motion otherwise.[572]

---

[569] Thomas E. Carlson & Jennifer Fraiser-Hayes, *The Small Business Provisions of the 2005 Bankruptcy Amendments*, 79 Am. Bankr. L.J. 645 (2005); Hon. James B. Haines, Jr. & Philip J. Hendel, *No Easy Answers: Small Business Bankruptcies After BAPCPA*, 47 B.C. L. Rev. 71 (2005); Richard Levin & Alesia Ranney-Marinelli, *The Creeping Repeal of Chapter 11: The Significant Business Provisions of the Bankruptcy Abuse Prevention and Consumer Protection Act of 2005*, 79 Am. Bankr. L.J. 603 (2005); Hon. A. Thomas Small, *If You Fix It, They Will Come — A New Playing Field for Small Business Bankruptcies*, 79 Am. Bankr. L.J. 981 (2005).

[570] Bankruptcy Code § 101(51D)(A). Debts to insiders and affiliates are excluded in calculating whether the debtor is within the $2 million threshold.

[571] Interim Fed. R. Bankr. P. 1020 provides a mechanism for debtors to declare their status in conjunction with their petition and establishes deadlines for objections to this designation.

[572] Bankruptcy Code § 1102(a)(3).

The exclusivity period, during which only the debtor may file a plan, is limited in cases involving small debtors, to a maximum of 180 days.[573] Further, no one may file a plan more than 300 days after the order for relief.[574] These time periods may be extended, but only if the debtor "demonstrates by a preponderance of the evidence that it is more likely than not that the court will confirm a plan within a reasonable period of time."[575]

In addition, the court is permitted to dispense with the necessity of a disclosure statement if it determines that "the plan itself provides adequate information."[576] Alternatively, the court may approve a simplified disclosure statement, submitted in accordance with a set of standardized forms. Moreover, the court may conditionally approve a disclosure statement on an ex parte basis, subject to final approval after notice and the opportunity for a hearing.[577] Acceptances or rejections of the plan may be solicited based on the conditionally approved disclosure statement, and the court may combine the disclosure statement hearing with a confirmation hearing after the requisite number of acceptances have been obtained.[578] This eliminates one of the major hearings that would otherwise ordinarily occur in a Chapter 11 case.

The 2005 Amendments also require the debtor to obtain confirmation of its plan within forty-five days of the time it was filed.[579] This period, like the period for filing the plan and disclosure statement, can be extended only upon a showing that confirmation is likely within a reasonable period of time.[580]

[C] Expanded Reporting in Small Business Cases

Accompanying these streamlined procedures are a bevy of additional reporting and record keeping requirements. Most of these duties are found in new § 1116. They include:

- appending the debtor's most recent balance sheets, statement of operations, and federal income tax returns to the debtor's petition;[581]
- attending an initial debtor's interview and other meetings and conferences with the United States Trustee, as further specified in the Judicial Code;[582]

---

[573] Bankruptcy Code § 1121(e)(1)(A). Prior to the 2005 Amendments, the limit for debtors who elected to subject themselves to the small business debtor rules, was 100 days. Debtors who did not wish to so limit themselves did not make the election.

[574] Bankruptcy Code § 1122(e)(2).

[575] Bankruptcy Code § 1122(e)(3)(A).

[576] Bankruptcy Code § 1126(f)(1).

[577] Bankruptcy Code § 1125(f)(3); *see* Fed. R. Bankr. P. 3017.1(a).

[578] Bankruptcy Code § 1125(f)(3)(C).

[579] Bankruptcy Code § 1129(e).

[580] Bankruptcy Code §§ 1129(e), 1121(e)(3)(A).

[581] Bankruptcy Code § 1116(1); *see* Interim Fed. R. Bankr. P. 2015(a)(6).

[582] Bankruptcy Code § 1116(2); 28 U.S.C. § 586(a)(7). Section 586(a)(7) codifies current practices of the United States Trustee's office.

- expediting filing of all schedules and statements of affairs that are not filed with the debtor's petition;[583]
- filing post-petition financial and other reports as specified by the Federal Rules of Bankruptcy Procedure or local bankruptcy rules;[584]
- maintaining insurance according to industry custom;[585]
- timely filing all relevant tax returns and other government filings and timely paying all post-petition taxes;[586] and
- permitting the United States Trustee or its designate to inspect the debtor's premises, books, and records.[587]

§ 19.15 Railroad Reorganizations

Much of our law of bankruptcy reorganizations is derived from early procedures that were developed to restructure the finances of the first great American businesses: the railroads. The great railroad reorganizations of the late nineteenth and early twentieth centuries presented unique issues, involving assets spread out over vast geographical areas and key components of the public interest. Thus, it is not surprising that the Bankruptcy Code retains special provisions, in Subchapter IV of Chapter 11,[588] to deal with railroad reorganizations. For a variety of reasons, railroad reorganizations have many distinct features. This section only highlights a few of the most notable among them.

First, in railroad reorganizations there is always a trustee. As soon as practical after the order for relief, the United States Secretary of Transportation submits a list of five qualified, disinterested persons who are willing to serve as the trustee. The United States Trustee appoints the case trustee from this list.[589] The fact that the trustee is selected from among nominees of the Secretary of Transportation reflects the strong public interest in railroad reorganization cases, but leaves one to wonder why similar provisions are not made for bankruptcies of domestic airlines, or large trucking companies, which are also key links in the nation's transportation system.

Second, the regulatory structures that govern the operation of the railroad remain largely in place. The Interstate Commerce Commission, the United States Department of Transportation, and state railroad regulatory

---

583 Bankruptcy Code § 1116(3).

584 Bankruptcy Code § 1116(4); *see* Bankruptcy Code § 308.

585 Bankruptcy Code § 1116(5).

586 Bankruptcy Code § 1116(6).

587 Bankruptcy Code § 1116(7); *see* 28 U.S.C. § 587(a)(7)(B) (LexisNexis Supp. 2006) (requiring the United States Trustee to conduct such an inspection where "appropriate and advisable").

588 Bankruptcy Code §§ 1161-1174.

589 Bankruptcy Code § 1163.

bodies play the role that the SEC plays in other Chapter 11 proceedings. Like the SEC, these bodies may appear and be heard on any issue, but they may not appeal.[590] Moreover, regulations that apply to railroads continue in force during the bankruptcy; and, with limited exceptions, the trustee is subject to the orders of any regulatory body.[591]

Third, as noted earlier, there is a greater emphasis on the "public interest" in railroad reorganizations. Both the court and the trustee are explicitly required, when applying some of the key provisions of Subchapter IV, to consider the public interest in addition to the interests of the debtor, creditors, and equity security holders.[592] At a minimum, this means that the ability of the public to have access to railroad transportation is to be weighed along with the more conventional interests of the stakeholders in the railroad.[593]

Finally, there is an absolute time limit on the pendency period. If a plan has not been confirmed within five years after the date of the order for relief, the court "shall" order the trustee to cease operations and liquidate the estate.[594] This puts considerable pressure on the debtor and creditors to come to terms over a plan. However, the case is not converted to Chapter 7. Instead, the Code applies Chapter 11's special railroad liquidation provisions which provide for the liquidation to proceed "in the same manner *as if* the case were a case under Chapter 7."[595]

The rights of unions are also treated differently and more favorably in a railroad reorganization. Collective bargaining agreements are protected by § 1167. It provides that neither the court nor the trustee may change the wages or working conditions of employees under a collective bargaining agreement that is subject to the Railway Labor Act, except as provided in that Act.[596] The procedures of provisions of § 1113, which apply to collective bargaining agreements in other Chapter 11 cases, do not apply in railroad reorganizations.[597] The Railway Labor Act requires much more elaborate procedures and considerable government involvement, including the power to order cooling off periods.[598]

---

[590] Bankruptcy Code § 1164.

[591] Bankruptcy Code § 1166.

[592] Bankruptcy Code § 1165.

[593] The court is not required to consider the public interest in all important matters. For example, it need not do so when making decisions under Bankruptcy Code § 363 (use, sale, and lease of property) or Bankruptcy Code § 364 (obtaining credit), even though these are among the most important decisions made.

[594] Bankruptcy Code § 1174.

[595] Bankruptcy Code § 1174 (emphasis added).

[596] Bankruptcy Code § 1167.

[597] Bankruptcy Code § 1113(a).

[598] *See generally* Railway Labor Act, 45 U.S.C. § 151 et seq. (2000).

Chapter 20

Family Farmers and Family Fishermen

§ 20.01 Goals of Family Farmer and Family Fishermen Reorganization[1]

Since 1986, the Bankruptcy Code has included a separate reorganization proceeding designed to assist financially troubled "family farmers." Chapter 12 was added because Chapter 11 proceedings were considered too complicated and expensive to facilitate the reorganization of family farm operations and because many family farms were ineligible for relief under chapter 13. They were ineligible because their level of debt was too high, because they were organized in corporate or partnership form, or because their income was too uncertain.[2]

Chapter 13 was initially enacted in partial response to the "farm debt crisis" that occurred in the mid 1980s.[3] The traditional congressional interest in saving family farms led to the enactment of a "temporary" chapter modeled largely on Chapter 13.[4] Chapter 12 was originally set to expire in 1993, but between 1993 and 2005 it expired and was re-enacted several times, usually retroactively.[5]

There have not been many cases filed under Chapter 12.[6] From the inception of Chapter 12 in 1986 through June 30, 1993, only about 15,000 Chapter 12 cases had been filed, and about half of those were filed before June 30, 1988. Only 348 cases were filed in 2006.

This is only a tiny percentage of all bankruptcy filings. In the year ending June 30, 1992, for example, overall bankruptcy filings were 972,490; of

---

[1] Patrick Bauer, *Where You Stand Depends on Where You Sit: A Response to Professor White's Sortie Against Chapter 12*, 13 J. Corp. L. 33 (1987); Janet A. Flaccus, *A Comparison of Farm Bankruptcies in Chapter 11 and the New Chapter 12*, 11 U. Ark. Little Rock L. Rev. 49 (1988-89); David Ray Papke, *Rhetoric and Retrenchment: Agrarian Ideology and American Bankruptcy Law*, 54 Mo. L. Rev. 871 (1989); Katherine M. Porter, *Phantom Farmers: Chapter 12 of the Bankruptcy Code*, 79 Am. Bankr. L.J. 729 (2005); Katherine M. Porter, *Going Broke the Hard Way: The Economics of Rural Failure*, 2005 Wis. L. Rev. 969; James J. White, *Taking From Farm Lenders and Farm Debtors: Chapter 12 of the Bankruptcy Code*, 13 J. Corp. L. 1 (1987).

[2] *See* § 6.02[B] Eligibility for Relief in Chapter 13, Individuals with Regular Income, *supra.*

[3] Katherine M. Porter, *Phantom Farmers: Chapter 12 of the Bankruptcy Code*, 79 Am. Bankr. L.J. 729, 730–33 (2005).

[4] *See generally* David Ray Papke, *Rhetoric and Retrenchment: Agrarian Ideology and American Bankruptcy Law*, 54 Mo. L. Rev. 871 (1989).

[5] Katherine M. Porter, *Phantom Farmers: Chapter 12 of the Bankruptcy Code*, 79 Am. Bankr. L.J. 729, 733 (2005).

[6] Katherine M. Porter, *Phantom Farmers: Chapter 12 of the Bankruptcy Code*, 79 Am. Bankr. L.J. 729, 740 (2005).

these only 1,634 (1.68%) were Chapter 12 filings.[7] In 2003, when over 1.6 million bankruptcy cases were filed, there were only about 750 Chapter 12 cases. Supporters of Chapter 12 have argued that, despite the low numbers, the Chapter has been a success. There is evidence that the success rate for Chapter 12 proceedings is high relative to Chapter 11 and 13 cases.[8] In 2005, despite the relatively few number of cases under its provisions, Chapter 12 was made permanent. At the same time, its provisions were extended to cover family fishermen.[9]

Chapter 12 is limited and its goals are fairly narrow: to provide a reorganization alternative to family farmers and their close aquacultural cousins, family fishermen.[10] It differs from Chapter 13 in that it always involves a business. Sole proprietors do sometimes use Chapter 13 to reorganize their business as well as their personal affairs. Nonehteless, Chapter 13 usually involves consumer debtors. It differs from at least the larger Chapter 11 cases in that it generally does not preserve the jobs and income of anyone other than a few family members who earn their income from the family farm. Fundamentally, its justification must rest on the belief that there is value to the preservation of family farming which merits special protection.

This chapter discusses the basic structure of Chapter 12, with special focus on provisions that are unique to it. It is relatively brief. Chapter 12 is usually given short shrift in bankruptcy courses because of the small number of Chapter 12 proceedings and because few of its provisions have been the subject of extensive litigation. There is good reason to believe that this lack of litigation indicates that the worst fears of the Chapter 12 critics have by no means come to pass.[11] While the propriety of a set of specialized rules for reorganizing family farms has been controversial,[12] Chapter 12

[7] Ed Flynn, *Bankruptcy by the Numbers: Chapter 12 Filings Level Out*, 13 Am. Bankr. Inst. J. 7 (March 1994).

[8] *See* Jonathan K. Van Patten, *Chapter 12 in the Courts*, 38 S.D. L. Rev. 52 (1993) (indicating a confirmation rate of 60% and a confirmed plan completion rate of 90%); *see also* Bruce Dixon, *Factors Affecting State-Level Chapter 12 Filing Rates: A Panel Data Model*, 20 Bankr. Dev. J. 401 (2003-2004).

[9] For a detailed discussion of the rules regarding eligibility for relief under Chapter 12, see § 6.02[B][5] Eligibility for Relief in Chapter 12 — Family Farmers and Family Fishermen, *supra*.

[10] In 2005, eligibility was expanded to permit family fishermen to take advantage of Chapter 12. *See* § 6.02[B][5] Eligibility for Relief in Chapter 12 — Family Farmers and Family Fishermen, *supra;* Katherine M. Porter, *Phantom Farmers: Chapter 12 of the Bankruptcy Code*, 79 Am. Bankr. L.J. 729, 735 (2005).

[11] Jonathan K. Van Patten, *Chapter 12 in the Courts*, 38 S.D. L. Rev. 52 (1993).

[12] *See generally* Michael J. Herbert, *Once More Unto the Breach, Dear Friends: The 1986 Reforms of the Reformed Bankruptcy Reform Act*, 16 Cap. U. L. Rev. 325 (1987) (criticizing Chapter 12); Carol Ann Eiden, *The Courts' Role in Preserving the Family Farm During Bankruptcy Proceedings Involving FMHA Loans*, 11 Law & Ineq. 417 (1993); William W. Horlock, Jr., *Chapter 12: Relief for the Family Farmer*, 5 Bankr. Dev. J. 229 (1987); James J. White, *Taking From Farm Lenders and Farm Debtors: Chapter 12 of the Bankruptcy Code*, 13 J. Corp. L. 1, 2 (1987) ("Congress was wrong to enact a law that redistributes wealth from existing mortgagees to existing mortgagors . . . [and will diminish] . . . the farm debtor's power to mortgage his land").

now seems likely to remain available to financially troubled family farmers and family-run commercial fishing operations for the foreseeable future.

§ 20.02 Filing, Conversion, and Dismissal

[A] Chapter 12 Filing

Chapter 12 petitions can only be filed voluntarily by the debtor.[13] Debtors are eligible for relief only if they are "a family farmer or family fisherman with regular annual income."[14] Individual debtors, corporations, and partnerships may qualify, depending on whether more than 50% of the ownership interests are held by members of the same family and their relatives.[15] As with Chapter 13, debtors are eligible for relief if their secured and unsecured debts are below the prescribed maximums. As explained in more detail elsewhere, these amounts are somewhat different for family farmers and family fishermen.[16] In addition, a specified portion of the debtor's income must be earned through the family farm or fishing operation.[17]

[B] Conversion and Dismissal

Chapter 12, like Chapter 13, is wholly voluntary; the debtor cannot be forced into it through an involuntary petition.[18] For the same reason, the debtor has an absolute right to convert a Chapter 12 case to a Chapter 7 case at any time.[19] This right to convert cannot be waived.[20]

This means that the Chapter 12 debtor who has come to the conclusion that the plan will not work or is too burdensome always has a ready exit. Any other party in interest, such as a creditor or the trustee, may request conversion of the case to Chapter 7, but only upon a showing that the debtor has committed fraud in connection with the case.[21] Further, because farmers cannot be the targets of an involuntary petition, creditors cannot force the debtor into Chapter 7.[22]

Similarly, debtors have a nearly absolute right to dismiss their case voluntarily. This right cannot be waived.[23] There is one exception to the

---

[13] Bankruptcy Code §§ 301, 303. Section 303 does not permit involuntary Chapter 12 petitions.

[14] Bankruptcy Code § 109(f).

[15] Bankruptcy Code §§ 101(18)(B), 101(19A)(B).

[16] *See* § 6.02[B][5] Eligibility for Relief in Chapter 12 — Family Farmers and Family Fishermen, *supra*.

[17] *See* § 6.02[B][5] Eligibility for Relief in Chapter 12 — Family Farmers and Family Fishermen, *supra*.

[18] Bankruptcy Code § 303(a).

[19] Bankruptcy Code § 1208(a).

[20] Bankruptcy Code § 1208(a).

[21] Bankruptcy Code § 1208(d).

[22] *See* § 6.03[C] Persons Against Whom an Involuntary Petition May Be Filed, *supra*.

[23] Bankruptcy Code § 1208(b).

debtor's right to dismiss. If the debtor previously converted a Chapter 7 or 11 case to Chapter 12, the debtor merely has the right to request that the case be dismissed. Dismissal in this case is not available as a matter of right.[24]

Any party in interest may request involuntary dismissal for cause, including such things as mismanagement, failure to file a plan, failure to commence payments under the plan, or termination of the plan according to its own terms.[25] In 2005, in an effort to provide additional protection for creditors who are owed support, the debtor's failure to pay a post-petition "domestic support obligation" was added as grounds to dismiss a case.[26] These provisions give children and former spouses protection against the interminable prolongation of a case in which there is no hope of success.

§ 20.03 Role of the Parties in Chapter 12

The roles of the parties in family farmer and family fisherman reorganization cases are strikingly similar to the roles of the parties in Chapter 13 cases. Creditors do not vote on the plan in either type of proceeding. This leaves cases largely under the control of the debtor and the standing trustee; creditors are relegated to a far more limited role.

[A] Chapter 12 Debtor-in-Possession

In Chapter 12, as in Chapters 11 and 13, the debtor remains in possession of the property of the estate while the case is pending. In other words, the debtors get to keep their family farm while they try to reorganize. Family fishermen are permitted to keep their boats and operate their commercial fishing operation.[27] Subject to whatever limitations the court might impose, a Chapter 12 debtor-in-possession has nearly all of the ordinary rights, powers, and duties of a Chapter 11 trustee.[28]

[B] Chapter 12 Trustees

Chapter 12, like Chapter 13, uses a standing trustee who is appointed to serve in all Chapter 12 cases in the district or division.[29] However, the Chapter 12 trustee plays a rather different and somewhat hybrid role. Like

---

[24] Bankruptcy Code § 1208(b).

[25] Bankruptcy Code § 1208(c).

[26] Bankruptcy Code § 1208(c)(10).

[27] Bankruptcy Code § 1208(c)(10).

[28] Unlike a trustee, the debtor-in-possession does not have the right to compensation under § 330 for performance of his duties as the debtor-in-possession. Bankruptcy Code § 1203. Likewise, the debtor-in-possession, unlike a Chapter 11 trustee, is not required to investigate the operations of the debtor or to file reports concerning the results of its investigation. *See* Bankruptcy Code §§ 1203 & 1106(a)(3)-(4).

[29] Bankruptcy Code § 1202(a).

the Chapter 13 trustee, the Chapter 12 trustee is a party in interest and as such is entitled to be heard on most matters. He carries out many of the same functions as a Chapter 7 trustee. In Chapter 12, however, the trustee is not empowered to advise or assist the debtor. The Chapter 12 trustee also has the broad investigatory powers similar to those given to a Chapter 11 trustee but not accorded to trustees in Chapter 13 cases.[30] In 2005, Chapter 12 was amended to charge the trustee with additional responsibilities in connection with the collection and enforcement of the debtor's domestic support obligations.[31]

The most significant potential difference between the role of a trustee in Chapter 12 and Chapter 13 lies in the fact that a Chapter 12 debtor-in-possession may under some circumstances be removed and replaced by the standing trustee. This cannot occur under Chapter 13.

In recognition of the fact that all Chapter 12 cases involve the operation of a business, Chapter 12 permits the court, upon request of a party in interest and after notice and a hearing, to replace the debtor-in-possession with the standing trustee.[32] This may only be done "for cause," which includes fraud, dishonesty, incompetence, or gross mismanagement on the basis of either the debtor's pre-petition or post-petition conduct.[33] A takeover of the estate is not necessarily permanent; the debtor-in-possession may be subsequently reinstated by the court.[34] The right to replace the debtor-in-possession with a trustee has been invoked only rarely.[35]

[C] Creditors in Chapter 12 Cases

Just as in Chapter 13 cases, creditors in Chapter 12 cases play a limited role. Unlike cases under Chapter 11, creditors do not vote on the plan. Their main roles are to file claims, to seek relief from the automatic stay to recover their collateral, and to object to confirmation of debtors' plans.

Secured creditors' efforts to obtain relief from the automatic stay in order to permit foreclosure on the debtor's real estate are somewhat different in Chapter 12 than they are in either Chapter 11 or 13 because of the special "adequate protection" rule of § 1205(b)(3), which is different from those that apply in other chapters. It defines "adequate protection" to include payment of the customary rental value of the land.[36] Also unlike Chapters 11 and 13, Chapter 12 debtors are permitted to modify the rights of claims secured by their residence, probably in recognition that on many traditional family

[30] Bankruptcy Code § 1202(b)(2).

[31] Bankruptcy Code § 1202(b)(6), (c).

[32] Bankruptcy Code §§ 1204, 1202(b)(5).

[33] Bankruptcy Code § 1204(a).

[34] Bankruptcy Code § 1204(b).

[35] In re Jessen, 82 B.R. 490 (Bankr. S.D. Iowa 1988).

[36] Bankruptcy Code § 1205(b)(3). In other respects, "adequate protection" has the same meaning as it does elsewhere in the Code. *Compare* Bankruptcy Code § 1305(b), *with* Bankruptcy Code § 361.

farms the debtor's residence is on the farm.[37] Creditors with security interests in farm equipment, fishing gear, and other personal property may seek relief from the stay and object to plan confirmation according to the ordinary rules that apply elsewhere in the Code, with only minor variations. Further, the purchase money security interest rules added to § 1325 by the 2005 Amendments (that limit the ability of debtors to strip down liens on cars and other personal property in Chapter 13 cases[38]) do not apply to cases in Chapter 12.

§ 20.04 Property of the Chapter 12 Estate

Under Chapter 12, the estate encompasses more post-petition property than under Chapter 7.[39] In this respect, Chapter 12 is similar to Chapters 11 and 13, where post-petition property is used to facilitate the debtor's rehabilitation. In particular, "earnings from services performed by the debtor after the commencement of the case" are explicitly made a part of the debtor's Chapter 12 estate.[40] Making these earnings part of the debtor's estate ensures that they are protected by the automatic stay, and subjects the debtor's ability to use these funds to the restrictions imposed by § 363.[41]

§ 20.05 Automatic Stay — Adequate Protection

The automatic stay and adequate protection rules in Chapter 12 are different from their counterparts in other reorganization proceedings. As explained in detail in an earlier chapter,[42] the automatic stay prevents creditors from taking a wide variety of actions against the debtor, the debtor's property, or property of the estate while a bankruptcy case is pending. Most importantly in this context, it prevents secured creditors from taking possession of their collateral or taking any other action to foreclose their security interests or mortgages.[43]

However, secured creditors may obtain relief from the automatic stay and foreclose on their interests unless they are "adequately protected" against

---

[37] Both parents of one of your co-authors grew up on farms during the Great Depression of the 1930s. Several of his aunts and uncles and many of his cousins are family farmers in western Ohio. He has visited the farms of these relatives many times and still does so for family gatherings. The hogs you might smell if you've ever stopped at the Interstate 70 rest area just inside the western border of Ohio belong to one of his uncles, whose farm was cut in half when the highway was built. This same co-author helped make hay one summer during college on one of his uncle's farms. This experience motivated him to study hard in school. The other co-author's grandmother spent the first six years of her life on a homestead in the Dakotas. When that farm failed (long before the advent of Chapter 12), her family farmed on the outskirts of Chicago.

[38] *See* § 18.08[F][6] Certain Purchase Money Security Interests, *supra*.

[39] Bankruptcy Code § 1207.

[40] Bankruptcy Code § 1207(b); *see* § 7.02[A][2] Debtor's Post-Petition Earnings, *supra*.

[41] *See* § 9.03 Use, Sale, or Lease of Estate Property, *supra*.

[42] *See* Chapter 8, The Automatic Stay, *supra*.

[43] *See* § 8.02 Scope of the Automatic Stay, *supra*.

any deterioration of their property interests that might occur while the case is pending.[44] If a secured creditor obtains relief from the stay due to a lack of adequate protection and forecloses on property the debtor needs to keep its business open, the debtor's effort to reorganize will come to a rapid halt. Thus disputes over whether secured creditors' property rights are adequately protected are, in reality, struggles over whether the debtor is able to reorganize at all.

[A] Adequate Protection in Chapter 12[45]

The first difference between Chapter 12 and its counterparts is a predicate to the second: § 361, which provides the general definition of "adequate protection" the for automatic stay and other purposes, does not apply in Chapter 12.[46] Instead, Chapter 12 contains its own, somewhat broader definition of adequate protection. Under § 361, three types of protection are recognized: periodic payments, the grant of a lien on property, or any other means that provides the indubitable equivalent of the creditor's interest.[47] Section 1205 repeats those three method of giving protection[48] and adds a fourth less demanding alterative: payment of the rental value of the farm. Section 1205(b)(3) thus provides that adequate protection can be provided to a secured creditor by "paying to such entity for the use of farmland the reasonable rent customary in the community where the property is located, based upon the rental value, net income, and earning capacity of the property."[49]

Secured lenders receive much less protection than they prefer under this provision, because it in effect freezes in place a single use of the property and gives protection only for the value of that use. If the lender could seize the property, it might be able to put the property to a more economically valuable use, perhaps including selling it for residential or commercial purposes.[50] This issue has not created much of a stir, suggesting that it,

---

[44] *See* § 8.06[B][1] For Cause — Lack of Adequate Protection, *supra*.

[45] Nancy H. Kratzke & Thomas O. Depperschmidt, *"Reasonable Rent" and Opportunity Cost in the Family Farmer Bankruptcy Act*, 39 Drake L. Rev. 863 (1990).

[46] Bankruptcy Code § 1205(a).

[47] Bankruptcy Code § 361; *see* § 8.06[B][1] For Cause — Lack of Adequate Protection, *supra*.

[48] Bankruptcy Code § 1205(b)(1)-(4). Note two probably insignificant differences. Subsections (b)(1), (2), and (4) make it clear that co-owners, as well as creditors, are entitled to adequate protection; this is certainly true under § 361 as well. In addition, subsection (b)(4), the catchall provision, does not state that the relief granted must be the indubitable equivalent of the claimant's interest. Although this apparently permits somewhat broader forms of adequate protection than are allowed under § 361, there does not appear to be much practical significance to it.

[49] Bankruptcy Code § 1205(b)(3).

[50] In the view of one critic of Chapter 12, who was the author of the first edition of this book: "The borrower, by paying rent based on what may be a low economic value use of the property, would be able to keep the lender from foreclosing and converting it to what may be a higher economic value use." Michael J. Herbert, *Once More Unto the Breach, Dear Friends: The 1986 Reforms of the Reformed Bankruptcy Reform Act*, 16 Cap. U. L. Rev. 325, 345–46 (1987).

like many of Chapter 12's perceived problems, has not caused much real world concern. In part this may be because farmland prices, which declined sharply in the early 1980s, have in more recent years been on the upswing. It also may be due to the fact that there are so few Chapter 12 cases, and not all of them generate adequate protection litigation. Indeed, to the extent land prices are stable or rising, there is no need to provide anything in the way of adequate protection. While there is some ambiguity in the statute, the generally accepted view is that, consistent with the Supreme Court's ruling in *Timbers of Inwood Forest*,[51] rent as adequate protection must be paid only when necessary to protect the creditor against a decline in the value of the property.[52] Thus, the issue may arise only rarely.

The addition of family fishermen to the scope of Chapter 12, on the other hand, increases the likelihood that adequate protection issues will become important in cases under Chapter 12. Debtors' principal assets in these cases are their boats. Fishing boats are far less likely to increase steadily in value than farm land. To the contrary, they are likely to depreciate in value, creating the same sort of adequate protection issues that arise in Chapter 11 cases. Here, however, the special adequate protection rule of § 1205(a)(3), which applies only to "farmland," has no effect.

[B] Chapter 12 Co-Debtor Stay

A second significant feature of the automatic stay in Chapter 12 is borrowed from Chapter 13: the co-debtor stay.[53] Section 1201(a) automatically stays all civil actions to collect consumer debts from co-debtors of the debtor.[54] The co-debtor stay is designed to protect the debtor from informal pressure from family members and friends who may have guaranteed one of the debtor's obligations. Thus, if the family farmer's parents guaranteed loans made to the debtor, the creditor may not put family pressure on the farmer by pursuing its claim against his parents.

However, the scope of the co-debtor stay is very limited. It does not apply if the debtor is a partnership or corporation, since a business entity has no consumer debts. Likewise, it does not apply to debts arising from the operation of the debtor's farm.[55] Not surprisingly, it does not apply if the co-debtor became liable as a commercial surety.[56] Further, the stay does not prevent the holder of a negotiable instrument that was signed by the co-debtor from presenting it and giving notice to the co-debtor of its

---

[51] United Sav. Assoc. of Tex. v. Timbers of Inwood Forest Assocs., Ltd. (In re Timbers of Inwood Forest Assocs., Ltd.), 484 U.S. 365 (1988); *see* § 8.06[B] Relief From the Automatic Stay, *supra*.

[52] *E.g.*, Zink v. Vanmiddlesworth, 300 B.R. 394 (N.D.N.Y. 2003); In re Anderson, 88 Bankr. 877 (Bankr. N.D. Ind. 1988); In re Turner, 82 B.R. 465 (Bankr. W.D. Tenn. 1988); *see* Jonathan K. Van Patten, *Chapter 12 in the Courts*, 38 S.D. L. Rev. 52 (1993).

[53] *See* § 8.04 Co-Debtor Stay in Chapters 12 and 13, *supra*.

[54] Bankruptcy Code § 1201(a).

[55] In re SFW, Inc., 83 B.R. 27 (Bankr. S.D. Cal. 1988).

[56] Bankruptcy Code § 1201(a)(1).

dishonor,[57] which is a formal necessity to preserve the creditor's rights under Article 3 of the U.C.C.

The co-debtor stay, like the automatic stay of § 365, terminates when the case is closed, dismissed, or converted to Chapter 7.[58] However, relief from the stay can be obtained, upon request, when the debtor's plan does not provide for payment of the debt,[59] where the creditor's interest would be irreparably harmed by continuation of the stay,[60] or where the co-debtor protected by the stay is the one who received the consideration for the claim held by the creditor.[61] Thus, relief from the co-debtor stay is quickly available where the debtor is liable only as a guarantor for a loan provided directly to someone else who is liable in his or her capacity as the principal obligor.

§ 20.06 Use, Sale, and Lease of Property

Section 363 generally permits the trustee to use, sell, or lease estate property, other than "cash collateral" in the ordinary course, without court permission.[62] Use or sale of cash collateral or of other property outside the ordinary course requires court permission.[63] In some circumstances, property can be sold free and clear of any liens on the property.[64] A Chapter 12 debtor-in-possession generally has the same right to use, sell, or lease property as debtors-in-possession under other chapters.[65] Section 1206 seems to limit this right by giving the right to sell property free and clear of secured creditors' interests solely to the trustee. However, the few courts that have interpreted this language have permitted the debtor to conduct the sale provided that the sale is approved by the trustee.[66]

Thus, a Chapter 12 trustee is permitted to sell part or all of the debtor's farm, or the debtor's commercial fishing equipment, including any fishing boats it operates, free and clear of a creditor's mortgage or security interest, provided that the creditor receives a replacement lien on the proceeds received from the sale. The sale must be approved by the court after notice and a hearing, at which the principal issue is mostly to be whether the price is sufficient.

---

[57] Bankruptcy Code § 1201(b).

[58] Bankruptcy Code § 1201(a)(2).

[59] Bankruptcy Code § 1302(b)(2).

[60] Bankruptcy Code § 1302(b)(3).

[61] Bankruptcy Code § 1302(b)(1).

[62] Bankruptcy Code § 363(c).

[63] Bankruptcy Code § 363(b), (c)(1).

[64] Bankruptcy Code § 363(f).

[65] Bankruptcy Code § 1203.

[66] *E.g.*, In re Webb, 932 F.2d 155 (1st Cir. 1991); In re Brileya, 108 B.R. 444 (Bankr. D. Vt. 1989).

§ 20.07 Chapter 12 Reorganization Plan

As is true with any reorganization proceeding, the key to Chapter 12 is the plan. The Chapter 12 plan rules are based very closely on the Chapter 13 plan rules.[67] Creditors are not given the right to vote on the plan, so there is little creditor participation in its formulation. Confirmation is based almost entirely on the debtor's ability to meet certain statutory mandates. As in Chapter 13, there is a time limit on the plan; a Chapter 12 plan may not extend for more than three years without court permission, and in no event may it extend for more than five years.[68]

[A] Required Chapter 12 Plan Provisions

The provisions that are required to be included in Chapter 12 plans are virtually identical to those required to be included in Chapter 13 plans.[69] The plan must provide for submission of a sufficient amount of the debtor's future earnings to the trustee for execution of the plan;[70] it must provide for full cash payment of nearly all § 507 priority claims;[71] and, if it separates claims into different classes, it must provide for identical treatment of each claim within a class.[72]

[B] Permissive Chapter 12 Plan Provisions

Additional provisions that are permitted to be included in a Chapter 12 plan are in most respects identical to those than can be included in a Chapter 13 plan.[73] The most significant difference is that a Chapter 12 plan may provide for the modification of a claim secured solely by the debtor's residence. Chapter 13 does not permit residential mortgages to be modified.[74] In addition, as noted above, there is nothing in Chapter 12 like the hanging paragraph at the end of § 1325(a)(9), and thus nothing in Chapter 12 prohibits bifurcation of partially secured claims liens on the debtor's personal property.[75]

---

[67] *See* § 18.06 The Chapter 13 Plan — Required Provisions, *supra*; § 18.07 Chapter 13 Plan — Permissive Provisions, *supra*.

[68] Bankruptcy Code § 1222(c). There is a limited exception to this: payments on secured claims and certain long-term claims may be stretched beyond the three-to five-year period. Bankruptcy Code § 1222(c), (b)(5), (9). There is no requirement, however, that payments on secured claims be stretched beyond the plan period. Appeal of Freund (In re Fortney), 36 F.3d 701 (7th Cir. 1994).

[69] *See* § 18.06 The Chapter 13 Plan — Required Provisions, *supra*.

[70] Bankruptcy Code § 1222(a)(1).

[71] Bankruptcy Code § 1222(a)(2). The 2005 Amendments added language that permits claims of governmental entities that arise from the sale of an asset used in the debtor's farming operations to be treated as non-priority claims.

[72] Bankruptcy Code § 1222(a)(3).

[73] *Compare* Bankruptcy Code § 1222(b), *with* Bankruptcy Code § 1322(b); *see* § 18.07 Chapter 13 Plan — Permissive Provisions, *supra*.

[74] *See* § 18.07[B][2][a] Residential Real Estate Mortgages, *supra*.

[75] *See* § 18.07[B][2][b] Certain Purchase Money Loans, *supra*; *see, e.g.*, Harmon v. United States, 101 F.3d 574 (8th Cir. 1996); Zabel v. Schroeder Oil, Inc. (In re Zabel), 249 B.R. 764 (Bankr. E.D. Wis. 2000).

Because of the limited duration of a Chapter 12 plan, which may never last longer than five years, § 1222(b)(5) and (9) permits the plan to cure any pre-petition defaults on long-term debts and to provide for the payment of any long-term secured claims over a period exceeding the duration of the plan.[76]

[C] Duration of Chapter 12 Plans

In most cases, a Chapter 12 plan must last a minimum of three years, and with court approval may be extended up to five years for good cause. The rare Chapter 12 debtor, who is able to pay his creditors' claims in full in less than three years, may obtain confirmation of a plan for whatever shorter period is necessary to fully satisfy his creditors claims.[77] However, most Chapter 12 debtors are unable to pay their creditors in full in less then three years. These debtors must submit all of their projected disposable income for three years for payments to creditors under the plan.[78] The plan may be extended for up to five years, for cause, with court approval.[79]

Chapter 12 also permits payments to secured creditors to extend beyond the duration of the plan, and thus beyond the three-or five-year limit, without any special court approval.[80] This permits family farmers and family fishermen to amortize secured claims over an extended period. This is particularly important with respect to real estate mortgages and claims secured by expensive farm implements. However, the proposed payment period may not be extended over such a long period that the creditor involved is left inadequately protected. If the useful economic life of the collateral is only seven years, extending the payment period for ten years, after the collateral is worthless, would deprive the creditor of its right to remain adequately protected.

[D] Chapter 12 Treatment of Priority Claims

Like Chapter 13, Chapter 12 also requires full payment of priority claims.[81] One exception is made for governmental claims that arise as a result of the sale, transfer, exchange or other disposition of any of the debtor's farming assets.[82] This will have its biggest impact on § 507(a)(8) income tax claims that arise from the sale of farm commodities, which are no longer entitled to automatic priority in Chapter 12, and the requirement of full payment that accompanies it.[83] An additional exception was added,

[76] Bankruptcy Code § 1222(b)(9).

[77] Bankruptcy Code § 1225(b)(1)(A).

[78] Bankruptcy Code § 1225(B)(1)(B).

[79] Bankruptcy Code § 1222(c).

[80] Bankruptcy Code § 1222(b)(9).

[81] Bankruptcy Code § 1222(a)(2).

[82] Bankruptcy Code § 1222(a)(2)(A).

[83] Neil E. Harl, *Major Developments in Chapter 12 Bankruptcy*, 16 Agric. L. Dig. 57, 58 (2005).

consistent with changes made to Chapter 13, for support claims that have previously been assigned to governmental agencies.[84] But this exception applies only if the plan provides for payment of all of the debtor's disposable income for a five-year period.[85]

[E] Chapter 12 Treatment of Unsecured Claims

Unsecured claims are given essentially the same treatment in Chapter 12 as they are in Chapter 13. The plan's treatment of unsecured claims is subject to two tests: the best interests of creditors test and the disposable income test.

[1] Best Interests of Creditors

The "best interest of creditors" test requires that the plan payments, when reduced to their present value, must be at least equal the Chapter 7 liquidation value of the unsecured claims.[86] Thus, unsecured creditors must receive what they would have received in a liquidation case, together with interest to compensate them for the delay in receiving payment under the plan. The best interests test thus operates the same way in Chapter 12 as it does in Chapters 11 and 13.[87]

For example, if a $10,000 unsecured claim has a liquidation value of $3,000 — that is, if in a Chapter 7 proceeding, the creditor would have received $3,000 — the debtor's Chapter 12 plan must provide for payments *worth* $3,000 to the creditor. Because the payments will most likely be distributed over time, the total actually paid must be more than $3,000 to compensate the creditor for the delay in receiving payment.[88] In other words, the payments need to include an interest component.[89]

The rate of interest that Chapter 12 debtors must pay to ensure that unsecured creditors receive the liquidation value of their claims is probably the same as that required to be paid in Chapter 13 cases. Some courts have relied on the Supreme Court's 2004 decision in *Till v. SCS Credit Corp.*,[90] regarding a similar issue on the appropriate rate of interest required to be paid to holder of secured claims under § 1325(a)(5).[91] If so, it must be

---

[84] Bankruptcy Code § 1322(a)(4).

[85] Bankruptcy Code § 1322(a)(4).

[86] Bankruptcy Code § 1225(a)(4).

[87] *See* § 18.08[E][1] Best Interests of Creditors, *supra*.

[88] *See* § 1.05[B][29] Present Value, *supra*.

[89] *E.g.*, In re Hansen, 77 B.R. 722 (Bankr. D.N.D. 1987); *see* Robert J. Kressel, *Calculating the Present Value of Deferred Payments Under a Chapter 12 Plan: A New Twist to an Old Problem*, 62 Am. Bankr. L.J. 313 (1988).

[90] 541 U.S. 465 (2004) (present value for secured claims under § 1325(a)(5)).

[91] *See, e.g.*, In re Bivens, 317 B.R. 755 (Bankr. N D. Ill. 2004); *see* Carmen H. Lonstein & Steven A. Domanowski, *Payment of Post-petition Interest to Unsecured Creditors: Federal Judgment Rate Versus Contract Rate*, 12 Am. Bankr. Inst. L. Rev. 421 (2004); *see generally* § 18.08[F][4][b] Payments Equivalent to Amount of Secured Claim, *supra*.

based on the prime interest rate, together with whatever upward adjustment is necessary to reflect the creditor's risk of non-payment. However, a few courts have rejected the use of the *Till* standard with respect to the best interests test, based partially on *Till*'s status as a plurality decision, and its applicability to secured rather than unsecured claims. These courts continue to require the use of whatever method they deployed before *Till* to pick the appropriate rate of interest, usually based on the market rate that would apply to a similar loan.[92]

[2] Projected Disposable Income[93]

The second test is the "projected disposable income" test.[94] It applies only if the plan does not provide for full payment of claims of unsecured creditors.[95] But as a practical matter, full payment is usually not feasible, making it necessary for virtually all Chapter 12 plans to comply with the disposable income test.

After the 2005 Amendments, Chapter 12's projected disposable income test is considerably different from the projected disposable income test applicable to many Chapter 13 debtors. In Chapter 13, debtors with household incomes above their state's median are required to submit the amount of their income that is available, after subtracting a set of presumed and actual expenses, to distribute to unsecured creditors.[96]

In Chapter 12, the amount required to be submitted for distribution to creditors depends on a calculation of the debtor's actual projected disposable income, based on whatever income the debtor has available after deducting amounts "reasonably necessary to be expended" for the support of the debtor and his dependents; amounts that must be paid to satisfy a domestic support obligation; and amounts that are necessary for the continuation, preservation, and operation of the debtor's farming or fishing business.[97] This is similar to the projected disposable income test that was used in Chapter 13 before BAPCPA's means testing rules were implemented and to the test that still applies to Chapter 13 debtors whose household income is below the applicable state median.[98]

Alternatively, the plan can be confirmed if "the value of the property to be distributed under the plan . . . is not less than the debtor's projected

---

[92] In re Cook, 322 B.R. 336, 345 (Bankr. N.D. Ohio 2005) (coerced loan approach based on current market interest rates for loans in similar situations). *Cf.* In re American HomePatient, Inc., 420 F.3d 559 (6th Cir. 2005) (applying § 1129(a)(5)); *see generally* § 8.09[F][4][b] Payments Equivalent to Amount of Secured Claim, *infra.*

[93] Melanie Fisher, Note, *Disposable Income Determination: Challenges in the Chapter 12 Family Farmer Context*, 18 J. Corp. L. 713 (1993).

[94] Bankruptcy Code § 1225(b)(1)(A).

[95] Bankruptcy Code § 1225(b)(1)(B).

[96] *See* § 18.08[E][2] Debtor's Projected Disposable Income, *supra.*

[97] Bankruptcy Code § 1225(b)(2).

[98] *See* § 18.08[E][2][b] Disposable Income for Debtors with Income Below the State Median, *supra.*

disposable income [for the duration of the plan]."[99] It is not entirely clear what this new language adds, other than perhaps to prevent the court from retroactively assessing the amount of the debtor's disposable income in cases where the "debtor's actual disposable income exceeds the projected disposable income on which the plan was based."[100]

[F] Secured Claims in Chapter 12[101]

Secured claims are given favorable treatment in other bankruptcy proceedings, and Chapter 12 is no exception. Secured claims are required to be paid in full, with compensation for any delay in receiving payment, to assure that the creditor receives the present value of its secured claim.[102] The interest rate required to be paid on secured claims is based on the same prime-plus formula adopted by the Supreme Court's plurality decision in *Till v. SCS Credit Corp.*[103] Liens on the debtor's property must remain in place until payments are completed.[104] The only exceptions are when the debtor surrenders the collateral to the secured creditor[105] or where the creditor acquiesces to the debtor's plan and accepts something less from the debtor.[106]

Chapter 12 differs from Chapter 13 by permitting secured claims to be paid beyond the three-to five-year duration of the plan.[107] Thus, the plan can provide for amortization of secured claims over long-term periods, provided the payments otherwise satisfy the cramdown standards of § 1225(a)(5)(B). For example, a claim secured by the debtor's combine[108] could be extended to be payable over seven years, even though the terms of the plan were to last only five years, and even though the contract with the creditor called for payments for only four more years.

---

[99] Bankruptcy Code § 1225(b)(1)(C).

[100] 8 Collier on Bankruptcy ¶ 1225.04, at 1225–26 to 30 (Alan A. Resnick & Henry J. Sommer eds., 15th rev. ed. 2006).

[101] William E. Callahan, Jr., Note, Dewsnup v. Timm *and* Nobelman v. American Savings Bank*: The Strip Down of Liens in Chapter 12 and Chapter 13 Bankruptcies*, 50 Wash. & Lee L. Rev. 405 (1993).

[102] Bankruptcy Code § 1225(a)(5)(B)(ii); *see* Thomas O. Depperschmidt & Nancy H. Kratzke, *The Search for the Proper Interest Rate Under Chapter 12 (Family Farmer Bankruptcy Act)*, 67 N.D. L. Rev. 455 (1991); Robert J. Kressel, *Calculating the Present Value of Deferred Payments Under a Chapter 12 Plan: A New Twist to an Old Problem*, 62 Am. Bankr. L.J. 313 (1988).

[103] 541 U.S. 465 (2004); *see* In re Torelli, 338 B.R. 390 (Bankr. E.D. Ark. 2006); *see generally* § 18.08[F][4][b] Payments Equivalent to Amount of Secured Claim, *supra*.

[104] Bankruptcy Code § 1225(a)(5)(B)(i).

[105] Bankruptcy Code § 1225(a)(5)(C).

[106] Bankruptcy Code § 1225(a)(5)(A).

[107] Bankruptcy Code § 1222(b)(9); *see* In re Dunning, 77 B.R. 789 (Bankr. D. Mont. 1987); Travelers Ins. Co. v Bullington, 89 B.R. 1010 (M.D. Ga. 1988), *aff'd*, 878 F.2d 345 (11th Cir. 1989).

[108] Farm combines are gigantic pieces of equipment. They sell for as much as $150,000.

§ 20.08 Confirmation of Chapter 12 Plans

In addition to the basic requirements concerning payment of claims, Chapter 12 plans are subject to most of the same requirements as Chapter 13 plans. The plan must comply with the mandatory provisions of Chapter 12 and with other applicable provisions of the Bankruptcy Code.[109] The debtor must have paid the filing fee and any other fees required by law or by the plan.[110] This now explicitly includes any domestic support obligations that became payable after the debtor's petition was filed.[111] Thus, deadbeat moms and dads are unable to evade making support payments while their cases are pending. In addition, as with Chapter 13 plans, the plan must have been proposed in good faith and not by any means otherwise legally forbidden.[112]

The plan must be feasible.[113] As with Chapter 13 plans involving individual debtors engaged in business, determining the feasibility of a Chapter 12 plan may be difficult. Plans based on unrealistic financial projections will not be confirmed.[114] The debtor must be able to supply the court with some reasonable assurances that the terms of the plan can be performed.[115] Likewise, plans based on unrealistic projection for the number of workers capable of operating the business, should not be confirmed.[116]

§ 20.09 Effect of Confirmation of Chapter 12 Plan

Confirmation of a plan binds the debtor, each creditor, and any equity security holders or partners of the debtor who are provided for in the plan, regardless of whether they have objected to the plan, accepted the plan, or rejected the plan.[117] Thus, the plan has res judicata effect on the parties as to all matters that were litigated or that might have been litigated in connection with obtaining confirmation of the plan.

Unless the plan provides otherwise, confirmation of a plan operates to vest all of the estate's property back in the debtor.[118] Of course, confirmation requirements with respect to claims of secured creditors' rights are

---

[109] Bankruptcy Code § 1225(a)(1).

[110] Bankruptcy Code § 1225(a)(1).

[111] Bankruptcy Code § 1325(a)(7).

[112] Bankruptcy Code § 1225(a)(1).

[113] Bankruptcy Code § 1225(a)(1); *see* Janet A. Flaccus & Bruce L. Dixon, *New Bankruptcy Chapter 12: A Computer Analysis of If and When a Farmer Can Successfully Reorganize*, 41 Ark. L. Rev. 263 (1988).

[114] *E.g.*, In re Torelli, 338 B.R. 390 (Bankr. E.D. Ark. 2006).

[115] In re Ames, 973 F.2d 849 (10th Cir. 1992), *cert. denied,* 507 U.S. 912 (1993); In re Clark, 288 B.R. 237 (Bankr. D. Kan. 2003).

[116] *E.g.*, In re Gough, 190 B.R. 455 (Bankr. M.D. Fla. 1995) (financial projections based on tripling citrus crop yield on expanded acreage without increase in labor force).

[117] Bankruptcy Code § 1227(a).

[118] Bankruptcy Code § 1227(b).

likely to require the plan to provide that secured creditors will retain their liens until full satisfaction of their secured claims.[119]

Like Chapter 13 plans, confirmation of a Chapter 12 plan does not automatically discharge the debtor. Instead, the debtor does not receive its discharge until completion of the terms of his plan.[120] Debtors who are unable to fulfill the terms of their plans due to circumstances beyond their control can receive a hardship discharge.[121] The availability of a hardship discharge is conditioned on the debtor's having already provided unsecured creditors with payments that are equivalent to what they would have received in a liquidation case, and upon the impracticability of modifying the plan.[122] The scope of a Chapter 12 discharge is discussed elsewhere.[123]

§ 20.10 Modification of Chapter 12 Plans

Debtors' plans are not set in stone. The debtor's proposed plan may always be modified prior to confirmation. After confirmation, the plan may still be modified, but court confirmation is required before the proposed modification takes effect.

[A] Modification Prior to Confirmation

Occasionally, it becomes necessary to modify a proposed plan before it has been confirmed. This usually occurs in response to the court's refusal to confirm the plan or because of the debtor's recognition that the plan is unlikely to be confirmed. The debtor is given a virtually unlimited right to modify the plan, provided that the modification does not violate any of the requirements for a plan.[124]

Once modified, the modified plan becomes "the plan."[125] In other words, for purposes of confirmation and other matters, it is the final version of the plan that controls.

[B] Modification After Confirmation

The plan may also be modified after confirmation. The rules regarding modification of the plan after confirmation depart somewhat from the principle that Chapter 12 cases must be entirely voluntary. Chapter 12 cannot be commenced involuntarily by a creditor;[126] nor may a creditor file a plan.[127] However, unsecured creditors and the standing trustee have the

---

[119] Bankruptcy Code § 1225(a)(5)(B)(i).

[120] Bankruptcy Code § 1228(a).

[121] Bankruptcy Code § 1228(b).

[122] Bankruptcy Code § 1228(b).

[123] *See* § 13.07 Chapter 12 Discharge, *supra*.

[124] Bankruptcy Code § 1223(a).

[125] Bankruptcy Code § 1223(b).

[126] Bankruptcy Code § 303(a).

[127] Bankruptcy Code § 1221.

right to propose modifications of the plan after confirmation.[128] To this rather limited extent, a Chapter 12 debtor may be forced into a plan he does not want — or, more precisely, a Chapter 12 debtor may be forced to choose between accepting and funding an unwanted plan, converting to Chapter 7, or dismissing the case altogether.[129]

A modification may be proposed by the debtor, an unsecured creditor, or the trustee at any time after confirmation but before completion of payments. The modification may (i) increase or decrease payments, (ii) extend or reduce the time for payments, or (iii) alter the distribution to a creditor to the extent necessary to take account of payments made outside the plan.[130]

To be confirmed, the plan must comply with the usual requirements.[131] However, because § 1229 conspicuously fails to refer to § 1225(b), a modified plans does not appear to be required to comply with the "disposable income" requirements of that section. Despite this, the 2005 Amendments specify that the plan may not be modified on the request of a creditor or the trustee "based on an increase in the debtor's disposable income, to increase the amount of payments to unsecured creditors required for *a particular month* so that the aggregate of such payments exceeds the debtors's disposable income for such month."[132] Likewise, the 2005 Amendments prohibit creditors or the trustee from obtaining an amendment during the final year of the plan, if the amendment would leave the debtor with "insufficient funds to carry on the farming operation after the plan is completed."[133] These provisions prevent creditors, or the trustee, from taking opportunistic advantage of temporary fluctuations in the debtor's income which make it seem like an adjustment to the plan is appropriate.

Any secured creditor who accepted or rejected the original plan is deemed to have accepted or rejected the modified plan, unless (i) the modification changes the creditor's rights, and (ii) the creditor changes its previous acceptance or rejection.[134] Since unsecured creditors do not vote on the plan, their view of the modified plan is irrelevant. The modified plan becomes "the plan," unless it is disapproved after notice and an opportunity for a hearing.[135]

---

[128] Bankruptcy Code § 1229(a).

[129] The debtor always has the right to convert to Chapter 7 and nearly always has the right to voluntarily dismiss the case. Bankruptcy Code § 1208(a), (b).

[130] Bankruptcy Code § 1229(a).

[131] Bankruptcy Code § 1229(b), (c).

[132] Bankruptcy Code § 1229(d)(2).

[133] Bankruptcy Code § 1229(d)(3).

[134] Bankruptcy Code § 1223(c).

[135] Bankruptcy Code § 1229(b)(2).

§ 20.11 Revocation of Chapter 12 Plan Confirmation

The rules regarding revocation of an order of confirmation must inevitably balance the interest of fairness to creditors with the interest of finality to the debtors and others. Thus, the timing and the substantive basis for revocation are both limited. Upon the request of a party in interest and after notice and an opportunity for a hearing, the court may revoke confirmation if it was procured by fraud. The request must be made within 180 days after the date the order of confirmation was entered.[136]

The potential grounds for revocation of confirmation are limited to proving that confirmation was procured through fraud.[137] Creditor confusion about the plan is not a sufficient basis to have confirmation revoked.[138]

If the order of confirmation is revoked, the court may either convert or dismiss the case under § 1207,[139] or if the debtor submits a modified plan, that modified plan may be confirmed.[140] If the modified plan is confirmed, the case continues under the new plan.

---

[136] Bankruptcy Code § 1230(a).

[137] Bankruptcy Code § 1230(a).

[138] In re Courson, 243 B.R. 288 (Bankr. E.D. Tex. 1999).

[139] Bankruptcy Code § 1230(b).

[140] Bankruptcy Code § 1230(b).

Chapter 21

Role of Professionals in Bankruptcy Proceedings

§ 21.01 Professionals in Bankruptcy Cases

Bankruptcy matters usually involve at least a few professional persons, such as lawyers, accountants, and appraisers. The simplest no-asset consumer case nearly always involves at least a lawyer for the debtor, even though a few hearty souls go into bankruptcy without one, possibly with the assistance of an unlicensed "petition preparer."[1] More complicated consumer cases involve a lawyer for the debtor, the trustee, and perhaps for a few secured creditors. In complex business cases there may be scores of lawyers for the debtor-in-possession, a creditors' committee, an equity security holders' committee, secured creditors, and unsecured creditors. There may also be accountants, appraisers, auctioneers, investment bankers, real estate agents, and other professionals whose assistance is necessary or at least useful to the proceeding. Their advice is rarely cheap.[2] Moreover, it would be impossible to conduct a difficult bankruptcy proceeding without people whose experience and expertise are sufficient to meet the challenges involved.

It is also necessary, when considering the proper role of a lawyer or other professional involved in a bankruptcy case, to deal with potential conflicts of interest that the professional may have. Especially given the fees demanded, it is imperative that the estate be provided with a full equivalent value in services. Part of that value is impartiality as between the various claimants against the estate. Ideally, a professional who represents the estate should be wholly committed to pursuing the interests of the estate (and thus, indirectly, the interests of creditors as a whole). It is for this, as well as knowledge and experience, that the professional is being paid from funds that, after all, belong to the creditors.

---

[1] Bankruptcy Code § 110(a)(1).

[2] Alexander L. Paskay & Frances Pilaro Wolstenholme, *Chapter 11: A Growing Cash Cow, Some Thoughts on How to Rein in the System*, 1 Am. Bankr. Inst. L. Rev. 331 (1993); Robert M. Lawless & Stephen P. Ferris, *Professional Fees and Other Direct Costs in Chapter 7 Business Liquidations*, 75 Wash U. L.Q. 1207 (1997); Robert M. Lawless et al., *A Glimpse at Professional Fees and Other Direct Costs in Small Firm Bankruptcies*, 1994 U. Ill. L. Rev. 847. *See also*, Daryl M. Guffey & William T. Moore, *Direct Bankruptcy Costs: Evidence from the Trucking Industry*, 26 Fin. Rev. 223 (1991); Michelle J. White, *Bankruptcy Costs and the New Bankruptcy Code*, 38 J. Fin. 477 (1983); Karen Hopper Wruck, *Financial Distress, Reorganization, and Organizational Efficiency*, 27 J. Fin Econ. 419 (1990); Elizabeth Warren & Jay Lawrence Westbrook, *Financial Characteristics of Businesses in Bankruptcy*, 73 Am. Bankr. L.J. 499 (1999).

For these reasons, the Bankruptcy Code regulates the employment of professionals whose fees are paid as administrative expense claims from the debtor's estate. The bankruptcy court must approve the employment of any professional hired by the trustee, the debtor-in-possession, a creditors' committee, or an equity security holders' committee. Professionals with conflicts of interest are disqualified from serving in these roles. Moreover, the fees professionals charge must be approved by the court before they may be paid.

§ 21.02 Employment of Professionals

The Bankruptcy Code imposes restrictions on the employment of professional persons whose fees are paid by the debtor's estate. Because professional's fees are entitled to administrative expense priority, reducing the amount that is otherwise available to pay pre-petition creditors, they can overwhelm the debtor's estate and transform Chapter 11 cases in particular into what one author characterized as a "feast for lawyers"[3] rather than a method of preserving the value of the debtor for the benefit of creditors.

Section 327 authorizes the trustee or debtor-in-possession to employ attorneys, accounts, appraisers, auctioneers, or other professional persons only after obtaining prior court approval.[4] Although the statute does not specify a standard, the test for whether the court should approve the estate's engagement of a professional is whether the person is "reasonably necessary" to assist the debtor or the trustee in administering the estate.[5] Further, professionals who are hired to provide services to the estate must not have conflicts of interest that would impair their ability to provide even-handed assistance to the estate for the benefit of all creditors.[6]

[A] Prior Court Approval[7]

Section 327 requires professionals to obtain prior bankruptcy court approval before they may be employed by the trustee or the debtor-in-possession.[8] Section 1103 similarly requires creditors' committees to obtain court approval to hire attorneys, accountants or other agents.[9] Bankruptcy

---

[3] Sol Stein, A Feast for Lawyers — Inside Chapter 11: An Expose (1989).

[4] Bankruptcy Code § 327(a). Although the statutory language refers only to the trustee, it applies with equal force to professionals hired by a debtor-in-possession. *E.g.*, In re Prince, 40 F.3d 356, 360 & n.2 (11th Cir. 1994).

[5] *E.g.*, In re Computer Learning Centers, Inc., 272 B.R. 897, 903 (Bankr. E.D. Va. 2001).

[6] Bankruptcy Code § 327(a). "Disinterested" means neutral; this differs from "uninterested" which means indifferent.

[7] Anthony Collins, Jr., Comment, *A Change of Disposition: The Evolving Perception of Pre-approval Requirements under 11 U.S.C. 327*, 28 J. Legal Prof. 133 (2003).

[8] Bankruptcy Code § 327(a); *see* In re Singson, 41 F.3d 316, 319 (7th Cir. 1994); In re Albrecht, 245 B.R. 666 (B.A.P. 10th Cir. 2000); In re Anicom, Inc., 273 B.R. 756, 761 (Bankr. N.D. Ill. 2002).

[9] Bankruptcy Code § 1103(a).

Rule 2014 specifies the procedure for obtaining court approval to hire these professionals.[10] It requires the professional to file an application with the court and to transmit the application to the United States Trustee. The application must specify:

- the name of the person to be employed;
- the facts showing the necessity for her employment;
- the reasons for her selection;
- the professional services she will render;
- any proposed arrangement for her compensation; and
- the person's connection with the debtor, creditors, and other parties in interest as well as with their attorneys and accountants or with the United States Trustee or any person employed by the United States Trustee.[11]

If a professional person is hired and works without prior court approval she may lose her right to compensation for her services, and may be compelled to disgorge any fees she received.[12]

[1] Employment of Professionals Must be Reasonably Necessary

The court should approve employment of a professional person if that person's skills and expertise are reasonably necessary for the effective administration of the estate. In most cases this is a fairly easy standard to apply. There is little dispute over whether it is reasonably necessary for a Chapter 11 debtor to engage an attorney or an accountant to assist with the case, though in some cases the court might question whether the debtor needs professional assistance with the task involved and whether the task might be performed by other employees. On rare occasions, the specific professional sought to be hired may be found unqualified to handle the matter.[13] Still, the trustee or debtor-in-possession must explain its reasons both for seeking to employ a professional for the task involved and for selecting the particular person she wishes to employ.[14]

One recurring point of contention is whether a trustee may employ a professional, such as an attorney, to perform tasks that might be an

[10] Fed. R. Bankr. P. 2014(a). Although the text of the rule refers only to the trustee and to a creditors' committee, a Chapter 11 debtor-in-possession has all of the rights, powers, and duties of a trustee. Bankruptcy Code § 1107(a).

[11] Fed. R. Bankr. P. 2014(a).

[12] *E.g.*, In re Federated Dep't Stores, Inc., 44 F.3d 1310 (6th Cir. 1995); *see* Stephen R. Grensky, *The Problem Presented by Professionals Who Fail to Obtain Prior Court Approval of Their Employment or Nunc Pro Tunc Est Bunc*, 62 Am. Bankr. L.J. 185 (1988).

[13] *See* In re Crayton, 192 B.R. 970 (B.A.P. 9th Cir. 1996) (attorney who was unqualified and incompetent to represent a Chapter 11 debtor was disciplined and required to disgorge fees he had charged).

[14] Fed. R. Bankr. P. 2014(a); *see* In re Computer Learning Centers, Inc., 272 B.R. 897 (Bankr. E.D. Va. 2001).

inherent part of the trustee's ministerial duties. For example, trustees are not usually permitted to employ an attorney or accountant to review the debtor's petition and schedules, unless the debtor's case is unusually complex. Nor may trustees employ professionals to prepare and distribute checks to creditors.[15] On the other hand, trustees are usually permitted to engage attorneys to pursue litigation to recover assets for the estate, to deny the debtor's discharge, or to litigate objections to claims, even though the trustee might herself be a licensed attorney and otherwise capable of performing these tasks.

The issue in these disputes is that the professional fees that are charged by the trustee's lawyer or accountant for her professional services transcend the compensation that otherwise is permitted to be paid to the trustee. Permitting the trustee to hire a lawyer, sometimes an attorney in the trustee's own law firm, might permit the trustee to recover more fees than are otherwise permitted by § 326 for performing the trustee's routine duties.

The trustee's compensation as trustee is based on a percentage of the amount that the trustee distributes to creditors.[16] In Chapter 7 cases, the trustee can receive up to 25% of the first $5,000, 10% of amounts between $5,000 and $50,000, 5% of amounts between $50,000 and $1 million, and 3% of amounts in excess of $1 million of the amounts that she distributes to creditors.[17] Amounts paid to professionals are above these limits and might benefit the trustee if the trustee either wishes to act as her own lawyer in the case, or if she wishes to employ her own law firm as the attorney for the estate.

[2] Nunc Pro Tunc Approval

Even though prior approval is normally required, courts sometimes approve the employment of professionals "nunc pro tunc" (now for then) — after they have been employed and rendered services to the estate without receiving prior court approval. Although this practice undercuts the requirement of prior court approval, some courts find it difficult to turn their backs on attorneys and other professionals whose services benefit the estate.[18] These courts, however, may refuse to authorize employment nunc pro tunc to permit the professional to receive compensation, unless the professional's failure to comply with § 327(a) was due to extraordinary circumstances.[19] In the view of some courts, mere negligence is not enough of an extraordinary circumstance to warrant nun pro tunc approval.[20]

---

[15] *E.g.*, In re Guterl Special Steel Corp., 316 B.R. 843, 861 (Bankr. D. Pa. 2004).

[16] Bankruptcy Code § 326(a).

[17] Unlike many other dollar amounts in the Bankruptcy Code, these thresholds are not automatically adjusted every three years to keep up with inflation.

[18] *See* In re Mehdipour, 202 B.R. 474 (B.A.P. 9th Cir. 1996).

[19] *See* In re THC Fin. Corp., 837 F.2d 389 (9th Cir. 1988).

[20] *E.g.*, In re Jarvis, 53 F.3d 416 (1st Cir. 1995); *see* Binswanger Cos. v. Merry-Go-Round Enters., 258 B.R. 608 (D. Md. 2001) (discussing conflicting authorities); *see also* In re Twinton Properties P'ship, 27 B.R. 817 (Bankr. M.D. Tenn. 1983), *aff'd,* 33 B.R. 111 (M.D. Tenn 1983).

Other courts take a more flexible approach and approve late applications for approval even where the professional's failure to seek timely authorization to be hired was due to simple negligence.[21]

Court approval of the professional's employment is not the same as court approval of the professional's fees. As explained below, §§ 328 and 330 impose further limits on the compensation of these professionals, whose fee applications must be approved separately.[22]

[B] Meaning of Professional Persons

Professionals whose employment must be approved by the court are those who take a central role in the administration of the estate and in the bankruptcy proceeding generally.[23] This includes attorneys for the trustee or the debtor-in-possession, as well as accountants, appraisers, and investment bankers engaged to assist with the reorganization process.

Other professionals, whose services would have been necessary even if a bankruptcy petition had not been filed, are not among those whose engagement must be approved.[24] Thus a Chapter 11 debtor-in-possession need not seek court approval to keep its in-house lawyers and accountants on the payroll. Section 327(b) makes this clear: "[I]f the debtor has regularly employed attorneys, accounts, or other professionals on salary, the trustee may retain or replace such professional persons if necessary in the operation of the business."[25] The Code does not contemplate court approval of these routine employment decisions that are made in the ordinary course of the debtor's operations.[26]

Despite this, anyone who might be regarded as a professional hired to assist with the reorganization should seek court approval before providing services to a trustee, a debtor-in-possession, or a creditors' committee. Otherwise, she runs the risk that her engagement will later be challenged as one that should have been approved by the court under § 327. Failing to obtain approval in advance may lead the court to deny the professional the right to any fees and to require him to disgorge any fees that she had been paid without court approval.

---

[21] *E.g.*, In re Triangle Chems. Inc., 697 F.2d 1280 (5th Cir. 1983); In re THC Fin. Corp., 837 F.2d 389 (9th Cir. 1988).

[22] *See* § 21.03 Professionals' Fees, *supra*.

[23] *E.g.*, In re D'Lites of America, 108 B.R. 352 (N.D. Ga. 1989).

[24] In re Johns-Manville Corp., 60 B.R. 612, 620–21 (Bankr. S.D.N.Y. 1986) (lobbyists hired in the ordinary course of the debtor's business).

[25] Bankruptcy Code § 327(b).

[26] *See generally* In re Yuba Westgold, Inc., 157 B.R. 869 (Bankr. N.D. Iowa 1993).

[C] Conflicts of Interest[27]

As indicated above, professionals hired by the trustee or a debtor-in-possession must have no conflict of interest with the interests of the estate. Section 327 requires that professionals neither hold or represent an interest adverse to the estate *and* be "disinterested."[28] Despite the statutory text, which plainly imposes a two-pronged test, courts often regard the "no adverse interest" and the "disinterested" tests as redundant.[29]

Section 101(14) defines a "disinterested person" as a person who:

> (A) is not a creditor, an equity security holder, or an insider;
>
> (B) is not and was not, within 2 years before the date of the filing of the petition, a director, officer, or employee of the debtor; and
>
> (C) does not have an interest materially adverse to the interest of the estate or of any class of creditors or equity security holders, by reason of any direct or indirect relationship to, connection with, or interest in, the debtor, or for any other reason.[30]

Thus, not surprisingly, creditors, owners, or their insiders may not be engaged as attorneys for the trustee or for the debtor-in-possession. This is frequently a problem in Chapter 11 cases because the law firm that seeks to represent the debtor-in-possession may be the same firm that represented the debtor prior to the case, either in connection with the debtor's efforts to negotiate a workout with its creditors or in connection with other matters. The debtor may owe legal fees to the firm, or may have paid those bills shortly before filing its petition and thus have made a preferential transfer to the firm.[31] The debtor-in-possession has a duty to recover that preference; its lawyers have an equal interest in leaving it be. Thus, a law

---

[27] John D. Ayer et al., *Ethics: Is Disinterestedness Still a Viable Concept? A Discussion*, 5 Am. Bankr. Inst. L. Rev. 201 (1997); Kurt F. Gwynne, *Intra-committee Conflicts, Multiple Creditors' Committees, Altering Committee Membership and Other Alternatives for Ensuring Adequate Representation under Section 1102 of the Bankruptcy Code*, 14 Am. Bankr. Inst. L. Rev. 109 (2006); Nancy B. Rapoport, Enron*and the New Disinterestedness — The Foxes Are Guarding the Henhouse*, 13 Am. Bankr. Inst. L. Rev. 521 (2005); Nancy B. Rapoport, *Turning and Turning in the Widening Gyre: The Problem of Potential Conflicts of Interest in Bankruptcy*, 26 Conn. L. Rev. 913 (1994); Nancy B. Rapoport, *The Intractable Problem of Bankruptcy Ethics: Square Peg, Round Hole*, 30 Hofstra L. Rev. 977 (2002); Grald K. Smith, *Standards for the Employment of Professionals in Bankruptcy Cases: A Response to Professor Zywicki's "Case for Retaining the Disinterestedness Requirement for Debtor in Possession's Professionals,* 18 Miss. C. L. Rev. 327 (1998); Todd J. Zywicki, *Mend It. Don't End It: The Case for Retaining the Disinterestedness Requirement for Debtor in Possession's Professionals*, 18 Miss. C. L. Rev. 291 (1998).

[28] Bankruptcy Code § 327(a).

[29] *E.g.*, In re Martin, 817 F.2d 175, 179 n.40 (1st Cir.1987); In re Filene's Basement, 239 B.R. 850, 857 (Bankr. D. Mass. 1999).

[30] Bankruptcy Code § 101(14).

[31] Jay Lawrence Westbrook, *Fees and Inherent Conflicts of Interest*, 1 Am. Bankr. Inst. L. Rev. 287 (1993); Nancy B. Rapoport, *Turning and Turning in the Widening Gyre: The Problem of Potential Conflicts of Interest in Bankruptcy*, 26 Conn. L. Rev. 913, 928–30 (1994); *see generally* Chapter 15, Avoidable Preferences, *supra*.

firm that represented the debtor before the petition is filed may find it necessary to waive any claim it has against the debtor or forego the opportunity to represent the debtor in the bankruptcy case.[32]

At first blush § 1107 appears to address this issue. It specifies that "a person is not disqualified for employment under section 327 . . . by a debtor in possession solely because of such person's employment by or representation of the debtor before the commencement of the case."[33] A court might use this language to permit law firms to represent the debtor-in-possession even though they are owed fees for pre-petition services. However, the statutory language speaks only to the debtor's prior employment of the attorney or other professional, it does not address the effect of a claim held by the professional that prevents it from being disinterested.[34] Courts that have carefully considered the relationship between §§ 327 and 1107 have adhered to the traditional view that an attorney who has a claim against the debtor may not serve as the debtor's counsel.[35]

Professionals are also disqualified if they represent an interest that is adverse to the estate.[36] This might suggest that an attorney (or a firm) that represents one of the debtor's creditors may not be employed as debtor's counsel or to serve as any other professional in the debtor's case. However § 327(c) provides that creditors' attorneys are not automatically disqualified from employment as a professional for the estate.[37] Creditors' attorneys are disqualified only if another creditor objects and if the court finds that "there is an actual conflict of interest."[38]

In some cases, the creditor's claim is so small compared to those of other more active creditors, that the attorney's representation of the debtor would not involve an actual conflict. If the creditor's claim is de minimis, or if the lawyer's firm represents the creditor in matters unrelated to the bankruptcy case, the court might find that there is no actual conflict. Where the proposed debtor's attorney represents a creditor in an unrelated matter, no actual conflict may occur, though the attorney must disclose the representation. She may also find it necessary to obtain everyone's consent to, and the court's approval of, the dual representation as a means of avoiding professional discipline.[39]

---

32 Patti Williams, Comment, *Bankruptcy Code Section 327(a) — New Interpretation Forces Attorneys to Waive Fees or Wave Good-bye to Clients*, 53 Mo. L. Rev. 309 (1988).

33 Bankruptcy Code § 1107(b).

34 *E.g.*, In re Microwave Products of America, Inc., 94 B.R. 971, 974–75 (Bankr. W.D. Tenn. 1989); In re Viking Ranches, Inc., 89 B.R. 113, 115 (C.D. Cal. 1988).

35 In re LKM Indus., Inc., 252 B.R. 589 (Bankr. D. Mass. 2000).

36 Bankruptcy Code § 327(a).

37 Bankruptcy Code § 327(c).

38 Bankruptcy Code § 327(c).

39 Regina S. Kelbon et al., *Conflicts, The Appointment of "Professionals," and Fiduciary Duties of Major Parties in Chapter 11*, 8 Bankr. Dev. J. 349 (1991); William I. Kohn & Michael P. Shuster, *Deciphering Conflicts of Interest in Bankruptcy Representation*, 98 Com. L.J. 127 (1993).

Another recurring issue is whether an attorney is disqualified from representing multiple debtors in cases involving related entities. The most obvious example involves representing an individual debtor and a corporation the individual owns in simultaneous Chapter 11 reorganization proceedings involving both.[40] Thus, if Harlan Wolff, the president and sole shareholder of Titanic Corporation, files his own Chapter 11 case while Titanic's separate Chapter 11 case is pending, it might appear to make sense for the same attorney to represent both Wolff and Titanic Corporation in their respective bankruptcy cases. A single attorney is likely to be familiar with the financial circumstances that led to the financial difficulties of both debtors, whose finances are likely to be intertwined with one another at least to some extent. Requiring these debtors to acquire separate counsel will likely lead to an expensive duplication of efforts that will reduce the amount available to distribute to their creditors.

On the other hand, the corporation may have claims against Wolff, based on his mismanagement of the corporation, or on his receipt of preferential or other payments that Titanic might wish to recover.[41] Further, it may develop that a trustee should be appointed in the Titanic case, or that Titanic can only survive if Wolff's stock in the company is cancelled, and all of the value of the company is distributed to its creditors. These, and other potential conflicts of interest strongly suggest different counsel for each debtor.[42]

Here, it is critical for the attorney who seeks appointment as debtors' counsel to fully disclose all of the connections she and members of her firm have that might lead the court to conclude that an actual conflict exists.[43]

As might be expected, the debtor's attorney is subject to especially strict scrutiny. Whether or not the debtor's attorney asks for compensation from the estate, the attorney must file with the court a statement regarding certain pre-petition transactions with the debtor. The statement must detail:

- compensation paid during the year prior to the petition for services related to the case;
- compensation promised during the year prior to the petition for services related to the case; and
- the source of the compensation.[44]

If the compensation is found to be excessive, the court can order it to be returned.[45]

---

40 *E.g.*, In re Lee, 94 B.R. 172 (Bankr. C.D. Cal. 1989).

41 *E.g.*, In re Interwest Bus. Equip., 23 F.3d 311, 316 (10th Cir. 1994); In re Wheatfield Bus. Park, LLC, 286 B.R. 412, 418 (Bankr. D. Cal. 2002).

42 *See, e.g.*, In re Lee, 94 B.R. 172 (Bankr. C.D. Cal. 1989).

43 I.G. Petroleum, L.L.C. v. Fenasci (In re W. Delta Oil Co.), 432 F.3d 347 (5th Cir. 2005) (failure to disclose indirectly held ownership interest in the debtor).

44 Bankruptcy Code § 329(a); *see* Fed. R. Bankr. P. 2017.

45 Bankruptcy Code § 329(b).

Moreover, an attorney or other professional who fails to reveal its conflict or to otherwise make an adequate disclosure may be denied fees or forced to disgorge fees it received before the information it should have disclosed came to light.[46] In the 1990s, a major New York law firm, with extensive experience in bankruptcy matters, was required to disgorge over $1 million in fees that it had received in the course of representing a debtor-in-possession, when the court held that it had not adequately disclosed its connections to the debtor in its initial application to be hired.[47]

§ 21.03 Professionals' Fees[48]

The payment of professional fees from the estate has long been one of the most difficult bankruptcy problems. Because creditors are unlikely to be paid in full and may include both those who have been gravely injured by the debtor's actions and some who have lost their jobs as a result of the debtor's financial trouble, it is sometimes uncomfortable to deal with demands from lawyers, accountants, and other professionals to be paid hundreds of dollars per hour for their work. On the other hand, the money wasted when a case is poorly administered may cost the creditors even more. Section 330 permits examiners, a Chapter 11 trustee, and professionals authorized to be hired under § 327, to receive "reasonable compensation for actual, necessary services rendered."[49] The court may also award them "reimbursement for actual, necessary expenses."[50] If approved, their fees are entitled to administrative priority expense under §§ 330(a), 503(b) and 507(a)(2).[51]

Before 1994, § 330(a) was clear that compensation could be awarded not just to the trustee, an examiner, or a professional person employed under § 327, but also to "the debtor's attorney." In 1994, the phrase referring to the debtor's attorney was eliminated from the statutory text. It was not until ten years later, in *Lamie v. United States Trustee* that the Supreme Court resolved the uncertainty created by this deletion, and ruled that a Chapter 7 debtor is not among those who are entitled to compensation from the estate.[52] Thus, Chapter 7 debtors' attorneys who expect to be paid must receive their fees in advance, as they will receive no compensation from the estate even in the few Chapter 7 cases in which assets are available to distribute to creditors. The applicability of *Lamie* to attorneys for debtors in Chapter 13 cases is not yet resolved. In Chapter 13, debtors' attorneys

---

46 Smith v. Marshall (In re Hot Tin Roof), 205 B.R. 1000 (B.A.P. 1st Cir. 1997).

47 In re The Leslie Fay Cos., 175 B.R. 525 (Bankr. S.D.N.Y. 1994).

48 Danielle Friedberg, Note, *The Ethical Ramifications of Section 330(a)(1) of the Bankruptcy Code*, 11 Am. Bankr. Inst. L. Rev. 289 (2003); Stephen J. Lubben, *The Direct Costs of Corporate Reorganization: An Empirical Examination of Professional Fees in Large Chapter 11 Cases*, 74 Am. Bankr. L.J. 509 (2000).

49 Bankruptcy Code § 330(a)(1); Fed. R. Bankr. P. 2016.

50 Bankruptcy Code § 330(a)(2).

51 *See* § 10.04[A][2] Administrative Expense Claims, *supra*.

52 Lamie v. United States Trustee, 540 U.S. 526 (2004).

are usually compensated under § 330(a)(4)(B) rather than § 330(a)(1).[53] However, some courts have questioned whether *Lamie* might be applied to prevent debtors' attorneys from recovering fees from the estate in Chapter 13.[54]

The Code's rules only apply to those who seek compensation from the estate. For example, a lawyer who is representing a creditor, and whose fees are not reimbursable from the estate, may (within the normal rules governing professional conduct) charge whatever the client is willing to pay.

A lawyer, accountant, or other professional who seeks compensation from the estate, and whose fee thus effectively comes out of the pockets of creditors generally, is subject to greater regulation. The usual rationale is the obvious one: the other creditors have not agreed to pay the lawyer anything, let alone what the lawyer is claiming. Even when there is a contract, however, such as an agreement with the trustee or the creditors' committee, the compensation provided for in that contract is subject to court review and the judge is not always obligated to award the amount provided for by the parties' agreement.

In reviewing professionals' fee applications, courts use a variety of approaches. Many courts use a test for what is reasonable that is derived from a pre-Code bankruptcy case, *American Benefit Life Ins. Co. v. Baddock (In re First Colonial Corp. of America)*.[55] It requires the court to "ascertain the amount of time involved and the rate at which the services should be compensated."[56] Courts consider a wide variety of factors including:

> (1) The time and labor required; (2) The novelty and difficulty of the questions; (3) The skill requisite to perform the legal service properly; (4) The preclusion of other employment by the attorney due to acceptance of the case; (5) The customary fee; (6) Whether the fee is fixed or contingent; (7) Time limitations imposed by the client or other circumstances; (8) The amount involved and the results obtained; (9) The experience, reputation, and ability of the attorneys; (10) The "undesirability" of the case; (11) The nature and length of the professional relationship with the client; and, (12) Awards in similar cases.[57]

Courts also use a "lodestar" approach that involves calculation not only of the ordinary market price for legal services, and the allowable number of hours, but also for the upward or downward revision of the amount derived if the services were exceptional or deficient.[58] Yet another method,

---

[53] In re Lewis, 346 B.R. 89 (Bankr. E.D. Pa. 2006); Boone v. Burk (In re Eliapo), 468 F.3d 592 (9th Cir. 2006); *see* Lamie v. United States Trustee, 540 U.S. 526, 537 (2004).

[54] *E.g.*, In re Moore, 312 B.R. 902 (Bankr. N.D. Ala. 2004).

[55] 544 F.2d 1291 (5th Cir. 1977).

[56] 544 F.2d at 1298–99 (5th Cir. 1977).

[57] 544 F.2d at 1298–99 (5th Cir. 1977).

[58] *See, e.,g.*, In re UNR Industries, Inc., 96 F.2d 207 (7th Cir. 1993); Gerard Di Conza, Note, *Professional Fees in Bankruptcy: The Use of the Lodestar*, 1 Am. Bankr. Inst. L. Rev. 463 (1993).

derived from the treatment of attorney's fees in class action suits, focuses on the success of the lawyers' efforts — that is, how much property was obtained for the creditors.[59]

In most cases, compensation is awarded at or near the end of the proceeding or when a plan is confirmed. However, professionals may request interim compensation while the case is pending. In cases that extend over several years, interim compensation must be awarded to enable professionals to meet their own financial obligations. Requests for interim compensation may first be made 120 days after the order for relief, and each 120 days thereafter.[60] Still, professionals who are accustomed to billing their clients every thirty days may find that interim compensation every 120 days imposes a serious constraint on their cash flow.

Application of these apparently simple rules has generated great controversy. One issue of considerable debate has been the degree to which the Code's standard for determining compensation diverges from the long-standing tradition of insisting on "economy of the estate." Under the old Bankruptcy Act, the courts tended to demand what amounted to the lowest possible fee for the service, on the theory that this would preserve as much of the bankruptcy estate as possible for the creditors. Critics of this approach deemed it penny-wise but pound-foolish since it could deprive the proceeding of the best qualified (and thus best-paid) professionals. The legislative history of § 330 was quite specific:

> Attorneys' fees in bankruptcy cases can be quite large and should be closely examined by the court. However bankruptcy legal services are entitled to command the same competency of counsel as other cases. In that light, the policy of this section is to compensate attorneys and other professionals serving in a case under title 11 at the same rate as the attorney or other professional would be compensated for performing comparable services other than in a case under title 11 . . . . Notions of economy of the estate in fixing fees are outdated and have no place in a bankruptcy code.[61]

The difficulty is determining what level of compensation is necessary to attract the most able lawyers, accountants, and others without in consequence turning the bankruptcy into a proceeding solely for their benefit.

In 1994, Congress expanded the statutory guidelines for awarding professional compensation. Under these guidelines, the court must consider various factors, including the time spent, the rates charged, the need for and benefits of the services, and whether the services were performed

---

[59] Christine Jagde & Mamie Stathatos, Note, *Professional Fees in Bankruptcy: Percentage-of-the-Recovery Method: A "Solvent" Response for Bankruptcy Proceedings?*, 1 Am. Bankr. Inst. L. Rev. 471 (1993).

[60] Bankruptcy Code § 331. The time period may be shortened by the court.

[61] 124 Cong. Rec. H1109 (daily ed. Sept 2, 1977) (statement of Rep. Edwards); 124 Cong. Rec. S17406 (Oct. 6, 1977) (statement of Sen. DeConcini); *see also* Mandy S. Cohen & Christopher C. Thomson, *Professional Compensation Reform: New Ideas or Old Failings?*, 1 Am. Bankr. Inst. L. Rev. 407 (1993).

"within a reasonable amount of time commensurate with the complexity, importance, and nature of the problem, issue, or task addressed."[62] On the other hand, the Code explicitly prevents compensation for services that are unnecessarily duplicative, services that were not reasonably likely to benefit the estate, or services that were not necessary to the administration of the case.[63]

§ 21.04 Key Employees

The 2005 Amendments impose new restrictions on compensation paid to insider employees to induce them to remain with the debtor's business. Before the 2005 Amendments, Key Employee Retention Plans (KERPS) were subject to court approval under § 363(b)(1) as transactions outside the ordinary course of business.[64] Court approval depended primarily on whether the incentive program was fair and reasonable within the "business judgment" of the debtor.[65] However, these plans were sometimes used to inappropriately reward high-paid executives whose misconduct had led to the debtor's financial difficulties.[66] As a result, after the 2005 Amendments, these employee retention plans are subject to further limits.

New § 503(c)(1) permits transfers to "insiders" that are made "for the purpose of inducing such person to remain with the debtor's business" only if:

- the compensation is "essential" to retain the employee because she has a bona fide competitive job offer "at the same or greater rate of compensation";[67]
- the employee's services are "essential to the survival of the business"; and[68]
- the proposed compensation is not grossly disproportionate to other similar transfers made to "nonmanagement employees" under very specific statutory criteria.[69]

The Code also restricts "severance payments" to insiders unless the payments are generally available to "all full-time employees" and are not more than ten times the severance packages that were supplied to nonmanagement employees in the year before the payment is to be made.[70]

[62] Bankruptcy Code § 330(a)(3)(A).

[63] Bankruptcy Code § 330(a)(4)(A).

[64] Bankruptcy Code § 363(b)(1); *e.g.*, In re U.S. Airways, Inc., 329 B.R. 793, 797 (Bankr. E.D. Va. 2005); *see* § 9.03[C] Use, Sale, or Lease Outside the Ordinary Course, *supra*.

[65] *E.g.*, In re Allied Holdlings, Inc., 337 B.R. 617, 721 (Bankr. N.D. Ga. 2005); U.S. Airways, Inc., 329 B.R. 793, 797 (Bankr. E.D. Va. 2005).

[66] *See* In re U.S. Airways, Inc., 329 B.R. at 797.

[67] Bankruptcy Code § 503(c)(1)(A).

[68] Bankruptcy Code § 503(c)(2).

[69] Bankruptcy Code § 503(c)(1)(C).

[70] Bankruptcy Code § 503(c)(2).

It also restrains other transfers or commitments outside the ordinary course that are "not justified by the facts and circumstances of the case."[71] This final restriction applies to "officers, managers, or consultants hired after the date of the filing of the petition" even if they are not subject to the rules for hiring "professionals" under §§ 327 and 328.

Debtors' efforts to sidestep these restrictions with compensation systems based on key employees' achievement of performance-based goals have been regarded with some skepticism by courts that have reviewed them. In *In re Dana Corp.*,[72] Bankruptcy Judge Lifland[73] refused to approve what was characterized as a "performance bonus" that would have paid certain executives a sizeable portion of the bonus if the value of the debtor's business actually declined by almost 25%. This made the proposed compensation package appear to be the type of Key Employee Retention Plan that § 503(c)(1) was designed to prohibit.[74] Likewise, the court regarded payments to be made in exchange for these same employees agreeing to a "no-compete" agreement as severance packages that were subject to § 503(c)(2).[75] Subsequent revisions to the employee bonus plan, which eliminated their objectionable features, resulted in their approval.[76]

§ 21.05 Regulation of Bankruptcy Lawyers as "Debt Relief Agencies"

The 2005 Amendments brought an additional layer of regulation of attorneys and others who provide services to financially troubled consumer debtors. Those who provide bankruptcy assistance to consumer debtors with less than $150,000 in nonexempt assets — primarily consumer bankruptcy attorneys — are now regarded as "debt relief agencies" and subject to government regulation.

[A] Debt Relief Agencies[77]

New §§ 526, 527, and 528 regulate the activities and communications of "debt relief agencies." A debt relief agency is: "any person who provides any bankruptcy assistance to an assisted person in return for the payment of money or other valuable consideration, or who is a bankruptcy petition

[71] Bankruptcy Code § 503(c)(3).

[72] 351 B.R. 96 (Bankr. S.D.N.Y. 2006).

[73] Judge Lifland is a particularly well-regarded judge who is active as a scholar and speaker on bankruptcy matters.

[74] 351 B.R. at 101–02.

[75] 351 B.R. at 102–03.

[76] In re Dana Corp., 358 B.R. 567 (Bankr. S.D.N.Y. 2006).

[77] Henry J. Sommer, *Trying to Make Sense Out of Nonsense: Representing Consumers Under the "Bankruptcy Abuse Prevention and Consumer Protection Act of 2005,"* 79 Am. Bankr. L.J. 191 (2005); Robert Wann, Jr., *"Debt Relief Agencies": Does the Bankruptcy Abuse Prevention and Consumer Protection Act of 2005 Violate Attorneys' First Amendment Rights?*, 14 Am. Bankr. Inst. L. Rev. 273 (2006).

preparer."[78] An "assisted person" is "any person whose debts consist primarily of consumer debts and the value of whose nonexempt property is less than $150,000."[79] "Bankruptcy assistance" means:

> any goods or services sold or otherwise provided to an assisted person with the express or implied purpose of providing information, advice, counsel, document preparation, or filing, or attendance at a creditors' meeting or appearing in a case or proceeding on behalf of another or providing legal representation with respect to a case or proceeding under [the Bankruptcy Code].[80]

The definition of "debt relief agency" contains several specific exclusions, one of which exempts any "author, publisher, distributor, or seller of works subject to copyright protection . . . when acting in such capacity." Nonprofit organizations exempt under § 501(c)(3) of the Internal Revenue Code are also exempt — this protects qualified credit counseling agencies and presumably most law school legal clinics from the regulations.[81] Exclusions are also available for creditors who are engaged in attempting to restructure debts owed to the creditor, banks, and officers, directors, employees, or agents of debt relief agencies.[82]

Thus, the Code's new restrictions apply primarily to consumer bankruptcy lawyers[83] and to non-lawyer bankruptcy petition preparers and others who assist consumer debtors in seeking relief under the Bankruptcy Code. However, one court has ruled that regularly licensed attorneys or those who are admitted pro hac vice are not debt relief agencies within the meaning of the term and are thus not governed by its regulatory provisions.[84] The court found the statutory language ambiguous because it did not specifically refer to lawyers or attorneys and held that bringing attorneys within the definition of a debt relief agency "would be a breathtakingly expansive interpretation of federal law to usurp state regulation of the practice of law."[85] Other courts disagree.[86]

---

[78] Bankruptcy Code § 101(12A).

[79] Bankruptcy Code § 101(3). This $150,000 threshold, unlike many other dollar figures in the Bankruptcy Code, is not subject to automatic adjustment every three years to keep up with inflation.

[80] Bankruptcy Code § 101(4A).

[81] Bankruptcy Code § 101(12A)(B).

[82] Bankruptcy Code § 101(12A).

[83] Hersh v. United States, 347 B.R. 19 (N.D. Tex. 2006); Olsen v. Gonzales, 350 B.R. 906 (D. Or. 2006); *see* Gary Neustadter, *2005: A Consumer Bankruptcy Odyssey*, 39 Creighton L. Rev. 225, 314 (2006); Catherine E. Vance & Corinne Cooper, *Nine Traps and One Slap: Attorney Liability Under the New Bankruptcy Law*, 79 Am. Bankr. L.J. 283, 288–89 (2005); *but see* In re Attorneys at Law and Debt Relief Agencies, 332 B.R. 66 (Bankr. S.D. Ga. 2005).

[84] In re Attorneys at Law and Debt Relief Agencies, 332 B.R. 66 (Bankr. S.D. Ga. 2005).

[85] 332 B.R. at 71.

[86] Olsen v. Gonzales, 350 B.R. 906 (D. Or. 2006).

[B] Restrictions on Debt Relief Agencies[87]

Most of the regulations proscribe conduct that is already illegal, such as assisting debtors in submitting false or misleading documents in a bankruptcy case.[88] Not surprisingly, any attempted waiver of these prohibitions is void.[89] Moreover, the Code creates specific remedies for violations of these rules, permitting debtors to recover actual damages and attorneys' fees from debt relief agencies that violate the Code's regulations.[90] It also gives state attorneys general the right to enforce its provisions on debtors' behalf.[91]

Other portions of the new regulations seem destined to impair the advice that debt relief agencies might sensibly provide to their clients. For example, § 526(a)(4) prohibits a debt relief agency from advising a debtor "to incur more debt in contemplation of . . . filing a [bankruptcy] case," even though borrowing additional funds may be a way for the debtor to attempt to avoid bankruptcy.[92] A number of District Courts have found this provision unconstitutional as a violation of the First Amendment.[93] Nonsensically, it also prevents attorneys advising debtors to pay "an attorney or bankruptcy petition preparer fee or charge for services performed as part of preparing for or representing a debtor [in a bankruptcy case]."[94] Read literally, this seems to prevent debtors' attorneys from advising their clients to pay for their lawyers' services.[95]

Debt relief agencies are also obligated to make an extensive set of disclosures to their clients (customers?), about their services and about bankruptcy and its alternatives.[96] Likewise, advertisements by those to whom the new moniker of "debt relief agency" is attached, are required to contain a set of very specific disclosures and detailed content, such as "We are a

---

87 Steven W. Rhodes, Thomas F. Waldron, Erwin Chemerinsky & Catherine E. Vance, *Ethics: New Challenges for Attorneys under the New Code*, 4 DePaul Bus. & Com. L.J. 567 (2006); George H. Singer, *The Year in Review: Case Developments under the Bankruptcy Abuse Prevention and Consumer Protection Act of 2005*, 82 N.D. L. Rev. 297, 306–10 (2006).

88 Bankruptcy Code § 526(c)(2); *see* Henry J. Sommer, *Trying to Make Sense Out of Nonsense: Representing Consumers Under the "Bankruptcy Abuse Prevention and Consumer Protection Act of 2005,"* 79 Am. Bankr. L.J. 191, 207–08 (2005) .

89 Bankruptcy Code § 526(b).

90 Bankruptcy Code § 526(c). The Code expressly preserves any rights the debtor has under state law. Bankruptcy Code § 526(c)(3).

91 Bankruptcy Code § 526(c)(3).

92 Gary Neustadter, *2005: A Consumer Bankruptcy Odyssey*, 39 Creighton L. Rev. 225, 315 (2006).

93 Hersh v. United States, 347 B.R. 19, 24–25 (N.D. Tex. 2006); Olsen v. Gonzales, 350 B.R. 906, 915 (D. Or. 2006); Zelotes v. Martini, 352 B.R. 17 (D. Conn. 2006).

94 Bankruptcy Code § 526(a)(4).

95 Robert Wann, Jr., *"Debt Relief Agencies": Does the Bankruptcy Abuse Prevention and Consumer Protection Act of 2005 Violate Attorneys' First Amendment Rights?*, 14 Am. Bankr. Inst. L. Rev. 273, 285 (2006); Catherine E. Vance & Corinne Cooper, *Nine Traps and One Slap: Attorney Liability Under the New Bankruptcy Law*, 79 Am. Bankr. L.J. 283, 306–08 (2005).

96 Gary Neustadter, *2005: A Consumer Bankruptcy Odyssey*, 39 Creighton L. Rev. 225 (2006).

debt relief agency. We help people file for bankruptcy relief under the Bankruptcy Code."[97]

The Code also requires debt relief agencies to enter into written contracts with their clients.[98] Thus, consumer debtors' attorneys must entered into written fee arrangements with their clients that lay out the fees the client is responsible for in clear and conspicuous language.[99] This written contract must be executed within five business days after the "first date on which [the debt relief agency] provides any bankruptcy assistance services to [a debtor]."[100] The Code is unclear how this requirement is supposed to apply in connection with clients who, after consulting with a bankruptcy lawyer, decide to delay engaging the lawyer.

Some aspects of the Code's restrictions and obligations on debt relief agencies are of questionable constitutionality.[101] On the other hand, the same courts that have regarded them as violations of attorneys' First Amendment rights have held that the Code's mandatory disclosure rules do not constitute unconstitutional "compelled speech."[102]

§ 21.06 Bankruptcy Petition Preparers

The Bankruptcy Code restricts the activities of unlicensed "bankruptcy petition preparers" who may also be subject to sanction for the unauthorized practice of law. A bankruptcy petition preparer is a person who is not an attorney or an employee working under the direct supervision of an attorney "who prepares for compensation a . . . petition or any other document . . . for filing by a debtor in a . . . bankruptcy court."[103]

These individuals must sign and print their names on any such documents they prepare.[104] They must also include their Social Security Number.[105] They are further required to provide their clients with a disclosure, in the form prescribed by the Judicial Conference, that informs the debtor that the petition preparer is not an attorney and may not practice law or give legal advice.[106]

---

[97] Bankruptcy Code § 528(a)(4), (b)(2).

[98] Bankruptcy Code § 528.

[99] Bankruptcy Code § 528(a)(1).

[100] Bankruptcy Code § 528(a)(1).

[101] Erwin Chemerinsky, *Constitutional Issues Posed in the Bankruptcy Abuse Prevention and Consumer Protection Act of 2005*, 79 Am. Bankr. L.J. 571 (2005); Gary Neustadter, *2005: A Consumer Bankruptcy Odyssey*, 39 Creighton L. Rev. 225, 311–37 (2006); Robert Wann, Jr., *"Debt Relief Agencies": Does the Bankruptcy Abuse Prevention and Consumer Protection Act of 2005 Violate Attorneys' First Amendment Rights?*, 14 Am. Bankr. Inst. L. Rev. 273 (2006).

[102] Hersh v. United States, 347 B.R. 19, 25–27 (N.D. Tex. 2006); Olsen v. Gonzales, 350 B.R. 906, 915 (D. Or. 2006); Zelotes v. Martini, 352 B.R. (D. Conn. 2006).

[103] Bankruptcy Code § 110(a).

[104] Bankruptcy Code § 110(b)(1).

[105] Bankruptcy Code § 110(c).

[106] Bankruptcy Code § 110(b)(2).

Petition preparers are precluded from supplying legal advice.[107] This specifically precludes petition preparers from advising the debtor:

- to file a petition;
- whether chapter 7, 11, 12, or 13 is appropriate for the debtor;
- whether the debtor's debts will be discharged in a bankruptcy case;
- whether the debtor will be able to retain her home, car, or other property,
- about the tax consequences of a bankruptcy case;
- how to characterize the debtor's property interests or debts;
- about bankruptcy rights and procedures.[108]

Similarly, bankruptcy petition preparers are precluded from using the word "legal" or similar words in any advertisement that they make.[109]

In addition, the Code permits the Supreme Court to establish the maximum fees that a bankruptcy petition preparer may charge for her services[110] and requires petition preparers to provide the court with a statement of the fees that they charged in connection with a filed petition, signed under the penalty of perjury.[111]

Violation of these rules subjects a bankruptcy petition preparer to potential fines, penalties, and injunctions.[112]

---

[107] Bankruptcy Code § 110(b)(2)(A).

[108] Bankruptcy Code § 110(e)(2)(B).

[109] Bankruptcy Code § 110(f).

[110] Bankruptcy Code § 110(h)(1).

[111] Bankruptcy Code § 110(h)(2).

[112] Bankruptcy Code § 110(i), (j), (k); *see* In re Duran, 347 B.R. 760 (Bankr. D. Colo. 2006) (injunction, $2,000 fine to the United States Trustee, and $2,000 actual and statutory damages to the debtor).

Chapter 22

International Bankruptcy

§ 22.01 Cross-Border Insolvency and its Theoretical Solutions

[A] Issues in Cross-Border Insolvency

Insolvency is a problem that is by no means limited to the United States. Businesses go broke all over the world, and courts must deal with it.[1] The enactment of modern bankruptcy laws has been seen by banks and international institutions as a critical part of the financial development of developing nations and countries with post-communist regimes.[2] As one scholar put it: "Today even the leaders of the People's Republic of China agree with the Founders of the American Republic that a bankruptcy system is central to fundamental economic reform.[3]

In an era of international business and multi-national firms, this inevitably creates problems of overlapping legal rules and legal systems.[4] However, because there is no overriding sovereignty to force any one nation's courts to defer to another's in either procedural or substantive matters, the

[1] European Bankruptcy Laws (David A. Botwinik & Kenneth W. Weinrib eds., 2d ed. 1986); Kevin P. Block, *Ukranian Bankruptcy Law*, 20 Loy. L.A. Int'l & Comp. L.J. 97 (1997); Shinichiro Abe, *Recent Developments of Insolvency Laws and Cross-Border Practices in the United States and Japan*, 10 Am. Bankr. Inst. L. Rev. 47 (2002); Samuel L. Bufford & Kazuhiro Yanagida, *Japan's Revised Laws on Business Reorganization: An Analysis*, 39 Cornell Int'l L.J. 1 (2006); Bruce G. Carruthers & Terence C. Halliday, *Negotiating Globalization: Global Scripts and Intermediation in the Construction of Asian Insolvency Regimes*, 31 Law & Soc. Inquiry 521 (2006); Juan M. Dobson, *Argentina's Bankruptcy Law of 1995*, 33 Tex. Int'l L.J. 101 (1998); Rafeal Efrat, *Global Trends in Personal Bankruptcy*, 76 Am Bankr. L.J.. 81 (2002); Klaus Kamlah, *The New German Insolvency Act: Insolvenzordnung*, 70 Am. Bankr. L.J. 417 (1996); Nathalie Martin, *The Role of History and Culture in Developing Bankruptcy and Insolvency Systems: The Perils of Legal Transplantation*, 28 B.C. Int'l & Comp. L. Rev. 1 (2005); Julia M. Metzger & Samuel L. Bufford, *Exporting United States Bankruptcy Law: The Hungarian Experience*, 21 Cal. Bankr. J. 153, 154 (1993); Pamela Bickford Sak & Tanya Senn, *The New Bankruptcy Law in Thailand*, 3 Asian Com. L. Rev. 50 (1998); Stacey Steele, *The New Law on Bankruptcy in Indonesia: Towards a Modern Corporate Bankruptcy Regime?*, 23 Melb. U. L. Rev. 144 (1999).

[2] *E.g.*, Angela C. Fleming, Comment, *Russia's Bid for Bankruptcy*, 5 J. Int'l Legal Stud. 145 (1999); Scott Horton, *The Death of Communism and Bankruptcy Reorganization*, 1994 Am. Bankr. Inst. J. 12; Henry N. Schiffman, *Bankruptcy Law Reform in Eastern Europe*, 28 Int'l Law. 927 (1994).

[3] Jay Lawrence Westbrook, *Universal Priorities*, 33 Tex. Int'l L.J. 27, 27–28 (1998).

[4] *See* Gabriel Moss, Ian F. Fletcher & Stuart Isaacs, The EC Regulation on Insolvency Proceedings: A Commentary and Annotated Guide (2002); Ian F. Fletcher, Insolvency in Private International Law (2d ed. 2005).

resolution of these problems is left to the vagaries of what is often referred to as "private international law."[5]

However, since the 1990s, cross-border insolvency law has emerged as an important branch of insolvency law.[6] The Council of the European Community has promulgated a regulation on cross-border insolvency cases,[7] and the United Nations Commission on International Trade Law (UNCITRAL) has developed a Model Law (the "Model Law") to address the issues that arise in these cases.[8] The Model Law was adopted in the United States as Chapter 15 of the Bankruptcy Code as part of the 2005 Amendments. In addition, the American Law Institute has developed a set of "Principles of Cooperation" for use by countries who are parties to the North American Free Trade Agreement.[9]

Scholars have identified several alternative approaches that are used to resolve these issues. Historically the predominant approach has been territorialism, in which local courts apply local law to seize control of and distribute assets within the scope of their territorial power. Sometimes this results in local creditors receiving more favorable treatment than foreign creditors. The advantage of such an approach is that it does not actually require a cross-border regime to wind up the affairs of a company. The problem with territoriality, however, is that it makes it devilishly difficult to reorganize an entity that does business in multiple jurisdictions. Over the past dozen years, scholars have proposed adoption of a more universalist approach, with the goal of resolving the difficulties of a financially troubled international business under a unified international bankruptcy law in a single forum. UNCITRAL's Model Statute and Chapter 15 of the Bankruptcy Code focus on the "procedural" aspects of such a universal vision, creating a regime under which courts across jurisdictions would cooperate with the court at the debtor's center of main interest ("COMI"). The issues dealt with under the Model Law are quite limited. They include:

- procedures for recognition of foreign representatives of foreign insolvency proceedings;

---

[5] Jay Lawrence Westbrook, *Theory and Pragmatism in Global Insolvencies: Choice of Law and Choice of Forum*, 65 Am. Bankr. L.J. 457 (1991).

[6] Jay Lawrence Westbrook, *Multinational Enterprises In General Default: Chapter 15, The ALI Principles, and the EU Insolvency Regulation*, 76 Am. Bankr. L.J. 1 (2002).

[7] This went into force as a "regulation" rather than a "convention." Council Regulation (EC) No 1346/2000 of 29 May 2000 on Insolvency Proceedings, available at europa.eu.int/eur-lex/pri/en/oj/dat/2000/l_160/l_16020000630en00010018.pdf. (last visited, April 4, 2007); Samuel L. Bufford, *International Insolvency Case Venue in the European Union: The Parmalat and Daisytek Controversies*, 12 Colum. J. Eur. L. 429 (2006); Principles of European Insolvency Law (W.W. McBryde, A. Flessner & S.C.J.J. Kortmann, eds.. 2003).

[8] U.N. Comm'n on Int'l Trade Law, Model Law on Cross-Border Insolvency with Guide to Enactment (1997) available at www.uncitral.org/pdf/english/texts/insolven/insolvency-e.pdf (last visited April 4, 2007); U.N. Comm'n on Int'l Trade Law, 30th Sess., at 3, U.N. Doc. A/CN.9/442 (1997) reprinted in 6 Tul. J. Int'l & Comp. L. 415 (1998); Cross-Border Insolvency: A Commentary on the UNCITRAL Model Law (Look Chan Ho, ed. 2006).

[9] *See generally* Am. L. Inst., Transnational Insolvency: Cooperation Among the NAFTA Countries: Principles of Cooperation Among the NAFTA Countries 9–10 (2003).

- procedures for granting and coordinating stays in pending cases;
- definition of relief available to a foreign representative;
- definition of the "main" proceeding as the proceeding initiated at the COMI;
- mechanisms to permit communication;
- principles for coordinating pending proceedings; and
- a rule to prevent double dipping.

It leaves to further developments the choice of law principles that will be applied in the various cases, as well as the substantive bankruptcy rules to be applied.

[B] Cooperative Territoriality[10]

In the absence of procedures for handling cross-border cases, the default is that cases involving multi-national debtors will be handled through a territorial approach under which courts in each country seize the assets within their own borders to pay local creditors.[11] This has been referred to, somewhat pejoratively, as the "grab rule."[12] Courts grab whatever assets are within its sovereign borders and administer them locally, sometimes for the exclusive benefit of local creditors. This results in piecemeal administration of a multinational corporation's property in multiple proceedings with duplicated expenses and inconsistent results.[13]

Assume, for example, that Globecom, Inc. is incorporated in the United States and has assets in both the United States and in Mexico. Under territorialism, the assets located in the United States would be administered in a bankruptcy proceeding in the United States according to U.S. bankruptcy law and the assets located in Mexico would be administered in a bankruptcy proceeding in Mexico according to Mexican bankruptcy law. Creditors with claims against these assets would file claims in the respective cases, and would understand that those assets would be administered under local law. Strict adherence to a territorial approach, however, creates a number of opportunities for abuse. The debtor, for example, might move assets from one country to the other in an effort to affect their distribution.[14]

---

[10] *See* Lynn M. LoPucki, *Cooperation in International Bankruptcy: A Post-Universalist Approach*, 84 Cornell L. Rev. 696 (1999).

[11] Lucian Arye Bebchuk & Andrew T. Guzman, *An Economic Analysis of Transnational Bankruptcies*, 42 J.L. & Econ. 775, 787 (1999); Ian F. Fletcher, Insolvency in Private International Law 12–14 (2d ed. 2005).

[12] Jay Lawrence Westbrook, *Chapter 15 at Last*, 79 Am. Bankr. L.J. 713, 716 (2005).

[13] Lucian Arye Bebchuk & Andrew T. Guzman, *An Economic Analysis of Transnational Bankruptcies*, 42 J.L. & Econ. 775 (1999); Jay Lawrence Westbrook, *Theory and Pragmatism in Global Insolvencies: Choice of Law and Choice of Forum*, 65 Am. Bankr. L.J. 457 (1991).

[14] Lynn M. LoPucki, *The Case for Cooperative Territoriality in International Bankruptcy*, 98 Mich. L. Rev. 2216, 2219 (2000).

Lynn LoPucki has proposed instead a system of "cooperative territoriality" in which parallel bankruptcy proceedings occur simultaneously in the affected countries, the parties negotiate, and the courts cooperate with one another to find a solution to the debtor's problems that produces the highest recovery for all.[15] In many cases under current law, the parties and courts negotiate a framework for cooperation on a case by case basis. These frameworks are generally referred to as "protocols."[16] Creditors' negotiations over the terms of the protocol occur against the backdrop of the consequences of failing to agree with its threat of piecemeal liquidation of the debtor's disparately located assets. One of the drawbacks of this cooperative system is that its informal nature might easily lead to a breakdown of the spirit of cooperation in response to local concerns.[17]

Under cooperative territoriality, bankruptcy courts of separate countries still administer the assets of multinational debtors located in their own countries, as if they were part of a separate estate. This necessarily involves the expense and inefficiency of parallel bankruptcy cases, but, according to its proponents, eliminates most of the uncertainties about choice of law and limits the opportunities for debtors to engage in forum shopping. In this respect, it provides creditors with greater certainty about the consequences of the debtor's bankruptcy.[18]

[C] Modified Universalism[19]

The alternative to territoriality is "universalism," in which a multinational entity is liquidated or reorganized in a single court with jurisdiction over all of the debtor's assets wherever they are located.[20] In a bankruptcy system operating on a theory of "pure universalism," courts in other countries would be bound by treaty to enforce the orders of the bankruptcy court in the debtor's home country, and distribute its assets according to

---

[15] Lynn M. LoPucki, *The Case for Cooperative Territoriality in International Bankruptcy*, 98 Mich. L. Rev. 2216 (2000); *see also* David Costa Levenson, *Proposal for Reform of Choice of Avoidance Law in the Context of International Bankruptcies from a U.S. Perspective*, 10 Am. Bankr. Inst. L. Rev. 291 (2002).

[16] *E.g.*, Stonington Partners, Inc. v. Lernout & Hauspie Speech Products N.V., 310 F.3d 118 (3d Cir. 2002); Maxwell Communication Corp. v. Societe Generale (In re Maxwell Communication Corp.), 93 F.3d 1036 (2d Cir.1996).

[17] *See* United States v. BCCI Holdings (Luxembourg), S.A., 48 F.3d 551 (D.C. Cir. 1995); United States v. BCCI Holdings (Luxembourg), S.A., 46 F.3d 1185 (D.C. Cir. 1995); United States v. BCCI Holdings (Luxembourg), S.A., 73 F.3d 403 (D.C. Cir. 1996) (United States used its criminal law to advance the priority of its claims).

[18] Lynn M. LoPucki, *Cooperation in International Bankruptcy: A Post-Universalist Approach*, 84 Cornell L. Rev. 696, 751 (1999).

[19] Andrew T. Guzman, *International Bankruptcy: In Defense of Universalism*, 98 Mich. L. Rev. 2177 (2000); Jay Lawrence Westbrook, *Multinational Enterprises In General Default: Chapter 15, The ALI Principles, And The EU Insolvency Regulation*, 76 Am. Bankr. L.J. 1 (2002); Jay Lawrence Westbrook, *A Global Solution to Multinational Default*, 98 Mich. L. Rev. 2276 (2000).

[20] Liza Perkins, *A Defense of Pure Universalism in Cross-Border Corporate Insolvencies*, 32 N.Y.U. J. Int'l L. & Pol. 787 (2000).

that country's laws.[21] Thus, in the Globecom, Inc. example above, a pure universalist system of international bankruptcy law would result in administration of Globecom's assets by one bankruptcy court according to one bankruptcy law.

However appealing this might seem, adoption of a system of pure universalism, in which the judgments of a court in one country were directly enforceable in other countries, is viewed by most as unlikely to develop in the near future.[22] In order for it to develop, the countries involved would need to have virtually identical bankruptcy laws. And they would have to be willing to cede authority to either an international court, or to a court in another jurisdiction. In a world in which American judges are criticized for relying on decisions in other countries as merely persuasive authority, such a system seems unlikely to develop.[23]

An evolving model, embodied in the Model Law and in efforts to harmonize substantive bankruptcy law, such as UNCITRAL's Legislative Guide for Insolvency Law,[24] is modified universalism. Under this approach, assets are collected and distributed on a worldwide basis under the supervision of the court at the debtor's center of main interest ("COMI"). For this system to work, however, the "main proceeding" at the COMI must obtain the cooperation of the various courts which have jurisdiction over the debtor's assets. Chapter 15 of the Bankruptcy Code, which is based on UNCITRAL's Model Law on Cross Border Insolvency and which was adopted as part of the 2005 Amendments,[25] represents a first step toward a modified universalist approach, which gives more deference to the "main proceeding" at the debtor's COMI than did former United States law under § 304 of the Code.[26]

Critics of modified universalism agree that pure universalism is unlikely to find sufficient political support to become a reality. Further, they contend that the modified universalism of the sort represented by Chapter 15 and the UNCITRAL model on which is was based suffers from the difficulty of identifying the home country of a large multinational corporation which might be incorporated in one country, have its headquarters and run its financial affairs from another country, and have the lion's share of its assets in a third country.[27]

---

[21] Lynn M. LoPucki, *The Case for Cooperative Territoriality In International Bankruptcy*, 98 Mich. L. Rev. 2216, 2221 (2000); Jay Lawrence Westbrook, *A Global Solution to Multinational Default*, 98 Mich. L. Rev. 2276, 2309 (2000).

[22] Lynn M. LoPucki, *The Case for Cooperative Territoriality In International Bankruptcy*, 98 Mich. L. Rev. 2216, 2221 (2000).

[23] *See* Roper v. Simmons, 543 U.S. 551, 607, 622–28 (2005) (Scalia, J. dissenting); *see* Rick Santorum, *The Internationalist Threat to America's Constitution*, Crisis, Dec. 2003, available at www.crisismagazine.com/december2003/hill.htm (last viewed Nov. 30, 2006).

[24] UNCITRAL Legislative Guide on Insolvency Law, available at www.uncitral.org/uncitral/en/uncitral_texts/insolvency/2004Guide.html.

[25] *See* § 22.03 Chapter 15 of the Bankruptcy Code, *infra*.

[26] David Costa Levenson, *Proposal for Reform of Choice of Avoidance Law in the Context of International Bankruptcies from a U.S. Perspective*, 10 Am. Bankr. Inst. L. Rev. 291 (2002).

[27] Lynn M. LoPucki, *The Case for Cooperative Territoriality In International Bankruptcy*, 98 Mich. L. Rev. 2216, 2221 (2000).

[D] Contractualism

Some scholars advance a third theory — "contractualism" — allowing a debtor and its creditors to precommit by contract to a particular bankruptcy regime.[28] There are a number of objections to contractualism. Some are procedural — how to ensure that a debtor chooses the same law to govern all of its contracts. Others run to the limits of contractualism itself. For example, not all of the creditors against a debtor are in a position to negotiate over the choice of insolvency law. These may include small claimants, or employees, for example. Indeed, not all creditors choose to do business with the debtor at all. There is no reason to think that a tort claimant should be bound to a debtor's choice of insolvency law. The final objection is regulatory. Many jurisdictions view it as their prerogative to regulate assets located in their jurisdiction, and/or contracts entered into in their jurisdiction. Contractualism would enforce private agreements regarding the choice of bankruptcy law that would apply in the event of a debtor's insolvency. This would allow debtors to contract around the regulatory provisions of local law.[29]

§ 22.02 Ancillary and Parallel Bankruptcy Proceedings[30]

The nomenclature of international insolvency law draws a distinction between two types of cross-border insolvency proceedings: ancillary proceedings and plenary proceedings.[31] "Ancillary proceedings" refers to a special proceeding in a domestic bankruptcy court that gives assistance to a bankruptcy case pending in a foreign jurisdiction. Thus, an ancillary proceeding is not a regular bankruptcy case in which the debtor's assets are collected and distributed according to the usual priorities.[32] Instead, the purpose of an ancillary proceeding is to assist the debtor's main bankruptcy proceeding that is pending in another country where the debtor's "center of main interest" is located.

---

[28] Robert K. Rasmussen, *Resolving Transnational Insolvencies Through Private Ordering*, 98 Mich L. Rev. 2252 (2000); Robert K. Rasmussen, *A New Approach to Transnational Insolvencies*, 19 Mich. J. Int'l L. 1 (1997); *see* David Costa Levenson, *Proposal for Reform of Choice of Avoidance Law in the Context of International Bankruptcies from a U.S. Perspective*, 10 Am. Bankr. Inst. L. Rev. 291, 296 (2002).

[29] Robert K. Rasmussen, *A New Approach to Transnational Insolvencies*, 19 Mich. J. Int'l L. 1, 4–5 (1997).

[30] *See* Evelyn H. Biery, Jason L. Boland & John D. Cornwell, *A Look at Transnational Insolvencies and Chapter 15 of the Bankruptcy Abuse Prevention and Consumer Protection Act of 2005*, 47 B.C. L. Rev. 23, 31–32 (2005); Jay L. Westbrook, *A Global Solution to Multinational Default*, 98 Mich. L. Rev. 2276, 2300 (2000); Jay Lawrence Westbrook, *Multinational Enterprises In General Default: Chapter 15, The ALI Principles, And The EU Insolvency Regulation*, 76 Am. Bankr. L.J. 1, 10–12 (2002).

[31] Am. L. Inst., Transnational Insolvency: Cooperation Among the NAFTA Countries: Principles of Cooperation Among the NAFTA Countries 9–10 (2003); *see* Jay L. Westbrook & Jacob Ziegel, *The American Insolvency Law Institute NAFTA Insolvency Project*, 23 Brook. J. Int'l L. 7, 8 (1997).

[32] *See* § 10.01 Meaning of Claims and Interests, *supra*.

Former § 304, which was repealed by the 2005 Amendments, permitted bankruptcy courts in the United States to administer an ancillary proceeding to assist with the administration of a foreign bankruptcy case. Under former § 304, a representative appointed in a foreign insolvency proceeding could petition to begin an ancillary proceeding in an American bankruptcy court. The ancillary proceeding was not a full-blown bankruptcy case. Instead, it provided a means of facilitating the foreign court's proceeding.[33] Under § 304, the American bankruptcy court could enjoin the commencement or continuation of actions against the debtor's property or against the debtor regarding the property,[34] enjoin the commencement or continuation of the enforcement of any judgment against the debtor respecting the property, or any act or proceeding to create or enforce a lien against the property,[35] order the property or its proceeds to be turned over to the representative of the foreign case,[36] or order other appropriate relief.[37]

New Chapter 15, enacted as part of the 2005 Amendments, also permits ancillary bankruptcy proceedings in the United States. It permits a bankruptcy court to recognize and cooperate with a "foreign main proceeding" involving a debtor who has interests or property in the United States.[38]

Alternatively, a debtor with a bankruptcy case pending in a one country might initiate a parallel plenary bankruptcy case in another country to administer the assets that are within the jurisdictional control of that country.[39] A parallel plenary proceeding is a full-blown bankruptcy case in which all of the usual rules and priorities apply. Judges in the parallel plenary cases usually attempt to coordinate their efforts to avoid inconsistent outcomes in the two cases. Chapter 15 also permits the opening of plenary proceedings,[40] but requires U.S. bankruptcy courts to cooperate with a parallel proceeding pending in another country and to defer to the "main proceeding."[41]

---

[33] *See, e.g.*, Interpool, Ltd. v. Certain Freights, 878 F.2d 111, 112 (3d Cir. 1989).

[34] Former Bankruptcy Code § 304(b)(1)(A).

[35] Former Bankruptcy Code § 304(b)(1)(B).

[36] Former Bankruptcy Code § 304(b)(2).

[37] Former Bankruptcy Code § 304(b)(3).

[38] Bankruptcy Code § 1517(b)(1).

[39] *See* Am. L. Inst., Transnational Insolvency Project, Court-to-Court Guidelines for Communications, available at www.iiiglobal.org/international/projects/ali.pdf (last visited Nov. 26, 2006); Jacob S. Ziegel, *Corporate Groups and Crossborder Insolvencies: A Canada-United States Perspective*, 7 Fordham J. Corp. & Fin. L. 367, 380 (2002).

[40] Bankruptcy Code § 1528.

[41] Bankruptcy Code § 1529.

§ 22.03 Chapter 15 of the Bankruptcy Code[42]

The 2005 Amendments to the Bankruptcy Code included a major revision of the rules relating to international insolvency cases. New Chapter 15 is based on the United Nations Commission on International Trade Law's (UNCITRAL) Model Law on Cross-Border Insolvency.[43] UNCITRAL's model law has been adopted by several other nations, including Japan (2000), Mexico (2000), Poland (2003), Romania (2003), Montenegro (2002), Serbia (2004); South Africa (2000), Great Britain (2006), British Virgin Islands, overseas territory of the United Kingdom of Great Britain and Northern Ireland (2005), and the United States (2005).[44] Some of those jurisdictions are also members of the EU, and are therefore governed by the EC Regulation on Insolvency for cases involving other EU countries.[45]

The purposes of Chapter 15 and UNCITRAL's Model Law are "to provide effective mechanisms for dealing with cases of cross-border insolvency."[46] They attempt to:

- promote cooperation between the courts and agencies of the United States and foreign countries involved in cross-border insolvency proceedings;[47]
- provide greater legal certainty for trade and investment;[48]
- promote fair and efficient administration of cross-border insolvencies that protects the interests of the debtor, creditors, and other interested persons;[49]
- facilitate the rescue of financially troubled businesses and thereby protect investment and preserve employment.[50]

---

[42] Evelyn H. Biery, Jason L. Boland & John D. Cornwell, *A Look at Transnational Insolvencies and Chapter 15 of the Bankruptcy Abuse Prevention and Consumer Protection Act of 2005*, 47 B.C. L. Rev. 23 (2005); M. Cameron Gilreath, Note, *Overview and Analysis of How the United Nations Model Law on Insolvency Would Affect United States Corporations Doing Business Abroad*, 16 Bankr. Dev. J. 399 (2000); Jay Lawrence Westbrook, *Multinational Enterprises in General Default: Chapter 15, the ALI Principles, and the EU Insolvency Regulation*, 76 Am. Bankr. L.J. 1 (2002).

[43] United Nations Commission on International Trade Law, Model Law on Cross-Border Insolvency, available at www.uncitral.org/uncitral/en/uncitral_texts/insolvency/1997Model.html; *see* Cross-Border Insolvency: A Commentary on the UNCITRAL Model Law (Look Chan Ho ed., 2006); André J. Berends, *The UNCITRAL Model Law on Cross-Border Insolvency: A Comprehensive Overview*, 6 Tul. J. Int'l & Comp. L. 309 (1998).

[44] *See* www.uncitral.org/uncitral/en/uncitral_texts/insolvency/1997Model_status.html (last viewed on Nov. 28, 2006).

[45] The European Union Regulation on Insolvency Proceedings appears at Council Regulation 1346/2000, 29 May 2000, on insolvency proceedings, 2000 O.J. (L160) 1–18 (effective May 30, 2001), as amended, available at europa.eu/eur-lex/en/legislation.pdf (last viewed on November 24, 2006). It applies in twenty-four of the European Union's twenty-five countries. Denmark is the only country in the EU where it does not apply.

[46] Bankruptcy Code § 1501(a).

[47] Bankruptcy Code § 1501(a)(1).

[48] Bankruptcy Code § 1501(a)(2).

[49] Bankruptcy Code § 1501(a)(4).

[50] Bankruptcy Code § 1501(a)(5).

The most significant features of Chapter 15 and the UNCITRAL model on which it is based are its provisions regarding "recognition" of a foreign bankruptcy proceeding by an American bankruptcy court, and those regarding the bankruptcy court's duties to cooperate with a foreign bankruptcy proceeding.

[A] Foreign Bankruptcy Proceedings: Main and Nonmain Proceedings

[1] Foreign Proceedings

Chapter 15 applies only in connection with a debtor who is the subject of a foreign proceeding.[51] A "foreign proceeding" is a

> collective judicial or administrative proceeding in a foreign country, including an interim proceeding, under a law relating to insolvency or adjustment of debt in which proceeding the assets and affairs of the debtor are subject to control or supervision by a foreign court, for the purpose of reorganization or liquidation.[52]

Thus, the mere fact that a lawsuit is pending against a debtor in a foreign country is not enough to trigger the Code's rules regarding cross-border insolvency cases. The foreign case must be a collective proceeding in which all of the debtor's assets are under court supervision for the purpose of reorganizing or liquidating the debtor's financial affairs.

This is different in two respects from the definition of foreign proceeding that was used before the 2005 Amendments. First, the new language requires the foreign proceeding to be "collective." A single secured creditor's foreclosure action is not a foreign proceeding, even though it might result in liquidation of the debtor's assets, because it is not a "collective" proceeding. Second, unlike former § 101(23), the foreign proceeding need not be pending in the debtor's "home" country, where its domicile, residence, principal place of business, or principal assets are located. Cases applying former § 304, which permitted ancillary proceedings to be initiated only if the foreign case was pending in the country of the debtor's main location, no longer control. However, to qualify as a foreign proceeding, the proceeding must be pending in a jurisdiction where the debtor has an "establishment."[53] An "establishment" is defined as "any place of operations where the debtor carries out a non-transitory economic activity."[54]

[2] Main Proceedings and Nonmain Proceedings

Chapter 15 distinguishes between two types of foreign bankruptcy proceedings: "foreign main proceedings" and "foreign nonmain proceedings."

---

[51] *See* Bankruptcy Code § 1502(1). For the purposes of Chapter 15, "debtor" means "an entity that is the subject of a foreign proceeding." Bankruptcy Code § 1502(1).

[52] Bankruptcy Code § 101(23).

[53] Bankruptcy Code § 1502(2), (4), (5).

[54] Bankruptcy Code § 1502(2).

A "foreign main proceeding" is a foreign proceeding pending in the country where the debtor has the "center of its main interests."[55] A "foreign nonmain proceeding" is a foreign proceeding pending in a country that is not the center of the debtor's main interests.[56]

The Code treats foreign main proceedings differently from foreign nonmain proceedings. As explained below, "recognition" of a foreign main proceeding results in the immediate imposition of the automatic stay and enjoins nearly every type of action a creditor might take to recover from the debtor against assets located in the United States.[57] Recognition of a nonmain proceeding authorizes the court to enjoin creditors' collection efforts as necessary to protect the debtor's assets or the interests of creditors generally, but does not result in an automatic injunction against collection activities.[58] Recognition of a foreign main proceeding also affects the debtors right to transfer its assets.

[3] Eligible Debtors

Chapter 15 imposes a few limits on who may be the subject of a Chapter 15 case. Chapter 15 does not apply to railroads, regulated financial institutions, or domestic insurance companies, who may not seek relief under Chapter 7.[59] Likewise, it excludes individual debtors (and their spouses) with debts below the limits imposed on debtors for relief under Chapter 13 who are either U.S. citizens or permanent residents.[60] Also excluded from eligibility are entities subject to the Securities Investor Protection Act of 1970, stockbrokers, and commodity brokers.[61]

[B] "Recognition" of Foreign Bankruptcy Proceedings

Section 1509 permits the debtor's representative in a foreign bankruptcy proceeding to petition an American bankruptcy court for "recognition" of the foreign case.[62] Before recognition, the foreign representative does not have access to American courts. The petition must be accompanied by a certified copy of the decision that commenced the foreign case and appointed the foreign representative, a certificate from the foreign court in which the case is pending that affirms the existence of the foreign proceeding and of the appointment of the foreign representative, or some other evidence acceptable to the bankruptcy court that the foreign case is pending and that

[55] Bankruptcy Code § 1502(4).

[56] Bankruptcy Code § 1502(5).

[57] Bankruptcy Code § 1520(a)(1); *see* Chapter 8, The Automatic Stay, *supra.*

[58] Bankruptcy Code § 1521(a).

[59] Bankruptcy Code § 1501(c)(1); *see* Bankruptcy Code § 109(b); *see generally* § 6.02[B][2] Eligibility for Relief Under Chapter 7 Liquidation, *supra.*

[60] Bankruptcy Code § 1501(c)(2); *see* Bankruptcy Code § 109(c); *see generally* § 6.02[B][6][c] Chapter 13 Debt Limits, *supra.*

[61] Bankruptcy Code § 1501(c)(3).

[62] Bankruptcy Code § 1509(a).

the applicant is the authorized foreign representative in the case.[63] The petition must also be accompanied by a statement that identifies all foreign proceedings with respect to the debtor that are known to the foreign representative.[64] This deals with the possibility that multiple cases are pending in several countries. If these original documents are not in English, they must be translated into English, along with any other documents the court requires.[65]

After notice and a hearing, the bankruptcy court is required to recognize the foreign proceeding if: (1) the foreign proceeding is either a foreign main proceeding or a foreign nonmain proceeding as those terms are defined in § 1502; (2) the foreign representative is an appropriate person or body; and (3) the petition is accompanied by the documents required by § 1515.[66]

This is considerably different from the application of former § 304. It permitted a bankruptcy court to grant relief, in the form of an ancillary bankruptcy proceeding, based on what would "best assure an economical and expeditious administration" of the debtor's estate consistent with six additional factors: (1) just treatment of holders of claims and interests; (2) protection of creditors in the United States against any prejudice and unfairness in the foreign proceeding; (3) prevention of preferential or fraudulent transfers of the debtor's property; (4) distribution of the estate's property in accordance with the bankruptcy code; (5) comity; and (6) providing the debtor with the opportunity for a fresh start.[67] Chapter 15 dispenses with this factor analysis, and requires the bankruptcy court to recognize most foreign proceedings, provided only that the application for recognition is legitimate.

The key exception to this is found in § 1506, which establishes a broad "public policy exception" to the rules in Chapter 15. It provides: "Nothing in this chapter prevents the court from refusing to take an action governed by this chapter if the action would be manifestly contrary to the public policy of the United States."[68] This is, however, a much more limited basis for refusing cooperation than the balancing test under former law.

While a petition for recognition is pending, the court may stay creditors' efforts to seize the debtor's assets and may entrust the administration of the debtor's assets to the foreign representative to preserve their value.[69] The court may also suspend the debtor's rights to transfer or encumber its assets, permit discovery, or grant nearly any relief that would be available to a bankruptcy trustee. However, this relief is not automatic — the foreign

[63] Bankruptcy Code § 1515(b).

[64] Bankruptcy Code § 1515(c).

[65] Bankruptcy Code § 1515(d).

[66] Bankruptcy Code § 1517; In re SphinX, Ltd., 351 B.R. 103 (Bankr. S.D.N.Y. 2006).

[67] Former Bankruptcy Code § 304(c)(1)-(6).

[68] Bankruptcy Code § 1506.

[69] Bankruptcy Code § 1519(a)(1), (2).

representative must apply for an order to protect the debtor's assets and the interests of creditors.[70]

[C] Effect of Recognition of Foreign Proceeding

[1] Stay of Other Proceedings

Upon recognition of a foreign main proceeding, the automatic stay of § 362 goes into effect.[71] As explained elsewhere, this stays virtually every type of collection activity a creditor might engage in,[72] including administrative and judicial proceedings against the debtor,[73] efforts to obtain possession of the debtor's property,[74] and even informal collection efforts.[75] It does not stay criminal prosecutions or other proceedings that involve the enforcement of a governmental police or regulatory power.[76] None of these actions would be barred by § 362 either. More importantly, however, the stay under Chapter 15 is territorial, reaching only assets and creditors within the United States. Therefore, nothing in § 1520(a) prevents a creditor from commencing an action against the debtor in a foreign country "to the extent necessary to preserve a claim against the debtor."[77] Thus, if a creditor would lose its rights against the debtor under foreign law if it failed to initiate a claim against the debtor in that country, the creditor may do so. Likewise, of course, creditors may file claims in the case.[78] Apart from this, the court also has the discretionary authority to stay actions concerning the debtor's property or liabilities beyond the limits imposed by the automatic stay,[79] except with respect to criminal or regulatory enforcement proceedings, or to the extent that the extension would overlap with the stay granted by another proceeding.[80]

Recognition of a foreign nonmain proceeding permits the bankruptcy court to stay any pending proceedings involving the debtor's assets and liabilities within the United States, but does not impose an automatic stay.[81] Whether the court should impose a stay to protect assets located within the scope of the bankruptcy court's authority depends on the extent to which this is "necessary to effectuate the purposes of [Chapter 15] and to protect the assets of the debtor or the interests of the creditors."[82]

---

[70] Bankruptcy Code § 1519.

[71] Bankruptcy Code § 1520(a)(1).

[72] *See* § 8.02 Scope of the Automatic Stay, *supra*.

[73] Bankruptcy Code § 362(a)(1).

[74] Bankruptcy Code § 362(a)(3).

[75] Bankruptcy Code § 362(a)(6).

[76] Bankruptcy Code § 362(b)(1), (4); *see* § 8.03 Exceptions to the Automatic Stay, *supra*.

[77] Bankruptcy Code § 1520(b).

[78] Bankruptcy Code § 1520(c).

[79] Bankruptcy Code § 1521(a)(1), (2).

[80] Bankruptcy Code § 1521(d). The foreign representative might still seek discretionary relief from such proceedings under § 105. *See* § 8.05 Discretionary Stays, *supra*.

[81] Bankruptcy Code § 1521(a)(1).

[82] Bankruptcy Code § 1521(a).

[2] Transfers of the Debtor's Property

Recognition of a foreign main proceeding invokes §§ 363, 549 and 552 all of which restrict a debtor's authority to freely transfer its property. As explained elsewhere, § 363 generally permits the debtor to use, sell, or lease its property in the ordinary course of business, but requires court authorization, consistent with principles of adequate protection of secured creditors under § 361, for the debtor to dispose of property outside the ordinary course or for the debtor to dispose of "cash collateral" even in the ordinary course of business.[83] Section 549 provides for the recovery of certain post-petition transfers.[84] Section 552 impairs the post-petition effect of security interests in after-acquired collateral.[85] These restrictions fall into place immediately upon recognition of the foreign case as a main case. Recognition also supplies the court with discretionary authority to suspend the transferability of the debtor's property beyond the limits imposed by these provisions.[86]

Recognition of a foreign nonmain proceeding gives the court discretionary authority to suspend the debtor's right to "transfer, encumber or otherwise dispose" of its assets.[87] However, the foreign representative of the nomain proceeding must seek this protection from the bankruptcy court in order to effectuate the purposes of Chapter 15 and to protect the debtor's assets and the interests of its creditors.[88]

[3] Authority to Operate the Debtor's Business

Recognition of a foreign main proceeding gives the foreign representative the authority to operate the debtor's business and to exercise the same authority to use, sell, and lease estate property that is normally enjoyed by a bankruptcy trustee or a Chapter 11 debtor-in-possession.[89]

Recognition of foreign nonmain proceeding does not instantly confer upon the foreign representative the right to operate the debtor's business, but it does permit the court to entrust "the administration or realization of all or part of the debtor's assets within the territorial jurisdiction of the United States to the foreign representative, or another person, including an examiner" as specified by the court.[90]

[4] Distribution of Assets

Recognition of either a foreign main or a nonmain proceeding permits the court to entrust the foreign representative with authority to distribute

[83] Bankruptcy Code § 363(a)-(d); *see* § 9.03 Use, Sale, or Lease of Estate Property, *supra*.

[84] Bankruptcy Code § 549; *see* § 14.05 Avoidance of Post-Petition Transfers, *supra*.

[85] Bankruptcy Code § 552; *see* § 10.03[B][4] After-Acquired Collateral, *supra*.

[86] Bankruptcy Code § 1521(a)(3).

[87] Bankruptcy Code § 1521(a)(3).

[88] Bankruptcy Code § 1521(a).

[89] Bankruptcy Code § 1520(a)(3).

[90] Bankruptcy Code § 1521(a)(5).

whatever of the debtor's assets are located in the United States.[91] The principle limitation on the court's authority in this regard, and perhaps a last vestige of § 304's multifactor test, is that the court must be "satisfied that the interests of creditors in the United States are sufficiently protected."[92]

[5] Trustee's Powers

Recognition of either type of foreign proceeding also permits the court to grant the foreign representative any additional relief that is ordinarily available to a bankruptcy trustee or to a debtor-in-possession.[93] However, the foreign representative may not exercise the trustee's avoiding powers under §§ 522 (avoidance of security interests and liens in exempt property), 544 (strong-arm clause), 545 (statutory liens), 547 (preferences), 548 (fraudulent transfers), 550 (remedies for avoiding powers), or 724(a) (lien for non-compensatory penalties).[94] To take advantage of these avoiding powers, the foreign representative must initiate a plenary bankruptcy proceeding under the appropriate chapter of the Bankruptcy Code pursuant to its authority under § 1511.[95]

[6] Additional Assistance

Bankruptcy courts are also authorized to provide "additional assistance" to a foreign representative, beyond the specific provisions contained in Chapter 15, so long as the court does not violate any specific limits it imposes.[96] In exercising discretion over whether to provide additional assistance, the court must consider the same factors that guided the court under former § 304.[97] This preserves some aspects of former § 304, the case law that developed under it, and the uncertainties with which it was associated, but it would appear to apply only where a court wishes to cooperate in a manner beyond that required by the statute.[98] The content of such additional relief is, however, difficult to conceive in the abstract.

[D] Rights of Foreign Creditors

Chapter 15 gives foreign creditors the same rights regarding the commencement of and participation in a case under Chapter 15 as domestic creditors.[99] It requires that notification be given to foreign creditors

---

[91] Bankruptcy Code § 1521(b).

[92] Bankruptcy Code § 1521(b).

[93] Bankruptcy Code § 1521(a)(7).

[94] Bankruptcy Code § 1521(a)(7).

[95] Bankruptcy Code § 1511.

[96] Bankruptcy Code § 1507(a).

[97] Bankruptcy Code § 1507(b); *see* § 21.03[B] "Recognition" of Foreign Bankruptcy Proceedings, *supra*.

[98] *See* Todd Kraft & Allison Aranson, *Transnational Bankruptcies: Section 304 and Beyond*, 1993 Colum Bus. L. Rev, 329, 339.

[99] Bankruptcy Code § 1513(a).

whenever notice is to be given to creditors generally or is required to be given to a specific class or category of creditors.[100] Chapter 15 further provides for adjustment of the normal mechanisms and time limits for providing notice to foreign creditors as may be appropriate under the circumstances.[101]

Foreign creditors have the right to appear in the bankruptcy case to the same extent as domestic creditors.[102] The priority rights of foreign creditors are not to be altered because of their status as foreign creditors,[103] with two limited exceptions. First, it maintains the "foreign revenue rule" which prevents allowance of certain claims of foreign governments.[104] This primarily limits the enforceability of foreign tax claims.[105] It also subjects the enforceability of such claims to any treaty that the United States might enter into with a foreign country.[106]

[E] Commencement of a Parallel Proceeding

Recognition of a foreign main proceeding authorizes the foreign representative to commence a voluntary case involving the debtor under §§ 301 or 302.[107] Naturally, this is permitted only if "the debtor has assets in the United States."[108] Such petition would probably be under Chapter 11 where the foreign representative may or may not manage the affairs of the debtor. Of course, if a Chapter 7 petition were commenced, a trustee would be appointed. Nothing in Chapter 15 appears to prevent the foreign representative from being selected as the trustee. Chapter 15 requires the efforts in a domestic case to be limited to the debtor's assets that are within the territorial jurisdiction of the United States.[109]

[F] Cooperation and Coordination with Foreign Courts and Foreign Representatives

A bankruptcy court in the United States must cooperate and coordinate its efforts with those of the foreign bankruptcy court in a foreign proceeding that the court has recognized[110] "to the maximum extent possible."[111] The

---

[100] Bankruptcy Code § 1514(a).

[101] Bankruptcy Code § 1514(d).

[102] Bankruptcy Code § 1513(a).

[103] Bankruptcy Code § 1513(b)(1).

[104] Bankruptcy Code § 1513(b)(2)(A).

[105] *See* Moore v. Mitchell, 30 F.2d 600 (2d Cir. 1929), *aff'd*, 281 U.S. 18 (1930); H.R. Rep. No. 109-31, at 111–112 (2005) *reprinted in* 2005 U.S.C.C.A.N. 88, 174.

[106] Bankruptcy Code § 1513(b)(2)(B).

[107] *See* § 6.02 Commencement of a Voluntary Case, *supra.*

[108] Bankruptcy Code § 1528.

[109] Bankruptcy Code § 1528.

[110] Bankruptcy Code § 1528.

[111] Bankruptcy Code § 1525(a).

court has express authority to "communicate directly with . . . a foreign court or a foreign representative, subject to the rights of a party in interest to notice and participation."[112] The trustee, debtor-in-possession, or examiner is similarly required to cooperate "to the maximum extent possible" with a foreign court or a foreign representative in a foreign case.[113]

This cooperation might be accomplished through a variety of means, including:

- appointment of a person to act at the direction of the court in connection with the cases;[114]
- communication "by any means . . . appropriate";[115]
- coordination of the administration and supervision of the debtor's assets and its operations;[116]
- approval or implementation of any agreement that might exist concerning coordination of the proceedings;[117] and
- coordination of concurrent proceedings involving the same debtor.[118]

"Coordination" refers to §§ 1529 and 1530.

A foreign representative of a foreign nonmain proceeding has standing to initiate an involuntary case under § 303.[119] However, an order for relief is granted under § 303 only if the petition is not controverted by the debtor, if the debtor is not paying its debts as they come due, or if a trustee, receiver, or other agent has been appointed in the past 120 days to take charge of substantially all of the debtor's assets.[120]

[G] Concurrent Proceedings

Chapter 15 provides rules governing concurrent bankruptcy proceedings in more than one country.[121] As noted above, once a foreign main proceeding has been recognized, the foreign representative may commence a voluntary case involving the same debtor, provided that the debtor is otherwise eligible for relief under the Bankruptcy Code.[122] When concurrent proceedings are pending, the bankruptcy court "shall seek cooperation and coordination" with the foreign proceeding.[123] If the case in the United

[112] Bankruptcy Code § 1525(b).

[113] Bankruptcy Code § 1526(a).

[114] Bankruptcy Code § 1527(1).

[115] Bankruptcy Code § 1527(2).

[116] Bankruptcy Code § 1527(3).

[117] Bankruptcy Code § 1527(4).

[118] Bankruptcy Code § 1527.

[119] *See* 6.03 Commencement of an Involuntary Case, *supra*.

[120] Bankruptcy Code § 303(h).

[121] Bankruptcy Code § 1529.

[122] Bankruptcy Code § 1528.

[123] Bankruptcy Code § 1529.

States is already pending when the foreign representative seeks recognition of a foreign proceeding, relief granted under §§ 1519 and 1521, restricting creditors' actions, must be consistent with whatever relief has previously been granted in the domestic case,[124] unless the foreign case is recognized as a foreign main proceeding.[125] If a foreign proceeding is recognized before a case is commenced in the United States, relief provided pursuant to recognition of the foreign case may be modified or terminated if it is inconsistent with relief in the domestic case.[126]

If more than one foreign case involving the same debtor is pending, which might easily occur with respect to financially troubled debtors with business activities in several countries, the court is similarly required to cooperate and coordinate with the foreign proceedings.[127] Proceedings in a domestic bankruptcy court must be consistent with proceedings in any foreign main proceeding that the bankruptcy court recognizes.[128]

---

[124] Bankruptcy Code § 1529(1)(a).

[125] Bankruptcy Code § 1529(1)(B).

[126] Bankruptcy Code § 1529(2)(A).

[127] Bankruptcy Code § 1530.

[128] Bankruptcy Code § 1530(1).

Chapter 23
Special Uses of Bankruptcy

§ 23.01 Special Uses of Bankruptcy

Bankruptcy can do more than discharge unpayable debt for the financially troubled. It can also be used as a tool to deal with many other difficult problems, particularly problems faced by business entities that are looking for ways to deal with diverse creditors while continuing a business, or for ways to sell complicated types of assets. In this chapter, we discuss a few novel uses of Chapter 11. Some of these uses of bankruptcy are relatively new. Others, notably substantive consolidation, have a long history. Some are specifically provided for in the Code. Others raise thorny issues of statutory interpretation.

§ 23.02 Mass Torts[1]

In modern industrial society, it is inevitable that some products will malfunction, workplace accidents will occur, and industrial processes will cause environmental harms. These mishaps may occur because of the bad luck, incompetence, or bad faith of an industrial enterprise. A sedative may have teratogenic properties that cause thousands of disabling birth defects. A commonly used mineral used to retard fires — and once used in baby powder — may cause a fatal lung disease. An intrauterine device may cause sterility. A commuter aircraft may crash. Any of these disasters may result in a "mass tort" — a situation in which a single act, transaction, or product generates tens, hundreds or even thousands of personal injury lawsuits. And, although the mass tort liability of the Roman Catholic Church in America does not stem from a single product or incident, it raises many of the same issues that arise in other mass tort cases together with its own set of unusual questions related to the religious nature of the debtors involved in several diocesan bankruptcy reorganization cases.

Inside or outside of bankruptcy, mass torts have tested state and federal procedural rules' capacity to administer justice. Proposals for reform include massive consolidation of actions; unified discovery, pre-trial, and trial; restrictions on the multiple award of punitive damages; and review of attorneys' fees. All are controversial.

Almost by default, bankruptcy has become a battleground in the struggle over tort law. A bankruptcy is a collective proceeding; in most cases it provides debtor and creditors with a single forum in which all controversies

[1] Alan N. Resnick, *Bankruptcy as a Vehicle for Resolving Enterprise-Threatening Mass Tort Liability*, 148 U. Pa. L. Rev. 2045 (2000).

can be decided before a single judge. True, that judge is generally unaided by a jury,[2] but the judge has the advantage of dealing with all matters concerning the debtor in one go. Moreover, the judge can provide for an equal distribution of available assets among all claimants, thus avoiding the possibility that those claimants who sue early will collect in full while those who sue late will get little or nothing. There is nothing in the Bankruptcy Code that prevents a debtor from using it to attempt a global resolution of mass tort issues, and a number of companies have attempted exactly that. Cases involving asbestos claims, IUDs, breast implants and commuter aircraft have found their way into Bankruptcy Court.[3]

[A] Future Claims[4]

One of the most difficult issues in many mass tort cases is how to deal with future claimants: those who have been exposed to the harmful effects of the debtor's conduct or product, but who have not yet discovered their injuries. In some cases, they have not manifested symptoms; in other cases they have not yet traced their illness or injuries to the debtor's product.[5] In some cases, they do not even know that they have been exposed to the source of the harm. Still others may not have yet been exposed to the defendant's product, but will be exposed to it and become ill, or injured as a result of its defects weeks, months, and perhaps years after the bankruptcy case concludes.

Bankruptcy cases involving the harmful effects of asbestos raise most of these issues. If a construction worker who installed asbestos becomes ill and is diagnosed with asbestosis before the manufacturer of the asbestos insulation product she installed files a bankruptcy petition, she undoubtedly has a claim, because she had a right to payment and thus a "claim" before the bankruptcy case commenced.[6] However, one of this creditor's co-workers, who had contact with the debtor's product at the same time, might not develop symptoms of her disease until after the case is pending. This might be an unmatured claim at the time of commencement, or not a claim

[2] *See* § 5.02[E] Jury Trials in Bankruptcy Litigation, *supra*.

[3] Kane v. Johns-Manville Corp., 843 F.2d 636 (2d Cir. 1988); Grady v. A.H. Robins, Co., 839 F.2d 198 (4th Cir. 1988); In re Owens Corning, Inc., 419 F.3d 195, 206 (3d Cir. 2005); In re Piper Aircraft Corp., 162 B.R. 619, 624 (Bankr. S.D. Fla.), *aff'd*, 168 B.R. 434 (S.D. Fla. 1994), *aff'd*, 58 F.3d 1573 (11th Cir. 1995).

[4] Larua Bartell, *Due Process for the Unknown Future Claim in Bankruptcy — Is this Notice Really Necessary?*, 78 Am. Bankr. L.J. 339 (2004); Ralph R. Mabey & Jamie Andra Gavrin, *Constitutional Limitations on the Discharge of Future Claims in Bankruptcy*, 44 S.C. L. Rev. 745 (1993); Sheldon S. Toll, *Bankruptcy and Mass Torts: The Commission's Proposal*, 5 Am. Bankr. Inst. L. Rev. 363 (1997); J. Maxwell Tucker, *The Clash of Successor Liability Principles, Reorganization Law, and the Just Demand That Relief be Afforded Unknown and Unknowable Claimants*, 12 Bankr. Dev. J. 1 (1995).

[5] *See, e.g.*, Grady v. A.H. Robins, Co., 839 F.2d 198 (4th Cir. 1988) (debtor did not discover that her injuries were related to the defendant's product until after the debtor's case was commenced).

[6] Bankruptcy Code § 101(5).

at all, depending on how claims are defined. Still others, who occupy the building, may not even be exposed to the harmful fibers until after the case is closed. Whether they should be permitted to participate in the case, through some representative, raises other difficulties.

Whether these parties have claims is important in several key respects. First, only those with claims are entitled to participate in the debtor's bankruptcy case by voting on a plan and receiving a distribution of the debtor's assets.[7] If the creditor's rights attached after bankruptcy, the creditor cannot participate in the case. Second, the automatic stay has its biggest effect on those whose claims arose before commencement of the case.[8] Those whose claims arose later may not be affected by the automatic stay.[9] Third, the debtor's liability on creditors' "claims" is discharged.[10] If the creditor's right to recover is not a claim, the debtor's liability is not discharged. On the one hand, the future claimant may prefer to allow his claim to "ride through" the bankruptcy, and assert it against the reorganized entity. On the other hand, it may not be assertable against the reorganized debtor, because it may not qualify as an administrative expense. Also, if the company is unable to reorganize, because of inability to resolve and contain its tort liability, the debtor may be forced to liquidate.[11] This may leave the future claimants with nothing.

Courts have developed several tests for determining whether future creditors hold claims.[12] One line of decisions focuses on the "right to payment" language in § 101(3), and restricts creditors with claims to those whose right to sue the debtor accrued under state law before the case began. Under this test, future claimants would not have a claim in the bankruptcy, and their claims could not be resolved through reorganization. Other courts adopt a broader view of claims and apply a "conduct test" under which the determination of whether a creditor has a claim depends upon when the debtor's conduct, which gave rise to its liability to the creditor, occurred. If the conduct, such as manufacture of the defective product, occurred before the petition was filed, the creditor has a claim in the debtor's bankruptcy case even though the creditor's cause of action did not accrue under conventional state rules, until after the petition was filed.[13] This test facilitate reorganization, but may deprive many claimants of their claims before they even know that they have them. A third test imposes a "due process" limitation on the "conduct" test. It treats the conduct as sufficient to give rise to the claim, but requires the creditor to have had some

---

[7] *See generally* § 10.02 Claims of Creditors, *supra.*

[8] Bankruptcy Code § 362(a); *see* § 8.02 Scope of the Automatic Stay, *supra.*

[9] *See* Grady v. A.H. Robins Co., 839 F.2d 198 (4th Cir. 1988).

[10] Bankruptcy Code § 524(a); *see* § 13.09 Effect of Discharge, *supra.*

[11] *See* Schweitzer v. Consolidated Rail Corp., 758 F.2d 936 (3d Cir. 1985); Frederick Tung, *Taking Future Claims Seriously: Future Claims and Successor Liability in Bankruptcy*, 49 Case W. Res. L. Rev. 435 (1999).

[12] *See* In re Hoffinger Industries, Inc., 307 B.R. 112 (Bankr. E.D. Ark. 2004).

[13] *See, e.g.*, Grady v. A.H. Robins Co. (In re A.H. Robins Co.), 839 F.2d 198 (4th Cir. 1988).

relationship with the defendant or its product before the case commenced for the creditor to have a cognizable claim in the debtor's bankruptcy case.[14] Under this test, those who are not exposed to the debtor's defective product until after the bankruptcy case is commenced, do not have claims, and their claims are not, therefore, discharged.

[B] Claims Trusts[15]

A key issue in many mass tort liability bankruptcy cases is how to handle the settlement of creditors' claims. Since its use in the Johns-Mansville bankruptcy,[16] cases involving mass tort claims have usually relied on a trust for the settlement of present and future claims.[17] The mechanism is now officially sanctioned by the Bankruptcy Code for use in cases involving liability related to exposure to asbestos.

Section 524(g) permits the court to create a qualified settlement trust funded by the debtor's stock or bonds and to issue a "channeling injunction" that requires present and future claimants to pursue their claims against the trust rather than against the reorganized debtor. By either funding the trust with stock or defining the precise scope of the debtor's liability, § 524(g) provides the assurance that prospective investors need to supply the funds to finance the debtor's reorganization.[18] Without this protection, investors would be reluctant to get involved with the reorganization, out of a fear that indeterminate future liabilities arising from the debtor's past would make further reorganization necessary. While 524(g) authorizes trusts and channeling injunctions for asbestos claims, it is not, by any means, clear that such channeling injunctions will work for cases not covered by that section.

---

[14] In re Piper Aircraft Corp., 162 B.R. 619, 624 (Bankr. S.D. Fla.), *aff'd*, 168 B.R. 434 (S.D. Fla. 1994), *aff'd*, 58 F.3d 1573 (11th Cir. 1995).

[15] Susan Power Johnston & Katherine Porter, *Extension of Section 524(g) of the Bankruptcy Code to Nondebtor Parents, Affiliates, and Transaction Parties*, 59 Bus. Law. 503 (2004); Linda J. Rusch, *Unintended Consequences of Unthinking Tinkering: The 1994 Amendments and the Chapter 11 Process*, 69 Am. Bankr. L.J. 349, 389–90 (1995) (explaining channeling injunctions under § 524(g)).

[16] Kane v. Johns-Manville Corp., 843 F.2d 636 (2d Cir. 1988); Marianna S. Smith, *Resolving Asbestos Claims: The Manville Personal Injury Settlement Trust*, 53 Law & Contemp. Probs. 27 (1990).

[17] *See* Eric D. Green, James L. Patton, Jr. & Edwin J. Harron, *Future Claimant Trusts and "Channeling Injunctions" to Resolve Mass Tort Environmental Liability in Bankruptcy: The Met-Coil Model*, 22 Emory Bankr. Dev. J. 157 (2005).

[18] Sander L. Esserman & David J. Parsons, *The Case for Broad Access to 11 U.S.C. § 524(g) in Light of the Third Circuit's Ongoing Business Requirement Dicta in* Combustion Engineering, 62 N.Y.U. Ann. Surv. Am. L. 187 (2006).

[C] Estimation of Future Claims[19]

Cases involving mass tort claims present difficult issues concerning the number and amount of valid claims against the estate. To avoid running the risk that the trust established to satisfy mass tort claims is insufficient to pay those claims, the fund must be adequately funded. Otherwise, there is a risk that their claims will receive a disproportionally small portion of the debtor's residual value in violation of bankruptcy's core principal of equal treatment of creditors of the same class. Accordingly, the size and extent of tort victims' present and future claims must be estimated.

The Code explicitly provides for the estimation of creditors' future claims. Section 502(c) provides:

> (c) There shall be estimated for purpose of allowance under this section —
>
> > (1) any contingent or unliquidated claim, the fixing or liquidation of which, as the case may be, would unduly delay the administration of the case; or
> >
> > (2) any right to payment arising from a right to an equitable remedy for breach of performance.[20]

Bankruptcy Rule 3018(a) further provides that the court may temporarily allow claims for the purpose of permitting creditors to vote on a proposed plan. In addition, courts have utilized the estimation of claims for the purpose of determining the feasibility of plans[21] and for determining the amount of any distribution under a proposed plan.[22] Thus, the court may estimate the extent of mass tort claims as necessary for the purpose of permitting present and future creditors to vote on the debtor's plan.

Although § 502(c) permits and indeed requires the court to estimate creditors' claims, it is conspicuously silent about the appropriate method for doing so. This void has led courts and commentators to suggest a variety of methods.[23] The most common of these approaches is the "discounted value model"[24] in which the face amount of the claim is discounted by the probability of the claimant prevailing under applicable nonbankruptcy law.

In cases involving unspecified future claims, courts rely on expert testimony. In the A.H. Robins, Inc. Dalkon Shield bankruptcy case, the court relied on expert testimony to estimate the amount of existing and future tort claims at $4 billion.[25] When the trust established by the debtor's

---

[19] David S. Salsburg & Jack F. Williams, *A Statistical Approach to Claims Estimation in Bankruptcy*, 32 Wake Forest L. Rev. 1119 (1997).

[20] Bankruptcy Code § 502(c).

[21] *E.g.*, In re Farley, Inc., 146 B.R. 748 (Bankr. N.D. Ill. 1992).

[22] In re Rusty Jones, Inc., 143 B.R. 499, 505 (Bankr. N.D. Ill. 1992).

[23] David S. Salsburg & Jack F. Williams, *A Statistical Approach to Claims Estimation in Bankruptcy*, 32 Wake Forest L. Rev. 1119, 1130–52 (1997).

[24] *E.g.*, In re Farley, Inc., 146 B.R. 748, 753–54 (Bankr. N.D. Ill. 1992).

[25] Menard-Sanford v. Mabey (In re A.H. Robins Co.), 880 F.2d 794 (4th Cir. 1989).

plan eventually shut down, it had paid out only 75% of that amount. By contrast, the Johns-Manville trust's initial funding proved inadequate to pay the unexpectedly large volume of claims that arose.[26]

[D] Bankruptcy of Religious Organizations[27]

Several American Diocese of the Roman Catholic Church have experienced financial difficulties arising from liabilities they faced in relationship to the child-abuse scandals that came to light in the late 1990s.[28] As of late 2006, this has led four of these diocese to file Chapter 11 petitions.[29] Along with the usual problems that arise in bankruptcies prompted by mass tort claims, diocesan bankruptcies raise numerous difficult management and property questions not usually encountered in bankruptcies of secular organizations.

Peculiar issues emerge in cases that involve debtors with the unusual organizational structure of the Roman Catholic church. Foremost among these are the constitutional implications of applying the bankruptcy code to bankruptcies of Catholic diocese in the normal fashion. Appointment of a trustee to take over the affairs of a diocese might violate the First Amendment's Free Exercise Clause.[30] At the same time, bankruptcy court involvement in the diocesan debtor's affairs could result in a constitutionally improper entanglement of the government into church matters, in violation of the principle of separation of church and state.[31]

Consider, for example, whether it would be appropriate for a trustee to take over the management of the diocese, either due to gross mismanagement or fraud on the part of the bishop[32] or because the Chapter 11 case is involuntarily converted to a liquidation cases under Chapter 7.[33]

---

[26] www.mantrust.org/history.htm (last viewed on April 24, 2007).

[27] Jonathan C. Lipson, *When Churches Fail: The Diocesan Debtor Dilemmas*, 79 S. Cal. L. Rev. 363 (2006); Felicia Anne Nadborny, Note, *"Leap of Faith" into Bankruptcy: An Examination of the Issues Surrounding the Valuation of a Catholic Diocese's Bankruptcy Estate*, 13 Am. Bankr. Inst. L. Rev. 839 (2005); Roundtable Discussion, *Religious Organizations Filing for Bankruptcy*, 13 Am. Bankr. Inst. L. Rev. 25 (2005).

[28] *See* www.bishop-accountability.org/resources/resource-files/timeline/2003-01-12-Goodstein-TrailOfPain.htm (last viewed, April 24, 2007).

[29] Petitions have been filed in Tuscon, AZ, Spokane, WA, Portland, OR, and Davenport, IA. Information about these cases, including links to the diocesan webpages, is available at Bankruptcy Protection and the Sexual Abuse Crisis, www.bishop-accountability.org/bankrupt/ (last visited April 24, 2007). Other dioceses that have suggested the possibility of filing are Boston, MA, Los Angeles, CA, Covington, KY, and Belleville, IL.

[30] Ryan J. Donohue, Comment, *Thou Shalt Not Reorganize: Sacraments for Sale: First Amendment Prohibitions and Other Complications of Chapter 11 Reorganization for Religious Institutions*, 22 Emory Bankr. Dev. J. 293 (2005).

[31] Jonathan C. Lipson, *When Churches Fail: The Diocesan Debtor Dilemmas*, 79 S. Cal. L. Rev. 363, 365 (2006).

[32] Bankruptcy Code § 1104; *see* § 19.03[D] Appointment of Trustee or Examiner, *supra*.

[33] Bankruptcy Code § 1112; *see* § 19.05[B] Involuntary Conversion or Dismissal, *supra*.

Although there is precedent for it,[34] appointment of a trustee to manage the affairs of a religious organization for the benefit of its creditors might violate the Free Exercise Clause.[35]

Diocesan bankruptcy cases also give rise to difficult and perhaps unique property issues concerning ownership of parish property.[36] Catholic diocese are divided up into numerous local parishes, each with its own church, school, and congregation. If parish property is owned by the bankrupt diocese, the liquidation value of the debtor is considerable. If the only property the diocese owns is the land occupied by the diocesan cathedral, the bishop's residence, and his offices, its value may be meager, at least compared to the extent of claims against the diocese.[37] Moreover, resolution of these issues may necessitate an inquiry into the details of canon law that entangles the court into what otherwise might be viewed as purely church matters.[38]

§ 23.03 Employees' Rights

[A] Rejection of Collective Bargaining Agreements[39]

For many companies, the liability that drives them into bankruptcy, or the cost that renders them unable to pay their debts is the employee payroll. In the U.S., airlines, steel manufacturers and other large companies have sought to use bankruptcy to renegotiate their obligations to unionized employees. Shortly after the Bankruptcy Code was amended in 1978, the Supreme Court held in the *Bildisco* case that a collective bargaining

[34] *E.g.,* In re United Church of the Minister of God, 74 B.R. 271, 280 (Bankr. E.D. Pa. 1987) (appointment of Chapter 11 trustee); *see also* Late Corp. of the Church of Jesus Christ of Latter-Day Saints v. United States, 136 U.S. 1 (1890) (receivership for church property).

[35] Jonathan C. Lipson, *When Churches Fail: The Diocesan Debtor Dilemmas*, 79 S. Cal. L. Rev. 363, 400–03 (2006).

[36] Daniel J. Marcinak, Comment, *Separation of Church and Estate: On Excluding Parish Assets from the Bankruptcy Estate of a Diocese Organized as a Corporation Sole,* 55 Cath. U. L. Rev. 583 (2006); Allison Walsh Smith, Comment, *Chapter 11 Bankruptcy: A New Battleground in the Ongoing Conflict Between Catholic Dioceses and Sex-abuse Claimants*, 84 N.C. L. Rev. 282, 315–30 (2005).

[37] *Compare* Committee of Tort Litigants v. Catholic Diocese of Spokane (In re Catholic Bishop), 329 B.R. 304, 318–20 (Bankr. E.D. Wash. 2005) (diocese estopped from asserting ownership right to parish property) *with* Munns v. Martin, 930 P.2d 318, 319–20 (Wash. 1997) (en banc) (diocese owns parish property)..

[38] Jonathan C. Lipson, *When Churches Fail: The Diocesan Debtor Dilemmas*, 79 S. Cal. L. Rev. 363, 385–90 (2006); Allison Walsh Smith, Comment, *Chapter 11 Bankruptcy: A New Battleground in the Ongoing Conflict Between Catholic Dioceses and Sex-abuse Claimants*, 84 N.C. L. Rev. 282, 315–30 (2005).

[39] Bill D. Bensinger, *Modification of Collective Bargaining Agreements: Does a Breach Bar Rejection?*, 13 Am. Bankr. Inst. L. Rev. 809 (2005); Daniel Keating, *The Continuing Puzzle of Collective Bargaining Agreements in Bankruptcy*, 35 Wm. & Mary L. Rev. 503, 526–34 (1994); Michael D. Sousa, *Reconciling the Otherwise Irreconcilable: The Rejection of Collective Bargaining Agreements Under Section § 1113 of the Bankruptcy Code*, 18 Lab. Law. 453, 469 (2003).

agreement was an executory contract that might be rejected under § 365.[40] If a collective bargaining agreement has no status apart from that as executory contract, then, like any executory contract, it can be rejected. There will, of course, be a claim for breach, but that claim is just another general unsecured claim, payable only in depreciated bankruptcy dollars.[41] If a debtor can cut its labor costs by $500,000,000, and is forced to pay only $50,000,000 to do so, it is still substantially ahead.

During the 1980s this led a number of companies to file Chapter 11 with an eye toward rejecting their union contracts. This tactic aroused outrage, especially, but not exclusively, from organized labor. The Supreme Court, however, ruled that it was permissible; that nothing in the Bankruptcy Code or other federal law bestowed special bankruptcy privileges on union contracts.[42]

Congress quickly responded with a compromise. It accepted the basic principle that collective bargaining agreements could be rejected. However, it decided that these contracts should be given special status and special protection.

Congress' response to the collective bargaining agreement problem is embodied in § 1113.[43] It imposes special substantive and procedural rules for the rejection of collective bargaining contracts. The procedural requirements attempt to force both sides to attempt negotiation of a mutually satisfactory new deal. In this respect, it reinforces the bargain model of both Chapter 11 and of collective bargaining law. Section 1113's substantive provisions require the court to determine whether a new deal is necessary to save the debtor. In this respect, § 1113 models itself to a degree on Chapter 11's cramdown rules.

After the petition is filed, but before filing an application to reject a collective bargaining agreement, the debtor-in-possession[44] must make a proposal to the employees' representative — their union. This proposal must be based on the most complete and reliable information available; it must encompass those "necessary modifications" in the agreement as are "necessary to permit the reorganization."[45] The union must also be given all relevant information necessary to evaluate the proposal.[46] From that point on, § 1113 contemplates that the debtor-in-possession and the employees will negotiate with one another. In the somewhat rosy scenario of the

---

[40] *NLRB v. Bildisco & Bildisco*, 465 U.S. 513 (1984). *See* Chapter 11, Executory Contracts and Unexpired Leases, *supra*.

[41] *See* § 11.04 Rejection of Executory Contracts, *supra*

[42] NLRB v. Bildisco & Bildisco, 465 U.S. 513 (1984).

[43] Section 1114, enacted under the Retiree Benefits Bankruptcy Protection Act of 1988, has parallel provisions for dealing with the payment of insurance benefits to retired employees.

[44] Section 1113 refers to both the debtor-in-possession and the trustee. But, as a practical matter, § 1113 will most often be invoked by a debtor-in-possession. Section 1113 does not apply in Chapter 7 liquidation cases.

[45] Bankruptcy Code § 1113(b)(1)(A).

[46] Bankruptcy Code § 1113(b)(1)(B).

Code, "the trustee shall meet, at reasonable times, with the authorized representative [of the employees] to confer in good faith in attempting to reach mutually satisfactory modifications of such agreement."[47]

If those negotiations fail, the debtor-in-possession may seek court authorization to modify the agreement unilaterally.[48] This requires court approval. The court approves only if (1) the requirements regarding the proposal and the negotiating process were met,[49] (2) the authorized representative of the employees has refused to accept the proposal without good cause,[50] and (3) the balance of equities "clearly" favors rejection of the agreement.[51]

The first of these standards requires the court to find that the proposed modifications are necessary. But, courts have not agreed about what "necessary" means.[52] In *Wheeling-Pittsburgh Steel Corp. v. United Steelworkers of America*,[53] the Third Circuit held that necessary meant "essential."[54] Other courts, such as *Truck Drivers Local 807 v. Carey Transportation, Inc. (In re Carey Transportation, Inc)*,[55] take a more flexible approach that focuses on the debtor's long-term prospects rather than on whether the modifications are essential to prevent an immediate liquidation.[56] This

---

[47] Bankruptcy Code § 1113(b)(2); *see, e.g.*, In re Delta Air Lines, 351 B.R. 67 (Bankr. S.D.N.Y. 2006) (debtor negotiated in good faith despite its refusal to agreed to a "snapback" provision that would reinstate the terms of the original collective bargaining agreement upon recovery of the airline industry).

[48] *See* In re American Provision Co., 44 B.R. 907, 909 (Bankr. D. Minn. 1984) (establishing a widely cited nine-part test for when the debtor may reject a collective bargaining contract); *see* Jeffrey Berman, *Nobody Likes Rejection Unless You're a Debtor in Chapter 11: Rejection of Collective Bargaining Agreements Under 11 U.S.C. § 1113*, 34 N.Y.L. Sch. L. Rev. 169, 173 (1989).

[49] Bankruptcy Code § 1113(c)(1).

[50] Bankruptcy Code § 1113(c)(2).

[51] Bankruptcy Code § 1113(c)(3).

[52] In re Family Snacks, Inc., 257 B.R. 884 (B.A.P. 8th Cir. 2001); Donald B. Smith & Richard A. Bales, *Reconciling Labor and Bankruptcy Law: The Application of 11 U.S.C. § 1113*, 2001 L. Rev. Mich. St. U. Det. C.L. 1145 (2001); *see generally* John F. Wagner Jr., Annotation, *Requirements for Obtaining Court Approval of Rejection of Collective Bargaining Agreement by Debtor in Possession or Trustee in Bankruptcy Under 11 U.S.C.A. §§ 1113(b) and (c)*, 89 A.L.R. Fed. 299 (1988).

[53] 791 F.2d 1074 (3d Cir. 1986).

[54] 791 F.2d at 1088–94; *see also* In re Royal Composing Room, Inc., 62 B.R. 403, 417–18 (Bankr. S.D.N.Y. 1986); In re Pierce Terminal Warehouse, Inc., 133 B.R. 639, 646–47 (Bankr. N.D. Iowa 1991); *see generally* David Keating, *The Continuing Puzzle of Collective Bargaining Agreements in Bankruptcy*, 35 Wm. & Mary L. Rev. 503, 527 (1994).

[55] 816 F.2d 82 (2d Cir. 1987); *see also* United Food and Commercial Workers Union, Local 328 v. Almac's, Inc. (In re Almac's, Inc.), 90 F.3d 1, 5–6 (1st Cir. 1996); Sheet Metal Workers' Int'l Assoc., Local 9 v. Mile Hi Metal Sys., Inc. (In re Mile Hi Metal Systems, Inc.), 899 F.2d 887, 22 C.B.C.2d 611 (10th Cir. 1990).

[56] Christopher D. Cameron, *How "Necessary" Became the Mother of Rejection: An Empirical Look at the Fate of Collective Bargaining Agreements on the Tenth Anniversary of Bankruptcy Code Section 1113*, 34 Santa Clara L. Rev. 841 (1994); Carlos J. Cuevas, *Necessary Modifications and Section 1113 of the Bankruptcy Code: A Search for the Substantive Standard for Modification of a Collective Bargaining Agreement in a Corporate Reorganization*, 64 Am.

more flexible standard is often paired with the requirement of § 1129(a)(11) that a plan of reorganization be confirmed only if confirmation is not likely to be followed by the liquidation of, or the need for further financial reorganization of the debtor.

When weighing the equities, the courts have often considered six issues:

1. The likelihood and consequences of liquidation if rejection is not permitted;

2. The likely reduction in the creditors' claims if the agreement remains in effect;

3. The likelihood and consequences of a strike if the agreement is avoided;

4. The possibility and likely effect of employee claims for breach of contract if the agreement is avoided;

5. The cost-spreading abilities of the various parties, taking into account the number of employees covered by the agreement and how their wages and benefits compare with those of others in the industry; and

6. The good or bad faith of the parties in dealing with the debtor's financial problems.[57]

The degree to which this provision adequately addresses the problems of collective bargaining agreements is debatable. The power of the provision is undercut by the fact that labor claims receive no special priority in a Chapter 7 case. Therefore, if the debtor liquidates, § 1113 does nothing for the employees. On the other hand, the company cannot reorganize without its employees, and the employees cannot benefit from § 1113 unless the reorganization is successful.

Employees' pension benefit plans are frequently part of the employer's collective bargaining contract with their employees.[58] Where employees' pension benefit plans are governed by collective bargaining agreements, § 1113 comes into play as well. However, an extra layer of complication is introduced here. Employee benefit plans, whether or not they are covered by a collective bargaining agreement, are also governed by ERISA, and many are guaranteed by the Pension Benefit Guarantee Corporation. As such, termination of employee benefit plans can be quite complicated.

Bankr. L.J. 133 (1990); Daniel Keating, *The Continuing Puzzle of Collective Bargaining Agreements in Bankruptcy*, 35 Wm. & Mary L. Rev. 503, 526–34 (1994); Mitchell Rait, *Rejection of Collective Bargaining Agreements under Section 1113 of the Bankruptcy Code: The Second Circuit Enters the Arena*, 63 Am. Bankr. L.J. 355 (1989); Jay M. Rector, Comment, *Bankruptcy — How Necessary is "Necessary" Under Section 1113?* Truck Drivers Local 807 v. Carey Transportation, 13 J. Corp. L. 941 (1988).

[57] Truck Drivers Local 907 v. Carey Transportation, Inc., 816 F.2d 82, 93 (2d Cir. 1987).

[58] Amy Lassiter, Note, *Mayday, Mayday!: How the Current Bankruptcy Code Fails to Protect the Pensions of Employees*, 93 Ky. L.J. 939 (2004-05).

[B] Retired Employees' Health Insurance Benefits[59]

Section 1114 provides special protection for insurance benefits of retired employees whose benefits are not covered by a collective bargaining contract governed by § 1113. Companies operating in Chapter 11 must meet the statutory standards of § 1114 to eliminate health insurance coverage provided to retired employees, even if the company could have terminated their coverage if it was not in Chapter 11. Section 1114 provides that a Chapter 11 debtor-in-possession "shall timely pay and shall not modify any retiree benefits."[60] Unpaid benefits are entitled to administrative expense priority under § 503.[61] Benefits may not be modified or eliminated unilaterally by the debtor. Instead, changes may be made only with the consent of the retired employee's representative[62] or approval by the court.[63]

In some cases, of course, modification may be necessary for the survival of the business. Modification or termination of retired employees' health benefits may be necessary to preserve the jobs of current employees. Employers may obtain court authorization for temporarily or permanently altering or eliminating health benefits for retired employees. Temporary modification of retired employees' health benefits is permitted if the court determines that such "interim modifications" are "essential to the continuation of the debtor's business or in order to avoid irreparable damage to the estate."[64]

Unilateral modification is permitted, but only after the debtor-in-possession has proposed adjustments "based on the most complete and reliable information available at the time . . . which provides for those necessary modifications . . . that are necessary to permit the reorganization of the debtor and assures that all creditors, the debtor, and all of the affected parties are treated fairly and equitably."[65] After such a proposal is made, the debtor-in-possession is admonished to "meet at reasonable times, with the [retired employees'] authorized representative to confer in good faith in attempting to reach mutually satisfactory modifications of such retiree benefits."[66] This duty to negotiate in good faith is based on the model established by § 1113 for modification of collective bargaining contracts, described above.

---

[59] Daniel Keating, *Bankruptcy Code § 1114: Congress' Empty Response to the Retiree Plight*, 67 Am. Bankr. L.J. (1993); Daniel L. Keating, *Good Intentions, Bad Economics: Retiree Insurance Benefits in Bankruptcy*, 43 Vand. L. Rev. 161 (1990); Donald R. Korobkin. *Employee Interests in Bankruptcy*, 4 Am. Bankr. Inst L. Rev. 5 (1996); Susan J. Stabile, *Protecting Retiree Medical Benefits in Bankruptcy: The Scope of Section 1114 of the Bankruptcy Code*, 14 Cardozo L. Rev. 1911 (1993).

[60] Bankruptcy Code § 1114(e)(1). The rule applies with equal force to a Chapter 11 debtor under the management of a trustee.

[61] Bankruptcy Code § 1114(e)(2); *see* § 10.04[A][2] Administrative Expense Claims, *supra*.

[62] Bankruptcy Code § 1114(e)(1)(B).

[63] Bankruptcy Code § 1114(e)(1)(A).

[64] Bankruptcy Code § 1114(h)(1).

[65] Bankruptcy Code § 1114(f)(1)(A).

[66] Bankruptcy Code § 1114(f)(2).

The 2005 Amendments provide additional protections for retired employees whose benefits were modified in the six months before the debtor's bankruptcy petition. If the employer was insolvent at the time of the pre-bankruptcy modification, the court may order the employer to reinstate the benefits to their original status, unless the court finds that the "balance of the equities clearly favors [the] modification."[67]

Section 1114 does not apply to benefits for current employees. Nor does it apply to well-compensated retired employees whose gross annual income in the twelve months before the debtor's petition was over $250,000, unless the retired employee demonstrates that she is unable to otherwise obtain medical insurance coverage.[68]

§ 23.04 "Single Asset" Real Estate Cases

Real estate booms are frequently followed by economic busts. The 1980s and early 1990's witnessed one of the most spectacular boom and bust cycles ever. Spurred in large measure by tax laws enacted in 1982 (and perhaps in part by lax regulation of lending institutions), developers put up commercial and residential buildings at a dizzying pace. In 1986, however, the favorable tax treatment of passive real estate investments came to an abrupt end. This, coupled with the huge overhang of already built but barely needed property, brought on a collapse of rental and resale values. Insolvent developers and developments reached for their lawyers in an effort to stave off foreclosure. In many of these cases, the debtor had only one major asset, a building, and only one major creditor, the financial institution from which it borrowed to build.

Single asset real estate cases are those involving a debtor whose sole principle asset is "real property constituting a single property or project . . . which generates substantially all of the gross income of a debtor . . . and on which no substantial business is being conducted by the debtor other than the business of operating the real property and activities incidental thereto."[69] The paradigm frequently involves a limited partnership that owns a single asset, usually an office building or an apartment complex. Consider an example involving Downtown Realty Partners, Ltd., a limited partnership that owns a downtown office building, subject to a mortgage in favor of State Bank. Only a portion of the office space in the building is occupied and many of the tenants are behind on their rent. Other similar buildings in the same community face the same problems, driving down the rent that the partnership can charge from any new tenants that it attracts.

Vacant space, defaulting tenants, and low rents have left Downtown Realty Partners unable to make the regular monthly payments due to State Bank. As its financial circumstances worsened, Downtown Realty has not

[67] Bankruptcy Code § 1114(l).

[68] Bankruptcy Code § 1114(m) (formerly located in § 1114(l)).

[69] Bankruptcy Code § 101(51B).

even been able to pay the interest that accumulates on the debt each month. In this worst case scenario, the total debt owed rises each month as the unpaid interest is added to the principal sum due to the bank. The bank is seriously dissatisfied with the situation, as it has its own cash-flow obligations to meet. Bank regulators are also likely to disapprove and may put pressure on State Bank to do something to correct the situation. Eventually, the Bank will bring a foreclosure action.

Faced with the prospect of losing its only asset and convinced that the economy will eventually improve, Downtown Realty is likely to respond by filing a Chapter 11 petition. This stops the foreclosure proceeding dead in its tracks. Better yet, assuming that the property is worth less than the amount of the total debt owed to the bank, it stops interest from increasing the amount of the debt owed to the bank.

Because the value of the land and building are based on the stream of revenue that they produce, Downtown Realty's office building is likely to be worth considerably less than the amount of the debt owed to State Bank. With a rising mortgage debt and a declining market value of the collateral, the bank is probably undersecured. The property, once worth $12 million, is now worth only $8 million. And the debt, once only $10 million, is now $15 million. Downtown Realty would like to write down the amount of the debt to the $8 million current market value of the collateral, and begin making payments based on its current financial capacity. State Bank prefers to get out from under the entire deal by foreclosing on the property. Single-asset real estate debtors in this situation usually have few other unsecured creditors. They may owe a few utility and maintenance bills, but these claims are likely to be small in comparison to the bank's large unsecured deficiency claim.

Here, Chapter 11 is not being used to preserve value. The building will remain an office building with tenants, no matter who owns it. The debtor is hoping that it might be able to either delay the foreclosure and negotiate with the bank to reduce the bank's claim on any guaranty or other recourse liability. Or the debtor may be hoping to take advantage of Chapter 11 cramdown to retain ownership of the asset by stripping the bank's lien down to the value of the collateral and making a negligible payment of the unsecured portion of the mortgagee's claims. Thus, the debtor's plan might call for paying the bank only $8 million, with interest, perhaps over a twenty to thirty year period, during which the bank might retain a mortgage on the land securing its $8 million claim. The $7 million unsecured balance would be classified separately from the claims of other unsecured creditors and receive only partial payment. Holders of other far smaller unsecured claims will be paid in full.

The bank is likely to vote against the plan, but as long as it is receiving the liquidation value of its unsecured claim and provided that the equity interest holders are contributing new value to the plan and the property has been exposed to the market to ensure that the price being paid is fair, the court might confirm the plan.[70]

[70] *See* § 19.11 Confirmation over Objection of Impaired Class — Cramdown, *supra*.

Here, the debtor and the bank are fighting over who will enjoy the benefit of any future increase in the value of the building. If the plan is confirmed, and the market improves, Downtown Realty's owners will reap the benefit of the appreciated value and the increased rental income received from new tenants. If State Bank is permitted to foreclose and keeps the building long enough for the building to appreciate in value, it will obtain the benefit of that appreciation. Of course, the bank might simply want to cut its losses. It may believe that the local economy will continue to decline and further reduce the value of its collateral. It may not want to keep the building, thus perhaps sending good money after bad, but if it gets the building, it can at least sell it for its current value and obtain at least partial payment on what is at present a "non-performing" loan. This in turn may facilitate the bank's efforts to repair its own financial status and improve its capital position. Such improvements may get the bank out of hot water with the regulatory authorities and enable it to make new and (it is to be hoped) better loans.

Before 1994, the Code contained few provisions to deal with this problem. The most obvious provisions were § 1111(b), and the absolute priority rule of § 1129(b), which are discussed elsewhere.[71] However, § 1111(b) does not address the real desire of the creditor to terminate the bankruptcy, seize the collateral, and retain or resell it, and the absolute priority rule may or may not be subject to the "new value" exception. Creditors have taken several approaches in their efforts to prevent single-asset real estate debtors, like Downtown Realty Partners, to speculate on the real estate market at their creditors' potential expense.

Some have sought to have the stay lifted by arguing that the case was not filed in "good faith."[72] One court recently listed a multi-factor test for determining whether a case should be dismissed as filed in bad faith:

1. The debtor has only one asset.
2. The debtor has few unsecured creditors whose claims are relatively small compared to the claims of the secured creditors.
3. The debtor has no employees.
4. The debtor's one asset is the subject of a foreclosure action as a result of arrearages or default on the debt.
5. The debtor's financial condition is, in essence, a two-party dispute between the debtor and secured creditors, which can be resolved in the pending state foreclosure action.
6. The timing of the debtor's filing evidences an intent to delay or frustrate the legitimate efforts of the debtor's secured creditors to enforce their rights.

---

[71] Bankruptcy Code § 1111(b); *see* § 19.07[C][2] The 1111(b) Election, *supra*.

[72] In re Springs Hospitality, Inc., No. 06-13331, 2006 Bankr. LEXIS 1804 (Aug. 22, 2006, Bankr. D. Col.).

7. The debtor cannot meet current expenses including the payment of personal property and real estate taxes.
8. The debtor has little or no cash flow.[73]

Another approach is to challenge the classification scheme of the debtor's plan which segregates the secured creditor's unsecured deficiency claim from the claims of other unsecured creditors.[74] Another approach has been to question the propriety of the new value exception to the absolute priority rule.[75] More central is an attack on the whole proceeding as lacking good faith because of the lack of any realistic chance for a successful reorganization.[76]

In 1994 and again in 2005, legislative changes to the Code added ammunition to the creditors' arsenal. The 1994 amendments carved out a special rule for relief from the automatic stay in "single asset real estate" cases. It originally defined these cases narrowly as those in which substantially all of the gross income of the debtor is generated by a single property or project, other than a property that consists of 1 to 3 residential units, where the aggregate noncontingent liquidated secured debts are $4,000,000 or less. The 2005 Amendments expanded the definition in dramatic fashion, by removing the $4 million ceiling on the amount of secured debt.[77] In these cases, the court is directed to grant relief from the automatic stay to permit a secured creditor's mortgage foreclosure action ninety days after the order for relief unless the debtor has either filed a plan that has a reasonable possibility of being confirmed within a reasonable time or has commenced making monthly payments to keep up with regular interest that is accruing on the mortgage debt.[78] This puts considerable pressure on single asset real estate debtors who are not earning sufficient income from rent or other income to keep up with the interest that is accumulating on the debt while the case is pending.

§ 23.05 Consolidation of Cases of Related Debtors[79]

Except for spouses, who may file joint bankruptcy proceedings,[80] each individual or entity in bankruptcy is treated separately. This is ordinarily

[73] *Id.*

[74] *See* § 19.08[D][2][c] Classification in Single-Asset Real Estate Cases, *supra;* Kenneth N. Klee, *One Size Fits Some: Single Asset Real Estate Bankruptcy*, 87 Cornell L. Rev. 1285 (2002).

[75] *See* § 19.11[C] New Value Exception to Absolute Priority Rule, *supra.*

[76] *See* § 19.10[B] Plan Proposed in Good Faith, *supra.*

[77] Bankruptcy Code § 101(51)(B). Family farmers are excluded from the definition.

[78] Bankruptcy Code § 362(d)(3); *see* § 8.06[B][4] Single-Asset Real Estate Collateral, *supra.*

[79] Chauncey H. Levy, *Joint Administration and Consolidation*, 85 Com. L.J. 538 (1980).

[80] *See* § 6.02[D] Joint Petitions, *supra*. Joint filing does not mean that the cases are substantively consolidated; substantive consolidation of joint husband-wife cases is analyzed in much the same way as substantive consolidation generally. *E.g.*, Reider v. Federal Deposit Insurance Corp. (In re Reider), 31 F.3d 1102 (11th Cir. 1994); Robert B. Chapman, *Coverture and Cooperation: The Firm, the Market, and the Substantive Consolidation of Married Debtors*, 17 Bankr. Dev. J. 105 (2000).

true even if related debtors go into bankruptcy at the same time. For example, real estate developers commonly set up many related corporations and partnerships. Each development project involves different companies, although all of them are under the direct or indirect control of the same developer. The developer's financial failure may result in the developer's personal bankruptcy as well as the bankruptcy of numerous related companies. In most cases, each of those bankruptcies will be dealt with separately, even though there is overlapping ownership, control, and debt among the various entities affected by the developer's collapse.

However, cases involving related debtors are sometimes handled differently, in one of two possible ways. First, it is common for the court to order "administrative consolidation" of cases involving related debtors. This is also sometimes referred to as "joint administration" or "procedural consolidation." In this type of purely administrative consolidation, the cases are handled together procedurally, but the various debtors' assets and debts are kept separate from one another just as they would have been if the cases were not jointly administered.[81] Far more rarely, bankruptcy courts exercise their plenary powers to order "substantive consolidation" of related debtors in which their assets are pooled together and creditors' claims are satisfied from the same consolidated fund.[82]

The purpose of joint administration is to make administration of multiple related cases more efficient without affecting the substantive rights of creditors.[83] Substantive consolidation, on the other hand, vitally affects creditors' substantive rights. Accordingly, it is "to be used sparingly."[84]

[A] Administrative Consolidation

Administrative consolidation is, as the name suggests, simply a method of simplifying procedures to increase convenience and reduce the costs of estate administration. Bankruptcy Rule 1015(b) specifically permits the court to order a joint administration of two or more estates if the petitions are pending in the same court and the petitioners are spouses; a partnership and at least one of its general partners; two or more general partners of the same partnership; or a debtor and an "affiliate."[85] Joint administration of cases involving married debtors is routine.

---

[81] *See generally* Gill v. Sierra Pacific Constr., Inc. (In re Parkway Calabasas Ltd.), 89 B.R. 832, 836 (Bankr. C.D. Cal. 1988).

[82] *See* William H. Widen, *Prevalence of Substantive Consolidation in Large Bankruptcies from 2000 to 2004: Preliminary Results*, 14 Am. Bankr. Inst. L. Rev. 47 (2006).

[83] In re Cooper, 147 B.R. 678, 682 (Bankr. D.N.J. 1992).

[84] Union Sav. Bank v. Augie/Restivo Baking Co. (In re Augie/Restivo Baking Co.), 860 F.2d 515, 518 (2d Cir. 1988) (quoting Flora Mir Candy Corp. v. R.S. Dickson & Co. (In re Flora Mir Candy Corp.), 432 F.2d 1060, 1062 (2d Cir. 1970), and Chemical Bank Trust Co. v. Kheel (In re Seatrade Corp.), 369 F.2d 845, 847 (2d Cir. 1966)); *see* William H. Thornton, *The Continuing Presumption Against Substantive Consolidation*, 105 Banking L.J. 448 (1988).

[85] Fed. R. Bankr. P. 1015(b).

"Affiliate" is defined in several ways, but includes a variety of situations in which a person is likely to have effective control of a business entity by reason of equity or property ownership. The most common situation described in the rule is ownership of at least 20 percent of the voting equity of the debtor.[86] A corporation that is wholly owned by one individual is an affiliate of that individual. Likewise, a wholly owned subsidiary corporation is an affiliate of the parent corporation. Most closely held corporations, owed by family members or former business partners, are affiliates of their owners.

However, joint administration is very limited. It does not consolidate the debts or the assets of the debtors, which remain separate. It merely permits such things as the appointment of a single trustee, the use of "a single docket . . . including the listing of filed claims, the combining of notices to creditors of the different estates, and the joint handling of other purely administrative matters that may aid in expediting the cases and rendering the process less costly."[87] Even these actions are permitted only to the extent that they do not materially affect the interests of the creditors of the different estates. Rule 1015(c) specifies that "[p]rior to entering an order [for joint administration] the court shall give consideration to protecting creditors of different estates against potential conflicts of interest."[88] For example, in some cases it might be necessary to have separate trustees because there are disputes between the debtors' estates. If a parent and subsidiary have both filed bankruptcy petitions, and the subsidiary has a claim against the parent, permitting the same person to serve as trustee in both debtors' cases would create an inappropriate conflict of interest for the trustee.

In short, administrative consolidation does not affect the fundamental legal distinction between the debtors. In the end, each debtor is liquidated or reorganized separately with each set of creditors receiving payment from the assets or future income of the debtor against whom their claims are made. In many of these cases, each debtor will owe money to a largely similar group of creditors, and in some cases one debtor will be a co-obligor with another debtor, but the debts will be paid (or more likely not paid) by the debtor or debtors who actually owe them, not by the group as a whole.

[B] Substantive Consolidation[89]

Substantive consolidation is the bankruptcy equivalent of piercing the corporate veil and removing the legal barrier between two entities that keeps their assets and debts separate from one another. The key difference

---

[86] Bankruptcy Code § 101(2)(A).

[87] Fed. R. Bankr. P. 1015 advisory committee notes.

[88] Fed. R. Bankr. P. 1015(c).

[89] Seth D. Amera & Alan Kolod, *Substantive Consolidation: Getting Back to Basics*, 14 Am. Bankr. Inst. L. Rev. 1 (2006); Douglas G. Baird, *Substantive Consolidation Today*, 47 B.C. L. Rev. 5 (2005); Mary Elisabeth Kors, *Altered Egos: Deciphering Substantive Consolidation*, 59 U. Pitt. L. Rev. 381 (1998).

between administrative and substantive consolidation is that in the former, each debtor's assets and liabilities are kept separate; when cases are substantively consolidated, the legal distinctions between the separate entities are eliminated.

Substantive consolidation entails the elimination of legal distinctions between entities. If the bankruptcy cases of Titanic, Inc. and its sole shareholder, Harlan Wolff, are consolidated, their separate assets will be combined and their separate creditors will compete with one another to receive a distribution from the common fund. In substantive consolidation, there is a single liquidation or reorganization; all creditors of each entity are paid, if at all, from the property of the consolidated entity.

Sorting out the exact dimensions of the consolidated estate can be complicated. Consider for example, a case in which the assets and debts of three separate corporations, Titanic, Inc., Olympic, Inc., and Brittanic, Inc. are substantively consolidated. Suppose that Titanic has $10 million in debt and $4 million in assets, Olympic has $12 million in debt and $3 million in assets, and Brittanic has $1 million in debt and only $100,000 in assets. Of Titanic's assets, $2 million is a debt owed to it by Olympic, and $500,000 is a debt owed to it by Brittanic. Conversely, of Olympic's $12 million in debt, $2 million is its debt to Titanic, and of Brittanic's $1 million in debt, $500,000 is its obligation to Titanic. These are netted out upon consolidation because an entity cannot owe money to itself. What remains are the groups' "real" obligations — the debts it owes to outsiders; and its "real" assets — its tangible property plus claims it has against outsiders.

Netting out the intragroup transactions in this example, Titanic's assets drop to only $1.5 million, Olympic's debt drops to $10 million, and Brittanic's debt drops to $500,000. After consolidation, the new entity has $20.5 million in debt owed to others and $4.6 million in assets available for distribution to these creditors.

Substantive consolidation, like piercing the corporate veil, makes shareholders liable for corporate debts.[90] Although many substantive consolidations involve corporations and their individual or corporate shareholders, many of them involve consolidating the estates of multiple subsidiaries of the same parent or other related entities. Moreover, many piercing cases merely involve giving creditors of the corporation access to the assets of the corporation's owner. Substantive consolidation gives creditors of all the consolidated entities access to the assets of all the consolidated entities. As such, it may significantly affect the distributions to creditors of the various debtors. For example, one debtor may be asset rich and debt poor (or even solvent), while other consolidated debtors may have considerable debt and few assets. Substantive consolidation will benefit the creditors of the asset poor entity at the expense of the creditors of the asset rich entity.

There is also a family resemblance between substantive consolidation and equitable subordination.[91] Under equitable subordination, creditors claims

[90] *See* In re Owens Corning, Inc., 419 F.3d 195, 206 (3d Cir. 2005).

[91] Bankruptcy Code § 510(c)(1); *see* § 10.05[B] Equitable Subordination, *supra*.

are accorded a lower priority than they otherwise would be entitled to, usually because of the creditor's misconduct.[92] Equitable subordination is a less drastic remedy than substantive consolidation, because it leaves intact the legal identities of those involved. It also focuses more precisely than substantive consolidation on redressing misconduct; one of the difficulties of substantive consolidation is that it can have a severe impact on the rights of third parties who were in no way involved in the misconduct that gave rise to the remedy.

Despite its long history,[93] substantive consolidation is not expressly authorized in the Code. Nor are there any guidelines for its application in the Code or the Rules. Instead, it is generally considered part of the court's general equitable powers under § 105, which broadly permits the court to enter "any order, process, or judgment that is necessary or appropriate to carry out the provisions of [the Bankruptcy Code]."[94]

Substantive consolidation is arguably a remedy for dealing with several distinct problems. Sometimes substantive consolidation is in fact an extreme form of administrative consolidation that is used where it is simply not feasible to administer the estates separately. Sometimes it is a method of dealing with abuse or fraud. Still other times, it is voluntarily invoked by the debtor. Although there is a good deal of overlap in the facts examined and the rationales used in these various circumstances, they are to at least some degree analytically distinct.

Substantive consolidation because of administrative necessity arises when there is no feasible way to have a separate administration. Consider the practical difficulties that would arise if Titanic Corp., Olympic Corp., and Brittanic Corp. are all engaged in the same business, all have an identical group of creditors, have never kept separate books and records, and are managed by the same people. Affiliated companies sometimes even use invoices and purchase orders interchangeably with one another, depending on whose stationary was most convenient. It may be impossible for them to determine which company owns what or owes what. In this situation, substantive consolidation may be a practical necessity. At best, it would be extravagantly expensive to sort this out, with little benefit for the creditors.[95] Whether the actions of the companies were fraudulent, abusive, or merely incompetent is not really relevant, because there is no alternative other than to substantively consolidate the companies' estates into one.

However, most of the serious disputes over substantive consolidation involve situations in which it is possible to separately administer the debtors' cases. Consolidation is usually sought by creditors of at least one

[92] *See* In re Owens Corning, Inc., 419 F.3d 195, 206 (3d Cir. 2005).

[93] *See* Reider v. FDIC (In re Reider), 31 F.3d 1102, 1105–08 (11th Cir. 1994); In re Bonham 229 F.3d 750 (9th Cir. 2000); Mary Elisabeth Kors, *Altered Egos: Deciphering Substantive Consolidation*, 59 U. Pitt. L. Rev. 381, 386–97 (1998).

[94] Bankruptcy Code § 105(a).

[95] *See, e.g.*, Chemical Bank v. Kheel, 369 F.2d 845 (2d Cir. 1966) (estimated cost of untangling the financial affairs of affiliates might exceed the entire value of the estate).

of the related entities (usually one with many debts and few assets), who contend that consolidation is the only way to save them from the effects of the various debtors' misconduct. Typically, these cases involve situations in which one or more of the debtors either (1) misled creditors about whom they were dealing with or (2) was grossly underfinanced by those in control of the debtor group. There are also cases in which there is outright fraud.

Creditors can be misled, intentionally or unintentionally, when the debtor group has failed to make clear to creditors which member of the group is obligated on its debts. If, for example, Titanic, Olympic, and Brittanic are all subsidiaries of Ocean Group, Inc. and all use similar or identical stationary with the name of Ocean and its three subsidiaries on it for all documents, correspondence and payments, creditors might not be sure who they are dealing with in any single transaction.

Consolidation is also sometimes ordered when one or some of the affiliated debtors are seriously undercapitalized. Thus, HoldCo Inc. might operates as the parent of two companies: Franklin Fabrications Inc. and Franklin Sales, Inc. Franklin Fabrications manufactures items and sells them to HoldCo which resells them, in turn, to Franklin Sales, Inc. Franklin Sales, Inc. sells the goods on the open market. HoldCo has set the prices it pays Fabrications and the price that it charges to Sales so that HoldCo appears to make money, regardless of whether this causes the subsidiaries to make or lose money. In fact, the price it pays Fabrications is sometimes less than the cost to Fabrications of manufacturing the goods, and the price it receives from Franklin Sales is sometimes more than the items can be sold for on the market. As a result of these practices, when all three companies go into bankruptcy, all of the unencumbered assets are in HoldCo's name. Neither Franklin Fabrications nor Franklin Sales have assets to distribute to their creditors. These creditors are likely to seek substantive consolidation, claiming that HoldCo's actions amount to a misuse of its subsidiaries to the detriment of their separate creditors.

Although situations of these two types are found in most substantive consolidation cases, courts have not developed specific rules that would indicate whether consolidation is necessary. Instead, they take a case-by-case approach which has resulted in a list of factors that are present in many cases where substantive consolidation has been ordered. An early substantive consolidation case, dealing with the consolidation of a parent and one of its subsidiaries, identified the following factors:

1. The parent owns or controls the sub,
2. The corporations have the same directors or officers,
3. The parent provides financing for the sub,
4. The parent created (incorporated) the sub,
5. The sub has grossly inadequate capitalization,
6. The parent pays salaries and expenses of the sub, and subsidizes losses,

7. The sub conducts little or no business with any entity other than the parent,

8. The sub has few or no assets except those it received from the parent,

9. The parent refers to the sub as a department or division, rather than a separate corporation,

10. Directors and officers of the subsidiary act in the interests of the parent, and under the parent's orders, and

11. Corporate formalities (such as separate books and records, shareholder and director meetings) are not maintained.[96]

Other cases have added to the list without necessarily increasing clarity. Additional factors identified include such things as fraudulent transfers between companies in the debtor group, intercorporate guarantees, the use of consolidated financial statements, commingled assets, and the difficulty of sorting out the property and debts of the various entities.[97]

Modern cases focus on a more narrow set of principles that encompass the factors that these traditional cases commonly articulate. In *In re Augie/ Restivo Baking Co., Ltd.,*[98] the court said that these various factors are nothing more than variations on two more fundamental consideration: (i) whether creditors dealt with the entities as a single economic unit and did not rely on their separate identities in extending credit; and (ii) whether the affairs of the debtors are so entangled that consolidation will benefit all creditors.[99] Other cases have focused on the "substantial identity" of the affiliated debtors and whether the benefits of consolidation heavily outweigh the harm.[100]

The United States Supreme Court's 1999 decision in *Grupo Mexicano de Desarrollo, S.A. v. Alliance Bond Fund, Inc.*,[101] has led some to question the continued vitality of the doctrine of substantive consolidation, at least in the absence of express statutory authority for the bankruptcy court's authority to order it.[102] In *Grupo Mexicano,* the Court held that federal district courts lack the equitable power to enjoin a prejudgment transfer of a debtor's assets, because such an equitable remedy did not exist when the federal courts were created under the Judiciary Act of 1789. Despite questions about the impact of *Grupo Mexicano* on the bankruptcy court's

[96] Fish v. East, 114 F.2d 177 (10th Cir. 1940).

[97] *See* In re Bonham, 226 B.R. 56 (Bankr. D. Alaska 1998).

[98] Union Sav. Bank v. Augie/Restivo Baking Co. (In re Augie/Restivo Baking Co., Ltd.), 860 F.2d 515 (2d Cir. 1988).

[99] 860 F.2d at 518.

[100] In re Auto-Train Corp., 810 F.2d 270, 276 (D.C. Cir. 1987).

[101] 527 U.S. 308 (1999).

[102] Daniel B. Bogart, *Resisting the Expansion of Bankruptcy Court Power Under Section 105 of the Bankruptcy Code: The All Writs Act and an Admonition from Chief Justice Marshall*, 35 Ariz. St. L.J. 793, 810 (2003); J. Maxwell Tucker, Grupo Mexicano *and the Death of Substantive Consolidation*, 8 Am Bankr. Inst. L. Rev. 427 (2000).

authority under § 105(a), courts have continued to regard it as a viable solution to the problems it addresses.[103]

[103] *See* In re Owens Corning, Inc., 419 F.3d 195, 208 n.14 (3d Cir. 2005); Douglas G. Baird, *Substantive Consolidation Today*, 47 B.C. L. Rev. 5, 20–21 (2005).

TABLE OF CASES

[References are to pages and footnotes.]

A

[References are to pages and footnotes.]

B

[References are to pages and footnotes.]

[References are to pages and footnotes.]

C

[References are to pages and footnotes.]

[References are to pages and footnotes.]

[References are to pages and footnotes.]

D

[References are to pages and footnotes.]

E

F

[References are to pages and footnotes.]

[References are to pages and footnotes.]

G

[References are to pages and footnotes.]

H

[References are to pages and footnotes.]

I

J

[References are to pages and footnotes.]

K

[References are to pages and footnotes.]

L

[References are to pages and footnotes.]

M

[References are to pages and footnotes.]

[References are to pages and footnotes.]

N

[References are to pages and footnotes.]

O

[References are to pages and footnotes.]

[References are to pages and footnotes.]

Q

R

[References are to pages and footnotes.]

S

[References are to pages and footnotes.]

[References are to pages and footnotes.]

T

[References are to pages and footnotes.]

[References are to pages and footnotes.]

U

V

[References are to pages and footnotes.]

W

[References are to pages and footnotes.]

X

Y

Z

TABLE OF STATUTES, RULES AND REGULATIONS

[References are to pages and footnotes.]

B

[References are to pages and footnotes.]

B—Cont.

Bankruptcy Code—Cont.

B—Cont.

Bankruptcy Code—Cont.

[References are to pages and footnotes.]

B—Cont.

Bankruptcy Code—Cont.

[References are to pages and footnotes.]

B—Cont.

Bankruptcy Code—Cont.

[References are to pages and footnotes.]

B—Cont.

Bankruptcy Code—Cont.

[References are to pages and footnotes.]

B—Cont.

Bankruptcy Code—Cont.

[References are to pages and footnotes.]

B—Cont.

Bankruptcy Code—Cont.

[References are to pages and footnotes.]

B—Cont.

Bankruptcy Code—Cont.

B—Cont.

Bankruptcy Code—Cont.

[References are to pages and footnotes.]

B—Cont.

Bankruptcy Code—Cont.

B—Cont.

Bankruptcy Code—Cont.

[References are to pages and footnotes.]

B—Cont.

Bankruptcy Code—Cont.

[References are to pages and footnotes.]

B—Cont.

Bankruptcy Code—Cont.

[References are to pages and footnotes.]

B—Cont.

Bankruptcy Code—Cont.

[References are to pages and footnotes.]

B—Cont.

Bankruptcy Code—Cont.

[References are to pages and footnotes.]

B—Cont.

Bankruptcy Code—Cont.

Bankruptcy Reform Act of 1978

Bankruptcy Rules

B—Cont.

Bankruptcy Rules—Cont.

C

Code of Federal Regulations

E

Employee Retirement Income Security Act of 1984

I

Internal Revenue Code

[References are to pages and footnotes.]

I—Cont.

Internal Revenue Code—Cont.

S

U

Uniform Commercial Code

U—Cont.

Uniform Commercial Code—Cont.

[References are to pages and footnotes.]

U—Cont.

Uniform Commercial Code—Cont.

Uniform Consumer Credit Code

U—Cont.

United States Code

[References are to pages and footnotes.]

U—Cont.

United States Code—Cont.

[References are to pages and footnotes.]

U—Cont.

United States Code—Cont.

United States Constitution

U—Cont.

United States Constitution—Cont.

United States Treasury Regulations

STATE STATUTES: ALABAMA/ ALASKA

Alabama Code

ARIZONA/ARKANSAS

Arizona Revised Statutes

CALIFORNIA/CANAL ZONE

California Civil Code

California Code of Civil Procedure

COLORADO/CONNECTICUT

Connecticut General Statutes

[References are to pages and footnotes.]

DELAWARE/WASHINGTON, D.C.

Delaware Code

FLORIDA/GEORGIA

Florida Constitution

Florida Statutes

HAWAII/IDAHO

Idaho Code

ILLINOIS/INDIANA

Illinois Compiled Statutes

Indiana Code

IOWA/KANSAS

Iowa Code

Kansas Statutes

MAINE/MARYLAND

Maine Revised Statutes

MICHIGAN/MINNESOTA

Michigan Compiled Laws

Minnesota Statutes

MISSISSIPPI/MISSOURI

Missouri Statutes

NEW YORK

New York Civil Practice Law and Rules

OHIO/OKLAHOMA

Ohio Revised Code

[References are to pages and footnotes.]

INDEX

[References are to page numbers.]

A

[References are to page numbers.]

[References are to page numbers.]

[References are to page numbers.]

[References are to page numbers.]

[References are to page numbers.]

[References are to page numbers.]

E

[References are to page numbers.]

[References are to page numbers.]

I

[References are to page numbers.]

[References are to page numbers.]

O

[References are to page numbers.]

[References are to page numbers.]

[References are to page numbers.]

[References are to page numbers.]

R

[References are to page numbers.]

S

[References are to page numbers.]

U